HUGH THOMAS

The Golden Age

The Spanish Empire of Charles V

PENGUIN BOOKS

PENGUIN BOOKS

Published by the Penguin Group
Penguin Books Ltd, 80 Strand, London WC2R ORL, England
Penguin Group (USA) Inc., 375 Hudson Street, New York, New York 10014, USA
Penguin Group (Canada), 90 Eglinton Avenue East, Suite 700, Toronto, Ontario, Canada M4P 2Y3
(a division of Pearson Penguin Canada Inc.)
Penguin Ireland, 25 St Stephen's Green, Dublin 2, Ireland (a division of Penguin Books Ltd)
Penguin Group (Australia), 250 Camberwell Road, Camberwell, Victoria 3124, Australia
(a division of Pearson Australia Group Pty Ltd)
Penguin Books India Pvt Ltd, 11 Community Centre,
Panchsheel Park, New Delhi – 110 017, India
Penguin Group (NZ), 67 Apollo Drive, Rosedale, Auckland 0632, New Zealand
(a division of Pearson New Zealand Ltd)
Penguin Books (South Africa) (Pty) Ltd, 24 Sturdee Avenue,
Rosebank, Johannesburg 2196, South Africa

Penguin Books Ltd, Registered Offices: 80 Strand, London WC2R ORL, England

www.penguin.com

First published by Allen Lane 2010
Published in Penguin Books 2011

003

Typeset by Palimpsest Book Production Limited, Falkirk, Stirlingshire
Printed in Great Britain by Clays Ltd, St Ives plc

A CIP catalogue record for this book is available from the British Library

ISBN: 978-0-141-03449-2

www.greenpenguin.co.uk

MIX
Paper from
responsible sources
FSC
www.fsc.org FSC® C018179

Penguin Books is committed to a sustainable
future for our business, our readers and our planet.
This book is made from Forest Stewardship
Council™ certified paper.

To Vanessa
A constant inspiration

Contents

BOOK II
Peru

BOOK III
The Indies as a Treasure House

BOOK IV
Counter Reformation, Counter Renaissance

BOOK V
The Indian Soul

BOOK VI
Envoi

Appendices

List of Illustrations

ENDPAPERS

List of Maps

Preface

This book, though complete in itself, is the second in a series of volumes which I am writing about the Spanish empire. The first volume was *Rivers of Gold*, published in 2003. I am now at work on a third volume which takes the extraordinary story to 1580, when Spain ceased to expand her responsibilities. King Philip II decided in that year not to try to conquer China.

A word about nomenclature: Carlos I and V are rendered 'Charles' as a matter of course. In *Rivers of Gold*, I elected to speak of Ferdinand king of Aragon as 'Fernando'. I have maintained that usage here. 'Moctezuma' is rendered 'Montezuma', the English translation of the name. I have found it so spelled by Spaniards several times in the sixteenth century; On the other hand, I have rendered the Aztecs by their more accurate designation 'Mexica'. I have as a rule rendered the capital, 'Mexico City', by the Spanish usage 'Mexico'.

I have some acknowledgements: first to Stuart Proffitt and his colleagues at Penguin London. They were patient, meticulous and a pleasure to work with. Stuart showed himself a publisher from whom I gained as much from his friendship as I did from his expertise and judgement. I am grateful too for his work on the text to Martin Davies, an excellent and learned editor. My editorial thanks also go to my agent, my imaginative friend Andrew Wylie and his remarkable assistants. Teresa Velasco typed and retyped the manuscript with care and accuracy. I owe her and Cecilia Calamante a great deal for their hard work on my behalf.

To sum up one's indebtedness to other writers is difficult. But I should be singularly ungrateful were I not to put on record how much I owe to: Manuel Fernández Álvarez whose work in the sixteenth century is an example to us all; and to *The Conquest of Peru*'s great historian, John Hemming, whose research and writings have placed all students of the matter under a lasting obligation. John Hemming also corrected the proofs and saved me from many mistakes. My wife Vanessa also read the proofs with attention. I am also grateful to James Lockhart for his remarkable study *The Men of Cajamarca* and his earlier work on *Spanish Peru*. Like everyone who has worked on Peru in the sixteenth century, I have been much assisted by the work of Guillermo Lohmann, whom I used to see at eight o'clock in the morning on the steps of the Archivo de Indias waiting for entrance to the *salón de lectores* in the old building of Herrera in Seville. He was always at his table before I was at mine. Other works which were of great value to me included Marcel Bataillon's *Erasme et l'Espagne* and José Martínez Millán's *La Corte de Carlos V.*

Hugh Thomas

A NOTE ON CURRENCY

The usual item of currency was the maravedí, a piece of copper worth a ninety-sixth of a gold mark, which in turn was equivalent to 230.045 grams. A ducado (ducat) was worth 375 maravedís, 1 real was 34 maravedís, 1 peso was 450 maravedís, and 1 castellano was 485 maravedís. A cruzado was an old coin, sometimes gold, sometimes silver and occasionally copper, of different values. An escudo was worth 40 reales, and a cuento had an indeterminate value.

PROLOGUE
A Tale of Two Cities:
Valladolid and Mexico

I

Valladolid

*If a war threatens, popes must use all their efforts either to secure
a settlement without bloodshed; or, if the tempest in human affairs
makes that impossible, to urge that the war is fought with less
cruelty and does not last long.*

Erasmus, *Enchiridion*

Charles of Ghent, Karl von Habsburg, king of Spain and emperor in
Germany, duke of many lands, and lord of many more beyond the
ocean, reached his temporary, many-towered capital of Valladolid, in
north-west Spain, at the end of August 1522. Already a much travelled
monarch though still only twenty-two years old, he had come from the
Low Countries with 2,000 people and over 1,000 horses – an entourage
which had seemed too large for the English when Charles had on the
way visited his uncle by marriage, Henry VIII (half had, therefore, been
left in Calais). Henry signed his letters *'votre père, frère, et cousin et bel
oncle Henry'*.[1] This court included chambermaids, butlers, grooms and
tapestry cleaners, as well as soldiers and clerks, courtiers and counts.

Particularly important in the court of Charles V was the keeper of
tapestries, Gilleson de Warenghien, whose family had been in the royal
Burgundian service for several generations. For in those still chivalrous
days, kings travelled with tapestries. When Charles's aunt Margaret
arrived in Spain in 1497 to marry the Infante Juan, she was met at the
port of Santander by 120 mules laden with plate and tapestries.[2]

Charles had reached Spain at that noble port of Santander on the
north coast, which was said to have been founded by Noah; and the
emperor and his entourage entered Valladolid over a big bridge across
the river Pisuerga, deep, rapid and clayey, just where the smaller torrent,

ins it. Charles then crossed the Paseo de las Moreras, ...k, before passing the substantial new palace of the multi- ...family, the Benaventes, on the edge of what had been, till a ...n before, the Jewish quarter. Charles had stayed with the ...ntes on his previous visit to the city in 1517. Now he went to stay in ...e rambling mansion of the Enríquez, his Spanish cousins. (Charles's great-grandmother had been an Enríquez, a semi-royal noblewoman who had been the mother of King Fernando the Catholic; Charles in consequence was the last king of Spain to have had commoners as near cousins.) The Enríquez's dwelling was in the centre of Valladolid, in the Calle de las Angustias.[3] The remainder of the court lodged in rented houses, mostly to the east of the town, near the supreme court.

There is a fine picture of Valladolid in the sixteenth century in the collection of drawings by the Flemish artist Anton van den Wyngaerde. Wyngaerde, who came from Antwerp, worked, as a young man, in the Netherlands, in middle life in England and Italy and, later, in Spain, where he became an official artist to King Philip II. He sketched most of the towns of Castile and did the work so carefully that, in 1572, he retired to Madrid with his hands crippled. His drawings form a fine topographical guide.[4]

Valladolid was a place of churches, convents and private palaces, some of which had become the seats of public buildings. For instance, the supreme court (*audiencia*) was established in 1479 in the palace of the once powerful Vivero family built by the chief accountant to King Juan II, Alonso Pérez de Vivero, who was murdered in 1453, a violent time in Spanish history almost forgotten by the 1520s. Pérez de Vivero's son, Juan, had had the same task in the household of Enrique IV. The family were converted Jews, *conversos*, like most high officials of the Trastámara dynasty who supplied the royal dynasty of Castile from 1369 to 1516. These officials served the Crown well, and Juan de Vivero had enabled King Fernando to meet Queen Isabel in his palace, and then to marry there, in the Sala Rica.

There must have been about 400 *señorial* houses in Valladolid in the early sixteenth century. They were stone buildings often in white-washed mudéjar style, but it was easy to see that the Renaissance, which took so long to reach Spain, had come to Valladolid. Windows seemed larger than they were elsewhere, doors were carefully placed in the centre of façades. Italian-style medallions depicting individuals could sometimes be seen above the main entrances. Patios were bigger than in other cities, as were the façades. At first sight, the palace of the Benavente looked like a medieval fortress but, on examination, the courtyard had an air of the Renaissance with acanthus leaves at the tops of pillars, with medallions recalling old Benavente family members and a plateresque frieze. Soon there would also be a Renaissance garden, organized by the count-duke, who had been one of the Regents of the country during the recent time of troubles.

Other noblemen were building in Valladolid, as it was becoming evident that the town was, for the time being at least, the capital of the newly united kingdom of Spain. Thus the marquises of Astorga, Villa-franca, Denia, Viana, Villasantes, Poza and Villaverde (marquis was a title much more used in Spain than in England)[5] had imposing buildings, with their coats of arms over their main doors; so did the counts of Miranda and Ribadavia. These edifices were mostly in the west of the town and, since they were new or even still being finished, they had an invigorating effect on the citizenry. The owners did not live continuously in them, but they provided both curiosity and employment for many of the 40,000 or so inhabitants of the city, a figure which made the town the largest in Castile. The noble houses had often to lodge the court; and, if some courtiers such as the Chancellor Gattinara, Juan de Vergara, the enlightened secretary to Alfonso de Fonseca, archbishop of Toledo, or the royal secretary, Alfonso de Valdés, might have been a pleasure to have as guests, others would have been merely demanding.

Even more striking to the eye than the palaces were about thirty convents or monasteries – half for women, the rest for men – as well as a *beaterio* (house for the pious) for Dominicans and, later, an oratory for the fathers of San Felipe Neri.[6] A foreign traveller would have been impressed to have found so many large buildings in the hands of religious professionals. Of these, the biggest was the Jeronymite foundation established in the mid-fifteenth century and now surrounded by gardens. When Charles had been in residence before, in 1517, some of its monks had preached against the Flemings who seemed to surround the monarch.[7] Almost as large was the Franciscan monastery, built in the late thirteenth century, in the Plaza del Mercado near the Plaza Mayor. The garden of that building occupied all the nearby land.[8] Then there was the rambling thirteenth-century monastery of the Dominicans, with its magnificent church of San Pablo, in the centre of the town.

San Pablo had been begun in the thirteenth century and had been much expanded by María de Molina, the astute widow of King Sancho IV of Castile (she died in Valladolid in 1321). The façade of the church had been rebuilt by the theologian Cardinal Torquemada[9] in the 1460s, and the church was added to by Fray Alonso de Burgos, using two famous architects, Juan Guas and Simon of Cologne. Burgos, like Torquemada a *converso,* was a coarse, immoral but clever Dominican who had been for a time confessor to Queen Isabel. He became bishop of Cuenca and then of the rich diocese of Palencia, in which Valladolid lay. His sermons were a pleasure to hear. Perhaps that was because he had lived for years in a cell cultivating a solitude which inspired him later to speak well. It was in the church of San Pablo in 1517 that the nobility of Spain had sworn homage to Charles of Ghent, led by the Count of Oropesa, carrying a sword of justice.[10] Three archbishops, seven bishops, eight dukes, five marquises, twenty-one counts, two viscounts, five *comendadors* (commanders) and seven archivists of military orders had mounted the three steps before the altar to subject themselves to the king. That homage had been a religious as much as a political ceremony, and was concluded by the oath of Charles, sworn on a cross and the Bible. The *Te Deum* was then sung. It was an occasion for celebration, and many noblemen who did not swear homage came simply to observe.

Other important churches in Valladolid included Santa Clara, founded by a friend of that saint in 1247, though the new buildings were of the 1490s; Santa María la Antigua, with its beautiful pillars and square Romanesque tower; and Santa María de las Huelgas,[11] a convent for Cistercian nuns built to the east, outside the town, on the site of the palace of María de Molina. The beautiful church of Santiago, recently built by the merchant Luis de la Serna, would soon be adorned on its reredos by a marvellous picture by the best Spanish painter of those days, Alonso Berruguete (son of Pedro), *The Adoration of the Magi.* Berruguete had been born in Paredes de Nava, forty miles to the north of Valladolid, a little town with which another Spanish Renaissance master was associated, the poet Jorge de Manrique, whose father was count of Paredes.[12] He had been in Rome when the famous Greek marble sculpture of Laocoön had been discovered in 1506 on the Esquiline Hill, perhaps the greatest archaeological discovery of the Renaissance – a sight which excited him all his life.

The Emperor Charles made Berruguete notary of the chancellery in Valladolid, a sinecure which gave him the leisure to paint. Charles's aunt Margaret of Austria would surely have approved of the arrangement since it gave her patronage a purpose.

We should also not forget the convent of regular canonesses of Saint Agustín had been founded at the little town of Portillo, outside the walls to the south-east, with the aim of serving the souls of the poor in hospitals. Close at hand was an Augustinian monastery founded in the early fifteenth century by a famous Constable of Castile, Ruy López Dávalos, the first of the great family of Dávalos to impose himself on the history of Spain; and there was also a Cistercian monastery with a church which was known for its fine altars and its Tuscan columns, in the Plaza de la Trinidad.

The Benedictine monastery had been a royal palace which was given to the monks by King Juan I at the end of the fourteenth century; and the church had been commissioned by Alfonso de Valdivieso, bishop of León. A small chapel had been added by Inés de Guzmán, the widow of the chief accountant Alonso Pérez de Vivero. The stalls in the main church were well carved by Andrés de Nájera, an illegitimate offspring of the great noble family of that surname ('we do not descend from kings but kings descend from us' was a famous boast of the dukes of Nájera). The church known as 'the Colegiata' was expanded on the insistence of its Abbot Juan, and a town councillor of another great family, Nuño de Monroy, thought the plans were incomplete. The church of San Andrés was famous for being the burial place of those executed by the state – Álvaro de Luna, the long-lived first minister of King Juan II in the fifteenth century, among them.

Valladolid had its secular life like any modern city. Printing had begun there in 1481, the first press being that at Nuestra Señora del Prado, which started by publishing Bulls of Indulgence.

For members of the court with less intellectual tastes, Valladolid had other charms. The women, thought the Venetian ambassador in the 1520s, Andrea Navagero, were beautiful even if, as the Flemish courtier Laurent Vital commented, they were heavily painted.[13] The Count-Duke of Benavente had an elephant. There were, in these happy days before the Reformation, many fiestas: '*Tout est prétexte à fêtes*.'[14] There was much dancing in summer along the banks of the river Pisuerga and many celebrations for Christmas, Holy Week (especially Holy Thursday when the procession leaving the church of Magdalena was spectacular) and Corpus Christi, not forgetting the night of San Juan in July, the day of the Assumption in August and the Nativity of the Virgin Mary in September. On Good Friday, two brotherhoods (*cofradías*) would set out – those of 'Our Lady at the Foot of the Cross' and 'the Prayer in the Garden of Olives'. The second of these processions had in the early sixteenth century over 2,000 pilgrims (*nazarenos*) and several beautiful floats, including a model of the Last Supper and a Saint Veronica. All these splendid religious occasions were excuses for music and dancing, as well as for bullfights.[15] Plays were often performed, especially the brief sketches of everyday life known as *sainetes*.

The university, an already ancient foundation (it was established in 1346), but in the past dominated by the Church, was by 1522 full of humanists. Law, medicine, theology and 'Arts' could all be studied there. New chairs were being founded regularly. It was then, with its 1,000 students, the third university of Spain in size, following Salamanca and Alcalá.[16] The best modern student of Valladolid, the French historian Bennassar, tells us that in the sixteenth century no other city in Castile had such a strong intellectual spirit. No doubt there were, as in most Spanish institutions of learning, two ways of looking at the classical authors: the Sicilian Lucio Marineo, Peter Martyr and the Geraldini brothers were among those who thought of the beauty of the poetry; others, like Nebrija, Diego de Muros and Diego Ramírez de Villaescusa, prized poetry for the truth it expressed.[17]

When one mentions intellectual matters in 1522, it is a short step to talk of Erasmus. That humane Dutch scholar had declined to come to Spain, but his ideas had arrived and infiltrated every place of learning and theological institute. Erasmus himself was still optimistic about the evolution of both European society and religion: had he not written 'I could almost wish to be rejuvenated a few years because I see a golden age dawning'? He pointed out that all the princes in Europe were in agreement and were leaning towards peace. 'I cannot but feel,' he went on, 'that there will be a new revival and in part a new unfolding of law-abiding behaviour and Christian society, but with a cleansed and genuine literature. We owe it to their pious minds that we observe the awakening and arising of glorious minds . . .'[18]

Alas, the optimism was premature. All the same, the books of Erasmus enjoyed extraordinary popularity in Spain. No other country had a comparable experience:

at the emperor's court, in the towns, in the churches, in the convents, even in the inns and on the high roads, everyone has the *Enchiridion* of Erasmus (the *Handbook of a Christian Soldier*) in Spanish. It had been read till then by a minority of Latinists; and even those did not always understand everything. But now it is read in Spanish by people of every kind.[19]

Erasmus had come to see the need to consider the problems of the Christianization of the new realms in the Americas. In a note of a conversation added to *Ichthyophagi* in 1526, he reflected on the smallness of the territory controlled by Christians. His interlocutor asks: 'Have you not seen all those southern banks and the multitude of islands marked by Christian symbols?' 'Yes,' replied Erasmus's character, Lanio, 'and I have learned that from there one can bring back plunder. But I didn't hear that Christianity had been introduced.'[20]

While Erasmus was optimistic, many simpler Christians could believe that a new, tolerant and intellectually rewarding Catholicism was imminent. Valladolid could believe it too. Many of its cultivated citizens spent their hours of leisure reading one or other of the famous novels of chivalry with which Spain was awash at that time. *Amadís de Gaula* was still the favourite, but there were the sequels (*Las Sergas de Esplandián, Lisuarte de Grecia*), a new series (*Palmerín de Oliva*) and the historian Oviedo's *Don Claribalte*.

In respect of dress, Flemish courtiers were surprised in Valladolid at the heavy chains of gold and the bright colours of the clothes. Women wore damask skirts and jackets. Feminine dress in the 1520s favoured narrow shoulders and a narrow waist with large trains to the floor. Men showed a taste for luxury as much as women, for they wore silk, brocade, velvet damask and taffeta. Not surprisingly, in Valladolid there was an army of tailors – in 1560 there would be one tailor per 200 inhabitants – not to speak of hosiers, braid-makers, shoemakers and jewellers. The most important jewellers of the town were the Arfe family from Germany. Enrique Arfe and his son Juan not only designed beautiful objects to wear but also refined the art of making gold and silver vessels for religious purposes.

As will be easily imagined in a town with an expensive if itinerant court, a large army of both black and Moorish slaves was to be found in Valladolid, as well as a colony of 'new Christians' of both Muslim and Jewish descent. The section of the city called Santa María, just east of the Calle Santiago, was the *morería*, the Moors' ghetto, and there was a substantial number of builders there, many of them Muslims, working on noblemen's new palaces. Nowhere in Castile did the poor get better treatment than they did in Valladolid, no doubt because there was so much work and because there were so many charitable foundations.[21] Sometimes there were accusations about Muslim secret propaganda, including the suggestion that a prophet had emerged in the community.[22] Life in Valladolid was well summed up by the ambassador of Charles V's brother Fernando, Martín de Salinas, in whose thoughtful prose we hear of bishops, dukes, kings and friars.[23]

And the empire in America? There were two buildings in Valladolid which would remind the friars, the noblemen, and even the king, that it existed: the colleges of San Gregorio and of Santa Cruz. First, at the side of the great church of San Pablo stood the college of the first named, begun in the late 1480s. The initiator of the project was Diego Deza, Columbus's friend from Zamora who afterwards became archbishop of Seville and Grand Inquisitor. Enrique de Egas – a Brussels architect who had built the *hostal* in Santiago de Compostela as well as reconstructing the cathedral at Toledo – Juan Guas and Gil Siloé contributed to the design, while Philippe Vigarny created the tomb there of Bishop Alfonso de Burgos, the refounder of San Pablo. Vigarny was the most interesting of these men. A Burgundian, he came to Burgos in his late twenties in 1498 and is considered by historians of art as 'one of the three foreign masters who taught the Spaniards perfect architecture and sculpture'.[24] He created a chapel in the cathedral of Granada where his 'delicate chisel' sculpted the tombs of King Fernando and Queen Isabel.[25] Already by 1520, he had an effective partnership with Berruguete. It was probably them who inspired the medallions in the Italian style on San Gregorio's which so impressed the Flemish courtiers who accompanied King Philip the Handsome and Queen Juana when they heard mass there in 1501.

What drew the attention of the court to the New World, to the conquistador, was the façade of the college of San Gregorio. It depicts hairy natives with clubs in their hands such as the adopted Vallisoletano Columbus said that he had found in the Caribbean. These were referred to as *maceros* or wild mace-bearers. The primitiveness of the scene was compensated for by a family tree of the royal family and one of Alfonso de Burgos as well as a depiction of that bishop kneeling before St Gregory.

In this college in the sixteenth century the Dominicans gave seven years' instruction in philosophy, logic, theology and study of the Bible. Among those who studied there were later famous theologians who would insist that the Indians in the New World had souls (such as Fray Francisco de Vitoria and Fray Domingo de Soto); civil servants who administered the new empire (such as Fray García de Loaisa, soon to be the long-serving president of Charles's Council of the Indies); and the first bishop of Lima, Fray Vicente de Valverde. Also among the 'old boys' of this college would be Fray Bartolomé de Carranza, the archbishop of Toledo who was so unfortunate in his intellectual trajectory.

The College of Santa Cruz nearby was as elegant a foundation as that of San Gregorio but its style was dramatically Renaissance, as one would expect from a building provided by the 'Third Monarch of Spain', Pedro González de Mendoza, archbishop of Toledo till his death in 1494. But here we see no sign that the cardinal wished his students to recall the achievements of his protégé, Columbus, which he had himself so furthered. It is González de Mendoza whom we should recall, as we consider Charles V's other realm, that in New Spain, since relations of the cardinal, Mendoza upon Mendoza, would play as large a part in bringing Spanish order there as they did in bringing the Renaissance to the mother country.[26]

There was one more connection with the New World in Charles's court in 1522. Among those who came to Valladolid with the emperor was Jean Glapion, his French confessor-counsellor. He had been born in La Festé-Bernard in the province of Maine, and had spent many years in the Franciscan convent in Bruges. He was enlightened and austere, light-hearted and pious, a dependant of Charles's aunt, the many-sided Archduchess Margaret. When he became Charles's confessor, he sought to persuade him to leave the handling of the ideas of Luther to Erasmus, to whom he was devoted. Glapion accompanied the emperor in his meetings with the main committees which governed the realms. But then in 1520 Glapion and a colleague in the Franciscan fraternity, Fray Francisco de los Ángeles, hearing of Cortés's discoveries, volunteered to go to New Spain to convert Indians. Pope Leo X, in his bull of April 1521, *Alias felicis recordationis*, had approved. But Fray Francisco was named general of the Franciscan order and Glapion became a counsellor of the emperor as well as his confessor. Whether he would have continued to think of going to New Spain is impossible to know. Glapion had an important role in the formation of imperial decisions from 1520 to 1522, including the nomination of officials. Alas, that fascinating Franciscan died in September 1522, leaving his place to a more conventional confessor-counsellor, García de Loaisa.[27] Had Glapion lived, the history of Spain, Europe and the Catholic Church would have been more tolerant, open to new ideas, and, indeed, more Erasmian.

Valladolid was in 1522 already a great metropolis. Places like it would soon be under construction throughout the Americas. There would soon be, in the New World, the same confusion of palaces and churches, monasteries and markets, squares and streets, often with the same names as those in Valladolid. Spain carried to the Indies the urban tradition of Rome and the Mediterranean. It remains.

2

Charles king and emperor

History is 'a great mistress', a leader 'even among our great teach-
ers' and our surest guide to 'an honest and virtuous life'.
Budé quoted in Quentin Skinner, *Foundations*

The Emperor Charles articulated the urban tradition of Spain and many
other lands. Though only twenty-two in 1522, his experience was considerable. He had been named after his great-grandfather, Charles the
Rash (*le Téméraire*), the last duke of Burgundy, a Christian name familiar in France but almost unknown at that time in Spain.[1] Charles had
been born in 1500 on 25 February, then the day of St Matthew, the
evangelist who played a part in his life; he often sought protection in his
memory.[2] His own birthplace, Ghent, had once been the capital of the
medieval counts of Flanders, centre of a cloth industry as well as of the
Burgundian principality and, as 'Charles of Ghent', the emperor had
learned to behave in his childhood and youth as a Burgundian nobleman. But Burgundy was itself in those days a complex international
organization: it was the premier French duchy with a German monarch
and a Flemish heart. Flemish was Charles's first language.

Charles was himself an international man, though among his thirty-
two immediate ancestors there was only one German, a Habsburg,
alongside a great gallery of Castilians, Aragonese and Portuguese. He
even had, in John of Gaunt (Ghent), Duke of Lancaster, 'time-honoured
Lancaster' in Shakespeare's *Henry IV*, an English forebear. Still, multinational though he seemed, Charles's childhood had been Flemish. His
Spanish mother, Joanna the Mad, Juana *la Loca*, lived a long way away
in Tordesillas, Castile; his father, Philip von Habsburg, the Fair, was
unavailable since he died in 1506. But Charles had in his father's clever

sister Margaret an effective substitute for a mother. Regent of the Low Countries – in effect queen – she was twice widowed, having married the Infante Juan, the son and heir of the monarchs of Spain, and then the Duke of Savoy, whose memory and that of herself she would preserve in the exquisite church of Brou, near Bourg-en-Bresse.[3] She had a palace in Mechelen which boasted the first Renaissance façade in the Netherlands, a building where the transition from late-medieval gothic to the Renaissance can be most clearly seen, for the styles stand in relation to each other in almost perfect symbolical balance.

There, in the shadow of the fine cathedral of Saint Rumbold, she maintained an elegant court, surrounded by poets, musicians and painters. She collected both pictures and unusual, beautiful and exotic objects. She painted, wrote poems, played chess and backgammon, and her library was famous as one of the first great collections of books after the recent invention of printing. Her librarian was a poet. She knew that, in courts, there had to be painters such as, in her case, the excellent Bernard van Orley from Brussels and the brilliant Albrecht Dürer from Nuremberg – not to speak of the prince of tapestry-makers, Peter van Aelst from Enghien. Margaret was confirmed by her nephew Charles in her semi-regal place, and she signed herself to him as 'your very humble aunt'. Her influence over him was profound. She was suspicious of France. But she taught her nephew, above all, that a court could be a *salon*.[4]

Charles was subject to at least two other influences: first, that of the tutor whom Margaret had found for him, Adrian of Utrecht, dean of St Peter's in Louvain, a member of the order of the Brethren of the Common Life, a pious, ascetic society founded in the northern Low Countries at Deventer, at the end of the fourteenth century. Proto-humanists, I suppose they should be named. Adrian was the son of a ship's carpenter, and could tell Charles how ordinary people lived. From Adrian, 'Charles acquired the popular easy-going and simple ways which made him so beloved by his Flemish subjects'.[5] The Brethren of the Common Life was one of those new Catholic bodies determined to simplify the Church's life, which, had they enjoyed greater success, might have rendered the Reformation unnecessary. The order had a cult of indigence, of which deprivation Adrian sought also to remind his famous pupil.[6] Some of the most remarkable men of the time were brethren – such as Mercator, the inventor of mapping,[7] and Thomas à Kempis, who was close to these men with his *Imitation of Christ*.

Adrian had, however, found himself able to accept worldly appointments. From being a mere doctor of theology at the University of Louvain, he became its chancellor. From being tutor to Charles, he became, first, the Flemish ambassador to Castile, and then Regent there, in Charles's absence, after May 1520. Though he was unable to control the revolution which followed in that year,[8] something extraordinary then occurred. For in January 1522 the cardinals in Rome unexpectedly named him pope. The Florentine historian Francesco Guicciardini, who lived at the time, recalled that Adrian had been proposed 'without anyone having any inclination to elect him but just to waste the morning. But then came several votes in his favour, the Cardinal of San Sisto began to speak in support of him in an almost perpetual oration, whereupon several cardinals began to move to his cause . . .' Others followed,

> more by impulse than by deliberation, with the result that, that same morning, he was elected pope by a unanimous vote, those who chose him not being able to give any reason why, amidst so many travails for the church, they should elect a foreigner from a 'barbarous country' who had not won any favour either because of his achievements in the past or from conversations which he might have had with cardinals, who scarcely knew his name, and who had never been in Italy.[9]

Adrian himself wrote to a friend that 'he would have preferred to be a canon of Utrecht than become pope'.[10]

Elected in January, Adrian took a long time to reach Rome. Indeed, he arrived only at the end of August, and a plague broke out immediately – a bad omen, it was understandably thought. Adrian was mocked in the Vatican because he liked beer more than wine and because he refused to commission Cellini, the great Tuscan jeweller and sculptor, to do anything. He caused consternation by refusing to countenance nepotism. A large placard was placed on the door of the Vatican announcing 'This palace to let'. Another poster denounced the cardinals who had elected Adrian: 'robbers, betrayers of Christ's blood, do you not feel sorrow to have surrendered the Vatican to German fury?' 'This pope of ours knows no one,' wrote a courtier, Girolamo Negri, 'the whole world is in despair.'[11] The cardinals had voted for him because they thought that they would do well to have a tutor of the new emperor in the Vatican. But Charles had not tried to back him. Indeed, he seems to have preferred Wolsey, the ambitious English cardinal.

Adrian was a politically stupid choice. He was insensitive to the classical antiquity surrounding him in Rome, which he regarded as the debris of paganism. He would have preferred a simple, small house to a palace. He had other concerns: one of his first decrees was to forbid the wearing of beards in the Vatican.[12] True, he celebrated mass daily and spoke Latin well, if without polish, but he was inexpert in politics. The marvellous historian of the popes, Ludwig von Pastor, wrote that 'Adrian's single-hearted anxiety to live exclusively for duty was to Italians of that age like an apparition from another world, beyond the grasp of their comprehension'.[13]

Another influence on the Emperor Charles in his early years was Guillaume de Croÿ, Sieur de Chièvres. Coming from a powerful Flemish family which had served all the great dukes of Burgundy in the preceding century, he became Charles's 'governor and grand chamberlain' in 1509. His influence was a contrast to that of Adrian; but it was considerable for he stood for the Burgundian tradition even more than did the Archduchess Margaret. 'The truth is,' Charles told the archbishop of Capua, 'as long as he lived, Monsieur de Chièvres governed me.' He slept in Charles's bedroom and had his eyes on him all day. Charles told the Venetian ambassador to Spain, Gasparo Contarini (a writer and a future cardinal), that he had early learned the value of Chièvres and 'for a long time subordinated his will to his'.[14] He was artful but observant, a hard master. When asked by the French ambassador, Genlis, why he made Charles work so hard when he was only fifteen years old, Chièvres replied: 'Cousin, I am the defender and guardian of his youth. I do not want him to be incapable because he has not understood affairs nor been trained to work.'[15] Trained to work! Can there be anything more important to gain from an education?

Chièvres was very interested in promoting his family interests. But all the same, it was he who gave Charles the chivalrous education which meant so much to him, who told him about the use of arms, about riding, and about such heroic writings as that of the elaborate courtier Olivier de la Marche. La Marche, an official from Franche-Comté, had been captain of the guard to the still much regretted Charles the Rash. He wrote notes about the etiquette and ceremonial of the court, giving pride of place to the famous Burgundian order, the Golden Fleece. He also wrote an allegorical poem about Charles the Rash in 1482, *Le Chevalier délibéré*, and memoirs which were much read in the sixteenth century.

La Marche was the author of a book describing codes of behaviour in different countries of Europe which the Emperor Maximilian and probably his daughter Margaret read. La Marche, who seems to have seen life as one long challenge with recurrent dangers, presented the memory of Charles as important in the young Emperor Charles's make-up; for 'no one', wrote the Dutch historian Huizinga, 'had been so consciously inspired by models of the past or manifested such a desire to rival them' as that duke.[16] The same could have been said of Charles the emperor. Like his ancestor, Charles was proud of the order of the Golden Fleece, which gave him a sense of the importance of valour, loyalty, piety and even simplicity.

In Valladolid in 1522, Charles still seemed the lanky, gangly, curiously featured youth with the ever open mouth, painted often by his aunt Margaret's favourite portraitist, Bernard van Orley. He had a pronounced Habsburg jaw[17] and one ambassador thought that it looked as if his eyes had been pasted on to too long a face. He was thin. The Venetian Contarini describes him as 'of a middle height neither tall nor short, more pale than rubicund, a fine leg, good arms, his nose rather sharp but small, restless eyes with a serious look neither cruel nor severe'.[18] He was certainly not yet the wise man we see in the masterpieces of Titian – the standing figure with the dog, the seated monarch wearing the Golden Fleece, much less the armoured knight at the battle of Mühlberg. But then Charles remained contradictory in his physique as he did in other things.

As a young man his negative qualities seemed to dominate. His confessor, Glapion, told Contarini that Charles remembered too much the injuries which people did him; he was not able to forget easily.[19] Talking seemed to bore him and was not something which he could do without difficulty.[20] Alonso de Santa Cruz said that he was 'a friend of solitude and a critic of laughter'.[21] To one courtier, de Longhi, his temperament seemed in the 1520s a mixture of passivity and impatience.

Charles soon started to impress his contemporaries with what Ramón Carande, the great historian of the early twentieth century, would describe as 'his extraordinary psychological penetration'.[22] His magisterial biographer, the German Karl Brandi, thought that he became eventually 'imperial in word and deed, in look and gesture ... Even those who have long been in attendance on him were astonished not only at his youthfulness, but at his energy, severity and dignity.'[23]

He began to seem, to courtiers and civil servants, magnanimous, liberal, generous. If still apparently unhealthy, and slow in his movements as in his speech, even ugly in person, Charles had something powerful about him, the weight of a leader. He never moved among men with natural ease but his personality was beginning to reflect his high sense of honour and his sureness of purpose. As his brief volume of memoirs suggests, he had become earnest and questioning. Some of this was already evident at Valladolid in 1522.[24]

Charles was a Burgundian nobleman thanks to Chièvres; Adrian of Utrecht made him pious; his aunt Margaret gave him a sense of politics and of art, as well as a concept of public service which all the Habsburgs had. This combination of influences instilled in him, as Karl Brandi put it, 'serious principles and a desire to confirm them; a courtly bearing; the ideal of knightly honour and that of fighting for the Christian faith in the style of the code of the Golden Fleece'. Burgundy also made him conscious of the political benefit of a rigorous court ceremonial.

He had already by 1522 an appetite for stylish dressing: he seemed *'muy rico y galán'*. He was a good sportsman, and his grandfather, the Emperor Maximilian, had said that 'he was glad that he was making such progress as a huntsman for, were it not so, it might have been supposed that the boy was a bastard, not his grandson'.[25] From early in life he expected to be buried at the beautiful charterhouse of Champmol, outside Dijon, with the tombs of his ducal Burgundian ancestors by Claus Sluter, and always hoped to be able to win back from France that part of Burgundy; he would tell Philip, his son, 'never to forget our duchy of Burgundy which is our ancient heritage'.[26]

Charles, like all members of his family, liked music. At Margaret's court he learned to play the clavichord. He delighted in listening to his aunt's violin and tambourin players, as well as her fifes and choristers, and loved to hear good music in his chapel.[27] A childhood friend, Charles de Lannoy, from a family as distinguished as the Croÿs (his grandfather, Hugues de Lannoy, had been a founding member of the order of the Golden Fleece), remarked that to like music was effeminate. Charles challenged him and chose lances and heavy horses for the duel. The exchange was dramatic. Though Charles won in the end, his horse fell and he always bore the marks of his injuries. Lannoy continued as Charles's chamberlain (*caballerizo mayor*) and, in March 1522, became viceroy of Naples.[28]

Karl Brandi thought that only Charles could have conceived the glory of the windows in the cathedral church of St Gudule in Brussels: 'in window after window, as though raised midway between heaven and earth, they stand in brilliant colour and ceremonial pomp, royal brides and bridegrooms, two by two kneeling in adoration ... who but Charles could have conceived and ordered thus?'[29] It seems likely, though, that the inspiration was his aunt Margaret's, at least for five of the windows of the great choir designed by the clever court painter Bernard van Orley. A final window, treating graphically the Last Judgement, was the contribution of Érard de la Marck, prince-bishop of Liège, a friend of Charles's and one of the few European aristocrats of the Church to have been influenced by a knowledge of the New World. This donor bishop is depicted in the front of the scene carrying a cross.[30]

Though intellectually well prepared, in his youth Charles always associated with young aristocrats such as Lannoy, John Frederick of Saxony, the elector Palatine with whom Charles's sister was so unwise as to have fallen in love, Frederick von Fürstenberg and Max Sforza, all of whom became his pages and all of whom considered it more important to be able to splinter a lance without losing one's seat on a horse than to construe a Latin sentence. They would play an important part in Charles's life, particularly John of Saxony.

Though Charles had many kingdoms, he spoke only French and Flemish fluently. He began to learn Spanish in 1517 but in 1525 the clever Polish ambassador to Spain, Dantiscus, wrote that he still found that language difficult and that he seemed at that time to have no German (Poland had something like a family pact then with the Habsburgs). He never learned Latin well, despite the lessons of Adrian of Utrecht and despite his later often repeated belief that it was essential that his son, Philip, should learn it. It was said that if someone addressed him in Latin and he did not know what was said, he would reply, 'This man takes me for Fernando' (a reference to his grandfather, the king of Aragon). But if he did understand what had been said, he would state, 'This man is illiterate, he speaks really bad Latin.'[31] In the end his Spanish improved, but his German was never good and his Latin was always bad, though he could understand Italian.

Charles lacked in his childhood any connection with his Spanish inheritance. Courtiers, such as Juan Manuel, intriguing and malicious, and friendly churchmen, such as Alonso de Fonseca, archbishop of

Santiago, or Ruiz de la Mota, bishop of Palencia, had limited influence in comparison with the archduchess, with Croÿ and with Adrian of Utrecht. The chronicler Santa Cruz thought that he found it hard to have confidence in Spaniards.[32]

But Erasmus presented him in 1516 with his *Education of a Christian Prince*, while Antonio de Guevara's *The Dial of Princes,* published in 1529, became the most widely read book of the entire sixteenth century in Europe, second only to the Bible. For Charles, historical knowledge became 'the nurse of practical wisdom'. Those who have the best understanding of the past may be said to have 'the best title to act as advisers to princes'.[33] Guillaume Budé, the French scholar, thought that reading history led to an understanding of the present and the future as well as of the past.

In respect of his politics, it has been said that it is hard to see whether Charles was more a monarch of the Middle Ages or of modern times. He would twice challenge King Francis to a single combat whose outcome, he considered, would have settled all their differences. Charles did not warm to nationalism, nor even patriotism, but loyalty to the Habsburg family was a different matter. He disliked the idea of having a fixed capital: 'kings do not need residences', he once told his son, Philip, when the two had passed an uncomfortable night at the royal pavilion at El Pardo.[34] In these ways, Charles seemed still a medieval monarch. But all the same he knew, from the advice of Mercurino Gattinara, the benefits of an organized civil service, and his rearrangements of his governmental committees would have reflected well on a post-Renaissance prince.

The public servants who worked for Charles at that time included many Flemings or Burgundians, such as Gattinara, from near Stresa, in Piedmont, who had first been with Charles's aunt, Margaret, as a legal adviser. Gattinara, chancellor from 1522, was indeed the most influential of these officials. He was clever if pernickety, being fond of disputing the finer points of the uses of the subjunctive, but he combined such attention to detail with broad vision. He also gloried in talking of Charles's imperial role in powerful, frequent memoranda; and his advice touched many lesser things such as recommending Charles to have his hair cut short, and to grow a beard like that worn by Hadrian.[35]

The Emperor Charles and his chancellor were not on the kind of warm terms that a great emperor and his most important public servant should be; Charles evidently wearied of Gattinara's continual grandiloquence. Early in 1523, in Valladolid, Gattinara wrote to his master that he thought Charles was in danger of following the path of his grandfather Maximilian who, despite his many gifts, was called 'the bad gardener' because he would never harvest his fruit in the right season. A proper budget of income and spending should be prepared. The Cortes (parliament) in Spain should seek a new source of revenue. He, Gattinara, would draft speeches for Charles whenever necessary. But he wanted Charles to adopt a 'forward policy' in Italy:

> I implore you, in the name of God, that, neither in council nor elsewhere, neither in jest nor in earnest, do you make it known before your going to Italy that you intend to take personal possession of Milan. Do not hand over the citadel to the Spaniards, do not take away the town secretly from the Duke. Such things must not be spoken of, be it ever so secretly, since walls have ears and servants tongues . . .

and, if Charles continued to go on as if daily expecting God to work miracles for him, then he, Gattinara, would beg to be excused from further involvement in matters of finance or war. Otherwise, he would like to remain in the royal service till the day that Charles was crowned in Italy. Then indeed he would be able to say, '*Nunc dimittis servum tuum domine.*'[36]

In April 1523, still in Valladolid, Gattinara wrote to Charles about his own position: he wanted to have his powers either reaffirmed or withdrawn. He had noticed that the chancellors of England and France were paid four times what he was. He complained that he sometimes had to wait two hours for an audience with Charles, while the emperor saw people whom Gattinara considered nonentities. The chancellorship, he feared, was being reduced to a tavern sign. In another note at much the same time, Gattinara told Charles: 'If your Majesty were to add to all your gifts the wisdom of Solomon, you would not be able to do everything yourself.'[37] God had advised even Moses to seek assistants. Nor should Charles embark on anything unless he could be sure of carrying it through. The ordinary costs of government should be distinguished from extraordinary costs, such as war.

Gattinara, nothing if not a Lombard, believed that he who controlled Northern Italy had the key to world power. The emperor's coronation there would put the seal on his achievements. A Roman diplomat wrote: 'Let the emperor rule Italy and he will rule the world.'[38] Mean-time, the love of (all) his subjects should be for Charles an 'impregnable fortress', as Seneca had put it. Their friendship should be cultivated, their complaints heeded. Charles should arrange that, if unpopular actions were needed, others would take responsibility. The emperor should not have to perform trivialities.

Then Gattinara touched on policy in the Indies. He asked whether the emperor believed that the natives should be converted to Christian-ity. Counsellor Gérard de la Plaine (Señor La Roche), a Burgundian much used by Charles for diplomatic missions, had said that the Indians had been treated not as men but as beasts. That should surely not be permitted. Charles was responsive to that kind of suggestion. Had he not listened to, and largely sided with, Bartolomé de las Casas in 1518, had he not himself proposed that the Indians sent home by Cortés in 1519 should be given warm clothes cut by the best tailors in Seville?

In July 1523 Charles held a Cortes at Valladolid. As usual repre-sentatives (*procuradores*) were present from half the cities of Castile. In a long speech written for him by Gattinara, Charles admitted mistakes but blamed them on his youth. He cited Caesar, Trajan and even Titus, who all believed, so he said, that the pursuit of peace was the greatest of foreign policies. Gattinara also spoke, declaring the divine origin of the royal power. God after all had the heart of kings in his hand. He did not explicitly mention the Indies, but he did speak of the need to continue the conquest of Africa.[39] The Cortes were impressed and voted for the grant of ducats for which Charles had asked, though the quantity was smaller than on any other occasion in Charles's reign.[40]

In politics, Charles was as much a mixture as he was in blood. At one moment he seemed liberal, humane, tolerant; at others he bridled at the slightest criticism. His consideration of the defeated rebels after the war of *comuneros* (parliamentarians who challenged the state) in 1522 was a model of wisdom for any age: fewer than a hundred perished in con-sequence in Castile, and some of those died of disease in prison.[41] The high point of this second stay of Charles in Valladolid was a ceremony outside the church of San Francisco on All Saints' Day 1522, when he proclaimed a general pardon for all who had been engaged in that conflict – apart from twelve *exceptuados* for whom Charles retained an aversion. Considering that the rebels had mounted, for whatever rea-son, a serious attack on the authority of the Crown and had even offered power to the king's poor, nervous mother, Juana, such clemency was remarkable.

In the 1520s Charles was convinced, above all by his chancellor, Gattinara, that he had a superhuman position in Christian society. Gattinara had hailed Charles in 1519 as the 'greatest emperor since the division of the empire in 843'. He was assured, and came himself to think, that God had chosen him to be the supreme universal monarch. Charles believed that he was the second sword of the Christian Commonwealth, with the Vicar of Christ, the pope, the first. He knew 'the confessional nature of his crown'.[42] The empire implied an inalienable mission, one over other kings, and a right to demand their support for his declared crusade against Muslims – either the sultan's army in Hungary or the fleet of Barbarossa at sea. Gattinara told him that the climax of the universal monarchy was at hand and that he hoped that Charles would lead the entire world back to 'a single shepherd', presumably as in Roman days.[43] The rest of the world would be conquered or fall into a subservient place.[44] Gattinara's powerful dreams were intoxicating. They sometimes convinced Charles; but often they were rejected by him.

The idea that Charles had a grand place in what Pope Julius II had called 'the world's game' was widespread. In 1520 Cortés would urge that Charles should think of himself as a 'new emperor' of New Spain no less than of Germany.[45] He would go further in 1524 by referring to Charles as 'Your Majesty to whom the whole world is subject'.[46] Perhaps Cortés derived this notion from his own captain, Jerónimo Ruiz de la Mota of Burgos, who was a cousin of that tutor of Charles's who had talked of the matter in a speech at Corunna in 1520. His titles reflected this idea in their first line: *'por la divina clemencia, emperador semper augusto'*.[47] In the 1530s a bishop of the remote see of Badajoz would pray that the Christian princes 'would all join with Your Sacred Majesty as monarch and Lord of the world in order to exterminate and persecute the pagans and infidels'.[48] Thus even in New Spain, a conquistador of no great importance, Juan de Ortega, from Hernando Cortés's home town of Medellín, in testimony on behalf of his leader in 1534, spoke of the Emperor Charles as 'his majesty the Lord of the world'.[49] Earlier, at the time of his election as emperor in 1519, Charles's friends argued that his greatness, resting on such mighty foundations as the crown of Spain and the empire, might mean that, having achieved the imperial crown, he could make all Italy and a great part of Christendom into 'a simple monarchy'.[50]

Charles's attitude to the Church was ambiguous. He saw himself first and foremost as the protector of Christianity. Thus he was always a devoted, even a rigid, Catholic. He heard mass daily, sometimes twice.[51] But he was not very interested in dogmatic matters and often quarrelled with popes, even when, as in 1522, that dignitary was an old friend. He would even urge war against popes, as he did the second Medici pope, Clement VII, in 1527. In his early days he had quite radical views about Church reform. He read with apparent pleasure such destructive dialogues on the papacy as those of Alfonso de Valdés, a brilliant new secretary from Cuenca.

Valdés was a public servant of quality. He was in 1522 still merely a notary in Gattinara's office, but he would soon become controller-general of the entire secretariat. He had been a protégé of Peter Martyr and had a quasi-religious enthusiasm for Erasmus. His dialogue, *Mercury and Charon*, written at the end of the 1520s, relates how the first-named thought that the fact that all Christendom seemed to be at war was the consequence of the machinations of the emperor's enemies. But Mercury's reflections were constantly interrupted by the arrival of souls ferried across the river Styx by Charon. These souls were mostly ignorant, not evil, and were astonished to find themselves on the way to damnation after a life of nothing worse than conventionality. Perhaps Valdés was influenced when choosing his subject by the great painting of Charon crossing the Styx by the Flemish master Joachim Patinir, a few years before?[52] It was a rare example of a classical theme at the service of Christianity.

Valdés wrote, as an Erasmian, not against the principles of Christianity but against the Church and the Curia. He looked on himself as the proselytizing counsellor of the monarch, the *Erasmista* who sought to convert his master into an enlightened despot.[53] Rebellion against bad kings was always necessary. Meantime Charles had obtained a great concession from the papacy, in the bull *Eximiae devotionis affectus* of 1523, which gave him and his successors as kings of Spain the right of presentation and patronage of all archbishops and bishops of Spain and its empire.[54]

Charles always had a tolerant side: even in his last will, written at a time when pain and exhaustion caused him to seem unbending, he would suggest that inquisitors should be given canonries and thus not have to live off goods confiscated from accused persons.[55] He often seemed an Erasmian inclined to compromise with the Reformation: in theology, he was prepared to yield on the matter of the articles of the faith, the doctrine of justification, the use of the chalice for the laity – even the idea of marriage for priests.[56] But he never wanted it to seem that he had been advised to these things by people such as Valdés. He always thought that the popes were mistaken not to interest themselves in the internal reform of the Church which his preceptors in Flanders had taught him was necessary and which most German princes, including most Catholics, wished to see.

As for the Church in Spain, Charles would soon appreciate the 'tremendous efficacy' of the power of the Inquisition at the service of the Church and the Crown. Charles came to realize the benefit of a tribunal which sought to guarantee the unity of the Christian faith, thus making possible the secular utopia of the universal Christian empire. But in 1522 that was not so; he was unenthusiastic about the institution and remembered that his father, Philip, had toyed with the idea of its abolition and had requested Pope Leo X to finish it off. Then he appears to have thought that the Inquisition could be put to good use.[57] Presumably it was for that reason that in September 1523 he confirmed the remarkable appointment to the position of *inquisidor-general* of an old friend, an Erasmian, Alonso Manrique de Lara, the half-brother of the great poet Jorge Manrique, author of those most famous lines: 'Our lives are rivers/which flow out at the sea/which is death/there go their lordships/whose rights end there.'[58]

Bishop of Badajoz in 1499, Alonso Manrique spent much of his time converting Muslims to Christianity, many of whom took the name of Manrique. Imprisoned by King Fernando as 'destructive', he eventually succeeded in reaching Flanders, where he attached himself to Charles's court. There he presided at the mass in 1516 in the cathedral church of St Gudule in Brussels which preceded the acclamation of Charles as king of Spain. Befriended by Cardinal Cisneros (Regent of Spain in 1516), who saw him as a responsible Spaniard, he was translated to the diocese of Córdoba, where he took the memorable initiative of inspiring the construction of a Christian cathedral in the centre of the great Mezquita. There he went out of his way to encourage Magdalena de la Cruz, prioress of the Clarisas, who claimed surprising gifts of communication with saints. At Corunna in 1520, he was named chief chaplain of the emperor, and was part of the delegation with the emperor at his coronation in Aachen in October of that year.

Manrique was following Charles's ideas in these actions despite the opposition of his new confessor, the Dominican García de Loaisa. In his last years, however, Charles regretted having given a safe conduct to Luther at the Diet of Worms, the last major discussion between Protestants and Catholics, in 1520 and would murmur in Spanish 'Muerto el perro, muerta la rabia' ('If you kill the dog, you finish with rabies too').[59] He allowed García de Loaisa and other conventional prelates to push Manrique de Lara to one side, persuading him to devote all his time to his archbishopric of Seville and leaving the business of the Inquisition for the council to manage.[60]

Already in 1522 people talked constantly to Charles of his need to marry. An heir was necessary. It seems possible, however, that he had a mistress in Spain in the surprising shape of Germaine de Foix, the improbably young widow of his grandfather Fernando the Catholic. Had not that grandfather requested in his will that Charles should concern himself with her? The conclusion that there was at the least an *amitié amoureuse* between the two was argued by Fernández Álvarez, while Lorenzo Vital recalled that the emperor had a little wooden bridge made from his lodgings to hers which enabled him to visit her secretly.[61]

In 1522, after Charles had left Flanders, a girl whom he had lightheartedly seduced in the Netherlands, Joanna van der Gheest, daughter of a tapestry-maker of Oudenaarde, gave birth to a baby girl, who was recognized by her father as his daughter. This was the future Margaret of Parma who, having been looked after and educated by her namesake the archduchess, would thirty years later become Regent in Brussels.

Two other girls were apparently born to Charles at this time: first, Juana de Austria, daughter of one of the ladies attached to Henry of Nassau, who would be brought up in the convent of Augustinians in Madrigal de las Altas Torres and remain a nun there; and second, Tadea, an Italian daughter of Orsolina della Penna, 'the beauty of Perugia', who reached the imperial court of Brussels in 1522, and later lived in Rome, being still alive in 1562.[62] There is also a possibility that Isabel, daughter of Germaine de Foix, King Fernando's widow, was the child of the emperor. She was still living in 1536.[63]

Charles was an astonishing figure. None of his predecessors had his ambitions. His grandfather Maximilian was a Renaissance prince and revelled in his Burgundian antecedents, but he was no intellectual statesman, rather he was a German politician. Charles was a multinational king served by Savoyards such as Gattinara. He was the dominant statesman of his time and took his grandeur for granted. The New World seemed something that he deserved and needed, but he was not surprised by it. New Spain seemed a natural development.

3

Cortés and the rebuilding of Mexico/Tenochtitlan

I assure your Caesarian majesty that these people are so turbulent
that at any novelty or opportunity for sedition, they rebel.

Letter from Cortés to Charles V, 1524

Hernando Cortés's life was triumphant in a way that has rarely been known by any captain of men.[1] Cortés, who looked on himself as Charles's agent, had both discovered and conquered a great empire: a regime marked by a sophisticated culture allied to barbarism. In 1522 he was the commander of a small successful Spanish army of about 2,000 men, which had the assistance of numerous native allies who relished the chance of rebellion and revenge against their old suzerains, the Aztecs (the Mexica).[2] He was surrounded by a praetorian guard of about 500 horsemen and 4,000 foot, all the latter being Indians.[3] He had no title to any command but nevertheless had all power in the ruins of the old Mexican capital, Tenochtitlan, which became generally referred to as 'Mexico' in 1524. The New World was an echo of the old: Cortés was a great European commander who conquered a new people. He gave the place the name 'New Spain', no less, which would remain with it for 300 years.

His chief captains – the Alvarado brothers; Gustavo de Sandoval; Andrés de Tapia; Francisco Verdugo; Ponce de León's son, Juan González Ponce de León; Alonso de Ávila; the captain of his bodyguard, Antonio Quiñones – were his political subordinates as well as his military deputies. One or two of these commanders had good connections in Spain: for example, Jerónimo Ruiz de la Mota was the first cousin of the Emperor Charles's preceptor, the bishop of Palencia; and Bernardino Vázquez de Tapia was the nephew of a member of the Council of Castile,

Pedro Vázquez de Oropesa. Several of Cortés's best connected commanders had returned to Spain to spread news of what he had done: Francisco de Montejo of Salamanca, for example, and Alonso Hernández Portocarrero, a cousin of the Count of Medellín and a nephew of Cespedes, the judge of the exchange market in Seville; and Diego de Ordaz of León, who had returned to Spain the previous year, in search of preferments of his own.

Cortés knew that what he had done was astonishing, and he had begun to conduct himself in the shadow of Alexander the Great, Julius Caesar and even the Argonauts. The defeated Mexica had been humbled, and several members of the late Emperor Montezuma's family had accepted the Spaniards as their new rulers. Montezuma's son, Don Pedro Montezuma, who must be supposed to have been his heir, and his daughter, Doña Isabel, whose Mexican name was Techuipo, were the foremost of these collaborators. There was also Cihuatcoatl (his secondary name was Tlacotzin), the majordomo of the old government, who was now working with Cortés in the ruined city of Tenochtitlan. The other defeated rulers of old Mexico, such as the monarch of Tlacopan and Tacuba, Tetlepanquetzaltzin, along with his colleague, the monarch of Texcoco, Ixtlilxochitl, and above all the tragic Cuauhtémoc, Montezuma's successor as the ruler of Tenochtitlan, were prisoners of Cortés. Cuauhtémoc had been tortured in the immediate aftermath of the Spanish victory by the royal treasurer, Julián de Alderete, to make him reveal the whereabouts of hidden gold and other treasure, and Cortés had accepted that, for he badly needed something to offer his victorious but restless fellow conquistadors. But he does not seem to have initiated the cruelty.

Cortés was the despot of the new territory which he had conquered. A great many people had died in the fighting between May and August 1521, mostly Mexican natives, but perhaps 500 Spaniards as well. That had not been Cortés's intention: he had wanted control, power, authority, not bloodshed nor massacre.[4] He had thought that he could overwhelm the empire of the Mexica by kidnapping its ruler and that Charles the emperor would rule New Spain through Montezuma. This scheme had been made impossible by Pánfilo de Narváez, Cortés's rival, and fighting began between Indians and Spaniards after Pedro Alvarado thought he could prevent an Indian uprising by striking first. In the event he brought the rising on.

In early 1522 Cortés was still awaiting a reaction from Charles to the news of his astonishing victory, details of which he had sent by letter – a manuscript letter, like everything from the Indies.[5] The delay was not surprising since, though the surrender of Tenochtitlan had been on 13 August 1521, a report of the final conquest of the Mexica did not reach Spain till March 1522.[6] Charles was still in the Low Countries and did not return to Spain till the summer of that year.

Cortés had planned that his report would be accompanied not only by Alonso de Ávila; his secretary, Juan de Ribera; and the chief of his bodyguard, Quiñones, but by a substantial treasure seized from the Mexica: 50,000 pesos in gold, of which the Crown would receive 9,000, many large pearls, much jade, several obsidian mirrors framed in gold and even three jaguars. There were also many presents of mosaics made of woven feathers, turquoise, cloaks, cotton cloths, painted maps, ornamental shields, and elaborately constructed parrots and crickets of gold or silver. These were all to go to friends of Cortés, to Spanish officials, to noblemen and sacred places – both monasteries and churches. Many conquistadors would take the opportunity to send gold to their relations back in Spain. Most promising of presents in the long run perhaps was a rubber ball, such as used by the Indians in their strange but elaborate wall games, which would constitute one of the Americas' most notable gifts to the Old World. Alas, much of this treasure was seized between the Azores and Spain by French adventurers led by the piratical Jean Florin, acting on behalf of his master, Jean Ango, and the expedition home also suffered other setbacks.[7]

Before Cortés's detailed account in a 'third letter' reached the court, however, in November 1522, Charles the king and emperor had made several critical decisions. After the emperor's meeting with the members of the Council of Castile who had come to deal with matters relating to the Indies, Cortés was, on 11 October 1522 (that is, a month before his report arrived), named *adelantado* – commander-in-chief with pro-consular responsibilities – *repartidor* (distributor) of Indians and also governor and captain-general of New Spain. That seemed to represent a political triumph for Cortés, since it formally released him from any subservience to his old master, the governor of Cuba, Diego Velázquez. It was also a victory since it accepted Cortés's grand name for the new land, 'New Spain' – a designation which indicated the supranational character of this new monarchy of Castile. It seemed too to give Cortés complete command: 'governor' and 'captain-general' were substantial titles.[8]

The territory covered by Cortés's appointment was, however, vague; no one knew where his dominions began and ended.[9] But it was assumed that at the least he would control the allies who had helped him so much in his conquest; not just the lords of the valley of Mexico who had been liberated from the yoke of the Mexica but also the Totonaca and the Tlaxcalteca and most of the 500 other tribes established in the mainland of old Mexico.

A decree issued four days after his main instructions told Cortés about the proper treatment of the Indians and talked of grants of government money to finance representatives (*procuradores*) to represent New Spain in Castile.[10] This decree had the advantage of accepting Cortés's view of the coming of Narváez to New Spain in 1520: 'the journey of Pánfilo de Narváez and his fleet was the reason for the rebellion and temporary loss of the great city of Tenochtitlan-Mexico ...'[11] Charles also wrote warmly to Cortés, praising his achievements.[12] The latter could no longer complain about a lack of appreciation at home, though these royal communications and the emperor's letter did not reach New Spain till September 1523. This was partly because of the curiously dilatory conduct of the messengers, Cortés's cousins, Rodrigo de Paz and Francisco de las Casas, who took an unconscionably long time to set off and decided to travel via Cuba, where they took the bad news of the success of 'Cortesillo', as Cortés was called there, to Diego Velázquez. He was naturally distressed.

The Emperor Charles accompanied his praise for Cortés and his acceptance of him as his governor in New Spain with the nomination of four officials whose task would be to 'assist' Cortés in the administration of the new provinces: a treasurer, Alfonso de Estrada; a factor, or general administrator of the new empire, Gonzalo de Salazar; an inspector of administration, Pedro Álvarez de Chirino; and an accountant, Rodrigo de Albornoz.

These men were important. Estrada had been in Flanders, admiral at Málaga and then *corregidor* (representative of the government) in Cáceres. He was a permanent councillor in his native city, Ciudad Real. He boasted that he was an illegitimate son of the late King Fernando – and perhaps he was. Salazar was a Granadino, but his family was originally from Burgos. He had been an attendant in the royal household and went to New Spain with quite a retinue. Álvarez de Chirino came from Úbeda and was seen as the agent of the principal royal secretary, Francisco de Cobos, who now dominated that city politically and socially. The fourth official, Rodrigo de Albornoz, was probably from Pardiñas, Lugo, and appears to have held some minor position in the court of Spain. He was asked by the Italian courtier Peter Martyr, who still advised the king on matters relating to the Indies though he was nearly eighty, to send home reports by cipher on Cortés's activities. Martyr once talked of Cortés's craftiness, his avarice and his 'partially revealed tyranny'.[13]

The nomination of these four courtly men to New Spain certainly showed that the Crown was taking the conquests of Cortés seriously. Yet they were obviously intended to control that conqueror and prevent him from undue assertion of his own authority. But these councillors, like Paz and Las Casas before them, took a long time to reach the new province. Long before they arrived, Cortés had embarked on his magnificent work of art, Spain's greatest achievement in the Americas in the sixteenth century, the rebuilding of the city of Mexico/Tenochtitlan.[14]

Cortés had been advised by some of his friends and fellow conquistadors to rebuild the capital of New Spain in a place removed from the lake of Tenochtitlan, say at Tacuba or Coyoacán. They had learned that the old capital was exposed to the dangers of flooding, which had occurred on a large scale in 1502. Since the environs were swampy, there would always be difficulties with water supply. The critics argued that Coyoacán would be a more suitable site for a capital, as Cortés had surely appreciated since he had established his residence there on the southern shores of the lake in a large, cool, spacious mansion built for him immediately after his victory in 1521.[15] But in January 1522 Cortés went ahead with his plan to rebuild on the old site regardless. Some of his enemies thought that he must be trying to arrange defences in order to resist any attempt to detach him from power. The motive behind Cortés's decision, however, was that he did not want to leave the legendary site of Tenochtitlan as a monument to past glory. The Indians wanted to rebuild too, and a good workforce could therefore be easily assembled.

The essential part in the reconstruction was played by a 'geometrician' named Alonso García Bravo, who had been born in Rivera, on the road between Málaga and Ronda in Andalusia, and had educated himself in matters of town planning even before he left Castile in 1513 with Pedrarias (Pedro Arias Dávila). He reached New Spain with the expedition of Francisco de Garay and subsequently joined Cortés's army. He took part in several battles as a conquistador, but then went to Villa Rica, Veracruz, having been asked to design the fortress planned for that town – two storeys, said Andrés de Rozas, a Burgalés, in evidence to an inquiry into the life and achievements of García Bravo.[16]

The success of García Bravo's building at Veracruz led Cortés to ask him to direct the reconstruction of Tenochtitlan.[17] Bravo went up to the capital in the summer of 1522 and studied the ground with Cortés himself, inspecting the damage done to a city that had been fought over fiercely. To prevent the Indians dropping rocks on his men from above, Cortés had ordered the destruction of lines of two-storey buildings, sometimes with the use of artillery. But, though the two main shrines of ancient Mexico, in the heart of Tenochtitlan and in Tlatelolco, had been badly damaged, the causeways, the main streets and the remains of many buildings were all evident.

García Bravo's first commission was to build a fortress with two towers, at the eastern end of the city, adjacent to the ruins of the old *templo mayor*. This was a lacustrine station called Atarazanas where Cortés could keep his thirteen brigantines, built under the direction of the clever but embittered Sevillano Manuel López, which had played such an important part in assuring the Spanish victory over the Mexica. The towers were built under the supervision of Cihuacoatl, now a rather improbable collaborator with the victors: one, high, had lodgings within it; the other was designed to shelter the boats. Cortés's enemies later argued, foolishly, that the construction of the towers was an act directed against the royal power.

In planning the main reconstruction, García Bravo proposed to accept the basic structure of the old Mexican city with its walled centre, which in the past had contained the sacred precinct with a great pyramid, which could be seen from all sides, and its sanctuaries. The sacred precinct was approached by three causeways – to the north, the west and the south; to the east, there was no communication with the mainland. The causeway to the north was planned for aesthetic reasons since the direct way (via Tepeyac, now the site of the shrine to the Virgin of Guadelupe) would have been a parallel road a little to the east. To the south, beyond the walls of the city, there was a large marketplace where

Indian buyers and sellers were busy within days of the conquest on 13 August 1521.

Around this open space there were the palaces of the old noblemen. Within the walls, in the past the streets had often been of water, in the Venetian style. In the centre, those canals were straight, though, as in Europe, there were twisted ways beyond the grand heart of the city. To the north of the sacred precinct, outside the walls, the city of Tlatelolco had its own large market and the remains of its pyramid. Perhaps Santa Fe, the artificial city built outside Granada by Fernando and Isabel in 1491, was an inspiration for the new city of Cortés and García Bravo, though it was smaller.[18]

If the great temples of Tenochtitlan and Tlatelolco were in ruins, that was not true of many others. Fifteen years later, in 1537, the bishops of Mexico, Guatemala and Oaxaca wrote to Charles the emperor in Spain to say that many Indians were still using their old temples for prayer and worship, though not for sacrifice, which had come to an abrupt end in 1521. Cortés permitted the old worship to continue though he would encourage the proselytization by, first, the Franciscans, and then the Dominicans. The bishops asked the king for support for the destruction of those buildings and the burning of any idols within them, and for an agreement that the stones of the old temples be used for making new churches. The king, or the Council of the Indies, wrote back the following year that indeed these buildings should be destroyed 'without scandal' and the idols should be burned. The stone of the old temples should certainly be used for building churches.[19]

Cortés decided to preserve the two main palaces of Montezuma as government buildings, one as the national palace, where he, the viceroys and, even later, the presidents of independent Mexico would live and have their offices. The other, which he had used as his headquarters in the happy months in the city from November 1519 to July 1520, would become the national pawnshop. In addition, he and García Bravo made an important decision: in the heart of the city there would be a Spanish quarter, where the conquistadors and *pobladores* (the name usually given to later arrivals) would be allotted plots on which to build or reconstruct substantial houses, following the so-called '*traza*', a word meaning 'plan'. Between 1524 and 1526, in consequence, the town council of Mexico/Tenochtitlan allocated 234 *solares* (plots), as well as 201 orchards or gardens in the city.

Beyond the *traza*, the old Indian districts would be maintained without change, even if they would receive a Christian prefix to their names: they would henceforth be San Juan Moyotlan, Santa María Cuepopan, San Sebastián Atzacualco and San Pablo Zoquipán. Each of these districts would have a church, an *'iglesia de visita'* as the expression was, under the direction of Franciscans, who, from 1522, had their headquarters in a large straw-roofed building a block away from the causeway to Tacuba, the future convent of San Francisco. Each of these Indian quarters would be governed much as in the past by a local 'elder' referred to by the conquerors as a *'señor'*. Meantime, Tlatelolco would be left to its own devices, as a separate town under a new name, 'Santiago'.

Rebuilding of the district within the *traza* began in the summer of 1522. García Bravo tried to ensure that water would be piped to every dwelling, that all houses would be built according to a pattern, and that all major roads would be fifteen *varas* wide.[20] The layout of old canals would be approximately followed though some would be re-dug, while others would be filled in.

García Bravo was assisted in these arrangements by a well-born conquistador, Bernardino Vázquez de Tapia. Born in Torralba near Oropesa, Vázquez de Tapia was the nephew of Francisco Álvarez, abbot of Toro and *inquisidor* of Castile. His father was on the Royal Council of Castile.

The Franciscan monk Motolinía thought that 400,000 Mexica were working in the city in 1524 under the direction of the high priest Tlacotzin, who had by then assumed the name of 'Juan Velázquez' in preference to his Mexican designation. More people, Motolinía asserted, worked there 'than those who had worked on the building of the temple of Jerusalem'.[21] They included many from the nearby town of Chalco, in the valley, who were specialists in building and plastering and whose ancestors had probably worked on the original construction of the great city. Several secondary architects came to work under García Bravo, such as Juan Rodríguez, whose task was to adapt Montezuma's palace to serve Cortés.

Prominent Mexica such as Montezuma's son, Don Pedro Montezuma, helped the Spaniards to recruit the workers. Motolinía recalled the latter singing and chanting, which had been the usual procedure in the old days during all such building projects, 'all day and all night (*los cantos y voces apenas cesaban ni de noche ni de día*)'.[22] The historian of imperial architecture George Kubler pointed out that, however distressed the Indians might have been at their defeat, they were delighted, and probably won over, by the new mechanisms brought to New Spain by the conquerors – mostly the consequence of the wheel – such as pulleys, carts and wheelbarrows, and also mules and nails, chisels and iron hammers. To have a beast of burden constituted a wonderful revolution in technology, but the nail seemed almost as important, while the pulley had a special fascination.[23] These were the stupendous contributions which Spain made to the technology of the New World.

By the summer of 1523 a new city was taking shape. For political reasons the place needed to be grand and imposing, for it had to reflect the power required and acquired by both conquerors and conquered. Mexico/Tenochtitlan had not been a mere pavement of mud huts, it had been a great city of a European size – a capital of a kind that Spain itself did not yet have. Throughout the year, the surroundings of the city were alive with workers carrying cut stone and large tree trunks. The striking arches in the great square were beginning to be admired because the European arch which the ancient Mexica had never known was now to be seen everywhere in the capital.

By early 1524 one could see the beginnings of monasteries and churches too, chapels crowned with cupolas, as well as private houses with battlements and buttresses, nail-studded doors and grilled windows. A temporary cathedral was under way. Already the trees of orchards could be seen rising over walls. A gibbet and pillory, reminders of civilization in one sense, were not forgotten.

Cortés was accused by his critics of having been interested primarily in building palaces for his followers. But, by 1526, thirty-seven churches were also being erected.[24] One of Cortés's secretaries, Juan de Ribera, a rather unreliable Extremeño, probably from Badajoz and possibly a cousin, who had come first to New Spain as a notary with Pánfilo de Narváez, would give an account to Peter Martyr of the great effort in New Spain of the master conquistador: 'he is striving at this moment to restore the ruins of the great lake city damaged in the war: the aqueducts have been revived, the destroyed bridges and many ruined houses have been rebuilt and, little by little, the city is taking on its former appearance'. Ribera added that the old commercial life had also recovered: markets and fairs could be seen again, 'boats come and go as actively as before; and the multitude of traders seems to be as great as during the time of Montezuma'.[25] In addition, two hospitals had been built, one specifically for lepers – San Lázaro near Tlaxpana – and one for all other diseases.[26]

Soon after the great business of the restoration of Tenochtitlan had begun, Cortés wrote another letter to the Emperor Charles, expressing his distress that his previous letters had received no answer, and explaining that, in the circumstances, he had been 'almost forced' to grant *encomiendas* to his fellow conquistadors because of his need to do something for those who had helped to achieve the great victory over the Mexica. He could not unfortunately offer them gold or pearls enough to retire to Spain! He had discussed the matter with his captains, including, we assume, such beneficiaries of his decisions as the Alvarados, Tapia and Sandoval. He commented: 'I entreat Your Majesty to approve.'[27]

Encomienda was a medieval term, indicating not a grant of land but a grant by the governor, or captain-general, of the labour and tribute of a certain number of Indian natives, *naturales*, living in a specific place. There were precedents in the reconquest of Spain from the Muslims, and the scheme had been used in the Spanish dominions of the Caribbean. Several of Cortés's men had been its beneficiaries in Hispaniola or in Cuba, in some cases both. The grant of an *encomienda* satisfied the desire of conquistadors for a lordship. It did not indicate territory but in some circumstances led to it. The *encomienda* would have a controversial history throughout the sixteenth century since the Crown soon wanted to argue that the grant applied only to one generation; the *encomenderos* wanted it for several generations if not indefinitely.

The first *encomendero* in New Spain appeared in April 1522: a relatively unknown conquistador, Gonzalo de Cerezo, who, though he had gone to New Spain with Narváez, had become a page of Cortés. He received the *encomienda* of the important town of Cholula and had helped to carry wood from Tlaxcala to Texcoco to make Martín López's brigantines. Later, he made a fortune in commerce and played a significant part in the early life of the colony.[28] Other early *encomenderos* were the golden-haired leader Pedro de Alvarado, who obtained the *encomienda* of Xochimilco; Francisco de Montejo (actually then in Spain), who was granted the rich silversmiths' town of Azcapotzalco; and Alonso de Ávila, who accompanied Cortés's letter of 22 May to Spain and was captured by the French on the high seas; he received Cuauhuitlan, Zumpango and Xaltocan. Cortés allowed himself Coyoacán, the builders' town of Chalco, Ecatepec and Otumba, the scene in 1520 of a great battle.

An essential activity in these early days was the Spanish attempt to implicate numerous leaders of old Mexico in their plans. Thus Cortés gave the ancient city of Tula to Pedro, son of Montezuma. Tacuba with 1,240 houses and several hundred *naturales* went to Isabel, Montezuma's daughter and an ex-mistress of Cortés.[29] It was understood that the surviving monarchies and leaders in society would be accepted as such by the conquerors, provided they did not direct themselves against the Christian religion.[30] This rule would be observed for many years in the empire. The indigenous lords would have to accept the absolute prohibition of polygamy and of human sacrifice. *Encomenderos* would have the right to the labour of the people in the place concerned, and receive appropriate produce. In return, the *encomendero* would concern himself with the religious life of the people in his district. He would not live there, but in a plot in Mexico/Tenochtitlan allocated to him within García Bravo's *traza*. Here was the link between the urban and agricultural arrangements in New Spain which reflected what had been done in the Caribbean colonies (Hispaniola, Cuba, Puerto Rico and Jamaica) and in Pedrarias's domain in Darien and Panama. These plans would be copied elsewhere in the Spanish empire in South America.

In 1522 Cortés sent back to Spain a map of Tenochtitlan which was published in the Latin editions of his second and third letters to Charles V. It had, some modern authors point out, both fantastical and realistic features. This Latin production was completed in Nuremberg, the capital of German printing at that time. It was 'a capricious representation of the Aztec capital' in the style of the so-called 'islands' in the *Isolario*, in which there were illustrations of the most famous islands in the world. Benedetto Bordon produced at least four editions after one in Venice in 1528. In one there was a plan of Tenochtitlan deriving from Cortés's map.[31] We are approaching the era of good maps after all.

4

Christianity and the New World

The people owe you much but you owe them everything. Even if your ears have to hear the proud titles of 'invincible,' 'inviolable,' and 'majesty' ... do not acknowledge them, but refer them all to the Church to which alone they belong.

Erasmus, *Enchiridion*

In his third letter to the Emperor Charles, which reached Spain in November 1522, Cortés sent a request for more churchmen to be sent to New Spain. At that time there were still only four there: two secular priests, Fr Juan Díaz, of Seville, who had been on Cortés's expedition throughout, and Fr Juan Godínez, and two monks, Fray Pedro Melgarejo de Urrea, a Franciscan, also from Seville, and Fray Bartolomé de Olmedo, a Mercedarian from near Valladolid. A little later Fray Diego de Altamirano, a Franciscan and a cousin of Cortés, and Fray Juan de Varillas, another Mercedarian, perhaps from his name also a distant cousin of Cortés, arrived in New Spain. They had, as they knew, multiple responsibilities.

The request in the letter of Cortés for further friars to be sent was supplemented by another letter signed also by Cortés, Fray Melgarejo and Alderete, the treasurer. After speaking of the good services which Cortés and all the conquistadors had performed: 'We besought His Majesty to send us bishops and clerics from every order that are of good life and sound doctrine that they might aid us to establish more firmly our Holy Catholic Faith in these parts.' The writers went on to request the king to grant the government of New Spain to Cortés for he was 'such a good and loyal servant of the Crown'. The letter ended on a wise note: 'We beg him also not to send us lawyers because by coming to this land they would put it in turmoil . . .' Such direct language was characteristic of the time. The letter writers also hoped that Bishop Fonseca would not 'meddle' any more in Cortés's affairs and that Governor Velázquez in Cuba would be arrested and sent back to Spain.[1]

Christianity had, of course, been engaged in the conquest of the Indies from the beginning. The Cross was the symbol of conquest as well as of conversion. Columbus had had priests on his second voyage,[2] and priests accompanied most of the conquistadors in the West Indies. There were two bishops in Santo Domingo by 1512, a third in Puerto Rico, and another bishop, Fray Juan de Quevedo, was appointed to Panama in 1513. Quevedo had taken a good suite of priests and canons. His remarkable argument with Las Casas in the presence of King Charles has been amply described.[3] So have the controversies in Santo Domingo following the marvellous sermon of Fray Antonio de Montesinos. The conquistadors were in some ways the reincarnation of those Spaniards who recovered Spain itself from the Moors; but they also saw themselves winning new lands for Christianity against the natural allies of the sixteenth-century Muslims.[4] The pope's decision to grant rights in Africa and the Indian Ocean in the fifteenth century to Portugal and to allocate to Spain a new zone of influence in the Indies had given the frame to all the conquests. In a bull of July 1508 Pope Julius II gave King Fernando the right to appoint bishops to all cathedrals and to present other ecclesiastical benefices.

In 1517 Cardinal Cisneros, Regent of Spain, received a letter from Las Casas suggesting that the Inquisition be sent to the Indies.[5] Cisneros agreed. The pope made concessions. First, Alonso Manso, bishop of Puerto Rico, was named *inquisidor-general* of the Indies. The bishop had been *sacristán mayor* at the court of the Infante Juan in the 1490s and had ever since been a protégé of Archbishop Deza. Then the bull *Alias felicis recordationis* of 25 April 1521 gave a licence to two Franciscans to go to New Spain: Fray Francisco de los Ángeles (really Quiñones), a brother of the Count of Luna in Seville, and Fray Jean Glapion of Flanders, the emperor's confessor. But they did not carry through the assignment because the former became general of his order and the brilliant Glapion died in Valladolid before he could arrange his voyage.

So in 1523, three other Franciscans went to Mexico/Tenochtitlan: Johannes Dekkus, Johann van der Auwern (Juan de Ayora) and Pedro de Gante.[6] The first-named had once been a subsidiary confessor to the emperor, as well as a professor of theology in Paris. He had taken the place of Fray Jean Glapion at Bruges. The second claimed to have Scottish forebears and was even said to be an illegitimate son of King James III of Scotland.

Fray Pedro de Gante was born about 1490 in Ayghem, a part of Ghent near the abbey of St Pieter. He never mentioned the names of his parents but was perhaps the illegitimate son of the Emperor Maximilian. He wrote to the Emperor Charles in 1546: 'Your Majesty and I know how close we are and how the same blood runs in our veins' and in 1552 did so again in similar style. After Fray Pedro's death in 1572, Fray Alonso de Escalona, provincial of the Franciscans, would tell King Philip of Spain that he had been 'a very close relation of your most Christian father, thanks to which we had been able to receive many and large grants'.[7] The way that letter is phrased rather suggests that Fray Pedro was a brother of Charles, and we know for certain of two illegitimate sons of Maximilian, both bishops in their maturity.[8]

Pedro de Gante studied at the University of Louvain, then became a lay brother at the Franciscan monastery of Ghent where he spent several years. He left there in 1522 with the emperor, his supposed brother or nephew, and in May of the following year embarked for New Spain where he and his two comrades arrived on 13 August 1523, the second anniversary of the conquest of Mexico/Tenochtitlan. Perhaps his decision to go to the New World was influenced by the failure of Glapion to do so. He spent three years in Texcoco where he founded a school of San Francisco behind the chapel of San José. Here he developed workshops for blacksmiths, tailors, carpenters, cobblers, masons, painters, designers and candlestick-makers. This vocational work was of great importance for the Mexica.

Pedro remained in New Spain all his life and taught thousands of Mexicans how to read, sew and write. He deliberately fostered the fusion of Spanish and Indian ways. Thus, if he were to observe an Indian ceremony, he would compose a Christian song for it. He drew new patterns for Indian cloaks in a Christian dance: 'in this way, the Indians first came to show obedience to the Church'. Considered beautiful to look at by his innumerable friends, Habsburg or not, Pedro was a majestic figure, worthy of his alleged ancestry. He remained a lay brother and never accepted ordination and so never had a grand position. All the same, the second archbishop of Mexico, the Dominican Fray Alonso de Montúfar, would say that 'Pedro de Gante is archbishop of Mexico, not me.'

Several officials of the Inquisition were soon named for the New World. In 1523 the first *auto-de-fe* was celebrated in the Indies: Alfonso de Escalante was condemned in Santo Domingo. Escalante had been the notary of Santiago de Cuba, no less, where his house had been the site of the place's foundry. He had also been a witness in Diego Velázquez's investigation of 1519 into the conduct of Francisco de Montejo. All the same, he was burned as a practising Jew,[9] his execution preceded by the usual vile torments which marked the Inquisition at the time.

That same year Pope Adrian VI conferred special privileges on the Franciscans in the New World. Every three years they would be able to elect their own superior, who would have all the powers of a bishop except those of ordination. The consequence was the departure for New Spain of twelve further Franciscans early in 1524.

These men reached Santo Domingo in February, Cuba in March, and Veracruz on 13 May of that year and began to walk barefoot up to Mexico/Tenochtitlan. They were not just ordinary Franciscans but men from the province of San Gabriel in Extremadura, a reformed section of the order which sought to reflect in their lives the poverty of the evangelists, or of the first centuries AD. They were radical reformers, usually of good birth, whose principles caused them to clash with ordinary settlers. This millenarian sect had been founded by Juan de Guadalupe in the new monastery of Saint Francis in Granada in 1493. Soon there were six such monasteries, five in Extremadura and one in Portugal.

These new Franciscans were led to New Spain by Fray Martín de Valencia, from Valencia de Don Juan, some fifteen miles south of León on the banks of the river Escla, on the way to Benavente. He was fifty years of age when he reached New Spain and, though one of the most pious of men, did not have the ability to learn a new language. He strove to compensate for that by praying in public places so that, by imitating him, the Indians might come to God, because, as he himself said, 'the natives are very prone to do what they see others doing'. They were, that is, excellent mimics. All the same, he is said to have beaten Indians in order to hasten their learning which he considered too slow. Not long before his death, he thought that he ought to sail across the Pacific to seek 'men of great capacity in China'.[10]

Once while preaching in Spain of the conversion of infidels, he experienced a vision about a great multitude being converted. Exclaiming three times 'Praised be Jesus Christ', he was assumed by his brother Franciscans to have lost his senses and was locked up till he explained that his vision was leading him to a mission of conversion.[11]

The other Franciscans included Fray Luis de Fuensalida who, from his name, must also have come from Old Castile. He had a most humane view of the task ahead of him. He knew that Christianity was a creed for all the world, and those who refused to accept that fact were men who had never taken the trouble to learn any Indian language (a thrust, perhaps, at Fray Martín), had never preached to them nor confessed them. He praised the Indians' fear of God and seems to have considered that their piety exceeded in many respects that of Spaniards.[12] In order to catch the imagination of the Indians whose souls he desired to capture, he would one day write a play in Nahuatl, in the form of a dialogue between the Archangel Gabriel and the Virgin Mary. The archangel was depicted presenting the Virgin with letters from patriarchs in limbo asking her to receive her ambassadors. He was the first Spanish cleric to be able to preach in Nahuatl and was offered the bishopric of Michoacan, which, however, he declined.[13]

Fuensalida was the second-in-command of this remarkable expedition. He was a friend of Cortés, whose cause he supported in his *residencia*,[14] defending him against the accusations of, for example, the Dominican Fray Tomás de Ortiz who, like most members of his order, was an opponent of the captain-general.[15]

Of the other friars, the most interesting was Fray Toribio de Paredes, born in Benavente, from which place he took his name before assuming the name 'Motolinía', which signified 'poor man' in Nahuatl – he apparently heard himself being so referred to.[16] He was a clever, passionate and noble individual who expressed his admiration for old Mexico's grandeur but his repulsion for its religion. His walk made a great impression on him: 'some of the villages [in New Spain],' he said, 'are on the tops of mountains, others are on the floors of valleys, so religious people are obliged to climb up into the clouds and at times they must descend into the abyss. Since the country is rough, and because the humidity causes it to be covered in mud in many places, there are slippery places where it is easy to fall.'[17] Motolinía wrote extensively of his experiences, and both his *Memoriales* and his *Historia* remain of great value.[18]

The other Franciscans included the aged Francisco de Soto, the austere Fray Martín de la Coruña, the able Fray Juan Suárez, who became the first 'guardian' of the monastery of Huejotzingo, Fray Antonio de Ciudad Rodrigo, Fray García de Cisneros, who was the inspiration for the imaginative college of Tlatelolco, the jurist Fray Francisco Jiménez and two lay brothers, Fray Andrés de Córdoba and Fray Juan de Palos. These were great men who took a lead to ensure that New Spain became a glowing province of Christianity.

The twelve walked up barefoot to Mexico/Tenochtitlan. Cortés, however, had roads swept for them and huts were built whenever they wanted to sleep. The journey was disagreeable because the weather was hot, they were always crossing ravines or streams, while mosquitoes and snakes did not relax their attacks. These Franciscans went first to Tlaxcala and then, in mid-June, were received in Mexico/Tenochtitlan by Cortés on his knees, a gesture which much impressed the old Mexican rulers such as Cuauhtémoc who saw it. When they arrived, the twelve naturally attached themselves to the three other Franciscans who were already in the capital.

Soon afterwards, they held a general meeting, attended by probably all fifteen Franciscans then in New Spain. They agreed to build four houses (in Mexico, Texcoco, Tlaxcala and Huejotzingo) for which they would obtain the financial support necessary from the captain-general. Each would have four friars, and each would direct both teaching and conversion over a large territory.[19] These friars had already engaged in formal conversations with Mexican priests hoping to convert them. They had answered: 'Is it not enough that we have lost? That our way of living has been lost? That we have been annihilated? Do with us as you please. That is what we answer, our Lords, all that we reply to your words!'[20]

The only texts available about how this early instruction was carried out are the sermons preached by the Franciscans and some conversations reported by Fray Bernardino de Sahagún in his Florentine Codex.[21] The catechism proper is missing but the preliminary discourses are interesting. The friars said to the Mexican priests:

> Do not believe that we are gods. Fear not, we are men, as you are. We are merely the messengers of a great lord called the Holy Father who is the spiritual head of the world and who is filled with pain and sadness by the state of your souls. Yours are souls which He has charged us to seek out and to save. We desire nothing better and, for that reason, we bring you the book

of the Holy Scripture which contains the word of the only true God, the Lord of Heaven, whom you have never known. That is why we are here. We do not seek gold nor silver nor precious stones. We seek only your health.

You, on the other hand, say that you have a god whose worship has been taught you by your ancestors and your kings: is that not so? You have a multitude of gods, each with his own function. And you yourself recognize that those gods have deceived you. You insult them when you are unhappy, calling them whores and fools. And what they demand of you, in sacrifice, is your blood, your heart. The images [of those sacrifices] are loathsome. On the other hand, the true and universal God our Lord Creator and dispenser of being and of life . . . has a character different from your gods. He does not deceive. He does not lie. He hates no one. He despises no one. There is no evil in Him. He regards all wickedness with the greatest horror, forbids it and prevents it, for He is perfectly good. He is the deep well of all good things. He is the essence of love, compassion and mercy . . . Being God, He has no beginning and no end, for He is eternal. He created heaven and earth, and hell. He created for us all the men in the world and also all the devils whom you hold to be gods. The true God is everywhere. He sees all, He knows all. He is altogether admirable. As a man, He is in His royal palace and here below, on earth, He has His kingdom which He began with the beginning of the world. He would have you enter it now . . .

The Mexica replied by saying that it seemed unjust to call on them to abandon ceremonies and rites which their ancestors had praised and held to be good. They were not yet learned enough to discuss the propositions of the Franciscans, but they wanted to call together their priests and discuss the matter. When they did so, these priests 'were greatly troubled and felt sad and fearful and did not answer'. Next day, they returned and the leaders said that they were very surprised to hear the Franciscans claim that the Mexica's gods were not gods for their ancestors had always thought them so, had worshipped them as such, and they were the ones to teach their descendants to honour them, with sacrifices and ceremonies. It could be a folly to set aside ancient laws which had been introduced by the first inhabitants of these places. They thought that it would be impossible to persuade the older men to abandon their old customs. They threatened their own rulers with the wrath of the gods and said there would be a popular rising if the people were told that their gods were not gods. They repeated that it was difficult enough to have to admit defeat and they would prefer to die rather than have to give up their gods.[22]

In 1525 Tzintla, the Caltzontzin monarch in Tzintzuntzan, begged Fray Martín de Valencia to send him some friars. He did so, under Fray Martín de la Corunna, though Tzintla must have been shocked at Fray Martín's insistence on destroying his temples and his idols.

This was a harsh time. Christian opinion was divided. Several friars were optimistic about the possibilities of conversion, generous and patient (Pedro de Gante, Motolinía); others, like the first Dominican to come to New Spain, Fray Tomás de Ortiz, had opposing views. Fray Tomás testified to the Council of the Indies:

> the Indians are incapable of learning . . . They exercise none of the humane arts or industries . . . The older they are, the worse they behave. About the age of ten or twelve, they seem to have the elements of civilisation but, later, they become like brute beasts . . . God has never created a race more full of vice . . . the Indians are more stupid than asses.[23]

What seems evident is that all the main orders, the Augustinians as well as the Dominicans and Franciscans, were allies of the Crown in their frequent clashes with *encomenderos*.[24]

In 1525 Peter Martyr wrote in almost his last letter:

> To tell the truth we hardly know what decision to make. Should the Indians be declared free and we without any right to exact labour of them unless their work is paid? Competent people are divided on this point and we hesitate. It is chiefly the Dominican order who, by their writings, drive us to an adverse decision. They argue that it would be better, and would offer better security for both the bodily and spiritual good of the Indians, to assign them permanently and by hereditary title to certain masters . . . It may be shown by many examples that we should not consent to give them their liberty [for] these barbarians have plotted the destruction of Christians wherever they could.[25]

The frame of all these Christian activities was, of course, ultimately provided by Rome. Unusual things were occurring there at that time. Pope Adrian VI, the last non-Italian pope till John Paul II, reached the Vatican only on 29 August 1522. His first consistory caused astonishment. For the first expressed the hope that the Christian princes could unite against the Ottoman Turks. Then he turned to the Curia. He spoke as if he thought that, in all the palaces of the cardinals, iniquity reigned. He urged the cardinals to be content with an annual income of 6,000 ducats and generally rebuked the lifestyle of the Roman court.[26]

Alas, in December, the Ottomans captured the fortress of the knights of St John at Rhodes and the Grand Master was forced to surrender. Where would the Turks stop? The question seemed urgent. All the same, the states of Germany were reluctant to help. Adrian exclaimed: 'I should have died happy if I had united the Christian princes to withstand our enemy.' He added: 'Woe to princes who do not employ the sovereignty conferred on them by God in promoting his glory, and defending the people of His election, but abuse it in internecine strife.'[27] Adrian continued in that style. For example, in January 1523 he was denouncing Luther and his extraordinary posture in Germany: 'We cannot even think of anything so incredible that so great, so pious a nation should allow an apostate from the Catholic faith which for years he has preached, to seduce it from the way pointed out by the Saviour and his Apostles sealed by the blood of so many martyrs.'[28]

The swift reform of the Church was not to be: Adrian succumbed to a harsh illness in September 1523. Thirty-five cardinals quickly assembled in the Sistine Chapel, the French ones arriving in riding clothes. Who would the next successor to St Peter be? Wolsey? Or Giulio de' Medici – a nephew of Lorenzo de' Medici – who was believed to be the Emperor Charles's candidate and who indeed had been the favourite three years before? The conclave continued for several weeks. On this occasion the cardinals made no mistake about their choice of successor, and on 19 November Cardinal Medici, the favourite, was elected as Clement VII. The Duke of Sessa, son-in-law of the *Gran Capitán*, who was now imperial ambassador in Rome, commented a shade optimistically: 'The pope is entirely your Majesty's creature. So great is your Majesty's power that you can change stones into obedient children.'[29]

Neither Adrian nor Clement had a serious concern for the New World. They had to accept the nomination of bishops and Franciscan and other missions there, but they did not yet see the vast opportunities opening up there for Spain, for Europe and for Christendom. The nominations to sees had, of course, political consequences, as Charles the emperor knew better than anyone.

5

Charles at Valladolid

Here people believe that His Majesty wants to reform his council and his household (Aca se cree que SM quiere reformar sus consejos y sa casa)

Martin de Salinas to Francisco de Salamanca, treasurer of the Infante Fernando, Valladolid, 7 September 1522

Charles the emperor was in Valladolid for a year from September 1522 to August 1523 – an unusual immobility for a monarch not just used to travel but one who grew up in a world of journeys which his predecessors, Isabel and Fernando, had practised all their lives. Charles spent most of this time in the rambling palace of the Enríquez family, though twice, in September 1522 and in April 1523, he went down to Tordesillas to see his mother, the doomed Juana, in the convent of Santa Clara there. Once or twice, too, he went for a retreat from the world to the celebrated monastery of the Bernardines (Cistercians) at Valbuena del Duero, a day's ride to the east.

Charles had set about reforming the administration of his realm, first reordering the number of officials attached to the Council of State which was principally concerned with foreign affairs and depended in 1522 on an inner caucus headed by Gattinara, who was the motor of all administrative reforms.[1] Other members were Charles's gallant friend Henry of Nassau, who was Great Chamberlain in the Low Countries. Though light-hearted and charming personally, he it was who was responsible for introducing the rigid formalities of Burgundian ceremony into the Spanish court. He had commanded the imperial army in 1521 and accompanied Charles in 1522 to Spain, where he served as president of the new Spanish finance council. Despite becoming enormously fat, he married a Spanish heiress, Mencía de Mendoza, Marquesa de Cenete, one of the two sisters whom the Governor of Cuba, Diego Velázquez, would joke with his friends in Santiago de Cuba by saying he would one day wed. The wedding was a royal occasion in Burgos in June 1524. Mencía was well connected as well as very rich and had a famous salon in the Low Countries in the 1530s, encouraging Flemish painters and writers. The historian Oviedo spoke of her warmly as 'very cultivated, knowledgeable and gracious, an echo of the marquis her father whom no knight in Spain of the time could equal in good manners and benign disposition'.[2]

Charles consulted two other Burgundians frequently: Charles de Poupet, Lord of La Chaulx, and Gérard de la Plaine, Lord of La Roche. Poupet had been born in Burgundy's golden age, in 1460. He had served Philip the Handsome in Spain but most of his life was spent in Flanders. He was back in Spain to treat with Cardinal Cisneros, the regent, and then Adrian VI when he had just been named pope. He had already seen the positive qualities of the great Cortés.[3] He had been for a time a preceptor, as well as a member of Charles's inner council.

The Lord of La Roche, Gérard de la Plaine, had been in Germany to confirm Charles in his imperial title, had been in England as ambassador, and would soon join Henry of Nassau on the Castilian finance committee.[4] He was a grandson of Margaret of Austria's great friend Laurent de Gorrevod, who had been the lucky contractor of the African slave trade to the Spanish Indies in 1518, and was also a member of the Council of State.

The two Spanish members of Charles's inner circle in early 1522 were Bishop Ruiz de la Mota, a native of Burgos of *converso* origin, and Juan Manuel. The former had been chaplain and preacher to Queen Isabel and then in Flanders to the Emperor Maximilian. He had been a tutor of sorts to the Emperor Charles too. Back in Spain he had at a meeting of the Cortes in Santiago coined the phrase 'the new world of gold' to describe New Spain. Named bishop of the then rich diocese of Palencia, Ruiz de la Mota had little opportunity to enjoy being on the supreme council of the empire, for he caught a fever in England on his way back to Spain and died in Herrera de Pisuerga near Aguilar de Campoo in September 1522. Some say that he was poisoned. That was a setback for the interests of the Indies, for Ruiz de la Mota had a first cousin who was with Cortés at Tenochtitlan.[5]

Juan Manuel for his part had much property in Spain, including the fortress of Segovia. He was son of a counsellor of the same name who had worked for kings John II and Henry IV of Castile, and was a bastard member of the royal family. His first important post had been as ambassador of the Catholic Kings in 1495 to Philip the Handsome in Flanders, who married Juana *la Loca*. He worked to prevent the growth of French influence with the Habsburgs. He accompanied Philip to Spain in 1506 and was the architect of his triumph there. Then he remained in Flanders throughout Charles's childhood. Juan Manuel played his cards so successfully that he became the first Spaniard to be given the Order of the Golden Fleece. His patience in Flanders was rewarded when in 1520 he became imperial ambassador in Rome, where he helped to ensure the papacy of Adrian of Utrecht, with whom he was, however, on bad personal terms. Charles the emperor asked him to return to Spain, which he did in February 1523, and began to serve on the Council of Finance. The chronicler Jerónimo Zurita wrote of him that he was both 'valiant and astute and, although small of stature, full of imagination and a great wit, very discreet and a great courtier, of a sharpness so alive . . .'[6]

The Council of State which had responsibility for all Charles's kingdoms in the 1520s had upon it in 1519 six Flemings or Burgundians (Gattinara, Gorrevod, Plaine, Lannoy, Henry of Nassau and Charles de Poupet), or seven if one adds to the list the confessor-councillor Glapion. There were just two Castilians, Ruiz de la Mota and Juan Manuel. It is easy to understand that this large number of 'bureaucrats from Brussels' must have seemed an imposition in Spain. Even the secretary was a Saxon, Jean Hannart, who had worked for Maximilian as well as for Charles. In 1524 he was accused of corruption and replaced by a clever Burgundian, Juan Alemán, sieur de Bouclans, who assumed the role of controller-general of the realm of Aragon which gave him responsibility for Naples.[7] Charming and intelligent, despatching much work with alacrity, Alemán made himself indispensable to both Gattinara and Charles in 1522, when the former was away many months in Calais. Alemán and Gattinara had both served their time at the *parlement* of Dôle, the former as a mere clerk, the latter as president. By 1526, Alemán seems to have already become more a rival of Gattinara than a protégé.

This group of men with the two secretaries met every other Monday and was Charles's best source of advice. He would also see the members on other occasions, including at private meetings.

Castile was at that time governed by a series of councils, of which the Royal Council of Castile was the most important.[8] It met every Friday, as it had done in the time of King Fernando. The Flemings dominated the Council of State which concerned itself with foreign policy, the Council of Castile dealt with the detailed administration of Castile. It constituted the real government of the country – a cabinet, as it would be termed in a later age. The president in 1522 was the bishop of Granada, Antonio de Rojas y Manrique, from an important Castilian family which had members in Cuba and would have them later in Peru. Antonio de Rojas had been preceptor of the emperor's brother, the Infante Fernando, whom his grandfather and namesake, the king of Aragon, had seemed to favour as his heir. In 1522 Rojas was prominent among those seeking, in Gattinara's shadow, to improve the working of the administration. He earned particular attention in a report made by the meticulous Extremeño Galíndez de Carvajal, who wrote in 1522 that he was a faithful public servant, with clean hands and zealous of doing justice. Sometimes he was impatient and indignant, but, Galíndez commented: 'I believe one could not find a better man for the job which he has.'[9]

There were from 1523 or so seven other councils; that of War, which met every alternate Wednesday except when the country was actually in conflict; of the Inquisition; of the Military Orders; of Accountancy (*Contaduría Mayor*); and of Aragon. Then there was a council for raising money as well as spending it. This latter Council of Finance was new. Most of these bodies had in the 1520s some Flemish membership: for example, the president of the Council of Finance was Henry of Nassau. And finally, there was a Council of the Indies, a new committee which previously had been a group of councillors of the Council of Castile managed by Rodríguez de Fonseca, the omni-competent bishop of Burgos, but was now more formally independent. The date when this body began to have a separate function is not quite clear; but something close to such an institution was in being by 1520.[10] Nevertheless it never lost its close relation to the Council of Castile.

The first president of the Council of the Indies was not Rodríguez de Fonseca, who for so long had been the Crown's 'Minister for the Indies without the name',[11] but the general of the Dominicans, Fray García de Loaisa, who had succeeded Jean Glapion as confessor of the emperor. He was also bishop of El Burgo de Osma, a bleak town with a fine cathedral whose splendid grille had been recently paid for by the cardinal arch-bishop of Toledo, Alonso de Fonseca.

The other members of the Council of the Indies were Pietro Martire d'Anghiera, or Peter Martyr, the Italian humanist who in the 1490s had educated so many members of the Castilian nobility. He had always had a consuming interest in the Indies, and on his own insistence was the Vatican's chief informant on the subject in Spain; Luis Cabeza de Vaca, bishop of the Canary Islands; and Gonzalo Maldonado, bishop of Ciudad Real. Dr Diego Beltrán was the only full-time councillor.

It was these men, with Francisco de Cobos as secretary, who in these years took the critical decisions in respect of Spain's American empire. They named the governors (later the viceroys), approved new exped-itions (*entradas*) and decided on the salaries of judges. They appointed minor officials, listened to complaints and heard appeals. They gave themselves sinecures and benefits in the New World though no member of the council had any first-hand idea of what the Indies were really like. Francisco de Cobos was chief 'founder' of the Indies, an office which brought him a handsome salary. With his concern for foundries because of their financial implications to the state, Gattinara, the imperial chan-cellor, collaborated with enthusiasm from the beginning.[12]

Of these men the president was of course the most important. García de Loaisa is elusive and there is no biography of him.[13] Gattinara, who was not a good judge of men, had apparently suggested him for the office.[14] García de Loaisa came from Talavera de la Reina where his father, Pedro, had been a councillor and had studied in Salamanca, where he became *corregidor*. His mother was a Mendoza, though it does not seem that she derived from the main branch of that influential family. García de Loaisa early entered the Dominican order. He became prior of St Tho-mas in Ávila, the exquisite if simple church in which could be found the delicate white marble sepulchre of the Infante Juan, the only son of Fern-ando and Isabel, and Charles's uncle,[15] and then prior of the formidable San Pablo in Valladolid, the most remarkable of Dominican houses in Castile. García de Loaisa was general of the order by 1518.[16] His subse-quent success seems to have derived from his ability to win over rebel *comuneros* in 1521–2.[17] He was offered the archbishopric of Granada, and refused it – presumably because of the problems presented by the Muslim population. He settled for Burgo de Osma, which was then a rich diocese. But he was the chief preacher at court from 1523.

A tranquil, discreet and far from adventurous man, García de Loaisa had reprimanded his colleague, Fray Pedro de Córdoba, for allowing the famous sermons of Montesinos in Santo Domingo to be given (see *Rivers of Gold*, chap. 21). For the presidency of the Council of the Indies, he would be paid 200,000 maravedís a year. He had been for a time also *inquisidor-general*, when he aspired to reduce the Inquisition to its medieval size.[18] He lived at court and the meetings of the Council of the Indies were held in his lodging there. Of course, his work as the emperor's confessor enabled him to be well informed. The Austrian historian Pastor wrote of him that, though he was a great ecclesiastic and a man of 'high moral character, being full of energy and loyalty to the emperor', he was 'wanting in the qualities of statesmanship'. He showed 'a lack of consideration and a rigid hardness ... which gave general offence'. He had no tact, and would show his vehement nature even to the pope. But that was in the future. In 1524 he seemed an honest man, a contrast with his predecessor, Rodríguez de Fonseca, but he was also a churchman, at a time when bishops were thought to be the right men to rule empires.

García de Loaisa was firm to the point of intolerance about Protestantism. He was in no way an Erasmian and so found himself in opposition to such shining lights of the age as the humane archbishop Alonso de Manrique, who succeeded him as inquisitor in 1523, and to Alfonso de Valdés, the Erasmian secretary to Gattinara. He was brave in relation to his master the emperor. Thus he wrote to Charles deploring the fact that he, the emperor, 'had lowered himself to try to persuade heretics that they take account of their errors ... Your Majesty closes his eyes because you don't have force at your disposal to punish them.'[19] He later reflected rather bleakly about the Reformation: 'force alone suppressed the revolt against the king [the war of the *comuneros*]. Force alone will suppress the revolt against God.'[20] He once urged Charles

> to raise himself from the deep pits of sin to embark on a new book of conscience ... You should rest assured that God gives no one a kingdom without laying on him an even greater duty than on ordinary men to love Him and to obey his commands ... In your person indolence is perpetually at war with fame. I pray that God's grace will be with you in government and that you will be able to overcome your natural enemies, good living, and waste of time.[21]

Charles later wrote of García de Loaisa, perhaps appropriately in view of these last comments:

> he would do better to go back to his clerical duties rather than live at court. If his health were not so bad, he would have been outstanding in politics. He has always advised me very well. But his feeble health and his inability to get on with the Cardinal of Toledo [Tavera, for many years president of the Council of Castile] are two great drawbacks.[22]

Though García de Loaisa had never been to the Indies, he was not quite isolated from the reality of imperial life since his first cousin, Fray Francisco García de Loaisa, knight of San Juan and till recently ambassador to the Ottoman empire, was even in 1522 preparing to lead an expedition to the Straits of Magellan and then the Moluccas. His purpose was to seize the Moluccas for Spain from Portugal. The pope had decreed, and the two governments had agreed, in 1494, that the world to the west of the line of the treaty of Tordesillas should be given to Spain, that to the east to Portugal. But there had been no discussion of where, in the east, the west was to begin. Spain now believed that the west was theirs, the Moluccas included. Francisco García de Loaisa wanted to prove the point and an expedition set off from Corunna on 24 July 1525, with seven ships, one of which was commanded by the remarkable El Cano who three years before had returned in command of Magellan's *Victory*. The journey did not prosper. But at least it gave the president some personal knowledge of some of the affairs over which he was to preside.[23] Meantime discussions were held in Valladolid about the dividing line with Portugal. Peter Martyr reported them with his customary competence.[24]

The other members of this first Council of the Indies are less important. Thus Luis Cabeza de Vaca, from Jaén, had been, while in the Netherlands, the Emperor Charles's instructor in reading and writing Spanish as well as in the history of Spain. An Andalusian and related to the resolute explorer Álvaro Cabeza de Vaca, he returned to Spain with Charles in 1517. He seems always to have been trusted by the emperor but, apart from later hearing of the life of the Indies from his cousin Álvaro, he had no direct personal connection with them. But his grandfather, Pedro de Vera, had been the conqueror of Grand Canary, and it was thus appropriate that he should be named bishop of the Canaries in 1523 – one of the few Spanish bishops to live in his diocese.

Another member of the Council of the Indies was Gonzalo Maldonado, of Ciudad Rodrigo, a protégé of Alonso de Fonseca, who secured
his nomination as bishop of his native town in 1525. He was used in
several unexpected missions by Charles the emperor, who, for example,
sent him from Parma in 1529 to seek special financial support from
Genoese bankers. Such a role was not then inconsistent with that of a
provincial bishop.[25]

The last member of this first Council of the Indies was Peter Martyr,
the humanist from Lake Maggiore. He had been named after St Peter the
Martyr, the first martyr of the Dominican order, who had been canon-
ized after his murder between Como and Milan in 1252 and had been
the object of a cult in fifteenth-century Lombardy. Our Peter Martyr
descended from the ancient counts of Anghiera but his branch of the
family was unsuccessful, and Count Giovanni Borromeo, a rich man
from a great family, paid for his education. In the late 1470s Martyr went
to Rome and worked for several cardinals before he became secretary to
Francesco Negri, governor of Rome. He became friendly with Cardinal
Ascanio Sforza, the richest cardinal after Rodrigo Borgia. A brilliant
young intellectual, he was then taken up by Iñigo López de Mendoza, son
of the Marquis of Santillana, who had gone to Rome as Spanish ambassador. Martyr went back to Spain with López de Mendoza.

In 1487 he gave some lectures in classical literature at Salamanca,
and his new friends begged him to remain, to which he agreed. Cardinal
Sforza asked him to send regular letters about what was going on in
Spain, and he did so, writing to the pope as well as to Sforza. His letters,
which talked interestingly of Columbus and other adventurers in the
New World, were eagerly awaited in Rome, their arrival constituting a
literary event of the first magnitude. The King of Naples would request
a copy from Cardinal Sforza, and Pope Leo X would have them read
out at dinner. Martyr wrote in Latin which he treated as a living, not a
dead, language, though he sometimes used Italian or Spanish words,
thereby incurring the mockery of several cardinals.[26] He seems at some
point to have lost the ear of López de Mendoza, his first Spanish patron,
who began to think him verbose. But he continued to lecture with success at Salamanca[27] and he taught classics to young scions of the nobility
in Spain: a list of his pupils was a 'who's who' of the up-and-coming.[28]
Martyr became chaplain of the royal household and then ambassador
to the Ottoman Sultan Bayazid, who sympathized with the Muslims

expelled from Granada and threatened to treat similarly the Christians in the Levant, not to speak of the Franciscans of Palestine. Martyr seems tactfully to have persuaded the Sultan of the benefit of good relations with Spain.

Given that success, it was not surprising that the royal secretary, Miguel Pérez de Almazán (a *converso* from Aragon who became secretary for international affairs to Isabel and Fernando, and was a favourite of the latter), should ask Peter Martyr to seek to promote similar good relations between King Fernando and King Philip the Handsome. After the death of Fernando, however, Martyr wrote hostilely to Rome of the austere Cardinal Cisneros, whom he disliked.[29] He was later, under the Emperor Charles, as hostile to the 'Flemings' as any Spaniard, though he admired Gattinara. He was among the first men in Spain to realize the importance of Cortés's conquests. Later he acted as interpreter to Adrian of Utrecht (from Latin into Spanish) when he was the Regent in Spain and perhaps hoped for a reward from him when he became pope. But Adrian did not give presents.

From 1523 Martyr enjoyed the benefits of the archpriestship of Ocaña, one of Queen Isabel's favourite towns, about forty miles south of Madrid (an archpriest is a senior secular priest). He spoke of Jamaica, where he had a title and rights, as if he had been married to it: 'my spouse', he called it. 'I am united to that charming nymph,' he commented, adding: 'nowhere in the world is there such an enjoyable climate'.[30] One supposes that he had talked to those who had been there.

Martyr had endless curiosity. He would ask people with experience of the Indies to dine with him. 'I have often invited this young Vespucci [Amerigo's nephew] to my table,' he wrote, 'not only because he has real talent but because he has taken notes of all that he has observed during his journey.' He said about Sebastian Cabot, who had become *piloto mayor*, chief pilot, in 1518 in succession to Díaz de Solís: 'Cabot frequents my house and I have sometimes had him to my table.'[31]

Martyr's fellow Italian, for years a professor at Salamanca, Marineo Siculo, said that, when he dined with Martyr, he observed the beautiful chairs with much enthusiasm, for they were of a 'perfection and unequalled art'. He had gold and silver in abundance, and also manuscripts and other things all piled up with some negligence.[32]

Francisco de los Cobos was the secretary to the Council of the Indies from its beginning. Just as interested in his own financial prosperity as

the late Bishop Rodríguez de Fonseca had been, he had little interest in
the New World over whose fate he had such a powerful influence. He
was the essential cabinet secretary to Charles V, meticulous, dry, competent, interested in women, unimaginative. He had been born in 1490;
his father was Diego de los Cobos Tovilla, who fought in the last battles
of the war against Granada. Oviedo, in his book of anecdotes *Quinquagenas*, wrote that the family originally did not have a penny.[33]

García de Loaisa wrote to the emperor that Cobos 'knows how to
make up for your carelessness in dealing with people . . . He serves you
with the highest loyalty and he is extraordinarily prudent, and he does
not waste your time saying clever things, as others do, and he never gos-
sips about his master and he is the best-liked man we know.' To Cobos
himself he said that he had read his letter to the pope: 'His Holiness gets
more pleasure from hearing your letters than from all those which the
ambassador shows him because he says that they are cordial . . . with a
lot of meaning . . . great discretion and no deceit.'[34]

A modern historian wisely wrote that Cobos was 'intelligent and
resourceful, an indefatigable worker, an expert diplomat, charming to
talk to, with some pretensions to be a humanist, a good writer of letters,
but, at the same time, hard, vengeful, and above all greedy for gain'.[35] In
his own time, López de Gómara, biographer of Cortés, recalled that
Cobos was 'fat, good-looking, merry and gay and so pleasant in conversation'. He added, though, that 'he was diligent and secretive . . . he was
very fond of playing the card game *primera* and of conversation with
women'.[36] He never seems to have read anything; he never mentioned
Erasmus in his letters, in which there was no discussion of any of the
great issues of the day.

According to Las Casas, he was 'good-looking and well-built', and 'soft
in speech and voice'. Bernardo Navagero, the second Venetian ambassador of that surname, thought 'Cobos is very affable and very skilful. The
greatest difficulty is getting to see him but, once you are in his office, his
manner is so engaging that everyone goes away completely satisfied.'

Cobos had gained his entrée to the court through Diego Vela Allide,
Mayor de los Cobos, who was the husband of his aunt and accountant
and secretary to Queen Isabel. From the beginning his rise was steady.
By 1503 he was named a royal notary at Perpignan, and became chief
accountant (*contador mayor*) of Granada in 1508. That year he became
a councillor of Úbeda, thereafter his headquarters in Andalusia.

Cobos was in Brussels for most of the time of Cisneros's regency. Oviedo thought that it was Ugo de Urriés, Charles's secretary for Aragonese affairs, who introduced him to the all-important Chièvres with whom he worked. The king wrote to Cisneros: 'he came to serve us and has been and is here in our service'. But his name does not figure among those whom Cisneros disliked.[37] He became formally a secretary to the king on 1 January 1517, receiving 278,000 maravedís as salary, a sum which was greater than that of other secretaries. Charles wrote to Cisneros saying that he had appointed Cobos 'to take and keep a record of our income and finances and what is paid out and consigned to our treasurers and other persons, that all is done in conformity with what you have established and discussed'.[38] Cobos took responsibility for the Indies after Charles's return to Spain in September 1517.

Las Casas describes him as

> surpassing all the others [among the Spanish secretaries] because M. de Chièvres [Croÿ] became fonder of him than of any of the others, since in truth he was more gifted than them, and he was very attractive in face and figure ... He was also soft of voice and speech and so he was likeable. He was likewise greatly helped by the information and experience he had in all the years of the kingdom[39]

By September 1519 Cobos had become a knight of Santiago, by November of that important year (important in New Spain, that is) he was named *fundidor* and *marcador* of Yucatan. In May 1522 this appointment was extended to cover Cuba, Coluacán and San Juan de Ulloa (New Spain). He made a good marriage with María de Mendoza y Pimentel, daughter of Juan Hurtado de Mendoza and María Sarmiento, counts of Rivadavia, in October 1522, soon after Charles's return. She brought a dowry of 4 million maravedís, a million coming from the town of Hornillos near Valladolid, next to the rich Jeronymite monastery of La Mejorada. María was a relation of the Count-Duke of Benavente, Velasco, the constable, and of Enríquez, the admiral of Castile.

By 1522, Cobos had begun to have serious responsibilities for the Indies though he never went near them. He had a licence to sell African slaves which he leased. It was he to whom the Emperor Charles V gave Cortés's famous silver phoenix and he who sadly had it melted down.[40] In 1527 he was named by the king *fundidor* for the entire coast of the Gulf of Mexico from Florida to Pánuco and from Panama to the Gulf of Venezuela. In November 1527 Charles gave Cobos and Dr Beltrán the right to export another 200 slaves each to the New World and, the following month, they agreed with Pedro de Alvarado to export 600 Indian slaves to work the mines in Guatemala, each of the three to pay for a third of the slaves at ten pesos a head and share in the profits. This committed Cobos to finding 900,000 maravedís.

Member of the Council of Castile in 1529, commander of León in succession to Fernando de Toledo and from then on, Cobos became the emperor's chief adviser. He soon had an accumulated income of 6,688,200 maravedís, a very large sum for that date: judges in the supreme court in Mexico (the *Audiencia*) were at that time paid only 150,000 maravedís.[41] At this time, he was building a family of assistants to whom he was as loyal as they were to him: for example, Alonso de Idiáquez, a mediocre individual whom Cobos trusted; his nephew, Juan Vázquez de Molina; Juan de Samano, longtime co-secretary of the Council of the Indies; and Francisco de Eraso, an aristocrat whom the Duke of Alba called 'cousin'. To them, he was *el patrón* who dominated the administration. The most interesting of these men was Samano, who in 1524 had been named chief notary of the government of New Spain. Because of Cobos's frequent absences, he was in fact the real secretary of the Council of the Indies for more than thirty years. But he was uninspired.

Cobos was soon also the controlling figure in the new Council of Finance which had been founded in 1523. From then on, he was busy outmanoeuvring the chancellor, Gattinara.

His money enabled him now to begin to commission great buildings; for example, the chapel of San Salvador at Úbeda, designed by Andrés Vandelvira, the gifted pupil of Siloé and future architect of the cathedral at Jaén.

Cobos owed his success to his decisive personality, his charm and his indefatigable industry. Many years later Charles wrote of him to his son Philip:

> I hold Cobos to be loyal. Up till now he has had little passion in his life. I think that his wife bores him and that explains why he has begun to have many affairs [such as that with the pretty Countess of Navallara in Mantua] ... He has experience of all my affairs and is very well informed about them ... He is growing older and is easier to manage ... The danger

with him is his ambitious wife. Do not give him more influence than I have sanctioned in my instructions ... above all, do not yield to any temptation he may throw in your path. He is an old libertine and he may try and arouse the same tastes in you. Cobos is a very rich man, for he draws a great deal from bullion in the Indies, as also from his slate mines and other sources ... do not let [those appointments] become hereditary in his family. When I die, it would be a good moment to recover those rights for the Crown. He has great gifts for the management of finance. Circumstances not he, nor I, are to blame for the deplorable condition of our revenues.

Another essential adviser of Emperor Charles in those years was Cardinal Juan Pardo de Tavera, archbishop of Toledo and for many years president of the Council of Castile. He was born in Toro in 1472 and his father Arias Pardo was a Gallego. Juan was named a canon of Seville in 1505 and in November of that year became a member of the Council of the Inquisition. In 1507 he was president of the town council of Seville and sustained his uncle, the influential archbishop Deza, in his local disputes. He was his protégé *par excellence*. Bishop of Burgo de Osma till 1523, member of the Royal Council of Castile already with Fernando the Catholic, he was named archbishop of Santiago in 1524, where he remained for ten years. A man learned in law, he was rarely in his bishopric, but lived mostly at court. That did not prevent him giving benefices and other prizes to his relations, which infuriated the local clergy of Santiago. Clever, if taciturn, and narrow in his approach, he opposed most of Charles's universal policies. He became a cardinal in 1531. He was the chief of the *Africanistas* in Charles's councils, hoping for conquests in Africa, rather than in the Indies.[42] After Manrique de Lara fell from favour in 1529, Tavera took most of the decisions in respect of the Inquisition, whose *inquisidor-general* he would eventually become.[43]

Tavera was an efficient administrator. When later he became *gran inquisidor* he cut the number of informants, demanded regular hours of work for the employees, concerned himself with the need to ensure good food for the prisoners, and limited investigations of purity of blood to the children and grandchildren of suspects.[44]

Dr Diego Beltrán, the one permanent official on the Council of the Indies and also a councillor from 1523, is a more shadowy figure. He was probably of *converso* origin.[45] He belonged to the 'Fernandine party' at court in 1506. His first mission seems to have been to act as *juez de residencia* in respect of the *corregidor* of Granada in 1506.[46] He began to work in the Casa de la Contratación in 1504. He moved to Brussels along with other ambitious civil servants and then went back to Castile to prepare for the coming of Charles in whose Council of Castile he figured as early as 1517. He was in Spain during the dark days of the war of the *comuneros* between 1519 and 1522, but he was considered a dangerous individual who was said to have sold state secrets to the Count of Benavente. He was even supposed to have lent money to the *comuneros*.[47] But all the same Peter Martyr evidently thought highly of him, asking: 'In the Spanish world, who is there more exquisite?'[48] In March 1523 he became the first salaried member of the Council of the Indies. He was, it turned out, a great gambler, for which reason he needed much money. Dr Lorenzo Galíndez de Carvajal, an older and much more austere courtier, wrote of him harshly: 'he is certainly cultivated (*tiene buenas letras*) and he is sharp. Yet his defects are so many that, even publicly, one could say that there is not enough paper to write them down.' He added: 'Neither in his birth nor in his way of living, nor in his habits, nor in his faithfulness to the secrecy of the Council, is he worthy to be a counsellor of a great lord, much less that of a great king and emperor.'[49] In fact, Beltrán was already corrupt, for twenty years later, when his career was being investigated, he confessed to having had financial dealings with Cortés. Cortés at one point before 1522 had needed assistance in the council and perhaps Beltrán helped to achieve it, for payment, with which the conqueror of Mexico was usually ready.[50]

Another source of advice in the shadow of Charles's court was a group of bankers, known as 'the four evangelists'. These were Juan de Fonseca and Antonio de Rojas, both archbishops, and Juan de Vozmediano and Alonso Gutiérrez, both financiers of verve. Alonso Gutiérrez of Madrid, of which city he was treasurer, though he was also apparently a *veinticuatro* ('twenty-four' was a name used for a councillor in Seville), where he had lived since 1510, was a *converso*.[51] He was a councillor of Toledo. Treasurer of the Casa de la Moneda as of the Hermandad, in which capacity he had been found resolving the question of the payment to the knights whose horses were taken by Columbus in Hispaniola in 1493. He was one of those who received the national taxes, and had many minor financial activities, such as being the *contador* of the orders of Santiago and Calatrava.[52] He became accountant of the income of

the order of Calatrava in 1516, and from 1519 to 1522 he was accountant of all the feudal grants. Later he was the link between the court and
the famous German bankers, the Fuggers. He assisted López de Recalde
in 1518 in selling the licence to old associates of both of them to carry
the 4,000 slaves to the New World.[53] He seems to have made money by
buying up cheaply possessions confiscated from the *comuneros* after
their defeat. In 1523 Gattinara wanted him as treasurer in the new
Council of Finance but he was outmanoeuvred, by Cobos probably. He
appears to have been the accountant in 1523, then '*canciller*' in 1524. In
1530 he is mentioned in a letter of Charles to the empress as being '*muy
servydo*'[54] and Charles wrote to him also in 1530 thanking him for his
efforts to find money.

In 1531 the Inquisition became interested in Gutiérrez.[55] But he
remained chief accountant of the order of Calatrava till his death in
1539. He received from that order 350,000 maravedís of which 1,500
were in cereals, half in wheat, half in barley.[56] The precise influence of
Gutiérrez is impossible to judge. But he was always at court, always
ready to advance money and always becoming richer.

Charles did not give up all his time to work and study. His brother
Fernando's representative at court, Martín de Salinas, wrote to his treasurer, Salamanca, in March 1523 that the news at court was that to give
entertainment the emperor devoted a lot of time to playing canes and to
jousting, and Cortés in New Spain knew well that rulers danced as well
as issuing ordinances.[57]

6

Cortés in power

Those who have written about your kingdoms in Peru, as well as
the conquest, as writers, they don't write what they saw but what
they heard said.

Pedro Pizarro, *Relación del Descubrimiento y*
Conquista de los Reinos del Perú

Meanwhile, in New Spain Cortés ruled from August 1521 until October
1524. He acted as an absolute monarch and was an active one. Within
a few months of his victory over the Mexica, he was already inspiring
other journeys of discovery and conquest, even before the news of his
triumph had reached Spain and long before the Council of the Indies
had pronounced on what it wanted to see in the new empire of New
Spain. Thus in early 1522 he sent the oldest member of his expedition,
his fellow Medellinés Rodrigo Rangel, to Veracruz to bring back Pánfilo
de Narváez. Narváez, still a prisoner from his expedition to New Spain
in 1520, had talked to Cristóbal de Tapia, the agent of the friars of Hispaniola and of Bishop Rodríguez de Fonseca, and assured him that
Cortés had not reached the end of his luck. So Tapia should return to
Castile and tell the court what was going on in New Spain. Then Narváez
agreed to go up to Mexico. Cortés received him well in Coyoacán and
Narváez was generous in his reaction: 'the least of the things which you
and your valiant soldiers accomplished in New Spain was defeating
me'. He added: 'Your Excellency and your soldiers deserve the greatest
favours from His Majesty.'[1]

Cortés reported to Charles V that, in his time in Mexico/Tenochtitlan,
he found a gunsmith among his followers. This was Francisco de Mesa
of Mairena, Seville, who worked with Rodrigo Martínez who had

directed Narváez's artillery. He was asked by Cortés to work for him as early as September 1521, three weeks only after the final victory. They found copper and tin at Taxco, about eighty miles south-west of Mexico/Tenochtitlan, and later iron. At that time, Cortés had thirty-five bronze cannons, seventy-five lombards and other small guns, many of which had been sent to him since the conquest. For ammunition, they had saltpetre and sulphur obtained by Francisco de Montaño, an imaginative conquistador from Ciudad Rodrigo who had himself lowered into the volcano of Popocatépetl in search of those products.[2]

Cortés despatched his most successful commander and fellow Medellinés, Gonzalo de Sandoval, to Tuxtepec, halfway between Veracruz and Oaxaca, and then to Coatzacoalcos on the Caribbean coast. Sandoval was a good soldier and a fine horseman, whose mount, Motilla, was the best horse in Cortés's army. Still in his teens at the beginning of the campaign against the Mexica in 1519, Sandoval rose to be a superior commander since Cortés knew that he would always do well what he was asked to do. He was not impetuous and unpredictable, as was Pedro de Alvarado, with all his gifts. Sandoval now had to fight an indigenous monarch with some bowmen at his disposal before he was able to set up a Spanish settlement on the river Coatzacoalcos, some twelve miles from its mouth. This he named Espíritu Santo after a settlement near Trinidad in Cuba where he had lived.

It seems that this region was populated by Indians who worshipped stone and clay idols for which they had special sanctuaries (*casas diputadas a manera de hermita*). The word '*coatzacoalco*' means 'the sanctuary of the serpent'.[3] The territory was well provided with maize, beans, sweet potatoes and pumpkins, as well as many tropical fruits, game and fish.[4] Sandoval divided this newly conquered land between several followers of Cortés: Francisco de Lugo, of Medina del Campo; the turbulent Pedro de Briones; the Genoese Luis Marín of Sanlúcar; the Extremeño Diego de Godoy; and, last but not least, the chronicler Bernal Díaz del Castillo. These men came from very different parts of Spain: Lugo was an illegitimate son of Alfonso de Lugo, Lord of Fuencastín in northwest Castile, and a distant relation of Diego Velázquez of Cuba. Briones, a native of Salamanca, was one of the few conquistadors in Mexico to have fought in Italy. He had been, Bernal Díaz wrote sharply, 'a good soldier in Italy according to his own account'.[5] Luis Marín's father had been born Francesco Marini in Genoa, and was one of the many bankers from that city to establish themselves in Andalusia at that time, especially in Sanlúcar de Barrameda. Luis Marín had become a close friend of Sandoval during the campaign against the Mexica. A brother of his had been killed in the company of Narváez.[6] Diego de Godoy had been born in Pinto, to the south of Madrid, though his name suggests that his family must have been from Extremadura. He was one of several notaries on Cortés's expedition and had been a companion of his predecessor Grijalva. Finally, there was Bernal Díaz del Castillo, who would become the great chronicler of the conquest. He was a native of Medina del Campo, home of Montalvo, the author of *Amadís de Gaula*, whom Díaz must have known as a child.[7] He had probably been on two expeditions to New Spain before that of Cortés, those of Hernández de Córdoba and of Grijalva.[8]

Espíritu Santo, a small place, became a base for the subsequent penetration of Guatemala and Yucatan.[9] Díaz married a Spanish lady named Teresa Becerra, with whom he settled in Guatemala after its conquest by Alvarado. There he planted oranges and wrote his legendary work.[10] The Spaniards who settled there were pleased with the salt, pepper, cotton fabrics, sandals, jade, gold, amber and large green quetzal feathers which were all to be found in the region.[11]

These conquistadors did not have an easy time, though. They would approach several *pueblos* where they assumed there would be friendly Indians and propose peace – of course on their terms: an offer of vassaldom to the Emperor Charles being invariably included. Often they were attacked. Díaz del Castillo was wounded in the throat. Luis Marín returned to Mexico/Tenochtitlan to ask help from Cortés, who sent him back to Coatzacoalcos with thirty soldiers led by Alonso de Grado, from Alcántara, one of the most interesting of Cortés's critics at the earliest stage of his campaign. Bernal Díaz del Castillo, his companion in 1522, said of him that he was well informed, with good conversation and a fine presence, but 'more of a troublemaker than a fighter'.[12] He was an *encomendero* in Buenaventura, Hispaniola. Despite his reputation, and despite his constant quarrels with, and punishments by, Cortés, the latter allocated him Techuipo (Isabel), daughter of Montezuma, as a wife.

Having assured himself of the subservience of Coatzacoalcos, Sandoval and his friends set out in the spring of 1523 to conquer what is now the state of Chiapas. They had twenty-seven horsemen, fifteen crossbowmen, eight musketeers and a black gunner with a cannon.

They led seventy foot soldiers and rather more than that number of native Mexicans, principally from Tlaxcala. There was a good deal of sporadic fighting against the Chiapanec Indians, armed with fire-hardened javelins and bows and arrows, as well as long lances with cutting edges. These Indians had good cotton armour, plumes and sheathed wooden *macanas* (swords), slings for stones, and also lassoes for catching horses, and they sometimes used burning pitch against their enemies, as well as rosin[13] and blood and water mixed with ashes. There was a battle at Ixtapa, twelve miles from San Cristóbal, which became the capital of Chiapas. The Indians killed two Spanish soldiers and four horses, and wounded Luis Marín, who fell in a marsh – these were victories of bows and arrows.

In the end, the Indians were defeated and the Spaniards sat in triumph on the battlefield, eating cherries which they found nearby. Some Xaltepec Indians who were enemies of the Chiapanecs assisted them with guides over the fast-flowing river Chiapas. That help enabled Grado and Marín to surround the town of Chiapas itself, where they summoned the chiefs and asked them to give tribute to the Emperor Charles – which they did. They found three gaols with wooden railings full of prisoners with collars round their necks. The Spaniards freed them and then went on to conquer Chamula, whose siege was more difficult. Díaz del Castillo entered first and was accordingly allocated the town by Cortés (he already had Teapa as an *encomienda*).[14] As frequently occurred in those days, the defeat of the Indians was followed by a dispute between the Spaniards; arguments between Marín, Grado and Godoy, the notary, led to the despatch of the difficult Grado as a prisoner to Mexico/Tenochtitlan under armed guard. Godoy and Bernal Díaz then quarrelled as to whether the prisoners should be branded as slaves.

In the summer of 1522 Cortés also despatched his lieutenant Cristóbal de Olid to Michoacan.[15] It was a small empire – or is that a contradiction in terms? – of about twenty cities, roughly coterminous with the modern state of Michoacan. The people called themselves the Purépecha, but the Spaniards knew them as the Tarascans; Cortés had received an embassy from them led by Tashovo, the brother of the Cazonci, the ruler there. They were the only people of the region to possess advanced metallurgical techniques such as gold-plating, casting, soldering and cold hammering, which enabled them to produce remarkable copper masks, copper bells shaped as turtles or fish, lip plugs of laminated turquoise and, above all, copper weapons. With these they had withstood the Mexica in the past, and decimated them in the 1470s; the Mexica had died 'like flies which fell into the water'.[16]

Olid, from Baeza in Andalusia, had an excessively turbulent temperament but was a magnificent fighter; Bernal Díaz del Castillo considered him a veritable 'Hector' (classical comparisons were frequent at that time) in hand-to-hand combat. He had allowed himself to be courted for a time in 1521 by Cortés's enemy Cristóbal de Tapia, and Cortés had reprimanded him. He had a beautiful wife, Felipa de Araúz, who joined him in New Spain in 1522.[17] He went up to Michoacan with 130 foot soldiers, 20 horsemen and 20 crossbowmen. He had with him Cortés's great friend Andrés de Tapia and his cavalry commander, Cristóbal Martín de Gamboa, who had fought with Ovando in Hispaniola, where he had a good *encomienda*. Martín de Gamboa had sailed to New Spain with Grijalva in 1518 and had been among those who had urged him to establish a settlement near Veracruz. He fought all the way up with Cortés in the conquest of Mexico and had been the first to reach the edge of the lake at Tacuba after the attack of the Noche Triste on the causeway. Afterwards he had returned and, by brilliant horsemanship, saved several of his comrades from being killed by the Indians – Sandoval, Antonio de Quiñones and even Pedro de Alvarado, whom he carried for a while on his horse after his famous 'leap'.[18]

When Tzintzicha, the Cazonci, heard that a detachment of Spaniards was making its way towards his principality, he very sensibly fled from his capital city of Tzintzuntzan. He had previously had good relations with two Castilians, Antonio Caicedo and Francisco Montaño, the last of whom was the hero of Cortés's singular recovery of sulphur from the volcano of Popocatépetl.[19] But the Cazonci realized that those two Spaniards were different from the 150 or so who rode up so nonchalantly with Olid. Finding Tzintzuntzan empty of authority, Olid had no hesitation in sacking the Cazonci's palace and destroying his idols, even though he was well received by Tashuaco, the Cazonci's brother, and an Indian leader, 'Pedro' Curiángari. Afterwards the Cazonci bravely returned and declared himself astonished that the Spaniards were so interested in gold. Why did they not prefer jade, as the Tarascans did? Olid had him sent to Tenochtitlan with 300 loads of gold. He was fêted there and became, for a few years, a willing collaborator of Spain, alongside Tashuaco and Curiángari.

This conquest concluded, Olid moved west to the Pacific coast, leaving Juan Rodríguez de Villafuerte, a Medellinés and friend of Cortés, a Michoacan. Olid joined Sandoval and, after avenging a minor defeat suffered by Juan de Ávalos and Juan Álvarez Chico at Zacatula on the Pacific, he and Sandoval established a shipyard at what immediately became known as the Villa de la Concepción de Zacatula. Blacksmiths, marine carpenters and sailors were despatched from Veracruz with anchors, rigging and sails, these being carried across the centre of old Mexico by 1,600 bearers recruited by the Cazonci. Within months, brigantines and caravels were being built. Cortés would later report to the Emperor Charles that his plans for a fleet on the Southern Sea were more ambitious than anything else he was working on in the Indies. His schemes would surely make Charles 'lord of more kingdoms and realms than up till now we have in our nations heard of'.[20] Perhaps that would entail a new claim to China.

For the moment, however, Cortés contented himself with prizes nearer at hand. Thus Miguel Díaz de Aux, an experienced settler of Santo Domingo, son of the enterprising conquistador who had famously discovered a 'nugget of gold' with Francisco de Garay, went with Rodrigo de Castañeda, by this time a good interpreter, to conquer Taxco where they knew that iron could be found – and, indeed, had been founded. Then, on 5 February 1524, Cortés sent the elderly Rodrigo Rangel and Francisco de Orozco, a conquistador from Cobos's city of Úbeda, southwards to Oaxaca to fight the Zapotecs and the Mixtecs and their long flint-headed lances. They took 150 foot soldiers and four pieces of artillery.

Oaxaca was marked by tropical coastlands, the humid region of Papaloapan, a large temperate valley and high mountains with a colder climate. The two peoples in this territory were the Zapotecs, centred on the ancient site of Monte Albán, and the Mixtecs, creators of Mitla. The Zapotecs were admirable architects; the Mixtecs were better known for their production of beautiful smaller objects such as turquoise mosaics, jade and gold jewellery, polychrome pottery and carvings in hard stone. But there was an extraordinary palace of many courts at Mitla, and something similar at Yagul. The Mixtecs were known too for their pictographic books, which the great scholar Ignacio Bernal thought the 'most important feature of Mixtec culture'.[21]

The conquistadors from Spain would soon have become aware of many characteristic elements of local culture in Oaxaca – for example, funerary paintings, a style of writing which became associated with figures known as *danzantes*, fine ceramics (Monte Albán 'grayware', cream ware and the coarser brown and yellow ware), jadeite (a variety of jade) and much lapidary, copper and gold work. Of these crafts the extraordinary ability of the people of Oaxaca as goldsmiths stands out. From them, the Mexica seem to have learned the art of working metals. The Franciscan Sahagún later attributed the invention of metallurgy to the Toltecs.[22] But that legendary origin should not displace the real achievements in Oaxaca, which were brought there from Panama and Costa Rica[23] or possibly Peru.[24] We know about the quality of Zapotec and Mixtec gold (and, to a lesser extent, silver) work from the opening in the 1930s of the famous Tomb 7 in Monte Albán. But Spaniards of the sixteenth century had much broader knowledge because of the abundance of such objects known to have been in the old royal treasury of Mexico. Many pieces were melted down to be sent back to Spain, but enough were sent back in their original form to dazzle men as sophisticated as Albrecht Dürer.

Oaxaca had perhaps about 1,500,000 people in 1519, established in some twenty or so towns which paid tribute to the central city, which was ruled by a monarch or *cacique* who was independent of, but allied to, the Mexica. Mitla would seem to have been, anomalously, ruled by a priest, whose subjects were accustomed to pay to Tenochtitlan tributes of gold dust, gold discs, cotton mantles, turkeys, rabbits, honey and slaves.

Like others of the region, in the past this society had had no draught animals, nor did they have the wheel. The only form of conveyance was that by men and women. War was continuous, the *macana* (sword) was in perpetual use. The main conflicts were against the Mexica. The purpose of the latter was to capture slaves and, by winning a victory, gather tribute. The religion of the region was comparable to that in Mexico/Tenochtitlan but human sacrifice was on a far smaller scale. All religious ceremonies were elaborate and marked by the usual marriage between music, dancing and the consumption of *pulque*, a fermented drink made from the agave cactus. The main crops were maize, chilli, sweet potato and squash; turkeys, bees and dogs were bred and many other animals were used for food. A native tobacco was used for medicinal purposes.

Ancient Oaxaca had a sophisticated society in which a trained priesthood educated the public into an ancestor cult, a culture of sacrifice, ceremony and a respect for the calendar. The society was built on the idea of a settled agriculture supplemented by hunting and fishing. The local priests and nobility led their people in traditional ways.

The venture of Cortés, led by the elderly Rodrigo Rangel, to absorb this society was completely successful. At that time Cortés himself had gone down to Veracruz to inspect the old sites of the towns on the coast. He wanted a good port on the Gulf of Mexico. In the end, he found one a few miles from the first place where he had landed in 1519, to which he ordered the town of Medellín to move. This became La Antigua, on the river Canoas.

Rangel died shortly after his success, of syphilis.

Meantime on midsummer day 1523, 24 June, Francisco de Garay, governor of Jamaica and veteran of Santo Domingo, where he had arrived in Columbus's second expedition in 1493, mounted a fleet of twelve ships with nearly 150 horsemen and 850 Castilians, as well as some Jamaican Indians, to go to Pánuco on the Bay of Mexico. He had in his army 200 musketeers and 300 crossbowmen and stocked his ships with merchandise, taking care before he left to receive the permission of the *audiencia* of Santo Domingo to mount an expedition in an area already conquered by Cortés. According to Díaz del Castillo, Garay was inspired to act by a series of conversations with Cortés's brilliantly intelligent pilot, Antonio de Alaminos.[25] He had, too, been fascinated by the idea of establishing a settlement in the region for many years. Garay had known Cortés in Hispaniola. So it was not surprising that the conqueror of the Mexica should write to Garay encouraging him to come, saying that, if he encountered difficulties with the Huastec Indians, he, Cortés, would help him. Garay thought that Cortés's offer was treacherous and continued with his plans, which he divulged to no one.

Garay reached the river Palmas to the north of the river Pánuco, and founded a city which he bombastically named 'Vitoria Garayana'. Councillors and magistrates were appointed from among several aristocrats with Garay's troops (Alonso de Mendoza, Fernando Figueroa, Gonzalo Ovalle and Santiago de Cifuentes).

Then Garay set off by land to Pánuco, while that old hand in the territory, Juan de Grijalva, directed the fleet along the coast. The land journey was a terrible ordeal for men used to the relative comfort of Jamaica: the march was long, the heat overpowering, the mosquitoes relentless, the forest trackless, the suffering appalling. Many men deserted, walking desperately away from the expedition into the jungle to seek relief, never to be seen again. Morale collapsed. Garay sent his lieutenant, Gonzalo de Ocampo, to San Esteban del Puerto where Cortés's representative, Pedro de Vallejo, a survivor of Narváez's expedition, greeted him. Ocampo was experienced in the Indies and had a brother, Diego, an equally experienced conquistador who had fought in both Hispaniola and Cuba before going to New Spain with Cortés. Vallejo sent a messenger to Cortés requesting instructions, while telling Garay that he could not possibly feed so many newcomers. So Garay established himself at nearby Tlacolula, where he unwisely told the Indians that he had come to punish Cortés for having harmed them. This ill-judged comment led to an affray between a number of Garay's men and Vallejo's, in which the latter, more experienced in the land and more accustomed to the climate, though less numerous, emerged triumphant. But all the same numbers were on Garay's side. Surely they would eventually win any pitched battle against Cortés's men.

But Cortés was favoured still by fortune, as Narváez had predicted would be the case for some time yet. In September 1523 Rodrigo de Paz and Francisco de las Casas, Cortés's cousins, at last reached New Spain with the news that the emperor had named him captain-general and governor. With the letter of appointment came an instruction to Garay not to settle in Pánuco but, if he wanted to stay in New Spain, to go down to Espíritu Santo or, better, beyond it. Cortés immediately despatched Diego de Ocampo and Pedro de Alvarado to inform Garay of these orders together with a notary from Tordesillas, Franciso de Orduña, to enforce the decree.[26]

Garay's men were still melting away through desertion and he, at that time still in his Vitoria Garayana, had fallen ill. His ships were seized by Vallejo, his artillery by Alvarado. In those circumstances, Garay had no alternative but to accept to go up to Mexico as Cortés's guest. It was a humiliating conclusion to his great adventure. Cortés and Garay embraced and exchanged reminiscences of old days together fifteen or more years before in Santo Domingo. But on Christmas Day 1523, after dining with Cortés at the house of Alonso de Villanueva – a friend of both Garay and Cortés – Garay died of a stomach complaint. Going into Garay's room, Alfonso Lucas, one of his friends, and probably a Sevillano, heard the governor of Jamaica at midnight shouting 'without doubt I am mortal'. He was.[27]

Within a few months, however, Cortés had himself to repair to Pánuco, for the Huastecs were celebrating what they believed to be their skill in expelling Garay and wreaking vengeance on his followers. The Huastecs, who were Maya-speaking, were enemies of the Mexica. They were highly licentious and had a luxurious way of life since, in their tropical land, they could grow plenty of food, while the cult of *pulque* made them strong drinkers. They had created much three-dimensional sculpture and were serious players of the famous ball game of the region.

Cortés swiftly established Spanish control in Pánuco and then, to his and his companions' shocked horror, came upon the faces of several men who had in 1523 come to the region with Francisco de Garay. The skin had been flayed and cured as if it had been glove leather. This gruesome discovery concentrated the minds of all the conquistadors.[28]

Cortés established Vallejo as his commander in the region in the new settlement of San Esteban del Puerto, which soon had over a hundred inhabitants, of whom twenty-seven were horsemen and thirty-six musketeers or crossbowmen. Juan de Burgos, a merchant of that city, who would become an enemy of Cortés, maliciously suggested that Cortés had ordered the Huastecs to kill as many as possible of Garay's men, but the accusation contains no truth.

Later the Crown sent a letter of complaint to the *audiencia* in Santo Domingo for having granted Garay permission to embark upon an expedition in an area already conquered by Cortés.[29]

At much the same time, Cortés's most turbulent lieutenant, Cristóbal de Olid, returned from both Michoacan and Zacatula and was pestering Cortés for new employment. He set off for Hiberas to found a settlement because he believed that there was much wealth there: he had heard that the nets used for fishing in those parts were a mixture of gold and copper, so he assumed that they were rich. Cortés told the Emperor Charles that 'many pilots believe that there is a strait between that bay and the other sea [the South Sea] and this is the thing which I most desire to discover because of the great service which I am certain your august majesty will receive thereby'. A new settlement under Cortés's direction would also presumably be a way of restructuring the territory of Pedrarias in Central America.

So Olid set off from Tenochtitlan on 11 January 1524 with six ships, with good guns and 500 men, of whom 100 were crossbowmen. Cortés assumed that Olid and Alvarado would meet if no strait divided them, for the latter had already begun a land journey to Guatemala. Two clerics accompanied Olid, to root out sodomy and human sacrifice 'in a friendly manner'. All houses where Indians were being fattened for human sacrifice were to be broken open and the prisoners freed; crosses were to be established everywhere.

Cortés sent Olid to Hiberas via Havana. There, Cortés hoped, he would pick up Alonso de Contreras, from Ordaz, Toledo, one of those who had accompanied him to New Spain in 1519, with horses, pigs, cassava (roots) and bacon. But Olid called on his old master, Diego Velázquez, then on his deathbed, who, despite his condition, encouraged Olid's rebellious instincts.

Some other Spaniards from Cuba accompanied Olid to Central America, where he immediately set himself up in opposition to Cortés. His settlement of 3 May 1524 was at Naco on the river Chamelecón, in Hiberas, thirty miles south of Puerto de Caballos, on the Gulf of Honduras.

When he heard of this unilateral declaration, Cortés's first reaction was fury; Peter Martyr in old, not New, Spain said that 'his neck swelled' at such bad news. But Díaz del Castillo, who was with Cortés at the time, wrote that he became very thoughtful but, since he was at heart high-spirited, he did not permit such matters to get the better of him.[30] Then he despatched a loyal force against Olid, under his cousin Francisco de las Casas, with five ships and 100 soldiers.[31] They reached Triunfo de la Cruz in Hiberas in good time and sought to land. Olid tried to prevent them and there was a short sea battle between Las Casas and Olid. The latter must have felt surrounded by enemies since he had had some days before to send two companies of men down the river Pechin to try to stop, or even seize, Gil González de Ávila, an eternal adventurer who was the elder brother of Cortés's friend Alonso de Ávila and who was making his way northwards from Panama.[32] So he offered a truce to Cortés's cousin Las Casas, who agreed to stay for a time aboard his ship. But alas for a peaceful solution! A storm pushed Las Casas on to the shore and he lost thirty men and all his arms. He was now a refugee with Olid, and soon found himself joined in his confinement by Gil González de Ávila and Juan Núñez de Mercado, an ex-page of Cortés, who were seized as they struggled northwards.

Olid was delighted by these unexpected events and wrote to Velázquez in Cuba boasting that he had outmanoeuvred everyone (Velázquez had died by April, before he could read the letter). He sent one of his captains, Pedro de Briones, a veteran of the Spanish wars in Italy, to establish his supremacy in some nearby settlements. But Briones was not to be trusted, for he planned to rejoin Cortés in Mexico. At that point Las Casas and Gil González decided to kill Olid, which was easy enough since, though more prisoners than refugees, they had not been chained. They found some scriveners' knives and then, while González de Ávila was talking to Olid, Las Casas seized the latter by the beard and tried to cut his throat. González de Ávila added some thrusts of his own but Olid was strong and broke away to hide in a thicket. Las Casas proclaimed: 'To me, those for the king and Cortés against the tyrant Olid!' No one supported the latter and he was soon betrayed. A charge of rebellion was swiftly brought against him in an arbitrary trial. Las Casas demanded a sentence of death for rebellion and Olid, one of the great men of the conquest of Mexico, was accordingly beheaded forthwith in the square of Naco. The victors founded a city there, which they named Trujillo, for Las Casas was from that city in Extremadura. Both he and González de Ávila then began to prepare to return to Mexico.

These events so successful for Cortés occurred in September 1524, but, not knowing of them, he decided on an expedition of his own against this new enemy. His aim was to punish Olid. This was a controversial decision and one which he must have later bitterly regretted. Why he thought it necessary is a mystery. Why at least did he not wait till he had heard the result of Las Casas's expedition? He was advised against leaving Mexico/ Tenochtitlan by all his friends there. He did not listen to them. Perhaps he was bored with problems of administration and coveted a return to campaigning.

At all events, and for whatever psychological reason, the great conqueror of Mexico set off for Hiberas by land on 12 October 1524, a month after Olid had been done to death. He left Alfonso de Estrada and Rodrigo de Albornoz, the royal treasurer and the accountant, as lieutenant governors to act in his stead while he was away. The chief magistrate would be Alonso de Zuazo, an experienced lawyer who had just completed the *juicio de residencia* of Diego Velázquez in Cuba. Two other royal officials (Gonzalo Salazar and Peralmíndez de Chirino) accompanied Cortés, as did the unfortunate Cuauhtémoc, last of the Mexican rulers, and his colleagues, Tetlepanquetzaltzin and Coanacochtzin, the Huey Tlatoani, or rulers, respectively of Tacuba and Texcoco.

Others in his train were the resilient interpreter Marina, the reliable Sandoval, the unpredictable Alonso de Grado, the fortunate Juan Jaramillo, Luis Marín, Pedro de Ircio and Bernal Díaz, all of whom had accompanied him in 1519.

Cortés took with him also a large personal staff which included a majordomo, two *maîtres d'hotel*, a steward, a shoemaker, a butler, a doctor, a waiter, two pages, eight footmen and five musicians. His followers included, so he himself reported, nearly a hundred horsemen and thirty foot soldiers, with perhaps 3,000 Indian followers.[33] Cortés's cousin Rodrigo de Paz would remain behind as majordomo of his property in Cuernavaca and Coyacán.

Soon after Cortés had abandoned the heartland of old Mexico, Salazar and Peralmíndez Chirino left the expedition to return to Mexico. The bad relations between Estrada and Albornoz had been reported to Cortés who assumed that the return of these two other officials, whom he believed loyal, would make everything easier in the great city whose rebuilding he had begun so well.

After Espíritu Santo and Coatzacoalcos, Cortés found himself in new country. The expedition passed through the centre of the Yucatan Peninsula; bypassing Copilco, where there was much cacao and good fishing; stopping briefly at Anaxuxuca, Chilapa, Tepetitán, Zagoatan, Istapan ('a very large town on the banks of a beautiful river, a suitable place for Spaniards to settle') and Teuticacar ('a most beautiful town with two very fine temples' in one of which pretty virgins were regularly sacrificed). Cortés had many bridges built of brushwood, sometimes of timber. Occasionally they had to cross marshes by bridges, including one built by Indians from Tenochtitlan, experiencing 'much distress through hunger'. Many curious conversations were held with Indians in canoes, and sermons were given by Cortés via Marina on the virtues of Christianity. Indian chiefs such as Apasolan became Christians and burned their idols. Sometimes mass was celebrated accompanied by sackbuts and flageolets. Cortés received many gifts of gold and girls, honey and beads, fallow deer and iguana. There were jungles which the expedition had to cross on their knees, and there were flat pasture lands. They encountered high inland seas over 100 miles in diameter, and endured nights of torrential rain amid plagues of mosquitoes. There were 'fearful northern gales', there were days when the expedition was carried onwards only by powerful currents in vast rivers, and there was the unmasking of an alleged plot of Cuauhtémoc, Coanacochtzin of Texcoco, and Tetlepanquetzaltzin of Tacuba and their subsequent execution by hanging at Izancanac on Ash Wednesday, 28 February 1525 (two senior Mexicans, Cihuatcoatl, or 'Juan Velázquez', and Moyelchuitzin, or 'Tapia', seem to have betrayed their colleagues' conversations about possible rebellion).[34] Guanacalin, prince of Texcoco, and Tacitetle, his equivalent in Tlatelolco, were left frightened but uncharged.

Cortés met merchants of the Mexican commercial centres of Xicalango and Los Terminos selling cacao, cotton materials, dyes, torches, beads made from shells, sometimes gold mixed with copper. The expeditionaries ate dried maize, cacao, beans, pepper, salt, hens and pheasants, as well as dogs bred for food. Sometimes they travelled by raft, each one of which carried about seventy bushels of dried maize as well as quantities of beans, peppers and cacao with which the Spaniards loaded them, as well as ten men.

Eventually, after many privations, the expedition reached Nito at the corner of Yucatan and Honduras and there they encountered some eighty Spaniards including twenty women who, unarmed and without horses, seemed to be dying of hunger. They had been left behind by Gil González de Ávila, who had returned to Panama. Cortés's own expedition was short of food and perhaps all might have starved to death had it not been for the unexpected arrival of a ship from Santo Domingo with thirteen horses, seventy pigs, twelve casks of salted meat and some thirty loaves of bread 'of the kind used in the islands' – that is, presumably, cassava bread. Cortés began to build a caravel and a brigantine which would re-establish his relations with those outposts. Of course, he found out about the fighting between Olid, Las Casas and González de Ávila, as well as the death of the first of these. He complained fiercely about the trade in Indian slaves which continued on a large, ever growing scale in those days, in the Bay islands off Honduras, and explained how he had freed those slaves previously seized by Rodrigo de Merlo of Cuba. Cortés was now presenting himself as the friend of the Indians.

In the meantime, many strange, disturbing, quite unexpected things were going on in Mexico/Tenochtitlan. At first, Cortés's absence seemed not to matter. Thus on 1 January 1525 a meeting of the town council of the city was held in the house of Licenciado Alonso Zuazo, Cortés's legal friend. Present were Gonzalo de Salazar, the majordomo, and Pedro Almíndez Cherino, the inspector, sent back to Mexico to maintain order while Cortés, the governor-general and *adelantado*, was on his journey. Also there were Gonzalo de Ocampo, Garay's majordomo who had become mayor in Mexico; Cortés's cousin Rodrigo de Paz, the chief magistrate, who had brought the good news of his governor-generalship; and Bernardino Vázquez de Tapia, the well-born conquistador from Talavera de la Reina, who had been with Cortés throughout the campaign of the conquest and had not yet revealed himself the bitter critic of the great conquistador that he would soon turn out to be. These Spanish conquerors then elected for the following year two mayors, four town councillors and a public spokesman.

Leonel de Cervantes, who had been with Narváez and had just returned from Spain with his marriageable daughters, became one of the mayors, as did Francisco Dávila, who had known Cortés since 1508 in Cuba. The councillors were Gutierre de Sotomayor, Rodrigo de Paz, Antonio de Carvajal and Juan de la Torre, while Pedro Sánchez Farfán, from a famous family of lawyers (*escribanos*) in Seville, became the spokesman. Carvajal, de la Torre and Sánchez Farfán had all been in Cortés's army during the conquest; the last-named had been for several years a prisoner of Indians in Cuba. There was thus nothing unexpected in the names of the new members.[35] They seemed much as they had been in the past and they duly distributed 211 shares of land in 1525, of which 114 were urban but 97 were orchards (*huertas*). Several shares were granted for the establishment of mills and one was given to a woman, Isabel Rodríguez, wife of Miguel Rodríguez of Guadelupe, who had cured the wounds of '*los enfermos de la conquista*'.[36] But more trouble was afoot.

During the course of 1525, the temporary rulers of New Spain, especially Peralmíndez Cherino and Gonzalo de Salazar, convinced themselves that, since they had had no news from or of Cortés, he must be dead. On 22 August the town council formally decided to that effect. On 15 December Rodrigo de Albornoz wrote to the Council of Indies a hostile letter about Cortés, whom he accused of having been 'consumed by avarice and a tyrant'.[37] When Rodrigo de Paz, Cortés's cousin, protested against the self-assumed authority of Salazar and Peralmíndez, he was peremptorily imprisoned in the new fortress of the Atarazanas. He was asked where Cortés's 'treasure' was, but denied that it existed. He was tortured and soon killed. It was an extraordinary development, aggravated by the seizure by Salazar and Peralmíndez of much of Cortés's property. A rule of terror was established. Juana de Mansilla, wife of a conquistador who was with Cortés, sustained the view that Cortés and her husband were still alive, and she refused to remarry. She was condemned to ride through the city on a donkey with a rope round her neck and to be whipped. Others of Cortés's friends took refuge in the monastery of San Francisco. Judge Zuazo escaped to Cuba. The legitimacy of the new empire seemed to be on the verge of collapse.

Then on 28 January 1526 Martín Dorantes, one of Cortés's grooms, who came from Béjar, reached Mexico with his master's order displacing Chirino and Salazar. He talked in the monastery of San Francisco to Jorge de Alvarado and Andrés de Tapia. After a struggle, Cortés's party regained control. A few months later the city council received a letter from Cortés himself, in which he explained that he had arrived at San Juan Chalchicueca, Veracruz. The council members read this on 31 May, the Day of Corpus Christi, as they prepared to leave the new makeshift cathedral in procession. This missive led the council to revoke the grants of *solares* in the city and *huertas* outside it which had been made by Salazar and Peralmíndez Chirino.[38]

After an absence of over a year and a half, Cortés returned on 19 June to the city which he had conquered and had then rebuilt. In a letter to the Emperor Charles he described how the population 'welcomed me as if I had been their father'. Presumably he meant the Indians as well as the Spaniards in the place. The treasurer Estrada and the inspector Rodrigo de Albornoz rode out in fine array (despite the fact that Albornoz had written so critically of Cortés the previous year) to meet him; the majordomo Salazar and the inspector Peralmíndez Cherino, hid in their houses. Cortés went first to the monastery of San Francisco, where he was effusively greeted by all his friends who had taken refuge there, and was told by old associates, such as Francisco Dávila, his friend since Cuba, of what had happened in his absence. Almost his first move was to rescind his grant of the *encomienda* of Tacuba to Peralmíndez Cherino and to give it formally to Isabel Montezuma on the occasion of her new marriage, to Alonso de Grado.[39] His next action was to arrest Salazar and Chirino and hold them both in a wooden cage.

Cortés had not been back more than two weeks before a new crisis arose for him personally. This was the arrival at Veracruz of Luis Ponce de León as judge of his *residencia*. This was a normal procedure for retiring administrators. A distant relation of the great Sevillano family of his name, this official was young, with a high reputation for integrity. Named *juez de residencia* of Cortés in November 1525, he set off for New Spain in February of the following year in a fleet of twenty-two ships. According to Peter Martyr, he was told that, if he should find Cortés alive, 'he should overwhelm him with flattery and seek to inspire him with truly loyal sentiments'.[40] He waited for two months in Santo Domingo for a ship to take him to New Spain. When he arrived at Veracruz, he heard that Cortés had been there only a few days before.

Ponce de León went up to Mexico/Tenochtitlan in haste. He was given a banquet on the way, at Ixtapalapa, where he was offered presents, which he refused, and blancmange, which he ate. He and Cortés then met in the monastery of San Francisco in Mexico in the presence of Estrada, Albornoz and most of the council of the city. A *residencia* of Cortés was proclaimed on 4 July. This meant in theory that all executive power passed to the judge. Cortés, a stickler for correct conduct and with his own legal training in mind, prepared for the transfer of authority and handed to Ponce the *vara*, the staff of office. But Ponce was ill, allegedly because of the blancmange he had eaten at Ixtapalapa. He must have been the first man to die from eating blancmange. For he and several of his travelling companions did succumb, on 20 July, and there were many who accused Cortés of poisoning them. The Dominican Fray Tomás Ortiz was the first to spread this rumour in the sixteenth century, though he only arrived in New Spain with twelve colleagues on 2 July.

Before he died, Ponce had placed his authority in the hands of an elderly lawyer, Marcos de Aguilar, who accompanied him. He passed him the *vara* of office. Aguilar, a native of the fine Roman city of Écija, between Seville and Córdoba, had gone out to the Indies in 1509. He had become chief magistrate in Santo Domingo and always supported the Columbus family, for which imprudent loyalty he was briefly imprisoned in 1515. He continued as *alcalde mayor*, but was then expelled at the royal request for being a '*persona escandalosa*'. What could that have signified? Homosexuality? Probably not, for he had an illegitimate son, Cristóbal, by an indigenous girl.[41] To live with an indigenous girl was not a scandal, since almost everyone had at least one such liaison. Drink? Not a scandal at that time!

At all events, he assumed the title of *justicia mayor* in Mexico, and for nine months exercised authority, though he knew nothing of Mexico and was so badly crippled that he had to be fed.[42] Cortés conducted himself arrogantly but correctly. Aguilar for his part began the business of arranging Cortés's *residencia*: the assembly of witnesses, the preparation of questionnaires and of counter-questionnaires, the hiring of notaries who, it was hoped, would write down all that was said by retired warriors with ease and grace. It continued for years.

Among those who would be witnesses was Jerónimo de Aguilar, a cousin of the Justicia, and an essential ally of Cortés since he had interpreted Spanish into Maya, leaving the final process of translation of Maya into Nahuatl for the Indian Marina.

But then once again death intervened. In March 1527 Licenciado Marcos de Aguilar followed his legal leader into the grave. This was the fourth swift death met by Cortés (his wife, Garay and Ponce being the previous ones); the accusations that he was in some way concerned were even more numerous.[43]

Aguilar had named the treasurer Estrada his successor as *justicia mayor*. But Cortés's captain, the resolute Gonzalo de Sandoval, was called on by the town council to assist him, and that captain moved into the *justicia mayor*'s suite for a few months till Estrada received a notice from Spain that he alone was to rule New Spain. But Sandoval was not to take the *residencia* of Cortés which was delayed *sine die*.

Despite that concession, Cortés began to see that he was being sidelined in the arrangements to manage his own conquests. He seems never to have recovered from the privations of his journey to Hiberas. A particularly unpleasant challenge to him had been the nomination in November 1525 of a courtier, Nuño de Guzmán, as governor of Pánuco.

Son of Hernando Beltrán de Guzmán of Guadalajara, chief magistrate of the Inquisition, Nuño de Guzmán seemed a typical representative of the old bureaucracy in Spain. Juan, Nuño's elder brother, was a Franciscan who was later on the point of going to New Spain to become the general commissar of the order. A younger brother was Gómez Suárez de Figueroa, a courtier who had served the emperor in Italy. Gómez was to be an outstanding ambassador in Genoa for many years and, as such, treated often with bankers there on Charles's behalf. He would ship some of Titian's magnificent pictures to Spain as presents to Charles from the Duke of Ferrara.

Nuño de Guzmán set off from Spain in May 1526 with two ships and a galleon with thirty servants, a tailor, a chemist, a surgeon, a housekeeper and a number of grooms. But he had to remain several months in Santo Domingo because of illness, and then went to Cuba (still known as Fernandina), where his kinsman Gonzalo de Guzmán poisoned his mind against Cortés.[44] Nuño sailed from Cuba to Pánuco in August, and he moved into a quickly reconstructed palace in the main town which was still called Vitoria Garayana by the local Spanish residents. Almost immediately he encountered difficulties with the colonists.

In these days people from all parts of Spain were arriving in the New World, in particular New Spain. 'Foreigners', that is non-Castilians, were permitted to come between 1526 and 1538, which meant that all inhabitants of the extensive monarchy of Aragon were allowed to venture there. Jews, Moors, gypsies and heretics were in theory forbidden, but it was in those years fairly easy to evade the regulations, and we find many new Christians entering the New World. Perhaps 1,000 to 2,000 immigrants would come every year, more men than women of course.[45]

BOOK I
Valladolid and Rome

7

Charles: from Valladolid
to the fall of Rome

The year 1527 was full of atrocities and events unheard of for
many centuries: falls of governments, wickedness of princes, most
frightful sacks of cities, great famines, a most terrible plague
almost everywhere.

Guicciardini, *The History of Italy*

Between 1523 and 1529, Charles the emperor, Charles of Ghent, was
above all Charles the king, of Aragon of course as well as Castile and its
substantial entanglements overseas. He had, remarkably, been in Valladolid a year from July 1522 to 25 August 1523 when he set off for
Navarre, and then Aragon, specifically Monzón, in the mountains
between Barbastro and Lérida, where the river Segre joins the Cinca, and
where kings of Aragon customarily held their local parliaments (*Cortes*).
Thereafter he was in Catalonia, Andalusia, Seville and Granada. By 1524
his travels seemed to combine to make him king of Spain indeed.

Charles, however, had his personal difficulties – above all with his
mother. In January 1525 his cousin Fadrique Enríquez, the admiral of
Castile, wrote to him to say that he had visited Queen Juana and that
she had complained to him of her ill-treatment by the Marquis de Denia,
who was both his and her close relation.[1] The dry and callous marquis,
Bernardino Diego Sandoval y Rojas, was governor of Tordesillas and,
therefore, warder-in-chief of Juana *la Loca*. Dealing with him at that
time, Juana had been lucid, but 'in the rest of her conversation, she
wavered'.[2]

Charles was also short of money. The Polish ambassador, Dantiscus,
thought in February 1525 that he had never seen the court 'so poor' as
it was then. 'Money is procured by unprecedented methods and all is

sent to the army in Italy. The Emperor is suffering from an extreme penury,' he added in his diary, when he received the order of the Golden Fleece for his own monarch, the cultivated Sigismund I of Poland. Conversation between Charles and Dantiscus was in German and Italian. Dantiscus was himself suffering from poverty despite being in receipt of a good income from Poland. With only sixty ducats a month, he could not live as an ambassador needed to: he could afford only six or seven horses and ten servants.[3]

Yet happier times were coming. Peter Martyr, in what turned out to be his last letter to Rome,[4] spoke of two vessels arriving at Seville from New Spain, commanded by Lope de Samaniego, who would later play a part in the administration of the overseas empire, with two tigers on board, and a culverin made of silver sent by Cortés before he left Mexico/Tenochtitlan the previous October.[5] Dantiscus reported good news about the Indies, such as the 'discoveries of new islands', which he did not name but which he said were 'abundant in gold, spices and perfumes' (aromas). He reported that, in just one day in New Spain, 70,000 men and women had received the sacrament. He added that, since there had been a severe drought, the Spaniards had persuaded the Indians there to form a procession preceded by a cross, whereupon it began to rain and the crops were saved. 'These Indians were more human than those who had been previously discovered [in the Caribbean] and the journey to their islands was shorter than the way of the Portuguese.'[6]

On 10 March even more remarkable news reached the Emperor Charles: in pursuit of triumphs in Naples, his army in Italy, led by the reliable Antonio de Leiva, the courtly Charles de Lannoy (viceroy of Naples), the treacherous French Constable de Bourbon and the brilliant Francisco de Ávalos, who had become Marquis of Pescara, had defeated the French at Pavia. The king of France, the unscrupulous charmer Francis I, had even been captured.

Lannoy received King Francis's sword in person, but the victory was particularly the work of Ávalos, one of the most admirable gentlemen-warriors of the age. Captain-general of the light cavalry of Spain in 1512 when still only twenty-two, he had been captured and wounded by the French at Ravenna that same year. He was known 'for his strong frame, his fine large eyes which though usually soft and mild' in expression, 'shot fire' when he was roused.[7] In 1524 he had skilfully covered the Spanish retreat from France and had given back to France the body of the valiant captain Bayard before the battle of Pavia.[8] Connected indirectly by blood ties to Cortés, he inherited an Italian title but spoke only Spanish.[9]

In 1509 Ávalos had married in sumptuous style the beautiful poetess Vittoria Colonna (later the great friend of Michelangelo), who forgave him his many absences and infidelities. He was a Renaissance man, for his life was full of extraordinary feats, his attitude to noble ardour and desire for glory being awoken by his heady reading of romantic novels. The playwright Torres Naharro (a very Italianate Spaniard) dedicated his *Propaladia* to him in 1517.[10] Vittoria Colonna wrote him poems: '*Qui fece il mio bel sole a noi ritorno/Di regie spoglie carco e ricche prede . . .*' The last chapter of Machiavelli's *Prince* suggests that many Italians agreed with his idea of patriotism. His wounds at Pavia distressed him, and he was bitter at the lack of recognition by the emperor. But Isabella, Duchess of Milan, wrote: 'I would that I were a man, signor, if for nothing else than to receive wounds in the face as you have done, in order to see if they would become me as well as they do you.'[11] His last months were tarnished by the suspicion that he was toying with the idea of backing Italian nationhood, through the machinations of the gifted patriot Girolamo Morone.[12] He died of his wounds in December 1525.

The emperor remained in Spain, and with the king of France in his control seemed to have the world at his feet. His brother Ferdinand wrote enthusiastically: 'Your Majesty is now monarch of the whole world.'[13] Again, that tempting phrase!

But the strategic problems seemed as serious as ever: what was to be done with Francis? How was Charles to handle his ally Henry VIII of England, who, he was coming to realize, was self-obsessed? Gattinara thought that his emperor should now claim the whole of his Burgundian inheritance: 'Burgundy no more, no less.' Perhaps, too, he should demand Provence from the Constable of Bourbon. A general council of the Church should surely be called, and the emperor should organize it, for Pope Clement could only organize excuses.

But nothing happened. The Council of Castile was divided. Gattinara wanted acquisitions, solutions hostile to France, and most of the other Flemings took that view. So did the Duke of Alba. But Lannoy and Ávalos, the victors in battle, advised a conciliatory treaty with France, as did the emperor's confessor, García de Loaisa.[14] At a mass held to give thanks for the victory at Pavia, a Dominican gave a sermon asking for a common front against the infidel, and preached 'universal concord'.[15]

The humanist philosopher Vives, then at Oxford, urged tolerance, for it was a wonderful chance 'to do good, to gain merit before God and glory before men'.[16]

The indecision of Charles after Pavia was due first to the confusion in the imperial chancellery headed by Gattinara who, though a fine intellect and an able official, was also always suspecting plots against him. For example, in July 1525 at Toledo the Venetian ambassador, Gaspar Contarini, reported that, in the presence of the governor of the Bresse, Laurent de Gorrevod, Henry of Nassau and Adrien de Croÿ, Gattinara had complained to the emperor that others were usurping his authority. Charles asked Gattinara to put his quarrel in writing. He did so in a fierce denunciation of secretarial corruption, which seems to have included not only the by now irreplaceable Cobos but also his own protégé, Lalemand, who was beginning to displace Gattinara himself.[17] At another meeting in Toledo, at which were present Cobos and Hugo de Moncada, prior of Messina, crafty, cruel and bold, as well as Gattinara, Charles explained that the chancellorship in Spain was different from what Gattinara imagined. The chancellor was the supreme adviser to the king, not the head of the civil service. Gattinara immediately asked leave to retire from the court. Charles sadly agreed to this request, then repented of his agreement and sent Laurent de Gorrevod to make things up. Gorrevod called on Gattinara while the president of the Council of the Indies, García de Loaisa, asked Gattinara to dine with the king.

Charles greeted his long-time adviser with affection and declared how much he loved him. They settled down to dine amply on beef and beer, as was then the emperor's custom.[18] It now seemed that Gattinara had been upset by the destruction caused by imperial troops to his own territory in Piedmont. He had written to Charles: 'the abuses which your troops commit are so abominable that the Turks and infidels would not do them and, instead of naming you "liberator of Italy", people will be able to say that you have introduced the greatest tyranny that ever was'.[19] No doubt Charles was aware of these scandals but he did not like to hear of them from his chancellor, of whose tirades, and even of whose exhortations, he was wearying.

Meanwhile, Francis I, held fast in the castle of Pizzighettone, between Cremona and Piacenza, persuaded Lannoy that it would be best if he were sent to see Charles in Spain. However, when he arrived as a prisoner in Madrid, Charles did not hasten to see him. Only when he heard that he was seriously ill did Charles visit him, and then only briefly.[20] After a month, Margaret, Duchess of Alençon, a sister of Francis and a cultivated, beautiful Renaissance princess, arrived in Madrid to open negotiations on Francis's behalf. She was a poet, playwright and neoplatonist as well as a reformer in so far as the Church was concerned, and that side of her is well expressed in her play *Le Miroir de l'âme pécheresse*. She later married the king of Navarre, Henri d'Albret, and was the grandmother of Henry of Navarre. Charles received her with courtesy, and negotiations followed in Toledo.

One reason for Charles's lack of attention to Francis and the treaty of peace to be made with him was that he had now decided, as he told his brother Fernando in June 1525, to marry the Infanta Isabel of Portugal. Like every bachelor monarch in those days (and later days, too), Charles had been constantly advised on his need for marriage, and had settled eventually on the merits of his first cousin, the Infanta who was daughter of King Manuel of Portugal by a Spanish princess María, who was herself the daughter of Fernando and Isabel. The English princess, Mary, who had also been considered, was too young, being only nine years old in 1525, and Charles had been persuaded that his marriage could not wait. He adopted a rather worldly view of such a wedding: 'My marriage,' he wrote in a private notebook (he was the first monarch to confide thus), 'will be a good reason to demand a great sum from the Spanish kingdoms.' He knew that the Portuguese princess was rich. He reflected that, once she was queen and empress, he could make her his Regent whenever he left Spain: 'In that way I ought to be able to set out for Italy with the greatest splendour and honour this very autumn.'[21]

A marriage with a Portuguese princess would also help to cement the good relations which Castilian monarchs had wanted with Portugal since the days of Isabel.[22] The courtier Alonso Enríquez de Guzmán, eccentric and indiscreet but modern-minded and articulate, had gone to Lisbon to tell the king of Portugal of Charles's victory. On his return, Charles told him: 'Don Alonso, you have performed this service well. Now tell me of the people whom you met in Lisbon.' He replied:

> Sire, I saw a fat monarch, rather short, with a very small beard, youthful and not very discreet [that was King John III the Pious who had been king

since 1521] . . . I saw the queen, his wife, who seemed very well prepared and on the spot, honourable and wise [that was Charles's sister]. Then I saw an infanta very self-possessed (*bien ansi*) and more (*más*), and more, if one can say so, who seemed to look like you, sir.[23]

This was the emperor's cousin and future wife, whom he came to love deeply. She was beautiful.

The negotiations with Francis I over peace and those with the Portuguese royal family over marriage overlapped with one another. On 24 October wedding arrangements were agreed between the infanta and Charles, whose titles now included that of 'monarch of the isles of the Canaries and of the Indies, the isles of the mainland and the Ocean Sea'.[24] The infanta would bring a handsome dowry: 900,000 'doblas de oro castellanas'.[25]

On 19 December Lannoy produced a list of fifty articles which the king of France would have to agree with Charles, the most important of which was that Francis would accompany Charles on a crusade. The king of France would be released when his two elder but still small sons, Henry and Charles, were exchanged as hostages for him. France would renounce all claims to Milan, Naples and Genoa, and abandon her overlordship of Flanders and Artois. Francis also assented, in somewhat hesitant terms, to the cession of Burgundy to Charles.

A dramatic scene unfolded in the king's room in Toledo where this was agreed, with Lannoy, Moncada and Lalemand being present on Charles's behalf, and France's ambassador, the bishop of Embrun, as well as Anne de Montmorency, the Constable of France. Charles agreed to let his sister Leonor, the widow of King Manuel of Portugal, marry Francis. It seemed a moment of great promise, even if Gattinara the chancellor did not agree and did not countersign the peace.

The emperor and the king then celebrated at the Alcázar in Toledo. They were joined by the ex-queen, Germaine de Foix, and the Marquess of Brandenburg, whom she would soon marry; Mencía, the Marquesa de Ceñete, rich wife of the Count of Nassau and granddaughter of Cardinal Rodríguez de Mendoza, Columbus's patron; and Leonor, the future queen of France. Dantiscus thought she had lost her looks since he had last seen her at Brussels,[26] and wondered whether she had also lost her purpose. Immediately afterwards Leonor and Francis went north to Burgos to await the arrival of the future hostages, his sons by his first marriage.

Charles, on the other hand, went with the court south to Seville where, on 10 March 1526, he found the Infanta Isabel already waiting. To his relief, he discovered that she spoke excellent Spanish, which he too had come to speak adequately by then. They were formally betrothed by Cardinal Jacopo Salviati, the papal legate to Spain, and married in the Alcázar almost immediately afterwards.[27] The celebratory ball was opened by Charles's favourite Fleming, Charles de Poupet, lord of La Chaulx, who had had so much to do with the negotiation of the marriage.[28]

The Alcázar had been redecorated beforehand with Genoese motifs, an appropriate embellishment for a place which owed so much to that Ligurian city. Dantiscus reported to King Sigismund that the wedding was not allowed to cost much because it was Lent. Also, the court was in mourning for Charles's other sister, the queen of Denmark. No ambassador seems to have been invited.[29]

The court remained in Seville for a few months and in June left for Granada, a city which had by then been ruled by Castilians for thirty years. Here the court remained till December and did welcome ambassadors. The stay was a prolonged honeymoon for Charles and his bride, Isabel; their heir, Philip, was conceived in September.[30]

But the court now received much bad news. First, no sooner had King Francis I become free than he forged a new and entirely unexpected alliance at Cognac with Pope Clement VII, which became known as 'the Papal League'.[31] The papal legate, Salviati, left Granada in haste. Francesco Maria Sforza in Milan and the rulers of both Florence and Venice, Duke Alessandro and the doge, gave support to Charles. The emperor was astonished at what he saw as Pope Clement's perfidy, yet Clement now wrote to Charles denouncing him for disturbing the peace. A reply was drafted by the brilliant Alfonso de Valdés, Charles's new secretary for Latin correspondence, who was the son of an old Christian who had committed the mistake – or had the good taste – to marry a *conversa*.[32] A convinced Erasmian, Valdés sought to influence his master, Charles, to that end through the drafts of his speeches and his writings – as modern speech-writers often do also. Valdés had an idea of empire which would have made Charles a reformer precisely by becoming an Erasmian. In his dialogue, *Ánima*, he wrote: 'the first thing I did was to give everyone to understand that I had such influence with the king that I could do anything that I wanted to with him and that he could do nothing without me'.[33] He was a natural ally of Alonso de Manrique, the *inquisidor-general* who thought that he had royal support to use the Holy Office for humane purposes.

Charles was present in Granada at the lodgings of Gattinara on 17 September 1526 when the letter for Clement was handed to the new nuncio, a man amply competent to judge the weight of such documents, for he was none other than the Mantuan writer Baldassare Castiglione, who had earlier been ambassador to Leo X in Rome on behalf of the Duke of Urbino. In 1519, he had also been the Gonzagas's representative in Rome before going to Spain in 1524. He became naturalized there and was soon named bishop of Ávila. He was in 1526 at work on his dialogue *The Courtier*, which would be published in Venice in 1528 and prove a great success for many generations. Castiglione really did not want to send Clement VII such a sharp communication as was suggested but Charles insisted: 'My Lord Nuncio, after you accept that paper for His Holiness, in which I report several unjust accusations, I take occasion to express myself yet more fully by word of mouth and I can but hope that, hereafter, the pope will resume towards me the attitude of a good father towards a devoted son.'[34] The emperor added that he wanted to see peace not only in Italy but in the whole world, for only thus could the Turks be defeated. But if the pope acted not as a father but as an enemy, not as a shepherd but as a wolf, Charles would have to appeal to a general council of the Church.[35] The nuncio reluctantly agreed to pass on this comment to his master in Rome.

Castiglione's conversations with the Emperor Charles continued at Granada. Charles admired him. On 17 August Castiglione reported that a French representative had, in the presence of himself and the Venetian ambassador, Gaspar Contarini, explained how the new Papal League had been founded. The emperor was angry and said to the Frenchman: 'Had your king kept his word, we should have been spared this. He has cheated me, he has acted neither as a king nor a nobleman. I demand that, if he cannot keep his word, the most Christian King should again become my prisoner. It would be better for us to fight out this quarrel hand to hand, rather than to shed much Christian blood.' This challenge to a hand-to-hand duel was a typically chivalrous Caroline gesture. At that time it still seemed to many people that Spaniards counted for nothing in the formulation of the policy of Charles V: policy was the work of a narrow group of Flemish counsellors.[36]

Gattinara said that perhaps those who put their trust in France to the neglect of Italy now had something to answer for. In order to gain support from the German princes, including his brother Ferdinand, Charles offered a general pardon to all who had differed from him at the Diet of Worms in 1521. On 20 August a brief reply came from Pope Clement. Charles seemed not to be angry, Castiglione noticed with pleasure. Gattinara prepared another reply in twenty-two pages – which Valdés, with the pride of the official speech-writer, claimed that he himself had drafted. This was *Pro divo Carolo ... Apologetici libri duo*. Gattinara presented it to the Council of Castile in the house in Granada of the Centurioni, the Genoese merchants. It seemed in the circumstances excessively Erasmian, for it tried to destroy the political pretensions of the papacy and to reduce the pope's role to a pastoral mission.[37]

Then, however, news of a further disaster broke: the sunny world of Granada in the days of the royal honeymoon was transformed in September by terrible news from Hungary. On 29 August Sultan Suleiman in Hungary had smashed the Christian kingdom there at Mohács. King Louis (Charles's brother-in-law), two archbishops, five bishops and many noblemen were killed. New, accurate Turkish artillery played a large part in the defeat. The blow was utterly unexpected. A week later Suleiman was in Buda. Where could the Turkish army be halted? At Vienna? Louis's widow, Charles's sister, Mary, was distraught. She did what she could to ensure that her brother, Fernando, who had married her sister-in-law, King Louis's sister, Anne of Hungary, should succeed her dead husband. There was for once a powerful Christian reaction: nobles, prelates, cities, all the institutions of the realm were ready for a supreme effort. 'Once more,' says a modern historian, 'Castile showed her European and Christian vocation.'[38]

All the same, Gattinara's reply to Pope Clement was despatched. The document denounced Clement for disloyalty and justified Charles in his unforgiving treatment of Reggio, Modena and Milan. The language was often sarcastic, for it remarked that it was scarcely credible that any Vicar of Christ should acquire any worldly possessions at the cost of a drop of human blood – was that not a contradiction of the teaching of the Gospel?[39]

In the event the Archduke Fernando was finally elected king of Bohemia, but most of what was left of Hungary was physically seized by a Transylvanian nobleman, John Zápolya, with whom, and with whose heirs, the Habsburgs would maintain an intermittent civil war for two generations.

After their long stay in Granada, the king, queen and court left the city on 5 December and made for Úbeda, where they for a time lodged in the grand new house of the secretary, Cobos. It was here that Charles signed a contract with Francisco de Montejo which allowed him to conquer and colonize Yucatan. This represented a cancellation of an older grant of Yucatan to Laurent de Gorrevod, who had been allocated the right in 1519. On 7 December an edict was issued in Granada, to which the Inquisition, established at Jaén, had been transferred. The edict set out to eliminate much of the local culture and identity – the Arabic language, traditional dress and costume, jewellery and baths.

A week later Charles also signed an agreement with another veteran of New Spain, that experienced conquistador Pánfilo de Narváez, to 'discover, penetrate and populate' the territory from the river of the Palma (near Pánuco) to the cape at the southern point of Florida – the entire coastline of modern Texas, Louisiana, Mississippi and Florida.[40] Narváez needed a new mission and here was one to which he seemed suited.

On 12 December the bishop of Badajoz spoke of Charles as 'monarch and lord of the whole world with the aim of persecuting and exterminating the pagans and the unfaithful'.[41] In Andalusia no one flinched at the use of 'exterminating'. Before leaving Granada, the emperor had decreed that the people of that city should abandon Moorish dress – though they would have six years to wear out the clothes they had already. Charles named Gaspar de Ávalos and Antonio de Guevara to act as visitors to check against the continuation of Moorish customs.[42] These men were successful in resisting such interventions as those of the Count of Ribagorza, who had been deputed by the Aragonese Mudéjars to try to preserve their old status.[43] Now these dignitaries as well as some Granadinos presented pleas on behalf of the conservatives. Some had fought well for the royalists in the war of the *comuneros*.

The court travelled from Úbeda to Valladolid, stopping on the way at Madrid, the small city in the centre of Spain which Cardinal Cisneros had made his temporary capital. There Charles and Isabel remained until they went to the nearby monastery of Abrojo for Holy Week.

In Italy the morale of the imperial army which had beaten Francis at Pavia was low. Payment to the soldiers was scandalously behind. The chivalrous Ávalos had died of his wounds. A Cortes was held at Valladolid where the nobles declared that, if the king were to take part personally in a war against 'the Turk', their lives were at his disposal, but they refused to be taxed to provide money for a campaign. The prelates, too, claimed that they had no money to give and the *procuradores*, representing the towns of Castile, maintained that the country was too poor for any such extravagance. The mendicant orders said that their mission was to pray for victory, though the Jeronymites did agree that they would sell their silver chalices if it became evident that it was the Christians who had really made peace first. The Benedictines also offered 12,000 doubloons, while the military orders volunteered one fifth of their pensions.

Charles was considering the implications of these disappointments when yet more bad news came – this time from Italy. The previous autumn the private army of the Colonna family had entered Rome, and the pope had fled to his Castel Sant' Angelo on the Tiber. It was reported that the old papal palace in the Vatican had been stripped, and that even the wardrobe and the bedroom of the pope had been ransacked.[44] Given this encouragement, the unpaid imperial army took the hint. In May 1527 it too entered Rome, its commander, the Constable of Bourbon, having given the order for the assault. The chaos was widespread. Most movable objects, such as the gold cross of Constantine, the golden rose presented to Pope Martin V and the tiara of the reforming Pope Nicholas V, disappeared. The abbot of Nájera said that nothing comparable had been seen since the destruction of Jerusalem.[45] No one was safe. Perhaps 4,000 were killed. Bourbon himself was also killed (perhaps by a shot from Cellini's arquebus) – a death which the courtier Castiglione saw as a sign of divine fury against his army.[46] The library in the Vatican was saved only by the intervention from his sickbed of the Prince of Orange, who had also been wounded. The Sistine Chapel became a stall for horses.[47]

Charles the emperor, learning of the event in mid-June, said that he had not wanted this *dénouement* and we cannot doubt that he rejected the cruelties practised by his army. All the same, the pope in Castel Sant' Angelo was now his prisoner, just as Francis I had been. Charles wrote to Bourbon before he knew of his death that what he wanted most was 'a good peace' and he hoped that the pope would come to Spain to help to achieve it.[48] Gattinara remained in touch. His gifted secretary,

Alfonso de Valdés, wrote in his dialogue *Lactancio y un arcediacono* that Rome got no more than it deserved.[49]

Charles then gave himself up to the pleasure of celebrating at Valladolid the birth of his heir, the Infante Philip, the *Hispaniarum princeps*, in the house of Bernardino Pimentel, of the great family of the Count-Duke of Benavente, just opposite the church of San Pablo. The emperor had with him for the first time the beautiful set of tapestries depicting virtues made in honour of his coronation in Aachen in 1520.[50]

Also in June Francisco de Montejo, that most experienced conquistador who would have benefited from all those virtues himself, left Sanlúcar with his expedition of four ships and 250 men for Yucatan,[51] and Pánfilo de Narváez left for Florida with his 600 men in three ships.[52]

Intellectual Spain settled down in Seville that month to discuss the importance of the works of Erasmus, under the benign chairmanship of the Grand Inquisitor, Alonso de Manrique de Lara, the liberal churchman to whom Erasmus had dedicated his *Enchiridion militis Christiani*. Its Spanish translation by the famous preacher Alonso Fernández de Madrid, canon of Palencia and archdeacon of Alcor, and issued from the press of Miguel de Eguía, printer of Alcalá, now had a popular success without precedent in the history of Spanish printing up to that time.

Manrique, a cousin of the Duke of Nájera, was a half-brother of the poet Jorge Manrique. The new Grand Inquisitor had become a friend of Charles during his childhood in the Netherlands and had presided over the mass in the cathedral of St Gudule proclaiming Charles king of Spain in 1516.[53] Earlier, Manrique had been bishop of Badajoz where he had spent much of his time converting Muslims, many of whom took the name of 'Manrique'. He had been a strong *felipista*, a supporter of the late King Philip, and later was imprisoned by Fernando, but he was also a correspondent of Cisneros, who made him bishop of Córdoba. He was with Charles at his coronation at Aachen and was named archbishop of Seville, as well as Grand Inquisitor, by Charles in 1522. A modern historian calls him '*un hombre ilustre, cortesano, erasmista y abierto*'[54] – adjectives impossible to apply to later grand inquisitors.

All the great names in the Spanish Church were at the discussions of Erasmus's ideas in Seville – Antonio de Guevara, author of *The Golden Book of Marcus Aurelius*, which he was still pretending that he had discovered in the library of Cosimo de' Medici in Florence; Francisco de Vitoria, the famous jurist, then still at San Esteban, the Dominican monastery in Salamanca; Bishop Siliceo, young but already known as a hard-line anti-Semite – to hear the Grand Inquisitor give a powerful defence of his Dutch friend. This was the second such discussion, for there had been something similar, on a lesser scale, in March.

Manrique made the effort to try to convert the Inquisition into an agent for the diffusion of Erasmian ideas – a most remarkable epoch in the history of that institution. Perhaps Bartolomé de las Casas had similar hopes for the Holy Office when in 1517 he had urged Cisneros to support its establishment in the New World.

The Council of the Inquisition firmly maintained their support for Erasmus. The Augustinian Fray Dionisio Vázquez, looked upon as the greatest of preachers at that time and renowned in Italy as much as in Spain, even made an elegy about the great Dutchman.[55] After all, even the pope had praised Erasmus. But great dangers lay ahead for all friends of the Rotterdam thinker. The greatest derived from the fact that the Spanish bureaucracy had adopted a harsh line in most matters following the transfer to Granada of the supreme court there in 1505, and this was rendered more so after the Inquisition of Jaén was also sent to Granada in 1526.

8

Four brothers in a conquest: the Alvarados and Guatemala

> *I again fitted out Alvarado and dispatched him from this city*
> *[Mexico] on the sixth of December in 1523. He took with him*
> *120 horsemen and with spare mounts a total of 160 horses*
> *together with 300 footsoldiers, 130 of whom crossbowmen and*
> *arquebusiers.*
>
> Letter from Cortés to Charles V, 1524

Heady theological uncertainties seemed far away from the practical politics of New Spain. For another remarkable expedition was mounted by Cortés and led by the brilliant, brutal, unpredictable, fascinating and brave Pedro de Alvarado, an Extremeño from Badajoz – to the Tehuantepec peninsula and subsequently to Guatemala. Far away Guatemala may seem, but the Spaniards were conquistadors from Extremadura. In November 1522 Alvarado had obtained a large *encomienda* in watery Xochimilco, just to the south of Mexico/Tenochtitlan and then one in Tututepec in Tlaxcala.[1] He had been employed by Cortés since the conquest of Mexico/Tenochtitlan in August 1521, in a variety of ways: in Veracruz, in relation to Cristóbal de Tapia, the king's representative (or the bishop of Burgos's), sent ineffectively in December 1521 to seize command from Cortés; then in Pánuco in 1523 to deal with the unexpected arrival of Francisco de Garay. Now this complex and usually successful Extremeño wanted a theatre of conquest for himself.

Cortés was always anxious to give his close friends a chance to fulfil themselves. With Alvarado in particular, he was always generous, for he had known him since their childhood together in Extremadura, and throughout the conquest of Mexico. Alvarado's reckless valour (with his own life, as well as those of others) and insolent pride impressed

Cortés, who was prudent, cautious, cultivated and patient: it was the charm of opposites. Alvarado, often known as Tonatiuh, 'son of the Sun' (or sometimes just 'Sun', '*el Sol*'), to the native Indians because of his fair hair, height, good looks and blue eyes, was the most popular of the many brave men whom Cortés had in his army.[2] In December 1523 he gave Alvarado the mission to go to Guatemala to see if indeed, as he had been told, there were there 'many rich and splendid lands inhabited by new and different races'.[3] Presumably he had also been informed that the region was fertile, that it produced both cotton and cacao, and that it had once contained the wild forebears of such plants as maize, tomato, avocado and sweet potato. Díaz del Castillo wrote that Cortés had asked Alvarado 'to try and bring the people [of Guatemala] to peace [with Spain] without waging war and to preach matters concerning our holy faith by means of the interpreters which he took with him'.[4] He took the opportunity to say that Alvarado was 'very well made and active, of good features and bearing, and both in appearance and speech so pleasing that he seemed always smiling'.[5] He was an excellent horseman, liked rich clothes and always had round his neck a small gold chain on which hung a jewel, and he wore also a ring with a good diamond. Díaz del Castillo's criticism was that he talked too much and sometimes cheated at *totoloque*.[6] Others would complain that he was insensitive to the feelings of Indians, whom he treated as beneath contempt.[7] Several of his soldiers in this journey to Guatemala later testified to his brutality

Alvarado set off. The distance was, of course, considerable. Even now to travel by land from Mexico to Guatemala is a challenge. Aldous Huxley wrote of the journey between Oaxaca and Chiapas with awe. And he did not travel by foot or on a horse, as Alvarado did, seeing for himself the long line of the Pacific coast.

Alvarado took with him about 330 men, of whom 120 were horsemen, the rest infantry. He had four pieces of artillery which he arranged to be pulled by Indians[8] and he had a strong force of crossbowmen and musketeers. It was a family expedition from the beginning. With him rode his brothers, Jorge, Gonzalo and Gómez, who had all accompanied Cortés on his dramatic journeys, as well as two nephews, Diego and Hernando de Alvarado, and his future son-in-law, Francisco de la Cueva. He had a chaplain in the shape of Fr Bartolomé de Olmedo, the Mercedarian who had been with Cortés and who was responsible for 2,500

conversions before the end of 1524, when he died.[9] All of them worshipped Pedro de Alvarado. In addition, Alvarado had with him a
substantial number of 'natives' from central Mexico (perhaps 6,000 or
7,000 men, according to Antonio de Luna, in an enquiry (*pesquisa*) of
1570), including, it would seem, both Mexica and people from Tlaxcala, the Spaniards' chief allies. There seem also to have been a number
of black African slaves.[10]

Alvarado took a month to reach Soconusco, a territory well known
for its chocolate and, then as now, for its beautiful, large women. Jorge
de Alvarado was allocated the place as an *encomienda* by his brother,
Pedro (Cortés himself had had it for a year or two).[11] It had been fully
conquered by the Mexica only in the early years of the century in the
days of Montezuma, but it had been sending semi-annual tribute to the
Mexica in Tenochtitlan for forty years before that.[12] It was known for
its supply of beautiful green feathers from the quetzal bird. Probably the
plumage in the famous headdress in Vienna derived from birds from
here.

The Alvarados were now on the verge of entering present-day
Guatemala. At that time, there were three dominant peoples there: the
Quichés, the Cakquichels and the Tzutúhil. All were similar in social
structure to the Mexica, and their priests said that they and their leaders
originally came from Tollan and Teotihaucan. Beyond were a warlike
tribe called the Mam. Archaeologists argue that there had been three
waves of invasion from the north. These northern invaders had brought
with them the idea of cremation rather than burial, they used caves (in
which they deposited deities) for worship, they had a cult of war, they
had good metallurgical traditions, they had experimented with a
bicephalous system of government in the style of Rome or Sparta, they
preferred *tortillas* to *tamales*, and they had regular commercial relations
with Tenochtitlan. They fought with grenades of pottery sometimes
filled with fire, sometimes with wasps or hornets, they decapitated prisoners and they had bark on which to write painted genealogical books.
The people wore cotton clothing – the women sarongs, the men loin-
cloths. They had brought down from old Mexico the god of rain, Tlaloc,
and some of his companions in the pantheon of Mexican deities, such
as Xope Totec, the terrifying flayed fertility god, and Xolotl, the evening
star, who was Quetzalcoatl's half-brother, while their calendar contained,
as did that of Tenochtitlan, a sacred cycle of fifty-two years. They did not

celebrate human sacrifice on anything like the scale that was practised in the sixteenth century by the Mexica, which makes one realize that the legends suggesting that practice had much increased in the last generations before the arrival of the Spaniards were probably right. Famous opponents were the only ones to be routinely killed.[13]

Though the Quichés and the Cakquichels were plainly related, they had fought each other for years over possession of cacao and cotton fields. That was what characterized them. Had the Spaniards not come, the region would probably have been eventually conquered by the Mexica.[14]

The land, Alvarado reported to his leader, Cortés, was so thickly populated that 'there are more people than Your Excellency has governed till now'.[15] Like all comments at that time on populations, or the size of armies, that was an exaggeration. But archaeologists have found pyramidal mounds of old Guatemala in which there were 15 million shards, perhaps from about 500,000 vessels, suggesting that the mounds must have been built in the early Christian era by 10–12,000 labourers.

The country included the Cuchumatan highlands, the most dramatic non-volcanic region of Central America. The name may signify 'that which has come together with great force', but it can also mean, in Nahuatl, the 'place of the parrot hunters'. There were also the jungle lowlands of Petén, and a chain of active and geologically young volcanic peaks which can be seen from the sea and which inspired Disraeli's famous comment about the aged Whig cabinet of 1870.[16]

Guatemala was the land of *Popol Vuh*, a poem composed in the fourth century AD about the creation of the world. By 1500 it probably had as many versions as there are dialects of Maya, but the one which has survived is that of one of the leading clans of the Quichés. The book which contained it was traditionally said to have been obtained as a result of a journey to the Atlantic or Caribbean coast and would be consulted by the lords of the Quichés when they sat in council. The Quichés referred to the volume as 'the light which came from near the sea'. Other names for it were 'Our place in the shadows' or 'The down of Life'. Repetitive, contradictory and often incomprehensible to the modern reader, *Popol Vuh* has about it an unquestionable profundity which makes it a landmark of indigenous literature.

The existence of this remarkable poem, along with high-class pottery, elaborate sunken ball courts with vertical walls and dance platforms for the performance of religious and historical music dramas as well as the

Annals of the Cakquichels[17] made Guatemala one of the most sophisticated of the countries which the Spaniards set out to conquer.

Once beyond Soconusco in January 1524, Alvarado sent messages to the lords of Guatemala asking them not to impede his progress but to submit themselves to him as the representative of Charles the emperor. If they resisted, he declared, he would make war on them. He understandably received no reply. Such communications were relatively easy, since Nahuatl was understood in many Quiché and Cakquichel towns. So Alvarado's mercenaries from Tlaxcala or Tenochtitlan could talk together easily and secure supplies at least of maize made into *tortillas*, or into drink (*atole*) or even boiled into a leaf (*tamale*), as today.

Alvarado moved on, passing Zapotitlan, the land of the *sapodilla* plum. Afterwards, the journey became more difficult since they were obliged to continue along the coastal plain, the *llanura costera*, between the sparsely populated Sierra Madre de Chiapas, which rises to about 1,500 metres at its border with Oaxaca and to 3,000 metres on the south-east frontier into Guatemala and the Pacific Ocean. The mosquitoes never left the Spaniards, who suffered more thereby than if they had met ferocious enemies[18] – though they encountered some of those too. On 19 February they struck inland and up the hillside. This was the first time that any European had seen, much less visited, these Pacific-facing hills.

The *pueblos* of the mountains were small clusters of twenty-four to thirty-six mud-walled dwellings with palm-leaf roofs. The only certain item in these houses was a tripodal *metate* for grinding corn – rounded or rectangular slabs of hard igneous rock whose grinding surface would have been worn in the centre. The villages were usually undefended, there were no avenues or fine plazas, nor, indeed, any kind of urban planning. What they did have, though, was much superb monochrome and bichrome pottery made into bowls, pots, incense burners with three legs, as well as figurines and whistles.

Popol Vuh seemed to have forecast the Spaniards' arrival: 'And it is not clear how they crossed the sea, They crossed over as if there had been no sea. Where the waters were divided, they crossed over.' The Quiché people were, therefore, on a war footing. They fell on Alvarado's indigenous mercenaries with enthusiasm. Their temporary success was set back by Alvarado's horsemen. But the Quichés had heard of the menace of the horsemen and recovered to attack the Spaniards from above, in a valley under the volcano Santa María, approximately where there is now the city of Quezaltenango (Xela in Maya). The attack was eventually held and pressed back, the Quiché leader Tecum Um'an being killed, perhaps by Alvarado himself. The Maya insisted that Tecum Um'an immediately became a god, in the shape of an eagle with quetzal plumes.[19] The legendary ability of many Quiché to become animals impressed even Alvarado.

After the battle, the Spaniards rested several days there, only to be attacked again, by another Quiché army numbering, so Alvarado grandly put it, 12,000. This was also defeated by a clever Spanish combination of artillery and cavalry. After this, the Quichés agreed to seek peace and invited Alvarado to negotiate with them at Utatlán, their main city, a characteristic hilltop fortress town, known for the legend of the so-called 'marvellous kings' Gucumatz, who died in 1425, and Quicab, who died in 1475.[20] Those mythical individuals have reminded some archaeologists of the great god Quetzalcoatl in Mexico (Ehecatl, in Guatemala), and there were in Guatemala certainly the circular temples with which that deity had been associated in Tenochtitlan. There were ceremonial plazas and buildings which served as tombs, painted temples and good avenues alongside pyramids, as in Teotihaucan. The fine pottery included many figurines.

The Spaniards duly went to Utatlán in March, by then knowing of the tribal hatreds between the Quichés and the Cakquichels, with the latter of whom Alvarado had just made an alliance and who were said to have provided him with 4,000 men. But he found the city closed. Rightly afraid of being trapped with his horses and all his followers if he were to go inside, he camped outside the walls. There he received a visit from two lords who emerged from inside Utatlán. The discussions went badly and Alvarado imprisoned them. This infuriated the other Quiché leaders, who ordered an attack. Alvarado responded by putting the city to the torch and, in the fire, amid sporadic fighting, the leaders whom he had captured were burned.[21]

Alvarado was later accused of inhumanity in this instance. A number of Spanish witnesses were later asked in lawsuits in Spain if they knew that when 'the said Pedro de Alvarado was the captain ... at Utlatan [sic] and at Guatimala [sic] ... certain lords came in peace and the said Pedro de Alvarado seized them and burned them for no good reason other than that he wanted to know if they had any gold'.[22] The accusations never ended. But Alvarado was never charged.

In April 1524 Alvarado turned on the Cakquichel who, from their capital at Quahtematlan, had observed with pleasure the defeat of their Quiché enemies. All the same, they were fearful of the Spaniards with their guns, horses and, not least, terrifying war dogs. These indigenous leaders urged Alvarado to take his army against the people of Atitlán, another town of the Cakquichels, who had already shown their hostility to Spaniards by killing four messengers who had come to propose a pact. So on 17 April 1524 Alvarado led towards Atitlán a detachment of sixty horse, 150 foot soldiers and a large unit of Cakquichels. After a skirmish with Tzutúhil Indians by a lakeside, they reached their destination with ease. But the city was deserted, for the people were justifiably terrified. Alvarado did, however, manage to find some Indians and sent them to tell their lords that he would make peace with them if they returned and declared themselves vassals of the king of Spain. The lords quickly accepted this condition, but whether they understood what they had undertaken is doubtful; the word 'vassal' is not easily translated.

In May Alvarado embarked on a new journey, to the south of Guatemala to Panatcat, where some of his indigenous allies, especially those who had come with him from Texcoco, were caught off guard and slaughtered. Alvarado punished the town by burning it. He continued onwards, passing through Atepac, Tacuilulá, Taxisco, Moquisalco and Nancintla, and across the river now known as the Paz, into what is now El Salvador. Everywhere the meeting between the Spaniards and the *naturales* was similar: the former were received in peace, the *naturales* then abandoned the town and fled to the hills, where they planned their resistance. The only serious battle was at Achiutla, the gateway to El Salvador, where about 6,000 fighters launched a serious attack and killed many of Alvarado's indigenous allies. No Spaniards died but some were wounded, including Alvarado himself. An arrow went through his leg and left him for a time crippled, one leg seeming for a long while shorter than the other. For several months his life was at risk because of infection.

Alvarado eventually continued into El Salvador, putting up with further attacks at Tlacusqualco and halting at Cuzcatlán, the most important of these towns, where the Spaniards would shortly found a settlement which they named San Salvador. One of Alvarado's soldiers, Román López, would testify later that, as they made their way to this city, the population of all the towns en route 'came out in peace and Alvarado then burned them and made slaves of the people and branded them'. Pedro González de Nájera, who had come to New Spain with Narváez, said the same: 'this witness was with Pedro de Alvarado and was present when those concerned were burned because they desired to burn them'.[23] The lords in Cuzcatlán offered food, fruit, cloaks – and obedience. But they then fled to the hillside as usual.

After two and a half weeks the Spaniards moved on to Ixmide, which they reached on 21 July. There they soon decided to found Santiago de los Caballeros de Guatemala, the day of Saint James, Santiago, being 25 July. It would become the main city of the colony, though it underwent several changes of site (one can still see the narrow causeway which Alvarado and his men used to storm the old town). Alvarado gave this new city several municipal councillors or *alcaldes ordinarios* (Diego de Rojas from Seville and a son of Leonora de Alvarado, Baltasar de Mendoza), while his brother Gonzalo became the *alguacil mayor* or chief magistrate. Thus the ways of Spain were once again transferred to a new site in an unknown country.

Here, eight months after leaving Mexico, Alvarado and his men rested. All his surviving indigenous troops except the loyal people of Tlaxcala made their way homewards. But 'Tonatiuh' imposed on his Cakquichel allies a tribute in gold which he said they had to pay even though they were helping him so substantially. The lords of the Cakquichels refused and recommended all their people to abandon the cities and take refuge in the hills. The friendship between them and Alvarado was thus severed.

Once again old hatreds were the best allies of the invaders. The Quichés and the people of Atitlan were happy to fight against their Cakquichel enemies, even under new circumstances. The Cakquichels had, however, learned new tactics from their months of alliance with the Spaniards, whom they forced to return to Quezaltenango. Diego de Alvarado, nephew of Pedro, took two years to reduce Cuzcatlán while his uncle Gonzalo conquered the territory of the Mames between Chiapas and the Quichés. Gonzalo de Alvarado was named by his brother Pedro to conduct this campaign after it became evident that an abortive plan to burn the Spaniards at Atitlan in 1524 had been suggested to the Quiché leader, Chugna Huincelet, by the Mam Caibil Balam. Chugna was killed but his son Sequechul wanted to avenge him. Sequechul offered to guide Gonzalo to 'the great and rich territory' of the Mames, which boasted what he explained was an abundant treasure.

For a year or so the initiative for further conquests lay with Gonzalo de Alvarado, not Pedro, who took many months to recover from the wound to his leg. Gonzalo had been in the Indies since 1510 and with Cortés throughout the great campaigns of conquest. He was devoted to his famous family and had even married into it since his wife, Bernardina, was his niece, being the daughter of his brother Jorge.

In July 1525 Gonzalo de Alvarado left Tecpán for the country of the Mames with forty horsemen, about eighty infantry and 2,000 or so Mexica and Quiché Indians, who acted either as porters or warriors in the early stages of the battles. He was delayed by the onset of rains. He went first to Totonicapán, on the edge of the Mames land, then to what the Spaniards named the 'Río Hondo', deep river, and seized the town of Mazatenango, which they rechristened San Lorenzo. Marching beyond that *pueblo* towards Huehuetenango they met a Mam army from Malacatán. But Gonzalo de Alvarado charged at it with his horsemen and the Mam leader Cani Acab was killed by the Spanish commander himself with his lance. As so often after the death of a leader, the native resistance collapsed and Gonzalo occupied Malacatan, whose inhabitants were swiftly accepted as vassals of the king of Spain.[24]

The next Mam town to be occupied was Huehuetenango, where fine birds such as the quetzal, parrot and cotinga could be found to provide feathers for headdresses and cloaks. The inhabitants fled first to the fortress town of Zaculeu with ravines on three sides. This had been an important centre of Mam culture for a thousand years. It had been captured by the Quichés in the early fifteenth century, but seemed to have recently asserted its independence.

Gonzalo de Alvarado demanded its peaceful surrender:

Let it be known [to Caibil Balam] that our coming is beneficial to his people because we bring news of the true God and of the Christian religion sent by the pope, the vicar of Jesus, as of the emperor king of Spain so that you may become Christians peacefully of your own free will. But if you should refuse our offer of peace, the death and destruction which will follow will be your own responsibility.[25]

Gonzalo gave his opponents three days in which to consider his offer. But no answer came. Instead, a Mam army arrived from the north to relieve Zaculeu. Gonzalo left his deputy, Antonio de Salazar, who had been with Narváez in New Spain and subsequently in most of Cortés's battles round the lake of Tenochtitlan, to continue the siege.[26] Gonzalo turned on the relief force, though by now his men were hungry and without much hope of food until Zaculeu was taken. The native Spanish mercenaries were as usual held by the Indians, who were then forced into defeat by the horsemen. Gonzalo returned to Zaculeu with starvation threatening; his surviving Indian auxiliaries were forced to eat dead horses. But then Juan de León Cardona, whom Pedro de Alvarado had made captain of the conquered Quiché territory, sent him a substantial shipment of food. Zaculeu surrendered in September 1525 and Gonzalo assumed the command of all the western Cuchamatan.

By then, Pedro de Alvarado had recovered sufficiently from his wound to be able to contemplate a new expedition of his own, this time into Chiapas, seeking to meet his old commander and comrade, Cortés, who was then en route for Hiberas to punish the wilful Cristóbal de Olid. Chiapas, it will be recalled, had some years before been conquered by Sandoval. Alvarado wanted Cortés's support for his claim formally to become governor of Guatemala. But the dense jungle, the colossal rivers and the majestic mountains made any thought of meeting Cortés impracticable.

Alvarado returned to Guatemala, where he found that several of his settlements, such as San Salvador, had been destroyed. He had become attached to Guatemala and its people, even though he had treated them so harshly. Perhaps the astonishing variety of landscape and vegetation of the well-watered narrow coastal plain along the Pacific appealed to him, improbable though it may seem. Brutal men can have a soft side. Perhaps he liked the cypresses, the high fertile valleys, the temperate climate, the volcanic stone for grinding stones and the sharp knives, the availability of lime for mortar. There was obsidian for weapons and iron pyrites with which to make looking-glasses. In the streams there was a little gold as well as copper, and also abundant fresh fish, with shellfish at the coast. There was bark for making paper, silk and cotton for quilted armour, tobacco, pumpkins for music, bees for honey. Some Spaniards were impressed by the diversity of gods in Guatemala, as well as by the ritual invoked on all occasions of celebration and by the speed with which Catholic saints were identified with local gods. Certainly this was a territory much richer than Alvarado's home town of Badajoz in Extremadura.

Hearing that Francisco de Montejo, a comrade of the early days of the campaign in New Spain, had been granted the governorship of Yucatan, Alvarado determined to return to Mexico/Tenochtitlan and then to Spain to obtain a similar nomination for himself in Guatemala. He had by then taken 'such a fancy to this land of Guatemala and its people that he decided to stay there and colonise. So he laid the foundation for Santiago de Guatemala and prepared a cathedral.'[27] He also established *encomiendas* and a town council for his new city, and then went through the motions of requesting its members' permission, as commander, to leave for Spain. In his absence his brother Jorge became acting governor from August 1526.

Though the conquest of Guatemala was far from complete, Alvarado had made his mark there, and would be remembered as 'Tonatiuh', son of the Sun. The Quiché lords would perhaps echo the prayer of the lords in *Popol Vuh*: 'Heart of Sky, heart of earth, give me strength, give me the courage, in my heart, in my head, for you are my mountain and my plain.'[28]

9

Charles and his empire

*I counted from a mosque [in Cholula] four hundred and more tow-
ers in the city and all of them are mosques.*

Cortés from Cholula to Charles V, 1519

Some modern historians have fallen into the trap of thinking that the
Emperor Charles paid little attention to his transatlantic possessions.[1]
These suppositions are not borne out, even considering his activities in
Valladolid in 1522. For example, we hear that, early in that year, he
prolonged for another four years the lucrative monopoly of Laurent de
Gorrevod, the Savoyard governor of Bresse and protégé of the Archduchess Margaret of Austria, for the sale of black African slaves in the
empire.[2] From November 1523, this arrangement was annulled and
the import of slaves to the Indies was permitted along new lines: 1,400
a year were allowed to Santo Domingo, 700 to Cuba, 600 to Mexico,
500 to San Juan and Castilla del Oro, and 300 to Jamaica. Gorrevod
was compensated by receiving the duty (*almorifazgo*) on the 1,400
slaves destined for Santo Domingo. That demanding but blunt and
simple tax was always changing. In 1524 it was introduced on all goods
entering New Spain and 50,000 pesos were raised by it in the next seven
years.[3]

Then, as we have seen, in October 1522, only three months after his
return to Spain for his second stay, Charles, as we have seen, was persuaded to send four important officials to 'assist' Cortés in the
government of Mexico; and there was also the reception of the world
travellers El Cano and Pigafetta when they came back from the round-
the-world journey which they had undertaken at Charles's cost, on the
initiative of the dead Magellan.[4] From 1523, first as an emergency, the

Crown seized all precious metals sent home from the Indies; then, as a matter of course, all such private gold was automatically turned into *juros* (periodic payments at a fixed rate of interest).[5]

It is true that in the 1520s the Spanish income from the Indies was still modest, amounting in 1520 to 1525 to a mere 134,000 pesos; the Crown's share was 35,000. In comparison, between 1516 and 1520, the figure was 993,000, with the Crown's share 260,000.[6] Between 1526 and 1530 the income was over a million pesos, of which the Crown's share was 272,000. Very soon, events in Peru would transform this situation for the better.

In 1526 Charles was persuaded to grant the government of Yucatan and Cozumel, which had often been visited by Spaniards but not yet conquered, to Francisco de Montejo, the hidalgo from Salamanca who had represented Cortés in Spain in the early days of his great adventure.[7] Montejo had been a friend of Diego Velázquez, the governor of Cuba, before that expedition began, but had become one of Cortés's allies in consequence of his achievements. Montejo's character was not grasping: he wanted glory more than gold. Now he was requesting a theatre of operations for himself.

The same year it became normal for those who undertook to grow sugar in the Indies to obtain a government loan, as Juan Mosquera did in February 1523 in Cuba. Mosquera was a notary (*escribano*) as well as an *encomendero* in Santo Domingo, where he was once 'visitor', that is, an occasional inspector, and where he had the luxury of a stone house. He was said to have been 'a man of very low manners, very passionate and the enemy of good men'.[8] His sister married Francisco de Molina, cousin and protégé of Cobos, whose daughter, María, would marry Luis Colón, the third admiral. Mosquera's laudable aim was to achieve free trade for the settlers in Cuba with other islands in the Caribbean.[9]

Another imperial concession of this time was to Licenciado Lucas Vázquez de Ayllón, an old hand in the Indies. Born in Toledo, he was the son of a councillor of that city, Juan de Ayllón, known as 'the Good'. He had gone out to the Caribbean in 1504, in Ovando's day, and to begin with, dedicated himself to agriculture and to mining, becoming *alcalde mayor*, chief magistrate, in Concepción in Santo Domingo. Perhaps he was a *converso*.[10] He made money on a property at Chicora, where he owned several hundred Indians.[11] In 1505 he appears as a university graduate in support of the able judge Alonso de Maldonado. Back in Spain for a year or two, he returned to Santo Domingo in 1509 to take the *residencia* of Ovando. In 1512 he was named judge, in the first supreme court, or *audiencia*, of the Indies.

This appointment did not prevent him from continuing to deal in indigenous slaves from the lesser Antilles, many of whom were destined for the icy-cold pearl fisheries of Cubagua, off Santa Margarita. He was moreover a financial backer of Juan Bono's expedition for slaves to Trinidad in 1516 and he also had for a time a monopoly of selling slaves from the Lucayos (the Bahamas, or 'useless islands').[12] His headquarters was Puerto Plata on the north coast of Hispaniola, where he had by 1522 a half-share in a new sugar mill. Thinking perhaps of the labour needed in that enterprise, he commented that it was 'far better that these Indians became slave men than free beasts'.[13] Difficult though it may be for a later age to envisage such a dilemma, the choice was almost a normal one in the sixteenth century.

Vázquez de Ayllón was the leading figure in the destruction of the free population of the Bahamas as well as a leading colonist of Santo Domingo, where he married Juana, daughter of Esteban de Pasamonte, treasurer of the island after the death of his uncle Miguel.

This Vázquez had been sent to Cuba by the court of Santo Domingo, of which he remained a member, to detain Narváez's fleet against Cortés in 1520. But he was thwarted by Narváez and, after a stay in New Spain as unfortunate as it was brief, he returned in a long sea journey to Santo Domingo.[14] Back in Castile, he was an influential witness testifying against Diego Velázquez in favour of Cortés. He became a knight of Santiago. Now he pursued his new adventure in Florida, which he was told was ruled by a giant (*'señoreado de un hombre de estatura de gigante'*). He went back again to Santo Domingo and spent his fortune on the Florida expedition, which he would not embark upon till 1526.[15]

The early decisions of the Council of the Indies included: a licence to allow merchants from ports other than Seville to trade with the Indies without registering in the Casa de la Contratación (the board in Seville which managed relations with the New World);[16] a contract for Santa Marta on the north coast of South America for Rodrigo de Bastidas, Cortés's backer, an adventurous *converso* merchant of Triana; blanket permission to all subjects of the Spanish world to go to the New World without distinction as to whence they derived;[17] and a ban on future conquistadors seizing people from the West Indies or the mainland except for those who might be needed as interpreters. This was a benign plan which was not carried through. A similar fate had befallen one of the most liberal orders to emerge from the Council of the Indies before it had formally taken shape, when it was decreed on 8 March 1523 that henceforth no war should be made against the Indians nor should any harm or damage come to them.[18] This was an early manifestation in Spain of the ideas of Fray Bartolomé de las Casas who, at this time, was still in his Dominican house in Santo Domingo studying for his subsequent crusade.

In July 1523 Charles gave a coat of arms to Tenochtitlan, or Mexico, as it was by then increasingly known. It was a great accolade, for no such concession had previously been made in the Caribbean. The device was characteristic: a shield coloured blue like water to recall the great lake on which the city had been built; and a gilded castle in the centre of it connected to the mainland by three causeways or stone bridges. A lion guarded each of these bridges, and its arms lay on the castle as a memory of the victory which the Christians had gained. The border of the design consisted of ten ears of green prickly pears with thistles.[19] The grant was signed by the Emperor Charles and also by Cobos, Hernando de Vega, Dr Beltrán, Dr Galíndez de Carvajal, and Domingo de Ochandiano, the new treasurer of the Casa de la Contratación (in succession to his dead uncle Sancho de Matienzo).[20] Neither Vega nor Galíndez de Carvajal would be members of the Council of the Indies, but they had been for many years members of that of Castile.

Significantly 1523 saw the publication in Toledo of what became a popular novel, *Clarín de Landanís* by Jerónimo López, as well as *Raimundo of Greece* by Francisco Bernal in Salamanca. The latter treated of a powerful king of Egypt named Cleopatro; a wise lady, Piromancia, who lived in Alexandria; and a duke, Pirineo, who lived in India. The kings of Scotland and Norway make fleeting appearances.[21] All the signs are that this work too became popular, and that it inspired, as well as amused, the court.

The Council of the Indies was in being by April 1526,[22] when it announced that, as it was in Seville for the wedding of the king emperor, it was going to investigate the activities of the Casa de la Contratación, which continued to be based there. There had been many rumours of corruption. The council asked the chief magistrates of nearby maritime towns (Sanlúcar, Palos, Moguer, Puerto de Santa María, Niebla) and the *corregidores* of Cadiz and Jerez de la Frontera to proclaim this enquiry by town crier.

The council, which undertook to make a report within thirty days, began by taking statements from witnesses. All the leading pilots were consulted. But the council took longer in their work than they had promised, and in November 1527 they announced that, having finished the accounts of the Casa itself, they would examine those of the officials and the treasure fleets' accountants. In the end, they found only one official guilty of corrupt practice: Juan López de Recalde, whose offences were listed by Juan de Aranda from Burgos (an old colleague as *factor* of the Casa over many years but López's bitter enemy). They did, however, find much evidence of incompetence. For example, the administration of the goods of people who had died in the Indies was spectacularly badly managed.

López de Recalde's condemnation was a blow to the Casa de la Contratación. He had been a power in Seville since the institution's foundation (and had been its accountant since 1505). It was he who, in 1518, had initially bought Gorrevod's grant of a monopoly of slaves for the Spanish empire, though he had resold it immediately.[23] He had been the chief assistant to Rodríguez de Fonseca in organizing the king's fleet to Germany in 1520[24] and the great friend in Andalusia of numerous successful Basque merchants.[25] He was married to Lorenza de Idiáquez, a sister of Alonso de Idiáquez, who was Cobos's majordomo and who would play a considerable part in bureaucratic policies in the next twenty years. López de Recalde's denunciation by Juan de Aranda (who had organized Magellan's expedition and defrauded the participants) marked the end of the power of the Fonsequistas in the Casa.

For the moment the only consequence of this investigation was the building in August 1520 of a chapel in the Casa de la Contratación where prayers for the souls of the dead explorers could be offered beneath the Flemish painter Alejo Fernández's beautiful picture *The Virgin of the Mariners*.[26] However, Dr Beltrán and Dr Maldonado stayed in Seville, with Juan de Samano, to continue to examine the business of the Casa de la Contratación.[27]

In November 1526 the Council of the Indies met in Granada in the

Alhambra. Charles, unusually, was presiding. Present were the three bishops who had the strongest voices on the council (García de Loaisa, Maldonado and Cabeza de Vaca), together with Cobos, Dr Beltrán, Juan de Samano and Cortés's distant relation, Dr Lorenzo Galíndez de Carvajal, who was a member of the Royal Council and Cabinet of Castile and who had much curiosity about the Indies. There was also Urbina, secretary to the chancellor, in the absence of his master, Gattinara himself.[28]

The council took what seems to read now as a remarkably humane decision. Talking of 'the disorganised greed of some of our subjects who go to our Indies . . .' and of 'the bad treatment which they show to the Indians native to those islands and on the mainland', not to speak of the 'great and excessive labour which they provide for them in mines to find gold' and 'in the pearl fisheries and in other farming', it accused the conquistadors of 'making the Indians excessively and immoderately tired, not giving them enough to wear or to eat, treating them cruelly and with the reverse of love, much worse than if they were slaves'. That had been the cause of the death of 'a great number of the said Indians on such a scale that many of the islands and part of the mainland remain barren and without any population'.

In addition, there were so many Indians who fled from the mines that 'it was a great hindrance to the enterprise of trying to arrange the conversion of the said Indians to our Catholic faith'. 'Too many captains, moved by the same greed, forgetting the service of our Lord God, went to kill many of those Indians in the discoveries and conquests and also seized their goods without the said Indians giving any cause for such a thing.'

As for the so-called '*requerimiento*' (Requirement): 'when the captains of the King discovered or conquered a new territory, they were obliged to proclaim immediately to its Indian inhabitants that they had been sent to teach good customs', to 'dissuade them from such vices as eating human flesh and to instruct them in the holy faith and preach it to them for their salvation'. A list of wrongs done to the natives followed. Every leader licensed by the Crown to carry out an expedition was to take with him a copy of the *requerimiento* and have it read by interpreters as many times as might be necessary. Every expedition henceforth also had to be accompanied by two churchmen, priests or friars, approved by the Council of the Indies, to instruct the Indians in religious matters, to protect them from the rapacity and cruelty of (some) Spaniards and ensure that the conquest was justly carried out. War was to be waged only after the ecclesiastics had given their consent in writing; and any such conflict had to be fought according to the methods permitted by law and the Christian religion. In addition, no one could make a slave of any Indian under pain of losing all his goods.[29]

This remarkable declaration remained the formal rule for the conduct of Spaniards in the New World for two generations. It was written into all capitulations and grants of opportunities from that day on, including, for example, the grant already mentioned to Francisco de Montejo in respect of Yucatan on 8 December 1526. That did not mean, however, a complete end to trading in Indian slaves. Thus on 15 November of that year Charles the emperor agreed to allow Juan de Ampiés to take Indians from the 'useless isles' off Venezuela – Curaçao and Cubagua, for example.[30] The same day he gave an *amplio permiso* for any subject of his from anywhere in Europe to go to the New World.[31] This was a special benefit to Germans who wished to share in the banquet of the Indies.

These Caroline decrees did not pass without challenge. The Cuban settlers, for example, thought that Indians might be made to wash for gold in rivers but not in mines. Even that led to complaints: Rodrigo Durán, the *procurador* of Santiago de Cuba, said that, if the royal order even as modified were carried out, many settlers would leave the island. The settlers in Cuba described mining as easy work and insisted that 'their' Indians preferred it to clearing land. Also, the settlers argued, workers were well fed at the mines on cassava bread and pork every day, whereas Indians in *encomiendas* had meat or fish only once a week. Ruin would surely follow any attempt to put these laws into effect.[32]

Rome continued to play a decisive part in the administrative history of the Indies. Thus in October 1523 the Flemish Erasmian Bishop Juan de Ubite, a Dominican, in Cuba was permitted to move his cathedral from the eastern extremity of Baracoa to 'the most powerful place on the island – namely, Santiago'.[33] (The King gave half his share of tithes in Santiago towards the completion of the cathedral.) Then in 1524 Pope Clement created a new patriarchate of the West Indies: its first incumbent would be Antonio de Rojas y Manrique, Bishop of Palencia, one of the richest Spanish dioceses, of which Valladolid was part.[34] This was a time when the Rojas family seemed to be filling every empty benefice, secular or ecclesiastical, in Spain. Bishop Antonio had been president of the Council of Castile for several years.[35]

Diego Colón, son of the legendary Christopher, had meantime returned to his governorship in Santo Domingo in 1520. He found the intrigues in that colony even worse than those in Seville. The chief intriguer remained the royal treasurer, the *converso* from Aragón, Miguel Pasamonte, who had dominated the colony since his arrival there in 1508.[36] Despite Pasamonte's evident disposition to conspire, Díaz del Castillo wrote well of him: 'personally worthy, of great good sense (*cordura*), honest to a fault, chaste all his life'.[37]

After three years of revived proconsular life in Santo Domingo, Diego Colón and his wife, María de Toledo, niece of the Duke of Alba – they had all the appurtenances of royalty – returned to Spain in October 1523, and two months later Charles, or rather the Council of the Indies, finally brought to an end the regime of the Columbus family in the New World. The title of Admiral of the Ocean Sea was suspended; the rights of the family too. All that the Columbuses retained was their dukedom of Veragua, a territory allegedly close to Panama. María de Toledo, however, retained her financial interests in the Caribbean. Having been a prominent dealer in Indian slaves, she became so in Africans. For the moment, she also kept her husband's income from the New World. Why the trade in blacks was permitted and the one in Indians discouraged is one of the mysteries of those days.

Diego Colón's departure required the appointment of a new governor of Santo Domingo. The government was for a time in the hands of a president of the court, and the choice of the Council of the Indies fell on Dr Sebastián Ramírez de Fuenleal, a reliable public servant from a tiny village south of Cuenca, Villaescusa de Haro, who had been a judge in the Alpujarra mountains during the Muslim rebellion there in 1500, after which he had become an *inquisidor* in Seville.[38] Despite that role, which must have tried him, Ramírez de Fuenleal showed himself a humane proconsul; at that time, many liberal churchmen still sought to enter the Holy Office in order to humanize it. 'There is no doubt,' Ramírez once declared, 'that the natives have sufficient capacity to receive the faith and that they greatly love it.' He also thought that 'they had sufficient capacity to carry on all mechanical and industrial arts'.[39]

Ramírez took a long time to reach Santo Domingo; indeed he arrived only in December 1528. In the meantime, Pasamonte enjoyed, as he had so often before, *de facto* authority. He used this interregnum to allow many of his friends to trade in Indian slaves, granting licences, including a new one to Vázquez de Ayllón, to Francisco de Lizaur, another old hand who had been Ovando's secretary, and to Diego Caballero, a *converso* merchant originally from Sanlúcar de Barrameda.

But the leaders of these entrepreneurs were by now probably Juan Martínez de Ampiés and Jacome de Castellón. The former was an Aragonese friend of Pasamonte who had been the factor of Santo Domingo in 1511. He had given evidence of a rather harsh sort to the legal enquiry mounted by the Jeronymites in 1517, agreeing that Indians were 'lazy, luxurious, gluttonous and with a disinclination to have any affections if left in liberty'. Despite that, in 1524, Ampiés sent an armada to bring 800 Indian slaves to Santo Domingo from islands off Venezuela, and in 1525 he sent another expedition to the same region. His agent, Gonzalo de Sevilla, had a tolerant attitude to Indians in principle, an attitude which caused him to clash with a fellow traveller, Martín de Baso Zabala.

All these slaving expeditions were the consequence of the use of captives in war or from kidnapping. There was none of the negotiation which by then characterized the purchase or exchange of African slaves. Ampiés himself spent eight months making friends with people in Curaçao and Aruba and soon convinced himself that only he could establish good relations with the South American Indians. He had a plan to take some of the chiefs of the Indians in what became Venezuela to Santo Domingo, educate and convert them and then send them back to their old homes as *agents provocateurs*. Ampiés would put up some of these tragic leaders in his own house in Santo Domingo. In order to protect his own interests on the South American coast, he also built a fortress on the island of Cubagua, optimistically naming it Nueva Cádiz, which soon became a centre of the pearl trade.

Cubagua, a small barren island off Santa Margarita, had been identified as a possible pearl fishery as early as 1502 by Rodrigo de Bastidas, the *converso* businessman who made a fortune in Santo Domingo. Within a few years, several Spanish adventurers had established pearl beds around the island, which was already mercilessly overfished. Spaniards did not know then that pearl fishing should be confined to the months of February, March and April. They did realize, though, that the pearls were of good quality, if inferior to those of the East. The 'Blanca Rosada' dominated.[40] Las Casas recalls what hard work fishing for pearls was: it meant diving deep in cold water, a task which even the toughest Indians performed under duress.

The other entrepreneur of importance was Jacome de Castellón, the natural son of a merchant of Genoa, Bernardo Castiglione, and a Sevillana, Inés Suárez. At the time of his birth, the commerce of Seville and south-west Andalusia was dominated by Genoese, as were the early beginnings of trade in the West Indies. Jacome's elder brother, Tomás, had represented the family in Hispaniola to begin with, but he had then gone to Puerto Rico, where he built the first sugar mill on the island and exploited the salt beds at San Juan. A cousin, Marcos de Castellón, had an olive farm near Seville.

Jacome went out to the Indies for the first time in 1510, being then eighteen. He became a partner of another Hispano-Genoese, Jerónimo Grimaldi, with Diego Caballero. Together they kidnapped Indian slaves from the Bahamas or from the mainland. By 1522 he was captain of a flotilla of his own which went regularly to Cumaná on the mainland just beyond Cubagua where, like Ampiés, he built a fortress and where he became chief magistrate (*alcalde mayor*) and received a salary in consequence. All the same, he continued to live in Santo Domingo. When he was granted a coat of arms in 1527, it depicted a fortress with the heads of four Indians bordering it.[41] By the 1530s he, like his brother Tomás, would have a sugar mill, 'La Española', near Azúa de Compostela.[42]

The seizing, branding and carriage of Indians as slaves from the Bahamas and northern South America seemed to be the major activity for Spanish entrepreneurs in the 1520s. But Ampiés and Castellón were unable to carry on after 1526 since the Crown allocated the geographer Fernández de Enciso most of the zone and then began to favour the German Welsers to whom the Emperor Charles owed money.

Diego Caballero, however, received a contract (*capitulación*) in 1525 for the discovery, development and settlement of the coast of Maracaibo, from Cabo de la Vela to Cabo de San Roman. It was thought that Lake Maracaibo might lead to – or even be – the great strait to the Pacific, or Southern Sea, of which so much had been said. That was one reason for the interest of the Welsers of Augsburg.

10

Pedrarias, Panama and Peru; Guzmán in New Spain

> *The good soil discovered is the most abundant and possible to populate with Christians that you have ever seen ... it has very fine gold.*
>
> Pizarro to Pedro de los Ríos, governor of Panama, 1527

Pedrarias Dávila was still the controlling genius in Spain's dominions in Panama and Nicaragua, though he was now well over seventy years of age. He had survived every challenge to his authority and outlived his benefactors, including King Fernando, as well as his enemies, such as Núñez de Balboa. It was said that he had made a pact with the devil to enable him to live so long. The judge of his *residencia*, Juan Ruiz de Alarcón, persuaded the governor to agree that he had discovered the Southern Sea at his own cost and founded there the city of Panama.[1] No friend of Núñez de Balboa would have agreed with such a claim but Balboa had now been forgotten; indeed, in Pedrarias's *residencia*, the name of Balboa did not figure. Perhaps because Pedrarias had arranged a new allocation of 10,000 Indians there, he was judged favourably: eighty-three *encomenderos* benefited.

The most recent distribution of Indians, it is true, particularly favoured Pedrarias himself, since he would have the services of 500 of them. Among the less well favoured were resourceful men such as Diego Almagro, probably from the town of that name in New Castile, who received a new grant of twenty Indians, just off Panama, in addition to the eighty which he already had on Susy; the priest Hernando de Luque, a Sevillano from Morón de la Frontera, in the sierra near Seville, who received seventy Indians; and the illiterate giant, Francisco Pizarro, from Trujillo in Extremadura, who also gained 150 Indians, on the island of

Taboga some fifteen miles off Panama. Of these last dependants of Pedrarias we shall soon hear more.

This allocation caused intense resentment, and a new lieutenant-governor of Panama, Licenciado Hernando de Celaya, who had already been named governor by the Council of the Indies in succession to Pedrarias, reduced the old adventurer's share of Indians to 378. The sudden death of Celaya followed. His friends were not slow to draw a malign conclusion about Pedrarias's responsibility.

Soon, Gil González de Ávila, the royal accountant in Santo Domingo, came to Panama. Like so many officials in the Indies in the early days, he attracted royal notice first through having been employed in the household of the much mourned Infante Juan. He was then a *contino*, courtier, a favourite of the corrupt but competent Bishop Rodríguez de Fonseca and he had gone to Hispaniola in 1509 with Diego Colón. He was one of those who, with Pasamonte, promoted the idea of taking Indians as slaves from the Bahamas. Elder brother of Alonso de Ávila, that successful captain of Cortés, he went first to Darien with Pedrarias. After several journeys back and forth to Spain, he reached Panama in 1522 and proposed an expedition to the west to explore the land. Gil González and his companion Andrés Niño, a shipowner of a family of seamen of Moguer, went to Spain and gained a licence to explore 3,000 miles of the coast of the Southern Sea. That permit ordered Pedrarias to give them the ships which Balboa had had built near Panama. Pedrarias was reluctant to comply, royal decree or not, until he was offered a good financial share in the expedition.[2]

At much the same time, the governor gave permission to a companion of his, Pascual Andagoya, to make a journey to the south. Andagoya was a Basque from a town of that name in Álava, the son of a hidalgo, Joan Ibáñez de Arza.[3] Andagoya had gone to the Indies in 1514 as a *criado* (follower) of Pedrarias, who left him a horse and 6,000 maravedís in the will he made before leaving Spain. Andagoya eventually established himself happily in Panama, becoming a town councillor in 1521, and married a señorita Tovar, who had been in the train of Isabel de Bobadilla, Pedrarias's wife. He once wrote: 'being already rich, I requested permission of the Governor Pedrarias to explore the coast beyond the bay of Saint Miguel' – that is, towards Peru, then known as 'Birú', of whose wealth he had heard rumours. It seemed that there might be another rich empire there, even comparable to that of New Spain.

Andagoya therefore set off and, after clashing with the Chocama, encountered a subordinate of the ruler, the Inca from 'Biru'. But then an accident upset the canoe in which he was travelling, he swallowed a lot of water and narrowly escaped drowning. He returned to Panama to recover. It was three years before he could ride again. He reported to Pedrarias what he had seen. It is not clear what happened to him but obviously he was struck by a serious setback which removed him from the list of those who might first exploit Peru.[4] The governor decided to act immediately to prevent anyone else becoming interested. He asked another friend, Juan Basurto, to prepare an expedition, but Basurto died. The field was then opened up to others.

Some indication of who these others might be was already evident in 1524, for, in May of that year, Pedrarias himself joined with three successful and rich *encomenderos* of Panama to explore 'Birú': Francisco Pizarro, Diego de Almagro and Fr Hernando Luque.

Pizarro, from Trujillo in Extremadura, was a distant cousin of Hernán Cortés, whose grandmother Leonor had been a Pizarro.[5] Almagro was a companion and friend of Pizarro, whose origins were similar to his own, while Luque was a Sevillano, who may have been a *converso*. Between them these three had a half-share of the planned expedition in three ships, the other half being in the hands of Pedrarias. Pizarro had a reputation for leadership, endurance in difficult circumstances and physical strength; he was also easy and popular with his men. The fact that he was illiterate seemed less important. It was suggested that he had in his youth looked after swine which, considering the importance of those animals in the economy of Extremadura, would not have been improbable.[6] Almagro was also illiterate. Luque could read and write, and indeed preach. He was one of the eleven churchmen who had accompanied Fray Juan de Quevedo, the first bishop of Panama, to the New World. The Peruvian historian Busto considered that Luque had an unusual gift for business.[7]

These men prepared their expedition carefully and in November 1524 Pizarro set off in three small ships with fewer than 200 men, from Panama down the Pacific coast, leaving Almagro to find reinforcements. It did not seem a very promising enterprise; they had with them only four horses, one fighting dog and no arquebuses, crossbows or artillery.[8]

Actually Spain had already made a mark on Peru, since in 1524 smallpox had been carried there from Castile, even though no Spaniard had yet been in the country.[9]

Before this, in January 1523, Gil González and Andrés Niño, convinced that wealth lay to the north, not the south, had departed northwards towards Guatemala from the Isle of Pearls off Panama with four small vessels. Like all early explorers in this region, they hoped to light upon a strait to the Pacific. They sailed nearly 2,000 miles and, in the next eighteen months, discovered several new Indian kingdoms. But no strait appeared. At the end of this time, their ships were so damaged by worm that they had to continue by land. They went into the interior about 300 miles further up the Central American coast with a hundred men, and Gil González de Ávila received presents worth over 100,000 pesos. This was land adjacent to Alvarado's Guatemala, with the same customs, gods, costumes and language. Over 32,000 natives received baptism voluntarily, wrote Peter Martyr, as usual exaggerating.[10] Gil González reported that, in this part of Central America, all the carpenters' tools were made of gold, but he too must have been mistaken, confusing copper for gold. They passed through land where the rivers were alluvial and wound up their journey at a place which they named San Vicente at the foot of the volcano of Chichontepec in the valley of the Joboa. A little further on, Gil González came upon a local Maya lord named Nicoiano, whom he persuaded to accept baptism and who, in consequence, gave him six gold figures of gods, each over a foot high. Nicoiano spoke of another lord named Nicaragua who lived about 150 miles to the west and Gil González continued there, persuading him to become a Christian, along with 9,000 of his people. Nicaragua gave the Spaniards 15,000 pesos in the form of gold necklaces. Gil González presented him in return with a silk jacket, a linen shirt and a red hat.

A long conversation followed during which Nicaragua said that the total destruction of the human race would soon come, brought on by man's many crimes and unnatural lusts. This lord asked all kinds of interesting questions of Gil González de Ávila which the conquistador must have found surprising: what was the cause of heat and cold? Were dancing and drinking acceptable? Did men have souls? Gil González delivered a good sermon describing the benefits of Christianity and the evils of human sacrifice.[11] He was made aware that these Indians were terrified of the Spaniards' beards.

Gil González and his comrades were also astounded at the high level of culture of these Indians. They were particularly impressed by their large palaces, and considered that their ceremonial centres with 'an urban disposition' would have given them little to envy in the world of Spain.[12] Still, every so often, to recall their essential 'barbarism', they would sacrifice girls to the nearby volcanoes.

Gil González moved on to Lake Nicaragua, which was supposed to be the site of the entrance to the strait so long sought, and named it the Sweet Sea (*El Mar Dulce*). Niño, meantime, was still exploring the coast by sea. He reached the Gulf of Choluteca in what is now Honduras, to whose sea outlet he politely gave the name of Fonseca after the bishop of Burgos, which it retains.

Both conquistadors then returned to Panama, claiming to have baptized 82,000 Indians, bringing 112,000 pesos of gold with them. Pedrarias predictably claimed a fifth of that for himself, but González returned to Santo Domingo with his treasure without bidding him, or indeed anyone, goodbye. He sought reinforcements there and despatched Andrés de Cerezeda to Spain with presents for Bishop Fonseca and a request that he, Gil González de Ávila, should receive a governorship in Nicaragua independent of Pedrarias.

But the latter was not prepared to abandon anything. He sent a letter of protest to the Crown via his son, and another via Gaspar de Espinosa, a *licenciado* (graduate lawyer) and bachelor of arts who had been chief magistrate under Pedrarias. Espinosa had been named the *juez de residencia* (judge of enquiry) for Balboa in 1514 and did not let Pedrarias determine his actions. Indeed he had begun to see that Balboa was a remarkable leader, as did Bishop Quevedo. Espinosa led an expedition into Coiba in 1517 and killed thousands.[13] The historian Deive says that he was '*el más cruel y despiadado*' (the most cruel and ruthless) of the captains of Spain.[14] He was though later given an *encomienda* of Indians which led him about 1522 to a lawsuit against the civil servant Salmerón.[15] He returned to Spain the next year to argue with the court over the damage done to Pedrarias by Gil González's expedition.

Pedrarias despatched Francisco Hernández de Córdoba[16] to Nicaragua and Costa Rica to take possession of the region. Hernández de Córdoba, who was perhaps a distant relation of the *Gran Capitán* who shared his name, had come out to the Indies in 1517. Following a contract between Pedrarias, Juan Téllez, treasurer of Panama, and Hernández de Córdoba, with the support of other conquistadors, the latter set off by ship in the course of 1524. He and his men made for the Costa Rican coast to the south of Nicaragua, landing at Urutina on the Gulf of Nicoya near where a year earlier González de Ávila had rested his expedition. Hernández de Córdoba founded several towns: Bruselas (named after Brussels), for example, near Puente de Arenas, Granada on Lake Nicaragua, near the Indian settlement of Jalteba, Segovia and León la Vieja, which would soon become the capital of the new settlement. Among the first thirty Spanish settlers there were men with brilliant futures in Peru, such as Sebastián de Benalcázar and Hernando de Soto, who became chief magistrate of this new city. There was complete uncertainty among these isolated Spaniards in respect of their northern frontier: who would they have to defeat in order to establish their 'independent' regime? Olid? González de Ávila? Alvarado? Cortés himself? Or perhaps Pedro Moreno, the *fiscal* of Santo Domingo who, acting for the supreme court of that city, had been sent to Central America to find out where these and other conquistadors actually were.

Hernández de Córdoba heard that González de Ávila was planning a return expedition to those same Central American lands. In fact he had already returned with his friend Andrés Niño to Honduras and settled at Puerto de Caballos, hoping to prove to the Indians that Spaniards did not die. They soon came into contact with Hernández de Córdoba, and the two small Spanish armies fought two pitched battles. Eight Spaniards and thirty horses died.

Hernández de Córdoba pressed the new municipalities of the places which he had founded to recognize him as their governor. His usurpation of authority was not universally accepted, in particular not by Hernando de Soto, a brilliant horseman from Jerez de los Caballeros – the same city that had given birth to Balboa – who had married Pedrarias's daughter, Isabel. In consequence Soto viewed Hernández de Córdoba's actions as destructive. Córdoba imprisoned Soto but a friend, Francisco de Compañón, freed him, and the two rode back to complain to Pedrarias, who mounted an expedition to seize the Lake of Nicaragua. To that generation of conquistadors the lake seemed a 'paradise of God', in the words of Las Casas, who relished not only the beautiful dark water but the rich black soil and the long row of volcanoes near the sea.

In these years a number of powerful persons were trying to assert themselves in too small a space in Central America, but they were soon to find a way to prosperity and advancement if not happiness. Pedrarias, aged but brutal to both his fellow countrymen and the Indians, remained, however, apparently impossible to remove.

*

The politics of Central America in the late 1520s is the central element in the preparations for the conquest of Peru. Most of the characters in that drama emerge from what happened in Panama and in Darien – in particular the dynamic figure of Francisco Pizarro.

In 1528, however, Pedrarias remained the dominant authority in the territory, as he had been for fourteen years. He had taken up his new office of governor of Nicaragua on Holy Saturday 1528, and found anarchy there. Diego López de Salcedo, a nephew of the governor of Hispaniola, Fray Nicolás de Ovando, with whom he had first come to the Indies in 1502, had illegally seized power as governor of Honduras with no permission from the Council of the Indies. And there was also a rebellion of Indian leaders. Pedrarias's chief followers were Francisco de Castañeda, who acted as chief magistrate and lieutenant governor, though he was no friend of Pedrarias; the treasurer Diego de la Tobilla, who was later a chronicler of these events; Alonso de Valerio was inspector (*veedor*); while Diego Álvarez de Osorio was both the first bishop of Nicaragua and founder of the monastery of the Merced and a Franciscan monastery in León (Nicaragua).

López de Salcedo eventually surrendered to Pedrarias and, after some months in the new fortress of León, was sent home to Spain. His lieutenant was Gabriel de Rojas, a member of the famous family of Cuéllar in Castile (Gabriel was a brother of Manuel de Rojas, then governor of Cuba). Pedrarias continued to be reproached even by his own men, such as his *alcalde mayor*, Castañeda, but it made no difference to his conduct. He was defended by Martín de Estete, whose brutality towards Indians was without parallel.

At that time the traffic in slaves still seemed the only way to make any money in Central America. Among those active in the commerce were Hernando de Soto and Juan Ponce, who collaborated with the *alcalde* Castañeda, and 'their' Indians were sold not only in Panama but in the Caribbean. Ponce's galleon *San Jerónimo* habitually carried 450 *piezas* (that is, full-grown slaves), Soto and Ponce's *La Concepción* could carry 385.

Soto and Ponce were also already showing interest in 'Birú'. But Pedrarias, having been persuaded to sell his own interests in Pizarro's dramatic project there for 1,000 pesos, was reluctant that anyone under his command should engage in it. If Soto and Ponce went to Peru, he argued, Nicaragua would lose her best men.

Francisco Pizarro's friend, the pilot Bartolomé Ruiz de Estrada, arrived in the *Santiago*, looking precisely for new projects for 'Birú'. Pedrarias banned all contact with him. But Ruiz himself met Soto and Ponce and almost certainly undertook to provide ships in return for a major role in what Pizarro was planning. Soto also agreed to supply thirty or forty men, mostly debtors, and perhaps 300 slaves. Then in August 1526 Pedrarias gave permission to Ponce to ship slaves for his estate at La Posesión in the *San Jerónimo*, but Soto had to agree to stay on in León. On 15 October Ponce left La Posesión in the *San Jerónimo* carrying 402 slaves, with the royal *factor* Alonso Pérez on board. Once in Panama, however, he seized the opportunity to discuss with Pizarro's friends his and Soto's hope to participate in the promising Peruvian adventure.

We recall how in 1522 Pascual de Andagoya had sailed 200 miles south of Panama in the Pacific Ocean and ascended the river San Juan; we have observed how Francisco Pizarro, Diego de Almagro and Fray Hernando de Luque bought Andagoya's ships and secured the financial support of Licenciado Gaspar de Espinosa, the second most important man in Castilla del Oro after Pedrarias. In 1524 Pizarro himself sailed south along the Pacific coast from Panama with eighty men and four horses to reach Puerto de Ayuno, where his comrade Almagro lost an eye in a skirmish with Indians at Pueblo Quemado. Then in March 1526 Pizarro set off on a second voyage south with fewer than 200 men and a few horses in two small ships captained by his friend the pilot Bartolomé Ruiz de Estrada, who was so experienced in dealing with Pizarro. Crossing the Equator for the first time in the Southern Sea, they came in contact with Peruvian civilization – though they were still far to the north of where modern Ecuador gives way to Peru. They encountered a balsa raft travelling northwards, fitted with sails of cotton, which was preparing to trade Peruvian artefacts: silver and gold, cotton and woollen cloaks, other clothing in many colours, not to speak of tiny weights with which to measure gold. The sight of sails heartened the Europeans, for neither the Mexica nor the Maya had enjoyed such a benefit. Eleven of the men on that raft leapt into the ocean to avoid capture but three were held by the Spaniards, to be trained as interpreters, the conquest of Mexico having taught Spaniards that a good interpreter is more valuable than 1,000 soldiers.

In June 1527 Pizarro caused his men, now reduced to eighty, to turn back north to take shelter on Gallo Island, a barren spot, off Panama near Perequeté. He sent Almagro to Panama for supplies, and Bartolomé Ruiz carried a letter to the new governor in Castilla del Oro, Ríos, insisting that his encounter with the balsa raft showed that 'Birú' was full of riches: 'very fine gold', he reported.[17] In August other letters were sent by Pizarro's men about their hunger, their despair and their physical determination to survive; some of them claimed that they were being detained on the expedition against their will.[18] Governor Ríos gave permission to those who wished to leave the expedition to do so. Many left in the boats sent by the governor under the command of Juan Tafur, who had brought a message from Ríos's wife, Catalina de Saavedra: she wanted to buy cotton cloth from Peru.

Pizarro held a meeting of his followers on the beach. He told the eighty or so Spaniards still with him that they were all free to leave, but he appealed to them to stay. He reminded them of the riches carried by the raft. He drew a line with his sword in the sand, and proposed that those who preferred the glory and the gold of an adventure in Peru to the misery and obscurity of Panama should cross the line. Only thirteen did so: five Andalusians, two Castilians, three Extremeños, a Cretan, a Basque and one whose origins are unclear.[19] The rest had heard too many promises of wealth and glory.

Pizarro sent his remaining boat back to Panama under his follower Carbayuelo to bring back Almagro, while on Gallo Island he and his thirteen followers did what they could to survive. They made a canoe out of a ceiba tree and went fishing daily, catching excellent fish. They killed animals called *guadaquinajes*, which were bigger than hares, and gave good flesh to eat. There was little other food, but 'mosquitoes enough to make war against the Turks'. After a month or so, some of Pizarro's men thought openly that 'death would be the end of our sufferings'.[20]

Back in Panama, Almagro and Luque are said by the chronicler Pedro Cieza de León to have allowed many tears to fall when they read the sad letters brought back from Gallo Island – though those two hardened conquistadors did not often weep. It was said that Pizarro had personally sent back a couplet which ran:

> *Oh my lord governor look well and take pains*
> *For there goes the knife and the butcher remains.*

Ruiz eventually set off back to Gallo Island, where he found Pizarro in despair. He suggested that all the men should return to Panama in six months' time. Pizarro agreed but said that first they should together sail to the south and see what the coast of Peru was like. Ruiz agreed to do this, leaving behind the most debilitated of the Spaniards.

In the next few months Pizarro and Ruiz made their way to Tumbes, a town on the coast, where they were well received and then to the island of Santa Clara and the river Santa to the south of the modern Trujillo, just north of Chimbote. The Andalusian Alonso de Molina here gave a *cacique* two pigs, a cock and two Spanish chickens, and the Cretan Pedro de Candia gave an exhibition of shooting with an arquebus. Antonio de Carrión, a Castilian, then took possession of the land in the name of the king of Castile. The unimpressed Indians gave many presents: llamas, pottery, fine cloths, metals and also some more boys to be trained to act as interpreters.

Pizarro's expedition in 1527 may have reached as far as the mouth of the river Chincha, well to the south of the modern capital, Lima. There were several stops on the way back, for example at Tumbes, where Alonso de Molina was left behind to learn Quechua. Pedro de Halcón from Seville fell in love there and asked to be allowed to remain too. A sailor of Ruiz's named Cunés decided to stay on for a similar reason at Pinta. The rest returned to Panama, where they were well received by the governor, Ríos.

The story of 'the thirteen of Gallo Island' kept Panama agog for a long time with tales of llamas, gold, cotton cloaks and other wonderful textiles. For a while Pizarro was silent. Then he too talked with his old friends, Almagro, Luque and Espinosa. It was agreed that an expedition should be mounted to establish settlements in Peru. Nothing was said of conquest, but it was understood that, if the people of Peru were to refuse the king's command, transmitted by the famous Requirement, they would be made dependent – in the most humane way possible, of course. Pizarro would be governor, Almagro *adelantado*, Luque bishop and the pilot Ruiz *alguacil*.

Luque, however, thought it essential to send a representative to Castile to receive the Crown's formal approval for the expedition. He thought that Diego del Corral, an experienced Castilian from Hoz de Ovejar, in the province of Burgos, would be the best man to do this; Almagro believed the right man was Pizarro himself. He was popular with many; Oviedo wrote of him that he was a 'good person with a good temperament, if slow and deliberate in conversation'.[21] Luque was doubtful, since he considered Pizarro 'a consummate warrior but one with little culture and little informed of the subtleties of rhetoric'. In the end, Pizarro went to Spain, accompanied by Diego del Corral and Pedro de Candia, the Cretan artilleryman.

In 1528 Pizarro was in his fifties, and very experienced in the Indies, where he had arrived in 1502 with Ovando. He was tall, lean and strong. Like Ovando and, indeed, Cortés and Núñez de Balboa, he was an Extremeño, the illegitimate son of a well-known soldier and aristocrat, Gonzalo Pizarro, who had fought in Navarre as well as in Italy. Pizarro's mother, Francisca González, had apparently been a servant girl who had worked in the convent of San Francisco in Trujillo for Sister Beatriz Pizarro de Hinojosa, a distinguished member of the family. Francisco may also have been in Italy with his father in the 1490s but, in his early days in Santo Domingo, he was just one more impoverished soldier – though impressed by Ovando.[22] When he received a coat of arms in 1537 it was recalled that he had served in Italy.[23] He reached Darien before Pedrarias went there and worked under Núñez de Balboa, though it was he who arrested him in 1519. He also was second-in-command to other captains.

Pizarro showed himself incomparably tough and a good leader, one loved by those who served with him. He could neither read nor write, and his horsemanship was modest since he had not been brought up with horses. The gossip and memoirist Alonso Enríquez de Guzmán, described him as 'a good companion without any vanity or pomposity'.[24] Garcilaso, the half-Peruvian chronicler who wrote so well, said of him that he was 'kindly and gentle by nature and never said a hard word of anyone'.[25] He once saved an Indian servant from death by leaping into a river, exposing himself to great danger. When reproached for taking such a risk, he replied that his interlocutor obviously did not know what it was to be fond of a servant.[26] He was old-fashioned and practically never departed from the clothes which he had worn in his youth: a black cassock with a skirt down to the ankle, with white deerskin shoes and a white hat, his sword and dagger worn in an old-fashioned way,[27] though he would later often use a fur coat which his cousin Cortés sent him from Mexico. He often wore napkins round his neck since he spent much of his life in time of peace playing bowls or some ball game such as nine-pins and 'they served to keep the sweat from his face'.

Despite all these good qualities, like most conquistadors he was quite prepared to be cruel to enemies, and to kill Indians in a ruthless manner in order to achieve a psychological advantage, thereby compensating for his inferiority in numbers.[28]

His friend and eventual rival, Almagro, was a few years younger than Pizarro, also illiterate, and, in 1528, must have been in his late forties. He appears to have been born in Bolaños de Calatrava, on the road from Manzanares to Ciudad Real. He was probably the illegitimate son of a Gallego hidalgo, Juan de Montenegro, by Elvira Gutiérrez, a servant girl in Almagro. Elvira perhaps had Moorish blood, a fact which later exposed Almagro to fierce insults. He lived for a time with his mother's cruel brother, Hernán Gutiérrez, and fled to find his mother married to a shopkeeper named Celinos in Ciudad Real. Almagro then went to Toledo, where he served Licenciado Luis González de Polanco, one of the court magistrates (*alcaldes de corte*) of the Catholic Kings and a long-lived councillor of the Crown in Castile. He had a violent fight with another boy and fled to Seville. There, in 1513, he joined the expedition of Pedrarias in the humblest of fashions, as a page, and was then involved in many of the *entradas* (military expeditions) in Castilla del Oro, becoming an intimate friend of Pizarro in about 1515.

Almagro had different qualities from Pizarro. He was apparently 'so excellent a woodsman that he could follow an Indian through the thickest forests merely by following his tracks and, although that Indian might have a league's advantage, Almagro would catch up'.[29] He was always swearing and, when angry, he treated those who were with him very badly, even if they were gentlemen,[30] but his soldiers loved him for 'his liberal disposition'. Enríquez de Guzmán thought him 'generous, frank and liberal, affectionate, merciful, correct and just-minded, very fearful of God and the King'.[31] He also forgave debts as if he were a prince, not a soldier. To look at, Cieza says, he was 'a man of short stature with ugly features, but of great courage and endurance'.[32]

Almagro never got closer to the court than Toledo in his teens. For that reason he played a lesser part than did Pizarro in the manufacture of the myth of the empire. It is uncertain if the emperor knew his name except as one who challenged and disputed royal authority. Yet he played an essential role in imperial politics in his lifetime.

It seemed for a time likely that Pizarro and Almagro had a third partner, the cleric Hernando de Luque; that now seems improbable. But the
first two were linked in those days of exploration by their joint membership of a so-called '*compañia*', a society made up of a group of men each
of whom was in charge of his own equipment and weapons and received
in return a previously stipulated share of the spoils, which went by
the name of the Compañía del Levante. Pedrarias the governor seems
to have taken an interest and some money was probably provided for
the expedition by the rich settler Gaspar de Espinosa, from Medina de
Rioseco, who had much experience in Panama, and who acted through
his son Juan who was for a time Almagro's secretary.[33]

Charles the emperor received news regularly from Cortés in New Spain,
from Santo Domingo, from Governor Rojas in Cuba, from Pedrarias in
Panama and from the north coast of South America. As for New Spain,
the *cabildo* (town hall) in Mexico/Tenochtitlan was continuing to allocate town and country properties, and that *cabildo* remained a mixture
of new men and experienced conquistadors who had been through all
the battles of Cortés.

Twelve Dominicans had arrived in New Spain in July 1526, led by an
enemy of Cortés, Fray Tomás Ortiz, to add their presence to the well-
established Franciscans. Ortiz was also, it seems, an enemy of Indians.
He and three other friars soon became ill, and returned to Spain as fast
as they could. This left Fray Domingo de Betanzos, a Gallego, with a
deacon, Fray Vicente de las Casas, as the spokesmen for the Dominican
order.

After living modestly in lodgings for a while, the Dominicans moved
in 1529 to a monastery being built specially for them at Tepetlaostoc,
just outside Tenochtitlan, where Miguel Díaz de Aux, an entrepreneur
from the days of the conquest, received an *encomienda* in 1527.[34] To
begin with their impact would be less than that of the Franciscans
because they were not interested in founding schools and were unenthusiastic about the idea of teaching Latin to the natives.

All the same, the latter's interest was increasingly secured: there is a
record of October 1526 of an indigenous marriage along Christian lines
when 'Don Hernando', brother of the 'señor' Cacama of Texcoco, and
seven companions were married. Several well-known conquistadors,
among them Alonso de Ávila and Pero Sánchez Farfán, were present,

with gifts and, 'the jewel most appreciated', much wine. After the mass in the monastery there was a banquet and a ball attended by 2,000 people.[35] This wedding was, however, less imposing than that of Techuipo, fovourite daughter of Montezuma, who married Pedro Gallego de Andrada, her previous Spanish husband, Alonso de Grado, having died. Most surprisingly she had a daughter, Leonor, by Cortés, some months after this marriage.[36] Pedro Gallego was a poet from Seville, and had a daughter, Juana Andrada. Later he had an inn on the road to Veracruz, as well as the *encomienda* of Iscuincuitlapilco.

When Nuño de Guzmán arrived at San Esteban del Puerto in Pánuco in May 1527, some sixty or seventy Spaniards were living there, in thatched houses surrounding a brick church, also with a thatched roof, and a pomegranate-coloured council house. Guzmán summoned the Spaniards and read out his instructions in the church.[37] He dismissed most of the town council immediately and replaced them with men who had come with him. He told the *caciques* that he was in Pánuco as representative of the king of Castile, who was his own supreme mentor, though there was always God in heaven. One should honour God by making Him presents. If one lived a Christian life on earth, one would one day live in His presence in heaven. If not, one would go to an inferno of eternal fire and burn for ever. To ensure that they went to heaven, the Indians would have to build a large church in Pánuco and go to it regularly to beg forgiveness. In their souls, these *caciques* had to bear complete obedience to the king of Castile and to Guzmán in his name. They were to fulfil their duties to their new Spanish master but not more. If their master asked more, he was to be reported to Guzmán, who would punish him.[38]

Seeing that their new commander was going to be demanding, and would cost them something, several *encomenderos*, such as Cortés's friend and fellow Medellinés Antonio de Mendoza, who had been lieutenant-governor in Pánuco, left, taking their sheep and slaves with them. It was Mendoza who had returned to Castile with Diego de Ordaz on Cortés's behalf in 1521, carrying the letter of the commander to the emperor written in October 1520.[39] One *encomendero* who did not leave now was Diego Villapadierna of Matlactonatico, who told the Indians to avoid giving any presents to Guzmán since, he said, Cortés would soon come there to sweep him away. But Villapadierna it was who suffered, since he was soon tried for conspiring with Cortés to make him king of

New Spain, an idea which was far from the captain-general's imagination. He was sentenced to the pillory, a fine of fifty pesos, and the loss of his *encomienda*.[40]

Similar punishments were meted out to others who challenged the new authority. For example, Guzmán had three of his compatriots hanged from an avocado tree for allegedly mistreating Indians, when they had in fact merely tried to prevent Guzmán presenting his commission in Mexico/Tenochtitlan. Guzmán also approved a slave trade in Mexican Indians (Huastecs, principally) from Pánuco to the West Indian islands, the business being organized in 1527 by one of the new governor's intimates, Sancho de Caniego, who had come to New Spain with him. Guzmán set the prices: no one, for example, could pay more than fifteen slaves for a horse. Slaves were not to be traded for items such as wine or cloth, only for livestock. Caniego was cruel: on the slightest provocation, he would beat an Indian to death.[41] Nor were Spaniards much better off: Caniego put the ex-*comandante* of San Sebastián del Puerto in irons and kicked him to death.[42]

Still, Guzmán tried also to be positive about 'his' Indians. In August 1527 he decided that no Indian women were to be seized by the Spaniards (and several Spaniards were hanged for flouting this injunction), that no Spaniard was to seize agricultural produce from Indians, that vagrants were to be given permanent homes, and that Spaniards should limit the number of their bearers. None of them was to be made to carry more than an *arroba* (25 pounds) in weight as well as his food. Nor were Spaniards to keep swine or livestock within half a league (say, a mile and a half) of an indigenous settlement's fields. Blasphemy was roundly condemned. Guzmán was a characteristic man of his time: with his black side and his benign one, and thus has to be judged at two levels. He also invited Fray Gregorio de Santa María, a Carmelite who had landed in Pánuco on his way to Tenochtitlan, to remain in his territory, which Santa María did for a time.

Guzmán abandoned Pánuco at the end of 1527 when he accepted an invitation to preside over the new supreme court of New Spain. The evidence is that this appointment was made to ensure that the Crown had a representative tough enough if necessary to oppose Cortés, whose motives in New Spain had been made to seem so suspect by his many enemies at court at home. Bishop García de Loaisa, president of the Council of the Indies, was responsible. There were to be four judges of first instance, named in Spain. One was Juan Ortiz de Matienzo, who had already had a long experience of Indian matters, having been one of the first four judges of Santo Domingo in 1511. That task had not prevented him or his colleagues, such as Vázquez de Ayllón, from engaging in commerce, including buying ships to obtain slaves on the mainland or in the 'useless islands'. Ortiz de Matienzo was the nephew of Sancho de Matienzo, the first treasurer of the Casa de la Contratación. By the time he gained this benefice in New Spain, he was old and unable to challenge the dominance of Guzmán, even if he had wanted to.

A second supreme court judge was Licenciado Alonso de Parada, who also had much experience in the New World: he had been a *juez de residencia* in La Concepción, Santo Domingo, in 1515. A native of Salamanca, he acquired an *encomienda* in Santo Domingo and then in Cuba and was subsequently commander of the supplementary flotilla of ships of Narváez which were wrecked in Yucatan. He had been a notary in Santiago de Cuba and had witnessed the oath by Cortés there to obey Diego Velázquez before the former embarked on his expedition in 1519.[43] He seems to have been an ally of Olid against Cortés in 1524.

Just before nomination to Tenochtitlan, Parada had been in Spain, where he wrote a memorandum on the nature of the empire. He told the Council of the Indies that in Santo Domingo there were no churches whose roofs were not thatched and that there were in that colony seven or eight sugar mills. Parada suggested that to work these mills, as well as the similar ones in the Canary Isles or Madeira, slaves were necessary. Spain should arrange with the king of Portugal a regular supply of black slaves – for the Portuguese, of course, dominated the west coast of Africa where such labour could be found. He thought half these slaves should be women.[44]

A third judge was Diego Delgadillo, who had been born in Granada and had always been a critic of Cortés. He did not have an impeccable personal record since he had kidnapped two Indian girls who had taken refuge in the Franciscan monastery in Mexico.

The fourth supreme court judge was Licenciado Francisco Maldonado, a Salamanquino who did not seem to think that his presence in his post was necessary for his office. He did not arrive in New Spain till 1529 and died soon after.

The supreme court was supposed to hear civil as well as criminal cases. Among the cases the court heard very early on was the strange affair of the young Tlaxcalteca, Cristóbal, who was killed by his father, Acxotecatl, for trying to convert him to Christianity. A parallel case was that of Hernando Alonso, a blacksmith whom the Dominicans found guilty of such Jewish practices as forbidding his wife to go to church during her menstrual periods and carrying out a baptism according to Jewish rites. Alonso was found guilty and was later burned in Mexico/ Tenochtitlan, the first conquistador to suffer such a fate.[45]

When Guzmán went up to Tenochtitlan, he was succeeded in Pánuco by Licenciado Pedro de Mondragón, a judge who must have had some humane feelings since he refused a pardon for a Spaniard who had violated an Indian girl aged eight; though he felt guilty the rest of his life because he thought that he had been too harsh.[46]

In his new palace in Cuernavaca, Cortés in the meantime began to realize that, despite his stupendous services and his remarkable letters about his achievements (his fifth letter to Charles V was written in September 1526),[47] he would never overcome his difficulties with his rivals unless he had overt royal support. Guzmán had behaved unacceptably in Pánuco. The treasurer Alfonso de Estrada, now the supreme authority in Mexico, was distinctly unfriendly, though he had been explicitly told that he could not be the *juez de residencia* against Cortés; and Estrada's assistant, Juan de Burgos, an experienced trader who had sailed a *nao* full of supplies to Cortés in New Spain from the Canary Isles in 1521, was equally hostile.

In April 1528 the Emperor Charles had ordered Cortés to return to Spain[48] and he was advised to comply by supporters of his, such as the Duke of Béjar, who had befriended the Cortés family. So Cortés decided to go home for the first time since his initial journey to Santo Domingo in 1506, over twenty years before. He left almost immediately, delegating power over his property in New Spain to his cousin Licenciado Juan de Altamirano, Pedro González Gallego and Diego de Ocampo. He took with him Gonzalo de Sandoval and Andrés de Tapiés, a large collection of treasure and works of art, plants and minerals, as well as numerous Indians, headed by two sons of Montezuma (Don Pedro Montezuma and Don Martin Cortés Netzahualcecolotl), and a son of Maxixcastin, 'Don Lorenzo', of Tlaxcala. There also came eight Indians who could play elaborate games with their feet.[49] He arrived at Palos, Columbus's port in 1492, in May 1528. There, at the monastery of La Rábida, Sandoval fell ill. He was too weak to prevent the theft of his gold and died soon afterwards.

The news reaching Spain from Panama and Darien was that Pedrarias had punished the rebellion, as he put it, of Hernández de Córdoba by having him executed. González de Ávila had died. This last information led Isabel de Bobadilla to secure the re-nomination of her husband, Pedrarias, as governor and captain-general of Nicaragua.

Florida, meantime, remained an unsuccessful venture for the Spaniards. Vázquez de Ayllón set out from Puerto Principe in Santo Domingo in mid-July 1526: the first expedition which he led in person. He had three good ships – his flagship *La Bretona*, the *Santa Catalina* and the *Chorruca* – as well as a brigantine which carried 500 men and about eighty horses. His comrades included Fr Antonio de Cervantes, a Dominican, Fray Pedro de Estrada and Fray Antonio de Montesinos, a cousin of the great preacher of that name. He reached a river which he called the Jordan, where the *Bretona* ran aground, though other vessels navigated it successfully. He decided, however, that it was a bad place for a colony and, instead, went further north to a river which seems to be in what is now New Jersey. There Ayllón died and all his plans came to an end. His expedition limped back to Santo Domingo.

There were other journeys in these years: for example, Sebastian Cabot's voyage from La Corunna to the river Plate and then the river Paraguay. He was *piloto mayor* for the Casa de la Contratación and was in search of the mysterious great white chief of the region (*el gran cacique blanco*). In the estuary of the Plate he came upon Diego García who had come on a similar journey from Seville. They could not agree on whose rights were at stake but continued together all the same, leaving behind a small garrison at Espíritu Santo, the site of the future Buenos Aires. Sailing up the Paraguay and the Pilcomayo they were severely attacked, and so returned, to find all the Spaniards whom they had left at Espíritu Santo dead and the garrison destroyed. They thereupon went back together to Spain, and there embarked on a lawsuit against each other which, like so many at that time, never ended.

Cabot was one of the half-dozen great men of the new generation of conquering explorers. But great man though he was, his standing never approached that of the conqueror of New Spain nor that of the Extremeño Pizarro, who knew that his mission lay in Peru.

11

Three giants of their time:
Charles, Cortés, Pizarro

> *Though your goodness rouses great hopes in me, I shall never*
> *cease to fear until you have bid farewell to this most unjust and*
> *dangerous world and have withdrawn to a monastery as to a safe*
> *harbour.*
>
> Erasmus, *De Contemptu Mundi*

In 1528 the three greatest men of the age were in Spain: Charles, king
and emperor, and his two most important subjects, Hernando Cortés,
conqueror of New Spain, and Francisco Pizarro, the future conqueror
of Peru. Charles was still at war with King Francis of France and had
sent Balthasar Merklin, vice-chancellor of the empire, to urge the German princes to arm against that country. Heralds from England as well
as France had appeared in Burgos with a declaration of war for 'the
safety and soul of Christendom'. Charles had replied with a challenge to
a duel with Francis, whom he accused of failing to meet the code of
honour to which they both subscribed. Francis accepted the challenge,
and demanded a time and place for the duel. Afterwards rational counsellors on both sides dissuaded their monarchs from such a personal
test.

At the same time, Charles was preparing to visit Italy, where he hoped
to be crowned by the pope, perhaps in Bologna. That meant the preparation also of his Empress Isabel for her work as Regent. Charles sent her
advice on her bearing, as well as on affairs of state. She was to have a
meeting of the Council of the Realm every Friday. He issued a general
authority for the queen.[1] He told her the president of the Royal Council of Castile was now Don Juan Pardo de Tavera, the archbishop of
Santiago (he received the cardinalate in 1531), and explained something

of Tavera's cautious, correct and cultivated personality and that he was an enemy of the exuberantly liberal Erasmian Alonso de Manrique, the *inquisidor-general*. Tavera is now remembered for his magnificent hospital at the gates of Toledo. Technically the hospital of San Juan Bautista, it was also known as 'the hospital outside the walls' (*hospital de Afuera*). It is the great building of the Toledan Renaissance, designated as a hospital for all ailments, perhaps as a copy or at least as a successor to the great hospital of Santa Cruz in Valladolid. Like Santa Cruz, Tavera's hospital began as a mortuary as well as a clinic. It was begun in 1540; the first architects were Alonso de Covarrubias, and then Hernán González de Lara. Afterwards there was the exquisite Nicholás de Vergara, who was working in the towers of the hospital in the 1570s.

In April 1528 the court was in Madrid. In May Infante Philip was recognized in the church of the monastery of San Jerónimo in Madrid as heir to the throne. In September Charles addressed both the Royal Council of Castile and the Council of the Realm, telling their members that he intended to go to Italy to be crowned emperor by the pope. He would also seek to persuade the pontiff to call a general council of the Church so as to give a formal answer to Luther.[2] Charles did not ask the councils for their permission to go to Italy, he merely told them that he was going. Gattinara later explained that there were many who tried to prevent Charles's departure. They hated the idea of important decisions being made by the unknown Empress Isabel as Regent. The Grand Duchess Margaret of Burgundy, like the empress, was also urging Charles not to go to Italy.[3] She believed that all his efforts, and money, should be spent on defending Europe against the Turks.

But the plan to be crowned had its idealistic side. Erasmian ideas for the future of the Church were constantly heard. Could not the Church show itself tolerant as well as generous, Fr Antonio de Guevarra asked nobly in a speech which Charles delivered in Madrid announcing a rendezvous with the pope in Bologna. Charles imagined that he was going to Italy for a spiritual renovation as well as a coronation.

Only a little before Cortés's return to Spain in May 1528, his erstwhile lieutenant, Pedro de Alvarado, received from the Crown the title of governor and *adelantado* of Guatemala at 562,500 maravedís a year, and was named to the order of Santiago, an honour which he had in his youth pretended to have received in his father's stead. Before setting off for his new appointment in Guatemala, Alvarado now married a cousin of the Duke of Alburquerque, Beatriz de la Cueva. (That conquistador had earlier been married to an elder sister of hers, Francisca, who had died.)

The court at that time was at the mercy of contrasting reports about Cortés. Alvarado and Fray Diego de Altamirano spoke in favour of him, while Estrada and Albornoz, as well as the Dominican Fray Tomás de Ortiz, were hostile. In the circumstances, Charles thought that the best he could do was appoint a cousin of his, Pedro de la Cueva, one of his majordomos, *comendador mayor* of Alcántara and a relation of Alvarado's wife, to go to New Spain with 300 armed men ready to cut off Cortés's head and those of his friends if Cortés turned out to be guilty of the serious crimes of which the Dominicans had accused him (murder of his wife and associates).

When Cortés returned to Spain, it was difficult to know how to treat him. Columbus too had returned with a train of treasure, having discovered a new world and was given prizes. Since Cortés had done something just as remarkable, the question was, should he be given a title, a pension, a European command?

Landing in Palos with an escort of fifty persons, Cortés went first to the Franciscan house of La Rábida, Columbus's favourite retreat nearby. It is sometimes said that Cortés met his distant cousin Francisco Pizarro there, but that meeting, if it occurred, could not have been in May 1528 since Pizarro was then still in Panama; if it happened at all, it must have been later in Toledo.

Cortés travelled from La Rábida to Seville, where he stayed with the Duke of Medina Sidonia in his palace in the west of the city.[4] The duke gave him good horses with which to continue his journey to the court in Toledo. The conqueror of the Mexica went on, perhaps stopping to salute his mother at Medellín, and then remaining for some days at the Jeronymite monastery of Guadalupe, where he is said to have flirted with Francisca de Mendoza, sister of Cobos's wife. But with the support of his now dead father, Cortés had already been formally engaged to Juana Ramírez de Arellano, niece of the Duke of Béjar, a marriage which would ensure his entry into the aristocracy, as it would ensure the further enrichment of a great Castilian family, the Zúñiga, of whom the duke was the leading member. Everywhere Cortés offered presents, not least to the Mendoza sisters. His gift to the monastery of Guadalupe was a replica of the scorpion that had once bitten him in Pátzcuaro, its golden body covered in emeralds, pearls and mosaics.[5]

Cortés was presented to the emperor at Toledo by his prospective father-in-law, the Duke of Béjar, by Fadrique Enríquez, the Admiral of Castile, and by Cobos. Cortés talked of his conquests, his travels, his Indians, his jaguars and his privations. But Charles had little time to spare: he was preoccupied with his disputes with the king of France, and with his first serious attack of gout. It was Cobos who was charged to inspect Cortés's treasures. But when Cortés, still in lodgings in Toledo, seemed to be on the verge of a serious illness (brought on, said Díaz del Castillo, by his reacquaintance with heavy Spanish dinners), the emperor, 'accompanied by much of the nobility' went to visit him – a great honour.[6]

Charles asked Cortés three questions: what demands did he make for grants? What kind of policy did he support for dealing with the indigenous populations? And how could the royal income be increased from New Spain?[7] In reply, Cortés said that he wanted his concession of 25,000 Indians to be confirmed by the cession to him of twenty places in New Spain which he listed.[8] He thought that Spain should aim at the 'conservation and perpetuation of the natives' through their good treatment by 'the pastors of the Church'. To increase the royal income, the land conquered had to be divided among the Spaniards as if it had been Castile. Cortés suggested that taxes should be paid when land was bought or sold, and that the main cities of New Spain should be reserved for the Crown. The royal reaction to these responses was that Cortés seemed to be demanding large grants and the few people in Castile who knew something of the geography of New Spain were naturally astonished – especially when they realized that some of the places concerned (Texcoco, Tehuantepec and all seaports) had been assumed to be royal holdings. The matter of what power Cortés would have over his vassals was also at issue: would it be only a matter of civil justice or criminal jurisdiction too?

The conqueror of the Mexica remained on and off at the court of Spain between May 1528 and March 1530. His first public appearance was at mass in Toledo – presumably in the cathedral, where he arrived late and sat himself down next to Henry of Nassau, in the emperor's stall. That was considered an act of arrogance, when it was in fact the scarcely less pardonable one of ignorance.[9]

Thereafter, along with his following, Cortés travelled with the court to Monzón, to Saragossa and back to Toledo. After several months, in July 1529, in Barcelona, the emperor named him Marquis of the Valley of Oaxaca and confirmed him as captain-general of New Spain as well as of the Southern Sea.[10] These titles were curious since Oaxaca was the most doubtful of Cortés's claims, and oceans usually were guided by an admiral, not a captain-general. All the same, though Cortés soon lost political control of Oaxaca, he was always referred to as Marquis of the Valley. It escaped no one's attention that he was not again named 'governor' of New Spain, the title he had received in 1522. Charles spoke of this in a letter to him in April 1529 saying that, of course, he knew that Cortés could perform that gubernatorial role but 'it was not convenient' (*pero no conviene*).[11] But Cortés did receive some other and unexpected benefits: for example, the supreme court of New Spain was ordered to respect his property, it would pay the costs of an expedition to the Moluccas, and various debts would be forgotten.

During this prolonged stay in Spain, Cortés also sent an associate, Juan de Rada (sometimes, Herrada), to the Vatican with rich presents of precious stones and golden jewels as well as two foot-jugglers. Pope Clement was delighted and made Rada a count Palatine; and he issued a bull legitimizing three of Cortés's bastard children.[12] Another bull conceded to Cortés the trusteeship of the hospital of Concepción de Jesús. The pope also allowed him to receive the tithes of lands which he owned, to be devoted to the building of churches and hospitals.

Cortés's stay in Spain was concluded by his long arranged marriage to Juana Ramírez de Arellano at the duke's castle of Béjar in April 1529. Cortés gave his new wife a present of five emeralds worth, it was said, 100,000 ducats. One emerald was made into a rose, another a hunting horn, one a fish with eyes of gold, one a bell, with a pearl as the clapper, and the last was a cup with a golden stem and the legend '*Inter natos mulierum non surrexit major*'. A group of Genoese who saw these emeralds in La Rábida offered 40,000 ducats for just one of them. It is said that the empress heard of the present and implied that she would like it herself. Cortés told her that he had already given it to Juana, who held on to it. The only one of Cortés's fellow conquistadors from Mexico present at the marriage in Béjar seems to have been Diego de Ordaz, who wrote of it in a letter to his nephew, Francisco Verdugo, in New Spain.[13]

It is characteristic of the sixteenth century that, though monarchs were often painted, and sometimes, as with Charles V, by great painters, lesser men were usually ignored by them. But Cortés was depicted at least twice by the German painter from Strasbourg Christoph Weiditz. Weiditz came to Spain in the train of the accomplished Polish ambassador Dantiscus – a happy recollection of a time when rich Poles could afford poor German artists in their entourage. His first portrait of Cortés was a sketch in pencil and watercolour of the conquistador standing next to his coat of arms. This must have been painted about 1528 during Cortés's stay in Spain. It is a light work and surely does not capture the real Cortés. It gives him a blond beard, which clashes with accounts by chroniclers who (for example, Bernal Díaz del Castillo) reported that his beard was black. Weiditz became a friend of Cortés and also did a medallion of him of which there are several copies. It is a sombre depiction, more mature and serious than the painting. There seems to have been a third work by Weiditz, for Dantiscus talks of it in a letter to his friend the Polish chancellor, Szydlowiecki, in Cracow.[14] Afterwards, a portrait was painted by the hispanized Fleming Pedro de Campaña (Peter de Kemperer) for the Italian art lover Paolo Giovio. This was painted about 1546 but has vanished. Various copies were, however, made.[15] Later portraits were of course painted, but no more in his lifetime.[16]

From all these portraits we see Cortés as a shrewd, thoughtful, serene, calculating individual of power and authority: a suitable representation of a Renaissance general who was also a proconsul.

In the weeks before he left Toledo for Italy on 8 May 1529, Charles also saw Francisco Pizarro, who had reached Spain in January of that year from Nombre de Dios on the coast of Panama. Between there and Spain, he had stopped in Santo Domingo. Then he arrived at Sanlúcar de Barrameda and thence went up to Seville, where he was rudely received by the geographer Martín Fernández de Enciso, who claimed that he owed him money from the time long ago that they had been together in La Antigua, Darien.[17] Pizarro and his comrades were soon behind bars, but the Council of the Indies released them on payment of a fine from the money which they had brought with them.

Among Pizarro's companions, it will be recalled, was, first, Licenciado Diego del Corral, a veteran of the early days of Darien, and an enemy of Balboa, if much liked by Pizarro; he seemed a good person to argue Pizarro's case for him. He was by then rich and had an Indian mistress by whom he had had many children. The second companion of Pizarro in Spain was Pedro de Candia, a giant Cretan who had been an artilleryman in the Spanish army since 1510. Greeks were often used in that capacity in those days. He had served in Asia Minor, in Italy and in Spain itself, and had gone to the New World in 1526 in the train of the new governor of Panama, Pedro de los Ríos. By that time he had a Spanish wife, who lived in Villalpando, Zamora, a town between Benavente and Valladolid. His accounts of his adventures in Peru were heard in Spain with astonishment by an amazed Spanish audience.

Pizarro spent about a year in Spain after January 1529. He presented himself and his companions at court in Toledo, arriving with several Indians, llamas and many cases full of interesting objects from Peru, including the all-important gold.

The Council of the Indies had since 1523 been formally headed by the conventional Bishop García de Loaisa but, since he was also the royal confessor, the king took him with him to Rome where he lingered some years without activity, as holy men can easily do in the Vatican, so that the president *de facto* was the Count of Osorno, García Fernández Manrique, a rather hard civil servant who would remain in place till 1542. He was distantly related to the royal family through an Enríquez grandmother, and was also, by his mother, a grandson of the first Duke of Alba.[18] Osorno was a balanced man in public life but foolish in private.[19] He was the first secular aristocrat to exert an influence on American matters. He had considerable experience, having been a page of the Infante Juan, in the army with the Duke of Alba in the conquest of Navarre, then *corregidor* in Seville, before becoming president of the Council of the Orders. The emperor eventually found him too bureaucratic, but for the moment, the substitution of a count for a cardinal seemed a relief.[20] He was a close friend of Cardinal Pardo de Tavera, which at the time meant a great deal in Spanish administrative politics.

The other councillors of the Indies who interviewed Pizarro were Gonzalo Maldonado, bishop of Ciudad Rodrigo; Luis Cabeza de Vaca, bishop of the Canary Islands; and Licenciado Juan Suárez de Carvajal, previously a justice of the supreme court of Valladolid and once married to a niece of president García de Loaisa. More recently he had been bishop of the distant diocese of Lugo in Galicia.

Also present were Pedro Manuel, the son of Juan Manuel, the long-time courtier and feline ambassador, supporter of both Philip and Charles in Flanders, who had been concerned with the Moluccas; and Gaspar de Montoya, of Miranda del Ebro, who had worked with Pardo de Tavera and was the author of a shrill defence of Catherine of Aragon against Henry VIII. Another member of the council was Rodrigo de Castro, who had been judge of the chancellery of Granada. He was another protégé of Pardo de Tavera who, though formally president of the Council of Castile, appeared to have been indirectly in control of that of the Indies too, as if that were still its dependant and not a separate institution.

Pizarro told the Council of the Indies all that he had seen in South America. He wanted the council's approval of his grand project for the conquest in Peru. The councillors listened and were impressed by the hardships endured by the tall Extremeño. They consulted Charles and, in July, Pizarro was granted the governance and other formal support that he wanted in the new, if still unknown, land. He was awarded the title of *adelantado mayor* of Peru, which was to be named 'New Castile', as well as the captaincy-general and governorship of whatever land he should conquer.

By this agreement (*capitulación*) of 26 July 1529, Pizarro was to be allowed to 'continue the said discovery and conquest and settlement of the province of Peru up to 200 leagues [600 miles] along that coast',[21] a limitation which would later give rise to controversy and even civil war among Spaniards. There was a passage about the captaincy-general and governorship of Peru with a lifetime salary of 725,000 maravedís a year – an income which put Pizarro well above what Pedrarias had received (that had been 366,000) for the same office, and there had been no inflation to speak of. That salary would be gained in the land to be conquered and Pizarro would have to pay from it a chief magistrate (*alcalde mayor*), ten shield bearers, thirty foot soldiers, one doctor and an apothecary. He would also have to pay for the journey of the friars whom he would take with him.

There were some other appointments: Pizarro, recalled the chronicler Cieza, 'secured the most and best for himself without remembering how much his partner [Diego de Almagro] had suffered and deserved'.[22] So Pizarro forgot about the *adelantamiento* which Almagro had expected. Almagro would become lieutenant-governor of the fortress of Tumbes, a town visited by him and Pizarro on their earlier journey; and Luque, the priest who had also contributed to the financing of the future expedition, was to be bishop of the town and protector of the Indians in that province. Actually at this time Tumbes was desolate since there had been fighting between it and nearby Puna, which the latter city had won.

Other nominations for the journey to Peru included Bartolomé Ruiz de Estrada, the able pilot who would become *piloto mayor del mar del sur* and town councillor of Tumbes at a salary of 75,000 maravedís a year. He had already worked for Pizarro and Almagro for several years. Candia, Pizarro's Cretan companion in Spain, was named chief of artillery of the expedition at 60,000 maravedís a year. He too would become a councillor of the phantom city of Tumbes.

All those who had been with Pizarro on Gallo Island, 'the thirteen of fame', were to be named hidalgos or, if they were that already, 'knights of the Golden Spur'. That brought Pizarro's expedition fully into line with new chivalrous romances such as the *Amadís de Grecia*, published in Cuenca in January 1530 by Cristóbal Francés.[23]

Pizarro's contract was signed by the Empress Regent ('*Yo la Reina*'), Osorno, who was acting president of the Council of the Indies, and the long-serving salaried member of the council, Dr Beltrán. Cobos's nephew, Juan Vázquez de Molina, also signed on behalf of his uncle, away with the emperor on his way to Italy. Vázquez would soon profit by his association with the empress, for he would shortly become her chief secretary.[24] Though Pizarro had brought to Spain some Indians from the periphery of the Inca empire, as well as one or two animals, it was still surprising that the Crown should interest itself in the financing in a modest way of the adventure.[25]

Gold from Peru would carry a tax of 10 per cent for six years, 20 per cent after that. Other taxes (*almojarifazgo, alcabala*) were delayed. Pizarro would have six months in which to prepare his expedition, and he could take 150 men from Spain itself and another 100 from the Americas, though he was prohibited from taking with him new Christians (converted Jews or Muslims), gypsies, foreigners and lawyers.

Pizarro went 'home' to Trujillo and recruited four of his brothers. There seem to be no records of that visit though the priest Fr Pedro Martínez Calero recalls meeting him then.[26] The outstanding recruit was Pizarro's brother Hernando, of whom Oviedo wrote that he was the only legitimate one and legitimate in his pride.[27] He was only twenty-five.

Trujillo at that time had about 2,000 *vecinos*, citizens with full rights; of these about seventy were hidalgos, while 213 of the population belonged to the town nobility.

Others recruited at this time included a Franciscan, Fray Vicente de Valverde; Pedro Barrantes, a distant cousin; Francisco de Ávalos, of the great family of the Marquis of Pescara; and Juan Pizarro de Orellana, who were also distant cousins.[28] Pizarro surely visited bankers in Seville, such as the Illescas brothers or Francisco García or Diego Martínez,[29] and perhaps saw one or two of the famous Genoese who were to be found in Seville – men such as Andrés Lomelín or Cristóbal Centurión, Juan Jacob Spinola or Jerónimo and Gregorio Cattaneo – not to mention Florentines such as Jacob Boti. Then Pizarro went down to Sanlúcar de Barrameda, Seville's port, and bought four ships, on which he would leave for the New World, with 185 men in all.[30] Six of these passengers were Dominican friars. Alonso de Riquelme became treasurer of the expedition, García de Salcedo inspector and Antonio Navarro accountant.

On the way Pizarro was awarded at Seville the much prized Order of Santiago as a knight. The expedition travelled via the Canaries as usual, stopping at Gomera, and at Santa Marta on the north coast of South America, where the governor, García de Lerma, promoted the fancy that Peru was full of serpents, lizards and wild dogs. This news dissuaded some weak hearts from continuing. The rest went on to Nombre de Dios, where the news of Pizarro's success in Spain had preceded him and where Diego Almagro and Bartolomé Ruiz, the pilot, as well as the priest Luque, awaited the returning Pizarro with fury at what seemed the neglect of their interests.

This was incidentally a promising moment in the history of the Spanish empire, for in January the Council of the Indies had opened up commerce in the New World to eight new ports – Corunna, Bayona de Galicia, Avilés, Laredo, Bilbao, San Sebastián, Málaga and Cartagena – a great step forward, though, to ensure taxes were paid, all ships had to return to Seville.[31]

Isabel, the Empress Regent, was in 1528 beginning to exert an influence. Serene and pale-cheeked, very intelligent and responsible, she had been brought up by her mother's confessor, Fray Gracia de Padilla, and by Fray Hernando Nieto, men who had introduced into Portugal the austere interpretation of religion known as the *Observancia*. Another influence in the same direction was Guiomar de Melo, later the queen's chief attendant. Her *mayordomo mayor* was the Count of Miranda, another Zúñiga, the elder brother of Prince Philip's tutor. Though she was Regent in Charles's absences, 'Her Majesty is pained by the emperor's departure, for fear that he will stay longer than he says, and she is right, for her life is very dreary when he is not here.'[32] The empress took the partings from her husband very hard but consoled herself 'with the consideration that the absence of her husband whom she so dearly loved, was for the service of God, for the benefit of Christendom and for the faith'. She did in 1529 have a well-prepared council of regency in the shape of Miranda, Tavera and the ultra-experienced Juan Manuel, though her household was much smaller than the large enterprises associated with the Burgundians.

When Charles arrived by sea in Genoa, via Monaco and Savona (which the French had once planned to make an alternative outpost for their control of Liguria), the city had arranged for him to be greeted with cries from 200 small boats of 'Carlo, Carlo, Impero, Impero, Cesare, Cesare', and he landed by a long specially built pier hung with tapestries and cloth of gold. A great ball appeared with an eagle on top which showered scent, and a boy symbolizing Justice handed the emperor the keys of the city. This entrance had been made possible for Charles by the opening in 1527 of this commercial city to him by Admiral Andrea Doria, who had changed sides from France to the empire. Charles had even sailed across the northern Mediterranean in one of Doria's boats. (He had departed from Barcelona in great style too: as his armada left harbour, the crew of the flagship called out his motto '*Plus ultra, plus ultra*', and the cry was echoed on the other galleys.[33]) Charles was then greeted by three cardinals sent by the pope, by the Duke of Ferrara and by Alessandro de Medici, last of the main line of that great family (and even he was illegitimate).[34]

Charles's success in Italy seemed even more striking since his dear aunt Margaret and Louise de Savoie, the mother of Francis I, signed in August the so-called '*paix des dames*' which was largely favourable to Charles. It was a confirmation of the Peace of Madrid of 1526, save that the recovery of Burgundy was omitted. Francis recognized Charles as sovereign in Flanders and Artois and renounced all his old claims to Milan, Genoa and Naples. The young French princes who had been hostages in Madrid were released on the payment of a vast ransom. The emperor's sister Leonor was confirmed as queen of France.

The emperor went on to Bologna where in November he at last met Pope Clement. Here too Charles had a great welcome. There were inscriptions everywhere: '*Ave Caesar, Imperator invite*'. Every statue in Bologna was garlanded, there were triumphal arches and portraits of Caesar, Augustus and Trajan. These imperial allusions did not, however, seem to embrace the territories which had been won in the New World. New Spain was not considered. For weeks Charles and Clement were in discussion in public.[35]

Spain was concerned in Bologna for two reasons: first, it was the seat of the famous college of San Clemente founded in the fourteenth century to welcome Spaniards by Cardinal Gil Álvarez de Albornoz, also called the College of the Spaniards; and, secondly, because Saint Dominic himself had died and was buried there.

On St Peter's day, 22 February 1530, Charles received the iron crown of Lombardy and, two days later, the imperial coronation was held on St Matthew's day, Charles's birthday, in San Petronio in Bologna, the largest church in the city, with its light – then as now – superior to that in the Duomo in Florence. It was begun in 1390 in emulation of other large churches in the Gothic style and is the most highly developed creation in Gothic church architecture in Italy. Charles's presence is still recalled in the small chapel of Sant' Abbondio which, however, was reconstructed in 1865. We know nothing of the impression made on the emperor by the other twenty-one chapels, of which one or two – the Chapel of the Magi, for example – contained fine pictures. Perhaps Gattinara showed these to Charles; certainly at least the great door of the Basilica decorated by the Sienese sculptor Jacopo della Quercia. Of the German princes, only the Elector Palatine was present. He carried the orb of empire, the Marquis of Montferrato the golden sceptre, the Duke of Urbino the sword of honour and the Duke of Savoy the kingly crown. These were great Italian noblemen.

The Spanish delegation was also large and distinguished. It included the poet Garcilaso de la Vega and his great friend the young Duke of Alba.

Charles's head was anointed with oil by Cardinal Farnese, the most senior of the cardinals and Clement's eventual successor. The pope officiated. For the last time in history, the two highest dignitaries of Christendom were present together in their robes. The historian, collector and papal favourite Paolo Giovio stood in a doorway and, in a resonant voice, proclaimed: '*Rex invictissime hodie vocaris ad coronam*

Constantinopolis.' Charles smiled and waved aside the aspiration to the recovery of the East.[36] The people of Bologna shouted: 'Impero, impero.' The Spanish contingent called out: 'Spain, Spain.'[37] Gattinara, now a cardinal, felt his work as chancellor had finally been sanctioned the moment the imperial crown of Charlemagne was placed on Charles's head.[38] He died soon after and with him vanished the supreme proponent of the idea of Charles as universal monarch. In his baggage Gattinara left a map of the world. He had no successor.[39]

Six months later, at the beginning of December 1530, the governess of the Netherlands, Charles's cultivated, intelligent and competent aunt, the Archduchess Margaret, also died, in her princely palace at Mechelen, aged fifty. Her death was an accident deriving from a poisoned foot caused by broken glass in her embroidered slipper. Her successor in Flanders would be Charles's sister Mary, the former queen of Hungary.

Margaret's library alone – containing pictures as well as books – would have entitled her to a grand place in international society. Only the collections of Cardinal Albert of Brandenburg, of Hernando Colón or the Elector Frederick the Wise of Saxony competed. Her career was a reminder that the sixteenth century had as many women in high places as the twentieth.

For twenty years Margaret had planned her sepulchre at the church which she had built at Brou outside Bourg. Gattinara had advised her in its construction,[40] and FORTUNE INFORTUNE FORT UNE, her mysterious motto, is reproduced everywhere on its tombs, walls, woodwork and stained glass. There already rested the remains of Margaret's second husband, Philibert of Savoy, and the tomb of her long dead mother-in-law, Margaret of Bourbon. The three tombs were the work of the Swiss sculptor Conrad Meyt. Margaret's feet lay on a stone greyhound. There too would be in future the coffin of Laurent de Gorrevod, governor of Bresse, the first to enjoy a large monopoly to carry black slaves to the New World, a grant which he sold and whose proceeds presumably helped to finish the exquisite church.

Margaret had been Charles's best adviser, as her letters to him make clear. It was a tragedy for him and his causes that she died so young and was not present for the later conquests made in his brilliant days.[41]

12

The Germans at the banquet: the Welsers

No rural household numbers less than forty men and women
besides two slaves attached to the soil

Sir Thomas More, *Utopia*

A curious manifestation of the early days of the Spanish empire was the implication in it of a German banking family, the Welsers, one of the oldest business families of Augsburg. One optimistic genealogist said that their name 'Welser' showed that they descended from Justinian's general, 'Belisarius'.[1] From the fourteenth century, they specialized in luxurious and expensive but scarcely military products: linen, cotton, hemp wool and velvet; they also had a connection with the import from the East of silk, ginger, cloves, cinnamon and saffron. Four Welsers agreed to establish a trading company in 1473. One of them, Anton, in 1480 married a Völhin von Memmingen whose family were boat builders and had Spanish investments. The Welsers then developed interests of their own in the Canary Islands and set about making sugar there on the island of La Palma. They also built a sugar factory on the Portuguese island of Madeira, and had representatives in India by 1505. The Fondaco dei Tedeschi, a building on the Grand Canal provided by the Venetians for the Germans who traded there, was their headquarters in Venice, and there they sold spices. In Amsterdam they were to be found at the inn known as The Golden Rose. They had agents everywhere, selling pepper in Lisbon, saffron in Saragossa.

Unlike their rivals, the Fuggers, who were strong Catholics, the Welsers were neutral in the religious quarrels of the sixteenth century. Some of them were even Protestants. In 1519 the future Emperor Charles borrowed nearly 150,000 ducats from them to bribe the seven imperial electors to vote for him (less than half what the Fuggers made available, but still a large sum).[2]

Apparently, the Welsers saw Cortés's Mexican gold in Brussels when it was exhibited in 1520 and were impressed. They bought 480 quintals of cloves which had been brought back to Spain by El Cano in 1522 from the Philippines, and in 1524 they established a branch 'factory' in Seville specially dedicated to trade with the Americas. Their *factor* there was the most powerful German merchant in Spain at that time, Lázaro Nuremberger, who arrived in Seville in 1520 and married a daughter of the famous printer Cromberger.[3] In June 1526 the Welsers set up a similar institution selling pearls from Cubagua in Santo Domingo. The factors were two merchants, Jorge Ehinger and Ambrosio Alfinger, from the city of Ulm. Jorge was the brother of several distinguished merchants by then established in Constance, among them Heinrich, who signed the letters lending money to Charles in 1519. Ambrosio Alfinger came from a family which had been prominent in the guild of tailors in Ulm. He had invested heavily in Cabot's voyage of 1526 to the river Plate, and his father had made a fortune through the cloth trade.

The Emperor Charles was usually short of money. He asked the Welsers in 1526 for a new loan. They agreed, the collateral to be 'the island of Venezuela'. In 1528 they arranged a contract to manage the settlements in that place, and they also secured the succession to Gorrevod's grant of the import of African slaves into the Spanish empire.[4] They had been led to assume that the large lagoon of Maracaibo would lead to the magic strait, on the way to the Southern Sea, about which there was such fascinated speculation for so long. Subsequent loans were made by the Welsers to the Crown in Burgos on 22 November, 20 December and 30 December 1527.[5] More loans of the same kind were made in early 1528 by the merchants of Burgos.

The acceptance of these Germans as a power in the Indies was brought closer in early 1528 when the king and the Council of the Indies signed a contract (*capitulación*) which gave Jorge Ehinger and Jerónimo Seiler the responsibility for sending an armada to assist in maintaining order in Santa Marta, the new settlement near the mouth of the river Magdalena in what is now Colombia. Seiler was one further powerful German-speaking banker to become engaged in the Indies. A native of the lovely city of Saint-Gallen in Switzerland, he was ennobled by Charles V in

1525 and had succeeded Nuremberger as the chief factor of the Welsers in Seville in 1528.

The contract of 1528 obliged the Welsers to send an expedition with 300 men to Santa Marta within a year and to build three fortresses there at their own expense. They were to take with them fifty German 'master miners' who would supervise the exploitation of gold in Santo Domingo and find new veins of that metal. The Welsers had experience, after all, of this kind of contract, since they had married into a silver-mining family in the late fifteenth century.

Santa Marta was a perplexing town in the expanding radius of Spanish interests. It had been discovered as a useful place for trade by Rodrigo de Bastidas, that son of a *converso* merchant in the Triana, across the river from Seville. Bastidas was a man experienced in voyages and in the Caribbean. He seems to have first gone to the New World in 1500. Then captain on the *nao Santa María de Gracia*, he explored the Gulf of Urabá and the river Hacha and was probably the first conquistador to bring back pearls from the Americas. After 1504 he was resident in Santo Domingo and assisted Cortés in February 1521 with reinforcements in three vessels. Among those who travelled thus to New Spain were the Franciscan Fray Melgarejo and the royal treasurer, Julian de Alderete.[6] Already rich by 1510, he abandoned the sea and became a merchant in Santo Domingo, assisting Cortés with reinforcements from there in February 1521. Old but still full of enterprise, he persuaded the Crown to make him the first governor of Santa Marta in 1524. He ruled there autocratically and was overthrown by his own followers in 1526. Bastidas was sent back to Santo Domingo but died on the journey – whether or not his end was hastened by his sometime subordinates, as was rumoured. Then Santa Marta lived a year or two without an effective ruler (though Bastidas's deputy, Palomares, assumed that he was in control). Finally, the Council of the Indies appointed a businessman, a man similar to Bastidas, García de Lerma, as governor.

Lerma, like Bastidas, had played an important part in the Indies before he was named governor. His own economic activity began with his interest in a gold mine in Puerto Rico. Oviedo summed him up well: 'He is short of money but not of words.'[7] Lerma had been a page in the household of Diego Colón in 1510, and he went to Flanders on Colón's behalf in 1516, where he became a courtier and a friend of Charles, who later always treated him well. He intrigued successfully to obtain a monopoly of the pearls of Cubagua and became inspector (*veedor*) of the north coast of South America, in succession to Francisco Vallejo, where he concerned himself in trading brazilwood. In Santa Marta as governor he seems to have acquired an immediate reputation as a hard taskmaster.

The Welser business in Santo Domingo was asked to organize the despatch of slaves to the New World and did so, but Licenciado Serrano, a rising lawyer in the Welsers' factory, wrote: 'the Germans bring in very black blacks, so much so that, despite the great necessity that we have for them, no one buys'.[8] (Later, 'very black' Africans rather than paler ones enjoyed a vogue among slave buyers.) There was evidently a profitable collaboration between Governor Lerma and Ehinger, the Welser factor: Ehinger estimated the value he had to make to help Lerma maintain order at 6,000 ducats, while Lerma used his influence at court to preserve Ehinger's monopoly of slaves.[9]

These arrangements did not work very well for the employers of slaves. In 1524 Alonso de Parada, a friend of Diego Velázquez who in 1528 became a judge in the *audiencia* in New Spain, proposed a contract whereby the king of Portugal would provide slaves to the king of Spain in a good cousinly exchange.[10] Actually Charles gave another small grant to take slaves to the New World to his secretary for American affairs, Francisco de los Cobos: 200 black slaves exempt from all taxes. Of course no one expected that that licence would be taken advantage of by Cobos in person, and, sure enough, he sold it to Seiler and Ehinger in Santo Domingo and also gave a share to three Genoese – Leonardo Catano, Batista Justiniani and Pedro Benito de Basinana. In February 1528 Ehinger and Seiler received a licence to introduce 4,000 slaves in the next four years, a third of them to be women.[11] This was in effect a continuation of the old grant to Gorrevod.

The Welsers profited. The new grant of Venezuela to them from the Gulf of Aljófar to Cape Vela was based on a sketch map by the veteran geographer Fernández de Enciso, who had received a contract for the governorship of '*tierra firme*', that is Venezuela. The contract was worked out by Ehinger, Seiler, Gessler, a new employee of the Welsers in Seville, and also Bartolomé Welser and his associates in Augsburg, who controlled several large warehouses in Andalusia. The contract not only gave the Welsers the right to trade in 'metals, herbs and spices' between the Indies and Spain but allowed them to arrange their commerce directly between the Indies and Flanders – something never granted before and, indeed, refused to the city of Santo Domingo the previous year.[12]

The agreement with the Welsers did not mention their name but spoke of the factors in Santo Domingo, Alfinger and Ehinger. They were, as usual in these circumstances, to be governor and captain-general for life; they would also be in perpetuity the captains (*alcaides*) of the two fortresses they would build. The task of these men would be first to found two Spanish *pueblos* with 300 citizens each and introduce miners.[13] The Germans would be free of taxes for six years, they could introduce cows as they wanted and take with them a hundred pine trees from Tenerife to plant. The governor could enslave all Indians who were shown to be rebels, but no one else.

All the enterprising Spanish merchants of Santo Domingo, who had already been extensively trading with the north coast of South America, were distressed by this arrangement. For the 1,500 miles of coast from Urabá to the mouth of the Orinoco were depopulated because so many Indians had fled into the interior to escape enslavement. There were in 1528 only two settlements, Santa Marta and Coro, as well as one improvised fortress at Cumaná.[14]

The experienced Juan Martínez Ampiés had been permitted by the supreme court in Santo Domingo (the judges were Alonso de Zuazo and Juan Espinosa) to go to Coro, which clearly needed an injection of life. His journey was delayed by a shipwreck in Saona, an island off Hispaniola first visited by Columbus, and by a request by the judges to reinforce the fleet because of a recent French attack on San Germán in Puerto Rico. (It had ruined San Germán's short-lived prosperity.) Ampiés fell on the French fleet by surprise and killed thirty of their sailors in what must have been the first European–Caribbean sea battle. Then he went on with fifty men to Coro via Higuey in Puerto Rico and Curaçao, just off the coast of Venezuela. His aim was to prevent the Welsers from establishing themselves on the Colombian–Venezuelan coast. He hoped that they (whose representatives in Santo Domingo he knew) would content themselves with the coast from Coquibacoa to Santa Marta, while he, Ampiés, would hold on to the longer shore between Coquibacoa and Coro. Ampiés succeeded in persuading an ally of the past, the chief Manaure, to receive him with affection. Manaure even became a Christian.

In January 1529 Alfinger set off by sea from Santo Domingo with fifty men of his own for Coro, where he arrived on 4 February. All seemed desolate; Ampiés was living in a stone house which he had built for himself on the island of Curaçao, and Lerma was in Santo Domingo too, awaiting his own journey to Santa Marta, some of his men being among Alfinger's troops.

Alfinger was horrified at the misery of Coro. His putative capital consisted of a few incomplete and dull buildings on the edge of a dusty plain. This was not what he had expected when his contract had been negotiated. The fact that Ampiés had abandoned his pretensions was little consolation – he had proclaimed himself *justicia mayor*, and was now claiming to have founded Coro only in order to export brazilwood. It was Alfinger who without enthusiasm now laid out the town in Spanish metrical style with grants of sites (*solares*) to appropriate settlers. Alfinger found that Ampiés had left nothing behind him and was even stirring up the Indians against him. He seized him when he returned and put him in a ship bound for Santo Domingo with orders not to return to Coro under any circumstances. In this, Alfinger was eventually supported by the Council of the Indies, whose members declared that they would condemn anyone new going to 'Venezuela' if he did not have the permission of the German governor.

Among those who had reached Santo Domingo with the miners was a remarkable man who would cast his mark on the history of South America: Nicolás Federman, like Alfinger originally from Ulm. Federman had been born about 1505, so in 1529 would have been in his mid-twenties. His father, Claus, had a property with a mill next to the church in Ulm. Nicolás had been educated at the famous Fondaco dei Tedeschi in Venice, which was assuming educational significance. He then began to work for the Welsers, who sent him to Seville. Thence he went to Santo Domingo, where it was felt he could help Alfinger, who was still away, now supposed lost, on his expedition to Maracaibo.

Federman reached Santo Domingo in December 1529, and went post-haste to Coro. He assessed the situation quickly and returned to Santo Domingo to seek supplies. He persuaded another employee of the Welsers, Sebastián Rentz, also of Ulm, to help him. He was assisted, as well as hindered, by the arrival of three ships direct from Spain under the command of Juan Seissenhofer (Juan Alemán to the Spaniards).

Alfinger had not been idle. Once he had settled in Coro, he began preparing an expedition to Maracaibo, the entrance to which lagoon he had seen on his first journey to Venezuela. In August 1529 he had taken 180 men out of the 300 whom he had brought from Santo Domingo. He found sweet water and concluded, in consequence of some primitive calculations, that the lagoon must be about 600 miles in circumference. He was convinced that this lagoon led to an even bigger sheet of water which in turn opened on to the Southern Sea. He and his friends ascended a mountain apparently called Coromixy which marked the entry to a province where the men had beards and the houses were made of stone with, it seemed, the Southern Sea only fifteen miles away. Hugo de Vascuna, one of Alfinger's captains, reported that there was a valley there called Unyasi where there were large 'sheep' – the llamas found in the land of 'Biru'.

Alfinger crossed the mountains of Jideharas south of Coro, to find the east side of the lagoon, founding the settlement of Maracaibo on 8 September. He also founded a less long-lasting settlement which he named 'Ulma' after his own faraway city in Germany. But he did not find a way to the Southern Sea.

Alfinger returned to Coro after losing a hundred men, mostly to Indian attacks, for the Indians on that coast were by then strongly opposed to Spain, having lost so many of their number to slavery, a trade in which Alfinger, like Ampiés in his time, and other Spanish captains concerned with the north coast of South America, also interested himself. Coro soon began to compete as a slaving port for that trade with Cubagua. Of course, Alfinger and his German fellow controllers needed Spanish lieutenants for this undertaking. In December 1529 we hear for the first time of the word 'Venezuela' being applied to the entire territory of the settlement, and Alfinger was being spoken of as its 'governor'.[15]

Further confusion was sown in the mind of Alfinger. Diego de Ordáz, Cortés's companion and a veteran of the campaign in Mexico in 1519–20, persuaded the Council of the Indies to let him explore and exploit the eastern end of Venezuela precisely as far as what he called the river Marañón, though it would seem better now to call it the Orinoco. Ordáz was to be allowed to take 250 men and would receive the habit of the order of Santiago.[16]

There were other more domestic disputes for Alfinger to try to settle. For example, the prices in the colony seemed far too high – above all for wine, but also for soap and for horses. Further, neither Alfinger nor his colleagues in Santo Domingo had been able to fulfil the demand for slaves to work there, neither Indian nor black slaves. The bishop of Santo Domingo would write shortly to the Emperor Charles (1530) that the very survival not just of his island but also of Puerto Rico and of Cuba depended on the provision of African slaves. He suggested that these colonies should be able to import them without licences,[17] and there was much support for this demand. In 1529 Ehinger sought and obtained a new contract for the carriage of slaves to the New World. He was helped by a temporary alliance which he made in Medina del Campo, that great market city of Castile, with Rodrigo de Dueñas, whose large Castilian fortune was based on the import of cinnamon.[18]

Agitation in favour of an extension of the slave traffic continued. For example, in 1527 Alfonso Núñez, a merchant of Seville, on behalf of a Portuguese, Afonso de Torres, undertook to sell to Luis Fernández de Alfaro, a backer of Cortés, ex-ship's captain and surely from his name a *converso*, one hundred black slaves, of whom four fifths were to be men. They would be procured in the Cape Verde islands, the Portuguese slave market off Africa, and sold in Santo Domingo.[19] Two years later, Fernández de Alfaro himself went to buy slaves in the Cape Verde islands. He had by then arranged a contract of his own, with Juan Gutiérrez of Triana, to supply another hundred black slaves to Santo Domingo.[20] There were lesser merchants who undertook the same kind of service to Puerto Rico.[21] The first merchant of Seville implicated in the African trade on a large scale was, however, Juan de la Barrera, who, returning in 1530 from the Indies already wealthy, soon became one of the richest of traders with establishments for the sale of slaves and other items in Cartagena, Honduras, Cuba and New Spain. He would himself regularly make the journey Seville–Cape Verde–Veracruz in one of his own boats.[22]

These procedures, and this route, marked an innovation. Until now, black slaves of African origin had usually been taken to the Americas from Europe, where they had probably been born in Portugal or Spain. But now slave ships began to sail direct from Africa to the New World, following the precedent of *Nuestra Señora de Begoña* belonging to a Genoese merchant, Polo de Espinola of Málaga, which left São Tomé, off what is now Nigeria, in 1530, with 300 slaves bound direct for Santo Domingo.[23]

Clearly, too, many of the slaves taken from Spain or Portugal to the Spanish empire now came from Africa, as is testified by the belief that all the difficulties encountered in disciplining them derived from Muslim *wolofes*, a term used to describe a Muslim tribe in West Africa – an anxiety which led to a ban in 1526 on the import of such slaves. In 1530 and 1532 rules were written against the shipment of *ladinos*, as slaves directly shipped from Spain were called, because they, too, were supposed to be potentially irresponsible. The Germans who had secured the contract for carrying slaves from Seville entered negotiations with the Casa da Mina in Lisbon. They reached an understanding that these slaves would be sent from São Tomé, in the gulf of Guinea. In 1530 King João III of Portugal gave permission to ships' captains to send slaves regularly from both the Cape Verde islands and São Tomé.[24] He does not seem to have hesitated a moment before agreeing to this, any more than King Fernando the Catholic had hesitated in 1510 about arranging for slaves to be sent to Santo Domingo. If these monarchs gave the matter any thought at all, they would have supposed that a slave in Christian hands would be much better off than a free African in Africa.

The first boat to travel from Guinea direct to the Caribbean was the *San António*, whose captain, Martin Afonso, took 201 slaves, branded 'G' for Guinea, from São Tomé in November 1532, a consignment which he delivered to the royal factor in San Juan de Puerto Rico, Juan País.[25] It was the forerunner of 300 years of such traffic. In 1533 nearly 500 slaves were taken direct from São Tomé to the Spanish Indies and, in 1534, about 650 were sent, even though at that time the royal factor at São Tomé was sending more than 500 slaves a year to the Portuguese castle of Elmina and 200–300 a year to Lisbon.[26]

A decree from King Charles in 1526 had repealed the slaving provision in the more tolerant code of Alfonso el Sabio, the *Siete Partidas* of the thirteenth century which provided that a slave who married would become free. Already the complexities of black slaves marrying free Indians had begun to preoccupy agile state lawyers.[27]

Thereafter black slaves, tied to their masters or no, would play a decisive part in most European ventures in the Americas.

13

Narváez and Cabeza de Vaca

Who will count the gold which entered Spain from this quarter?
                                                    Pedro Cieza de León

Bent on founding a new settlement in Florida, Pánfilo de Narváez, with his Segovian upbringing, his deep voice and his long experience of fighting in the Indies, set off from Sanlúcar de Barrameda with 600 men in five ships on 17 June 1527. On board there were five Franciscans, headed by Fray Juan Suárez, the commissary of the expedition. Other important participants were: Alonso Enríquez, the accountant; Antonio Alonso de Solís, the *factor*; and Álvaro Núñez Cabeza de Vaca, the treasurer. There was too, as often in those days, a Greek sailor; this one was named Doroteo Teodoro. There was a captain, Valenzuela, a relation of Narváez's wife, María de Valenzuela. A Spaniard named Esquivel, another named Velázquez de Cuéllar, and an Alanís as notary completed the crew. It was thus a typical expedition of the late 1520s.[1]

Of these men, Cabeza de Vaca would make history on this voyage. His extraordinary surname means literally 'head of a cow'. It derives from the legend that King Sancho of Navarre gave the name to an ancestor, the shepherd Martín Alhaja, who marked a path for the Christian armies at the battle of Las Navas de Tolosa in 1212. Álvaro Cabeza de Vaca was brought up in Jerez de la Frontera by his uncle, Pedro de Vera, and Beatriz Figueroa, his aunt. He became a chamberlain in the household of the Duke of Medina Sidonia, who sent him to Valladolid with urgent messages during the war of the *comuneros*, and he also fought in Seville for the royal forces. Then he was in Italy with the imperial army.

He married María de Marmolejo before he joined Narváez. He was a cousin of the Cabeza de Vaca who was even then bishop of the Canary Islands and on the Council of the Indies.

After stopping in the Canaries, as was *de rigueur* in those days, Narváez's expedition reached Hispaniola by mid-August. There Narváez tried, unsuccessfully, to recruit more men. Instead of gaining new adherents, 140 of Narváez's men preferred the local scene, being 'influenced by the offers and promises made to them by the people of the islands'.[2] Florida, after the journeys of Ponce de León and Vázquez de Ayllón (about both of which people in Santo Domingo were informed), did not now seem so inviting, and more attractive rumours of a rich new country to the south of Panama were already beginning to be current.[3] With the remainder of his men, Narváez set off for Cuba, where they stayed for the winter of 1527 to 1528.[4] Narváez had not lived in Santo Domingo since 1511 but he had been in Cuba most of the time between that date and 1520, so he had many friends there to draw upon. He had a son in Cuba too, Diego Narváez, as well as his wife, María de Valenzuela, who managed his estates. One of his friends was Vasco de Porcallo de Figueroa, now of Trinidad, where he had a large *encomienda*, which he treated as an estate rather than as a grant of individuals. He had been in New Spain in Narváez's disastrous expedition there of 1520 and had a bad name for mistreating Indians. He went with Cortés to Spain in 1527.[5] He offered to supply Narváez.

Narváez set off for Trinidad but in the event waited at Cabo de Santo Cruz, and Cabeza de Vaca returned with a captain named Pantoja to Trinidad to obtain the supplies. They encountered a fierce storm, and Cabeza de Vaca went alone to see Porcallo but a hurricane almost destroyed the place while he was there; the houses and the church were blown down and Cabeza de Vaca says that he had to link arms with several others to avoid being blown away. Narváez then assembled his fleet outside Jagua, a town in Cuba which he had himself established in 1511.

In February 1528 Narváez, Cabeza de Vaca and the rest of the expedition set off for Florida with the experienced Diego Muriel as their chief pilot. Muriel had already been to the west coast of Florida and had also been with Narváez on his disastrous expedition to New Spain in 1520.[6] He left behind in Havana one of his captains, Álvaro de la Cerda, with forty men and twelve horses. Another storm caught them off Havana and they were near Florida rather sooner than they had expected or desired. They found themselves in a bay which seems to be Moore Haven on Thursday, 12 April. Narváez landed there on Good Friday and the following day he raised the flag of Castile and took possession of the land in the name of the distant emperor. He was then proclaimed governor of Florida by his men and Cabeza de Vaca, as treasurer, and Alonso de Solís, as *veedor*, presented their credentials to him. After that, forty-two thin horses were landed, in a very poor way after such a bad journey. Alonso Enríquez exchanged some Spanish goods for venison from local Indians who had first made threatening gestures and then left, abandoning a large hut which could have sheltered 300.

Narváez immediately wanted to investigate the interior and he set off with Cabeza de Vaca and forty men, with six of the healthier horses. They found what seems to have been Tampa Bay, where they spent the night. They then returned to the fleet and Narváez sent a brigantine back to Havana to seek more provisions from Álvaro de la Cerda. He also seized four Indians whom he asked to lead him to where maize was grown, but found there that the sought-after cereal was far from ripe. They came upon some cases belonging to traders from Castile with their bodies inside, each covered with painted deerskin. There was also some gold, and some feathered objects which looked as if they had originated in New Spain, home of feather mosaics. The Indians explained that these objects came from Apalache where there was everything which the Spaniards might want. Enríquez burned these reminders of previous Spanish defeats to avoid demoralization.

The Castilians, meantime, disputed what the right course would be: Cabeza de Vaca believed they should re-embark and seek a better harbour, but Fray Juan Suárez thought quite differently, explaining that Cortés's fief of Pánuco was only about thirty miles away to the west. Narváez agreed. He suggested that Cabeza de Vaca should remain with the ships while he went ahead. Cabeza refused, saying that he preferred to risk his life than lose his honour. A Captain Carvalho stayed behind with the ships. But Pánuco was in fact over 1,000 miles off.

The expedition set off, meeting a river which they crossed with difficulty. They made rafts for the supplies and some Spaniards swam. Two hundred Indians were waiting on the other side, but the Spaniards captured some of them and they led them to their settlement where they at last found ripe maize. Cabeza said that they should now seek the sea again, but Narváez refused to commit his men to such a journey. Cabeza went ahead on his own but found only a river with oyster shells which cut the explorers' feet through their boots. In the end it was an expedition led by Valenzuela that found the sea, if only a small bay.

The expeditionaries continued their journey, which was generally westward in direction though it was by now quite unclear where they were going. They occasionally met and made friends with, as they supposed, Indian chiefs, such as a certain Dulchanchellin, who was attended by men playing reed flutes, and with him they exchanged beads and hawksbells for deerskins. The aim was to find a good place for a settlement but one did not appear. Occasionally they obtained maize, sometimes a Spaniard (as Velázquez de Cuéllar) was drowned, sometimes horses were killed. Occasionally, there were golden moments as when 'we saw that we had arrived at a place where they told us that there was an abundance of food and also gold [so that] it seemed that a large part of our weariness and hunger had been lifted from us'. The abundance included pumpkins and beans. They encountered such interesting animals or birds as rabbit, hare, bear, geese, hawk, sparrowhawk, heron, partridge, teal and duck. While up to their necks in a lake which they could not cross in any other way, they were attacked by 'tall, naked, handsome, lean, strong and agile Indians' with powerful bows which they managed 'so surely that they never miss anything'.

Narváez sent Cabeza de Vaca with about sixty men again to seek the sea. He found it at the Bay of the Cross (or Mobile Bay). The whole expedition set off for there but the journey was long and there were many who were sick (perhaps a third of them). Cabeza de Vaca noted: 'most of the horsemen began to steal away in the hope that they could find some recourse for themselves by abandoning the governor and the invalids'. But 'those who were hidalgos could not bring themselves to do this without telling the governor and we, the officials (the *veedor*, the *tesorero*, the *contador*), reproached them and they agreed to stay'. Then Narváez asked each man separately their advice 'about this evil land and how to get out of it'.

At the sea, they built boats, but that meant making nails, saws, axes and other tools out of stirrups, spurs and crossbows. They made rigging from the tails of horses, sails from shirts, oars from juniper wood. The Greek Doroteo Teodoro made pitch from pine trees. They tanned the hides of dead horses to obtain pails for water. The building of boats began on 4 August and by 20 September they had five of them, each 22 cubits long.[7] On 22 September they ate the last of the horses and embarked, with Narváez on the first ship with forty-nine men. Forty-eight men sailed with Andrés de Dorantes, forty-eight with captains Téllez and Peñalosa, and forty-nine with Cabeza de Vaca. They set off, with no one on board having any knowledge of navigation, for none of these conquistadors were sailors. The boats were loaded so high as to give scarcely a hand's breadth above the water.

After seven days, they landed at an island which seems to have been in the delta of the Mississippi. They sailed on in a westerly direction and ran short of water (the horses' hides rotted) as well as of food and reached an island without sweet water. They began to drink sea water, five men becoming almost insane as a result. At last they arrived at an Indian port where there were canoes, fresh water and cooked fish, all of which the Indians offered Narváez, apparently because they admired his sable coat. But at midnight the Indians attacked, Narváez was injured, the Greek Doroteo Teodoro deserted. It was observed that the Indian canoes seemed to be cutting off the Spaniards from the open sea so the flotilla of five boats set sail again. Cabeza de Vaca was swept out into the Gulf of Mexico but he managed to return and saw again three of the boats, including Narváez's. Cabeza de Vaca caught up with him but as the governor's boat carried 'the strongest and healthiest people among us, there was no way whereby the others could follow him'. Cabeza was able to ask Narváez for a line so that he would not be left behind and also to ask for orders. Narváez said that 'this was no time to give orders to others, each of us must do what seems best to save his life and that was what he intended to do'. So saying he drew away with his boat. No one ever saw him again. It became known that he remained on board his ship that night when there was no food and, in the course of the evening, the ship was blown out to sea without anyone seeing him go. 'And no one learned any more of him' ('*Nunca más supieron de el*').

It was a tragic end to the life of a resolute adventurer whose ambitions were boundless even if his capacity was limited. He was good-hearted, optimistic and resourceful but also ruthless and cruel. Some years later his lieutenant, Pantoja, was killed by Porcallo's brother Sotomayor for abusing the Indians. They all ate each other after their deaths, Esquível being the last to die.

For a time Cabeza de Vaca sailed alongside the boat of Téllez and Peñalosa but, on the fifth day of sailing, a storm separated them.

> Next day all the [49] men in my boat were lying heaped upon one another, so near death that few were conscious. Not five men were able to stand. When night fell, only the mate and I were capable of sailing the boat and, at nightfall, the mate told me to take over, for he thought that he would die that night ... At midnight I went to see if he was dead but he was better.

At daybreak this boat was flung on to the shore and nearly all the ship's company revived. They found themselves with fresh water on an island which they called Malhado, island of ill fortune. There they were given food by Indians for which the Spaniards offered more hawksbells and beads. These Indians had their nipples pierced and a reed was driven 2.5 inches through them. Their lower lips were also cut open. Their staple food was the swamp potato but in the summer they also ate fish.

The Spaniards decided to set off again but waves overwhelmed the boat. Fray Juan Suárez drowned and the others were flung naked on to the shore. It was now November 1528 and Indians emerged from a village and offered to take the survivors into their houses. There was a general disposition to accept such kindness but the few of Cabeza's conquistadors who had been in New Spain (such as Alanís and Dorantes) refused because they thought that the concession was certain to lead to their being sacrificed. The Indians had built a hut for their unexpected guests with beds of reed mats inside it. The Indians danced and made revelry though, wrote Cabeza, 'for us there was neither pleasure nor revelry nor sleep, for we were waiting to know when they were going to sacrifice us'.

Matters began to improve when Cabeza's men discovered that another of Narváez's five ships had docked nearby, that of Dorantes, whose men, remarkably, were still clothed. The two groups pooled such resources as they had. Cabeza and Dorantes decided to try to spend the winter on this island. They despatched a boat under Álvaro Fernández with three other strong men to try to reach help in Havana, but they must have been wrecked on the way. Very cold weather came upon the survivors. Five Christians who had had to camp on the beach ate each other's bodies. By then only fifteen from the two boat crews were alive. A stomach complaint hit the Indians, who were tempted to kill the remaining

Spaniards, but abandoned the idea when they considered that, if the Spaniards were so strong, they would surely have saved more of their own people.

The Indians tried to make the Spaniards into medicine men. Cabeza was unenthusiastic but the Spaniards felt that they had to accept. They established their authenticity by arranging to blow on the part of the body where there seemed to be pain and then they made the sign of the cross. They recited a Pater Noster and an Ave Maria. This cure sometimes worked.

Cabeza de Vaca soon went to the mainland where he survived for a month eating blackberries. He became ill, and the survivors of the expedition visited him. Then he returned to the island of Malhado, where the Indian chiefs prescribed hard labour for him and the other survivors. His first task was to seek swamp potatoes under water. He eventually became a trader, procuring sea snails, shells, fruit, hides, flints for arrowheads, dried reeds, glue and tassels of deer hair. But commerce was limited since those Indians were constantly at war with their neighbours. In these circumstances, Cabeza became famous among the Indians of the Mississippi delta. He remained there almost six years.

14

Ordaz on the Orinoco; Heredia at Cartagena

Those who do military service for the world pant, sweat, and
endure the tumult of battle for many years. And for what perish-
able and worthless concerns, and with such uncertain hope!

Erasmus, *Enchiridion*

Several of the captains who had accompanied Cortés in his years of struggle against the Mexica wished to have the opportunity of achieving something similar themselves. In particular Pedro de Alvarado who, as has been seen, was carving out for himself a principality in Guatemala; Francisco de Montejo in Yucatan; Pánfilo de Narváez, the tragic Segovian, who would die in a storm off the Mississippi; and finally Diego de Ordaz, who embarked on a great adventure on the river Orinoco.

Diego de Ordaz had been born in Castroverde de Campos, a small town in north-western Castile near Medina de Ríoseco, surrounded by flat, fertile land and fed by the river Valderaduey. Castroverde is a remote place and it is at first sight astonishing that so determined a conquistador should have come from it. Ordaz was, however, a blood relation of other conquistadors who had accompanied Cortés, such as Cristóbal Flores from Valencia de San Juan, a friend of Cortés who was punished by him for blaspheming. Ordaz was an uncle too of Francisco Verdugo, one of the many men of Cuéllar to take part in Diego Velázquez's enterprises, and who had left Spain with Ordaz in 1510. It seems likely that Ordaz had been present at the disastrous battle of Turbaco, in what is now Colombia, where the Spaniards were defeated and the veteran explorer Juan de la Cosa was killed.

Diego de Ordaz and his brother Pedro also took part in the conquest of Cuba: Diego became majordomo to the governor, Diego Velázquez.

He was notorious for leaving behind his brother Pedro in a swamp in the south of the island, but he survived and went on to volunteer to join Pánfilo de Narváez in his expedition to New Spain in 1520.

Ordaz had joined Cortés's expedition in 1519. Velázquez thought of him as one of 'his' men on the journey and he was asked to keep an eye on Cortés on Velázquez's behalf. Ordaz was captain of one of the expedition's ten ships and Cortés sent him to obtain supplies from Jamaica. Later Ordaz tried to kidnap Cortés by asking him to dine on board his ship at Havana, but Cortés wisely refused the invitation. Ordaz's brigantine in Yucatan went in search of the lost Andalusian, Jerónimo de Aguilar. He seems to have plotted against Cortés in Veracruz, and was arrested, condemned to death but then pardoned (as captain-general Cortés had the right to issue such condemnations).[1] Ordaz had no doubts about Cortés's lack of morals: 'the Marquis has no more conscience than a dog', he later wrote to his nephew Francisco Verdugo.[2]

Ordaz's next exploit was to climb the volcano Popocatépetl and he was able from that height to observe and, later, describe the beautiful site of Mexico/Tenochtitlan on its lake.[3] It was the first mountain ascended in the Americas. The Spaniards, therefore, knew which route to take to the Mexican capital. Understandably, Ordaz took a volcano as his coat of arms. He lost a finger in the fighting 'on the bridges' in 1520. Later that same year Cortés, who now trusted him, sent him back to Spain to support his cause at court. Ordaz was not much missed in the last battles around Tenochtitlan, for he was no horseman and he stuttered in speech.[4] But he was one of the conquistadors who interested himself in the achievements of the Indians and, later in Spain, requested his nephew Verdugo to send him some feather mosaics which the Mexica arranged so artistically.[5] He was also a good letter-writer, as those to Verdugo would show.

In 1524 we find Ordaz branching out into new activities of his own. He was then owner of two thirds of the ship *Santa María de la Victoria*, which sailed with merchandise for the Americas from Santo Domingo. But, like all the successful captains in New Spain, he had his *encomiendas*: Teutla, Huejotzingo, Caplan, Chiautla. In 1529 the Crown also gave him the peninsula of Tepetlacingo on the Lake of Mexico.[6] Then he went back to old Spain and was the only conquistador from New Spain present at Cortés's second wedding in 1529 in Béjar.[7]

This was the background of the Castilian who, in May 1530, obtained a contract to 'discover, conquer and populate' the towns which were to be found between the river Marañón[8] and the Cape de la Vela (of the sail) in what is now western Venezuela, on the west side of the peninsula of Güiria.[9]

Ordaz was able to organize a new expedition of 500 men.[10] He also had thirty horse. His captains were the famous and persistent Gil González de Ávila as chief magistrate, Jerónimo Dortal as treasurer and Juan Cortejo as captain-general, while Alonso Herrera was *maestre de campo* (marshal). Of these men, the first-named had by then been active, as we have seen, in innumerable ways in the Indies over twenty years. Alonso Herrera, who came from Jeréz de la Frontera, had been in Mexico in the last stages of the conquest. He had then been sent by Cortés to suppress a rebellion of the Zapotecs in Oaxaca in 1526: 'he was a practical man experienced in military matters with a singular capacity to attract young soldiers'. Thus it was that he persuaded one hundred men to go with them, including three brothers named Silva. They sold all they had in order to go with Ordaz, whom they joined late, in the Gulf of Paria, in the galleon of a Portuguese merchant which they had stolen, or rather persuaded the daughter of the merchant to make over to them without payment.

Most of the money for this expedition was found by two Italian bankers established in Seville, Cristóbal Franquesín and Alejandro Geraldini.

There was an obvious ambiguity between Ordaz's licence and that already assigned to Welser's men, the Germans Micer Enrique Eyniger and Jerónimo Seiler. It was also feared in Spain that Ordaz might touch the land of the most serene king of Portugal, 'our brother' – that is the territory which became Brazil. In the other direction, Ordaz would control the entire coast of Venezuela. How did that square with the existing concessions to the Germans? In this territory Ordaz would become governor and captain-general for life and receive a salary of 725,000 maravedís a year. Out of this, he would, as the custom then was, have to pay a chief magistrate, thirty infantrymen, 110 squires, a physician and an apothecary. He would be able to grant such *encomiendas* as he thought fit, and receive twenty-five mares from the Crown which he would pick up in Jamaica. He would also receive 300,000 maravedís for artillery and munitions. He would have the right to carry with him fifty black slaves, of whom a third would be women.

The ambiguity in Ordaz's licence was mitigated by the fact that he had no intention of interfering with the Germans on the northern coast of South America. He wanted to explore the great river Orinoco which he believed led to a land where extensive supplies of gold were to be found.[11]

Ordaz's fleet of two large *naos* and a smaller ship which he called a '*carabelón*' sailed from Sanlúcar on 20 October 1531. He had been maintaining his expedition at his own cost already for two months.

They stopped at Tenerife to pick up another hundred men, about forty horses and some mares. Then, after a storm which dispersed the ships, they reached the Cape Verde Islands on 26 December, and sailed easily across the Atlantic to make landfall in the Americas sixty miles east of the river Orinoco. Perhaps that was just inside the territory now known as Guyana. No European before had seen this wild green landscape. Ordaz sent out a launch, a *chalupa*, with thirteen men on board. But three days later it returned, having been unable to land because of the mud. They then found some islands which they named San Sebastián, and from there sailed up the river for eight days, 'but all the land which appeared was flooded'. They could find nothing which suggested that there was any settlement in the neighbourhood. On one of these islands they left a wooden cross to help guide those who would follow them.

This is how Ordaz's account appears in a later investigation in Santo Domingo. But some chroniclers talk of a wreck of the two caravels which formed part of the flotilla and of how everyone aboard them took to small boats as best they could and left their colleagues to a, in some cases, terrible fate. It was sometimes said of those who disappeared at this stage that they had in fact sailed on upriver and discovered a magical golden land, 'El Dorado', but the only certain thing is that nothing more was heard of them. A small group did set off in two little boats to look for Ordaz and his flagship, but they in turn found themselves swept northwards into the Gulf of Paria. One of the boats was lost there with all hands.

Ordaz, meantime, having indeed gone north to where he knew there was water, also found himself in the Gulf of Paria and, after another forty days, on the island of Trinidad (so christened by Columbus on his third voyage). He had only one barrel (*pipa*) of water left. He and his men waited four days there to gather more water and grass for the horses. Then they reached land in the gulf, presumably to the west of the channel already known to Spanish captains as the Dragon's Mouths. There they were approached by Indians in two canoes. Ordaz gave them some good shirts of that staple Holland cloth which had played such a part in relations between Spaniards and Indians.[12] He also gave them some Venetian glass beads which had played a similar role.

These people talked a great deal; Ordaz and his friends considered that a good sign. But here the expedition came into contact with Antonio Sedeño, an aggressive ex-notary like Cortés and a man who had made a fortune selling Carib slaves. In 1530 he had been named governor of Trinidad, though the island had not yet been conquered. He had gone to the South American mainland and started to build a fortress. This caused him to seem as much a threat to Ordaz as Ordaz was to him. One of Sedeño's lieutenants tried to seize Ordaz but Jerónimo Dortal got the better of him and, on 14 June 1531, Ordaz established the *pueblo* of San Miguel de Paria.

He sought then to establish the different responsibilities in the zone of the Orinoco: Sedeño in Trinidad, the Germans in Venezuela and even the pearl fisherman Pedro Ortiz de Matienzo in Cubagua. But Ordaz's Spanish rivals were unyielding. It was anyway hard to reach any agreement about land in a continent where the distances were enormous, knowledge modest and hatreds intense.

Advised of the real route of the river Orinoco, Ordaz began to sail up its delta on 23 June in his splendid galleon. What a sight it must have been! He still had over 350 men with him, though some of them derived from Sedeño and Ortiz de Matienzo.

He sent Alonso Herrera ahead. He found the Indians on the first large settlement on the bank, probably Uyapari, unfriendly (*'fuera de amistad y concordia'*). Most of the people in these *pueblos* were warlike bowmen and fighters (*'flecheros y guerreros y muy belicosos'*). Ordaz soon caught up with Herrera and proceeded to scrutinize (*tantear*) other *pueblos*. In one of these, which he and his friends named Tuy after the pretty Portuguese–Spanish border town, they learned that on the other side of the mountains there was a large province called Guyana. Ordaz sent there one of Sedeño's men, Juan González, who returned with the bad news that the way was difficult for horses, the sterile land being sharp under foot.

Ordaz now decided to continue up the Orinoco on land, leaving at Uyapari twenty-five sick men under the command of Gil González de

Ávila. But after several weeks' march, and having travelled about 600 miles – an astonishing distance – to the site of the modern Puerto Ayacucho, it became impossible to go any further. The jungle was too intense, the heat unbearable, the mosquitoes triumphant, the diseases merciless. Carib Indians attacked regularly. Ordaz withdrew to the confluence of the Orinoco and the river Meta. Some Caribs persuaded the gullible Spaniards that there was gold high up the Meta. Ordaz and his men went some way up the tributary by boat, but rapids and currents prevented them going very far. Ordaz decided to return to Paria, a rough spot which by then seemed to him a memory of tranquillity. His idea was to re-enter the zone of the Meta with its golden promise later, overland via Cumaná. But there were further difficulties. Gil González de Ávila, veteran of so many odd encounters in the Indies, was halted and imprisoned by Ortiz de Matienzo. Ordaz eventually found himself in Cubagua with a mere thirty men. Ortiz de Matienzo captured him too, and despatched him under guard to Santo Domingo. The judge there released him. Ordaz tried to recruit new men for his journey back to the Orinoco, but was refused permission to do so. He accordingly determined to return to Spain with the same intent. He set off but died on 22 July 1532, halfway across the Atlantic, poisoned, according to Fray Pedro de Aguado, a historian of Venezuela, by Ortiz de Matienzo.[13] He was not the first of Cortés's contemporaries to die in suspicious circumstances.

In 1532 another contract was made by the Crown for the conquest and settlement of a part of the territory which had been left with the German Welsers, namely the land between Darien or the Gulf of Urabá and the mouth of the river Magdalena. The arrangement was made by the only Madrileño among the leading conquistadors, Pedro Fernández de Heredia.[14]

Heredia was a small-time businessman who left for the New World to escape his creditors. His first visit to the Indies was financed by his wife, Constanza Franco, who had inherited a fortune from her first husband. On that first voyage of 1532, Heredia went to Santo Domingo and founded a sugar mill and plantation at Azúa de Compostela, where Cortés had served as a notary in his youth, on land which he inherited from a cousin.[15] There he and his brother, Alonso, busied themselves in the Indian slave trade from the north of South America, indeed from the territory close to Cartagena where he would receive his contract in 1532. Heredia went to Santa Marta, where he was for a time lieutenant-governor to Pedro de Valdillo, who himself took over from Álvarez Palomino in 1528. He must have seen that no one was taking any notice of the zone between Darien and the river Magdalena. Then he returned to Spain where he pursued his plan of gaining his grant of Cartagena, which he obtained in August 1532.[16]

In September 1532, only a month afterwards, Heredia left Sanlúcar with a single galleon, a caravel, a *fusta* (light rowing boat) and 115 men. Again his wife, Constanza, seems to have been the principal backer. They sailed via the Canaries, then Puerto Rico (the island of Mona), on to Santo Domingo, where Heredia enrolled more men, including some left over from Ordaz's unhappy expedition to the Orinoco. At Azúa, where Heredia had had his plantation, they secured a new caravel. Then they went to Santa Marta, where the commander looked for interpreters who spoke the language of the natives in Cartagena. Finally, early in 1533, probably on 14 January, Heredia and his expedition disembarked on the Colombian coast in the Bay of Cartagena.[17]

Soon after their landing, Heredia was joined by his brother, Alonso de Heredia, who sailed in with reinforcements from Guatemala, where he had been with Pedro de Alvarado. Together the brothers mounted expeditions from Cartagena southwards into the territory of the Cenu people, and towards Urabá. Some further Spanish settlements were founded, in unpromising circumstances: San Sebastián de Buena Vista in the Gulf of Urabá, for example, Villa Rica de Madrid in Cenu territory, and, some way up the Magdalena, Santa Cruz de Mompox, whose remarkable colonial architecture can still be appreciated by the adventurous traveller.

Cartagena was difficult to turn into a successful colony. Partly that was because the supply of food was poor – the land nearby was marked by marsh and swamp. Sugar plantations and mills were founded but, for the time being, Heredia granted no *encomiendas*. The territory, which seemed to lie between two rivers, was soon to be viewed as no more than a bridge to Peru. The governor of Santa Marta, at that time still García de Lerma, the businessman converted into proconsul, believed that Cartagena should be a dependency of his own city. Thwarted in that, he placed every obstacle in Heredia's way, even seeking to avoid his training interpreters in Santa Marta to assist him.[18] The

Spanish settlers in that city were always raiding Cartagena for Indians whom they could sell in 'the islands', that is, the West Indies. On the other hand, the people in Cartagena considered the charm of their city to be its proximity to the provinces of the Cenu, who could be used as a workforce. All the same, they were soon using black African slaves for all the hard work when *encomiendas* were in the end founded.[19]

Almost before Cartagena had time to settle down, Juan de Padilla, a judge in Santo Domingo, came to carry out the *residencia* of Heredia, and a second and, in the end, a third such enquiry were commissioned. That was, of course, the Crown's decision in Spain. Heredia was accused of neglecting the defence of Cartagena, of the division of the land nearby into *encomiendas* which favoured his own friends, of defrauding the royal treasury and of forgetting the need to maintain public morality.[20] All these accusations seemed unfair, premature and inappropriate and it transpired that the *residencia* had been introduced because Heredia was a mere commoner without the pretensions of a Montejo, the aristocratic Alvarado or even Pedrarias.

Heredia later had great difficulties with his wife, who claimed that his adventures in the Indies had left her with no money. He eventually set sail for Europe but only in 1554; his fleet was wrecked off the Azores in January 1555 and he and over one hundred others drowned. By that time Cartagena de las Indias was a much valued port in an empire which seemed to command two oceans, the Ocean Sea (Atlantic) and the South Sea (Pacific).

15

Cortés and the supreme court in New Spain

*You know, don't you, that to the right hand of the Indias there is
an island called California which is populated by black women?*
García Rodríguez de Montalvo, *Sergas de Esplendián*

Cortés returned in July 1530 from old to New Spain with no illusions.
In his absence there had been a political earthquake. Guzmán, the president of the *audiencia*, arrived in the capital of New Spain in December
1528, and there had appeared too the saintly, austere, intellectually
determined, strong-minded and unbending first bishop of the Mexicans,
Juan de Zumárraga, a Basque Erasmian of originality and strength of
character. He was of the great generation of liberal Spanish bishops
such as the inquisitor Alonso Manrique de Lara and Alonso Fonseca,
archbishop of Toledo. He had met the emperor in the Jeronymite monastery of El Abrojo and Charles had asked him to eliminate the witches
of Navarre – a task which he was said to have carried out to perfection.
Nominated to Mexico in consequence of this triumph, Zumárraga proclaimed himself one who believed that the Indians were rational beings
whose souls could be saved; he was a Utopian as well as an Erasmian.[1]

Zumárraga at once entered upon quarrels in Tenochtitlan with the
supreme court, whose members, he thought, were neglecting their duties,
spending their time 'promenading in public gardens'. But Zumárraga
was in a weak position since he had left Spain hastily, before his confirmation in office, so that it was easy enough to argue that he was just
a 'religious' like so many others. Zumárraga presented his authority as
'Protector of the Indians'; the court agreed to give him all necessary
powers, but argued that he had delegated his authority. The judges also
insisted that Indian complaints were their business and that Zumárraga's

task was just to teach the catechism. They threatened the new bishop with exile, and the leading Indians, seeing how things were going, fled from their protector. Zumárraga denounced the judges in a sermon and threatened to report them to the Emperor Charles.[2]

There then came the curious affair of Huejotzingo, a town on the eastern slopes of the volcano Itzaccíhuatl, some six miles from both Tlaxcala and Cholula. Cortés had taken the place as an *encomienda* in 1524. In 1528 the Indians there complained that, in addition to their tribute to him, they were being forced to pay dues to the court, including to the Crown's representative, García del Pilar, an experienced conquistador who had accompanied Cortés throughout the campaign leading to the conquest. He had the reputation of being the first Spaniard to know Nahuatl. Zumárraga, apprised of the problem, asked the court for a schedule of the tributes. Guzmán told Zumárraga that the court was not answerable to him and warned him that, if he persisted in his trouble-making, he would have him hanged, as Charles had hanged Bishop Acuña of Zamora after the war of the *comuneros*. Guzmán sent a magistrate to arrest the complaining Indians of Huejotzingo. Zumárraga warned the Indians in time and they took refuge in the new Franciscan convent in their town. Fray Motolinía was the 'guardian' of the convent and soon Fray Jerónimo de Mendieta would be writing his books in his cell there.

Zumárraga then set out himself for Huejotzingo, followed by the magistrate, who proceeded to arrest the Indians and take them to Mexico. A town meeting was held in Huejotzingo calling on a Franciscan, Fray Antonio Ortiz, to go to Mexico to insist that the court respect justice. He preached thus at a pontifical mass chanted by another Erasmian, Fray Julián Garcés, the Dominican bishop of Tlaxcala. Guzmán tried to silence Ortiz, and an *alguacil* on his orders expelled him from the pulpit. Next day, Garcés's vicar-general announced that all those concerned would be excommunicated – that is, both Guzmán and the magistrate. Guzmán ordered the vicar-general exiled and despatched another magistrate to escort him to Veracruz. The vicar-general went to the church of San Francisco in Tenochtitlan, where Cortés's friends had used to foregather, and which Guzmán then had surrounded. Zumárraga returned to the capital and persuaded the two junior members of the *audiencia* (Delgadillo and Ortiz de Matienzo) to go to Huejotzingo to perform a penance and recite a *Miserere*.[3] They did go and withdrew a document which they had previously issued denouncing the Franciscans. But Guzmán sought his revenge by giving orders to hold up all the bishop's letters to Spain. That seems certain to have become normal practice.[4] One missive, though, reached its due destination. It was a letter to the Emperor Charles which recalled how many in Mexico had looked forward with pleasure to the coming of the new supreme court. It would surely be a breath of fresh air and a legal respite after the rough rule of Estrada. But the supreme court had seemed well disposed to nobody. Helped by the interpreter García del Pilar, Guzmán was robbing the land.

Zumárraga also reported that Pánuco had become a slave emporium, for many Indians were kidnapped there and shipped to the West Indies.

Guzmán, probably aware that he would soon be relieved of his responsibilities as president of the court, cleverly turned his attention to the conquest of the north-west. He had remarked that only fifty miles from the capital, the Chichimecas (a wild Indian people) were still in control. To mount an expedition against them, many horses were seized from private individuals, 10,000 pesos were taken from the treasury and 400 men were dragooned to take part. Juan de Cervantes was designated lieutenant of the captain-general in Pánuco and ordered to drive north from there at the same time as Guzmán himself drove north-west. He hoped that they would together fulfil a 'grand design' of an empire running from sea to sea, north of New Spain. Guzmán asked the Crown to approve his title as governor of 'Greater Spain'.

The Crown refused to concede that but agreed that the new territory might be called 'New Galicia', and Guzmán was named its governor in February 1531. But his larger ambition failed because the distances were too great. Guzmán did, however, conquer what became the future states in 'Mexico' of Jalisco and Sonora, founding Compostela and Guadalajara in the first, San Miguel and Chiametla in the second.

While these negotiations continued, the Council of the Indies in Valladolid was coming to terms with the fact that it had made a mistake in relation to the government of New Spain[5] and took the unusual step of meeting in November 1529 in conjunction with the Councils of Castile and of the Treasury (*hacienda*). Archbishop Pardo de Tavera, the head of the Council of Castile, presided. The letters of Zumárraga, a man known to be of a just spirit, had distressed all who had read them. The councillors studied an *información* critical of Guzmán, and Guzmán's response in rebuttal.[6] The council decided to change the com-

1. Charles V aged about twenty-two, by the Master of the Magdalene
legend, with the Golden Fleece round his neck.

2a. Mercurino Gattinara,
Chancellor to Charles V,
who dreamed of world
power for his master.

2b. Gonzalo Pérez was
Charles V's chief
secretary in the 1540s.

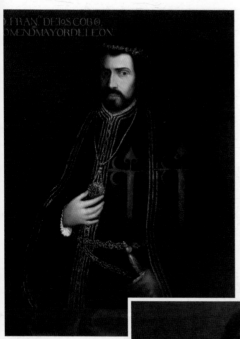

3a. (*left*) Francisco de los Cobos – reliable, covetous, patient.

3b. (*below*) Granvelle, chancellor to Charles V in all but name, who, like many servants of the Habsburgs, came from Franche Comté.

4a. (*above*) The Empress
Isabel of Portugal was
named regent of Spain by
Charles V during his
many absences. (Titian)

4b. (*right*) The
Archduchess Margaret of
Austria, who was the
governess of the
Netherlands as well as of
Charles V. (School of
Bernard van Orley)

5a. (*above*) Clement VII, the second Medici pope, whom Charles ruined at Rome in 1527. (Sebastian del Piombo)

5b. (*left*) Paul III, Alessandro Farnese, though preoccupied with his family, also concerned himself with American Indians. (Titian)

6a. Quiroga, Bishop of Patzcuaro, tried to apply More's principles in *Utopia* to New Spain

6b. The Erasmian Zumárraga, first bishop and then first archbishop of Mexico, was Mexico's first prince of the church.

D₂ Antonius Đ Mendoça. 1ᵃ. noua Hispaniᵉ Pro
Rex et dux Generalis ꞏAño. 1535ꞏ

7. Antonio de Mendoza, first viceroy of New Spain, a great
aristocrat who organized an empire.

8a. (*above*) A Spanish galleon full of passengers.
Galleons carried gold, silver, passengers and crews
across the Atlantic throughout the sixteenth
century.

8b. (*below*) Lombards were an early type of
artillery, which terrified natives all over
the Americas.

position of the court there and then. In the long run, they thought, there should be a viceroy, but in the interim a new court would serve. Both Gattinara and Pardo de Tavera, as well as García de Loaisa, took it upon themselves to suggest names of candidates to the presidency, but the matter was difficult to decide because a man of great integrity was required, though he would not be receiving a large salary. A further discussion was held on 10 December 1529 when the Count of Osorno and some members of the Council of the Treasury agreed that the new president of the court in New Spain should be a prudent, strong *caballero* with, if possible, a fortune in Castile. But such a person was hard to find.[7]

The empress, who was present, suggested a clever young Gallego, Vasco de Quiroga, whose father had been governor of the priory of San Juan in Castile. Tavera was Quiroga's father's friend and had always been helpful to the family. In 1525 Quiroga had been *juez de residencia* of a *corregidor* in Orán, Alfonso Páez de Ribera. At court, Quiroga later became friendly with Bernal Díaz de Luco, the secretary to Pardo de Tavera, and it was with him that Quiroga discussed a controversial passage in Antonio de Guevara's play *El Villano en el Danubio*. Perhaps it was this Bernal Díaz de Luco, as well as the queen, who suggested Quiroga as a judge.

Two other nominations were Antonio de Mendoza, the son of Fernando the Catholic's favourite public servant, the Count of Tendilla, the notably liberal governor of Granada. Eminently a *caballero* and not an intellectual, Mendoza had been a victorious commander, if on a small scale, in the war of the *comuneros* and then an emissary in Hungary. Apparently when chamberlain to the empress regent in Saragossa in 1529, he had told her that he would like to go to New Spain in some capacity.[8]

Things were still going politically from bad to worse in Mexico itself. Perhaps to distract attention from his other failings and setbacks in late 1529, Guzmán led a large and well-equipped force up to Michoacan. He was accompanied by the old monarch of the realm there, the *cazonci*, who had been a compliant dependant of Spain since Cortés sent Sandoval to take him up to Mexico/Tenochtitlan in 1523. In February 1530 Guzmán had the *cazonci* tried, tortured and then executed for organizing an attack on the Spaniards near the beautiful Lake Chapala.

The surviving *oidors* (judges of the supreme court), Diego Delgadillo and Juan Ortiz de Matienzo, were conducting themselves equally badly in the city of Mexico itself. Two conquistadors, García de Llerena and

Fray Cristóbal de Angulo, had been imprisoned by an episcopal court in the Franciscan convent in the capital. Both had offended the judges, who had the two men arrested and put to torture in the common gaol. Zumárraga and the superiors of both the Franciscan and Dominican orders with numerous friars made their way in procession to that building to demand their release. Zumárraga lost his temper and Delgadillo's guards chased away the procession. Zumárraga threatened to suspend all religious services in the city unless the prisoners were released in three hours. The judges then ordered Angulo to be hanged and quartered and sentenced Llerena to have a foot cut off and be whipped a hundred times. Services were indeed suspended, the Franciscans left their convent for Texcoco, and the horrifying sentences seem to have been carried out. Negotiations began between Fray Garcés, the bishop of Tlaxcala, and the Dominicans acting for the judges. Services were carried out for Easter 1530 but suspended once more on Low Sunday. The judges, who had not begged for absolution, remained under excommunication.[9]

But now they were to be removed. On 12 July a new court for New Spain was at last chosen. The president would be Bishop Ramírez de Fuenleal, at that time president of the *audiencia* in Santo Domingo, a responsible and hard-headed civil servant who showed that he could work effectively with Zumárraga. The other members were: Juan de Salmerón, who had been a judge in relation to Pedrarias in 1522; Alonso Maldonado, a great gambler and games player, who had married a daughter of Francisco de Montejo and whose interests in Yucatan and elsewhere he supported; and Francisco de Ceynos, who had once been prosecutor in Spain for the Council of the Indies. These men assumed office on 12 January 1531 and their arrival marked a fundamental change in the anarchic rule of the cruel Guzmán, who, however, managed to remain for a time as governor of his vast realm of New Galicia (Jalisco, Zacatecas, Aguascalientes and part of San Luis Potosí).

The first action of the new court was to remove the restriction which the old one had imposed on the movements of Cortés, who had been forbidden to approach the city which he had fought, destroyed and rebuilt. He had brought his mother, Catalina, and his new wife, Juana, to see the sights but they had been able to observe the city only from afar: a telling commentary on how the world has often treated the memory of its greatest men. Another initiative by the court was to seek to gather together all the sons of Spaniards by Indian women to give them a Spanish education.[10] This *audiencia* was asked by the Council of the Indies gradually to eradicate the *encomienda*, an instruction which clearly contradicted an order of October 1529 to the first supreme court to allow *encomiendas* in perpetuity. But we must not expect consistency as yet in Spanish imperial administration. The *encomienda* was confirmed as a system of labour and of land-holding in 1535.[11]

16

Montejo in Yucatan

> *Hernando Pizarro gave his word that ... good soldiers are not to*
> *be judged by their horses but by the valour of their persons. Who-*
> *ever showed himself brave would be rewarded in conformity with*
> *his service; for not to possess horses was a matter of fortune and*
> *no disparagement of persons.*
>
> Cited Sir John Elliott, *Empires*

Francisco Montejo was an accomplished conquistador from Old Castile
with experience in Cuba, Panama and New Spain. He knew something
of the two oceans already under Spanish control and he had helped in
the conquest of Panama as well as of New Spain. On 8 December 1526
he obtained a contract from the emperor, while he and the court were
still in Granada, for the conquest and settlement of Yucatan and of
Cozumel, a delectable island surrounded by deep blue water, off the
Mexican mainland, where both Grijalva and Cortés had stopped before
embarking on their serious adventures. Montejo was given the titles of
adelantado, governor and captain-general, designations intended to continue for two generations. He would have a salary of 150,000 maravedís
as governor and another 100,000 as captain-general.

Up to that point there was nothing unusual in the contract. Other
terms in it, however, were unexpected. Thus Montejo would be asked to
found two *pueblos*, inhabited by a hundred men each, both with fortresses in 'the most convenient and most necessary places'. Montejo
would have to finance his own army, but would not have to pay any
taxes. He and his heirs were granted 'in perpetuity' 4 per cent of all
income generated in Yucatan, and only one tenth would have to be paid
to the Crown for three years after the conquest. Then the figure would

fall to a ninth and slowly thereafter to a fifth. Each of the conquerors with Montejo would receive two *caballerías*[1] of land and two *solares* in the towns. Montejo would be able to name town councillors – as captains of these expeditions usually could – and it was assumed that they would be chosen from among his closest followers. A bishop would be named for Yucatan within five years, and from then on a tithe would be gathered to support the clergy and to build churches. Montejo was entitled to enslave Indians if they refused to accept the benefits of Spanish rule. Neither Jews nor Muslims, nor indeed criminals, were to be allowed to go to Yucatan. Finally the humane ordinance of November 1526 was written into Montejo's contract, which was signed by the emperor and by all the court bureaucracy of the Indies – Cobos, as well as the three bishops who then participated in the Council of the Indies (Osma, Ciudad Rodrigo and the Canaries), that is, García de Loaisa, Maldonado and Cabeza de Vaca.[2]

Montejo was of a good family established in Salamanca. He was born some time between 1473 and 1484 and so was of the same generation as his one-time commander, Cortés. He was a man of medium height, with a cheerful countenance, a good horseman and of an open-handed nature. He usually spent more than his income, as the censorious Bernal Díaz del Castillo put it.[3] He went to live in Seville in the early 1500s, where he seduced Ana de León (daughter of the Licenciado Pedro de León, who was probably a *converso*), by whom he had a son, who took his name and later became famous as Francisco de Montejo, '*el Mozo*', the boy.[4]

Montejo the father went to the Indies in 1514 with Pedrarias, who sent him ahead to recruit volunteers in Santo Domingo.[5] Disappointed by what he found in Darien and Panama, Montejo went to Cuba, where a personal friendship with Diego Velázquez enabled him to establish a large farm near what is now the pretty port of Mariel. There he met Hernández de Córdoba returning from New Spain looking very 'badly treated'. Montejo himself was a member of Grijalva's expedition to New Spain and captained one of his *naos*. Then, like Ordaz, he went as one of Diego Velázquez's friends in Cortés's expedition in 1519, but he seems to have been easily persuaded by Cortés to work with him – at a salary of 2,000 pesos, said Díaz del Castillo.[6] He started late in 1518 from Santiago in his own ship and caught up with Cortés at Havana, where he sold the latter 500 rashers of bacon.[7] He went across to

Cozumel, an island which he says, in the *residencia* of Cortés, that he had visited 'many times' – a claim which, by 1530, may have been the case.[8] At Veracruz, Cortés sent him north to look for a good harbour at a time when he himself was carrying out his *coup de main* against the friends of Velázquez. When Montejo returned, he was rewarded for his lack of complaint by being named first magistrate of Veracruz. He then went back to 'the kingdoms of Castile', as he put it, on Cortés's behalf, accompanied by another hidalgo, a cousin of the Count of Medellín, Alonso Hernández Portocarrero.

On the way, Montejo stopped off at his Cuban property at Mariel, where he and Hernández Portocarrero took on bread, meat and water. They remained for three days during which Montejo committed what a modern historian calls 'an unpardonable indiscretion': he could not resist showing his old friend and neighbour Juan de Rojas the breathtaking treasures that he was taking back to Spain – 'an infinite amount of gold so much so that there was no ballast in the ship except for gold', as a servant on Montejo's property put it, grossly exaggerating.[9]

Montejo's crossing of the Atlantic back to Spain in 1520 was interesting since the great pilot Antonio de Alaminos took a route between Florida and the Bahamas along the line of the Gulf Stream (the usual route was still through the Windward Islands). Governor Velázquez later criticized that route as being dangerous but it became commonplace within a short time. Indeed, Alaminos pioneered it.

Leaving Cuba on 26 August the conquistadors stopped again at Terceira in the Azores Islands, which must have been well known to Alaminos, and were in Spain by November. Then Montejo and Hernández Portocarrero embarked on a long struggle at court to establish the respectability of Cortés, whose enemies, above all Diego Velázquez, were active, powerful and unforgiving.

After the Crown found in favour of Cortés, thanks largely to Montejo and partly also to Cortés's father, Montejo was named *alcaide*, or commander of Villa Rica de la Veracruz.[10] He returned to New Spain in 1524 but went back once more to Castile quite soon with 60,000 *pesos de oro*,[11] having obtained from Cortés the valuable *encomiendas* of Azcapotzalco, Matlactlan and perhaps Chila, worth 1,500 pesos a year. Montejo was at that time the *procurador*, or official representative, of New Spain in Castile. There he sought his contract for Yucatan, in which pursuit he was supported by Pánfilo de Narváez and some others of his point of view. Having talked to Jerónimo de Aguilar, the interpreter, who had spent some years in Yucatan as a prisoner, Montejo had been led to believe that the territory in his contract was rich. Having obtained Charles's permission in December 1526 he was able to set off from Sanlúcar in June 1527, with 250 followers.[12]

This group included one important veteran of the wars in New Spain, Alonso de Ávila, who must have remembered Cozumel from his time there with both Grijalva and Cortés. Ávila had had an even more complicated life than Montejo recently; he had gained Cortés's respect but Cortés did not trust him because he had been a protégé of Bishop Rodríguez de Fonseca. Returning to Castile in 1522 in one of Cortés's famous treasure fleets, Ávila had been seized off the Azores by the French. He endured three years as a prisoner in France and then spent 'all which I had in my patrimony' as a ransom.[13] Famous but penniless, it is understandable that Ávila should seize the chance of recovering his fortune under Montejo.[14]

Montejo secured four good ships, on which he loaded cannon, some small arms and horses as well as meat, flour, biscuits, wine, oil: enough food for a year. The other expeditionaries with Montejo included men from most parts of Spain. If there was as usual a majority of Sevillanos (Pedro de los Ríos as lieutenant governor, Pedro de Añasco as a captain), there were also Pedro de Lugones of Ciudad Rodrigo, Pedro González of Madrigal de las Altas Torres, Hernando Palomar, the chief magistrate, who came from Andújar, and, from Montejo's own Salamanca, Pedro Gaitán. There was one Basque at least, Andrés de Calleja, and one Fleming, Roberto Alemán, who exceptionally was permitted to take his wife, Talina. The chief pilot, Antón Sánchez Calabares, was said to have been a veteran of New Spain but it is hard to identify his past services. There was a surgeon, Íñigo López, and two pharmacists, Pedro Díaz de Ocaña and Pedro de Arenas, from Toledo. Juan Láinez was to appraise the gold and silver which they expected to find. There were several merchants, such as the Catalan Juan Ote Durán, who was to present some of the famous Holland cloth to the Maya chiefs. The churchmen were Juan Rodríguez de Caraveo, Montejo's personal chaplain; Pedro Fernández, who was priest to the expedition; and a Carmelite, Gregorio de San Martín. The character of the Christian impulse in Yucatan can be gathered from a later declaration of Fray Rodríguez de Caraveo: 'In six years I baptized many heathen Indians ... I made them give up witchcraft and the diversity of gods whom they worshipped and have given them to understand that there is only one omnipotent God and how there is the Pope our Holy Father on earth.'[15]

Montejo was drawn to Yucatan less, it would seem, by the precious metals and jewels which he expected to find (though there were admirable jade objects there)[16] than by the realization that Yucatan could be turned into a good agricultural–pastoral province, and commerce and industry could be developed. The Maya even in the sixteenth century were skilful makers of good textiles. They had time and wealth enough for the production of ornaments, as shown by their special preoccupation with headdresses.

Montejo was a man of vision and wisdom as well as of ambition. His attitudes towards the Indians were comparatively humane. He must have known before he sought, and obtained, his contract that Yucatan was, as Bishop Landa would put it later, 'a very flat land with no mountains for which reason it cannot be seen from ships till they are close inshore'.[17]

On his way to Yucatan, Montejo, as was customary, stopped at Santo Domingo to obtain more horses and soldiers, but he did not then seek an interpreter, though he should have known of the special value of such people from his experience with Jerónimo de Aguilar and 'Doña Marina' – who for a time had been the mistress of his companion in Spain in 1520, Alonso Hernández Portocarrero. But he did add to his expedition in Hispaniola Gonzalo Nieto, whom he made chief lieutenant (*alférez mayor*). Nieto had been at the *comuneros'* battle against the Crown at Villalar in 1520, he had served against France, and he had been in New Spain with Luis Ponce and in Florida with Ayllón.

The fleet continued along the southern coast of Montejo's old home, Cuba, and made for Cozumel, just as Grijalva and Cortés had done. Montejo paid attention to the *cacique* there, Naum Pat, who over the previous ten years had become quite used to Spaniards.

Montejo and his little army then crossed to the mainland. Gonzalo Nieto raised a standard and shouted the word 'Spain' three times, adding 'In the name of God, I take possession of this land for God and the king of Castile'[18] – approximately at the site of the delightful Playa del Carmen. There Montejo established a settlement which, after his own birth place, he named 'Salamanca' – 'Salamanca de Xelhá', the last part of the name commemorating the previous Maya settlement there. The historian Oviedo commented drily that this was in a palm grove 'near a swamp in the worst place of all the province. In that bad place the ships were unloaded and a large house swiftly constructed to act as a residence for Governor Montejo.'[19] Several Spaniards then set about learning Maya, among them Montejo himself and Fray Rodríguez de Carvajal, who recognized that his work of conversion would be far easier if he knew the language of his proposed flock. Pedro de Añasco of Seville turned out to be the best short-term interpreter.

In a matter of weeks, difficulties arose. Despite the fact that Montejo had been assured that he had enough food for a year, supplies were soon used up and Indian substitutes seemed inadequate, despite the assistance of the local *cacique* of Zama. It seems that Montejo's men disliked tortillas, and anything made from maize. The conquerors even began to be short of clothes. Montejo sent a ship up to Veracruz to buy more but the master died there and his ship sailed off to Cuba instead of back to Yucatan.[20] Montejo began to seize food from the Indians, an act which, of course, damaged relations. In an effort to avoid any attempt at desertion, Montejo did what Cortés had done; he destroyed his boats after the Catalan Juan Ote Durán plotted to leave with the seamen on the *San Jerónimo*.

Early in 1528 Montejo set out on a journey to find a better port than Salamanca de Xelhá. Though he was different from most of his contemporaries because of his preoccupation with agriculture, his technique was much the same as theirs. He would march towards an Indian *pueblo*, out of which the natives would emerge in a friendly fashion carrying presents of maize, turkey and beans. The Spaniards would be astonished at the large number of idols which they observed everywhere, on the streets and temple steps, as well as in the shrines and temples themselves. Most were made of clay. Fray Diego de Landa, later the first bishop of Yucatan, would comment: 'There is not an animal or insect of which they did not make a statue.'[21] Montejo would then receive the Indians as vassals. Indians who did not receive the Spaniards in peace would surround them close to their *pueblos* on the road and would quickly build half-moon palisades and prepare an ambush. Naum Pat of Cozumel was helpful to Montejo, however, and offered to test out the ground ahead of the Spaniards on several occasions. This enabled the latter to ensure his safe arrival at Mochí, a place of one hundred 'good houses', with temples and shrines of stone. There they received chickens, tortillas and *fisol*, a drink of fermented maize and honey. This town, like many others in Yucatan, had four ceremonial entrances at the cardinal points. But inside it was not laid out in regular streets. In the centre of the town there was a raised temple in a plaza, surrounded by the houses of the rich – not unlike cities of Spain.

Montejo continued on to Belma, perhaps the 'Ecab' or the 'Gran Cairo' which he and Ávila would have recalled from their previous visit ten years before with Cortés. The *caciques* there were friendly, they summoned their neighbours and looked at the horses. Montejo obliged with an impressive horse show at which the natives were more afraid than impressed.[22] Here the Spaniards were given jewel-encrusted necklaces of gold, which cheered them greatly. Montejo did not, however, accept what was offered him since he did not wish to give the impression that he had just come for gifts.[23]

In his travels Montejo was still looking for a place to establish a settlement which could act as his capital. After Salamanca de Xelhá, he was impressed by Conil, a large commercial town in north-east Yucatan, with ample supplies of fresh water from springs close to the sea, with a good port and a generally friendly population – and perhaps as many as 500 houses.[24] Here a man of great strength in the suite of the Indian lord of Chicaca seized a cutlass from a black boy belonging to Montejo and tried to kill the commander, who defended himself with his own sword till his men came 'and the disturbance was quietened'.[25]

They moved west via Cachí, with its large square, and entered sweet-smelling Sinsimato, in the land of the warlike Chikin-cheel, pervaded with a scent of the resin copal. Then they reached Chuaca, the main city of the *cacique* of the Chikincheel, with its many ponds and artificial watercourses, with some buildings of carved stone and thatched roofs. The temples and other shrines were characterized by their fine workmanship. This territory had been ancient Maya land in the past, so it is understandable that the level of craftsmanship should have been high.

The *cacique* received Montejo in friendly fashion and the latter therefore abandoned his customary caution. But next morning he and his army found the town abandoned and they themselves surrounded by 'bowmen who aimed well (*buenos punteros*)', as Oviedo put it.[26] Battle was engaged at first light. The Indians painted their faces to make themselves look frightening and had the weapons Montejo was used to in New Spain – wooden bows and arrows with slender shafts and very hard stone heads. They also had the same *macanas* (swords) as the Mexica, with sharp stones set in wooden frames.

Montejo showed much personal courage as he and his men with their superior weapons and their horses ensured they checked and then pressed back the Maya. Then they moved on to Ake, a rival town to Chuaca, but nevertheless ready for war as the lords there had told their subjects that the Spaniards were coming to steal their wives.[27] When Montejo arrived, the people of Ake first abandoned their city and then prepared an assault on it.

The Spaniards entered Ake and prepared to defend themselves there. They were attacked the following day by what seems to have been a large force but they fought well, killed many Maya and suffered no losses themselves. At dusk, Montejo received the submission of the lords of Ake without any retribution. He and his men then continued their journey to Loché, where they encountered a *cacique* who kept a curtain of thin cloth between himself and the Spaniards when he talked to them.

Montejo moved on along the coast towards Campeche. On the way, he divided his men into two sections, one group being asked to cut across the peninsula back to Chetumal, making their way through cacao and copal groves, till they reached the salt pans near the eastern coast.

To the explorers' surprise, they encountered no golden city in the interior of Yucatan. There was neither gold, nor silver, nor emeralds; nor indeed did there seem to be markets. There were in the northern towns fine cloths which were sold in Campeche itself, said to boast 2,000 homes, or in Champoton, to its south, where the first Spanish expedition in 1517 had been defeated and its commander, Hernández de Córdoba, fatally injured. Cortés's legendary interpretress Marina had originally come from Champoton. Montejo found that all these settlements had a deep *cenote* (natural well) which descended to the water table below. There was no other water supply, no rivers and many of the disputes and wars between these Maya villages, even wars between provinces, were about water or access to remote *cenotes*. Most *cenotes* were close to the houses of lords.[28] Maize was, as in New Spain and Guatemala, the principal food and indeed provided the main alcoholic drink. The Indians ate turkey, duck and even little dogs. The temples in the places were usually of stone but the houses, including those of the lords, were always of wattle and adobe. Many such settlements were remote: 'only birds could visit them freely', recalled Fray Lorenzo de Bienvenida, one of the first eight Franciscans who later came to Yucatan.[29]

Inga Clendinnen has described the geographical background:

> Scattered through the forest were the villages or towns, each sustained by cleared patches ... where the Indians grew their maize and other basic crops. But without local knowledge of the vague tracery of paths webbing the forest it was easy to pass them by ... There were no vantage points in that flat land from which distances gained could be measured [or] future objectives identified. What small elevations there were revealed only the grey forest stretching to the rim of the horizon.[30]

In these months Montejo learned something of the structure of Maya society. It naturally had much in common with Alvarado's Guatemala. He may, however, not have appreciated the extent to which, torn apart by wars, it had declined absolutely in quality. For example, the rich or upper class could still read and write, but neither letters nor important contracts were written down. Much Maya science and learning had been forgotten.[31]

Among the lords there was something similar to primogeniture. Montejo gathered that sometimes *caciques* were subservient to a principal lord. Later, when Montejo's son demanded that the lord of Chichen Itza accept the Emperor Charles as his overlord, that ruler said that they already had lords enough.[32] Montejo found that the entire peninsula of Yucatan spoke the same Maya language but that there were many variations of dialect and vocabulary (Chontal, Yucatec Maya, Chol and Chorti competed). Bishop Landa much later (in the 1560s) discovered that the lords of Yucatan, like the Spaniards, were interested in the ancestry of their families. Those who shared a patronymic regarded themselves as members of the same family and so avoided intermarriage, as if they were Christians limited by the rules of consanguinity. Bishop Landa, a curiously ambivalent witness because his deep interest was balanced by his fanatical intolerance of 'heresy', would comment:

> before the Spaniards ... the natives had lived together in towns in a politic fashion and they had kept the land very clean and free from weeds and [in the towns] had planted good trees. In the middle of the towns, there were temples with beautiful squares and, around the temples, were the houses of lords and priests.[33]

In most of these towns there were professionals: potters, carpenters, sorcerer-surgeons, bead manufacturers and, above all, merchants, who exchanged, in Tabasco or on the river Ulua near Veracruz, salt, cloaks and slaves for cacao and stone beads. Slaves were an important commodity and a stimulus here, as in the old world too, to wars. The Maya counted their beads and other things in their usual eccentric style – by fives up to twenty, by twenties up to 100, by hundreds up to 4,000 and by 400 up to 8,000 – and usually did their counting on the floor.[34]

Harvesting was a common activity but hunting was done in packs of about fifty men. They sowed, Landa commented, in many places so that, if one sowing failed, another harvest could replace it. Such social activities had communal consequences, making for economic collaboration in all spheres, and everyone was expected to master the basic skills necessary for collective life. Most Maya lived in multigenerational groups of father and sons, married and unmarried, and it was a group of related males who usually went to work in the *milpa*, their system of crop rotation. Children's names echoed those of their parents: thus the son of Chel and Chan would be called Na Chan Chel. The Spaniards had a comparable tradition.

The invaders found that the Maya admired a special type of facial beauty where the hair was brushed back to extend the curve of the nose in a single straight line. To enhance this elongated line, newborn babies often had their heads bound between two boards while they were still soft. The Maya also considered that to be cross-eyed was beautiful and this deviation was encouraged by mothers who hung from the foreheads of their children a little black patch contrived to reach down between their eyebrows. Whenever the child raised his eyes, this patch moved in front of them, the process assisting the cross-eyed deformity to develop. Another family habit was to burn the faces of children with hot cloths to prevent the growth of beards and other bodily hair. At that time most men used mirrors made of obsidian, though women did not. Clothing for both sexes was a strip of cloth the width of a hand, wound round the waist several times.

Houses in Yucatan had roofs of straw or palm leaves, the former sloped steeply to carry off the rainwater. The Indians built walls in the middle of their simple houses to divide them into two, and usually slept in the back part. In front, the roof would be low, for protection against both heat and rain – and also against human enemies.

The Maya appear to have considered the Spaniards uncouth warriors with their codpieces and their breastplates in quilted cotton in imitation of Mexican armour. They seemed a new version of the Itzá, a group of soldiers who, led by Kukulcan, the feathered serpent (Quetzalcoatl among the Mexica), came down from central Mexico in the tenth century to establish themselves at the well of Chichen.

The Maya, like the Mexica, were addicts of sacrifice, but on a smaller scale. Thus they made sacrifices of their own blood, sometimes cutting pieces from the outer part of their ears. They also sometimes made a hole in the penis and passed thread through it. Women might draw the hearts out of animals and offer them whole to their gods. Sometimes the Maya might sacrifice individuals by shooting them with arrows, 'turning the place in his chest above his heart into a hedgehog of arrows'. Sometimes they might give the chest of a captive a blow with a stone knife, make a deep incision, and, as happened in Mexico/Tenochtitlan, plunge in a hand to draw out the heart and give it to the priest, who would anoint the face of an idol with the fresh blood. Then they would throw the body down the steps of the temple. Officials (or were they priests?) would pick up the corpse and flay it except for the hands and feet. Then the priest might strip naked and cover himself with that skin, while others danced before him. Montejo and Antonio de Ávila had had experience of this kind of behaviour over ten years since 1518, but newcomers from Castile were shocked. It was the ruthless ghoulishness of these scenes which caused the Spaniards to harden their hearts and assure themselves that they were right to insist on bringing Christianity to the New World. All the same, the number of human sacrifices – again, as in Guatemala – was apparently decreasing.

From Champoton and Campeche, Montejo and his sixty remaining men, his vanguard, cut across about 150 miles of the peninsula to rejoin his first settlement and those whom he had left behind at Salamanca de Xelhá. Did he pass by such ancient sites as Uxmal, Chichen Itza, Coba and Tulum? It is not clear. He would now have seen that the peninsula was a vast plain with thin soil, most of which was covered by dry scrub forest, with no large rivers but many wells. The land was sparsely populated but the Indians may have numbered 300,000 in 1520.[35]

After some weeks of reconsideration and stocktaking, Montejo decided to set off for the south of his peninsula, making for the Bay of Ascension which had been so named by his old captain Grijalva in 1518 (it had been Ascension Day). They made for the town of Chetumal in a combined land-and-sea operation: Montejo went by boat, Antonio de Ávila by land. Alonso de Luján remained behind at new Salamanca to build a ship so he could follow. The plan was for all three sections of Montejo's expedition to meet at or near Chetumal, one of the richest Mayan towns on the west of the bay, characterized by the cultivation of bees, in large apiaries. Much maize and cacao also was grown there. It was at Chetumal that Montejo came across an unexpected stranger: Gonzalo Guerrero.

Guerrero, a Spaniard from the small town of Niebla, on the river Tinto about twenty miles upriver from Palos, had accompanied Diego Colón to the Indies in 1509. He seems to have been literate. Bored with life in Santo Domingo, he set off with Diego de Nicuesa for the South American mainland, but was shipwrecked. Saved from being fattened and eaten, he and Jerónimo de Aguilar, who later became Cortés's interpreter, settled down in Yucatan. Guerrero found a Maya girl by whom he had several children. He was a slave but nevertheless became a military adviser to Na Chan Can, the *cacique* in Chetumal. Fray Diego de Landa believed he taught the Indians 'how to fight, showing them how to build fortresses and bastions'.[36] He was said to have advised the Maya to attack Hernández de Córdoba in 1517. In 1519 he had refused to return to Spanish life, as Jerónimo de Aguilar did, saying to him:

> Brother Aguilar, I am married and have three children, the Indians treat me as a chief and as a captain in war. You go [back] and God be with you but I already have my face tattooed and my ears pierced. What would the Spaniards say if they saw me in this guise? And look how handsome those boys of mine are! For God's sake give me those green beads which you brought and I will give them to my sons and I shall tell them that my brothers have given them to me.

Guerrero's Maya 'wife' said to Aguilar, 'be off with you and don't give us any more trouble'.[37]

Eight years later, in 1527, Guerrero received a letter from Montejo. It read:

> Gonzalo, my special friend and brother! I count it as your great good fortune that I have arrived and I have learned of you through the bearer of this letter. I remind you that you are a Christian created by the blood of Christ

our Redeemer to whom you should give infinite thanks. You have a great opportunity to serve God and the emperor in the pacification and baptism of these people and, more than that, to leave your sins behind you with the grace of God and so benefit and honour yourself. I shall be your good friend in this and you will be treated very well. Thus I beseech you not to let the devil influence you to decline what I ask, so that he will not possess himself of you forever. On behalf of His Majesty, I promise to do very well by you and fully to comply with what I have said. On my part and as a gentleman [*como hombre hidalgo*], I give you my word and pledge my faith to make my promises to you without any reservation whatever ... and I shall make you one of my principal men, and one of the most dearly loved and select of these parts. Consequently, I beg you to come to this ship or the coast without delay to do what I have suggested and help me carry out this work of conversion by giving me your advice and opinions which seem the wisest.[38]

Guerrero, however, could not be persuaded to rejoin his compatriots. He wrote on the back of this letter: 'Señor, I kiss your lordship's hand. As I am a slave, I have no freedom. I have a wife and children, even though I remember God. You, my lord, and the Spaniards will find in me a very good friend.'

But in truth Guerrero remained an enemy. Thus he seems to have ensured that news passed to Antonio de Ávila coming down the coast with reinforcements included the story that Montejo had died; and news reached Montejo that Ávila was dead.

Montejo sailed down to Honduras where he briefly put in on the river Ulua, eminently navigable in that territory. Perhaps he went there out of curiosity. He then sailed north again to Salamanca de Xelhá to find it deserted, so he assumed that Luján, Ávila and their men were lost. But further north still, at Cozumel, he received the news that they were alive. Montejo crossed to the mainland for a meeting with those old comrades.

In the summer of 1528 he went back even further than Cozumel: he returned to New Spain in his ship *La Gavarra* to seek reinforcements. He still had his valuable *encomiendas* near Mexico and he thought that he would be able to borrow a substantial sum of money on their security and so persuade about another seventy-five or a hundred new soldiers to accompany him, including his own half-*converso* son, Francisco Montejo, *el Mozo*, who had been brought up at court in Spain and had accompanied Cortés to Hiberas in 1524. He also bought another ship, which he loaded with supplies, but it sank in a storm in the harbour of Veracruz. Undaunted, he bought yet one more vessel, and made an arrangement with a rich ship-owner, Juan de Lerma, perhaps related to García de Lerma, the pearl king of Cubagua, who agreed to make his ships available for trade in Yucatan – perhaps in return for eventual trading privileges there, though no document proves it. Lerma later became treasurer of Yucatan and also *veedor* of Hiberas.

The supreme court, headed by the odious Nuño de Guzmán, arrived in New Spain while Montejo was in Mexico.[39] But Guzmán had no enmity for such a well-born conquistador. That determined Montejo to return to Yucatan from the west: proximity to New Spain would be a help. He went back via Tabasco and Acalán. Guzmán agreed to help him and made him chief magistrate of the former.[40]

Before returning, Montejo wrote (on 20 April 1529) to the Emperor Charles the first of many reports about Yucatan: 'All the towns have an orchard for fruit, but are a little rough for our horses. I found many signs of gold (*hallé mucha nueva de oro*).' The great difficulty was that 'there is no port and, for that reason, I wonder whether I could not be given the river Grijalva as part of my grant'. So he said that he would found a few towns in the west, perhaps one precisely on the Grijalva, another in the mountains and a third at Acalán. Then he would send ships to the islands (the West Indies) for more men, horses and livestock.[41]

In April 1529 Montejo set off for Tabasco with his son, *el Mozo*, as his second-in-command and Gonzalo Nieto as his general factotum and *alcalde mayor* of Tabasco. Montejo *padre* went by land with twenty-five men, among them Baltasar Gallegos, who had been sent back to New Spain by the settlers of Santa María de la Victoria on the Grijalva, a colony which had been founded in 1519 at the suggestion of Cortés but whose existence had been threatened by Indians and which took a long time to attract residents.[42] Montejo arrived at Santa María in time to prevent its complete disintegration. He sent for Antonio de Ávila's men in Salamanca de Xelhá, where they had been busy capturing Indians probably to enable Montejo's backer, Juan de Lerma, to sell them in the West Indies. These troops, if that is what they were, sailed back around the head of the peninsula to meet Montejo at Guayataca, west of Xicalango.

Montejo was at that stage hoping to make Xicalango, on the lagoon of Términos, his forward base for the conquest of Yucatan. The Indians seemed complacent. Leaving his son, *el Mozo*, there, Montejo turned back west and soon overcame the populous districts of Tabasco along the river Copulco. Then, with Ávila again as his second-in-command, he moved up the river Grijalva into the mountains with about a hundred men, his horses being carried upstream on rafts. He reached Teapa at the foot of the mountains of Chiapas. There were what Blas González, one of his captains, called 'excessive tribulations'.[43] But Montejo himself later described how, 'at a cost of much effort, both for myself and to all the soldiers', he conquered and pacified 'all the provinces of the Río Grijalva'. Some thirty Spaniards were killed, a high number for those days. But Montejo successfully carried through the institution of the *encomienda* there – a remarkable achievement in the circumstances.

Montejo had planned to return to Santa María de la Victoria and then go on to establish a settlement at Acalán, but he learned that another Spanish force under Juan Enríquez de Guzmán, one of Alvarado's captains in Guatemala, was coming up northwards from Chiapas, hoping to conquer the border areas. The two met and reached a rough agreement as to where Alvarado's domain of Guatemala should stop and that of Montejo begin. Enríquez de Guzmán suggested that Montejo should make his way to Acalán via Alvarado's new city, San Cristóbal de las Casas. Montejo agreed, but he was ill and sent Ávila on the journey in his place, while he returned to Santa María de la Victoria.

Ávila had a long and weary march through the mountains, first to San Cristóbal, then to Acalán. It was the rainy season and the suffering of the Spaniards in these jungles was considerable. On the river Usumacinta, Ávila loaded his horses on to canoes attached to one another, the forelegs in one canoe, the hind legs in another. They descended a cascade between cliffs of such a height that 'to those who were there, it would not have seemed worse to voyage in the shadows of Mount Athos'.[44] Later they came across the remains of a bridge built by Cortés on his way to Hiberas, but it was too much in decay for Ávila and his men to profit from it. They still had to use canoes provided for them by some friendly natives of Tenosique. They continued on towards Acalán, which had been an important trading port for the Indians in the days of Montezuma and before. Ávila sent a message to the ruler of the town saying that he hoped to be welcomed since he intended no injury. But the natives did not believe him because Cortés, when passing there a year or two before, had said the same but had carried off the *cacique* and 600 bearers who were never seen again.[45] So they fled.

Ávila described Acalán as a city of about 1,000 people with good buildings of stone and white stucco, with thatched roofs. It was on a river which the Spaniards had already christened the Candelaria and which flowed into the lagoon of Términos. After a day or two, the *cacique* returned with a train of about 400 people – so Ávila reported – and swore fealty to the emperor. He brought presents of birds and supplies. All the same, Ávila seized and chained him for he feared treachery, since his own force was so small. He must have been influenced by the precedent of Cortés in relation to Montezuma.[46]

Shortly the rest of the population of Acalán returned and began to serve the Spaniards with relative enthusiasm. Ávila now freed the *cacique* and his followers and, in the tradition of Montejo, began to allocate *encomiendas*. He gave Acalán the name of Salamanca de Acalán to recall Montejo's birthplace.

Despite its excellent communications, Acalán was, however, not to be the capital city of the new Yucatan which Montejo wanted to establish. There was no gold, the population was small, the supplies of food poor. Ávila became interested in another town, Maztalán, a little to the east, where the Spaniards remained for a few weeks, before they began to think of Champoton, the town whose people had defeated Hernández de Córdoba in 1517, as a capital.

Champoton, like Acalán, was a town of many stone houses with thatched roofs. It was on the sea, and from it many canoes set out daily to fish. Just offshore, there was an island filled with idols where the fishermen went to pray and to make offerings. The people were the Cuohes, of whom a large detachment went to greet Ávila on his arrival. Montejo had previously sent messengers there and the Spaniards found that a special district had already been prepared for them – a square, houses with stables and enough food to last a month. Every day the Spaniards could eat turkey, ample maize and good fish. The *cacique* said that he wanted to become a Christian. So his island was abandoned and his idols thrown into the sea.[47]

Montejo, meantime, was having difficulty confirming his control of the passage from New Spain to Yucatan. A previous chief magistrate of Santa María, Baltasar de Osorio, had succeeded in persuading the *audiencia* in Mexico to restore his own control of Acalán, going back on the decision to give it over to the Montejos. He even managed to seize part of Montejo's property in Tabasco and he persecuted Montejo's followers. Though Montejo succeeded in securing the reversal of some of these judicial decisions, he was obliged to delay his new plans for the conquest of Yucatan. When finally he felt able to set out again, he reached only as far as Xicalango. He and his followers were in poor morale, men deserting from his side, and he himself believing that Ávila was lost. Fortunately Montejo's mercantile backer, Lerma, came to the rescue by sending several ships full of men, supplies, horses and clothing bought in Cuba.[48]

Learning that Ávila was still alive in Champoton, Montejo repaired there himself in the early days of 1531. On his way he completed his organization of the port of Xicalango. Ávila and Montejo agreed to establish their real base not at Champoton, with its bad memories of defeat in 1518, but at Campeche, some forty miles north. The people there could support a Spanish settlement and there were well-populated places nearby capable of being the centre of *encomiendas*. Campeche might also turn out to be a most useful port. So Montejo went ahead, and optimistically read the Requirement to a number of local lords. He explained that all Christians worshipped God in heaven, asked the lords to permit his clergy to preach the Gospel and told them to recognize him as the representative of the Emperor Charles. A number of local lords accepted, or pretended to accept, these requests. Then Montejo proclaimed the foundation of a new Spanish city, which predictably he called Salamanca de Campeche.

Here he set about making plans for the conquest of the rest of the peninsula, which was still largely unknown to the Spanish explorers. He sent Ávila back across the centre of the country to Chetumal with fifty men who included Alonso Luján and Francisco Velázquez, a mining specialist. Montejo's nephew, a third Francisco Montejo, son of one of his brothers, was with this party. They went from Campeche to Maní where the Xui Maya made themselves friendly, continuing to Cochuah, Chablé and then Bacalar, where the treacherous Guerrero had influence. Ávila requested the lords in Chablé to go to Chetumal to explain that he wanted peace, but the messengers returned with the reply that 'the people there were not interested in peace but desired war, and would give us chicken in the form of lances, and maize in the form of arrows'.[49]

All the same, arrived at Lake Bacalar, Ávila and his men obtained canoes to go across to Chetumal. The town was deserted. Ávila determined to establish a new settlement, which he named Villa Real. He was planning this when the news came that the Maya, assisted if not led by Guerrero, were about to attack. Ávila struck first and destroyed an Indian encampment. He took sixty prisoners and suffered no losses although the *cacique* and Guerrero, if he had indeed been there, escaped. The Spaniards did find gold and turquoise masks at this place and Ávila sent those prizes back to Montejo with six Spaniards. They were, however, all killed en route at Hoya.

Ávila returned to Bacalar. He became aware that a general rebellion was being mounted by the lords of a place named Macanahaul. Chablé also came out in revolt, but Ávila cleverly surprised his enemies by attacking the town from the rear. Afterwards he returned to Villa Real at Chetumal but everywhere there were rumours of rebellion. It became evident that any idea of alliance with the Indians of Chablé would fail since the project was 'false and with evil intent'.[50]

Ávila met another conflict at Cochuah where the town was destroyed by a hurricane. After its capture, he found the wells filled in with earth and stones. One well twelve feet deep was dug out and two Indian boys were let down into it by straps made from horses' harnesses to bring up water. Ávila decided to return to his Villa Real – a difficult journey through swamp and maquis, and also susceptible to frequent attacks by Maya. Oviedo reported that one of the Spanish sentinels saw a vision of Santiago, accompanied by six or seven knights with a divine scent: '*Santiago glorioso, nuestro patrón de España, es este socorro que Dios, por su misericordia, con su Apóstol nos envía.*'[51]

A sighting of Santiago was, of course, a good sign – even if it was one traditionally balanced by the appearance of the Moorish knight Alfatami on a green horse. All the same, by the time the news reached Villa Real, Ávila's force was reduced to forty men, of whom ten were maimed in the arm or in the leg; they were able to call on only four horses.[52]

Alonso de Ávila sent a message to Montejo to tell him that, though in poor condition, he and his men had survived. The messenger, a captured *cacique*, was to return in a month to report whether all was or was not well with the *adelantado*. Yet after that month there was no news. It transpired that neither the *cacique* nor his son had taken the message. Instead, he and his friends plotted an attack to destroy Ávila once and for all. What should the Spaniards do? They had no food, and they had seen no brigantine on the coast which might help. They assumed that Montejo believed them dead.[53] Could they evacuate Villa Real? If so, how?

In the end, Ávila decided to go to Honduras by canoe. They encountered a furious sea: 'such a manner of coast as had never been seen before', commented Oviedo, exaggeratedly.[54] They met several merchantmen in large boats but, though they sometimes seized them, they could not rely on such piracy as a source of food. After seven months of escapes and privations, Ávila reached Puerto de Caballos on the Bay of Honduras. That seemed a good place for a settlement since it was fertile and well peopled. The Spaniards were also impressed by the river Ulua, which boasted groves of cacao on both its banks. Here, though, a storm destroyed their canoes. So they went on to the town of Trujillo by land where they were well received by Andrés de Cerezeda, the acting governor of Hiberas, and his treasurer, Juan Ruano. Ruano had been an enemy of Cortés, who looked on him as responsible for Olid's treachery.[55] After some painstaking negotiations, they set sail on a merchant ship which had come from Cuba and set off for home or, rather, for Campeche.[56]

Montejo had passed the long months of waiting to hear of Ávila's accomplishments in almost continual fighting. First, with forty-five soldiers, including nine horsemen, he was attacked by a large force led by Nachi Cocom, whose main objective was to capture Montejo himself. A great number of Indians penetrated his camp, some seized his horse and its reins, some caught him by the arms. He would probably have been captured had it not been for Blas González, who 'set upon them and killed many'.[57] Thus, as another Spanish combatant, Pedro Álvarez, would put it 'the victory of our Holy Faith was gained'.[58]

In the middle of the year 1532 Montejo embarked on a new campaign in the east and north-east of Yucatan. His persistence seemed as remarkable as his patience. He appointed his son to lead it. *El Mozo* brought a galleon to carry his men from Tabasco, the invaluable Lerma organized supplies, and he set off with 200 men, leaving a number to guard Campeche with his father in command. *El Mozo*'s aim was to establish Spanish control wherever possible without fighting; he was to make allies whenever he could. In this respect, he landed in the *cacicazgo* of Ceh Pech whose support he received and who urged him to go on to Chichen Itza, an ancient temple which was hallowed ground to the Maya. The remains of the place could be made into excellent fortresses. Ávila named it Ciudad Real after the city of Castile where he had been born. But that did not prevent the *caciques* from giving a haughty negative answer to the reading of the Requirement: 'We already have kings oh noble lords! Foreign warriors, we are the Itza!'[59]

These Indians were from the proud tribe of Cupul, headed by Nacon Cupul, who was determined to expel, if not destroy, the Spaniards. At a parley with *el Mozo*, Nacon tried to kill him there and then and *el Mozo* saved himself with difficulty. Nacon was himself soon killed, but the Cupul then refused absolutely to deliver any supplies to *el Mozo*, so the Spaniards seized them. This worsened relations further and the Cupul, though leaderless, mounted a new attack, killing ten or twelve of *el Mozo*'s men, as well as ten horses and all the Indian slaves who were serving the Spaniards. *El Mozo*, with his large force of 150–170 men fended them off but a much bigger attack was to follow, after a siege. *El Mozo* retaliated but, though he killed many Indians, he could not break through their cordon. He determined to escape in darkness, as Cortés had done in Mexico/Tenochtitlan, and was more successful than Cortés, for the Spaniards managed to give the Indian besiegers the slip. They then turned successfully on the Maya vanguard who pursued them, and completed their escape thanks to an Indian ally, An Kin Chef.

Ávila managed to return to Campeche, travelling by sea in a Cuba-based merchant ship. He and the Montejos together sought to re-establish their Ciudad Real at Dzibilkan on the coast. They were there when the intoxicating news came of the discovery of Peru: 'Because of this news, and the slight reward which they had in ... this country [Yucatan], the citizens made off against my will.'[60] It was not surprising that the depleted army of Montejo could not maintain itself. Again they evacuated an advanced settlement and returned to Campeche.

Montejo now penned a gloomy despatch to the king:

There is [in Yucatan] not a single river, though there are lakes. The entire land is covered by thick bush and is so stony that there is not a single foot of soil. No gold has been discovered nor is there anything else from which advantage can be gained. The people are the most abandoned and treacherous in all the lands discovered until this time, being people who never yet killed a Christian except by foul means ... in them I have failed to find the truth touching anything. With the news from Peru, the soldiers will not remain here any longer.[61]

It seemed in 1534 that seven years of continuous conflict in Yucatan were thus ending in failure. The Spaniards had a base in Campeche, little more. Their efforts to establish Spanish power on the eastern seaboard of the peninsula had failed. Montejo *padre* by now had only thirty men at his disposal, which was not enough of a force to conquer such a large country full of high-spirited and alert natives. He had made the mistake of dividing his men too often and did not seem to realize that Indians often gave their verbal loyalty to Spain only as a temporary expedient. In Yucatan there were many governments, not just one, as there had been in New Spain, whose tactics Montejo remembered. The defeat of one *cacique* left his neighbours untouched; and the Maya weapons had turned out to be superior to those of the Mexica. They had strong bows, more straight than curved, flint-tipped arrows, lances and darts, and swords of hard wood with razor-sharp flakes of obsidian which could inflict serious wounds. The arrows, made from reeds growing in lagoons, were often five palms long. The bow strings were made successfully from the local hemp. They also had little copper hatchets which could be used both as weapons and for working wood.[62] As for defence, they had shields made of carefully woven reeds lined with deerskin. They also had jackets of quilted cotton; a few lords even had wooden helmets. Priests and sometimes others went to war in animal skins.[63] Finally, the Indians' tactics had been intelligent. Realizing early on that their vast superiority in numbers could not make much of an impact on the Spaniards, they defended their towns in these 'harsh, stony and dry lands' as the Mérida Council described the region in 1561, and then destroyed them, fleeing into the forests or the unconquered south.

17

To pass the sandbar

*Now that we have passed your sandbar, be pleased to have us
return and pass over it again with a good and safe voyage.*

Prayer to Our Lady of Barrameda

The connection provided between Charles's empire in Europe and the
'new world of gold' (the phrase of the courtly Bishop Ruiz de la Mota)
in the Indies was of course shipping. The trade to the Indies was tacked
on to the already thriving maritime commerce between Seville, Sanlúcar
de Barrameda, the Canary Islands and Portugal. The large correspondence between officials, emigrants, merchants and captains who
maintained the empire was all seaborne. The most complex machine of
its time, as a modern historian described the sixteenth-century *nao*,[1]
was a fortified warehouse which had to be loaded and unloaded as well
as steered across the ocean. It was also, as Dr Johnson put it 200 and
more years later, very like a gaol with all, even grandees, living in conditions which on land would be usually considered intolerable.[2]

In the reign of the Emperor Charles, between 1516 and 1555, some
2,500 ships left Spain for the Indies, an average of about 60 a year;
1,750 returned. That meant that 750 were lost, or (a few of them)
destroyed in battle. The ships which crossed the Atlantic in 1504 numbered 35, in 1550, over 200.[3]

The small size of these vessels is what holds the attention first
and foremost. The Genoese and Venetians might have carracks of
over 1,000 tons; some of them were always in Portuguese or Spanish
waters in those days. The great 'Admiral of the Ocean Sea' thought
a boat as big as 70 tons too large for coastal exploration. Nor could
anything over 200 tons have sailed easily up, or down, the often

shallow and risky fifty miles of the river Guadalquivir which led to and from the port of Seville (8 per cent of losses of these fleets were on the river!).

At first, ships might take on their cargoes in ports other than Seville but, even so, they were required, before they crossed the Atlantic, to go up the Guadalquivir and register with the officials of the always bureaucratic Casa de la Contratación (the essential institution of Spanish commerce with the Indies). Even in the first half of the sixteenth century larger vessels were unable to ascend the Guadalquivir without unloading their cargo eight leagues (twenty-four miles) below or south of the city. This procedure was supervised by an official known as the 'visitor', who in the first instance was a certain Pedro de Aguila. After a while this individual was appointed directly by officers of the Casa, and that body decided that it should have a permanent resident at Cadiz since that port was becoming the effective nerve, the jugular vein of the trade to the Indies.

Captains might choose eccentric ports from which to sail but the rule was that they had to return to the Guadalquivir. The government relied on the payment of customs and other taxes, and it also required that gold and silver be paid to them in a regular fashion. Even so ships sometimes returned to other ports such as Málaga or Vigo, or even Lisbon. On their way out to the Indies almost all stopped in the Canaries, a most convenient watering and victualling station for ships on their way west or east, with tolerant attitudes by the Spanish authorities towards English and other foreign merchants.

The average tonnage of ships in these years was just under 100 tons. Columbus's vessels had been 60, 70 and 100 tons. Ovando's fleet in 1502 had all been between 30 and 90 tons; Díaz de Solís's three ships in 1508 were 90, 60 and 35 tons respectively; Pedrarias's in 1514 averaged 80 tons. Magellan's expedition of 1519 left with the largest ship being 120 tons and the *Victoria*, the survivor, was 75 tons.[4] Between 1521 and 1550 average tonnage would rise to between 100 and 150. Afterwards, ships increased in weight, but rarely in the sixteenth century did a ship exceed 200 tons – even though in 1509 there was an *ordenanza* which established a minimum of 80 tons.[5]

Such vessels might carry sixty passengers and twelve crew, and also perhaps eighteen mares and twelve calves. If they were adapted for military use, there would be four great cannons, two at each end of the ship, but perhaps a dozen smaller cannons (falconets, *versos*, culverins) would be on each side on a second deck.

A ship of 100 tons would probably be 54 feet long, 15 feet wide, and 7½ feet deep in the hold from keel to the lowest planked deck. Most ships had a single deck, though sometimes there were awnings (*toldos*) or bridges (hence a 'bridge') connecting with what was known as 'the chimney', sometimes as 'the castle'. They could be much larger. For example, the great merchants Portinari in Holland constructed a boat 130 feet long and 36 wide.[6]

To begin with, most of these ocean-going ships were known as caravels, *carabelas*, a word used in Spanish coastal waters since the early fifteenth century. The word *nao* was often used interchangeably. Caravels were rarely mentioned after 1530. The Portuguese usually gave them triangular or lateen sails; the Spaniards preferred square or round sails on the main masts.

The galleon was much bigger than the caravel and eventually became the typical Atlantic ship. It was first mentioned in a list of ships registered in 1525. A galleon might be up to 500 tons, and would have a crew of fifty or sixty, and perhaps a company of 120 or 150 soldiers.

There were many other smaller ships. For example, the *burcho*, a large launch, powered by rowers, was much used in the fifteenth century off Africa. A slightly smaller vessel, also a launch, was the *falúa*, with two masts. There was too the brigantine, a small boat suitable for travelling on rivers or with sail. Sometimes it was covered, sometimes it was open, as convenient. Most expeditions of importance had one or two of these accompanying the larger craft. We also find *filibotes, pataches, fragatas* and *urcas*, small useful little ships comparable to the English pinnaces.

All these vessels would dock in Seville in the strangely rough port known as the Arenal, a sand bank between the river and the cathedral which was the centre of trade and provisioning. The Arenal was dominated by the Golden Tower, the Torre de Oro, an Arab defence bastion on which there was, in the sixteenth century, a crane which had been constructed to facilitate the unloading of stone for the building of the nearby cathedral and which was afterwards used for landing merchandise. But because of the primitive nature of the port, the rest of the lower river, almost as far as Sanlúcar, fifty miles down at the mouth of the river, constituted an informal shipyard.

These ships cost, perhaps, 500 ducats if between 60 and 70 tons or about 3,000 maravedís (8 ducats) a ton.[7] On top of the cost of the vessel, the crew of, say, ten sailors and eight cabin boys, as well as apprentices and pages, were probably paid an average of 1,000 maravedís each. The total cost of a ship of this kind about to depart on an expedition, therefore, might be 180,000 maravedís.

The social standing of a man who set off for the sea was low at whatever level he joined his ship. All the same, an experienced mariner who had been a page or an apprentice could look forward to a professional life as a sailor, his credentials being confirmed by a document attesting to his expertise.

Shippers or captains gained something, too, from passengers, who played a decisive part in financing most outward voyages. The average number of passengers per caravel in the first half of the sixteenth century was perhaps twenty. For example, in November 1514 the passengers on board a ship owned by Andrés Niño paid 8 ducats (3,000 maravedís) to go to Santo Domingo;[8] while Cortés paid 11 ducats for the same journey in 1506.

No ship carried much in the way of furniture. The captain's cabin would have a few chairs, but there would be no others. The chests of the sailors did, however, serve as seats as well as trunks, and even sometimes as beds. They were customarily fastened down on the deck by ropes.

These vessels usually had short lives, perhaps only four years. The problem was the *broma*, a small sea-worm which seemed especially aggressive in hot waters. To guard against it, there could be caulking, which meant covering the vessel with resin, and then later a leaden top coat. Interestingly, the masters on Pedrarias's fleet of 1514 were the pioneers of the technique, invented by a certain Antonio Hernández. But lead was expensive, it often wore out, and it was heavy.[9]

Pilots had to have a licence from the *piloto mayor* (in the Emperor Charles's day Juan Díaz de Solís, Sebastián Cabot, Alonso de Chaves, Rodrigo Zamorano and Antonio García de Céspedes), which meant an apprenticeship under that official's direction. A pilot had to be Spanish by birth or by naturalization, had to have had six months in the profession and six months on a course of cosmography, as well as have a precise knowledge of the route. Every ship had to have two pilots. All would probably have read Fernández de Enciso's geography and, later, Pedro de Medina's *Arte de Navegar*; and later still other works by Martín Cortés (no relation to Hernando) and Escalante de Mendoza.

The average journey from Cadiz to Vera Cruz was 90 days, a minimum of 55, with a maximum of 160. The return journey was longer, averaging 128 days, a minimum of 70 and a maximum of 298.[10]

Most of the ships' expeditions were collaborative financial enterprises, the shipowners having to provide incentives for men to enrol. Thus large parts of the ship were reserved for *quintaladas*, the space in quintals in which the officers and crew could ship goods to the New World. The captain could perhaps ship ninety quintals, the boatswain thirteen, sailors a mere three and a half.

The great shipowners were financiers such as Cristóbal de Haro of Burgos, who already thought in the 1520s that it would be better to give sailors an income in cash rather than space for merchandise on the ships.[11] A typical mercantile family were the Almontes of Seville who were *conversos*, as many of the shipowning families seem to have been.[12]

Masters of ships were often part-owners of their vessels, and they would arrange to be paid two and a half times what was received by a sailor. A master could also ship a certain amount of merchandise free. He would travel in a good cabin where he would have a silver dinner service and probably be waited on by African slaves. He would hire the crew and be responsible for the safe delivery of the cargo.[13] An admiral or major commander, such as Hernando de Soto, would travel with an escort of say twelve 'gentlemen of honour'.

As a rule there would be a mate or boatswain (*contramaestre*) who, with his short thick cable, the *rebenque*, for beating lazy apprentices, would control the ship if the captain was a soldier without maritime experience. There would usually be a notary, a carpenter, a caulker, a cook-steward and as many seamen as necessary – the maximum being forty for a large galleon (but seventy on naval vessels).

The level of literacy was low on ships. Captains and generals would scarcely know more than how to sign their names. Most masters would have been able to do it, though perhaps 17 per cent could not do even that; nor could 25 per cent of pilots. A minority of officials such as boatswains and stewards could do so, but only 21 per cent of sailors.[14]

Wages and salaries were usually partly paid before a journey. Sometimes these advances, up to 20 per cent of the expected income, were handed out months before departure. Sailors might receive only 100 to

300 pesos for a year's voyage. Surprisingly little, it might be said, for a journey in an immensely complicated craft with its hundreds of pulleys, cables and rigging, often overcrowded and sailing in conditions of great danger. Sailors on royal naval vessels were paid less than others (1,500 maravedís or 4 ducats a month).

Men of the sea were usually paid less than skilled labourers on land. But many who went to Seville in the sixteenth century in the hope of finding work in the city had to fall back on going to sea instead. They might be compensated by the fact that sailors could rise in the ranks by becoming a ship's officer.

Many increased their wages by stealing from stores: carpenters would steal wood, boatswains rope, stewards provisions. Admirals would carry illegal passengers and contraband.

In his history, Pablo Pérez-Mallaína has several excellent paragraphs devoted to his idea that wages paid to the Renaissance sailor made him less well off than his medieval equivalent, who would customarily have had an interest in the enterprise of the ship.[15]

Most sailors slept on the deck in sacks or on mattresses filled with straw. Some would bring small pillows with them. The fact that a third of the crew would at any one time be likely to be on some kind of guard duty created space. Masters and captains often had good beds, however. It was a mark of their superior status. They would also have copper chamber-pots.

Passengers, too, would sleep on bags, which were often also sacks filled with straw. Hammocks, though used by Indians, were as rare as beds. Rich passengers might create little private rooms under the awnings, with panels nailed together by the ship's carpenter. Many hulls ended up as a labyrinth of small cabins.

A ship's latrines were usually set up on a wooden grating jutting out at the prow over the sea. Officers would have their own latrines, 'gardens', on the poop deck. The stench was normally overpowering. Dirty clothes remained dirty for most of the journey.

Storms were appalling experiences which might necessitate many sailors spending hours pumping water out of the ship to prevent it from sinking. If pumping did not work, every weight would be thrown into the sea. Sometimes masts would have to be cut down to prevent them breaking the ship. Waves of great size could strike a terrifying blow on the keel, opening up the hull to floods of water. Fire was also a cause of shipwrecks. Divers would have to be ready with tarred canvas 'palettes', or lead ones, to patch the outside of ships below the level of water.

Many sailors were citizens of Triana, a town across the river from Seville in the shadow of an Arab castle which the Inquisition had begun to use as a prison. In 1561 a census indicated that out of thirty-four pilots in Seville, thirty-one lived in Triana.[16]

Seville was still a growing city, by far the largest port of the south of Spain, rising in population from 40,000 in 1500 to double that by 1550. Many of the new citizens were from Old Castile or Extremadura. Other ports nearby were tiny in comparison: Puerto de Santa María, Moguer, Palos, Cadiz had about 4,000 citizens each, but until 1558 were not permitted to engage in transatlantic trade.

The international aspect of this Atlantic traffic should be remembered. A surprisingly large number of new citizens of Seville were foreigners. Italians, principally Genoese but also some Florentines, had dominated the commerce of Portugal from the fourteenth century, and much of it affected Spain. The first discoveries in the Canary Islands were, as emphasized in *Rivers of Gold*, carried through with Genoese capital. Many of the first sugar mills in the Caribbean and other investments had Genoese support or were initiated thus. The Genoese knew all about money, insurance and investments, loans and mortgages. Bankers and merchants from Genoa looked upon themselves as Spaniards: the Marini became the Marín, the Centurioni the Centurión.

In addition, many sailors on the ships were often not Spanish. Fifteen per cent of those who sailed with Pedrarias were born abroad. At least ninety out of the 265 on Magellan's voyage were foreigners, mostly from Portugal or Italy. Greeks, French, Flemings usually managed a representative or two on a big expedition. Portuguese sailors often pretended to be Spaniards – easy enough if they said that they were Gallegos since the languages of Galicia and Portugal are close. An Italian could pose as a Catalan. All the same, the Spanish control of this vast enterprise cannot be underestimated. Before the seventeenth century Spain and Portugal were the only colonial powers to speak of, and Portugal's imperial greatness was displayed mainly in the East.

During most of the reign of Charles V, ships bound for and coming from the Indies sailed independently. Would-be emigrants on a permanent basis would have to make a detailed application to the Casa de la Contratación as well as pay for their food en route and their fare.

The increasing danger at sea from France caused some to argue as early as the 1530s that commercial vessels should sail in fleets. The first French corsair was apparently a pirate of 1506.[17] In 1543 the Spanish fleet was accompanied by ships of war for protection.[18] In 1564, after further French intrusions, these anxieties would mature into a regular organization whereby two escorted merchant fleets a year would head for New Spain: in April for Cartagena de las Indias and in July for Nombre de Dios (after 1585 Portobelo). Both fleets would usually stop after about a week or a little more in the Canaries for supplies and water, or to allow sailors to recover from seasickness, then sail direct for the West Indies. The fleet for New Spain would usually travel via Puerto Rico to San Juan de Ulúa opposite Vera Cruz; the fleet for Cartagena would not as a rule make a stop in the Americas. San Juan de Ulúa was inhospitable but convenient, and both merchandise and crews would be shipped from there to the mainland by barge.

On return journeys, both the northern and the southern fleets usually sailed home via Havana, the best harbour in all the Americas. Both would wait there for a naval escort. Then the return across the Atlantic would begin, usually via the Azores, still Portuguese, from whence it would be usual to expect another month's voyage to Castile. Welcomed home they might then well be, but many seamen would have to be sent off to the special maritime hospital of Buena Aire in Triana.

Regular voyages across the Pacific incidentally began in the 1560s and were a fearful experience on most occasions. There were often battles with the French or pirates attempting to board the ships, when cannon would be fired and all manner of objects thrown: flaming arrows (*alacranes*), gunpowder, tar and oil mixtures (*alquitranes*) and pieces of iron with four sharp points (*abrojos*).

The main items of trade by 1550 were, first, wine, olive oil, *eau de vie*; then complementary products such as vinegar, olives, raisins, almonds, spices, wax; then clothes; metal objects such as agricultural machinery, nails and nail-making equipment; leather, soap, glass, medicines, even works of art. Mercury was a Spanish state monopoly but much used in securing good silver. In the sixteenth century, textiles – many from Rouen or Angers – constituted over 60 per cent of all imports into the Americas. Then there were paper, rosaries, pens and strings for violins. Slaves, however, were thought of as an item of commerce second to none.[19]

Colourings or dyes, such as cochineal and indigo, seem to have constituted about half the imports, these being the American products most easily sold. At the end of the sixteenth century, leather, tobacco, ginger, pearls and brazilwood were also important.

The ships on both the Atlantic and the Pacific would be stocked with sacks of biscuit, salt and firewood, *pipas* of wine and of water, *botijas* of oil and vinegar, *botas* of salt meat, salt fish and beans or rice, dozens of cheeses. The staple elements in the diet of a sailor were biscuit, water and wine, and the usual daily rations on a transatlantic ship would probably have been a pound and a half of biscuit, and a litre of both water and wine, 5 oz of a mixture (*menestra*) of horse beans and chickpeas, and 5 oz of salt fish – probably *tollo* (dogfish), *pargo* (red snapper), or *bacallao* (cod). Some days the *menestra* would be replaced by 2 oz of mixed rice and oil, and 8 oz or even over a pound of salt pork. Two ounces of cheese might sometimes be distributed, particularly when storms or possible battles made it unwise to light the stove.[20]

Masters would expect grander menus: white rather than black biscuit, roast chicken, dried fruit, good wine. Fresh fish would be frequently found in the sea and most sailors would have a fishhook and a line. About 4,000 calories a day was adequate for the efforts demanded.[21]

Most seamen wore loose-fitting clothes, usually blue – trousers known as *zaragüelles* or *greguescos*, capes or jackets called *capotes de mar* or *chaquetillas*, such as those sketched by the Strasbourg painter Christoph Weiditz. Most travellers would carry a knife in their belts.

Fray Antonio de Guevara tells us that at sea there were three diversions – not that he was a man of great maritime experience – gaming, talking and reading. The first included gambling at dice or card games such as *triunfo del basto, malilla, parar, treinta por fuerza* or *cientos*, and also chess. The second included many kinds of books, some religious, such as the *Libro de la Oración y la Meditación* of Fray Luis de Granada, the most widely read book in Spain in the sixteenth century; some technical, some chivalrous such as *Amadís de Gaula* or one of its successors. The third included seductions of both boys (by sailors) and the few women travelling – female servants or perhaps widows. Homosexuality naturally played its part.

The commerce with the Indies was every year more and more governed by laws. Thus, to begin at the beginning, on 10 April 1495 a decree was proclaimed giving the right to all Spanish subjects to establish, exploit or carry out commerce in the New World under prescribed conditions.

On 6 May 1497 another decree stated that participation in commerce was to be under the direction of the Crown. A few years later, on 6 September 1501, a further decree, which principally concerned the new proconsul of Santo Domingo, Nicolás de Ovando, proscribed foreigners from going to the Indies.

All the same, at this time any ship which kept to the rules had the liberty to travel freely and whenever convenient.

A decree of 12 October 1504 spoke of the need for commerce to be directed by Isabel from her realms. On 10 December 1508, Spanish merchants were able to register their merchandise at the Canary Isles. The following year it was laid down that all ships whose captains wanted to would be able to load their merchandise at Cadiz.

In 1510 the ordinances for the Casa de la Contratación instructed that body not to allow foreigners to go to the Indies and not to allow ships to go to the Indies without a permit that would entail three inspections: an official *visitador* (visitor) would have to inspect a ship before any permissions were granted; then there would be a look at the loaded ship, in Seville; finally there would be a general search at Sanlúcar, seeking to ensure that the vessel was not overloaded and therefore dangerous.

From the beginning, all merchants who wanted to send goods to the Indies had to pay taxes known as *almojarifes de Indias* and obtain a licence from the Casa de la Contratación. Similar permits were needed in the Indies both for the outward and the homeward journey. All goods, above all gold but also brazilwood, had to be registered, any smuggler being required to pay four times the value of the amount seized. The property of anyone dying in the Americas would be carefully listed and later sold in a regulated way. All such regulations were published by Andrés de Carvajal, one of the many of that surname who played a part in the Indies.

In 1513 there was another striking change: the Casa de la Contratación was ordered to send two caravels to Cuba to defend the coast there against French pirates; and in 1521 a little squadron of four or five ships was charged to patrol the waters off Cape St Vincent in Portugal. From 1514 the hulls of many ships were to be protected by a sheathing of lead, a good defence against ship-worm.

Next year there was a protest against the monopoly of trade enjoyed by Seville. In 1518 we hear of officials in the shape of visitors, Diego Rodríguez Comitre and Bartolomé Diaz, and a subsequent decree forbidding them from having any financial connection with any vessel engaged in commerce with the Americas. Though like most officials they would buy their offices, they were well paid and expected to be experts in ship-care such as careening. They would eventually carry out the prescribed three inspections of every ship, ending at Sanlúcar de Barrameda, sometimes checking that all priests had regularized their passage. They were later concerned with loading, and were also concerned with the need to prevent smuggling.[22]

On 5 April 1522 orders were given to the officials of the Casa de la Contratación not to permit any stranger of any sort to travel who had not given proof of identity. Also excluded were non-Catholics and Jews, Moors and the children, even grandchildren, of those who had publicly worn a San Benito in consequence of the punishments of the Inquisition. On 14 July of that same year numerous further ordinances were proclaimed: thus every ship of 100 tons was obliged to carry at least fifteen mariners, including a gunner, eight apprentices or cabin boys (*grumetes*) and three pages (*pajes*). There would have to be four large iron guns, provided with three dozen shot each, and twenty-four swivel guns (*pasavolantes* and *espingardas*, six dozen shot for each of them); two hundredweight of powder, and ten crossbows with eight dozen arrows would be provided, along with four dozen short lances, eight long pikes and twenty shields. Naturally every soldier carried a sword, usually at his own expense.

On 15 January 1529 a decree at Toledo again reserved all commerce to the people of Castile, but also named nine ports in addition to Seville from which ships could sail: Corunna, Bayona, Avilés, Laredo, Bilbao, San Sebastián, Cartagena, Malaga and Cadiz. In September 1534 it was insisted that no ship, unless it were new, might leave for the Americas without being careened first. The crew as well as the ship had to be examined by the pilot-major. The upper deck and main cabins had to be kept free of merchandise; only provisions, artillery and passengers' chests were permitted above deck. But it turned out that first-rate ships were more rarely sent to the Americas than seemed likely.

Voyages to the Indies were by now dominated by rules. Very often, however, the regulations insisting on these limitations were not kept.

Bureaucratic rules are meant to be broken and in the Spanish Empire as in other such undertakings were frequently only an indication of what the civil servants in Seville hoped might happen. Captains, bosuns, passengers and sailors exploited the rules as best they could.[23]

In 1537 a royal fleet was sent to the Indies to guarantee the safe despatch of its treasures. In 1538 the Casa de la Contratación authorized merchants to collaborate in a consulate with a prior and two consuls. In 1540 there was a reference to the idea that all ships active in the Indies would have to be Spanish.

From 23 August 1543 the annual departure of the fleets was formalized, with only ships of 100 tons or more being allowed to take part, two annual fleets of at least ten ships lifting anchor, one now sailing in March and the other in September. In 1552 it was decided temporarily to suspend convoys and to arm all ships against possible foes. Ships were classified in three categories: from 100 to 170 tons; from 170 to 220; and 220 to 320. Armaments were mostly of brass. Crossbows were being supplemented by the more efficient arquebus.

Henceforth a ship of the first category would have eighteen mariners, the second two twenty-eight and thirty-five mariners. The first ship would carry two gunners and eight apprentices, with two cabin boys; the second category of ship would have four gunners, twelve or fifteen apprentices and four cabin boys. But soon the government returned to the convoy system.

A *cédula* (decree) of 3 April 1558 abrogated the rule of obligatory return from Puerto Rico and Santo Domingo to Seville. From 1561 ships which were damaged and might not be able to pass the sandbar at Sanlúcar were also allowed to discharge merchandise at Cadiz.[24] Special naval vessels were allocated to the defence of the treasure fleets from now on and were paid for by a duty on exports and imports known as the *avería*, which was managed by a *contador de averías*, of whom there were six by the end of the century.

Colonists to the New World were encouraged by the Crown in numerous ways. For example, those on their way to Santo Domingo or Tierra Firme (Venezuela) were now given maintenance and free passages from the day that they arrived in Seville until they disembarked in 'America'. They were all provided with the land, livestock, plants and agricultural implements they needed. They were for twenty years free of the tax known as *alcabala* and other taxes except tithes to the Church.

Doctors and apothecaries would in principle be provided. Special prizes were offered for good husbandry: 30,000 maravedís would be given to whoever produced 12 pounds of silk, and similar payments were made to those who produced comparable quantities of cloves, cinnamon and olive oil.

Long before that arrangement, however, Spain had become preoccupied by a new territory to the south, namely a land known to the conquistadors of Darien and Panama as 'Birú'.

BOOK II
Peru

18

Birú

It rarely happens that new islands emerge out of the sea. But should that occur and some new island ... appear, it should belong to him who first settles it.

King Alfonso X, *Las Siete Partidas*

The kingdom of old Peru, like Mexico, was the heir of many traditions and was made up of the coming together of many small entities. The Chavin culture had dominated central Peru in the time of the classical Greeks. In the north, there had been the Moche, much of whose pottery has survived, depicting most of the facts of life including love and war. In the south, inland on the dry peninsula of Paracas, the Nazca were the most civilized of the Incas' predecessors, being responsible for elaborate, interesting and sophisticated textiles, much preserved in graves in the deserts there.

About AD 1000 an empire known as that of Tiahuanaco was established, beginning on the shores of the high inland lake of Titicaca. This fell apart since there was no mechanism for maintaining its unity. Other sophisticated urban societies had a brief hour of glory at Wari (or Huari) in the Ayacucho basin and at Tiwanaku south of Lake Titicaca. There was also Chan Chan, city of the Chimu renowned for their smiths.

The Incas emerged from the valley of Cuzco about the time of the establishment of Tiahuanaco, though, to begin with, the idea that they might soon dominate the whole of Ecuador and Peru as well as half of Chile would have seemed as absurd as to suppose at the same time that the Castilians were about to conquer the Americas. Their descendants thought that the Inca had emerged from 'the House of Windows' at the 'Inn of Dawn'.

The Incas progressed gradually up the valley of the river Urabamba adding tribe after tribe to their roll of dependants, sometimes by arms, sometimes by diplomacy. The mythical third Inca – the ruler was so called – about AD 1400 carried the tribe's authority to beyond Lake Titicaca, with expeditions to the eastern forests as well as to the Pacific, and beyond La Paz to include what is now Bolivia. The polities of the Nazca and Arequipa came into Inca control in the fifteenth century and, in the next hundred years, the seventh Inca, who took as an additional name that of the god Viracocha, defeated and absorbed the till then powerful Chanca at the battle of Xaquixaguana, a turning point in the history of the country. Then Pachacuti, 'the best all-round genius produced by the native races of America', in the words of the archaeologist Sir Clements Markham, established in the early fifteenth century what seems to have been something which deserved the name of 'empire', comprising much of the coastal plain and an important part of the Andes. Pachacuti's four sons directed large tracts of well-farmed coastal valleys and imposing towns more impressive than anything which the Incas had up till then controlled (hence the kingdom was usually known as 'the Four Parts Together' or Tawantinsuyu). It was an entity of about eighty provinces. Pachacuti was the Ch'in emperor of the New World. His son Tupac Yupanqui added much of Ecuador to the Inca empire in the second half of the fifteenth century and conquered half of Chile.

The last independent ruler of Peru was Huayna Capac who reigned from 1498 till 1527 and who seems to have been inactive, being perhaps ill from syphilis.[1] He exercised his power through his elegant use of Quechua, which had been spoken throughout the northern Andes before the expansion of the Incas, who adopted it.[2] He may have died from smallpox, a disease from the old world which certainly seems to have killed his eldest son. Huayna's weakness was that he left two sons: Huascar, his son by his first wife, and Atahualpa, a son by his second wife, a princess of a northern tribe, the Carab Sapri, conquered by a recent Inca. Huayna apparently considered dividing his large kingdom into two, leaving the northern part to Atahualpa, the southern to Huascar – a sensible policy it might seem. But both sons wanted everything. Hence the civil war which divided both the Inca family and the honorary Inca nobility though, about the time that the Spaniards arrived, Atahualpa had won and his senior generals Quizquiz and Rumiñavi in Quito had seen their position enhanced. The family of the defeated Huascar had been cruelly killed, while Huascar himself was forced to watch. When the Spaniards arrived, Atahualpa was going south on the main Inca highway on his way to be crowned in Cuzco.

Peru and old Mexico were powerful monarchies which knew nothing of each other. Both were relatively recent in power, having accumulated their positions in the fifteenth century. Both had rulers taken from the same royal family throughout their histories. Both had dominating religions with priestly castes. The Incas worshipped the moon as well as the sun. Some coastal societies in Peru (the Chimu) thought that the moon was more important than the sun. The Mexica and the Incas included savagery and high culture in their ceremonials and customs, but the violence in Mexico was never seen in Peru. In neither society is there any evidence that anyone had a sense of humour, whereas the Spaniards were always laughing. Both had settled capital cities – Tenochtitlan and Cuzco – something which at that stage Spain had not. Both had sophisticated systems of landholding. Both the Mexica and the Inca were peoples who had succeeded in exerting their dominance over neighbouring tribes to whom they had themselves once been subordinate, and war and fighting were persistent with them both. Both the Inca and the Mexica used stones in fighting and both employed slings which could accurately fling a stone the size of an apple some hundred yards. Both also used battle axes with bronze or stone blades which were sometimes effective in war against the Spaniards, though they were nothing like so destructive against the Spanish steel sword. Some Peruvians had throwing sticks shaped like Mexican *atlatls*, and both societies had bows and arrows. These weapons had been used in the campaigns to create the Inca and Aztec empires. At Tumbes the Spaniards admired the Peruvians' 'long arrows, spears and clubs'.[3]

The rise in Peruvian power had been slower than that of the Mexica, but nevertheless the great conquerors of the two dynasties were fifteenth-century contemporaries. Both the ruling houses of Mexico and Peru were large family autocracies, not unlike the Saudi royal family of today. In neither country did primogeniture play a part. The best man was expected to gain power. (The Scots Law of Tanistry laid down that kind of arrangement in the tenth century and before.) In Mexico a succession was less of a crisis than it was in Peru because the reigning emperor (*huey tlatoani*) would select his successor soon after his own enthronement. All important positions were filled by members of the royal house.

Both the Mexica and the Incas thought that they were 'chosen peoples'. The Inca rulers, like the Mexica, were in one respect comparable to the English monarchy after Henry VIII: they were at the summit of the national religion, though the 'king' was not a high priest. The two monarchies were both absolute ones: the power of the ruler was unquestioned. Both rulers were in constant touch, it was said, with the sun. The popular adulation attached to the monarch was exorbitant and protest or dissent unthinkable.

Both Peruvians and Mexica made fine cotton clothes including tunics and cloaks, deriving from sophisticated weaving, and both, on occasions, wore feathers arranged as cloaks or in headdresses. The Incas valued their cloth so highly that they burned it rather than allow it to fall into Spanish hands.[4] Both empires used languages, the Mexica Nahuatl, the Inca Quechua, which seemed to be *lingua francas* in the territories concerned, though the Incas also had a private language for use within the royal family. Both societies liked alcohol and some drugs: the Peruvians had *chicha*, a mild beer made from maize, while the Mexica had *pulque* made from the agave cactus; the Incas enjoyed coca rather than the elaborate range of hallucinogenic drugs available to the Mexica from mushrooms. As a staple food the Mexica had maize, the Peruvians had the potato,[5] and both supplemented their diet[6] with fish (anchovies, sardines, tuna, sea bass, salmon off the coast of Peru) and birds, while the Peruvians also ate dried llama meat and guinea pig. The Peruvians would organize great hunts for vicuña, guanaco, roe deer, mountain fox, hares and puma, as the Inca Manco would show to Francisco Pizarro in 1534. Though both societies made elaborate pottery, neither had the benefit of the potter's wheel. Perhaps in the Mexican case that convenience was not far away. Nor had either any means of writing, though the Peruvians used so-called '*quipus*', knots and rows of coloured strings which represented mathematical units.[7]

The Spanish conquerors recorded what they observed of the old societies with much attention to detail. The greatest of these writers was the Franciscan Fray Bernardino de Sahagún in Mexico, who interpreted the old world which had already passed away by recalling the voices of the Indians themselves to tell of what used to happen. Relations of Montezuma, such as Ixtlilxochitl, also wrote accounts of great interest; and in Peru, Titu Cusi Yupanqui, second son of Manco Inca and an ebullient administrator of his reserves, made a historical record of a similar sort for Augustinian missionaries.

There were, moreover, similar expressions of anxiety in both Peru and New Spain about the future before the arrival of Cortés at Veracruz and of Pizarro at Tumbes. Peruvians were said to have heard prophecies of an ex-king that the empire would be overcome by bearded people who would preach the virtues of a new religion. But this seems to have been a late sixteenth-century church tale. Some news of the fate of Central America under the brutality of Pedrarias may have filtered down to Peru before 1530, just as some information about the Spanish actions in the West Indies reached Mexico before 1519. The Peruvians had suffered from one or two Western diseases, such as bubonic plague, before 1530, though they were unaware of their provenance. They also had a legend which predicted cataclysm: a *pachakuti*, a turning-over of time and space such as, according to a convenient myth, had occurred four times before the 1530s.

There were, of course, differences between these two indigenous societies. The most important one was that ancient Peru had no commercial life while Mexico enjoyed a lively one: Mexican merchants also played an important part in informing the rulers, the 'emperors', about other places, as if they were secret agents. A related difference was that there was no private landholding in Peru. The peasants farmed elaborate, productive and even beautiful terraces but they were held in common. Never was there a more pervasive government than that of the Incas. Personal liberty was practically non-existent. Blind obedience and unquestioning self-abnegation had forever to be accorded. But if much was demanded of the subject, much was done for him. Marxists have talked of 'Inca communism' and they may have been correct thus to designate the Peruvian social structure in which almost everything was supervised by officials. Aztec society was much less controlled. The last emperor Montezuma's remark about the necessity of dealing harshly with his people if they were going to be ruled effectively is well known.[8]

Mexico had no domestic animals. Peru on the contrary had the alpaca, the guinea pig and the llama, which the Spaniards thought were large sheep. The Inca used them to carry light loads – up to fifty or sixty pounds – but also to give their wool and meat. They could last several days without drinking. They were the heart of the Inca economy and herds were carefully bred to ensure that they were always there. Alpaca wool was invaluable. Otherwise both communities employed men as runners and porters. Both used wooden rollers to assist the movement of great stones or lumps of masonry, especially the Peruvians.

Another difference was that the Peruvians had sails on their rafts and canoes, which the Mexica and Mesoamerican people, such as the Maya, do not seem to have had. The Peruvians used the sea as a means for trade more than the Mexica did. Yet a high percentage of Andeans (perhaps two thirds of the population) lived at heights over 9,000 feet and most communication was by land.

The Mexica had remarkable artistic achievements to their credit: for example, their painting, poetry and sculpture – monumental and tiny, relief and in the round. In these matters, the Peruvians were more limited and no pre-Hispanic poetry is known from Peru.[9] Both societies prized gold and silver jewels, but the Peruvians had more of them. Both had a process for creating metals of quality out of ore, but the Peruvians produced more elaborate gold ornaments than the Mexica did.

The Inca built magnificent roads and suspension bridges, far superior to anything then found in ancient Mexico or, thought the Sevillano chronicler Pedro Cieza de León, in old Europe.[10] There was an elaborate network of storehouses which held food, arms and clothing on the roads. Along these roads the state's llamas and human porters travelled incessantly.

The Peruvians had devised a decimal system of numbers to enable the accurate gathering of tribute. Inca decimal administrators were, at the time of the coming of the Spaniards, painstakingly taking over the business of collecting tribute from the old chiefs who had calculated before with more conventional methods.[11]

The Inca capital of Cuzco was much smaller, less elaborate and less grand than Tenochtitlan in Mexico, but both cities boasted stone or stone-faced houses as well as streets well washed by streams, with sewers. The main square at Cuzco had something in common with the Zócalo in the centre of Tenochtitlan, though it was smaller. In the architectural use of stone the Inca were, however, superior to the Mexica. The Inca did not have the arch but they paid much attention to the exactness of the fitting of the joints between the huge stones. These essential elements in construction were manoeuvred into place by teams of men using wooden levers.[12] Throughout the age of the Inca, people depended on home-made chipped stone tools, for scraping, chopping, cutting and even drilling.

Inca religion was simpler than that of Mexico. Human sacrifices occurred but on a lesser scale than in ancient Mexico – the victims in Peru being usually beautiful boys and girls, often prisoners of war. Still, the death or investiture of a ruler could inspire the sacrifice of hundreds.[13] Local deities survived conquest by the Inca. As in the empire of Montezuma, effigies of the gods of conquered tribes were taken to the capital almost as hostages for their peoples.

The dead were not left to rest, but played a part, in Peru. Pedro Pizarro, a cousin of the conquering band of Extremeño brothers, who had been brought up in Toledo, recalls how, when he arrived in Cuzco, the citizens took out the coffins of the dead into the main square and placed them in a row, according to their age. There the citizens sat, ate and drank *chicha*. They made fires before the dead from dry wood and burned in them what in the past they had given to the dead. In front of the coffins, they placed large pitchers of gold, silver or pottery which they filled with *chicha*. When these were full, they emptied them into a round vessel of stone in the middle of the plaza.[14]

The priests in Peru, headed by Villac Umu, the high priest, often produced a small covered bundle which they assured observers was the sun itself. This was guarded by men with lances decorated with gold, 'the arms of the Sun'. The precious object was placed on a bench in the plaza and offered feathers or cloaks, and food which was afterwards burned. The ashes of the sun's dinner were then thrown into a round stone trough shaped like a teat.

Viracocha was the name for the supreme Inca deity; the word actually meant 'foam of the sea'. Cieza de León, one of the most responsible of Spanish chroniclers, said that he thought that this Viracocha was a tall white man, large of stature, with a white robe reaching to his feet, tied with a belt. His hair was short, he carried something which looked like a breviary and he wore a crown. But Juan de Betanzos said that he was a tall man, with a belted robe. The Indians explained that he travelled constantly till he came to the sea, where he spread his cloak, moved on it over the waves, and never appeared again. Atahualpa's nephew pointed out that the Spaniards appeared from the same sea into which the creator god had disappeared. Perhaps it was the same sea where the Mexican god Quetzalcoatl had also vanished.

The sun in old Peru had a palace covered with gold which was guarded by 200 women who were supposed to be chaste but, Pedro

Pizarro tells us, they often 'involved themselves with the male servants and guardians of the Sun'. Nearby was a garden filled with golden representations of maize stalks, trees, fruit and vegetables.

This was the land which now became the subject of Spanish attention, even obsession, particularly in the isthmus of Panama–Darien, one which seemed at first sight similar to that which Cortés had conquered in New Spain.

19

Pizarro's preparations

*Yet surely Master More ... wherever you have private property,
and all men measure all things by money, there it is scarcely possible for a state to have justice or prosperity.*

Thomas More, *Utopia*

Pizarro spent a year in Panama and Darien preparing his expedition to
Peru. He knew little of the politics of the place; far less, say, than a
reader of the last chapter.

He had organized his endeavours in a Peruvian company, or Compañía del Levante, with Diego de Almagro, Hernando de Luque and one
or two others such as Diego de Mora and Gaspar de Espinosa. There
were three ships, jointly owned by Hernando de Soto, Pizarro, and
Hernán Ponce de León, about 180 men – no women – and about thirty
horses: 'as many Spaniards and horses as his ships would hold'.[1] The
expedition was financed by Pizarro himself and Almagro; Hernando
de Luque had a minor investment but he was not a partner on the same
level as the other two leaders.[2] Pizarro had paid for the horses and several black African slaves for the expedition and the ships seem to have
been stocked with food, water and armaments by their masters. His
captain and pilot was his friend Bartolomé Ruiz (de Estrada), who, as
we have seen, came from that nursery of good sailors, Moguer, on the
river Tinto. He had also worked for Almagro and had recruited men for
the journey. But Pedro Pizarro said that those participating had to pay
their own expenses, including money for their passage; and Jerónimo de
Aliaga, a clever and literate lawyer from Segovia, also explained that he
paid for everything himself.[3] There were other investors: for example
the rich *licenciado* Gaspar de Espinosa, a native of Medina de Río Seco,

the city of the semi-royal family of Enríquez. Pizarro was the captain-in-chief, as it were the commander of a company such as was often seen in those days.[4] His power was limited by royal officials appointed to ensure that the Crown received a fifth of all income or loot, but he was able to leave them behind in reserve.[5]

The important men on the journey were the Pizarro family. Of these, Hernando, then about thirty years of age, was the only legitimate brother, and was twenty years younger than Francisco. Oviedo, who knew him, said that Hernando was 'a heavy man, but tall of stature with thick lips and tongue, and the tip of his nose was fleshy and red'.[6] His cousin, Pedro Pizarro, however, said that he was 'a man of good stature, valiant, wise and brave, albeit a heavy man in the saddle'.[7] Garcilaso de la Vega, the most imaginative, but not the most accurate, chronicler of those days, thought him 'rough and ill-tempered'.[8] Enríquez de Guzmán said that Hernando was a 'bad Christian with no fear of God and less devotion to the king . . . a great and boastful talker'.[9] Being legitimate, he inherited a large house in Trujillo and also the nearby village of La Zarza some miles south, which had long been a Pizarro holding. Hernando had accompanied his father, Gonzalo Pizarro, in the war against France in Navarre and so had knowledge of both courts and royal armies. He was one of the two men on the expedition to Peru who had some kind of experience of war in Europe (the other was the Cretan Pedro de Candia).[10] His education had also given him some grasp of finance which he would put to good effect during the next few years. He could be witty and was articulate. His letter of 1533 to the *audiencia* in Santo Domingo makes him one of the best eyewitnesses of what occurred in Peru in those years.[11] He was his brother Francisco's chief confidant, and intensely disliked Almagro, whom he now met for the first time and whom he called 'the circumcised Moor'. The bad relations which developed between Francisco Pizarro and Almagro were worsened by the attitude of Hernando Pizarro.

The other Pizarro brothers with Francisco were in 1531 still too young to count for much. Yet it was already obvious that Juan Pizarro, still in his twenties, was 'affable, magnanimous, impetuous – and popular';[12] 'the flower of all the Pizarros', Cieza de León, the chronicler, called him.[13] He had been brought up by his aunt Estefanía de Vargas, but he lived with the other Pizarros.

Then there was Gonzalo Pizarro, a little younger than Juan, of whom he was a full brother (their mother was María Alonso, probably a maid in the Pizarro house). He loved hunting and was good at it; he was well proportioned with a striking face, always graceful, and had a capacity for camaraderie which enabled him to make friends easily. Garcilaso said of him that 'his nature was so noble that he endeared himself to strangers' and that 'he was full of nobility and virtue and ... [so] was beloved and respected by everyone'. He was also a fine rider, a good shot with both arquebus and crossbow and, it was claimed, 'the best lance which crossed to the new world'.[14] Pedro Pizarro said of him that he was valiant, with a good countenance and a fine beard but 'knew little'.[15] His day, however, would come.

In the early stages of Pizarro's expedition, Pedro de Candia from Crete had a strong influence. Physically a giant, he had been in the Spanish army since 1510 as an artilleryman, a position for which the Greeks were then known. He had been one of Pizarro's elite 'thirteen' at Gallo Island. Pizarro had always liked him, often asking him to dine with him. He took him with him in 1528 to Spain, where his tales of Peru were too extravagant for comfort and Pizarro had to ask him to be quiet.

Pizarro left Panamanian waters on 27 December 1530 without Almagro, his nominal partner, who, fatally for himself, undertook to follow later, and without his first ship, which was captained by Cristóbal de Mena, a native of Ciudad Real like Almagro, of whom he was a close friend. He had been an *encomendero* and a councillor in Nicaragua.

The journey to 'Birú' was long-drawn-out. The Spanish expeditionaries sailed south under Bartolomé Ruiz's direction, and their first port of call, thirteen days after leaving Panama, was the Bay of San Marcos at the mouth of the river Esmeraldas, in the extreme north of the country which we now know as Ecuador, not Peru. The names had been given to the places by Bartolomé Ruiz, without much reflection, during Pizarro's previous expedition.

They had intended to sail to Tumbes but that seemed impossible because of a strong south wind, so men, materiel and horses were all disembarked. After a preliminary look for the emeralds which Bartolomé Ruiz assured his comrades were to be found in substantial quantities, the force then moved southwards by land along the coast. Here there were new difficulties, with mosquitoes and a severe shortage of water. The Spaniards took formal possession of the place following the reading of the Requirement, in the town of Cancebi, whose inhabitants were not enthralled at hearing the threatening-sounding, if incomprehensible, declaration. The expedition by land continued, with Pizarro trying to educate his men in the complexities of a new landscape. There were certainly immense difficulties. The land was barren but intersected by large rivers, which Pizarro and his men crossed by making rafts of wood, rushes or osiers, built according to the captain's instructions. Pizarro was a real example, for 'he often carried the sick over rivers on his back, being experienced in such tasks and he went about them with a patience and a courage that stimulated the others' spirits'.[16]

These Spaniards' first obvious act of pillage was at the town of Coaque, which they reached on 25 February 1531. They found a place of about 400 houses, where they were met by very surprised Indians, who had not realized that they were threatened in any way. Pedro Pizarro recalled that the Spaniards attacked suddenly without warning for, 'had it been otherwise, they would not have captured the quantity of gold and emeralds which was found there'.[17] Pizarro distributed this treasure 'in conformity with each man's merits and services'. There was, it seems, 'a shameful mistake on the part of certain members of the expedition who did not know their value ... Others scorned the emeralds saying that they were glass.'[18] They also seized about 2,000 pesos of gold and silver and Pizarro ordered Hernán Ponce de León, with one of his ships, and some of his treasure, to go back to Panama in order to show what he had found and encourage the people there to volunteer to join him.[19] Bartolomé de Aguilar, one of Pizarro's recruits from Trujillo, also returned. While waiting in Coaque, Pizarro seized the local chief of the town, but appears to have treated him humanely, with the result that the chief ordered his people to supply the Spaniards with the food that they wanted. But then the Spaniards 'bothered and offended the natives so much that ... they took to the forests'.[20] The news spread about 'the arrival of bearded men who came in floating houses'.[21]

The Spaniards remained at Coaque seven months.[22] That was a mistake. A strange disease of growths (*verrugas*) developed. It was either Oroya fever or Verruga Peruana – probably the latter. The attacks began with pains in the muscles, bones and joints, followed by the growth of large nodules or boils like nuts.[23] No one knew how to treat these things and many died. Garcilaso says that 'at first a wart appeared as large as a black fig. It hung from some kind of stem, produced a great deal of blood and caused pain and nausea. The growths could not be touched and made the appearance of the sufferer most repulsive.'[24] Pedro Pizarro suggested that the fault lay with some unusual fish which the Indians gave the conquistadors to eat. But it could also have been the woollen mattresses which the Indians had and which seemed to ensure that, if the Spaniards threw themselves down on them, they rose crippled: if the arm or the leg were doubled up during sleep, 'it could not be straightened without great difficulty'.[25]

At Coaque, Pizarro was joined by reinforcements. But still Almagro did not come; he was apparently continuing to seek 'supplies and men'. One cannot avoid supposing that he may have been waiting to see how the expedition would turn out. But those who did come now included the royal treasurer, Alonso Riquelme, the official supervisor García de Salcedo, who came from Zafra, and the royal accountant, Antonio Navarro.[26] The whole force set off on 12 October for the south, again by land. They crossed the Equator just short of Pasao where they came upon excellent fields of maize and where the chief gave Pizarro some girls; both were welcomed. The expedition soon found itself in Puerto Viejo, on what is now the Bay of Manta.

Here, Cieza tells us, the Spaniards realized for the first time that the great Inca kingdom, their object and their destination, had been torn apart by the civil war between the brothers Huascar and Atahualpa. Spaniards, of course, with their memories of La Cerdas fighting Trastámaras, knew all about such wars. News of the arrival of the expedition reached the Inca princes. Atahualpa, who had, to begin with, been his brother's viceroy for Quito, commented that, since there were so few Spaniards, perhaps they could serve him as superior servants (*yanaconas*). But the rumour spread fast that the Spaniards wanted 'to rule over them and take their land'.[27]

Moving down the Pacific coast, the Spaniards were provided by the Indians with food and water. They passed some strange places and sights. At Mataglan, for example, not far from the modern Guayaquil, the chief was a woman and, according to Juan Ruiz de Arce, a conquistador from Alburquerque, the people were all homosexuals.[28] Here a Spaniard named Santiago was killed and Pizarro caused the chief to punish those responsible. One of these was tied to a pole and left to die.

Pizarro was shortly joined by a new Spanish force from Panama led by Sebastián de Benalcázar. He probably came from a place which his surname reflected, even if it was slightly differently spelled: Belalcázar, a village in the Sierra Morena. He was from a family of muleteers and, like Pizarro, was illiterate. He probably went out to the Indies in 1505, first to Santo Domingo in the days of the iron proconsul Ovando. He joined Pedrarias in Panama and served with Gaspar de Espinosa in a brutal expedition to Azuero, in Central America, in 1519.[29] He was present at the execution of Núñez de Balboa. He became an *encomendero* of Natá, Panama. By then he had already known Almagro and Pizarro for some years. Cieza considered that he was 'a man of little knowledge, poor origin and a low intellect'. But all the same he was brave and instinctively clever in battle, liberal in his relations with his men and had real qualities of leadership which were to serve the Spanish cause well, virtues which he had in common with Pizarro himself. He also realized sooner than other Spaniards how the Cañari Indians could become Spanish allies against the Inca.

Benalcázar came to Peru with thirty men: among them Juan de Porrás, a thirty-year-old from Seville, who would be Pizarro's chief magistrate;[30] Rodrigo Núñez de Prado, of a well-known Extremeño family related to Cortés, who had gone to the Indies with Pedrarias, was an *encomendero* in Panama and would become *maestro de campo*;[31] and Alonso Romero, an illiterate sailor from Lepe near Huelva, who had already spent twenty years in the Indies, in Santo Domingo, Honduras and Nicaragua. He would be the new royal lieutenant and carry the standard of Spain. Fabián García Moyano, Benalcázar's twin brother, arrived with the first conquistadora in Peru, his sister, Anastasia. Pizarro's expedition was thus staffed by adventurers from families which had distinguished themselves in Spain in the fifteenth century. But none of those with Pizarro had been in New Spain with Cortés, even if Cortés's memory was fresh among them.

Pizarro, Benalcázar and their friends moved on to Santa Elena, where they suffered a serious shortage of water. Many of the men were disaffected and wanted to go back to a town which they had left a few days before, Puerto Viejo. Pizarro refused to allow it, saying that to turn round would look like a defeat. They continued to the island of Puna in the Gulf of Guayaquil, where they remained four months. The local chief was, to begin with, benign but, after a few days, he ordered and persuaded his men to rise and try to destroy the visitors. Their attack began with the organization of a great noise which was said to be a preparation for dancing but turned out to be a mobilization. Some conquistadors were wounded, among them Hernando Pizarro. But the attack ended quickly when the Spaniards took the chief Tumala prisoner with several of his lieutenants.[32] Nothing the Indians could do had the slightest effect on the Spaniards' swords and horses.

Here in Puna on 1 December 1531 the expedition was enhanced by the arrival of further reinforcements from Panama. This was a force of nearly one hundred in two ships, led by Hernando de Soto, a hidalgo from Jerez de los Caballeros, Extremadura, who had gained much credit for his conduct in Nicaragua and who had helped to finance Pizarro's ships.[33] Soto is considered 'dashing'[34] and he was certainly brave. He was small in build but, says Pedro Pizarro, 'dextrous in warfare and affable with soldiers'.[35] He probably went first to the Indies in 1513 with Pedrarias, whose daughter, Isabel, he later married. He explored part of what is now Colombia in 1517. He had a company with Hernán Ponce de León from 1517. In the 1520s he was in much brutal conflict in Central America and gained good *encomiendas* in León. To chart his trajectory among the squabbling conquistadors in that new territory is a hard task, but we know that he and Hernán Ponce de León were busy there selling slaves from Nicaragua to the Caribbean and to Panama also. Before they set off, Soto concluded an informal agreement with Pizarro whereby he would receive the lieutenant-governorship of 'the main Peruvian city' – Cuzco, we assume. Pizarro promised good *encomiendas* too. Soto's hundred men were financed by himself, or by some of those taking part, who sold their property in order to be able to participate.

In Puna Pizarro and his friends encountered obvious signs of the Peruvian civil war between the two royal brothers, Huascar and Atahualpa. Thus they met 600 prisoners from the port of Tumbes across the water which had seemed very important to the Spaniards on their previous visit. The local chief, Tumbalá, sued for peace and presented the Spaniards with gold and silver gifts. He also gave them rafts, which were maliciously devised to disintegrate by allowing the ropes that held the timbers together to unfasten when they had been at sea a few minutes.

Pizarro's expedition now counted nearly 400 Spaniards and one woman, Benalcázar's sister. They were hated by the local Indians, who could not understand their motivation. Those Indians devised a deer hunt. While the Spaniards were watching the conclusion, it was supposed,

the Indians would fall on them. But by a fatal weakness in Peruvian discretion, one of the Indians revealed this scheme to Pizarro's Quechua
interpreter, 'Felipe', a boy who had been captured in 1527 and trained
in Spanish.[36] Pizarro seized sixteen chiefs who had been engaged in the
plot. A large body of Indians then tried to attack the Spaniards – 3,500
of them, according to Cieza: 'They attacked in three directions, with
determination and boldness.' The Spaniards awaited the charge with
horses and shield-bearers well placed. The Indians as usual made little
impact, many were killed and they wounded only two conquistadors
and three horses. Pizarro requested Tumbalá to order his men to call off
the battle. He refused, saying that wild beasts would not make them
accept peace with people who had done them such damage. But there
was for the moment no more fighting, and the Spaniards assembled a
great quantity of cloth, as well as gold and silver in sheets as if ready for
use as linings of the interior walls of temples.[37]

The expedition set off by raft and ship from Puna to Tumbes. Pizarro
assumed that the people of that port would help him since he had
returned 600 prisoners there. But on the contrary the Indians under
Quillemin, their chief, organized a conspiracy to kill all the Spaniards
there and then. One small raft-borne expedition included a certain Hurtado, who was captured and murdered when he landed, with two boys,
whose eyes were gouged out and penises cut off. But the Indians did not
have the courage to attack the main body of Spanish expeditionaries.
Cieza says that the Indians wanted to leave 'without hearing the snort-
ing of the horses'.

Pizarro found Tumbes abandoned because in the civil war the place
had been laid waste. The temple of the Sun remained there, painted with
large pictures which Miguel de Estete claimed were of a 'rich variety of
colour'.[38] (Estete was from Santo Domingo de la Calzada, a well-known
halt on the pilgrim route from France to Santiago. He was a notary and
had come to Peru with Benalcázar.) This temple had in 1527 much
impressed Alonso de Molina and his description of the sheets of silver
and gold there, confirmed by Candia, was one of the decisive reports
which led to Pizarro's expedition in 1530.

Pizarro and his men camped in two fortresses in Tumbes, one of
which he commanded himself, the other being controlled by his brother
Hernando. An expedition was sent out to 'punish' the murder of Hurtado. This found few Indians upon whom to wreak revenge but the

Spaniards pillaged what they could, stealing llamas as well as other treasures and, with them, they returned to the camp. But Pizarro's anger remained and he ordered Soto, his newest captain, to pursue the local Indians where he could.[39] Soto was always adept at finding Indians to kill and he drove one enemy leader, Quilterosa, into the mountains. Then the Peruvians agreed to beg pardon for what they had done and to offer peace, because they realized that otherwise Pizarro would destroy their settlements. They therefore asked the Spanish commander to have mercy on them in the name of the Sun. Pizarro agreed. Drily, he commented that 'he needed them to give him guides and to help the Spaniards to carry their baggage'.[40]

At some point in the empty city of Tumbes an Indian came up and said that he had no wish to flee since it seemed to him that the new arrivals, being 'men of war and of much power', were destined to conquer everything and that, for that reason, he had not wanted to flee with all the others. He begged that his house be not sacked. Pizarro told him to put a white cross on it and instructed his men that no one was to attack a place so marked.[41] This was the Indian who told Pizarro for the first time of Cuzco and its great riches.[42] At this time Pizarro learned too of such great centres of Peru as Vilcas, with its stone temple and many open squares, and Pachacamac, whose magnificent buildings were said to be coated with gold and silver.

The chiefs of Tumbes, having been sought by Soto and his seventy horsemen, then appeared and thanked Pizarro for his patience with them. They had been convinced of the Spaniards' superior qualities by seeing the horsemen ride uphill![43] At a town nearby which the Spaniards christened San Miguel, because it was then Saint Michael's day (10 April), these chiefs offered a rich booty of gold and silver jewellery. Thereafter the chief Quillemesa was *'mucho nuestro amigo'*.[44] At that time there was a half-hearted rebellion against Pizarro by Soto, who wanted to go up to conquer the Peruvian second city of Quito. Soto was betrayed by Juan de la Torre, a survivor of the famous 'Thirteen' of 1527, and thereafter Pizarro made a point of ensuring that Soto was customarily accompanied by his brothers, Juan and Gonzalo, who acted as a combination of gaolers and bodyguards.[45]

The news which Pizarro heard of the dazzling riches of Peru and its interior caused him to change his strategy. He had intended to proceed to the heart of the country, including Cuzco for example, by continuing down the coast, but then he learned that Atahualpa was at that time not far off in Cajamarca, in the mountains some fifty miles from the sea. Pizarro resolved to seek a meeting with this ruler of the country, who had won the civil war against his elder brother, Huascar. Pizarro left Tumbes on 16 May 1532, leaving behind twenty-five sick Spaniards and fifteen others, under Captain Antonio Navarro, who had been the accountant of the expedition for the last year. He also left there two other royal officials, Alonso Riquelme and García de Salcedo, and, as his own representative, his half-brother, Francisco Martín de Alcántara, a younger son of his mother, whose devotion to him was lifelong. Pizarro made his first grants in this settlement to these stay-behinds, and he planned squares, public buildings and some private houses in San Miguel, this first Spanish city of Peru.[46] Four soldiers and two Franciscans also returned from Tumbez to Panama.

Pizarro's army, now of about 200 men, of whom half were horsemen, pressed on through fertile lands. Thus Miguel de Estete reported:

> The Tallan river is heavily populated with pueblos and has a very good fruit-growing sector, of a better kind than Tumbez. There is an abundance of food and native livestock. All the area to the sea was being well exploited because it seemed to have a very good port.[47]

They continued to cover about four to six leagues, twelve to eighteen miles, every day, passing through Huauillas, Silar, Cerro Prieto, Jagay Negro and the banks of the rivers Chira and Poechos. They saw many most unusual people, such as the Tallares, who, according to Pedro Pizarro, dressed in cloaks of cotton with woollen shawls round their heads which they tied under the beard. The women had lip ornaments, as the Mexican natives had also had. They worshipped the sun and would send it a large supply of dried lizards to eat.[48] They were great drinkers and ate maize, their priests dressed in white and fasted by abstaining from salt as well as garlic. They cultivated watermelons and other fruit. They tended llamas, were fishermen and shellfish enthusiasts, and danced and made music. They were polygamous as well as patriarchal, their leaders lived in adobe palaces and their lords travelled by hammock. Coming originally from the mountains, they now lived on the coast. Their conquest by the Incas in about 1470 had not yet led to them speaking Quechua.[49]

In this zone the Spaniards noted an Indian who wore the ample cloak of the desert as well as a great shawl on his head and shoulders, carrying a basket full of wares. He spent the whole day in the Spanish camp seeking to sell his objects yet, at the same time, he was admiring the work of the expedition's blacksmith, Juan de Salinas, the shaving by the expedition's barber, Francisco López, and the horse-taming by the skilful Hernán Sánchez Murillo, from Villafranca de los Barros, between Mérida and Zapa.[50] Hernando Pizarro guessed that this Indian was more than he appeared at first sight. Indeed, he turned out to be Apoo, a spy of Atahualpa, to whom he reported that the Spaniards were not gods, but bearded robbers who came out of the sea and who could probably be both conquered and enslaved.[51] There were only 190 of them.

Atahualpa seems to have thought it best to allow these 'robbers' to advance and then he would seize them and make them work for him. It was surely for that that the gods had sent the Spaniards.[52] Apoo made the Spaniards show him their swords, and he pulled the beard of one, who gave him many blows in return.[53]

Then Pizarro received a messenger from the Inca Huascar, the defeated prince of the civil war, who, since they had given out that they had come to Peru to undo injustices, asked for Spanish protection. Pizarro rather drily replied that he was always ready to put such things right.[54]

This was a hard march, even if some presented it as if it were a carnival. There was much sun, little shade, much sand and no water except what was carried. Yet they encountered one vast royal house which had an abundance of fresh water, and both the soldiers and the horses refreshed themselves. They saw too a river and a beautiful and cheerful valley through which the broad highway of the Inca passed, with elegant resting places and marked by brilliantly contrived swinging bridges.[55]

Pizarro sent Soto and Benalcázar ahead on horses to explore. They found ample provisions and gold in many temples. The Indians attacked them but Soto's force responded very effectively, the local people still having no answer to Spanish swords.

Atahualpa's captain Ciquinchara sent Pizarro a present of some duck and two model earthenware fortresses through Soto. He also sent *chicha*, Peruvian beer, and tiles of gold. Ciquinchara stayed with Soto till he returned to Pizarro; who, in his turn, sent to Atahualpa the typical Spanish present of a good Holland shirt of fine white linen, two crystal glasses from Venice (only slightly less typical), some pearls from Panama and a random collection of scissors, knives, combs and mirrors from Spain.[56]

The expedition was still in the pretty valley of the river Puira on 8 October 1532, at Serrán on the 16th, and then passed several towns at the foot of the sierra on the 19th. From there Pizarro sent an emissary to Atahualpa. At the same time he held an open meeting of his followers at which he declared that his intention was 'to carry this barbarous people to their union with Christianity without doing them any damage'.[57] In the mountains Atahualpa asked his secret agent all kinds of sensible questions, including whether the Spaniards ate human beings, and received the correct reply: 'I have seen them eat nothing but sheep [llamas], lamb, duck, pigeon, and venison and with these they eat tortillas of maize.' As they marched south Soto was sent inland on a reconnaissance to Cajas on the main Inca road. He took over 500 women from their 'convent' in the main square and allowed his men to rape them (the evidence is that of Diego de Trujillo, an eyewitness).[58]

On 15 November 1532 Pizarro and his men made their way to Atahualpa's city of Cajamarca through plantations of cotton. At this time, Atahualpa, with a large army of, it was said, 40,000 soldiers, was at some baths at Kónoj about four miles outside Cajamarca. Here there was a palace with two towers rising from a courtyard where there was a pool in which the Inca was taking the waters. There were two pipes, one of cold, one of hot water. The Spaniards could easily identify with such a spa.

20

Cajamarca

The courtier's chief purpose and end to which he is directed must be to provide the ruler with sound political advice and to ensure that the public seeks honour and profit.

Castiglione, *The Courtier*

The Pizarros and their expedition of by now 168 men, of whom sixty-two were horsemen, reached Cajamarca by what the Romans would have called 'forced marches'. The last part of the road had been harsh: Hernando Pizarro, every day more important because of his superior education and his experience in a European army, later said that if the Inca had taken any trouble 'they could have stopped us easily'.[1] But the Inca took no such trouble. He had a big army with him. It was the last day of one of his fasts. He was looking forward to seeing these strange animals, horses, of whom he had heard so much.[2] It was reported to Atahualpa that the Spaniards needed these mounts because usually they could not walk uphill. Another report was that when they had to walk uphill, the Spanish foot soldiers hung on to the horses' tails.

One conquistador, Juan Ruiz de Arce, from Alburquerque in Extremadura, from a family of petty hidalgos which had long fought for the Christian cause in Castile, said that, from the hillside over which they had come, the Indian encampment beyond Cajamarca looked like a beautiful planned city. But, he commented, it would have been a serious psychological mistake to display any kind of fear, 'so we descended into the valley and entered the city'.[3]

Cajamarca lay in a fertile flat valley with complicated water courses, a temple of the Sun and sacred buildings full of women chosen either for their birth or their beauty. Their main task seems to have been to make *chicha* for the Inca.

Pizarro's first action on reaching Cajamarca was to despatch his brother, Hernando, with Soto and fifteen horsemen to go and ask Atahualpa to come and visit them. With them went one of the native interpreters whom Pizarro had seized on his first visit to Peru and trained in Spain. As to which one it was, the chroniclers differ: Garcilaso declared that it was Felipillo, Pedro Pizarro that it was Martinillo. Whoever it was, he was not up to the task and must be considered partly responsible for the tragedy which followed for he rendered Spanish words barbarously, giving some of them the opposite meaning to what was intended, so that he not only upset the Inca but angered the Spaniards. Whichever interpreter it was also found it difficult, after two years' absence, to render the speech of the Inca adequately and his mistranslations irritated Atahualpa: 'what does this fellow mean stammering from one word to another and from one mistake to the next as if he were dumb?'[4]

The Inca said that he knew that the Spaniards were gods, sons of Viracocha, that is, and messengers from the long-lost god king Pachacuti, and that their arrival had been foreshadowed by his father, Huayna Capac. So he, Atahualpa, had decreed that no one should take up arms against them. All the same, he wondered why the Spaniards were always talking of perpetual peace while often killing people. For example, he had heard from Marcavilca, the chief of the Poechos on the river Zuracan, how Pizarro had put several chiefs into chains.[5]

Hernando Pizarro replied by saying that his brother Francisco loved Atahualpa. That was why he had gone so far to find him. He wanted Atahualpa to know that, if any enemy should appear, he, Francisco Pizarro, would send ten horsemen to destroy them. That should be adequate. Even the turbulent tribe, the Chachapoyas, would be beaten easily.[6]

At this, Atahualpa invited the Spaniards to drink *chicha* with him and Hernando accepted, comforted by this sign that the new world had something at least in common with the old. Atahualpa also asked the visitors if they would like to stay the night, but they refused, explaining that they had to return to their friends in Cajamarca. Atahualpa said that they and those friends could stay in the centre of Cajamarca, where there were three large dormitories which might suit them.

Before they left the spa, Hernando performed in front of the Inca on a small horse which had been trained to rear. Like most of Pizarro's horses, this beast was small, of Arab stock from Andalusia, hardy and intelligent. Atahualpa was very interested. The other Hernando, Hernando de Soto, gave the Inca a ring from his finger as a sign of peace. Atahualpa promised to pay the Spaniards a return visit the following day, with an escort of several thousand men. Pedro Pizarro commented that one or two of Atahualpa's followers who had shown signs of fear were executed 'to encourage the others'.[7]

On the return of Hernando Pizarro's mission, he and his brother Francisco examined the main square in Cajamarca. Each side was about 200 yards long. On three sides there were low buildings, each with twenty gates. The fourth side had a low wall of adobe with a tower and gate in the centre. Pizarro and his men moved into the buildings on the first three sides but left the fourth unattended.[8]

The Spaniards present at Cajamarca have been carefully studied by James Lockhart in an admirable work.[9] Most knew something of fighting and knew something of horses, but only two or three had any experience of war in Europe: Hernando Pizarro, Candia from Crete, perhaps Martín de Florencia, perhaps also Francisco Pizarro who, late in life, claimed to have had some kind of European military experience.[10] Of the hundred or so men whose past is known, about half had been in the Indies for five or more years. All the captains (Pizarro, Soto, Benalcázar) had been there for twenty or more years, while Cristóbal de Mena and Juan de Salcedo had been there for ten years. Most of those who had been in the Indies for any length of time had, like Francisco Pizarro and Soto, been companions of Pedrarias. None of the men with Pizarro had been with Cortés in New Spain.[11] Practically nobody except Pizarro himself had spent any time in the West Indies. Most of the rank and file were in their twenties, but the captains were mostly in their thirties; Candia said that he was forty. Pizarro was exceptional: having been born about 1479, he was in his fifties.

Of those whose origins we know something, thirty-six came from Extremadura (fourteen from Trujillo), thirty-four came from Andalusia (mostly Seville), seventeen were from old Castile and fifteen from new Castile. Two had Italian surnames (Pinelo, Catano) but, by that time, many men with such names were considered Spanish: the Pinelos had been major entrepreneurs in Seville for two generations; almost certainly they were merchants as well as soldiers. The men with the grandest names were Juan Morgovejo and Juan de Valdivieso, both of whom came from León. There was only one man who certainly had been at a university, the priest Valverde, but Morgovejo, Valdivieso, Estete, Aliaga, Luis Maza and Pedro de Barrera may also have done so. So perhaps had Hernando Pizarro. About three quarters of this Spanish army were literate: 108 could sign their names, 33 could not; perhaps 36 out of the 168 were hidalgos and could read and write. One in ten were notaries. Two seem to have had Muslim blood: Juan García and Miguel Ruiz. Four may have been *conversos*, including Juan de Barbarán, from Illescas between Madrid and Toledo, and Jerónimo de Aliaga. There seems to have been a small unit of maybe thirty African slaves at Pizarro's orders.

The Spaniards in Cajamarca did not know what their plan for the following day should be. Pedro Pizarro wrote of real doubt among the rank and file: 'we took many opinions,' he said,

> as to what should be done. All were full of fear, because we were so few and so far away from home that we could not be reinforced. All assembled in the Governor's [i.e. Pizarro's] quarters to debate what should be done next day. There was [in this discussion] no distinction between great men and unimportant ones, nor between foot soldiers and horsemen. All carried out their sentry duties fully armed. On that night all were gentlemen. The Spaniards had no knowledge whatever as to how the Indians would fight.[12]

At the same time Miguel de Estete thought that the 'campfires of the Indian army [being so many] were a terrible sight. Most were on the hillside and they seemed like a star-studded sky.'[13] There were moments of alarm, even anxiety, effectively contained by Pizarro's comforting self-confidence.

John Hemming suggests that it was agreed among the Spaniards that Governor Pizarro himself should decide on the spur of the moment the course of action to be taken the next day.[14] It seems likely, though, that the brothers Pizarro had in truth already decided what to do. They remembered Cortés's successful seizure of Montezuma. Surely they had decided to act similarly in respect of Atahualpa?

Probably Pizarro wanted Atahualpa to be absolutely at his disposal. He had a dais made for the Inca to sit upon: 'He would be asked to sit there in the square of Cajamarca and then order his men to return to their camp.'[15]

Pizarro prepared also for a battle. He organized his modest cavalry in two groups, one under his brother Hernando, the other under Soto.[16] Candia was to control the artillery as well as a detachment of trumpeters.

Pizarro himself, always a foot soldier, would lead the infantry with his brother Juan as his deputy. When Atahualpa arrived in the square, Candia was to fire his guns and have trumpets blown. At that signal, the cavalry, bells attached to the bridles of the horses, would ride out of the long building where they stood in readiness.

Naturally things did not go according to plan. Atahualpa made no appearance in the morning. Indeed he did not come to Cajamarca till the late afternoon, as the sun was sinking. He was accompanied by about 500 men – so it was said – carrying small battle axes, slings and pouches full of stones under their tunics.[17] Adorned with jewels (including emeralds round his neck) and many highly coloured parrot feathers the Inca was carried on a litter with silver ends. The work of carrying the litter was performed by about eighty nobles – that is the Castilian estimate – surrounded by others in chequered clothing who were busy singing and sweeping away rubbish in front of the Inca, including straw and feathers.[18] These nobles were armed with slings. The lord of Chincha, a prominent courtier, was present too, also it seems on a litter. Pedro Pizarro reflected that it was 'a marvel to see how the sun glittered' on the gold and silver of the litter of Atahualpa. He had explained to his court that the Spaniards were ambassadors of God and so it was not necessary to carry offensive arms.

Only one Spaniard came to greet the Inca: Hernando de Aldana, an Extremeño from Valencia de Alcántara, close to the Portuguese frontier, who had already learned a little Quechua – to Atahualpa's astonishment. But shortly the Dominican Fray Vicente de Valverde also came out to address Atahualpa through the interpretation either of Felipillo or Martinillo, probably the first. One native source explained that Atahualpa was surprised by Valverde's uncouth appearance: perhaps he had not been able to shave for a time.[19] The Dominican gave Atahualpa in effect a rough version of the famous Requirement giving a short history of Christianity, and insisted that the Inca should begin to pay tribute to the Emperor Charles V and become his vassal. He should hand over his kingdom to him and repudiate his gods. Valverde also said: 'If you obstinately seek to resist, you may rest assured that you and all your Indians will be destroyed by our arms, even as the Pharaoh of old and all his host perished in the Red Sea.'[20] Presumably that abstruse biblical reference was not understood by the unfortunate Inca.

There followed a moment of confusion. According to Garcilaso de la

Vega, Valverde by mistake dropped his day-book and his cross. Pedro Pizarro, however, said that Atahualpa had asked to see these objects and, unable to open the book, perhaps because it was locked, threw it on to the ground. Or did he throw it to his relations? Anyway, Atahualpa fumbled and this gave the Christians what they later considered a good excuse for their extraordinary conduct.[21]

Candia's moment had come. He fired two guns, the trumpets were sounded. The cavalry streamed out of their quarters at a gallop. The infantry followed, their steel swords mercilessly active. Though they were in a vast majority over the foreigners, the Indians had no idea of what to do. Most panicked, broke through the adobe wall on the square's fourth side and fled into the country. The Spanish horsemen followed and caused many further deaths. In the square, hundreds were quickly killed. No Spaniards appear to have died, but the Indians slaughtered were without number: Garcilaso believed 5,000 Indians died that afternoon. Other Spanish chroniclers made similar estimates: Trujillo thought in terms of 8,000, Ruiz de Arce 7,000, Mena 6,000–7,000, Xerez 2,000.[22] If we accept the lowest estimate, Xerez's, it still must seem a vast number to be killed by fewer than 200 Europeans.

Atahualpa was not killed but captured by Pizarro himself, having been wounded by Miguel de Estete, the notary from Santo Domingo de Silos, who had wanted to kill the Inca with a knife.[23] Almost all the nobility of old Peru was killed, however, and Atahualpa, the Inca, became a frightened prisoner, held at first in the temple of the Sun and then in Pizarro's own lodgings in one of the palaces in the square.

The explanation for this massacre must be sought in the mood of anxiety and apprehension among the Spaniards who, even outnumbered, believed that they had to fight in order to live. They felt extreme unease when surrounded by a large horde of a quite different race from themselves. Thereafter they assumed that violence worked, and that terrible day in the square of Cajamarca was not forgotten. Indeed it would be repeated. The barbarity of the Spaniards was due to their fear, their isolation and their uncertainty, but that does not justify their disgraceful behaviour, for which Francisco Pizarro must take full responsibility. His achievement was, it is true, a triumph of European warfare. Nevertheless the probability is that even Xerez exaggerated and that casualties did not exceed 1,000 at most.

21

The end of Atahualpa

*It is better for a ruler to be feared than loved. Better to rely on
punishment than considerateness.*

Machiavelli, *Discourses*

It must seem improbable that anything new can be said of the imprisonment of Atahualpa, last independent Inca in Peru. Such great historians
as Prescott and Hemming have admirable pages on this matter in their
famous books. Macaulay in an essay of 1840 pushed aside any such
pretensions when he made his famous comment that every schoolboy
knew who strangled him.[1] Yet little is clear in history.

Atahualpa was afraid that he would be killed the day following his
capture (13 November 1532). He was led to think that the Pizarros and
their expedition really favoured his defeated brother Huascar.[2] That
explained to him what had occurred the previous day. Atahualpa realized
that he had been deceived by his agent, Apoo, about the Spaniards' capacity to fight. Having been fully informed by Apoo, and others, of the
Spaniards' preoccupation with gold, he told the interpreter Martinillo
that he would give Pizarro a quantity of gold and silver. Pizarro came to
ask how much that would be. Extremeños such as Pizarro liked to have
such questions clear. Atahualpa replied that he would fill the room where
they were talking with gold 'as high as he could reach with his hand on
the wall'.[3] He made 'a line on the wall' (*hizo una raya en la pared*).[4] This
room was apparently 22 feet long by 17 feet wide by 11 ½ feet high.
That would mean a gift of 3,000 cubic feet.[5] This present would be procured in two months. An *escribano* (notary) wrote everything down
(was it Francisco de Xerez?).[6] Pizarro seems to have promised Atahualpa
his life if these undertakings were fulfilled but this detail seems a little

unclear, as events were to show.[7] Perhaps that was merely the implication of Pizarro's comments.

The Spaniards settled down to wait. Some went with Hernando de Soto to see again Atahualpa's camp, which they found full of troops behaving as if nothing had happened. Instructed by the Inca, they made the sign of the cross as a mark of surrender. Soto and his men ransacked the Inca's camp at Cajamarca and seized what is said to have been 80,000 pesos of gold, 7,000 silver marks and fourteen emeralds.[8] These thefts were independent of the promises to fill the room where Atahualpa was. A little later, three Spaniards set off for Cuzco, of which Pizarro and his friends by now had heard a great deal. These were Martín Bueno, Pedro Martín de Moguer and Juan de Zárate. They were carried in hammocks by Indians on Atahualpa's orders.[9] At the same time, Atahualpa had established his general Quizquiz also at Cuzco to ensure the collection of the ransom – if that is what it was. Publicly he continued to conduct himself as the leader of the empire, consulting advisers, appointing new officials (necessary after the killings in the square), receiving messengers from the outer provinces, issuing orders. The mood was much as it had been in New Spain in November 1519 after the kidnapping of Montezuma; except that, at that stage, Cortés had killed no one.

The Spaniards reached Cuzco after a journey of two months.[10] They were lodged in a round-towered palace known as Huayna Capac (the building was called after the man; it was later replaced by the Jesuit building). They found a great deal of treasure.[11] The Peruvian general Quizquiz had 30,000 men in the capital. Another general Chalcuchima was at Jauja with 35,000 men. Atahualpa had asked these soldiers to guarantee the safety of the Spaniards on their journey. He had also ordered that the gold was to be taken from the temple of the Sun in the capital, though nothing which had anything to do with Huayna Capac was to be touched. The Spaniards who were there removed 700 gold plates from the temple with crossbars which they had brought with them. Each plate was about three or four palms long, each weighed 4½ pounds.[12] The Spaniards seized a sacrificial gold altar weighing 19,000 pesos and a gold fountain weighing 12,000 pesos.[13] Of course they did not neglect to take possession formally of Cuzco, 'the navel of the world', as it was known in Quechua, in the name of the Emperor Charles.

Yet one more expedition was that of Francisco's tough legitimate brother, Hernando, to Pachacamac, passing near what would become the city of Lima. He arrived on 5 February 1533. He was accompanied by two of Atahualpa's captains, the Inca Mayta and Urcos Guaranga, who told the conquistadors of the whereabouts of a large temple there on top of a stepped pyramid of adobe.[14] Miguel de Estete recalled the shrine in the heart of the temple being a small room of cane wattle characterized by posts decorated with gold and silver leaf. But on top of the pyramid was the kind of rough, small, dirty cavern such as the conquistadors in New Spain had encountered on the summit of the pyramids in Mexico/Tenochtitlan. There was a post in the centre of the cavern on top of which there had been placed the uncouth head of a man. Hernando Pizarro stole a quantity of gold from there, then destroyed the shrine. But he also spent some time looking for further treasure which he believed had been hidden in the vicinity. He apparently had the support of Atahualpa for these actions, since the Inca was angry with the priests and gods of Pachacamac because they had falsely predicted that Huayna Capac would recover from his last illness, that Huascar would defeat Atahualpa and that Atahualpa himself would be well advised to fight, not to welcome, the Christians.[15]

This journey was of considerable importance for in the course of it, Hernando Pizarro found sweet potatoes for the first time, saw holes in the ground being made by foot-powered ploughs, and observed thatched huts and terraces in the valley. Returning, he encountered the Peruvian general Chalcuchima at Jauja. They had several hours of conversation. Hernando explained that Atahualpa himself wanted Chalcuchima to return with him. The general said that, if he were to leave Jauja, it would declare for Huascar. But the next day he unwisely changed his mind and agreed to go to Cajamarca with Hernando. These Spaniards also travelled in hammocks carried by Atahualpa's Indians, who at first gave the horses gold to eat, insisting that that was better for them than the iron bits to which they seemed accustomed. They also sometimes shod the horses with silver.[16]

On his way back to Cajamarca with gold, Hernando Pizarro met Huascar Inca, now a prisoner of Atahualpa. Huascar greeted the Spaniards with enthusiasm and told them that if he, not Atahualpa, had been the victor in the civil war he would have filled the room in Cajamarca to its top, not just up to the line which his brother could reach. Soon after that, Atahualpa had his brother Huascar killed, perhaps because, contrary to what he said to Soto, that prince claimed that some of the gold offered to the Spaniards was his. Pizarro by that time believed that Atahualpa was a bastard younger brother of Huascar.[17]

The Spaniards who remained in Cajamarca became impatient. They passed the time gambling, seducing the virgins of the temple, studying the Inca's personality and observing his grand habits.[18] Some came to think the Inca was 'the most educated and capable Indian who had yet been seen in the Indies'. He 'seemed very anxious to learn our ways', wrote Licenciado Gaspar de Espinosa from Panama 'and even plays chess rather well (*xuega el ajedrez harto bien*). By having him in our power, the whole land is calm.' But he was also cruel and intolerant.

It was once believed that a second expedition, headed by Hernando de Soto and Pedro del Barco, also went to Cuzco. The mistake was made by a chronicler, Agustín de Zárate, and copied by Garcilaso de la Vega. There is no evidence for it.

The Spaniards saw that Atahualpa seemed to be convinced that he was a divine monarch for he was 'in constant touch with the sun, his father. He was guarded by women, he was surrounded by beautiful objects and he and everyone around him wore very fine, soft clothing.'[19] Once Atahualpa challenged Pizarro to put up a powerful Spaniard who could wrestle and defeat one of his own giants. Alonso Díaz, a Spanish blacksmith, did so and 'strangled the giant [only] with a great effort'.[20] Who could say that the chivalrous novels were not being relived? One Spaniard gave Atahualpa a beautiful piece of Venetian glass. The Inca admired it and said that surely nobody but kings would use such a thing in Spain. The donor said that not only kings but common people and lords also would use one. Whereupon Atahualpa deliberately dropped the glass, which, of course, broke.[21]

Provincial leaders continued to call on Atahualpa though he was a captive. The nobility, the *orejones* (ear men), so called since they wore golden plugs in their ears, maintained their privileges and rights: to chew coca, to use special bridges and roads, to enjoy fine cloths, good ornaments and the company of beautiful ladies, and even permission for incest.[22]

The gold for Atahualpa's ransom from Cuzco and Pachacamac began to arrive, usually in large jars capable of carrying two *arrobas* worth, on some days 20,000 pesos, others 30,000, occasionally even 60,000. Completion depended on the collection of sheets of gold from the temple of the Sun at Cuzco. Sometimes the gold came shaped as exquisite and realistic stalks of maize, hibiscus blossoms, palm leaves, trees ripe with fruit or even life-size deer.

These shipments occurred at a fortunate moment for the expedition since, on 15 April, Almagro, the lost ally, at last reached Cajamarca from Panama. He had 150 to 200 men with him, as well as fifty horses. He came angry, impatient and restless. For he appeared at a time when it was too late for him to share in the spoils. Almagro's new force settled down alongside the Pizarros' experienced one, but they remained two separate undertakings with long-term difficulties between them which were to fester. Almagro had one priest with him, Fr Francisco de Morales.[23]

Ten days later, on 25 April, Hernando Pizarro returned from Pachacamac, with a large caravan of treasure, bringing with him the tragic figure of the general Chalcuchima, who remained yet another prisoner of Pizarro. He was constantly asked the whereabouts of his secret supply of gold, but denied that he had any such thing. The general was tortured by Soto, Riquelme and Almagro, to no avail.

In early May the melting down and assaying of the gold in Pizarro's hands began. The total value counted was apparently over 1.5 million pesos' worth, which was far more gold than had ever before been found in the Indies. Francisco Pizarro had decided that all but the king's fifth would go to the 165 men of Cajamarca. The cavalrymen who had been allocated 8,000 pesos each, the infantrymen 4,000. Furious, Almagro argued that he and Francisco Pizarro should each take half of the whole and that then they should give to each of their followers 1,000 or 2,000 pesos.[24] He got nowhere with these reasonable demands. Hernando Pizarro meantime busied himself with the organization of *encomiendas*, the details of which he arranged on 8 May with his majordomo, Crisóstomo de Hontiveros, a native of Ávila and a very skilful accountant.[25] Hernando was always busy with his finances.

In June Pizarro's division of the treasure followed. First, the hoard was parcelled out into shares of 4,440 gold pesos and 181 silver marks, worth altogether 5,345 golden pesos (at that time a peso of gold was reckoned as being worth 450 maravedís). Indian smiths did the melting down of the priceless gold and silver objects in nine large forges under the direction of a notary from Córdoba, Gonzalo de Pineda, now a close adviser to Francisco Pizarro and presumably connected with the successful mercantile Italo-Sevillian family of Pineda in Seville.

Over eleven tons of precious metals were fed into the forges to produce eventually 13,420 pounds of 22½ carat gold and 26,000 pounds of silver. Much of this had been in the form of jewellery whose details are now lost. Two hundred and seventeen shares were carefully divided according to Pizarro's judgement of the contribution of the individual concerned. The rough idea was that an infantryman would receive one share, a cavalryman two, and captains more still but, in the end, all was decided by a committee of *repartidores* headed by Francisco and Hernando Pizarro, including Pineda, the master of the forges; Pedro Díaz, a silversmith who weighed the silver, though he had not been himself in the fighting at Cajamarca; and two other captains, Hernando de Soto and Miguel de Estete, whom we have met as a chronicler. These men ensured that there would be no treasure for Almagro nor for any of his followers.

The apportionment was thus nothing if not biased: Francisco Pizarro received thirteen shares, as well as 'the Governor's jewel', Atahualpa's golden seat worth two shares. Hernando Pizarro received seven shares, Juan Pizarro two and a half shares and his brother Gonzalo the same. These allocations were enough to make the people concerned very rich. In round terms, 135 and a fraction of the 217 shares went to the 62 horsemen, 81 to 105 infantrymen. The Pizarro brothers received 24 shares out of the 217. Almost certainly some of the gold and silver allocations were left out of the calculations.[26] Benalcázar had a small share but no doubt he received more than was officially registered. Pizarro also divided among his followers the Indian chiefs and all who were encamped at Cajamarca and whose lands would soon become *encomiendas*.

Soon after the division of the treasure, Hernando Pizarro left Peru for Spain to tell of the great conquest which had been carried out. He took with him a substantial quantity of gold and silver and 100,000 castellanos for the king which, his enemies were quick to point out, was less than half the royal fifth. He carried also thirty-eight beautiful vessels of gold and forty-eight of silver. He also took fifteen or twenty men with him; Francisco Pizarro prevented more from leaving on the ground that he could not afford their loss. Of those who were left, seven were older men and could not be expected to last long in Peru – though none was as old as Francisco Pizarro. One or two were sent home as possible critics or even enemies (Cristóbal de Mena of Ciudad Real, a friend of Almagro but a leader of the expedition of Pizarro to begin with; and

Juan de Salcedo, a captain of infantry from Talavera de la Reina).[27] Some who went back with Hernando did so for precisely opposite reasons: that they were friends of the Pizarros and could help to propagate their cause; for example, Juan Cortés of Trujillo, who had been Pizarro's bodyguard, *escudero*, at Cajamarca. He had already shown that he had a head for figures and he now returned to manage the Pizarros' money in Trujillo. There was also Martín Alonso, who was probably a relation of the younger Pizarros and who came from La Zarza, the village owned by the Pizarros near Trujillo. He was a reliable dependant of that family, and received a double share of gold and silver.

When Atahualpa heard that Hernando was returning to Spain his heart sank. He had just seen a large green and black comet which he believed meant that his death was certain. He had been on easy terms with Hernando and thought that nothing would go wrong for him if he were still second-in-command. He had no such confidence in Almagro, nor in the royal treasurer, Alonso de Riquelme. But though those men were unhelpful to Atahualpa's cause, his downfall may have been due to the Peruvian interpreter, Felipillo. By that time Atahualpa believed that he should be set free because, of course, the great 'ransom' had been paid. At the very least, he said, he should be allowed to go to eat and drink with his subjects. But Felipillo had apparently fallen in love with one of the Inca's favourite ladies, a certain Cuxirimay, 'very fair skinned and beautiful', and wanted him out of the way for that reason. He now is said to have alleged falsely that the Inca was planning to escape and organize a new campaign against the Spaniards, with his surviving general in Quito, Rumiñavi.

Pizarro is believed to have taken this tale seriously. Sentries were doubled. He had made plans to go to Cuzco. But how would the Inca be guarded while the Spanish army was on its way? Could he be left with a guard in Cajamarca? Surely, that would be difficult to arrange. But to take Atahualpa to Cuzco would also have risks. Felipillo was incompetent as an interpreter. For example, he did not understand Christianity and there were few direct translations of the holy words used in connection with it. Yet he was supposed to explain the Gospel to the Inca.

Pizarro sent a small detachment of his followers towards Quito under the command of Soto, with the chronicler Estete and three other conquistadors – Rodrigo Orgóñez, Pedro Ortiz de Cariaga and Lope Vélez de Guevara. The first was apparently a *converso* veteran of the

Italian wars as well as a lieutenant of Almagro's;[28] the second was a combatant at Cajamarca and probably a native of Ampuero in Cantabria; the third was a native of the town of Palos and an admirable horseman who had been in many of the combats of the 1520s in Central America before coming to Peru as a companion of Soto. The aim of this little expedition was to see if Rumiñavi was really on his way with an army towards Cajamarca.[29]

These adventurers would soon return with the news that there were no signs whatever of Rumiñavi being on the move. But in their absence, the rumours of Atahualpa's 'rebellion' grew in intensity. Almagro made no bones about being in favour of killing him. Would it not be the easiest way out of a dilemma? But the Inca argued that the Spaniards were behaving foolishly, for there was not an Indian in the country whom they could hope to manage without his assistance. Since he, the Inca, was their prisoner, what did they fear? If the Spaniards were motivated by a desire for more gold (and Almagro, having been left out of the division of April, certainly was), he would give them twice what they had already received. Pedro Pizarro says that Atahualpa saw the governor – that is how Francisco Pizarro was now always designated – weep: he could not give Atahualpa his life because he could neither be guarded indefinitely nor released.[30]

The Inca submitted to a trial of a sort. Pizarro and Almagro were the judges, Sancho de Cuéllar, presumably a member of that family of conquistadors from the city of Diego Velázquez, was the notary. Atahualpa was condemned to death by Pizarro who, allegedly against his will, commanded that he should be killed and his body burned.[31]

The Spaniards were divided about the wisdom of the judgement. At least fifty expeditionaries were hostile. Some of them had wanted the clever young lawyer Juan de Herrera as Atahualpa's advocate.

Atahualpa heard his sentence with resignation. He was told by the priest Valverde of the inestimable benefits which he would encounter in heaven, and how he would save his soul for eternity if he were to ask to be received as a Christian.

On 26 July 1533, trumpets greeted Atahualpa as he was brought into the centre of the same main square of Cajamarca where he had been captured the previous year. He was tied to a stake. Valverde briefly instructed him in the articles of the Christian faith and the Inca then formally requested baptism and that was administered to him by Valverde, who named him 'Francisco'.[32] Then he was garrotted. Pedro Pizarro explained that Atahualpa had told his wives and other Peruvians that, if he was not burned, he would eventually return to them. He left his small sons to be looked after by Pizarro. Afterwards, two of Atahualpa's sisters 'went about giving utterance to lamentations accompanied by the beating of drums and by singing and by accounts of their royal husband-brother'. They explained to Pedro Pizarro that, since the Inca had not been burned, he would return to them, but Pizarro told them that the dead do not return. 'They wailed till all the *chicha* was drunk.'[33] Almagro's priest, Fr Morales, presided and took off Atahualpa's head band indicating royalty.

Pizarro organized a solemn funeral. The Inca was buried in the newly built church of Cajamarca. But the manner of his death excited an immediate argument. Soto, for example, when he returned from his journey to Quito, was furious that such an important decision should have been carried out in his absence. He thought the Inca should have been sent alive to the Emperor Charles. Espinosa, the clever governor in Panama, later wrote that the Inca's guilt should have been established clearly before he was killed. He believed it would have been better if he had been exiled to another Spanish territory: Panama, for example, where he could have been treated as if he had been a great noble of Castile.[34] Others thought that it would have been easier to convert Peru to Christianity if the Inca had not been killed – if, indeed, his baptism had not been followed by his execution. Later too, the Emperor Charles wrote to Pizarro: 'we note what you say about the execution of the cacique Atahualpa'. Charles accepted that Atahualpa had probably ordered a hostile mobilization. Nevertheless 'we have been displeased by the death of Atahualpa since he was a monarch and particularly since it was done in the name of justice'.[35]

22

News from Peru

I reached this port of Sanlúcar today, Wednesday January 14,
from New Castile which is the land which Francisco Pizarro con-
quered on behalf of Your Majesty. I have to inform Your Majesty
of what has been done in that country to serve you. I bring for
Your Majesty your share, some 100,000 castellanos [of gold] and
five million of silver.

Hernando Pizarro, 14 January 1534

In the winter of 1533–4 the standing of the Spanish empire had at first
seemed low. Charles the emperor and king was in Monzón in December
with the Cortes of Aragon, which always met in that remote valley. The
meeting lasted so long that neither king nor court reached the local
capital of Saragossa till the last day of the year.

The Council of the Indies told the emperor that, in Hispaniola, the
reinvigorated Fray Bartolomé de las Casas, now an active Dominican,
emerging from several years of retreat in his monastery, was refusing
absolution to *encomenderos* on grounds of their heretical status. They
also informed Charles that Las Casas had persuaded a colonist on his
deathbed to leave his goods to the Indians as restitution for past wrongs.
In Cuba there was a rising of black slaves in the region of Bayamo. In
New Spain the supreme court was in control, for a viceroy had not been
named. The condition of the new realm was much superior to what it
had been under Guzmán; there was a large Spanish population but it
was difficult to imagine the place's future.

Some aggressive expeditions were still proceeding. For example, in
October 1533 Gerónimo Dortal, veteran of Ordaz's journey on the Orinoco, who had up till then been responsible for a small stretch of the

coast of Venezuela, filled three ships with men in Spain, and horses and weapons bought in the Canaries, and set out aiming to pass by the Gulf of Paria and, first sailing up the Orinoco, reach the river Meta, which he was convinced was the key to the world of gold which he thought of as 'Eldorado'.[1] Then it became generally known that, at the end of 1533, a new armada had been sent from Hispaniola to the *tierra firme* by Judge Zuazo, Juan de Vadillo and Rodrigo de Infante to look for slaves. These were all responsible settlers, especially the first-named, who had now been in the Indies, in one position after another, since 1517. Vadillo too was a *licenciado* and judge;[2] Rodrigo de Infante was a *converso* who was already a judge in Hispaniola and would soon be interim governor of Santa Marta.

Spain was then stirred into a new mood of enthusiasm for the Indies by the unexpected arrival in Seville of the *nao María del Campo*, owned by Soto and Hernán Ponce de León, with Hernando Pizarro on board. On 9 January 1534 the chronicler Cieza, still a boy, saw many pieces of gold and silver being unloaded from that ship on the Arenal outside the city. Cobos ordered the Casa de la Contratación to impound all the gold and silver. Hernando is said to have brought 153,000 pesos of gold and 5,048 marks of silver for the king alone. Private soldiers sent back 310,000 pesos. In fact, between the end of 1533 and the middle of 1534, ships arrived in Seville bringing over 700,000 pesos in gold and nearly 50,000 marks in silver belonging to the Crown or to private persons.[3] Hernando went to Toledo, taking samples of his gold and silver jewellery, also some unusual animals such as llamas and even nuggets of gold. He met the Emperor Charles and the court, first at Calatayud. The king and Cobos ordered all the jewels to be melted down. Hernando expostulated. Charles agreed to exhibit the treasure for some weeks but no longer.[4]

Henceforward the magic glint of Peruvian treasure lit the imagination of king, courtiers and common people. Henceforward, too, there was a general disposition to believe all that was said of the New World. One historian wrote that, if seventy ships had arrived at Laredo with 10,000 Amazons on board, to seek fathers for their children to whom they would give 50 ducats, with the girls being sent back to the New World, the boys to stay in Spain, the tale would have been believed. Meantime the treasure of the Pizarros was looked after by two faithful friends, Martín Alonso and Juan Cortés. In 1534 two new chivalric novels, *Lidamor de Escocia* by Juan de Córdoba, and *Tristan el Joven* by María Luzdivina Cuesta Torre, were published in Castile. It was not easy to distinguish between what was said in those books and what was reported by Hernando Pizarro, whose account was, if anything, the more unbelievable. Hernando asked the king many things for his brother, for example (an echo of what had been granted to Cortés) the service of 20,000 Indians for himself and his descendants in perpetuity, and the title of marquis, without it being evident of what place exactly he was to be such.[5]

Charles the emperor was preparing in Barcelona for the conquest of Tunis – an expedition which would not have been possible if the monarch had not received so much gold from Peru. For example, twenty-two cartloads of gold arrived in Barcelona from Seville on 29 April, and twenty heavily laden mules came on 22 May. The Genoese bankers who had advanced credit were also repaid in American gold. The consequence was that the expedition to Africa was the most impressive ever mounted by the Christian powers in the western Mediterranean.

The emperor's brother Fernando, the ruler of Austria, always interested in the Indies, was given a silver nugget worth 212 castellanos by Cobos the same year.[6] The penniless courtier Enríquez de Guzmán, who set out from Sanlúcar for the Indies in September 1533, was suddenly supposed to have for the first time made a wise decision.[7]

Those were the years, too, when Mercator and Gaspar van der Neuvel were busy sketching their idea of a new printed terrestrial globe – their intention was to 'publish a globe or sphere of the whole world on which the recently discovered islands and lands will be added . . .'[8] The cosmographers would be protected from copyists. To fulfil his charter's instruction, Mercator had to make a sphere the likes of which nobody at court would have seen before, a globe of exquisite beauty crammed with the latest geographical data: new coastlines, hundreds of place names, even stars.

The new enthusiasm for the Peruvian adventure was not confined to the mother country; it shook the Caribbean too. Antonio López wrote that Yucatan was emptying because of the news from Peru. Officials in Puerto Rico explained that the reports were so extraordinary that even men of fifty who had settled down to their modest *encomiendas* as if their highest lot was indeed to plant the bergamot, became suddenly restless. In Santa Marta, the governor, García de Lerma, wrote that 'the greed of Peru was gripping everyone'. Greed was to be found in Spain also. Thus Hernando Pizarro was allowed by the royal officials to take some of the pieces which he had brought to show Charles V. But the latter again confirmed the order for the smelting down of almost everything.[9]

The Council of the Indies proclaimed that no one could leave for Peru unless he were a substantial merchant or a married man ready to take his wife with him. But this rule was to no avail. No one obeyed it.

Among the most restless was Pedro de Alvarado, the second-in-command of Cortés in New Spain, now the governor of Guatemala, who had been told by a friend of his, García Holguín, a Cacereño who had played an important part in the last stages of the conquest of Tenochtitlan, that the possibilities for enrichment in Peru were limitless. Alvarado was quick to take action and, by 23 January 1534, he had gathered an expedition which he hoped would share in the pleasures of the great Peruvian adventure. He left *La Posesión*, his *finca* (estate) in Guatemala, with twelve ships, on which he planned to carry 500 Spaniards from his province, including 119 horsemen and 100 crossbowmen, to sail down the west coast of Central America to Peru. He was said to have also taken several thousand Indians from Guatemala. His chief pilot was a typical seaman of that day, Juan Fernández, who combined low birth, illiteracy and intelligence. He had earlier been 'captain-master' to the Pizarros on their galleon the *San Cristóbal*.[10] As his chief chaplain Alvarado took Fray Marcos de Niza, an intelligent Franciscan who had been born in Nice and who had already interested himself in learning several native languages. He had been in Santo Domingo and Nicaragua before joining Alvarado in Guatemala.

The expedition landed in Ecuador in late January 1534. By then the condition of the old Peruvian kingdom had fundamentally changed. First, the people of Cajamarca had witnessed the coronation of a new Inca, Tupac Huallpa, a younger brother of Huascar and Atahualpa, in that same main square of the town where the latter had died. Under the patronage of Francisco Pizarro and his brothers, the chiefs of the country assembled, wearing white plumes. A great feast followed, accompanied by singing, dancing and drinking of *chicha* on an epic scale. Francisco Pizarro wore a white silk shirt, the Spanish royal standard was raised and the Requirement was read out by Fr Valverde.

Then, on 11 August, Pizarro led the main body of his followers from Cajamarca on the way to Cuzco. Almagro accompanied him, the force totalling perhaps 350,[11] including most of Almagro's men. It also included, as a captive, the Inca general Chalcuchima. A few Spaniards were left behind to maintain the royal presence in Cajamarca, including the notary Sancho de Cuéllar, Francisco Chaves, of a family in Trujillo connected to the Pizarros, and Hernando de Haro, the last two of whom were known to have opposed the execution of Atahualpa.[12]

Pizarro's journey was by Cajabamba, Huamachuco and the valley of Huaylas where, on 31 August, the expeditionaries crossed a gorge using one of the Incas' best suspension bridges. Pedro Sánchez de Hoz, a notary whom Pizarro had named as his secretary, described how the bridge trembled, how the horses were afraid – as indeed were some of the conquistadors. They waited a little more than a week at this bridge to ensure the passage of the entire expedition and the equipment, then marched on to Recuay below Mount Huascarán and continued, via Jauja and Bombón on Lake Chinancocha.

There Pizarro divided his army. He decided to press ahead himself to Cuzco with seventy-five to a hundred horsemen and thirty foot, a force which included Almagro, Juan and Gonzalo Pizarro, Soto and Candia, as well as the well-guarded Chalcuchima; and he left behind the artillery with the infantry, the tents and such treasure as they had obtained on the journey. The command of this reserve force would lie with the royal treasurer, Riquelme.

Pizarro was no horseman but he survived well enough in this new venture all the same. A local Indian commander killed several of his rivals, Pedro Pizarro reported, by making these leaders put stones on their heads which were then hit by another stone, so flattening the heads 'as if they were tortillas'.[13] There was a skirmish with Indians when the Spanish advantage in weapons (swords, steel-tipped lances, armour, horses) as usual told against the Peruvians' superiority in numbers and local knowledge backed by slings with stones, javelins, maces and stone clubs. Just short of the settlement known as Bombón, Riquelme founded a city at Jauja with an initial establishment of eighty citizens from men of his command. He had with him the new Inca, Tupac Huallpa, but he died – poisoned by Chalcuchima, according to the Inca's friends. The inhabitants there were busy hunting down the followers of Atahualpa.[14]

Pizarro's journey was a remarkable one. He took the route to Cuzco of his brother Hernando earlier in the year, and some who had been with Hernando accompanied Francisco. They crossed magnificent wild land and came to several fine bridges. Pedro Sancho de Hoz recalled a stop at Parcos at the summit of the mountainside. From there Pizarro divided his men yet again, sending the best horsemen ahead under the resourceful Soto. This group included Pedro Pizarro, the future chronicler, Diego de Trujillo and Juan Ruiz de Arce, as well as Rodrigo Orgóñez, Juan Pizarro de Orellana and Juan de Pancorvo. Of these men, Diego de Trujillo came from the town of that name and was very much a dependant of the Pizarro family, having been recruited there in 1529 by Francisco; Pancorvo must have come to Peru with Almagro; and Pizarro de Orellana was another distant cousin of the Pizarro family, a hidalgo, and, like Diego de Trujillo, had been born in Trujillo where he had been recruited by Francisco Pizarro in 1529. He had been with Hernando Pizarro to Pachacamac and recalled the hillside there glittering with gold. Francisco Pizarro remained in a new rearguard with Almagro, Pedro Sancho de Hoz and Miguel de Estete. The small Spanish force was now strung out over 200 miles in four groups, scarcely a wise disposition.

Soto had been determined to be the first Spaniard of the new expedition to enter Cuzco. Pedro Pizarro said that he had 'the evil intention' of wishing to do this.[15] But to achieve it he had to cross the canyon of the Apurimac where, at Vilcaconga, he was attacked and nearly destroyed by an Indian army under Quizquiz, who had by then learned much about Spanish tactics. The Spaniards lost five men immediately.[16] They would have been in grave difficulties had it not been for the arrival of reinforcements under Almagro. His trumpeter, Pedro de Alconchel, cheered them greatly with his horn as it resounded, like that of Roland, across the high valleys. This was the most serious battle which the Spaniards had had to fight since the death of Atahualpa. (Alconchel had been one of Pizarro's recruits in Extremadura, though he came from La Garganta de Béjar, in the Sierra de Gredos.)

Pizarro had been encouraged by the discovery of several slabs of silver at Andahuaylas. 'While I was looking for maize,' wrote his page Pedro Pizarro, 'I entered by chance a hut where I found these slabs of silver ... ten in number [with] a length of 20 feet each, a width of one foot and a thickness of three fingers. These had been intended to build a house for an idol named Chino.'[17] Afterwards, Pizarro joined Almagro and Soto, and the reconstituted Spanish force of 350 moved on to Jaquijahuana (now Anta) about twenty miles from Cuzco. Here on the river Apurimac, the Pizarros were greeted by Manco Capac, the youngest brother of Huascar and Atahualpa,[18] who gave Francisco Pizarro a golden shirt. The prince also gave a vivid, but surely inaccurate, commentary on the cruelties practised by Atahualpa. This new friendship enabled Pizarro to enter the city of Cuzco with Manco Capac at his side. He imaginatively told Manco that he had come to Peru for no other purpose 'than to free you from the slavery of the men of Quito'.

Atahualpa's general, Quizquiz, remained a threat. When Pizarro saw smoke rising in the distance, he sent horsemen forward to prevent any destruction before he reached the capital. There was a brief skirmish between Quizquiz and Pizarro. The two armies rested at night on two nearby hillsides, but the Indians lost heart for, at dawn, Quizquiz had disappeared.[19] So on 15 November 1533 the Spaniards entered Cuzco without resistance and were well received by such authorities as there were there.[20]

Cuzco, wrote Pizarro's page Pedro Pizarro, lay in a hollow between two ravines through which two brooks ran, though one, which passed through the central plaza, had only a very little water. The city

> was dominated by a strong fortress with terraces and flat places on top of a hill with two high round towers, surrounded by walls of stone so large that it seemed impossible that human hands could have set them in place . . . They were so well fitted together that the point of a pin could not be inserted into a joint.

In this redoubt, Sacsahuaman, 10,000 Indians could be concealed, the place being full of arms, lances, arrows, darts and clubs, as well as helmets and shields. Pizarro's secretary, Sancho de Hoz, thought Cuzco 'so grand and beautiful that it would be worthy of being seen even in Spain since it is filled with palaces of lords. No poor people live there . . . the majority of the houses are of stone. The houses are made with great symmetry.'[21] Cieza de León recorded: 'in all Spain I have seen nothing which can compare with these walls and the laying of their stone'.[22] There were great labyrinths which even Pedro Pizarro, who was there for months, never understood completely.[23]

The journey of the Spaniards, said Murúa, had not been very interesting![24] All the same they now quartered themselves in old Inca palaces with vast halls, central courtyards and impressive stone walls.

Francisco Pizarro, for example, settled in the one-time 'Casana' palace of the Inca Huayn Capac which Garcilaso says was capable of holding 3,000 people. Soto took over Amarucancha, a building of red, white and multi-coloured marble, with two towers and a large, beautiful thatched hall. The young Gonzalo Pizarro took the house of the Inca Yupanqui, while Almagro selected the newest Huascar palace. Valverde, the chaplain of the expedition, installed himself in the palace of Suntur Huasi which eventually became the site of the new Spanish cathedral. All these leaders collected a great deal of treasure in these edifices, this time more silver than gold.[25] They seized women and children. Mancio Sierra de Leguizamón made off with the gold image of the sun from its temple; he lost it in a night of gambling soon after. Most of the Spanish soldiers, however, camped in the main plaza of Aucapata or in a shed nearby. There was looting and ravaging on a large scale.[26]

The temple of the Sun at Coricancha would eventually become the Dominican convent, but the palaces of Hatun Cancha, Hatun Rumiyoc and Pucamara became the stables for the Spanish cavalry.

Pizarro proclaimed Cuzco a Spanish city but he accepted Manco Inca as the ruler of the empire and encouraged the Inca to found an army to defeat Quizquiz. After a few weeks he had what was said to have been 5,000 men who, with the troubleshooter of Spain, Hernando de Soto, soon set off to look for that general. They were actually held in the wild country of Condesuyos on the Apurimac but Quizquiz seems to have been depressed by this third failure to defeat the Spaniards and soon retreated towards Quito, leaving Pizarro in control of Cuzco and its surroundings.[27]

The next manifestation of Spanish power was a denunciation of Chalcuchima by Pizarro, who thought him responsible for the continued restlessness of the Indians. Manco Capac supported this theory and asserted that Chalcuchima had revealed to Quizquiz details of Spanish plans for fighting. He had certainly told Quizquiz that the Spaniards were mortal, that they were wont to dismount in bad passes and even to hand their lances to their servants to be carried. Their horses tired there. So, he said, they should be attacked in such places. Manco Capac handed over to Pizarro three messengers who, he alleged, had taken this news to Quizquiz. Pizarro denounced Chalcuchima, who denied any such contact. But Pizarro believed, probably rightly, that he was lying, and he was accordingly burned to death in the main square of Cuzco. Valverde failed to persuade him to become a Christian first and so be killed without pain.[28]

An early festival in the square at Cuzco was the coronation of Manco Capac as Inca at the end of December 1533. There was the usual ceremony of a parade of mummies, a feast, and much singing and dancing over thirty days, and drums were heard throughout the city at night. The Spaniards were astounded at the drinking by both men and women that resulted in two large drains running with urine throughout the day for a week.[29] This coronation was more traditional and more elaborate than that of the short-lived Inca Tupac Huallpa at Cajamarca, and it lasted much longer. Pizarro used the occasion by ordering Pedro Sancho de Hoz to read out the Requirement once again. The Inca implied that he had understood. Manco Capac drank from a golden cup with Pizarro. He also brought out all the bodies of his ancestors on litters. Once again the Spaniards raised their now famous standard and greeted it with trumpets. The Peruvians sang songs which, among other things, expressed their gratitude to the Spaniards for expelling their Atahualpine enemies. Manco Capac, though he asked for the return of his empire, said that he was entirely happy to let the Spanish priests preach Christianity. Pizarro accepted what Manco Capac said and implored him to wear the traditional scarlet fringe of the Inca in the ceremony.[30]

This kind of festival was a characteristic of the life of the nobility (orejones). There were sometimes festivals with fasting, which meant doing without salt, garlic and chicha, not to speak of walks to see the god Guanacaure, an idol of stone who was worshipped a mile and a half outside the city. Meantime, porters were placed on the main roads outside Cuzco to prevent thefts of gold and silver. Pedro Pizarro described how there were large storehouses for tribute above the city: 'all in such vast quantities that it is hard to imagine how the natives can ever have paid such tribute on so many items'.[31]

Diego de Trujillo, one of Pizarro's most dedicated followers, reported that the priests at the temple of Coricancha reproached him and other Spaniards: 'How dare you enter here?' they demanded. Trujillo explained: 'Anyone who enters here has to fast for a year beforehand, and must enter barefoot, and bear a load; but we Spaniards paid no attention to what was said and went in.'[32]

Pizarro embarked on a division of the spoils of the city of Cuzco. He sought to do this in an orderly manner, as usual reserving a fifth of the treasure for the Crown, which was accumulated in a shed attached to the palace which he had seized and listed by Diego Narváez.

The melting down, the work of Jerónimo de Aliaga, began on 15 December 1533. The treasurer of the expedition, Riquelme, was still at Jauja, otherwise no doubt he would have been in command. Pizarro authorized new gold and silver marks. The value of the treasure seized in Cuzco was even more in aggregate than that which had been gathered for Atahualpa's ransom at Cajamarca. The temple of the Sun had lost a great deal of gold for Atahualpa's ransom, but there was still much left. The conquistadors with Pizarro were astonished at other vast store-houses of several generations' collections of cloaks, weapons, feathers, sandals, knives, beans, shields and cloth. But the golden image of the Sun itself which had been in that edifice was lost for ever.[33] Still, there was plenty of gold left: many storehouses were found with fine clothing, coarser clothes, stores of wheat, coca, sunflowers which looked like pure gold, a very slender feather grown on their breasts by small birds ('hardly larger than a cigar', reported Pedro Pizarro), mantles with mother-of-pearl spangles, sandals, copper bars, golden slippers, lobsters and spiders made of gold, and pitchers of both pottery and gold.

The coronation of Manco Capac was the signal for the establish-ment of large *encomiendas* for the conquistadors in or attached to Cuzco. The conquistadors of Cajamarca – 'first conquerors', as they were known – occupied all the municipal offices; sometimes they received huge benefits. In Cuzco, where there were to be over eighty *encomiendas* in a few years, no one received fewer than 5,000 vassals; one received 40,000.[34]

These dispositions affected Jauja as well as Cuzco. But the former was threatened by Quizquiz and his alarmingly itinerant army. So Soto and Almagro returned to save that staging point, as well as the lives of the treasurer, Riquelme, and his eighty or so men. This relief travelled slowly because Quizquiz had cut many essential bridges, but before Soto and Almagro arrived, Jauja was relieved by the support for Riquelme of 2,000 Huanca Indians who were hostile to Atahualpa and the men of Quito. Still, one Spaniard was killed and almost all the others were wounded, Riquelme included.

Other unexpected help was afforded by Gabriel de Rojas, an old hand in Pedrarias's Nicaragua. He came from the well-known family in Cuéllar whose mansion was next to that of the Velázquezes. Alonso de Mesa, a young conquistador from Toledo (where he had probably been recruited by Pizarro in person), was also helpful. He had joined the expedition in 1529 when barely fifteen years old.[35] These men's small following performed wonders. Rojas also brought the news, both alarming and encouraging to Pizarro's expedition, that Pedro de Alvarado, with his large army, had landed at Puerto Viejo in what is now Ecuador and was striking up towards Quito.[36]

Benalcázar at San Miguel was the most disturbed of Pizarro's men at this news since he was the commander closest to Alvarado. He also had his own plans for the conquest of Quito which – quite without foundation – was assumed to be very rich. He took his own decision and set out from San Miguel for Quito with his 200 experienced foot soldiers and sixty-two horsemen. The Indians were far from quiescent, however, and Atahualpa's general, Rumiñavi, headed a powerful army against Benalcázar.[37] Once again in the conquest of Peru (or in the conquest generally), Indian allies, in this case Cañari Indians, made a major contribution to the Spanish cause. Benalcázar skilfully forced Rumiñavi to a pitched battle at Teocajas on 3 May 1534 in open land where his well-led cavalry could act much as it wished. Rumiñavi had upset what remained of the Inca upper class by drugging them and killing their children. He had women in Quito burned alive for laughing when he described the Spaniards' codpieces.[38] Oviedo reported that 50,000 Indians took part, making many efforts to trick the Spanish horses – traps for horses, for example.

Despite such attacks, Benalcázar's Spaniards reached Quito on 22 June. He was disappointed because Rumiñavi had already seized such treasure as there was there. He had kidnapped surviving members of Atahualpa's family and what was said to have been several thousand other women. He sought to set fire to Quito after he had left it.

Benalcázar conducted himself with his usual ruthlessness: he killed all the women at the village of Quinche, where the men of military age were with Rumiñavi. He was joined by Almagro who, though he criticized him for leaving San Miguel, was pleased that he had conquered Quito and had done so in his, Almagro's, name, as well as that of Pizarro.

Shortly after, Benalcázar was joined by yet a third conquistador army, that of Alvarado, which passed through jungle and across mountains with great difficulty, due to a shortage of food and because of the cold in the high Andes. The coastal Indians whom Alvarado had assembled died in great numbers. His cruelty to the Indians whom he encountered was legendary, for they 'repeatedly tortured Indians in order to be informed of the route'.[39]

Alvarado was eventually faced by Almagro. For a time there was a risk of a battle between the two Spanish armies at Riobamba, but a prolonged discussion convinced Alvarado that he would be unable to prosper, much less emerge as a leading captain, in a Peru which was so much better known by Almagro, the Pizarros and Benalcázar. Much to the surprise of his fellow Spaniards, Alvarado agreed to sell his ships and artillery to the Pizarros for 100,000 castellanos. He would go back to Guatemala but his men would remain in Peru under the command of Almagro and Pizarro. An agreement to this end was reached on 26 August 1534. The two captains then went to Quito where with Benalcázar they founded a new Spanish city.

Almagro and Alvarado went to see Pizarro. On the way they encountered Quizquiz, the morale of whose army collapsed when they heard that Quito was lost. There was a mutiny and Quizquiz was killed by one of his own captains. Benalcázar forced Quizquiz's ex-rival and superior Rumiñavi to take up a fortified position near Pillaro. There the Indians soon dispersed after they had exhausted their supply of missiles. Rumiñavi was betrayed to Benalcázar, whose captains Alonso del Valle and Miguel de la Chica captured him. A third Peruvian commander, Zope Zopahua, was captured on the mountainside and executed in Quito's main square with Rumiñavi.[40]

Alvarado met Pizarro at Pachacamac. After friendly embraces, Pizarro gave Alvarado the promised 100,000 castellanos for his ships and his guns, and offered places to Alvarado's men in his army. Several of Alvarado's relations remained with Pizarro, including his brother, Gómez de Alvarado, who had fought all the way through the campaign in New Spain, and García and Alonso, his nephews. Alonso would play a large part in the politics and combats of Peru in the future. Alvarado then returned to Guatemala after confessing a failure of the first magnitude. It was not something to which the 'son of the Sun' was accustomed. 'What a disgrace for the Alvarados!' commented his cousin Diego, who had been his camp master.

Meanwhile in Peru the allocation of gold and silver continued: many poor conquistadors became newly rich entrepreneurs overnight. Thus, in Cuzco in March 1534, a quantity of silver estimated to be four times what had been distributed in Cajamarca was allocated by Pizarro with the help of Valverde according to their judgement of each soldier's merits, extra shares being given to those who seemed to deserve it. Those who had remained in Jauja and had returned with Benalcázar to San Miguel were included. These decisions were generally accepted as fair by the conquistadors; Francisco Pizarro was even recognized as being just by the Spaniards.

Pizarro went ahead in March 1534 with a ceremony refounding Cuzco as a Spanish city. He divided it among eighty-eight of his soldiers, naming two *alcaldes* and eight councillors. Each soldier would have the ample provision of a length of 200 feet of housing in a street of the city. The founding documents insisted that the Indians should be treated as 'brothers' because they were descended from 'our first ancestors'.

Manco Capac was to be recognized as the leader of the Indians. Pizarro went through the motions of building a city wall and a church from existing material taken from unoccupied palaces and warehouses. At the same time he ordered the Spaniards to stop asking for gold and silver, for he believed that, if they were continually refused, they could be tempted to rebel.

Pizarro and Manco Capac set off back to Jauja on the way to Cajamarca. The former had the idea to found another Spanish city there. He left his brother Juan Pizarro, then twenty-four years of age, as acting governor in Cuzco. The Indians would have Paullu Inca as their leader in Manco Capac's absence; he was a member of the royal family who had decided almost immediately that collaboration with the conquerors was not only desirable but essential.

Francisco Pizarro did establish Jauja as a Spanish city on 25 April 1534. He distributed the property among fifty-three Spaniards who had been there a year by the chance of having been left in the place by Pizarro on his first outward journey to Cuzco.

Pizarro went on in August 1534 to the ancient site of Pachacamac to seek the Indian treasure said to have been hidden there. On his way back, he saw Indian porters struggling to carry European supplies up to the conquistadors in Cuzco. There and then he decided to move the capital to the coast. It was a decision of genius. He discussed the idea in Jauja and selected a point named Lima at the mouth of the river Rimac.

To begin with it was known as Ciudad de los Reyes, City of the Kings, because it was founded soon after Epiphany, on 17 January 1535.[41]

At the same time, the governor gave a general licence to Spaniards to leave Peru and about sixty conquistadors did avail themselves of the opportunity to return. They did so as rich men, for some went back with 40,000 pesos, none with less than 20,000.[42] Their return journey was in some cases a triumphal progress, for some stopped in the isthmus or at one or other of the Caribbean islands. They dazzled those whom they met with their golden jars and figurines, and their stones filled many in those places 'with [a desire for] fame and wealth'.[43] Admittedly, the money of the conquistadors was usually held for a time by the Casa de la Contratación in Seville and the returning millionaire would be allocated an annuity (*juro*), which would give him an income. The negotiations might oblige the returning adventurer to spend several months in Seville. He would probably obtain a coat of arms. Then he would return to his old home, where he might live very well. Take the case of Juan Ruiz de Arce in Alburquerque. He had pages, lackeys, negro slaves and horses. Twelve squires served him at his table, laid with splendid tableware. When he went hunting, he took many horsemen, and gave them dogs, falcons and hawks.[44] Ruiz de Arce reported after meeting the empress:

> She received us very well, thanking us for the services we had rendered, and offering to reward us; and so great was her kindness that anything we wished was given to us and there was not one disappointed man among us ... There were twelve of us conquistadors in Madrid and we spent a great deal of money ...[45]

This was a major change. Few had returned rich from New Spain. Indeed, nearly all of Cortés's followers remained in the country which they had conquered.

Pizarro now considered that his conquest of the Inca empire was complete. He had contrived an excellent friendship with Manco Capac. The surviving Indian noblemen and the conquistadors who had decided to remain in Peru shared a great hunt in honour of Pizarro: 10,000 Indians took part as beaters or hunt advisers and 11,000 animals (vicuña, guanaco, roe deer, fox and puma) were killed.[46]

The Spaniards who had taken part in this extraordinary conquest were amazed at what they had done. They could not comprehend how they were still alive or how they had overcome the hardships they had suffered. How could they have survived such long periods of hunger?[47]

The Inca world was never integrated into the political theory of Europe. The Inca was definitely a monarch but he was not regarded as such as a rule by the theorists and officials of the old world. The only person to see the Inca in imperial terms appears to have been Charles V, who did make a comparison between monarchs of the old world and those of the new one. There are, however, no allusions to the emperors of the Mexicans or the Inca in European theoretical discussions of monarchy.

23

The battle for Cuzco

My sons and brothers! We are going to ask those whom we regard
as children of our god Viracocha for justice for they entered our
country declaring that their main purpose was to do justice all
over the world.

Garcilaso de la Vega, *El Inca*

The conquest of Peru was complete. But the ambitions of the conquerors had not by any means all been resolved. Almagro in particular
had to be satisfied. That was one of the matters which Hernando Pizarro
tried to settle in Spain. On 21 May 1534 a contract (*capitulación*) signed
by the Council of the Indies granted Almagro the right to assume the government of 200 leagues (600 miles) of territory to the south of Pizarro's
Peru. He would have the titles of governor and *adelantado* of those
lands as well as chief magistrate and be captain-general there: not only
himself but his heirs.[1]

This contract, in effect, made Almagro the conquistador of Chile.
Chile was believed at that time likely to be as rich as Peru, if not richer.
The geographical boundary of the grant, however, was unclear. How far
inland did it stretch? Where exactly did the 200 leagues begin? The contract spoke of the lands and provinces on the coast of the Southern Sea
to the south, 'those 200 leagues beginning from the limits of the government which had been entrusted to Francisco Pizarro'. Hernando Pizarro
figured in the contract as the representative of Almagro, which must
have seemed inappropriate to anyone who knew them both since Hernando always spoke critically of Almagro.[2]

There was one particular uncertainty in Almagro's contract: the place
of Cuzco in Spanish official thinking. It was so far to the south that it

could be argued, as Almagro would, that it was in his zone. But Pizarro had conquered it. So it surely was his to exploit.

Almagro, who had been a difficult ally of Pizarro in Cuzco, set off for Chile in July 1535. He took with him nearly 600 Spanish foot soldiers, 1,000 Indian auxiliaries and 100 negro slaves.[3] Pizarro gave financial backing, perhaps made possible because he had reopened the furnaces in Cuzco to enable him to accumulate more gold and silver. Almagro took with him Paullu Inca, the representative of the Inca collaborators in Cuzco, and a high priest of the Peruvians, whom the Spaniards called Villac Umu. The Spaniards included most of those whom Almagro had himself brought to Peru such as the *converso* Rodrigo Orgóñez, a fine horseman who had fought in Italy, perhaps even at the battle of Pavia, before coming to the Indies in the 1520s. Soto had offered himself in that place but Almagro preferred Orgóñez, who was more of a friend. There were also most of the better known men in Alvarado's expedition who had stayed on in Peru, such as Juan de Saavedra of Seville and Alvarado's brother Gómez, another conquistador of New Spain.

This army made heavy weather of the long journey to central Chile but eventually Almagro established himself in the fertile valley of Aconcagua. Thence he sent off several secondary expeditions, such as that of Saavedra, who went to the Bay of Valparaiso, where he laid the foundations of a city, and that of Gómez de Alvarado, who went even further south to the valley of the Maipo. How wonderful it was for Spain to discover such promising agricultural land, and so beautiful too! But these conquistadors had eyes only for precious metals, of which Paullu Inca alone knew the whereabouts.

Some months after he had reached Aconcagua, Almagro was reinforced by Ruy Díaz and Juan Herrada, accompanied by about a hundred Spaniards and a large number of Indian bearers. Díaz had gone to Peru with Almagro, and Herrada was a Navarrese who had been with Cortés in Hiberas. He had been so much in Cortés's confidence that he had gone on his behalf to Rome in 1529 to present the pope with gifts from the New World.[4] He had then gone to Panama and to Peru with Almagro, to whom he became majordomo.

Herrada brought more than just much needed reinforcement. He brought the contract between the Crown and Almagro about his territory to the south of Pizarro's realm. Almagro and his friends studied this *capitulación* carefully – though since the former could not read, he had to rely on the reading aloud of Ruy Díaz and others. These conquistadors, none of them men favoured by Pizarro, were ambitious and wanted much more wealth than they had obtained. They painfully read through the twenty-five paragraphs of the document, which they believed gave Almagro not just the control over the valleys of Chile, where anyone could see that good wine could be grown, but over Cuzco too, where gold and silver could be found in such quantity.[5] Almagro's advisers (Rodrigo Orgóñez, Gómez de Alvarado, Diego de Alvarado, a cousin of the famous band of Alvarado brothers who had conquered Guatemala after taking such an important part in the conquest of Mexico) urged Almagro to return to Cuzco 'and govern'.[6] That is precisely what he decided to do.

Francisco Pizarro, meanwhile, was planning his new capital, Lima, La Ciudad de los Reyes. The city was beautifully laid out with a large square in the centre surrounded by fine cool houses, but it had a hot damp climate which made it more unhealthy than distant Cuzco, about 300 miles away, where Soto, Pizarro's man of all work, had been despatched as lieutenant-governor. Pizarro himself gave the impression now of being a retired peaceful proconsul concerned with urban planning.[7] He had a well-established household: in late 1534 his mistress, 'Doña Inés Yupanqui', previously known as Quispe Sisa, a half-sister of Atahualpa, had given him a daughter, Francisca. He was, naturally, busy apportioning *encomiendas*.

Further afield the church of San Francisco in Quito, about 1,000 miles to the north, was being built as a focal point for northern Peru in the grounds of the palace of Huayna Capac. It was intended to be what it still is, a magnificent commemoration of a great religion. The architect was Fray Jodoko Ricke, the Peruvian counterpart of Pedro de Gante in New Spain. He was the counterpart in every sense for, like Pedro de Gante, he, too, was supposed to have Habsburg blood.

San Francisco was Italianate in style. (The exterior staircase was inspired by the palace of Nicholas V in the Vatican.) It was one more sign that the Renaissance had reached Spanish America. The building took many years: the main cloister in a very Andalusian style was still being built in 1573, the church was finished only in 1575 and the towers were not complete till the eighteenth century. The elaborate façade would be the model for many others.[8] Like many Franciscan foundations, it was to be a place of education as well as prayer – a centre of training for artisans as well as one of worship.

In 1535 Pizarro had to face several accusations of corruption and arrogance made by some of his collaborators to Bishop Tomás de Berlanga who noted these things in his detailed report as to how the Pizarros were coping with their mission in Peru.[9] Pizarro was also visited by an old ally, Gaspar de Espinosa, who came down to Peru from Panama, aged seventy, with his daughter and 200 men.[10]

The absence of Almagro did not in the long run bring Cuzco the peace which Pizarro might have expected. That was partly because Manco Capac had been flattered by Almagro, partly because of intrigues within the Inca family. Was Manco Capac really the right man for Peru in this perilous moment? Manco apparently persuaded a resourceful Basque, Martín Cote, to lead a Spanish gang to murder a cousin of his, Atoc-Sopa, who, some thought, had a good claim to Manco's position. Afterwards, Manco Capac hid in Almagro's house. Spanish followers of Pizarro are then supposed to have robbed Manco's own empty palace. Almagro complained but Pizarro took no action. Cote then joined Almagro. Apparently the commander asked him to guard Paullu Inca, who seemed now to be a dangerous element among Almagro's followers.[11]

The first months after Almagro left for Chile were relatively calm. Francisco Pizarro believed that he could safely leave Cuzco to found another Spanish city, to be called Trujillo, between Piura and Lima, about 250 miles to the north of the latter city.

Hernando de Soto meantime decided to return to Spain to seek a new, independent field of action for himself. He had been disappointed not to have been at least second-in-command on Almagro's journey to Chile, and indeed he would have liked the command itself and is said to have offered Almagro 200,000 pesos for the post. But, thwarted, he packed up and returned to Seville, leaving behind his beautiful Peruvian mistress, Tocto Chimpu, daughter of Huascar, with their daughter, Leonor the *mestiza*.[12]

In these circumstances, the affairs of Cuzco were ruled by Juan Pizarro and his younger brother Gonzalo. Juan Pizarro had many qualities. Cieza, we remember, called him 'the flower of all the Pizarros'. Pedro Pizarro, the page, said of him that 'he was valiant and very courageous, a good fellow, magnanimous and affable'.[13]

Gonzalo Pizarro also began for the first time to make an impact on his fellow Spanish conquerors. The youngest of the Pizarro brothers, he was, as we have said, graceful, handsome and well proportioned. He could read and write. He had a great capacity for camaraderie and for friendships. Garcilaso said of him 'his nature was so noble that he endeared himself to strangers'.[14] But López de Gómara, Cortés's biographer and confessor, who did not know him personally, said that he was rather dull of understanding.[15] He did in these months achieve a new personality and his magnetism played a major part in events. People were prepared to put all their hopes in him and look on him as their new start.

Late in 1535 Manco Capac became increasingly restless under Spanish control. Perhaps things would have been different had he been looked after by men older than the young Pizarro brothers. But these Spaniards subjected him sometimes to mocking rudeness even though they permitted such gatherings as the eight days' festival of the Sun – a great ceremony in which all the major figures of the Inca nobility were concerned. Fray Bartolomé de Segovia, an emissary of Alvarado to Pizarro, who was present, described how

> they brought out all the effigies from the temples of Cuzco onto a plain just outside it, in the direction of where the sun came up. The richest effigies were put under finely worked feather canopies. When the sun rose, the Inca began to chant, there were offerings of meat which were consumed in a great fire, much *chicha* and coca were offered in sacrifice, llamas were let loose, and Manco broke the earth with a foot plough, so inaugurating the ploughing season.[16]

Manco had decided on a radical uprising. He summoned a secret meeting of all Peruvian leaders, especially the chiefs of southern Callao, and explained to them the indignities he had had to suffer. He determined to leave Cuzco immediately. But it was hard to keep a secret in old Peru. Servants (*yanaconas*) were present and informed Juan Pizarro of what was being planned. Manco Capac, it seemed, had already left in a litter. Riding hard, Juan and Gonzalo Pizarro caught up with him at night and, in the morning, they found him hiding in reeds near Lake Muyna. They took him back to Cuzco in chains. Manco Capac later accused some of the Spaniards (Alonso de Toro, Alonso de Mesa, Pedro Pizarro, Francisco de Solares and Gregorio Setiel, all of whom but the last had been at Cajamarca) of urinating on him, of burning his eyelashes and sleeping with his wives. All these accused men were strong supporters of the Pizarros, and had been with the expedition from the beginning –

indeed, all had been recruited by the governor in Spain in 1529. Probably they had been drunk when they were at their most offensive.[17]

This behaviour, or the rumour of it, had its consequences. The only general of the Inca who remained was Tiso. He went to Riquelme's *encomienda* at Jauja, and to Bombón, and encouraged revolts with promises of advancement.

Hernando Pizarro had now returned to Peru after his journey to Spain. He had done little after presenting his treasure, and himself, to the emperor in 1534 apart from visiting Trujillo to see his family. He returned with two ships full of Spanish goods for profitable sale to his friends and his brother's men. He assumed, justifiably, the airs of a great general. In Cuzco, relations between the two peoples improved after his return as *corregidor*. He not only released Manco but showed every possible kindness to him, partly because he had been asked to do so by the Emperor Charles.[18] But the conduct of Spaniards towards Indian women continued to cause intense resentment among male Indians, who saw the most attractive of their girls disappearing into Spanish households.

During Holy Week 1536 Indian resentment came to a head. On Holy Wednesday Hernando Pizarro gave permission to Manco Capac to accompany his best-known priest, Villac Umu, to perform some religious ceremonies in the nearby Yucay valley. He promised to return with a large golden statue of Huayna Capac. In fact, he had gone for a final meeting to coordinate attacks by his followers against the Spaniards. He made what the chronicler Murúa described as a 'general appeal' to all the provinces (of the Inca empire).[19] Perhaps he chose this moment because he knew that Francisco Pizarro and Soto were both away.

On Easter Saturday, 21 April, Hernando Pizarro was told that a major rebellion of Indians was now inevitable. He recognized his misjudgement in releasing Manco Capac and despatched his brother Juan with seventy horsemen to disperse the Indians. Hernando rode out himself with his usual energy and found himself on top of the Yucay valley looking down on a colossal assembly of Indian warriors. Some chroniclers, such as Mena, speak of 100,000 Indians in the encampment.[20] Below, Villac Umu, a real warrior priest, was pressing for an immediate attack, but Manco wanted to wait till all his Indians had gathered. This did not prevent the latter doing whatever they could to murder those Spaniards whom they encountered on the way to or from their *encomiendas*.

About thirty were killed, including Martín de Moguer, one of the first three Europeans to have seen Cuzco.[21]

At the same time Villac Umu occupied the fortress of Sacsahuaman overlooking the city and also destroyed Cuzco's irrigation canal. That action flooded the fields near the city as well as depriving those in the city, including the Spaniards, of water.

Faced with the likelihood of an immediate attack, Hernando prepared his defence as best he could. He divided his cavalry into three bands of twenty-five men each, one commanded by his brother Gonzalo, one by Hernán Ponce de León and another by Gabriel de Rojas – an Extremeño, a Sevillano and a Castilian from Cuéllar. Hernando Pizarro himself, Juan Pizarro (taking the formal rank of *corregidor*) and the treasurer Riquelme remained at the centre of the defence in the heart of Cuzco. In addition to the seventy-five horsemen, there were nearly 200 foot soldiers. All withdrew to the main square of Cuzco where 'owing to its great size, they could more easily dominate the enemy than in the [smaller side] streets ... the infantry were in the middle and the cavalry stayed on each side'.[22] But this must have seemed a tiny force in comparison with the vast horde of Indians. The infantry were, to begin with, under the direction of Alonso Enríquez de Guzmán, a new arrival from Spain, an experienced soldier though not as experienced as he made himself out to be in his engaging memoir.[23] Thus a regular siege began, the Spaniards numbering a little less than 250 with fewer than half mounted.

The Indians, wrote Pedro Pizarro, held the Spaniards in the main square. The latter 'obtained water from the stream which ran through that square and gained maize from the adjacent houses which they cheerfully sacked. Some Indians returned to their Indian masters by day but at night brought food to the Spaniards.' The besiegers, however,

> began to set fire to all parts of Cuzco, by which they gained many parts of the town [for] we Spaniards could not go out through them. We gathered ... in the plaza and in the houses adjoining it such as the Hatun Cancha. Here we were all collected, some [sleeping] in tents ... To burn down the houses where we were, [the Peruvians] took stones and threw them into a fire where they became red-hot. They wrapped these up in cotton and threw them by means of slings into houses which they could not reach ... Thus they burned our houses without us knowing before we understood how ... at other times they shot flaming arrows at the houses which soon took fire.[24]

'It looked as if a black cloth had been spread over the ground for half a league round Cuzco ... At night there were so many fires that the scene looked like a very serene sky full of stars ... [with] much shouting and the din of voices.'[25]

An early mounted counter-attack was organized by Gabriel de Rojas but, though many Indians were killed, their numbers prevented any continuing thrust and several groups of cavalrymen were surrounded, one such having to leave behind Francisco Mejía, an Extremeño, to be killed with his horse.

The main Indian attack was on 6 May. The Indians moved down the narrow streets to occupy that part of Cuzco known as Cora Cora, which overlooked the north corner of the main square, making a withering fire of hot stones on two places held by the Spaniards: the hall of Subur Huasi, the one-time palace of the Inca Viracocha and already the main church of the city; and the Hatun Cancha, where many Spaniards had plots for their town houses. But the Indians failed to burn the Spaniards' dwelling places despite their being roofed with straw – a failure which they attributed to a decision of the gods.

Garcilaso de la Vega reported that the conquistadors were saved on this occasion by Santiago himself on his usual white horse, but Murúa insisted that that knight was the Basque Mancio Sierra de Leguizamón. He reported, though, that the Virgin Mary did appear on this day in the sky, dressed in a blue cloak.[26]

Despite this setback the Indians had captured nearly the entire city, and the Spaniards were left with little more than the main square and the houses around it. The Indians were protecting themselves effectively by the pits which they devised against the horses and used slings to good effect, as well as *ayllus*, three stones tied to the ends of llamas' tendons, to entangle horses' legs. Hernando Pizarro was advised by some of his men to escape in the direction of Arequipa but he held on, partly persuaded that he had a chance of victory by using the Cañari Indians, the old enemies of the Incas. Their assistance was essential in a night attack on the wicker palisades behind which the Indians sheltered as they advanced.[27]

Comforted by this limited success, Hernando Pizarro instructed his brother Juan to lead an attack on the fortress on Sacsahuaman which, with its polygonal masonry, dominated the city. Juan Pizarro decided to move on a night of full moon when he suspected the Inca and his men would be celebrating. He advanced with fifty horsemen, among them his brother Gonzalo, and about a hundred friendly Cañari Indians, but they faced a fierce onslaught of stones from above as they went forward. Juan Pizarro was wounded in the head, rendering him unable to wear a helmet. He then led a frontal attack, which was successful, but he died in the effort, being again hit on the head by a stone. Many were wounded but Hernando led a force scaling up ladders at night, with Hernán Sánchez of Badajoz becoming the hero of the hour, since he climbed steadily up a steep ascent. Alonso Enríquez argued that 1,500 Indians were killed in this onslaught, including one brave *orejón* who threw himself off the tower rather than surrender. Hernando Pizarro then garrisoned Sacsahuaman with fifty Spanish foot soldiers and a hundred Cañari Indians.

Hernando Pizarro wanted now to send fifteen cavalrymen to tell his brother Francisco that the resistance was continuing in Cuzco, but they asked not to be sent since they considered that the Spanish position could not be sustained without them. Thwarted in that venture, Hernando Pizarro decided to strike at Manco Capac's headquarters at Ollantaytambo in a fertile valley some fifty miles away. It had been a royal property of importance and consisted of a series of residential structures and a temple complex built round a large carved rock. It was surrounded by terraces. There were canals.[28]

The Spaniards found this place well fortified and the Indians there amply supplied with stones to throw at them or to send down by sling. Manco Capac also had jungle bowmen from the other side of the Andes as allies. Some Indians had learned by now how to use captured Castilian swords, shields, even lances, culverins and arquebuses, though it was not that knowledge which caused Hernando Pizarro to withdraw but the diversion by the Indians of the river Patacancha to flood the valley.[29] A smaller Spanish contingent headed by Gonzalo Pizarro routed another army of Indians, and Pedro Pizarro recalled rounding up 2,000 llamas.

Still the fighting in Cuzco continued brutally and the two sides were surprisingly unyielding. Alonso Enríquez de Guzmán commented:

This was the most dreadful and cruel war ... Between Christians and Moors, there is usually some fellow feeling and it is in the interests of both sides to spare those whom they take alive, because of the ransom. But in this Indian war there is no such fellow feeling. We give each other the most cruel deaths we can imagine.[30]

The Peruvian historian José Antonio Busto assures us that in this fighting about 1,000 Spaniards died.[31]

Francisco Pizarro in Lima learned quickly through Indians of the fighting in Cuzco and he organized several relief expeditions: thirty men were despatched under Francisco Mogroviejo de Quiñones; seventy horse under Gonzalo de Tapia, a relation of the Pizarros; and sixty men under Diego Pizarro, another kinsman. He also called back some of his captains from new expeditions: for example, Alonso de Alvarado, a nephew of Pedro, with whom he had come to Peru, from the conquest of the Chachapoyas; Gonzalo de Olmos from Puerto Viejo;[32] and Garcilaso de la Vega from San Mateo. Olmos was accused in 1542 of giving the bureaucrat Beltrán two emeralds and two golden vases in return for favours granted. Beltrán said that they were worth only 220 ducats. He had apparently founded Villa Nueva de Puerto Viejo in the name of Pizarro.

Pizarro also sent his half-brother, Francisco Martín de Alcántara, to warn the Spanish settlers along the coast of the Indians' campaign. About 1,500 Spaniards altogether were isolated at different points in the vast territory of Ecuador–Peru. But all these cautions took time to be effective. In the meantime, the few Spaniards left in Jauja after the foundation of Lima had mostly been killed by Quizo Yupanqui, a new Peruvian commander. Smaller forces of Spanish fighters met similar ends: thus the seventy horse under Gonzalo de Tapia were destroyed in a gorge on the upper river Pampas; Diego Pizarro was killed with sixty followers near the river Parcas; sixty horse led by Alonso de Gaeta and Francisco de Godoy y Aldana, an Extremeño from Cáceres, were defeated and nearly all killed. These were extremely difficult times for the Pizarro mission, comparable to the moment when Cortés had been forced in 1520 to withdraw at night in disorder from the Mexica capital of Tenochtitlan.

Manco Capac apparently wanted his new general, Quizo, to go on to Lima, not only to kill the Spaniards there but to burn all their buildings. Only Francisco Pizarro would be spared, for Manco wanted him as a prisoner – for what disagreeable purpose one can only guess.

But the tide had now turned. Quizo took his army to San Cristóbal, a hill overlooking Lima, but he was held there by good Spanish cavalry tactics. Some Indians opposed to the Incas, not just the Cañari, fought well for Spain. Quizo inspired a general attack, promising that the fourteen or so women inside the city would be given to them – Indians all. But the Spanish cavalry killed that resilient commander and the mountain Indians who had accompanied him felt ill at ease in the close climate of the coast. In any case, the coastal Indians could not make common cause with their comrades from the mountains. Divisions among the indigenous people were, as usual in the Americas, responsible for the natives' defeats.

Further assistance came to the Spaniards in Peru in late 1536 from an unexpected quarter. First Diego de Ayala of Toledo took a letter from Pizarro to Alvarado, of all people, appealing for his help. Hernán Cortés despatched Rodrigo de Grijalva, probably a son of Grijalva, the second conquistador of New Spain, with a quantity of weapons to Peru. Gaspar de Espinosa, the persistent governor of Panama, also sent supplies. Cortés himself would have liked to have gone to Peru and he did what he could to arrange it.[33] The new president of the supreme court in Santo Domingo, Alonso de Fuentemayor, bishop too of that city, sent his brother Diego with 100 cavalry and 400 foot including 200 Spanish-speaking black Africans, while the governor of Nicaragua sent his brother, Pedro de los Ríos, with men, arms and horses on a big ship. Juan de Berrio sent four shiploads in February 1537.[34] All this help was, however, slow to arrive and slower still to make any impact on events. Nor should we be in any doubt that the willingness of so many from elsewhere in the Americas to assist the Spanish mission in Peru derived from an expectation of gold as well as of glory.

More significant perhaps than the promised reinforcements from abroad was the gathering of a new Spanish army led by Alonso de Alvarado who had come back easily enough from the conquest of the Chachapoyas. His army probably amounted to 350 men including 100 horsemen and 40 crossbowmen. He was challenged by a small Indian force led by Illa Tupac, of whom 100 were captured. Alvarado had some of them killed, others mutilated. Two Indian chiefs who hated the Inca were with him throughout and they relished these cruelties. Gómez de Tordoya of Badajoz brought 200 men to help him. They moved on slowly to Cuzco.

By the time they got there, the situation had been transformed: Almagro was about to arrive on his return from Chile.

24

Almagro

Almagro arrived in the vicinity of Cuzco in March 1537. He was bitter and resentful at his failure to find precious metals in the south. 'New Toledo' was fertile but poor; Potosí, on the way, had not yet been discovered as the wonderful mountain of silver it would soon become. Almagro's failure had been marked by brutalities to Indians, who in consequence tried to avoid working for him. Gangs of Spanish horsemen would hunt down these reluctant serfs as if they were game, and kidnap their wives and children as if they were toys. Any Spaniard who stood up for Indians would be mocked.[1]

In spite of that this journey was much assisted – perhaps had even been made possible – by the presence among the Spaniards of Paullu, Manco Capac's half-brother, who had in every way furthered the expedition by acting as its guide and preparing the ground for reception by local leaders.[2]

The difficulty now was that still no one really knew if Cuzco was legally in Almagro's jurisdiction or that of Pizarro. It was not easy to work out what the royal decree of 21 May 1534 was trying to say. Perhaps it was too much to expect the *letrados*, clergymen and noblemen of the Council of the Indies sitting in Valladolid, who had no experience of Peru, to set this matter straight. But it left a real uncertainty.

As he approached Cuzco from the south, Almagro learned that his comrade Pizarro's Peru was at war with Manco Capac. The state of affairs was very confused, but he was led to believe that Manco Capac now had the advantage in the conflict. However, though Hernando Pizarro was short of food, that was actually the reverse of the facts at that point.

Almagro began to correspond with the Inca from the safety of the headquarters of his army and, at Urcos, only eighteen miles from Cuzco, he sent two emissaries to him (Juan Gómez Malanes and Pedro de Oñate, both of whom had been with him from the beginning).[3] Through them, Almagro assured Manco Capac that, if he would surrender to him, he would punish the Spaniards guilty of abuse towards the Inca. Manco replied that he had suffered much from the Pizarros. While Oñate was with Manco, an Indian runner came with a note from Hernando Pizarro telling Manco not to trust Almagro – a somewhat bizarre message since Manco and Hernando had been fighting one another for nearly a year. The Inca asked Oñate to prove his enmity with the Pizarros by cutting the messenger's hand. Oñate obliged, severing the fingers.

Another friend of Almagro, Ruy Díaz, soon made his appearance. Manco asked him: 'If I were to give the Christians a great treasure, would the king withdraw all the Christians from the land?' Ruy Díaz asked how much treasure Manco would give. Manco took a *fanega* of maize and, picking one grain, said: 'As much as this grain is the quantity of the gold and silver which you have found for the Christians, and what you have not found is as this *fanega* from which I have taken this grain.' Ruy Díaz seems to have been nonplussed by this proposition and replied that 'even if you were to give the king all these mountain peaks made in gold and silver, he would not remove from this land the Spaniards who are now in it'. Manco answered: 'Get you away, Ruy Díaz, and tell Almagro that he may go where he will, for I am bound to die and all my people too, till we have made an end of the Christians.'[4] The exchange seems to have led Manco to change his mind about Almagro and he ordered one of his commanders, Paucar, to attack him. He also imprisoned Ruy Díaz, had his beard cut off and had guavas fired at him, which may have been more disagreeable than it sounds. He did not know how bad the relations were between Almagro and the Pizarros and assumed that, in the end, Almagro's 450 men would be a good reinforcement for Hernando Pizarro's 200.

So Manco decided to call off his siege of Cuzco, attributing his setback to the gods, and withdrew first from Calca, then to the mountain and fortress city of Ollantaytambo, and next to the upper Vilcabamba valley, specifically to the forest of Antis Vitcos, all the while pursued by Spaniards. He took with him the golden statuette of a small boy, Punchao, wearing a royal headband with solar rays issuing from his head and shoulders, while lions and serpents projected from his body.[5] The fighting was severe in Ollantaytambo, though the Indians held out effectively against Hernando Pizarro.

Then Paullu sent a message to Manco saying that Almagro seemed in truth ready to help Manco fight the Pizarros. He suggested that they kill Francisco, Hernando and Gonzalo Pizarro and 'afterwards the surviving Peruvians could live quietly with no one to injure them (después vivirían quietos sin que nadie los injuriase)'. This apparent treachery to the Spanish cause did not prevent Almagro from sending his lieutenant Orgóñez to capture Manco. Orgóñez succeeded in sacking the Sun temple at Vitcos, but Manco escaped further into the mountains.

Almagro was approaching Cuzco. He had first to meet the reinforcement army of 500 men under Alonso de Alvarado, but he managed to defeat it on the Abancay bridge, even capturing Alvarado himself with several of his captains, such as Gómez de Tordoya of Badajoz. Cuzco was then at his feet. Hernando Pizarro sent a messenger to try to bring over Almagro's troops by playing on the ambitions of Alonso de Saavedra, who was now his commander. Saavedra refused.[6] Next, Hernando suggested to Almagro that he should set himself up in one part of Cuzco while he and his brothers would remain in another. But Almagro demanded that Hernando give up all Cuzco to him. A battle between Spaniards seemed inevitable, despite the efforts of Diego de Alvarado, a cousin of the great Pedro, 'a model of good sense and discretion, an accomplished gentleman in all respects'[7] – and, it must be said, an unusually tolerant figure for a member of that family.

On 18 April 1537 Almagro and his men entered Cuzco by three separate gates, drums and fifes playing. Almagro's men shouted his name when they walked into the palace of Pizarro, which they set on fire. He put to the torch the roof of the house of Hernando Pizarro, who was captured with twenty of his men, including his brother Gonzalo. These prisoners were walled up in a round tower at the palace of Huayna Capac, which had only one small window through which food could be introduced. Almagro told the Pizarros that 'they, with their insolence and arrogance, were the chief reasons for the rebellion of Manco'.[8] He had in some way been apprised of the news that the Pizarros would never forgive the death in action of their brother Juan. He staged a ceremony in Cuzco in which Manco Capac was deprived of the imperial crown and gave the royal fringe – that is, the imperial crown – to his brother Paullu Inca.[9]

Hearing of these events, Francisco Pizarro sought an accommodation with Almagro. He was always inclined to compromise if he could. Licenciado Gaspar de Espinosa, the experienced ex-governor of Panama who had come down to Peru the previous year, was asked to act as an intermediary. But unfortunately he died. Almagro set off to face Francisco Pizarro, taking Hernando Pizarro with him as a prisoner. Francisco organized his army of 800 with care: 200 of his men were horsemen, and the future conqueror of Chile, Pedro de Valdivia, renowned as a brilliant captain, was his chief commander.[10]

Several further efforts were made to arrange a reconciliation between the two sides. Almagro's representatives were, however, not loyal. For example, Fray Francisco de Bobadilla, a Mercedarian, treacherously sided with the Pizarros, having been asked to act for Almagro.[11] A committee was set up to establish a line between Pizarro's and Almagro's land. This included the clever if footloose courtier Enríquez de Guzmán. But they could make no progress. Still, Diego de Alvarado skilfully negotiated the release of Hernando Pizarro. Most realized that he would disturb the situation. It was true. The two conquistadors met south of Lima at Mala but nothing transpired. Then Francisco Pizarro proposed that Almagro should be given good land at Arequipa and Chencas, but Almagro wanted the city of Cuzco or nothing.

Everything now seemed to be leading towards the tragedy of a civil war. In the preparations, no one seems to have noticed that the unreliable interpreter Felipillo had been killed, though an Almagrista, because he had joined the rebel Villac Umu, an ally of Manco Inca.

The critical battle occurred at Las Salinas (the salt mines), outside Cuzco, on 26 April 1538, where the road goes uphill, leaving a swamp on one side and a narrow but flat stretch of the land on the other. Enríquez de Guzmán, still with Almagro, wrote that, though the encampments of the two armies were close, one was in summer, the other in winter, for Almagro was at Huaytara in the sierra while Pizarro was below. In the sierra it rained or snowed half the year, while on the coast there was no water.

Almagro could not fight at Las Salinas because he was suffering from a fever. He left his command to Orgóñez who had with him four infantry captains: Cristóbal de Sotelo, Hernando de Alvarado, Juan de Moscoso and Diego de Salinas. In addition he had two cavalry detachments, led by Juan Tello and Vasco de Guevara on one side, Francisco de Chaves, from a well-known family of Trujillo, and Ruy Díaz, on the other.

Hernando Pizarro's cavalry was also divided into two, led by Diego de Rojas and Alvarado on one side and himself with Gonzalo, his brother, on the other. His infantry was controlled by Diego de Cerbina (pikes) and Castro from Portugal (arquebuses). Thus an Alvarado was to be found on both sides – a characteristic feature of those tragic days.

First Orgóñez ordered Guevara to attack the Pizarros' pikemen and arquebusiers. But they were by then established in the swamp which held up the cavalry of Almagro. They charged all the same. Hernando Pizarro and Pedro de Lerma, one of Almagro's more important commanders, were met with lances and Hernando was wounded. Almagro's commander was blinded before being killed, and Enríquez de Guzmán was wounded when his horse fell into a ravine.

Victory lay eventually with the Pizarros. About 200 were killed on each side, including Moscoso, Salinas and Hernando de Alvarado. Ruy Díaz and Lerma were killed after the battle, the latter treacherously. Almagro was captured after the battle too, and imprisoned in one of the round towers where he had previously placed Hernando Pizarro and Gonzalo.[12] Hernando Pizarro thought of sending him to Spain but he heard that Gonzalo de Mesa, one of his own captains, planned to rescue him on the way to Lima. So, after a perfunctory trial, Hernando sentenced Almagro to death. He appealed against this but without success. On 8 July 1538 Almagro, already over seventy-five, was strangled in his cell, then publicly beheaded in the square of Cuzco, and buried in the main church, the only witness of the funeral being his favourite African slave.[13] His dead body lay for a while naked in the square and a Pizarrista examined it carefully to see if he had been, as was rumoured, a sodomite. Gonzalo de Mesa, Almagro's would-be rescuer, was also beheaded. These executions were carried out by Alonso de Toro, *criado* of the Pizarros and a native of Trujillo. He soon became lieutenant-governor of Cuzco, but was murdered in 1546.[14]

From this time onwards, as few noticed, the general use of heavy field artillery began in Peru and thousands of *encomienda* Indians were employed carrying big guns round the country. Salinas was the last major battle fought in medieval fashion, with lances and swords playing a decisive part. It was not, however, a chivalrous occasion.

25

Pizarro, triumph and tragedy

This doctor is worth a Peru.

Mozart, *Così Fan Tutte*, Act I

Fray Vicente Valverde, the Valladolid- and Salamanca-educated Dominican who was the only churchman to have accompanied Pizarro throughout, had returned to Spain in 1534, and now returned having been named first bishop of Peru. He was escorted by a retinue of fifty soldiers and a hundred arquebusiers and crossbowmen led by Andrés Jiménez. Valverde had received instructions in Spain to be a model bishop: to see to it that *repartimientos* (parcels of land) were moderate, to ask for accounts from the officials, to ensure that the payment of the royal fifth was honestly done and to collect tithes. The Crown hoped to establish a truly separate authority here.[1] In 1539 Valverde sent a long report to the king in which he urged the Crown to defend the Indians against his Spanish friends, whom he described as 'so many wolves'. Yet the indigenous people, he said (as he had said on other occasions), were very ready 'to receive the doctrine of the holy Gospel'.[2] The Pizarros had always been friendly with the Dominicans and the Mercedarians.

It was not a propitious moment to write thus for, now that Almagro was dead, Manco Capac was planning a new rebellion. He had as his main commander Illa Tupac, a general who had attacked Pedro de Alvarado in 1537. Their plan was to inspire many small-scale local risings, causing much damage. The decisive moment seems to have been when a people called the Conchucos fell on Trujillo by the sea, and carried out much torture or killings of travellers. Manco himself was pursued by a commander of Pizarro's, Illán Suárez de Carvajal, who belonged to an important family of public men. (His brother, Juan Suárez de Carvajal, was on the Council of the Indies.)[3] But Manco Capac turned successfully on this enemy and twenty-four out of thirty men were soon killed.

Francisco Pizarro himself took command in new counter-attacks. His main interest, however, was still to found new settlements. For example, in full campaign, he founded San Juan de la Frontera at Huamanga under Francisco de Cárdenas.[4] Pizarro also went to Charcas and to the famous inland lake, Titicaca. He learned there that rebellious Indians were busy trying to destroy a pontoon bridge of boats across the lake to the south. It was there that Pizarro received a request from one of his most brilliant men, Pedro de Valdivia, 'the perfect captain', as he was known for his good qualities. Valdivia asked Pizarro for permission to go and explore, and also conquer, the land abandoned by Almagro. 'Seeing my determination,' Valdivia wrote later to the king, 'he graciously opened the door to me.'[5] But such grants were not without their cost. At the same moment as giving him *carte blanche* in Chile, Pizarro withdrew his earlier grant of the valley of Canela and its silver mine.

The Pizarro family were busy establishing their control in the centre of Peru, east of the conquered lands. Thus Hernando found and took for himself the mines which the Indians had begun at Porco. Gonzalo occupied the entire valley of Cochabamba.[6] Francisco established himself and his family in equally excellent estates.

Feeling that his conquests had now been completed, Hernando Pizarro again took leave of his brothers. To Francisco he declared:

> Look, your lordship, now I am going [again] to Spain and consider that safety lies first in God and then in your lordship's life ... do not permit those who wish it to gather ten people together within fifty leagues of wherever your lordship may be, for if you let them assemble, they are certain to kill you. If they kill your lordship, I shall be sure to conduct our business badly and no memory of your lordship will remain.[7]

With that unexpectedly modest statement, he set off for Spain with the intention of justifying before the Council of the Indies his already much criticized execution of Almagro. He travelled via New Spain, avoiding Panama since he was afraid of being seized or killed by his enemies there.[8]

Francisco Pizarro had aged during the crisis over the Almagros. The emperor had named him 'Marquis', as he had named Cortés, but he was allowing Pizarro to choose his title, leaving it up to him as to of what place he would be 'Marquis'.

Pizarro despatched his brother Gonzalo accompanied by their cousin, Pedro the chronicler, and Paullu to seek out Manco in his new refuge beyond Vilcabamba. They went as far as horses could take them, then continued on foot. With Pedro del Barco temporarily in control of the expedition, the Spaniards were ambushed by Indians who killed five of them. Gonzalo retreated and his brother Francisco sent more troops to assist him. Next day they reached Manco's secret redoubt, while another section of their forces went into the forest nearby without the Indians' knowledge. Gonzalo sought to negotiate but his emissaries were Huaspar and Inquill, two brothers of Manco's queen, Cura Ocllo. Here the Indians tried unsuccessfully to experiment with arquebuses.

Manco Capac escaped downstream with three followers. The Spaniards then embarked on persecution. For example, Cura Ocllo herself was captured; she tried to avoid rape by smearing filth over herself. Manco sent a messenger inviting Francisco Pizarro to meet him at Hucay, with three or four followers. Pizarro sent a pony, a black slave and some other presents. Manco Capac had all of them killed. Pizarro's reply was to order the brutal murder of Cura Ocllo by shooting arrows at her. She made no complaint at the evident pain.[9] Her body was put in a basket in the river Yucay so that it would be found by Manco's people. Pizarro then executed several of his grander prisoners, such as the general Tiso. Among others killed were Villac Umu, the high priest, who had been fighting Pedro de los Ríos in the Condesuyo for at least eight months. These enemies of the Spanish were killed by being burned.

After this there were no more large-scale Indian rebellions. Alonso de Alvarado returned to the conquest of the Chachapoyas north of Cajamarca, and his relatively humane treatment of Indians secured for him a reasonable reception. He founded the town of Rabantu. But in Huánaco a new and inexperienced Spanish force under Alonso Mercadillo was busy terrifying the natives in the hope of finding gold. There were many complaints, causing Pizarro to order his brother Gonzalo to stop there on his way to becoming governor of Quito. Another rebellion which had to be quelled was on the road to Chinchaysuyo, which was the responsibility of Alonso de Orihuela. In July 1539 two *encomenderos* were killed in the Callejón de Huaylas. Francisco de Chaves, one of Pizarro's most successful but more brutal captains, swept through the valleys to carry out fearful reprisals, killing children as well as women.

Franciso Pizarro meanwhile was busy founding two new towns, La

Plata and Arequipa. There he and his secretary, the much disliked Antonio Picado (he had accompanied Pedro de Alvarado to Peru in 1534), made themselves unpopular by cutting back large *repartimientos* which had already been allocated. Picado was also hated because he unjustifiably desired that all should show reverence to him. Pizarro was busy as well with the *encomiendas* which he had awarded to himself, above all those in the valley of the Yucay where coca was grown.

In the summer of 1541 several plots against Francisco Pizarro were reported to him; perhaps a priest betrayed the secrecy of the confessional. News came, too, that Hernando Pizarro had been indicted in Spain as a result of complaints by Diego de Alvarado on account of the execution of Almagro. Diego, either poisoned or worn out by his exertions, died soon after, but Hernando was seized and arrested. Though by now immensely rich, he spent the next quarter century as a prisoner, if a privileged one, at first in Madrid in the Alcázar, then in the Castillo de la Mota just outside Medina del Campo. He could receive guests, children, mistresses and food from the town; he could buy houses and properties (and did so), but it seemed an extraordinary end for a great conquistador who with his brothers had won so much of South America for the Spanish Crown.[10]

La Mota is a formidable brick castle on the south side of Medina, which had always been a royal city. Famous for its great annual fairs in the late fifteenth and early sixteenth centuries, it had been the favourite city of Queen Isabel the Catholic, who died there. She once said that, if she had had three sons, she would have liked one to be king of Castile, another to be archbishop of Toledo and the third to be a notary in Medina del Campo. La Mota had been the prison of numerous dangerous persons, such as Cesare Borgia, the Italian adventurer, who made a daring escape from it in 1506.

Francisco Pizarro continued to walk about Lima, the new city which he had created in Peru near the sea. The Almagrists were busy with complaints and plots, though it had been his brother Hernando, not he, who had executed the elder Almagro. Manco Capac lived on in secrecy in Vilcabamba. Gonzalo Pizarro led an attempt to destroy that Indian claimant to the throne. Pizarro was told by the mayor of Lima, Dr Velázquez, that 'those of Chile', that is, the friends of Almagro, had determined to attack 'the Marquis' (as the governor was now known) at mass on Sunday, 26 June 1541. These Almagrists seemed in a majority, and they sensed Pizarro's alarm. They emerged from the house of a *mestizo* son of Almagro, with ferocious declarations: 'Down with the traitor and the tyrant who has killed the judge whom the emperor has sent to punish him.'[11] Actually that official had not arrived. Nor had the young Almagro taken much interest up till then in avenging his father. He was Almagro's son by a Panamanian. Pizarro consulted his friends Francisco de Chaves and Juan Blázquez, the deputy governor. The latter said: 'Have no fear, while I have in my hand this staff, none will dare to attack you.' The three concocted a plan: Pizarro would pretend that he was ill, so he would not go to mass. Then in the afternoon he would order his cavalry to seize the young Diego Almagro and some of his friends.[12]

When the hour of mass came, the Almagrists assembled to kill Pizarro on his way to church. When he did not appear, they despatched a Basque priest, Domingo Ruiz de Durama, to Pizarro's house to see what had happened.[13] Pizarro invited the priest in and asked him to celebrate mass. He heard mass with Dr Velázquez, the mayor; Francisco de Chaves, his deputy; and Francisco Martín de Alcántara, his half-brother, who was usually in attendance on him. Hearing a tumult in the square, Pizarro asked Chaves to go and see what was going on. Chaves, ill-prepared, went outside to ask the crowd's intentions. Forty men appeared at Pizarro's door, including some who were looked on as 'those of Chile'. The Indian servants fled. So did Dr Velázquez. Pizarro had no armour, just a sword and a shield. He, his half-brother and two pages defended the door as best they could but Martín de Alcántara, Chaves and the pages were soon killed. Pizarro was left alone. He was surrounded and struck in the throat. He apparently made the sign of the cross with his thumb and index finger, and died kissing the hand which had made the sign.[14] He was about sixty-five.

Juan de Rada, the most prominent enemy of Pizarro, inspired the young Almagro to mount a horse and ride round Lima to say that there was no other governor of that city than he. The houses of Pizarro and his staff, including the feared secretary, Antonio Picado, and his half-brother, were sacked. Picado was soon apprehended and also killed after horrible tortures. A friend of Pizarro, Juan de Barbarán of Trujillo, and his wife, with some black slaves were brave enough to haul Pizarro's body to the church which the dead governor had built. There they buried him, with Diego Almagro's permission. Barbarán also made it his business to look after Pizarro's children and he disposed of many of his possessions. 'The Chileans' went into the square and shouted that Diego Almagro *hijo*, the son, aged twenty-one, was now king of Peru. That *mestizo* had himself sworn in more modestly as the governor, and named Rada as his captain-general. Various others assumed perilously fragile posts as judges or captains. There were still 'monarchists', and they soon rallied, their captain-general being Pedro Álvarez de Holguín with Alonso de Alvarado, Garcilaso de la Vega and Pedro Ansúnez as the main captains. A new civil war was now certain.

Pizarro died rich. He had allocated to himself 30,000 Indians in his numerous *encomiendas*, and he had about 400 Spaniards working for him, a large staff of '*criados*', a word encompassing many subordinate activities but essentially 'dependants'.[15] Most of them were from Extremadura and the part played in his life by men from Trujillo was always notable. In Peru Pizarro's special interest had been his *encomiendas* in the valley of Yucay, which included the Ceja de Selva where coca was grown, and which had been reserved for the personal use of the Inca rulers. Pizarro also had *encomiendas* at Chuquiago, Puna, Huaylas (very good agricultural land), Chimu, Conchucos, Lima and Chuquitanas. He had mines at Porco with a partner, García de Salcedo, who became the companion of his daughter Francisca. He also had a mine at Collao where his majordomo was in 1535 paid 5,000 pesos a year.

Hernando and Gonzalo Pizarro held *encomiendas* in the neighbouring valley of Tampu.[16] Bishop Berlanga, who was known for introducing the banana to the colony of Santo Domingo, had commented: 'it is publicly said that Your Lordship and your brothers and officials have as many Indians as His Majesty and all the other Spanish conquistadors'.[17] They could not hold them very easily, however.

26

Vaca de Castro in Peru

*Mrs Pipchin had a way of falling foul of all meek people; and her
friends said who could wonder at it, after the Peruvian mines!*
Charles Dickens, *Dombey and Son*

Peru was much too rich to be left with no governor. So, within months
of the murder of the marquis, a name came forward in the Council of
the Indies to take his place. It was not the name of Hernando Pizarro, as
would have seemed logical, given his prominence in the conquest: Hernando
was in prison in Medina del Campo. Nor was it the name of
Gonzalo Pizarro who, as governor in Quito, was in Amazonia seeking
cinnamon and was passed over, though he was Francisco's legal heir.
The name suggested as a temporary governor was Cristóbal Vaca de
Castro, a Leonés who had been judge of Valladolid.

Cobos and García de Loaisa had earlier recommended him to act as
governor of Peru alongside Pizarro and, though no one had worked out
what that might mean in practice, he was already on his way – to Quito
if not to Lima. The assumption was that, sooner or later, a viceroy would
be named, as had occurred in Mexico, and, when that happened, Vaca
de Castro would step aside in an honourable fashion.

Vaca de Castro asked three men to act for him till he reached Peru: a
Dominican, Fray Tomás de San Martín; Jerónimo de Aliaga, Pizarro's
educated disciple; and Francisco de Barrionuevo. The first was the provincial
or leader of the Dominican order in Peru and was a humane and
warm-hearted individual who would play a decisive part later on in the
creation of the university of San Marcos in Peru. Aliaga, from Segovia,
we have met earlier. He had recently been inspector of the treasure
seized in Cuzco. Finally, Barrionuevo was a remarkable conquistador

who had been in Florida with Ponce de León, in Cubagua looking for pearls, and in Santo Domingo charged with defeating the rebellion of the Indians led by Enriquillo.[1] He and his nephew Pedro had built the first stone house on the pearl island, Cubagua. He had also been in Tierra Firme which he used as a base to become a merchant in Peru. He entered into a commercial agreement with one of the largest entrepreneurs, Antonio de Ribera, a magistrate also, and with him shared the profits of a mine.[2] He owned a good sugar mill in Puerto Plata on the north coast of Santo Domingo. Thus he was concerned in a broad sweep of Spanish imperial adventures and he was rightly called 'one of the most fascinating men in the history of America' by the German historian Enrique Otte.[3]

The letter from Vaca de Castro explaining the designation of Fray Tomás, Aliaga and Barrionuevo was received by the first-named in the new Dominican convent in Lima, given to the Dominicans by Francisco Pizarro, a makeshift building at that time but already in the magnificent site which would make the completed edifice a triumph of colonial architecture.[4] The city council of Lima welcomed the arrangements with alacrity but then apparently abandoned the city, for Diego de Almagro *hijo* was suspected of wanting to burn down the whole settlement. But, when Vaca arrived and began to wear the appropriate robes of an acting governor, many fairweather friends and allies of the young Almagro deserted him.

Some of 'the Chileans', survivors of Almagro's journey to Chile, suggested that they or Almagro should kill the remaining Pizarrists whom they had as prisoners in their power, among them Pedro Pizarro the chronicler. A recently arrived *licenciado*, Rodrigo Niño (son of Hernando Niño, *regidor* of Toledo), advised against such actions and instead the people concerned were imprisoned on a boat in the port of Arequipa, under the captaincy of Pedro Gómez. Gómez, however, had his price. The Pizarrists found that it was 500 ducats, with which they bought their freedom.[5]

Vaca de Castro went to Quito, then to Trujillo. Both Pizarrists and ex-Almagrists crowded his drawing room. Soon an army sprang up at his disposal. The commander would be Gómez de Tordoya of Badajoz, who had been a friend of the marquis and had been hunting when he died. When the news came of Pizarro's death, he said: 'Now is the time for war and blood, not for hunting and pastimes.' This was, however, still a time when wars seemed to be a gentlemanly activity second to none.[6]

Soon Vaca reached Lima. There he named Barrionuevo his chief lieutenant, while Juan Vélez de Guevara, a lawyer from Jerez de la Frontera, became captain of his increasingly important arquebusiers. They awaited the arrival of Almagro *hijo* in trepidation for his force was large. But they need not have worried, since he was still in Cuzco and his two chief lieutenants, García de Alvarado and Cristóbal Sotelo, had fallen out so badly that the former killed the latter in the main square of the city.

It is significant that none of these brawling conquistadors had been colleagues of the Pizarros in the great battles of the early days; they were new men with less than five years' experience in the country. García de Alvarado, for example, had come down to Peru with his kinsman Pedro de Alvarado in 1535. Now, to save himself, he decided to kill young Almagro, his putative commander. He invited him to a banquet and Almagro accepted. At the last minute, though, suspecting the worst, Almagro declined, saying that he was ill. Alvarado went to taunt him, and apparently persuaded him to change his mind. As they left for Alvarado's lodging, Alvarado said to him, 'You are under arrest.' Almagro, however, remarked, 'But you are not under arrest but dead,' and he killed him there and then.[7] Then Almagro with his 250 horsemen set off against Vaca de Castro, whose numbers were three times that.

They met in June 1542 at Huamanga in some fields called Chupas. Before the armies fought, Vaca de Castro, usually prudent, sent two of his men, Diego Mercado and Francisco de Idiáquez, to offer terms, including a general pardon. The intrepid Almagro said that he would accept the compromise, provided the pardon included all his followers and that he, Diego de Almagro, would be named governor of a new kingdom of 'New Toledo', that is Chile, as well as of its gold mines. Vaca, who knew that many of Almagro's men were unenthusiastic about the idea of a battle, also sent Alonso García to offer terms privately to many captains but, though he was disguised, he was unmasked by Diego, who had him hanged. Almagro then prepared for battle. Vaca, proclaiming a list of Almagro's crimes, did the same. It was one more tragic event in the tragic early history of Peru.

Vaca had as his main commander García de Alvarado's cousin, Alonso de Alvarado. His other captains were Álvarez Holguín; Gómez de Alvarado, who had been with Cortés throughout the campaigns in

New Spain; Pedro de Vergara and Vélez de Guevara. Nuño de Castro led his arquebusiers. Vaca de Castro, who delivered a fine speech beforehand, remained in the rear.[8]

Almagro had with him Pedro Suárez, who had fought in Italy. Other captains were Diego de Hojeda, Martín de Bilbao, Juan de Oña, Diego Méndez, Pedro de Oñate, Juan Balsa and Juan Tello de Guzmán. Suárez told Almagro that he could win any battle now simply by using artillery – which, in his case, may have been so, since his guns were controlled by Pizarro's one-time artillery king, Pedro de Candia, who had made an astonishing series of changes of front in recent years.[9] But Candia now betrayed yet another leader and aimed his guns high so as deliberately to cause no damage. Almagro realized what was going on, and had him executed as a traitor. Pedro Pizarro says that the real battle did not begin till darkness fell, and adds that the royalist infantry sang a song of victory amid the confusion and the cavalry of Almagro was disheartened by this.[10]

Then Pedro Suárez reported that he told the young Almagro, 'My Lord, if your Lordship had followed my advice, we should have won a victory today. But you took other counsel and so we shall lose. I do not want myself to be on the losing side so that, since your Lordship won't let me win on my terms, I'll do so on the other.' With that he cantered over to join Vaca de Castro. There were other such actions in this battle. Almagro's arquebuses, however, continued to do much damage, killing several important royalists such as Gómez de Tordoya and Álvarez Holguín.

The fighting continued into the night till Almagro *hijo* admitted his defeat and rode back disconsolate into Cuzco, where he was shortly detained by Rodrigo de Salazar, who had once been his deputy, and Antón Ruiz de Guevara, whom he himself had named a magistrate. Next day, Vaca went into Cuzco, where he had Almagro *hijo* beheaded in the same place where his father had died. Like his father, he was buried in the Mercedarian church. Some Almagrists, however (Diego Méndez, for example), escaped into the forest where they were welcomed by Manco Capac.

This victory inaugurated some years of relative serenity in Peru. Vaca de Castro governed with rectitude. He divided those Indians who had no masters among those who had no Indians but had done well on his behalf in the war. Vaca's laws were generally received with favour by the

Indians, who admitted that they were comparable to those of their own monarchs in the past.[11] There were, of course, Spanish complainers, such as Hernando Mogollón, who had done well but received no Indians; Vaca agreed with his self-appraisal and gave him an *encomienda*. Vaca also sent deserving captains to remote places to win new conquests: Vergara to Pacamura; Diego de Rojas, Nicolás de Heredia and Felipe Gutiérrez to Musu; Vélez de Guzmán to Muyupamba; and Alonso de Monroy to help Valdivia in Chile. But though Vaca at last seemed to have found a peaceful settlement, there were still many tragedies ahead.

For a time, however, the surviving members of the Pizarro family were not engaged in these battles since the surviving putative leader, Gonzalo, was physically far away from the centre of power.

Gonzalo Pizarro and Orellana
seek cinnamon and find the Amazon

*You shall understand, Sancho, that Spaniards and those who
embark themselves at Cadiz to go to the Indies, one of the greatest
signs they have to know whether they have passed the equinoctial,
is that all men that are on the ship, their lice die on them . . .*

Cervantes, Don Quixote

In late 1540 Francisco Pizarro had named his younger brother, the
charming and valiant Gonzalo, governor of Quito. This gave Gonzalo
control of the north of the old Inca empire. Atahualpa had had his supporters there. Pizarro had also given Gonzalo an *encomienda* which
included the Cañari people, Spain's best friends among the indigenous
population. Gonzalo behaved curiously, however, in his new position.
He took up his office formally on 1 December 1540, but immediately
devoted himself to arranging an expedition whose aim was to try to find
cinnamon on the eastern side of the majestic Andes.

Cinnamon was native to Brazil, though it is generally believed that
the quality of the product there is inferior to that found in the old world,
for example in Ceylon. To produce cinnamon, the bark of the tree is
powdered, macerated in sea water, then distilled. The resulting golden
aromatic oil with its distinctive smell and taste had by the sixteenth
century already become much sought after in cookery. The search for
cinnamon was the incentive for the expedition which Gonzalo Pizarro
now mounted.

He left Quito in February 1541 with nearly 200 Spaniards, a large
number of Indian porters – though surely not approaching the figure of
4,000 given by chroniclers – many llamas as beasts of burden, about
200 pigs to supply bacon on the way and a large number of fighting dogs,

without which, at that time, no Spanish army was complete. At that time Gonzalo Pizarro was powerful because of his association with his brother, the marquis, but his own qualities of leadership also seemed magnetically attractive. So, as the conquistador Ortiguera would one day put it, 'there followed him in that undertaking a large number of the noblest and most prominent people of the realm'. Ortiguera added: 'it was a great achievement to have been able to bring them together and with them 260 horses', as well as a good number of arquebuses and crossbows, munitions, other implements of war, slaves and Indians; a 'magnificent body of men and one well prepared for any adventure'.[1]

They began by going east over the Andes where Gonzalo reported: 'we came to some very rugged and wooded country with great ranges out of which we were obliged to open up roads anew not only for the men but also for the horses'. At least a hundred Indians died from cold, crossing the Andes. They continued thus till, sixty leagues (180 miles) to the east of Quito, they found themselves in the flat lands of the jungle in the headwaters of the Napo, a large meandering river with a big flood plain,[2] in a province which they named Zumaco, where it was supposed that the cinnamon trees grew.

From Zumaco, Gonzalo and his men went down into the beautiful valley of the abundantly flowing river Coca, and followed it down to where there was a stretch of narrows. Here Gonzalo built a wooden bridge over which he could carry his expedition to the north side. There the men remained for several weeks.

At this point they were joined by a smaller force led by another Extremeño, Francisco de Orellana. This conquistador, though his name is from a place in the beautiful valley called the Serena, was born, like the Pizarros, in Trujillo and, like them also, was a distant cousin of Hernán Cortés.[3] He was in Nicaragua by 1527 and probably was among the lion-hearted men who came down to Peru with Alvarado in the company of Pedro Álvarez de Holguín, another Extremeño friend of the Pizarros. Orellana established himself at Puerto Viejo and afterwards went as a senior captain to help the Pizarros at Lima and at Cuzco. He became 'ensign-general' of the 700 men sent by Hernando Pizarro to Cuzco and lost an eye at Las Salinas. At some point in these undertakings, he gained a rough knowledge of Quechua. Then he was sent by Francisco Pizarro to re-establish the settlement at the port of Guayaquil and La Culata which had been founded by Benalcázar but then destroyed

by Indians. He became a link between the *tierras del sur* and the Ecua-
dorian plains.

Discussions began as to how one could go directly from Quito overland to the Mar del Norte, or the Atlantic. A pioneer in this field had
been Gonzalo Díaz de Pineda, who was the first Spaniard (or European,
for that matter) to cross the great range of the Andes.[4] Orellana soon
became captain-general and lieutenant-governor in this province –
lieutenant, that is, to Francisco Pizarro. In these offices Orellana emerged
as a strong opponent of sexual deviations: he had two compatriots
burned for sodomy and their goods confiscated.[5] Gonzalo Pizarro then
became his overlord.

Gonzalo Pizarro expected Orellana to assist and accompany him and
he was anxious to do this, though he had to go down to Guayaquil first
on the Pacific coast. Thus he was too late to accompany Gonzalo in February and caught up with his commander only at the end of March.
They met at Quema, about 400 miles east of Quito. But Orellana and
his twenty-three companions were near starvation and, as was said at
the time, no one had more than a sword and a shield as weapons. Quema
had a savannah about six miles long and about a mile broad, so it was
a reasonable place for a rest. Gonzalo Pizarro interrogated, brutally,
several Indian chiefs whom he expected to be able to tell him about the
country ahead but, though they said that there was good land to be
found, where the population was large and wore clothes, most knew
only of forests usually inundated with water. Pizarro pressed on, however, seeking food and fertile land, while Orellana rested.

On his journey of reconnaissance, Gonzalo Pizarro left his horses
behind. He was away seventy days and found a few cinnamon trees. The
cinnamon here was not in the bark, however, but in the form of flower
buds, a sample of which Gonzalo sent back to the king. A small detachment led by Gonzalo's camp master, Antonio de Ribera, a man from an
aristocratic family in Soria, went ahead further to discover settlements
with houses on the bank of what they thought was a new river (which
turned out to be the Napo), and, indeed, people wearing clothes. Gonzalo
captured some fifteen canoes from these Indians: 'in these,' he recalled,

we went up and down the main river in search of food and there we built
[also] a brigantine to protect and to accompany the canoes, because we
were compelled to cross over from one side of the river to another and,

without this [brigantine], the men of the expedition could not have been kept in condition both from the point of view of food and from the point of view of carrying weapons and munitions for the arquebuses and [whatever was necessary] for the crossbows and iron bars and pickaxes, [not to speak of shoes for horses]. But I was informed by Indian guides that ahead of us lay a great uninhabited region where there was no food whatsoever.[6]

Orellana had by this time joined Gonzalo Pizarro. He had been against building the brigantine, but once the decision had been made against his own judgement, he busied himself, as the *de facto* second-in-command, in finding iron for nails and wood for timber and so on. There was no shortage of wood, lianas for cordage, resin nor indeed of metal for nails.

With the canoes and this brigantine, the *San Pedro*, Gonzalo Pizarro and his men reached the junction of the rivers Coca and Napo. The equipment, the supplies and the sick were here placed on the brigantine, and Juan de Alcántara (presumably, from his name, an Extremeño) was put in command. The rest of the expedition struggled with their horses along the banks of the river though the undergrowth was thick and there were marshes and tributaries flowing into the river Napo which meant they had to build bridges. The adventurers found little food and by that time all the pigs of the expedition had been eaten. They continued thus for forty days and covered another 150 miles.

Orellana told Pizarro that he had been able to talk to guides whom he considered reliable (his Quechua was by then reasonable), who had said that the uninhabited region ahead was indeed vast and that there was no food whatever to be had until the point

> where one great river [the Amazon itself] joined that down which we were proceeding and that, from that junction, one day's journey up the other river, there was an abundance of maize. And captain Orellana told me that, in order to serve His Majesty, and for love of me, he was willing to go in search of that food where the Indians said that it was and that, if I would give him the brigantine *San Pedro* and the canoes manned by sixty men, he would go in search of that food and bring it back.[7]

Gonzalo trusted Orellana since he had been such a friend of the Pizarro family for so long. They both came from Trujillo. So Pizarro agreed and allowed him fifty-seven men, but specified that Orellana had to be back with him in twelve days.[8] This was the crucial moment of Orellana's life, the origin of his glory and of the terrible accusations which would be made against him. For Orellana sailed off in the brigantine, with about ten canoes tied to its sides, with the plan of turning back with such food as he had procured, but he never returned.

Orellana took with him on the *San Pedro* many heavy objects, such as most of the clothing and bedding of the expedition, munitions, spare weapons, a small quantity of food, but probably not, as was afterwards alleged by Gonzalo Pizarro and his friends, emeralds and gold. On their second day out, still on the Napo, the *San Pedro* hit a fallen tree in the middle of the river and much damage was caused. Had they not been close to the shore the ship would have been destroyed. But Orellana and the crew hauled the *San Pedro* to the side of the river, mended the hole in its side and continued their journey. The river there had a fast current so that they found themselves travelling sixty or seventy-five miles a day, the river always increasing in width as so many smaller streams were entering it, especially from the right or the south.

The first three days they travelled without seeing any settlement. As they had by then long distanced themselves from where they had left Gonzalo and since they had so little to eat and their route seemed so unclear, Orellana and his leading companions began to talk quite soon of their return and how they would cope with the tremendous current against which they would have to row. Fr Carvajal, the chaplain of the expedition, recorded that it seemed from very early on necessary to choose between two evils: one, which the captain and most of his fellow leaders thought the lesser danger, was to continue on and follow the river; the other, which seemed to spell certain death, was to try to return upstream. To go back by land appeared impossible.

So they continued onwards with no idea what they would encounter. They did realize that the river would eventually meet the Atlantic but no one had any knowledge of how far that point would be. Food was now almost non-existent, and the Spaniards were reduced to cooking shoes, belts and other leather clothes, sometimes seasoned with herbs. But no one knew which herbs were edible, and some found themselves poisoned in consequence and at the point of death 'because they became like mad men and did not possess sense'.[9] They did still have, it is true, some maize and wine but Fr Carvajal was attempting to preserve the latter so that he could celebrate mass.

Conditions in one sense began to improve. For after New Year's Day 1542 Orellana's Spaniards started to hear the distant beat of drums. It became slowly evident that they were not far from an Indian *pueblo*. Then, after several weeks of seeing nobody, they came upon four canoes full of Indians. Orellana sailed the *San Pedro* fast down river to find what he and his companions assumed to be the *pueblo* of Aparia. This was probably near the confluence of the Napo and the Curaray, a black-water river which is the Napo's largest tributary. There Orellana addressed the assembled local elders in Quechua and told them not to be afraid because he and his friends would do nothing wrong or evil. The chief was pleased and asked whether the Spaniards needed anything. 'Only food,' replied Orellana and in a short time they were brought a selection of meat, including game, and fish of many types. There was also maize, yucca and sweet potato.

After they had eaten, Orellana called a meeting of his fifty-odd companions. He told them he favoured returning up the river by boat to rejoin Gonzalo Pizarro, however difficult that might seem. But most of his companions thought that it would be 'disastrous for us if we were to go with Your Lordship back up the river'.[10] They hoped that Orellana would not put them in the awkward situation where they would be compelled to disobey him and in which they would appear traitors, adding that, on the other hand, they would be ready to follow him on any other route by which their lives might be saved. They concluded by saying that

> they had been assured by the seamen who are here, or in the boat, or in the canoes, that we are some 600 miles or more by land from the expeditionary force of governor Gonzalo, all without road or settlement but, on the contrary, with very wild and wooded regions which we have come to know well from experience.

Like most Spaniards at that time, those who thought like this committed their views to paper, and they signed the document where one can see the names of the Dominican friar, Gaspar de Carvajal; the notary, Francisco de Isasaga; and several Enríquezes, Gutiérrezes and Rodríguezes.

Next day, 5 January 1542, Orellana called the notary Isasaga and declared that, though it was against his wish, the expedition would indeed continue, provided that they waited where they were for a time to see whether Gonzalo Pizarro and his friends would catch them up.

For since they had on board many objects which belonged to the men with Gonzalo, they might otherwise risk being accused of being thieves. This scene before a notary in a spot so remote that there could have been no European for over 1,000 miles, on the edge of a river which had never before been visited by any European, illustrates an astonishing side of the great Spanish adventure.

Later there was much argument about this conversation. Some, such as Toribio de Ortiguera, recalled thinking that they could with ease have sailed back up the river. Others, such as Pedro Domínguez Miradero, thought that the currents and the rains would have prevented them going any distance upstream at all. Yet others said that the brigantine could not have gone back, and that left only the canoes which they thought would have been easily overwhelmed. Orellana himself seems to have become dominated by the desire to see where the rivers on which he had embarked reached the sea. In the meantime, he took possession in the name of the king of the *pueblo* in which they were and gave it the name of 'Victoria'.

Fr Carvajal noted:

> We stayed in that *pueblo* longer than we should have done, eating whatever we could find (the Indians had stopped bringing food regularly) in such a way that, thereafter, we went ahead with great speed and we discussed again whether there was some way of finding out what was going on in Gonzalo Pizarro's camp.[11]

Orellana agreed to give 6,000 castellanos to any group of his men willing to return to give news to Gonzalo, and he promised them two black slaves also. But only three men volunteered, and they did not go.

The Spaniards left this Amazonian *pueblo* on the day of the fiesta of Candelmas, that is, 2 February, which commemorates the purification of the Virgin. They rowed their way further down the Napo past a point where the turbulence of the waters was intense to an area infested with mosquitoes. There a chief named Irrimorrany visited them, bringing food, including turtles and parrots. On 11 February, some hundred miles beyond where the Napo meets the Curaray, Orellana and the *San Pedro* finally came upon the Amazon proper, not far from what is now Iquitos, at a place now called Francisco de Orellana.

At the next halt they received food in abundance such as turtles, sea cows, roast monkeys, roast cats and partridges. Orellana gave a sermon to the Indians explaining that the Spaniards were Christians and vassals of the 'emperor of the Christians and the king of Spain, Charles'. 'We,' Orellana insisted, 'were children of the sun.'[12] The Indians of that region seemed pleased to hear that interesting claim.

Orellana set about making another boat to substitute for the *San Pedro*, which had now deteriorated. Juan de Alcántara, the Extremeño, and Sebastián Rodríguez from Galicia, neither of whom had experience of such tasks, promised to make the necessary nails, which they did: 2,000 were ready in twelve days. They also made bellows from buskin and built a forge. Timber was cut, cotton was used as oakum to fill in cracks in the wood, resin from trees was used as tar and the new vessel was ready in about forty days. Diego Mexía, a carpenter, was the director of these operations. He wrote it was 'a wonderful thing to see the happiness with which our comrades worked. There was no one amongst us who was accustomed to such work but, all the same, they conducted themselves as if they had been professionals.'[13] The Spaniards bore in mind that the Amazonian Indians cut wood only in the last quarter of the moon's cycle to avoid the rotting which they believed occurred if they cut at other times. Thus it was that Orellana and his expeditionary force spent Lent 1542.

On the Amazon in April – the *San Pedro* having been repaired – Orellana travelled fast with his two ships. When the river broadened, it was impossible for them to land and sleep. They again became short of food. On 6 May, however, they succeeded in shooting a vulture with a crossbow and a large fish was caught the same day. From then on, Fr Carvajal wrote,

> we endured more hardships and more hunger and passed more uninhabited regions than before because the river led from one forested territory to another and we found no place to sleep nor could any [more] fish be caught, so we were reduced to our customary fare of herbs and occasionally roasted maize.[14]

On 12 May they reached the junction of the Tefé with the Amazon and a great number of canoes suddenly appeared, full of warriors. Orellana prepared for battle but, alas, the powder for his arquebuses seemed damp, so he had to rely on crossbows. There followed a confusing conflict: half the fifty Spaniards found themselves quickly in the water but Orellana and Alonso de Robles, with the other half, captured a riverine *pueblo* and seized a good quantity of food, including turtles in corrals, much fish, some dried meats and biscuit. This they placed on their new brigantine and set off down the river again, the arquebuses now able to be used since the munitions had become drier. Still the Indians pressed hard and there were some difficult moments, Orellana being nearly killed just before his assailant was himself killed by a Spaniard with an arquebus.

The two ships soon reached Omagua, which was the first territory where neither Orellana nor any of his friends could communicate with the natives, since the language spoken bore no relation to Quechua. There were other surprises. For example, the Indians of this region were skilled potters and Fr Carvajal thought the pottery there was 'superior to that of Malaga'.[15] It is now known as 'Guarita ware'. The Spaniards also found two giant idols elaborately decorated with feathers. Here was a riverine town about six miles long, whose lord, Paguana, received the Spaniards hospitably. The Indians awaited them in their houses as if it were the most normal thing to welcome foreigners, though they had never before met such people as the Castilians. Carvajal wrote that 'from this *pueblo* there were many roads running inland, with many llamas, and there seemed a good deal of silver about'. The people seemed happy and wore clothes with bright colours. They evidently ate fruit of all kinds: there were pineapples, pears, cherries and avocados.[16]

Another riverine town also seemed to continue for miles, every section with its own embarkation point. The houses here were designed for living on the land but the people had large dwellings in trees, 'like magpies' nests', with everything ready for when the river was in flood.[17] Some towns gave the Spaniards 'much war'; others supplied them with food. In others, the people fled. Thus it was that Orellana and his men reached the junction of the Amazon proper with what they called the Black river, the Río Negro, as it has been known ever since, because its waters were as 'black as ink' and for more than sixty miles after joining the Amazon it preserved its menacing dark colour.[18]

After the union of the two immense rivers, Orellana and his expedition met an extraordinary variety of towns. There was one with two towers, several with temples to the Sun, and one where an Indian explained through signs that the people were 'subjects of the Amazons whom they served only with the feathers of parrots, which they used as linings of the roofs of their houses'. It turned out that there was here a lady who ruled the whole territory, directing the wars of these women with zest and verve.[19] It was this improbable experience that led Orellana to christen the river which they soon would know so well as 'the Amazon'.

Soon after this they came to another great confluence where the Amazon met the river Madeira. In one of the towns here they captured as a potential interpreter an Indian girl, who told them that inland there were many Christians, among them two white women – left behind, it seemed, in 1531, eleven years before, by Diego de Ordaz. In this territory of the 'Amazonas' they were attacked fiercely by bows and arrows, including poisoned arrows such as one which wounded Antonio Carranza and another which killed García de Soria. In this battle, the Spaniards found themselves facing about ten naked women who were white skinned, tall, with big heads.

In the next town, which was surrounded by a temperate land which the Spaniards thought would be good for cattle, wheat and fruit trees, Orellana asked an Indian who the women were who had attacked his expedition. The Indian replied that there were seventy *pueblos* inhabited only by women. Orellana asked if these women had children. The reply was that 'the lord who lived next door carried the women to his own land, his men impregnated them and returned them to their own residence. If they had a son, he would be killed but, if they had a daughter, she would be well looked after and trained for war.'[20] One can only imagine that the Spaniards heard in this conversation what they expected to hear. The historian Oviedo commented that these were not real Amazons for they had two breasts; a real Amazon did not have a right breast since it would get in the way of her bow.[21]

Soon after that Orellana and his friends noticed that the river was becoming tidal and realized that they must be approaching the sea. The land was clear of woods, the high banks and savannah were replaced by lowlands, and soon they were plainly in the estuary of the mighty river, surrounded by islands instead of mainland. By this stage of the journey, they lacked anchors and used stones instead, but sometimes the tide picked them up and carried them back in an hour or so to where they had been that morning. Here one of the brigantines was damaged by a floating log, and the other one at the same time was left high and dry on the riverside. There they were attacked by Indians in great numbers, but they withstood them. They found a beach where they could haul out and repair their vessels. New rigging was made out of vines and sails out of the blankets in which they had been sleeping, and in two weeks both ships were adequately restored. But these last days in the Amazon were days of penance because of the hunger from which they suffered, for they did not eat anything save what could be picked up on the edge of the river – a few snails and some tiny crabs.

Then at last they were able to sail out of the mouth of the great river. It was, as they all knew, 25 August, St Louis's day, 244 days since they had separated from Gonzalo Pizarro. They had lost fourteen men in that time. Fr Carvajal noted:

> we rested a day making ropes and, as the rest of the things with which we fitted ourselves out were imitations, and made by men without experience and unaccustomed to such professions, they lasted only a short time. So it was necessary to keep working and fitting ourselves out at random. In this way in one place, a sail was made and in another a rudder, in a third a pump, and in one further instance some rigging. In the case of each of these things, so long as we did not have them, we were in great danger.

Carvajal went on to say that he was leaving out a 'list of many other things which we lacked such as pilots and sailors and a compass . . . and without them there was no man, however devoid of common sense, that would thus dare to go to sea except ourselves'.[22]

They emerged into the Atlantic by sheer chance in a zone which the Treaty of Tordesillas had given to Spain, not to Portugal.

Meantime, Gonzalo Pizarro was at the confluence of the Napo and the Coca, at least 1,600 miles away as the crow flies. It took him a long time to realize the truth of what had happened. He later accused Orellana of treachery, claiming that Orellana had

> shown the greatest cruelty in which any faithless man could indulge, abandoning Gonzalo Pizarro and the rest in those wildernesses among so many rivers and without food and caught in vast uninhabited regions, also carrying off all the arquebuses and crossbows, the iron materials of the whole expeditionary force. After great hardship, that expeditionary force did arrive at the junction of the Rivers Coca and Napo.[23]

Gonzalo never considered what might have happened to prevent his friend's return, and since then his view has been widely canvassed. Even the historian Oviedo, who came to know Orellana afterwards, seems to have thought that he should, and could, easily have returned to where Gonzalo Pizarro was waiting.[24] Few appreciated that the force of the currents made a return virtually impossible.

Gonzalo went on in his accusation:

And paying no heed whatever to what he owed to the service of Your Majesty, and to do what was his duty as he had been instructed by myself, instead of bringing back the food, he [Orellana] went on down the river without leaving any arrangements [to inform me] . . . And when my expeditionary force, having gone that far and seen that there was no relief for them in the way of food . . . they became greatly discouraged, because for many days they had eaten nothing but palm shoots and some fruit which had fallen from trees and which they found on the ground, together with all kinds of noxious wild beasts which they had been able to find since they had eaten in this wild country more than 1,000 dogs and more than 100 horses.

First Gonzalo Pizarro forced his men down to where the rivers met, and having been told that food was to be had up the river which the Coca joined he went there and indeed found food in abundance. 'There they rested' and then, realizing that Orellana and their other friends had gone for good, they went back to where they had left him and began the long dispiriting return to Quito.

This was one of the worst journeys in the history of the empire. Lost in forests without paths, in heavy tropical rain, Gonzalo's men floundered slowly west, many barefoot, suffering as much from the thorns and the roots as from the mosquitoes and wild animals, often having to clear the way with their swords. It rained so much that days went by without their ever seeing the sun. The Spaniards were always drenched and such clothes as they had rotted, so that they had no alternative to going practically naked. All the 4,000 or so Indian porters had died, and two thirds of the Spaniards as well. About eighty of them reached more open land which they knew to be close to Quito, where there was game and birds. Unshod, they walked into that city, kissing the earth and there eating with such passion that most nearly died of a surfeit. Gonzalo Pizarro said:

> At the cost of great suffering and with the loss of everything which we had taken with us, we returned to Quito with only our swords and a staff in hand. To Quito from where we turned back must have been more than 800 miles and a much greater distance by the route by which we returned.[25]

Quito was far emptier than it had been when Gonzalo had left it, for half the population had gone to the war against Almagro. All the survivors of Gonzalo's expedition needed new clothes but tailors were hard to find. Six suits were brought out by the citizenry to greet Gonzalo, but he and his close friends did not wish to wear what could not be worn by their companions. So half-naked, they went to the cathedral to give thanks for their survival, in scenes of great emotion. Then the bitterness at Orellana's action took shape with a vengeance.

28

Orellana and 'New Andalusia'

The nearer the church the further from God, and all is not gold which glistreth.

Cervantes, *Don Quixote*

The extraordinary journey of Orellana was, meantime, continuing. Leaving the Amazon they soon found themselves north of the estuary, in the alarming Gulf of Paria. Once in it, like most sixteenth-century travellers there, they found it very difficult to leave it. Fr Gaspar de Carvajal described how this took seven days 'during all of which time our companions never dropped the oars from their hands and during all these seven days, we ate nothing but some fruit resembling plums called *hogos*'. Carvajal added:

> having escaped from this prison, we proceeded for two days along the coast [of Guiana] at the end of which, without knowing where we were, or where we were going, nor what was to become of us, we made landfall in the island of Cubagua [on 11 September 1542] and then in the city of Nueva Cádiz, where we found our company and the small brigantine which had arrived two days before.[1]

Most of the survivors, about forty all told, returned to Peru. In no time, Carvajal found himself in charge of the Dominican house in Cuzco – a foundation which had become rich because of the many sacks of coca leaf given to it by Hernando Pizarro. But Orellana and some of his close associates bought a ship in Trinidad and went first to Santo Domingo, then to Spain via Portugal. In Santo Domingo Orellana met the historian of Spain in the New World, Oviedo, who eventually wrote a good, clear and detailed account of the journey down the Amazon.[2]

Orellana was delayed some days in Portugal and then went to Valladolid, which he reached in May 1543. The secretary of the Council of the Indies, Juan de Samano, wrote to the king's principal secretary, Cobos:

> There has arrived from Peru one who came out by going down a river which he navigated for a distance of 1,800 leagues and emerged at the Cape of St Agustin; and because of the particulars which he has brought with him covering his voyage, Your Lordship will not hear him without fatigue. I shall not relate these particulars since he will shortly come himself.

In the margin of this letter Cobos made a note: 'Would like an account sent to H. M.'

Orellana's account was based on the notes of Fr Carvajal. It was widely read, sometimes with disbelief. People laughed at the idea that there were Amazons, and López de Gomera, Cortés's chaplain and biographer, commented that 'women can shoot perfectly well with a right breast still there'. He added that others beside Orellana had told this same story about Amazons ever since the Indies had been discovered. There was also anxiety as to whether the river on which Orellana had travelled was in Portuguese territory according to the Treaty of Tordesillas. The Prince Regent Philip accepted Orellana's version of what had happened: 'owing to the current, you were all carried down the said river for over 600 miles to a place where you could not turn back'. In fact, the course of the Amazon (Orellana's river) is to the west of 48° longitude and, therefore, well within the Spanish zone as laid down by the pope at Tordesillas.

Orellana also faced the bitter criticism of Gonzalo Pizarro, who had reported that 'he ran off with a brigantine and canoes filled with men and property belonging to him and, as a consequence a certain number died of hunger'. Orellana, however, wrote a note to the king about the great size and wealth of the country which he had seen and across which he had travelled. He ended by stating that the natives inhabiting the land alongside the Amazon were intelligent and so 'will be able to come into a knowledge of our Holy Catholic Faith'. Because of that, he beseeched the king 'to see fit to give it to me as territory to be held by me as governor in order that I may be able to explore it and colonise it on behalf of Your Majesty'.[3]

The Council of the Indies was more cautious in respect of this demand than it would have been a generation before: 'it may be a rich country,' it conceded, 'and one by which Your Majesty might be rendered a service'. The council agreed, however, that 'it would be advantageous to the service of Your Majesty that the banks of the river be explored and settled and taken possession of within the shortest time'. The council noted that the Portuguese had built flotillas to go up the Amazon from the coast and that the king of France was also interesting himself in these regions. It was, however, the view of a majority on the council that the business of exploration and colonization should be entrusted to Orellana. The minority opinion was confined to the untrustworthy Dr Bernal, who thought that Orellana was inappropriate as a commander since he was poor. Nor did Bernal believe that Orellana could live up to the instructions which would be given to him. The land would be stirred up and people would come to hate the Christian religion. Bernal thought that a peacefully inclined captain should be sent to the Amazon, not with soldiers in attendance but with clergymen, 'who would try out all the good and most feasible means for bringing the land round both to the service of God and to obedience to Your Majesty'.[4]

Another member of the Council of the Indies was now Licenciado Gutierre Velázquez de Lugo, a typical member of the bureaucracy of Spain of the time, being a relation of the Velázquezes of Cuba and a brother of Alonso de Lugo, judge of Granada, as well as apparently related to the chronicler of Medina del Campo, Bernal Díaz del Castillo.[5] Velázquez, who had never left Spain, assumed that any new expedition on the Amazon would begin from Peru, approximately, indeed, from where Orellana had started off. Orellana, he thought, should take 180 men from Spain, of whom seventy would be cavalrymen.[6]

In the end, in February 1544 Orellana did receive a contract from the Crown 'to discover and populate the lands which are called New Andalusia'. Who suggested this name is not evident from the surviving papers, but it must have been someone on the council, presumably not Orellana himself.

Orellana's new territory would extend many miles from the mouth of the Amazon. A city would be founded at its mouth and another at some distance inland at a place where he, the royal officials and the friars thought best. Orellana would be *adelantado*, that coveted title, also governor and captain-general.[7] He would take with him 200 infantrymen, 100 horse, 8 friars and 8 African slaves, as well as material to build brigantines in which to sail up the river. Orellana's salary would be 5,000 ducats a year, to be paid for from the profits of the lands conquered and settled, together with a twelfth of the royal revenue, provided it was not more than one million maravedís each year. He would be exempt from taxes.

Orellana was warned:

> if some governor or captain shall have explored or colonised some section of the river bank and shall be on it when you arrive, you should not do anything in detriment to his interests ... even though you may find this to be within your jurisdiction as governor, so that we can avoid those disturbances which have arisen out of such situations in Peru and elsewhere.

He was instructed to keep to the rules which had been agreed with the 'most serene King of Portugal' as to the division of the Indies and also with regard to the Moluccas and the Spice Islands.[8]

There were several minor instructions: no Indians were to be carried on Orellana's boats 'unless it be an occasional Indian boy whom the Spaniards ... may have brought up [to be an interpreter]' and, even for that, authorization had to be given by the viceroy of Peru. Orellana was told that neither he nor any member of his party should take away from the Indians 'any married woman nor child nor any woman whatsoever, no gold nor silver nor cotton nor feathers nor precious stones nor any other article unless it be by bartering and by payment'. But when the food which the expedition was to take from Spain ran out,

> they shall be entitled to ask the Indians for some with offers of barter and, in cases where this may fail, then they may appeal to them for the said food with entreaties and kind words and means of persuasion, in such a way that they shall never go so far as to take it by force except after all these means, as well as others which the inspector and the friars together with the captain may advise, shall have been tried out.

It was also stipulated that in no way whatsoever was war to be waged against the Indians unless it was to defend themselves, with the restraint that the situation might demand. For His Majesty was sending Orellana and his men 'solely to teach and instruct the Indians' – not to fight but 'to impart to them a knowledge of God and our Holy Catholic Faith and the obedience which they owe to Your Majesty'. Finally, 'no occasion is to be allowed to arise serving as an excuse wherewith the

Spaniards may hold Indians or maltreat them or prevent them from becoming Christians'.[9] These provisions were written after the passage of the New Laws of 1542.

From May to November 1544 Orellana was busy in Spain recruiting men for his expedition. He found that there was in Seville a shortage of sailors who wanted to take part, nor was there any Castilian who knew the region of the Amazon at all. So Orellana decided that he would do well to take Portuguese sailors 'because they are experienced in small, well-fitted out vessels' and told the emperor that he wanted to be able to take as many Portuguese pilots as he desired. Then guns could not be found unless the emperor provided them. In September 1544 we find a letter written from Valladolid by Prince Philip (the Regent) to Orellana saying that, through Fr Pablo de Torres, he had become informed of the preparations for the great journey and of its excellent prospects. As to Torres, because he was so experienced and so good 'it would be wise to get advice from him in whatever you undertake'. The prince added: 'Be warned against taking any Portuguese because it is believed that they would be a source of trouble.'

When, a few weeks later, Fr Torres reported that Orellana seemed to be running out of money, the prince wrote to the friar: 'there is no possibility of our helping out with any money at all. I am telling, too, the Casa de la Contratación not to allow on this expedition anyone of whom you disapprove. But it is perfectly all right to take stallions as well as mares.' He was in agreement that arms should be neither given nor sold to the Indians. But general Spanish opinion was that there was advantage in the Spaniards giving attention to the teaching of the Indians to be artisans. We read of Orellana writing to the king at the end of October to say that his stepfather, Cosme de Chaves of Trujillo, was helping with the expedition to the extent of 1,600 ducats and that Genoese merchants were going to assist with another 2,500, thanks to the dealings of Vicente del Monte. This letter received a sharp answer, addressed to Orellana 'Governor of the province of New Andalusia'. The prince said that he had 'learned that Orellana was entering into a contract for aid from various merchants ... we do not consider that to be true because we don't think that you could do such a thing'. And he added: 'You must not go against what Fray Pablo says.'[10]

At the end of November 1544 Orellana reported something else: 'in order the better to perpetuate myself, I have become married'.[11] His wife was Ana de Ayala, who agreed to travel with him to New Andalu-sia, along with 'a few sisters-in-law'. This seems to have made Orellana unpopular. But not as much as his nomination of a Genoese camp mas-ter did.

By now the preparations for the voyage back to the Amazon were almost complete but relations on board and in the dockyard in Seville continued bad. Cristóbal de Maldonado, the chief constable on board and in effect in control of discipline, was on bad terms with Orellana, whom he knew well, having been with him on the Amazon. Orellana hired as pilot a good sailor from Cadiz, Francisco Sánchez, who, however, did not know the coast of Brazil. A Portuguese who did know it was also hired, but it took time to secure approval for his participation.

Fr Pablo de Torres reported ill of these preparations. He wrote that, when he arrived in Seville, he found the whole expedition to New Anda-lusia in a 'very disorganized and even desperate condition'. One of the ships was damaged so that it had to be replaced by another, smaller one. To those who complained, Orellana said that he planned to take on the horses which he needed in the Canary or the Cape Verde islands and that he already had all the materials necessary to build small boats *in situ*. Seville was outraged at the fact that not only were many of the sailors Portuguese but also some of them were even English, Germans or Flemings. The master of the flagship (the *capitana*) came from Dubrovnik! Torres was unable to examine the expedition's accounts, which were kept secret by Orellana and his Genoese friends. Orellana seemed to have managed everything so badly that 'no organiser of an expedition would have let him go from here to Naples', much less the Amazon. Fr Torres wrote:

> I do not wish to relate the infinite errors ... which have been perpetrated in connection with the enterprise. The man who has completely ruined things has been [Vicente] del Monte, who has made himself rich out of the money of the Genoese through deals, and the *adelantado* [Orellana] has been putting up with all this. How could the fleet be well fitted out if to his own wife, who is excessively poor, they have given jewels, silks and embroi-deries and if the Genoese have not handed over the 3,000 ducats in small change; and if the *adelantado* and Del Monte had money in their pockets while the rest of the expedition is perishing from hunger and thirst.

It seems to have been the incompetence of Orellana which most shocked Fr Pablo, who wrote to the Prince Regent Philip: 'I assure Your Highness that he is not carrying enough water to reach the Canaries nor jars in which to secure any if it takes them fifteen days to get there ... and also the deck of the ship on which the *adelantado* is sailing is full of women (*llena de mujeres*).'[12]

Nevertheless, on 11 May 1545 the voyage began: four ships with 400 foreign soldiers on board. The journey was slow since Orellana chose to stop three months in Tenerife, and then spent two months in Portugal's Cape Verde islands. In the latter, ninety-eight members of his expedition died and fifty remained there because they were too weak to continue. Orellana also left behind one of his ships because he needed some of its equipment to repair the other vessels. In November he at last set off on the relatively short voyage from the Cape Verde Islands across to Brazil. But bad luck still dogged him: another ship with seventy-seven men on board, as well as eleven horses, foundered and was lost. Despite the long stay in the Cape Verde islands, water became short.

Finally Orellana reached one of the mouths of the Amazon. He started upstream immediately, despite his men's requests for a rest. There was at once a shortage of food and all the dogs and horses were eaten. Another fifty men died. One of the two caravels was wrecked, and those on board took refuge on an island where the natives were unusually friendly. In the next three months they built a new brigantine. Orellana, his wife and Fr Pablo set off on this vessel looking for the main river Amazon, leaving Diego Muñoz and thirty or so men behind. They eventually built their own boat using some of the timber and nails from the one which had foundered. In this craft they went upriver in search of Orellana, but there was no sign of him. So they returned to the sea. Six of them ran away because they believed that the territory was promising for agriculture, and four others absconded because they feared going on upstream in a small boat. The rest continued, though they were marooned one night in a mangrove swamp and driven mad by mosquitoes. Led by Francisco de Guzmán, they found a cultivated zone with cassava and maize as well as sweet potatoes, yams, ducks, chickens and also a turkey. Thus fortified, they had the energy to sail back up the South American coast through the Gulf of Paria to the island of Margarita.

After some time there they were joined by Ana de Ayala, without her husband, and twenty-five others. She reported that Orellana had not succeeded in finding the main channel of the Amazon and that, having fallen ill, he had decided to abandon the project of founding New Andalusia. He had made up his mind to seek gold and silver instead. But when, more prosaically, he was looking for food, he and his expedition were attacked by Indians in canoes. They bombarded the Spaniards with arrows; seventeen of them died. Orellana also died shortly afterwards, whether from grief over this loss or from his fever was unclear. It was November 1546.

Of the whole expedition which had set out from Sanlúcar in May 1545, only forty-four survived, including Orellana's widow, Ana. New Andalusia was not to be. But all the same Orellana is remembered as the involuntary architect of the geographical unity of a continent and the heroic survivor of one of the greatest journeys. Gonzalo Pizarro remembered him too – for other reasons.

29

The defeat of the viceroy

Oh Indies! Oh conquistadors full of work in the simplicity of those
times, where you had an excellent name and found eternal fame.
Dorantes de Carranza, *Nueva España*

Vaca de Castro's apparently calm control of turbulent Peru lasted till a
formal successor, a viceroy, was appointed from Spain. That was in February 1543 and the nominee was Blasco Núñez Vela, whose earlier life
had been spent as a captain of the fleet in several voyages to the Indies.
He had also been *corregidor* of Cuenca and of Malaga. His maritime
qualities may have been superlative; he may have been privately enchanting, for he was known to have been passionate in his feelings; he may
have been a good administrator, but he was politically inept. The Council of the Indies (García de Loaisa, García Fernández Manrique, Juan
Suárez de Carvajal, Juan Bernal Díaz de Luco and Gutierre Velázquez
de Lugo) made an error in nominating him to such an important post.
When he was named viceroy, it became immediately known that it
would be his responsibility to carry into effect in Peru the New Laws on
the administration of the empire and the benign treatment of Indians.[1]
(For the New Laws see Chapter 42.)

This news shocked the old conquistadors of Peru, above all the *encomenderos*. These men, often rich and comfortable, turned to the last of
the Pizarros, Gonzalo, to represent and lead them. Since his return from
the Amazon, Gonzalo had been living in luxury on his estate in Charcas
in what is now Bolivia. He had planned an expedition in 1542 but had
been distracted from that by his wish to avenge his brother Francisco.
The following year he set out with his son Francisco to deal with the
Paez Indians who had obstructed him on his earlier journey to the

headwaters of the Amazon, precisely at Timaná. In his absence he left Juan Cabrera as his acting governor. Cabrera then was named to carry out an expedition to the cinnamon forest.

Throughout 1542, however, Gonzalo seemed the man whom the *encomenderos* thought could lead them against the New Laws which they considered both unfair and absurd. Some of his friends urged him to seize the opportunity to carry out a 'unilateral declaration of independence', even make himself the first Spanish king of Peru, and marry an Indian princess.

In this electric atmosphere, Núñez Vela, the first viceroy, arrived at Nombre de Dios in the Gulf of Darien, accompanied by new judges of the supreme court of Peru, namely, Diego de Cepeda, who came from Tordesillas; Lisón de Tejada, from Logroño; Licenciado Álvarez; Pedro Ortiz de Zárate, from Orduña, in the Basque country; and Agustín de Zárate, his accountant. He was also accompanied by a host of friends, relations and a retinue of hopeful courtiers, among whom were the brothers of Santa Teresa, who as *conversos* thought that they had to escape Spain if they could. The new administrators separated from the fleet bound for Mexico in what is now Costa Rica. From Nombre de Dios the viceroy travelled overland to Panama, where he liberated many Indians who had been brought as slaves or servants from Peru. There were protests from the 'owners' but the viceroy told them that Charles the emperor had specifically requested that that should be done.

The rest of the viceroy's journey was beset with bad luck. First, his judge, Ortiz de Zárate, could not leave Panama because of illness. He tried, though, to persuade Núñez Vela to enter Peru '*blandamente*', innocently, and not to attempt to execute immediately the New Laws agreed in Spain – at least till the supreme court was in place. Then he could proclaim such laws as he thought right but even then, if there was opposition, it would be as well to consult the emperor again. If Charles once more directed the viceroy to enact the laws, he would be in a better position since he would by then have established himself.

The viceroy was angry at these suggestions, which he thought feeble, and set off impetuously without waiting for the judges. He went first to Tumbes, then south to Trujillo, insisting on declarations there about the New Laws. The people of Trujillo appealed against him, many of them supposing that their toils had been wasted if they were to expect no one to look after them when they were old. But Núñez Vela went ahead and sent a message to the interim governor, Vaca de Castro, ordering him to lay down his authority.[2] By then 'all Peru was full of the viceroy's harshness', as Garcilaso later put it. But Núñez Vela's train continued onwards to Lima. The town council decided on a grand reception, but there were to be no Indian slaves present. An anonymous wit wrote on the back wall of the main inn: 'Whoever seeks to throw me out of my house, I shall throw out of the world.'[3]

Núñez Vela was received about ten miles from Lima where many had gone out to meet him, headed by Vaca de Castro, Bishop Loaisa (not to be confused with his namesake and cousin), the bishop elect of Quito, Díaz, as well as the town council, headed by the Basque Benito Suárez de Carvajal, brother of Illán and Juan. The viceroy publicly swore that he would always act in the interests of all Peruvians. Celebrations followed in the cathedral. The next day Núñez Vela went to Pizarro's palace and had Vaca de Castro arrested and put in the common prison. The viceroy accused his predecessor of abetting the plots of Gonzalo Pizarro, an unjust accusation. If blame were to be found for such events, the finger should point rather at the viceroy himself, for it was he who was to blame for coming to Peru in such an impetuous way, publishing all that he was going to do against the *encomenderos*.[4] He seemed an absurd figure in demanding so much ceremony and ritual from his attendants.

Meantime Gonzalo wrote to the viceroy on behalf of the cities and the *encomenderos* to protest against the New Laws. The viceroy seemed obtuse. The judges of the supreme court eventually arrived in Lima. This further complicated matters, for they soon took up the cause of Xuarez de Carvajal, a factor whom the viceroy had had killed because a body of soldiers had been spotted leaving his house on their way to see Gonzalo Pizarro.[5] The matter was further complicated by the bad behaviour of two Almagrists, Diego Méndez and Gómez Pérez, who had escaped from Vaca de Castro to go and live in the circle of Manco Capac. They suggested that Manco Capac should be permitted to return to Cuzco where he could be expected to serve the new viceroy. Núñez Vela was pleased with that idea, but before he could act, Gómez Pérez and Manco Capac had a dispute over manners. The former threw a ninepin ball at Manco which hit him on the head and killed him.[6] Life in the new Peru was nothing if not short.

Now those Spaniards who were settled in Peru took the law into their own hands. The settlers of Huamanga, Arequipa and Chuquisaca all implored Gonzalo Pizarro to be their *procurador*, or representative, against the viceroy. In La Plata the settlers made a similar request to Diego Centeño, one of Pedro de Alvarado's followers, who by now was Gonzalo's deputy. Both went to Lima with armed men and, with the viceroy in Cuzco, prepared an independent army. Gonzalo recovered the *encomiendas* and other property of his brother Francisco which Vaca de Castro had seized. He also took gold and silver from the royal chest and soon had 400 settlers and as many as 20,000 Indians at his behest. He took prisoner those who had sided in recent events with the viceroy and hanged several of them, such as Pedro del Barco, Gómez de Luna from Badajoz and another former follower of Pedro de Alvarado, as well as Martín de Florencia who had been at Cajamarca. Diego Maldonado, held to be the richest of the *encomenderos* in Peru and so known as 'the Rich', was placed naked on a donkey and tortured with ropes and water.[7] Gonzalo also ordered other injustices, such as the execution of his cousin Pedro Pizarro. But he was talked out of that unwise idea by his experienced, eccentric and artful master of the horse, Francisco de Carvajal. Gonzalo also permitted Vaca de Castro to escape in a ship to Panama.

Gonzalo Pizarro now sought to order his army in an efficient style. His commander was Alonso de Toro from Trujillo but not from a grand family; his cavalry was commanded by Pedro Puertocarrero, a relation of the counts of Medellín (and remotely of Hernán Cortés); his arquebuses by Pedro Cermeño from Sanlúcar de Barrameda; while the captains of pikemen were Juan Vélez de Guevara[8] and Diego Gumiel. Hernando Bachicao, who pretended to be a count and was savage in all his actions, captained Gonzalo's artillery. That arm was becoming the decisive weapon of war. All these men were powerful independent conquistadors with long histories of achievement.

Gonzalo and his men mounted the great hill of Sacsahuaman overlooking Cuzco, and awaited the viceroy, who had a slightly larger army of 600 Spaniards, with 100 horse and 200 arquebusiers. Its basis was Vaca's army, and many of its men had known their opponents intimately for a generation: Alonso de Montemayor from Seville as captain of cavalry; Diego Álvarez de Cueto, the viceroy's brother-in-law, Martín de Robles who, like F. E. Smith, the great English lawyer, was ruined by his inability to keep a witty remark in his mouth, and Pablo de Meneses as captains of arquebusiers. The viceroy's own brother, Núñez Vela, was captain-general, while Diego de Urbina, a Basque from Orduña, was his commander.

For a time the two armies fenced with, rather than fought, each other. Gonzalo was despondent at the size of his opponent's force and realized the risk which he was taking in choosing to fight against the emperor's envoy, which could be perceived to be against the emperor himself. But he was cheered by the adherence to his cause of Pedro de Puelles, another of those who came to Peru from Guatemala with Pedro de Alvarado, with forty horsemen and twenty arquebusiers. He was also encouraged by the complete confusion in Lima, resulting in charges and counter-charges between viceroy and judges of the supreme court. Núñez Vela was for a time under arrest as a result of the judges' decisions, then sent to an island two leagues off, allegedly for his own safety.[9] Afterwards he was able to leave for the apparently safe port of Trujillo.

On 6 October 1544 Gonzalo Pizarro triumphantly entered Lima. His van was led by Bachicao, and he was backed by no fewer than twenty-two pieces of artillery, carried by Indian porters – a colossal array for Peru. There followed thirty arquebusiers, fifty artillerymen, Diego Gumiel and 200 pikemen, then Juan Vélez de Guevara and Pedro Cermeño's arquebusiers. Finally, three companies of infantrymen preceded Gonzalo Pizarro riding a fine white horse. He in turn was followed by three sections of cavalry led respectively by Antonio Altamirano, another distant cousin of Cortés, Pedro de Puelles and Pedro Puertocarrero. Gonzalo repaired to the house of Judge Zárate, where that official and his judicial colleagues received his oath of allegiance. They then went to the council chamber where Gonzalo was received with due ceremony as 'Procurator General of Peru'. No one in Spanish America had had such a grand entry into a city as Gonzalo. There was no battle. The presence of artillery and arquebuses on such a substantial scale was remarkable, and a formidable innovation.

Gonzalo now found himself governor of Peru in view of the rights of conquest held by his brother Francisco and on the nomination of the judges. He acted, however, more as a monarch than as a governor. He gave satisfaction to merchants as well as *encomenderos*. Of course, there were some settlings of old scores. For example, Diego de Gumiel, head of the pikemen in the *joyeuse entrée*, made a minor complaint and was strangled by Francisco de Carvajal. Carvajal declared with his special black humour: 'Make way for Captain Diego de Gumiel who has sworn never to do it again.'[10] Garcilaso commented: 'there were no rejoicings without executions and no executions without rejoicings'. Yet there were many more conventional celebrations: bullfights, games, jousts and even some poems were specially written. After a few weeks Gonzalo Pizarro, a man with no sense of bitterness, gave a general pardon to all who had taken up arms against him. The exceptions were Sebastián Garcilaso de la Vega, an aristocrat related to the poet of that name, who had also come to Peru with Alvarado, and who hid for a time in a grave in the Dominican convent, and a Licenciado Carvajal, who fled to the north. Gonzalo sent Dr Tejada and Francisco Maldonado as *procuradors* to represent his cause in Spain, escorted by Hernando Bachicao as far as Panama. On the only ship there was Vaca de Castro, still a prisoner who, with a kinsman, García de Montalvo, seized control before it could leave harbour. In the end, a brigantine was found and Bachicao and the *procuradors* left on it.

Núñez Vela, surprisingly free and still determined to impose his viceroyalty, was now making for the first Spanish city of Peru, Tumbes, in order to try to raise men. He then went to San Miguel (in modern Ecuador). He was certain that reinforcements would rally to him, for he was strategically well placed to receive such help. He could not avoid some further skirmishing. Jerónimo de Villegas from Burgos and Gonzalo Díaz de Pineda, acting for Pizarro, captured one of the viceroy's men, Juan de Pereina, and cut off his head. The viceroy in revenge pursued and dispersed them, and afterwards Gonzalo Díaz was killed by Indians as he wandered lost.

Gonzalo Pizarro himself set off in March 1545 to deal, as he supposed, with the viceroy's challenge, now with about 600 foot and substantial cavalry. He left behind in control of Lima with eighty men, Lorenzo de Aldana, originally from Cáceres who, like so many, had come with Pedro de Alvarado to Peru. There were other ambiguities: Gómez de Luna in La Plata unwisely remarked that sooner or later the emperor would rule again – a comment which led to his execution by Francisco de Almendras, Gonzalo's great friend, who was a native of Plasencia. Friends of Luna, such as Diego Centeno, organized a rising which resulted in some sporadic bloodshed in Lima. But everyone knew that all depended on the dealings between the viceroy and Gonzalo Pizarro.

The viceroy withdrew even further northwards to Quito, then fled to

Popayán, which is far into what is now Colombia. There, he built forges and had new arquebuses made. He wrote to Benalcázar and Juan Cabrera asking for their help. Gonzalo put it about that he was planning now to withdraw from Quito in order to deal with the rising of Diego Centeño. The viceroy believed this and made as if to return to Quito. But Gonzalo had made a feint. The viceroy returned to Quito and was astounded to find Gonzalo still outside the city. All the same, though weary, he prepared for battle. His captains of infantry were Sancho Sánchez de Ávila and Juan Cabrera, while Benalcázar fought for him with Cepeda and Pedro de Bazán as captains of cavalry. The arquebusiers skirmished. Then Gonzalo's evil genius, Francisco de Carvajal, attacked the viceroy's right. The viceroy's cavalry, despite the presence of Benalcázar, responded haphazardly and were destroyed by the arquebusiers. Gonzalo rode into the centre of the fighting with a hundred horsemen. Cabrera and Sancho Sánchez were killed, as was Alfonso de Montalvo on Gonzalo's side. Nuñez Vela, wearing an Italian shirt, was knocked to the ground by Hernando de Torres. His execution was carried out by a black slave and his head was taken to Quito where it was displayed for months. Two hundred of the viceroy's men were killed but only seven of Gonzalo Pizarro's. Most of these men were buried on the field but the viceroy himself and other leaders were interred in the new cathedral of Quito. The wounded were pardoned, Benalcázar was sent back to Popayán, and others went to join Valdivia in Chile.[11] Another who died was Santa Teresa's brother, Antonio de Cepeda. Of the old leaders, Diego de Cepeda was with Gonzalo, Licenciado Álvarez was dead, Tejada had gone to Spain, Zárate was in Lima alone and Centeño was in the south, but had so few friends with him that his whole force could hide in a cave.

These unprecedented political disputes overshadowed some important economic events. In 1542–3 there was a gold rush near Cuzco and another one in 1545–6.[12] In 1545 the silver mines at Potosí were stumbled upon by 'Don Diego', son of a minor Indian *cacique* in the region of Cuzco. Don Diego had already been first at the mine of Porco, which was no distance from Potosí. Then he found Potosí and within months 7,000 Indians were working there. It was a discovery which soon transformed the country – indeed the empire.

The Spanish miners, with chains of gold round their necks, would spend their new wealth on 'fountains in which flowed the best European wines and on dark *mestizo* girls in silk shoes and pearls for laces, their hair kept in place by rubies . . . and the streets would be covered by silver'. Every kind of embroidery, brocade, silk, gold, tapestries, looking glasses from Venice and pearls from Panama could soon be bought.[13]

At this time there were probably some 4,000 Spaniards in Peru, living in 274 *encomiendas* scattered throughout the colony – probably 86 at Cuzco, 45 at Trujillo and Lima, 34 at Huánaco, 37 at Arequipa, 22 at Huamanga and 5 at Chachapoyas. There were perhaps 1,550,000 tributary Indians. So at least suggested the census of 1540.[14] The missionary orders, the Dominicans and the Mercedarians, numbered about a hundred.

30

Gonzalo and Gasca

No one can foresee the future which is known only to God. Cowards may weep over tomorrow's misfortunes but you know better than I that though battles be lost and soldiers slain, brave knights may still win victory's crown of glory.

Tirant lo Blanc

Gonzalo Pizarro now had Peru at his feet. That was certain. But what should he do with it? The advice to which he primarily listened was that of a dangerous but curious and talented individual, Francisco de Carvajal, an experienced conquistador who had become known in his old age as 'the devil of the Andes'. He was apparently born Francisco López Gascón in 1464 at Rágama, a bleak village in old Castile between Peñaranda de Bracamonte and Madrigal de las Altas Torres, and took the name of Carvajal since he had been a protégé of the cardinal of that name in Italy – or had wanted to be.[1] In the early years of the sixteenth century, he went to Italy to fight under the command of 'El Gran Capitán', Ferdinand's most successful commander, González de Córdoba. He was said to have been at Pavia in 1525 – but then very many who went to the Indies were rumoured to have been present at that legendary battle. Then he went to New Spain. After a few years there he was among those sent by Viceroy Mendoza to help the Pizarros in Peru against Manco Capac. He appears to have conducted himself well and had risen to be *alcalde* in Cuzco by 1541. He later fought effectively for Vaca de Castro as captain of the pikemen at Chupas and, as we have just seen, for Gonzalo Pizarro at Quito. By then he was apparently well into his eighties.

Carvajal dressed always in a purple Moorish burnous and a hat of black taffeta. He had a formidable name as a witty, cruelly courteous and competent soldier who was never shocked by his own or other men's brutality. He killed men pitilessly but accompanied his actions with jests and humorous sallies. For example, on one occasion he said that, since the doomed man was so rich, he would allow him to choose from which branch of a tree he would like to be hanged. Gonzalo Pizarro once asked him to 'calm these people down', referring to the citizens of Lima who had fled from him. Carvajal replied: 'I promise your lordship that I'll quieten these men down so effectively that they will come out to meet you.' Their bodies were soon hanging on poles on the road into Lima.[2]

In 1546, after the death of the Viceroy Núñez Vela, Carvajal is said to have addressed Gonzalo Pizarro in Lima along the following Shakespearean lines:

Sir, when a viceroy is killed in battle and his head is cut off and placed on a gibbet and the battle is fought against the royal standard, there is no pardon to be hoped for and no compromise to be made, even though your lordship may make ample excuses and show himself more innocent than a suckling or a babe. Nor can you trust their words or promises, whatever assurances they give, unless you declare yourself to be king and take the government on yourself without waiting for another to give it to you and put a crown on your head and allocate whatever land is unoccupied among your friends and supporters. And as what the king gives is adequate for two lives, you should take it as a perpetual title and make dukes, marquises and counts and set up military orders, with similar names and titles to those in Spain, and name other saints and patrons and insignia, as you think fit. Give the knights of the new orders incomes and pensions to keep themselves and to let them live at ease. With this approach, your Lordship will attract to your service all the Spanish nobility and chivalry in this empire, fully rewarding those who have conquered it and who have served your lordship. And, to attract the Indians, and make them so devoted that they will die for your lordship, as they would have done for their Inca monarchs, take one of their princesses to wife and send ambassadors to the forest where the heir of the Incas lives and bid him come forth and recover his lost majesty and state, asking him to offer you as your wife any sister or daughter whom he may have. You know how much this prince will esteem kinship and friendship with you and you will gain the universal love of all the Indians by restoring their Inca and, at the same time, make them genuinely willing to do whatever their king orders them on your behalf, such as bringing supplies, etc.

In short, all the Indians will be on your side and, if they do not help your enemies with supplies and porters, no one can prevail against you in Peru ... The Inca will govern his Indians in peace as his ancestors did in the past, whilst your Lordship and your officials and captains will govern the Spaniards, and have charge of military affairs, requiring the Inca to tell the Indians to do whatever you command. Your Lordship will receive all the gold and silver which the Indians produce in this empire, for they do not regard it as wealth ... With all the gold and silver which they are reputed to have, your lordship can buy the entire world if you want to. And pay no attention if they say you are a traitor to the king of Spain. You are not. For no king can be a traitor. This land belongs to the Incas, its natural lords and, if it is not restored to them, you have more right to it than the king of Castile, for you and your brothers conquered it at your own expense and risk. Now by restoring it to the Inca, you are simply doing what you should have by natural law [*ley natural*] and in seeking to govern it yourself as its conqueror and not as a vassal and subject of another, you are doing what you owe to your reputation, for anyone who can become a king by the strength of his arm should not remain a serf. It all depends on the first step and the first declaration.

I beg your lordship to consider the import of what I have said about ruling the empire in perpetuity so that those who live and shall live will follow you. Finally I urge you, whatever may happen, to crown yourself and call yourself king, for no other name befits one who has won an empire by his strength and courage. Die a king and not a vassal.[3]

Carvajal's speech, as reported by Garcilaso de la Vega, may owe much to imagination – but it was perhaps the approximate truth.

Carvajal was supported in this appeal by three men high in Gonzalo Pizarro's favour at the time: Pedro de Puelles, Hernando Bachicao and Diego de Cepeda. We learned of them earlier, but now was their hour.

These three are said to have repeated the theme of Carvajal's speech: the land of Peru they thought was theirs and they could share it, since they had won it at their own expense. They would ally with the Turks if Gonzalo was not given the governorship of Peru and Hernando Pizarro not released from his prison in the Castillo de la Mota in Medina del Campo.

Gonzalo himself was tempted by the ideas of Carvajal but at the time he never lost hope that Charles the emperor would make him governor of Peru. In these months he seemed to have no enemies in Peru, he treated everybody so kindly, referring to all his captains as 'brother'. He called Carvajal 'father'. He ate at a long table laid for a hundred people, with two empty places always beside him so that he could summon whoever he wished to dine with him.[4]

Yet time was not on Gonzalo's side. His rebellion disturbed Charles V, distressed by what seemed an imperial setback.[5] In Spain they were considering the despatch of someone new, a clever man ready for everything, 'to put Peru in order'. In the Council of the Indies, the name which attracted everyone was Antonio de Mendoza, viceroy of New Spain, but they realized that it could not be as he was still fully occupied in his current post in New Spain. In the council, the Duke of Alba supported the idea of pursuing the rebels without quarter. The duke and Dr Guevara thought it essential to send some gentleman to Peru in whom the king would have personal confidence because of his family and blood. A Velasco or a Mendoza would be ideal. But the majority of the council thought a *letrado*, a man of the pen and of learning, was the right person.[6] And eventually the latter argument won the day. At the end of May 1545 the council decided in favour of sending to Peru Pedro de la Gasca, a lawyer who was at that time visitor-general of public officials in the kingdom of Valencia, where he was concerned with the incursions of Muslim pirates from the north of Africa. He had defended Valencia successfully against the Turkish admiral Barbarossa. He was known as a hard man and had political experience. He was a protégé of the powerful secretary, Cobos, and had always been favoured by Cardinal Tavera. Already in his late fifties, he would celebrate his sixtieth birthday before he reached Peru.

Gasca was a typical bureaucrat of the age of Charles the emperor, for, like so many, he derived from a family of public servants. He took his name from his mother's family, his maternal grandfather having been *corregidor* of Congosto. His brothers included Juan Jiménez de Ávila, *corregidor* (representative of the government) of Malaga, later *proveedor* (supplier) of the royal galleys; another was a judge in the chancellery of Valladolid, and would later be a member of the Royal Council of Castile; a third was, again a very usual circumstance, a canon in Palencia. Pedro de la Gasca's career was also a characteristic one until he went to

Peru. He had attended Cisneros's famous University of Alcalá de Henares and had been taught by the great grammarian Lebrija. He had taken part in the war of the *comuneros* on the royalist side. In 1528, he became rector of the university of Salamanca but he was there for a short time only, because of some mysterious controversy which turned out to be less an ideological matter than an affair of personalities. He had several other lucrative assignments before becoming in 1540 judge of the Council of the Inquisition in Valencia.[7] There he had shown the qualities of efficiency and leadership which were to stand him well in Peru.

To look at, Gasca was a person of no importance, but Garcilaso rightly wrote of him that he was 'a man of much better understanding than his appearance suggested'.[8]

Gasca studied Peru carefully before he agreed to accept the commission to go there. He made unusual requests, which were, unusually, granted. He wanted full powers, including the right to grant life and impose death; he wanted to be free to name new men for the right places and to be able to concede *encomiendas*.[9] He wanted no salary but insisted that all his expenses had to be paid.

Gasca set off from Sanlúcar on 26 May, on the way visiting his brother, Abbot Francisco Jiménez de Ávila, his mother in Barco de Ávila, then his brother Juan in Malaga. He took with him a suite of thirty, including two new judges, Licenciado Andrés Cianca of Peñafiel, Valladolid, and Íñigo de Rentería. The first would become Gasca's chief legal adviser; the second was an old friend, having been with him in the 1520s in Salamanca. There were also Alonso de Alvarado, whom we met earlier as a captain of the Pizarros against Almagro, and Pascual de Andagoya, the first Spaniard to go to Peru, long before Pizarro became interested. Andagoya had been a long time recovering from his near-drowning in 1522 and, in the interim, had performed other tasks such as being deputy governor in Panama.[10] Also with Gasca was Francisco Maldonado, who had gone back to Spain on Gonzalo Pizarro's behalf to explain what he had done or was doing, and seems then to have changed sides. Thus Gasca was likely to be well advised once he got to Peru.

Gasca's party touched at La Gomera in the Canaries, as was then usual for America-bound ships, and made landfall at Santa Marta, where they were well received by the governor of New Granada, Miguel

Díaz de Armendariz. They then went on to Nombre de Dios where they arrived on 27 July with little display, crossing the isthmus to reach Panama on 13 August, where they learned for the first time of the death of the viceroy. One of Gonzalo's captains, Hernán Mejía, offered to bring many of his colleagues over to him.[11] But Gasca also met a small delegation of high-placed churchmen and others who were on their way to Spain to request the emperor to make Gonzalo governor. They changed sides, too, when they met the new royal emissary who, despite his feeble appearance, clearly had nerves of iron and real qualities of leadership.

These churchmen were important. Fray Jerónimo de Loaisa was archbishop of Lima and brother of the new archbishop of Seville, the *inquisidor-general* and sometime president of the Council of the Indies; Fray Tomás de San Martín was the provincial of the Dominicans in Lima, and had already once been acting governor of Peru; and Lorenzo de Aldana had accomplished much since he, with so many other great captains, had arrived in Peru in 1534 with Alvarado. Gonzalo had made him governor in Lima during his own absence in the north. Gasca shortly made him commander of his navy. Another churchman with them who made this act of royal loyalty was Martín de Calatayud, bishop of Santa Marta near Cartagena. Finally among these eminent turncoats was Gómez de Solís, who had been *maestresala* to Gonzalo.[12] These men were influenced by Gasca's decision to declare a general pardon and his undertaking to delay implementation of the New Laws; and thus they deserted the leader 'who had raised them up', in Garcilaso's words.[13]

One of those who came with Gasca was Pedro Hernández Paniagua Loaisa, a cousin of both Cardinal Loaisa in Spain and of the archbishop of Lima. He had been on the municipal council of Plasencia in Castile and now was sent by Gasca to take a letter to Gonzalo Pizarro. This explained that he had heard of the late viceroy's intractability over the New Laws. He also said 'we are assured that neither you, nor any who has followed you, has any inclination to be disloyal to us'.[14] In another letter Gasca told Gonzalo that he was certain that it would be impossible for him to resist the attack of a powerful army formed in the name of the emperor. Another clever letter from Gasca to Gonzalo declared that 'His Majesty and the rest of us in Spain have never regarded what you have done as rebellious or disloyal to the king but simply as a defence of your just rights.' Henceforward, though, Gonzalo should fulfil His Majesty's demands, 'thereby performing what was due also to God'.[15]

Gonzalo discussed these missives with Francisco Carvajal and with Cepeda. Carvajal thought them excellent and thus became in favour of collaboration with Gasca. Cepeda thought that they were deceitful documents, a way of trying to secure Gonzalo's surrender without the use of force; thereafter trials and executions could begin.

Gonzalo was foolishly in favour of Cepeda's view. All the same, he thought it right to have a meeting of eighty settlers, a majority of whom supported Carvajal. One or two told Hernández Paniagua that they would now support Gasca in any discussion or dispute. Hernández Paniagua thought that Gasca would have confirmed Gonzalo in the governorship of Peru if he had had real evidence that the majority of settlers wanted it. But there were difficulties: one of Gasca's representatives, Fray Francisco de San Miguel, was detained at Tumbes by Gonzalo's men, who told the friar that the king was bankrupt and needed their money. Paniagua spiritedly replied: 'The city of Naples alone is worth more than three Perus.'[16] He left Lima with a bland reply from Gonzalo to Gasca in which the former pledged anew his loyalty to the Emperor Charles and described how 'for sixteen years he and his brothers had worked for the royal crown of Spain to whose glory they had added so much'.[17] At the same time, sixty Spanish residents wrote to Gasca suggesting that he go home because, they said, they had no need of his presence; nor had they any need of any royal pardon from him since they had done nothing wrong.[18]

Gasca could now see that the surrender of Gonzalo would be a complex matter. He set about organizing the skeleton of an army and, on 10 April 1547, set off for Peru from Panama with 820 soldiers in eighteen ships and a galliot. Despite bad weather and heavy winds, the new army reached Manta on 31 May and went on to Tumbes on 30 June. Several groups of settlers in nearby towns proclaimed their loyalty to the Crown and told Gasca so. After waiting a month at Tumbes, Gasca wrote to Charles the emperor suggesting that a new viceroy be named immediately. He again proposed Antonio de Mendoza, the viceroy in New Spain.[19] Then he continued down the coast as far as the mouth of the river Santa before starting into the mountains.

Gasca was all this time accompanied by both Alonso de Alvarado and Bishop Loaisa, who knew the land well by now. He had before that named Pedro de Hinojosa as the commander of his forces. Hinojosa came from a notable family from Trujillo, one of whose members, Alfonso, had in the fifteenth century led an important regiment in the war of Granada, with which Cortés's father had served. Pedro had been among those recruited by Francisco Pizarro in 1529 and had been for a time Gonzalo Pizarro's naval commander. In Jauja, Hernando de Aldana was named mayor. Others taking a major part in this new crusade were Benito Suárez de Carvajal, who had fought for the Pizarros for a long time and had been responsible for the death of Blasco Núñez Vela after the battle of Añaquito. He was now *alférez mayor*, chief lieutenant, with Gasca. Two other old supporters of the Pizarros were Pedro de Villavicienzo and Gabriel de Rojas, by that time over fifty, with a record, since he arrived with Alvarado in 1534, of remarkable inconsistency. He had been trusted by Hernando Pizarro, whom he later captured on behalf of Almagro, but was himself imprisoned by Hernando after the battle of Las Salinas. Later Hernando had made him commander in Cuzco seeing in him someone 'very experienced and prudent in war'.

On 20 July Gonzalo Pizarro wrote to the emperor saying that, if there were any fighting, the fault would be all Gasca's, not his, because he would never do anything which His Majesty would dislike.[20] By now, however, Gonzalo had begun to find his position falling apart. As soon as many of his followers heard that Gasca had at least delayed if not cancelled the New Laws in Peru, and had proclaimed a pardon, many of his leading supporters made it evident that they would be willing to repudiate the leadership of Gonzalo.

Still, the latter assembled his army. Carvajal was the overall commander, to whom a company of arquebusiers was attached. His captain of cavalry was the ex-judge Cepeda; his standard was borne by Antonio de Altamirano, a member of a famous family in Mérida and related to the great Cortés. Some captains had chosen as their heraldic devices Gonzalo's name surmounted by a crown. Carvajal insisted that each soldier should have a badge indicating to what company he belonged. Cepeda drew up a document insisting that Pedro de Hinojosa had committed treason in giving Gonzalo's ships to Gasca and Gasca was accused of the same for having received them. He announced that both would be hanged, drawn and quartered when they were captured.

As this army took shape there were some terrible moments for Gonzalo. Thus the standard-bearer, Altamirano, was killed by Carvajal personally on suspicion of desertion. Pedro de Puelles deserted and was killed by a gang of Spaniards led by the hunchback Diego de Salazar, who immediately himself crossed to Gasca. Gonzalo hanged a common soldier whom he observed wearing two shirts which he interpreted as a sign that he was ready to desert. Gonzalo announced then that if only ten friends stood by him, he would reconquer all Peru. But every day brought a new setback: Lima declared for Gasca, some of Gonzalo's men began to think that they could preserve their lives only by fleeing to the forest of Anti or going to join Valdivia in Chile.[21] Gonzalo had also sent some of his best men against Diego Centeño, who was still sheltering near Lake Titicaca. Reading of these and other manoeuvres is like hearing of an elaborate game whose rules have not yet been decided.

Gonzalo and Gasca fought two battles. The first at Huarina, on the shores of Titicaca, was won by the former. Carvajal was Gonzalo's commander as usual, and he still had with him 400 skilled fighters, among them Juan de Acosta and the experienced Hernando Bachicao. For once his arquebusiers had a decisive effect, though the cavalry of the two sides fought fiercely. Bachicao seems to have changed sides in the middle of the battle but then changed back again. Gonzalo's camp was sacked but Centeño's infantry were too busy doing the sacking to be able to fight afterwards. Then the victorious captains returned to Cuzco to seek supplies and reinforcements. There they were diverted by feeling that they needed to execute, in some cases brutally, both Spaniards and Indians whom they thought were not in favour of Gonzalo.

In these moments of hesitation, Gasca recovered. He despatched Alonso de Alvarado back to Lima to seek artillery, clothes, arms, craftsmen capable of making arquebuses and powder, pikes and helmets. He sent two commanders to assemble the remains of Centeño's forces, and captured one of Gonzalo's friends, Pedro de Bustamante, and had him strangled. He then organized a new army with the same commanders (Hinojosa, Alonso de Alvarado, Benito Suárez de Carvajal, Pedro de Villavicencio), but whose captains included such old-stagers as Gómez de Alvarado of Mexican fame, and Pascual de Andagoya. Rojas was his captain of artillery. Gasca had with him Loaisa, the archbishop of Lima, as well as the bishops of Cuzco and Quito, not to speak of the provincials of the order of Saint Dominic and of the Mercedarians.

Gasca left Jauja for Cuzco on 29 December 1547 with about 1,900 men, including 400 horsemen, 700 arquebusiers and 500 pikemen. This was the most formidable army which had yet been assembled in the New World. They spent the three months of the Peruvian winter at Antahuailla. Many of Gonzalo's men joined him, and Gasca was specially pleased by the adhesion of Pedro de Valdivia from Chile to help him. He said that he valued Valdivia more than 800 good soldiers. Gasca wrote a long letter to Gonzalo on 16 December 1547, with a meticulous response to all the comments made by Pizarro to the emperor in his letter of 20 July.[22]

Given this swelling success, Gonzalo's friend the ex-judge Cepeda suggested to his leader that he should accept peace terms with Gasca. Gonzalo consulted several of his captains: Bachicao, Juan de Acosta, Diego Guillén and Juan de la Torre, but they considered themselves invincible and advised Gonzalo not to treat. Carvajal then returned and had Bachicao strangled for deserting in the middle of the battle of Huarina. He also had strangled María Calderón, who had railed against Gonzalo's intransigence. Her body was hung outside her window.

For the moment, Gonzalo seemed well enough. He entered Cuzco triumphantly: flowers, bells, Indians greeting him as the Inca, trumpets. The chronicler Garcilaso de la Vega saw it all as a boy. He observed, too, Carvajal, old but indomitable, entering the city on a large dun-coloured mule.

Gasca moved towards Cuzco with his great army, and reached the river Abancay. Then he faced the river Apurímac. Where should the army cross? There were three or four bridges. The road was almost impassable for men in any kind of formation because of the sharpness of the mountains on both sides of the river. Gasca, advised by the imaginative Valdivia, pretended to build bridges at four new places so that Gonzalo would not know which section he would use. Carvajal commented: 'Valdivia is in this land or else it is the devil.' He had known Valdivia in Italy, perhaps even heroically at Pavia. Gasca decided to cross the river at Cotapampa, near Jaquijahuana where the battle was supposed to have been.

Carvajal advised Gonzalo how to react. He should destroy everything living on the northern bank of the river and, playing on the inexperience of half of Gasca's army, fall on them while they were crossing. But, for reasons now difficult to understand, Gonzalo preferred to rely on the counsel of Juan de Acosta, who had accompanied him on his cinnamon journey and who lazily permitted the enemy to cross at night while he slept. Had Carvajal's advice been followed, Gonzalo would have had a chance of victory. Now, however, there was little that he could do. He fell back on Sacsahuaman, where Gasca could only attack from the front and where Gonzalo hoped to be able to destroy his enemy with heavy artillery fire. He had become bewitched by the effectiveness of artillery. At the end of March Gonzalo wrote desperately to Fr Francisco de Herrera, then a priest in his own *encomienda* of Charcas: 'God is fighting for us, your excellency must believe that, we can conquer the world.'[23] Desperate words!

At Sacsahuaman the battle was not to be, for Gonzalo's army was melting away. Even Diego de Cepeda, of all people, abandoned Gonzalo, as did Garcilaso de la Vega. The pikemen dropped their weapons and took to their heels; the arquebusiers did the same with their weapons. Carvajal was for once uncertain what to recommend. Gonzalo took the hint. He rode towards the enemy and, coming up with Villavicencio, said: 'I am Gonzalo Pizarro, I wish to surrender to the emperor.' He preferred to surrender honourably than to flee in dishonour. He was taken immediately to Gasca, who asked him if he thought it had been right to have stirred up the country against the emperor and to have made himself governor against the will of His Majesty, as well as to have killed a viceroy in a pitched battle. Gonzalo replied that the judges of the supreme court had bidden him become governor and he had himself authorized these actions in the light of the power vested by His Majesty in his brother, the marquis. As to the Viceroy Núñez Vela, the judges had ordered him to be expelled from Peru. He, Gonzalo, had not killed the viceroy. But the relations of those whom the viceroy had killed had been obliged to seek revenge. Everything which he had done had been at the instance of his fellow residents.

Gasca replied that Gonzalo had shown himself most ungrateful for the grants which the king emperor had made to his brother Francisco. The grants had raised the Pizarros from the dust and enriched them all, though they had all been poor before. In any case, Gasca claimed, Gonzalo himself had done nothing in respect of the actual discovery of Peru.

Gonzalo replied:

My brother alone was enough to discover the country but all of us four brothers were necessary for its conquest. We and our relations and friends did what we did at our own risk and expense. The only honour which His Majesty gave to my brother was to make him a marquis. He did not lift us from the dust since the Pizarros have been noblemen and gentlemen with our own estates since the Goths came to Spain. If we were poor, that explains why we ventured out into the world and won this empire and gave it to His Majesty, though we might have kept it, as many others have done who have won new lands.

Gasca considered these words and said to his advisers: 'Take him away, he's as much a rebel today as he was yesterday.'[24]

Meanwhile, Carvajal, seeing the game was up, fled on a pony. It fell into a stream, pinning one of its rider's legs under it. Some of his men who were also fleeing found him and took him to Gasca in the hope that he would pardon their own misdeeds if they handed in such a prisoner.[25] Carvajal was taken to a makeshift gaol which Gasca had set up, where his guards at first put lighted torches between his shirt and his back until Diego Centeño, who had known him well, put a stop to that torture.[26]

The following day, 10 April 1548, Gonzalo Pizarro, Carvajal, Juan de Acosta, Francisco Maldonado, Juan Vélez de Guevara, Dionisio de Bobadilla and Gonzalo de los Nidos – all the leaders of the Pizarros who had not deserted – were executed. Carvajal was treated especially harshly, being dragged from prison to an execution yard by a horse and there hanged. The heads of the dead were cut off and sent for exhibition to numerous places in Peru. Gonzalo's body was buried in Cuzco alongside that of Almagro in the Mercedarian church. His house was razed to the ground. Of course, he lost all his valuable *encomiendas*. Another whom Gasca executed was Francisco de Espinosa, nephew of the famous Licenciado Espinosa who had served as Gonzalo's *maestresala*.[27]

Gasca was greeted in Cuzco with the ceremonies usual for the reception of great men, which had included Gonzalo Pizarro only a short time before. There were bullfights and shows of tilting. Alonso de Alvarado and the judge Andrés de Cianca punished those of Gonzalo's supporters who had not given themselves up. Some were hanged, some quartered, some were condemned to serve in Gasca's galleys, some were flogged.[28] The floggings caused a scandal, for the Indians, still secretly worshipping their dead, had not seen Spaniards beaten before.

Soon the Spanish victors would turn their imaginative attention to the Peruvians whom they had so roundly defeated. In the 1550s, for example, Juan Polo de Ondegardo, a Spanish magistrate, would begin profound enquiries into the nature of the Inca religion. He established that the Incas worshipped at over 400 shrines in or near the city,[29] and also found in 1558 that the descendants of the Inca were still worshipping their ancestors' mummies.

One element in Gasca's success should not be ignored: 'The desire of the Spaniards to see the things of their own land in the Indies has been so desperate,' wrote Garcilaso de la Vega, 'that no effort or danger has been too great to induce them to abandon the attempt to satisfy their wishes.'[30] They wanted wine, oranges, horses and dogs, guns and swords, wheat bread and salt beef. So a true break with the old Spain was never really contemplated.

Gasca hoped to persuade the heirs of Manco Capac, headed by the five-year-old Sayri-Tupa, to come out of their secret encampment in the jungle at Vilcabamba and he made some headway in this.

Hernando Pizarro, the eloquent victor of Cuzco, was in the Castillo de la Mota just outside Medina del Campo, city of imagination (Bernal Díaz del Castillo) and of fantasy (*Amadís de Gaula*), and there he remained till May 1561. He lived comfortably but was confined all the same.[31] At first he lived with Isabel Mercado of Medina del Campo. Then in 1552 he married his niece Francisca, the daughter of Francisco Pizarro, who was then aged seventeen. The idea of such a marriage had occurred at one time to Gonzalo Pizarro.

Once married to such a very rich girl, Hernando devoted his time to centralizing the management of his family's estates in Peru, part of which had been administered by royal officials after the final defeat of Gonzalo Pizarro. When eventually Hernando and Francisca left La Mota, free, in 1561 they went to live at La Zarza, the village outside Trujillo which had always belonged to the Pizarro family, of which Hernando was now the head. They embarked there on 'a strategy of reconstruction of their finances', and built a new palace in the main square of Trujillo (which still survives). They lived in the light cast by the coat of arms granted to Francisco Pizarro and inherited Francisco's marquisate, which from 1576 was named as 'of the Conquest'. Hernando died two years later, a survivor of extraordinary deeds into what seemed a calmer age. Francisca married again, to Pedro Arias Portocarrero, son of the count of Puñonrostro, and lived until 1598.[32]

Hernando's fortune was large. About 1550 it was almost as big as that of Cortés – 32,000 pesos a year in comparison with the family of Cortés's 36,800 (the latter was in 1560), and the figure for Hernando's income does not take into account the product of his mercantile adventures and mines.[33] In the end Hernando had gained control of most of the estate (including the Porco mines) that the Pizarro brothers had acquired during the conquest.

Valdivia and Chile

*Are you not aware, Christian Soldier, that when you were initi-
ated into the mysteries of the life-giving feast, you enrolled in the
army of Christ.*

Erasmus, *Enchiridion*

In April 1539 Francisco Pizarro, apparently triumphant in all Peru over
both the Indians of the region and his Spanish rivals, made a journey of
exploration to Charcas and Lake Titicaca. Among the followers and
friends with him was Pedro de Valdivia, who had recently been his
maestre de campo and who had been asked to lead the army against
Almagro. After his victory at Las Salinas, Pizarro gave him the valley of
Canela, 'the cinnamon valley', in Charcas as an *encomienda* and the
rich silver mine of Porco. Pizarro probably thought of him as an entirely
reliable captain who could be counted upon in all circumstances. It was,
therefore, probably an unwelcome surprise when Valdivia asked for
permission to explore and conquer the land to the south which had
been abandoned by Almagro. But Pizarro, wrote Valdivia himself, 'seeing my determination graciously opened the door to me'.[1] His new
command of course meant that he was lost to Peru.

Valdivia was a military man and the descendant of military men. He
seems to have been born in 1497, the son of Diego de Valdivia, and
came from a village such as Castuera or Campanario in the beautiful
valley known as the Serena in Extremadura from where many of Cortés's
lieutenants originated. His home town was about twenty miles from
Cortés's birthplace in Medellín and not far from the home towns of all
the great conquistadors. He entered the army about 1520 and fought in
Italy under Henry of Nassau, then Prospero Colonna, finally at Pavia

under Pescara. He seems in those campaigns to have been a simple soldier. He then married Marina Ortiz de Gaete of Zalamea, also in the Serena, and lived an impoverished life with her, without children. He apparently met Pizarro in Trujillo in Extremadura in 1529.

Valdivia left Spain in 1535 and spent an unprofitable year or so with Federman in Venezuela.[2] He then went to Peru and earned the nickname of 'the perfect captain', for he inspired high regard among his men. His motives in wishing to go to Chile seem, and probably were, simple. He later wrote to the Emperor Charles:

> I have no other wish than to discover and to settle lands for Your Majesty and no other interest, together with the honours and favours which you may be pleased to grant me, than to leave a memory and the good report which I won in war as a poor soldier in the service of an enlightened monarch who, putting his sacred person every hour against the common enemy of Christianity and its allies, has upheld, and upholds, with its unconquered arm its honour and God's.

Valdivia said that he aspired to be a governor, a captain, a father, a friend, a geometrician, an overseer 'to make channels and share out water, a tiller and a worker at the sowings, a head shepherd, a breeder, a defender, a conqueror and a discoverer'.[3]

Valdivia had difficulties from the beginning with the nature of his command for he owed his commission to Francisco Pizarro, not to the king nor to the Council of the Indies. Another conquistador, Pedro Sancho de Hoz, who had joined Pizarro in Panama and been at Cajamarca, where he received one full share of gold together with a quarter share for secretarial work (he was for a time Pizarro's secretary), was a rival. He had been concerned in all the great dramas in the conquest of Peru: as a clerk at the execution of Atahualpa, and as a notary at the creation of the new Spanish city of Cuzco. He was a good writer whose account of the discovery of Cuzco by the Spaniards is second to none.[4] He also wrote the texts of many of the first *encomiendas* in that city. Sancho de Hoz himself had one. Pizarro seems to have dismissed him as his secretary in early 1535, for telling Fray Tomás de Berlanga, the Dominican vice-provincial and later bishop of Panama and then Peru, that Pizarro had not paid the king's fifth on the silver which he had used to buy Pedro de Alvarado's ships.

Sancho de Hoz was back in Spain in 1536 and seemed as rich as all those who had been at Cajamarca. He went to live in Toledo and married Guiomar de Aragón, who was perhaps a child of a royal bastard. Then he persuaded the Council of the Indies not only to make him chief notary of mines in Peru but also governor of the territories leading to the straits of Magellan and to allow him to penetrate south of Peru as captain-general 'of the people who go on the expedition and those found in the discovered territory'. However, when he returned to Peru he found that Valdivia had also been given the right to penetrate the south. Pizarro commented: 'Pedro Sancho has come back from Spain as stupid as when he went.' But Sancho de Hoz was persistent in his demands and caused no end of difficulty.

Pizarro sought to be the mediator between Valdivia and Sancho de Hoz. He adopted a twentieth-century solution by inviting them both to lunch. Pizarro asked Sancho to show his credentials. These indicated that he had indeed been asked by the Crown to explore the seas, the coasts, the ports to the south of Peru but – a most curious qualification – 'without entering into the confines and territories of those portions which have been given in government to other persons'.[5] Pizarro was tactful – it was one of his remarkable characteristics. He pointed out that, in any expedition, Valdivia's ability to lead men in battle would be most helpful; and he thought that Sancho de Hoz could contribute to the success of the enterprise because of his wealth and his capacity for administration. He asked them to form a partnership. They agreed, though it was said that Pizarro gave Sancho de Hoz too much wine. The agreement read:

I, Pero [Pedro] Sancho de Hoz will go to the city of Los Reyes [that is, Lima] and from there I shall bring fifty horses and mares ... and I will bring two ships loaded with necessary things ... including 200 shields. And I, Captain Pedro de Valdivia, say that, in order to serve His Majesty better in the expedition which I have begun, I accept the said company.[6]

But despite this agreement, there was always ambiguity. Was Valdivia the subordinate of Sancho de Hoz? Or was Sancho his subordinate? Pizarro gave the latter some kind of document but its contents are unknown. Perhaps it was destroyed by Valdivia when Sancho de Hoz tried to kill him. Valdivia once wrote to Hernando Pizarro that he formed two partnerships in Peru, one with Francisco Martínez, one with Sancho de Hoz, but he implied that they were both commercial relationships.[7] Martínez, it is fair to say, was merely a successful merchant in Cuzco.

In January 1540 Valdivia set off on his expedition. He seems to have been accompanied by only seven men, although the figure twenty was also mentioned. These included Luis de Cartagena, perhaps a member of the famous *converso* family of that name, as his secretary; Juan Gómez de Almagro, the *alguacil mayor* (chief magistrate), who had married Colluca, daughter of Atahualpa; and his father, Diego Almagro's brother, Alvar. In addition to his seven Spaniards, Valdivia took a large escort of Indian servants, and also his beautiful and resolute mistress, Inés Suárez. Pizarro had asked him what he planned to do with her when he left for Chile. 'I will carry her with me if your excellency gives me leave.' 'How will you manage that if your wife is still living in Spain?' asked Pizarro. 'Inés is my servant,' Valdivia answered. In fact his relationship with Inés was based on more than love. Valdivia had always been a gambler and was wont to go to Francisco Martínez de Peñalosa's *bodegón*, or bar, in Cuzco operated by the mulatto Pinillos. It was there that he had rescued Inés, then a widow from Palencia, who was being molested by a certain Fernán Núñez. She had come to the Indies to look for her husband, first in Venezuela, then in Peru. She was allowed a small *encomienda* in Cuzco. She turned out to be brave, intelligent and resourceful.

There was a rather gloomy send-off, with a complete absence of the shining armour, the plumes, the banners and the trumpets frequent on such occasions. 'This [absence] coupled with the presence of a servile people jaded, dust-covered and sweaty, left the impression of a drove of slaves guarded by a few horsemen of low rank, instead of an expedition marching to conquer one more kingdom for the European Emperor Charles.'[8]

One companion who was not present was Sancho de Hoz. The explanation was that he was in prison in Lima for debt; the rich often suffer from financial conundrums. So, naturally, his two ships with their horses and shields were missing.

The route taken by Valdivia was the one by which Almagro had returned. He travelled about 'twelve leagues' a day. Almagro's brother, Alvar, fell from his horse and died, and there were other difficulties. But, as Valdivia went south, he was joined by others: for example, at Arequipa, Fr Juan Lobo and Alonso de Monroy, a member of that remarkable family of Extremadura from whom Cortés descended, attached themselves and their destinies to him. At Tarapacá seventy soldiers came in from the sea, including two new priests – one was Fr

Rodrigo Marmolejo – and two Germans, Juan Bohon and Bartolomeus Blumenthal, who, in Spanish circles, called himself Bartolomé Flores.

After leaving Arequipa, Valdivia was soon in the desert of the north of Chile. The story of the expedition's crossing of this famous obstacle was, according to one historian, 'an epic not yet well written. Historians have gathered a thousand details but have not yet captured its spirit.'[9] Valdivia adopted the technique of sending out small troops of his followers to break up any band of Indians that might be forming and to seek Spanish reinforcements.

The difficulty at this stage was not so much the Indians as Sancho de Hoz, who arrived at Valdivia's headquarters by riding fast and light with a few horsemen, some of his wife's grand relations and some friends. This group had determined to kill Valdivia when they caught up with him, but when they reached Valdivia's camp near Atacama, they found that their enemy was away on a reconnoitre and only Inés Suárez was there. She gave the newcomers dinner and discussed with her own friends what should be done. They learned that Sancho de Hoz planned to seize and kill Valdivia. Next morning Valdivia's lieutenant, Gómez de Don Benito, wanted to start the journey early. Sancho de Hoz told Don Benito that the site had been badly chosen for a camp. 'Who are you to say this to me,' asked Don Benito, 'for I am in command by order of Captain Valdivia?' Next day the latter appeared with ten horsemen, and he was immediately apprised of Sancho de Hoz's arrival and of the rumour that he planned to kill him.

Valdivia went to Sancho de Hoz and said: 'You repay badly, friend Sancho, the affection that the Marquis Pizarro and I hold for you.' He arrested him and a brief trial followed. He was imprisoned, while his comrades were ordered to return to Cuzco with neither horses nor arms. The two Guzmán brothers, who were relations of Sancho de Hoz's wife, and Juan de Ávalos, an Extremeño from Garrovillas, accepted the order and did in fact make their way back on foot and then by sea. They were fortunate since Valdivia's first idea had been to hang them and he even had gallows built for the purpose.[10] Sancho de Hoz was kept under guard and for a time in handcuffs for the rest of Valdivia's journey. Valdivia would have liked to have executed him but he did not want to kill someone whose relations could claim that he was the Crown's representative. But Sancho de Hoz did sign a declaration, witnessed by Alonso de Monroy and Juan Bohon, releasing Valdivia from any partnership with him, though he paid for the horses which Sancho had sold him.[11]

The expedition continued across the desert of Atacama. There was a constant shortage of food and even more so of water till Inés Suárez's white horse by accident ate a prickly pear, the red fruit of the cactus which became a major source of sustenance. It was Inés also who discovered a spring in an unpromising desert zone. There was a fierce wind, sometimes stinging sleet, once a dust-storm. At last they came upon the green valley of Copiapó. There the army rested for two months. Valdivia took possession of the land to the south of it and gave it the promising name of 'New Extremadura'.[12] They raised there a large wooden cross and Valdivia told the local Indians that he was going to instruct them in Christianity.

Several stragglers caught up with the expedition, including men such as Gonzalo de los Ríos and Alonso de Chinchilla. Some of these newcomers seemed ready for a new rebellion, as Inés Suárez and some others told an unbelieving Valdivia. Juan Ruiz de Torbillo was heard to say: 'If it had been left to me to do, I should have killed Pedro de Valdivia by now.' He was arrested and hanged.

When Valdivia was again absent one day reconnoitring, Chinchilla and Gonzalo de los Ríos rode into the camp at the head of twenty horsemen and announced that they had come to kill Valdivia. Sancho de Hoz was delighted but the redoubtable Inés arrested both leaders. On his return, Valdivia gave them a choice: continuing under guard or going back to Peru. Chinchilla, astonished at that merciful concession, cravenly told him all his plans and he was held with Sancho de Hoz till they reached their journey's end. The expedition continued but there were more and more Indian attacks on stragglers, sometimes killing horses or more often Indian bearers. Valdivia forced a pass into the valley of the Mapocho on 13 December, Santa Lucía's day, and they called the hill which commanded the place by that name.[13]

A good analysis has been made of the 154 men who in the end accompanied Valdivia. Among them there were 26 Andalusians, 17 were Extremeños, 16 came from New Castile, 15 from León, while 12 were Basques and 1 was from Asturias; 41, or more than a quarter, were illiterate; 11 were called hidalgos *de solar*, that is, they had property, 23 were ordinary hidalgos; 14 had been with Almagro in 1535.[14] None of these things was surprising except that it is strange that there were no Gallegos. The geographical breakdown is very similar to that in Peru and in Mexico.

No sooner had Valdivia decided that the valley of the Mapocho was the obvious place for his capital city than he suffered a serious attack by

Indians, whose numbers seemed at first to compensate for the Spanish swords and horses. The Spaniards were held and appear to have been almost defeated till the Indians threw down their arms and fled due to the arrival, so legend tells, of a new conquistador on a white horse who came out of the sky with a naked sword: Santiago![15]

The subsequent victory meant that Valdivia could establish himself at the foot of Santa Lucía. He adopted a clever technique of sending out horsemen regularly in all directions so that, as he told the Emperor Charles, the Indians 'believed that the Christians were many, so most of them came in and served us peacefully'.[16] They even helped the Spaniards to carry logs and clay to build their first houses.

Valdivia finally founded Santiago de Chile in the valley of the Mapocho on 12 February 1541. The municipality of the new city proclaimed him captain-general and governor, thereby detaching itself and him from Pizarro. There was quite a ceremony. The whole camp gathered; Valdivia appeared in full armour, carrying in his left hand the standard of Castile. He took possession of the place in the name of the emperor and king. Cavalrymen galloped past. Valdivia declared that anyone who challenged his claim to be governor should give him battle and he would defend his right to the title with his life. He drank water from the river Mapocho, offered it to his senior captains and tossed what was left in the air. He then planted a cross before which all knelt in thanks. It was like a scene from *Amadís*. They were over 1,500 miles from Lima.

The only one of Valdivia's captains who was absent on this spectacular occasion was the German conquistador Bartolomé Flores. He came in some days later to say that he had engaged in battle an Indian *cacique* named Talagante. He had captured a son of that potentate whom, in keeping with Valdivia's chivalrous rules, he had handed back. Talagante was very pleased and asked Flores to return and visit him. He gave him four princesses, one of whom was his daughter, perhaps his heiress. Inés took charge of these ladies and had them baptized. They lived with or married Spaniards, one of them being the ancestress of the Lisperguer family in Chile.

The building of Santiago de Chile began on 20 February 1541. The designer, or architect, was the one-eyed Pedro de Gamboa. There were nine streets each 12 *varas* (a *vara* is 835 millimetres and 9 *décimas*) wide, in blocks 138 *varas* wide. Each block was divided into four lots (*solares*). One block was reserved for a square on the west side of which there would soon be a church – a cathedral. This was traditional Spanish urban practice. On the north side of the square in Santiago there would be both the governor's house and the prison. A municipality (*cabildo*) with a headquarters on the south side was formed in March 1541, with two magistrates, six councillors, a *mayordomo*, a notary and a *procurador*. All of them were men with well-known names, the chief magistrate being an old associate of Valdivia's, Francisco de Aguirre.

Though his name was Basque, Aguirre came from Talavera de la Reina. A man of great energy, he was proud and irascible, if cultivated, and he liked to live, so we are told, '*rumbosamente*', which perhaps we can translate as 'lavishly'. He fathered fifty *mestizo* children to whom he gave exotic names: Marco Antonio, Eufrasia, Floridan. But he eventually married his cousin, María Teresa de Meneses.

One of the first councillors was one of Valdivia's Germans, Juan Bohon. Luis de Cartagena was the notary, as he had been of the expedition. Valdivia, as ever disdainful of danger, or not believing that it existed, made councillors of two friends of Sancho de Hoz: Antonio de Pastrana (*procurador*) and Martín de Soller. The council took their oaths on 11 March and municipal life began.

Valdivia sought to make the survival of Santiago easier. He went out of his way to try to soothe the Indians and to some extent he succeeded. It was now that his name as 'the perfect knight' came to be known and used. His conduct in general was a contrast with that of most conquistadors. He was for a while even popular among his Indian conquests. But, Valdivia had learned, Manco Inca

> had sent to warn them, the people of Chile, that they should hide all the gold, sheep, clothing stuffs and food, for since we sought all this, [they thought] that, if we did not find such things, we would go away. And they did this work of obstruction so thoroughly that the sheep were eaten and the gold and all the rest hidden or burned; and they did not spare their own clothing but left themselves bare.[17]

Sancho de Hoz's friend Antonio de Pastrana urged the reluctant Valdivia to accept the nomination as governor by the municipality. He thought that would be a way of eventually ridding Santiago of Valdivia because he would, if he accepted the nomination, be seen in Spain as committing treason. On 10 June Pastrana's plan seemed to have worked for Valdivia called an extraordinary meeting of the town hall (a *cabildo abierto*) at which he presented a petition signed by nearly all the inhabitants of Santiago demanding that he should become governor. This document was presented to the 'perfect knight' as he was leaving mass. Valdivia said 'since you have seen my replies and are not satisfied with them . . . you in one voice say it and I alone contradict it, so I might be mistaken . . . And so I accept the office of governor elected by the town hall and so I shall entitle myself until His Majesty commands something else.'[18]

Thus Antonio de Pastrana's cynical plot was, in the short term anyway, a success. Valdivia, however, went to the notary, Luis de Cartagena, and had him write down that 'this election was not of my wish and since I do not know if in doing it I am doing a disservice to my King, let everyone be a witness for me in what way I have accepted it. Nor do I reduce the obedience that I owe to the illustrious marquis Don Francisco Pizarro if he lives'.[19] Valdivia later explained what had happened to the Emperor Charles in a letter which seems accurate in its summary.[20]

But Valdivia was still not governor and captain-general in the reckoning of the Council of the Indies. The rumour, and then the news, of the death of Francisco Pizarro affected his position in Chile, for Pizarro had been his first mainstay and protector; Valdivia regarded himself as Pizarro's lieutenant. As soon as he had confirmation of Pizarro's death, Valdivia wrote to the emperor suggesting that he should take care to ensure that Pizarro's children 'could support themselves as such'.[21]

Soon after this, the Indians made a major onslaught on the new Spanish town of Santiago, attacking under two leaders coming from two directions. Valdivia wrote one of his excellent letters to the Emperor Charles informing him that he had himself dealt effectively with the attack with ninety men but that, in the second battle, with Alonso de Monroy in command, the Indians had burned down the new Santiago entirely and killed all the animals so that

> we were left only with the arms at our sides and two small pigs, one suckling pig, a cock and a hen, and about two handfuls of wheat. In the end, when night came, the Christians summoned up so much courage, together with what their commander Monroy put to them, that, though all were wounded, with the good wishes of Santiago himself, they found the energy to fight and kill many . . . And with this, the war began in earnest.

Valdivia continued:

seeing the plight we were in, it seemed to me that, if we were to hold on to the land and make it Your Majesty's forever, we must eat of the fruits of our hands as in the beginning of the world ['*la primera edad*']. So I set about sowing. I divided my men into two groups. We all dug, ploughed and sowed, being always armed and the horses being saddled always by day. At night one half of us kept watch. And I with the other half moved at the time eight to ten leagues [twenty-four to thirty miles] around the town breaking up bands of Indians . . . [till] I built up the town again.

In one of these expeditions in the neighbourhood of Santiago Valdivia captured the local *toqui*, or *cacique*-in-chief, Michimalongo – or rather one of his followers, Rodrigo de Quiroga, did. To save his life, Michimalongo led the Spaniards to some gold mines in the so-called Malga district. It was from those mines that the people of the Mapocho had dug the gold which they paid to the Incas. The Spaniards were delighted and began to calculate how many sacks they would need, some putting on airs as if they were already rich, thinking that in a short time they would be able to go to Spain, establish a country estate and – who knew? – obtain a marquisate.

Work began at Malga, with a hundred Indian *yanaconas* obtained from Santiago. Michimalongo offered his own army of miners who numbered 1,200 (there were also 1,500 women). Valdivia left there two Spanish captains, Pedro de Herrera and Diego Delgado, who had engaged in mining in Peru, together with fifteen soldiers, under Gonzalo de los Ríos. Then Valdivia went down to the coast near Santiago to seek a place where he could conveniently build a brigantine with which he could communicate with Peru by sea. He found a likely harbour at the mouth of the river Canconagua at Concón, where there was also plenty of wood. Work on the vessel began.

Then two crises arose for Valdivia. First, Alonso de Monroy sent a message to explain that yet another plot was being planned by Sancho de Hoz. The plan was to kill Valdivia, Inés, Monroy and all their friends. Sancho de Hoz would then seize the gold of Malga and return to Peru to join Diego de Almagro who had now, it seemed, triumphed over the Pizarros. Valdivia returned to Santiago and with his usual insouciance made light of the rumour. But then a quarrel broke out in the house of Monroy. In the confusion, the lamps inside were destroyed. Inés Suárez, who was there, brought another light which revealed Sancho de Hoz being held by Monroy himself, Chinchilla engaged in a duel with Juan Gómez, one of Valdivia's captains, and the priest, Fr Juan Lobo, defending himself with a stool against Pastrana.

As if that fracas were not enough, Gonzalo de los Ríos and a black slave named Valiente at this moment rode in from the gold mine at Malga bringing news that the Indians working in the mines had rioted, killed all the Spaniards except for themselves and then had gone down to the coast to throw the gold which had been mined into the sea.

Valdivia now feared another general assault – with reason, since the woods near Santiago were reported to be full of Indians bent on his destruction. He went out to the north of his city and captured seven *caciques*, who confirmed that an attack was probable. But he could not return in time. Inés Suárez and Monroy organized the resistance. The Spaniards were pressed back to their main square, most houses except that of the magistrate Francisco de Aguirre were soon on fire, most of the Spanish population were wounded, but Inés cut off the heads of the seven *caciques* whom Valdivia had captured earlier and exposed them. The gory display inspired dismay in the attackers who held off their assault. Sancho de Hoz appeared to redeem himself by fighting well with a lance, even if he had to do so manacled. Afterwards he was pardoned.

Valdivia returned and the Indians withdrew. There was, however, practically no food. Some argued for the abandonment of Santiago and a withdrawal to Peru, but even that did not seem feasible with no supplies. The recently established fields of maize were worked at double intensity. A harvest of twelve *fanegas*, or bushels, of wheat was forthcoming but was immediately put back into the soil. Hunger was the characteristic of this first year at Santiago.

The old Spanish houses were swiftly rebuilt but this time, to safeguard against the effects of fire, not with wood and straw roofs but with adobe bricks.

A fort too was built, 1,600 feet square, requiring 200 bricks a *vara* long and a *palmo* high.[22] The likelihood of another Indian attack was assumed to be considerable by everyone concerned. In that event the children of the Spaniards and their Indian servants could take refuge there.

32

Valdivia's consummation

Can it be that only the design for a holy life is without the benefit of a system of rules? Indeed there is in general an art and a discipline of virtue, in which those who exercise themselves diligently will be inspired by the Spirit.

Erasmus, *Enchiridion*

In December 1541 Valdivia sent back to Peru his most reliable subordinate, Alonso de Monroy, presumably a cousin of Hernando Cortés, to seek new clothing, men, horses and ammunition. He went by land with five men, taking the best horses with new horseshoes. Some of these horseshoes were made of gold as iron was so short. Valdivia wrote to the emperor:

> Since I know that no man would stir to come to these lands owing to its bad report, unless someone would go from here to bring them and take gold to buy men . . . And since the land they had to traverse was at war and there were great wildernesses, they would have to go lightly equipped and unsheltered by night, I have arranged . . . to send [to Peru] no less than 7,000 pesos of gold

– gold from Malga – to impress the Peruvians. Valdivia also wrote a letter for Monroy to take to Pizarro.[1] Then, reported 'the perfect knight',

> we went through the next two years in great want. Many of the Christians had sometimes to dig up roots for food . . . There was no meat and Christians who found fifty grains of maize a day thought themselves well off. And he who had a fistful of wheat did not grind it to take away the husks . . . I chose to have thirty or forty mounted men always about the plain in

winter; and when the food which they took with them was finished, they came back and others went out. And so we went about looking like ghosts and the Indians called us '*cupias*', which is the name which they give to their devils for, whenever they came in search of us (and they know how to attack at night), they found us awake, armed and, if need be, on horseback.[2]

Monroy and his party of five men meantime journeyed on to Peru till they reached the valley of the Copiapó. There, early in 1542, they were surprised by Indians and four of the six were killed. Monroy himself and Pedro de Miranda, who survived, were made prisoners. They were led to the *cacique* Andequín, who had a Spanish adviser in Francisco de la Gasca, earlier one of Almagro's men, who had been captured some years before. He had won the admiration of the Indians by playing the flute well and so he was given three wives who presented him with many children. Gasca ensured that Monroy and Miranda were well treated; their lives were saved, if not their possessions. After several months Monroy and Miranda began to teach Andequín to ride. One day, they drew further and further away from the Indian settlement, then Miranda stabbed the *cacique* and he and Monroy forced Gasca to flee with them to help them on their way – three men on two horses.[3] But he soon escaped.

After further difficulties, Monroy and Miranda reached Cuzco in September 1542. Vaca de Castro was in power by that time, but his authority was fragile. He received Monroy and Miranda well, but he had no money nor indeed time for them: 'Being so busy, trying the guilty, bringing peace to the land, rewarding services, sending out captains to make further discoveries, he could do little.' He promised to send a ship of supplies to Valdivia once he had restored order in Peru. But that moment was a long time coming. Monroy, with the persistence of an Extremeño, did meet two rich men who were interested in his story: one was Cristóbal Escobar Villarroel, a merchant who had been in the Indies since 1531 and who offered 5,000 castellanos to equip seventy horsemen. The other was Fr Gonzalo Yáñez, a priest who lent Monroy a similar sum, with which he returned to Chile.

On his journey back, Monroy stopped at Arequipa where he met an old friend of Valdivia's, Lucas Martínez Venegas, who was also willing to help him. 'Look for a ship, señor Monroy,' he said, 'in which to put the things most needed by your governor. I have only one ship, the *Santiaguillo*, and I would rather not give that to you since I need it for my mines. But if you do not find a ship on the nearby coast, I am prepared to give it to you even though I should lose much by it.'[4] Monroy was not one to hesitate. He took the *Santiaguillo*, and filled it with arms, ammunition, ironware, clothing, food and wine. They left for Chile in May 1543 with Lucas Martínez on board but, because of the adverse winds and their ignorance of the route, the captain did not arrive till September.[5] On their arrival in Santiago, they found 118 Spaniards there – near-skeletons they seemed. But what a wonderful change the *Santiaguillo* brought about.

Monroy, who travelled part of the way by land, did not reach Santiago till December. His arrival was another infusion of life into the moribund colony. But he brought back no confirmation of Valdivia as governor; he remained to his frustration just the lieutenant-governor.

Thereafter, Valdivia told Emperor Charles that the Indians did not attack any more,

> nor came within four leagues [twelve miles] round this town and they all withdrew to the province of the Promaoces and would send daily messages bidding me to come and fight them and bring the new Christians who had come, for they wanted to see if they were as brave as we were; and if they were, they would submit to us but if not, not.[6]
>
> When all the men and horses of Monroy had recovered, I went forth with them to seek the Indian strongholds. I found them but the Indians all fled ... leaving all their villages burned down and abandoning the best stretch of land in the world so that it looks as if it never had an Indian in it.[7]

Soon after, Valdivia, still with no further communication from Peru, began to grant *encomiendas*. In order to make that easier, he founded a second settlement in the north, where colonists coming in from Lima or Cuzco could rest on the last stretch of their journey. The need for this was confirmed by the fate of a boat belonging to an Italian, Juan Albert. Juan Albert sailed on south, passed Valparaiso and, somewhere south of that port, Indians killed all his crew, as well as a black slave who was scrubbed to death to see if he washed white.[8] Valdivia meanwhile sent the German Juan Bohon and thirty horsemen to found a settlement in the Coquimbo valley, in the north near the Andacolla mines. Valdivia himself joined him and they called the place La Serena after everyone's happy memories of that magical valley in Spain south of the river Guadiana. They found there plants which yielded a good pitch, like a wax, that could be used for careening boats.[9]

The colony was again reinvigorated by another arrival from Peru: this was Juan Calderón de la Barca, in the *San Pedro*, a vessel owned and piloted by Juan Bautista de Pastene from Genoa, who afterwards would be a strong adherent of Valdivia, who sent him down the coast to explore the land south of Magellan's strait. This was seen as an important extra journey, Pastene being accompanied by a treasurer (Jerónimo de Alderete, probably a relation of the Alderete from Tordesillas who had held that post in New Spain at the end of the conquest there), a chief clerk (Juan de Cárdenas) and Rodrigo de Quiroga. Alderete and Cárdenas were to take possession of all the land in the name of the emperor and give names to ports and rivers, islands and districts (Valdivia, Concepción, Osorno – after the acting president of the Council of the Indies) and load the ship with sheep and food for their return. The *San Pedro*'s voyage would be followed by that of the *Santiaguillo*, which would sail to the river Maule to assist Valdivia in a more local contest. Both expeditions brought back good news of the fertility of the land in the south, the number of natives, the crops grown, the size of the towns and the good harbours.

Valdivia was concerned with the gold mines too, using Peruvian Indians to work in them, guarded by a Spanish contingent of armed men. In the next nine months they would produce 60,000 castellanos' worth of gold. Valdivia sent one of his would-be assassins, Antonio de Ulloa, back to Spain to represent him before the monarch in the Council of the Indies – a very odd choice by the naïve Valdivia, one cannot but think, for Ulloa was a close friend of La Hoz's. Valdivia also sent Monroy back again to Peru by land, and Pastene by sea, to seek more supplies. Valdivia had further dealings with the equally naïve Michimalongo, to whom the still determined Inés Suárez offered looking-glasses, combs, Venetian glass, beads and trinkets. Michimalongo in reply presented Inés with a white feather from a bird which lived high up in the snows and did not burn if passed through a flame.

It was at this stage on 4 September 1545 that Valdivia sent Charles the emperor a very enthusiastic description of Chile: 'this land,' he insisted, is such that there is none better in the world for living in and settling down in ... it is very flat, very healthy and very pleasant ... it has four months of winter [but] it is only when the moon is at the quarter that it rains for a day or two ... on all other days, the sun is so fine that there is no need to draw near the fire. The summer is so temperate with such delightful breezes that a man can be out in the sun all day long without annoyance. It is a land most abounding in pastures and fields and yielding every kind of livestock and plant imaginable; much timber and very fine [too it is] for building houses, endless wood for use in them; the mines being rich in gold, the whole land being full of it. And whoever wants to take it, there they will find a place to sow and a site to build on and water, grass and wood for their beasts.[10]

He added that, as a result of the expedition of Almagro, Chile had acquired an evil name but did not deserve it.[11]

Valdivia wrote too a curious letter to Hernando Pizarro (also dated 4 September 1545) telling him that there were 15,000 Indian families between Copiapó and the valley of the river Maule. Assuming an average of five persons in each family, the total population would accordingly have been 75,000. But Valdivia added that an equal number had died in the intervening years since the conquest of Chile had begun. So one might assume that the total population would have been 150,000 in 1540. But these are guesses; no one knows how accurate Valdivia was, and no one knows how many are to be assumed in a single family.

In early 1546, while Gonzalo Pizarro was still dominating Peru, Valdivia was driving down to conquer the immediate south of his new country. He had sixty horsemen, 150 Indians as porters and a black ex-slave, Juan Valiente, as doctor. South of the river Maule, they encountered hostile Indians. Many who were captured were asked to put to their fellows a request that they surrender to Valdivia but, instead, 300 Indians came to bar the Spaniards' path. The conquistadors fell on them and killed fifty. Valdivia says that they reached Quilacura later that day, where they discovered that a surprise attack was being mounted by 7,000 Indians. The onslaught was cleverly foiled by the Spaniards, but the Indians fought well, 'packed together as if they had been Germans'. Rodrigo de Quiroga killed the *cacique* and routed this force with the loss of only two horses, though many Spaniards were wounded. Having reached the river Brobio, they returned to Santiago at the end of March 1546.[12]

There they encountered some disquiet. The settlers there had fully expected Valdivia to have established a new city in the south so that the *vecinos* (neighbours) of Santiago had been busy reassigning the *encomiendas* locally. Now Valdivia ordered that all property be returned to those who had had it before his departure – which caused much grumbling.[13] Valdivia worked anew on the divisions, and some nineteen persons found themselves actually dispossessed, the number of *encomenderos* being cut from sixty to thirty-two. Those who gained were the men of the *cabildo* (the town council), the church, the most powerful conquistadors – and Inés! The dispossessed were assured that they would be assigned wonderful property in the beautiful south, but only *when* it was conquered.

Sancho de Hoz was among those dispossessed. Still longing for authority in Santiago, or the *vara de dos palmos*, the symbol of mayoral authority, he approached and won the sympathy of several other discontented men. Thereupon, he sent a message to Valdivia to tell him that he was dying and begging him to visit him. The plan was that once Valdivia entered Sancho's house, a friend of his, Julio Romero, would stab him. Valdivia agreed to go but insisted on taking several of his friends. Sancho de Hoz asked Francisco de Villagrán to join his plot. He went to Inés, who immediately informed Valdivia, who in turn at last arrested Sancho.

Shortly afterwards the German Juan Bohon rode in from La Serena to inform Valdivia of further treachery. Pastene, the Genoese friend of the 'perfect captain', had just arrived back in the port. Bohon said, and Pastene confirmed it, that on their outward journey to Peru, their ship had reached Los Reyes in the record time of twenty-four days. There they had news of the war between Núñez Vela and Gonzalo Pizarro. When they arrived, the faithful Monroy died and Antonio de Ulloa, instead of going to Spain, had rather joined Gonzalo Pizarro, supporting Aldana, who had (as we remember) been made chief justice by Gonzalo. Ulloa tore up the letters and papers which had been given him by Valdivia for the Emperor Charles. He obtained an order that enabled him to steal all the gold which had been carried for the viceroy by the now deceased Monroy, and Pastene, the loyal Genoese, was restrained from leaving Los Reyes. Ulloa also gained permission to seize what was being held of Valdivia's money in Pastene's ship. But Pastene was saved by Gonzalo's evil genius, Francisco de Carvajal whom he had known, as he had known Valdivia, in Italy.

Ulloa arrived in Gonzalo's camp just in time to take part in his rebellious activities at the battle of Añaquito. But by then Carvajal had heard of the plans of Aldana and Ulloa to carry out a '*maldad galalonesa*', that is, a crime in the style of Galalón in the chivalrous novel *The Twelve Peers*. Carvajal might be a scoundrel but he was a literate scoundrel. He told Pastene that 'Aldana and Ulloa are aiming at . . . Valdivia's death so that they [and their friends] may govern. And they want to make use of my lord the governor's friendship with Pedro de Valdivia to gain what they want.'[14] Carvajal sent Pastene to Quito to see Gonzalo Pizarro, who authorized him to collaborate with the treacherous Antonio de Ulloa in search of supplies.

Pastene returned to Los Reyes where he found Ulloa busy loading the *San Pedro*. He showed Ulloa his letter from Gonzalo Pizarro, but, despite that, Ulloa sailed down to Arequipa, forcing Pastene to buy another vessel for 1,000 pesos, which left him with the responsibility to pay another 7,000 once he rejoined Valdivia. Valdivia's name was held in such high standing that the seller of the ship knew that even such a large debt would be sure to be honoured. Pastene found thirty men to sail with him and went down to Tarapacá, whence Ulloa had already sailed south, planning to kill Valdivia and rearrange the *encomiendas* under Gonzalo's rule. Pastene, however, overtook Ulloa, who invited him to confer. But Pastene, realizing that he would be killed, declined the invitation. Ulloa then returned north in order to fight on behalf of Gonzalo.

Valdivia, still preoccupied by his legal position (was he governor or lieutenant-governor?), sent Juan de Ávalos, from the family of the victor of Pavia, an old friend, north to Peru to clarify matters. He took with him, as any responsible well-to-do conquistador then did, 60,000 castellanos in gold, as well as copies of the letters which Ulloa had seized.[15] A little later, having received no answer, Valdivia realized that he ought to return to Peru himself. He left Francisco de Villagrán as his deputy and Francisco de Aguirre as the administrator.

Valdivia had been away from Peru seven years and was determined to resolve the question of his gubernatorial status. He left Valparaiso with as much money as he could secure. He is supposed to have told all Spaniards who wanted to return to Spain with what they had accumulated in Chile to put their possessions on board his boat. They did so. He gave a dinner on the shore, and then, with Jerónimo de Alderete and Juan de Cárdenas, left for the ship to take them to Peru, leaving the diners aghast. One of them, Juan Piñelo, outraged, swam after the boat but was thrown back into the sea. The defenders of Valdivia argued that this was just a change of plan, and that view was sustained by Gasca in a later enquiry. But the money seized thus came to be known as the 80,000 *doradas*, sea bream, netted by Valdivia 'as easily as St Peter brought up his net so full that it broke'.[16]

Valdivia intended to go back to Spain to establish his position. On leaving Santiago, the city which he had founded, he wrote to the *cabildo* there:

> I am leaving for the court of His Majesty, to present myself before his exalted person ... to tell him all that his subjects and I in these provinces have done for him; and to ask and request that it be to his service to grant to me this government in order to be better able to serve him and to reward the persons who have helped me conquer this land.[17]

There were, however, a few who thought that he might instead be going to Portugal 'to live off the gold which he had stolen'. That would have been out of character, but not impossible in such extraordinary circumstances.

Valdivia set off for Peru, intending to go to Spain, with a handful of loyal friends. At La Serena he received the news that Gonzalo Pizarro had won the civil war in Peru. But a little more to the north, at Tarapacá, he heard that Gasca was recapturing the country. Valdivia had no doubts about siding with the Crown, despite his old friendships with Carvajal and Gonzalo Pizarro. Gasca was delighted to welcome him, 'knowing him to be a man of great diligence and experience and courage and to whom great credit is given in this land in matters of war'. The 'perfect captain' became one of the three most important members of Gasca's army, alongside Alvarado and Hinojosa and, as we have seen, it was he who was concerned in deciding the crossing of the river at Jaquijahuana and rebuilding the bridges broken by the Pizarristas.[18] This was a decisive contribution to Gasca's triumph.

Valdivia's participation in the battles against Gonzalo Pizarro led on 23 April 1548 to his tardy but welcome nomination by Gasca as governor and captain-general of 'New Extremadura', by which was to be understood Chile. His dominion lay between Copiapó at 27 degrees in the north and 41 in the south which gave him not only Santiago but the towns of Concepción, Valdivia and Osorno, as well as nearly 1,000 miles of sea coast. In the interior the concession was for 100 leagues (300 miles), which gave him the entire southern Andes and much of the flat lands of what would become Argentina.

Valdivia set off triumphantly to Santiago. Gasca gave him two ships – unprecedented largesse from the effective authority in Peru. Valdivia loaded them and sent them by sea under Jerónimo de Alderete down to Atacama, where he planned to greet him himself. Valdivia set off for there with 120 men but was overtaken by Hinojosa, his fellow general, who compelled him to return to Peru to face charges made by Antonio de Ulloa, the treacherous Pizarrista, who had successfully manoeuvred himself into becoming commander of Gasca's ports. The accusations were that Valdivia had taken with him some Indian *yanaconas* from Peru and also some ex-Pizarristas who had been condemned to perpetual imprisonment or to the galleys (such as Luis de Chávez); and Valdivia had refused to allow Ulloa to inspect his ships.

Valdivia returned and met Gasca at Callao on 20 October 1548. The bizarre investigation then began. Almost immediately, a letter from the *cabildo* at Santiago reached Gasca to tell him that, in the prolonged absence of Valdivia, they would like Francisco de Villagrán to be named as governor. But they preferred Valdivia. If he were alive, 'please do us the favour of sending him back to us as soon as possible, because it is conducive to the peace and tranquillity of this land; and if Your Excellency does not favour us by sending him, our loss would be great'.[19]

In Valdivia's absence, the ineffable Sancho de Hoz, the thorn in his side in Santiago for so many years, had sought to take advantage of the discontent caused by the rearrangement of the *encomiendas*. He had been living outside Santiago but he had friends in the city such as Hernando Rodríguez Monroy, who committed the mistake of formulating a new plot with Fr Lobo and Alonso de Cordoba. They went immediately with their news to the subgovernor, Villagrán, who, more determined than Valdivia had ever been in matters of rebellion, arrested Sancho de Hoz and his friend Juan Romero and had them both executed there and then. Valdivia would probably have hesitated and given them a pardon again.[20]

Despite the death of Sancho de Hoz, there remained friends of his in the *cabildo* in Santiago and also some in Gasca's circle in Peru. They accused Valdivia of murder, immorality (living with Inés) and sometimes tampering with the box for the royal fifth. Gasca talked to some of these conspirators. For example, to Vicente del Monte, who had come with Valdivia to Peru; to Diego García de Villalón, the captain of the *Santiaguillo*; to some passengers on other ships from Chile; and to Bernardino de Mella, who had ridden back with Monroy to Chile in 1543.[21]

Most admitted that there was discontent in Chile. Some thought that Sancho de Hoz had had a good claim to much land. Others believed that Valdivia had been excessively generous to Sancho de Hoz, and yet others that his eventual execution had brought peace. Some said that Valdivia had given them a charge on his land in return for his seizure of their gold. Six out of eleven witnesses considered that Valdivia's return would benefit Chile. Mella said that Gasca ought to send Inés Suárez back to Spain because she was mad. Other accusations were levied against Valdivia. He defended himself well, saying that Inés was his maid and that Pizarro himself – Francisco, not Gonzalo – had given him permission to take her.

Gasca's judgement was solomonic: Valdivia was confirmed as governor and captain-general but within six months he had to break his relationship with Inés: either send her away or marry her to someone else. He had within a year to pay off all loans forced by him; he had to permit all who wanted to leave to do so; he had to ensure that all *encomiendas* had enough Indians to support them; and anything borrowed from the king's box had to be replaced. Except for the clause about Inés, the punishments were logical. Some of Valdivia's friends tried to persuade him to act against Gasca. Valdivia refused and went overland to Arequipa. There he became ill, but recovered, thanks to two later famous nurses, María del Encio Sarmiento and Juana Jiménez. He went thence to Aruca and took a ship to Valparaíso, where he arrived in April. There he remained till June.[22]

He discovered immediately that La Serena, his port of entry 250 miles north of Santiago, had been destroyed. The Indians had entered the town at night and placed an assassin in front of every door. When the alarm was given, the Spaniards were killed on their doorsteps. All Juan Bohon's men and settlers had been massacred, except for two who survived to tell how not only the settlers but their animals were killed.

Villagrán was sent back to La Serena to recover the place with sixty men, and thirty horse, under himself by land and thirty arquebusiers by sea under Diego de Maldonado. The sea party arrived first but were forced back on to their ships. Villagrán arrived the following day, and the two groups were able to hold back the Indians. A rebuilding of the town then began. The incident had inspired consternation in Santiago; there was general fear of an Indian attack, especially in the mines of Malga. The miners wanted six armed horsemen to protect them; Valdivia sent only four and the mines were closed.

Valdivia's return to Santiago had many bizarre aspects. His friends were now established in the town council: Alderete became treasurer again, Esteban de Sosa was the accountant, Vicente del Monte was the overseer and Pedro de Miranda was the official spokesman. Valdivia himself, through his agent, Juan de Cárdenas, had already sworn to respect the laws and rights of all settlers, and he now made a triumphal entry with Indians carrying myrtle and cinnamon before him. He found that Inés Suárez, having evidently heard of her condemnation by Gasca, had left Valdivia for Rodrigo de Quiroga, whom she subsequently married.[23]

Just as soon as Valdivia had returned to Santiago, another hundred men under well-established leaders appeared in the capital, led by Francisco de Villagrán. Valdivia was then tempted by a new idea for an attack in the south, but first he sent Francisco de Aguirre to assist to rebuild La Serena. Then he set off himself for the south in a hand chair carried by Indians, because he had broken his hip when his horse fell. With Alderete as his second-in-command, he as usual sent small units ahead to find out the lie of the land. Then he moved down to attack the Indians on the rivers Laja and Biobio, both of which flow into the Pacific, and at what would become Concepción, where a fort was now established (3 March 1550). There was a ferocious reply by the Indians. Alderete responded successfully and many prisoners were taken.

Valdivia wrote to the emperor that he had defeated the Araucanian Indians – 'the finest and most splendid Indians that have ever been seen in these parts'. Some 1,500 or 2,000 had been killed, and he had cut off the noses and hands of another 200 for 'their contumacy in rejecting his offers of peace'.[24]

Valdivia was supported by his Genoese ally Pastene, who arrived with food at his fortress in Concepción. He went in search of further supplies and information and reached as far as the island of Santa María off Talca and close to Concepción. Valdivia's land party then continued, to found a settlement at what became La Imperial (founded as such in March 1551) and then Valdivia itself, a new town also, like almost all those founded by the governor, on the coast; and he also founded Vila

Rica between Concepción and Valdivia in April 1552. This was a highly successful expedition. The towns survive till the present day in their old sites.

Valdivia continued his advocacy of Chile as the best place in Charles's American empire: 'the land has a fine climate and every kind of Spanish plant will grow in it better than [in New Spain]'.[25] He thought that southern Chile was 'all a town, a garden and a gold mine'. He argued too that there were 'more Indians in southern Chile than in Mexico'.[26]

Obviously Valdivia was hoping to establish his or Spanish imperial control over the whole of the southern part of the continent. He was, he wrote, sending the faithful Francisco de Villagrán from Villarrica across the Andes to 'the northern sea', the Atlantic. He had sent Francisco de Aguirre to the north to add El Barco to the empire. He himself had been recently into the mountains and discovered there a high lake, presumably Lake Ranco. He was also thinking of sending Alderete to explore the strait of Magellan from the south.

Villagrán's journey to the Atlantic was not a success. He did cross the Andes near Chile but he found the way ahead blocked by two rivers (perhaps the Almuinó and the Limay) so he returned to Villarrica. There he learned that the Indians had risen at Pucuseo between La Imperial and Villarrica. He sought to save the garrison, though its commander, Alonso de Moya, was killed. From Villarrica, Villagrán went down to Concepción, where he found Valdivia, to whom he gave an account of his journey. Everyone else was engaged in a gold rush since that intoxicating metal had just been discovered nearby.

Valdivia returned to Santiago to speed up the departure for Spain of Alderete: he was to try to bring to Chile Valdivia's wife, whose presence had been demanded by Gasca. In Santiago, Valdivia wrote his last letter to the Emperor Charles:

> Most sacred Caesar, Your Majesty being so taken up with the service of God and the defence and the upholding of Christianity against the common enemy the Turks and the Lutherans, it would be more fitting to help by deeds rather than distract by words. Would to God that I could find myself in Your Majesty's presence with much money and that you might use me in your service, even though I am not useless where I am.[27]

Valdivia soon returned to the south of Chile where he considered his mission was to bring the entire land to submission. He founded Los

Confines between Concepción and La Imperial. Then he built forts at Purén and Tucapel, where his captain Alonso Coronas advised him that another general rising of Indians was about to begin. He also reported that a one-time stable boy, Lantaro, an Indian who had worked with the Spaniards, was teaching the Indians how to fight on horseback. Captain Martín de Ariza was obliged to abandon the fort at Tucapel by Indians who hid their guns in bundles of grass brought in precisely for the horses. Tucapel was burned.

On Christmas Day 1553 there was one of the few battles on fixed lines between Indians and Spaniards, outside Tucapel. Lantaro had arranged to follow Valdivia's route carefully, then to force the outnumbered Spaniards into the marshes. Valdivia drew up his men in three companies. He ordered his first unit to charge and rout the Indians. They held firm. Then he sent in his second company. Still the Indians did not flee. Leaving ten men to guard the baggage Valdivia then led his own company against the enemy. Their ranks held. 'Gentlemen,' asked Valdivia of his captains, 'what shall we do?' 'What does your lordship wish us to do except fight and die?'

Valdivia withdrew the horsemen guarding the baggage, hoping that the enemy would be distracted by the chance of loot; it was usually a successful tactic. But Lantaro had anticipated that and there was no weakening on the Indians' part. Shortly they advanced, pressing the Spaniards into the nearby marsh. They were killed one by one. Valdivia had a strong horse and might have escaped, but he refused to abandon Fr Bartolomé del Pozo who was on foot. Both were captured.[28]

According to Góngora Marmolejo, Valdivia was disarmed and undressed and then tied up by the Indians. They built a fire in which they roasted slices of his arms cut off with mussel shells and ate them. Other tortures followed till they finally cut off his head.[29]

Thus died the 'perfect captain', the most humane and tolerant of the conquistadors, and the father of Chile, a society which, buffered behind the *despoblado* desert of Atacama, was more free of the diseases of Peru and the north than anywhere else on the continent. But the country was to be at the mercy of both famine and pestilence in the late 1550s.

BOOK III
The Indies as a
Treasure House

33

Carolus Africanus

*The best remedy would seem to be a good war. How can we
arrange that? I have no means of sustaining my army. . . . The King
of England does not look on me as a true friend and does not
advise me adequately as to what he is going to do.*

Charles V autobiographical note, February–March 1525

The news of the thunder and fury of all these conquests and battles,
slaughters and sufferings, arguments and denunciations in the New
World reached Europe eventually and was absorbed by the officials and
others who served the Crown in regard to the Indies. But they had different priorities. The decision of Ferdinand, the emperor's brother, to
become king of the Romans in 1531, seen by many as the end of the
idea of universal monarchy, was a decisive consideration, but it had, of
course, an impact on American policy too. The frame of the extraordinary achievements in the Americas was provided by the Crown, after all.
Charles V might be at Innsbruck or Augsburg, in Toledo or Valladolid,
Rome or Bologna, on the Mediterranean or in a palace in Flanders; he
might be considering the Turkish threat (was Erasmus right to argue in
his *Consultatio de bello Turcis inferendo,* that the true victory over the
Turks would be to make them Christians?) or how he could outmanoeuvre that 'monster' (that *'bellaco'*, as Diego de Ordaz, the conqueror
of the Orinoco, put it) Luther or defeat the German princes; but, at any
moment, the emperor might be interrupted by the faithful secretary,
Cobos, with a request for a contract for a new adventurer from Seville
or Extremadura who wanted to go to the Indies to conquer and settle a
new desert or jungle, to be called, say, New Extremadura or even New
Badajoz. Charles might want to concentrate on the question of how to

persuade the pope to call a general council of the Church, but news from New Spain might interrupt his consideration of episcopal and religious reform.

Charles travelled continuously – surely no ruler has ever travelled so much – and he was 'most fond' of maps, as Dantiscus reported.[1] Gout already tortured him, but the Council of the Indies was always in communication, and other informal advisers were always writing to him. So were conquistadors themselves, such as Valdivia, 'the perfect knight', as he was known, or indeed the great Cortés. Decisions affecting the Americas had to be made. Of course, Charles would give the island of Malta to the Knights of St John who had been expelled by the Turks from their old home at Rhodes. That was an easy decision. But who should be sent to Peru to face and defeat Gonzalo Pizarro? A lawyer or a gentleman? That was a more difficult decision.

Charles is often held to have had no profound interest in his American empire. That is not so. True, his first attention was always paid to the cause of Germany and the Protestant revolt and to the growing disorganization in the Low Countries themselves. But all the same he had often listened to Las Casas's pleas about the treatment of the Indians and, from the moment that Charles saw the shivering Totonaca sent from Mexico to Andalusia by Cortés in 1520, he was concerned with the health of his new subjects. He was also very interested in the provision of gold and silver from the Indies, which helped to finance his wars in Italy. The twentieth-century Spanish historian Ramón Carande pointed out that 'without the Indian payments, his adventures [in Italy] would have been few'.[2] Even though preoccupied by the Diet of Augsburg in 1530, the empress signed the decree of August of that year which forbade any new enslavement in Charles's realms: 'no person shall dare to make a single slave whether in peace or in war ... whether by barter, purchase, trade or on any pretext or cause whatsoever',[3] and Charles advised his son, Prince Philip, in 1544 and 1548, always to concern himself with the quality of governors and viceroys: 'do not cease to keep yourself well informed of the state of these distant lands, for the honour of God and for the sake of justice. Combat the abuses which have arisen there.'[4]

In 1534 the Moorish admiral Barbarossa had captured Tunis. Charles, who had some knowledge of strategy, thought that threatened the entire western Mediterranean – Spain as well as Italy. He thereupon began to gather a considerable army and navy. To finance this conflict, he called a meeting of the Cortes to seek more money, and remained in Madrid all the winter of 1534–5, seeing the controllers of the military orders.

While these preparations were beginning, the news came in September of the death of Pope Clement VII, a great relief to Charles. He was succeeded by Cardinal Farnese, the oldest of the cardinals and the only one to date his cardinalate to the days of Alexander VI. Farnese was proclaimed Pope Paul III and he immediately announced his support for Charles's plea for a general council of the Church.

Two senior counsellors, Tavera and Cobos, were against any campaign against Barbarossa, but their protests were ignored. Charles had, after all, a new source of finance – namely, Peruvian gold. For, as we have seen, Hernando Pizarro had returned in the winter of 1534 with his extraordinary news and presents from Peru. One hundred and eighty-five thousand ducats of the treasure of Pizarro were held in the castle of La Mota at Medina del Campo (a castle which Hernando, ironically, would come to know only too well).[5] Cobos said that the king could also count on 800,000 ducats seized from private individuals who had brought that sum from the New World.

On 13 May 1535 all the forces which Charles was committing trooped past the emperor outside the gate of Perpignan at Barcelona, while the royal treasurer, Pedro de Zuazaola, and Juan de Samano, the secretary of the Council of the Indies during most of the reign of Charles V, sat at a table writing down names and numbers.[6] Never before had he seemed the leader of a real crusade. Charles unfurled a banner of Christ crucified and called to the assembled men, noblemen, soldiers and camp followers: 'Here is your captain-general, I am your standard bearer.' Seventy-four galleys, thirty minor ships and 300 transport were assembled under the command of Andrea Doria, the brilliant admiral from Genoa, assisted by his young Spanish disciple, Álvaro de Bazán. The Marquis de Vasto, son of the Marquis de Pescara of Pavia renown, commanded the troops in Doria's fleet, the Emperor Charles agreeing to submit himself to that command.[7]

On 10 June the fleet set out for Africa and, five days later, it lay at anchor before the ruins of Carthage. On 14 July the fort of La Goleta was stormed. That was Charles's baptism of fire. Was he in a mêlée, was his horse killed under him? Such details are obscure. On 21 July, however, we know that Charles entered Tunis, triumphantly releasing 20,000

Christian captives. He captured eighty-two vessels of Barbarossa's fleet. The following month he gave back Tunis to his friend Muley Hasán, whom Barbarossa had dispossessed as king. The king emperor returned to Sicily on 22 August as 'Carolus Africanus'. A banner described him as 'Champion of Europe and of Asia', and another proclaimed; 'Long live our victorious emperor, conqueror of Africa, peacemaker of Italy'. Much booty was obtained. People began to talk of Charles as if he had become a combination of Saint Louis, Scipio and Hannibal. Turkish fashions had a short sway.

Charles was in Palermo for several weeks before leaving to make a triumphal entry into Naples. Splendid sculptures welcomed him at the Porta Capuana (Giovanni da Nola building on the work of the Florentine Giuliano da Maiano). The leaders of Europe flocked to congratulate him.[8] There were dances, masked balls, even bullfights. In December Cobos gave a dinner for the art collector Paolo Giovio, and it was probably then that he gave Giovio a pre-conquest codex from New Spain which may have been a present from Cortés. A treasure from the New World thus won pride of place in the city of Tancred.[9]

While Charles was spending the winter in Naples, the Council of the Indies recommended that the trade in African slaves in the New World should be thrown open, relieving the practitioners of all duties save payments of taxes.[10] Charles considered this but he was preoccupied. He had set off northwards for Rome but on 2 April he met the pope at Sermoneta, the most southerly town of the Monti Lepini, so he was diverted. Two days later, the emperor celebrated a triumphal entry into Rome 'con gran demonstración de alegría', Charles reported to the empress in Spain.[11] Over 200 houses and even three or four churches had been pulled down to make possible la grande entrée.[12] The vicar of the pope came to meet the emperor. Then, surrounded by noblemen such as the dukes of Alba, Guasto and Benavente,[13] Charles rode down a new street (now the Via di San Gregorio) to the Arch of Constantine. He crossed the bridge over the Tiber to be greeted by the pope at St Peter's. The two talked. Though Charles failed to persuade the pope to side with him against France, a special congregation of cardinals at last agreed to summon a general council; Charles was so pleased that he arranged to thank the pope formally on 17 April.[14]

On that day Charles met the pope, the cardinals, the ambassadors and other Roman officials, and harangued them for an hour in Spanish without notes. He launched a real challenge to the king of France,[15] promising again that, if Francis wanted him to fight personally, he could do so, armed or unarmed, 'in shirt sleeves or in armour, with a sword or with fists, on land or on sea, on a bridge or on an island or in a closed place, in front of our armies or wherever he liked'.[16] The prize would be Burgundy if he, Charles, won; Milan, if Francis won. Cobos and Granvelle were not consulted before their master made this chivalrous gesture.[17] They were dismayed. If such challenges could be made in Europe, what if a Peruvian made the same in the Americas? The French bishop of Mâcon complained that he could not understand what was said. Charles made a defiant reply about the virtues of the Spanish language.[18]

The speech by the emperor was seen everywhere as aggressive because of being in Spanish. The twentieth-century scholar Ramón Menéndez Pidal argued that it proclaimed Spanish as the common tongue of diplomacy.[19] But there was no such purpose in Charles's declaration.

There was agreement on the need for a general council of the Church. On 4 June 1536 it was decided it should meet at Mantua in May 1537. But when the Protestant Germans refused to attend a meeting in Italy, the scheme was cancelled. Alas, if the Protestant community had only brought themselves to make the journey to the enchanting Palazzo del Te at Mantua the unity of Christendom might have been preserved!

War with France was decided upon instead. The emperor moved up to Sarzana, the first Genoese town to the east on the Gulf of Liguria, the city of Pope Nicholas V, who had given Portugal its place in Africa and India. There he was greeted by Doria, who had agreed to fight for Charles. The plan was for a joint land and naval attack on France such as had been so successful at Tunis the year before. Anselmo de' Grimaldi came out to meet Cobos and Granvelle and, a few weeks later, Cobos and another Genoese banker, Tomasso Forne, arranged a loan with Grimaldi for 100,000 scudi.

Even in these circumstances, the news from the Indies remained insistent. But on 30 May 1536 Granvelle, in effect now chancellor of the empire in all but name, wrote: '*Tout se porte bien en Espagne.*'[20] In July 1536 Charles crossed into France, but it was a disastrous campaign thanks to Anne de Montmorency's scorched earth policy. Aix-en-Provence was besieged but the attempt to take it failed.[21]

In September Charles decided to withdraw. Montmorency, always in favour of an alliance with the emperor against the heretics, wrote to Granvelle that Francis was prepared to seek a lasting peace. But, though Charles returned to Genoa, no peace was signed. On 14 November 1536 Charles also admitted how much he was relying on the gold from the Indies: '*Et sommes attendant et en espoir qu'il viendra du côté de Perou, qui pourra servir au propos.*'[22] Considering the significance of Genoa in opening up the New World, it was appropriate for the emperor to be there.

Two days later the court sailed for Palamós in Catalonia, where they arrived on 5 December. There, the remorseless succession of decrees affecting the New World continued. Charles gave his assent in January 1537 to the despatch of the press and type to enable a son of Cromberger to set up a branch of his successful family business in Mexico, even if for a time only government printing and Christian textbooks were undertaken.[23]

The initiative to establish a branch of Cromberger in Mexico was largely that of Bishop Zumárraga. As a Franciscan, he had had much to do with the Crombergers before he left Spain. In 1529 we find him owing Jacob Cromberger money and then Jacob authorized him and Licenciado Marroquín to take over the fortune of a certain Diego de Mendieta in Mexico. Zumárraga soon decided that the establishment of a printing press would greatly assist the business of evangelization. Back in Spain in 1533, Zumárraga talked with the Council of the Indies about the plan and in 1534 the emperor gave the bishop permission to spend a fifth of the income of the diocese for three years to establish a printer.[24] The nucleus of this would be the published works of Cromberger. As for the printer in Mexico, the Crombergers sent an Italian from Brescia, Giovanni Paoli, to establish their branch.[25] He set himself up in one of the houses owned or controlled by the bishop, and was formally registered as a citizen of Mexico, as 'Juan Pablos'. There he supervised the publication of *Manual de Adultos*, the first book which we know for sure was published in Mexico.[26] The Cromberger family soon acquired other interests in Mexico, principally in the silver mines of first Taxco and then Zacatecas.[27]

On 21 December 1537 Bishop Zumárraga had written from Mexico to Charles urging that a large college (say, for 500 boys) should be established in each diocese in New Spain and a second one for girls. The instruction for boys should be extended to include Latin grammar, while girls should be educated from six to twelve, when they should be married.[28] Lord Macaulay would have approved. So did Charles after a time.

As far as officials in Seville are concerned, we are aware of a constant pressure on the emperor to control and limit the scale of operations. Thus in 1538 we read of a decree on the petition of both the officials of the Casa de la Contratación and the merchants of Seville which made the rules to exclude foreigners from the navigation to the Indies more strict.[29]

But in Europe the battles for peace continued. At the end of 1537 there were talks about ending the Franco-imperial war at the little town of Fitou on the French frontier between Leucate and Salsas, with Granvelle and Cobos, present on the one hand, and Montmorency and Jean, cardinal of Lorraine (a Guise and brother of the founder of the house), on the other. Charles was at Perpignan, Francis at Montpellier. The officials' discussions centred on the restoration to the empire of Savoy, Milan and Hesdin in the Pas-de-Calais, which Francis had wanted handed to him as a preliminary to further negotiations. Later, there was also discussion of Navarre, Tournai and even Asti. The talks went on into 1538. The emperor again suggested a personal meeting between himself and Francis. But Francis was reluctant.

Nevertheless the pursuit of an understanding between France and the empire continued: in May 1538 the emperor arrived at Villefranche, near Nice, as usual in his friend Doria's fleet. He sent M. de Bossu with thirteen galleys to Savona, Columbus's town, where the pope was waiting. The pope then went to the Franciscan house of Les Cordeliers near Nice, and next day Charles had an hour's talk with him there. They met again in a pavilion built between Nice and Villefranche. On 28 May Francis arrived at Villeneuve, west of Nice, with his son Henry's consort, Catherine de' Medici, Queen Leonor, Charles's sister, and a bodyguard of 10,000 Swiss. On 29 May Cobos, the duke of Alburquerque and Granvelle called on King Francis and met Queen Leonor, and there was a similar courtesy call by Montmorency and the Cardinal de Lorraine to the emperor. Then on 2 June Francis had his first meeting with the pope, in a house which had been specially prepared for him between Nice and Villeneuve. On 4 June the French and imperial commissioners met the pope for the first time and, later, the queen visited Charles. The pier at Nice collapsed and many grand men and women fell in the water (including the archbishop of Santiago). Even the emperor was thrown in but he managed to save his sister Queen Leonor. Though Charles still did not meet the French king on that occasion, the pope did arrange a ten-year truce.

Queen Leonor eventually persuaded her brother to meet Francis at the castle of Aigues-Mortes in a lagoon near Montpellier, west of the Rhône. They talked a long time while a dance went on outside. Perhaps they could arrange a crusade together? Francis embraced the proposal with the same exaggerated enthusiasm which he had shown before for the idea and then quickly forgot about it.

All the same, there was a celebration in Mexico, organized by Luis de León of Rome, to mark the end of the war with France. This took place there in the viceregal palace, whose corridors

> were transformed into bowers and gardens and, for each course, there were stewards and pages and a full and well-arranged service . . . together with much music of singers and trumpetry, and all sorts of instruments, such as harps, guitars, vihuelas, flutes, dulcimers, and oboes . . . huge pastries were full of live quail and rabbits, whose escape afforded much amusement. There were also jesters and versifiers, and fountains of white wine, sherry, and red wine. Over 300 men and over 200 women were present and the banquet lasted till two hours after midnight when the ladies cried out that they could no longer stay at the table and others that they were indisposed. Everything was served on gold and silver, none of which was lost since the authorities placed an Indian guard next to every dish. But silver salt cellars, table cloths, napkins and knives did disappear . . .

The viceroy, Antonio de Mendoza, and Cortés, now on reasonable terms celebrated together. Thus, less than twenty years after the great conquest of New Spain, did the New World give full recognition of the old one.

34

The Indies finance Europe

I wished your Highness to know all things of this land which are
so many and of such a size that one might call oneself the emperor
of the kingdom with no less glory than of Germany which by the
grace of God your sacred Majesty already possesses.

Letter from Cortés to Charles V, 1519

Charles the emperor was back in Spain in 1538, first in Burgos, then in Valladolid, and there he or the empress issued more decrees affecting the Indies; for example, one to encourage bachelors in the Indies to marry, giving preference indeed in *encomiendas* to those with families. Another decree ordered an ecclesiastical tribunal to examine a Tarascan catechism and take special heed that the terms used did not present difficulties for the teaching and practice of their religion.[1] It almost began to seem as if the American empire was becoming a priority among the imperial authorities.

But the emperor in Spain was as busy with difficult noblemen as he had been in Germany. Thus, in October 1538, he summoned the Cortes of Castile at Toledo. Charles had with him not just the *procuradores* of the towns but the nobility – ninety-five grandees and nobles – and the clergy. He explained that the total revenue of the realm was just over 1,000,000 ducats, but more than half was mortgaged in advance. The Crown had decided, therefore, to levy a new tax, the *sisa*, which would be paid by everyone, like the *alcabala*[2] but bigger. Opposition to this proposal was led by the Duke of Béjar, son of Cortés's great friend and benefactor, and in the end Charles dropped the idea.

This meeting of the Castilian Cortes was notable for bad tempers on all sides. The three estates assembled in different buildings in the city. The nobles refused to accept the secretary designated by the court and, whenever he appeared in the chapter house of the monastery of San Juan de los Reyes, he was expelled by angry noblemen crying: 'Leave us, leave us, here we have no need of any secretary.'[3]

It was here, according to Sepúlveda, that Charles said: 'It's now that I understand the little power that I possess.'[4] Sandoval reported that Charles told the Constable of Castile: 'I should like to throw you out of the window,' to which the constable (Velasco) replied: 'Your Majesty should take care for, even if I am small, I weigh a lot.'

At this time, the idea of fighting the Turks so filled Charles's mind that he set to work in haste to solve all other problems.[5] He was not deflected by a good letter of advice from his sister Mary in the Netherlands:

Your Majesty is the greatest prince in Christendom but you cannot under-take a war in the name of all Christendom until you can be sure to carry it to victory. Such an enterprise could not be carried out save over many years and would cost inexhaustible money. Where could this come from? France, Venice, Naples, the Netherlands? Could you really go and leave us unpro-tected? The Turks cannot be conquered unless their whole empire falls. So great a prince as you must only triumph. Defeat is the ultimate crime. Win the love of the German princes, make France a friend, not an enemy. March across France, settle your last accounts with the king there, then visit your Netherlands, then Germany and at last Italy. Gain the support of all! This is the advice which in all humility I offer you.[6]

Charles had to endure the death of his beloved wife, the Empress Isabel, in childbirth in 1539. Her death was the tragedy of Charles's middle life.

Yet Charles still had to decide such tedious matters as the rivalries between the Casa de la Contratación, the Council of the Indies and the city council in Seville. It was agreed in 1539 that, in all civil cases relat-ing to commerce with the Indies, communication with them, and navigation to and from them, the Casa de la Contratación only could act, and the municipal council could not intervene. Appeals from the Casa de la Contratación could be made to the Council of the Indies but any such appeals up to a value of 40,000 maravedís were to be decided by the Court of the Steps – the steps on the cathedral where business-men settled their affairs and where Alonso de Céspedes as judge had made such an impact in the early sixteenth century.[7]

In civil cases relating to the Indies, the petitioner could choose between the Contratación and the municipal court, always supposing that the accused was in Seville. Criminal cases could only be heard first by the Casa de la Contratación, but criminal cases involving death would be heard by the Casa and passed to the council for sentencing.[8]

These considerations did not prevent Charles from planning once more to go to Flanders and Germany, leaving the reliable Cardinal Tavera as Regent (after the empress's death), eventually with the help of Cobos and García de Loaisa. Francisco de Borja, Marqués de Llombay, great-grandson of Pope Alexander VI, was viceroy of Catalonia. Granvelle, Vázquez de Molina and Idiáquez were now the chief secretaries of the emperor outside Spain, in effect the ministers for foreign affairs.

We follow Charles in 1541 to the Diet of Regensburg, where the German princes assembled. There the Venetian Cardinal Contarini, dominating the Catholics, spoke with the authority of one experienced in the affairs of the Indies because of his old *nunciatura* in Spain. Also there was the new prophet of intolerant Protestantism, Jean Calvin from Geneva. There were some good signs. Philipp Melanchthon, for example, was conciliatory. Charles, longing for reconciliation, intervened often. But still, in the end, there was no peaceful solution. Charles withdrew and eventually saw the pope at Lucca in the bishop's palace. He received papal blessing for a new expedition against the Ottomans.

For this an armada of sixty-five galleys and 450 other ships was made ready with 24,000 troops, including none other than the Marquis del Valle de Oaxaca, Cortés himself. But he had no command. How could a conquistador direct European troops? The Duke of Alba assembled the fleet in Majorca under Doria, the troops under Ferrante Gonzaga. They left Majorca on 13 October 1541 and arrived off Algiers on the 20th. On 23 October Charles began to disembark on a treacherous spit of land to the east of that city. The infantry was landed but bad weather prevented the cavalry and artillery following. A storm came up on 24–25 October and there seemed no way of saving the ships without throwing overboard food and armaments. Even so, fourteen galleys were lost. Charles landed again to the west of Algiers, but the disembarkation of provisions seemed impossible. Cortés told Charles that, if the emperor turned back, he personally could show how to conquer the city. But, if it had not been for the storm, Algiers could easily have been captured. Cortés, for all his talents, was not a master of the weather.

On 2 November Charles ordered the now almost starving troops to be re-embarked.[9] He was held up for days at Bugia, west of the city. He returned defeated to Cartagena on 1 December, then went on to Valladolid via Ocaña, Toledo and Madrid.

Back in Valladolid, Charles found the Council of the Indies again in low morale. The trouble was that various cities, such as Córdoba, Madrid and Guadalajara, had complained of the slow pace with which it despatched its business. In the Cortes, someone had written, perhaps under the influence of Las Casas: 'We beseech His Majesty that he remedies the cruelties which are done to the natives in the Indies and, in that way, God will be served and the Indies preserved.'[10]

In February 1542 Charles, contemplating these problems, held a new Cortes, this time at Valladolid. Most towns yielded to royal pressure and granted a subsidy of 400,000 ducats a year for the crusade, substantial bribery probably being used to achieve this.[11] The king told the Cortes what he had been doing. He saw Las Casas, who came on the recommendation of Bishop Zumárraga. Of course, Charles had met him often in the days of his first visit to Spain in 1517–18,[12] but their present encounter was equally important. Las Casas again made a profound impression, not only on the emperor, but on all to whom he talked. He had, after all, been to the places which they had only discussed. Charles was shocked by Las Casas's new *memoriales* about the condition of Indians. Those documents led to the reorganization of the Council of the Indies and then to the New Laws, essentially a project of Las Casas.[13]

At that time, Spain alone of Charles's dominions was at peace. Taxes remained high. Direct taxes (for example the *alcabala*), the revenues of the knightly orders, the grants of the Vatican on Church lands, the *cruzado*, and money from indulgences, as well as income from the West Indies, generally reached 240,000 ducats a year.[14] Some Arab taxes remained unaltered, such as the silk tax of Granada and income from ports and islands. Sometimes there were extra revenues such as the dowry paid by the king of Portugal for Isabel; or the king of France's ransom of his sons for a million ducats. In 1540 the 282,000 ducats which derived from 'Indies treasure' were a major item in the Crown's total income of 1,159,923 ducats.[15]

But the difficulties were many because there was never enough money at the start of a war. Bankers were called in, loans were raised at high interest, Crown lands and some sources of revenue were mortgaged.

The future income of the Crown was thus crippled. Charles contracted debts haphazardly as the need occurred. This is why by this time the Spanish Crown, articulated by Cobos or other secretaries, was coming to think of the Indies as a new treasure trove to finance its European designs. The Crown seems to have raised two thirds of its revenue from the Indies in 1543.[16] This was exceptional but it was an indication of what might be expected in the future.

There were, however, obstacles to the Indies being able to confirm this financial role. In consequence of accusations of corruption, the Council of the Indies suspended its activities till February 1543. Dr Juan de Figueroa carried out an investigation. He was, Cobos said, 'a man of sound learning, very honest and in official matters nothing will deflect him an iota from that which is right'.[17] Figueroa found that the only permanent long-term member of the council, Dr Beltrán, was a flawed individual. He had requested benefits in Peru from the Pizarros for his two sons, Antonio Beltrán and Bernardino de Mella. The latter was named chief magistrate, *alguacil mayor*, of Cuzco, while the former received good Indians in Arequipa. Those benefits were illegal. Beltrán was accused of having received, in return for support or for favours, money from Almagro and Cortés and, from Gonzalo de Olmos, a cousin of his wife, two emeralds and two beakers of gold.[18] The Emperor Charles was outraged.

True, Beltrán defended himself: the money which came from Almagro had not been for him but for someone else to whom he had given it. The bribes of Cortés had gone astray, and he denied any contact with Hernando Pizarro. The presents from Olmos, he claimed, were worth only 220 ducats. But Beltrán was not believed and he was condemned to loss of office and of salary. He also lost all his special grants, and he was sentenced by the magistrates in the court to pay a fine of 17,000 ducats which almost ruined him (it was twice what he was said to have received in bribes). Suárez de Carvajal, bishop of Lugo, was also found guilty but the papers of his part of the enquiry have been lost, so it is not clear of what he was accused. He was deprived of his bishopric and fined 7,000 ducats.[19] The Emperor Charles strongly opposed tolerance in both these circumstances.

So in the winter of 1542-3, Beltrán withdrew to the monastery of Our Lady of Grace in Medina del Campo. There this first civil servant of the Indies made an appeal but no one wanted to listen to him. Juan de Samano, with whom he had collaborated for twenty years, said he could do nothing. The council in its new shape wrote to the emperor asking for a pardon but Charles instructed the magistrates to maintain their sentence.

Afterwards, the council for the first time received a set of rules to govern their functioning. These were prepared by Cardinal García de Loaisa, Dr Figueroa and Dr Hernando de Guevara (speaking on behalf of the Council of Castile) with the help of Fray Domingo de Soto, Granvelle and Cobos and were publicly announced in a contract signed by Charles, Samano, García de Loaisa, Dr Guevara, Dr Figueroa and Ochoa de Luyando on 20 November 1542).[20]

Another important innovation came in 1543: at the express petition of merchants in Seville, from then on ships bound for the Indies were to sail together in convoys for safety. No vessel of less than ten tons was to be cleared for departure to the Indies. The minimum fleet was ten vessels and two such fleets would leave a year, one in March, one in September. This, to begin with, applied only in time of war but, given that French pirates were active at all times, the ruling was maintained in peace. In January 1546 all merchant vessels, not just those for the Indies, were instructed to arm themselves and sail in convoys.[21] Over the years these arrangements would be further developed.

Alas for the papal hopes of peace with France. On 10 July 1542 that country declared war. The declaration was inspired by the designation by the emperor of his son Philip as Duke of Milan. That caused a crisis in the Netherlands. Queen Mary of Hungary, as Regent, led the defence herself with the Prince of Orange. Antwerp beat off a rebellion of Gelderland, but there was much destruction. Then the French mysteriously withdrew. The Netherlands suffered from the lack of a general: such men as Roeulx and Arschot seemed inappropriate, Orange was considered too young, De Boussu, whom Charles liked, was thought too greedy, while the Landgrave Philip of Hesse had never fought a serious adversary.

Charles left Monzón in October for Barcelona. He had written to Pope Paul hoping that he would cease dealing with France and the empire as if they were equal powers. At Barcelona, Charles welcomed his son Philip for his first visit to the city. On 8 November 1542 Philip made a formal entry into the Catalan capital (having arrived secretly and in disguise the previous night) and, on the 9th, received the homage of the councillors, and of the multi-competent Francisco de Borja, the viceroy. The following day Charles departed for Genoa, leaving Philip, aged sixteen, as Regent, to be advised as before by Fernando de Valdés, archbishop of Seville, a hard and unbending churchman from Salas in Asturias who was the new Grand Inquisitor. The Council of the Indies would still be chaired by García de Loaisa but, in his frequent absences, the experienced ex-judge of the *audiencia* in Santo Domingo and Mexico, Ramírez de Fuenleal, would preside.

Charles's two letters from Palamós to Philip on how to conduct himself as Regent have a deserved place in history. It was now that Charles told his son not to give himself over too much to the pleasures of marriage (Philip had married his cousin Maria of Portugal in November 1543). In respect of the empire, Charles enjoined Philip to 'remember how many lands you will be called on to govern, how far apart they are, how many different languages they speak ... and you will see how needful it is to learn languages'. Latin, Charles insisted, was indispensable, though he himself had never mastered it.

In August 1543 Cobos wrote to the emperor: the difficulty of finding money was so great that there had never been anything like it. He assured Charles 'that there is no way that it [more money] can be found, for there is none ... To find 18,000 ducats every 30 days for the defence of Perpignan, Fuenterrabía, San Sebastián and Navarre, as well as Malaga and Cartagena has been, and is, extremely difficult ... I am very truly perplexed.' In the end, he raised 420,000 ducats, much of it from a shipment of gold and silver from the Indies, and there were some loans from private persons. Tavera lent 16,000 ducats, Cobos himself advanced 8,000, but other rich men refused. The Duke of Alba said that he would serve the emperor 'pike in hand', but not in any other way.[22]

But such difficulties did not act as a brake on Charles who, in July 1544, led his armies under Orange, Este, Gonzaga and Granvelle into French Burgundy. He besieged Saint-Dizier on the way to Vitry-le-François. King Henry VIII of England was ready at Boulogne. Charles proceeded with the slogan 'on to Paris'. He did not besiege any city but drove on. There was panic in the capital. The cardinal of Lorraine, the Guise of the Church, indicated that France was interested in negotiation. On 31 August a conference at St Amand, to the north of the Marne, articulated a serious effort to make peace. This led in September to the Peace of Crépy. The public terms included: first, France would send 10,000 men, of whom 600 would be cavalry, against the Turks. Secondly, both sides would restore all conquests made since the Truce of Nice of 1538. Thirdly, Stenay on the Meuse in the Ardennes was to be given back. The king of France's son, Charles, Duke of Orleans, was to marry the Infanta and inherit the Netherlands on Charles's death; or he could marry the Archduchess Ana and have Milan. More importantly, France would abandon its policy of encroaching on Spain's empire in the New World and would not attack any more treasure fleets.

There were also some secret clauses: Francis would help Charles to reform the abuses of the Church; France would support the planned general meeting of the Church at Trent; France would do what it could to encourage the return of the German princes to the Catholic fold; Francis would give Charles the diplomatic help that he had promised against the Turks; France would support the return of Geneva to the Duke of Savoy; Francis would not make any peace with England from which Charles was excluded and, if Charles were to go to war with Henry VIII and England, France would support him.[23]

On 14 September 1544 treaties along these lines were signed in the abbey of Saint Jean-des-Vignes in the vineyards of Soissons. The peace was to be confirmed by a visit in October of the queen of France, Charles's sister Leonor, to Brussels, her birthplace, accompanied by her stepson (the Duke of Orléans) whom the emperor already treated almost as a son, and by Madame d'Estampes, the king's mistress. Charles had with him his sister Queen Mary of Hungary; his Austrian nephews, the archdukes Maximilian and Ferdinand; and Ottavio Farnese, his son-in-law, the pope's son who had married his illegitimate daughter, Margaret of Flanders. There were balls and tournaments: 'at the reception, it seemed as if they [the emperor and his sister,] would never have done with kissing and embracing each other'.[24]

These celebrations were followed by discussions in Spain as to whether Charles should maintain himself in Milan or in the Low Countries. The Italian party was headed by the Duke of Alba, who was the new governor of Milan, supported by the Count of Osorno, who saw in Milan the essential point of entry to Germany, as well as the key to the defence of Naples, while Flanders was difficult to govern, easily open to French attack and had never done anything for Spain. The opposing view was held by Tavera.[25] Nothing was decided. Spain continued with pretensions to both places.

Another consequence of Charles's continued preoccupation with war was that, when at last that so desired general council of the Church opened at Trent, in the far north of Italy, in the winter of 1545, his representative, Francisco de Toledo, a disciple of Fray Domenico de Soto and a lecturer at Salamanca, had a free hand to decide what he thought best.

Cobos wrote sycophantically of Philip to the Emperor Charles:

> King Philip ... is already so great a monarch that his knowledge and capacity have outstripped his years [then sixteen], for he seems to have achieved the impossible by his great understanding and his lofty comprehension. His diversions are a complete and constant devotion to work and the affairs of his kingdom. He is always thinking about matters of good government and justice, without leaving room for favouritism nor for idleness, nor for flattery nor for any vice ... where it is necessary to hold meetings, he listens to the opinions of each one with the greatest gravity and attention ... he is frequently closeted with me for hours at a time ... afterwards, he does the same thing with the president of the council [the *inquisidor*] Valdés to talk about justice and the Duke of Alba to talk about war ... I am astonished at his prudent, well considered recommendations.[26]

Charles wrote in 1546 to his son Philip that he was determined to take the field against the German princes. He proposed to borrow the money needed for these campaigns from bankers in Nuremberg, Augsburg, Genoa and Antwerp. The security? Why, the shipments of gold and silver from the Indies of 600,000 scudi. He hoped that Cobos would undertake the negotiations. He was optimistic: in 1545 the emperor's fifth (his share of the treasure of the Indies) had been 360,000 ducats.[27]

Cobos anyway acted quickly: on 22 May he and the Castilian Council of Finance – Juan Suárez de Carvajal, Fernando de Guevara, Cristóbal Suárez, Francisco de Almaguer – signed a contract for a loan with the agent in Spain of the Fuggers, still the richest bankers in Germany.[28] Of these the first named was the ruined bishop of Lugo; Guevara was a Basque from Treceño, who had been for years in Bologna as rector of the Spanish School there, then on Charles's Council of the Realm from 1515 and his interpreter (Guevara knew Italian and Latin, possibly French and German). He was president of the Mesta, the collective established to preserve sheep's health and rights, a member of the Inquisition in Aragon, and had been a member of the Empress Isabel's council. Cristóbal Suárez had been named to the Council of Finance in 1525 and he became chief accountant in 1531. Almaguer had been a protégé of Juan López de Recalde. Cobos admired his qualities and made him his deputy. Cobos also raised money by diverting some funds already allocated, but he wrote to the emperor that the financial situation was still difficult: 'we are at the end of our tether unless God our Lord in His mercy and Your Majesty can find a remedy'. Cobos suggested 'a counsel of despair': to seize all the cash in Spain and ship it to the emperor by galleys to provide ready money in Genoa where it was so needed. The mad plan was approved by Philip and the council. Philip then wrote to his father: 'these kingdoms are so bare of gold – you cannot find a scudo – that there will be no lack of complaints and outcries . . .' But somehow they did gather 180,000 scudi by 10 October.[29]

Long before that, in June, Charles had written to his sister Mary:

> All my efforts . . . have come to nothing. The heretic princes and electors have decided not to attend the Diet in person; indeed they are determined to rise in revolt immediately the Diet is over, to the utter destruction of the spiritual lords and to the great peril of the king of the Romans and ourself. If we hesitate now, we shall lose all. Thus we have decided, I, my brother and the duke of Bavaria, that force alone will drive them to accept reasonable terms. The time is opportune, for they have been weakened by recent wars. Their subjects, the nobility in particular, are discontented . . . Over and above this, we have good hope of papal help of an offer of 800,000 ducats or more. Unless we take immediate action, all the estates of Germany may lose their faith and the Netherlands could follow.
>
> After fully considering all these points, I decided to begin by raising war in Hesse and Saxony as disturbers of the peace and to open the campaign in the lands of the duke of Brunswick. This pretext will not long conceal the purpose of this war of religion but it will serve to divide the protestants from the beginning. Be assured I shall do nothing without careful thought . . .[30]

The letter was an implicit order to the Netherlands to mobilize.

35

Federman, Jiménez de Quesada
and the quest for Eldorado

*Between the province of Santa Martha and that of Cartagena there
is a river which divides these territories; it is called the Magdalena
and it is known because it is a great river but also because it runs
with great fury and impetus into the sea, carrying sweet water out
for a league's distance.*

Jiménez de Quesada's account, 1536

In 1529 there were several German subjects of the emperor in Venezuela
connected more or less directly with the banking house of Welser:
Ambrosio Alfinger and Sebastián Rentz (both from Ulm), Nicolás Federman, Georg Ehinger from Konstanz and Juan Seissenhofer, often known
as Juan Alemán, who came from Augsburg. Alfinger was formally the
governor of Venezuela. While he went on an expedition in the Andes, he
allowed himself to be briefly substituted by Seissenhofer and then, when
he returned, he handed authority over to Federman while Alfinger went,
at the end of July 1530, to rest in Santo Domingo.[1]

Federman, who was, of course, a citizen of Ulm, had courage, energy
and originality. He spent the early days of his new post looking for pearls
off the peninsula of Paraguana. Then, on 13 September 1532, he set off
with a hundred Spaniards on foot, sixteen on horses and about a hundred
porters from the nearby tribes on his own expedition into the interior,
leaving Bartolomé de Santillana as his deputy. His objective was to seek
the 'Mar del Sur', the Pacific, by which route it would surely be a short
distance to the Spice Islands. It later seemed that Federman's activity
clashed directly with the instructions of Alfinger to stay where he was.

Federman's aim was to go due south from Coro. He journeyed
through the territories of three unknown peoples, the Xideharas, the

Ayamanes – who were so small in build that they seemed to be dwarfs – and the Xaguas, and encountered several towns. The illness of many of his men forced them to travel in those humid valleys in hammocks, 'more like hospital patients than men of war',[2] but Federman strove to ensure that his sick colleagues were treated as if they were great lords. He wanted the Indians to think that the Spaniards were immortals, immune to all diseases.

As usual with Spanish adventurers of this kind, Federman met many difficulties. For instance, his accountant Antonio Naveros made an unwise comment criticizing him,[3] was sent back in chains to Coro and was killed by a poisoned arrow in his throat. That was a serious setback to the Welser cause in Venezuela: Oviedo had looked on Naveros as an excellent person and Licenciado Tolosa said he was of a calm disposition.[4]

On his way south Federman reached the large *pueblo* of Acariagua on the river Tocayo, where he had a serious battle in which almost all the Spaniards were wounded. So he returned to Coro. Alfinger, who by then had returned from Santo Domingo, was furious with Federman for undertaking a grand journey without his permission and decided to send him back to Europe. Federman accordingly returned to Seville, in the company of his friend Sebastián Rentz. He even made his way back to Augsburg, where he wrote his *Historia Indiana* to inform the Welsers of what was happening. At first he was ordered to stay away from the Indies for four years, but he then negotiated a new contract for seven years, for which he would receive a small salary.

Meanwhile Alfinger made another fruitless journey west to look for the elusive strait of whose existence he remained convinced. He went to the Lake of Maracaibo and on to the mountains of Perija and reached the banks of the river Magdalena. But there was no strait. Alfinger was killed by Indians in May 1533. When news of his death reached Spain, Federman was named Alfinger's successor in July 1534 with the titles of governor and captain-general of Venezuela.

Federman's rise to the governorship was confused by the fact that for a time another German, Georg Hohermuth von Speyer (known among Spaniards as 'Espira'), from the ancient ecclesiastical city of Speyer, was a rival in Venezuela. But Federman was restored to his posts before he left Spain.

Federman's second departure for Venezuela from Sanlúcar was marked by an astonishingly lavish ceremony. There were shawms, bagpipes and drums; processions of priests with candles; bandsmen with trumpets and trombones; Dominican friars, barefoot Franciscans; eleven columns of horsemen, arquebusiers, fighting dogs, shield-bearing captains and soldiers with axes wearing deerskins to ward off poisoned arrows. There followed flags, units of infantrymen, shoemakers, tailors, builders and the whole troop of Federman's army, which included Flemings, Englishmen, Albanians, even Scots, as well as Germans and Castilians. They went in procession to the convent of the barefoot friars to swear loyalty to the emperor, as well as the governor.[5] Provisions on the journey would be generous (a pound of meat three times a week; on other days fish).

The expedition reached Santo Domingo and then made for Coro. For a year or two, Federman negotiated his way more or less successfully through a jungle of conflicting interests in northern Venezuela. The municipality of Coro clashed with Federman, whose activities it sought to limit. Federman, like other German governors in Venezuela, looked on his post primarily as one which could give a justification for journeys of discovery: Espira, who was looking for the apparently rich territory of Xeriva, set off for the interior and was not seen again for three years; Antonio de Chaves, another Spanish adventurer, made his way along the coast to the mouth of the Magdalena; and Federman himself tried to found a port on the river Hacha, on the way to Santa Marta beyond Maracaibo.

Life in Coro declined sharply and the population of this new Spanish 'city' fell to a mere 140, of whom two thirds were ill. Bishop Bastidas, son of Rodrigo, who came from Santo Domingo as acting governor in the absence of the Germans, painted a gloomy picture:

> it was part of my infirmity to have to see the place's great poverty. And we went to our church and there found poverty and ruin. Everything both smelled and appeared of sovereign impoverishment. . . . The *pueblo* has got fifty cottages, or a few more, and there are not four *bohíos* [small native huts] which could be described as reasonable. The church is covered with the poorest kind of straw . . . and at present people do not have shirts with which to dress themselves.[6]

Later there were denunciations of cruelty. For example, Federman was accused of transporting his Indians in a long chain with their necks in irons and of cutting off their heads when they were ill or tired.[7] This evidence emerged during a *residencia* which had to be interrupted by the judge, Dr Navarro, because he ran out of paper.[8]

Federman then resolved on an extensive new journey of discovery. This would go due south from Coro along roads where he had been before, but then seek a crossing of the Andes a long way to the south of his last expedition's concluding point. Again the aim was partly, or perhaps wholly, the search for 'the strait'.

Federman set off with about 200 men and 500 bearers. The first stage of the journey was from the eastern foothills of the Andes to the valley of the river Tocuyo. Here he encountered troops of Juan Fernández de Alderete who had rebelled against Governor Dortal in the Paria territory and were seeking what they had heard, from the survivors of the late Diego de Ordaz's expedition, were the rich lands of the valley of the Meta. Federman took over these troops but seized the goods of the leaders, whom he sent back to Coro. He had a similar encounter with an expedition of Diego Martínez, who had explored the rather more remote peninsula of Guajira. His goods, too, were seized.

Federman crossed the river Pauto, a tributary of the Meta, and then sent a lieutenant, Pedro de Limpias, to seek a pass over the Andes to the west. He could not find one. Federman divided his little army into three but they were united again at Aracheta, the future San Juan de los Llanos. The rumour was that, between the rivers Meta and Guaviare, an entrance could be made to a magical territory known as 'El Dorado', where all Spanish dreams would be fulfilled.

In February 1539 Federman was on the upper river Guaviare, where he found many objects of gold and realized that these came from 'the other side of the sierra', that is, from the Indians who inhabited the Chibcha high plateau. This realization gave Federman an even stronger motive to seek to scale the cordillera of the Andes. He performed this feat in forty days, of which twenty-two were through barren country, including a wide plain of intense cold where seventy of his Indians died as well as forty of his 130 horses. When he reached the summit, he had only 160 soldiers and seventy horses. Here, he assumed, was the land of his expectations. It was not, however, 'the strait' to the Southern Sea. But it was a magic land of gold. Alas, the land could not be his – without argument at least. For Federman immediately discovered that the territory had been occupied for two years by another Spanish expedition, from Santa Marta, under the leadership of Gonzalo Jiménez de Quesada.

*

Gonzalo Jiménez de Quesada was a native of Córdoba, a city which gave fewer conquistadors to the Indies than any other large city of Andalusia. Jiménez de Quesada's father was a lawyer and his mother came from a famous family of dyers. A maternal uncle, Jerónimo de Soria, had been president of the dyers' guild in Córdoba, but had difficulties when he started using a cheap dye which, it was said, damaged the good cloth of the city. So Gonzalo, with his brothers Hernando and Francisco, decided to go to the Indies to recover their fortunes. Perhaps they were *conversos*. The 'evidence' for that, such as it is, derives from a quarrel which Gonzalo once had with a certain Lázaro Fonte, who accused him of being Jewish. When he sought to become governor in the Indies, the Council of the Indies even said that one reason against him was that he was descended from people who had been 'reconciled'.[9]

Gonzalo, like his father, was by education a lawyer. Probably he had attended the university of Salamanca and certainly for a time he worked in the supreme court of Granada. He then went to Santa Marta, no one seems to know exactly when; probably about 1534.

Jiménez de Quesada found Santa Marta in bad shape. There was a shortage of horses, arms, supplies of food and houses. The inhabitants, it is true, received supplies on a modest scale from the *cacique* of Bonda. The governor, Pedro Fernández de Lugo, however, seemed incompetent, greedy and miserly, even though he came from a family of conquistadors who were probably also *conversos*.[10] He gave Jiménez de Quesada a characteristic contract (*capitulación*) on 22 January 1535. This was in the first instance in the east from the meridian line which crosses the Cabo de la Vela; in the west, the line which runs from the mouth of the Magdalena; and, in the south, the unknown coast of the Southern Sea. Jiménez de Quesada was named as commander and captain-general and provision was made as to who should succeed him if he were to die. His brother Hernando was named chief magistrate.

His expedition left Santa Marta on 5 April 1536 with 600 men, including seventy mounted. Another 200 men were to be asked to sail up the Magdalena in support, under the captaincy of Diego de Urbina, on three brigantines and a pinnace (*fusta*). But this small fleet was dispersed on the open sea before it even reached the Magdalena: the pinnace was sunk and its crew drowned; the brigantines took refuge in Cartagena. A hundred miles up the Magdalena, Jiménez de Quesada waited fruitlessly for these ships, on which he had placed his supplies.

In the end, his men had to continue without food, eating any herbs and berries which they could find. As usual, the mangrove swamps extended down to the river's edge, and the continual difficulty posed by tributaries of the Magdalena, as well as the mosquitoes, combined with the lack of food, made the journey very difficult. About 200 miles up the river, they were met by two new brigantines sent under Diego Hernández Gallego by Fernández de Lugo when he heard of the setbacks met by Urbina's three vessels.

Reaching La Tora at the point of confluence of the rivers Magdalena, Opon and Carrare, the expedition followed the Opon. Jiménez de Quesada sent a mounted expedition ahead to find out the nature of the territory and where the Opon rose. This unit, captained by Juan de Céspedes, a Sevillano,[11] and Juan de San Martín as inspector, came back to report that the land was well populated. The whole force – only 230 foot and 70 horsemen, for 300 had died or otherwise fallen by the way – camped in La Tora and then ascended the Opon, leaving the ships below under Diego Hernández Gallego with thirty-five healthy men and twenty-five sick ones. About fifty miles up, they were welcomed by the first Chibchas, dressed in cotton cloaks, who offered them food. They entered the valley of the Opon and came upon abundant food and even some gold. In the far distance they could see the Chibcha plateau.

News was brought to them from the valley which they had left behind that Hernández Gallego had been attacked by Indians and had lost a brigantine and half his men, and so had decided to return to Santa Marta. A new (interim) governor, Jerónimo Lebrón, sent a flotilla of four brigantines with food to restore Jiménez de Quesada, but they never found him since he was by then enriching himself on the Chibcha plateau.

For on reaching La Grita in March 1537, Jiménez de Quesada found in one day over 1,000 pesos of fine gold and 73 of a lower grade. Two or three days later his party reached Guachetá, where they found their first emeralds. Moving southwards, every day meeting new peoples, such as the Lemguarque, the Conumba and the Suesca, they found more gold and emeralds, and then on 22 March they even discovered salt, another important item of commerce. On 28 March they skirmished with natives sent by a chief known as Bogotá, but they went ahead first to besiege and then to enter the capital which had the chief's name. He fled to mountains nearby, taking with him his main treasure, but was later killed there. By that time the Spaniards had seized about 4,600 pesos of good gold as well as over 500 emeralds. Jiménez de Quesada then despatched Pedro Fernández de Valenzuela to the emerald reserves of Somondoco.

Jiménez de Quesada meantime began to explore the cordillera of Tunja, where a rich chief was said to be. On 20 August the Spaniards found there another 140,000 pesos of fine gold, 14,000 pesos of low-grade gold and 280 emeralds. In October they seized even more: nearly 200,000 pesos of fine gold, 30,000 of low grade and over 800 emeralds. The rumour then reached them that to their south-east there was a rich region called Neiva, abundant in gold mines. The Indians of Pasca were said to descend there to trade their many products for gold. The Spaniards, therefore, abandoned Tunja, though part of their army under Jiménez de Quesada's brother Hernando remained. The rest went on under their established commander to Pasca and the plateau of Sumapez, to camp in Neiva, where they were offered gold but not in the quantity that they anticipated.

Now came a division of the booty, decided by the commander, Jiménez de Quesada, and the inspector, Juan de San Martín. This was a great moment for all concerned, since the wealth almost equalled the great riches brought from Peru. The royal fifth was decided as being 38,259 pesos of fine gold, 7,257 of low-grade gold, nearly 4,000 of scrap (*oro de Chatalonia*) and 360 emeralds of varying sizes. All debts were paid out of the scrap gold. The army was divided into captains, horsemen and soldiers. Those who had come up the Magdalena under Diego Hernández Gallego were excluded, since they had not participated in the extraordinary struggles along the great river. There were payments to the surgeon and for the cost of arquebuses. Jiménez de Quesada insisted on contributions being made to the two dilapidated churches of Santa Marta – La Mayor and La Merced.[12]

Each 'share' of the treasure, it was determined, would be worth 510 pesos of fine gold, 576 of low-grade gold and five emeralds.

The leaders decided that the absent governor in Santa Marta would receive ten shares, Jiménez de Quesada nine, his captains four, the sergeant-major three, the lieutenants two, each captain's lieutenant half a share, lieutenants of horse three, horsemen and clerics two, arquebusiers 1½ and one each for the workmen and the infantrymen. Those who had died on the journey were allocated nothing, nor would their heirs receive anything; but 200 pesos were left to pay for the masses for the 500 who had died since the expedition had begun.

Jiménez de Quesada wanted to settle this high territory and establish himself and his soldiers there. He decided to go home to Spain to have himself proclaimed *adelantado* of the area, taking with him his own money and the royal fifth. He would leave his brother Hernando in command. First, however, he allowed himself to be diverted by a *cacique*, Sagipa, who came to ask for Spanish assistance against his old enemies, the Panches. Jiménez de Quesada set off with a group of horsemen and some infantry, promising his help in return for being told the whereabouts of the dead *cacique* of Bogotá's treasure. Sagipa agreed and presented Jiménez de Quesada with many gifts such as plumes, snail shells (*caracoles*) and bells of bone (*cascabeles*). But no gold came. Jiménez de Quesada, disillusioned, chained up Sagipa, though giving him free access to his people. Nothing transpired. The conquistadors in a democratic impulse elected Gonzalo de Luza as their *procurador*. Through an interpreter he told the *cacique* Sagipa that he would be tortured if the treasure did not appear. Gonzalo de Luza said that he needed 10 million pesos in gold, and 10,000 emeralds. Jiménez de Quesada named his brother Hernando as the defender of the chief. Having heard the arguments, he nevertheless sentenced Sagipa to torture. The *cacique* was raised by a beam to which his hands were tied – 'lightly' apparently and 'only twice'. But Sagipa returned in a bad condition to his prison. There was then a fire in the improvised Christian section of Bogotá which was attributed to Sagipa who, in order to save himself from further torture, agreed to lead Jiménez de Quesada to the place where he believed that the *cacique* of Bogotá had buried his gold. But there seemed to be nothing there.

Jiménez de Quesada lost his temper and submitted Sagipa to further tortures, such as burning his feet, a favourite torment of the conquistadors, as we saw happen to Cuauhtémoc in New Spain. The consequence was that a few days after returning to the camp Sagipa died. Later there were enquiries as to whether Jiménez de Quesada had tortured him to death.[13] There was real doubt: a witness of Jiménez de Quesada's, 'Don Gonzalo indio', said that he had dined with Sagipa the night before he died and that all that he complained of was that his head ached.[14] Jiménez de Quesada gave a document to two of his colleagues, Pedro Fernández de Valenzuela and Diego de Segura, which enabled them to mount a defence on the *cacique* Sagipa's behalf at the Council of the Indies. It was a matter which would be debated for many years.

In the meantime, Jiménez de Quesada still hoped to return to Spain to confirm his status as an independent governor and *adelantado*, but he had to postpone his journey again, for two reasons. First, because of the battles which he had to fight against a ferocious and apparently indomitable tribe, the Panches; and secondly, because in mid-1538 he received astonishing news: not only that Federman had reached the eastern cordillera no distance away but also that the even more threatening Sebastián de Benalcázar was in Neiva, about 150 miles south of Bogotá. He had driven up from Peru, his reputation as a fighter second to none.[15] Jiménez de Quesada, isolated and even incommunicado for three years, now found himself confronted by two Spanish armies which were well furnished with arms and horses, while he had little fighting capacity except for his swords.

Benalcázar had left Quito early in 1538 and made his way north with about 500 men well equipped for war. He reached what is now Popayán, then climbed up through modern Colombia along the river Magdalena to Neiva. He still had about 300 men with him, to which his own great name as one of the conquerors of Peru added much. On the way he had founded four towns, including a settlement at Popayán, where he had left altogether 300 men. From Neiva, hearing of Federman's journey, he sent messengers to Jiménez de Quesada hoping to concert action with him against the unexpected German from Venezuela.

For Federman it was a hard blow at the end of an atrocious journey of two years to find that the territory which he, on the Welsers' behalf, had coveted as part of Venezuela was being occupied by others. But he was realistic. He made a remarkable concession. He subscribed to an agreement by which he would leave his men under Jiménez de Quesada's control, or that of his brother Hernando, but he and the former would go to Spain on the same ship, to seek judgement from the Council of the Indies as to who would rule the country. The Welsers later thought that for Federman to have left his men in 'New Granada' exceeded his authority. But Bogotá was an advantageous place and some of Federman's men had anyway come from Santa Marta or, as we have seen, from Paria and he thought that they would not have accepted an order to return to Coro by the way that they had come. The decision was a good one for Federman even though, in a pitched battle against Jiménez de Quesada in the style of the Spaniards in Peru, he would probably have won, since Jiménez de Quesada's army was in poor shape. Federman's men would now help to establish a sound nucleus of Spaniards in Bogotá with magistrates, councillors, notaries and other officials.[16]

Jiménez de Quesada soon also reached an agreement with Benalcázar, the text of which was lost. But a revision drawn up by Fr Domingo de las Casas was agreed. Benalcázar went on to Bogotá – 'Santa Fe de Bogotá', it had become – met Federman on 20 June, and set off with both his rivals in a brigantine down the Magdalena. They went first to Cartagena where they met a judge, Juan de Santa Cruz, appointed to carry out a *residencia* of Pedro de Heredia, governor of that port, and they gave him much information about the Indians whom they had encountered and whom Jiménez de Quesada believed he had conquered. They also explained how they had granted *encomiendas* to fellow conquistadors in Bogotá, and how one or two chiefs had been similarly favoured, as if they had been Spaniards. For example, the chief Quencubansa had been allotted a town in the Panche province of Tamanjuaca.

In Cartagena, the three conquistadors of Bogotá awaited a ship to take them to Castile. While they waited, Jiménez de Quesada found himself in a lawsuit with his ex-subordinate, Diego Hernández Gallego, in respect of the first flotilla of brigantines which had sailed up the Magdalena without finding his army. But eventually the three returned to Spain, Jiménez de Quesada and Benalcázar going together direct, Federman travelling via Jamaica. The first-named took with him 11,000 pesos of gold in twenty-one bars, as well as nine boxes of emeralds and one necklace (*cordel*) of emeralds.

The circumstances of the return of these conquistadors were highly discouraging for them. Bartolomé de las Casas was at that time winning his debates against the *encomenderos*.[17] Jiménez de Quesada also found that he had suits mounted against him by Alonso Fernández de Lugo, the heir of Pedro Fernández de Lugo, a brutal but influential proconsul himself, being the brother-in-law of Cobos no less.[18] The treasurer of Santa Marta, Pedro Briceño, and the new governor there, Jerónimo Lebrón, sued Jiménez de Quesada and he was ordered to pay them 5,300 pesos of gold and some emeralds. Till he had paid it he was to remain in the Casa de la Contratación's prison in Seville. In addition, he was to pay 1,000 pesos as taxes to the king. Jiménez de Quesada appealed through his skilful lawyer, Sebastián Rodríguez, to the Council of the

Indies but, when he appeared before that august body, he was further accused of illegally bringing into Spain 150,000 pesos of gold and of having had his own secret supply of emeralds. He found to his astonishment that he had numerous creditors, such as Marcos Griego, who owned a boat which had been used by Pedro Fernández de Lugo, and Martín de Orduña, the factor of the Welsers in Santa Marta.[19]

Eventually Jerónimo de Soria, Jiménez de Quesada's uncle, and Pedro Bueno, both of Córdoba, offered bail and Jiménez de Quesada was released, still in possession of his gold and emeralds. The Council of the Indies at first decided in favour of the conqueror of Bogotá as the next governor there. However, Dr Bernal and Gutierre Velázquez (who was related to the Lugos), both members of the council, opposed the nomination and they were in the end supported by the emperor. It was now that the question of Jiménez de Quesada's supposed Jewish blood was brought up.

How disillusioned that conquistador must have been, thinking that he was going to return home as a great conqueror of new territory, only to find himself tied down by petty denunciations. All the same, his new province took shape in his absence. Santa Fe de Bogotá was named a city (in which there would be eight councillors, two magistrates and a constable), and the Dominicans agreed to send friars (Fray Tomás de Vicente was the first provincial).

Jiménez de Quesada went to France, apparently (or so his enemies said) to sell his emeralds there, and did not return to Spain till the end of 1545. He busied himself with his defence of Charles V, 'Antijovio', a pamphlet denouncing the Italian historian Paolo Giovio, who was collecting material for his own history.

New accusations were made against Jiménez de Quesada. He was not praised for conquering a rich territory. Instead, he was denounced with his brother Hernando for bringing about the deaths of the *caciques* Bogotá and Sagipa, as well as for other cruelties against the Indians. In Bogotá itself, Alonso Fernández de Lugo appeared as the new governor and declared both the *encomiendas* and the division of treasure made by Jiménez de Quesada to be illegal. He sent Hernando Jiménez de Quesada home to Spain, and a third brother, Francisco (who had joined them from Peru), was despatched under guard. New legal disputes followed. But events in Santa Marta and Cartagena were nothing to what was brewing in Castile.

Jiménez de Quesada was subjected to numerous accusations about his emeralds. Many witnesses appeared before him, including his interpreter in the Chibcha plateau, an Indian now known as 'Don Gonzalo de Huesca', who had by now mastered Spanish perfectly. In his own defence, Jiménez de Quesada presented an interesting questionnaire in which there were sixty-three questions. In question 22 we hear that the *cacique* Bogotá had made 'a very cruel war' against Jiménez de Quesada and question 41 was a chance for a friend of the conqueror, Antonio Díaz Cardona of Seville, to say that Jiménez de Quesada had 'treated the Indians of the new realm of New Granada very well indeed and that witness never saw or knew of or heard talk of such cruelties administered to the Indians except in war'.[20]

On 5 February 1547 his trials ended and Jiménez de Quesada was found innocent of all the serious charges. Of the minor charges, he was found guilty of asking his soldiers for money when he was contemplating a return to Spain, a 'crime' for which he was condemned to pay 100 ducats and have his offices suspended for one year. For the torture and subsequent death of Sagipa, he was fined another 100 ducats and called on to accept the suspension of all his offices for another seven years, as well as exile for a year. The accusation that he had thrown two Indians to be devoured by dogs was left undiscussed for the time being. The heirs of Sagipa would be able to sue Jiménez de Quesada for all the trouble that that death had caused them.

Juan de Oribe, another skilful lawyer, appealed against these judgements and persuaded the Council of the Indies to reduce the fines from 100 to 50 ducats. There only remained outstanding the accusation that Jiménez de Quesada had somehow secreted 12,000 ducats. That accusation dominated the rest of his life – and also that of his heirs.

In July 1547 an *audiencia* was established for the new realm of New Granada. Jiménez de Quesada, at last triumphant in his own country, was named marshal (*mariscal*) and received a coat of arms. He also became *adelantado* on the death of Fernández de Lugo. In April 1548 he was allowed to introduce fifty black slaves into his new country to work for him only and granted an income of 2,000 ducats a year, as well as receiving three large *encomiendas* with a promise from the Council of the Indies that they would be perpetual grants which would continue to his children. His prohibition on working in any official position was cut from seven years to two.

Having written his *Epítome de la Conquista del Nuevo Reino de Granada* for the Council of the Indies, Jiménez de Quesada returned to New Granada at the end of 1550. The *Epítome* is the best account of a conquest in the New World after the letters of Cortés and Valdivia.

Meantime Jiménez de Quesada's colleague (as he now had negotiated himself to be), Nicolás Federman returned to Spain via Jamaica, whence he wrote a letter to Francisco de Ávila about his extraordinary travels. He also sent 1,344 pesos to Pedro de Limpias, who had decided to remain in Venezuela. By February 1540 Federman was back in Seville. He made his way by land to salute Balthasar Welser, his supposed leader, then in Ghent. It seems that he wanted to be named governor of Venezuela by the emperor himself rather than by the Welsers, but the return of Las Casas to imperial favour removed that possibility. Instead Federman had to negotiate a new agreement with the Welsers, for his first one had been for ten years from 1533 and his time would soon run out. The Welsers demanded accounts. At that time in Flanders it was assumed that all new conquistadors came back vastly rich from the Indies. But they would never concede the size of their colossal wealth. Federman refused to present any accounts.

The ensuing drama marked an astonishing transformation in Federman's life. First, he was seized in his house in Ghent. Then he was imprisoned in Antwerp and his goods confiscated. His case passed from one court to another. Eventually it went to the Council of Flanders, where proceedings were conducted in either Latin or Flemish, with Spanish and German ignored. Everything was done to favour the Welsers. Federman sought to get his case transferred to the Council of the Indies and in that the Crown of Castile supported him. Federman was eventually freed from prison in Antwerp on a bail of 8,000 ducats. The Flemish authorities refused to obey the order of release and demanded that Federman hand over to them an emerald worth 100,000 ducats as well as 15,000 ducats in gold which they claimed he had received from Jiménez de Quesada. Federman denied it but the consequences were his continued imprisonment and the retention of his goods by the Flemish authorities. Everything which Federman was said to have brought from the Americas was apparently deposited in the bank of Cristóbal Raizer, the factor of the Fugger family in Seville.[21]

On 22 September 1540 the president of the Council of Flanders appeared in the prison of Antwerp and asked Federman if he could substantiate his statement that the Welsers had committed a fraud in the New World. If he did not prove the declaration, he would have to be physically beaten by one of the Welsers. Federman accepted the charge. Immediately the emperor, who had learned of Federman's astounding triumphs, ordered that the prisoner be sent to Spain. Federman arrived in February 1541 in Madrid. The Council of the Indies then insisted that they had exclusive competence in relation to the suit between the Welsers and Federman. The Welsers complained and demanded the return of the accused to Flanders. That was refused. Federman was allowed a new delay till the end of 1541.

In August 1541 he admitted in Madrid, at a court where the king's Regent, Philip, presided, that his complaint against the Welsers had been made only to secure his departure from prison in Flanders. He then had transferred to him the income from his *encomienda* in Bogotá which had been allocated to him by Jiménez de Quesada. By that time he was in Valladolid, under house arrest; and there death surprised him in February 1542.

Thus the conquest of the plateau on which Santa Fe de Bogotá was established brought almost as much tragedy to the conquerors as to the conquered. The long years of exile of Jiménez de Quesada were a sad commentary on his remarkable achievements. The lawsuits of Federman were if anything more destructive to him than the jungles of the eastern Andes. The only one of the three conquerors who met so unexpectedly in Bogotá in 1540 to survive and prosper thereafter was Benalcázar, who was named governor of Popayán. His fame as a conqueror of Peru ensured him that designation. Illiterate but brave, he was one of the great survivors of the age of the conquests.

36

The great walk of Cabeza de Vaca

The Myth of the Giant admonishes us not to do battle with the forces of Heaven.

Erasmus, *Handbook of the Christian Soldier*

Cabeza de Vaca was a great survivor, the only remaining conquistador from Narváez's expedition of 1528. He had become famous among the Indians of the delta of the Mississippi. He acted for many months as a trader of shells (which were used as knives), hides, ochre (used by Indians to paint their faces), flints for arrowheads, tassels of the hair of deer, glue from pine trees and dried reeds. He was also considered a doctor. He was always planning to move on west to Pánuco (about 700 miles south-west of the Mississippi estuary) and New Spain, but the companionable presence of Lope de Oviedo constrained him. Lope de Oviedo was a strong and vigorous conquistador and Cabeza wanted him to accompany him. Lope de Oviedo was always saying that he would indeed go west, but could not think of doing so till the following year.

Eventually they set off and crossed the Mississippi. Immediately they were on the western bank they met Indians who assured them that they were close to a band of Christians who had been living there for some years. These turned out to be Andrés Dorantes, Alonso del Castillo and the slave Estebanico, also survivors of Narváez's expedition. Dorantes was a native of Béjar in northern Extremadura, the town where Cortés had married; del Castillo came from Salamanca; Estebanico was probably a Berber. The five planned to set off for Pánuco but, just as they were ready to leave, Lope de Oviedo said that he had to collect some of his favourite Indian women to go with them. He left his friends – and no one saw him again. Presumably the women persuaded him to stay.

Cabeza de Vaca was held for several months as a slave to a family of one-eyed Indians (as he explained it). Many times, he recalled, with these people, 'they said that we were not to be sad because soon prickly pears would be brought to them and, in the end, they did come'. These people had many strange characteristics; for example, they would set the forest afire to force lizards and other such creatures to come out, which they would kill and eat. They trapped deer by surrounding them with fires and depriving them of grazing places. The animals would be forced to go where the Indians could then kill them in order to eat them. From the deerskin they made cloaks, shoes and shields. They made fires against mosquitoes though they were bitten by them all the same.

Cabeza, Estebanico, del Castillo and Dorantes agreed to escape from their Indian masters under cover of the new moon. They did so and entered the territory of the Marcame Indians, whose language they seemed to be able to speak. The night they arrived some Indians came to del Castillo and told him that they had dreadful pains in their heads, imploring him to cure them. Del Castillo made the sign of the cross and commended them to God, whereupon the Indians said that all their pains had left them. The same occurred on other occasions. This comforted the Spaniards as much as it did the Indians for it reinforced their beliefs. 'It inspired us to give many thanks to Our Lord that we might more fully know His Goodness,' recalled Cabeza, 'and have the firm hope that he would free us and bring us to where we might serve Him. For myself, I always had faith in His mercy that he would release me from that captivity.' Cabeza carried out a comparable 'medical' feat by removing an arrow of deer bone which was close to one Indian's heart. 'This cure,' Cabeza said, 'gave us fame everywhere in the land.'

Cabeza also told that the Indians spoke of an evil spirit named Mala Cosa who would come to houses with a firebrand and take what he wanted and sometimes, with a sharp knife, tear out the entrails of people whom he did not like. He would appear at dances – sometimes dressed as a man, sometimes as a woman – and he could lift up a house and let it crash when he wanted. He was often given food but he never ate anything, and it was said that he lived in a crack in the earth. The Spaniards told the Indians that if they could only believe in God, demons like Mala Cosa would never return and, indeed, as long as they were in the town, no one did see him.

Then Cabeza de Vaca and his three friends moved on. They were always hungry and naked except at night, when they had deerskins to keep them warm. They shed these skins twice a year as if they had been snakes.

The journey of the four Spaniards across what later became Texas was remarkable because a large body of Indians attached itself to them, each Indian carrying a club. Eventually, Cabeza wrote later, they began to find villages where there were permanent houses, whose inhabitants ate squash, beans and maize, as well as deer or hare. One day Alonso del Castillo saw a buckle from a sword belt hanging round the neck of an Indian with the nail of a horseshoe sewn on to it. Where did it come from, del Castillo asked. 'From heaven,' was the reply. They asked more questions and, after a while, learned that

> those who had brought it were men who wore beards like us and who had come from Heaven and reached the river [Mississippi] and that they had horses, lances and swords and they had wounded two of their people with lances. Where had they gone? They said that they had gone to the sea and thrust their lances under the water, and that they had followed them and later the Indians saw them floating in the water going towards the sun.

After that Cabeza de Vaca's expedition kept hearing of Christians. They saw many places deserted because 'the people there feared the Christians, even though it was fertile and beautiful'.[1]

> They brought us blankets which they had hidden for fear of the Christians and gave them to us and even told us how, on many occasions, the Christians entered the land and destroyed and burned the villages and carried off half the men and all the women and children and that those who had managed to escape were wandering and in flight. We saw that they were so frightened, not daring to stay in any place and that they neither wanted nor were able to sow crops nor cultivate the land but rather were determined to let themselves die, for they thought that was better than waiting to be treated with such cruelty as they had endured.[2]

After a few more weeks, Cabeza de Vaca and Estebanico, going ahead but accompanied by eleven Indians, encountered one of these mysterious Christians, Lázaro de Cárdenas, and three mounted Spaniards at Los Ojuelos, a day's journey from Tzinaba on the river Petatlan, somewhere in what is now Sinaloa. Cabeza had thus crossed all the modern Mexican peninsula. While Cárdenas took the walkers to meet his own captain, Diego de Alcaraz, Estebanico was sent back to fetch Andrés Dorantes and Alonso del Castillo, who arrived with an escort of 600 Indians. Cabeza de Vaca had many arguments with Alcaraz, who at first wished to enslave these Indians that Cabeza had brought; but in the end, they sent the Indians home and promised they would not be attacked.

The walkers carried on to Compostela further south. The news of their coming began to circulate. In July they reached Mexico, where they were sumptuously received both by Cortés and by the Viceroy Mendoza, though for months they were unable to wear clothes and preferred to sleep on the floor rather than in a bed. There were great celebrations: jousting with canes and bullfights. After spending the autumn and winter of 1536 in the capital, the four adventurers went down to Vera Cruz in the spring of 1537, where they boarded a ship to Spain on 10 April, stopping at Havana, Bermuda, the Azores and finally Lisbon before reaching Sanlúcar. They had some difficulties with French pirate ships but arrived in Castile at last, in time to greet and wish 'God speed' to Hernando de Soto, a veteran of Peru, who was resolved to return to the New World and to conquer as much of North America as he could.

37

Soto in North America

*The rarest thing of all in men who have made history is greatness
of soul.*

Jacob Burckhardt, *Reflections on History*

The most glittering of expeditions led from Spain in the late 1530s was
that of the Peruvian conquistador, the reckless, brave and enterprising
Hernando de Soto, who had been in the vanguard of Pizarro's triumphs
and who, on 20 April 1537, secured a contract in Seville to conquer and
settle the land between the river de las Palmas in Mexico and the south-
ernmost keys of Florida. He would be named the governor of Cuba. As
adelantado of Florida, he would be allowed to take 1,500 men with him
and would receive 500 ducats a year from the Spanish government. In
addition, Soto had his 180,000 cruzados from the treasure of Peru. He
would take a large household with him, among whom there were several Peruvian veterans, as well as his new wife, Isabel de Bobadilla, a
daughter of Pedrarias.

Cabeza de Vaca had recently come back to Castile to report that
Florida was the richest of countries, but had added that, though he
wished Soto well, neither he nor Andrés Dorantes could accompany
him because they 'did not wish to divulge certain things which they had
seen lest someone might beg the government in advance'.[1] No one knew
what that mysterious message meant. Some of those who decided to go
to the Indies with Soto (Baltasar Gallegos, Cristóbal de Espíndola) told
Cabeza de Vaca that they did so because of his strange words.

The court smiled on Soto. Many close to the monarch planned to
accompany the expedition: for example, the Osorio brothers. Francisco
and Antonio spent a great deal on outfitting: indeed, the 130,000

castellanos which Hernando lavished on his expedition was six times what Pedrarias had spent twenty years earlier. Soto himself paid for many of the men. He bought the galleon *La Magdalena* of 800 tons for 1,212 ducats from a famous shipbuilder of Triana, the galleon *San Juan* for 1,410 ducats. He took 800 quintals of biscuit and a quantity of salt beef. His ships were well stocked with olive oil, water and wine, as well as 'steel, iron for bridles, spades, mattocks, panniers, ropes, baskets, arquebuses, gunpowder, crossbows, swords, chainmail, bucklers, boots, sacramental vessels for use at mass, beads and other goods for gifts – and iron chain links and collars for slaves'.[2] Horses, seed and other provisions would be bought in Cuba.

Soto had, too, a pair of outstanding commanders: his infantry would be led by Francisco Maldonado, the cavalry by Pedro Calderón. Soto had a personal guard of sixty halberdiers led by Cristóbal de Espíndola, a future official of the Inquisition in New Spain. Soto probably expected to conquer all the lands to the north in America.

The expedition sailed from Sanlúcar in April 1538, leaving in great style. As usual in expeditions like this, they stopped for a few days in the Canaries, where they were greeted by the governor dressed in white. There the governor's daughter, Leonor de Bobadilla, joined them to travel as lady-in-waiting to her cousin, Isabel, the wife of Soto. (Leonor was soon seduced by Nuño de Tovar, one of Soto's senior captains, who later married her, and was rather curiously dismissed by Soto in consequence.)

Soto reached his Cuban governorship in June 1538, making landfall at Santiago. There the flagship, the *San Cristóbal*, hit the shoals of Smith's Key and it was feared that all was lost. Many left precipitately in small boats, some distinguished men in panic, thinking that 'it was no time for gallantry'. But only the wine was lost.

Soto landed in Santiago on the 7th amid much celebration. He and his friends were pleased by what they saw for there were many Spaniards in the town, living in well-built houses of which some were of stone and some roofed with tiles. Most had walls of board and dried grass roofs. The many country houses nearby often boasted fig trees, pines, guavas, bananas and sweet potato from which bread was made; some had orange groves. There were wild cattle. Already Santiago and Havana (in the west of the island) had seventy or eighty Spanish households each, another six towns had thirty to forty dwellings in each. All had not only a church, but a priest and, in Santiago, there was already a small Franciscan monastery. While Soto was in Cuba a tax was introduced for 'defence against rebels, wild Indians and the French'.[3] This demand was much resented.

In Santiago, then the capital city of Cuba, Soto presented his credentials as governor to the city council, and so there were the usual celebrations such as balls and masquerades, horse races and bullrunning. A new bishop, Diego Sarmiento, who had previously been rector of the Carthusian monastery of Las Cuevas in Seville, reached Santiago at much the same time as Soto. He too was fêted. After some weeks, the new governor rode to Bayamo, eighty or so miles to the west, on a new roan horse which was a present from the people of Santiago. Then he rode on to Puerto Príncipe, another 150 miles further west, where Vasco de Porcallo, who had been in Narváez's expedition to New Spain, joined him as captain-general. Soto went on by land to Havana, which would be his point of departure, and which had already been established for ten years on the north coast of the island, not the south where it had originally been founded.[4] Las Casas recalled that, at that time, the forest was so dense that one could ride from one end of the island to the other without leaving the shade. At Havana Soto's wife, Isabel, joined him, after a rough journey by sea from Santiago.

Soto was convinced that the expedition to Florida was going to make him the richest man in the world. He left nothing to chance. Thus he sent ahead Juan de Añasco, his accountant, who was a good geographer and from one of the great families of Trujillo in Extremadura, to explore the coast of Florida. Añasco sailed with fifty men in two pinnaces. Avoiding the swamps on the southern tip of Florida, they made for places on the Gulf of Mexico such as Charlotte harbour (then referred to as La Bahía de Juan Ponce de León) or Tampa Bay (Bahía Honda). In the second of these, Añasco kidnapped four Indians, who were later to serve as interpreters. They assured their eager and gullible captors that 'much gold existed in Florida'.[5]

Meantime, Soto was shown something of the reality of the Caribbean by a rising of Indians, near Baracoa in eastern Cuba, joined by some African slaves. Bartolomé Ortiz, the chief magistrate of Santiago, despatched a small force to crush the revolt but these men were murdered by their Indian guides. It took some time for the rebellion to be subdued.[6]

Soto was busy in Havana organizing the details of his expedition. He was short of ready money and sent a message in consequence to an old friend in Panama, Hernando Ponce de León, who had done so much to assist the conquest of Peru, to ask for 10,000 ducats. Alonso de Ayala sold a ranch in Panama belonging to Isabel de Bobadilla for 7,000 pesos. Ponce de León took ship to Havana, where he remained for a time as the virtual prisoner of Soto, who extracted 8,000 castellanos from him as well as a pair of silver stirrups. Ponce de León then left for Seville where he concealed what remained of his treasure to avoid tax and bought a large house. Soto, too, was investing in land, in Cuba, where he established plantations in Cojímar and Mayabeque, both close to Havana.

Soto finally set off on the last stage of his great journey to Florida in May 1539. He had by then nine ships (five *naos*, two caravels, two pinnaces) in which he carried 600 men as well as about 130 sailors. Among the 600, there were about 240 horsemen. Vasco Porcallo de Figueroa, who had first gone to the Indies with Pedrarias and who had been a close friend of Diego Velázquez as well as a companion of Cortés with Narváez, became deputy leader. The supplies were apparently considerable: 3,000 loads of cassava, 2,500 shoulders of bacon and 2,500 *fanegas* of maize. Soto left his wife, Isabel, as deputy governor in Cuba with the experienced if elderly Juan de Rojas as her deputy. It was Juan de Rojas who, years before, had glimpsed the treasure which Cortés's friends Francisco de Montejo and Hernández Portocarrero were taking back from Veracruz to Spain, and who told Diego Velázquez of its quality. Rojas had also invested in Cortés's expedition in 1519 and had been largely responsible for moving the town of Havana from the south to the north coast of Cuba in the late 1520s. These Spaniards, together with Bartolomé Ortiz, the supreme magistrate of Santiago, found themselves in a bitter dispute with the settlers of Cuba, for the Crown wanted to set all the Indians free in practice while the latter tried to prevent it.

On 25 May Soto's fleet saw the land of North America and, on 30 May, they reached what seems to have been Tampa Bay, which they named Espíritu Santo.[7] This was not uninhabited land, for it was only two leagues (six miles) from Hirriga, the town of the Indian chief Ucita, established where the town of Ruskin, Florida, stands now. All the horses were safely disembarked.

Soto's deputy, Vasco Porcallo, set off immediately to reconnoitre. Coming up against six Indians who sought to resist him with bows and arrows, he killed two of them, but the others fled into marshes in which the horses could not survive. Soto set off in a pinnace and established himself in another small town, Ocoto, whose inhabitants had fled. At the same time the Indians who had been captured by Añasco to be guides or interpreters fled too. Ocoto consisted of seven or eight houses made of timber but covered with palm leaves, all built on a rise apparently to facilitate defence. There was a temple on top of which a wooden chicken gazed out through golden eyes; inside it there were rough pearls. Soto and Porcallo, with Luis Moscoso, slept in the chief's house. The rest of the Spanish force cut down the nearby wood within a crossbow shot to ensure defence. They began to build a palisade of earth and timber.

The natives who had fled from Soto's first settlement and who had earlier attacked were Timúcan Indians. They worshipped the sun, built their chief's palaces on high earth mounds, tattooed their bodies with pictures of birds and snakes as well as geometric designs and were led by chiefs who ruled clusters of townships. Most had black hair, brown skin, strong arms and black, cheerful eyes. They were excellent runners. They fought with six-foot longbows with which they fired deadly arrows of cane or reed tipped with sharp stones or even fishbones capable of penetrating chain-mail and shields.

In June 1539 the expedition had an unnerving experience. Baltasar Gallegos, its chief constable, set out with about forty horsemen and eighty foot soldiers to explore the land to the north of Ocoto. They encountered twenty red-painted Indians wearing plumes and carrying longbows. These the Spaniards began to cut down, but one of them suddenly proclaimed himself to be Juan Ortiz of Seville, a veteran of Narváez's expedition who had returned to Cuba but then returned to Florida. There he was captured by Indians who placed him on a grill and started to roast him. He had been saved by the daughter of the chief, who had never been helpful to him afterwards since his mother had been stoned to death by Narváez. He had lived with the princess for nine years and had become Indianized: he wore a grass skirt and a breech cloth, had had himself tattooed and carried a longbow.

Ortiz successfully re-established himself as a Spaniard and became Soto's chief interpreter. He begged Soto and his colleagues not to pursue his Indian friends as if they were deer since they had 'given me my life'. He also gave them the unexpected news that there was no gold, so far as he knew, in Florida. This disquieting information had a predictable effect on the commitment of Vasco Porcallo to Soto and he soon returned to Cuba.[8] His first aim had probably been to find slaves for his plantations in Cuba, but he left his son Lorenzo Suárez to continue with the expedition.

With Ortiz's bad news in the forefront of his mind, Soto now left on a new journey of investigation. His aim was still to find a good place for a settlement of Spaniards which was also rich in, above all, gold. Espíritu Santo did not, however, seem the ideal candidate for that destiny. But the chief of a nearby town, Urriparacuxci, assured him that, at Ocale, some way to the north, the Spaniards would find all the treasure that they could carry. He added that, at Ocale, the Indians even wore hats of gold when they made war. Baltasar Gallegos was sceptical but Soto, a simpler soul, became enthusiastic. Spaniards in the New World were always being deluded by such aureate dreams.

Soto left half his men with Pedro Calderón de la Barca in Espíritu Santo and set off through Florida in a north-westerly direction. Ocale turned out to have maize, but no gold. Eventually Soto and his friends found themselves in the territory of the Apalache Indians, whose main settlement lay in the modern Tallahassee. There may have been 100,000 Apalaches.

The Apalaches, like most of the native Indians in the New World before the Christians came, worshipped the sun, grew maize, ate shellfish, built cities with pyramids on which they placed temples, and lived in round houses. They played a kind of *pelota* with a hard buckskin ball the purpose of which was to secure entry to a goal on top of which a stuffed eagle was placed. If you hit the eagle, you scored two points; if the post, one. Here Soto reassembled his forces. Calderón came up from Espíritu Santo. The Spaniards were delighted with the fertility of the Apalache territory, even if the promised gold was not to be seen. So Soto sent back a message to Havana with orders to restock him with supplies and then come back next year to meet him in the vicinity of Tallahassee. If they found nothing, Soto made clear that he would keep cruising as far as the Mississippi, which he knew about from previous journeys of discovery.[9]

On 3 March 1540 Soto and his small army turned their backs on the known world of the Gulf of Mexico and set off for a newly described magic kingdom named Cofiachequi. This was a long way to the north-east, across the rivers Ochlockonec and Flint, in what is now South

Georgia. The Spaniards crossed these waterways with difficulty, using chains of Indians to haul them over rivers on rafts. They stopped at Capachequi where the Indians attacked stragglers. Then they met Lower Creek Indians living in good houses made from trunks of cedar or pine wood in large towns surrounded by palisades built along the rivers, with a well-developed agriculture and making good pottery, baskets, jewellery and even statuary. The women wore blankets woven from fine thread, and jewelled necklaces, earrings, pendants, amulets and beads made from shells, bone and wood.[10]

The apparently civilized town of Toa was deserted when Soto arrived. The king of the place ordered his men to offer the Spaniards lodging as well as food. Soto was now facing complaints from his men; some were restless at the endless journeys. Where were they going? Soto explained that he had come to teach the Indians 'to understand the sacred faith of Christ . . . that they should know Him and be saved'.[11] He also asked the Indians to give obedience to the emperor and king of Castile and to the pope, the supreme pontiff and vicar of God. Soto added that he was himself the son of the Sun.

Brightly dressed Ichisis Indians led Soto's expedition towards their capital, probably Lasmar near what is now Macon, Georgia. Rodrigo Rangel, Soto's secretary, recalled that here they were greeted by innumerable women in white who gave the Spaniards omelettes made of maize as well as spring onions. Several hundred Indians, Mississippians, seem to have lived here in a town encircled by a log palisade about 1,200 feet long. On this Soto raised a large wooden cross.

Soto moved on to the river Oconce, where he was met by some Indians from Atamaha. A ruler named Camumo received the adventurers in his capital, which seems to have been close to what is today Milledgeville, Georgia. Soto gave him a feather which had been coloured silver. Camumo said: 'You are from heaven, and with this feather that you give me I will eat, I will go to war, I shall sleep with my wife.' Camumo then asked to whom he should give tribute, to Soto or to Ocute, who was a king on the river of that name to the north. Soto rather surprisingly said that Camumo should pay tribute to Ocute. Then he went on to the town of Ocute. The chief there gave the Spaniards rabbits, partridges, maize bread, hens and many small dogs, and provided several hundred porters who were loaded with food.

They carried on to Cofiachequi, guided by an Indian who claimed to be taking them to a new El Dorado in the north. They soon reached the river Savannah, which was 'broader than the shot of an arquebus'. The men crossed it tied to one another. It is astonishing that Soto was able to maintain discipline and order. Not only that, he asked four of his captains to lead eight horsemen each in different directions to establish exactly where they were. In their absence, Soto killed his pigs, which enabled him to allow each man half a pound of pork every day for a short spell.

Juan de Añasco returned to Soto's headquarters to say that he had found a good town some thirty-six miles away. He brought back grain and some horns of cattle, as well as an Indian girl and a boy. This town was Himahi, which may have been near Columbia, South Carolina. They found there fifty *fanegas* of maize, some mulberries and other fruit, as well as roses. They then continued their way to the mysterious Cofiachequi about twenty miles east of Himahi near what is now Lugoff, South Carolina, where Soto met a queenly ruler of the tribe. This lady – Garcilaso characteristically insisted that she was a beauty – is said to have come out to meet Soto in a canoe with an awning. She gave him some pearls as large as hazelnuts. Soto gave her a ruby ring which he usually wore on his finger. In return she offered food and lodging, and the Spanish expedition, quickly moving from pessimism to joy, became optimistic again.

It turned out that Cofiachequi had recently experienced a serious plague which much reduced the population (this seems not to have been the direct responsibility of European invaders). The queen apparently controlled the land between the Blue Ridge mountains and the Atlantic. Her people wore 'excellent hides which had been very well tanned' as well as 'blankets of sable', and breeches and buskins with black garters, tied by laces of white hide. The soldiers of this principality are said to have worn breast plates made from raw and hairless hides, perhaps buffalo. 'They were,' wrote Elvas, 'more well-mannered' than the other Indians whom the Spaniards had met in Florida. Rodrigo Rangel recalled seeing a substantial temple on high ground at a town called Tamileco. This, Garcilaso noted, was well decorated with giant figures carved from wood. There was also, Rangel recorded, 'a large, tall and broad palace'.[12] The queen gave Soto the town of Ilap, about fifty miles northeast of the modern town of Cheraw, which was a generous gesture, considering that she herself was short of food.

Alas, the 'gold' in the queen's palace turned out to be copper, the 'emeralds' were glass, and the 'silver' was mica. The best treasure was some Castilian iron axes surviving from Vázquez de Ayllon's expedition there.

Some Spaniards would have liked to have established a colony here in what one day would become South Carolina. But, Elvas commented, 'the Governor's purpose was to seek another treasure like that of Atahualpa' and 'he insisted that they keep going'. For 'he had no wish to content himself with good land and pearls'. Many wondered whether Soto had lost his senses. But his magnetic attraction as a leader remained, and no one would oppose him even when he now insisted on going on to Chiaha, a territory which was either Hickory in North Carolina or Dandridge, Tennessee. They came upon the Appalachian mountains, which seemed to Soto a sure sign that gold was close at hand. Here in the foothills the expedition rested for three weeks. Soto asked the chief in Chiaha for women. The population fled. In the end, the chief supplied porters, but not women.

The Spaniards at this point still numbered about 550 with a large army of carriers, most of whom were treated more as slaves than as servants. During the summer of 1540 they slowly headed for what they believed to be the southern coast, in what is today the state of Alabama. Soto's tactic in these days was to insist on being received by a ruler, kidnap him, demand food, porters and women, and then move on. The technique worked well across Alabama. For instance, the ruler of the Coosa assisted Soto with porters thinking, probably correctly, that that was the best way to rid himself of such demanding visitors.[13]

How to treat Soto was much on the mind of the next ruler whom they met, the giant Tascalusa of the Atahachi in south-west Alabama, who knew something of Spaniards from a Greek, Doroteo Teodoro, who had fled to him many years before from the expedition of Narváez.[14] Tascalusa was of a different mould from other monarchs since he seemed to have hundreds of servants, while a nobleman always stood in front of him with a sunshade on a pole as, in his vast headdress, he addressed large audiences from a balcony – almost like a modern Mexican politician.

On 10 October Soto reached the outskirts of Atahachi. He sent Luis de Moscoso to greet Tascalusa. Moscoso made a successful display of horsemanship, and then Soto came up. Tascalusa offered dinner. Afterwards Soto requested the king to give him women and porters in order to carry their burdens onwards on the next stage of the journey. Tascalusa declined, explaining that he was not accustomed to serve anyone. At that point, as Doroteo Teodoro should have told him would be likely to occur, Soto detained him. The two then rode through Atahachi, the king in his litter, the conquistador on his horse. Tempers were worsened by the death of two Spaniards at the hands of Indians, and Soto was even angrier when he was informed that the Indians were preparing an attack at Mabila, his next point of call.

The Spaniards travelled there with Tascalusa remaining in virtual freedom. Three to four hundred Indians in ceremonial feathers were ready to greet them. It was a substantial town, for there were eighty large houses and stockades with towers. Soto and Tascalusa walked to a place of honour in a square, most of the former's army being left outside. Tascalusa succeeded in meeting his captains and they decided to act immediately against Spain. Cristóbal de Espíndola observed that the houses around the square were full of soldiers, and Baltasar Gallegos tried to persuade one of Tascalusa's captains to fetch the king. He refused and Gallegos cut off his arm. At that Tascalusa gave the signal to move against the Spaniards.

Soto was trapped in a fortress-like town with his horsemen unable to move freely. Five of his guards were killed instantly, Gallegos was wounded. All the porters deserted. This became the most serious battle in which the Spaniards had been engaged since their landing in North America. But Soto managed to find a mount and escaped, so the Spaniards were able to besiege the town and they set the houses nearest to them on fire. It seems that, in this combat, Tascalusa and his son and heir were burned to death. About twenty Spaniards were killed and 250 were wounded. Twelve horses were also killed, and almost all the baggage was lost. Soto remained outside this doomed city of Mabila for several weeks, his men forced to cover themselves in native blankets, not Spanish dress.

Next the expedition went south again, crossing the river Alabama. They found maize at Talicpacam but not enough, while at Mozulixa, the Indians disappeared without leaving any food or indeed showing any signs of life. Soto seized food at two villages belonging to the Apafalya people, capturing a chief whom he afterwards used as a guide. Crossing the cold river Tombigbee, the Spaniards reached the capital of the Chikkasahs which had twenty houses and was full of maize. The people fled, the chief presented Soto with 150 rabbits, some skins and blankets. This friendly tactic was a ruse, for the Chikkasah Indians sought to steal Soto's pigs and horses. In fact they did kill about 400 pigs and nearly sixty horses, as well as eleven Spaniards. It took two months for Soto's 450 Europeans to organize their defences once more.

Shortly they reached the Mississippi near what is now Memphis. The mouth of that great waterway had been observed years before, in 1520, by Alonso Álvarez Pineda. Now Soto saw a fleet of canoes with painted warriors on board wearing white plumes in their hats, led by a chief from a town called Aquixo. This dramatic appearance suggested once again to the credulous invaders that they might be on the edge of a land of gold.

On 18 June 1541 Soto carried his men across the Mississippi, going first to Aquixo, then to Casqui, where they found buffalo, maize, walnuts, plums and mulberries. Soto was making for Pacaha, which he besieged and then broke into while it was being abandoned. The chief escaped and hid successfully, leaving Soto to observe the fine pottery made in the place, the elaborate system of irrigation, the blankets and deerskins, the shirts and the leggings of hide and cassocks. They stayed in this town for a month making local forays. They were probably then near what is now Helena, fifty miles south of Memphis.

They continued down the Mississippi, reaching the river Arkansas in mid-September. In Tula they encountered a people who deformed their heads at birth to make them longer, and pricked their faces and lips with flint needles in order to colour them black. They used long lance-like poles against buffalo, which served also as defensive weapons. They had the eccentricity of weeping profusely as a greeting.

Soto and his army spent the winter of 1541–2 near Redfield on the river Arkansas, because rumours of wealth in that territory had reached them. There were, however, only beans, dried plums and nuts. In the spring they went south again to follow the Mississippi. Soto sent Juan de Añasco ahead to report how far off the sea might be. He rode fifty miles down the river but saw no sign of it. Unlike Orellana in somewhat similar circumstances on the Amazon, he returned. Soto was gloomy at his apparent isolation. He told a local chief that he was son of the Sun; at which the chief replied that if he were really a god, he should dry up the great river.[15]

In the spring of 1542 Soto abandoned his mission. He died soon after. Did he die from exhaustion or was there a fever or other infirmity? It is impossible to say, but he was not old. We hear, though, that Baltasar Gallegos had sought to console him by speaking of the shortness of life in this world attended as it was by so many afflictions. God showed particular favours to those whom he called away early. Sweet were the uses of adversity. Elvas commented that Soto 'died in a land and at a time that could afford him little comfort in his illness'.[16] Before he died, Soto named Luis de Moscoso as his successor.

Moscoso buried Soto first at the gate of the town but then, to avoid questions from Indians, his body was committed to the great river. Moscoso told the local chief that Soto had not died but had gone to the skies. All the same, he immediately set about selling Soto's mobile property: two male slaves, two females, three horses and 700 pigs. He made it evident that he had no more interest in Soto's enterprise. On the contrary, he longed 'to be again where he could get his full measure of sleep rather than govern and go on conquering a country so beset for him by hardships'.[17]

It appeared sensible to march westwards; in that direction as all knew lay New Spain. They were surprised not to discover the gold, silver and cotton which Cabeza de Vaca had assured the Emperor Charles was to be found on the way, but they concluded that that was because they were marching into the interior whereas Cabeza had gone along the coast. Some grieved to return to civilization; they would rather have continued to live in the hope of riches in peril than leave Florida poor.

Moscoso hoped to reach New Spain in the summer of 1542, but the country in Texas was too dry to maintain the army, so they returned to the Mississippi near Guachoya, where Soto had died. Here they spent the winter making rafts to float down the river.

The expedition, by then numbering 311, eventually reached Pánuco by boat in September 1543. Viceroy Mendoza welcomed them and gave orders that they should be fed as they required. The news was soon taken to Havana. Thus what had been assumed there was confirmed: Soto was dead. Isabel, his widow, was disconsolate.

Soto's expedition was one of the oddest of the Spanish adventures in the New World. It would have seemed heroic had it had a true destination. As it was, Soto and his constantly dwindling band of experienced Spaniards and their horses travelled on and on, always expecting to find a new Peru or a new Mexico, with Soto himself and his senior colleagues always believing in stories that, fifty leagues ahead, there was just such a realm with vast resources of gold, not just maize and persimmon, or other delicacies such as watercress, cabbages, chestnuts and grapes, not to speak of 'symmetrical and tall' girls of the Macanoche tribe or the robust Mochila ladies. Many self-deprecating comments had been made to the Spaniards: 'I entreat you to forgive me for the error I committed in not waiting to greet and to obey you since the occasion should have been for me (and is one) a matter of pride'[18]; or 'very high, powerful and good master. Think what must be the effect of me and mine of the sight of you and your people . . . What pride was ours when the fierce brutes of your horses entered with such speed and fury into my country . . . I hope you will tell me who you are, whence you come, and what it is you seek.'[19]

The Spaniards were often cruel. Several times we read 'of those made captive, the Governor sent six to the chief with their right hands and their noses cut off'.[20] Or, 'the Governor having been led for two days out of the way ordered that the Indian [guide] should be put to the torture when he confessed that his master, the chief of Nondaco had ordered him to take them in that manner . . . He was commanded to be cast to the dogs.'[21] It is hard to sympathize with Hernando de Soto. Yet his plight was genuine. Sometimes the distress was caused by 'the intolerable torment of a myriad of mosquitoes';[22] the sails of their vessels might seem covered with them at daylight. We cannot forgive him his brutalities. But neither can we forget his multiple tragedies.

38

The lure of the Indies

> *It is the awareness of this great mystery that removes the person-*
> *ality of the great artist in whom all is fulfilled to such a vast height*
> *of distance from us.*
>
> Jacob Burckhardt, *Reflections on History*

We are in Venezuela. The great expedition of Federman had long vanished into the Andes. The few Spanish settlers at Coro maintained an
austere life only interrupted from time to time by demands for slaves
from the Caribbean islands which they could not meet.[1]

Coro remained important as a place from which expeditions could
be mounted. Hence the arrival there of Philipp von Hutten. He came
from a powerful family in Frankfurt, the second son of Bernard von
Hutten who had once been the imperial representative at Königshofen,
and his character had apparently been shaped by an excessive diet of
romantic novels. Philipp's benefactor in his early youth had been the
emperor's friend Henry of Nassau, and Philipp was for a time a companion of Prince, later the Emperor, Ferdinand. He went to the New
World still in his twenties in 1535 (he had been born in 1511 at Birken-
feld, Frankfurt) in search of honour: 'After having passed a great part of
my life among friends, I want to come back with my name and my family honoured, so that no one laughs at me.'[2] He had a lot to live up to.
A von Hutten had led the army of the Emperor Frederick Barbarossa
against the Hungarians; he was a cousin of the humanist reformer and
rebel Ulrich von Hutten, who had died so young; and his eldest brother
was Maurice, bishop of Eichstatt. The Indies were for Philipp the back-
drop against which he hoped to display his personality, the ideal of a
Renaissance man. 'God is my witness', he wrote to his brother the

bishop, 'that, in this journey, I have not been for a second moved by a desire for wealth, rather I have been affected by a strange dream. It seemed to me I could not die in peace without having seen the Indies (*No hubiera podido morir tranquilo si no hubiese visto las Indias*).'[3]

He went on Federman's first, unfortunate expedition to the plains in which three quarters of the soldiers died. He came to admire Federman, whom he had met in Seville. 'I believe,' he noted, 'that the future of this province depends on him.' He wrote to his brother, the bishop: 'I ask you to think that it would be an honour for you and for our friends if I came back heavily laden with debts for, for the moment, I cannot expect to bring any other booty.' His letters then take on a darker character: 'If you could know what an effort and danger the riches from here entail, and how many thousands of Christians the Indies have cost and how many fleets one loses before one finds a Peru . . . !' He added:

> It is a great comfort to those who are here in the desert [a green desert of jungle, not of sand] to receive a letter from home . . . I well know that, with this long drawn out journey, I have given my parents a sad and restless old age . . . You cannot believe what a good cook hunger makes. Please wish me a glass of wine which I have not drunk for almost four and a half years, except for the drop I receive in the chalice when I take communion.[4]

Hutten achieved some success in Venezuela. In 1540 he was in Barquisimeto when he received news of the death of Espira. Hutten had been part of the small army led by Lope Montalvo de Lugo, Espira's favourite captain. He returned to Coro, where he met Bishop Bastidas, who had brought 200 men including 150 horsemen. Bastidas named Hutten captain-general to pursue the plans of Espira, a nomination Hutten received with much happiness. At the same moment, he, however, heard from Germany that his father had died.

He set off in August 1541 for what he fondly expected would be 'El Dorado', the source of fabulous gold supplies, with a hundred horsemen and a few foot soldiers. He took with him as his second-in-command Bartolomé Welser the Younger, the son of Bartolomé Welser, as well as Fray Frutos de Tudela. He expected to join or indeed absorb the army of Montalvo de Lugo but that captain, horrified by the nomination of Hutten as captain-general, had left for New Granada. So the two Germans Hutten and Welser went ahead by themselves.

They crossed the river Opia by canoe and entered the territory of the

Guaypiés Indians. They proceeded along the base of the Andes, and soon arrived at San Juan de Llanos, where they supposed Jiménez de Quesada had been. They moved west and seem to have found the source of the river Uaupés, a tributary of the Amazonian river Negro. Pedro de Limpias, a skilled linguist and experienced explorer, who could not bear having an inferior position to the spoiled Bartolomé Welser, went for a three-month reconnaissance down the river Guaviare, which eventually joins the Orinoco. The entire expedition then went on to a town apparently called Macatoa, where the chief told Hutten that 'alongside a certain range of mountains which could be observed on clear days, there were vast towns of rich people who possessed enormous wealth'.[5] Once again, an Indian chief was seeking to divert a potential conqueror with a tale of wealth just round the corner; and as usual, the diversion worked, for Hutten and his army made for where they had been directed.

These were the Omagua people. In the centre of the town there was a fine house in which, the explorers were assured, were wonderful objects, including a woman made of gold who was the natives' goddess. Hutten, with a friend, Arteaga, made to seize two Indians who, however, defended themselves well and wounded both the conquistadors. The Spaniards retreated to the jungle, where Diego de Montes operated on the two captains to save their lives (he investigated the interior of an Indian to see how such wounds affected the body). Hutten reached the conclusion that he did not have enough men and resolved to return to Cora to recruit reinforcements.

The journey of nearly 1,000 miles took them from January to May 1545. They reached the river Pauto, whence Hutten sent on Welser in command of twenty men, alongside Pedro de Limpias, who had been on one of Federman's expeditions. Relations between Welser and Limpias were still bad, however, and, anyway, the former did not want to go to Coro. He suggested that they go to Cubagua, where there were by then good houses and from where they could return to Santo Domingo and escape for ever the fortunes of Venezuela.

In Hutten's absence, there had been both natural and human catastrophes on the coast of Venezuela. In 1541 a hurricane had destroyed Cubagua, which had become prosperous because of the pearls found there. Two years later, in July 1543, French pirates in five big ships fell on the ruins and seized what remained there.[6] In addition, a decision had been taken in the Council of the Indies to take a *residencia* in Coro and in particular of the actions of Hutten. A judge (*oidor*) of Santo Domingo, Cervantes de Loaisa, was appointed. But illness prevented him from going. Instead he sent Juan Frías, prosecutor of the supreme court in Santo Domingo, to be governor of Venezuela once the *residencia* was over; and Juan de Carvajal, one more member of the vast family of that name who played such a part in the history of the Americas, *relator* (*rapporteur*) of the *audiencia*, would be his lieutenant in Coro. He accompanied the nomination with a sensible proviso: Carvajal was not to be allowed to go into the interior of Venezuela as so many governors or their lieutenants had done.

Carvajal went to Coro and found the place utterly miserable. The settlers seemed primarily in pursuit of Indians, particularly Caribs, so that they could send them to be sold as slaves in Santo Domingo. The few remaining natives had unsurprisingly an implacable hostility to all Spaniards.

This must have played a part in Carvajal's inability to survive there. He went by ship eastwards along the coast as far as to enter the valley of the river Tocuyo, where he founded a new town, Nuestra Señora de la Concepción de Tocuyo, more or less at the mouth of the river. This was a more fertile region. He even felt able to grant *encomiendas*, with the help of the skilful Juan de Villegas.

Limpias, meantime, bade Welser goodbye at Barquisimeto and, with five friends, went immediately to Carvajal's camp, where he was given a safe conduct as well as a pardon for breaking with Hutten. But both Hutten and Welser followed Limpias and clashed violently – in words, that is – with Carvajal. At first, it is true, they dined together and even watched a play of canes. Carvajal suggested that Hutten suspend his march to Coro and that they both collaborate in the government. Then Carvajal said that he wanted to go to the so-called valley of Pamplona, which was known to be full of riches, and suggested to Hutten that he for his part should go to the island of Margarita, the centre for pearls, and buy some horses there with money borrowed from his own soldiers. Hutten refused and said that he had to go to Coro in order to report to the Crown on his expedition. Carvajal asked Hutten to present himself at his camp tent and to place himself at his, Carvajal's, orders. Hutten replied: Señor governor,

already you know that I and these gentlemen and brothers have been marching for five years in order to carry out the full discovery of this territory, where
we have lost many friends, horses and clothes. And we come here ruined and
poor, sick, tired and indebted; and as my followers have been friends, I would
like them to go with me to the port whence we set off [Coro] and there we can
recover, for there is the judge of the *Residencia*. I wish to give my testimony
and give an account to His Majesty and to the *Belzares* [Welsers] who have
this government. I beg your excellency not to disturb us.

The feelings of his soldiers for Hutten were mixed, for they had suffered
great privations without much reward. They saw in their mind's eye the
possibility of having to voyage again to distant lands in search of mythical
El Dorados. The Germans seemed to bring bad luck. Carvajal seemed better organized. At least he could provide food. Carvajal said to the soldiers:
'I hope you will be a witness of the fact that this is the government of the
emperor. Here the Welsers are nothing, it is His Majesty who rules.'

Hutten replied: 'Already I have said that these [the Welsers] hold the
land on behalf of His Majesty.'

Carvajal responded with: 'Stop talking.' He said to the notary: 'Take
heed that I order that he goes a prisoner to his tent and does not leave it.'

Hutten answered: 'Take heed that I stand by what I have said, which is
that I do not recognize Señor Carvajal as the judge, for I am the captain-
general of His Majesty.' He insisted again that he had to go to Coro in
order to make a report about his journey to the king and to the Welsers.

Carvajal said: 'To the king you have to tell this story and not to the
Welsers.'

Hutten returned: 'To the king I say I shall give my first account and
then to the Welsers.'

Carvajal replied: 'You are not captain-general, indeed you are nothing
where I am and, therefore, both you and Captain Bartolomé Welser must
go as prisoners to your tents (*posadas*) and treat them as a prison.'

Hutten retorted that Carvajal had power only because it was believed
that he, Hutten, was lost and had died in his expedition.

This remark caused an uproar. Carvajal went forward to seize the
two Germans himself but they, supported by ten of their soldiers, drew
their swords to defend themselves. Carvajal withdrew and Hutten and
Welser went to their lodgings. They were soon surrounded by Carvajal's
men. Welser attacked Carvajal lance in hand, but his horse was killed.

Nevertheless the Germans set off that night with some supporters on the hundred or so miles to Coro. On the way, an agreement, arranged by Carvajal's notary, Juan de Villegas, was reached between Carvajal, Hutten and Welser: the latter were to be permitted to go to Coro. But on the second night of their journey, Carvajal attacked and seized both the Germans in their hammocks. He ordered an African slave to cut off their heads with a machete, refusing them the right of absolution: 'they can make their confession in heaven', he grimly commented.[7]

So ended the brutal implication of Germany in the Spanish empire.

The conclusion of this chapter of tragedy is quickly told. At the end of 1545 Licenciado Frías finally reached Coro to carry out his task as *juez de residencia*. He found the port practically deserted, and food almost non-existent. The Council of the Indies had changed their policy, however, and had named Juan Pérez de Tolosa, a lawyer of Castile, in Frías's stead, at a salary of 645,000 maravedís a year. All other governors, lieutenant-governors and chief magistrates were suspended. The *residencia* was to be completed in ninety days.

Pérez de Tolosa reached Santo Domingo on 27 May 1546. He was told that Venezuela was in chaos. On 9 June he arrived there to see for himself. He found Coro, as Frías and indeed Carvajal had found it, in a deplorable state, for there were only fifteen settlers there; the rest had gone to Santa Marta or to Bogotá. He wrote:

> the poverty of those who are to be found in this city . . . is so great that if it were not for the little I have brought of clothing and footwear I could do nothing. There is no gold, nor silver, nor money and no food except for fish and good things obtainable from hunting.

Three weeks after Pérez de Tolosa arrived, he began his investigation of Carvajal, using Juan de Eldua as magistrate. Carvajal was accused of conducting himself as a governor and a captain-general without authority, of removing the colony from Coro to Tocuyo without permission, of robbing peaceful Indians of their goods and of executing Hutten and Welser without trial. Pérez de Tolosa had Carvajal arrested and all his men accepted the judge as the new governor. Carvajal presented a long questionnaire with witnesses. He explained that the executions of the Germans were the consequence of their disobedience to his government. He did not improve his cause by saying that 'if Prince Philip had committed the crimes of Philipp von Hutten, he would also have had his head cut off'. And he also admitted to saying that 'no one in these parts who has a house can do without having women, Spaniards or Indians, it does not matter which'.[8]

Carvajal did all he could to save his life, but on 16 September he was condemned to be 'taken from the public gaol where he is to be tied to the tail of a horse; and from this square, he will be taken to the pillory and the gallows; and there he will be tied from the neck with a cord of esparto grass . . . so that he would die naturally'.

The Hutten and Welser families thought that it had been the desire of Carvajal and his friends to rob the two Germans of the treasure which they had brought back from 'El Dorado'. That had obviously been the motive for their arrest and execution. Bartolomé Welser's father, also Bartolomé, told Bishop Maurice von Hutten that they brought back great riches.

Thereafter the government of Licenciado Pérez de Tolosa was correct. He confirmed Carvajal's *encomiendas* in Tocuyo and organized several journeys into the interior. He sent his brother Alonso on one of these to the Sierra de Mérida, as it is now known, but he took care not to go himself. He declared Juan de Villegas free from blame in relation to Hutten and Welser, and sent him in mid-1547 to the Valle de las Damas in order to see if a settlement could be established there; and he did find a good new route from the interior to the coast. Pérez de Tolosa took a close look at the coast of Venezuela but left his brother and Villegas to investigate the interior further. When Pérez de Tolosa died in 1549, Villegas became his successor and, in most senses, inaugurated the colonial era in the country. He founded a road to New Granada which passed over the headwaters of the rivers Apare, Sarara and Oro. There were no further disastrous expeditions into the southern jungle. Tocuyo became in effect the new capital.

Perhaps, though, the best memorial of this era in Venezuela is to be found in the small German city of Arnstein, near Würzburg in Bavaria. There Philipp von Hutten is remembered in the church of Maria-Sondheim in a tomb ordered by his brother Bishop Maurice. Philipp was a victim of his own generous illusions. Nothing in his tragic life shows more vividly the extraordinary connection between the new and the old worlds and between reality and the world of fantasy as expressed in the chivalric novels.

BOOK IV
Counter Reformation, Counter Renaissance

39

Buenos Aires and Asunción: Pedro de Mendoza and Cabeza de Vaca

Some day things will be as God wills and the Twelve Peers will rule.

A member of Pedro de Mendoza's
expedition to the River Plate, 1536

The capital of the Portuguese colony in Brazil would soon be Olinda, a name taken straight from that of a princess in *Amadís de Gaula*. Yet the Spaniards were slow in developing relations with, much less conquering and settling, the territory which they believed to be theirs but which lay beyond the Portuguese colony in Brazil. Their interest there had, however, been awoken by the ill-fated journey of Vespucci's successor as *piloto mayor* in Seville, Juan Díaz de Solís, in 1515. Díaz de Solís had been looking for a strait into the Southern Sea. Like so many adventurers of that time, he found many other things while not finding the strait. Díaz de Solís, as we have learned, was captured by the Querandi Indians on the banks of the river Plate (de la Plata), though that was not yet its name in 1515. With those companions who had landed with him on the island of Martín García, he was killed and then eaten, slice by slice, in full view of those who remained in the boats.[1] Those survivors of the expedition understandably did not choose to continue their search for the strait and returned home as fast as they could. The river Plate was then named by the Spaniards 'the Solís'.

The next to risk those waters was Sebastian Cabot, who sailed from Sanlúcar in 1526. He was himself *piloto mayor* in succession to Díaz de Solís and, now that Magellan had shown the way, it was thought right that he should direct a new expedition to the Spice Islands by Magellan's route. The expedition of García de Loaisa had made an effort to do so but had been a failure. Cabot left Sanlúcar on 5 April 1526 with three *naos* and a caravel. He explored the estuary of the river Plate, as well as the river Parana and, on the river Carcaraña, he built a fort near where the town of Rosario now stands. He sent some silver home to the king; hence the name of the great river. 'Río de la Plata' it had become by 1530 and so it has remained, though the English, as is their wont, mistranslated it.

Cabot carried out several minor expeditions up the rivers of this territory and they remain his great achievement. But he was supposed to be heading for the Spice Islands and these he did not reach. Indeed, he never went further than the estuary of the Plate. This was partly because of the arrival there of another Spanish expedition, that of Diego García of Moguer, with two caravels. García claimed to have secured the right to explore and colonize the whole region. The quarrels between Cabot and García brought an end to both expeditions, as the two returned to Spain to engage in a lawsuit without end to decide the matter. Since Cabot had been expected to go to the Spice Islands, he found himself in some disgrace, 'without glory', and was sent for two years' exile in Orán.

After such small expeditions whose aims had been far beyond the Río de la Plata, it was notable that, in 1535, a major expedition should at last be sent to the region under the leadership of Pedro de Mendoza. It must seem right that the conquistador who first established himself in a permanent fashion on the Plate and founded a colony which eventually became a great nation should have been a Mendoza, the family which dominated Spanish history in the early sixteenth century. It is, however, obscure from what branch of the family of the dukes of Infantado, Pedro de Mendoza derived. He was probably an illegitimate son of Íñigo López de Mendoza, Count of Tendilla, for he was born in Guadix while Spain was still at war a few miles away in Granada.[2] He seems to have lived a good deal at the court, as shown by the terms in which the king addressed him: 'You, Don Pedro Mendoza, *mi criado y gentil hombre de mi casa*' and to have served in Italy, being present in his thirties in 1527 at the sack of Rome, where he is said, probably falsely, to have increased his fortune. His interests were extravagant and, without proving his capacity for such a mission, he succeeded in having himself named *adelantado* of the region: 'to go and conquer the lands and provinces which there are in the river Solís which is called La Plata where Sebastian Cabot was'. He had no knowledge of where he was going.[3]

Mendoza left Sanlúcar in September 1535 with fourteen ships and no fewer than 2,150 men. His expedition was full of high-ranking persons known at court, such as the sea captain Juan de Osorio; the chief magistrate, Juan de Ayolas, who came from Briviesca, Castile; the Cáceres brothers; and Pérez de Cepeda de Ahumada, a brother of Saint Teresa of Ávila, who left Spain to avoid persecution as a *converso*. More important still was Diego de Mendoza, Don Pedro's brother, who acted as admiral of the fleet. Various wives, daughters and sisters of the adventurers sailed too. Oviedo wrote that the expedition was fit to make a 'goodly show in Caesar's army in any part of the world'.[4] On a ship which belonged to Flemish merchants established in Seville travelled Ulrich Schmidt, who wrote an unreliable account of the expedition. Another vessel was hired by the Welsers and carried Sebastian Neidhart, a German from Nuremberg, the captain and *factor* being another German, Heinrich Paeime.[5]

The expedition encountered a storm halfway across the Atlantic, and the ships were dispersed. Some went to Rio de Janeiro instead of Río de la Plata, but most of the expedition had reassembled in the river Plate by New Year's Day 1536. On 22 February Mendoza, in the name of the emperor, established the first serious settlement at what he named 'El Puerto de Nuestra Señora del Buen Aire'. One of the most remarkable Spanish cities thus had its beginning. The name derived from the 'Virgin of Buenos Vientos', protector of sailors, which used often to be placed in caravels in the centre of the compass.

Some months passed during which the Spaniards began to establish their settlement. The Indians who had eaten Díaz de Solís appropriately gave them some food, but ceased doing so by May. In June Mendoza sent his brother Diego to 'punish' the Querandi Indians for this. There was a fierce battle, which the Spaniards won, but Diego de Mendoza was killed, along with four nephews of his and Pedro's. Soon after, the settlement itself was attacked by an army of natives, who were driven off but not before they had burned four of the *adelantado*'s ships. Mendoza then had the settlement resited with new buildings built along the entry of the river Riachuelo into the estuary. He went to rest at a site found by his lieutenant, Juan de Ayolas, and which he named Buena Esperanza. There he left two lieutenants, one characteristically being an Alvarado (one more nephew of Pedro) and the other a Dubrín. Then his kinsman, Gonzalo de Mendoza, arrived from Brazil, bringing an ample supply of food as well as another 150 men. (Gonzalo was the son of the Count of Castrogeriz and had been with Pedro at the beginning. He had gone to Brazil in search of supplies the previous year.)

Now the rule of Pedro de Mendoza was approaching its conclusion. Illness seized him and he decided to return to Spain. He took two ships. He left a hundred Spaniards in Buen Viento (Buenos Aires) under Juan Ruiz Galán. At the same time Alvarado and Dubrín were in the pampas at Buena Esperanza while Juan de Ayolas had been sent up the river Paraguay – successfully, since he reached a place where he established a settlement at Candelaria, soon to be called Asunción, as it was formally founded on the feast of the Assumption, 15 August 1536. Ayolas left behind there as the interim governor Domingo Martínez de Irala, a Basque from Vergara who, like him, had come out with Mendoza. Ayolas was, however, killed by Payaqueses on his way back to Buenos Aires. Pedro de Mendoza too died at this time, not at the hands of Indians but of a fever on his ship on the way back to Spain in May 1537.

The achievement of Mendoza was modest because soon after he departed, Buenos Aires was attacked by Indians twice and burned. In 1541 the place was abandoned, and the inhabitants left for Asunción. All the same, Pedro de Mendoza was the founder of the new colony which eventually was looked upon as a jewel in the Spanish diadem.

It now seemed necessary in Seville to appoint a new governor in the far south of South America, and the man of the hour in Castile was Álvaro Cabeza de Vaca, hero of the extraordinary walk across North America, who had just published his account of his journey. He also plainly wanted to return to the Indies. Probably he had been adversely affected by his experience, but then he had always been tactless if persistent. His affection for Indians was proverbial and, at the time of his nomination to succeed Mendoza, seemed to be fashionable – a man in the mould of Las Casas.

Cabeza de Vaca at first expected to be able to gain the position of *adelantado* of the region between Florida and New Spain or, as the Council of the Indies would then have put it, between Cape Miedo and the Río de las Palmas. But Hernando de Soto had obtained that grant. Cabeza, therefore, devised a new territory for himself. It would be the unknown land between the Río de la Plata and Santa Catalina, that is, the part of the continent of South America which lay south or south-west of the Portuguese dominion which would become Brazil. Cabeza de Vaca had not been to this territory, but all the same he secured nomination as its '*adelantado*, captain-general and governor' as well as 'chief magistrate'. The King Emperor Charles signed this *capitulación* (contract) on 18 March 1540.[6]

Eight months later Cabeza de Vaca left Sanlúcar de Barrameda with three ships and 400 men but, there was a storm, and the fleet was delayed, leaving Cadiz only on 2 December.

The journey was longer than usual, but then they were going to unknown places. They stopped on the way in both the Canary and the Cape Verde islands and Cabeza de Vaca secured some supplies there without paying for them. They arrived at Santa Catalina off Brazil at the end of March. To Cabeza de Vaca's astonishment, he found on the island a Franciscan, Fray Bernaldo de Armenta, living alone, who had come there from Buenos Aires. From Santa Catalina Cabeza de Vaca sent a small expedition to Buenos Aires to assist its revival as a Spanish dependency. But since it was already the South American winter, it seemed unsuitable to travel far by the river Plate, so they pusillanimously returned. Their return coincided with the arrival of nine further Spaniards from Buenos Aires.

Cabeza de Vaca now discovered that most of those Spaniards who had survived from Mendoza's expedition had established themselves high up the river Paraguay at Asunción. He sent ahead his friend Pedro Dorantes from Béjar (presumably a cousin of that Dorantes, Andrés, with whom he had crossed America) to find out what the territory was like and himself began a journey to Asunción with 250 men and twenty-six horses.[7]

This was another great walk for Cabeza de Vaca. He took four months to reach Asunción from Santa Catalina and attained his destination without losing any man or horse. On the way the adventurers saw extraordinary sights, such as the waterfall of the river Iguazú.[8] At one point Cabeza and his followers lived off worms: 'in the hollows of these [bamboo] reeds there were white worms, *calandra palmarum*, about the length and thickness of a finger. The people eat these, obtaining enough fat from them to fry them very well.'[9]

In Asunción Cabeza conducted himself as a man of the new enlightened era of Las Casas, and tried to make his fellow settlers pay taxes and treat Indians as human beings. This caused fury and he was opposed by

Martínez de Irala, who had been serving as interim governor. The position was rendered more complex by the fact that Cabeza de Vaca was attracted, even seduced, by stories of fabulous wealth in the South American interior. The myth of Alejo García and his journey to the fabulous white chief was current, almost as if it had been a real chivalrous novel.[10] Cabeza organized a new expedition into the interior after hearing promising news along those lines from Martínez de Irala. They sailed up the river Paraguay from Asunción almost to its source. But they found nothing, and the white chief was notable for his absence. They went back after a year, ill, poor and unhappy.[11]

On their return to Asunción, the quarrel between Cabeza de Vaca and Martínez de Irala became a public one. Even though the great walker had been tolerant to Martínez de Irala and named him his *maestre de campo*, eventually Martínez de Irala felt that he had to act against what he argued to be an improperly designated governor. Basing himself on his local authority, which Cabeza had never replaced, Martínez de Irala arrested his governor and sent him home to Spain in chains on a caravel, accompanied by his notary, Pedro Hernández. Officers on board the ship (Alonso Cabrera, García Venegas) thought this too great a dishonour for Cabeza de Vaca, who was not only the hero of North America but had, after all, been named governor by the king. At least Cabeza could return as a free man. They reached home on 15 August 1545.

In Spain things went ill for him. After some months' delay, he appeared before the Council of the Indies, where he was accused of thefts of food and horses in the Canary and Cape Verde islands on his way out to South America. The prosecutor, Marcelo Villalobos, also presented a series of accusations made by the settlers in Asunción, who spoke with one voice about Cabeza de Vaca's hard stand on taxation and soft attitude towards Indians. He suddenly found himself not a hero of the empire but an accused prisoner. He said that he was 'poor, lost and bankrupt'. He was duly arrested and, though released under provisional freedom after a mere month in gaol, he never recovered his health nor his morale. Living in Madrid, he devoted his time to collecting material for his defence. Three years passed.

The Council of the Indies eventually found against Cabeza de Vaca. His punishment was to be stripped of the grandiose titles granted him in 1540, to be prohibited from returning to the Indies, and to accept that settlers in Asunción could pursue private petitions against him. He was also, remarkably for the national hero that he really was, condemned to forced labour in the galleys of Algiers. He appealed against this and managed to secure the removal of that punishment. He died poor in Valladolid in 1556, a victim of his weaknesses, leaving behind only the memory of his astonishing achievements.

Domingo Martínez de Irala, now established in Asunción, very far indeed from Buenos Aires, was the master of the field in the region of the river Plate. He had come to the Indies for the first time with Mendoza, then had accompanied Ayolas up the Paraguay, and had been with him at the foundation of Asunción. At Ayolas's death, he was named governor – nothing more, no *adelantado*-ship nor captaincy-general – of the Spaniards in the Río de la Plata. He was unceasingly active in the fortification of Asunción, naming a town council and controlling the countryside.

Another Spanish proconsul, Diego de Sanabria, soon arrived with orders to establish himself in the Spanish ports on the Atlantic coast, to the south of the Portuguese colony of San Vicente, where in fact many Spaniards had taken refuge.

Later Martínez de Irala had to contend with new rivals for authority in those remote plains, namely, Gonzalo de Mendoza and then Diego de Abreu. But he survived these difficulties – though it seems probable that he had Abreu assassinated when he saw that he could not control him peacefully. For some years afterwards this tiny colony lived in approximate peace – untouched by the journeys through what became northern Argentina of some conquistadors from Peru led by Diego de Rojas, Felipe Gutiérrez and Nicolás de Heredia, including some 200 wanderers in search of riches and fertile land, among them women, slaves and Indian bearers. But Rojas was killed, Gutiérrez discredited and Heredia, a notary, eventually died in the Peruvian civil war, so nothing came of that promising incursion. Martínez de Irala, the least remarkable of all these conquistadors in the south-east of the continent, proved the most enduring. His grandson, Ruy Díaz de Guzmán, wrote the first authoritative history of his achievements.[12]

A characteristic of his government was the swift development of a mestizo society based on the fact that Spanish women were rare and unusual. The percentage of natives who acted as wives to the conquistadors was far higher than anywhere else in South America. The mestizos were, therefore, more numerous.[13]

40

New Spain
with Antonio de Mendoza

> *To the third question answered that after the said lord Viceroy came to this New Spain, this witness used and exercised an authority from the accountant Rodrigo de Alborñoz, that is office of chief financier for about two years more or less ...*
> Juan de Burgos, *Información* of Antonio de Mendoza

In April 1535 Antonio de Mendoza was named viceroy of New Spain. He would also be president of the *audiencia* in succession to the wise Ramírez de Fuenleal. Cortés, the conqueror who had made New Spain possible and had given the place its name, would remain captain-general at the viceroy's pleasure – a title without weight in these strange circumstances.[1]

Mendoza was to represent the person of the monarch, to administer equal justice to his subjects of all races, and his vassals, and to be active in everything to ensure the 'peace, quiet and prosperity' of the Indies. He was to help in the conversion of Indians to Christianity, and govern his viceroyalty according to his best understanding. He was to have general authority over all appointments to ecclesiastical positions within his viceroyalty, even bishoprics, as the pope had agreed. He was to visit all the towns of New Spain so far as he could. He should carry out a census. Existing indigenous temples, 'heathen' temples, should be sought out, for who knew whether they had gold and silver there. Abuses of the Indians should, however, be investigated and punished.

Mendoza's salary would be 3,000 ducats as viceroy, 3,000 as president of the supreme court. This was a substantial increase in comparison with what was paid to Guzmán or to the governor of Cuba. Numerous grants of land, wood, water and grazing rights completed his emoluments. As he was not formally a *letrado*, a university-educated lawyer, he could not vote in the supreme court of which he was president but, all the same, his signature was necessary to make decisions of the court binding. He was the first viceroy of Spain in the New World.

In his letter of appointment to Mendoza, the emperor suggested various ways of increasing the royal income from New Spain. Gold and silver could be sought more intensively than theretofore. There should be payments of tithes direct to the Church to avoid having to pay civil servants to count what was due to the great institution. Perhaps silver mines might be directly run by the Crown instead of it taking a fifth from those privately run. The viceroy was also to help two German entrepreneurs, Enrique and Alberto Girón, to develop saffron and blue dyes.[2]

Defence had to be considered. The Spaniards were to be concentrated in one part of the city of Mexico and a second fortress was to be considered for the causeway to Tacuba, to balance that existing in the shipyard to the east of the city. Mendoza should establish a mint.[3] The viceroy could distribute *encomiendas* if he thought fit.

The beneficiary of all these provisions, Antonio de Mendoza, was the son of Íñigo López de Mendoza, the Count of Tendilla, who had been a successful ambassador to the Vatican and then a most effective, if liberal, governor of Granada. It would seem certain that his father's determined tolerance and grand style influenced Antonio. Viceroys in Mendoza's view had to live like kings – but just kings. His mother, Francisca Pacheco, was the daughter of Juan Pacheco, the Marquis of Villena, who was the dominant nobleman in the reign of King Enrique IV of Castile. A sister of Antonio de Mendoza's mother, his aunt Beatriz, was that Countess of Medellín who had employed Cortés's grandfather as *mayordomo*. Beatriz's brother, the Marquis of Escalona, after a politically equivocal youth became known in his old age as the enlightened 'old marquis' who kept a benign Erasmian court at his house in Escalona in the foothills of the Gredos mountains. Antonio de Mendoza's brothers and sisters included the all-too-famous María who married the hero of the *comuneros*, Juan de Padilla, and she herself was a heroine of that war after her defence of Toledo against the Crown; his brother, Francisco, was an ambassador and viceroy of Naples; and another brother, Diego Hurtado de Mendoza, would be the accomplished ambassador to Venice and Rome who would write a history of the last Spanish war against the Moors in the Alpujarra mountains in the 1560s. Of course, the viceroy's paternal grandfather was the famous Íñigo, first Marquis of Santillana, grandfather-in-chief to the Spanish aristocracy in its golden age.[4] The memory of the great cardinal Rodríguez de Mendoza survived.

Antonio de Mendoza was born in 1492 in Alcalá la Real, a picturesque town between Jaén and Granada, built on a conical hill. Having been taken from the Moors by Alfonso XI in person, it acquired the suffix 'Real', royal, in 1340. Visitors are shown a tower, La Mota, or *el farol*, which Antonio's father built to be a light guiding those Christians who had escaped from Granada. This town was the headquarters of the Spaniards fighting the Moors and, when Antonio was born there, it was at 'the front'.

Mendoza's childhood was mostly passed at Granada just after its conquest by the Castilians. Eminently an aristocrat, he was brought up to despise the *letrados*, who, as civil servants, increasingly dominated the Spanish government. In 1521 Mendoza was at Huéscar with 500 foot and a hundred horsemen and defeated the *comuneros* there. In 1526 he went to Hungary as an emissary of the Emperor Charles to his brother Ferdinand, the king of the Romans, just after the terrible battle of Mohács, with some letters of credit worth 100,000 ducats. He was in England in 1527 and encountered King Henry VIII at Greenwich. Then he became chamberlain of the empress, to whom he said that he would be interested in going to Mexico. In 1530 he went as the personal messenger of the queen regent to the emperor, who was then at Bologna. He was named viceroy in April 1535, an appointment made by the empress.

The country for which he assumed responsibility was in a far better condition than it had been when the second supreme court had taken over. Then it had seemed as if the president of that body's predecessor, the first court's president, Nuño de Guzmán, was seeking to link the province of New Galicia, which he was busy conquering, with his old responsibility of Pánuco in order to create a big new realm for himself. The disorder in the city of Mexico was also considerable. The trade in slaves in Pánuco was out of control, despite its illegality.[5]

Because Guzmán had seized 10,000 pesos from the treasury of the city of Mexico in order to conquer New Galicia, the second supreme court confiscated all Guzmán's property in the capital, as well as all that in Pánuco.[6] Certain prominent settlers in New Spain thought that

Pánuco should be merged with New Spain as a province. This business of the disentangling of Pánuco from its union with the rest of Guzmán's realm occupied much of the early 1530s.

The second supreme court found itself immediately in difficulties over recent decisions in Spain. For example, on 2 August 1530 an ordinance had been proclaimed in Madrid on the subject of enslavement. It was resisted by all officials of the Spanish Crown in the Indies. It stated that 'no person should venture to make a single new slave whether in peace or in war . . . whether by barter, purchase, trade or any pretext or cause whatever'. The penalty for a breach of this law would be the loss of all wealth and of Indians so enslaved. Within thirty days, everyone who owned (Indian) slaves was to register them and prove that they were true chattels. After that, there was to be no more enslaving.[7]

In August 1531 the supreme court of New Spain wrote to the Crown saying that, if the law about slaves were enacted, the colonies would soon be in rebellion, once the Indians learned of their freedom. No Spaniard would want to help to put down such a rebellion, for there would be no reward for his efforts. The Council of the Indies, therefore, hesitated over its policy.

There had, however, been some positive new policies. One was the foundation of Puebla de los Ángeles in Tlaxcala, in 1531. It was to be a city of workers, not of *encomenderos*. Its creator was Alonso Martín Partidor, who had arrived in New Spain in 1522 and married a *conquistadora*, María Estrada Farfán, who had accompanied Narváez, and indeed had been at the Noche Triste, the classic battles on the causeways and at Otumba.[8] She had first been married to Pedro Sánchez Farfán, who had died, and she had inherited the *encomienda* of Tetela.[9] Martín Partidor received the enthusiastic help of 7,500 Tlaxcalteca. To encourage people to live in this new city, the Crown gave numerous fiscal benefits to settlers there so that, by the time of Mendoza's arrival as viceroy, there were eighty-two *vecinos* in Puebla, among them thirty-two conquistadors of the first wave.[10]

New Spain was increasingly conformist. In 1533 a large Augustinian convent was built in the city of Mexico, reflecting the arrival in May of seven friars of that order. The Mercedarians also built their own refuge, appropriately, considering the role played by the Mercedarian friend of Cortés, Fray Bartolomé de Olmedo, in the conquest of New Spain.

Dr Ramírez de Fuenleal had reached New Spain only in September

1531, but there had been an immediate transformation in how political matters were managed there. The new judges petitioned the Crown to increase their number, for, they said, they found that their work needed twelve hours a day, the *residencia* of their predecessors was itself a Herculean task and they were absorbed all the time with the conversion of the natives and with the regulation of relations with the Church. It seemed that only Vasco de Quiroga was up to the burdens involved, and even he was more interested in the problems of the Church than those of general administration. The other judges, Alonso de Maldonado, Juan de Salmerón[11] and even Fuenleal were old and tired.

This supreme court, it is true, enacted some astonishing reforms. For example, Indians were formally to have equal rights with Spaniards and they were to be trained in Spanish methods of administration. The two 'republics', as it was put at first, were to be treated equally. Perhaps the most surprising innovation was a decree of 10 December 1531 by which officials in New Spain were instructed to keep a ledger in which they were to register the balance between good and bad conduct of each *encomendero* every two years.[12]

Of the members of the second *audiencia* the most remarkable was Vasco de Quiroga, 'Tata Vasco', as he was universally known, a son of a Gallego nobleman who had become governor of the *priorazgo* of San Juan in Castile.[13] 'Tata Vasco', who was born in Madrigal de las Altas Torres in the late 1470s, was a lawyer, having attended the university of Salamanca. He was judge of the *residencia* against Alfonso Páez de Ribera, who had been denounced by two Savoyard merchants for seizing their goods when he was *corregidor*. Quiroga then lived at the court, where he became friendly with Juan Bernal Díaz de Luco, a Sevillano who became bishop of Calahorra, a protégé and then secretary of Archbishop Tavera, and later a member of the Council of the Indies.[14] With him, Quiroga is said to have discussed the role of Spain in the Indies in the criticism included in Antonio de Guevara's *El Villano en el Danubio*.[15] (Here an uncivilized peasant astonishes the Senate by his wisdom in condemning the greed of his conquerors.) Perhaps it was Díaz de Luco who suggested Quiroga as judge in New Spain, but the empress also favoured it.

Quiroga went to a monastery to seek divine guidance as to whether he should accept his nomination. The voices of the monks spoke favourably for going ahead. Once in New Spain, he set about planning his first *pueblo-*hospital, of Santa Fe at Tacubaya. His aim was to create a place where

Indians would be educated by friars to live in a Christian way, to carry out conversions and to effect benevolent missions among the sick. He explained all this in a letter to the Council of the Indies in August 1531.[16]

We need to recall that this was the era of the humanist Juan Maldonado, who, in a tower on the walls of Burgos in 1532, evoked a Christian America. The worst savages would acquire in ten years the purest of orthodox faith. Being blessed by Nature, they could live an idyllic life free from both fraud and hypocrisy. There was no false modesty or decorum, only shame for morally reprehensible actions. Men and women mixed together in games like brothers and sisters. The shops were so well supplied that the customers helped themselves. Such heavy agricultural labour as was needed was carried out by all.[17] Quiroga had a similar view, since he said: 'Not in vain but with much cause and reason is this called the new world because in its people and in almost everything it is like the first golden age.'[18]

In 1533, still a member of the supreme court, he went up to Michoacan to find out what was happening there. He reported how surprised he was to find the natives so capable of juridical expression and the conquistadors so evil, for they were already exploiting indigenous people in copper mines. So he founded his second *pueblo*-hospital in Santa Fe de la Laguna, near the old capital of Michoacan, Tzintzuntzan. There was a protest by *encomenderos*. For example, Juan Infante said that he had received land there from Cortés himself; actually it was from Estrada.[19] Here in 1535 Quiroga would say firmly that 'the people of this land and of the new world generally are almost all of one quality, very mild and humble, timid and obedient. They should be brought to faith by good Christian influence not by war and fear.' He strongly opposed the use of Indians as slaves, which he thought an invention of the devil. He said: 'those who allege Indian vices have their own profit in mind. I have never seen the abominations charged by those who desire to defame them . . . [but] persons who have Indians serving them use them not as men but as beasts and worse.'[20] Thus Quiroga began his mission in a quite new mood. By this time, incidentally, he had already sent a legal brief to the Council of the Indies suggesting that the life of the native Indians should be regulated by placing them in villages,

> where by working and tilling the soil they may maintain themselves with their labour and may be ruled by all good rules of policy and by holy and

good and Catholic rules; where there may be constructed a friar's house, small and not costly, for two or three or four brothers who may not leave their task till such time as the natives have acquired the habits of virtue.[21]

He suggested that the laws of which he had read in Sir Thomas More's *Utopia* should be introduced. Thus a city of 6,000 families – each composed of from ten to sixteen couples – would be ruled, regulated and governed as if it were a single family. Each magistrate would control thirty families and each governor would preside over four magistrates. These could be chosen by a method copied from *Utopia*. The supreme court would appoint a mayor-in-chief or *corregidor*.[22]

Quiroga wanted to establish 'a priest in each district' and talked hopefully of 'the simplicity and humility of the aborigines; men who went barefoot, bare-headed but long-haired as the Apostles were'.[23]

At the end of 1531 there had been a remarkable occurrence which affected for ever all relations between Spaniards and Indians. The Indian Juan Diego 'met' the Virgin Mary on the hill of Tepeyac just outside Mexico, on the north of the town. She appeared three times and left a picture of herself on a shroud which was taken to Zumárraga, who organized a chapel there. Cortés supported Zumárraga in his identification. No matter that the sceptics about the matter included Franciscans and their brother fraternities, the Dominicans and Augustinians, who pointed out that the hill of Tepeyac had been a Mexican holy site before the conquest. The belief grew and the consequent cult soon began to seem of the greatest importance for the Christian faith of the Indians. It remains so and transformed Mexican and Christian history.

There were also more practical ideas afoot. Early in 1533 Gaspar de Espinosa, the richest and most influential settler in Panama, later a great entrepreneur in Peru, suggested to the Council of the Indies that a canal might be dug from the Pacific to the Atlantic. This would be at the level of the river Chagres, near the line of the canal which was eventually built by Ferdinand de Lesseps in the twentieth century. But Espinosa died before he could do anything to help to carry this great project to fruition.

In July 1532 the supreme court in New Spain informed the empress that they were sending the description and account of the land and the people of the conquistadors and settlers. The viceroyalty, they considered, should be divided into four provinces. In November 1532 ex-judges Matienzo and Delgadillo sailed for Spain, taking with them a wooden box containing the depositions of the supreme court and descriptions of the land.

Such was the New Spain to which Antonio de Mendoza, now forty-three years of age, would devote the next fifteen years – in effect the rest of his life. He arrived at Veracruz in October 1535 with a large number of followers and relations. It was as if he were really a monarch. Spanish viceroys in Galicia, Navarre or Naples, though they had that title, never had enjoyed such style. Mendoza was greeted at Veracruz by two members of the municipality of Mexico, Gonzalo Ruiz and Francisco Manrique, soon to be supplemented by Bernardino Vázquez de Tapia and Juan de Mansilla, both old associates of Cortés. Mendoza then went up to the city of Mexico, where, on 14 November, he was greeted with trumpets, acrobats, the public crier and the whole of the town council. Indigenous Mexicans made very good acrobats, as is evident to this day.

The viceroy was an absolute monarch. His rule was apparently supposed to extend throughout the Spanish Indies as far as the northern frontier, if that is not an inappropriate word, of Peru – that is, it included Colombia and Venezuela. In theory his domain thus included all Central America, Florida, California, the Antilles and the north coast of South America from Urabá or Darien to the mouth of the Amazon.[24] But even absolute monarchs have their limitations and in the case of the viceroy these came in the shape of the supreme courts, above all those in New Spain and in Santo Domingo, and later those of Guadalupe and Guatemala. The Antilles were considered a government within the viceroyalty of New Spain but were virtually independent of it in all matters save that of defence.[25]

In Mendoza's day the supreme court in New Spain sat daily from 8 a.m. till 11 a.m. On Mondays, the viceroy would attend all day. On Mondays, Wednesdays and Thursdays, there were also sessions in the afternoons, from 2 to 7 p.m., mostly given over to the affairs of the Indians. There were then hearings until 10 p.m. and on Saturdays till 9 p.m., after which there would be a visit to the prisons. On Tuesdays and Fridays from 8 a.m. till 11 a.m., the viceroy would be present as the informal president of a court. The *rapporteurs* would also be present, and every day the last hour would be given over to petitions. On

Tuesdays, Wednesdays and Thursdays, the judge would receive petitions from Indians in his own house, working with a notary and one of a vast number of translators. The judges were all men well connected in Castile and would bring their wives and children with them. They would be expected to conduct themselves as if they had been members of an aristocracy.

Mendoza's arrival in the city of Mexico came soon after a decision by the empress and the Council of the Indies that settlers in New Spain would henceforth be able to buy land in Mexico from indigenous owners. The buyer had first to establish that the land was empty, but, if he did that, he could purchase innumerable acres for very little. This decision in Valladolid on 27 October 1535 was the real beginning of the history of the great estates of New Spain.[26]

One limitation on the viceroy's power was that he could not grant sites for building in established cities. That was for the local council to decide upon. He could not even give permission to build churches or monasteries; nor could he grant titles of nobility. He could not increase salaries, certainly not his own, nor could he extend his own term, although that term did not have a date of completion.[27]

The *audiencia* had become the most important institution before the arrival of Mendoza, but now it lost much of its political power and became largely judicial. The court, where each judge was paid 500,000 maravedís a year, was still supposed to control the actions of the viceroy but it did not do so in the days of Mendoza, who conducted himself as a benign monarch more than a public servant. Mendoza's court – Alonso de Tejada, Francisco de Loaisa, Gómez de Santillán in place of Alonso de Maldonado, and Antonio Rodríguez Quesada – had to take the *residencia* of its predecessor, but there were no complaints except, bizarrely, against Quiroga, who was accused of having built his two hospital villages of Santa Fe on land belonging to Indians. But he was easily able to prove the benefit to the indigenous people.

In Santa Fe Quiroga established the common ownership of property; the integration of large families; the systematic alternation between urban and rural people; work for women; the abandonment of all luxury; the distribution of the products of common labour according to the needs of the people; and the election of judges by families.[28] Of the new judges, Tejada was once described as the first great promoter of land values in the New World. He was specially concerned in flour mills in Otumba.[29] Loaisa had the unusual privilege of being allowed into the municipality in Mexico City, an arrangement which was a considerable benefit for the Crown.

Beneath the viceroy and the supreme court there was no administration except the municipalities, which in character were transplanted direct from old Spain, and were usually known as *cabildos*. They had a variable number of councillors, but in the city of Mexico there were twelve of them, six elected each year. There were also two magistrates (*alcaldes*), while the town councillors themselves would name the others.

Mendoza had at first hoped to leave exclusively Indian towns to their native lords, but there was much confusion in this regard because some of them had their power from before the conquest, others had been nominated by *encomenderos* or churchmen. It also seemed that such indigenous lords, following the spirit of Montezuma's encouragement to his subordinates to be harsh, often treated their people worse than the conquistadors did.

The dominant figure in New Spain on the arrival there of Mendoza was the bishop of Mexico, Juan de Zumárraga, whose early life and struggle against Guzmán and his circle has already been discussed.[30] He was high-minded and resolute, and he and Fray Martín de Valencia destroyed over 500 temples in New Spain and smashed 20,000 idols.[31] Valencia added that there were already twenty Franciscan monasteries in New Spain, even if most were no more than large huts.[32] By 1532, on the other hand, the first cathedral of Mexico was completed, the builders using much of the stone of the old pyramids in the construction. Martín de Sepúlveda, the architect (he had worked on the rebuilding of Tenochtitlan as a master of works, having originally come with Narváez to Mexico), had built an aisled rectangular building with a flat wooden roof and wooden supports.[33]

Perhaps this explains the enthusiastic attitude which the supreme court had towards the Indians' capacity for Christianity. At the first ecclesiastical *junta* in the city of Mexico at which Ramírez de Fuenleal had presided, with Zumárraga in attendance, the learned good men proclaimed that there was no question but that the natives had sufficient capacity, that they greatly loved the doctrine of the faith, and that they were 'able to carry on all mechanical and agricultural arts'. The

Indian, they thought, was a rational being entirely capable of governing himself.[34]

Almost the first radical decision taken by Mendoza was one to suspend a despatch to New Spain of a large new consignment of black slaves which had been ordered and which he had wanted. The reason was not altruistic: the explanation was the discovery of a conspiracy of black slaves such as had led to a ferocious rebellion in Puerto Rico in 1527, in Santa Marta in 1529, in Santo Domingo in 1522 and in New Spain itself in 1523. The last occasion had seen a threatening alliance of Zapotecs in the neighbourhood of Oaxaca with the blacks. This was none the better for having been seen as idealistic by some romantically minded Spaniards, such as the poet Juan Castellanos. Castellanos later wrote a poem in which figure the lines 'Skilful are the Wolofs and very combative, with a foolhardy presumption to be gentlemen.'[35]

All the same, some black slaves fled their masters and the viceroyalty of Mendoza did see the establishment of a small colony of escaped Africans in the forest near the mines of Tomacustla in Veracruz, living as robbers and beginning the long history of banditry in the country.

The key to Mendoza's rule in Mexico was his court of thirty to forty gentlemen, *caballeros*, who served both as his bodyguards and his private office. This was headed by Agustín de Guerrero, his majordomo and also chancellor of the supreme court and keeper of the official seal, which could not be removed from the courtroom and without whose stamp no document could be looked on as legal. His assistant, Juan de Salazar, became almost as powerful. Luis del Castilla, a descendant of King Pedro the Cruel in the male, if illegitimate, line, was also of constant assistance to the viceroy. He had first come to New Spain in 1529 as a companion to Juana de Zúñiga, Cortés's second wife, his distant cousin. Earlier he had fought against both the *comuneros* and the French. He received an *encomienda* at Tututepec in 1534 and lived sumptuously, as perhaps a king's bastard cousin should: 'Even the servants drank from silver,' commented Dorantes de Carranza admiringly.[36] But he gave away a great deal to the poor, especially to the Spanish poor in New Spain.

Mendoza had sixty Indian servants and insisted that they were taught music and everything to do with 'minstrelsy'. He received the harvests from numerous ranches – one in the valley of Matalcingo, five near Maravatio, in Michoacan, two near Tecamachalco, including the site of Cortés's victory after the Noche Triste at Otumba; and one, a ranch for

438

horses, in the valley of Ulizabal. These ranches produced the meat and the wool needed in the viceroy's household.

Mendoza lived in the city of Mexico in the great house of Axayactl which Cortés had converted into a Spanish palace, next to the one-time 'holy' precinct of the ancient Mexicans. He lived there with his son, Francisco, and his sister, María (later viceroys were not allowed to take their families with them). Mendoza's wife, Catalina de Vargas y Carvajal, apparently died before he left for Mexico.

Mendoza rose early and would listen to petitioners at all hours, not just those prescribed by the supreme court. He was always friendly, if always brief. He travelled continuously, as if he had been a king of Castile. He was able to grant *corregimientos*, *encomiendas* and Indians. No act of a town hall had validity unless he approved it. He could proclaim laws and, in that respect, was dependent only on the approval of the distant Council of the Indies.

From all these discussions, Cortés the conqueror was excluded. Mendoza as viceroy found the overpowering personality of that great conqueror difficult to manage. But he had been excluded from consideration at court in Spain. He had been made a marquis, he had married an aristocrat, he had a family, he had become rich. What more, people asked in Valladolid, did he want? There was just a sense that the court was afraid of Cortés. He had done too much to be easily pleased by any second-rate position. Cortés's resentment at this was expressed by him in a memorandum to Charles the emperor in June 1540. Having alluded contemptuously to an expedition northwards of Fray Marcos de Niza, he went on to talk of his own discovery and conquest of the land and how he had sent four fleets at his own cost (300,000 ducats) in order to discover the north.[37]

It was not just Marcos de Niza whose plans had offended Cortés. There was the fact that Pedro de Alvarado had also secured a contract to search for islands – those of Santa María off Puerto Vallarta (as it later became). He took 600 men and twelve ships from Guatemala, met and negotiated with Mendoza's friends Luis del Castilla and Agustín Guerrero and worked out an agreement whereby Alvarado would have a quarter share in the profits of the viceroy's expeditions, while Mendoza could have a half interest in Alvarado's fleets. This looked like an effective prohibition on Cortés from making further conquests, and Cortés's protest was serious.

But the viceroy had his own problems. For example, there was the Mixton war, a serious Indian rebellion probably provoked by the brutality of many *encomenderos* in the north of New Spain. The viceroy, who had been preoccupied by the new plans of Francisco Vázquez de Coronado and Fr Marcos de Niza (which he had backed), thought, however, that the rebellion was by the wild Chichimeca Indians from the far north, with a new religion, brought to them by 'messengers of the devil'.[38]

There was also much brutality attached to work in the mines, for example those at Oaxtepec, where Fr Motolinía, who, it is true, usually exaggerated, said the work was so destructive that for 'half a league around it one could not walk without stepping on dead men and bones and so many birds came to scavenge that they darkened the sky'.[39] Rumour had it that the Indians were dancing round a pumpkin when a gust of wind carried it away and the sorcerers said that that meant that the Indians should rise against the Spaniards.[40]

At all events, in this region to the north of the viceroyalty, ancient rulers and some of their families assembled on the hill of Tepetiquipaque and revived their ancient religious practices, including human sacrifice. Several local *encomenderos* were forced to leave, some (such as Toribio de Bolaños) were wounded and fled to Tlatenango, where Diego de Ibarra, assisted by four Franciscans, sought to establish an armed force to fight the rebellion.[41] There ensued the most serious conflict between Christians and Indians since the conquest.

The indigenous rebels were cheered by mysterious messages from the alleged devils of the old days. For example, in the valley of Tlatenango a messenger declared:

> we are the messengers of Tecoroli [the devil, according to the Spaniards]. Accompanied by his ancestors, whom he has revived, he is coming to seek you. He will make you believe in him, not in [the Christian] God, on pain of never seeing the light again and being devoured by wild beasts. Those who believe in Tecoroli and renounce the teaching of the friars will never die, but will become young again and have several wives, not just one, as the friars order and, however old they may be, they will beget children. Whoever takes only one wife will be killed. Tecoroli will come to Guadalajara, Jalisco, Michoacan, Mexico and Guatemala, in fact wherever there are Christians, and will kill them all. After that, you will be able to go home and live happily with your ancestors, suffering no more hardship or pain.[42]

Among the leaders of the rebels was Tenemaxtli, who had once had a mission to take the catechism to the converted. Under his leadership, the rebels burned the churches at Tlatenango and at Cuzpatelán. They also burned the convent at Juchilpa. Christian Indians were made to do penance for the time that they had been Christians, washing their heads to free themselves from the memory of the cross. They killed Fray Juan de Esperanza at Tequila outside Guadalajara and Fray Juan Calero near Etzatlan, and Fray Antonio de Cuéllar was assassinated near Ameca.[43]

Diego de Ibarra, an able conquistador, was persuaded to face the rebels. He had only seventeen Spanish horsemen but he had about 1,500 Tonalá Indians who had always opposed the Mixton people, and he also had the more doubtful support of some Cascan Indians. Some of the Tonalá told of a planned ambush by the Cascanes in a cedar-lined gully where the Spaniards would be unable to use their horses effectively. Ibarra had several Cascanes executed but, all the same, they attacked, wounded Ibarra and some others, as well as some of the precious horses. The Spaniards retreated first to Suchipala, then to Guadalajara, rescuing numerous compatriots en route (for example, Fray Bobadilla at Teul). By then the rebels were established throughout the area of the river Tololotlan.

Mendoza at first thought that this rebellion was a local affair. Then he realized that the threat was colony-wide and he hastened to Guadalajara. There he sent out a peace mission headed by Fray Martín de Jesús, and guarded by Ibarra. Its failure convinced Mendoza that force had to be used. He assembled together a council in Guadalajara, with Licenciado Francisco Marroquín, the bishop of Guatemala, Ibarra who was recovering, and Cristóbal de Oñate, who had been Nuño de Guzmán's deputy in New Galicia and had founded Guadalajara in 1531, naming it after Guzmán's birthplace. They resolved to despatch Oñate with fifty horsemen against the Mixton camp on a hillock. The Indians fought well, and thirteen Spaniards were killed as well as six black slaves and a large number of Indian allies. This battle was the signal for many further revolts throughout New Galicia and Jalisco.

The continued threat persuaded Mendoza to call on Luis del Castilla and Pedro de Alvarado to abandon their planned journeys of discovery in the Pacific. They landed near Colima and made for Guadalajara with a hundred horsemen and an equal number of foot soldiers, which put paid to any Indian advance on that city. Mendoza also sent a hundred men from Mexico under Íñigo López de Anuncibay and ordered another member of the large Alvarado family to move in from Michoacan with thirty horse and a huge number of Mexican foot, perhaps 5,000.

There followed a meeting under Oñate's direction in Guadalajara to formulate a plan of action. Pedro de Alvarado, impatient to return to his voyage of discovery, told his colleagues that they were children in their timidity and declared that, with his experience, he would soon personally defeat these Indians. Oñate sought to dissuade Alvarado but the latter reminded all his comrades of their lack of experience in comparison with his. Refusing Oñate's offers of help and certainly not waiting for support from Mexico, he then set off for the hill of Nochistlán and reached it on 24 June 1541.

Alvarado had with him a hundred foot soldiers, a hundred horsemen and several hundred Indian allies. First he sought to negotiate his enemy's surrender, then mounted a direct assault which was repelled with losses. Alvarado rallied, his infantry attacked without the help of cavalry, and the rebels fought them with great force. Alvarado tried unsuccessfully to rally his men again and he dismounted to prevent a headlong retreat. It was raining and the ground had become a bog. Alvarado led his horse backwards, but his secretary, Baltasar Montoya, who had come out with him in his most recent return to the Indies, slipped, and Alvarado was flung into a ravine with his horse on top of him. Oñate, watching from a nearby hillock, saved the day, prevented a complete catastrophe, and carried the wounded Alvarado back to Guadalajara. There Alvarado went to the house of his cousin, Juan del Camino, and there, victim of the impetuosity which had always been his hallmark, he died in June 1541. The first great ally of Cortés in his conquest of Mexico was thus removed, leaving a reputation for success in spite of danger, bravery in spite of cruelty, and good looks, which inspired admiration among his enemies, in place of prudence.

The Indians then besieged Guadalajara. The assault of 50,000 Mixton was beaten off with difficulty. Beatriz Hernández, surely the same *conquistadora* who had come to New Spain from Cuba with the great Cortés, was the heroine of this siege. There were several successful sorties, in one of which the tireless apostle Santiago was said yet again to have appeared on his white horse.

Mendoza sent the judge Maldonado to report on the situation in Guadalajara. He returned to say that Mendoza himself was needed.

Though he had little military experience except in the war of the *comuneros*, it was assumed that a Mendoza could automatically command men in battle. This was the great challenge to, or test of, his viceroyalty.

The viceroy did go up to Guadalajara with 180 horse, a large number of friendly Indians, perhaps several thousand, and a good quantity of artillery, the new weapon of the day.

The innovations of Mendoza's army were not only the substantial number of guns, but the fact that friendly Indian noblemen, of Mexican origin, were encouraged to use Spanish weapons, including swords, and to ride on horseback.

Mendoza travelled via Michoacan. He met Ibarra and Juan del Camino at the Tlazazalca tower near Cuina and invested that fortress, then feigned flight, returned to the hilltop, defeated the enemy easily and condemned the Indians whom he captured to death or to slavery; he seems to have felt an exemplary series of punishments was essential.

> Many of the Indians taken in the conquest of the said hill were put to death in his presence and by his orders. Some were placed in line and blown to pieces by cannon. Others were torn to pieces by dogs while others still were handed over to negroes [sic] to be put to death. These killed them by knife thrusts.[44]

After this repression, Mendoza was able, at Acatic, Istlean and Cuyutlán, to negotiate peace. He moved on to Nochistlán. Fray Juan de San Román, Fray Antonio de Segovia and Diego de Ibarra sought a truce without success. Mendoza settled down to a siege, cutting off the town's supply of water and battering down the resistance with artillery. The Indians offered peace at last but Mendoza chose to launch an assault, on the ground that anyone who offers peace can be more easily defeated. He triumphed. He moved to Mixton hill, where the bulk of the enemy had gathered. Ibarra and Francisco Maldonado made a new offer of peace, but it was rejected. Mendoza then moved to Suchipala where 800 Indians appeared, to sacrifice chickens to the rain god Tlaloc and to sing hymns. He again sent Ibarra to propose peace but he was again turned down.

Mendoza spent the next three weeks besieging the Mixton camp. There were daily proposals of peace and also daily enfilades of artillery. The Indians on Teul deserted and betrayed an oath not to disclose the way to the top of their hill. The hill soon fell, once the viceroy's horsemen made their presence powerfully felt on the summit but they purposely permitted the Indians to escape, hoping to save lives and so spare the *encomenderos* the loss of all their Indians. This broke the back of the revolt. The captives were divided up as slaves and the war ended by the capture of Ahuacatlan.

Mendoza returned to Mexico where his victory was celebrated solemnly, with rejoicing and many festivities. A general rising of Indians, which had seemed for a time a real possibility, was thus avoided. The viceroy was afterwards accused of causing unnecessary cruelty, a charge that he successfully fended off.

During these celebrations the news came that Diego da Almagro the younger had rebelled in Peru. Mendoza wrote: 'it would appear that the Marques del Valle [Cortés] would be a very good person to remedy the problems down there, because of the experience he has of that kind of matter and I would help him as much as possible'.[45] It seemed that the viceroy was seeking a way to rid himself of the brooding marquis. But if that was so he was unsuccessful. Anyway the crisis in Peru lasted a short time only.

Mendoza's victory over the Mixton Indians coincided with many steps taken to demonstrate that the Spanish presence in New Spain was no ephemeral phenomenon. Nothing, for example, could be less transitory than the beginning of the great cathedral of Patzcuaro, the inspiration for which came from Bishop Quiroga, who sought to create a building as big as the cathedral of Seville on the model of the cathedral of Granada. The plan which Quiroga requested of Hernando Toribio de Alcázar was to have five naves culminating in a great central chapel. The construction began and went on for twenty years, but thereafter the pace of building declined.

Another confirmation of Spanish grandeur was Mendoza's insistence on sending Ruy López de Villalobos on an expedition from Acapulco to the islands off Asia discovered by Magellan, who had died there – thereby incurring the ire of Portugal.[46] Villalobos's expedition was intended to found a colony in that archipelago, but he and his friends established themselves in a land which was claimed by Portugal and the Emperor Charles eventually told Mendoza that he accepted the Portuguese map-making and that he would have to abandon the settlement which had been founded. Mendoza wrote to Juan de Aguilar that he hoped that one day he or one of his sons might be permitted to stand on the line of demarcation between Spanish and Portuguese interests armed with a sword in order to demonstrate what belonged to them.[47] A Spanish ship from this expedition under Álvaro de Saavedra landed in Hawaii and two Spaniards were said to have remained to marry into the royal line of those islands. All the same, Villalobos gave the Philippines their name in honour of Prince Philip. Villalobos did not return to New Spain, staying in the Moluccas protected by Saint Francis Xavier.

Another expedition was despatched by Mendoza up the west coast of California, under a Portuguese, Juan Rodríguez Cabrillo, with a Valencian, Bartolomé Ferrelo, as chief pilot. They left Navidad in June 1542, were at Cabo San Lucas on 3 July and, by the end of September, in San Diego (which they called San Miguel). They continued north, dropped an anchor in Cuyler's Bay, and rounded Port Concepción in early November, being already north of San Francisco, whose superb harbour they did not see. Their furthest northern point was approximately Fort Ross, where they turned south again, resting in Cuyler's Bay, where Rodríguez Cabrillo died in early January 1543. Ferrelo took over and determined to sail north again. He got as far as the river Rogue, halfway to what is now Canada. This was a triumph of navigation, for they had returned successfully to Navidad by 14 April 1543.[48] We can look on it as one more triumph by Viceroy Antonio de Mendoza.

Meantime, Vasco de Quiroga, a bishop after 1537 and, consequently, richer, was still busy in his attempts to use *Utopia* as a guide to good governance. We know a good deal of Quiroga's thinking since he was never silent about his meditations. Thus we hear that after his first reading of *Utopia*, Quiroga came upon the account by the philosopher Lucian (born about AD 120) in the form of a dialogue about the *Saturnalia*, as translated by More with the help of Erasmus. This led Quiroga to suppose that 'the simple people of New Spain would be found capable of dwelling in the state of innocence of the golden age' as indicated by Lucian. These people were ready for whatever one might make of them. The task of civilization in the New World should therefore consist not in transplanting the old culture among the newly discovered peoples but in raising them to the standards of primitive Christianity. More's *Utopia* would be the instrument of the elevation.[49]

41

Coronado and the seven
magic cities of Cibola

No one has ever seen me saddened by reverses or cheered by
triumphs.

Tirant lo Blanc, 90

By the late 1530s successive expeditions by conquistadors had revealed
an outline of the geography and much of the social organization, such
as there was, between New Spain and Guatemala on the one hand and
Panama on the other. Those 1,000 miles of isthmus, mountain and lakeside no longer held grandiose secrets. It was quite a different story with
the territory to the north. So it was logical that the Viceroy Mendoza,
as curious as he was intelligent, should seek an expedition north of
New Spain, and north of New Galicia, and of anywhere known to the
conquistadors.

The first such journey was led, unusually, by a clever Franciscan, Fray
Marcos de Niza. Born in Nice – hence his name – he went, already a
member of his order, to the New World in 1531. First in Santo Domingo,
then in Nicaragua and Guatemala, later he went to Peru with Pedro de
Alvarado, where he was the leader of the first Franciscan mission. He
returned soon after to Guatemala and became vice-commissioner of the
Franciscans in New Spain.

In 1536 he was sent by the viceroy as head of a small expedition of
discovery to the north. The main part of his group remained in Culiacán
while he went on with the legendary Estebanico, Cabeza de Vaca's black
companion across half the continent, and a lay brother, Onorato, across
half the continent. They left Culiacán with some Indian bearers on 7
March 1537.[1] Then Onorato became ill and was left behind. Estebanico
went on ahead. He found interesting places such as Hawaikuh in what

is now New Mexico. He found two large crosses there and reported the place to be one of 'the seven cities of Cibola', a legendary concept which had come to dazzle settlers in New Spain. '*Cibola*' is a word used by Spaniards as a translation of 'bison', but in the hands of the new citizens of New Spain it signified something magical – an echo of the fantastical novels that played such an important part in forming the conquistadors' imagination.

Estebanico, though a man of resilience, was not one of any delicacy. He mistreated all the Indians with whom he came into contact. His ruthless insensitivity now led to a rebellion in the expedition, causing the murder of his entire group, including himself, except for three members who escaped by accident.

Fray Marcos de Niza was informed of these developments and himself went ahead in Estebanico's footprints. He wrote back to the viceroy: 'Judging by what I could see ... the settlement [of Hawaikuh] is larger than the city of Mexico. It appears to me that this is the best and largest of all the lands which have been discovered.'[2] The viceroy and monarch should by that time have been used to such extravagant commentaries about new places. But like everyone else engaged in the expansion of the empire, they had an unfailing appetite for good news. Hawaikuh was actually a hamlet in comparison to the city of Mexico. At all events the myth of Cibola was now launched. The Indian settlements concerned were the villages of the ancestors of the Zuni Indians in New Mexico.

In order to stay alive, Fray Marcos divided all the goods which he had with him among his Indians and persuaded, or induced, them to remain with him till he reached the village where Estebanico had been killed. There Fray Marcos raised a cross and then returned to Culiacán.

At the end of 1539 the viceroy decided to follow up this voyage of enquiry with another more powerful one at whose head he placed a great friend, Francisco Vázquez de Coronado, a man who seemed 'wise, skilful and intelligent'. Vázquez de Coronado was a native of Salamanca and had come to the New World with Mendoza himself. He soon set about marrying the beautiful and rich Beatriz de Estrada, daughter of the treasurer Alfonso de Estrada. Vázquez de Coronado had first of all been named investigator in the affair of Nuño de Guzmán in the *residencia* mounted against him as governor of New Galicia.

The expedition which Viceroy Mendoza wanted Coronado to lead was elaborately organized. He had, for example, Lope de Samaniego, an experienced old hand in New Spain as his general. Samaniego had gone first to New Spain as agent or representative of Peter Martyr and had returned to Spain as guard of the famous silver phoenix of Cortés. Then he went back to New Spain as *alcaide*, or commander, of the fortress of Atarazanas. The captain of Coronado's infantry was Pablo de Melgosa, his captain of horse Hernando de Alvarado, probably a nephew of the great Pedro. Coronado had altogether about 580 conquistadors with him and perhaps 2,000 Indians, most of them camp followers, porters, or cattle- or swine-herds. Fray Marcos de Niza would travel as the priest-in-charge. Among the captains was Juan de Zaldívar, a pioneer of New Granada, a future pioneer too of silver mining in Zacatecas. His house in Mexico was one of the best in New Spain and was always full of guests and visitors. Zaldívar was already married to María de Mendoza, a daughter of Cortés's reliable Genoese lieutenant, Luis Marín, of Sanlúcar de Barrameda.

Mendoza ordered an expedition by sea to escort Coronado and he asked his chamberlain, Hernando de Alarcón, to lead it. He did so, sailing up to the extreme north of the Gulf of California with three ships, the *San Pedro*, the *Santa Catalina* and the *San Gabriel*. He set off up the river Colorado, hoping there to meet Coronado. He did not find him but probably reached as far as Yuma, some fifty miles inland, before he turned back. He then returned to Santiago, in Colima, having at the least established that 'California' was not an island.

Coronado's expedition set off gaily, pennons and lances to the fore, on 23 February 1540, Viceroy Mendoza giving his blessing by accompanying it for the first two days. At Chiametla, Samaniego was wounded in the eye by an arrow but his men were rallied by Diego López of Seville. At that stage the danger seemed to be the cold, rather than the Indians. The vanguard of Juan de Zaldívar, for example, reported that the excessively low temperature had frozen to death some of the Indians with him. Reaching Culiacán, Coronado determined to press ahead with Tristán de Arellano, one of his high-born captains (a cousin of the Count of Aguilar and so of Cortés's second wife), and fifty horse and to leave the main body of the army under Fernandarias de Saavedra. Pressing on, Coronado captured Fr Marcos de Niza's town of Hawaikuh, while Pedro de Tovar and García López de Cárdenas seized several villages belonging to the Moqui Indians. They became the first Europeans to look into the Grand Canyon. Cárdenas spent several days searching for a passage down to the river in the canyon, which from above seemed to be a mere six feet across but, when they got down into the valley, turned out to be half a league wide.

After three days Pablo de Melgosa, with Juan Gallego and another who was among the lightest and most agile of men, made an effort to descend at the least difficult place and 'so went down till those who were above could not see them any more. They returned about four o'clock in the afternoon on account of the great difficulties, because what seemed to be easy from above was not so.'[3]

The whole army marched on to winter in the valley of the Rio Grande in the country of the Tigeux tribe. On the way they passed Chichilticale, 'where the wilderness begins', according to Coronado. They had expected this town to be one of the magic cities of Cibola but it turned out to be 'full of tumbledown houses of red earth' without roofs.

In the spring of 1541 the army of Coronado set out for the city of Cibola as they supposed it to be. When they arrived, Melchor Díaz would remain in charge while Juan Gallego would return to Mexico with a report for the viceroy. Fray Marcos de Niza and Tristán de Arellano would stay in the town of Señora with the weakest men, while Melchor Díaz took twenty-five strong and competent soldiers into country which turned out to be very cold indeed. It was said that there were giants there, one hundred of whom, young and old, slept in one large cabin, each carrying a *tizón* (firebrand) as they moved about. They found there a message from Hernando de Alarcón buried near a tree fifty miles up the river Colorado, which for a time they called the Tison. They also saw at Chichilticale rocky-mountain sheep and prickly pears. They were caught in a tornado which turned to snow. Finally they reached the presumed magic city, their destination, Cibola of their dreams.

Coronado sent in a small troop headed by Pedro de Tovar with Fray Juan de Padilla. The natives offered them presents of copper, cloth, dressed skins, pinenuts and turquoise mosaics, 'but not many'. The place seemed to be governed by an assembly of the oldest men. The Spaniards found it poor and small, for it was no more than 'a crowded village of small houses, one piled on top of the other without courtyards', which looked as if they had been scrambled together. 'Such were the curses that some hurled at Fray Marcos de Niza that I pray that God will protect him from them,' Fray Juan de Padilla wrote, adding: 'To tell the truth, I do not know why we have come here.' It is true that there was some food, which the Spaniards seized; and there were about 200 native soldiers, who did nothing.

The adventurers, sadly disillusioned, continued with their expedition. They reached a town on the river Sonora – which Cabeza de Vaca, passing that way, had called 'Corazones' because the Indians there had offered him the hearts of animals. Rodrigo Maldonado went to look for Hernando de Alarcón's ships but found only the very tall Indians ('giants') of whom mention has been made. Hernando de Alvarado, accompanied by Fray Juan de Padilla, made a special journey to see the bison of Cicuye of which he had been told. He took twenty companions via Acoma, a large village on a rock where he was offered corn, pine-nuts, deerskin, bread made from maize and cockerels.[4] They went on with a chief whom they nicknamed '*Bigotes*' (Moustaches) to Tigeux, where they were at least welcomed with flutes and drums. An Indian slave whom they nicknamed 'the Turk', for the simple reason that he looked like one, told Alvarado and Padilla that his country, which lay ahead, was full of gold and silver so that 'they need not look at cows'. When they returned to Coronado to tell him this good news, the Turk went on to add that in his country there were rivers with fish as big as horses, canoes with twenty rowers and sails and, on the hillside, golden eagles; everyone ate off gold plate and the chief lived under a tree with golden bells.

Coronado found this story promising, and they set off for the Turk's country. What can explain such fancies? On the way they were rejoined by Tristán de Arellano who had demanded of a local *cacique* 300 pieces of cloth, which 'he needed' because of the cold. The *cacique* told him that was impossible because the demand would have to be discussed by each town of the region. In the end the people seem to have taken off their own cloaks to provide the right quantity of cloth.

The army reunited. Gloom rather than enthusiasm characterized the conquistadors. In one village a Spaniard was accused of having violated an Indian's wife. That village and others nearby then closed themselves in behind palisades. Spanish horses chased Indians as in a bull-run, and were shot at with arrows. Coronado ordered García López de Cárdenas to surround the village where the violation had occurred. Coronado, Zaldívar and others seized the upper section of the place but López de Cárdenas did not seem to realize they had done so, and killed 200 Indians whom he had made prisoners. There followed a siege of Tigeux for fifty days with many Indian deaths and some Spanish ones. Here the good faith of the Turk was seriously criticized, for a Spaniard named Cervantes swore that he had seen the Turk talking to the devil, who had appeared in a pitcher of water. The Turk asked Cervantes how many Spaniards had been killed at Tigeux. 'None,' was the answer. 'You lie,' said the Turk. 'Five Christians have been killed at Tigeux.' That was the truth but how could he have known it if he had not been in touch with the devil?

The next adventures of the expedition of Coronado were varied and interesting. His followers became experts on the way to capture bison and were impressed at how easily they could be herded and by their vast numbers. They also noticed that the women painted their chins as well as their eyes. They had to endure hail which destroyed tents, battered helmets, broke china plates and cups, and terrified horses. Some Spaniards were lost when they went out hunting on their own. Then they reached Quivira, the Turk's town, of Wichita Indians. There the Turk had to admit that he had been lying all the time: there was no gold or silver to be found – nor it seemed had such metals ever been heard of. Coronado sent out captains in numerous directions but 'found only roses, muscat grapes, parsley and marjoram'. The Turk was garrotted, a victim of the conquistadors' credulity as well as of his own fantasies.

But the Spaniards did in the end find a territory, somewhere, we may suppose, in what is now New Mexico, where there was treasure in the shape of beautiful glazed earthenware with many figures of different shapes, as well as bowls of shining metal which looked like silver in the distance.

Coronado passed the winter at Tigeux, where Pedro Tovar joined him carrying letters from Mendoza. They whiled away the time with games. Coronado had a race with Rodrigo Maldonado, but was thrown so badly by his horse that for a time his recovery seemed improbable. Weary of the unpromising search for the magic towns, the adventurers began their return to Mexico, marked by a minor rebellion deriving from a protest headed by Pedro de Ávila. Fray Juan de Padilla stayed on at the Turk's town of Quivira and Luis de Escalona did so at Cicuye. The former was martyred within months and we must assume that the latter was also soon killed.

By June 1542 Coronado and his men had reached Culiacán and went on as fast as they could to Mexico, where the commander, 'very sad and very weary, completely worn out and very shamefaced, went to kiss the hand of the viceroy'.[5] He travelled on a litter and reached the capital of New Spain with barely a hundred men, for the rest had deserted. Suárez de Peralta, nephew by marriage of Cortés, recalls seeing the return of the expedition, with the viceroy receiving his old friend in great sadness.[6]

Yet Coronado had two achievements to his credit: he had learned much of the size of the continent and he had laid to rest the tales that there were wonderful rich new Perus and Mexicos to the north of New Spain. He later returned to his governorship of New Galicia but was soon dismissed because of poor management. A *residencia* later conducted against him by the judge Tejada talked not only of serious abuse of funds but also of mistreatment of Indians on a large scale. Coronado pleaded extenuating circumstances. He was arrested, but allowed to remain free till his appeal was heard by the Council of the Indies. He knew as well as Viceroy Mendoza that it would be a long time before the matter was resolved.

42

Montejo and Alvarado
in Guatemala and Yucatan

*The ominous thing is not the present war but the era of wars upon
which we have entered . . ., how much, how very much, that men
of culture loved, will they have to cast overboard as a spiritual
luxury?*

Jacob Burckhardt, *Reflections on History*

For several years after the conclusion of Francisco Montejo's unsuccessful attempts at the conquest of Yucatan in the early 1530s, the position
there remained confused. Montejo continued as titular governor and
maintained an interest in the territory, but he spent most of his time in
Mexico, seeking new support in men and money for his far-reaching
ambitions. In 1535 he was named governor, in addition, of Hiberas. His
wish was to exchange that remote territory for Chiapas, then ruled by
Pedro de Alvarado as part of his Guatemala. That would enable Montejo geographically to consolidate his interests better. Alvarado had just
returned from his humiliation in Peru. Impetuous in politics as in battle,
he agreed instantly. The Viceroy Mendoza also agreed.

Alvarado went immediately to this, for him, new territory. He founded
a town, San Pedro de Puerto de Caballos (now San Pedro Zula), a little
south from the Gulf of Honduras, and overwhelmed the natives in
Zompa. He sent Juan de Chávez to found a city at the remote cape,
Gracias a Dios, on the extreme east of the peninsula of Honduras. He
was not, however, a good peacetime governor, for he permitted every
kind of brutality against the Indians. He returned to Spain in August
1536 in order to tell the king of his achievements in New Spain as
Cortés had done earlier. He travelled via the Azores and Lisbon, then
made straight for the court. There he seems to have convinced the

Emperor Charles that it would be good to send a fleet to sail regularly across the Pacific to the Spice Islands. Álvaro de Paz, a relation of Cortés, said that Alvarado deliberately sought new contracts 'for the discovery of the west, for China and for the Spice Islands'.[1] Perhaps he was in fact thinking of an invasion of China. A friend of Alvarado's, Álvaro de Loarca, later recalled that he had said that he would set off for China in consequence of a definite contract he had arranged with the Crown ('and I heard say that the said *adelantado* was going to China in consequence of a certain contract which he had arranged in Spain with His Majesty'.)[2] This may have been a wild embroidery of the truth but Alvarado was capable of anything.

Alvarado returned to the Indies from Spain in January 1539 with three ships – the *Santa Catalina*, the *Trinidad* and the *Santa María de Guadalupe* – and, on board, he had not only a new wife (Beatriz de la Cueva, a sister of his dead first wife, Francisca), but also Andrés de Urdaneta, who had accompanied Loaisa on his abortive journey round the world. He was to assist him in building a Pacific fleet in Guatemala. They stopped at Santo Domingo and reached Puerto de Caballos in Honduras in April. For a time, then, Alvarado continued as governor of Hiberas with Guatemala, though it was known that he was thinking of the Pacific Ocean and of China. But he was distracted and went up to assist the Viceroy in his battle against the Chichimecas in Jalisco with the disastrous consequences which have been noticed.[3]

Alvarado left Guatemala to his new wife, Beatriz, and, for a while, she acted as the 'first woman governor' in Spanish America. It is astonishing that, given the concern in the twenty-first century with women in politics, she is not remembered better.[4] But she lasted as governor only a year, till 1542, when she was killed in a flood and earthquake in Santiago, Guatemala, with her daughter Ana. Her father, Luis de la Cueva, had been related to the famous dukes of Alburquerque, as he was to Cobos, who seems to have helped to arrange her marriage.

Guatemala enjoyed a certain continuity of Spanish rule after Alvarado's death. But that was not the case in Hiberas. Early in 1542, the authorities there wrote to Montejo asking him to take over the governorship, since there was chaos in the territory. The disputes between the town halls had been rendered worse by the nomination of the supreme court in Mexico of one of its judges, Alonso Maldonado of Salamanca, as acting governor of Hiberas as well as of Guatemala. Later, in 1544, he would become president of a new short-lived supreme court, that of 'Los Confines', the Frontiers, a tribunal later briefly established at Gracias a Dios. Maldonado had married the daughter of Montejo, a fellow citizen of Salamanca, and, therefore, it was not hard to see where his loyalties would lie. He was a man of many interests since, in addition to being a judge, he loved racing and would hold horse races in his garden in Mexico. He it was who in 1546 would write to the king that it would be for the well-being of the state if Bartolomé de las Casas were assigned to a monastery in Spain rather than a bishopric in the Indies.[5]

Montejo in these years seems to have dreamed of a large territory at his disposition, extending from Yucatan as far as Tabasco near Villahermosa in the north to the Bay of Fonseca in the south on the Pacific. He hoped that Honduras would become the commercial centre of the whole region. Guatemala would presumably adhere in due course. But still, Yucatan itself remained unconquered. Montejo commissioned his son, *el Mozo*, to complete this process.

By that time much had occurred to alter the balance of forces in Yucatan. For example, in 1535 or 1536, five Franciscans went there, headed by the interesting figure of Fr Jacobo de Testera, a well-connected churchman, who was a brother of the chamberlain to the king of France. Testera went to the Indies in 1529, was custodian of the Franciscan mission by 1533, visited Francisco Montejo *el Mozo* in Campeche and, after returning briefly to Castile, sent an enlarged mission to Yucatan, headed by the famous Motolinía, to carry out proselytization there and in nearby kingdoms. Among Motolinía's twelve followers, four later made their mark there: Fray Juan de Herrera, Fray Melchor de Benavente, Fray Lorenzo de Bienvenida and Fray Luis de Villalpando.

Testera himself was powerful because of the strength of his personality more than for his learning. Yet, though he knew no Indian language, he preached with Indian pictures (hieroglyphs) and was very effective.

Motolinía secured permission from Montejo, then in Gracias a Dios, to let Lorenzo de Bienvenida enter Yucatan by a southern route on foot via the Golfo Dulce in the Pacific. But in the end Villalpando, Benavente and Herrera went to Yucatan via Chiapas and Palenque. Four other Franciscans arrived in Yucatan direct from Spain: Nicolás de Albalate, Ángel Maldonado, Miguel de Vera and Juan de la Puerta, the last named becoming commissar and going to the site of the future Mérida where he met Bienvenida. Villalpando, meantime, learned Maya, and remained in the west of the territory, carrying through the conversion of what he claimed were 28,000 Indians. He also prepared a Maya dictionary and grammar.

In Champoton, on the coast of the Gulf of Mexico, Montejo *el Mozo*, now a relatively mature conqueror and *administrador*, received these Franciscans politely, welcoming them to his house so that the Indians would also respect and worship the Christian deities.[6] *El Mozo* had a church built for the Franciscans in Champoton and told the natives that the friars had arrived to instruct them in the true faith and lead them to a better life. This was in keeping with the firm instructions of his high-minded father: 'You must strive to see that the people who go with you shall live and act as true Christians, keeping them from evil and public sins, and not allowing them to blaspheme God nor His Blessed Mother nor his saints.'[7]

In 1540 Montejo *el Mozo* was gathering a new army together. Unlike those who had accompanied his father ten years and more before, these men seemed chastened individuals, knowing that Yucatan, unlike Peru, could boast embroidered cloths though not gold, and that there was honey, wax, indigo, cacao and slaves: all good exports.[8]

El Mozo returned from his army-raising to Champoton and there met a cousin, a nephew of his father, of the same name as them, Francisco Montejo '*el Sobrino*', the nephew. They both went up to Campeche which they re-established as a Spanish town under the name of San Francisco. They had been reinforced by 250–300 well-equipped soldiers and many, perhaps 1,000, Indian auxiliaries, including some Mexicans from Montejo senior's rich *encomienda* near the city of Mexico at Atzcapotzaltongo.

El Mozo's plan for the conquest of Yucatan was a slow process of penetration by the manipulation of a series of *pueblos* founded by the Spaniards on Indian bases, each of which would be self-supporting and with a well-ordered system of supply. Every column which attacked in Yucatan would have a means of communication to avoid isolation. The subjugation of any district beyond simple penetration would not occur till sufficient forces had been gathered. Each town would have the citizens needed to ensure its permanent success. The surrounding district would be brought under control before the town was properly settled.

This 'admirably conceived system' was described by the learned

North American historian R. S. Chamberlain as 'Roman' in its efficiency. *El Mozo* as well as his father, the *adelantado*, worked on the strategy. The columns were instructed to advance in three sections: mounted troops in the centre, with on either side well-armed foot soldiers. In pitched battles, the impact was as decisive as ever, for the Maya were never to find any real defence against the horse. The *Relación de Mérida*, a full account of the conquest published later, repeats the old story that 'at the beginning, they thought that the man and mount were all one animal'.⁹ Firearms, swords, daggers, lances and crossbows ensured the Spaniards their usual superiority. Though they often stood their ground very well, the Maya also never overcame their fear of artillery.¹⁰

The expedition left Campeche in the autumn of 1541, and a captain was sent to Tihó, a typical Indian town, which would become the present-day city of Mérida. There they came upon the remains of the old fortifications which had been thrown up during the previous Spanish occupation of the 1520s. Though the chief welcomed them and received them well, the Indians, reported one of the conquistadors, had 'haughtiness and stubbornness in their souls'.¹¹

The disputes among the Maya themselves had in the years between continued unabated, with the Cocom of Sotuta in what seemed like permanent war with the lords of Maní. The former had killed many important leaders of the Xiu people. The inhabitants of the peninsula had also wasted much of their maize during their endless wars with the Spaniards and such a famine fell on them that they were apparently reduced to eating the bark of trees, especially the tender '*kumche*'. The Xiu offered sacrifices to their gods to escape the persecution visited on them by, for example, throwing slaves into the *cenote*, the large deep natural well of Chichen Itza.

There were some resolute enemies of the Spaniards: for example, Hin-Chuy, a priest from Peba, a small *pueblo* near Tihó who preached a war of extermination against them – so much so that they were told at one stage that 'more Indians than a pelt of a deer has hairs' were threatening them.

Still, on 6 January 1542, Mérida was finally founded. The name was chosen because 'on its site they found buildings of worked lime and stone and with many mouldings', which, as Extremeños recalled, was the case in the Roman city of Mérida in Spain. Seventy soldiers were named residents and soon there was a town council. A geometrician, a friend of Alonso de Bravo who had laid out Mexico/Tenochtitlan after 1521, was asked to design the new town and a Franciscan, Fray Francisco Hernández, was requested to build the church.

There was an immediate Maya attack. The seventeenth-century historian Fray Diego de Cogulludo thought that as many as 60,000 Maya fell on the Spaniards and 'only sword-thrusts could defeat our enemies'. The natives who survived, however, fled away for ever and never again offered an open pitched battle.[12]

El Mozo sent out small bands of Spanish horsemen in all directions to carry the war into outlying districts, while the Indians sought to destroy everything which might be useful to the Spaniards. But the battle of Mérida had broken the Maya resistance. *El Mozo* occupied Techoh and Dzilam. The local chieftains were now under control.

El Mozo and his cousin next made plans for the general area of Conil in the north-east. They hoped that Conil would become a centre of commerce. They also proposed to move against Chikin-cheel and Ecale, two other regions on the far north-east of the peninsula. Independently *el Mozo* moved against interior chieftains such as Sotuta, to whom he read the *requerimiento* without, however, much success. He also defeated the proud Nachi Cocom, who was obliged to accept the formal overlordship of the Spaniards. *El Mozo* allowed him to retain his traditional authority, but as a vassal now of the king of Spain. Like other natives, whether he really understood the concept must be doubtful.[13]

Meantime, *el Mozo* despatched his uncle, Alonso López, to Calotmul and the south-east of Yucatan. Here he encountered more Xiu, who had not followed their kinsmen of Maní into an alliance with Spain. He managed to control Calotmul though without glory. Then in 1543 *el Mozo* led a well-equipped expedition into Cochuah, in the east, which had a long sea-coast. Montejo *el Sobrino* was more concerned with the north-east, where he established Valladolid in 1543, with a forceful leader named Bernaldino de Villagómez as chief magistrate. He had been *el Sobrino*'s field commander and was the younger brother of Jorge de Villagómez, who had been Cortés's chief magistrate in Xochimilcho and then in Tlaxcala, where he had befriended the son of the old ruler Maxixcastin and even accompanied him to Spain with Cortés in 1528. Thus Villagómez was part of the new aristocracy of New Spain. Once more, forty or fifty soldiers were named residents of the new town. This was a successful settlement because, so a *relación* put it, it is healthier and drier than Chuaca: 'It is the best town there is in the Indies ... [It] is surrounded by a large and rough, stony, region covered with bushes ... There are two wells of fresh water ... Captain Montejo laid out this town north, east and east-west and gave it broad streets ...'[14]

The *caciques* of Saci concerted a new attack on behalf of many towns whose efforts they organized, but Saci itself was seized for *el Sobrino* by Francisco de Cieza with only twenty Spaniards. An incipient revolt at Mérida was forestalled by Rodrigo Álvarez. *El Sobrino* then continued through Ecab where Cortés had first met the Maya in conflict, and on to Cozumel, an island to which he crossed with no opposition. Only a storm gave him reason to complain.

With his father's agreement Montejo *el Mozo* then gave the command in the south-east, Chetumal, first to Jorge de Villagómez, then to Gaspar Pacheco, his son Melchor and his nephew Alonso. They reached Chetumal early in 1544. The Indians resisted, and one of the cruellest campaigns against them began. Gaspar Pacheco and Melchor were successful in re-establishing Spanish control but they resorted to many acts of savagery. The Montejos were unable to restrain them. The Franciscan Fray Bienvenida denounced the Pachecos: 'Nero was not more cruel than this man [Alonso Pacheco],' he reported.

> Even though the natives did not make war, he robbed the province and consumed the food of the natives who fled into the bush in fear ... since, as soon as this captain captures any of them, he sets the dogs on them. And the Indians fled from all this and did not sow their crops, so that they all died of hunger ... There were once *pueblos* of 500 and 1,000 houses but now one of 100 is considered large. This captain with his own hands killed many with the garrotte, saying: 'This is a good rod with which to finish these people' and, after he had killed them, he might say: 'Oh, how well I finished them off.'

Yet there were benign acts of education, too, which must now seem more significant. For example, in the mid-1540s 2,000 Indian boys in the Franciscan school in Mérida were already being taught to read and write Maya in European script. They also learned what Christianity was and how to sing in choirs. A Franciscan house was set up at Oxkutzcab in Maní, the land of the Xiu, the Spaniards' allies. There was a school attached to it by 1547.

The Spanish military success, the foremost modern historian of these events, Inga Clendinnen, has explained, was primarily due to 'their superb discipline under pressure'. They understood the meaning of a light formation, they were aware of the value of every life, but they had the capacity to move through territory with no scruple about the cost of their actions. The crossbows, the muskets and the mastiffs all counted. Horses enjoyed their usual success when the terrain suited. Nor should one forget the three feet of Toledo steel which, in Yucatan as in New Spain and Peru, were in the right hands devastating.

The Maya were nevertheless often strong and brave. They were innovative, too. For example, they devised pits to trip up horses. But their traditions were against them in a war with Europeans for, like the Mexica, their aim in conflicts was traditionally to take prisoners and to seize booty. The Spaniards were difficult to deal with partly because they brought new diseases as well as new weapons, and the diseases led to destruction of populations. For example, the town of Champoton, where Cortés had fought and Hernández de Córdoba had been defeated, declined from 8,000 in, say, 1517, to 2,000 in 1550. Perhaps the population of all Yucatan declined from 300,000 in 1517 to less than 200,000 by 1550.

The Spanish towns in the late 1540s numbered four, headed by Mérida, with seventy families. There were forty-five families in Valladolid, forty in Campeche, while Salamanca de Bacalar had about twenty. These Spanish families in Yucatan lived in houses with courtyards, Spanish in design, certainly, but with 'an ineradicable Indian flavour',[15] for now the Spaniards on land often slept in hammocks to keep cool and, like the Indians, *their* Indians included, would wake to the sound of women grinding maize on stone slabs. Only the most common Spaniards would marry Indian women, the others would have Indian mistresses till their real wives, old or new, came from Spain.[16]

Now that the Spaniards seemed well established in Yucatan and the surrounding territories, the work of conversion to Christianity could proceed apace. A significant role was played by Bartolomé de las Casas, who was appointed bishop of Chiapas at the end of March 1544. Chiapas at that time comprised Coatzacoalcos, Tabasco, Champoton and Cozumel, as well as Soconusco, Verapaz and Chiapas itself – a large diocese.

Las Casas had travelled from Spain via Santo Domingo.[17] We hear of his arrival in Campeche from the visitor Tello de Sandoval.[18] The captain of the ship on which this great friend of the Indians sailed from Sanlúcar refused to take him any further than Hispaniola unless he received further payment. But Fray Francisco Hernández, chaplain to *el Mozo*, gave him money to enable him to go on to Tabasco and then to 'Ciudad Real de Chiapas'. Las Casas was well received in Mérida, however, and stayed with *el Mozo*, despite being threatened with death by Pedro de Mazariegos, a disgruntled conquistador from Ciudad Real in Castile. Las Casas in those years made no bones about saying that the Mexica and the Incas were as intelligent as the Greeks and the Romans. In 1544 he argued that the discovery of America was a providential decision to provide American Indians with the means of salvation. From the moment he arrived in Yucatan he set about preaching the faith without any consideration of the need for conquest. He infuriated the colonists by all his decisions in favour of the Indians – his pastoral letter of 20 March had been a striking innovation along those lines. He even refused to confess Spaniards unless they said that they were willing to hand back land taken from Indians. He would advocate the complete enforcement of the New Laws of 1542 for the protection of Indians and continued to admonish the colonists in unmeasured terms. The colonists of Yucatan, for their part, refused to recognize Las Casas's spiritual jurisdiction over their peninsula, tried to cut him off from supplies of food, and refused to pay tithes. Las Casas was thus encountering the greatest difficulty in the most important part of his diocese.[19]

Then disaster struck. At full moon on 8 November 1546 a great Maya revolt erupted. It had been carefully coordinated by the *caciques* of the Cupal – the heart and soul of the revolt – the Cochau, Solita and Vayonil–Chetumal Indians. All these peoples had formally accepted Spanish masters, but only after much protest and all longed for the day of revenge – the priests especially. They found the *encomienda* system unacceptable, with its obligations on the Indians to work a certain number of years for the conquistadors.

The Maya's greatest attack was against the Spaniards in the new city of Valladolid. There conquistadors, their wives and their children were slaughtered: some were crucified, some roasted over copal, some shot to death by arrows as if they had been Saint Sebastian, some had their hearts torn out as in a Mexican sacrifice. Bernaldino de Villagómez, the chief magistrate of the town, was dragged by a rope through the streets over which he had so recently presided, and then his head, legs and arms were cut off and carried throughout the peninsula by swift Indian couriers in order to excite the population to greater fury. They killed not only the Spaniards but all who had worked for them, as well as those Indians who would not join the rebellion. They slaughtered animals owned by Spaniards – horses, cattle, chickens, dogs and cats. They also uprooted European plants and trees.

Some *encomenderos* were found on their properties. The rebels seized them and killed many, along with their families, smoking some to death as if they had been dried meat.

The Spaniards resisted by coming together as best they could. Even in Valladolid a few organized resistance under Alonso de Villanueva, while the council of Mérida raised as many as they could to go to help Valladolid under the leadership of Rodrigo Álvarez, the reliable secretary of Montejo *el Mozo*. Francisco Tamayo Pacheco took forty men and 500 loyal Indians from there to Valladolid and relieved the garrison. Francisco de Bracamonte moved against the Indian chief Sotuta but waited at Cheguan for reinforcements. *El Sobrino* also set off for Valladolid, where Tamayo Pacheco was now the commander. He sought to break the siege and eventually did so, while Juana de Azamar, wife of Blas González, acted as the nurse of the garrison, after her brother and all his family had been killed on their *encomienda*:

> I being of but slight age was with my husband, living in our home which we refused to abandon. I gathered into our house many wounded and ill soldiers and, with great care, I healed them and cared for them till they were cured ... for there were then no doctors in this town. I likewise encouraged them not to leave this land but to remain for the service of His Majesty.[20]

The three Montejos – *el Padre, el Mozo* and *el Sobrino* – met in Champoton to discuss how to crush the rebellion. *El Mozo* assumed general responsibility for a broad military answer, while *el Sobrino* was charged with reconquering the district of Cupal, the heart of the revolt. He and Tamayo Pacheco stormed the religious centre of Pixtemax, whose fall was to prove decisive for the eventual Spanish recovery. *El Sobrino* then turned against the province of Cochant, with Hernando de Bracamonte from Medina del Campo. They had a relatively large force with which they brought all Cochant under Spanish control.

Juan de Aguilar was then sent to relieve the Spaniards in Salamanca de Bacalar: 'if it should prove that the natives greet you in peace, receive and protect them in accordance with how His Majesty commands'.[21] Aguilar was successful, the settlers there naming him their military captain, and he and they then moved against the island fortress of Chamlacan. Aguilar persuaded the chief there to surrender and to accept Spanish authority.

By March 1547, after a winter of fighting, the revolt had been quelled. Hundreds of Indians had been burned at the stake, the *caciques* and priests believed most responsible had all been captured and executed, among them Chilam Anbal, a priest who had claimed that he was the son of God. Only Chikin-cheel remained to be conquered and Montejo the proconsul sent Tamayo Pacheco, who had proved such a successful commander, to bring that province to obedience.

The campaign to suppress the revolt was carried out more brutally than previous ones mounted by the Montejos. Even the usually just *el Sobrino* committed some acts of cruelty, for he used dogs and killed some Indian women. But after the end of the emergency, the elder Francisco Montejo took legal actions against some intemperate captains.[22] Also after the revolt, *el Sobrino* summoned the surviving chiefs and addressed them, first assuring them that he would rule with justice and for the benefit of the whole province and, second, asking them why they had risen in rebellion. They replied, no doubt accurately, that it had been the responsibility of their priests.[23]

The Montejos then mounted a serious campaign to capture anew the loyalty, 'the hearts and minds', of the Indians. They invited the chiefs to their houses, and sought in a hundred ways to gain their goodwill. Fr Villalpando preached in Maya about the essentials of Christianity and invited these lords to send their sons to Christian schools. This educational revolution was among the most noble and successful of Franciscan enterprises – and one which had no obvious precedent in the old world. That initiative seems to have been an immediate success. Some important chiefs became Christians. Villalpando and Benavente thereafter went to Maní where they established another similar school in the monastery.

These moves at last helped to secure the political tranquillity of Yucatan. There were still difficulties to be tackled in the Golfo Dulce where the different competences of the Montejos, the supreme court of 'the

Frontiers', and the Franciscans seemed certain to lead to conflict, but they were resolved eventually in 1550.

Montejo *padre* the proconsul has received high praise for what he did in Yucatan. For example, R. S. Chamberlain, the best student of the conquest of the last generation, wrote: 'he was a great conquistador and had all the qualities of a good administrator. He could fight implacably but he could negotiate. He could be both magnanimous and stern. He was far from ruthless. He always sought good relations with the Indians.'[24] In addition, he introduced sugar cane into Yucatan.

His daughter-in-law Andrea del Castillo, the wife of *el Mozo*, is remembered for her comment that 'No less of a *conquistadora* can I say that I am; and, many times, the principal women of my quality when they find themselves in such conquests are as good fighters as men are.'

BOOK V
The Indian Soul

43

Las Casas, Pope Paul and the Indian soul

I have the hope that the Emperor and King of Spain overlord and master Don Charles V of the name who begins to understand the cruelties and treasons which have been committed against those poor people ... will extirpate the ills and give a remedy to this new kind which God has given him.

Las Casas, *The Destruction of the Indies*

The isthmian highway at Panama had become the vital link in transport between Peru and Spain, the goal of pirates, but it remained for a long time nothing but a primitive mule path maintained by fifty black slaves. To build and maintain forty miles of road over mountains covered with tropical forest, through swamps and jungles in one of the most deadly of climates, imposed a big demand on a new community. The inhabitants of Panama suggested that goods might best be carried five leagues to the upper reaches of the river Chagres and then floated down to the Caribbean: eighteen leagues (fifty miles) to the river's mouth. They urged that Nombre de Dios be moved west towards the mouth of the river. But even the Chagres was only explored for the first time in 1527 by Fernando de la Serna, the mariner Pedro de Coro and a notary, Miguel de las Cuesta.

In 1534 a new governor, the persistent Francisco Barrionuevo, ordered a warehouse where the river joined the sea. A third of the cost would be borne by the king, the rest by a tax on local merchandise. Efforts were made to improve the overland route, at least in summer, and much hope was placed on the efforts of Bernardino Gozna and Diego de Enciso, who were to be allowed unlimited export of wool from Peru to Spain provided that they contributed to the maintenance of the trans-isthmian highway. When the level of the river Chagres was high, the transit could be accomplished in three or four days, but, at other times, eight to twelve days were needed. To transfer goods from the mouth of the river to Nombre de Dios was only a matter of eight to ten hours.

The *tierra firme* fleets carried their cargoes to Nombre de Dios even if that port, a little to the east of what is now Colón, was never more than makeshift. The bay was shallow, full of reefs and open to the sea. The town of Nombre de Dios was not walled and consisted of 150 wooden houses, with a sandy beach in front and the jungle behind. Fever raged. Between the arrivals and departures of fleets the population was reduced to about fifty households, the east providing the best natural harbour on the Caribbean side of the isthmus, but just as unhealthy. The removal of the port from Nombre de Dios took ten years because of the need to reroute the road from Venta Cruz.

The river San Juan was mapped in 1521 by Alonso Calero, but its direction was west–east and so linked Lake Nicaragua to the Atlantic but not the Pacific. Alonso de Saavedra and Gaspar de Espinosa both proposed a scheme for a canal, it seems, but the project was set aside.

Panama in the west had most of its three to four hundred buildings in wood, even the churches. Most of the 500 inhabitants were of Andalusian origin and were merchants or transportation agents, the few exceptions being engaged in pearl fisheries, or ranching or agriculture. The carrying of goods across the isthmus provided most of the income of the city. Prices were high. Some merchants maintained stables of pack animals for use on the highway to Cruces and Nombre de Dios; others had large flat boats on the river Chagres, directed by slaves. There were probably 400 negroes. The cathedral of 1521 had but one canon, even if there was a supreme court in the town.

In 1521 there were three monasteries but all together there were only eighteen inmates. By 1607 there were five and a hospital with forty-five monks and twenty-four nuns. There were still no more than 372 dwellings of which only eight were of stone (these were the town hall and the council chamber and six private houses). In 1607 there were 550 European households, of which fifty-three were not Spanish, being mostly Portuguese or Italian, together with a hundred thatched huts occupied by about 3,700 negro slaves of whom 1,000 were concerned in transport. There were, in addition, sixty-three colonists of creole birth.

But fleets by then came only every two or three years. Brokerage licences sold in 1580 for 6,550 pesos in 1607 were worth only 4,200 pesos. The town crier who in 1575 would be hired for 2,200 pesos, in 1607 was worth only 150. The rents of the main meat market had fallen from 700 to 200 pesos a year. There were only 250 or so foot and eighteen horses available for the militia. The harbour in Panama was shallow and exposed, and the tides were so great that all larger ships resorted to nearby Perico, two leagues to the west, which was partly enclosed. In 1575 sixty-ton vessels could approach at high tide but in 1607 even small boats had difficulties.

Such was the frame against which the high dramas of Las Casas's middle career were played out.

Bartolomé de las Casas, we should remember, became a Dominican in 1522 and entered the Dominican convent at Puerto Plata on the north side of Santo Domingo after his disappointments in South America in early 1523. He then spent nine years in meditation and preparation for the next stage in his extraordinary life. He began writing his *History of the Indies*, which remains among the finest, as well as the most personal, of sources for events in the Americas between 1492 and 1525.

He emerged from his self-imposed silence, aged about fifty, in 1531 and, on 1 January of that year, wrote a pamphlet in favour of the peaceful conversion of Indians: 'that is the true path, gentlemen, that is the way to convert the people in your charge. Why, instead of sending among them peaceful sheep, do you send hungry wolves?'[1] He wrote to the king along those lines a few weeks later.[2] He went as a visitor to the Dominican house in Puerto Rico and then accompanied Dr Ramírez de Fuenleal, the new president of the supreme court of New Spain, to Mexico. But he was soon sent back to Santo Domingo, where he returned to his convent at Puerto Plata.

About that time, Las Casas met the official historian of the Spanish empire, Gonzalo Fernández de Oviedo, who then lived in Santo Domingo. Oviedo, despite spending most of his life in the Caribbean, believed that the thick skulls of the inhabitants of Hispaniola indicated a bestial and ill-intentioned mind, and he saw no chance of their being able to absorb Christianity; to think otherwise was to beat one's head against a wall.

Oviedo devotes a polite chapter to Las Casas in his *History*, in which he says that he was a fine man but had been accused of some financial irregularities.[3] It seemed that he had quarrelled with an old friend, Pedro de Vadilla, who had wanted to contest the will of an uncle who had left a fortune to the indigenous people.

Las Casas found himself temporarily back in the cell of his convent, but then he went out to meet both the Indian rebel, Enriquillo, and Tomás de Berlanga, then on the first stage of his journey to Guatemala as bishop. Las Casas went to the Dominican house of Granada in Guatemala. There Licenciado Francisco Marroquín, bishop of Guatemala, asked Las Casas to assist him in the peaceful conversion of Tuzuhitlan, which he did, setting a text about the splendour of Christianity to music. Las Casas then finished his pamphlet *De unico vocationis modo*, whose main thesis was that to evangelize was the only way to secure real victories over the Indians. Fray Bernardino de Minaya, who, as a deacon, had helped to found the glorious gilded Dominican monastery in Oaxaca, New Spain, sent Las Casas's ideas to the newly elected Pope Paul III (previously Cardinal Alessandro Farnese).

This was a time when churchmen were beginning seriously to advocate the cause of Indians. In 1533, for example, Julián Garcés, bishop of Tlaxcala, every year more Erasmian, made a remarkable announcement: the time had come, he said, to speak out against those

> who have judged wrongly these poor people, those who pretend that they are incapable and claim that their incapacity is a sufficient reason to exclude them from the church . . . That is the voice of Satan . . . a voice which comes from the avaricious throats of Christians whose greed is such that, in order to slake their thirst for wealth, they insist that rational creatures made in the image of God are beasts and asses.[4]

He added that the children of some Indians spoke better Latin than the children of many Spaniards. Garcés, by then an elderly Aragonés, erudite and well-read, had once been confessor to Rodríguez de Fonseca. He had founded a hospital in Perote and had always concerned himself with the sick. His personality had evolved remarkably.

Much the same would be declared a few months later by Fray Jacobo de Testera, the French-born Franciscan in the city of Mexico. He denounced the devil who was seeking to persuade people that the Indians were incapable and also those who were too fastidious and lazy 'to undertake the labour of learning their languages and who lacked the zeal to break through this wall of language in order to enter their hearts'. He added:

how can anyone say that these people are not capable when they construct such impressive buildings, make such subtle creations, were [long before Spain arrived] silversmiths, painters, merchants, able at presiding at meetings, good at public speaking, adept in the exercise of courtesy, in fiestas, marriages, and other solemn occasions . . . able to express sorrow and appreciation when the occasion requires it? They can even sing plainsong [Gregorian chant] contrapuntally to organ music and teach others how to enjoy religious music, [and some] preach to their people the sermons which we teach them.[5]

Soon after his announcement here cited, the same Bishop Garcés wrote to the pope asking him to take up the cause of the Indians and, simultaneously, Dr Ramírez de Fuenleal sent letters to protest that he had heard in Mexico that Dr Domingo de Betanzos, the Gallego who had once been a friend of Las Casas, had said that Indians were incapable of assimilating Christian doctrine.

The first time that Bartolomé de las Casas was engaged as a Dominican in controversy as to how to treat natives was in 1533 when the judges of Santo Domingo complained to the Council of the Indies that the friar had been refusing absolution to *encomenderos*. He had also persuaded a colonist in Santo Domingo to leave all his goods to the Indians as restitution for his past misconduct. That same year, 1533, Las Casas, still in his monastery of Santo Domingo, protested about two slave expeditions from Puerto Plata to the South American mainland, one despatched by the judge Zuazo (that was financed by the royal accountant, Diego Caballero) and the other by Jácome Castellón, one of the many Genoese–Spanish sugar merchants. The supreme court supported Las Casas. Two hundred and fifty or so Indians brought back from northern South America were distributed as *naborias*, servants, and afterwards, it was understood, they would be freed.

But all through the 1530s these slaving expeditions continued – Las Casas or no Las Casas – along the north coast of South America. Slaving in those days was still what brought the most profit of all commercial undertakings. With the sale of Indians, ships, armaments, tools and provisions for expeditions into the interior of the continent could be financed. There were already thirty-four sugar mills in Santo Domingo whose efficient working required labour. Black slaves were reckoned superior to Indians because they worked harder, something specially noticeable in the hot climate. But they were not easy to secure and, where there was a shortage of Africans, Indian slaves could serve.

By then an exchange of letters had begun between the senior Dominican thinker Fray Francisco de Vitoria and Fray Miguel de Arcos over the former's concern about the treatment of natives in Peru. Erasmus himself was not silent since, in 1535, his *Ecclesiastes* pointed out that those who talked of the decay of Christianity could be reminded of the great new territories in Africa, Asia and 'what should one say of the countries hitherto unknown, which are being discovered in the Americas every day?'[6]

Vitoria, probably born about 1480, was the essential leader in a new Thomist revival. He entered the Dominican order in 1504 and then went to the Collège de Saint Jacques in Paris. There he remained for nearly eighteen years, first as a student, then as a lecturer on Aquinas's *Summa Theologiae*.[7] In 1523 he went back to Spain and was soon elected to the Prime Chair of Theology in Salamanca, a position which he held till his death in 1546. Vitoria published nothing, so that his views can only be discovered by reading his manuscript lecture notes. But he had an immense impact as a teacher and when he died thirty of his students held professorships in Spain.

In 1535 Las Casas was heard complaining about what he had heard of 'the Germans'' actions in Venezuela: 'This is not the path my lord' – he was writing to someone at court in Spain – 'which Christ followed. This is ... rather a Muslim practice, indeed worse than what Muhammad did.'[8] His comments perhaps reflected the attitude of the clever, benign and beautiful Empress Regent Isabel who, having heard that many Indians from the region of Coro, Venezuela, were being kidnapped and sold in Santo Domingo, ordered them to be returned. However, the German controllers of the 'colony' of Venezuela did nothing to put the royal order into effect. But these complaints had to be judged against the impression made by the publication, in 1535 precisely, of much of Oviedo's *History*, giving a generally negative picture of the Indians' capacity.

At this moment the obstinate but shrewd Pope Paul III (Alessandro Farnese) took an important stand on the matter of how to treat natives. He came from an old family from near Bolsena, itself near Orvieto. His lovely sister, Giulia, was the chief cause of his rise at the court of Alexander VI for 'it is certain that Alexander VI had given the dignity of cardinal not to him but to his sister'.[9] Surrounded by his family and ambitious for them, Paul III enjoyed the life of a Renaissance prelate, and his papacy was a time of remarkable tranquillity. Titian's painting shows him with two grandsons, of whom one, Ottavio, Duke of Camerino, married Margaret, an illegitimate daughter of Charles V by a Dutch girl; the other became another Cardinal Alessandro Farnese.

When elected pope, he was, as we have seen, then the oldest cardinal. His first action was to offer Erasmus a cardinal's hat, which he declined.[10] Guicciardini says that 'he was a man gifted with learning and, to all appearance, good morals, who had exercised his office as cardinal with greater skill than that whereby he had acquired it'. He completed the palazzo Farnese in Rome, 'with the cornice of all cornices', with the help of Antonio da Sangallo. Pasquino the pamphleteer put up a notice in the Vatican: 'Alms are requested for this building.' He also built a palace for the popes in the garden of the monastery of the Franciscans facing the Corso in Rome, now, alas, replaced by the monument to King Victor Emmanuel.

Pope Paul was influenced by such intelligent and humane correspondents in the New World as Fr Minaya and the bishop of Tlaxcala, Julián Garcés. In his bull *Sublimis Deus* of 1537, the pope recalled that Christ had said: 'Go ye and teach all nations ... He said all, without exception, for all are capable of receiving the doctrines of the faith.' So

the enemy of the human race [that is, the devil] who opposes all good deeds in order to bring men to destruction, beholding and envying this, invented a means never before heard of, by which ... he inspired those who ... have not hesitated to preach abroad that the Indians of the West and South, and other people of whom we have recent knowledge, should be treated as dumb brutes, created for our service, pretending that they are incapable of receiving the catholic faith. ... We who, though unworthy, exercise on earth the power of our Lord ... consider, however, that the Indians are truly men and that they are not only capable of understanding the catholic faith but, according to our information, desire exceedingly to receive it.

Desiring to provide an ample remedy for these evils, we define and declare that ... the said Indians, and all other peoples who may be discovered by Christians, are by no means to be deprived of their liberty or of their property, even though they may be outside the faith of Jesus Christ; and that they may, and should freely, and legitimately, enjoy their liberty and the possession of their property; nor should they be in any way enslaved; should the contrary happen, it shall be null and of no effect ... the said Indians should be converted to the faith of Jesus Christ by preaching the word of God and by the example of good and holy living.[11]

This bull, despite its benevolence, infuriated the Emperor Charles, for he thought that it infringed his powers. But Paul's intention had been benign. His subsequent bull *Altitudo divini consilii* found Franciscans at fault when they did not administer the complete ceremony of baptism to the Indians. Henceforth, the pope declared, they should not omit the smallest parts of the ceremony except the rites of salt, the ephphatha,[12] the wearing of white robes and the candles. For it was good that the Indians should be impressed by the grandeur of the ceremony.[13] Pope Paul's interest in these matters, whatever his motives were, helped to dictate events.

In early 1540 Cardinal García de Loaisa, the long-serving president of the Council of the Indies, held a meeting in Valladolid to discuss seriously how to treat Indians. He had with him Dr Ramírez de Fuenleal who, as we know, had been a successful and noble president of the *audiencias* in both Santo Domingo and Mexico. He was now bishop of Tuy, a pretty city in Galicia on the riverine frontier with Portugal, about as far as anyone could be from anything to do with the Indies. Also present were the commander Juan de Zúñiga, younger brother of the Count of Miranda, Prince Philip's *mayordomo* and a great friend of the Emperor Charles whom he served well;[14] the Count of Osorno (García Fernández Manrique), who had been acting president of the Council of the Indies for much of the 1530s; Licenciado Gutierre Velázquez, a kinsman of the first governor of Cuba, Diego Velázquez, whom we have mentioned before, and related too to the great chronicler Bernal Díaz del Castillo; Cobos; and the eternal bureaucrat, Dr Bernal.[15] Fray Bartolomé de las Casas was by then again in Spain and he sent a memorial to García de Loaisa as to how to bring to an end the 'vexation of the Indians', proposing the winding up of all *encomiendas*.

The discussion, led by García de Loaisa in 1540, lasted off and on almost two years. It began with six interesting questions put by the president who, it will be remembered, was for many years confessor to the king:

How should those who had treated Indians badly be punished?
How could Indians best be instructed in Christianity?
How could it be guaranteed that Indians would be well treated?
Was it necessary for a Christian to take into account the welfare of slaves?

What should be done to ensure that governors and other officials
    carry out the government's orders to be just?
And, how could the administration of justice be properly organized?

The answers of one of those present, Pedro Mercado de Peñalosa,
who owed his advance in the bureaucracy to being son-in-law of the
mayor Ronquillo of Valladolid, are preserved. He wanted six lettered
scholars sent from the Spanish supreme court to take a *residencia* of all
the similar institutions in the New World. From then on, he thought
that no Indians would be enslaved.[16]

At that time there were many royal orders in Spain designed to
assist or, where necessary, complete plans for peaceful conversion. For
example, the Franciscans had been asked to provide Las Casas with the
names of Indians who had musical talent and could write arrangements
for psalms.

An equally important development was the extraordinary experiment
associated with the new Franciscan house at Tlatelolco, the town which
had been Tenochtitlan's immediate neighbour on the island to the north.
It had been independent till the 1470s and then had been effectively
absorbed by the Mexica's capital till the conquest. There had been a
good deal of fighting there in 1520–21. Within a mere quarter of a century after the fall of old Mexico, the dedicated and meticulous Franciscan
Fray Bernardino de Sahagún, who had come out to New Spain in the
1520s, presided over an attempt to educate there the sons of Mexica
noblemen. This was the Colegio Imperial de Santa Cruz de Santiago de
Tlatelolco, founded on 6 January 1536. Spaniards and friars of other
orders who observed the founding of this institution

> laughed broadly and jeered at us, thinking it beyond all doubt that no one
> could be clever enough to teach grammar to people of such small aptitude. But
> after we had worked with them for two or three years, they had attained such
> a thorough knowledge of grammar that some understood, and not only spoke
> and wrote Latin, they even composed heroic verses in it.... It was I [Sahagún]
> who worked with these pupils for the first four years and who introduced them
> to the Latin language. When the laymen and [regular] clergy were convinced
> that the Indians were making progress, and were capable of prospering still
> more, they began to raise objections and to oppose the enterprise.[17]

This school was not like Pedro de Gante's institution, which was concerned with apprenticeship. It was a centre of learning comparable to the Jesuit College in Goa and had the support of Bishop Zumárraga. It was from the beginning trilingual (Spanish, Nahuatl and Latin). The syllabus reflected the seven liberal arts, and the teachers were enlightened Franciscans. The aim was to educate the future elite of the indigenous population in both European culture and Christian theology. Another of Santa Cruz's functions was to serve as a seminary for indigenous priests. Bishop Zumárraga wrote in 1538 that he had 'sixty Indian boys already able to do Latin grammar and who know more grammar than I'.[18] But the indigenous priests did not as a rule want to become Catholic priests because they did not wish to renounce marriage.

Some Spaniards were seriously perturbed by the consequences of this programme of education, arguing that the case of Don Carlos Ometochtl, a Mexican condemned for seeking to revive the ancient religion, showed the risks. (Ometochtl was executed in 1540.) On the other hand, on 10 December 1537 Viceroy Mendoza wrote to the emperor that not only had the old indigenous lords accepted these changes but he, the viceroy, had decided to re-establish, Christianized and Hispanized, the solemn ceremonies by which they, the 'Tecles', became aristocrats or leaders.[19] Mendoza even founded an Order of Tecle Knights which would regularize the methods of education for these Indian 'señores'.[20] These new Indian aristocrats would be transformed into a new rung of the Spanish social hierarchy.

The emphasis given to conversion by the three main religious orders in these years was notable. The Franciscans were more concerned with linguistic and even ethnographic studies, for that is what Sahagún's great book, *The General History of the Things of New Spain*, written between the 1550s and 1580s, really was. The Franciscans were optimistic about the possibilities of training Indian clergy. The Dominicans were more doubtful, and generally more pessimistic about the capacities of Indians. The Augustinians were more interested in building monasteries and were perhaps more competent at organizing indigenous communities, and even more interested in securing a real training for their novices.[21] Nevertheless, the three orders could collaborate and, on the suggestion of Bishop Zumárraga, they met regularly in New Spain to discuss their different experiences.

Zumárraga is a man of great interest because, at the same time as being the promoter of the College of Santa Cruz, as later of the university of Mexico, an admirer of Thomas More as of Erasmus, he was also a fierce opponent of indigenous religions. Several challenges were made which put Zumárraga on his mettle: not simply by don Carlos, earlier mentioned, but also by Marcos Hernández Atlaucatl, judge of Tlatelolco. These were met with firmess, decision and in effect ruthlessness.

From this time on there were few years which did not see some kind of a publication in Spain by Las Casas for the next half century. In 1542, for example, he completed his 'A Remedy for Existing Evils'. In this, he insisted that the pope had wanted to do the Indians a favour, not do them harm, by granting them to the king of Spain. The Indians, he said, 'are free and they do not lose that status on becoming vassals of the king of Spain'.[22] The same year he completed 'A Very Brief Account of the Destruction of the Indies', in which claimed that 15 or 20 million Indians had been killed by the Spaniards. That was a vast exaggeration. Yet the book was presented to the Emperor Charles and became the most famous of Las Casas's works, being translated into all the main European languages, often with horrifying illustrations.[23] In it, he argued that the pope had had no right to give the Indies, much less Indians, to the Christian rulers. There was no justification for the numerous aggressive *entradas*:

> All wars which are called conquests are and were very unjust, and are characteristic of tyrannies, not wise monarchies. All the lordships of the Indies we have usurped. For our kings to achieve their principality in the Indies validly and correctly, that is without injustice, would necessarily require the consent of the kings and the people concerned.[24]

Cieza de León, the best of the chroniclers of the conquest of Peru, was roughly in support. 'I knew from experience,' he said,

> that there were great cruelties and much injury done to the natives ... All know how populous the island of Hispaniola [Santo Domingo] used to be and how, if the Christians had treated the Indians decently, and as friends, there would be many more of them there now ... There remains no better testimony of the country having once been so peopled than the great cemeteries of the dead and the ruins of the places where they lived. In *tierra firme* [that is, Venezuela, in the region of Coro] and Nicaragua there is not an Indian left. Benalcázar was asked how many Indians he found between Quito and Cartago ... 'There are none.'[25]

Did the king ever consider abandoning the Indies? That was improbable, especially after Francisco de Vitoria had begun to insist that 'Spain should not leave the Indies till they were capable of being maintained in the Catholic faith.'[26] Even cities accepted that Spain had a role to fulfil.

From the middle of 1542 there ensued a string of humane regulations. Thus on 21 May a royal decree forbade 'any captain or any other person to make slaves of Indians, even if they were captured in a just war. No one was to be sold at all.' A special section of that decree condemned practices which might lead to the death of slaves '*así indios como negros*' – a very rare reference at that time to black slaves – while looking for pearls off Venezuela. The decree insisted that the life of those slaves was more important than any benefit which might be gained from the pearl fisheries.

This order clashed with the views of the noble Vitoria who, in his *Reflexiones de Indios* of that same year, thought that the capture of Indians in a just war could result in slaves. Yet also in 1542 came the Franciscan Fray Alonso de Castro's treatise *Utrum Indigenae novi orbis* which argued that Indians should receive higher education. (Fray Alonso had taught for many years at the Franciscan monastery in Salamanca and had become famous for a chilling denunciation of Protestantism, *Adversus Haereses*, in 1534.) He added that the Bible should become generally available to Indians, a view which he shared with Bishop Zumárraga who, in his eloquent *Conclusio exhortatoria*, had urged that the Bible should be translated into the Indian languages so that it might be studied by everyone who could read in Mexico. He did not understand why 'our doctrine should be concealed from all except those who were called theologians. After all, no one could be called a Platonist if he had not read Plato. So no one could surely be called a Christian unless he had read the doctrine of Christ.'

Castro wrote his *Utrum*, incidentally, at the request of the Crown in consequence of arguments about the school at Tlatelolco.[27] That treatise was praised by all the prominent theologians of the day. For example, Vitoria thought that 'everything that has been said by the Rev. Father Alfonso de Castro seems to me to be both pious and religious'. Fray Francisco del Castillo and Fray Andrés Vega noted that

> many zealously but ignorantly attack the Church which they think that they are defending. They are of the same kind as those . . . who do not cease

to attack, ignominiously, and with Satan's means, the Church which has been established in the western islands and on the newly found continent, and which is nowadays growing in a wonderful way.

Then Fray Luis de Carvajal commented: 'it is ridiculous to admit [the Indians] to baptism and to absolution and the forgiveness of sins but not to a knowledge of the scripture'.[28]

At that time Las Casas was back in Spain seeking to inspire new laws about the treatment of Indians. He was accompanied by Fray Jacobo de Testera, who had come from New Spain with a letter from Bishop Zumárraga on the subject, as well as letters from several enlightened Dominicans. There were continual discussions on the matter in the Council of the Indies where García de Loaisa was as cautious as always, though he clearly realized that the majority of his colleagues were against *encomiendas*. Las Casas saw the Emperor Charles in Germany in 1541 and his strong, attractive personality, probably had an effect on his master as it had done before, in 1517.[29] Charles was a deeply religious man and could be easily persuaded by Las Casas to act in favour of the Indians.[30] Las Casas would also see Prince Philip very shortly.

Some time in the early part of 1542 a further series of meetings was held between García de Loaisa and Cobos. Probably other advisers were present: for example, Granvelle, the good Latinist and linguist from Burgundy who had become *de facto* chancellor of the empire, though he never had the title; Dr Juan de Figueroa and Dr Antonio de Guevara of the Council of Castile, of whom the first was said to have been 'a man of sound learning' in Cobos's judgement; the second, Guevara, was a brilliant writer and now bishop of Mondoñedo in Galicia, who had been the emperor's confessor. Dr Ramírez de Leal, with his experience in both Santo Domingo and in New Spain, and, as we have seen, now a bishop (of Tuy), was also called on to advise. They produced the so-called New Laws of the Indies.

These laws deserve much consideration. First, because they were just, and, secondly, because their proclamation in Peru and Mexico, as well as elsewhere in the Spanish imperial dominions, caused a crisis. The laws began with a personal statement by Charles. Already, years before, he had wanted to involve himself with greater intensity in the organization of the affairs of the Indies. Now he had settled to do so. We must assume that, though most of the rest of the text was written by Cobos and García de Loaisa, the emperor himself made a contribution.

In the text, dated 20 November 1542, there are forty paragraphs.[31] The first ones are modest statements about how the Council of the Indies should meet, and how often – three hours in the morning and in the afternoon, if necessary. Paragraphs 4 and 5 forbade relations or servants of members of the Council of the Indies from receiving any presents. This echoed Castilian procedure. Paragraph 6 prohibited councillors from indulging in any private business – that was a welcome change even if it was impossible to guarantee it. Then it was laid down that all criminal or civil cases in the Indies should usually be resolved by the colonial administration, but in cases where more than 10,000 pesos were at stake, an appeal could be made to the Council of the Indies or even to the king.

Paragraphs 20 to 40 constituted the heart of the laws and it was these which caused such difficulties in the empire. The Indians were declared free if they were vassals of the king, as had been specifically urged by Las Casas in 'A Remedy for Existing Evils'. In order to free the natives who had been enslaved against all reason, the law now would provide that the *audiencias* should act summarily and with true wisdom if the masters of Indian slaves could not show that they possessed them legitimately. The supreme court was to

> enquire continually into the excesses and ill treatment which are (or shall be) done to them by governors or private persons . . . henceforward [and this was a passage which caused outrage throughout the empire] for no cause of war nor in any other manner can an Indian be made a slave and we desire that they be treated as [vassals] of the Crown of Castile, for such they are.

Indians who 'until now have been enslaved against all reason and right were to be put at liberty'. Indians were not 'to carry heavy loads unless absolutely necessary and then only in a manner that no risk to life or health of the said Indians' may ensue. No Indian was to be taken against his will to the pearl fisheries 'since these have not been conducted in the proper manner [they were usually icy]'. As for *encomiendas*, those who held them without a proper title would lose them; those who held an unreasonable number were also to lose them. Those who had been engaged in Peru in the 'altercations and passions' between Pizarro and Almagro would have their *encomiendas* confiscated as would all royal officials and churchmen (including bishops), monasteries and hospitals. There would be no new *encomiendas* and, when the present *encomenderos* died, their lands would revert to the Crown. Their children would be looked after since they would be granted a sum drawn from their fathers' revenues – a very complicated compromise.

All Indians placed under the protection of the Crown would be well treated. 'First conquistadors' – that is, those who had first been involved in the conquest of the place concerned – would be preferred in royal appointments, all new discoveries were to be made according to certain rules, no Indians were to be brought back as loot to Spain or Mexico and the scale of tributes imposed on newly conquered Indians would be assessed by the governor. Indians living in Cuba, Hispaniola and San Juan (Puerto Rico) were no longer to be troubled for tribute but were to be 'treated in the same way as the Spaniards living in those islands'. No Indians would be forced to work except where no other solution was possible. Paragraph 33 of the laws declared that Spaniards could not have lawsuits against Indians.[32]

These laws, proclaimed in Spain in November 1542, were published in July 1543 and were received with *desasosiego* (disquiet) in New Spain. Even before they were published, they caused 'a true panic'.[33] So a series of visitors (*visitadores*) were sent to the New World to explain the Crown's thinking: Alonso López de Cerrato to the West Indies and then to Venezuela and the Gulf of Paria; Miguel Díaz to Santa Marta, Cartagena, Popayan and the river San Juan; Blasco Núñez de Vela to Peru; and Francisco Tello de Sandoval to New Spain. In addition to publishing and enforcing the laws, these officials were empowered to take a *residencia* of all royal officials, to act as judge on the supreme court concerned and were given a papal bull conferring the power to extend or to restrict bishoprics and to hold meetings of bishops to consider the welfare of the Church.

We know what happened to Blasco Núñez de Vela. Tello de Sandoval was much more prudent and the viceroy in Mexico had already begun to educate the colonists in what they should do and think. He ordered the New Laws to be proclaimed (*pregonado*) but he did not apply them.

Still, Jacobo de Testera, the 'custodian' of the Franciscans in New Spain, who had been recently to the mother country and had undoubtedly influenced the text of the laws, was received in Mexico City with vast enthusiasm by a large crowd of Indians

> who bestowed gifts, erecting triumphal arches, sweeping clean the street which Testera was to pass [as if he had been Montezuma, who had been

treated like that] and strewing on him cypress branches and roses, bearing him in a litter because he and the other Franciscans had informed the Indians that they had come to free them and restore them to the state in which they had been before they were placed under the rule of the king of Spain . . . the Indians went forth to receive Friar Testera as if he had been the viceroy.[34]

It may be to emphasize the accidental more than is necessary to recall that 1542 saw the foundation of the Archivo Nacional de Simancas and also the publication of Copernicus's *De Revolutionibus orbium coelestium*. Lovers of literature will insist that the publication of the collected poems of Boscan and Garcilaso de la Vega was as important as those events since, by introducing Italian verse forms, a flood of new Spanish poetry was made possible.[35] To those concerned with romantic geography, the publication of *Felix Magno* by Claudia Demattè in Seville should be remembered because it speaks again of Califa, the mythic queen of California.[36] More realistic monarchists were pleased that the Infante Philip announced his marriage to the Infanta Maria of Portugal. Those with a practical sense were no doubt more impressed by the decision in 1542 that the ships from Spain bound for the Indies were to sail henceforth in convoys of no fewer than ten vessels.[37]

We are, however, concerned with Dominicans as well as with treasure. Among the disciples of Francisco de Vitoria was Fr Domingo de Soto, who became a convert to Vitoria's version of Christianity.

After studying with Vitoria at the university of Paris, he followed Vitoria back to Salamanca in 1526, took over some of Vitoria's lectures when the latter was ill and in 1532 was elected to be professor of theology at Salamanca. He lectured there till 1545, when he resigned his chair to go to the general council of the Church at the request of the emperor. Soto played an important part in the first years of the work of the Council of Trent, both as imperial adviser and as representative of the Dominicans. It is comforting to realize that this great Catholic thinker, with his knowledge of the New World, was present at the council's meetings. Returning to Spain, he again became a professor at Salamanca in 1551, a position which he held till his death in 1560.

44

Controversy at Valladolid

One of the guardians, a horseback rider, explained that they were
slaves condemned by His Majesty to the galleys and so there was
no more to be said ...

Cervantes, *Don Quixote*

A formal 'visitor', Francisco Tello de Sandoval, reached New Spain in February 1544. A Sevillano, he had attended the university of Salamanca and afterwards had entered the bureaucracy of the Inquisition in Toledo. Then in 1543 he joined the Council of the Indies. He was a characteristic bureaucrat of the age, and had an inflexible nature. He would eventually become a bishop. He brought with him to New Spain not only an instruction to explain the New Laws to the settlers but a *provisión de visita* authorizing him to investigate the conduct of almost everyone: viceroy, judges of the supreme court, treasurer and their subordinates, down to the most insignificant officials in the poorest towns. In addition, he was named *inquisidor* of New Spain (Alonso López de Cerrato would be *inquisidor* of the Antilles).[1] He arrived with a financial adviser, Gonzalo de Aranda, who left a memorial.[2] The colonists wanted to go and greet him to reproach him for the New Laws, but the prudent viceroy Mendoza restrained them and welcomed Tello de Sandoval himself, accompanied by 600 officials and gentlemen of the supreme court and of the viceregal court. No grander reception could have been held in Seville or in Valladolid.

Tello repaired then to the convent of Santo Domingo in the city of Mexico where Bishop Zumárraga greeted him and where he installed himself. The very next day, a large number of the colonists and conquistadors besieged him with their complaints, but Tello dismissed them for the time being since he had not yet presented his credentials. Later he met Miguel de Legazpi, a Basque notary, and some others of the town council, as well as the chief prosecutor, to whom he talked reassuringly.

The following month Tello devoted to meeting people and listening to their anxieties. Then on 24 March he instructed the notary Antonio de Tuncios to proclaim publicly the New Laws on the treatment of Indians. The announcement was received with no enthusiasm. Tello was therefore persuaded by the councillor Alonso de Villanueva to stay the implementation of five of the provisions which specially distressed the settlers until an appeal could be made. Then the provincials – that is, the leaders – of the three main orders, the Franciscans, Augustinians and Dominicans, declared in favour of the *encomiendas*, and went to Spain to protest at the high-handed manner with which they were treated, as did three important councillors, the above-mentioned Alonso de Villanueva; Jerónimo López, a survivor of the conquest, who had reached New Spain in 1521 with Julián de Alderete; and Peralmíndez Chirino, the erstwhile enemy of Cortés. At this, Tello de Sandoval went out of his way to try to gain the support of the settlers, though, at the beginning, he was critical of Mendoza whose administration in Mexico he wished to challenge, for private reasons which are hidden from us.[3]

The day after the proclamation of the New Laws, Bishop Zumárraga invited all the leaders of the viceroyalty to take part in a mass which he celebrated in the cathedral. Tello attended and heard Zumárraga preach intelligently and eloquently. But, with the announcement of the New Laws, all business came to a stop in Mexico, wheat rose in price to eleven reales a *fanega*, maize to five reales; settlers went about saying that they would be obliged to kill their wives and their daughters 'lest they seek a life of shame'. Despite the fact that the viceroy and the supreme court judges distributed charity to the families of conquistadors to prevent their flight,[4] the first fleet returning to Spain after the proclamation carried thirty-five to forty families, 600 people in all.

The Dominicans mounted an effective counter-attack to the New Laws. The provincial Diego de la Cruz and the eloquent Fray Domingo de Betanzos, one-time friend of Las Casas, wrote to the Emperor Charles to say that Indians should not be encouraged to study

> since no benefit could be expected for a long time ... Indians are not stable
> persons to whom one can entrust the preaching of the Holy Gospel. They

do not have the ability to understand correctly and fully the Christian faith nor is their language sufficient and copious enough to be able to express our faith without great improprieties, which can easily result in great errors.[5]

So no Indian should be ordained a priest. This document was signed on 4 May 1544 by all the leading Dominicans in Mexico. A similar letter was written by the councillors of the city of Mexico and was signed too by several old conquistadors still on the town council: Vázquez de Tapia, Antonio de Carvajal, Jerónimo López and Gonzalo de Salazar, one of the officials sent in 1522 by the Emperor Charles.[6] They begged to be heard before the New Laws were put into execution.

Meantime the *procuradors* of New Spain reached Castile and immediately sought out Ginés de Sepúlveda, the able lawyer and polemicist who had become the prop and stay of the opponents of the New Laws. They could not seek out Las Casas even if they had wanted to, since that now famous preacher had been named bishop of Chiapas and was on his way to his see.

Both Alonso de Villanueva and Jerónimo López argued in the town council that the Indians would be better off if the *encomiendas* were given to the settlers in perpetuity. Surely that would be best too for the land concerned? They also thought that, since the leaders of the orders had given their views, individual friars should keep silent.[7] But it had become evident that those same leaders of the orders were more opposed to the New Laws than anyone expected. Thus Fr Diego de la Cruz, who had been the Dominican provincial for nine years, agreed that *encomiendas* in perpetuity should be granted, to avoid Spaniards abandoning agricultural projects. He did not think that the Indians would work hard even if the judges ordered it. The Indians were no longer afraid of horses. So he anticipated a revolt.

The viceroy sent a serene commentary to the Crown. He noted that even Tello had used Indian services, including slavery, when he had been in Mexico. The idea of personal services anyway had not been invented by Spaniards but had been used by the Mexica themselves. Even if His Majesty cut off the heads of the settlers, he could not make them enforce his laws, which actually destroyed his rents and his income and would in the end depopulate the country which really needed people. What should be done if there were to be a major rebellion? For the Spaniards would fight if there were indeed financial rewards in the form of the persons of the rebels as slaves.[8]

A meeting of the Council of the Indies was held in Spain to discuss these matters. The Duke of Alba, who came across from the Council of State – every day more important in the emperor's councils – having talked to churchmen from Mexico, advised the king to suspend the New Laws. He urged the grant of *encomiendas* in perpetuity, though without legal confirmation, so that 'the Spaniards there would always need some favour of the king of Spain'. He opposed the idea of pensions for conquistadors. The Indians should be subject to the Spaniards, of course, but they should be treated well, and not required to be slaves or even servants. If the troubles continued, they should be crushed by 'a large and powerful armada' – Alba's usual solution to political problems.[9]

The archbishop of Toledo, Cardinal Pardo de Tavera, thought that some reward should be given to conquistadors but that it should not be in the form of *encomiendas*. Licenciado Juan de Salmerón, who had spent several years as chief magistrate in Castilla del Oro and had been a judge in New Spain in the days of the benign second supreme court, thought that the New Laws were neither just nor practical. But only the most important Spaniards should be allocated Indians as slaves, the rest could have them just for themselves and one more generation. All *encomenderos* should always be available, thought Salmerón, to serve the king.[10] Dr Hernando Guevara, learned and imaginative as well as eloquent, believed that till the council received more information about both *encomiendas* and *encomenderos*, the New Laws should not be enforced. The Count of Osorno, who had acted as president of the Council of the Indies and whose name is preserved in one of the cities founded by Valdivia in Chile, backed the idea of *encomiendas* in perpetuity, though he considered that the *encomenderos* should have only civil jurisdiction. Cobos said that, though he had no experience himself of the Indies, he had noted that two out of the four members of the council who had opposed giving *encomiendas* in perpetuity had indeed been there. Dr Ramírez de Fuenleal, veteran of two supreme courts in the New World and now a bishop in Castile (he had been awarded the see of León), wanted to consider the New Laws themselves first. The trouble had been caused by individuals, not only by the injustice of the laws. He considered that the heir of a conquistador should receive two thirds of his father's property as an entailed estate.

Cobos argued simply that *encomiendas* should continue to be given to worthy Spaniards in the Indies and agreed with Alba that the New Laws should be temporarily suspended. García de Loaisa also supported the concept of *encomiendas* being granted in perpetuity, which he believed would guarantee an income for the king, the conversion of Indians and peace. Dr Bernal, Licenciado Velázquez and Licenciado Gregorio López supported pensions for conquistadors and 'moderate' pensions for other Spaniards who had served in the Indies for two generations. Conquistadors should not collect tribute and should not own property in Spain 'so that they would identify themselves with the [new] land'.[11] (Gregorio López was an Extremeño from Guadalupe whose uncle Juan de Sirvela had been prior of the Jeronymite monastery there. López had even married a Pizarro, but it is not clear that his wife, María, was related to the Peruvian conquerors.)[12]

On 3 July 1544 the Council of the Indies had told the emperor that dangers both to Indians and to the royal conscience were so great that no new expeditions should be licensed without his express permission and that of the council. Also a meeting of theologians was really needed to discuss 'how conquests may be conducted justly and with security of conscience'. Although laws had been promulgated on these matters

> we feel certain that these have not been obeyed, because those who conduct these conquests are not accompanied by persons who will restrain them and accuse them when they do evil. The greed of those who undertake conquests and the timidity and humility of the Indians is such that we are not certain that any instruction of ours will be obeyed. It would be fitting for Your Majesty to order a meeting of learned men, theologians and jurists with others according to your pleasure, to discuss and consider the manner in which these conquests should be carried out in order that they may be made justly and with security of conscience. An instruction for this purpose should be drawn up, taking into account all that may be necessary for this, and this instruction should be considered a law in the conquests approved by this council as well as those approved by the senior judges.[13]

The debate continued. Pamphlets were written by Las Casas and others discussing the injustice of these wars (in the Indies) 'according to all law, natural and divine'. Papers were contributed by Sepúlveda and others to the effect that the conquests were just, as well as wise.

All these views were passed on to the emperor, at the time in Germany, and some representatives of New Spain joined him to present their opinions in person. The Prince Regent Philip[14] wrote to his father that he had talked with representatives of the New World and with 'appropriate people' of both the Council of Castile and the Council of the Indies, but 'as the matter was so grandiose and of such weight and importance' he, Philip, did not think that he could take a decision on the subject, which was for his father to resolve.[15]

Philip added, though, that the Council of the Indies evidently wanted someone to put Peru in order. We have earlier talked of the controversy. Everyone thought that the ideal person would be Antonio de Mendoza but all realized that he was too valuable in New Spain to go. Alba and Dr Guevara considered it essential not to send some *letrado*, or university-educated civil servant, but a gentleman (*caballero*), a person in the confidence of the emperor, but everybody else thought that a *letrado* would be best.[16]

The conclusion of this difficult but important argument came on 25 October 1546, when Charles, now in his aunt Margaret's city of Mechelen, suspended the New Laws insofar as they affected *encomenderos* 'in order to avoid loss of revenue and perhaps the loss of New Spain itself'.[17]

Fray Domingo de Betanzos, the leading Dominican of New Spain, looked upon this suspension as a victory for himself. He had written in September that all laws promulgated on the supposition that the Indians were going to continue to exist were 'dangerous, wrong and destructive of all good in the republic'.[18] Laws which assumed that sooner or later the Indians would disappear altogether were sound and good. He added that he, like Bishop Zumárraga, longed to go to China where the 'natives were so much more intelligent than those of New Spain'.[19]

Las Casas, of course, differed. From Chiapas he had sent a message dated 15 September that all who pressed for the revocation of the New Laws deserved to be hung, drawn and quartered ('*merecen ser hechos cuartos*').[20]

The decision taken in Mechelen was against Charles's wishes. He had, however, been much disturbed by the rebellion in Peru of Gonzalo Pizarro, which was partly a protest against the New Laws.

The *encomenderos* in New Spain breathed a sigh of relief, so much so, indeed, that they set aside the second day of Christmas 1546 for a general rejoicing. That year they had suffered a destructive epidemic of smallpox which had killed thousands and there was a new revolt of black African slaves which frightened everyone.

The *encomenderos* were also confronted with the open quarrel between the two most prominent friends of the Indians, Las Casas and Motolinía. This occurred because a mere Franciscan friar such as Motolinía could not at that time baptize Indians. On one occasion he asked Las Casas to act in his stead, but Las Casas refused, because he thought that the Indian concerned was inadequately prepared. Motolinía, who believed that the Christian faith should be disseminated as quickly as possible, never forgave him. This caused Las Casas to lobby against Motolinía's claim for a bishopric.[21]

But no doubt the *encomenderos* had been pleased that García de Loaisa at last left the presidency of the Council of the Indies when in February 1546 he become *inquisidor-general* (he died soon after). He had been succeeded by Luis Hurtado de Mendoza, the elder brother of the viceroy.

Don Luis was one of those noblemen whose education had been formed by Peter Martyr. He was as much a Renaissance prince as his father had been in Granada (where Luis had been brought up) and as his brother was in New Spain. He had been much concerned in the building of the cathedral in Granada, Spain's most obvious Renaissance cathedral, designed by Pedro Machuca, who was said to have worked with Michelangelo. Luis Hurtado de Mendoza inspired, too, the plans for a Renaissance palace in the Alcázar in Seville, also designed by Machuca. He had been viceroy of Catalonia and captain-general of Navarre.

When he was named president of the Council of the Indies, Hurtado de Mendoza was in Regensburg with the court. The emperor told him of the great pressure being exerted by *encomenderos*.[22]

The establishment of the Mendoza brothers in the two most important places in the empire articulated perfectly both the importance of their family and the fact that, despite the prevalence of middle-class *letrados* in so many fields, the emperor preferred aristocrats in the leading positions. The Mendozas' younger brother, the cultivated and creative Diego, was in 1544 ambassador in Venice and moved to the all-important Rome in 1545. It was characteristic of him that he took both *Amadís* and *La Celestina* to read on his journey to Venice.

Actually in 1546 the viceroy, Mendoza, was enduring a serious personal crisis, since Tello de Sandoval had presented a list of forty-four accusations against him. The viceroy was accused of, in particular, favouring his friends: Luis del Castilla, his *mayordomo* Guerrero, the notary Turcios and others. He was also accused of receiving gifts in return for favours, of abusing Indians on his ranches, of neglecting to send royal revenues and of using the income of certain councils for an improper purpose. Mendoza was accused of forcing his sister María to marry Martín de Lucio, an elderly conquistador who had come to New Spain first with Pánfilo de Narváez.[23] More seriously, he was also said to have covered up a murder by a friend of his, Pedro Paco. Mendoza had his replies ready by 30 October 1546. He also drew up a counter-questionnaire of over 300 questions, to which most prominent citizens of Mexico replied. Then he successfully carried his case to the Council of the Indies. But, before that, the economy of New Spain had been transformed.

One of the hopeful conquistadors in Mendoza's New Spain was Juan de Tolosa, whom we assume to have been a Basque from Guipuzcoa. At any rate that is the origin of the surname, and Tolosa has been for generations an important stop on the way from San Sebastián to Burgos. Juan de Tolosa married Leonor, a daughter of the great Cortés by Isabel, the daughter of Montezuma. One day in early September 1546, Tolosa camped at the base of the Cerro de la Bufa near what became the town of Zacatecas in central Mexico and, in return for some meretricious trinkets brought from Spain, he received presents of a few stones which, according to a metal analyst in Nochistlán, turned out to be high in silver content. The mines nearby surpassed all previous such discoveries. Tolosa founded the town that was later Zacatecas, and he and some others turned the place into a silver town. Of these others, the most important were Cristóbal de Oñate, a hero of the war against the Mixton Indians, and Diego de Ibarra, who had also had a role in that conflict. Oñate soared far ahead of Tolosa in terms of achievement for, in the end, he owned thirteen silver mines, a hundred slaves and a magnificent residence with a chapel. At last it seemed that New Spain was going to justify the expense which its conquest had entailed. There were, of course, problems, one of which was that there was no river near Zacatecas, so the machinery of production had to be turned by horsepower – or by slaves. All the same, the news intoxicated the colony.

This knowledge arrived just in time for it to become known to the creator of New Spain, then living in a house in Seville, in the Plaza San Lorenzo. In October 1547 Hernando Cortés went to stay in the house outside Seville of a friend, Juan Rodríguez de Medina, and there on 2 December 1547, having made his will, he died, probably aged sixty-six.[24]

Cortés had transformed the history of Spain and the Americas. Nothing was the same again after his astonishing achievement of leading a few hundred Spaniards to triumph over a powerful indigenous monarchy. Matters might easily have gone differently had the Spaniards been led by a less intelligent commander who did not see, as Cortés had done, the importance of interpreters; who did not have the gift of serenity in difficult moments, as Cortés had; who did not believe, as Cortés did, that leaving aside gold and glory (important motives certainly), the Mexica would soon find the Christian God and the attendant saints, not to mention the Virgin Mary, irresistible. Cortés's tactic of kidnapping Montezuma was copied afterwards a hundred times, not just in Peru. His skill at transforming the Americas by using a small company of soldiers was an inspiration to other conquerors, who believed that, with a few cavalrymen, they too could capture a kingdom.

Yet this great conqueror did not seem quite at ease with his victory nor did his country help him to be so. The king of Spain, the Emperor Charles, never forgot that Cortés had in effect rebelled against Diego Velázquez, so he never gave Cortés the European command which might have transformed the history of Europe. Cortés's life was after 1525 full of disappointment and even sadness.

Several of the contemporaries of Cortés died at much the same time. For example, Cobos, the great secretary for the Indies and for most other things, died in his palace in Úbeda in May 1547. Other advisers such as Zúñiga, Pardo de Tavera, García de Loaisa and Osorno all vanished for good in the two years prior to Cortés's death.

Charles the emperor must have felt alone in 1550, when he would be faced by some of the most difficult moments of his life.

45

Las Casas and Sepúlveda

Some qualities are always good in any language . . .
Castiglione, *The Courtier*

Las Casas returned to Spain in 1547 and went to stay at the monastery of San Gregorio in Valladolid, the splendid palace-convent next to the church of San Pablo. He came with Fray Rodrigo de Andrada, who represented the Indian tribes of Oaxaca and Chiapas, and who wanted to represent them before the Council of the Indies. Las Casas had something more to his taste in his agenda: a riposte to Juan Ginés de Sepúlveda's latest dialogue, *Demócrates Segundo*. Las Casas insisted that that book should be examined by the universities of Alcalá and Salamanca.

Sepúlveda had just finished a great translation of Aristotle's *Politics*, as well as a new tract about how to treat Indians. This was rejected by the Council of the Indies but then was transferred for the approval of the Council of Castile which, as Las Casas said, knew nothing of the Indies. Las Casas supposed Sepúlveda assumed that 'men who knew nothing of Indian affairs would not notice the poison'. In fact, the Council of Castile referred Sepúlveda's latest treatise to the theologians at Salamanca and Alcalá, where they discussed whether to publish on many occasions. On mature consideration they found that the work was unworthy since the teaching in it seemed unsound. Dr Diego Covarrubias at Salamanca gave lectures criticizing the idea that the Indians' low culture justified the wars against them. He 'doubted whether American Indians should be looked on as among those people born to obey'.[1]

One who surprisingly seems to have remained aloof in the controversy was Bishop Quiroga who, in 1548, while still bishop of Patzcuaro,

the one-time capital of Michoacan, returned home temporarily to help
to work out the boundaries and rights of the bishoprics of New Spain.
While in Castile he wrote a treatise (now lost), *De debellandis Indis*,
about whether it was ever just to make war against the Indians. Apparently, Quiroga, in contradictory fashion, thought that war was usually
just since it brought Indians closer to Christianity.[2] Muslims had said
much the same of slavery.

Sepúlveda wrote to Prince Philip asking for a formal meeting of theologians to discuss his book, but Philip had left Valladolid for a European
tour before he had time to answer, and Sepúlveda instead went to Rome
where, for good or evil, his book appeared. In April 1549 King Charles
issued the extraordinary ruling that all conquests and expeditions
(*entradas* included) were to be suspended till the dispute between Las
Casas and Sepúlveda was resolved and it was clear if they were to be
looked upon as legal.

A declaration of April 1549 entitled 'The manner in which new discoveries are to be undertaken' elaborated on this matter. Churchmen
were to explain that they had come to the New World principally to
secure the friendship of the Indians and their acceptance of subjection
to the emperor and to God. Conquistadors had been enjoined not to
seize Indian women and were to pay for everything which they took
from Indian properties, at the low prices set by men of the Church. No
force was to be used by Spaniards except in self-defence and then only
in proportion to needs. Any breach of these rules would be severely
punished 'inasmuch as this matter is so important for the exoneration of
the royal conscience and of the persons who undertake these conquests,
as well as for the preservation and increase of these lands'. Perhaps this
remarkable declaration was drafted by Las Casas.[3] Whether that was so
or not, the very next month Las Casas was found writing to Fray
Domingo de Soto, now in the forefront of Spain's theologians and much
preoccupied by the matter of how to treat the Indians.

Las Casas agreed that the New World was far away but the issues
involved were close. He regretted that even pious missionaries offered
conflicting advice on what to do. He said that some friars had been
suborned by money from conquistadors, others did not learn the languages necessary to progress in conversion (Las Casas included!), and
yet others knew nothing of what had happened. One friar (perhaps
de Soto) had eaten the paper on which he had previously signed his

support of the perpetuity of the *encomienda*: 'Where else in the world,' Las Casas continued,

> have rational men in happy and populous lands been subjugated by such cruel and unjust wars called conquests, and then been divided up by the same cruel butchers and tyrannical robbers as though they were inanimate things ... enslaved in an infernal way, worse than in Pharaoh's day, treated like cattle being weighed in the meat market and, God save the mark, looked on as of less worth than bedbugs? How can the words of those that support such iniquities be believed?[4]

On 4 July 1549 the aristocrat Luis Velasco was appointed as Mendoza's successor as viceroy (the king had quietly pushed aside Mendoza's suggestion that his own son Francisco might be temporarily named in succession). Velasco was worthy of the charge, being of the family of the constable of Castile. He had been viceroy of Navarre and, like so many, had married a granddaughter of the first Duke of Infantado. Thus he was accustomed to grandeur and would soon establish a tradition of having forty people to dine every day.

Mendoza wrote to Velasco about the mission that he was leaving him. Everyone wished the government to conform to their own notions and the diversity of views was remarkable. Mendoza would listen to all kinds of advice and usually said that the ideas were good and that he would adopt them. His aim was to avoid sudden changes, especially in respect of the indigenous people, for so many changes had been made already that he wondered that the populace had not become insane. Though many gave advice, few gave help. The secret of good government was to do little, and that slowly, since 'most affairs lend themselves to being handled in that way and in that way alone can one avoid being deceived'. His chief concern was to maintain good relations between himself, the judges and the lesser officials.

Mendoza told Velasco that the Spaniards had respect for nothing said to them if they were not treated as gentlemen. The wealth from which the Crown's revenue derived came from them, of course: they had the silver mines, the mulberry trees for silk and the sheep. The Indians' production was of much less value. That had to be taken into account.

Mendoza told his successor that the Indians should be treated as sons of the Crown and both loved and punished in that spirit. Services and porterage should be done away with slowly, so as not to offend the Spaniards. Yet one had to accept many Indians were undoubtedly cunning and mendacious, and had a habit, when a legal case was decided against them, of bringing the matter up again once they thought that the judge had moved on or everyone had forgotten the matter. He, Mendoza, never punished Indians for lies, because he feared that they might then not come to him with their stories at all. He had regular hours for them on Mondays and Thursdays but he was also ready to see them at any time, notwithstanding their 'smell of perspiration and other evil odours. Many people thought that the Indians were humble, abused and misunderstood. Others thought that they were rich, idle vagabonds. Neither view was correct. The thing to do was to treat them as men like everyone else.'[5]

Meantime, Mendoza was named as viceroy of Peru. But if he seemed too ill, he could stay in Mexico and Velasco would go to Peru. The two could work that out together.

On 23 September 1549 Sepúlveda wrote to Prince Philip saying that 'by falsehoods, favours and machinations', Las Casas had succeeded in preventing his *Demócrates Alter* from being published, and any copies which reached the Indies were immediately confiscated. Las Casas – 'this quarrelsome and turbulent fellow' – had written a 'scandalous and diabolical confessionary' against Sepúlveda. He thought that his case ought to be debated before the Council of the Indies. But Las Casas, Andrade and others began to argue against the idea of holding *encomiendas* in perpetuity and managed to shake the opinions of some members of the council. Las Casas was able to delay a decision till the Emperor Charles returned from Germany. Bernal Díaz del Castillo, who came from Guatemala to assert the need for the heritability of *encomiendas*, returned to New Spain with this comment: 'in this manner, we proceed, like a lame mule, from bad to worse, and from one viceroy to another, from governor to governor'.[6]

In August 1550 the epic dispute between Sepúlveda and Las Casas came to a head in a formal confrontation in Valladolid in the monastery of San Gregorio.[7] It was an appropriate year. The best historians of the Spanish world have argued that it marked the culmination of Spanish civilization, though evil memories of the past were not yet quite erased. In New Spain, for example, a rebellion was mounted by the Zapotecs in Oaxaca by a leader who proclaimed himself to be Quetzalcoatl.

This encounter between Las Casas and Sepúlveda was set in motion by María de Bohemia and Maximilian of Austria, her husband, regents of Spain in the absence of both the Emperor Charles and the Prince Regent Philip.

A junta of fifteen was formed with seven members of the Council of the Indies: Luis Hurtado de Mendoza, Gutierre Velázquez, Gregorio López, Francisco Tello, Hernán Pérez de la Fuente,[8] Gonzalo Pérez de Ribadeneira[9] and Gracián de Briviesca;[10] four theologians: Domingo de Soto, Melchor Cano and Bartolomé Carranza, all Dominicans – and a Franciscan, Bernardino de Arévalo; two councillors of Castile: Licenciado Mercado de Peñalosa and Dr Bernardino de Anaya;[11] Licenciado Pedro de Pedrosa[12] of the Council of the Orders; and the bishop of Ciudad Rodrigo, Pedro Ponce de León.[13] (The Franciscan Fray Bernardino de Arévalo was ill from the beginning so that the junta was in effect a board of fourteen.) These men had to decide between the point of view of Juan Palacios Rubios, who had said that the pope had full authority and therefore so did the Catholic Kings, and that of the Dominicans, who denied all authority to the pope and therefore indirectly to the Catholic Kings.

Soto put the question:

> The purpose for which your lordships are gathered together ... is in general to discuss and determine what form of government and what laws may best ensure the preaching of and extension of our catholic faith in the new world ... and to investigate what organisation is needed to keep the peoples of the new world in obedience to the emperor, without damage to his royal conscience and in conformity with the bull of [Pope] Alexander [VI].

The central issue was the justice of making war against the Indians.

Sepúlveda spoke for three hours, essentially summarizing his work *Demócrates Alter*, in which he had indirectly accused Las Casas of heresy, for his character 'Leopoldo' was a German 'considerably tainted with Lutheran errors'. The character 'Demócrates' was represented as taking the opposing view.

Sepúlveda's arguments for the legality of the conquests were: first, on account of the gravity of the sins committed by the Indians, especially their idolatries and their sins against nature; secondly, on account of the rudeness of the Indians' nature, which obliged them to serve the Spaniards. Here Aristotle could be adduced, recalling his observation that some people are inferior by nature; the Indians are as different from Spaniards as monkeys are from men.

Sepúlveda quoted from *Demócrates Alter*:

compare then those blessings enjoyed by Spaniards, of prudence, genius, magnanimity, temperance, humanity and religion, with those of the '*hombrecillos*' among whom you will scarcely find even a vestige of humanity, who not only possess no science but who also lack letters and preserve no monument of their history except certain vague and obscure reminiscences of some things in some paintings. Neither do they have written laws, but barbaric institutions and customs. They do not even have private property.

As to the Spaniards, did not Lucan, Seneca, Isidore, Averroes and Alfonso the Wise testify to their intelligence and bravery from the days of Numantia onwards? Did not the brave Cortés subdue Montezuma and his hordes in his own capital? How can we doubt that those people – so uncivilised, so barbaric, so contaminated with so many impieties and obscenities – have been justly conquered by such an excellent, pious and just king as was Fernando the Catholic and he who is now the Emperor Charles and by a most humane nation and excellent in every kind of virtue?

The third reason for the conquest was in order to spread the faith which would be more easily done if the natives were first subdued; and finally, the conquest was to protect the weak among the natives themselves. Here Sepúlveda denounced human sacrifice and cannibalism.

There followed a discussion of the injunction in Luke 14:23 which so impressed Pope Paul: 'Go out into the highways and hedges, and compel them to come in, that my house may be filled.' Sepúlveda argued that the passage justified the prosecution of war to bring Indians into the fold. Las Casas could not say that that was wrong; for many emperors, and indeed popes, had fought for what they supposed were just causes.

When no danger threatened, preachers should go into new lands alone. In dangerous places, fortresses should first be built on borders and then the people would be slowly won over.

Sepúlveda added:

In prudence, virtue, and humanity, the Indians are as inferior to the Spaniards as children are to adults, women to men, as the wild and cruel to the most meek, as the prodigiously intemperate to the continent and temperate, and, as I nearly said, as monkeys to men.[14]

And don't think that, before the arrival of the Christians, the Indians were living quietly and in the Saturnian peace of poets. On the contrary, they were making war continuously and ferociously against each other with such rage that they considered their victory worthless if they did not satisfy their monstrous hunger with the flesh of their enemies. Their inhumanity was so much more monstrous since they were so distant from the unconquered and wild Scythians, who also fed on human flesh, for these Indians were so cowardly and timid that they scarcely withstood the appearance of our soldiers and often many thousands of them have given ground, fleeing like women before a very few Spaniards who did not even number a hundred.[15]

Sepúlveda argued that, 'though some of them [the Indians] show a talent for certain handicrafts, this is not an argument to take seriously ... since we see that some small animals, both birds and spiders, make things which no human industry can imitate completely ...' This was an argument later much used by Sepúlveda's friends. We may remember that Burckhardt would write that 'insect societies ... are far more perfect than the human state, but they are not free'.[16]

Las Casas appeared on the second day of the debate. He attacked the historian Oviedo almost as fiercely as he attacked Sepúlveda. His speech was intolerably long and wearied his audience. He read in full his *Argumentum Apologiae* ('Defence') which ran to 550 pages in Latin in sixty-three sections,[17] and that speech lasted five days.[18] Sepúlveda said that Las Casas only stopped because the jury could bear to hear no more.

Las Casas drew heavily on his *Historia Apologética*, in which he argued that American Indians compared very favourably with the European people of antiquity, were in some ways superior to the Romans – being more religious – and were better at raising their children (the educational system in ancient Mexico was certainly remarkable), provided a better education for the good life, their marriage arrangements were more reasonable, Indian women were devout and hardworking, and the temples in Yucatan were comparable to those of Egypt. He quoted Aristotle frequently, to outmanoeuvre Sepúlveda who, we recall, had translated that philosopher. Evidently Las Casas agreed with Aristotle that some men were born slaves, just as some men were born with six toes or only one eye; but he did not consider that the Indians were in that category. Indeed, he believed that all the peoples of the world are men ... all have understanding and will, all have five exterior senses, and four interior ones. All take satisfaction in goodness and feel pleasure with happy and delicious things, all regret and abhor evil ... No nation exists today nor could exist, no matter how barbarous, fierce or depraved its customs may be, which is not attracted and converted to all political virtues and to all the humanity of domestic, political and rational man.

Las Casas spoke as if the Indians, Mexica and Peruvians, as well as Tainos and Mayas, were all one people. In his *Historia Apologética* he did, in his universalism, anticipate Rousseau:

thus we see how they had important kingdoms, numbers of persons who live settled in a society, great cities, kings, judges, and laws, persons who engage in commerce, buying, selling, lending and the other contracts of the law of nations. So will it not stand proven that Dr Sepúlveda has spoken wrongly and viciously against peoples like these, either out of malice or in ignorance of Aristotle's real teaching? ... Even if the Indians are barbarians, it does not follow that they are incapable of government and have to be ruled by others, except to be taught about the Christian faith and be admitted to the sacraments. They are not ignorant, nor inhuman, nor bestial ... They cultivate friendship and are used to living in populous cities in which they wisely administered the affairs of both peace and war ... [They were] truly governed by laws which at very many points surpass ours and could have won the admiration of the sages of Athens.

Las Casas then talked of Indians' wonderful 'concern about their salvation and their soul ...' He insisted that the indigenous people had a simple sincerity and were 'moderate and meek'. He also argued that it has been implied that God had become careless in creating so immense a number of rational souls, and let human nature ('which He so largely determined and provided for') go astray in the almost infinitesimal part of the human race which they comprise.

Las Casas declared that even those who lived in highly developed states, such as the Greeks and Romans, could be called barbarians when their conduct was savage. Were the American Indians barbarian because they had no written language? Spanish missionaries had attested to the beauty of the Indian languages; Nahuatl, the tongue spoken by the Mexica, had much grace.

Barbarians were so either because of their wicked character or because of the barrenness of the region in which they lived. They lacked the reasoning and the way of life suited to human beings. They had no laws to live by ... they lived a life very much like that of brute animals ... Barbarians of this kind were rarely found in any part of the world and were few in comparison with the rest of mankind.[19]

Human sacrifice? Las Casas almost made a defence of that practice:

> Strabo reminds us that our own Spanish people, who reproach the poor Indian people for human sacrifice, used to sacrifice both captives and their horses ... There is no greater or more arduous step than for man to abandon the religion which he has once embraced ... There is no better way to worship God than through sacrifice.

Thus Las Casas recognized the good faith of the pagan in his religion even if it was idolatrous, and justified his activity of sacrifice because he was offering his most valuable possession, his life, to God.[20] He added: 'that it is not altogether detestable to sacrifice human beings to God is shown by the fact that God commanded Abraham to sacrifice to Him his only son'.[21]

After absorbing this remarkable declaration, the judges talked to the two disputants and then asked Fray Domingo de Soto to condense the arguments into a resumé.[22] This he did well, and the text was submitted to Sepúlveda, who replied to the objections of Las Casas. The judges then left, agreeing to meet again on 20 January 1551 after having studied the resumé.

January, however, presented difficulties for some of the judges. Bishop Ponce de León, for example, found that he had precisely at that time to visit his diocese. Fray Domingo de Soto, advised by Samano, wanted to abbreviate the session, and the presence of Fray Melchor Cano and Fray Bartolomé Carranza was doubtful because they both had to be at the Council at Trent. They wanted to give their opinions by letter.[23]

In early 1551 the judges decided that they needed more time in order to make their judgements. Lent intervened. Soto continued to try to avoid attending at all. Cano and Carranza as well as Miranda, bishop of Ciudad Rodrigo, remained at Trent.[24] Cano seemed to have the matter of the dispute on his mind there when, on the urging of the Jesuits led by Fr Diego Láinez, the powerful second general of that order, he supported a resolution at the congress stating that all men regardless of the colour of their skin have souls capable of salvation.[25]

In mid-April 1551 the second session of the debate at Valladolid finally began. Much of the discussion revolved round the interpretation of the papal bulls of gift to the Catholic Kings. Las Casas had written a considered reply to Sepúlveda in the interim, but the junta had not read it. Sepúlveda for his part prepared a paper on the issue of Alexander VI's donation: 'Against those who deprecate, or contradict, the bull and decree of Pope Alexander VI which gives the Catholic Kings and their successors the authority to conquer the Indies and subject those barbarians (and by this means convert them) to the Christian religion and submit them to their empire and jurisdiction'.

The judges then fell into confusion. Las Casas said that they had made a decision 'favourable to the opinions of the bishop [himself], though unfortunately the measures decreed by the council were not well articulated'. Sepúlveda wrote to a friend that the judges 'thought it right and lawful that the barbarians of the new world should be brought under the dominion of the Christians, only one theologian dissenting [presumably Soto]'. Much of the last session's records seem lost or 'at least have not come to light'.[26] Both sides claimed victory. Yet apparently most of the council approved the Las Casasian rules. So Las Casas seemed to have won.

For months afterwards the Council of the Indies strove to secure the judgements of the judges in writing. None of the written opinions have been discovered, except for that of Dr Bernardino de Anaya, who approved conquest in order to spread the faith and to stop the Indians' sins against nature, provided, though, that the expeditions were financed by the Crown and led by men 'zealous in the service of the king, who would act as a good example to the Indians and set off for the good of the Indians, not for gold'. He wanted a revised version of the *requerimiento*.

In his notes to his edition of 1555 of the *Siete Partidas*, the medieval law code of King Alfonso the Wise, Las Casas raised all kinds of interesting issues. Were the Spaniards justified in dominating the New World because they were the nearest to it? No, since Portugal was nearer. Because they were cleverer than other nations? No, the Greeks, the Africans (!) and the Asians were cleverer. Because Indians were idolatrous and committed unnatural crimes? Well, many Indians lived an orderly life in cities, in some respects superior to those of Spain. Superiority in arms? A nefarious argument! Las Casas published a little work about his difficulty with Sepúlveda, *Aquí se contiene una disputa o controversía*

(1552), to which Sepúlveda replied with *Proposiciones temerosas y escandalosas* which, like his *Demócrates Alter*, was not published till the nineteenth century.[27]

What Las Casas plainly wanted from the judges was a declaration that, 'when no danger threatened, preachers alone should be sent to the new world'. That is what the Catalan theologian and poet Ramón Lull had considered desirable in respect of the Muslims in the thirteenth century, and what Las Casas had tried to encourage in Alvarado's Guatemala – not unlike what the Jesuits would do in Paraguay, or in the missions later sent by Spain to California, New Mexico and Texas. Sepúlveda's doctrine was less clear. He was never satisfied that he was understood.

The Council of the Indies waited for the written statements of the advisers. They waited for ever. Perhaps the Crown did not want a clear-cut decision; a compromise might be better.

What happened in practice was that in Spain the benign friars won the intellectual argument, but in the Indies, 'on the ground', the settlers triumphed. Perhaps no one observed that at the time, since all was subsumed in the quarrels of Europe, the mother continent.

BOOK VI
Envoi

46

The Knight of the Black Eagle: Philip and his Flemish role

A prince who makes a deal with a fox is justified in learning to play the fox himself especially if the public welfare requires it.

Justus Lipsius, *Six Books of Policies*

War marked Europe in the late 1540s. It was the first time that a major European war had been fought in Germany. On one side was a Catholic emperor, standing not only for the unity of Christendom but for universal Christian power; on the other, the Protestant states, articulating special particularism. Charles, now a widower,[1] and usually melancholy in time of peace, was happy to be in an army again: 'There goes the happiest man in the world,' his brother Fernando's ambassador Martín de Salinas wrote in 1536 about the emperor and the war in Provence.[2] (It was Salinas who ensured that Ferdinand received so much information about the Indies.)[3]

On 26 June 1546 the Farnese pope, Paul III, signed a treaty agreeing to support Charles against the Protestants. But France and England had concluded a treaty on 6 June at Guînes, in the Pas de Calais, which freed them both from obligations to Charles. On 26 July an army of Protestant princes reached the Danube and threatened to cut off Charles who, in his litter, was carried to the river Inn and joined with papal troops on 13 August. The following day the Protestant Schmalkaldic League formally challenged him, sending him a herald in the traditional manner. Charles assembled his army of 30,000 infantry and 5,000 cavalry, then amalgamated these forces with the 5,000 cavalry of the Dutch Count Egmont van Buren.

The first battle was on 31 August at Ingolstadt, Charles taking part at the head of his men, supported by the Duke of Alba and Egmont.

Through his victory there, Charles won control of south Germany by the end of 1546. This was really the victory of Alba, then at his best as a commander.

At Christmas 1546 Charles was at Heilbronn in Württemberg. He was weary, having slept in forty different places since August. The following spring, in April, supported by his brother Ferdinand with his son Maximilian and by the treacherous Maurice of Saxony, he defeated the Elector John Frederick of Saxony at Mühlberg, near Leipzig, on the Elbe. (John Frederick had not been aware that Charles could ford the Elbe at Mühlberg.) Charles commented: '*Vine, vi y Dios conquistó.*' Alba brought the elector as a prisoner to Charles, who treated him scornfully. The emperor then continued north to Wittenberg, the scene of Luther's first challenge, which John Frederick surrendered on 4 June to avoid a siege. This marked Charles's greatest triumph and enabled him to summon a Diet at Augsburg. The battle of Mühlberg is known as the occasion for Titian's masterpiece; it is a notable example of a great victory inspiring a great picture.

Early in 1548 Charles wrote to his son the Prince Regent Philip, who was then just twenty-one:

Seeing that human affairs are beset with doubt, I can give you no general rules save to trust in God. You will show this by defending the faith. . . . I have come to the conclusion that a general council [of the Church] is the only way ahead . . . Peace will depend not so much on your actions as on those of others. It will be a difficult task for you to preserve it, seeing that God has bestowed so many great kingdoms and principalities on you. . . . You know yourself how unreliable Pope Paul III is in all his treaties, how, sadly, he lacks all [real] zeal for Christendom, and how badly he has acted in this affair of the council [of the Church] above all. Nevertheless, honour his position. He is old [he had been born in 1468 so he was eighty]. Therefore, take careful heed to the instructions which I have given my ambassador [the clever Diego Hurtado de Mendoza] in case of a [papal] election. . . . France has never kept faith and has always sought to do me harm. . . . Never yield to them so much as an inch. . . . Defend Milan with good artillery, Naples with a good fleet. Remember that the French are always discouraged if they do not succeed immediately in anything which they undertake. The Neapolitans, remember, are much given to revolt. Let them be constantly reminded how the French once sacked their city . . . You can never manage without Spanish troops in Italy ... To preserve peace, I have allowed my demands for our ancient hereditary land, for the duchy of Burgundy, to lapse. But do not altogether forget your rights there. ... And do not at any time be persuaded to renounce Piedmont ...

It was an emperor who wrote and one who did not forget his more remote possessions. For he went on to advise Philip to keep a watch over his fleet. It was his best defence against pirates in the Mediterranean, and it would also keep the French from interfering in the Indies. Philip should cultivate Portugal for the same reason. 'Do not cease to keep yourself well informed of the state of those distant lands,' Charles went on, 'for the honour of God and the care of justice. Combat the abuses which have risen in them.' He also urged Philip to marry again soon, since he would need more children, and suggested Elizabeth of Valois, daughter of the new King Henry of France, or Jeanne d'Albret, daughter of King Henry of Navarre, who was 'very attractive and clever'. The first-named was the one Philip chose.

And as for the Indies, take care to keep a good watch to see if the French want to send an armada there, dissimulating or otherwise, and ensuring that the governors of those parts keep a good look out so that, when it is necessary, they can resist the said French; ... and you should establish good intelligence with Portugal ... And as for the division of the Indians, about which there have been so many conflicting reports and advice, we have even consulted Don Antonio de Mendoza, the viceroy of New Spain, so as to be properly informed.[4]

The recipient of this letter was himself now on the move. Though quite unconvinced of the need to travel as his father had done, or in the same restless fashion, he had decided to visit his future dominions in the north of Europe. On 2 October 1548 Philip left Valladolid, ignoring the determined opposition of the Cortes to such a journey. With him were the Duke of Alba, both his own and his father's chief military adviser; Ruy Gómez da Silva, the future prince of Eboli, a Portuguese courtier who would become in effect a chief minister; his long-time secretary, Gonzalo Pérez; Honorat Juan, who had been his tutor in mathematics; the clever and original Fray Constantino Ponce de la Fuente[5]; and Juan Cristóbal Calvete de Estrella, the learned *maestre de pages* of the prince, who would write an account of the journey. (Vicente Álvarez, the steward, would also write a memoir.) Also accompanying them were the musician Luis Narváez and the blind composer Antonio de Cabezón. They were a strange gathering: Alba standing for the hereditary nobility; Silva for the *noblesse de robe*; Honorat Juan was a learned preceptor of the prince from the Borgias' town of Játiva; Ponce de la Fuente was 'Christophorus Fontanus', an Erasmian preacher, a *converso*, who as a result died in prison; while Calvete was Philip's Latin and Greek teacher, who wrote a fine account of Gasca's triumph over Gonzalo Pizarro.[6]

The prince's court spent three nights at Montserrat, then stayed at Barcelona with Estefanía de Requesens, widow of Juan de Zúñiga and Philip's foster-mother, and subsequently went to Rosas in the Ampurdan where, on 2 November 1548, they boarded a vessel in a fleet of fifty-eight galleys commanded by the unconquered Andrea Doria. Then they set off for Genoa, stopping at Cadaqués, Collioure, Perpignan, Aigues Mortes (where they waited six days because of the wind), Hyères and Savona, Columbus's father's town, where the Regent was introduced to the famous bankers Lomellini, Pallavicino and Grillo, all of whom, or their families, were to become important in the Indies.

Finally they arrived at Genoa itself (on 25 November), where Philip was lodged by Doria in his palace. On 19 December Philip left Genoa for Milan of which he was already the duke. His time there was filled with balls, theatres, tourneys, banquets and local tours. He also met the painter Titian for the first time. He set off for the Catholic Church's congress at Trent, where he was welcomed by the Elector Maurice of Saxony (his father's ally, though a Lutheran) and the cardinals of Augsburg and Trent. The council of the Church had actually gone to Bologna because of plague in Trent. Then, after five more days of celebrations, Philip and his party departed for the Netherlands via Bolzano and Innsbruck. This journey lasted six months. It was a serious education – the first time he had visited his northern European dominions.

By 13 February 1549 the princely party was in Munich, with its clean streets and small houses. There was much hunting and many dinners and picnics. Then at Augsburg they visited the all-important Fuggers, while at Ulm there was a joust on the Danube. At Vaihingen they were greeted by Prince Albert of Hohenzollern, who escorted them to Heidelberg, a Catholic enclave in a Protestant valley, where the prince had four days of hunting, picnicking, dancing and drinking. Then the expedition went on to Speyer, Luxembourg, Namur and finally Brussels, where the prince was welcomed by his aunt, the Regent María. There followed a formal reunion with the Emperor Charles at the royal palace.

As usual those days Charles was ill, but he nevertheless held many celebrations, balls, hunting parties and tournaments in honour of Philip, where he met all the grandees of the Low Countries, such as the prince of Orange and Count Egmont, both fatally associated with him later in life. On 12 July Charles and his son embarked on a tour of the Netherlands which lasted till the end of October. There was a formal swearing in of Philip as the heir, and also a celebration at the beautiful palace of Binche, between Charleroi and Mons, at the end of August 1549, where Philip saw *The Descent from the Cross* by Rogier van der Weyden, which he had copied by Michiel Coxcie[7] and which, many years later, he would buy. Probably he bought other Flemish paintings at this time, including some by Bosch and the popular landscapist Joachim Patinir.

Queen Mary of Hungary had held a carnival in 1540 to honour the Spanish conquest of Peru. But there was now a new chivalric feast based on the novel *Amadís de Gaula*, characterized by a storming of magic castles and liberation of prisoners. At a later stage in the 'chivalrous entertainment', knight after knight fails to defeat a certain 'knight of the black eagle'. They are imprisoned in a 'dark castle' till an unknown gentleman, who calls himself 'Beltenbrós' (the name adopted by Amadís during his amorous penance, in the '*Peña Pobre*'), defeats his adversary and reveals that he is the knight for whom this adventure is reserved by drawing forth an enchanted sword from a stone. This unknown, of course, turns out to be Philip.

In September there were two triumphal entries for Philip: first, into Antwerp, then Rotterdam.

The following year, with Philip still in the Netherlands, there were further celebrations. During a carnival in February at Brussels three famous Spanish preachers – Fr Agustín de Cazalla, Fr Bernardo de Fresneda and Fr Constantino Ponce de la Fuente – covered themselves with glory by delivering sermons. This was the last night that Philip spent in Brussels.

> That night His Highness did not go to bed. He stayed in the main square conversing with the ladies as they sat at their windows. A few gentlemen, young and even some old, accompanied him. The talk was of love, stories

were told, there were tears, sighs, laughter, jests. There was dancing in the moonlight to the sound of orchestras which played all night.[8]

These were happy days which were never to recur for Philip in the Low Countries.

An expedition which included Charles as well as Philip then went by boat to Louvain, Aachen, Cologne and Bonn, on the Rhine, though stopping at night on land. They went too to Mainz, Worms, Speyer, and Augsburg, where the imperial Diet met in July 1550. Here or nearby in southern Germany, Philip spent a year. He commissioned Titian's famous *Poesies*, as well as a portrait of himself by the Italian master.

At Augsburg there was discussion about the future inheritance of Philip, to whom Charles hoped to leave everything, in a last fling of his desire to maintain a Habsburg union, a single constitution, a single confession and a single ruler. But his patient brother, Ferdinand, the king of the Romans, wanted the imperial throne, as did Ferdinand's son Maximilian, who came from Spain, where he was co-regent, to argue his case. Ferdinand and Charles disputed in public. Eventually, in March 1551, a formal agreement between Charles and Ferdinand, drafted by the adroit Granvelle, specified that, after the former's death, the latter would be emperor, while Philip would be elected king of the Romans and be emperor after Ferdinand. He would be succeeded by his cousin Maximilian. Thus European power would remain in the hands of the Habsburgs, though it was not quite evident which line it would be.

In July Charles wrote to both the young Maximilian and his wife, María, in their capacity as regents of Spain, about the most important matter on his mind:

> The fleet which goes for the gold and silver of Peru will set off, we don't know when but we do know that any delay at all is very damaging . . . The people of the Council of Finance write about their problems and costs and what they have to provide this year, taking into account that, in addition to the 200,000 ducats which we permit ourselves to take from the gold and silver of Peru, another 500,000 will be needed for the settling of various other liabilities.[9]

Another letter dealt with the idea of contracting with the great admiral of Spain, Álvaro de Bazan, to guard the merchant fleets sent to the New World.[10]

Charles was again talking of gold from the Indies before the end of the year: thus, on 30 December, he wrote from Augsburg that

> La Gasca has brought 200,000 ducats from Peru, of which we will avail ourselves this year. There will be 85,000 ducats which will be remitted and have to be balanced against the fact that costs will amount to 91,716 ducats and another 60,000 ducats which, with interest, will add up to 84,200 ducats and the last slice of 20,000 ducats which, with interest, will make 20,800 ducats which all in would mean that, from the gold and silver of Peru, we would make either 376,000 or 403,570 ducats . . .[11]

Charles's interest in money was as perennial as his incapacity with dealing with it.

In fact, between 1551 and 1555, the Spanish Crown imported from the Indies over three and a half million pesos and private people over 6 million.[12] Charles, the mirror of chivalry and the inheritor of the great Burgundian traditions, spent hours puzzling over these sums.[13]

On 25 May 1551 Philip at last left Augsburg for Spain, travelling back via Mantua (where Gasca explained in detail what had befallen him in Peru, where he had left 346 rich *encomenderos* and about 8,000 colonists). Philip went on to Barcelona, where he arrived on 12 July and where he as usual stayed with Estefanía de Requesens. He only left on 31 July, setting off for Saragossa, Tudela, Soria and Valladolid, his birthplace and *de facto* capital, which he reached on 1 September.[14] No Spanish king had spent so much time abroad, no Spanish monarch would ever know so much of the way of living in other countries, no ruler of Spain was so well prepared to be an international emperor.

On 23 June 1551 the Emperor Charles sent general instructions to Philip for the government of the Indies. These included:

> that you examine all the offices which become free in the Indies in a spirit of justice, alongside the president and council of that enterprise, except for those in the Casa de la Contratación, the viceroyalties, the presidents of the *audiencias* and the office of *fundidor* and inspector of forges, as well as the other principal governors I would reserve for myself . . . All the other dignities and benefits should be guaranteed by the prince . . .

These declarations read like statements in the emperor's will.

The following month Charles wrote more optimistically from Augsburg: 'By letter from Seville on the 12th last, I have gathered that the fleet of the Indies has arrived in Sanlúcar with the galleons coming from all parts [that is, Peru, New Spain, the other Indies and the islands], and everything on board has been unloaded.'

Philip wrote back on 24 November:

> And inasmuch as we are talking of the Indies, they say that the latest reports which have been sent are satisfactory and that, from the treasure brought from Peru by the bishop of Palencia [Gasca], there remains to be taken to Barcelona only 130,000 ducats. And in respect of the other amount from the Indies, that is from '*tierra firme*' [Venezuela and Colombia], New Spain and Honduras, they say that only 80,765 ducats have yet to be delivered.[15]

The letter went into much detail as to how the money from the Indies should be spent.

In December Philip wrote again, from Madrid:

> What would be really sensible would be to establish a fleet to guard the coast of Andalusia, from cape Saint Vincent to the straits of Gibraltar, to ensure the safety of the vessels which go to and come from the Indies which is now the main route of the merchants in Seville and Andalusia and where damage can be done by the French. And this fleet could be paid for by a grant which Your Majesty could make and be financed by a tax which could be levied on all merchandise coming from the Indies.[16]

The armada of ships named to protect the merchant fleets was always exposed to illegal or even corrupt practice. Thus as much as a quarter of the galleons were carrying goods which overweighed them. The captains of these ships sometimes made 100,000 pesos from this illegal freight and more from the sale of offices on their ships to merchants. Captains were told that they were rendering their vessels unfit for fighting, but critics were told that so long as the gun decks were free, cargo in the hold made the ships steadier. The curious part of this story was that the captains carried their illegal cargoes above decks where they could easily be seen.

The captains and the admirals of these ships were thought to be of superior rank to the commanders of the fleets, for they received their appointments directly from the monarchs, whereas the flag officers were usually chosen by the officials of the Council of the Indies. Of course there were arguments about this. By the seventeenth century the *junta de*

9a. (*above*) Bartolomé de las Casas, the apostle of the Indies.

9b. (*left*) Portable altars were used everywhere in the new world.

10a. (*left*) The head of Francisco Pizarro with his mistress, in the Palace of the Conquest built by Hernando Pizarro.

10b. (*below*) Hernando Pizarro, second-in-command to his brother Francisco in the conquest of Peru, kneeling, in the Palace of the Conquest.

11a. (*left*) Inca architecture: a street wall built to last, in Cuzco.

11b. (*below*)
Inca walls: the fortress of Sacsahuaman, Cuzco, whose stones were put together with immense skill.

ESTOS MVДIHO5OS/RIENAVETVRAД₵ SДO3ЕRELIGIOSOS FVEPOLOSBRIMEROSFVNдAдORES дELAFREENE₵TA
ɅCLESIA SALLEROد ESɅANA ANدEIS24dIΛдELΛ₵OVERSIOдES·BΛBLO YLLEGAIO ΛESTATVΛMIERNESVIGILIΛVIGILI
ΓE₵OSTESдELMESMOΛNO₤.

RΛIOꝶ :ЕRΛFRΛ₵ISCO ·FRΛGΛR ·FRΛTORIVIO·FRΛFRΛ₵IS
РДI·ХIMENEꞆ ₵I₤вΛɔꝶꝶꝶꝶMOTOLIɴIA ·дESO₤O   FRΛ·MHGEL дE   FRΛ·MHGEL РFRΛYΛTОNIОIO ·FRΛIVΛ ·FRΛIVΛ· R·RΛLVIS
   VΛLEΓIΛ   дEIESOꝶ   SдECIVдΛδROдPICO дERIBΛS·XVΛRE₤ дEFVESΛ

12a. (*above*) The barefoot friars who
walked to Mexico from Veracruz, 1524.
Mural in the Franciscan monastery at
Huejotzingo.

12b. (*below*) Augustinian monastery of
Acolman, completed in 1560: plateresque
façade and open chapel in the centre.

13. The Franciscan monastery in Quito, built 1533–81, was
an inspiration for all the New World.

14. San Pablo, Valladolid, where Philip II was christened, where the nobility took an oath of loyalty to Charles V and where Las Casas debated with Sepúlveda.

15. Philip II, regent of Spain in 1542, king in 1556. (Moro)

16a. (*above*) Charles V
at Mühlberg: the great
battle picture of Charles
V, who was always at
war. (Titian)

16b. (*left*) The Jeronymite
monastery of Yuste in the
Gredos mountains, where
Charles V retired and
died.

guerra of the Council of the Indies presented their lists of eligible persons which were chosen by the king – or rather by his closest nominees.

There were two types of captain-general, those appointed to the title for life, and those named for a single voyage. Like most Spanish officials they bought these posts, or at least advanced the Crown a sum of money such as 100,000 pesos to be repaid in the Indies, with 8 per cent interest. They took an oath of loyalty before the Council of the Indies or before the president and officials of the Casa. The captain-general would concern himself in detail with the experience of his officers, their supplies and their equipment, and several appointments depended on these captains, for example the chaplains, the master carpenters, the caulkers, the physicians, the barber-surgeons, the quartermasters. The governor would have the choice of galleon after the general and the admiral, his ship being called the *gobierno*. Two companies of infantry, sometimes drawn from the Cadiz garrison, were usually assigned to the Mexican fleet. Each fleet carried an inspector (*veedor*) whose role was to see that all relevant laws were observed and that each man from the captain-general down performed his duties. He was royal watchdog for all occasions and was immune from all judicial process. Other officials included an accountant on each armada and a magistrate (*alguacil*) for each ship. These arrangements were all in place in the last years of the Emperor Charles.

In early 1552, Philip was at Madrid and Gasca, the victor of Peru who was becoming an imperial adviser of the first rank, was with the Princess María at Linz negotiating for Ferdinand with Maurice of Saxony. Ferdinand continued to show concern for the Indies, putting many questions to Gasca, who received as a present from Ferdinand eight richly worked plates; and Gasca bought a triptych to give to the church of Barco de Ávila very close to his birthplace.[17]

Despite his triumph at Mühlberg, Charles did not escape further difficulties. On the contrary. He spent the winter of 1551–2 in Innsbruck, the city associated with his grandfather Maximilian. In the spring of 1552 he heard that the Protestant princes, outraged by the emperor's treatment of their colleagues, would receive the backing of the new King Henry of France who, with Maurice of Saxony, who had once more changed sides, was ready to fall on the fortresses of Metz, Toul and Verdun. Charles was on the point of becoming a prisoner. On 3 March Charles sent a steward, Joachim de Rye, Sieur de Balançon, with instructions to his brother, begging him to try to persuade the princes to seek peace because the Turkish peril was surely far more grave. But Maurice of Saxony (now known in imperial circles as the 'kinglet') nevertheless sent his army against Charles and on 23 May entered Innsbruck. Charles and what there was of the court only escaped by fleeing south across the Brenner Pass into Italy in driving rain. Remarkably, Gasca was with his master in this crisis.[18]

Charles was now at war with France on every front. In April Metz was seized by the Constable of France, the brilliant and powerful friend of the late King Francis I, Anne de Montmorency. Metz was a city proud of being a 'Free City' but it was one *of the empire*. Francis, Duke of Guise (*le Balafré*), as governor ruthlessly pulled down the suburbs and even moved the body of King Louis the Pious from St Arnulf's outside the walls to the cathedral of Saint Etienne within the city.[19] Only in the autumn did troops come from Spain which enabled the emperor in person to besiege Guise in Metz, but the duke was a brilliant defender in a siege and Charles failed to recapture the place.

Philip wanted to go to help his father. He wrote in May from Madrid: 'I have no information about the news that Peru has sent to Panama and Nombre de Dios over 335,000 pesos.'[20] He wrote again in June, saying that he was anxious to ensure that the Spaniards who came back from the Spice Isles would be well received: 'let them be good informers about the state of those islands'.[21] Then in July the Casa de la Contratación reported that the treasure brought back by Gasca amounted to 1,906,082 escudos. Of these, 600,000 would be sent to Germany, 400,000 to the Low Countries, 200,000 to Parma, and only 200,000 to Castile, while 100,000 would be a loan to the pope.[22]

Given the increased reliance of the Spanish Crown on an income from the Indies, the Casa de la Contratación now received new rules of conduct, following the similar reorganization which we have seen of the Council of the Indies. The headquarters would still be in Seville, but there would be a daily mass, fixed hours of work (seven to ten in summer, eight to eleven in winter and, in the afternoons, Monday, Wednesday and Friday from five, or in winter from three). The officials who did not attend would be fined. They would have to live in the Casa and take an oath on introduction. The discussions of the afternoon would deal with licences to go to the Indies. Votes would be by a simple majority. Grave disputes would be referred to the Council of the Indies. Sections 27–30 forbade officials to receive gifts for any services and to do anything commercial in the Indies. Sections 45–88 dealt with the separate functions of each official. For example, the treasurer would be responsible for all the money in cash, the factor for all merchandise. Sections 121–6 listed those people forbidden to go to the Indies – Moors, new Christians or *conversos*, and descendants of those punished by the Inquisition. Prohibited merchandise included 'profane books and stories, books whose contents are untruthful'. (There was a specific decree repeating the banning of the import of romances into the New World; it was still thought that Indians might doubt the scriptures if they realized that the books were fictional. But this law had no effect.)[23] The only books permitted were those which dealt with Christianity and virtue. And, though scientific books were not banned, the Council of the Indies wanted strict censorship over both historical and geographical works dealing with the Indies.

Sections 144 to the end dealt with how ships should sail to the Indies. Two thirds of the water which was carried should be in well-prepared casks. The rest could go in clay pots, vats or pitchers, which were less good since they sometimes broke and water was wasted.

Ships of 100 tons (the minimum size) should have a crew of thirty-two, those of 250 tons should have sixty-four, including officers. Boats should be inspected when built, then when loaded. A third inspection of every ship should follow just before it left Sanlúcar de Barrameda for the Indies, in the presence of a judge

These rules (*ordenanzas*) were signed in August 1552 by Philip and countersigned by Samano, the secretary, by Luis Hurtado de Mendoza, still the president of the Council of the Indies, and by *licenciados* Gregorio López and Tello de Sandoval, Gonzalo Pérez de Ribadeneira and Gracián de Briviesca. All were members of the Council of the Indies; Tello had been in New Spain as we have seen, the other three were lawyers who had risen through the system, each with a spell of education at Santa Cruz de Valladolid. These rules were placed on every ship and widely distributed to colonial officials.

On 7 October 1552 Philip wrote to his father from Monzón, where he was attending the Cortes of Aragon, to say that, in respect of paying the expenses which he had previously listed, 'the principal recourse for those necessities is the Indies'.[24]

We find Charles replying from Metz that 'Insofar as the perpetuity of the *encomiendas* is concerned, we think that this is not the time to treat of that ... All the same, we think that we have done well by arranging a contract with Hernán Ochoa for the sale of 23,000 African slaves for the Indies.'[25]

On 12 November 1553 Philip wrote again to the Emperor Charles that every year more corsairs sailed out of France intending to sack Spanish imperial ports. In the previous July they had destroyed Palma in the Canaries.[26] Yet, had it not been for the sums which now regularly reached Castile from the Indies, Spain would probably have had to abandon northern Europe.

Most of the money sent legally by private persons from the New World to Spain was still turned into *juros*, those promises of a periodic payment at a fixed rate of interest for which responsibility was assigned to specific sources of the Crown's admiring bankers. Other money came in through the profits from businesses owned or founded by enterprising conquistadors. Much of this was illegal, and that method became increasingly attractive as the Crown imposed more and more restrictions on the legal means of entry. The fiscal Licenciado Juan Villalobos of the Council of the Indies accused Hernando Pizarro of having taken unregistered gold, silver and emeralds valued at 500,000 ducats on which the royal fifth had not been paid.[27] There were, alas, many illegal ways of proceeding – for example, Hernando Pizarro had an agent, Juan de Zavala, in Panama who devoted all his time to evasion of official rules.

47

The emperor at bay

If there is no way to avoid an engagement before I arrive I cannot enjoin you too strongly to inform me post haste.
Philip II, on the eve of the battle of Saint Quentin

Gold or no gold, northern Europe notwithstanding, the shadows were now darkening for the Emperor Charles. Nearly forty years of continuous struggle since 1516 had left him exhausted, and he was now always racked with pain from gout and other maladies. His failure at Metz at the hands of the Duke of Guise had been a serious setback. On 12 January 1553 he abandoned the siege, blaming the cold and disease affecting his soldiers. He retired to Brussels where he succumbed to melancholy, examining his collection of clocks. In September of that year a statement about his health was made by Nicolas Nicolai:

> In the opinion of his doctors, His Majesty cannot be expected to live long because of the great number of illnesses which affect him, especially in winter ... the gout attacks him and frequently racks all his limbs and nerves ... and the common cold affects him so much that he sometimes appears to be in his last straits ... his piles put him in such agony that he cannot move without great pain ... All these things, together with his very great mental sufferings, have completely altered the good humour and affability which he used to have and have turned him into a melancholic ... His Majesty will not allow anyone, lord or prelate, into his presence nor does he want to deal with papers ... he spends day and night in adjusting and setting his countless clocks and does little else.[1]

The possibility of abdication brought on by ill health became a continual preoccupation. The fact that no monarch of substance had

abdicated since Diocletian, also probably in consequence of ill health in
AD 305, was on his mind.[2] Charles was only fifty-three but seemed to
have reigned for centuries. The realistic but for Charles tragic peace of
Augsburg of September 1555 sealed his reign: the principle was '*cuius
regio, eius religio*'. Every state of the empire had the right thereafter to
decide its own religion.

Charles, too, was no longer the humane statesman concerned with
the well-being of his Indian subjects, with enlightened Erasmian confes-
sors such as Jean Glapion and liberal clergymen such as Alonso Manrique
de Lara at his side. Crushed by ill health, he had become intransigent,
obsessed by the Protestant heresy and concerned with the Indies only in
respect of the gold and silver which could be drawn out of them; and, it
is fair to add, distressed by his own failure to crush heresy and maintain
the Habsburg legacy undivided.

The Prince Regent Philip, on the other hand, was at the time preoccupied with his second marriage. Despite suggestions that Philip
might marry another Portuguese princess, in August 1553 Simon
Renard,[3] ambassador in London, mentioned the possibility of an English marriage for the prince to Queen Mary: 'She began to laugh not
once but several times and looked at me to suggest that she found the
idea very much to her liking.'[4] She was, after all, the daughter of Henry
VIII by Catherine of Aragon and had been used to consider the Emperor
Charles as her guiding light. Once in 1521 she had even been betrothed
to him; 'the pearl of the world' she had been proclaimed.[5] Charles
obtained Philip's (reluctant) approval, and made a formal request for
her hand. Mary asked Renard many questions and requested a portrait;
a copy of Titian's famous one in armour was sent to her. If Philip was
disposed to be amorous, she told Renard, such was not her desire for
she was 'of such an age that His Majesty knows of and had never har-
boured thoughts of love. Also she would love and obey Philip but, if he
wished to encroach on the government of her country, she would be
unable to allow it.'[6] It was therefore an astounding decision of Philip's
since at that time his only heir was Don Carlos, his son by Maria of
Portugal, and he and the empire needed more reassurance and, above
all, more *infantes*. The new marriage was not a decision welcomed by
Ferdinand, Charles's brother, the king of the Romans, who had already
sent a messenger, Martín de Guzmán, a courtier of the emperor, to propose a marriage of Mary with his own son, the Archduke Ferdinand of

Tyrol, then in his early thirties. Ferdinand had sent a portrait of him to London too.[7]

On 29 October 1553 Mary, however, swore to accept Philip as her husband. He was then twenty-six, eleven years younger than she. He was not enthusiastic and, since the death of his first consort, had had several pretty mistresses (Isabel Osorio, Catalina Láinez and above all Eufrasia de Guzmán). There was opposition in England too. The House of Commons requested Mary not to marry a foreigner. But she went ahead. On 12 January 1554 a marriage contract was drawn up between Mary of England and Philip. Philip would share all titles and responsibilities with Mary, but would relinquish everything if she died first. He would conform to English laws and customs, admit no foreigners to office in England, and not implicate England in his wars. It was an arrangement similar to that of Ferdinand with Isabel in 1479.

On 13 July 1554 Philip left Spain to marry Mary and this time his sister Juana of Portugal, recently widowed in Portugal, would be Regent in Spain.

The prince sailed from Corunna, apparently with 4,000 troops in seventy vessels, in bad weather; Silva, the prince of Eboli, said he nearly died of seasickness. They were met off the Isle of Wight by Lord Howard of Effingham, the Lord High Admiral, and father of the future English commander against the *armada invincible* in 1588, and entered Southampton on 20 July.[8] They were greeted by Henry, Earl of Arundel, a Catholic nobleman, who presented Philip with the Order of the Garter. Then they went to Winchester and on 23 July were met at the cathedral by the ambassadorial Stephen Gardiner, the bishop of Winchester, who introduced him to the queen. Though Mary was the daughter of Catherine of Aragon, she could not talk Spanish well, but she did speak French adequately. Charles sent, via Juan de Figueroa, '*un gentilhombre de la boca de la casa de Borgoña*', a special present to Philip – the throne of Naples – so he could marry as a king.

On 25 July, the day of Santiago, the wedding was held at Winchester. Philip was very affable, talking to the English crowd in the rain, drinking beer, promising to cut his retinue, taking some English nobles into his train, telling his people to try to adapt to English customs. 'He has shown such affability and such sweetness of temper as not to be surpassed,' reported Soriano, the Venetian ambassador.[9] Then they proceeded slowly to London by water, disembarking there on 18 August, and carried on to Hampton Court for 'what remained of the summer'. According to Andrés Muñoz, the Spanish nobles knew that they were in the land of *Amadís de Gaula* (much of which novel is set in England). 'There is more to be seen in England than is written of in those books,' he commented, 'because of the dwellings that there are in the country, the rivers, the fields, the beautiful flowered meadows, the cool fountains . . . a pleasure to see . . . above all, in summer.'[10]

The Spaniards found the English less appealing than the countryside, for they looked white and pink, and were quarrelsome. 'All their celebrations seemed to consist of eating and drinking, they think of nothing else . . . they have a lot of beer, and drink more of it than there is water in the river at Valladolid.' There were frequent robberies in the streets, the ladies of the court were 'quite ugly', and the queen had no eyebrows and, 'though she was a saint, she was short-sighted, and her voice was rough and loud'. Some Spaniards said that 'they would prefer to be in the slums of Toledo than in the meadows of Amadís'.[11] The king acted 'as if he were Isaac allowing himself to be sacrificed to the will of his father'.[12] Then in November Mary and Philip presided over a joint session of the English parliament in which a reconciliation with the Church of Rome was made law. Philip also dealt with imperial affairs. Thus in London he set up a committee of twelve, including the flawed Fray Bartolomé de Carranza and Fray Bernardo de Fresneda, to discuss the matter of *encomiendas*. He told his father that he thought they should concede these grants in perpetuity.

But there would be shadows in London too: on 1 February 1555 the first victim of persecution in England was burned at the stake. Many Spaniards were appalled. The ambassador in London, Simon Renard, wrote to Philip: 'I do not think it well that Your Majesty should allow further executions to take place.'[13] But the prince had no power in the English Church courts, even if he inspired his confessor, Fray Alonso de Castro, a Franciscan with a mission to preach to the Prince Regent from 1553 to 1556, in a sermon on 10 February to criticize the bishops of England for burning Protestants. The initiative was that of the Lord Chancellor Stephen Gardiner, who re-enacted the anti-heresy statute of 1401. Yet he, like Richard Sampson and Edward Foxe, had published acts in defence of King Henry's divorce and royal supremacy in the 1530s.[14]

The year 1555 marked the beginning of the end for Charles the emperor. On 22 October in Brussels he made Philip master of the Order of the Fleece. Three days later Charles summoned the authorities of the Low Countries. He abandoned Burgundy and the Netherlands (leaning on the arm of the Prince of Orange) in favour of his son. Philip came over from England. Charles spoke in elegiac mode of his travels, his troubles and his triumphs. Through his mind as he spoke there must have passed recollections of Luther at Worms, of Pope Adrian VI in Flanders and the happy gardens of his childhood with his clever aunt Margaret at Mechelen. He surely would have recalled meeting Cortés and Pizarro in 1529, Magellan in 1522, King Henry VIII in 1520 and 1522, and all the members of that brilliant Netherlandish court who accompanied him on his first visit to Spain in 1517, above all Chièvres.

He recalled for his audience his ten stays in Flanders, his nine journeys to Germany, his six sojourns in Spain, his seven voyages to Italy, four to France, two to England (to see Henry VIII, whom he had admired to begin with) and two to Africa, not to speak of several in the Mediterranean – his ceaseless travels which enabled him at least to know all the mysterious corners of his European empire as his ancestors had known their Spanish kingdoms.[15] He was surrounded as he spoke by the knights of the Fleece; Philip; his royal sisters, Leonor and Mary, both ex-queens; the young Ferdinand of Austria; Christine of Lorraine; and Emanuel Philibert, the new Duke of Savoy. It was he who introduced the emperor. Charles then spoke of his life and how everywhere he seemed to have failed. He commended Philip. There were abundant tears.

Mary of Hungary also abdicated from the Netherlands. She and the former queen of France, Leonor, would follow Charles to Spain, Mary taking with her a fine collection of pictures, books and tapestries (many of the pictures would find their way eventually to the Prado).

Early in 1556 Charles gave up Castile and Aragon, and later that year, in a letter of 12 September he handed his brother, Ferdinand, the imperial throne. (Not till February 1557 did the electors accept the abdication and the elevation of Ferdinand.)

On 12 September Charles also wrote to explain his decision to all the authorities and municipalities of the Indies. He said his bad health made his personal direction of the government impossible.[16] He also abandoned his mastership of the great knightly orders. The abdication was read in Latin by Fr Francisco de Vargas, chaplain of the royal family since 1549.

In January 1556 Philip had written to the same recipients accepting the Crown of Castile and León with everything belonging to them.[17] The heir to the throne, Don Carlos, son of Philip's first wife, Maria of Portugal, proclaimed his father in Spain: '*¡Castilla, Castilla por el rey Don Felipe!*'

Charles retired to Spain in September. The plan was that he would go to live at the Jeronymite monastery of Yuste, founded in the early fifteenth century on the site of two ancient hermitages, in the Gredos mountains. Thus he left Flushing with 150 followers on the Basque ship *Espíritu Santo* (known as the *Bertendona*), of 565 tons. Most of Charles's courtiers were made ill by the voyage.

Charles and his court reached Laredo near Santander on 28 September. It was still the famous port which it had been throughout the century. He was greeted by Pedro de Manrique, bishop of Salamanca, and by Durango, mayor of the court. They went to Burgos where Charles stayed two days in the famous Casa del Cordón, the house of the Constable of Castile, Pedro Fernández de Velasco. At Torquemada, the emperor was greeted by Gasca, now bishop of the rich diocese of Palencia; at Cabezón rather gracelessly by his grandson Don Carlos; at Valladolid by the Regent Juana; and at Medina del Campo by the rich merchant Rodrigo de Dueñas, a money broker, who gave Charles a gold chafing-dish filled with Ceylonese cinnamon – not Amazonian – the extravagance of which gift infuriated the ex-emperor so that he refused to allow Dueñas to kiss his hand – or so it was said.[18]

Charles then moved to a mansion belonging to the Count of Oropesa at Jarandilla, in the Gredos, about ten miles from Yuste. The count was hereditary protector of the convent of Yuste because of the actions in 1402 of an earlier count in defending the first Jeronymites there against marauding monks from other monasteries. Charles had not been to Yuste before, though he had been to Guadalupe in April 1525 and to Oropesa in February 1526. He had been to Salamanca, though, in 1534. The Prince Regent Philip had visited Yuste in May 1554, presumably to inspect its possibilities.

Charles remained at Jarandilla for three months before he moved, on 3 February 1557, to Yuste, which by then had been refurbished by Fray Juan de Ortega.[19] It is in a beautiful spot, surrounded by chestnuts, on the turbulent river Tiétar. During much of the year the nearby mountains are covered by snow, but the lower valley of La Vera is fertile.

The Jeronymites were an offshoot of the Franciscan order. As predicted by St Bridget of Sweden, two Franciscan hermits who had been living in the mountains of Toledo had presented themselves to Pope Gregory XI at Avignon and obtained the establishment of their new order. The brothers wore white woollen tunics and brown scapulars and mantles as allegedly worn by St Jerome, the symbolic inspiration of the order. Yuste was one of the first of their houses. The Jeronymites were known for the rigour of their observances, the munificence of their alms and the hospitality of their tables. They emphasized humility. All these attributes attracted the emperor, who had always admired them.

Charles had expected to remove himself from all business, but he conducted an active correspondence on many matters, especially those relating to heresy. He employed a staff of fifty, headed by Luis Méndez Quijada, his majordomo. He had with him religious books such as one by St Augustine and another by the fluent Fray Luis de Granada, scientific works such as the *Astronomicum Caesareum* of Peter Apian, historical works such as the *Commentaries* on Charles's own war in Germany by Luis Dávila y Zúñiga, and Olivier de la Marche's *Le Chevalier délibéré*, that 'mirror of chivalry' which he had had translated into Spanish. There were also two big books on which had been painted 'trees, grasses, men and other things from the Indies', a reminder that the Indies were still on the emperor's mind, though what books they were it is hard to know.[20] He had some clocks, such as one of ebony and sand, another of crystal, and several portraits of his wife, the Empress Isabel, of himself, of Prince Philip and even one of Queen Mary of England.[21] From his bed in the monastery, he could see the altar of the church and, having positioned himself well, could watch the host being raised during mass.

In August 1558 he became seriously ill with malaria and the gout which had for so long tortured him grew worse every day. He died on 21 September of that year, at 2 a.m. He had time to rehearse his funeral. Fray Bartolomé de Carranza was present at the end, as was the Count of Oropesa and his brother, and their uncle abbot Diego de Cabañas, Luis Dávila (to whom Charles had entrusted the bringing up of Don Juan, his bastard son by Frau von Blomberg of Regensburg), and his secretary for correspondence, Martín de Gaztelú.[22] His body was placed beneath the high altar of the monastery at Yuste but was removed from there to the Escorial in 1574.

Philip was in Flanders when he received the news of his father's death.

On 17 November Mary of England died without heirs. On 28 November Philip held a glittering funeral service in St Gudule in Brussels for his father and, on 2 December, another for his wife, the English Queen Mary.

At his death Charles left his empire in Europe restored. Spain, Italy, half of Germany and the Netherlands were under his control or that of his brother Ferdinand. The empire in the Indies, though no one used that term, was effectively under Spanish direction. Some parts of it were economically successful, especially after the use of an amalgam of mercury rendered the process of mining for silver much easier; Zacatecas and Potosí were becoming great sources of silver. Then in 1558 the Spanish Antilles produced 60,000 *arrobas* of sugar to be exported to Seville.[23] Great sums were still regularly paid to the Pizarro family, including the imprisoned Hernando, who often received an illegal income through agents. Part of this wealth derived from the cultivation of coca which was forty times larger than before the conquest.[24]

By the time of the death of Charles V, probably 15,000 African slaves had reached the Spanish empire. About 500 had been bought by Cortés, no less, to work on his sugar plantations in New Spain.[25] Already too there was a large subculture of lesser groups. For example, the children of African slave fathers and Indian women, *zambos*, were already making an impact on the society of the empire in both New Spain and Peru. The two large principalities based on those two regions were the seats of Spanish viceroyalties, and most of the rest of South America as well as the Caribbean was governed by Spanish commanders. There were untidy gaps in the texture of the empire and North America, despite the efforts of Hernando de Soto, was far from being a Spanish outpost. The administration of the Empire depended on the collection of income from the Crown's fifth of the precious metals and other products. Later there would be an imperial version of the 2 per cent Castilian sales tax known as the *alcabala*.

In 1559 another even more elaborate funeral was held for the Emperor Charles in the new cathedral in Mexico, a small edifice begun in 1525. On Cortés's orders stones from the old pagan pyramids had been used as the foundation. Inside this *iglesia mayor*, as it was known, was an aisled rectangle with wooden supports and a flat, wooden roof, on the site of its colossal successor cathedral, begun in the 1570s.[26]

The empty sarcophagus in Mexico of the king emperor was on two levels, in Doric style. A funeral urn was placed on the first level, and was covered with a black cloth and a cushion on which a crown rested. On the second level, the Austrian eagle spread gilded wings beneath a painted blue sky. This remarkable tribute took the architect Claudio Arcienaga, from Burgos – later the inspiration of the second cathedral of the city – three months to create. He had been busy since his arrival in New Spain in the late 1540s designing the viceregal palace on the site of the *casas viejas* of Montezuma. He had built the first university building in Mexico, as well as the beautiful staircase in the hospital of Jesus.

The funeral procession was led by Indian rulers in black cloaks, their hems dragging in the dust, carrying standards with embroidered coats of arms – their own and those of the dead emperor. After them came the leading men of different towns of New Spain, and many Indian noblemen, followed by 400 monks and priests and then by the second archbishop of Mexico, Alonso de Montúfar, a Dominican friar from Loja near Granada (where he had once been *inquisidor* of the Holy Office), attended by the bishop of Michoacan (still the remarkable Utopian Vasco de Quiroga) and the bishop of New Galicia (Pedro de Ayala, a Dominican from a famous family of Toledo).

Quiroga remained firm in his determination to create Utopia in New Spain.[27] He still believed that the Church in the New World could obtain the purity of customs lost among the Europeans, who were victims of ambition, pride and malice.[28]

At that time there were nearly 800 friars in New Spain and they had established between them over 150 religious houses. Many of them in their day had converted thousands of Indians. Had not the emperor's kinsman Pedro de Gante spoken in June 1529 of baptizing 14,000 in a day? Many of these friars must have been present at this funeral. So were the six bishops of New Spain (Mexico, Oaxaca, Michoacan, Chiapas, Guadalajara and Yucatan).

The secular part of the procession was headed by Bernardino de Albornoz, who carried the banner of the city. Coming from Paradinas near Segovia, he had become a councillor of the city, and magistrate (commander) of the fortress of Atarazanas. Albornoz was followed by two mace-bearers, dressed in black damascene and coats of mail on which the royal arms gleamed, in gold and silver. The city's treasurer, Hernando de Portugal, a descendant of the royal house of that country and sometime courtier (*contino*) in Spain, carried a crown on a damask cushion. The constable, Ortúno de Ibarra, carried a bare, unsheathed sword, and the inspector, García de Albornoz, brother of Bernardino, a crossbow. Luis del Castillo, the great friend of the late Viceroy Mendoza, also a member of an illustrious family, carried an imperial coat of mail.[29] Somewhere in the procession there would surely have been seen Alonso de Vilaseca, possessed of vast cattle ranches as well as rich silver mines in Pachuca, who had endowed a chair of theology at the university of Mexico, a liberal friend of Franciscans on the savage frontiers. Other benefactors of New Spain would have been present, such as the trustees of the two-storey hospital of the Immaculate Conception (later known as Jesus Nazareño), founded so soon after the conquest and maintained by a fraternity (*cofradía*) of which Cortés had been a leading member. (There was, too, Bishop Zumárraga's hospital del Amor de Dios.) Pedro de Gante would have been present, if only because of his establishment of the hospital for Indians known as San José.

Behind walked Viceroy Mendoza's successor, Luis de Velasco, an eminently noble and dignified figure, a cousin of the Constable of Castile, whose train was held by a chamberlain. He was married to Ana de Castilla, who had a weakness for the persecuted Archbishop Carranza. There followed other officials such as the judges of the supreme court, the *oidores*, the chief bailiff, the chief of the exchequer and the rector of the new university of Mexico. Velasco had in 1553 introduced a kind of rural guard in New Spain, a Santa Hermandad or police force comparable to what had been created in old Spain under Fernando and Isabel. We cannot doubt that this ceremonial viceroyalty was an advance on what existed before; as the great historian Burckhardt put it, 'the State founded on sheer crime is compelled in the course of time to develop a kind of justice and morality, since those of its citizens who are just and moral gradually get the upper hand'.[30]

Thus did Spain carry across the Atlantic well-tested ceremonies attended by aristocrats and great men and women.[31]

Laus deo.

APPENDICES

1. *The councils of Charles V*

COUNCIL OF STATE

GLAPION, Fr Juan de: 1522
GORREVOD, Laurent de: 1522–9
PLAINE, Gerard de la: 1522–4
LANNOY, Charles de: 1522–6
CROŸ, Adrien de: 1524–5
GATTINARA, Mercurino Arborio: 1522–30
NASSAU, Enrique de: 1522–38
POUPET, Charles de: 1522–30
MONCADA, Hugo de: 1523–8
VEGA, Hernando de: 1526
RUIZ DE LA MOTA, Pedro: 1522
MANUEL, Juan: 1522–35
FONSECA, Alonso de: 1526–7
TOLEDO, Fadrique de: 1526–7
ZÚÑIGA, Álvaro de: 1526–7
MERINO, Esteban Gabriel: 1526–34
LOAISA, García de: 1526–7
FLANDES, Luis de: 1527–55
ZÚÑIGA, Francisco de: 1528–36
PERRENOT, Nicolás (Granvelle): 1528–50
COBOS, Francisco de los: 1529–46
PADILLA, García de: 1529–42
FERNÁNDEZ MANRIQUE, García: 1535–46
ZÚÑIGA Y AVELLANEDA, Juan de: 1536–46
SILVA, Fernando de: 1538–45
VALDÉS, Fernando de: 1543–56

ÁLVAREZ DE TOLEDO, Fernando: 1543–56
HURTADO DE MENDOZA, Luis: 1546–56
VÁZQUEZ DE MOLINA, Juan: 1548–56
PIMENTEL Y ENRÍQUEZ, Bernardino de: 1548–51
FONSECA, Antonio de: 1554–6
NAVARRA, Pedro de: 1554–5
ROJAS, Antonio de: 1554–5
TOLEDO, García de: 1554–6

Secretaries

HANNART, Juan: 1522–4
ALEMÁN, Juan: 1524–8
COBOS, Francisco de los: 1528–46
VÁZQUEZ DE MOLINA, Juan (interim): 1539–56
IDIÁQUEZ, Alonso de (interim): 1529–47
PÉREZ, Gonzalo (interim): 1543–5, 1554–5 (Naples and Milan)

COUNCIL OF WAR

FERNÁNDEZ MANRIQUE, Luis: 1517–34
SANDOVAL Y ROJAS, Bernardo de: 1518–35
ENRÍQUEZ, Fadrique: 1520–21
FERNÁNDEZ DE VELASCO, Íñigo: 1520–21
VARGAS, Francisco de: 1520–22
MANRIQUE, Rodrigo: 1520–29
HURTADO DE MENDOZA, Diego: 1520–34
TÉLLEZ GIRÓN, Alonso: 1521–2
ROJAS, Diego de: 1521–2
GORREVOD, Laurent de: 1522–9
MONCADA, Hugo de: 1523–8
FERRAMOSCA, César: 1524–6
VEGA, Hernando de: 1526
FONSECA, Antonio de: 1526–7
ZÚÑIGA Y AVELLANEDA, Francisco de: 1528–36
ANDRADE, Hernando de: 1529–33
ZUAZOLA, Pedro de: 1533–6

FERNÁNDEZ MANRIQUE, García: 1535–46
ZÚÑIGA Y AVELLANEDA, Juan de: 1536–46
SILVA, Fernando de: 1538–45
ÁLVAREZ DE TOLEDO, Fernando: 1543–82
HURTADO DE MENDOZA, Luis: 1546–57
VÁZQUEZ DE MOLINA, Juan: 1548–59
PIMENTEL Y ENRÍQUEZ, Bernardino: 1548–51
NAVARRA, Pedro de: 1554–5
ROJAS, Antonio de: 1554–5
TOLEDO, García de: 1554–6

Secretaries

ZUAZOLA, Pedro de: 1518–33
VÁZQUEZ DE MOLINA, Juan: 1533–67
MARTÍNEZ DE ONDARZA, Andrés (interim): 1529–32
LEDESMA, Francisco de (interim): 1539–59

ROYAL COUNCIL AND CABINET OF CASTILE

Presidents

ROJAS MANRIQUE, Antonio de: 1514–24
PARDO DE TAVERA, Juan: 1524–39
VALDÉS Y SALAS, Fernando de: 1539–46
NIÑO, Hernando: 1546–52
FONSECA, Antonio de: 1553–6

Councillors

OROPESA, Pedro de: 1491–1529
ZAPATA, Luis de: 1498–1522
BAÑEZ (IBÁÑEZ) DE MÚJICA, García: 1498–1519
GALÍNDEZ DE CARVAJAL, Lorenzo: 1502–27
GÓMEZ DE SANTIAGO, Toribio: 1503–34
LÓPEZ DE PALACIOS RUBIOS, Juan: 1504–23
GONZÁLEZ DE POLANCO, Luis: 1505–42

VARGAS, Francisco: 1505–23

SOSA, Francisco de: 1506–20

CASTILLA, Alonso de: 1506–7, 1518–23

IBÁÑEZ DE AGUIRRE, Fortún: 1506–47

RODRÍGUEZ DE FONSECA, Juan: 1508–24

VEGA, Hernando de: 1509–26

CABRERO, Juan: 1510–28

COALLA, Rodrígo de: 1514–28

PADILLA, García de: 1516–42

RUIZ DE LA MOTA, Pedro: 1516–22

BELTRÁN, Diego: 1517–23

GUEVARA, Hernando de: 1517–46

VÁZQUEZ (VELÁZQUEZ) DE ACUÑA, Cristóbal: 1519–37

TELLO, Nicolás: 1520–23

MEDINA GARCIAVELA, Pedro de: 1523–32

VÁZQUEZ, Martín: 1523–34

CORRAL, Luis de: 1528–51

GARCÍA DE ERCILLA, Fortún: 1528–34

MANUEL, Pedro: 1528

MONTOYA, Gaspar de: 1529–36

GIRÓN, Hernando: 1529–44

DÍAZ DE LEGUIZAMÓN, Sancho: 1534–43

ESCUDERO, Diego: 1534–51

(YÁÑEZ DE) CASTRO, Gonzalo: 1535–6

GIRÓN DE LOAISA, Pedro: 1535–41

ÁLAVA ESQUIVEL, Diego de: 1536–44

MERCADO DE PEÑALOSA, Pedro: 1537–53

BRICEÑO, Jerónimo de: 1537–42

ALDERETE, Cristóbal de: 1538–47

VACA DE CASTRO, Cristóbal: 1539–64

RODRÍGUEZ DE FIGUEROA, Juan: 1540–59

GALARZA, Beltrán de: 1542–57

MARTÍNEZ DE MONTALVO, Hernando: 1542–60

ANAYA, Bernardino de: 1544–62

MONTALVO, Francisco de: 1544–50

SÁNCHEZ DE CORRAL, Juan: 1544–5

CORTÉS, Pedro: 1546–9

LÓPEZ DE OTALORA, Sancho: 1547–62

CASTILLO DE VILLASANTE, Diego: 1548–52

LÓPEZ DE RIBERA, Pedro: 1548–56

LÓPEZ DE ARRIETA, Pedro: 1549–63

GONZÁLEZ DE ARTEAGA, Jacobo: 1550–51

MENCHACA, Francisco de: 1551–71

GASCA, Diego (García) de la: 1552–72

VELASCO, Martín de: 1552–73

CANO, Fernando: 1554–9

PEDROSA, Pedro de: 1554–63

BRIVIESCA DE MUÑATONES, Juan: 1554–70

COUNCIL OF THE INQUISITION

Inquisitors-general

UTRECHT, Adriano de: 1516 (Aragon), 1518 (Castile)–22

GARCÍA DE LOAISA, Jofre: 1522–46

MANRIQUE, Alonso: 1523–38

PARDO DE TAVERA, Juan: 1539–45

VALDÉS, Fernando de: 1547–66

Councillors

AZPEITIA, Martín de: 1502–16 (Aragon)

SOSA, Francisco de: 1504–20 (Castile)

MONTEMAYOR, Fernando de: 1505–23 (Aragon)

GONZÁLEZ MANSO, Pedro: 1508–25 (Castile)

MAZUECOS, Fernando de: 1508–23 (Castile)

IBÁÑEZ DE AGUIRRE, Ortún: 1509–47 (Castile and Aragon)

RUIZ DE CALCENA, Juan: 1517–19 (Aragon)

HERRERA, Francisco de: 1518–24 (Castile)

MENDOZA, Francisco de: 1518–23 (Castile)

GONZÁLEZ POLANCO, Luis: 1521–8 (Aragon)

GUEVARA, Hernando de: 1524–9 (Aragon)

VALDÉS, Fernando de: 1524–35

SUÁREZ DE MALDONADO, Jerónimo: 1524–44

NIÑO, Hernando: 1525–39

NAVARRA, Francisco de: 1537–43

SALDAÑA, Toribio: 1537–40

GASCA, Pedro de la: 1541–53

TAVERA, Diego: 1544–55

ACUÑA Y AVELLANEDA, Pedro: 1546–8

PONCE DE LEÓN, Pedro: 1546–50

COBOS Y MOLINA, Diego de los: 1548–59

MONTALVO, Francisco de: 1549–50

CORTÉS, Pedro: 1549

CÓRDOBA, Diego de: 1550–58

GALARZA, Beltrán de: 1553–7

LÓPEZ DE OTALORA, Sancho: 1553–63

HERNÁNDEZ VALTODANO, Cristóbal: 1554–69

PÉREZ, Andrés: 1555–68

Secretaries

RUIZ DE CALCENA, Juan: 1502–17

URRÍES, Hugo de: 1518–44

GARCÍA, Juan: 1518–38

URRÍES, Jerónimo de: 1544

VÁZQUEZ DE MOLINA, Juan: 1546–

ZURITA, Jerónimo: 1538–80

COUNCIL OF THE INDIES

Presidents

GARCÍA DE LOAISA, Jofre: 1524–46

FERNÁNDEZ MANRIQUE, García: 1529–42

HURTADO DE MENDOZA, Luis: 1546–59

Councillors

BELTRÁN, Diego: 1523–42

MALDONADO, Gonzalo: 1524–30

CABEZA DE VACA, Luis: 1524–30
ANGLERÍA, Pedro Mártir de: 1524–6
MANUEL, Pedro: 1527–8
MONTOYA, Gaspar de: 1528–9
CORTE, Rodrigo de la: 1528–30
NÚÑEZ DE LOAISA, Álvaro: 1529
SUÁREZ DE CARVAJAL, Juan: 1529–42
ISUNZA, Francisco de: 1531
DÍAZ DE LUCO, Juan Bernal: 1531–45
MERCADO DE PEÑALOSA, Pedro: 1531–5
VELÁZQUEZ DE LUGO, Gutierre: 1535–51
LÓPEZ, Gregorio: 1543–56
SALMERÓN, Juan de: 1543–8
RAMÍREZ DE FUENLEAL, Sebastián: 1543–4
TELLO DE SANDOVAL, Francisco: 1543–58
PÉREZ DE LA FUENTE, Hernán: 1545–57
BRIVIESCA, Gracián de: 1549–60
PÉREZ DE RIBADENEIRA, Gonzalo: 1549–54
SARMIENTO, Juan: 1552–61
VILLAGÓMEZ, Diego de: 1554–59
VÁZQUEZ DE ARCE, Juan: 1554–71

Secretaries

CONCHILLOS, Lope de: 1508–18
COBOS, Francisco de los: 1518–47
SAMANO, Juan de: 1524, 1539–58

COUNCIL OF THE ORDERS

Presidents of Calatrava and Alcántara

NÚÑEZ DE GUZMÁN, Pedro: 1516–23
PADILLA, García de: 1523–42
CÓRDOBA, Hernando de: 1542–50

Presidents of Santiago

VEGA, Hernando de: 1506–26
FERNÁNDEZ MANRIQUE, García: 1526–46
TOLEDO, Enrique de: 1550–52
NAVARRA, Pedro de: 1553–6

Councillors

ALARCÓN, Luis de: 1498–1530
VARGAS, Francisco de: 1506–24
BARRIENTOS, Hernando de: ? –1549
TELLO, Nicolás: 1513–20
PADILLA, García de: c. 1520–23
CALVETE, Martín Tristán: 1514–17
LUXÁN, Antonio de: 1516–42
CÓRDOBA, Hernando de: 1524–42
FLORES, Diego: 1524–7
GARCÍA DE ERCILLA, Fortún: 1525–8
PERERO DE NEYRA, Diego: 1528–?
SARMIENTO Y ORTEGA, Juan: 1528–52
ANAYA, Bernardino de: 1534–44
ÁLAVA Y ESQUIVEL, Diego de: 1535–6
GONZÁLEZ DE ARTEAGA, Jacobo: 1540–50
ACUÑA Y AVELLANEDA, Pedro: 1542–6
PEDROSA, Pedro de: 1549–54
GOÑI, Pedro: 1542–60
ARGÜELLO, Íñigo: 1550–66
OVANDO, Nicolás: 1552–63
PÉREZ DE RIBADENEIRA, Gonzalo: 1554–72

COUNCIL OF THE TREASURY

Mayordomos mayores

CÁRDENAS, Diego de: 1507–42
ÁLVAREZ DE TOLEDO, Fernando: 1543–82

Contadores mayores

VELÁZQUEZ DE CUÉLLAR, Juan: 1504–17
FONSECA, Antonio de: 1504–32
CROŸ, Guillermo de: 1516–20
ZÚÑIGA, Álvaro de: 1520–31
COBOS, Francisco de los: 1539–47

Lugartenientes

VELASCO, Ortún: 1508–17
RÚA, Rodrigo de la: 1508–29
TELLO, Nicolás: 1517–20
GUTIÉRREZ DE MADRID, Alonso: 1520–31
PAZ, Sancho de: 1529–43
SUÁREZ, Cristóbal: 1531–49
ALMAGUER, Francisco de: 1543–64
LAGUNA, Francisco de: 1549–54
EGUINO, Antonio de: 1554–7

Charles V and his relations

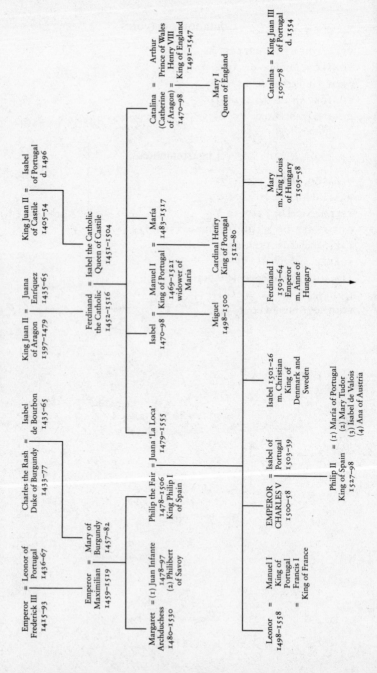

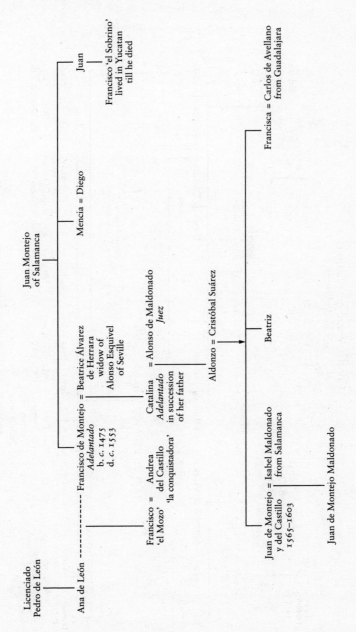

The Montejos

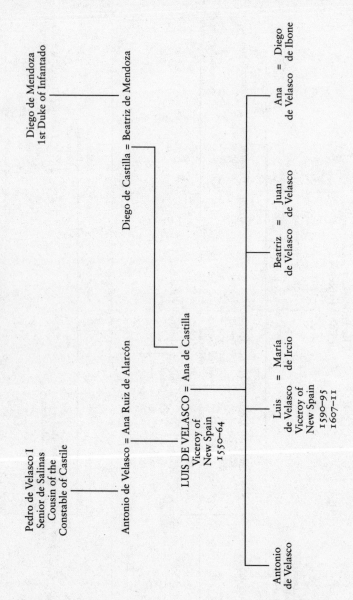

The Velascos

The Pedrarias

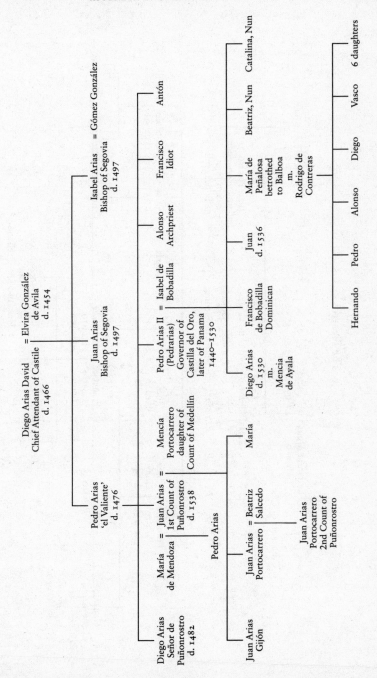

The Pizarros

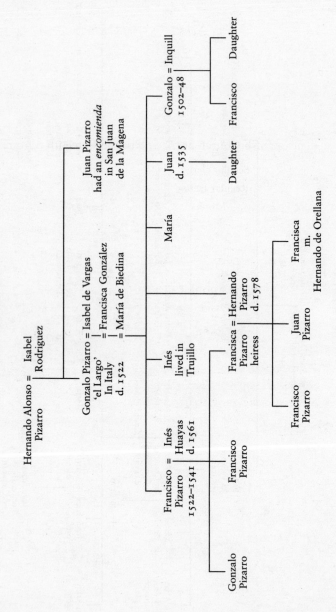

Hernando Alonso = Isabel
Pizarro   Rodriguez

Juan Pizarro
had an *encomienda*
in San Juan
de la Magena

Gonzalo Pizarro = Isabel de Vargas
'el Largo'   = Francisca González
In Italy   = María de Biedina
d. 1522

Francisco = Inés
Pizarro   Huayas
1522–1541   d. 1561

Inés
lived in
Trujillo

María

Juan
d. 1535

Gonzalo = Inquill
1502–48

Gonzalo
Pizarro

Francisco
Pizarro

Francisca = Hernando
Pizarro   Pizarro
heiress   d. 1578

Daughter

Francisco   Daughter

Francisco
Pizarro

Juan
Pizarro

Francisca
m.
Hernando de Orellana

3. Some statistics

The Spanish Church at the end of the sixteenth century

Secular clergy	33,087
Regular clergy	
Monks	20,697
Nuns	20,369
	74,153

(Census of 1591)

Population of the Americas *c. 1570*

	Whites	Negroes Mulattos	Indians
Mexico, Antilles, Central America 4,072,150	52,500	91,000	—
South America (Spanish and Portuguese South America) 4,955,000	65,500	139,000	—
	118,000	230,000	—

9,027,150
(Rosenblatt)

Division of June *1533 Cajamarca*

Cavalry	25,798 marcas de plata	610,131 pesos de oro
Infantry	15,061.7	360,994
	40,860.3	971,125

Gold

REVENUE FROM THE INDIES*
(PESOS OF 450 MARAVEDÍS)

Years	Crown	Private persons	Total
1516–1520	260,000	733,000	993,000
1520–1525	35,000	99,000	134,000
1526–1530	272,000	766,000	1,038,000
1531–1535	432,000	1,218,000	1,650,000
1536–1540	1,351,000	2,588,000	3,939,000
1541–1545	758,000	4,200,000	4,958,000
1546–1550	1,593,000	3,916,000	5,509,000
1551–1555	3,628,000	6,237,000	9,865,000

* Earl J. Hamilton, *El Tesoro Americano y la Revolución de los Precios en España,
1501–1650*, Barcelona, Ariel, 1975, p. 47.

REMITTANCES OF BULLION FROM NEW SPAIN, 1522–1601
(British Museum Add. Mss. 13,964, f. 196)

Year	Pesos	Weight	Gross	Year	Pesos	Weight	Gross
1522	52,709	4	9	1525	30,886	0	0
1523		?		gold	1,838	2	0
1524	99,264	5	8	gold in jewels	1,592	0	0

Year	Pesos	Weight	Gross	Year	Pesos	Weight	Gross
gold	1,145	2	0	1539	65,407	7	0
unregistered				1540	132,996	1	0
1526	20,387	1	1	1541	16,599	3	0
gold	1,145	2	0	1542	113,240	3	0
unregistered				1543	50,524	4	0
1526	20,387	1	1	1544	164,136	3	5
gold	5,542	0	0	1545	26,483	4	7
unregistered				1546		?	
1527	47,505	6	7	1547	20,497	6	9
gold	16,049	4	0	1548	115,996	9	0
unregistered				1549		?	
gold in	1,130	0	0	1550	236,344	3	4
jewels				1551	61,635	3	1
1528	33,015	3	6	low	1,253		
gold	16,558	0	0	grade	marcos		
unregistered				silver			
1529		?		1552		?	
1530	20,142	4	6	1553	165,039	0	0
1531	24,971	4	1	1554	165,636	0	10
1532	40,927	7	1	1555	207,118	4	2
1533	40,272	5	6	1556	433,914	2	7
1534	104,440	2	9	low	1,113		
1535	16,250	0	0	grade	marc.,		
1536	32,500	0	0	silver	4 onz.		
1537	33,108	6	6	1557	167,078	2	8
1538		?		1558	313,543	1	0

Ships

REGISTERED VESSELS SAILING TO AND FROM THE INDIES, 1504–55

Year	Outgoing	Returning	Year	Outgoing	Returning
1504 (from 14 Aug.)	3	—	1523	41	13
			1524	60	10
1506	22	12	1525	73	37
1507	32	19	1526	59	37
1508	46	21	1527	68	41
1509	21	26	1528	55	17
1510	17	10	1529	62	42
1511	21	13	1530	79	33
1512	33	21	1531	54	33
1513	31	30	1532	45	39
1514	30	46	1533	60	37
1515	33	30	1534	86	35
1516	42	10	1535	81	47
1517	63	31	1536	84	67
1518	51	47	1537	42	28
1519	51	41	1538	63	41
1520	71	37	1539	69	47
1521	33	31	1540	79	47
1522	18	25	1541	71	68

Year	Outgoing	Returning	Year	Outgoing	Returning
1542	86	64	1549	101 and (2)	73 and (2)
1543	72	56	1550	85 and (2)	72 and (7)
1544	22	54	1551	78	84 and (4)
1545	97	38	1552	72	53 and (8)
1546	79	65	1553	47	32 and (7)
1547	83	75	1554	3	24 and (11)
1548	89	73	1555	65	44 and (15)

Ships' Wages

Wages on Vessels in the India Navigation. Sixteenth Century

	Almirante San Nicolás of an armada guarding the Spanish coasts in 1543 against French corsairs	Carrack Santa María of the same armada (A de I, 40.3.1/13)	Similar Spanish vessel in the year 1544 (ibid.)	Armada of Sancho de Biedma, 1530–51 (A de I, 30.3.2)	Armada de Pedro de las Roelas, 1563–4 (A de I, 30.3.1)
General	—	—	—	—	1,875 ducats per year
Admiral	—	—	—	—	1,000 ducats per year
Captain	4,166 maravedis per month	—	—	100,000 maravedis per year	—
Master	6 ducats per month	—	—	—	—
Pilot	(2) 10 and 4 ducats per month	10 ducats per month	—	110–180 ducats per voyage	—
Notary	4 ducats per month	6 ducats per month	5 ducats per month	8 ducats per month	8 ducats per month
Doctor	—	4 ducats per month	—	12 ducats per month	8 ducats per month
Chemist	4 ducats per month	—	5 ducats per month	6 ducats per month	—

Magistrate	5 ducats per month	4 ducats per month	—	6 ducats per month	6 ducats per month
Lieutenant and Trumpeter	—	6 ducats per month	—	6 ducats per month	6 ducats per month
Corporal	—	4 ducats per month	—	—	—
Sergeant	—	—	—	—	4 ducats per month
Drummer	—	—	—	—	4 ducats per month
Artillery	—	4 ducats per month	5 ducats per month	4 ducats per month	4 ducats per month
Constable	4½ ducats per month	—	6 ducats per month	5 ducats per month	5 ducats per month
Soldier	—	2 ducats per month	—	2 ducats per month	2 ducats per month
Sailor	2 ducats per month	—	2½ ducats per month	3 escudos per month	—
Cabin boy	—	—	—	2 escudos per month	—

(continued)

Wages on Vessels in the India Navigation. Sixteenth Century (cont.)

	Almirante San Nicolás of an armada guarding the Spanish coasts in 1543 against French corsairs	Carrack Santa María of the same armada (A de I, 40.3.1/13)	Similar Spanish vessel in the year 1544 (ibid.)	Armada of Sancho de Biedma, 1530–51 (A de I, 30.3.2)	Armada de Pedro de las Roelas, 1563–4 (A de I, 30.3.1)
Page	—	1 ducat per month	—	2 ducats per month	—
Chaplain	—	4 ducats per month	—	2 ducats per month	20,450 maravedís per voyage
Bosun	4 ducats per month	—	5 ducats per month	—	—
Carpenter	4 ducats per month	—	5 ducats per month	—	—
Caulker	4 ducats per month	—	5 ducats per month	—	—

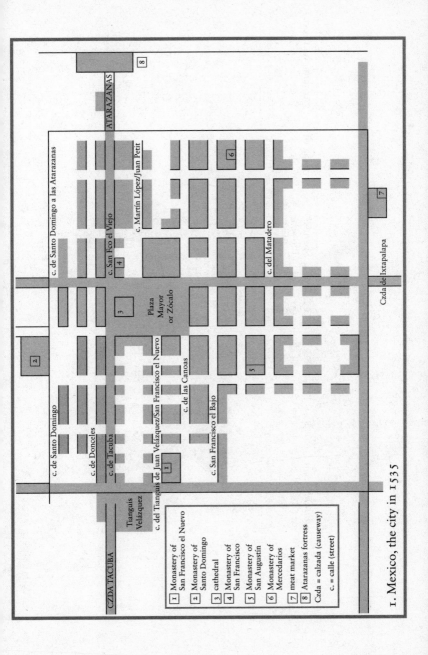

1. Mexico, the city in 1535

1	Monastery of San Francisco el Nuevo
2	Monastery of Santo Domingo
3	cathedral
4	Monastery of San Francisco
5	Monastery of San Augustín
6	Monastery of Mercedarios
7	meat market
8	Atarazanas fortress

Czda = calzada (causeway)

c. = calle (street)

CZDA TACUBA

ATARAZANAS

Tianguis Velázquez

c. de Santo Domingo

c. de Donceles

c. de Tacuba

c. del Tianguis de Juan Velázquez/San Francisco el Nuevo

c. de las Canoas

c. San Francisco el Bajo

Plaza Mayor or Zócalo

c. de Santo Domingo a las Atarazanas

c. San Fco el Viejo

c. Martín López/Juan Petit

c. del Matadero

Czda de Ixtapalapa

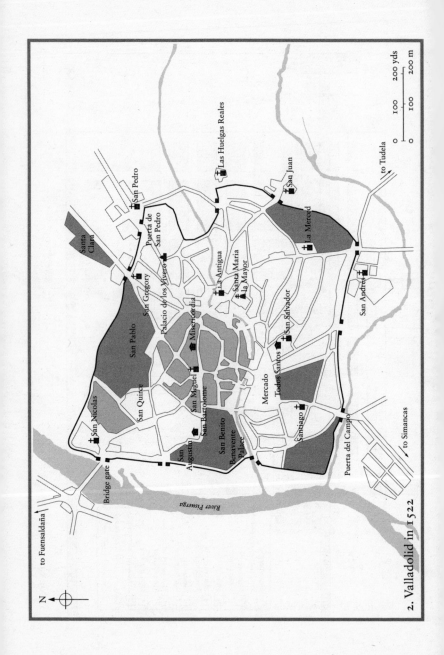

2. Valladolid in 1522

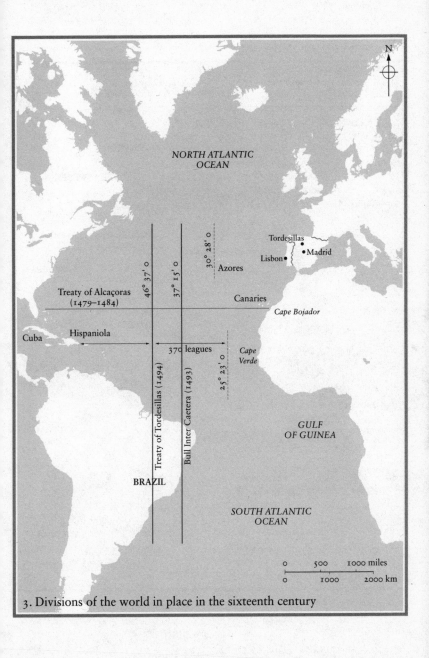

North

*NORTH ATLANTIC
OCEAN*

Tordesillas

Lisbon • • Madrid

30° 28' O

Azores

Treaty of Alcaçoras
(1479–1484)

46° 37' O

37° 15' O

Canaries

Cape Bojador

Cuba

Hispaniola

370 leagues

*Cape
Verde*

25° 23' O

Treaty of Tordesillas (1494)

Bull Inter Caetera (1493)

*GULF
OF GUINEA*

BRAZIL

*SOUTH ATLANTIC
OCEAN*

0	500	1000 miles
0	1000	2000 km

3. Divisions of the world in place in the sixteenth century

4. Charles V's Europe, 1522

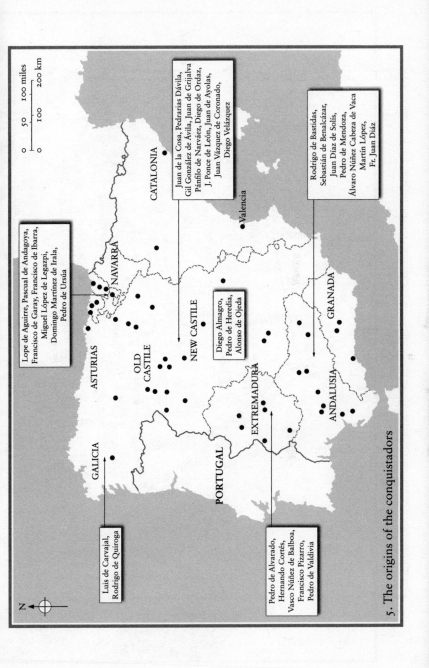

Lope de Aguirre, Pascual de Andagoya,
Francisco de Garay, Francisco de Ibarra,
Miguel López de Legazpi,
Domingo Martínez de Irala,
Pedro de Ursúa

Juan de la Cosa, Pedrarias Dávila,
Gil González de Avila, Juan de Grijalva
Pánfilo de Narváez, Diego de Ordaz,
J. Ponce de León, Juan de Ayolas,
Juan Vázquez de Coronado,
Diego Velázquez

Rodrigo de Bastidas,
Sebastián de Benalcázar,
Juan Díaz de Solís,
Pedro de Mendoza,
Alvaro Núñez Cabeza de Vaca
Martín López,
Fr. Juan Díaz

Diego Almagro,
Pedro de Heredia,
Alonso de Ojeda

Luis de Carvajal,
Rodrigo de Quiroga

Pedro de Alvarado,
Hernando Cortés,
Vasco Núñez de Balboa,
Francisco Pizarro,
Pedro de Valdivia

GALICIA
ASTURIAS
NAVARRA
CATALONIA
OLD CASTILE
NEW CASTILE
Valencia
PORTUGAL
EXTREMADURA
ANDALUSIA
GRANADA

N

0   50   100 miles
0   100   200 km

5. The origins of the conquistadors

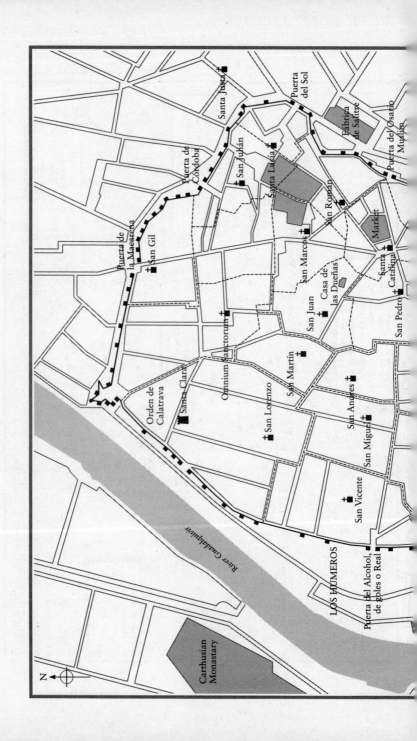

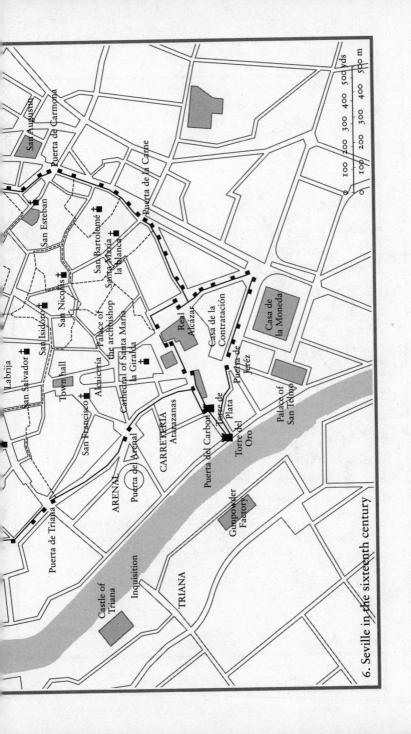

6. Seville in the sixteenth century

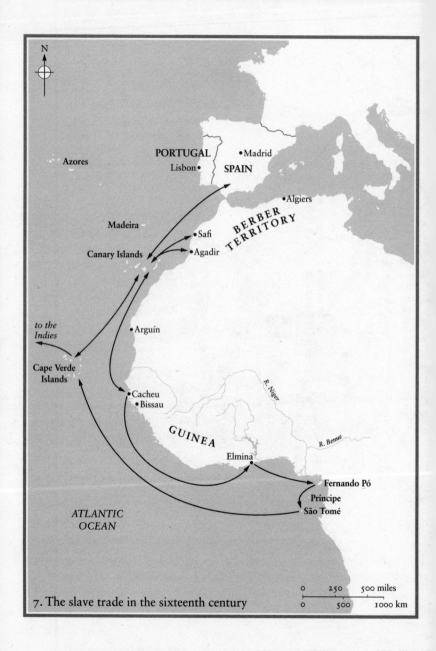

7. The slave trade in the sixteenth century

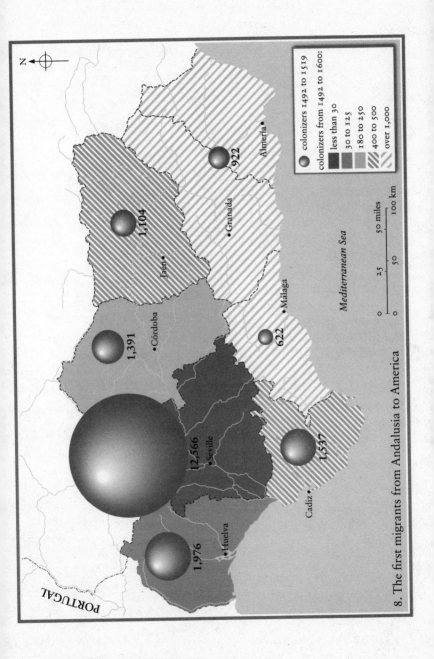

8. The first migrants from Andalusia to America

PORTUGAL

N

922
Almería •

1,104
Jaén •

• Granada

1,391
Córdoba •

• Málaga
622

12,566
Seville •

1,537
Cádiz •

1,976
Huelva •

Mediterranean Sea

0   25   50   50 miles
0   50   100 km

colonizers 1492 to 1519
colonizers from 1492 to 1600:
less than 30
30 to 125
180 to 250
400 to 500
over 1,000

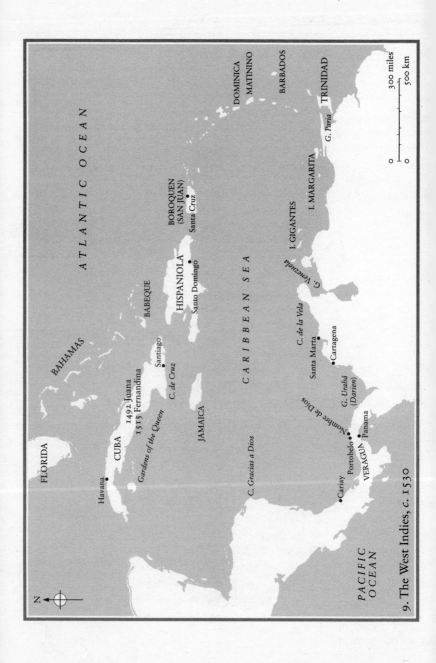

9. The West Indies, *c.* 1530

FLORIDA

ATLANTIC OCEAN

BAHAMAS

1492 Juana
1515 Fernandina
CUBA

Santiago
C. de Cruz

Havana

JAMAICA

Gardens of the Queen

BABEQUE

HISPANIOLA

Santo Domingo

BOROQUEN
(SAN JUAN)

Santa Cruz

DOMINICA

MATININO

BARBADOS

CARIBBEAN SEA

C. Gracias a Dios

Cariay

Portobelo
Nombre de Dios

Panama

VERAGUA

G. Urabá
(Darien)

Santa Marta
Cartagena

C. de la Vela

I. GIGANTES

G. Venezuela

I. MARGARITA

G. Paria

TRINIDAD

PACIFIC OCEAN

N

0   300 miles
0   500 km

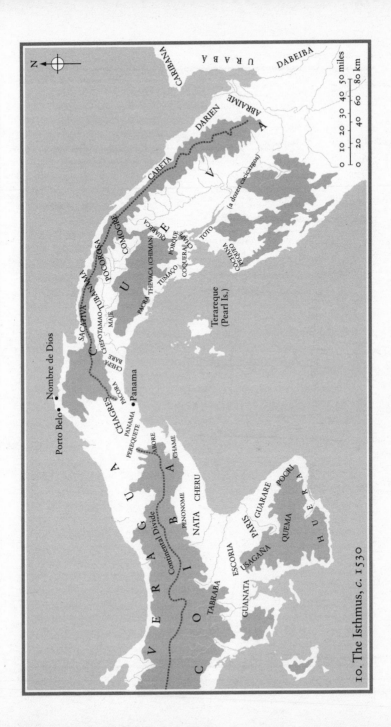

10. The Isthmus, c. 1530

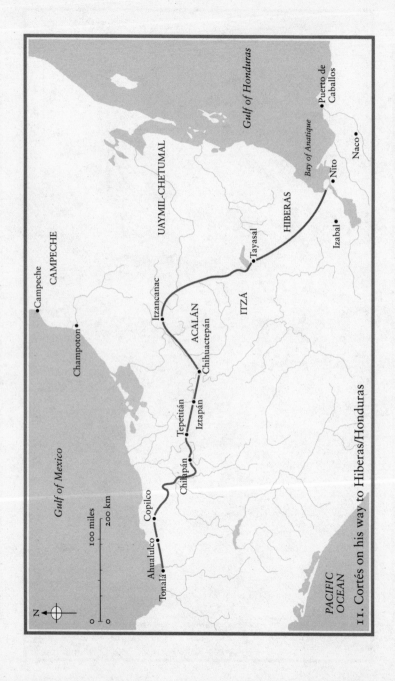

11. Cortés on his way to Hiberas/Honduras

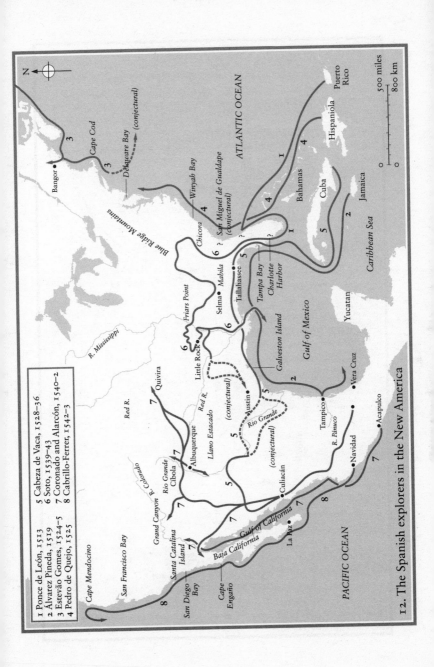

12. The Spanish explorers in the New America

1 Ponce de León, 1513	5 Cabeza de Vaca, 1528–36	
2 Álvarez Pineda, 1519	6 Soto, 1539–43	
3 Estevão Gomes, 1524–5	7 Coronado and Alarcón, 1540–2	
4 Pedro de Quejo, 1525	8 Cabrillo-Ferrer, 1542–3	

N

500 miles

800 km

ATLANTIC OCEAN

Puerto Rico

Hispaniola

Bahamas

Cuba

Jamaica

Caribbean Sea

Cape Cod

Bangor

Delaware Bay (conjectural)

Winyah Bay

Chicora

San Miguel de Gualdape (conjectural)

Blue Ridge Mountains

Friars Point

Mabila

Selma

Tallahassee

Little Rock

Tampa Bay

Charlotte Harbor

Galveston Island

Gulf of Mexico

Yucatan

Vera Cruz

R. Mississippi

Quivira

Red R.

Red R.

Llano Estacado (conjectural)

Austin

Rio Grande (conjectural)

Tampico

R. Pánuco

Acapulco

Navidad

Culiacán

Albuquerque

Cibola

Rio Grande

R. Colorado

Grand Canyon

Cape Mendocino

San Francisco Bay

Santa Catalina Island

San Diego Bay

Cape Engaño

Gulf of California

Baja California

La Paz

PACIFIC OCEAN

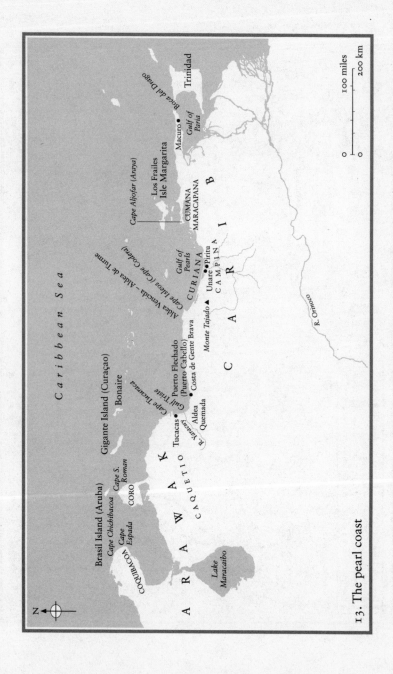

13. The pearl coast

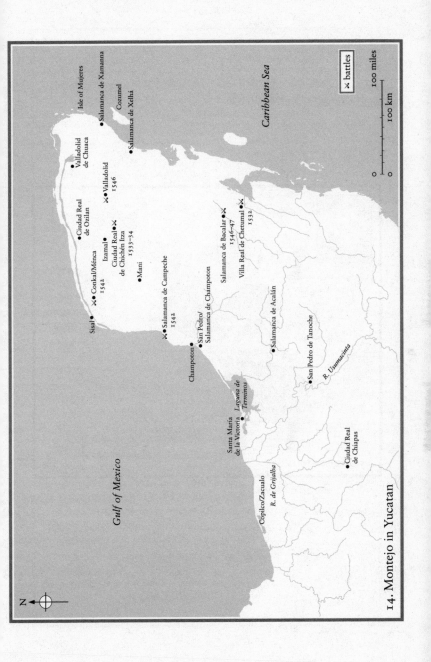

Gulf of Mexico

Isle of Mujeres

Salamanca de Xamanna

Cozumel

Valladolid
de Chuaca

Salamanca de Xelhá

Salamanca de Xamanna

×Valladolid
1546

Ciudad Real
de Ozilan

Conkal/Ménca
1542

Izamal

Ciudad Real ×
de Chichén Itza
1533–34

Maní

Salamanca de Bacalar
1546–47

Villa Real de Chetumal ×
1532

Sisal

Salamanca de Campeche
1542

San Pedro/
Salamanca de Champoton

Champoton

Salamanca de Acalán

San Pedro de Tanoche

Santa María
de la Victoria

Laguna de
Terminos

R. Usamacinta

Copilco/Zacualo

R. de Grijalba

Ciudad Real
de Chiapas

Caribbean Sea

× battles

0   100 miles

0   100 km

N

14. Montejo in Yucatan

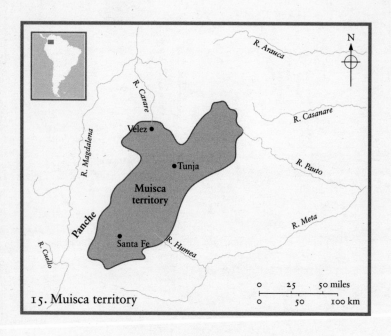

15. Muisca territory

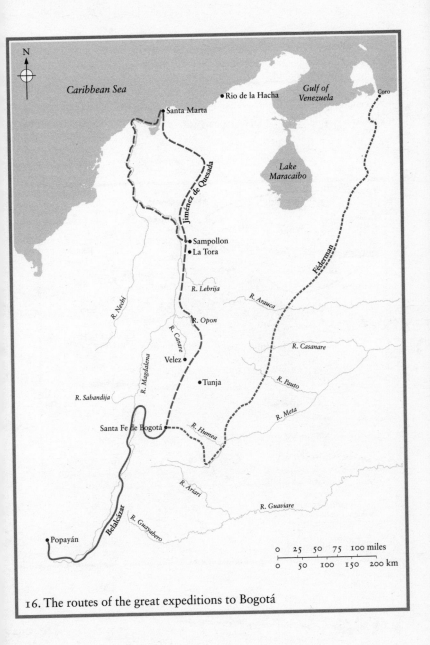

16. The routes of the great expeditions to Bogotá

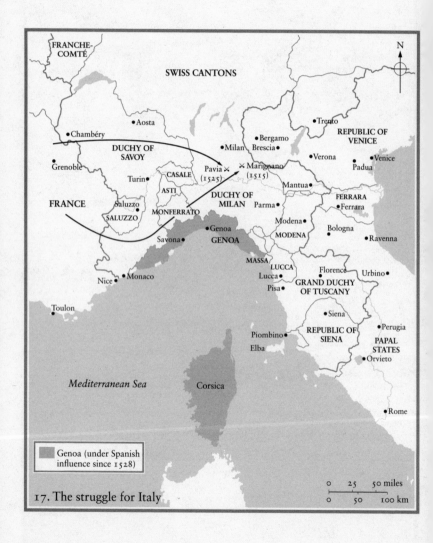

17. The struggle for Italy

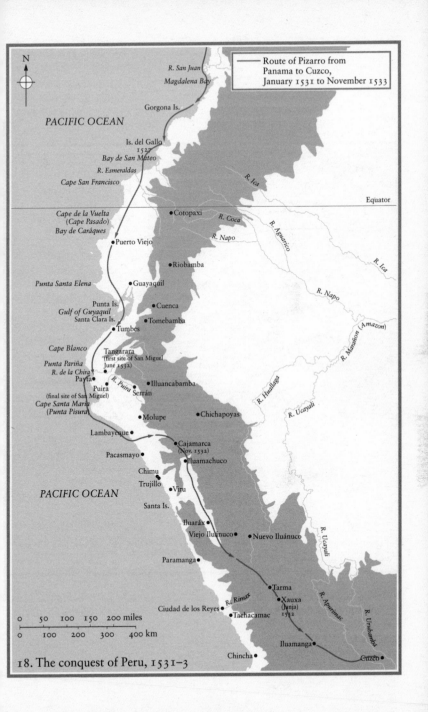

N

Route of Pizarro from
Panama to Cuzco,
January 1531 to November 1533

R. San Juan

Magdalena Bay

Gorgona Is.

PACIFIC OCEAN

Is. del Gallo
1527
Bay de San Mateo
R. Esmeraldas
Cape San Francisco

Equator

Cape de la Vuelta
(Cape Pasado)
Bay de Caráques
• Cotopaxi   *R. Coca*   *R. Aguarico*   *R. Ica*

• Puerto Viejo   *R. Napo*

• Riobamba

R. Napo

Punta Santa Elena
• Guayaquil

R. Marañon (Amazon)

Punta Is.   • Cuenca
Gulf of Guyaquil
Santa Clara Is.   • Tomebamba
• Tumbes

R. Huallaga
R. Ucayali

Cape Blanco
Tangarara
(first site of San Miguel
June 1532)
Punta Pariña
R. de la Chira
Payta •   • Puira   • Illuancabamba
(final site of San Miguel)   • Serrán
Cape Santa Maria   *R. Puira*
(Punta Pisura)
• Molupe   • Chichapoyas

Lambayeque •

• Cajamarca
(Nov. 1532)
Pacasmayo •   • Iluamachuco

Chimu •
Trujillo •   • Viru

PACIFIC OCEAN

Santa Is.

Iluaráx •
Viejo Iluánuco •   • Nuevo Iluánuco

R. Ucayali

Paramanga •

• Tarma
R. Apurimac
R. Rimax   • Xauxa
Ciudad de los Reyes •   (Jenja)
• Tachacamac   1533

R. Urubamba

Chincha •   • Iluamanga   Cuzco •

0   50   100   150   200 miles

0   100   200   300   400 km

18. The conquest of Peru, 1531–3

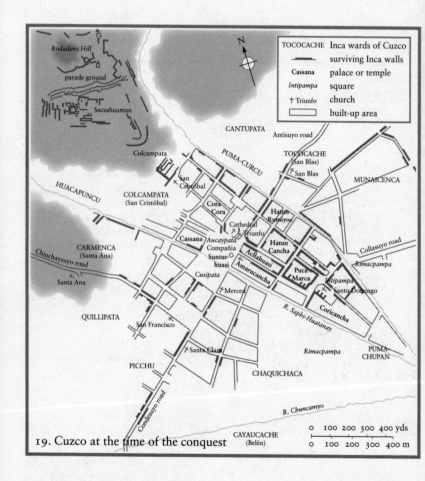

TOCOCACHE Inca wards of Cuzco
━━━ surviving Inca walls
Cassana palace or temple
Intipampa square
✝ Triunfo church
☐ built-up area

Rodadero Hill

parade ground

Sacsahuaman

Colcampata

CANTUPATA

Antisuyo road

PUMA-CURCU

TOCOCACHE
(San Blas)
✝ San Blas

MUNAICENCA

HUACAPUNCU

COLCAMPATA
(San Cristóbal)

✝ San
Cristóbal

Cora-
Cora

Cathedral
✝ Triunfo

Hatun
Rumiyoc

Hatun
Cancha

Collasuyo road

Rimacpampa

CARMENCA
(Santa Ana)

Chinchaysuyo road

Santa Ana

Cassana *Aucaypata*
Compañia
Suntur-
huasi

Cusipata

✝ Merced

Acllahuasi

Amarucancha

Puca
Marca

Intipampa
✝ Santo Domingo

QUILLIPATA

✝ San Francisco

Coricancha

R. Saphi-Huatanay

PUMA-
CHUPAN

PICCHU

✝ Santa Clara

Rimacpampa

CHAQUICHACA

Condesuyo road

R. Chuncamyo

CAYAUCACHE
(Belén)

0   100 200 300 400 yds

0   100 200 300 400 m

19. Cuzco at the time of the conquest

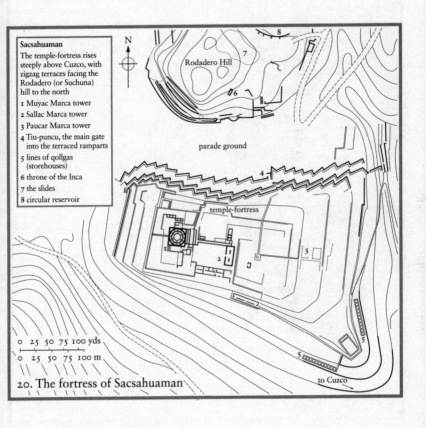

Sacsahuaman

The temple-fortress rises steeply above Cuzco, with zigzag terraces facing the Rodadero (or Suchuna) hill to the north

1 Muyac Marca tower
2 Sallac Marca tower
3 Paucar Marca tower
4 Tiu-puncu, the main gate into the terraced ramparts
5 lines of qollgas (storehouses)
6 throne of the Inca
7 the slides
8 circular reservoir

N

Rodadero Hill

parade ground

temple-fortress

0 25 50 75 100 yds
0 25 50 75 100 m

20. The fortress of Sacsahuaman

to Cuzco

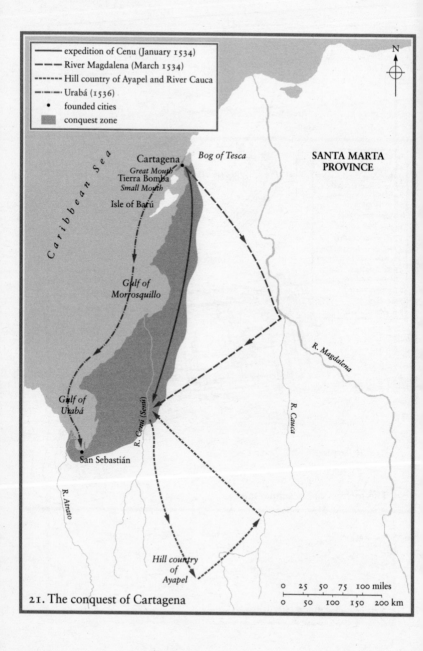

Legend:
- expedition of Cenu (January 1534)
- River Magdalena (March 1534)
- Hill country of Ayapel and River Cauca
- Urabá (1536)
- • founded cities
- conquest zone

N

Cartagena
Great Mouth
Tierra Bomba
Small Mouth
Isle of Barú

Bog of Tesca

SANTA MARTA PROVINCE

Caribbean Sea

Gulf of Morrosquillo

R. Magdalena

Gulf of Urabá

R. Cenú (Senú)

R. Cauca

• San Sebastián

R. Atrato

Hill country of Ayapel

| 0 | 25 | 50 | 75 | 100 miles |
| 0 | 50 | 100 | 150 | 200 km |

21. The conquest of Cartagena

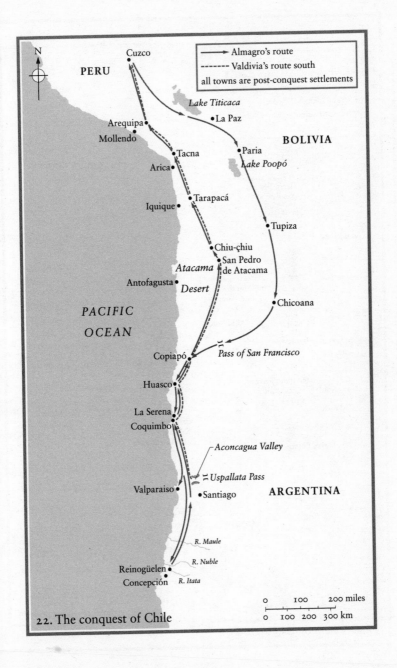

N

PERU

Cuzco

Lake Titicaca

La Paz

Arequipa
Mollendo

BOLIVIA

Paria
Lake Poopó

Tacna
Arica

Tarapacá

Iquique

Chiu-chiu
San Pedro
de Atacama

Atacama

Antofagusta

Desert

Tupiza

Chicoana

PACIFIC

OCEAN

Copiapó

Pass of San Francisco

Huasco

La Serena
Coquimbo

Aconcagua Valley

Uspallata Pass

Valparaiso

Santiago

ARGENTINA

R. Maule

R. Nuble

Reinogüelen
Concepción

R. Itata

Almagro's route
Valdivia's route south
all towns are post-conquest settlements

0   100   200 miles
0   100 200 300 km

22. The conquest of Chile

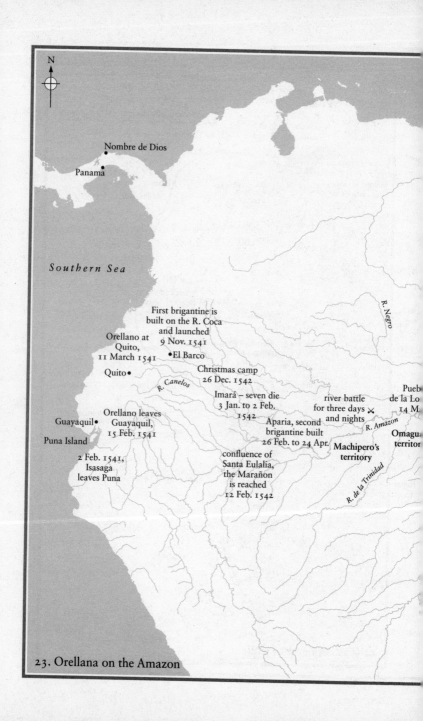

N

Nombre de Dios

Panama

Southern Sea

First brigantine is
built on the R. Coca
and launched
9 Nov. 1541

Orellano at
Quito,
11 March 1541
•El Barco

Quito•

Christmas camp
26 Dec. 1542

R. Canelos

Imarã – seven die
3 Jan. to 2 Feb.
1542

river battle
for three days
and nights

Pueb
de la Lo
14 M

Orellano leaves
Guayaquil,
15 Feb. 1541

Guayaquil•

Aparia, second
brigantine built
26 Feb. to 24 Apr.

R. Amazon

Puna Island

Machipero's
territory

Omagu
territor

2 Feb. 1541,
Isasaga
leaves Puna

confluence of
Santa Eulalia,
the Marañon
is reached
12 Feb. 1542

R. de la Trinidad

R. Negro

23. Orellana on the Amazon

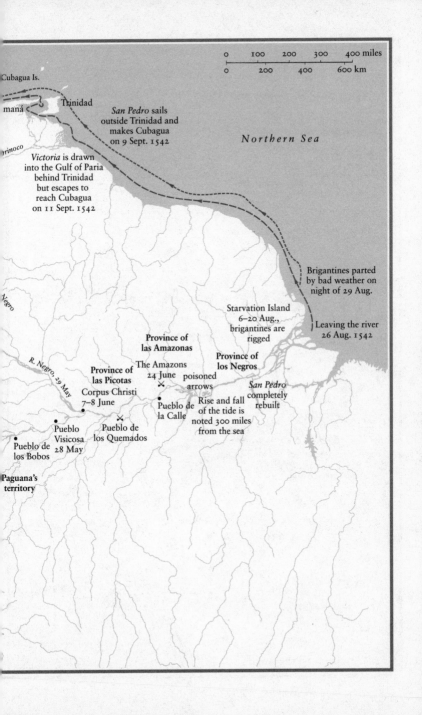

Cubagua Is.

maná

Trinidad

San Pedro sails outside Trinidad and makes Cubagua on 9 Sept. 1542

rinoco

Orinoco

Victoria is drawn into the Gulf of Paria behind Trinidad but escapes to reach Cubagua on 11 Sept. 1542

Northern Sea

0   100   200   300   400 miles
0   200   400   600 km

Negro

R. Negro, 29 May

Paguana's territory

Pueblo de los Bobos

Pueblo Visicosa 28 May

Pueblo de los Quemados

Province of las Picotas

Corpus Christi 7–8 June

The Amazons 24 June

Province of las Amazonas

Pueblo de la Calle

poisoned arrows

Rise and fall of the tide is noted 300 miles from the sea

Province of los Negros

San Pedro completely rebuilt

Brigantines parted by bad weather on night of 29 Aug.

Starvation Island 6–20 Aug., brigantines are rigged

Leaving the river 26 Aug. 1542

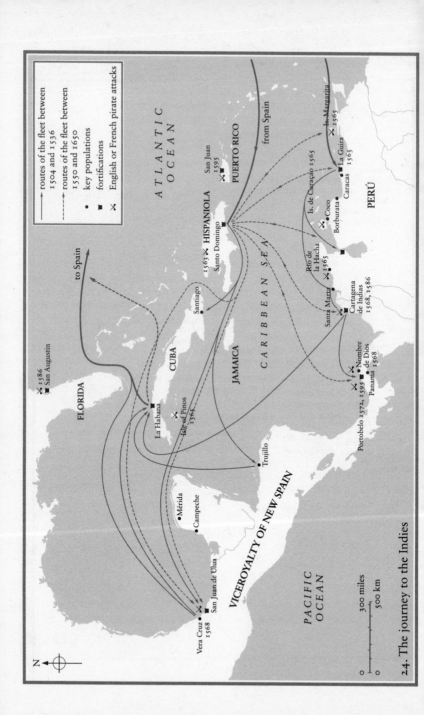

24. The journey to the Indies

routes of the fleet between 1504 and 1536
routes of the fleet between 1550 and 1650
key populations
fortifications
English or French pirate attacks

ATLANTIC OCEAN

N

from Spain

to Spain

FLORIDA

×1586
San Augustín

San Juan de Ulúa

Vera Cruz ×
1568

Mérida
Campeche

VICEROYALTY OF NEW SPAIN

PACIFIC OCEAN

300 miles
500 km

La Habana

Isle of Pinos
1561 ×

Santiago

CUBA

Trujillo

JAMAICA

PUERTO RICO

San Juan
1595 ×

HISPANIOLA

1565 × Santo Domingo

CARIBBEAN SEA

Is. de Curaçao 1565

La Guira
1565

Isla Margarita
1565 ×

Caracas

Coco
Borburata
×1565

Río de
la Hacha
×1565

Santa Marta ×

Cartagena
de Indias
1568, 1586

Nombre
de Dios
1568

Portobelo 1572, 1595 ×
Panamá 1568

PERÚ

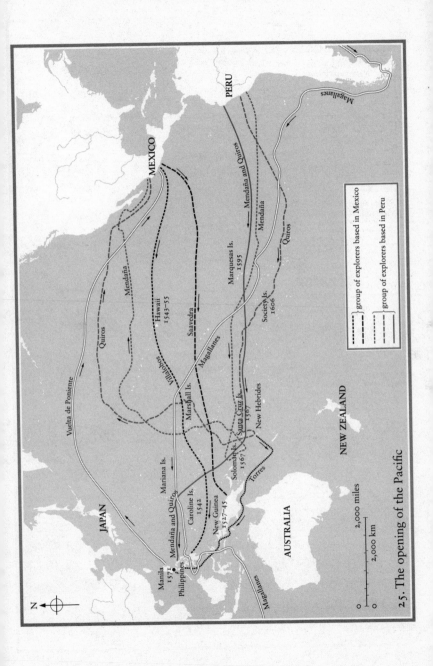

25. The opening of the Pacific

N

Dutch-speaking provinces

1 Flanders 2 Brabant 3 Malines
4 Limburg 5 Zeeland 6 Holland
7 Utrecht 8 Gelderland 9 Overysel
10 Drente 11 Friesland 12 Groningen

Walloon provinces

I Artois II Walloon Flanders III Cambrai
IV Tournia V Hainaut VI Namur
VII Luxembourg

Towns outside Habsburg territory

Liège, St Truiden (Bishopric of Liège),
Köln (Archbishopric electorate), Cleve,
Wesel, Emmerik (Duchy of Cleve),
Emden (County of Friesland)

— political frontier
‑‑‑ provincial frontier
···· linguistic boundary
▓ non-Habsburg territory

Emden

Groningen

Leeuwarden

11

12

10

Koevorden

Enkhuizen
Alkmaar • • Hoorn

Zwolle

9

Haarlem

Amsterdam

6

8¹

The Hague

7

Arnhem

Zutfen

Delft

Rotterdam

Groenlo

The Brill

Schoonhoven

Dordt

Cleve

Emmerik

Zierikzee

Geertruidenberg

Den Bosch

Wesel

5

Goes

Breda

8²

Gelder

Bergen-op-Zoom

Eindhoven

Venlo

Ostend • Sluis

2

Brugge

Ghent

Antwerp

Roermond

Grevelingen • Dunkirk

I

3 Malines/Mechelen

Köln

Yper

Brussels

Maastricht

Lille

II IV

V Nivelles

St Truiden

I

Douai

Mons

Namur

Liège

Arras

Valenciennes

VI

Cambrai

III

VII

0   20   40   60   80 miles

0 20 40 60 80 100 km

Luxembourg

26. The Netherlands in the 1550s

Bibliography

BIBLIOGRAPHICAL NOTE

For Valladolid in the 1520s there is Bartolomé Bennassar's *Valladolid au siècle d'or*. For Charles V, I still like best the biography of Karl Brandi translated by Veronica Wedgwood, *The Emperor Charles V: The Growth and Destiny of a Man and a World*. But there are also excellent works by Fernández Álvarez (*Carlos V, el César y el Hombre*), Federico Chabod (*Carlo V e il suo Imperio*), translated into Spanish by Rodrigo Ruza, and the former's great collection, *Corpus Documental de Carlos V*. Now we can also study the remarkable collective works of J. Martínez Millán (ed.), *La Corte de Carlos V*. The reconstruction of Mexico/Tenochtitlan is well analysed in Lucía Mier and Rocha Teran, *La Primera Traza de la Ciudad de México*, and there is also Jaime Montell's excellent *México, el Inicio*. Cortés's time in power, his journey to Honduras and his later life are to be seen in José Luis Martínez's careful biography, *Hernán Cortés*, and four accompanying volumes of documents. The Welsers have been magisterially studied by Juan Friede. The Montejos in Yucatan can be followed in Robert Chamberlain's admirable *The Conquest and Colonization of Yucatan 1517–1550*. For Pizarro and the conquest of Pizarro, there is now John Hemming's masterpiece, *The Conquest of the Incas*, and his more recent *Monuments of the Incas*, with admirable photographs by Edward Ranney. The work should be supplemented by James Lockhart's *The Men of Cajamarca*, and the same author's *Spanish Peru, 1532–1560*. New lives of Pizarro include J. A. Busto Duthurburu's *Pizarro*. A work of consummate skill is Guillermo Lohmann Villena's *Les Espinosa*. Other important secondary works on Peru include Rafael Varón Gabai's *La Ilusión del Poder: Apogeo y Decadencia e los Pizarro en la Conquista del Perú*, and the same author's *Francisco Pizarro and his Brothers*. Teodoro Hampe's brilliant biography of Pedro de la Gasca, *Don Pedro de la Gasca, 1493–1567*, deserves English and French translations. Valdivia's life has been well written and his companions are studied in Thayer Ojeda's *Valdivia y sus Compañeros*. For Jiménez de Quesada, there is the edition of his own memoir by Demetrio Ramos, *Ximénez de Quesada, Cronista*, and there is also Friede's *Gonzalo Jiménez de Quesada a través de Documentos Históricos, Estudio Biográfico, 1509–1550*. See too his *Vida y Viajes de Nicolás Federman*. Here we encounter another illuminating work by John Hemming, *The Search for El Dorado*.

De Soto in North America is splendidly recalled by David Ewing Duncan, *Hernando de Soto*, and the journey of Álvar Núñez Cabeza de Vaca is analysed well by Roberto Ferrando (ed.), *Naufragios y Comentarios*, and Enrique Pupo Walker, Berkeley, 1993.

Of the many works relevant to the life and work of Bartolomé de las Casas, there is Louis Hanke's deservedly famous *The Spanish Struggle for Justice in the New World*, and a new biography by Luis Iglesias Ortega, *Bartolomé de las Casas: Cuarenta y Cuatro Años Infinitos*. There is also the astonishing life of Las Casas by Manuel Jiménez Fernández. Its two volumes cover three years but illuminate an age. For ecclesiastical matters, I was guided by the great *History of the Popes* of Ludwig von Pastor, tr. by Mgr Ralph Kerr. The challenge of Erasmian thought is marvellously presented by Marcel Bataillon in his *Erasmo y España: Estudios sobre la Historia Espiritual del Siglo XVI*, translated from the French.

MSS DOCUMENTS

I have, as in previous works of mine, relied on several *legajos* (files) of the Archivo de Indias in Seville, especially the section called *Patronato*, and in particular *legajo* 150, which contains a mass of documents loosely referred to as *Informaciones de Servicios y Méritos*. I have also used the section called *Justicia*, where there are the texts of the various *residencias*, or judicial enquiries, taken for Cortes, Diego Velasquez, Pedrarias, etc.

BOOKS AND ARTICLES

This lists books and articles referred to in the notes of this volume. A full bibliography will be included at the end of volume III of this work.

ABBREVIATIONS

AGI – Archivo General de las Indias
APS – Archivo de Protocolo de Sevilla
BAE – Biblioteca de Autores Españoles
CDI – Colección de documentos inéditos relativos al descubrimiento, conquista y colonización de las posesiones Españolas en América y Oceania
CDIHE – Colección de documentos inéditos para la historia de España
CDIU – Colección de documentos relativos al descubrimiento, conquista y colonización de las antiguas posesiones Españolas de Ultramar

Indif. Gen. – Indiferente General
leg. – legajo

Aguado, Pedro del, *Historia de Venezuela*, written in 1581, 2 vols., Caracas, 1913, 1915

Aiton, Arthur, *Antonio de Mendoza*, Durham, North Carolina, 1927

Alberi, Eugenio, *Relazione degli Ambasciatore Veneti al Senato*, series I, Florence, 1839–63

Alvarado, Pedro de, *Residencia* of (1535), ed. José Fernando Ramírez, Mexico, 1847

Álvarez, Vicente, *Relation du beau voyage que fait aux Pays Bas en 1548 le Prince Philippe*, ed. M.-T. Dovillé, Brussels, 1964

Andagoya, Pascual de, *Relación y Documentos*, Madrid, 1986

Andrés, M., *La Teología Española en el Siglo XVI*, Madrid, 1977

Angulo, Diego, *Pedro Berruguete en Paredes de Nava*, Barcelona, 1946

Aran, Bellamy, *Pedrarias*, Madrid, 2009

Arranz, Luis, *Don Diego Colón*, Madrid, 1982

——, *Repartimientos y Encomiendas en la Isla Española*, Madrid, 1991

Bataillon, Marcel, *Erasme et l'Espagne*, Paris, 1937, masterfully translated by Antonio Alatorre and published as *Erasmo y España: Estudios sobre la Historia Espiritual del Siglo XVI*, Mexico, 1950

——, 'Novo Mundo e Fim do Mundo', *Revista de Historia*, 18, São Paulo, 1954

——, 'La rébellion pizarriste, enfantement de l'Amérique espagnole', *Diogène*, 43, July–Sept. 1963

——, 'Les Colons du Pérou contre Charles Quint 1544–1548', *Annales*, May–June 1967

Bauer, Brian S., *The Development of the Inca State*, Austin, 1998

——, *The Sacred Landscape of the Inca: The Cusco Ceque System*, Austin, 1998

Bejarano, Ignacio, *Actas del Cabildo*, Mexico, 1889

Beltrán de Heredia, Vicente, *Cartulario de la Universidad de Salamanca*, Salamanca, 1960

Bennassar, Bartolomé, *Valladolid au siècle d'or*, Paris, 1967

Bernal, Antonio-Miguel, *La Financiación de la Carrera de Indias, 1492–1824*, Seville, 1992

Blockmans, Peter and Mout, M.E.H.N., *The World of Charles V*, Amsterdam, 2004

Bonet Correa, Antonio, *Monasterios Iberoamericanos*, Madrid, 2007

Borah, Woodrow, 'The Cortés Codex of Vienna', *The Americas*, 2, vol. 19, 1962

Boyd-Bowman, Peter, *Indice Geobiográfico de Cuarenta Mil Poblados Españoles de América en el Siglo XVI*, 2 vols., Bogotá, 1964, Mexico, 1968

Brading, David, *The First America*, Cambridge, 1991

——, *Mexican Phoenix*, Cambridge, 2002

Brandi, Karl, *The Emperor Charles V: The Growth and Destiny of a Man and a World*, tr. C. V. Wedgwood, London, 1949

Braudel, Fernand, *The Mediterranean and the Mediterranean World in the Age of Philip II*, 2 vols., tr. Siân Reynolds, London, 1972, 1973

Brenan, Gerald, *The Literature of the Spanish People*, Cambridge, 1962

Brunke, José de la Puente, *Encomienda y Encomenderos en el Perú*, Seville, 1992

Burckhardt, Jacob, *Reflections on History*, London, 1943

—— *The Civilisation of the Renaissance in Italy*, London, 1950

Busto Duthurburu, J. A. del, *Diccionário Histórico-Biográfico de los Conquistadores del Perú, Los Trece de la Fama*, 2 vols., Lima, 1986, 1987

——, *La Tierra y la Sangre de Francisco Pizarro*, Lima, 1993

——, *Pizarro*, 2 vols., Lima, 2001

Cabeza de Vaca, Álvar Núñez, *Naufragios y Comentarios*, ed. Roberto Ferrando, Madrid, 1984

Cadenas y Vicent, Vicente de, *Carlos I de Castilla, Señor de las Indias*, Madrid, 1988

Campbell, L., *Renaissance Faces: Van Eyck to Titian*, London, 2008

Carande, Ramón, *Carlos V y sus banqueros*, 3 vols., 3rd edn, Barcelona, 1987

Carmack, Robert M., *Historia General de Centro América*, 2 vols., Madrid, 1993

Carolus, exhibition catalogue, Ghent, 1999, Toledo, 2001

Carolus V, exhibition catalogue, Barcelona, 1999

Carvajal, see Medina, José Toribio

Castañeda, Pedro de, *Spanish Explorers of the Southern United States*, New York,. 1998

Castello Yturbide, Teresa, *El Arte Plumaria en México*, Mexico, 1993

Cervantes de Salazar, Francisco, *México en 1554 y Túmulo Imperial*, Mexico, 1964

Chabod, Federico, *Carlos V y su Imperio (Carlos V e il suo Imperio)*, tr. Rodrigo Ruza, Madrid, 1992

Chamberlain, Robert S., 'The Lineage of the Adelantado Francisco Montejo and his Last Will and Testament', *Revista de Historia de América*, no. 8, April 1940

——, 'La Controversía entre Cortés y Velázquez', *Anales de la Sociedad Geográfica de Guatemala*, XIX, September 1943

——, *The Conquest and Colonization of Yucatan 1517–1550*, Washington, 1948

Chaunu, Pierre and Huguette, *Séville et l'Atlantique*, 7 vols., Paris, 1956 and onwards

Chevalier, François, *La Formation des grandes domaines au Méxique*, Paris, 1952

Chipman, Donald E., *Nuño de Guzmán*, Glendale, 1967

——, *Moctezuma's Children*, Austin, 2005

Cieza de León, Pedro, *Descubrimiento y Conquista del Perú*, ed. Carmelo Sáenz de Santa María, Madrid, 1986

Clendinnen, Inga, *Ambivalent Conquests*, Cambridge, 1987

Colección de documentos inéditos para la historia de España, ed. M. de Navarrete, 113 vols., 1842 onwards. This collection is referred to here as CDIHE

Colección de documentos inéditos relativos al descubrimiento, conquista y colonización de las antiguas posesiones Españolas de Ultramar, 25 vols., Madrid, 1884–1932. This collection is referred to here as CDIU

Colección de documentos inéditos relativos al descubrimiento, conquista y colonización de las posesiones Españolas en América y Oceania, ed. Joaquín Pacheco and Francisco Cárdenas, 42 vols., Madrid 1864–84. This collection is referred to here as CDI

Constant, G., 'Le Mariage de Marie Tudor et Philippe II', *Revue de l'histoire diplomatique*, 26, 1912

Conway, G. L. R., 'Hernando Alonso', Publications of the American Jewish Historical Society, 1928

Cooper, Edward, *Castillos Señoriales en la Corona de Castilla*, 3 vols., Salamanca, 1991

Cortés, Hernán, *Cartas de Relación*, ed. Angel Delgado Gómez, Madrid, 1993; English trs. by Anthony Pagden as *Letters from Mexico*, introduction by Sir John Elliott, New Haven, 1986

Covarrubias, M., *Mexico South: The Isthmus of Tehuantepec*, New York, 1947

Crane, Nicholas, *Mercator, the Man who Mapped the Planet*, London, 2002

Cuesta, Luisa, 'Una documentación interesante sobre la familia del Conquistador del Peru', *Revista de Indias*, no. 8, 1946–7

Cuevas, Mariano, S.J. (ed.), *Documentos Inéditos del Siglo XVI para la Historia de México*, Mexico, 1914

D'Altroy, Terence, *The Incas*, Oxford, 2002

Defourneaux, Marcel, *La vie quotidienne en Espagne au siècle d'or*, Paris, 1964

Deive, Carlos Esteban, *La Española y la esclavitud del Indio*, Santo Domingo, 1995

Delmarcel, Guy, *Los Honores: Flemish Tapestries for the Emperor Charles V*, Mechelen, 2000

Díaz de Guzmán, Ruy, *La Argentina*, edn of Enrique de Gandia, Madrid, 2000

Díaz del Castillo, Bernal, *Historia Verdadera de la Nueva España*, 2 vols., Madrid, 1982; tr. A. P. Maudslay, *The True History of the Conquest of New Spain*, 5 vols., London, 1908–16

Dios, Salustiano de, *El Consejo Real de Castilla*, Madrid, 1982

Dorantes de Carranza, Baltasar, *Sumario de Relación de las Cosas de la Nueva España*, new edn, Mexico, 1970

Duncan, David Ewing, *Hernando de Soto*, New York, 1995

Durán, Fray Diego, *Historia de las Indias de Nueva España*, 2 vols., Mexico, 1984

Dworski, R. J., 'The Council of the Indies in Spain', Columbia University thesis (unpublished), 1979

Eichberger, Dagmar (ed.), *Women of Distinction*, Leuven, 2005

Elliott, Sir John, *Empires of the Atlantic World: Britain and Spain in America 1492–1830*, New Haven, 2006

Enríquez de Guzmán, Alonso, *Libro de la Vida de*, ed. Howard Keniston, Madrid, 1960

Erasmus, Desiderio, *Collected Works*, 48 vols., ed. and tr. Robert D. Siler and Jane E. Phillips, Toronto, 2008

Estete, Miguel de, 'El Descubrimiento y la Conquista del Perú', ed. Carlos María Larrea, *Boletín de la Sociedad Ecuatoriana de Estudios Americanos*, vol. 1, no. 3, Quito, 1918

Ezquerra, Ramón, 'Los Compañeros de Cortés', *Revista de Indias*, no. 1, 1948

Fabié, Antonio María, *Vida y escritos de Bartolomé de las Casas*, Madrid, 1879

Federman, Nicolaus, *Indianische Historia: eine schöne kurz-weilige Historia, Nicolaus Federman des Jungers von Ulm*, Hagenau, 1557, tr. Juan Friede, in Joaquín Gabaldón Márquez, *Descubrimiento y Conquista de Venezuela*, Caracas, 1962, 155–250

Fernández Álvarez, Manuel, *Corpus Documental de Carlos V*, 7 vols., Salamanca, 1973–82

—(ed.), *Carlos V, el César y el Hombre*, Madrid, 1999

——, *Sombras y Luces en la España Imperial*, Madrid, 2004

Fernández de Enciso, Martín, *Suma de Geografía*, Seville, 1519

Fernández de Navarrete, Martín, *Colección de Viajes y Descubrimientos que Hicieron por Mar los Españoles*, ed. Carlos Seco Serrano, 3 vols., Madrid, 1959

Fernández de Oviedo, Gonzalo, *Historia General y Natural de las Indias*, ed. Juan Pérez de Tudela, 5 vols., Madrid, 1959

——, *Batallas y Quinquagenas de los generosos e illustres e no menos famosos Reyes*, 4 vols., Madrid, 1983–2002

Fernández Martín, Luis, *Hernando Pizarro en el Castillo de la Mota*, Valladolid, 1991

Fita, Fidel, S. J., 'Los Judaizantes Españoles en los Primeros Cinco Anos del Reinado de Carlos I', *Boletín de la Real Academia de Historia*, 33, 1898

Florentine Codex, *The General History of the Things of New Spain*, by Fray Bernardino de Sahagún, tr. Charles Dibble and Arthur J. Anderson, 12 vols., New Mexico, 1952 onwards; Spanish edn tr. Fray Angel Garibay, 4 vols., Mexico, 1956

Fontán, Antonio, and Jerzy Axer (eds.), *Españoles y Polacos en la Corte de Carlos V*, Madrid, 1994

Foronda, Manuel de, *Estancias y Viajes de Carlos V*, Madrid, 1895

Friede, Juan, *Documentos Inéditos para la Historia de Colombia*, 3 vols., I, 1509–28, Bogotá, 1955

——, *Gonzalo Jiménez de Quesada a través de Documentos Históricos, Estudio Biográfico, 1509–1550*, Bogotá, 1960

Friede, *Vida y Viajes de Nicolás Federman*, Bogotá, 1964

——, *Los Welsers*, Bogotá, 1965

Gachard, Louis-Prosper., *Retraite et mort de Charles Quint*, Brussels, 1854

——, *Relations des ambassadeurs vénitiens sur Charles Quint et Philippe II*, Brussels, 1855

——, *Correspondance de Charles V et d'Adrien VI*, Brussels, 1859

Galíndez de Carvajal, Lorenzo, *Crónicas de Castilla desde de Don Alfonso el Sabio Hasta los Católicos Don Fernando y Doña Isabel*, Madrid, 1875–8

García-Baquero González, Antonio, *La Carrera de Indias*, Seville, 1992

García Bravo, Alonso, *Alarife que trazó la Ciudad de México: Información de Méritos y Servicios de*, ed. Manuel Toussaint, Mexico, 1956

García Icazbalceta, Joaquín (ed.), *Colección de Documentos para la Historia de México*, 2 vols., Mexico, 1980

García Mercadal, J. (ed.), *Viajes de Extranjeros por España y Portugal*, Madrid, 1952

Garcilaso de la Vega, El Inca, *Royal Commentaries of the Incas*, tr. by Harold Livermore, 2 vols., Austin, 1966

Gasca, Pedro de la, *Descripción del Perú*, 1553, ed. Josep M. Barnadas, Caracas, 1976

Gerhard, Peter, *Geografía Histórica de la Nueva España 1519–1821*, tr. Stella Maestrangelo, Mexico, 1986

—— *La Frontera Sureste de la Nueva España*, tr. Stella Maestrangelo, Mexico, 1991

Getino, A., 'Dominicos Españoles Confesores de Reyes', *La Ciencia Tomista*, 14, 1916

Gil, Juan, *Los Conversos y la Inquisición Sevillana*, 5 vols., Seville, 2000–2002

Giménez Fernández, Manuel, *Bartolomé de las Casas, Biografía Crítica*, Santiago de Chile, 1954

——, *Bartolomé de las Casas*, 2 vols., Seville, 1953, 1960

——, *Breve Biografía de Fray Bartolomé de las Casas*, Seville, 1966

Ginés de Sepúlveda, Juan, *Obras Completas*, Pozoblanco, 1995–2008

Glave, Luis Miguel, *Trajinantes*, Lima, 1989

Gómez Pérez, María del Carmen, *Pedro de Heredia y Cartagena de Indias*, Seville, 1984

Góngora, Mario, *Los Grupos de Conquistadores en Tierra Firme, 1509–1530*, Santiago de Chile, 1962

González Palencia, A., and E. Mele, *Vida y Obras de Don Diego Hurtado de Mendoza*, 3 vols., Madrid, 1941

Goulding, Michael *et al.*, *The Smithsonian Atlas of the Amazon*, Washington, 2003

Granvelle, Cardinal, *Papiers d'état du*, ed. C. Weiss, Paris, 1841–52

Graziani, Antoine-Marie, *Un prince de la renaissance*, Paris, 2008

Griffin, Clive, *The Crombergers*, London, 1990, tr. as *Los Cromberger: La Historia de una Imprenta del Siglo XVI en Sevilla y México*, Madrid, 1991

Grunberg, Bertrand, *L'Univers des Conquistadors*, Paris, 1993

Guicciardini, Francesco, *The History of Italy*, tr. Sidney Alexander, New York, 1969

Guillén, Edmundo, *La Versión Inca de la Conquista*, Lima, 1974

Gussaert, Ernst, *Espagnols et Flamands*, Brussels, 1910

Hamilton, Earl J., *American Treasure and the Price Revolution in Spain 1501–1650*, Cambridge, Massachusetts, 1934

Hampe, Teodoro, *Don Pedro de la Gasca, 1493–1567*, Lima, 1989

Hanke, Lewis, 'Pope Paul III and the American Indians', *Harvard Theological Review*, XXX, 1937

——, *The Spanish Struggle for Justice in the Conquest of America*, Philadelphia, 1949

——, *Aristotle and the American Indians*, London, 1959

——, *All Mankind is One*, De Kalb, 1974

Haring, C.H., *Trade and Navigation Between Spain and the Indies in the Time of the Hapsburgs*, Cambridge, 1918

——, *The Spanish Empire in America*, New York, 1947

Harth-Terré, Emilio, 'Esclavas Blancas en Lima 1537', *El Comercio*, Lima, 3 June 1963

Harvey, L. P., *Islamic Spain 1250 to 1500*, Chicago, 1990; new edn 1993

——, *Muslims in Spain 1500–1614*, Chicago, 2005

Headley, J. M., *The Emperor and his Chancellor*, Cambridge, 1983

Helps, Sir Arthur, *The Conquerors of the New World and their Bondsmen*, London, 1848–52

Hemming, John, *The Conquest of the Incas*, London, 1970; new edn 1993

——, *The Search for El Dorado*, London, 1978

——, *Monuments of the Incas*, new illustrated edn, London, 2010

Henig, Stanley, 'Numbers Never Lie', unpublished manuscript in my possession

Herrera, Antonio de, *Historia General del Mundo, del Tiempo del Señor Rey Don Felipe II el Prudente*, 3 vols., Madrid, 1601

Huizinga, J., *The Waning of the Middle Ages*, tr. F. Hopman, London, 1924. There is a later translation by Rodney J. Payton and Ulrich Mammitzsch, *The Autumn of the Middle Ages*, Chicago, 1996

Iglesias Ortega, Luis, *Bartolomé de las Casas: Cuarenta y Cuatro Años Infinitos*, Seville, 2007

Jaquit, J., *Les Fêtes de la Renaissance*, Paris, 1960

Jeréz, Francisco de, *Verdadera Relación de la Conquista del Perú*, in *Historia-dores Primitivos de Indias*, ed. Enrique de Vedia, vol. 2, Madrid, 1946–7

Jones, R. O., *The Golden Age: Prose and Poetry*, London, 1971

Kagan, Richard, see Van der Wyngaerde

Kamen, Henry, *Philip of Spain*, New Haven, 1997

Kellenbruz, Hermann, *Los Fugger en España y Portugal hasta 1560*, Salamanca, 2000

Keniston, Ralph Hayward, *Garcilaso de la Vega*, New York, 1922

——, *Francisco de los Cobos*, Pittsburgh, 1958

Kubler, George, and Martin Soria, *Art and Architecture in Spain and Portugal and their American Dominions 1500–1800*, Harmondsworth, 1959

Láinez Alcalá, Rafael, *Pedro Berruguete, Pintor de Castilla*, Madrid, 1935

Landa, Fr Diego de, *Relación de las Cosas de Yucatán*, ed. Miguel Rivera, Madrid, 1985

Las Casas, Fr Bartolomé de, *Apologética Historia Sumaria*, ed. Juan Pérez de Tudela, 3 vols., Madrid, 1957

——, *Tratado sobre los Hombres que han sido hechos esclavos*, in *Opúsculos, Cartas y Memoriales*, BAE, Madrid, 1958

——, *Tratado de las Doce Dudas*, Madrid, 1958

——, *Los Tesoros del Perú*, ed. Angel Losada, Madrid, 1958

——, *Obras Escogidas*, ed. Juan Pérez de Tudela, Madrid, 1958

——, *Brevísima Relación de la Destrucción de las Indias*, ed. Consuelo Varela, Madrid, 1999

Laso de la Vega, M., *Doña Mencía de Mendoza, Marquesa de Cenete 1508–1554*, Madrid, 1942

Lavalle, Bernard, *Bartolomé de las Casas*, Paris, 2007

Lawley, Alethea, *Vittoria Colonna*, London, 1888

Lockhart, James, *Spanish Peru 1532–1560*, Madison, Wisconsin, 1968

——, *The Men of Cajamarca*, Austin, 1972

Lohmann Villena, Guillermo, *Les Espinosa: une famille d'hommes d'affaires en Espagne et aux Indes à l'époque de la colonisation*, Paris, 1968

——, *Los Americanos en las Ordenes Militares*, 2 vols., Madrid, 1975

——, *Las Ideas Jurídico-políticas en la Rebelión de Gonzalo Pizarro*, Valladolid, 1977

López, A., 'Confesores de la Familia Real de Castilla', *Archivo Ibero-Americano*, 31, 1929

López de Gómara, Francisco, *Hispania Victrix, Historia General de las Indias*, Saragossa, 1552, new edn, Madrid, 1846

——, *La Conquista de México*, Saragossa, 1552, new edn of José Luis Rojas, Madrid, 1987, Eng tr. L. B. Simpson, Berkeley, 1964

López de Jerez, Francisco, *Verdadera Relación de la Conquista del Perú, o Provincia del Cuzco, Llamada Nueva España* . . ., Seville, 1534

López de Mendoza, Íñigo, Count of Tendilla, *Correspondencia del Conde de Tendilla*, Madrid, 1974

López Rayón, Ignacio, *Documentos para la Historia de México*, 2 vols., Mexico, 1852–3

Loyola, Ignatius de, *Powers of Imagining*, collected works, ed. Antonio de T. de Nicholas, Albany, 1986

Lucía Megías, José Manuel, *Antología de Libros de Caballerías Castellanos*, Alcalá de Henares, 2001

Ludeña, Hugo, 'Versiones Temporanas sobre la Muerte de Don Francisco Pizarro', *Boletín de Lima*, 37, January 1985

Macdonald, Mark (ed.), *The Print Collection of Ferdinand Colombus*, 3 vols., London, 2004

Machiavelli, Niccolò, *Machiavelli and His Friends*, trans. by James Atkinson and David Sices, Da Kalb, 1996

Magalhães-Godinho, V., *Os Descobrimentos e a Economia Mundial*, Lisbon, 1963

Malfatti, Cesare V., *The Accession, Coronation and Marriage of Mary Tudor as Related in Four Manuscripts in the Escorial*, Barcelona, 1956

Marías, Fernando, *El Hospital Tavera de Toledo*, Seville, 2007

Marineo Siculo, Lucio, 'Don Hernando Cortés', in *De Rebus Hispaniae Memorabilibus Libri*, XXV, Alcalá de Henares, 1530, new edn of Miguel León-Portilla, *Historia*, 16, April 1985

Martín González, J. J., 'El Palacio de Carlos V en Yuste', *Archivo Español del Arte*, nos. 23–4, 1950–51

Martínez, José Luis, *Hernán Cortés*, Mexico, 1990, with four volumes of documents 1990–92

Martínez Millán, José (ed.), *La Corte de Carlos V*, 5 vols., Madrid, 2000

—— and J. Esquerra Revilla, *Carlos V y la Quiebra del Humanismo Político en Europa, 1530–1558*, 4 vols., Madrid, 2001

Martyr, Peter *De Orbe Novo*, trans. Francis MacNutt, 2 vols., New York, 1912; Spanish edn Ramón Alba, *Décadas del Nuevo Mundo*, Madrid, 1989

——, *Epistolario*, vols. IX–XI in *Documentos Inéditos para la Historia de España*, Madrid, 1953

——, *Cartas sobre el Nuevo Mundo*, Madrid, 1990

Medina, José Toribio, *El Descubrimiento del Río de las Amazonas*, 1894. (An English edition with invaluable appendices was published as *The Discovery of the Amazon* by the American Geographical Society in 1934. It includes an English translation of the account of Fr Gaspar de Carvajal)

——, *Cartas de Pedro de Valdivia*, Seville, 1929

Mena García, María del Carmen, 'El Traslado de la Ciudad de Nombre de Dios a Portobelo', *Anuario de Estudios Americanos*, 40, 1982, 71–102

——, *Pedrarias Dávila*, Seville, 1992

——, *Sevilla y las Flotas de Indias* (based on the accounts of Pedrarias's fleet which Professor Mena García found in AGI, Contratación, 3253), Seville, 1998

——, *Un Linaje de conversos en Tierras Americanas*, Salamanca, 2004

Menéndez Pidal, Ramón, *La Idea Imperial de Carlos V*, Buenos Aires, 1955

——, *La Lengua de Cristóbal Colón*, Madrid, 1958

Mexico, Splendours of Thirty Centuries, catalogue introduction by Octavio Paz, London, 1991

Mier, Lucía, and Téran Rocha, *La Primera Traza de la Ciudad de México*, 2 vols., Mexico, 2005

Molina Martínez, Miguel, 'El Soldado Cronista', *Anuario de Estudios Americanos*, 40, 1984

Montell, Jaime, *México: El Inicio*, Mexico, 2005

Morales Padrón, Francisco (ed.), *Primeras Cartas sobre América (1493–1503)*, Seville, 1990

Morán and Checa, F., *El Coleccionismo en España*, Madrid, 1990

Morel-Fatio, Alfred, *Historiographie de Charles Quint* (including a French translation of the autobiography of Charles, as well as the 1620 edition in Portuguese), Paris, 1913

Morison, Samuel Eliot, *The European Discovery of America: The Southern Voyages, 1491–1616*, New York, 1974

Mörner, Magnus, *La Mezcla de Razas en la Historia de América Latina*, Buenos Aires, 1969

Morrison, K. F., 'History *malgré lui*: A Neglected Account of Charles V's Coronation in Aachen', *Studia Gratiana Postscripta*, 15, Rome, 1962

Motolinía, Fray Toribio de Benavente, *Memoriales o Libro de las Cosas de la Nueva España y de los Naturales de Ella*, ed. Edmundo O'Gorman, Mexico, 1971

——, *Epistolario, 1526–1555*, Mexico, 1986

Munda, Salvatore, *El asesinato de Franciso Pizarro*, Lima, 1985

Muñoz, Andrés, *El Viaje de Felipe Segundo a Inglaterra*, Madrid, 1877

Muñoz de San Pedro, Miguel, *Tres Testigos de la Conquista de Perú*, Madrid, 1964

Muriel, Josefina, *Hospitales de la Nueva España*, Mexico, 1956

Murúa, Martín de, *Historia General del Perú: Origen y Descendencia de los Incas 1590–1611*, ed. Manuel Ballesteros-Gabrois, 2 vols., Madrid, 1962, 1964

Navarrete, see Fernández de Navarrete

Otte, Enrique, 'Aspiraciones y actividades Heterogéneas de Gonzalo Fernández de Oviedo, Cronista', *Revista de Indias*, no. 18, 1958

——, 'Cartas de Diego de Ordaz', *Historia Mexicana*, July–Sept. 1964

——, *Las Perlas del Caribe*, Caracas, 1977

——, *Cartas Privadas de Emigrantes a Indias*, Seville, 1988

Oviedo, see Fernández de Oviedo, Gonzalo

Palmer, Colin, *Slaves of the White God: Blacks in Mexico, 1570–1650*, Cambridge, Massachusetts, 1976

Paso, Francisco del, *Papeles de Nueva España*, 2nd series, 7 vols., Madrid, 1905–8

Pastor, Ludwig von, *History of the Popes*, tr. Mgr Ralph Kerr, vols. 5 to 20, London, 1898–1930

Pérez, Joseph, 'Moines frondeurs et sermons subversifs', *Bulletin Hispanique*, vol. 67, January–June 1965

——, *Carlos V*, Madrid, 1999

——, *Los Comuneros*, Madrid, 2001

Pérez-Mallaína, Pablo, *Spain's Men of the Sea*, tr. Carla Rahn Phillips, Baltimore, 1998

Pérez de Tudela, Juan, *Crónicas del Perú*, 5 vols., Madrid, 1963–5

——, *Documentos Relativos a Don Pedro de la Gasca y a Gonzalo Pizarro*, 2 vols., Madrid, 1964

—— Pérez Villanueva, J., and B. Escandell, *Historia de la Inquisición en España y América*, Madrid, 1984

Pietschmann, Horst, *El Estado y su Evolución al Principio de la Colonización Española de América*, Mexico, 1989

Pike, Ruth, *Enterprise and Adventure: The Genoese in Seville and the Opening of the New World*, Ithaca, New York, 1966

——, *Linajudos and Conversos in Seville*, New York, 2000

Pizarro, Pedro, 'Relación del Descubrimiento y Conquista de los Reinos del Perú', in *Colección de Documentos para la Historia de España*, ed. Martín Fernández de Navarrete, vol. V, Madrid, 1844, pp. 201–388, Eng. tr. Philip Ainsworth Means, The Cortes Society, New York, 1921

Polavieja, General Camilo, *Hernán Cortés, Copias de Documentos Existentes en el Archivo de Indias . . . sobre la Conquista de México*, Seville, 1889

Popol Vuh, *The Maya Book of the Dawn of Life*, tr. Dennis Tedlock, New York, 1996

Porrás Barrenechea, Raúl, *Cedulario del Perú*, 2 vols., Lima, 1944–8

——, 'Dos Documentos Esenciales sobre Francisco Pizarro', *Revista Histórica*, Lima, 1948

——, 'El Nombre del Perú', *Mar del Sur*, 6, no. 18, 1951

——, *Cartas del Perú 1524–1543*, Lima, 1959

——, *Las Relaciones Primitivas de la Conquista del Perú*, Lima, 1967

——, *Pizarro*, Lima, 1978

Puga, V. de, *Provisiones, Cédulas, Instrucciones para el Gobierno de la Nueva España*, Mexico, 1563; facsimile edn, Madrid, 1945

Quiroga, Vasco de, *Utopia en América*, ed. Paz Serrano Gassent, Madrid, 1992

Ramos, Demetrio, *El Consejo de Indias*, Valladolid, 1970

——, *Ximénez de Quesada, Cronista*, Seville, 1972

——, 'El Negocio Negrero de los Welser', *Revista de Historia de América*, 1, Jan.–June 1976, no. 8, Mexico,

Rayon, see López Rayón

Recinos, Adrián, and D. Goetz, *The Annals of the Cakchiquels*, Norman, Oklahoma, 1953

Resplendence of the Spanish Monarchy, Metropolitan Museum of Art catalogue, New York, 1991

Ricard, Robert, *La Conquête spirituel du Mexique*, Paris, 1933; tr. L. B. Simpson as *The Spiritual Conquest of Mexico, 1523–72*, Berkeley, 1966

Rivet, P., and H. Arsandaux, 'La Metallurgie en Amérique précolombienne', *Travaux et Mémoires Institut d'Ethnologie*, XXXIX, Paris, 1946

Rodríguez de Montalvo, García, *Amadís de Gaula*, ed. Juan Bautista Avalle-Arce, 2 vols., Madrid, 1991; Eng tr. Anthony Munday, Aldershot, 2004

Rodríguez Villa, Antonio, *El Emperador Carlos V y su Corte, según las Cartas de Don Martín de Salinas*, Madrid, 1903

Ryder, A. J. C., *Benin and the Europeans*, London, 1969

Salinas, Martín de, *El Emperador Carlos V y su Corte según las cartas de Martín de Salinas*, Madrid, 1903

Sampaio García, Rozendo, *Provisão de Escravos Negros na América*, São Paulo, 1962

Sancho de Hoz, Pedro, *Relación de la Conquista del Perú*, Madrid, 1962

Sandoval, Fray Prudencio de, *Historia de la Vida y Hechos del Emperador Carlos V*, 3 vols., Valladolid, 1604–6, Madrid, 1956

Santa Cruz, Alonso de, *Crónica del Emperador*, 5 vols., Madrid, 1920–25

Sanuto, Marino, *Diarii*, 58 vols., Venice, 1887

Sanz, Eufemio Lorenzo, *Comercio de España con América en la Época de Felipe II*, 2 vols., Valladolid, 1986

Sarabia Viejo, María Justina, *Don Luis de Velasco: Virrey de Nueva España, 1550–1564*, Seville, 1978

Sauer, Carl Ortwin, *The Early Spanish Main*, Cambridge, 1966

Saunders, A. C. de M., *A Social History of Black Slaves in Portugal*, Cambridge, 1982

Scelle, Georges, *La Traite négrière aux Indes de Castile*, 2 vols., Paris, 1906

Schäfer, Ernesto, *El Consejo Real y Supremo de las Indias*, 2 vols., Seville, 1935. New edn Antonio-Miguel Bernal, Madrid, 2003

Schick, Léon, *Un grand homme d'affaires au début du XVIème siècle: Jacob Fugger*, Paris, 1957

Schmidt, Ulrich, *Historia y Descubrimiento del Río de la Plata y Paraguay*, Tübingen, 1567, London, 1891

Schmitt, E., and F. K. von Hutten, *Das Gelt der Neuen Welt: Die Papiere des Welser-Konquistadors und GeneralKapitans von Venezuela Philipp von Hutten 1534–1541*, Hilburghausen, 1996

Scholes, France V., and Dave Warren, 'The Olmec Region at Spanish Contact' in Steward, J. (ed.), *Handbook of the Middle American Indian*, 3, Austin, 1965

Schwaller, John, 'Tres Familias Mexicanas del Siglo XVI', *Historia Mexicana*, XXXI, no. 2, Oct.–Dec. 1981

Segovia, Bartolomé de, *Relación de Muchas Cosas Acaecidas en el Perú*, BAE, Madrid, CCIX

Serrano, Luciano, 'Primeras Negociaciones de Carlos V con la Santa Sede 1516–18', *Cuadernos de Trabajo de la Escuela Española y Historia en Roma*, vol. 2, 1914

Serrano y Sanz, Manuel, *Historiadores de Indias*, 2 vols., Madrid, 1909

Service, Elman, *Spanish–Guarani Relations in Early Colonial Paraguay*, Ann Arbor, 1954

Simpson, L. B., *The Encomienda in New Spain 1492–1550*, Berkeley, 1966

Skinner, Quentin, *The Foundations of Modern Political Thought*, 2 vols., Cambridge, 1978

Sobaler, María A., *Los Colegiales Mayores de Santa Cruz, una Élite de Poder, 1484–1670*, Valladolid, 1988

Soisson, Jean-Pierre, *Marguerite, Princesse de Bourgogne*, Paris, 2002

Solano, Francisco de (ed.), *Proceso Histórico al Conquistador*, Madrid, 1988

Solorzano, Juan de, *Política Indiana*, 3 vols., Madrid, 1996

Spivakivsky, Erica, *Son of the Alhambra*, Austin, 1970

Steward, J. (ed.), *Handbook of the Middle American Indians*, several vols., Texas, 1973

Stirling, Stuart, *The Last Conquistador*, Stroud, 1999

——, *Pizarro, Conquistador of the Inca*, Stroud, 2005

Stirling-Maxwell, William, *The Cloister Life of the Emperor Charles V*, London, 1853

Studnicki Gizbert, Daviken, *A Nation upon the Ocean Sea*, Oxford, 2007

Suárez de Peralta, Juan, *Tratado del Descubrimiento de las Yndias y su Conquista*, Mexico, 1949

Tena Fernández, Juan, *Trujillo Histórico y Monumental*, Trujillo, 1967

Thayer Ojeda, Tomás, *Formación de la Sociedad Chilena y Censo de la Población de Chile en los Años de 1540 a 1565*, 3 vols., Santiago de Chile, 1939–41

——, *Valdivia y sus Compañeros*, Santiago de Chile, 1950

Thomas, Hugh, *The Conquest of Mexico*, London, 1993

——, *Quien es Quien de los Conquistadores*, Madrid, 2000

——, *Rivers of Gold*, London, 2003

Toussaint, Manuel, 'El Criterio Artístico de Hernán Cortés', *Estudios Americanos*, 1, 1950, 62

Tovar de Teresa, Guillermo, *et al.*, *La Utopia Mexicana del Siglo XVI*, Mexico, 1992

Tremayne, Eleanor E., *The First Governess of the Netherlands, Margaret of Austria*, London, 1908

Trujillo, Diego de, *Relación del Descubrimiento del Reino del Perú*, Seville, 1948

Valdés, Alonso, *Diálogo de las Cosas Ocurridas en Roma*, Madrid, 1956

——, *Obras Completas*, Madrid, 1960

Van den Wyngaerde, Anton, *Ciudades del Siglo de Oro: Las Vistas Españolas de Anton van den Wyngaerde*, ed. Richard Kagan, Madrid, 1986

Varón Gabai, Rafael, *La Ilusión del Poder: Apogeo y Decadencia e los Pizarro en la Conquista del Perú*, Lima, 1996

——, *Francisco Pizarro and his Brothers*, Norman, Oklahoma, 1997

——, and Auke Pieter Jacobs, 'Peruvian Wealth and Spanish Investments', *Hispanic American Historical Review*, 67, 1987

Varón Velasco, Balbino, 'El Conquistador de Nicaragua, Gabriel de Rojas', *Anuario de Estudios Americanos*, 1985

Vassberg, David, 'Concerning Pigs, the Pizarros and the Agropastoral Backgrounds of the Conquerors of Peru', *Latin American Research Review*, 13, no. 3, 1978

Vázquez, A., and R. S. Rose, *Algunas Cartas de Don Diego Hurtado de Mendoza, Escritas en 1538–1552*, New Haven, 1935

Vega, Juan José, *El Manco Inca, el Gran Rebelde*, Lima, 1995

Vergara, Alejandro, *Patinir*, Madrid, 2007

Vernon, Ida Stevenson Weldon, *Pedro de Valdivia, Conquistador de Chile*, Austin, 1946

Vila Vilar, Enriqueta, with Guillermo Lohmann Villena, *Familia, Linajes y Negocios entre Sevilla y las Indias*, Seville, 2003

Vilar Sánchez, J. A., *1526: Boda y Luna de Miel del Emperador Carlos V*, Granada, 2000

Villacorta, Antonio, *La Emperadora Isobel*, Madrid, 2009

'Vitraux des XVIème et XVIIème Siècles', Cathédrale des Saints Michel-et-Gudule, Brussels, 2009

Vives, Juan Luis, *Obras Políticas y Pacifistas*, ed. F. Calero *et al.*, Madrid, 1999

Walser, Fritz., *Die Spanischen Zentralbehörden und der Stadtrat Karls V Grundlagen und Aufbau bis zum Tode Gattinares*, Göttingen, 1959

Warren, J. Benedict, *The Conquest of Michoacan*, Norman, Oklahoma, 1984

Watts, David, *The West Indies: Patterns of Development*, Cambridge, 1987

Whitelock, Anna, *Mary Tudor*, London, 2009

Winship, G. P., 'The Coronado Expedition', XIVth Annual Report of the (US) Bureau of Ethnology, Washington, 1896

Wright, I. A., *The Early History of Cuba, 1492–1586*, New York, 1916

Yupangui, Diego, *An Inca Account of the Conquest of Peru*, tr. Ralph Bauer, Boulder, Colorado, 2005

Zavala, Silvio, *Las Instituciones Jurídicas en la Conquista de América*, Madrid, 1935

——, *Ideario de Vasco de Quiroga*, Mexico, 1941

——, 'Debate with Benno Biermann', *Historia Mexicana*, XVII–XVIII, 1968–9

——, *Recuerdo de Vasco de Quiroga*, Mexico, 1997

Zorita, Alonso de, *Historia de la Nueva España*, Madrid, 1909

Notes

The full title of books and articles mentioned here is given in the Bibliography above.

I. VALLADOLID

1. Tremayne, 217.
2. *Memorias*, Spanish Academy of History, vol. VI, Inventory of plate and jewels presented to the Archduchess Margaret, 3 April 1497.
3. The site is now occupied by the Teatro Calderón. From nobility to the stage would seem an agreeable translation for any building. On the main gate of the old house of the Enríquez, there is the rhyme:

> *Viva el Rey con tal Victoria*
> *Esta casa y su vecino*
> *Queda es ella por memoria*
> *La fama renombre y gloria,*
> *Que por él a España vino*
> *Año MDXXII Carlos*

It was signed *Almirante Don Fadrique, segundo de este nombre.*
4. These designs have been admirably reproduced with an introduction and essays on the places concerned by Richard Kagan, *Ciudades del Siglo de Oro: Las Vistas Españolas de Anton van den Wyngaerde*, Madrid, 1986.
5. *Marqués* originally meant someone who was a lord of some land within the territory of the kingdom.
6. García Mercadal, 455, tells us that there were thirty-nine religious houses in 1520 on the eve of dissolution. San Felipe Neri himself (1515–95) was in 1522 still a child in Florence.
7. See Joseph Pérez, 'Moines frondeurs et sermons subversifs'.
8. Later used by the Banco Castellano.
9. Uncle of the inquisitor Fray Tomás. The cardinal was the greatest Spanish theologian of the century.

10. The Counts of Oropesa were hereditary protectors of the Jeronymite monastery of Yuste where Charles V went in 1556 to retire and to die.

11. *Huelga* in the sixteenth century indicated not a strike, as it now does, but a fertile stretch of land.

12. For Berruguete see Angulo, *Pedro Berruguete en Paredes de Nava*, Barcelona, 1946 and Ricardo Laínez Alcalá, *Pedro Berruguete: Pintor de Castilla*, Madrid, 1935.

13. For Navagero, see the Nota Preliminar in García Mercadal, *Viaje por España*, Madrid, 1952, 835. For Vital, see the same, 706.

14. Defourneaux, 148.

15. These wonderful occasions are beautifully described in Bennassar's admirable history, especially p. 534.

16. See Inmaculada Arias de Saavedra, 'Las Universidades Hispánicas durante el Reinado de Carlos V', in Martínez Millán, *Carlos V y la Quiebra*, III, 396.

17. 'We don't seek and we should not seek only the purity of Latin but the knowledge of many other things' (Andrés, II, 48).

18. Letter of 26 February 1517 to Wolfgang Fabricius Capite quoted in Huizinga, *The Waning of the Middle Ages*, 31.

19. Bataillon, *Erasme*, 302.

20. Ibid., 484.

21. Bennassar, 116–19.

22. Harvey, *Muslims*, 112.

23. Salinas, *El Emperador Charles V y su Corte según las cartas de Don Martín de Salinas*, Madrid, 1903.

24. Kubler and Soria, 351.

25. Stirling-Maxwell, 126.

26. Sobaler, 136.

27. For Glapion, see Martínez Millán, *La Corte*, III, 178.

2. CHARLES KING AND EMPEROR

1. The only known 'Carloses' in Spain in the sixteenth century, apart from the king, were Carlos, prince of Viana, and Carlos de Valera, a captain in the Spanish–Portuguese war of the 1470s, and son of a *converso* historian, Diego de Valera.

2. The day of St Matthew was changed by the Council of Trent in the late sixteenth century.

3. As a child, she had been for a few years the first wife of King Charles VIII of France till he announced that he preferred to marry, for dynastic reasons, the last Duchess of Brittany. This crude rejection was the source of Margaret's dislike of France.

4. For Margaret, see Tremayne, *The First Governess of the Netherlands*, an old but worthy book.

5. Ibid., 154.

6. The founder was Geert Groote.

7. See Crane, 29.

8. See my *Rivers of Gold*.

9. Guicciardini, 330–31.

10. Letter of 15 February 1522 to Floris Wyngarden qu. Pérez Villanueva and Escandell, 444.

11. Cit. Pastor, IX, 115.

12. See Adrian's letter of 3 May 1522 to Charles from Saragossa, cit. Tremayne, 193.

13. Pastor, IX, 226.

14. Contarini, in García Mercadal, 677.

15. Chièvres is well studied by Manuel Jiménez Fernández in his great life of Las Casas.

16. Huizinga, *The Waning of the Middle Ages*, 77; Eichberger, 222.

17. For the family history, see P. Gargantilla Madera, *Historia Clínica del Emperador*, in Martínez Millán, *Carlos V y la Quiebra*, IV, 33ff.

18. Contarini in Alberi, II, 6off.

19. Ibid.

20. A description by Lorenzo Pasqualino in Sanuto, XX, 422; XXX, 324.

21. Santa Cruz, II, 374.

22. In preface to 1987 edition.

23. Cit. Brandi, 504.

24. This paragraph is based on Brandi, 394.

25. Maximilian qu. Tremayne, 117.

26. Granvelle, II, 124. The same in 1548 quoted Chabod, 46. Like so much of old France, the place was ruined in the Revolution, to no good end.

27. Mgr Anglés cit. Fernández Álvarez, *Carlos V*, 182. The clavichord had established itself in the fifteenth century as an instrument for use in the home.

28. For Lannoy, see Martínez Millán, *La Corte*, III, 225f. Lannoy was born in Valenciennes in 1487. He followed his father into work for the imperial family. He was with the Archduke Philip before he served Charles as 'supreme master of the horse'. He married Françoise de Montbel in 1510. He accompanied Charles to Spain in 1517 as chamberlain and member of Charles's council. Lannoy, Hugo de Moncada and Pescara were in favour of an agreement with France as opposed to the more belligerent line taken up by Gorrevod and Gattinara.

29. Brandi, 345.

30. 'Vitraux des XVIème et XVIIème Siècles', Cathédrale des Saints-Michel-et-Gudule.

31. Morel-Fatio, 154.

32. Santa Cruz, II, 37–40.

33. Skinner, I, 24, 220, 221.

34. Lhermite, I, 101.

35. For Gattinara there is a fine study by J. M. Headley. See also Martínez Millán, *La Corte*, III, 167f.

36. Manuel Rivero Rodríguez has a study of Gattinara's autobiography (written in the third person) in his 'Memoria, Escritura y Estado: la Autobiografía de Mercurino Arborio de Gattinara', in Martínez Millán, *Carlos V y la Quiebra*, I, 199ff.

37. Claretta qu. Headley, 41. Keniston thought the letter was written only in 1526. There are some stories in the memoirs of the Venetians Navagero and Contarini in 1525 about angry exchanges between the emperor and Gattinara.

38. R. Acciaiuoli in Desjardins, II, 861, qu. Pastor, X, 30–34.

39. Fernández Álvarez, *Carlos V*, 287, 288.

40. The grant was for 154,000,000 maravedís, 411,000 ducats. Valladolid in 1518 had granted 204,000,000 maravedís or 545,000 ducats. Juan M. Carretero Zamora, 'Liquidez, Deuda y Obtención de Recursos Extraordinarios', in Martínez Millán, *Carlos V y la Quiebra*, IV, 448.

41. See Joseph Pérez, *La Rebelión de los Comuneros*, 136.

42. As a 'Catholic King' of Spain. See Fernández Álvarez, *Carlos V*, 209.

43. Cited J. M. Headley in Martínez Millán, *Carlos V y la Quiebra*, I, 8.

44. Oviedo qu. Brading, 34.

45. In the second *carta de relación* of Cortés to Charles V, in Cortés, 159.

46. Letter of October 1524 in Pagden, 412.

47. Fernández Álvarez (ed.), *Corpus Documental*, III, 304.

48. '*Se junten con V. sacra majestad en amistad y paz verdadera como monarca y señor del mundo para que sean en exterminar y perseguir los páganos y infieles*' (ibid., I, 120).

49. Question 2 of *pequeño interrogatorio* in *Residencia* of Cortés.

50. Guicciardini, 305.

51. Qu. Fernández Álvarez, *Carlos V*, 165.

52. Patinir began to paint about 1515 and would die in 1524. He painted Charon in 1520. See Vergara, 161.

53. Fernández Álvarez, *Carlos V*, 374. See too the same author's fascinating *Sombras y Luces en la España Imperial*, 185.

54. Pastor, XVI, 355.

55. Brandi, 631. This was his fifth will, it appears.

56. Bucer qu. Brandi, 504. This was in 1541.

57. See Serrano, 300.

58. '*Nuestras vidas son los ríos que van a dar en el mar, que es el morir: allí van los señoríos derechos a se acabar y consumir.*'

59. See biography in Martínez Millán, *La Corte*, II, 225. Manrique lost much influence by defending Dr Juan de Vergara of Toledo. He died in 1538 leaving four bastard sons, one of whom, Jerónimo, became *inquisidor-general* at the end of the century.

60. See Lorenzo Vital, *Relación del Primer Viaje de Carlos V a España*, García Mercadal, 711.

61. See Fernández Álvarez, *Carlos V*, 97–9. Fernández Álvarez spent the best years of his life editing, very well, the papers of Charles V.

62. Ibid., 264–9.

63. Ibid.

3. CORTÉS AND THE REBUILDING OF MEXICO/ TENOCHTITLAN

1. In 1522 he was always known as 'Hernando', not 'Hernán'.

2. See chap. 39 of my *Conquest of Mexico*.

3. Martyr, II, 358.

4. See chaps. 16 and 17 of my *Conquest of Mexico*.

5. See Renate Pieper, 'Cartas, Avisos e Impresos', in Martínez Millán, *Carlos V y la Quiebra*, IV, 434.

6. See my *Conquest of Mexico*, 568ff.

7. See Cortés, 575, n. 119.

8. The second in 1520, the third in 1522, the other two subsequently (CDI, XXVI, 59). The *cédula* of 15 October 1522 speaks of '*las tierras y provincias de Aculuacán e San Xoan de Olua llamada La Nueva España*'.

9. See AGI, Justicia, leg. 220, no. 2, f. 128.

10. CDI, XXVI, 65–70.

11. Ibid., 66.

12. Ibid., 65–70. Text also in CDIHE, I, 97.

13. Martyr, *De Orbe Novo*, II, 406. The four men were to be paid: Estrada 510,000 maravedís; Albornoz 500,000; Álvarez de Chirino 500,000; Salazar 170,000.

14. Tenochtitlan began to be called 'Mexico' in 1523 or 1524.

15. I do not think that house has any connection with the old mansion shown nowadays to tourists as 'the house of Cortés'.

16. *Probanza* of García Bravo, p. 57.

17. Benítez, 7–9.

18. Instruction of 26 June 1523, José Luis in Martínez, docs. I, 270.

19. Cited in Toussaint, *El Criterio Artístico*,.

20. A *vara* was a measure of 835 *millimetres* and 9 *décimas*.

21. Motolinía in *Colección de Documentos para la História de México*, ed. by Joaquín García Icazbalceta, 2 vols., Mexico, 1980, 18.

22. Ibid., 19.

23. Kubler and Soria, 136.

24. Martyr, II, 418.

25. Ibid., 193, 358.

26. Muriel, 212.

27. See *Cortés*, ed. Delgado Gómez, 126.

28. The wife of Amerigo Vespucci, María Cerezo, may have been a relation. For the family's *converso* connections, see Gil, III, 500ff.

29. See Gerhard's splendid *Geografía Histórica de la Nueva España*, 252, 254.

30. These understandings would be reflected in laws of 12 July 1530, cited in de Puga, fol. 45.

31. See Crane, 63.

4. CHRISTIANITY AND THE NEW WORLD

1. Díaz del Castillo, II, 141.

2. See my *Rivers of Gold*, 129.

3. Ibid., chap. 30.

4. See F. de Solano, *El Conquistador Hispánico: Señas de Identidad*, in Solano *et al.*, 31.

5. The letter from Las Casas is in *Memorial de Remedios para las Indias* in *Obras Escogidas* by Pérez de Tudela, V, Madrid, 1958, 15. The text reads:

> Thus I beg your most Reverend Lordship . . . that you send to these isles of the Indies the Holy Inquisition, of which I believe there is a great need, because wherever we have newly to plant the faith, as in those lands, to ensure that there is nobody who sows any seed of heresy since there such people have been found and two people have burned as heretics and there remain more than fourteen; and these Indians who are simple people and then believe what may be said by some malign and diabolic person who brings there their damnable doctrine and heretical iniquity. Because it could be that many heretics have fled there from these realms [Spain] thinking thus to save themselves . . .

6. Bull of 9 May 1522, *Exponi nobis fecisti*.

7. *Artes de México*, no. 150, XIX, Mexico, 1972.

8. Leopoldo de Austria, bishop of Córdoba, and Jorge de Austria, bishop of Liège. Both were born about 1505.

9. Wright, 155; Cadenas, 176. See Fernández Álvarez, *Sombras*, 113ff.

10. Bataillon, 'Novo Mundo e Fim do Mundo'.

11. Motolinía, *Memoriales*, 178.

12. Ricard, 361.

13. Ibid., 365.

14. A *residencia* was the examination of an official after his resignation or dismissal. The term derives from the fact that the official concerned had to remain in his place of residence for thirty days.

15. His evidence in AGI, Justicia, leg. 224, pieza 462–4 was on 21 January 1535. See Greenleaf, who argued that the Inquisition was used against Cortés and his affiliates.

16. *Motolinía* = poor man or woman.

17. Ricard, 136, in García Icazbalceta.

18. The history, written in 1541, was published as *Historia de las Indias de Nueva España* by García Izcabalceta in *Colección de Documentos para la Historia de México*, I.

19. Mexico would for the time being control Toluca, Michoacan, Jilotepec and Tula; Texcoco would have authority over Otumba, Tepeapulco and Tulancingo; Tlaxcala would control Zacatlan, Jalapa and Veracruz; and Huejotzingo would exercise authority over Cholula, Tepeaca, Tecamachalco, Tehuacan, Huaquechula and Chietla. The last named is now the oldest religious house in the Americas.

20. *Coloquios*, qu. in my *Conquest of Mexico*, 587.

21. Sahagún was the great historian/anthropologist of old Mexico.

22. Ricard, 49, 50.

23. Qu. Hanke, *All Mankind*, 13.

24. See Horst Pietschmann, 108–9.

25. Martyr, *De Orbe Novo*, II, 275.

26. Pastor, IX, 92–3.

27. Ibid., IX, 175–6.

28. Ibid., IX, 135.

29. Ibid., X, 253.

5. CHARLES AT VALLADOLID

1. This was the view of Walser, 199–228, but opposed by Martínez Millán, in *La Corte*, I, 219. For this remarkable individual see my *Rivers of Gold*, 416ff.

2. Oviedo, *Batallas y Quinquagenas*, I, 141.

3. See my *Conquest of Mexico*, 341; also Martínez Millán, *La Corte*, III, 351.

4. See Martínez Millán, *La Corte*, III, 350.

5. Ibid., III, 377. For the Ruiz de la Mota family see Schwaller, 178.

6. J. Zurita, *Historia del Rey Don Hernando el Católico*, 12 v. Qu. Martínez Millán, *La Corte*, III, 264.

7. Hannart continued in the public service since, between 1531 and 1536, he was ambassador in France.

8. See Salustiano de Dios, 215.

9. See Heredia, II, 500; also for Rojas, Martínez Millán, *La Corte*, III, 369ff.

10. See Demetrio Ramos, 'El Problema de la Fundación del Real Consejo de Indias', in *El Consejo de Indias*; and Dworski, 143.

11. For whom see my *Rivers of Gold*, chap. 15.

12. Schäfer, I, 47.

13. Perhaps because the papers of the Dominicans in San Esteban in Salamanca are not yet in the public domain.

14. Headley, 126.

15. This beautiful grave was the masterpiece of the Florentine Domenico Fancelli.

The first *inquisidor-general*, Torquemada, who founded the monastery, is also buried there.

16. See Getino, 417–19, and López, 5–75.

17. See Pérez Villanueva, 447.

18. Fernández Álvarez, *Carlos V*, 208.

19. Joseph Pérez, *Carlos V*, 68.

20. Brandi, 395.

21. Cit. ibid., 294.

22. Ibid., 492. There is a good biographical essay in Martínez Millán, *La Corte*, III, 228–38.

23. See Juan de Areizaga's account of the journey of one of the ships, the *Santiago*, to Cortés in Mexico.

24. See Martyr, *De Orbe Novo*, II, 239.

25. Carlos Javier de Carlos Morales, in Martínez Millán, *Carlos V y la Quiebra*, IV, 411–13.

26. Martyr, *De Orbe Novo*, I, 254.

27. Martyr, *Epistolario*, 57, 83–4.

28. Among them were the dukes of Cardona and Villahermosa; Juan Carrillo; García de Toledo, the heir of the Duke of Alba; Pedro Hernández de Córdoba; Alfonso de Silva, heir of the Conde de Cifuentes; Pedro Fajardo, Marqués de los Vélez; Luis Hurtado de Mendoza, Marqués de Mondéjar (future president of the Council of the Indies); Pedro Girón; Pedro de Aguilar; Pedro de Mendoza and Álvar Gómez de Villareal.

29. This may have been written by the great grammarian Nebrija.

30. Martyr, *De Orbe Novo*, II, 345–6. 'My feelings for Jamaica are certainly sincere,' he said elsewhere, 'but perhaps exaggerated' (see ibid., 348).

31. Ibid., I, 338, 348.

32. Epist. Familiarium lib. XVII. See Martínez Millán, *La Corte*, III, 46f.

33. Oviedo, *Batallas y Quinquagenas*, II, 180: '*porque no tenía nada entonces Francisco de los Cobos*'. Other benefits went to Galíndez de Carvajal (mines near Valladolid); to the Conde de Zuñiga (mines at Belalcázar); and to Juan Vázquez de Molina. See Carande, II, 350.

34. Keniston, *Cobos*, 143.

35. This was Giménez Fernández, I, 283.

36. López de Gómara, 126.

37. Giménez Fernández, I, 283.

38. Keniston, *Cobos*, 33.

39. Las Casas, III, 170.

40. See my *Rivers of Gold*, 212.

41. Keniston, *Cobos*, 117.

42. Fernández Álvarez, *Carlos V*, 391–2.

43. The Renaissance hospital was founded by Tavera as a general hospital but also as a sepulchre for himself. It is an echo of Cardinal González de Mendoza's

hospital of Santa Cruz in Valladolid. The chief architect was Alonso de Covarrubias, assisted by Tavera's secretary, Bartolomé de Bustamante. Later architects included Nicolás de Vergara, father and son.

44. Pérez Villanueva, I, 523.

45. Giménez Fernández, II, 16, Dworski, 206; see too Fita, 307–48.

46. For *residencia*, see above, p. 600. A *corregidor* was a 'co-councillor' appointed by the Crown in municipal councils.

47. Salinas in a letter to the treasurer, Salamanca, 100, in Schäfer, I, 61.

48. Paso, IV, 170. This was in 1521.

49. CDI, XXIII, 425. Galíndez de Carvajal came from an Extremeño family, the Carvajals, but his father was the archpriest of Trujillo, and Lorenzo was his offspring with a Galíndez girl from Cáceres.

50. Beltrán also received money from Almagro and Pizarro. The whole interesting investigation is to be seen in AGI, Patronato, leg. 185, no. 34 of 1542.

51. Giménez Fernández, II, 264, 953.

52. See Carande, II, 85ff.

53. Ibid., 158ff.

54. Fernández Álvarez (ed.), *Corpus Documental*, I, 189.

55. Giménez Fernández, II, 953 n. 3, 191.

56. Kellenbruz, 356.

57. Salinas, 109.

6. CORTÉS IN POWER

1. Díaz del Castillo, IV, 208.

2. See my *Rivers of Gold*, 489, also for his astounding *Información de Servicios y Méritos*, in AGI, Patronato, leg. 54, no. 7 r1, of 11 August 1530.

3. Covarrubias, 38.

4. Scholes and Warren, part 2, 784.

5. Díaz del Castillo, IV, 229.

6. Información de Servicios of February 1532 of Luis Marín in AGI, Patronato, leg. 54, no. 8, r. 2. Included there is an unpublished testimony of Cortés. Antonio Arroyo had known Marín's father, Francesco Marín.

7. Bernal Díaz's father was a *regidor*, council member, of Medina, along with Montalvo.

8. Bernal Díaz del Castillo claimed to have been with Grijalva but there are some indications that that was not so.

9. See Gerhard, *Geografía*, 141.

10. Others with Sandoval included Rodrigo de Nao of Ávila, Francisco Martín of Vizcaya and Francisco Ximénez of Ynguejuela in Extremadura.

11. Scholes and Warren, 784.

12. '*Mas pendenciero que luchador*'.

13. Rosin is a resin produced by distilling oil of turpentine.

14. Díaz del Castillo, IV, 512; Gerhard, *The Southeast Frontier*, 124.

15. Warren, 216.

16. Durán, II, 284.

17. Probably at Zarauz.

18. An *Información de Servícios y Méritos* was published in the Archivo General de la Nación, XII, Mexico, 1927, 232. Cortés gave evidence, among others.

19. Warren, 295.

20. Cortés, 277.

21. Ignacio Bernal in *Handbook*, III, II, 809.

22. Florentine Codex, III, 113.

23. As was suggested by Alfonso Caso in a splendid essay in Scholes and Warren, part 2, 915.

24. As argued by Rivet and Ansandaux.

25. Díaz del Castillo, II, 246.

26. CDI, XXVI, 71–6.

27. Dr Ojeda and Dr Pedro López, neither of them friends of Cortés, both said that they believed his to be a natural death. See Martyr, *Cartas*, 279ff and Res. López Rayón, I, 284.

28. Díaz del Castillo, III, 26.

29. See Chipman, *Nuño de Guzmán*, 66.

30. Díaz del Castillo, IV, 368.

31. Cortés's relation with this Las Casas family was through his mother.

32. Gil González de Ávila had been a page with the Infante Juan, then a *contino* with King Fernando, later *contador* in Santo Domingo and, since 1521, 'general of the southern sea', a title which he received from Fonseca.

33. Cortés so reports. Bernal Díaz del Castillo thought that Cortés had 130 horsemen and 120 foot (IV, 364).

34. See Montell, 165ff.

35. Bejarano, 25.

36. Mier, 168.

37. Martyr, *De Orbe Novo*, II, 46: letter in García Icazbalceta, I, 484ff.

38. Mier, 195.

39. Ibid., 196. Grado would die in 1528. Cortés then gave Techuipo (Isabel) to Pedro Gallego de Andrada, before which Cortés himself gave Techuipo a child, Leonor Cortés Moctezuma. When Gallego died, Techuipo was married yet again, to Juan Cano of Cáceres.

40. Martyr, *De Orbe Novo*, II, 417.

41. Oviedo, *Batallas y Quinquagenas*, IV, 238.

42. Paso, I, 97.

43. Account by Bartolomé de Zarate in 1542 in Paso, IV, 132ff.

44. Letter of Bishop Zumárraga to the king, 27 August 1529, in García Icazbalceta, I, 39.

45. By 1570 the European population of Spanish America was said to be about 150,000.

7. CHARLES: FROM VALLADOLID
TO THE FALL OF ROME

1. Denia was related via the Enríquezes, of which family Admiral Fadrique was the head, and of whom the mother of King Fernando had been a member.
2. Fernández Álvarez (ed.), *Corpus Documental*, I, 83.
3. Qu. García Mercadal, 793.
4. Martyr, *De Orbe Novo*, II, 409. He died in 1524.
5. *Información de Servícios y Méritos* in AGI, Mexico, leg. 203, no. 13.
6. García Mercadal, 795.
7. The genealogical history of this great family remains to be written.
8. Bayard was Pierre du Terrail, seigneur de Bayard, '*sans peur et sans reproche*', who had been in Charles VIII's expedition. He was mortally wounded near Milan.
9. His blood relationship to Cortés is obscure.
10. These were plays and poems published in 1517 in Naples, 'the first things of Pallas'.
11. Lawley, 20.
12. Chancellor of Francesco Sforza, Duke of Milan.
13. Fernández Álvarez (ed.), *Corpus Documental*, I, n. xxi, 98.
14. See Guicciardini, 350, for his argument for 'a loving and brotherly liberation'.
15. Brandi, 162.
16. Vives to King Henry VIII, in Vives, 77.
17. Headley, 151ff.
18. App. I, Hermann Baumgarten, *Geschichte Karls V*, Stuttgart, 1885, 11/2, 707.
19. Headley, 6. See also Gussaert, 250ff.
20. See Sandoval, II, 209.
21. Qu. Chabod, 154–8.
22. Harvey, 15.
23. Guzmán, 72.
24. Fernández Álvarez (ed.), *Corpus Documental*, I, 104.
25. Martínez Millán, *La Corte*, I, 236.
26. Dantiscus in García Mercadal, 801.
27. Fernández Álvarez wonders why Seville was chosen, why the king travelled there via Extremadura and why the future queen was asked to wait.
28. Martínez Millán, *La Corte*, II, 351.
29. Dantiscus in García Mercadal, 789.
30. He was born on 21 May 1527.

31. See Guicciardini for the exchange of prisoners at Fuenterrabía on the border of France and Spain.

32. Bataillon, *Erasme*, 121.

33. Valdés, *Obras*, 126. For Charles and Manrique see M. Avilés, 'El Santo Oficio en la Primera Etapa Carolina', in Pérez Villanueva and Escandell Bonet, I, 443–72.

34. Cit. Brandi, 251.

35. Ibid.

36. Vettori to Machiavelli, in *Machiavelli and His Friends*, 346.

37. J. M. Headley, in Martínez Millán, *Carlos V y la Quiebra*, I, 31.

38. Fernández Álvarez (ed.), *Corpus Documental*, I, 121.

39. Pastor, XIV, 352ff.

40. Cadenas y Vicente, 68.

41. Fernández Álvarez (ed.), *Corpus Documental*, I, 120.

42. Harvey, *Muslims*, 58.

43. Ibid., 97.

44. Pastor, XIV, 332.

45. Bataillon, *Erasme*, 407.

46. Abbot of Nájera to the emperor, after 6 May 1527, cited in Rodríguez Villa, *Memorias*, 134–41.

47. With of course the ceiling of Michelangelo – finished in 1512.

48. Charles to Bourbon, 6 June 1527, in Rodríguez Villa, *Memorias*, 202–3. See comment by Martínez Millán in *Carlos V y la Quiebra*, 142.

49. See Fernández Álvarez, *Carlos V*, 371–2; Valdés, *Diálogo*, 14.

50. These had been commissioned by Charles's Aunt Margaret and designed by Bernard van Orley and Jan Gossaert. The tapestries are a visual mirror of princes and depict all the things needed by a good ruler: Fortune, Prudence, Virtue, Faithfulness, Fame, Justice, Nobility and Honour itself. Charles bought this series from the Fuggers, each tapestry being five metres high and eight to ten metres wide. The series was taken to Seville in 1526.

51. See chap. 9.

52. Paso, I, 104.

53. Núñez, *Castaways*, XV.

54. Bataillon, *Erasme*, 257; Brandi, 49–60, 64.

55. Pérez Villanueva and Escandell Bonet, 668.

8. FOUR BROTHERS IN A CONQUEST: THE ALVARADOS AND GUATEMALA

1. Alvarado led what seems to have been an expedition there with 200 foot, including twenty crossbowmen headed by Francisco de Orozco, and forty horse. The venture was characterized by Alvarado's swift execution of two Spaniards who apparently planned to kill their leader: Bernardino from the Spanish Levant and a pilot named Salamanca.

2. '*Persona de lo más estimada entre todos los capitanes que el dicho marqués tenía en su ejército*', AGI, Patronato, leg. 69, r.1. Interrogation of Leonor de Alvarado.

3. Cortés third letter, in *Cartas de Relación*, edited by Angel Delgado Gómez, Madrid, 1993.

4. Díaz del Castillo, II, 410.

5. Ibid., I, 295.

6. Ibid. A game played with quoits.

7. Among Alvarado's men in Guatemala there were several who had been with him throughout the campaigns in Mexico: Juan de León Cardona, for example, and Antonio de Salazar. Others were: his secretary, Antonio de Morales; Gonzalo Carrasco, who had been the lookout for Narváez at Cempoallan; Alonso de Loarca; Pedro González de Nájera and Francisco de Tarifa, both of whom had been with Cortés; and Francisco de Andrada.

8. Alonso de Loarca said that Alvarado '*traya trezientos y treynta hombres poco más o menos y este testigo fue uno de ellos*' (AGI, Patronato, leg. 69, r.1). But Pedro González de Nájera testified that there were over 500 men with Alvarado (ibid.).

9. Ezquerra, 45.

10. AGI, Patronato, leg. 35, no. 3, r. 1.

11. Jorge de Alvarado had always fought alongside his famous brother and even married a sister of Luisa, the Tlaxcalan mistress of Pedro. Gerhard, *The Southeast Frontier*, 130.

12. Stephan de Borleygi, in *Handbook of the Middle American Indians*, II, 282.

13. Ibid., II, 285.

14. 'There is no question,' says de Borleygi (II, 56), 'but that, by the end of the sixteenth century, these competing nations, weakened as they were by internal and external conflicts, would have fallen victim to the rapidly expanding and military confederation. Instead . . .'

15. Alvarado, 86.

16. 'One of those marine landscapes not very uncommon on the coast of South America. You behold a range of exhausted volcanoes. Not a flame flickers on a single pallid crest. But the situation is still dangerous. There are occasional earthquakes and, ever and anon, the dark rumbling of the sea' (Robert Blake, *Disraeli*, London, 1966). After Keats's inaccurate description of Cortés, this was the most famous declaration made about Latin America in the English language before 1914.

17. Recinos and Goetz, 216.

18. My mother, Margery Swynnerton, was on a train in 1917 between Basra and Kut-el-Mara in Iraq (Mesopotamia). Asked how she put up with being under Turkish fire, she replied: 'It was not at all agreeable but preferable to the mosquitoes in Basra.'

19. Letter of Alvarado to Cortés in Gutiérrez Escudero, 58. See *Handbook*, II, 1, 284.

20. Recinos and Goetz, 141–54.

21. Ibid., 62.

22. *Residencia* against Pedro de Alvarado.

23. *Residencia*, 25, 28. Francisco Flores, Bernardino Vázquez de Tapia, Rodrigo de Castañeda and Alonso Morzillo also testified to Alvarado's rough methods.

24. Fuentes y Guzmán, 259.

25. Recinos, 63.

26. Polavieja, 75.

27. Alvarado's attachment to Guatemala is thus reported by López de Gómara, *Hispania Victrix*.

28. *Popol Vuh*, 18.

9. CHARLES AND HIS EMPIRE

1. For example, the American empire is scarcely mentioned in *The World of the Emperor Charles V*, the admirable work of Blockmans and Mout.

2. See my *Rivers of Gold*.

3. Friede, *Los Welsers*, 123; Aiton, 73.

4. For which see my *Rivers of Gold*, chap. 36.

5. These *juros* played a key part in Spanish royal undertakings for the rest of the century.

6. See Appendix taken from Hamilton.

7. See my *Conquest of Mexico*, chap. 23.

8. Arranz, *Repartimientos*, 418. Mosquera, a controversial figure in Hispaniola, had a large *encomienda* of 257 Indians in Santo Domingo (ibid., 535).

9. Wright, 104.

10. A letter of Licenciado Zuazo to Croÿ says, '*quien dice que es converso*' (CDI, I, 308).

11. Indians according to Arranz, *Repartimientos*, 532.

12. Deive, 141; Otte, *Las Perlas*, 113. 'Useless' since no gold was found there.

13. Qu. Hanke, *The Spanish Struggle*, 44.

14. See my *Conquest of Mexico*, 353.

15. The *Información de Servícios y Méritos* of Vázquez de Ayllón is in AGI, Patronato, leg. 63, r. 24.

16. Ibid., leg. 170, r. 39.

17. AGI, Indif. Gen., leg. 421, lib. 2.

18. Cadenas, 212.

19. See the coat of arms of Cortés in the *Revista de Indias*, 1948, with its heads of dead monarchs.

20. Others who signed were Francisco Lizamar and Juan de Gomiel. The first must have been Francisco de Lizaur, ex-secretary of Nicolás de Ovando, for whom see my *Rivers of Gold*, 205.

21. Lucía Megías, 134, 275.

22. At this moment the council was composed of García de Loaisa, Dr Beltrán,

bishops Maldonado and Cabeza de Vaca, with Cobos and Samano as secretaries and Gattinara as an occasional visitor.

23. See my *Rivers of Gold*, 126.

24. Giménez Fernández, I, 59; Schäfer, I, 40.

25. Bernal, *Financiación*, 164. The Basque merchants were probably Nicolás Sánchez de Aramburu and Domingo de Alzola.

26. Schäfer, I, 95. Alejo Fernández had been born in Spain of Flemish origin. Perhaps he studied in Italy. In Seville he is known for four large panels in the cathedral, now in the Chapel of the Cálices (chalices): St Joachim and St Anne embracing; the Birth of the Virgin; the Adoration of the Magi; and the Presentation of Christ in the Temple in the same great building; and the depiction of Christ bound to a pillar in a chapel of piety.

27. Ibid., I, 80.

28. Cadenas, 225.

29. For the text of this document, see ibid., 28–33.

30. Deive, 136.

31. Friede, *Los Welsers*, 113.

32. Wright, 145.

33. Ibid., 122. Ubite was bishop of Cuba from 17 February 1517 till 4 April 1525. Was he the first bishop of Cuba or was Hernando de Mesa before him (see Wright, 121)? See Giménez Fernández, *Las Casas*, 96, n. 297 for this prelate. He had been preacher in the service of Queen Leonor of Portugal.

34. Pastor, X, 365.

35. See biographical article in Martínez Millán, *La Corte*, III, 369.

36. He was of a Muslim family.

37. Díaz del Castillo, II, 176.

38. See the biographical essay in Martínez Millán, *La Corte*, III, 353ff.

39. Cuevas, 1922, I, 230.

40. Otte, *Las Perlas*, passim. The main Spanish pearl fishermen in those days were Gonzalo Hernández de Rojas, Pedro de Barrionuevo, Pedro Ortiz de Matienzo, Juan López de Archuleta, who became *veedor* and a town councillor in Santo Domingo, and Juan de la Barrera. Each of these had two pearl-fishing canoes.

41. Ibid.

42. Oviedo, *Historia*, I, 109.

10. PEDRARIAS, PANAMA AND PERU; GUZMÁN IN NEW SPAIN

1. He had been governor of Soconusco.

2. Las Casas, III, 357.

3. Oviedo, *Historia*, V, 15.

4. Andagoya, 29.

5. On Trujillo, see Tena Fernández.

6. Vassberg, 48.

7. Busto, *Pizarro*, 168.

8. Ibid., 131. Hemming hazards that Pizarro had with him 'some 160 men'.

9. This was an unpleasant haemorrhagic version of the European disease.

10. Martyr, *De Orbe Novo*, 537–40.

11. The Ávilas seem to have come directly from Ciudad Real, but ultimately from Montalván in Ávila. The brothers were the sons of Alonso de Ávila, a *comendador* of the order of Calatrava, and Elena Villalobos.

12. Mena García, *Pedrarias*, 160.

13. Sauer, 252.

14. Deive, 139.

15. Mena García, *Pedrarias*, 148–50.

16. Not to be confused with his long-dead namesake who led the first expedition to New Spain/Mexico in 1517.

17. Pizarro to de los Ríos, 2 June 1527 in Porrás Barrenechea, *Pizarro*, 5.

18. Ibid., 6–18.

19. The Andalusians were Cristóbal de Peralta, Nicolás de Ribera, Pedro de Halcón, Alonso de Molina and García de Jerez; the Castilians were Francisco de Cuéllar and Antonio de Carrión; the Extremeños were Juan de la Torre, Rodríguez de Villafuerte and Gonzalo Martín de Trujillo; the Cretan was Pedro de Candia; the Basque was Domingo de Soraluce; and the unknown was called Paez or Paz.

20. Cieza de León, 74–6.

21. It is worth having the accolade in the original. Oviedo said he was '*buena persona e de buen animo*', also '*lento e espacioso, e al parecer de buena intención, pero de corta conversación e valiente hombre por su persona*' (Oviedo, III, lib. VIII, proemio 259).

22. See Lockhart, *The Men*, 140–41.

23. Porrás Barrenechea, *Cedulario del Perú*, II, 393.

24. Enríquez de Guzmán, 498.

25. Garcilaso, II, 895.

26. Ibid., 892.

27. Ibid.

28. See Busto, *La Tierra y la Sangre*.

29. Pizarro, 134.

30. Ibid., 341.

31. Enríquez de Guzmán, 161.

32. Cieza de León, 53.

33. Varón Gabai, *La Ilusión*, 20–23.

34. Gerhard, *Geografía*, 321.

35. Motolinía, *Memoriales*, 146 describes this ceremony.

36. Techuipo, 126.

37. *Cédula* from Enríquez de Guzmán.

38. *Residencia* of Guzmán, AGI, Justicia, leg. 234.

39. Díaz del Castillo, II, 298.

40. Gerhard, *Geografía*, 224.

41. Ibid., 219.

42. See AGI, Justicia, leg. 108, no. 2.

43. CDI, XII, 245.

44. Ibid., XL, 260.

45. Conway, 331. The details of this tragic case were revealed only in 1574.

46. CDI, XXVII, 130f.

47. Angel Delgado Gómez (ed.), *Hernán Cortés: Cartas de Relación*, 662.

48. The emperor had also asked the four officials whom he had sent to New Spain in 1522 to return and give an account of their actions.

49. The treasure included 1,500 marcos of silver, 20,000 pesos of superior gold, 10,000 of inferior gold, fine emeralds, cloaks of plumage and skin, obsidian mirrors, fans, as well as two jaguars and barrels of balsam.

11. THREE GIANTS OF THEIR TIME: CHARLES, CORTÉS, PIZARRO

1. Fernández Álvarez (ed.), *Corpus Documental*, I, 148.

2. Text in Santa Cruz, 454ff. Menéndez Pidal, *La Idea Imperial*, thought that the speech was written by Antonio de Guevara, Brandi thought that it was by Gattinara. See also Chabod, 117.

3. Brandi, 282, 287.

4. The Medina Sidonias' palace was on the site of the modern Corte Inglés. The square there is still known as the Plaza del Duque – but another duke.

5. This jewel vanished in the nineteenth century.

6. Díaz del Castillo, II, 367–8.

7. Memorandum of Cortés of 25 July 1528 summarizing the position.

8. Texcoco, Chalco, Otumba, Huejotzingo, Coyoacan, Tacuba, Cuernavaca, four townships in Oaxaca including Cuilapan, the isthmus of Tehuantepec, Tuxotla, Coataxla, Charo-Matalcingo, in Michoacan and Toluco. To these were subsequently added the *peñoles* of Xico and Tepeapulco in the Lake of Mexico, large sections of the city of Mexico/Tenochtitlan between the causeways of Chapultepec and Tacuba as well as the two big palaces of Montezuma next to the Zócalo where Cortés first lived.

9. Díaz del Castillo, II, 503.

10. CDI, XII, 381.

11. Fernández Álvarez (ed.), *Corpus Documental*, IV.

12. The children were Martín Cortés, the son whom he had by Marina; Luis de Altamirano, the son whom he had with Antonia Hermosilla; and Catalina Pizarro, whom he had with the half-Indian Leonor Pizarro in Cuba.

13. Otte, XIV, 53, 105–12.

14. Fontán and Axer, 324.

15. See my *Quien es Quien de los Conquistadores*, 77.

16. I am grateful to Julie Pastore for pointing this out to me.

17. Fernández de Enciso was author of *Suma de Geografía*.

18. He was the son of Pedro Manrique, Count of Osorno, and Teresa de Toledo, daughter of the Duke of Alba and María Enríquez, a first cousin of Fernando the Catholic.

19. Enríquez de Guzmán in Giménez Fernández, II, 975, n. 328.

20. See Martínez Millán, *La Corte*, III, 125–30.

21. The *capitulación* (contract) is in CDI, XIX, 18.

22. Cieza de León, 136–8.

23. Lucía Megías, 46.

24. The *capitulación* between Pizarro and the Empress Isabel was dated 26 July 1529 but signed only on 17 August.

25. Varón Gabai, *Francisco Pizarro and his Brothers*, 40.

26. AGI, Escribanía, 496A ff 685–6, v, 24 April 1566.

27. Oviedo, *Historia*, part III, lib. VIII, chap. 1, 265.

28. Other Extremeños recruited in 1529 were Diego de Aguero, Hernando de Aldama, Juan de Herrera, Francisco Peces (from Toledo), Lucas Martínez, Francisco de Almendras, Sancho de Villegas, Diego de Trujillo, Hernando de Toro, Alonso de Toro, the trumpeter Alconchel, the town crier Juan García, Francisco de Solares and Francisco González. See Lockhart, *The Men*. There was probably a number of European (white) slaves taken to Lima at this time as there had been such people taken to New Spain. See Harth-Terré.

29. Carande, I, 300.

30. Busto, *Pizarro*, 250.

31. Cadenas, 206.

32. Estefanía Requesens de Zúñiga reported so (1 March), Busto, *Pizarro*, II, 345.

33. See letter of Giovanni Batista dei Grimaldi to Ansaldo dei Grimaldi, a cousin in Genoa, cited in J. M. Headley, in Martínez Millán, *Carlos V y la Quiebra*, I, 35.

34. Pastor, X, 68.

35. All kinds of interesting conversations occurred in the exchanges of power: for example, the humanist Juan Ginés de Sepúlveda found that the young aristocrats from Spain who had come with Charles to Bologna were quite unable to reconcile the idea of piety with military efficiency and strength. This conversation was one which led Sepúlveda to write his dialogue *Demócrates* in 1535. Sepúlveda at that time was at the university in Bologna.

36. Cited in Morison, 684.

37. 'España' was a word already used in moments of stress and had been for two centuries.

38. See José Martínez Millán and Manuel Rivero Rodríguez, 'La Coronación Imperial de Bolonia y el Final de la Via Flamenca', in Martínez Millán, *Carlos V y la Quiebra*, I, 131–50.

39. As discovered by Valdés; see Manuel Rivero Rodríguez, 'Memoria, Escritura y Estado', in Martínez Millán, *Carlos V y la Quiebra*, I, 223.

40. In Tremayne.

41. The list of her possessions in her will included paintings by Roger van der Weyden, Michel Coxcie, Van Eyck and Hans Memling. There was also a treasure from the Indies, given to her by her nephew through Charles, Lord of La Chaulx (Poupet), then a councillor: '*Accoustremens de plumes, venuz des Indes, présentées de par de l'Empereur à Madame à Bruxelles, le XXe jour d'Aoust, XVCXXIII et aussi de par Mgr. de La Chaulx le tout estant en la dite librairie.*' Soon the collections of the Habsburgs would be enhanced by new treasures sent back by such conquistador families as the Welsers.

12. THE GERMANS AT THE BANQUET: THE WELSERS

1. This was the age of many touching genealogical inventions.

2. See my *Rivers of Gold, passim*; Schick, 178.

3. Otte, *Las Perlas*, 74–5.

4. CDI, I, 354.

5. This was a wonderful era for the lending of money. For example, in 1527 not just Charles but Pope Clement borrowed 195,000 golden scudi from the Genoese, Miguel Girolamo Sánchez of Barcelona and Ansaldo Grimaldi – the first being of the famous *converso* family, the second being the richest of the well-known banking family of Genoa (he later became a creditor of Charles also).

6. See my *Quien es Quien de los Conquistadores*, 299–308.

7. CDI, III, 77. '*Le faltaba dinero pero no palabras.*'

8. Muñoz de San Pedro, 78f, 247.

9. Ramos, *El Consejo*.

10. Sampaio García, 8.

11. Friede, *Los Welsers*, 121.

12. Otte, *Las Perlas*, 283.

13. Friede, *Los Welsers*, 118. The Maestro Pedro Márquez saw these poor miners arrive in Seville and then set off for Santo Domingo; most had been recruited in Silesia. Juan Ehinger, Juan Reiss and Jorge Neusesser went to Leipzig to arrange their passage, going with them down the Elbe to Hamburg and to Antwerp and then Seville. The miners were eight months in Santo Domingo before, exhausted, they applied to go home. They reached Antwerp and walked home to Silesia. Only eleven got back. They began a lawsuit against the Welsers.

14. Ibid., 149.

15. Ibid., 186.

16. García Bravo, 121.

17. Helps, III, 149–50.

18. Scelle, I, 178.

19. APS, VI, 1547. See my *Rivers of Gold*, 333.

20. Ibid., 162.

21. Ibid., 104.

22. See Otte, *Sevilla*, and Sanz, I, 316.

23. Characteristic of this slave traffic was a long lawsuit. Espinola found himself being sued by Esteban Justiniani, the representative of the Genoese, and by Agustín de Ribaldo, one of the purchasers of Gorrevod's licence of 1518, who took the affair to the Council of the Indies (AGI, Justicia, leg. 7, no. 3). Braudel, I, 146 gives the date wrongly as 1526. The lawsuit is in no. 4 of this *legajo*.

24. Saunders, 23.

25. Magalhães-Godinho, 550.

26. Ryder, 66.

27. CDIHE, IX, 239–42.

13. NARVÁEZ AND CABEZA DE VACA

1. The *capitulación* is in CDI, XII, 86ff, dated 8 March 1528. We learn from CDI, XXXV, 514 that María de Valenzuela was owed 300 pesos de oro by Diego Velázquez at his death in 1524.

2. Núñez, *Naufragios*, 5.

3. Friede, *Los Welsers*, 360.

4. *Castaways*, XV, 123.

5. CDI, XXVII, 391.

6. Morison, 513, 515.

7. A cubit was the length of a forearm.

14. ORDAZ ON THE ORINOCO; HEREDIA AT CARTAGENA

1. Polavieja, 272.

2. In one of the letters published by Otte, *Cartas Privadas*.

3. See his evidence in a *probanza* in Santo Domingo in 1521.

4. Díaz del Castillo, V, 254; I, 82.

5. Ordaz to Verdugo, in Otte, *Cartas Privadas*.

6. Paso, I, 152.

7. Letter to Verdugo in Otte, *Cartas Privadas*.

8. At that time the Orinoco was often known as the Marañón.

9. CDI, IV, 466.

10. Figures in Question V of *probanza* of July 1532 in CDI, IV, 466. Oviedo, *Historia*, II, 384 suggests 450.

11. Question VI of Ordaz *probanza*.

12. The cloth was so called because it was sent to Holland to be bleached.

13. See AGI, Patronato, leg. 74, no. 1, r. 10 of 1575. *The Información de Servícios*

y Méritos is in CDI, XL, 74ff. Hemming has a fine account of Ordaz's courageous journey in *The Search for El Dorado*, 9ff.

14. He may actually have been born in Sotodosos, Guadalajara.

15. Gómez Pérez, 307.

16. CDI, I, 586.

17. On landing, the expedition was led inland by twenty Indians to near Turbaco where Juan de la Cosa had suffered his disastrous defeat twenty years before. There were skirmishes and several Spaniards were killed. Heredia returned to his landing place and there founded the city of Cartagena de las Indias on what had been the site of an indigenous town. Immediately, as usual on this kind of occasion, magistrates and councillors were appointed. They had surnames to be found in all lists of this kind: Gabriel de Barrionuevo and Juan de Sandoval were the magistrates; the councillors were Juan de Peñalosa, Alonso de Saavedra and Luis de Soria; the official notary (*escribano de número*) was Miguel Sanz Negrete and Juan Velázquez was inspector. Carmen Gómez Pérez has published an analysis of conquistadors who were with Heredia. Most (48 per cent) were in their twenties, several (22 per cent) were under twenty. None had been in Cortés's expedition to New Spain. Of the 204 Spaniards who arrived in Cartagena, 26 came from Old Castile, 21 from Extremadura, 19 from Seville and 18 from Toledo.

18. Gómez Pérez, 108.

19. Ibid., 289.

20. Ibid., 319ff for list of witnesses.

15. CORTÉS AND THE SUPREME COURT IN NEW SPAIN

1. See cover of his edition of *Utopia* in Zavala, *Recuerdo*, 53–5.

2. Tension was not reduced by the arrival in early 1529 of another expedition of twenty Franciscans under Fray Antonio de Ciudad Rodrigo, which included the remarkable Fray Bernardino de Sahagún, who became the chronicler *par excellence* of old Mexico through his famous *General History of the Things of New Spain* (Florentine Codex). The ship also carried several of the Indians taken to Spain by Cortés; some have thought that Sahagún's learning of Nahuatl and study of ancient Mexican ways began on this vessel. García Icazbalceta so thought but the contrary view was taken by Antonio Toro, Wigberto Jiménez Moreno and Luis Nicolau d'Olwer. See *Quarterly Journal of the Library of Congress*, April 1969.

3. Psalm 51, from the words with which it begins.

4. Guzmán's agents at Veracruz, Juan Pérez de Gijón and Juan del Camino, interfered with the letters of at least three friars: Antonio de Aveñado, Juan de Angayo and Juan de Montemayor. Juan González, *alcalde* of Veracruz, testified in 1531 that Guzmán had ordered him to do this.

5. The Count of Osorno was the acting chairman and the other members were now Dr Beltrán, Bishop Maldonado, Bishop Cabeza de Vaca, Gaspar de

Montoya, Rodrigo de la Corte, Álvaro Núñez de Loaisa and Juan Suárez de Carvajal.

6. Chipman, *Nuño de Guzmán*, 228.
7. Schäfer, I, 26.
8. Aiton.
9. Ricard, 260. See also CDI, XLI, 5–6.
10. Morner, 55.
11. See CDI, XXIII, 423–5.

16. MONTEJO IN YUCATAN

1. A *caballería* was a measure of land which in Spain was equivalent to 60 *fanegas* or 3,863 acres. In Cuba it meant 1,343 acres; in Puerto Rico, 7,858. I assume that the Yucatan measure was close to the Cuban one.
2. CDI, XII, 201ff; CDI, XXII, 201ff.
3. Díaz del Castillo, V, 253.
4. See Gil, *Los Conversos*, II, 321.
5. I don't, however, find him in Carmen Mena's brilliant study of the expedition of Pedrarias.
6. Díaz del Castillo, I, 34.
7. Polavieja, 156–7.
8. See CDI, XIII, 86–91.
9. Robert Chamberlain, 'La controversía entre Cortés y Velázquez' in *Anales de la Sociedad Geográfica de Guatemala*, vol. XIX, Sept. 1943.
10. Paso, I, 57.
11. Fifth *carta de relación*, ed. Pagden, 440.
12. Paso, I, 78.
13. Ruiz de la Mota, evidence in his *Información de Servicios*, of which I have a copy.
14. See his *Información* in AGI, Patronato, leg. 54, no. 7, r. 6 of August 1531.
15. *Probanza* of Rodríguez de Carvajal in AGI, Indif. Gen., leg. 1204.
16. Consider the stolen jade mosaic mask of Palenque or the Leyden Plaque.
17. Landa, 29.
18. Ibid., 26.
19. Oviedo, *Historia*, III, 398.
20. *Probanza* of Ibiacabal in AGI, Indif. Gen., 1204, qu. Chamberlain.
21. Landa, 110.
22. Oviedo, *Historia*, III, 399.
23. Letter of Montejo to Charles the emperor, 13 April 1529, in CDI, XIII, 87; Oviedo, III, 399.
24. Chamberlain, *The Conquest and Colonization of Yucatan*, 49.

25. Landa describes, 51.
26. Oviedo, *Historia*, III, 402.
27. Chamberlain, *The Conquest*, 54.
28. Landa, 57.
29. Otte, *Cartas*, 70–82.
30. Clendinnen, 26.
31. *Handbook*, III, part 2, 675.
32. Clendinnen, 153.
33. Landa, 57.
34. Ibid., 72.
35. See *Handbook*, III, part 2, p. 661. The estimate of Ralph Roys.
36. Landa, 330.
37. 1928/2005 transl. of Díaz del Castillo has this on p. 91.
38. Oviedo, *Historia*, III, 404–5.
39. Montejo is amply treated in chap. 16.
40. Chamberlain, *The Conquest*, 73–4.
41. CDI, XIII, 87–91.
42. Chamberlain, *The Conquest*, 36.
43. AGI, Patronato, leg. 68, n. 1, r. 2.
44. Oviedo, *Historia*, III, 411. There is an interesting illustration in the first edition of Oviedo of a horse in these circumstances.
45. Chamberlain, *The Conquest*, 88.
46. See my *Conquest of Mexico*, 324.
47. Chamberlain, *The Conquest*, 92.
48. *Probanza* of Lerma in AGI, Santo Domingo, leg. 9.
49. *Relación* of Alonso de Ávila in CDI, XIV, 100: '*que las gallinas nos darían en las lanças y el maíz en las flechas*'.
50. CDI, XIV, 105: '*falsa y con mal propósito*'.
51. Oviedo, *Historia*, III, 420.
52. Ibid., 421.
53. CDI, XIV, 111: '*el señor Adelantado nos tenía por muertos*'.
54. Oviedo, *Historia*, III, 45.
55. *Hernán Cortés, Cartas de Relación*, tr. Anthony Pagden, 414.
56. Chamberlain, *The Conquest*, 127.
57. *Probanza* of Blas González, in AGI, Patronato, leg. 68, n. 1, r. 2.
58. Pedro Álvarez in AGI, Mexico, leg. 916.
59. Juan Martínez Hernández, *Crónica of Yaxkukul*, Mérida, 6–7.
60. *Probanza* of Francisco de Montejo in AGI, Patronato, leg. 65, no. 2, r.1, qu. Chamberlain, *The Conquest*, 161.
61. In CDI, II, 312.
62. Perhaps, says Pagden, there was a little gold mixed in too.
63. Landa, 81–3.

17. TO PASS THE SANDBAR

1. Pérez-Mallaína, 64.
2. Boswell, *Life of Johnson*, I, 348, 16 March 1759.
3. García-Baquero González, 226.
4. Mena, *Sevilla*, 241.
5. Bernal, 132.
6. Carande, I, 368.
7. Bernal, *Financiación*, 133.
8. Mena, *Sevilla*, 251.
9. Ibid., 212.
10. Chaunu, VI, 1, 178–231.
11. Pérez-Mallaína, 102.
12. Gil, I, 239–43. The senior member of the family, Antonio González de Almonte, had been *alcaide* of the Duke of Medina Sidonia and was punished in 1494. See too Vila Vilar and Lohmann.
13. Lockhart, *Spanish Peru*, 119.
14. Pérez-Mallaína, 231.
15. Ibid., 192.
16. Ibid., 15.
17. Haring, *The Spanish Empire*, 7.
18. See Haring, *Trade and Navigation*, I, 918.
19. This is to go ahead of time, but the supreme calculator, Earl Hamilton, estimated that, for 1560 to 1650, precious metals counted for 82 per cent of all the exports. Precious metals, remarked Pierre Chaunu, carried alone the weight of the Spanish empire.
20. This was the diet on Pedro Menéndez de Avilés's ships in 1568.
21. Pérez-Mallaína, 143.
22. See Haring, *Trade and Navigation*, 288ff.
23. See CDI, III, 513.
24. A fine of 100,000 maravedís would have to be paid by anyone who travelled without a permit. The arrangement was made final in 1604 when anyone travelling without a permit would also be punished by four years in the galleys or, if the person was someone of quality, to ten years in Orán. From 1614 ships leaving Seville could complete their cargoes at Cadiz. Seville maintained only the bureaucracy rather than the vigour of the real trade; and from 1664 ships could start off from Sanlúcar.

18. BIRÚ

1. On the indigenous nature of this disease see my *Rivers of Gold*, 151, 171–2.
2. D'Altroy, 44, suggests that the word 'Quechua' was imposed by the Spaniards. It meant 'valley speech'.

3. Pedro Pizarro, 155.

4. D'Altroy, 291.

5. In *The Conquest* John Hemming wittily suggested that the global potato harvest was in the twentieth century worth more than the treasure of the Incas sent home by the conquistadors.

6. Four hundred and seventy varieties of potato have been found (D'Altroy, 31).

7. A good account is in D'Altroy, 15ff.

8. See an interview with Jerónimo López, *c.* 1540.

9. D'Altroy, 192.

10. 'Oh! Can anything similar be claimed for Alexander or any of the powerful kings who ruled the world?', Cieza de León, *Descubrimiento y Conquista del Perú*, 213–14. See too D'Altroy, 243ff.

11. See D'Altroy for analysis, 233.

12. Hemming, *The Conquest*, 124–6.

13. D'Altroy, 172–4.

14. Pedro Pizarro, *Relación del descubrimiento*, 89–90.

19. PIZARRO'S PREPARATIONS

1. Francisco de Jeréz in *Verdadera Relación*, and Cieza de León, 146. But Diego de Trujillo and Cristóbal de Mena wrote that there were 250 men (*Relación*, 45 *Conquista de Peru*, 70) and Pedro Pizarro said that there were 200 (*Relación*, V, 171).

2. Raúl Porras and Rolande Mellafe exposed the idea that he was a partner on the same level as the others. See Porrás Barrenechea, 'El Nombre de Perú', *Mar del Sur*, 6, no. 18, 1951, 26. See also Lohmann, *Les Espinosa*, 206ff.

3. This conquistador, said to have *converso* origins, is the only one whose family still possess their home in Peru, which they obtained in 1535.

4. The notion of the small company perhaps with two or three members in search of commerce is considered well in Carande, I, 289.

5. See Lockhart, *The Men*, 75.

6. Oviedo, *Historia*, V, 33.

7. Pedro Pizarro, 341.

8. Garcilaso, II, 636. See Carande, I, 289.

9. Enríquez de Guzmán, 106.

10. See Luisa Cuesta, *Una documentación interesante sobre la familia del conquistador del Perú*, R de I, 8, 1946–7, 866ff

11. Hernando Pizarro, *Carta a oidores de Santo Domingo*, Panama. In Oviedo, *Historia*, V, 84–90.

12. Pedro Pizarro, 341.

13. Cieza de León, 370.

14. Garcilaso, II, 916, 972, 1076.

15. Pedro Pizarro, 146.

16. Garcilaso, II, 601.

17. Pedro Pizarro, 148–9.

18. Ibid.

19. Ibid., 150.

20. Cieza de León, 150.

21. See Guillén, 78.

22. Cieza de León, 152.

23. Ibid., 154 with notes.

24. Garcilaso, II, 662.

25. Pedro Pizarro, 151.

26. Others included Jerónimo de Aliaga, Gonzalo Farfán, Melchor Verdugo and Pedro Díaz.

27. Cieza de León, 159.

28. For Ruiz de Arce's account see Muñoz de San Pedro, 72–119.

29. Guillermo Lohmann Villena, *Les Espinosa*.

30. See Lockhart, *The Men*, 238.

31. For the Núñez de Prado of Medellín, see my *Conquest of Mexico*, chap. 30.

32. Pedro Pizarro, 167.

33. See Duncan; also Busto, I, 320.

34. The word is Hemming's, *The Conquest*, 27.

35. Pedro Pizarro, 166.

36. See Garcilaso, II, 820; Hemming, *The Conquest*, 302–4 gives much attention to him.

37. Garcilaso, II, 663.

38. Estete, 20.

39. Cieza de León, 176.

40. Pedro Pizarro, 167.

41. Ibid., 167.

42. Busto, I, 340.

43. Pedro Pizarro, 163.

44. Ruiz de Arce, 92.

45. Pedro Pizarro, 162.

46. Ibid., 165; Cieza de León, 88; Hemming, *The Conquest*, 27.

47. Estete, 21; Cieza de León, 181. Pizarro gave the name of San Miguel either because the archangel Michael had appeared in the sky during the recent battle or to recall his own baptism at San Miguel in Trujillo.

48. Oviedo, *Historia*, V, ii, 29.

49. Busto, I, 369.

50. Lockhart, *The Men*, 352–3.

51. Busto, *La Tierra y la Sangre*, 385.

52. Pedro Pizarro, 173.

53. Ibid., 172.

54. Garcilaso, II, 665.

55. Ibid.
56. Jeréz, 326; Mena, *Sevilla*, 81.
57. Oviedo, *Historia*, III, I, iv.
58. Diego de Trujillo, 46.

20. CAJAMARCA

1. Ruiz de Arce, cit. Lockhart, *The Men*, 346.
2. Oviedo, III, 84: '*el camino era tan malo que de verdad si así fuera que allí nos esperaran . . . muy ligeramente nos llevaran*'.
3. Ruiz de Arce, cit. Hemming, *The Conquest*, 32; Lockhart, *The Men*, 346.
4. Murúa, I, 206; Pedro Pizarro, 185.
5. Hemming, *The Conquest*, 34.
6. Ibid., 35, 549.
7. Pedro Pizarro, 176; Mena, *Sevilla*, 326.
8. Hemming, *The Conquest*, 37, 200.
9. Lockhart, *The Men*, *passim*.
10. Ibid., 140.
11. Lockhart says one had been in Mexico but in a 'marginal capacity'.
12. Pedro Pizarro, 36.
13. Estete, 28–9; Hemming, *The Conquest*, 36–7.
14. Hemming, *The Conquest*, 37.
15. Trujillo, 58.
16. Some chroniclers thought that there were three units of twenty horses each, the third being led by Benalcázar.
17. Pedro Pizarro, 86.
18. Hemming, *The Conquest*, 38–9.
19. Ibid., 39–41.
20. Garcilaso, II, 687.
21. Murúa, I, 269.
22. Garcilaso, II, 691. See Hemming, *The Conquest*, 551, 442–3; also 42–4.
23. Pedro Pizarro, 214.

21. THE END OF ATAHUALPA

1. 'Every schoolboy knows who imprisoned Montezuma, and who strangled Atahualpa' (essay on Lord Clive).
2. Hemming, *The Conquest*, 47.
3. Garcilaso, II, 693.
4. Murúa, 210.
5. Hemming made sense of these figures. See *The Conquest*, 48, 551, n. 48.

6. Pedro Pizarro, 187.

7. See below p. 250.

8. Ibid., 248; Hemming, *The Conquest*, 47.

9. Hemming, *The Conquest*, 64.

10. Lockhart, *The Men*, 196, looks on the expedition of Soto and del Barco as a myth. The rumour of Soto's expedition finds no backing in his biographer, Duncan.

11. Garcilaso de la Vega,

12. A '*palmo*' was the distance from the thumb to the little finger, the hand extended. A 'hand' is a good translation.

13. Ibid., 263; Hemming, *The Conquest*, 64–5.

14. Guillén, 58–9.

15. Hemming, *The Conquest*, 56.

16. See Lockhart, *The Men*, 285.

17. Murúa, II, 213.

18. '*La persona del cacique es la más entendida e de más capacidad que se a visto e muy amigo de saber e entender nuestras cosas; es tanta que xuega el ajedrez harto bien . . .*' Gaspar de Espinosa to Cobos, Panama, 1 August 1533, in CDI, XLII, 70.

19. Pedro Pizarro, 352.

20. Cit. Hemming, *The Conquest*, 55.

21. Murúa, II, 210.

22. Hemming, *The Conquest*, 52.

23. Ibid., 71.

24. Duncan, 156.

25. Harkness Collection in the Library of Congress, 2 vols., Washington, 1932, I, 7; see Lockhart, *The Men*, 299.

26. Ibid., 96–102.

27. Actually of Cazalegas, five miles east of Talavera de la Reina; Lockhart, *The Men*, 189.

28. See, for the Jewish connection of Orgóñez, CDIHE, VI, 126–30.

29. Oviedo, *Historia*, V, 122.

30. Pedro Pizarro, 247.

31. Ibid.

32. Sancho de Hoz, 127.

33. Pedro Pizarro, 220, 226.

34. Hemming, *The Conquest*, 80–81.

35. Cartas de Perú, *Colección de documents inéditos para la historia del Perú*, Lima, 1959, III, 64.

22. NEWS FROM PERU

1. CDI, IV, 466.

2. Vadillo had been *juez de residencia* for Gonzalo de Guzmán in Cuba.

3. Jeréz, 346. The actual figures were 708, 580 and 49,008.

4. Hemming, *The Conquest*, 89, with sources 559-60.

5. Garcilaso, II, 709.

6. Keniston, *Francisco de los Cobos*, 161.

7. Enríquez de Guzmán, 78.

8. Crane, 66.

9. See Varón Gabai and Jacobs, 665.

10. Not the Juan Fernández after whom Robinson Crusoe's island was named.

11. Garcilaso, II, 741.

12. Hemming, *The Conquest*, 90-93.

13. Pedro Pizarro, 230.

14. See Sancho de Hoz.

15. Pedro Pizarro, 236.

16. These were Hernando de Toro, Miguel Ruiz, Gaspar de Marquina, Francisco Martín and a certain Hernández.

17. Pedro Pizarro, 245.

18. Hemming, *The Conquest*, 118.

19. Ibid., 116.

20. Sancho de Hoz, 169.

21. Ibid., 88.

22. Cieza de León.

23. Pedro Pizarro, 273.

24. 'No aconteció cosa notable en el camino, ni tuvo cual dificultad ni contraste alguno' (Murúa, II, 224).

25. Ibid.

26. Lockhart, *The Men*, 80-81.

27. Ibid., 126, 137-8.

28. Sancho de Hoz, 164.

29. Estete, 54.

30. Hemming, *The Conquest*, 127-8.

31. Pedro Pizarro, 273.

32. See Muñoz de San Pedro, *Tres Testigos de la Conquista*.

33. Pedro Pizarro and Pedro Sancho, cit. Hemming, *The Conquest*, 134 thought that much of the treasure was probably stolen by Manco Capac's servants, the *yanaconas*.

34. See Brunke, especially his extraordinary Appendix 1.

35. See Lockhart, *The Men*, 227-9; Lohmann Villena, *Les Espinosa*. He became famous as the only man of Cajamarca to marry an Indian.

36. Hemming, *The Conquest*, 158.

37. The best account is in Oviedo, *Historia*.

38. Garcilaso, II, 741.

39. CDI, IV, 244.

40. Hemming, *The Conquest*, 168.

41. Ibid., 148–9.
42. Ruiz de Arce, *Advertencias*, III, qu. Lockhart, *The Men*, 55.
43. López de Gómara, *Hispania Victrix*, I, 231.
44. Ruiz de Arce, *Servicios en Indias*, ed. Antonio de Solar and José de Rújula, qu. Lockhart, *The Men*, 56.
45. Ruiz de Arce, *Advertencias*, qu. Lockhart, *The Men of Cajamarca*, 435–6.
46. Hemming, *The Conquest*, 142.
47. Sancho de Hoz, 162.

23. THE BATTLE FOR CUZCO

1. Cadenas y Vicente has the text, 76–81.
2. See Hemming, *The Conquest*, 223, 557, for the size and extent of the grant.
3. Ibid., 175–7.
4. Díaz del Castillo, V, 152.
5. The document is in Cadenas, 76–81.
6. Lucía Megías, 788.
7. The first *cabildo* of Lima consisted of the treasurer Riquelme, the inspector (*veedor*) García de Salcedo and the following Pizarristas: Rodrigo de Mazuelas, Alonso Palomino, Nicolás de Ribera *el Mozo*, Cristóbal de Peralta, Diego de Aguero, Diego Gavilán and the mayor Nicolás de Ribera. Mazuelas had represented Pizarro before the court, and he with Ribera became lifetime *regidors*. They were soon joined by Diego de Aguero and Nicolás de Ribera *el Mozo*. Antonio Picado who was now Pizarro's secretary, Crisóstomo de Hontiveros and Pizarro's half-brother Francisco Martín de Alcántara also became members, as did Martín de Ampuero. Other officials appointed in those days included Pedro de Añasco as *alguacil mayor* of Quito, Martín de Estete as lieutenant-governor in Trujillo and Antonio de la Gama, the same in Cuzco.
8. Bonet Correa, *Monasterios*, 159.
9. CDI, X, 237–332. A most interesting report.
10. Lohmann, *Les Espinosa*, 233–4.
11. See Vega, *El Manco Inca*.
12. She married later and lived in Cuzco.
13. Pedro Pizarro, 341.
14. Garcilaso, II, 916.
15. Ibid., 1076.
16. Bartolomé de Segovia, *Relación de muchas cosas acaecidas en el Perú*, BAE, CCIX, 82.
17. Hemming, *The Conquest*, 183–8.
18. Ibid.
19. Murúa, I, 233.

20. Pedro Pizarro, 300–301.

21. See above, p. 206.

22. Garcilaso, II, 799.

23. For Alonso Enríquez de Guzmán, see his self-romanticized memoir.

24. Pedro Pizarro, 304.

25. Ibid., 302; also Hemming, *The Conquest*, 190–91. Others killed at this time included Juan Becerril and Martín Dominguez.

26. Murúa, I, 235–6.

27. Hemming, *The Conquest*, 184–5. The Spanish captains in this attack included Pedro del Barco, Diego Méndez and Francisco de Villacastín. The first-named, from Lobón, Medellín, had come to the Indies with Gil González de Ávila, and went to Peru with Soto. Méndez was an Almagrista who was a half-brother of Rodrigo de Orgóñez.

28. D'Altroy, 137.

29. Hemming, *The Conquest*, 215.

30. Hakluyt, 101.

31. Busto, II, 287.

32. This individual was related to the wife of Dr Beltrán, the corrupt bureaucrat of the Council of the Indies, and owed such positions as he gained to that connection.

33. See Lohmann, *Les Espinosa*, 219; see his essay 'Hernán Cortés y el Perú' in *Revista de Indias*, 1948, 339.

34. Garcilaso, II, 839.

24. ALMAGRO

1. Molina Martínez, 167.

2. Hemming, *The Conquest*, 223.

3. Ibid., 225–6.

4. Pedro Pizarro, 349.

5. D'Altroy, 147.

6. Garcilaso, II, 823.

7. Alvarado in Oviedo, *Historia*, V, 167.

8. Murúa, I, 248.

9. Oviedo, *Historia*, V, 169.

10. Valdivia was from either Castuesa or Campanario in the Serena in Extremadura. Others were Antonio de Villalba as sergeant major, Diego de Ansínez and Alonso de Mercadillo being captains of horse, Diego de Urbina being captain of pikemen, and Pedro de Vergara and Nuño de Castro being captains of arquebusiers.

11. Enríquez de Guzmán, 186.

12. Garcilaso, II, 855.

13. Ibid., 860. For commentary see Busto, *Pizarro*, II, 325.

14. Lockhart, *The Men*, 359.

25. PIZARRO, TRIUMPH AND TRAGEDY

1. Instruction of July 1536 published in Porrás Barrenechea, *Cartas*, 177–95.

2. CDI, III, 92–137.

3. The two brothers were sons of Pedro Suárez de Talavera and Catalina de Carvajal. Juan's fortunes surely had something to do with the fact that he had married Ana, a niece of García de Loaisa. When his wife died he became a churchman and eventually bishop of Lugo.

4. Hemming, *The Conquest*, 239–41.

5. Valdivia letter in Vernon, 215.

6. Pedro Pizarro, 389.

7. *Mire vuestra Señoría que yo me voy à España y que el remedio de todos nosotros está despues de Dios en la vida de vuestra Señoría. Digo esto porque estos de Chile andan muy desvergonzados, y si yo no me fuera no habia de que temer. Y decía la verdad Hernando Pizarro porque temblaban dél. Vuestra Señoría haga dellos amigos dándoles en que coman los que lo quisieren, y à los que no lo quisieren no consienta vuestra Señoría que se junten diez juntos en cincuenta leguas alrededor de adonde vuestra Señoría estuviere, porque si los deja juntar le han de matar. Si à vuestra Señoría matan, yo negociaré mal, y de vuestra Señoría no quedara memoria. Estas palabras dijo Hernando Pizarro, altas que todos le oimos* (CDI, V).

8. Varón Gabai and Jacobs, 672. Hernando was arrested at Coatzacoalcos but released by the viceroy. Hemming, *The Conquest*, 251.

9. Pedro Pizarro, 404.

10. But Medina del Campo was the city where such great experts in fantastical journeys as Montalvo, the reviver of *Amadís de Gaula*, and Bernal Díaz del Castillo, had been born and lived. See Luis Fernández Martín, *Hernando Pizarro en el Castillo de la Mota*, Valladolid 1991.

11. Garcilaso, II, 886.

12. Pedro Pizarro, 418.

13. For Pizarro's house, see Busto, II, 352. It had a *ranchería* and a *corral* for Indian servants and black slaves.

14. See Salvatore Munda, *El asesinato de Francisco Pizarro*, Lima, 1985; also Hugo Ludeña, 'Versiones Temporanas sobre la Muerte de Don Francisco Pizarro', *Boletín de Lima*, 37, January 1985.

15. Well discussed in Varón Gabai and Jacobs, 82, 206ff.

16. Ibid., 661.

17. AGI, Patronato, 192, n. 1, r. 12, cited in Varón Gabai and Jacobs, 110.

26. VACA DE CASTRO IN PERU

1. CDI, I, 481.
2. Lockhart, *Spanish Peru*, 26.
3. Otte, *Las Perlas*. See also Schäfer, II, 177.
4. See Antonio Bonet Correa, 'Santo Domingo de Lima', in *Monasterios Iberoamericanos*, Madrid, 2007, 227.
5. Pedro Pizarro, 429.
6. Garcilaso, II, 902.
7. Ibid., 912.
8. Ibid., 921 prints what he believed to be a text.
9. Ibid., 922.
10. Pedro Pizarro, 321.
11. Garcilaso, II, 931.

27. GONZALO PIZARRO AND ORELLANA IN PURSUIT OF CINNAMON

1. Ortiguera in Medina, *Descubrimiento*, 313.
2. Michael Goulding *et al.*, *The Smithsonian Atlas of the Amazon*, Washington 2003, 206.
3. See Appendix to my *Conquest of Mexico* and Muñoz de San Pedro, *Revista de Estudios Extremeños*, January 1948.
4. See Medina, *Descubrimiento*, 238, n. 4 and Herrera, Dec. V, Bk X, ch. 14.
5. Medina, *Descubrimiento*, 42, n. 68.
6. Gonzalo Pizarro in Medina, *Descubrimiento*, 249.
7. Gonzalo letter, qu. ibid. 56.
8. Fifty-three names can be found in Oviedo, *Historia*, V, 237–8, but see Carvajal, 42, whose work speaks of fifty-seven men.
9. Medina, *Descubrimiento*, 71.
10. Ibid., 74.
11. Carvajal, 68.
12. Ibid., 53.
13. Medina, *Descubrimiento*, 55.
14. Carvajal, 116.
15. Ibid., 69.
16. Ibid., 71.
17. Cit. Hemming, *The Conquest*, 31.
18. Ibid., 72.
19. Carvajal, 77.
20. Ibid., 88.
21. Oviedo, *Historia*, V, 394.

22. Carvajal, 123.
23. Oviedo, *Historia*, IV, 393.
24. Ibid., V, 373ff.
25. Medina, *Descubrimiento*, 250.

28. ORELLANA AND NEW ANDALUSIA

1. Carvajal, 97.
2. Oviedo, *Historia*, V, 373-402.
3. AHN Simancas, Estado Leg. 61, f. 19, qu. Medina, *Descubrimiento*, 320.
4. Medina, *Descubrimiento*, 128, fn. 180.
5. See Martínez Millán, *La Corte*, III, 461-2.
6. Medina, *Descubrimiento*, 328.
7. Cadenas, 65.
8. Officials were named: Juan García de Samaniego as inspector, Juan de la Cuadra, keeper of accounts, Francisco del Ulloa, treasurer, Cristóbal Maldonado, chief constable, Vicente del Monte, revenue collector, while Fr Pablo de Torres would be inspector-general and have with him a secret package naming the succesor to Orellana if he died.
9. Medina, *Descubrimiento*, 326.
10. Ibid., 355-6.
11. Ibid., 336.
12. CDI, XLII, 268.

29. THE DEFEAT OF THE VICEROY

1. See below, especially chap. 43.
2. Garcilaso, II, 951-2.
3. Ibid., 963.
4. Pedro Pizarro.
5. Garcilaso, II, 992; see commentary by Hemming, *The Conquest*, 268.
6. Garcilaso, II, 970.
7. He apparently gave his wife the pearl known as 'La Peregrina', which eventually would be given by the actor Richard Burton to the actress Elizabeth Taylor.
8. He had been a lawyer in Jerez de la Frontera before he came to Peru in 1536.
9. Garcilaso, II, 996-1000.
10. Ibid., 1011.
11. Ibid., 1056, 1058.
12. Lockhart, *Spanish Peru*, 185.
13. Bartolomé Martínez y Vela cit. Stirling, *The Last Conquistador*, 130.
14. Puente Brunke, *Encomiendas y encomenderos en el Perú*, 141.

30. GONZALO AND GASCA

1. Busto, *Diccionario Histórico-Biográfico*, I, 323.

2. Garcilaso, II, 1008.

3. Ibid., 1073. See, however, G. Lohmann Villena, *Las Ideas Jurídico-políticas en la Rebelión de Gonzalo Pizarro*, Valladolid, 1977.

4. Garcilaso, II, 10, 83.

5. Lohmann, *Les Espinosa*, 11.

6. Fernández Álvarez, *Corpus Documental*, II, 399.

7. Gasca in Valencia is discussed in Teresa Canet Aparisi, 'La Justicia del Emperador', in Martínez Millán, *Carlos V y la Quiebra*, II, 175ff.

8. Garcilaso, II, 1084.

9. Instructions dated 10 February 1546 are in CDI, XXIII, 506–15. See also Shäfer, II, 26.

10. Andagoya, *Relación*, 29.

11. Hampe, 106; Garcilaso, II, 1091.

12. Garcilaso, II, 1091.

13. Ibid., 1092.

14. Letter in ibid., 1094.

15. Ibid., 1094–6.

16. Cit. Hampe, 136.

17. Garcilaso, II, 1160.

18. AGI, Justicia, leg. 451, no. 2, f. 10, cit. Pérez de Tudela, *Documentos*, I, 1369–71.

19. Cit. Hampe, 79.

20. Pérez de Tudela, *Documentos*, I, 368.

21. See below, chap. 34.

22. Pérez de Tudela, *Documentos*, I, 375ff.

23. Ibid., 119.

24. Garcilaso, II, 1196–7.

25. Ibid., 1197.

26. See Marcel Bataillon, 'La rébellion pizarriste, enfantement de l'Amérique espagnole', *Diogène*, 43, July–September 1963 and 'Les Colons du Pérou contre Charles Quint 1544–1548', 479–94. Also Lohmann Villena, *Las Ideas Jurídico-políticas en la Rebelión de Gonzalo Pizarro*, Valladolid, 1977.

27. See Varón Gabai, *Francisco Pizarro and his Brothers*, 149.

28. See CDI, XX, 487–537 for a list of condemned supporters of Gonzalo.

29. Brian S. Bauer, The *Sacred Landscape of the Inca: The Cusco Ceque System*, Austin, 1998, 16–19, cit. D'Altroy, 156, who discusses the implications with rigour and intelligence.

30. Cit. Elliott, 89.

31. See Luis Fernández Martín, *Hernando Pizarro en el Castillo de la Mota*, Valladolid, 1991.

32. For the Pizarros' holdings in Spain see Rafael Varón Gabai and Auke Pieter Jacobs, 'Peruvian Wealth and Spanish Investments', *Hispanic American Historical Review*, 67 (1987), 657–95. For their holdings in Peru, see Varón Gabai, *Francisco Pizarro and his Brothers, passim.*

33. Varón Gabai, *Francisco Pizarro and his Brothers*, 285.

31. VALDIVIA AND CHILE

1. Letter in Medina, *Cartas*, 88.

2. See chap. 35.

3. Medina, *Cartas*, 39–40.

4. See Berlanga in CDI, X, 237.

5. CDI, XXIII, 7. The key phrase was '*sin que entreis en los límites y paraje de las islas y tierra que estan dadas en governación a otras personas*'.

6. Medina, *Cartas*, 33.

7. Ibid., 82.

8. CDI, I, 460.

9. Ibid., I, 3.

10. CDI, II, 167.

11. Medina, *Descubrimiento*, 541.

12. Ibid., 566.

13. Vernon, 71.

14. Thayer Ojeda, *Valdivia y sus Compañeros*, 31.

15. Vernon, 73.

16. Letter of Valdivia to Charles of 4 September 1545 in Medina, *Cartas*, 312.

17. Valdivia to Charles V, in ibid., 186.

18. CDI, I, 297.

19. Ibid., I, 326.

20. Medina, *Cartas*, 21.

21. Valdivia to Charles V, 4 September 1545, in ibid.

22. Note a *braza* or *estado* = 2 *varas* = 1.67 metres or one fathom. A *palmo* is ¼ of a *vara* = 208 mm.

32. VALDIVIA'S CONSUMMATION

1. Medina, *Cartas*, 17.

2. Ibid., 28–9. There is a similar report of Cortés's behaviour in New Spain.

3. Ibid., 29.

4. Guillermo Pérez de Arce, 'Santiago Comienza una Nueva Vida', in CDHI, XV, 180.

5. CDHI, I, 8.

6. Medina, *Cartas*, 33.

7. Ibid., 35.
8. CDHI, XXV, 60.
9. Medina, *Cartas*, 49.
10. Ibid., 42–3.
11. Ibid.
12. Vernon, 115.
13. Ibid., 116.
14. Medina, *Cartas*, 160.
15. Garcilaso, II, 1092.
16. CDI, XXXVII, 122.
17. Actas del Cabildo, in *Historiadores de Chile*, I, 129.
18. CDI, III, 566.
19. Actas del Cabildo, in *Historiadores de Chile*, I, 154.
20. Vernon, 127.
21. Ibid., 126.
22. Ibid., 150.
23. Vernon, 159.
24. Letters, 199, 147.
25. Medina, *Cartas*, 225.
26. Letters to Charles V, 25 September 1551 in ibid., 223.
27. Ibid., 245.
28. Vernon, 214.
29. Marmolejo, 35.

33. CAROLUS AFRICANUS

1. Letter of 6 May 1543 from Lieven Algoet to Dantiscus in Fontán and Axer, 372.
2. Carande, III, 87.
3. CDHE, X, 41.
4. Letters of 1544 and of 1548. See Fernández Álvarez, *Carlos V*, 638 and Chabod, 158, 165.
5. See CDI, XX, 550, XLII, 158.
6. We see them so sitting in a famous tapestry in the series 'Los Honores'.
7. See Antoine-Marie Graziani, *Un prince de la Renaissance*, Paris, 2008.
8. There had been in the battles the Dutch painter Jan Vermeyen from whose sketches the famous tapestries in the Kunsthistorisches Museum of Vienna were later made.
9. Possibly this codex was what is now known as the Codex Borgia. It became known as such in the eighteenth century when Cardinal Stefano Borgia owned it though he did not really prize it. It is now in the Vatican Library. Coming originally from Tlaxcala, it depicts the gods in control of the ritual calendar.
10. Wright, 200.

11. Fernández Álvarez (ed.), *Corpus Documental*, III, 483.

12. Pastor, XI, 242.

13. Benavente was a count-dukedom.

14. Pastor, XI, 76.

15. *'Yo mismo con mis manos tomé en la Goleta estas cartas que tengo en la mano que las enviaba a Barbarroja en una fragata el rey de Francia en las cuales hay palabras de tan familiar amistad cuanto en ellas podra bien ver quien quisiere.'*

16. Joseph Pérez, *Carlos V*, 90.

17. Granvelle (Nicolás de Perrenot) (1486–1550) had become one of Charles's most important advisers in the 1530s with the title of *Consejero de Estado* after 1528.

18. Qu. Menéndez Pidal, *La Lengua de Cristóbal Colón*, 66.

19. Menéndez Pidal, *La Idea Imperial*, 31.

20. Asti, 30 May 1536, qu. Fernández Álvarez (ed.), *Corpus Documental*, I, 515.

21. Anne de Montmorency (1493–1567) became Constable of France in 1538. He was brought up with King Francis I. The Montmorencys had had for centuries the title of 'first barons of France'.

22. Charles to Nassau, Roeulx and Praet 14 November 1536, qu. Fernández Álvarez (ed.), *Corpus Documental*, I, 515.

23. See Griffin, *Los Cromberger*, 117.

24. The *cédula* is dated 21 May 1534 and was reproduced by Alberto María Carreño, in 'La Primera Biblioteca del Continente Americano', in *Divulgación Histórica*, Mexico, 4 (1943), 428.

25. Contract between Cromberger and Pablos signed 12 June 1539. See Griffin, 121.

26. Esteban Martín who was in New Spain in 1538 also has a claim to be the first printer of the country, but he seems to have been a protégé of Cromberger.

27. Griffin, 132.

28. Pastor, XIII, 298.

29. Bernal, *Financiación*, 152.

34. THE INDIES FINANCE EUROPE

1. Ricard, 56. It was now that to avoid confusion between the Indian word *'papa'*, used constantly for priests and the pope. Bishop Zumárraga ordered that the Latin Papa should never be employed, only 'pontifex'.

2. An inclusive sales tax of 10 per cent.

3. Joseph Pérez, *Carlos V*, 125: *'Marchese, no necesitamos aquí secretario alguno.'*

4. *De rebus gestis*, qu. Morel-Fatio, 61.

5. Brandi, 393.

6. Ibid., 414–15.

7. See my *Rivers of Gold*, chap. 30.

8. Schäfer, I, 100.

9. Joseph Pérez, *Carlos V*, 84.

10. Cuaderno general, no. 94, l.c., p. 255, qu. Schäfer, I, 78.

11. Keniston, *Cobos*, 250.

12. See my *Rivers of Gold*, chap. XX.

13. Consuelo Varela, introduction to Las Casas, *Brevísima Relación*.

14. Brandi, 461–2.

15. Other items were ordinary subsidies 268,000 ducats, extraordinary subsidies 125,867, *maestrazgos* 152,000, clerical subsidies 166,667 and Cruzada 125,900. See James D. Tracy in Blockmans and Mout, 73.

16. Brandi, 465.

17. Keniston, *Cobos*, 272.

18. Escribanía de Cámara, in AGI, leg. 1007, no. 19.

19. Schäfer, 82.

20. CDI, XVI, 397.

21. Wright, 226; Bernal, *Financiación*, 12.

22. Keniston, *Cobos*, 264.

23. Brandi, 521.

24. Ibid., 523–5.

25. A summary of the discussion in the *consejo de estado* between the archbishop of Seville, Tavera, Alba, Valdés, Osorno, Dr Guevara and the vice-chancellor can be seen in Chabod, 244–51.

26. Keniston, *Cobos*, 270.

27. Ibid., 300–301.

28. Ibid., 301.

29. All these quotations derive from Brandi.

30. Ibid., 548.

35. FEDERMAN, JIMÉNEZ DE QUESADA AND THE QUEST FOR ELDORADO

1. AGI, Justicia, leg. 56, cit. Friede, *Documentos Inéditos para la Historia de Colombia*, I, 178.

2. Friede, *Vida y Viajes*.

3. Ibid., 58.

4. Oviedo, *Historia*, III, 55.

5. See Kohler in British Museum, Add. Ms. 217.

6. Letter of 1 November 1537 in AGI Santo Domingo, leg. 218, qu. Friede, *Vida y Viajes*, 132.

7. Friede, *Vida y Viajes*, 161.

8. Ibid., 159.

9. See ibid., 19. There is no explicit mention of the family in Juan Gil's great work on the *conversos*.

10. He had been *adelantado* in the Canaries. He was a nephew of the conqueror and first governor of La Palma and Tenerife, Alonso Fernández de Lugo. See Gil, IV, 369, 371.

11. Céspedes seems to have been a *converso* and was related (probably nephew) to the one-time judge *de las gradas* (the money exchange) in Seville of his name.

12. AGI, Justicia, leg. 599, n. 2, published in Friede, *Vida y Viajes*, 136ff.

13. See question 6 of Questionnaire in AGI, Escribanía de Cámara, leg. 1006-A, Cuaderno 1, in DIHC, 1264, as in Friede, *Jiménez de Quesada*, 168. Evidence about the death of Sagipa was given by six Spaniards including two who 'were there'.

14. Friede, *Jiménez de Quesada*, 323.

15. CDI, I, 320, 523.

16. The text of the agreement of Federman with Jiménez de Quesada is in AGI, Justicia, leg. 1096, published in DIHC doc. 1245 and Friede, *Jiménez de Quesada*, 128.

17. CDI, XXIV, 333.

18. He had married Cobos's wife's sister Beatriz.

19. Friede, *Jiménez de Quesada*, 68–9.

20. Ibid., 304.

21. For Raizer see Kellenbruz, *Los Fugger en España y Portugal hasta 1560*, Salamanca, 2000.

36. THE GREAT WALK OF CABEZA DE VACA

1. Cabeza de Vaca, 107.
2. Ibid., 117.

37. SOTO IN NORTH AMERICA

1. Elvas, 136.
2. Garcilaso, II, 628.
3. Ibid., 168–70.
4. No sign remains of Old Havana on the south coast.
5. Elvas, 56; CDI, III, 417.
6. Wright, 220–22.
7. See Duncan, 243 for a discussion, and references to the work of Charles Hudson on the matter.
8. Oviedo, *Historia*, II, 163; Wright, 170–71.
9. Duncan, 307.
10. Ibid., 35.
11. Ibid., 38.

12. Qu. ibid., 330.
13. See discussion in ibid., 352ff as to where Coosa might be.
14. See above, chap. 13.
15. Elvas, 229.
16. Ibid., 244.
17. Ibid., 246.
18. Ibid., 228.
19. Ibid., 167.
20. Ibid., 229.
21. Ibid., 243.
22. Ibid., 263.

38. THE LURE OF THE INDIES

1. Otte, *Las Perlas*, 209.
2. Friede, *Los Welsers*, 376.
3. Ibid.
4. See Schmitt and von Hutten (eds.), *Das Gelt der Neuen Welt: Die Papiere des Welser-Konquistadors und Generalkapitans von Venezuela Philipp von Hutten 1534–1541*, Hildburghausen, 1996.
5. Aguado, I, 262.
6. Otte, *Las Perlas*, 394.
7. Friede, *Los Welsers*, 392–400.
8. Ibid., 405. See too CDI, V, 518–22.

39. BUENOS AIRES AND ASUNCIÓN: PEDRO DE MENDOZA AND CABEZA DE VACA

1. See my *Rivers of Gold*; for the scene on the river see Peter Martyr, *De Orbe Novo*, 241.
2. The date usually given for his birth, 1487, cannot be correct since at that time Guadix was still part of the Muslim kingdom of Granada. Guadix fell to the Christians in 1489.
3. CDI, XXII, 350ff. The contract was dated 21 May 1531.
4. Oviedo, *Historia*, II, 364.
5. See Hakluyt edition 1891, 2.
6. CDI, XXIII, 8.
7. Cabeza de Vaca, *Naufragios*, 33.
8. Ibid., 120.
9. Ibid., 115.
10. See my *Rivers of Gold*.
11. Cabeza de Vaca, *Naufragios*, 23.

12. See Enrique de Gandía's edition of Ruy Díaz de Guzmán, *La Argentina*, Madrid, 1986.

13. Service, 19-20. The admirable Henig has a fine chapter on the size of the Guarani population 'at contact' in his work 'Numbers Never Lie'.

40. NEW SPAIN WITH ANTONIO
DE MENDOZA

1. CDI, XXIII, 423ff, 454.

2. Ibid., 554.

3. A mint antedated Mendoza's arrival because one was established for silver and copper coin in May 1535 under the direction of a formidable gathering of officials.

4. See A. González Palencia and E. Mele, *Vida y Obras de Don Diego Hurtado de Mendoza*, Madrid, 3 vols., 1941; also E. Spivakivsky, *Son of the Alhambra*, Austin, 1970. There is also A. Vázquez and R. S. Rose, *Algunas Cartas de Don Diego Hurtado de Mendoza, Escritas en 1538-1552*, New Haven, 1935.

5. Chipman, *Nuño de Guzmán*, 237.

6. Ibid., 236.

7. CDHIE, X, 38-43.

8. See my *Conquest of Mexico*, chaps. 26 and 29.

9. Gerhard, *Geografía*, 303; CDI, XXVIII, 430.

10. Grunberg, 121. The Franciscan mission in New Spain, hitherto part of the 'province' of San Gabriel de Extremadura, became its own autonomous province of 'the holy Evangelist'.

11. Salmerón had been much involved in the foundation of Puebla.

12. Simpson, 125. CDIU, X, 975.

13. See the essays in Zavala, *Recuerdo de Vasco de Quiroga*.

14. Like many *letrados*, Díaz de Luco was the son of a curate, Cristóbal Díaz of Seville. He was provisor of Tavera at Toledo and became known for his *Doctrinae Magistrales*. He later became a Jesuit and was at the Council of Trent.

15. See the French translation of Guevara's Marcus Aurelius.

16. CDI, XIII, 420-29.

17. Zavala, *Recuerdo de Vasco de Quiroga*, 85.

18. CDI, X, 363. '*Con mucha causa y razón este de acá se llama Nuevo-Mundo (y es lo 'Nuevo-Mundo' no porque se halló de nuevo, sinó porque es en gentes y cuasí en todo como fué aquel de la edad primera y de oro)*' (1535).

19. See Gerhard, *Geografía,* 352.

20. See Zavala, *Ideario*.

21. CDI, X, 376.

22. Zavala, *Recuerdo de Vasco de Quiroga*, 90

23. CDI, XIII, 420-29.

24. Schäfer, II, 21. 'Governors' of these subordinate territories were appointed by the viceroy, subject to approval by the Council of the Indies.

25. Haring, *The Spanish Empire*, 85.

26. CDIU, X, 29ff. See François Chevalier, *Les grandes domaines au Méxique*, chap. I.

27. Solorzano, *Política Indiana*, III, chap. II.

28. Zavala, *Recuerdo de Vasco de Quiroga*, 92.

29. Aiton, 113.

30. CDI, II, 119.

31. Ricard, 37.

32. Pastor, XII, 297.

33. Kubler and Soria, 126.

34. Cuevas, 239.

35. '*Destros son los Gilofos* [Wolofs] *y muy guerreros con vana presunción de caballeros.*' Castellanos was a Sevillano who went to live in Santiago de Tunja, Colombia and whose best-known poem was his *Elegías de Varones Ilustres de Indias*, written in 100,000 verses, in 1589.

36. Dorantes de Carranza, 160; Gerhard, 389–90.

37. Memorial of 25 June 1540, *Documentos para la Historia de España*, I, iv, 210.

38. Aiton, 139–41.

39. Motolinía, *Memoriales*, 171–9.

40. Ricard, 272.

41. Fray Antonio de Segovia, Fray Martín de Veracruz, Fray Martín de la Coruña and Fray Pedro de la Concepción.

42. Ricard, 265.

43. Ibid.

44. Arthur Aiton, *The Secret Visita against Viceroy Mendoza in New Spain and the American West*, I, 20, qu. Hanke, *The Spanish Struggle*, 89.

45. Aiton, *Antonio de Mendoza*, 126.

46. Fernández Álvarez, *Corpus Documental*, III, 256.

47. CDI, III, 510.

48. Ibid., XIV, 165–91. This is not much more than a log. But the word 'California' is freely used, e.g.: '*Domingo à 2 días de julio, tuvieron visita en la California, tardaron en atravesar, por amor de los tiempos que no fueron muy favorables, casí cuatro días . . .*'

49. Zavala, *Recuerdo*, 56.

41. CORONADO AND THE SEVEN MAGIC CITIES OF CIBOLA

1. His instructions are in CDI, III, 325ff.

2. Qu. Winship, 'The Coronado Expedition', XIVth Annual Report of the (US) Bureau of Ethnology, 362.

3. Castañeda, 132.

4. CDI, III, 511.
5. Castañeda in Winship, 539.
6. Suárez de Peralta, 159.

42. MONTEJO AND ALVARADO IN GUATEMALA AND YUCATAN

1. Álvaro de Paz, *Información* in Patronato, leg. 69, r.1.
2. Ibid.
3. Peralmíndez to Juan de Samano in Spain, 28 July 1541, in Paso, IV, 25.
4. The sixteenth century seems to have found such designations as easy as the twenty-first.
5. Aiton, 101.
6. *Probanza* of Andrea del Castillo, AGI, Mexico, leg. 974.
7. AGI, Mexico, leg. 299.
8. Clendinnen, 29.
9. Chamberlain, *The Conquest*, 206.
10. Clendinnen, 204.
11. Diego Sánchez, *Probanza* in AGI, Patronato, leg. 69, no. 8.
12. Cogulludo, *Historia de Yucatán*, 3–7, cit. Chamberlain, *The Conquest*, 216.
13. The Nahuatl for '*vasallo*' seems merely to signify '*gente plebeya*': cuitlapilli, etc. See Molina, 116.
14. *Relación* de Valladolid, cit. Chamberlain, *The Conquest*, 231.
15. Clendinnen, 46.
16. Ibid., 43.
17. Where he had been lodged by the Virreina María de Toledo, taking the ashes of her father-in-law Christopher Columbus to the cathedral there.
18. Paso, IV, 223.
19. See AGI, Mexico, leg. 68.
20. *Probanza* of Juana de Azamar in AGI, Mexico, leg. 983.
21. Ibid., leg. 923.
22. Letter of 13 February 1547 by Montejo to Charles V, qu. Chamberlain, *The Conquest*, 252.
23. *Residencia* of Montejo in AGI, Justicia, leg. 244.
24. Chamberlain, *The Conquest*, 128.

43. LAS CASAS, POPE PAUL AND THE INDIAN SOUL

1. Las Casas, 1953, v. 48.
2. Antonio María Fabié, *Vida y Escritos*, II, 60–82.

3. Oviedo, *Historia*, I, 138. '*No estuvo muy en gracia de todos en la estimativa . . . a causa de cierta negociación que emprendió . . .*'

4. Garcés is one of the early heroes of the Church in the New World.

5. Ricard, 64.

6. Erasmus, *Ecclesiastes*, qu. Bataillon, *Erasme*, 252.

7. Getino, 28.

8. Lavalle, 128.

9. Guicciardini, 442.

10. Bataillon, *Erasme*, 535.

11. Cuevas, 84. See Hanke, 'Pope Paul III and the American Indians' in *Harvard Theological Review*, XXX, 65–102; and Alberto de la Hera, 'El Derecho de los Indios a la Libertad y a la Fe: La Bula "Sublimis Deus" y los Problemas Indianos que la Motivaron', *Anuario de la Historia del Derecho Español*, XXVI, Madrid, 1956.

12. A ceremony in which the celebrant pronouncing the word 'ephphatha', that is, be opened (Mark 7:34), touches the mouths and ears of the candidate for baptism.

13. Ricard, 93.

14. See Martínez Millán, *La Corte*, III, 477.

15. The meeting was also attended by Licenciado Pedro Mercado de Peñalosa, Dr Hernando de Guevara, Dr Juan de Figueroa, Licenciado Gregorio López and Jacobo González de Arteaga of the Council of the Orders. Perhaps there was also Licenciado Juan de Salmerón, fiscal of Castile.

16. Schäfer, I, 5.

17. Qu. Ricard, 226.

18. See AGI, Patronato, leg. 184, no. 27, cit. Jesús Bustamante Garcia in Martínez Millán, *Carlos V y la Quiebra*, IV, 15.

19. Ricard, 200.

20. Ibid.

21. Ricard, 285.

22. Las Casas, III, 325–452, cit. in Hanke, *The Spanish Struggle*, 89.

23. See Consuelo Varela's ed. and introduction to Las Casas, *Brevísima Relación*, 23.

24. Qu. Cadenas, 131.

25. Cieza de León, qu. Hanke, *The Spanish Struggle*, 90.

26. Cadenas, 131.

27. Cit. Hanke, *All Mankind*, 24.

28. Ibid.

29. See my *Rivers of Gold*, 430.

30. See commentary of Consuelo Varela in her introduction to his *Brevísima Relación*. He became bishop of Chiapas in March 1544.

31. CDI, XVI, 376ff. See Haring's commentary in *The Spanish Empire*, 565ff.

32. Qu. Shäfer, II, 245.

33. The expression is Schäfer's.
34. Hanke, *All Mankind*, 60.
35. Brenan, 47.
36. Lucía Megías, 265.
37. I. A. Wright; Bernal, *La Financiación*, 12.

44. CONTROVERSY AT VALLADOLID

1. That is, Cuba, Jamaica, Hispaniola, Puerto Rico, Cubagua and the coast of Venezuela as far as Santa Marta.
2. Letter of Gonzalo de Aranda to the king, 30 May 1544 in Aiton, 98.
3. See Aiton, 97; Garcilaso, II, 944.
4. Letter of Aranda, qu. Aiton, 98. See also AGI, Indif. Gen., 1530, 1624.
5. CDI, VII, 532–42.
6. Letter to Charles V, 19 February 1545 in CDIU, VI, 241–6.
7. AGI, Indif. Gen., leg. 1530ff 783–5.
8. Letter from the supreme court, 17 March 1545, qu. Aiton, 99.
9. Kamen, 29.
10. Martínez Millán (ed.), *La Corte*, III, 379.
11. AGI, Indif. Gen., leg. 1530.
12. Martínez Millán (ed.), *La Corte*, III, 238–40.
13. Qu. Hanke, *The Spanish Struggle*, 116–17.
14. For his regency see CDI, XVII, 9.
15. Fernández Álvarez, *Corpus Documental*, II, 398. This was when Gasca was chosen. See above chap. 20.
16. Fernández Álvarez, *Corpus Documental*, II, 399.
17. Ricard discusses, 136.
18. The word 'republic' had come to be used in the sixteenth century in Spain to indicate the state.
19. Wagner, 123, qu. Hanke, *All Mankind*, 27.
20. CDI, VII, 436.
21. CDI, VII, 262. Letter of Motolinía to the king, 2 January 1555. Nicolau d'Olwer wrote a most valuable life of Motolinía.
22. Puga, 479–80.
23. Aiton, 167.
24. For his birthday see my *Conquest of Mexico*, 117.

45. LAS CASAS AND SEPÚLVEDA

1. Perena Vicente, 205.
2. See Zavala, 'Debate with Benno Biermann'.

3. This was the suggestion of Hanke in *The Spanish Struggle*, 46.

4. Found by Marcel Bataillon in AGI, qu. Hanke, *All Mankind*, 64–5.

5. CDI, VI, 484–515.

6. Díaz del Castillo, II, 473.

7. It was 400 years before the text of the disputation was published. Only in the 1950s did Stafford Poole transcribe the Latin text and translate it – into English.

8. Pérez de la Fuente was the son of a *licenciado* from Fuentesaúco, Zamora, near Salamanca; he became a doctor of law and afterwards *juez de las gradas* of Seville.

9. Pérez de Ribadeneira was a Toledano, he studied in Santa Cruz, Valladolid, where he became *alcalde del crimen*. Two of his daughters married rich *encomenderos* in New Spain and in consequence he left the Council of the Indies.

10. Briviesca studied in the College of Santiago el Cebedeo, he worked on the establishment of the Archivo de Simancas and was a protégé of Luis Hurtado de Mendoza. He was later in the Council of Castile.

11. Anaya derived from the Salamanquino nobility, being related to Diego de Anaya, founder of the college of San Bartolomé. He was rector of the College of San Clemente in Bologna. Afterwards he was a judge in Navarre.

12. Pedrosa was a Segoviano, son of a public servant, studied at Santa Cruz in Valladolid and was attached to both the *audiencias* of Valladolid and of Granada, later becoming a *consejero* of the Council of the Orders.

13. This Ponce de León, son of the Marquis of Priego, brought up in Córdoba, was one of the many protégés of Cardinal Tavera. He later went to Trent as a Spanish delegate. He had a great library.

14. Did he say this? The text which Las Casas had when preparing his reply included this reference to monkeys, but the most complete version published omits it.

15. Qu. Hanke, *All Mankind*, 85.

16. Burckhardt, *Reflections*, 38.

17. The original is in the Bibliothèque Nationale de Paris.

18. Text prepared and translated into English by Stafford Poole as 'Defence against the Persecutors and Slanderers of the People of New World Discovered across the Seas'.

19. Hanke, *All Mankind*, 82.

20. Ibid., 94.

21. Ibid., 95.

22. Printed at Seville in 1552 and widely distributed in the Indies and even soon in Manila.

23. Shäfer summarizes, II, 268–9.

24. Losada, 280.

25. For the Jesuits, see vol. III of this work.

26. Hanke, *Aristotle*, 40.

27. See Baltasar Cuart Moner, 'Juan Ginés de Sepúlveda', in Martínez Millán, *Carlos V y la Quiebra*, III, 346.

46. THE KNIGHT OF THE BLACK EAGLE: PHILIP AND HIS FLEMISH ROLE

1. The Queen Empress Isabel had died after a miscarriage in May 1539.

2. Salinas, summer 1536.

3. See Borah.

4. Fernández Álvarez, *Corpus Documental*, III, 225.

5. On his tragic end see José Nieto, 'Herejía en la Capilla Imperial' in Martínez Millán, *Carlos V y la Quiebra*, IV, 213ff.

6. See Antonio Álvarez-Ossorio, 'Conocer el Viaje del Príncipe Felipe 1548–1549' by in Martínez Millán, *Carlos V y la Quiebra*, II, 53ff.

7. Coxcie was a Flemish painter born in the Archduchess Margaret's city of Mechelen.

8. Vicente Álvarez, *Relation du beau voyage que fait aux Pays-Bas en 1548 le prince Philippe* . . . ed. M.-T. Dovillé, Brussels, 1964, 119.

9. Fernández Álvarez, *Corpus Documental*, III, 222.

10. Ibid., III, 225ff.

11. Ibid., III, 252–3.

12. Earl Hamilton, *American Treasure*, table 19: 3,628,506 pesos for the Crown, 6,237,024 pesos for private people.

13. Fernández Álvarez, *Corpus Documental*, III, 259.

14. Kamen, 49.

15. Fernández Álvarez, *Corpus Documental*, III, 381.

16. Ibid., III, 393.

17. Hampe, 206.

18. Ibid., 207.

19. That monarch had been the last king of both France and Germany, and it was his division of the realms into three at the Treaty of Verdun in 843 which provided the agenda for modern European history.

20. Fernández Álvarez, *Corpus Documental*, III, 429.

21. Ibid., III, 445.

22. The escudos could be converted as 667,128,600 maravedís, or 1,482,508 pesos (Hampe, 198).

23. Jones, 54.

24. Fernández Álvarez, *Corpus Documental*, III, 505–6.

25. Ibid., III, 548.

26. Ibid., III, 626–7.

27. AGI, Justicia, leg. 1066, no. 4, cit. in Varón Gabai and Jacobs, 669.

47 · THE EMPEROR AT BAY

1. Memorial que embió Fco Duarte de lo que le dixo Nicolas Nicolai, qu. Kamen, 55.

2. For Diocletian's withdrawal to Salona, see Gibbon, chap. 13.

3. Renard was French, born in Vesoul, and had been persuaded by Granvelle to work for him and for Spain.

4. Constant, 36.

5. See David Loades, 'Charles V and the English', in Martínez Millán, *Carlos V y la Quiebra*, I, 263; Whitelock, 136.

6. Calendar State Papers, Spain, XI, 290, 4045.

7. With his commoner wife, Philippina von Welser, he would establish a collection, or *Kunstkammer*, in Ambras near Innsbruck, the Ferdinandeum, which would house many interesting Mexican objects, some from his great-aunt Margaret's collection.

8. William Howard, first Lord Howard of Effingham, was a great survivor, being Lord High Admiral under Queen Mary (1553–8) and Lord Chamberlain (1558–72) under Queen Elizabeth. He was a son of the second Duke of Norfolk and had studied, and been a protégé of Gardiner, at Trinity Hall, Cambridge.

9. Kamen, 57.

10. Muñoz, 97, 113.

11. Ibid., 77, 108, 118.

12. Sandoval, I, 222.

13. CDI, XIII, 138–9.

14. Skinner, II, 94.

15. For a remarkable study of Charles's journeys see Foronda, *passim*.

16. CDI, IV, 390ff.

17. Including the '*reinos de las Indias*'. He added: '*Acordándome de vuestra fidelidad y lealtad, y del amor y aficción especial que entre vosotros he conocido, mandaría mirar por lo que general y particularmente os tocare, haciéndo os merced al favor en lo que justo sea, como lo mereceis*' (Ibid., IV, 394ff).

18. Carande, III, 210.

19. For the emperor in Yuste, there is W. Stirling-Maxwell, *The Cloister Life of the Emperor Charles V*, London, 1853, especially pp. 8–15; and G. Gachard, *Retraite et mort de Charles-Quint*, Brussels, 1854–5. There is also J. J. Martín González, *El Palacio de Carlos V en Yuste*, Archivo Español del Arte, 1950–51.

20. Cit. Moran and Checa, *El Coleccionismo en España*, 56.

21. The list includes what is described as 'a portrait on wood by Thomas More of the Queen of England' – which would seem improbable.

22. Dávila had been with the emperor on nearly all his campaigns, about some of which, notably those in Germany, he wrote a book. He became Marquis de Mirabel.

23. Watts, 125.

24. Damián de la Bandera cit. in Glave, 84.

25. Palmer, 67.

26. Grunberg, 151.

27. See Zavala, *Ìdeario de Vasco de Quiroga*.

28. Zavala, *La Utopía*, 13, in *Recuerdo de Vasco de Quiroga*. It would be a mistake to overlook Quiroga's magnificent *Ordenanzas* for the two hospitals called Santa Fe which appear in his will of 1565.

29. The Castillas were illegitimate descendants of Henry IV's wild Queen Juana.

30. Burckhardt, *Reflections on History*, 39.

31. See Cervantes de Salazar, 46. There were also funeral services in Lucca, Bologna, Naples, Mainz, Rome, Florence, Valladolid and Augsburg, as well, of course, as Brussels.

Index

PENGUIN HISTORY

THE SPANISH CIVIL WAR
HUGH THOMAS

'A full, vivid, and deeply serious treatment of a great subject' *New York Times Book Review*

Since its first publication, *The Spanish Civil War* has become established as the definitive one-volume history of a conflict that continues to provoke intense controversy today. What was it that roused left wing sympathisers from all over the world to fight for a cause for which their governments would not give active support? In his famous history, Hugh Thomas presents an objective analysis of a conflict – where fascism and democracy, communism and Christianity, centralism and regionalism were all at stake – and which was as much an international civil war as a Spanish one.

'A prodigy of a book…about the most heroic and pitiful story of the twentieth century' Michael Foot

'A splendid book…he has the historian's most important quality, a tremendous appetite for detail and a grasp of the essential' Cyril Connolly, *Sunday Times*

'A great work…Professor Thomas has indeed now said the last word, and all the words, on the subject' *Times*

PENGUIN HISTORY

RIVERS OF GOLD: THE RISE OF THE SPANISH EMPIRE
HUGH THOMAS

'Splendid ... bold and strong in its outlines, rich in fascinating details' Paul Johnson, *Literary Review*

Inspired by dreams of riches and hopes of converting native people to Christianity, the Spanish adventurers of the fifteenth century convinced themselves that an Earthly Paradise existed in the Caribbean. This is the extraordinary story of the hundreds of conquistadors who set sail on the precarious journey across the Atlantic to create an empire that made Spain the envy of the world. In this epic history, Hugh Thomas brings Spain's early imperial achievements vividly to life, capturing the spirit of an ebullient age.

'Affirms Hugh Thomas's record as one of the most productive and wide-ranging historians of modern times' Paul Kennedy, *New York Times*

'So steeped is he in the spirit of the time, so familiar with its people and places that we almost feel he must have been there at the time' *Sunday Telegraph*

'As a historian, Thomas is master of the big picture...Rivers of Gold sweeps us restlessly on' Jonathan Keates, *Spectator*

PENGUIN HISTORY

CUBA: A HISTORY
HUGH THOMAS

'An astonishing feat…the author does more to explain the phenomenon of Fidel's rise to power than anybody else has done so far' *Spectator*

Hugh Thomas's acclaimed book explores the whole sweep of Cuban history, from the British capture of Havana in 1762, through the years of Spanish and United States domination, all the way up to the twentieth century and the extraordinary revolution of Fidel Castro. Throughout this period of over two hundred years, Thomas examines subjects ranging from sugar, tobacco and education to slavery, war and occupation. *Cuba* is the essential work for understanding one of the most fascinating and controversial countries in the world.

'Immensely readable. Thomas's notion of history's scope is generous, for he has not limited himself to telling old political and military events; he describes Cuban culture at all stages…not merely accessible but absorbing. His language is witty but never mocking, crisp but never harsh' *New Yorker*

'A brilliant history' *New York Times*

'Thomas seems to have talked to everybody not dead or in jail, and read everything. He is scrupulously fair' *Time*

PENGUIN HISTORY

THE PURSUIT OF ITALY: A HISTORY OF A LAND, ITS REGIONS AND THEIR PEOPLES
DAVID GILMOUR

'The best one-volume history of Italy now available ... has the same tonic, exhilarating impact as the thigh-slapping overture to a Verdi opera' Jonathan Keates, *Literary Review*

David Gilmour's captivating history tells the story of Italy from Virgil to Verdi and on to today. Filled with colourful figures, vivid detail and personal observations based on a lifelong love of Italy, this enormously engaging book also debunks many of the myths surrounding the country. Gilmour shows that Italy's glory comes not from a forced unified national identity, but from its regions, with their distinctive art, cuisine, civic cultures and traditions.

'Lucid and elegant, clever and provocative ... Tracing Italy's history from Romulus and Remus to the misdemeanours of Silvio Berlusconi, Gilmour develops his thesis with wit, style, and a great deal of learning' Dominic Sandbrook, *Sunday Times*

'A witty guide with an elegant prose style and a mind delightfully furnished with anecdotes and dictums, sensual impressions and conversations. Its prose smells of a convivial meal eaten below a pergola in the Pisan hills' Lucy Hughes-Hallett, *Sunday Telegraph*

'David Gilmour's elegantly written book is full of impressive insights ... a stimulating, up-to-date and reliable guide to modern Italian history' Tony Barber, *Financial Times*

PENGUIN HISTORY

THE GREAT SEA: A HUMAN HISTORY OF THE MEDITERRANEAN
DAVID ABULAFIA

'A towering achievement. No review can really do justice to the scale of Abulafia's achievement: in its epic sweep, eye for detail and lucid style.' Dominic Sandbrook, *Sunday Times*

For over three thousand years, the Mediterranean Sea has been one of the great centres of world civilisation: the teeming human activity here decisively shaped much of the course of world history. David Abulafia's *The Great Sea* is the first complete history of the Mediterranean from the erection of the mysterious temples on Malta around 3500 BC to the recent reinvention of the Mediterranean's shores as a tourist destination.

The focus of the book is on places and individuals, and emphasises their diversity – ethnic, linguistic, religious and political. Abulafia describes the teeming port cities that have been particularly influential or representative during particular periods – cities such as Amalfi, Alexandria, Venice, Trieste and Salonika – which he argues have prospered because of their ability to allow many different peoples, religions and identities to co-exist within sometimes very confined spaces right up to the twentieth century.

'Brocaded with studious observation and finely-tuned scholarship, the overall effect is mesmerising.' Ian Thomson, *Independent*

'A memorable study, its scholarship tinged with indulgent humour and an authorial eye for bizarre detail.' Jonathan Keates, *Sunday Telegraph*

'The greatest living historian of the Mediterranean' Andrew Roberts

PENGUIN HISTORY

VANISHED KINGDOMS
NORMAN DAVIES

'Norman Davies has the gift of all great historians – the ability to make us rethink the past' *Times*

How many British people know that Glasgow was founded by the Welsh in a period when neither England nor Scotland existed?

Europe's history is littered with kingdoms, duchies, empires and republics which have now disappeared but which were once fixtures on the map of their age - 'the Empire of Aragon' which once dominated the western Mediterranean; the Grand Duchy of Lithuania, for a time the largest country in Europe; the successive kingdoms (and one duchy) of Burgundy, much of whose history is now half-remembered - or half-forgotten - at best. This book shows the reader how to peer through the cracks of mainstream history writing and listen to the echoes of lost realms across the centuries.

'Davies is among the few living professional historians who write English with vitality, sparkle, economy and humour.' Felipe Fernandez-Armesto, *Sunday Times*

'Norman Davies possesses remarkable range, massive gusto and a spanking literary style. His ability to synthesise vast amounts of specialized material, to draw out arresting examples and comparisons, and to combine political, demographic, environmental and cultural analysis is always impressive.' Linda Colley, *TLS*

He just wanted a decent book to read ...

Not too much to ask, is it? It was in 1935 when Allen Lane, Managing Director of Bodley Head Publishers, stood on a platform at Exeter railway station looking for something good to read on his journey back to London. His choice was limited to popular magazines and poor-quality paperbacks – the same choice faced every day by the vast majority of readers, few of whom could afford hardbacks. Lane's disappointment and subsequent anger at the range of books generally available led him to found a company – and change the world.

'We believed in the existence in this country of a vast reading public for intelligent books at a low price, and staked everything on it'
Sir Allen Lane, 1902–1970, founder of Penguin Books

The quality paperback had arrived – and not just in bookshops. Lane was adamant that his Penguins should appear in chain stores and tobacconists, and should cost no more than a packet of cigarettes.

Reading habits (and cigarette prices) have changed since 1935, but Penguin still believes in publishing the best books for everybody to enjoy. We still believe that good design costs no more than bad design, and we still believe that quality books published passionately and responsibly make the world a better place.

So wherever you see the little bird – whether it's on a piece of prize-winning literary fiction or a celebrity autobiography, political tour de force or historical masterpiece, a serial-killer thriller, reference book, world classic or a piece of pure escapism – you can bet that it represents the very best that the genre has to offer.

Whatever you like to read – trust Penguin.

read more
www.penguin.co.uk

record

of

a

spaceborn

few

becky

chambers

HODDER

First published in Great Britain in 2018 by Hodder & Stoughton
An Hachette UK company

This paperback edition published in 2019

I

A CIP catalogue record for this title is available from the British Library

Paperback ISBN 978 1 473 64764 0

Typeset in Sabon MT by Palimpsest Book Production Limited,
Falkirk, Stirlingshire

Printed and bound in Great Britain by Clays Ltd, Elcograf S.p.A.

Hodder & Stoughton policy is to use papers that are natural, renewable
and recyclable products and made from wood grown in sustainable forests.
The logging and manufacturing processes are expected to conform
to the environmental regulations of the country of origin.

Hodder & Stoughton Ltd
Carmelite House
50 Victoria Embankment
London EC4Y 0DZ

www.hodder.co.uk

For Anne, who showed me I could.

With the exception of the prologue, the timeline in this book begins during the final events of *The Long Way to a Small, Angry Planet*.

....

FOUR STANDARDS EARLIER

TESSA

'Mom, can I go see the stars?'

Tessa looked up from her small workbench and down to her even smaller daughter. 'I can't take you now, baby,' she said. She nodded toward the cleanerbot she was trying to coax back to life. 'I want to finish this before your Uncle Ashby calls.'

Aya stood in place and bounced on her heels. She'd never in her life been still, not while sleeping, not while sick, not while she'd grown in Tessa's belly. 'I don't need you to go,' Aya said. 'I can go myself.'

The declaration was made boldly, laden with enough self-assurance that Tessa set down her screwdriver. The words *I don't need you* made a part of her shrivel in on itself, but then, wasn't that the point of being a parent? To help them need you less and less? She turned to Aya, and considered. She thought of how deep the elevator shaft to the family cupola was, how easy it would be for a bouncing almost-five-year-old to slip off the bench and fall a full deck down. She tried to remember how old she herself had been the first time she'd gone down alone, but found she couldn't. Aya was clumsy, as all people learning their bodies were, but she was careful, too, when she put her mind to it. She knew to buckle her safety harness on the ferry, to find an adult if she heard air hissing or metal groaning, to check for a green pressure light on any door before opening it. Aya was a kid, but a spacer kid, and spacer kids had to learn to trust themselves, and trust their ships.

'How would you sit on the bench?' Tessa asked.

'In the middle,' Aya said.

'Not on the edge?'

'Not on the edge.'

'And when do you get off of it?'

'When it gets to the bottom.'

'When it *stops*,' Tessa said. It wasn't hard to picture her daughter jumping off while still in motion. 'You have to wait for the bench to stop *all the way* before getting off of it.'

'Okay.'

'What do you say if you fall?'

'I say, "falling!"'

Tessa nodded. 'You shout it real loud, right? And what does that do?'

'It makes . . . it makes the . . . it makes it turn off.'

'It makes what turn off?'

Aya bounced and thought. 'Gravity.'

'Good girl.' Tessa tousled her kid's thick hair with approval. 'Well, all right, then. Go have fun.'

Her daughter took off. It was only a few steps from Tessa's table at the side of the living room to the hole in the centre of the floor, but running was the only speed Aya knew. For a split second, Tessa wondered if she'd just created a future trip to the med clinic. Her fears gave way to fondness as she watched Aya carefully, carefully unlatch the little gate in the kid-height railing around the elevator shaft. Aya sat on the floor and scooted forward to the bench – a flat, legless plank big enough for two adults sitting hip-to-hip. The plank was connected to a motorised pulley, which, in turn, was attached to the ceiling with heavy bolts.

Aya sat in quiet assessment – a rare occurrence. She leaned forward a bit, and though Tessa couldn't see her face, she could picture the little crumpled frown she knew had appeared. Aya didn't look sure about this. A steep, dark ride was one thing when held firmly on your mother's lap. It was another entirely when the only person taking the ride was you, and nobody would catch you, nobody would yell for help on your behalf. You had to be able to catch yourself. You had to be able to raise your voice.

Aya picked up the control box wired to the pulley, and pressed the down button. The bench descended.

I don't need you, Aya had said. The words didn't sting anymore. They made Tessa smile. She turned back to the cleanerbot and resumed her repairs. She'd get the bot working, she'd let her daughter watch ships or count stars or whatever it was she wanted to do, she'd talk to her brother from half a galaxy away, she'd eat dinner, she'd call her partner from half a system away, she'd sing their daughter to sleep, and she'd fall sleep herself whenever her brain stopped thinking about work. A simple day. A normal day. A good day.

She'd just about put the bot back together when Aya started to scream.

ISABEL

Isabel didn't want to look. She didn't want to see it, didn't want whatever nightmare lay out there to etch itself permanently into memory. But that was exactly why she *had* to go. Nobody would want to look at it now, but they would one day, and it was important that nobody forgot. Somebody had to look. Somebody had to make a record.

'Do you have the cams?' she asked, hurrying toward the exit.

Deshi, one of the junior archivists, fell alongside her, matching her stride. 'Yeah,' he said, shouldering a satchel. 'I took both packs, so we'll have plenty to— holy shit.'

They'd stepped out of the Archives and into a panic, a heaving chaos of bodies and noise. The plaza was as full as it was on any festival day, but this was no celebration. This was terror in real time.

Deshi's mouth hung open. Isabel reached out and squeezed his young hand with her wrinkled fingers. She had to lead the way, even as her knees went to jelly and her chest went tight. 'Get the cams out,' she said. 'Start recording.'

Her colleague gestured at his scrib and opened his satchel, and the camera spheres flew out, glowing blue as they absorbed sight and sound. Isabel reached up and tapped the frame of the hud that rested over her eyes. She tapped again, two short, one long. The hud registered the command, and a little blinking light at the corner of her left eye let her know her device was recording as well.

She cleared her throat. 'This is senior archivist Isabel Itoh, head of the *Asteria* Archives,' she said, hoping the hud could pick up her voice over the din. 'I am with junior archivist Deshi Arocha, and the date is GC standard 129/303. We have just received word of— of—' Her attention was dragged away by a man crumbling soundlessly to his knees. She shook her head and brought herself centre. '—of a catastrophic accident aboard the *Oxomoco*. Some kind of breach and decompression. It is believed a shuttle crash was involved, but we do not have many details yet. We are now headed to the public cupola, to document what we can.' She was not a reporter. She did not have to embellish a moment with extraneous words. She simply had to preserve the one unfolding.

She and Deshi made their way through the crowd, surrounded by their cloud of cams. The congregation was dense, but people saw the spheres, and they saw the archivists' robes, and they made way. Isabel said nothing further. There was more than enough for the cams to capture.

'My sister,' a woman sobbed to a helpless-looking patroller. 'Please, I think she was visiting a friend—'

'Shh, it's okay, we're okay,' a man said to the child he held tight against his chest. 'We're gonna be home soon, just hold on to me.' The child did nothing but bury xyr face as far as it would go into xyr father's shirt.

'*Star by star, we go together,*' sang a group of all ages, standing in a circle, holding hands. Their voices were shaky, but the old melody rose clear. '*In ev'ry ship, a family strong . . .*'

Isabel could not make out much else. Most were crying, or keening, or chewing their lips in silence.

They reached the edge of the cupola, and as the scene outside came into view, Isabel suddenly understood that the clamour they'd passed through was appropriate, fitting, the only reaction that made any sense in the face of this. She walked down the crowded steps, down as close as she could to the viewing glass, close as she could to the thing she didn't want to see.

The rest of the Exodus Fleet was out there, thirty homestead ships besides her own, orbiting together in a loose, measured cluster. All was as it should be . . . except one, tangled in a violent shroud of debris. She could see where the pieces belonged – a jagged breach, a hollow where walls and homes had been. She could see sheet metal, crossbeams, odd specks scattered between. She could tell, even from this distance, that many of those specks were not made of metal or plex. They were too curved, too irregular, and they changed shape as they tumbled. They were Human. They were bodies.

Deshi let out a wordless moan, joining the chorus around them.

'Keep recording,' Isabel said. She forced the words from her clenched throat. They felt as though they were bleeding. 'It's all we can do for them now.'

EYAS

'Do they know how many yet?' someone asked. Nobody had said much of anything since they'd left the *Asteria,* and the abrupt end of quiet startled Eyas out of wherever she'd been.

'Forty-three thousand, six hundred,' Costel said. He cleared his throat. 'That's our best estimate at this point, based on counting the evacuees who scanned in. We'll get a more accurate number once we— once we collect the rest.'

Eyas had never seen her supervisor this rattled, but his halting words and uneasy hands mirrored her own, mirrored them all. Nothing about this was normal. Nothing about this was okay. If someone had told her the standard before – when she'd finally shed her apprentice stripes – where accepting this profession would lead her, would she have agreed to it? Would she have continued forward, knowing how this day would unfold?

Probably. Yes. But some warning would've been nice.

She sat now with the other caretakers from her segment, twenty of them in total, scattered around the floor of a volunteered cargo ship, headed to the *Oxomoco.* More cargo ships and caretakers were on their way as well, a fleet within the Fleet. This ship normally carried foodstuffs, she could tell. The smells of spice and oil hung heavy around them, ghosts of good meals long gone. Not the smells she was accustomed to at work. Scented soap, she was used to. Metal. Blood, sometimes. Methylbutyl esters. Cloth. Dirt. Rot, ritual, renewal.

She shifted in her heavy exosuit. This, too, was wrong, as far a cry as there was from her usual light funerary garments. But

9

it wasn't the suit that was making her uncomfortable, nor the spices tickling her nose. *Forty-three thousand, six hundred.* 'How,' she said, working some moisture into her mouth, 'how are we supposed to lay in that many?' The thought had been clawing at her ever since she'd looked out the window thirteen hours prior.

Costel said nothing for too long a time. 'The guild doesn't . . . we don't know yet.' A ruckus broke out, twenty questions overlapping. He put up his palms. 'The problem is obvious. We can't accommodate that many at once.'

'There's room,' one of Eyas' colleagues said. 'We're set up for twice our current death rate. If every Centre in the Fleet takes some, there's no problem.'

'We can't do that, not all at once,' said another. 'You'd fuck up the carbon–nitrogen ratio. You'd throw the whole system out of whack.'

'So, don't do it all at once. A little at a time, and we . . . we . . .'

'See,' their supervisor said. 'There's the issue.' He looked around the group, waiting for someone to step in with the answer.

'Storage,' Eyas said, shutting her eyes. She'd done some quick math while the others spoke, much as she hated to reduce something this important to numbers. One hundred and eighty Centres in the Fleet, each capable of composting a thousand corpses over a standard – but not at the same time. A Human body took just under four tendays to break down fully – bones and all – and there wasn't space to lay in more than a hundred or so at once. Even if you could set aside the carbon–nitrogen ratio, you couldn't change time. You'd have to store tens of thousands of bodies in the interim, which the morgues could not handle. More importantly, you'd have to tell tens of thousands of families that they'd have to wait to grieve, wait to hold a funeral, wait their turn to properly say goodbye. How would you choose who went first? Roll dice? Pick a number? No, the trauma was great enough without adding anything smacking of preferential treatment to the mix. But then . . . what would they do? And how would those same families respond when told that the people ripped away from them would not be joining their ancestors' cycle – would not transform into nourishment for the gardens, would not fill the airways and stomachs of those who remained – like they'd always been promised?

She put her face in her hands. Once more, silence returned to the group, and this time, no one broke it.

After a while, the ship slowed and stopped. Eyas stood, the pain inside stepping back to make room for the task at hand. She listened to Costel give instructions. She put on her helmet. She walked to the airlock. One door closed behind her; another opened ahead.

What lay outside was an obscenity, an ugliness she would wrestle another time. She blocked out the ruined districts and broken windows, focusing only on the bodies floating between. Bodies she could handle. Bodies she understood.

The caretakers scattered into the vacuum, thrusters firing on their backs. They flew alone, each of them, the same way that they worked. Eyas darted forward. The sun was muted behind her tinted visor, and the stars had lost their lustre. She hit her stabilisers, coming to a halt in front of the first she would collect. A man with salt-and-pepper hair and round cheeks. A farmer, by the clothes he wore. His leg dangled oddly – possibly the result of some impact during the explosive decompression – and a necklace, still tied around his neck, swayed near his peaceful face. He *was* peaceful, even with his eyes half-open and a final gasp at his lips. She pulled him toward her, wrapping her arms around his torso from behind. His hair pressed against her visor, and she could see the flecks of ice woven through it, the crunchy spires the cold had sculpted. *Oh, stars, they're going to thaw*, she thought. She hadn't considered that. Spacing deaths were rare, and she'd never overseen a funeral for one. She knew what normal procedure was: vacuum-exposed bodies got put in pressure capsules, where they could return to normal environmental conditions without things getting unseemly. But there weren't enough pressure capsules for the *Oxomoco*, not in the whole Fleet. No, they'd be piling frozen bodies in the relative warmth of a cargo hold. A crude half-measure improvised in haste, just like everything else they were doing that day.

Eyas took a tight breath of canned air. How were they supposed to deal with this? How would they give these people dignity? How would they ever, ever make this right?

She closed her eyes and took another breath, a good one this time. 'From the stars, came the ground,' she said to the body. 'From the ground, we stood. To the ground, we return.' They were words for a funeral, not retrieval, and speaking to corpses was not an action she'd ever practised (and likely never would again). She didn't see the point of filling ears that couldn't hear. But this – *this* was the way they would heal. She didn't know where this body or the others would go. She didn't know how her guild would proceed. But she knew they were Exodan. They were Exodan, and no matter what threatened to tear them apart, tradition held them together. She flew back toward the ship, ferrying her temporary charge, reciting the words the First Generation had written. 'Here, at the Centre of our lives, we carry our beloved dead. We honour their breath, which fills our lungs. We honour their blood, which fills our hearts. We honour their bodies, which fuel our own . . .'

KIP

Not in a million years would Kip have wanted to be held up –
that was for *kids*, not eleven-year-olds – but he couldn't help but
feel kind of envious of the little droolers sitting comfy around
their parents' heads. He was too big to be held, but too short to
see over the forest of grown-ups that filled the shuttledock. He
stretched up on tiptoe, swaying this way and that, trying to see
something other than shoulders and shirt sleeves. But no, whenever he found a gap to look through, all there was beyond was
more of the same. Tons of people packed in tight, with kids up
top, making the view all the more impossible. He dropped his
heels down and huffed.

His dad noticed, and bent down to speak directly in Kip's ear.
'Come on,' he said. 'I've got an idea.'

It wasn't easy for them to push their way back out of the
middle, but they managed – his dad leading the way, Kip following
the grey-striped print of his father's shirt. It was a nice shirt, the
kind of shirt you wore to naming days or weddings, or if someone
important came to the hex for dinner. Kip was wearing a nice
shirt, too – yellow with white dots. He'd struggled with the
buttons, and his mom had had to help him get it closed. He
could feel the fabric tugging tight over his chest every time he
took a breath, just like he could feel his toes pressing against the
ends of his shoes. His mom had shaken her head, and said she'd
go over and see if his cousin Wymer had any bigger hand-me-
downs lying around. Kip wished he could get brand new clothes,
like the ones the import merchants hung outside their stalls, all

crisp and straight and without stitches where somebody else's elbows had poked through. But he could see stitches on his dad's shirt, too, and on most of the shirts they pushed past. They were still nice shirts, though, as nice as people could manage. Everybody wanted to look good for the Aeluons.

No matter whether the shirts were new or stitched, there was one thing everybody had on: a white band tied around their upper right arm. That was what people wore in the tendays after funerals, so other people knew to cut you some slack and give you some kindness. Everybody had them on now – everybody on the *Asteria*, everybody in the whole Fleet. Kip didn't know anybody who'd died on the *Oxomoco*, but that wasn't the point, Mom had said while tying cloth around his arm. *We all lost family,* she'd said, *whether we knew them or not.*

Kip looked back once they'd cleared the crowd. 'Where are we going?' he asked with a frown. He hadn't been able to see anything where they were, but the empty dock was far away now, and the ship would be arriving any minute. They weren't going to *miss it,* were they? They couldn't.

'Trust me,' Dad said. He waved his son along, and Kip could see where they were headed: one of the cargo cranes perched nearby. Some other people had already got the same idea, and were sitting in the empty gaps of the crane's metal neck. His dad put his hand on Kip's shoulder. 'Now, you should *never, ever* do what we're about to do any other time. But this is a special occasion, yeah? Do you think you can climb up there with me?'

Kip nodded. 'Yeah,' he said, his heart pounding. Dad didn't break the rules often. Ever, really. No way would Mom have gone for this. Kip was secretly glad she hadn't come.

They climbed up the crane's service ladder, then clambered along the fat metal supports. The crane was way taller than it had looked from the floor, and Kip was a little scared – not like *scared scared,* he wasn't a baby – but the climb wasn't hard. It was kind of like the obstacle course at the playground, only way bigger. Besides, he was with his dad. If Dad said it was okay, it was okay.

The other people already on the crane smiled at them. 'Pull up a seat,' one lady shouted.

Dad laughed. 'Don't mind if we do.' He swung himself into an empty spot. 'Come on, Kip.'

Kip pulled himself alongside, letting his arms hang over one support beam and his feet swing free below another. The metal below his thighs was cold, and definitely not designed for sitting. He could already tell his butt was going to go numb.

But the view . . . the view was awesome. Being far away didn't matter so much when you were up top. Everything looked small – the people in the crowd, the patrollers at the edges, the in-charge group waiting right at the dock. 'Is that the Admiral?' Kip said, pointing at a grey-haired woman in a distinctive green council uniform.

'That's her,' Dad said.

'Have you ever met her?'

'No.'

'I did, last standard,' said the friendly, shouting lady. She sipped something hot from a canteen. 'She was on my sanitation team.'

'No kidding,' Dad said. 'What'd you think?'

The lady made a *yeah, not bad* kind of face. 'I'd vote for her again.'

Kip felt a knot start to unravel itself, a mass that had been tangled in him ever since the crash. Here was his dad, climbing up a crane with him and chatting easily with strangers. There was the crowd, assembled in the smartest clothes they had, nobody crying or screaming anymore. There was the Admiral, looking cool and official and powerful. Soon, the Aeluons would be there, too, and they'd help. They'd make things right again.

The dock lights turned yellow, indicating an incoming vessel. Even up high, Kip could hear the crowd hush. All at once, there it was. It flew into the dock silently – a smooth, gleaming Aeluon skiff with rounded corners and pearly hull. It almost didn't look like a ship. Ships were angular. Mechanical. Something you bolted and welded together, piece by piece, chunk by chunk. This ship, on the other hand, looked like it had been made from something melted, something poured into a mould and polished for days. The entire crowd held their breath together.

'Stars, that's something,' Dad said quietly.

'Get 'em all the time over at cargo,' the lady said. 'Never get tired of it.'

Kip didn't say anything. He was too busy looking at the most beautiful thing he'd ever seen. He almost asked his dad what this kind of ship was called, but his dad obviously hadn't seen one before, and Kip didn't know the lady, so he didn't want to ask her. He'd look up Aeluon ships on the Linkings when he got home. He knew all the types of Human ships, and he also liked to know stuff about alien bodies, but he hadn't ever thought to learn about *their* ships. It was easy, in the Fleet, to think that Human ships were all there was.

A hatch yawned open. How, Kip couldn't say, because there weren't any edges on the outer hull to suggest doors or seams. The crowd broke into a cheer as three Aeluons stepped out. Kip had really wanted to see them up close, but even at a distance, they made his heart race. Bare silver heads he knew were covered in tiny scales. Patches on their cheeks that swirled with colour. Weird grey and white and black clothes that, he guessed, had never been anybody's hand-me-downs.

'Why are they wearing masks?' Kip asked. 'Can't they breathe oxygen?'

'They can, and do,' Dad said. 'But sapients who don't live around Humans tend to find us, ah . . . pungent.'

'What's pungent mean?'

'We stink, kid.' The lady laughed into her canteen.

'Oh,' Kip said. He wasn't sure how he felt about that. And the longer he sat there, the less he was sure how he felt about anything. His insides began to tangle themselves again as he watched the Admiral greet their otherworldly neighbours. Her uniform no longer looked cool, the crowd no longer looked smartly dressed, and the dock no longer looked normal, not with a big flying gemstone resting in the middle of it. The Aeluons were here to clean up a mess the Fleet couldn't, a mess that wouldn't have happened without busted ships and worn-out tech. They shook hands Human-style with the stinky, stitched-up council, and beneath Kip's excitement, beneath his wonder, a sadness spread.

He watched the Aeluons, and he felt ashamed.

SAWYER

The trick to living on Mushtullo was knowing which sunrise to wait for. Ressoden came up first, but only spacer merchants and little kids made the mistake of going out that early. Ressoden was dinky, capable of providing usable light but not enough warmth to burn off the cold. The pre-dawn fog carried the kind of insidious wetness that wormed its way to your bones, and you couldn't be blamed for deciding to wait for the third sun – big, fat Pelus – to banish the clouds entirely. But that, too, was a rookie mistake. You had about a half an hour after Pelus' appearance until the surrounding swamps started to evaporate, and the roasting midday air became thick enough to chew. The second sunrise – Makarev – was where it was at. Makarev held court for an hour and sixteen minutes, just long enough for you to get up and catch a tram to wherever it was you needed to go. Not too damp, not too muggy, not too hot, not too cold. You didn't need to layer, and you wouldn't show up to work with a sweaty shirt that wouldn't dry out. Ideal.

Sawyer pressed his palm against the inner wall of his capsule bunk, and he could tell that Makarev was just about there. His capsule was supposedly temperature controlled – and okay, sure, he hadn't frozen to death or anything – but the insulation was as cheap as his rent. He lay under his blankets, waiting for the wall to hit that level of warmth that meant . . . *now*. He sat up on his mattress and hit one of the buttons on the wall. The sink shelf slid out, a thick rectangle with a basin and a pop-up mirror and the almost-empty box of dentbot packs he needed to restock.

He rinsed his face, drank some water, cleaned his mouth, combed his hair into place. He pushed a different wall button. The sink retracted, and a larger shelf extended, holding a quick-cooker and a storage box full of just-add-water meals. He knew he had a long day at work ahead, so he opted for two packs of Magic Morning Power Porridge, which were still heating up when he checked his scrib and discovered he had no job to get to.

He didn't bother to finish reading the soulless form letter his (former) employer had sent. He knew what it said. Unforeseen funding shortage, blah blah, sincerely regret the abrupt notice, blah blah, wish you the very best of luck in future, blah blah blah. Sawyer fell back onto his pillow and shut his eyes. He was nineteen, he'd been working since twelve, and he'd had ten jobs by now. The math there was not in his favour.

'Great,' he sighed, and for a while, he considered staying in bed all day, blowing the extra creds needed to cool his capsule while Pelus was out. But now his creds were even more precious than before, and if he'd been laid off, that meant everybody else at the factory had, too. They'd all be descending on the commerce square, ingratiating themselves to business owners until one of them offered a job. That was how things worked with Harmagians, anyway. No résumés or interviews or anything. Just walk up and hope they like you. With other species, finding a job was a less tiring to-do, but Harmagian jobs were where the creds were at. There were jobs in his neighbourhood, probably, but Human-owned work didn't get you very far. Much smarter to head out to the square and try his luck. He could do it. He'd done it before.

With a weary will, he sat back up, ate his porridge, and put on clean clothes (these, too, were stored in the wall). He scooted off the end of his mattress and out the capsule hatch, planting his feet on the ladder outside in a practised way. He gripped his doorframe as he started to lower himself down, and immediately withdrew his hand with disgust. 'Oh, come on,' he sighed, grimacing at the grey gunk smeared across his fingers. Creep mould. The grey, greasy stuff loved the night-time fog, and it grew so fast you could clean it up before bed and find a fresh new mat in the morning, just like the one inching over Sawyer's tiny home now. He wiped his palm on an old shirt and resumed his exit, taking care to not get any of the gunk on his clothes. He had new bosses to impress, and this already wasn't his day.

It would be, though, he decided, hoisting his mood as he climbed down. He'd go out there, and he'd find a job. He'd find something even better than the job he'd had yesterday.

He headed out into Mushtullo's second morning, weaving his way through the neighbourhood. The narrow paved streets were as packed as the tall buildings that lined them, and the general flow of foot traffic was headed for the tram stations, like always. He saw a few other better-dressed-than-usual people in the crowd, and he quickened his step. Had to get to the square before the good stuff got snapped up.

Out of the corner of his eye, he spotted something out of the ordinary: a small crowd – old people, mostly – gathered by that little weather-worn statue of an Exodan homesteader over by the grocery. They were decorating the statue, laying wreaths of flowers and ribbons over it, lighting candles around its base, scrubbing creep mould off of it. Sawyer dimly remembered talk at work a few days before, something about a homesteader exploding, or decompressing, or something. Some horrible shit. He figured that was the reason for the crowd, and would've kept going on his way were it not for one face he recognised: Shani Brenner, one of the supervisors from the factory. She wasn't headed for the trams, she was helping some old – no, *ancient* – lady light a candle. Did she not know about the layoffs? Had she not checked her scrib?

Sawyer hesitated. He didn't want to waste time, but Shani was all right. She'd shared her lunch with Sawyer once, when he'd been short on creds. This day hadn't had a lot going for it yet. Maybe, Sawyer thought, helping somebody out would get the universe back on his side.

He changed course and hurried toward the statue. 'Hey, Shani!' he called with a wave.

Shani looked up, first with confusion, then with recognition. She patted the old woman (who was sitting on the ground, now), then met Sawyer halfway. 'Shitty morning, huh?' she said, rubbing the back of her neck.

'You heard,' Sawyer said.

'Yeah. Got a letter, same as I bet you did. No idea it was coming. Stingy bastards. I gave Tolged a thanks-for-being-my-boss gift three days ago and everything.'

Sawyer jerked a thumb toward the street. 'Aren't you going to the square?'

Shani shook her head. 'Not today.' She nodded to the statue. 'That's my grandma over there. You hear about the *Oxomoco*?'

'That homesteader that . . . ?'

'Yeah. She was born there. Came here when she was seven, but still. Roots, y'know?' Shani eyed Sawyer. 'You Exodan?'

'I mean . . .' Wasn't everybody, at one point or another? 'Like way, way back. I— I don't know what ship, or anything. I've never been.'

Shani shrugged. 'Still counts. Wanna come sit with us?'

Sawyer blinked. 'Thanks, but I—'

'There'll be jobs tomorrow,' Shani said. 'I'm not worrying about it, and neither should you. We'll both land on our feet, yeah? Things work out.'

Over Shani's shoulder, Sawyer could see other people joining Grandma Brenner on the ground. Some were weeping. Some held hands, or passed a flask around. Some were speaking in unison, almost like a chant, but he could only catch a few words. His Ensk was scattershot at best.

Shani smiled at Sawyer. 'Up to you,' she said as she walked away. She, too, sat on the ground, and held her grandmother close.

Sawyer did not join them, but neither did he turn back. There was no reason for him to stay, and yet . . . and yet. He imagined the jam-packed frenzy that awaited him at the commerce square, the lines of eager people desperate to impress. It was the antithesis of the scene in front of him, this quiet mourning, this shared respect. The idea of joining them felt awkward. He didn't want to intrude. He wasn't one of them, didn't belong there. But as he watched them share tears and songs and company, he wished that he did. He didn't have anything he was a part of like that. Even in grief, it looked like a nice thing to have. Maybe *especially* in grief.

He thought, as he rode the tram to the square, of the recited words he'd managed to make out. They circled his mind, over and over as he watched crowded neighbourhoods blur through mouldy windows.

From the ground.

FROM THE BEGINNING

Feed source: Reskit Institute of Interstellar Migration (Public News Feed)
Item name: The Modern Exodus – Entry #1
Author: Ghuh'loloan Mok Chutp
Encryption: 0
Translation path: [Hanto:Kliptorigan]
Transcription: 0
Node identifier: 2310-483-38, Isabel Itoh

[System message: The feed you have selected has been translated from written Hanto. As you may be aware, written Hanto includes gestural notations that do not have analogous symbols in any other GC language. Therefore, your scrib's on-board translation software has not translated the following material directly. The content here is a modified translation, intended to be accessible to the average Kliptorigan reader.]

———

Greetings, dear guest, and welcome! I am Ghuh'loloan Mok Chutp, and these words are mine. I hope my communicative efforts will be sufficient to make any time you spend on this feed here worthwhile. I shall exercise my skills to the best of my ability, with the aim of educating and entertaining you. If I fail in these endeavours, please accept my sincere apologies and know that such failings are mine alone and are not reflective of my place of employment, my schooling, or my lineage.

If you are unfamiliar with my work, allow me to provide a brief introduction. I am an ethnographic researcher based at the Reskit Institute of Interstellar Migration. I have worked in this field for twenty-two standards, and my focus is on transitory and orbital communities in the modern era. I am proud of my work thus far, with a few exceptions. I am confident that I am qualified for the task I will describe momentarily. I hope you will agree.

What do you think of, dear guest, when I mention the Exodus

Fleet? You could define the term literally: the collection of ships that carried the remnants of the Human species away from their failed planet. Perhaps the Fleet sparks some deeper association in you – a symbol of desperation, a symbol of poverty, a symbol of resilience. Do you live in a community where Humans are present? Do you know individuals born within one of these aged vessels? Or are you from a more homogeneous society, and therefore surprised to learn that the Fleet is still inhabited? Perhaps the entire concept of the Fleet baffles you. Perhaps it is mysterious, or exciting. Perhaps you yourself are Human, dear guest, and think of the Fleet as home – or, conversely, a place as alien to you as to the rest of us.

Whatever your background, the Fleet is a source of curiosity for all who do not have some personal connection to it. Unless you have a close Human friend or are a long-haul merchant, it is unlikely you have travelled there. While Humans living in GC territories and planetary colonies outnumber Exodans in aggregate, the Fleet is still where you will find the largest concentration of their kind outside the Sol system. Though many Humans have never set foot in the great homestead ships, the journey of the Fleet is a history they all consciously carry. That lineage has inextricably shaped every modern Human community, regardless of foundational philosophy. In one way or another, it affects how they think of themselves, and how the rest of us see them.

So what is the Fleet today? How do these people live? How do they view the GC? Why have they continued this way of life? These are the questions I will attempt to unravel in the time ahead. I, Ghuh'loloan, will likewise be a guest. As I write this, I am on my way to the Exodus Fleet, where I will be staying for eight tendays. I will be living aboard an Exodan homestead ship, interviewing Exodan citizens, and learning Exodan ways. Much was written about the state of the Exodan Fleet following first contact and leading up to GC membership, but little mainstream record has been made of them since. The assumption, I fear, is that their presence in multispecies communities means they have integrated into our varied societies and left their old ways behind. Nothing could be further from the truth. I cross the galaxy now in search of a more honest story.

It is my hope, dear guest, that you will join me.

TESSA

Received message
Encryption: 0
Translation: 0
From: Ashby Santoso (path: 7182-312-95)
To: Tessa Santoso (path: 6222-198-00)

Hey Tess,
I don't know if you've seen the feeds, but if you have, I'm okay.
If you haven't, some bad stuff went down at Hedra Ka, but again:
I'm okay. The ship's suffered a lot of damage, but we're stable and
out of immediate danger. I've got my hands full with repairs and
my crew, so I'll get on the sib when I can. I'll send a note to Dad,
too.
More soon, promise. Hug the kids for me.
Ashby

———

In the grand tradition of siblings everywhere, Tessa wanted to
kill her brother.

Not *permanently* kill him. Just a casual spacing to get her
point across, followed by a quick resurrection and a hot cup of
tea. *That*, she'd say, as he sat shivering on the floor, clutching his
mug like he used to when he was little. *That's what you put us
through every time you go off the map. We all stop breathing
until you get back.*

27

Tessa tossed her scrib across her desk and rubbed her eyes with her fingertips. 'Shit,' she breathed, furious and relieved. She'd seen the feeds. Of course, they hadn't said *which* civilian ship the Toremi had fired on, but Tessa had known where Ashby had been headed for the past standard, what he'd been hired to do. 'You stupid . . .' She exhaled, her eyes stinging. 'He's okay.' She inhaled, her voice steadying. 'He's okay.'

She'd gone to the cargo bay immediately after the news feed had wrapped up, despite her shift not starting for another two hours, despite her father telling her to stay home until they knew whether to relax or plan a funeral. Tessa had no stomach for how Pop had decided to deal with it: holding vigil in front of the pixel projector, watching every feed over and over until something new uploaded, smoking and muttering and tossing out anxious theories. She saw no point in sitting around waiting for news, especially when you had no idea when it would arrive. She'd addressed the fist squeezing her heart in her own way. She'd dragged Aya out of bed, given Ky a cake bite to keep him from fussing at the change in schedule, given Aya a cake bite so she wouldn't cry unfairness, and told Pop to get on the vox if anything changed.

You'd know if you stayed home, he'd grumbled, shoving fat pinches of redreed into his pipe. But she hadn't budged, and he hadn't pushed, for once. She'd patted his shoulder, and sent the kids across the way to the Parks' – who, as Tessa had figured, had been asleep, but that's what hexmates were for.

Aya had pestered her for an explanation every step toward the door. *Why are we up so early? Why can't I stay here? Do I have to go to school? Why was Grandpa mad at you? Is Dad okay?*

Your dad's fine, Tessa had said. That was the only question she'd answered directly. Every other query got a *because I said so* or an *I'll tell you later.* There was no way to say *your Uncle Ashby's ship may have been blown up by aliens and this is my way of coping* to a nine-year-old, and no way a nine-year-old would respond to that sentiment in a way that wouldn't freak out the two-year-old as well. Let the kids have a quiet morning. The grown-ups could worry enough for everyone.

Tessa stretched back against her desk chair, cracking the tight points between ribs and spine. She turned her head toward the wall vox. '224-246,' she said. The vox chirped in acknowledgement of a home address. 'Pop, is your scrib on?'

'No,' her father shouted back. He'd never grasped the concept that even though the vox was on the other side of the room, he didn't have to yell like he did with the old models. 'Why?'

Tessa rolled her eyes. *Why*, asked the man who'd been looping feeds all morning. 'Ashby wrote to us. He's okay.'

The vox relayed a long sigh, followed by a softly spoken 'shit.' He started shouting again. 'How's his ship?'

'He said stable. He didn't have time to write much, just that he's okay.'

'Is he still on board? *Stable* can change fast.'

'I'm sure Ashby knows whether or not his ship's safe.'

'These Toremi weapons they're talking about on the feeds, those things can really—'

'Pop, stop watching the feeds. Okay? They don't know what's going on either, they're just filling time.'

'I'm just saying—'

'Pop.' Tessa pinched the bridge of her nose. 'I have to get back to work. Go to the gardens or something, yeah? Go to Jojo's, get some lunch.'

'When are you coming home?'

'I don't know. Depends on how the day goes.'

'Okay.' He paused. 'I love you.'

Pop wasn't withholding or anything, but he didn't throw those three words around lightly. Tessa softened. 'I love you, too.'

The vox switched off, and she took another opportunity to clear her lungs. She stared out the workroom window, out into the cargo bay. Rows of towering shelves stretched on and on, full to the brim with wires and junk, attended by the herd of heavy-duty liftbots following assignments Tessa had punched into her terminal. There were stacks of metal, too, the pieces too big for the shelves, the pieces nobody'd had time to cut down. This was her domain, her project. It was her job to track comings and goings, to make sure everything got logged and weighed and described, to keep track of stuff the merchants and foundries weren't ready for yet, to wrangle the unintelligent machines who shuffled goods from where they had been to where they were needed. A complicated job, but not a taxing one, and one where you could count on most days going exactly the way you'd thought they'd go when you woke up. Compared to the constant familial chaos of home, she valued that.

When she'd first started working in cargo, way back in her twenties, Bay Eight had been a tidy place. She remembered the neatly packed bins of raw materials, the imported crates with exciting labels printed in multiple alien alphabets. Twenty years down the road, and you couldn't find a one of those in her bay anymore. Imports and processed stock were elsewhere. Bay Eight was one of three on the *Asteria* dedicated to the remains of the *Oxomoco*. Every homestead ship was made the same: a massive central cylinder full of vital systems, a flat ring of thousands of homes anchored around it, a cluster of chunky engines at the back. The *Oxomoco* didn't look like that anymore. Half of it was a ragged husk, dragged far from the Fleet's orbit but still out there, still scaring the boots off anyone who saw it grimacing through a shuttle window. The other half was in pieces, gathered and shoved away in cargo bays like hers. So now, instead of alien crates, she dealt with a never-ending backlog of support trusses, floor panels, empty oxygen tanks. Things that had been vital. Things that had been viewed as permanent. All it had taken was one malfunctioning shuttle, one unlucky trajectory, one stretch of fatigued bulkhead. Just one combination of small things that led to the deaths of tens of thousands, and to cargo bays packed with what was left of the place that had carried them.

Pop's words stuck in her head. *Stable can change fast.*

'M Santoso, you okay?'

Tessa looked over. Kip was peeking around the doorway, his pockmarked face scrunched in concern. She sighed and gave her head a light shake. 'Yeah,' she said. 'Yeah, I'm fine.' The scrunch persisted. Explanations that worked for a nine-year-old had no chance against a sixteen-year-old. Tessa gave an acknowledging smirk and waved him in. 'Just family stuff. Would you pour me some mek?' She paused. 'You can have one, too, if you want.'

The boy raised his eyebrows. 'My shift's not over.'

Tessa gave him a wry smile. 'You've got two days left with me, and we both know you're not going to apprentice here.'

Kip smiled sheepishly as he poured two mugs of mek from the brewer in the corner. 'Come on, M, I'm not *that* bad.'

'You're not,' Tessa said. 'You *could* be decent at managing inventory if you put in the practice. You've got the kind of logicky brain you need for sorting stuff. But we both know this isn't for you.' She accepted the mug with a nod, trying to brush away the lingering mental image of kicking Ashby in the shins. 'But that's the point of job trials, yeah? You've gotta find a good fit, and you won't know what you like and what you don't until you give everything a try. You worked hard for me, and you didn't slack off.' *Much*, she thought.

Kip sat down, a lanky assemblage of too-long limbs and patchy stubble. The kid would be handsome in a year or two, but puberty wasn't going to let him get there without a fight. 'What was your first trial?' he asked.

'Fish farms with my dad,' Tessa said. 'I lasted three whole days.'

'Did you not like killing them, or what?'

'No, that part was fine. It was more that Pop and I were gonna kill each other.' She took a sip of mek and *did not think about Ashby*. 'Have you thought about trying the food farms?'

'I did bugs,' Kip said.

'And?'

'I didn't like killing them.'

This surprised her not a bit. 'But you eat 'em, yeah?'

'Yeah,' he said, with the same goofy smile. 'I'm just good letting somebody else . . . y'know. Do that.'

'Fair enough,' Tessa said. Inwardly, she found that mindset silly. If you were okay with eating something, you had to be okay with it being dead. But Kip was a nice kid, and she wasn't about to make him feel bad for having a soft heart. 'Any idea what you want to try next?'

'I dunno. Not really.'

'You've got plenty of time. And besides, there's tons more for you to try. Always something to do in the Fleet, yeah?'

Kip's mouth smiled, but his eyes didn't. 'Yeah,' he said. 'I guess.'

Tessa took in the kid's face. She knew that look – that restless, empty-handed look. She'd seen it on her baby brother's face, just a standard or so before he packed his bags and tearfully promised them all he wouldn't disappear. He'd made good on that. They got letters and sib calls regularly. He visited when he could. He sent them more credits than any of them knew how to thank him for. But there was a room in the Santoso home that was used for storage now. There were a lot of rooms like it in the Fleet. Empty rooms had been a luxury once, Pop often said. Nowadays . . . nowadays folks could spread out more, take longer showers, hear their voices echo a little louder in the public walkways. She looked at Kip, drinking his mek, probably bored out of his mind. She wondered if his room would end up empty, too.

ISABEL

Isabel had worked in the *Asteria*'s Archives for forty-four years, but she never tired of days like this. These days were some of the best, and she'd prepared in kind. The assembly hall was most often used for lectures and workshops and so on, but today, it had been transformed. She and the other archivists had hauled out the decorations they'd long ago made for such occasions: hanging sunbursts made of scrap metal, bright streamers of recycled cloth. A long table stood waiting to the side, ready to receive home-cooked food and drink. Another table held new seedlings brought in from one of the nurseries, available for those present to bring home to their neighbourhood gardens. Floating globulbs hovered around the room's upper edges, radiating yellows, greens, and blues. Life colours. Growth colours. At the front of the room, by the big screen that projected the view of the starry black beyond the bulkhead, there was a podium. It was covered with streamers and fully-grown plants and, at the top, held Isabel's scrib. This was the most important piece of all.

The person being honoured there would not remember any of it, but the others present would, and they would relay the story one day. That, in a nutshell, was what Isabel's profession was for. Making sure everybody was a link in a chain. Making sure they remembered.

Guests began to arrive, festively dressed, carrying containers dewy with steam and fragrant with spice, syrup, toasted dough. Isabel would not need dinner after this. One of the finer perks of her job.

A boy pleaded with a man to let him have *just one* of whatever they'd brought to the shared table. The man told the boy to be patient. The lack of patience in his own voice indicated that this was not the first time this conversation had been had that day. Isabel smiled. She'd been in both their shoes.

Two musicians set up near the podium. Isabel knew them both, and greeted them warmly. She remembered when they'd been kids begging at the table, too. The same was true for many of the people entering the room, except for the ones she'd shared a childhood with so long ago. There weren't many faces here she didn't know.

The room filled, and at last, two people entered, carrying a tiny third. This was Isabel's cue. She walked to the podium, stepping with practised care in her formal robes. The hum of voices started to fade. She met eyes with one of the musicians and nodded. The musicians nodded to her, then to each other. *One and two and* . . . she saw them mouth. A sheet drum and a long flute leapt into merry action. The final voices disappeared, and the gathered bodies parted to allow the trio to make their way to Isabel.

The young couple stood before her, smiling, proud, perhaps a little shy. Their infant daughter wriggled in the woman's arms, more interested in the glint of her mother's necklace than anything else.

Isabel raised her head to the room as the song reached its end. Faces looked back at her, smiling, waiting. Everyone there knew exactly what would come next. She'd said the words hundreds of times. Thousands, maybe. Every archivist knew how to say them, and every Exodan knew their sound by heart. But still, they needed to be said.

Isabel's body was old – a fact it constantly reminded her of – but her voice remained strong and clear. 'We destroyed our world,' she said, 'and left it for the skies. Our numbers were few. Our species had scattered. We were the last to leave. We left the ground behind. We left the oceans. We left the air. We watched these things grow small. We watched them shrink into a point of light. As we watched, we understood. We understood what we were. We understood what we had lost. We understood what we would need to do to survive. We abandoned more than our ancestors' world. We abandoned our short sight. We abandoned our bloody ways. We made ourselves anew.' She spread her hands, encompassing the gathered. Mouths in the crowd silently mirrored her words. 'We are the Exodus Fleet. We are those that wandered, that wander still. We are the homesteaders that shelter our families. We are the miners and foragers in the open. We are the ships that ferry between. We are the explorers who carry our names. We are the parents who lead the way. We are the children who continue on.' She picked up her scrib and addressed the couple. 'What is her name?'

'Robin,' the man said.

'And what name does your home carry?'

'Garcia,' said the woman.

'Robin Garcia,' Isabel spoke to the scrib. The scrib chirped in response, and retrieved the citizen registry file she had created that morning. A blue square appeared on screen. Isabel gestured for the mother to step forward. The baby frowned as they manoeuvred one of her bare feet onto the square, pressing tiny toes and heel against it. The scrib chirped again, indicating that a new file had been added to the mighty towers of data nodes that stood vigil a deck below. Isabel read the record to the room. 'Robin Garcia,' she said. 'Born aboard the *Asteria*. Forty Solar days of age as of GC standard day 158/307. She is now, and always, a member of our Fleet. By our laws, she is assured shelter and passage here. If we have food, she will eat. If we have air, she will breathe. If we have fuel, she will fly. She is daughter to all grown, sister to all still growing. We will care for her, protect her, guide her. We welcome you, Robin, to the decks of the *Asteria*, and to the journey we take together.' She cupped the baby's head with her palm, weathered skin cradling new. She spoke the final words now, and the room spoke with her. 'From the ground, we stand. From our ships, we live. By the stars, we hope.'

SAWYER

He stood at the railing outside the dockside bioscans, luggage in hand, breathing in the recycled air. It was different than the air he knew, for sure. It wasn't what he'd call *good* air, not like what you'd get around a forest or a field. There was a slight metallic edge to it, and though the walkways were lined with healthy planters exhaling oxygen back his way, something about each breath just *felt* artificial. There was no wind here, no rain. The air moved because Humans told it to, and maybe in that, it had lost something along the way.

But Sawyer smiled. *Different* was what he was after, and everything he'd encountered in the twenty minutes since coming aboard was as different as could be. What struck him was the practicality of the architecture, the intense economy. On Mushtullo, people embellished. There were mouldings on the tops of walls. Roofs twisted and fences spiralled. Even the ships were filigreed. Not here. Nothing in the foundation of this vessel had been wasted on sentiment.

But while the ship's skeleton was simple, the people within had spent centuries fleshing it out. The metal walls were disguised with inviting paint: warm tan, soft orange, living green. On his way to the railing, he'd come upon an enormous mural that had stopped him in his tracks. He'd stood for a minute there, as other travellers split their busy stream around him. The mural was vibrant, almost gaudy, a spree of colour and curves depicting dancing Exodans with a benignly burning sun beneath their feet and a starry sky above. Myriad professions were on display – a farmer, a doctor, a tech, a musician, a pilot, a teacher leading children. It was an ordinary sort of theme, and yet there was something about it – the lack of actual ground, perhaps, or something in the sweeping style – that was undeniably foreign. You'd never see a mural like that on Mushtullo.

Sawyer let his reality sink in: he was in the Fleet. The Fleet! He was finally, actually *there*, not just reading reference files or pestering elderly folks for any scraps they could remember about what *their* parents had told them about the ships they'd left behind. He'd made it. He'd made it, and now, everything was right there for him to explore.

There were no other species in the crowd, and it left him both giddy and jarred. The only times he'd seen anything close to this many Humans in one place was on holidays or at parties, and even then, you'd be sure to see other sapients in the mix. There'd been merchants from elsewhere on the transport with him, but as soon as they reached a branching sign that read *Cargo Bays* on the right and *Central Plaza* on the left, all the scales and claws went right. Everyone around him now had two hands, two feet, soft skin, hairy heads. He'd never blended into a public group like this, and yet, he felt like he stuck out more than he ever had.

Sawyer had thought perhaps some part of him would recognise this place, that he'd feel himself reversing the steps his great-great-grandparents had taken. He'd read accounts of other grounders visiting the Fleet. They'd written about how connected they felt to their ancestors, how they felt immediate kinship with the people there. Sawyer hadn't felt that yet, and part of him was a touch disappointed. But no matter. He'd been there for all of twenty minutes, and the only person he'd talked to was the patch scan attendant. So far, he'd dipped a toe in the water. It was time to dive in.

He took an elevator down to the market floor, an expansive grid of shop fronts and service centres. It wasn't like other market-places he'd been to, where everything sprawled and piled as if it were alive. The Fleet, as he'd read and as had already proven true, was a place of orderly geometry. Every corner had been considered, measured, and considered again. Space efficiency was the top order of business, so the original architects had provided future generations of shopkeepers with defined lots that could be assigned and repurposed as needed. The end result was, on the surface, the tidiest trading hub Sawyer had ever seen. But once he got past the neat exteriors, the underlying business was bewildering. Dozens of signs, dozens of displays, hundreds of customers, and he had no idea where anything was.

He eyed the places that served food – all open-air (if that was the right term to use inside a ship), with shared eating tables corralled behind the waist-high metal walls that defined each lot's edges. Sawyer found himself drawn toward a cheery, clean cafe called *My Favourite*. The menu posted outside was in both Klip and Ensk, and the fare was things he recognised – beansteak skewers, hoppers, jam cakes. It looked like a respectable spot for a non-threatening meal. Sawyer pointed his feet elsewhere. That was a place meant for merchants and visitors. Tourists. He wasn't here to be a tourist. He was after something *real*.

He spied another eatery of the same size and shape. *Jojo's*, the sign read. Or it would have, if the pixels on the second *j* hadn't been twitching themselves nearly illegible. There was no posted menu. The only other signage displayed the hours of business, which were in Ensk numerals and Ensk numerals only. (Standard time, though. They only used Solar for age, or so he'd been told.) Behind the corral, some folks in algae-stained coveralls wolfed down whatever was for lunch. A group of five or six elderly folks were arguing over a game taking place on an old pixel board. Nobody had any luggage.

Perfect.

No one greeted Sawyer as he walked in. Few looked up. There were two people behind the counter: a wiry young man chopping something, and an imposing middle-aged woman peeling shells off steamed red coaster bugs. The woman was absorbed in a loud vid on a nearby projector – a Martian period drama, it looked like. She cracked each shell segment with speedy precision, without so much as a glance down at her work. Sawyer had no real way of knowing, but he got the unshakable sense that this was her place.

The woman gave a short, mocking laugh. 'This Solan shit,' she said in Ensk, shaking her head at the projector. The vid music hit a melodramatic crescendo as a character in a clunky exosuit succumbed to a sandstorm. 'Why does anybody watch this?'

'You watch it,' an old woman piped up from the board game table.

'It's like a shipwreck,' the shell-cracker replied. 'Once it starts, I can't look away.'

The scene changed. A tearful group of terraformers sat huddled in their dome. 'This damned planet,' one actor cried. He wasn't about to win any awards for this, but stars, he was trying. 'This damned planet!'

'*This damned planet!*' the woman repeated, laughing again. Her eyes snapped over as she noticed Sawyer at last. 'Hey,' she said, glancing at his bag. 'What can I get ya?'

Sawyer walked up to the counter. He was more or less fluent in Ensk, having crammed Linking language lessons hard over the past few years, but the only person he'd been able to practise speaking with had been the lady at the shoe shop back home, and her slang was about twenty years out of date. He screwed up his courage, and asked: 'Do you have a menu?'

Every person in Jojo's looked up. It took Sawyer a moment to realise – *accent*. His accent. He didn't have the distinctive snap of an Exodan, the silky smoothness of a Martian, the muddle of someone who did a lot of bouncing around. His face said *Human*. His vowels said *Harmagian*.

The woman blinked. 'No menu,' she said. She jerked a thumb back toward the wiry man, still chopping away. 'It's ninth day. That means we've got twice-round pickle on a quickbun and red coaster stew. Only, we're out of red coaster stew.' Exoskeleton crunched between her hands. 'I gotta make more, and that's gonna be at least an hour.'

'Okay,' Sawyer said. 'I'll have the other one.'

'The pickle?'

'Yeah.'

'You ever had twice-round pickle?'

Sawyer grinned. 'Nope.'

The woman grinned back, but it wasn't a good grin, not the kind of grin that shook hands with his own. This was a different look, a look that knew something he didn't. Sawyer felt his mood slip a bit. He was pretty sure the board game crew was still watching him.

'Okay,' the woman said. 'One pickle bun. Comes with tea.'

It took him a second to realise she was asking him a question. 'Tea would be great.' She searched for a mug by way of reply. Sawyer took a chance, trying to coax more conversation. 'Are you Jojo?'

'No,' the woman said flatly. 'Jojo was my mom.'

'And she was a lot nicer than this one,' an old man with a pipe added from the back.

'*Ch,*' the woman said, rolling her eyes. 'You only say that 'cause she slept with you once.'

'I would've thought she was nice even if we hadn't.'

'Yeah, well. She always was a sucker for ugly things.'

The board game crew cracked up – the old man in particular – and the woman grinned, a real grin this time. She filled a mug from a large decanter and set it on the counter as the wiry man silently assembled Sawyer's lunch. Sawyer tried to see what was going into what he'd just ordered, but the man's body blocked his view. Something was chopped, something was ladled, a few bottles were shaken. Twice-round pickle looked . . . involved.

The woman stared at Sawyer. 'Oh,' he said, understanding. He hadn't paid. He pushed back his wristwrap. 'Where should I, ah . . .' He looked around for a scanner.

The woman pursed her lips. 'Don't take creds,' she said.

Sawyer was elated. He'd heard about this – Exodan merchants who operated on barter and barter only. But there was a problem: that was as far as his knowledge of the practice went, and he didn't know what the protocol was. He waited for her to suggest an acceptable trade. Nothing came. 'What would be good?' he asked.

Another short laugh, like the one the sandstorm victim received. 'I dunno. I dunno what you've got.'

Sawyer thought. He'd only brought one bag of essentials and didn't have much he was willing to part with, not for the sake of a sandwich. He scolded himself for not planning for this with a bag of circuit chips or something. 'Do you need some help in the kitchen? I could wash dishes.'

Now *everyone* laughed. Sawyer had no idea what the joke was, but he was starting to wonder if the tourist cafe would've been the better option.

The woman leaned against the counter. 'Where are you from?'

'Mushtullo.'

'What now?'

'Mushtullo.' No response. 'Central space.'

She raised her eyebrows. 'Huh. You got family here?'

'No,' Sawyer said. 'But my family came *from* here.'

'*Oh*,' the woman said, as if she understood everything now. 'I see. Okay. You got a place to stay?'

'I figured I'd sort that out once I got here.'

'Oh boy,' the woman said under her breath. The wiry man handed her a plate, which she pushed across the counter. 'Here. On the house. The food of your ancestors.'

'Wow, you sure?' Sawyer said.

'Well, now I'm not.'

'Sorry, um . . . thank you.' He took both plate and mug. 'That's really kind.'

The woman resumed her shell cracking without another word. Sawyer looked around, hoping one of the groups might wave him over. None did. The algaeists were stacking up their thoroughly cleaned dishes, and the old folks had resumed their board game.

Sawyer dropped his bag in an empty chair and sat in another alongside it. He studied his food – a large mound of wet, shredded vegetables, piled on top of two halves of a nondescript bun, dressed with whatever Jojo's daughter's assistant had dashed on top of it. He lifted one of the halves. It leaked, sending purple liquid running down his forearm. He paused before opening his mouth. There was a smell, fetid and sharp, maybe a bit fishy. He thought of the other customers, chowing down with satisfaction. He took a bite. His throat tightened, his sinuses shot open, and his bravery died. The stuff tasted exactly as it smelled, only now it was inescapable, mingling with a bitter, tangy undercurrent he wasn't sure he wanted to identify. He couldn't taste the bread, but despite the sour liquid now dripping all over his hands, the texture was distractingly dry. The pickle didn't crunch, as he'd expected. It just softly surrendered.

It was, without a doubt, the worst thing he'd ever eaten.

Okay, he thought. *This is okay. It's an adventure.* Not the start he'd been hoping for, but it was a start, and that was something. He forced another bite of pickle, washing it down with a huge swig of tea (the tea, at least, was good). There was no way he wasn't going to finish his meal. This was a test. The locals were watching, his ancestors were watching, everybody back home who thought this plan of his was bonkers was watching. He would clean his plate, and find a place to stay, and everything would be great.

Sawyer heard the woman laugh again. He thought for a moment it was directed at him, but no. Another Martian terraformer had died.

KIP

Lunch breaks were the best part of Kip's day. No teachers, no job trials, no parents. Nothing that needed doing or that he might screw up. Kip savoured every second. This was *his* time, and he always did the same thing with it: get a choko and a hopper at Grub Grub, park himself on the bench facing the oxygen garden, and try to stretch out his brief bit of freedom as long as possible. Chane in biology class said Sianat Pairs could slow time with their brains, and Kip didn't think that was true, but if it was, he'd seriously trade an arm or something if it meant he could do that. Both arms, maybe. Maybe even his eyes. Okay, not his eyes. But limbs, definitely.

Somebody jumped him from behind, pulling his shirt up over the back of his head. '*Tek tem*, fucko!'

Kip had his shirt back down and a hand swinging before he could get a look at where it would land. Not a mean fist or anything – he'd never punched anybody for reals. Just a soft slap that wouldn't even hurt, much less bruise.

His hand landed in Ras' ribs. Ras shoved the slap away with one hand and grabbed for Kip's choko with the other. 'Gimme.'

'*Dosh*,' said Kip, stretching his drink out of reach. 'Fuck off.' In one fast move, he reached out and mussed Ras' hair.

Ras withdrew at that, as he always did. 'Aw, come on,' he said, combing away the minimal damage with his fingers. 'Uncalled for.'

Kip chuckled into his drink, scrunching his eyes tight. He wiped his hand on his pants, trying to get rid of the hair glue

43

remnants he'd picked up. Ras always put too much shit in his hair.

The scuffle ended as fast as it had started. He and his friend sat in an easy slump, watching the crowd for the unlikely chance of something interesting happening. Kip passed the choko bottle to Ras. Ras took a long pull of the sweet fizz and passed it back. It was a rhythm they fell into without any thought. There'd been a lot of shared snacks over the years. That was what had eventually led to them getting assigned work day and school day schedules that didn't overlap – too many passed-between packs of cake bites in class. *A persistent disruption to other students*, M Rebane had called him and Ras. Whatever. At least they still had lunch at the same time.

'You know Amira, at the tech shop?' Ras said.

'Yeah.'

'I think she likes me.'

Kip almost got choko up his nose. 'Okay.'

'Seriously,' Ras said. 'I saw her looking at me.'

Kip kept laughing. 'Okay.'

'What? I did!'

'Amira. From the tech shop.'

'That's what I said.'

'She's, like, twenty-five or something.'

'So?'

'So she probably just thought your hair looks stupid and couldn't stop staring.'

'*Remmet telli toh.*' Ras cuffed him, but grinned. '*Your* hair looks stupid.'

'Yeah,' Kip agreed. No argument there. Had he combed it this morning? He couldn't remember.

The crowd went back and forth, back and forth. Same faces, same patterns as every other day. 'What do you wanna do after work?' Ras asked.

'Don't you have history this afternoon?'

Ras shook his head with an expression that said he *did* have that class lined up, but there was no chance of him being there for it. 'Wanna go to the hub?'

'Nah,' Kip said. There weren't any new sims out, and they'd played all the ones worth playing. Ras was always down for *Battle Wizards,* but Kip was kind of sick of it.

'Wanna go look at the new transport pods?'

'We did that yesterday.'

'So? They're cool.'

Kip shrugged. New pods were the kind of thing that were cool only when you'd never seen them before.

'Okay,' Ras said. 'What do *you* want to do?'

Kip shrugged again. 'I dunno.'

Ras took ownership of the choko. 'You have a bad day or something?'

'It was fine. M Santoso kind of just let me hang out. Let me have mek during my shift.'

'That's cool.'

'Yeah,' Kip said, taking the choko back. 'She's all right.'

'I dunno why you're doing job trials anyway. Exams are coming up.'

This was Ras' grand plan, unchanged since they were twelve: take the qualification exams and get into university (the fastest ticket out of the Fleet – all there was at home were trade classes and apprenticeships). After that, get a cool job, get on a big ship, and make lots of creds. That was as good of a plan as any for Kip – and more than he'd ever been able to come up with on his own – but he wasn't as sure as Ras that he'd be able to come along.

'When I don't pass, I'm gonna need a job,' Kip said.

'You'll pass,' Ras said.

'I suck at tests.'

'Everyone sucks at tests.'

'You don't suck at tests.'

Ras didn't say anything, because he *didn't* suck at tests, just like he wasn't doing job trials because he knew he wouldn't need them. When Ras said he was gonna do a thing, the thing *happened*. Sometimes Kip was jealous of that. He wished he could be more like Ras. Ras always knew what to say, what to do, what was happening. Kip was real glad they were friends, but sometimes he didn't know what Ras got out of the arrangement.

'Hey, M Aksoy,' Ras called out. The grocery seller was walking past them, followed by an autocart carrying . . . ? 'What is that?'

M Aksoy turned his head, gestured at the cart to stop, and waved them toward him. 'Come on and see.'

Kip and Ras ambled over. Among the recognisable boxes – mek powder, root sugar, bottles of kick – there were three plex tanks full of water, like jellyfish tanks. But whatever was inside wasn't jellyfish, no way. They were long and wispy, covered in soft spines. They shivered their way through the water.

'Special order from the Archives,' M Aksoy said.

'Are they pets or something?' Ras asked. 'Some kind of science thing?'

'Nope,' M Aksoy said. 'They're called—'

'*Pokpok*,' Kip said, saying the word before he realised he knew it.

Ras turned his head. 'The hell'd you know that?'

Kip had no idea. Something from when he was little? Like something in a learning sim, or a Linking book, or . . . he couldn't say. He'd been a dork about that kind of stuff as a kid, and it had been a long time since that was his thing. But wherever *pokpok* had come from, the dusty old memory remained active. He could feel Ras looking at him, though, so he just shrugged and didn't say anything about the bit where he was pretty sure the swimming things were Harmagian food. Ras was real smart, and Kip didn't want to look stupid by saying something wrong.

'You're right, *pokpok*,' M Aksoy said. 'M Itoh has a Harmagian guest arriving today. These, apparently, are one of their favourite things to eat.'

Kip watched the *pokpok* wriggle around the tank, looking like spiky snot brought to life. He felt his nose pull into itself.

Ras mirrored his expression. 'Do they fry them or—'

The grocer's eyes crinkled at the edges. 'You know, I don't know if they cook them at all.'

Kip groaned with disgust. Ras looked at him. 'Give you twenty creds if you eat one.'

'You don't have twenty creds.'

The grocer laughed. 'One of these'd cost you well more than twenty creds, and they're not for you anyway. But here.' He reached into one of the crates on the cart, and pulled out two snack bags. 'Free sample, all the way from the independent colonies.'

Kip accepted the bag and looked at the label. *The One and Only Fire Shrimp*, it read in Klip. There was another line that ended in the word *hot*, but the word before it he didn't know. He pointed it out to Ras. They both used Klip all the time, but Ras was super good at it – *real* Klip, classroom Klip, not just a few words stuck into Ensk like everybody did (everybody who wasn't old, anyway). Ras was definitely going to university.

'*Soolat*,' Ras read. 'That's like, uh . . . horribly.'

'*Devastatingly*,' M Aksoy said. 'That's a better translation. *Devastatingly hot*. I don't know if they're any good, but if you like them, you know where to trade for more.'

'Thanks, M,' Ras said.

'Yeah, thanks, M,' said Kip.

The grocer gave them a nod and started back on his way. 'Hey, M,' Ras called after him. 'You said the Harmagian's gonna be at the Archives?'

'Far as I know,' M Aksoy called back as he disappeared into the crowd.

Ras looked at Kip. 'Ever seen a Harmagian before?'

Kip shook his head. 'Just in sims.'

'When you gotta be back at work?'

Kip shrugged. M Santoso hadn't given him a specific time

that he needed to be back, and given their conversation that morning, he didn't think she'd care too much if he was gone a while.

'Well, then, let's go.' Ras headed for the elevator to the transport deck.

Kip followed. Going all the way to the Archives just to look at an alien seemed like a stupid thing to do, but then, *everything* seemed like a stupid thing to do, and at least this stupid thing was a stupid thing that didn't happen every stupid day. He sighed.

Ras noticed. 'Yeah, I know, man.' He shook his head as they weaved through the crowd. 'The Fleet sucks.'

EYAS

A bot could have carried Eyas' load easily, but some things needed to be moved by hand. Not that it made any difference to the things being carried. Bots could've got them to the same place, and probably faster, too. That wasn't the point. The point was that some weights needed to be felt, and that hands convey a respect bots never could.

She pulled her wagon along, the canisters inside rattling slightly. The people she walked past recognised the sound, no question. Her cargo was unmistakable. Eyas sometimes wondered what it was like for merchants to carry boxes that passersby didn't know the contents of. Perhaps it felt a bit like a birthday, like having a good secret wrapped away. Eyas' canisters were no secret, but they were good all the same. They were undeniably good, even though some of the glances they received took a moment to sort themselves out.

'Thank you, M,' a woman said as she passed her. The woman was grey-haired, at least twice her age, and yet, still, 'M.' She had long grown used to that.

Eyas was tired, and not in the best of moods. She'd awoken with a headache and had skipped breakfast, which she'd regretted after a mere hour at work. She smiled and nodded at the woman anyway. That was part of her job, too. To smile. To be the opposite of fear.

She continued down the thruway, heading into the buzz of a neighbourhood market. The smells of crispy fish, warm starches, and fresh-cut veggies greeted her. Her stomach growled.

The environment shifted slightly as she moved through it, as it always did. She passed through the familiar blanket of long glances, murmured thanks, the occasional exhale. Someone appeared in her periphery – an older man, coming right toward her. 'M Parata,' the man said. He opened his arms wide.

Eyas didn't remember the man when she went in for the hug, but an image surfaced as she was squeezed tight. A face at a ceremony two – no, three – tendays prior. 'M Tucker,' she said. 'Please, call me Eyas.' She pulled back, leaving a friendly hand on the man's arm. 'How are you?' It was a difficult question, she knew, but simply saying *I care* was awkward.

'Oh, well,' M Tucker said. His face struggled. 'You know.'

'I do,' Eyas said. She did.

M Tucker looked at the cart. He swallowed hard. 'Is that Ari?'

Eyas raced through some math. 'No,' she said. 'Not for at least four tendays yet. If you'd like to come by then, I can prepare a canister for you myself.'

The man's eyes watered. He squeezed Eyas' upper arm. 'Do you like bean cakes?' he asked, gesturing back at his stall. 'I've got both sweet and savoury, fresh out of the oven.'

Eyas wasn't huge on bean cakes, but she had never, ever turned down a gift under these circumstances, and her stomach was willing to accept anything at this point. 'I'd love a sweet one.'

M Tucker smiled and scurried back to his workspace. He lifted a fat bean cake off a teetering stack and wrapped one end of it in a thin piece of throw-cloth. 'You have a good day now, M Eyas,' he said, handing over the bundle.

Eyas thanked him and continued on. She received more handouts before she reached her destination – a pack of vegetable seeds, which she had no use for but would keep for trade, and a mug of strong tea, which she desperately needed. She paused in her walk, sat on a bench, and consumed her gifted meal. The bean cake was fine, as far as bean cakes went, and the tea soothed a tightness she hadn't known was there. She found a nearby recycling station and put the mug and the throw-cloth in their respective bins, from which they would be collected, washed, and reused. She resumed her walk, dragging her own recycling along behind her.

Her destination was the oxygen garden, the central hub of any neighbourhood, a curved green assemblage of places to play and places to sit and plenty of room to think. She parked her wagon in its usual spot, put on her apron and gloves, and selected a canister. She stepped over a plex barrier into one of the planters, treading carefully around all that grew there. The grasses couldn't be easily avoided, but she did her best to not trample the flowering shrubs and broad leaves. She crouched down near a bush and unlocked the canister lid. The heady smell of compost greeted her, a smell she spent so much time alongside it was a wonder she noticed it anymore. She spread the stuff around the roots with her gloved hands, laying down handful after handful of rich black nutrients. She wouldn't have minded getting compost on her bare skin but, much like pulling the wagon, it was a matter of respect. Compost was too precious to be wasted by washing it from her hands. She was meticulous about brushing off her gloves before folding them back up, about doing the same with her apron, about shaking every last crumb out of the canister. Each bit had to make its way to where it had been promised it would go.

Eyas emptied every canister in turn, tending the recipient plants carefully. She made sure not to walk where she'd worked, and took care not to touch her face. She stuck a small green flag in each planter as she finished, letting others know the area had recently been fertilised. There was nothing about the compost that could harm a person, but it wasn't the sort of thing most would be comfortable accidentally sticking their hand in. It didn't matter that compost was just compost – nitrogen, carbon, various minerals. People got so hung up on what a thing *had been*, rather than what it was *now*. That was why publicly distributed compost was reserved for oxygen gardens and fibre farms, the only public places in the Fleet that used soil. You could use compost tea in aeroponics, sure, but the food farms got different fertiliser blends, ones that came from plant scraps, bug husks, fish meal. Some families did indeed use their personal compost canisters on food gardens at home; others recoiled from that practice. Eyas understood both sides. Clear divisions between right and wrong were rare in her work.

As she neared the end of her batch, she felt the shapeless tingle of someone's gaze. Eyas turned to see a little boy – maybe five or so – watching her with intense focus. A young man was with him – a father or uncle, who could say – crouched down to the child's height, explaining something quietly. Eyas didn't have to guess what the topic was.

'Hello,' Eyas said with a friendly wave.

The man waved back. 'Hi,' he said. He turned to the boy. 'Can you say hi?'

The boy presumably could, but did not.

Eyas smiled. 'Would you like to come see?' The boy shifted his weight from foot to foot, then nodded. Eyas waved him over. She spread some compost on her gloved palm. 'Did M here tell you what this is?'

The boy rubbed his lips together before speaking. 'People.'

'Mmm, not anymore. It's called *compost*. It used to be people, yes, but it's changed into something else. See, what I'm doing here is putting this onto the plants, so they grow strong and healthy.' She demonstrated. 'The people that turned into compost now get to be part of these plants. The plants give us clean air to breathe and beautiful things to look at, which keeps *us* healthy. Eventually, these plants will die, and they'll get composted, too. Then *that* compost gets used to grow food, and the food becomes part of us again. So, even when we lose people we love, they don't leave us.' She pressed her palm flat against her chest. 'We're made out of our ancestors. They're what keep us alive.'

'That's pretty neat, huh?' the man said, crouching down beside the boy.

The boy looked undecided. 'Can I see in the tube?' he asked.

Eyas made sure there wasn't any compost on the outside of the cylinder before handing it over. 'Careful not to spill,' she said.

The boy took the cylinder with two hands and a studious frown. 'It looks like dirt,' he said.

'It basically *is* dirt,' Eyas said. 'It's dirt with superpowers.'

The boy rotated the cylinder, watching the compost tumble inside. 'How many people are in this?' he asked.

The man raised an eyebrow. Eyas threw him a reassuring glance. It was not the weirdest thing she'd ever been asked, by far. 'That's a good question, but I don't know,' Eyas said. 'Once the compost reaches this stage, the . . . the stuff that makes it gets jumbled together.'

The boy absorbed that. He handed the canister back.

Eyas reached into her hip pouch and pulled out a flag. 'Would you like to put this in the dirt? It lets people know I've been working here.'

The boy took the flag, still not smiling. Eyas understood. It was a lot to think about. 'Where can I put it?'

'Anywhere you like,' Eyas said, gesturing to the dirt around them.

The boy considered, and chose a spot near a bush. He stuck the flag down. 'Does it hurt?' he asked.

'Does what hurt?'

The boy tugged at the edge of his shirt. 'When you get turned into dirt.'

'Oh, no, buddy,' the man said. He put a reassuring hand on the boy's back and kissed the top of his head. 'No, it doesn't hurt at all.'

ISABEL

Aliens did not make Isabel uncomfortable. In her youth – a period of her life she was sure her grandkids didn't truly believe had taken place – she'd spent three standards hopping tunnels, crashing in spaceport hostels, gobbling up every strange sky and unknown city until homesickness finally won the day. She'd bunked with a Laru for one leg of a trip, become the drinking buddy of a quartet of Aandrisks on another. That was a long time ago, to be sure, but she'd had contact with aliens since – merchants, mostly, when she ordered something special for import. But in recent years, she'd found herself in the odd, delightful position of being a person of interest to certain individuals from the Reskit Institute of Interstellar Migration. The Exodus Fleet had drifted back into academic fashion, and, as the head archivist of the *Asteria*, Isabel did not have to ask why they'd sought her out. Every homesteader had its Archives and archivists, but Isabel was the current oldest of her profession, and even among aliens, that counted for something.

She was biased, of course, having worked in the Archives for most of her adult life, but the files she kept watch over were nothing short of magic. The first Exodans had crammed old-timey server racks full to bursting with records of Earth and personal stories, and every generation since had added to their work. *What is it you're looking for?* she asked anyone who made the trip to the spiralling chamber of data nodes (the server racks had been retired well before her time). Art? Literature? Family history? Earthen history? Earthen life? Whatever topic you needed, if Humans deemed it worth remembering, the Archives kept it safe.

Her life spent in service to the past was why she now found herself doing a rather-out-of-the-ordinary task, something other than helping students or doing node maintenance or conducting record ceremonies. Today, she was meeting with an alien, and as transgalactic as her correspondence was, it had been a long time since she'd shared a room with one.

Ghuh'loloan had come straight from the shuttledocks to the Archives, and given what Isabel knew of her, she doubted she'd checked into her guest quarters yet. The Harmagian was the most enthusiastic of Isabel's Reskit Institute pen pals, and they'd been friendly colleagues for years. But this was their first time meeting in person, and, as was to be expected, Isabel found herself reconciling the person she knew from letters with the person now sitting before her. The dog-sized, speckled-yellow, wet-skinned person, lying legless on a motorised cart, with no feet and no bones and no real shape at all until you got to the wreath of grasping tentacles and smaller tendrils centred around a toothless maw, crowned with a pair of retracting eyestalks that made Isabel stare despite her best efforts.

Stars, it really had been a long time.

'I'm sorry I couldn't meet you at the dock,' Isabel said. 'Today's ceremony took a long time to clear out.' They were in her office now, at her meeting table, away from the towering technology and busy staff. Well, ostensibly busy. Isabel had seen more than a few of her peers undertaking tasks of dubious value that steered them conveniently past her office windows. Everyone wanted a glimpse of the visitor.

Ghuh'loloan flexed her facial dactyli. Isabel knew Harmagian facial gestures were important communicative cues, but they were lost on her. She could follow only her colleague's words, which dripped with a deliciously-burred accent. 'Nonsense,' Ghuh'loloan said. 'You have work, and I am the one disrupting it! I feel nothing but joy in sharing your company, for however much time you can spare.'

Harmagians, Isabel knew, had a tendency to lay it on thick. 'I'm looking forward to working together as well. Was your journey all right?'

'Yes, yes, entirely adequate. I've had better, but then, I've had plenty worse.' Ghuh'loloan laughed with a wavering coo. Her eyestalks studied something. 'Do you have trouble understanding me?'

'No, not at all.'

'But then—' Ghuh'loloan pointed a tentacle toward Isabel's face.

It took Isabel a moment to understand. 'Oh,' she chuckled, removing her hud. A faint border disappeared from her field of vision, an edge she barely noticed until it was gone. 'Sorry, I'm so used to having it on I often forget to take it off. I've even worn it to sleep, once or twice.'

'Ah,' Ghuh'loloan said. 'For filing, then, not translating?'

'For everything, really,' Isabel said, looking at the clear lens set in a well-worn frame. 'It's much faster than my scrib, and it keeps my hands free.'

'I wouldn't know,' Ghuh'loloan said in a good-humoured tone. She pointed at her delicate, swaying eyes, incapable of wearing Isabel's favoured gadget. 'But it sounds very useful.'

Isabel smiled. 'Well, I envy *that* a bit,' she said, nodding at Ghuh'loloan's cart. 'My knees aren't what they used to be.'

'I wouldn't know about knees, either.'

They both laughed. 'Would you like something to drink?' Isabel asked.

'Mek, if you have it.'

Isabel knew that she did, as the other archivists hadn't rioted. 'You take it cold, I assume?' She'd learned to do a Harmagian-style flash cold brew in the tenday before her colleague arrived.

But Isabel's new skill was to be untested. 'I do,' Ghuh'loloan said, 'but if I wanted cold mek, I would've stayed home. Please, make it for me as you'd make it for yourself.' She paused. 'Although, perhaps not *too* hot.'

Isabel nodded with understanding as she opened the tin of mek powder. Introducing scalding hot liquid to mollusk-like skin would not end well. She glanced over and laughed, seeing that Ghuh'loloan had opened a storage compartment on her cart and removed both scrib and stylus. 'Are we getting started?'

Ghuh'loloan curled the tentacles around her mouth. 'I had questions before I arrived, but after seeing these wonderful ships of yours with my own eyes – oh, I hardly know where to start! Everything. I want to know everything. Let's begin with the ships. I saw so many things on my way here that I wish to understand better.'

'You'll have to tell me what you already know about them, so I don't walk the same corridors twice.'

'No. My understanding may be flawed, and if I assume that I already know something, you won't know to correct my mistakes. Besides, it is such a rare opportunity to get information that is not filtered through a screen. Tell me of the ships as if I know nothing of them. Tell me as if I were a child.'

'All right then.' Isabel gathered her thoughts as the mek brewer rumbled. 'The original architects based everything around three basic principles: longevity, stability, and well-being. They knew that for the Fleet to have any chance of survival, the ships had to be something that could withstand both distance and time, something that the spacers within could always rely on, and something that would foster both physical and mental health. Survival alone wasn't enough. *Couldn't* be enough. If there were disputes over food, resources, living space—'

'That'd be the end of it.'

'That'd be the end of it. These had to be places Humans would *want* to live in. In that long stretch between leaving Earth and GC contact, we were utterly alone. Those who lived and died during that time only knew planets from stories. This' – she gestured at the walls – 'was everything. It had to feel like a home, rather than a prison. Otherwise, we were doomed.'

'Longevity, stability, well-being,' Ghuh'loloan repeated, writing on her scrib in her strange boxy alphabet. 'Please, go on.'

Isabel put her own scrib on the table between them and launched a sketch programme. Floating pixels followed her stylus as she drew in the air. 'Architecturally, every homesteader is the same. At the centre, you have the main cylinder, which is essentially life support storage. It houses the water tanks, the air tanks, and the batteries.'

'Now, the batteries,' Ghuh'loloan said, still taking notes. 'Those store kinetically harvested energy, yes?'

'Originally, yes, mostly. Well . . . right, let me back up. When the Exodans first left Earth, they burned chemical fuels to get going, just to tide them over until enough kinetic energy had been generated through the floors. They also had hydro-generators.'

'Water-powered?'

'Yes, using waste water.' The brewer dinged, and Isabel filled two mugs. 'As it flows back to the processing facilities, it runs through a series of generators. That system's still in use. It's not our primary power source, but it's a good supplement.' She placed the mugs between them, and considered bringing out the tin of cookies stashed away in her desk. She decided against it. Harmagians had famously finicky stomachs, and she didn't want to hospitalise her colleague over ginger bites.

Ghuh'loloan reached for the mug closest to her, eying the tiny wisps of steam. She gave the surface of the drink a few tentative raps with the tip of her tentacle – one, two, three. Apparently finding the temperature suitable, she wrapped a portion of her limb around the handle and brought the mug aloft. 'See, this is why I wanted to start with the basics. How fascinating. Might we be able to visit the water generators?'

'Absolutely,' Isabel said. Not a place she would've been excited to visit on her own, but Ghuh'loloan's enthusiasm was catching.

'Wonderful. But I'm getting you off-track. Do I correctly glean that kinetic energy is no longer your primary power source?'

'That's right. Once the GC gave us this sun, we started collecting solar power.'

'Yes, I saw the satellites as I flew in. Those were provided by . . . ?'

'The Aeluons.' Isabel's tone was matter-of-fact, but she felt a slump in pride. Her colleague had assumed correctly that the Exodans couldn't have built such tech on their own.

Lacking lips, Ghuh'loloan held the Human-style mug up, flattened her face back into her body so that it lay almost horizontally, and poured a little waterfall into her wide mouth. Her whole body shivered. 'Ho! Oh *ho*!'

'Too hot?' Isabel asked with dread.

'No— no, I'm just unaccustomed. What a feeling!' She executed a longer pour. 'Ho! That's . . . stars, that's *thrilling*. I may never take mek cold again.' She shivered once more, then cradled her mug between two tentacles. 'Oh dear, where was I?'

'Satellites.'

'Yes, and Aeluons. They provided you with artigrav, too, yes?'

'That's right.'

'A generous people,' Ghuh'loloan said. 'I wish I could say the same of mine.' She laughed. 'I suppose it is in your best interest that we did not win their war against us, eh?'

Isabel chuckled, but took that as a sign to steer the conversation back to the topic at hand. The war invoked was very old, very ugly history. Clearly, Ghuh'loloan didn't mind a bit of self-deprecation, but Isabel didn't want to cross the line from cultural ribbing into insult. 'Indeed. So, the main cylinder.'

'The main cylinder.'

'Unlike the habitat ring – which I'll get to – the cylinder interior was never designed for gravity, so you won't find artigrav nets there. Everything is arranged in a circle, around a central core.'

Ghuh'loloan set down her cup. 'Do you mean that when you go in there—'

'We have to work in zero-g, yes.'

'Incredible! I had no idea there were still species doing that. Not within the hull, at least!'

'Tamsin worked there, until some years back,' Isabel said, knowing her colleague knew her wife's name even though they hadn't properly met yet. 'I'm sure she'd be happy to talk to you about it.'

'Oh! Yes. Yes, that would be marvellous.' Ghuh'loloan scribbled furiously. 'Please, please, go on.'

'At the aft end of the cylinder – as much as anything can be aft in space – we have the engines. They're . . . they're engines.' She shrugged and laughed. 'Not my area of expertise.'

'And they don't get much use anymore.'

'We use them to correct orbital issues, but no, nothing like they did back in our wandering days. Now, the ring – that I can talk on for days.' She directed the pixels into shapes she walked through every day. 'Six hexagons, each joined to another around the main cylinder.'

'And this used to spin, before artigrav.'

'Right. It was a big centrifuge.'

'Was that not unpleasant?'

Isabel shrugged. 'I don't know. I've only ever lived in artigrav. I'm sure there's an account of how centrifugal gravity felt.' She made a mental note to go searching for that.

Ghuh'loloan made a note as well, on her scrib. 'So, six hexagons comprise the ring.'

'Six hexagons. And within those, you find more hexagons. Let's start small and work our way up.' She thought for a moment. 'Ah, I have just the thing.' She accessed an animated image file intended for young kids. A lone hexagon appeared. 'Okay, so we start with a single room. A bedroom, let's say.' She gestured. The hexagon shrank, and was joined by six others, creating a mathematical flower. 'Six rooms, surrounding a seventh room. This is a home.' The geometry expanded again. 'Now you have six homes, surrounding a common area. We call this, predictably, a hex. You'll hear this term a lot. Somebody's hex is their primary address.' Another expansion. 'Six hexes surround a hub. This forms a neighbourhood.'

'And in a hub, you will find . . . ?'

'Everyday services. Grocery stands, a medical clinic, tech swaps, cafes, playgrounds, that kind of thing.' She gestured again. 'All right, here's where it starts to get big. Six neighbourhoods to a district. The space in the centre is the plaza. The amenities here vary from district to district, but in general, this is where you find your big stuff: schools, recycling centres, entertainment, long-term medical facilities, council offices, marketplaces, big gardens.'

'We are in a plaza now, yes?'

'Yes. And from there . . .' The image blossomed into one final shape – six triangles comprised of six districts each, arranged around a final colossal hexagon. 'So, all of this' – she circled it with her hands – 'is a deck.' The middle area is the nucleus. That's where you get farms and manufacturing. At the centre of everything is, well, the Centre.'

'Where you dispose of your dead.'

'I . . .' Isabel chose her words carefully, knowing her colleague hadn't meant any offence. 'I'm not sure we'd use the word "dispose", but yes.'

'And then above and below the residential deck, you have . . . ?'

'Directly above, the transport deck, where you can hop from district to district in a pod. Below, waste processing. And below *that*, observation.'

'Yes, I'm very excited to see your viewing cupolas. I don't know of any other ship architecture quite like that. Most have windows on walls, not the floor.'

'That goes right back to the need to prevent fighting over living space. If some people have rooms with a view and others don't, you're going to have problems. And if centrifugal gravity is pulling our feet toward the stars, then you *can't* have windows on most walls. The only people who could would be the ones with homes on the edges of each deck, and that . . . well, that would invite trouble.'

'Ahhhhh. Yes, I see. I see.' Ghuh'loloan's eyestalks traced over her notes. 'Six homes to a hex, six hexes to a neighbourhood, six neighbourhoods to a district, thirty-six districts to a deck, four decks to a . . . ?

'Segment.'

'A *segment*. And six segments to a homesteader.'

'You've got it.'

The Harmagian studied the children's images again. 'It's rather beautiful, in a way. Nothing wasted, nothing frivolous. Simple exponents.'

Isabel smiled. 'It's like a . . . oh dear, I only know the word in Ensk.' She shifted linguistic gears. '*Honeycomb*.'

Ghuh'loloan flicked her mouth tendrils. 'I don't know that word. My Ensk is poor enough that I'd call it non-existent.'

Isabel gestured at her scrib and accessed another image file. '*Honeycomb*. It's a structure made of interlocking hexagons. Incredibly strong and space-efficient.'

'Ahhhh. I've seen configurations like this, but I don't know that there is an easy word for them in Klip. Or Hanto, for that matter. *Honeycomb*.' She stretched her face forward toward the image. 'Wait, is this . . . organic? What is this?'

'A relic from Earth. A communal insect species built nests with walls of this shape out of . . . spit, I think. I don't know off-hand.'

'How strange. Well, I am looking forward to seeing your own *honeycomb* nest.' Her tendrils changed, taking on a slight slackness. 'Will my presence be intrusive for the families there? I am not overly familiar with Human social custom when it comes to the home.'

'They know you're coming, so it won't be any trouble. In fact, I was hoping you'd join me for a meal at my home tonight. I had originally thought of taking you to a restaurant, but—'

'Bah, restaurants! At some point, yes, I would enjoy that, but on my first day here, I would much rather be *your* guest than someone else's.'

Isabel took serious note of that term – *guest*. She'd done research on that front before Ghuh'loloan's arrival, spurred by a slight shift in her colleague's letters. Once arrangements for the visit to the Fleet had been made, Isabel found herself no longer being addressed as *dear associate* but *dear host*, and Ghuh'loloan's phrasing had become deferential. This was an important thing, Isabel had learned, as was the entire concept of *hosts* and *guests* in Harmagian culture. By anybody's definition, hosts were expected to be accommodating and guests to be gracious, but Harmagians put considerable stock into everyone performing those roles well. A bad host would be shunned – or, as the rules extended to merchants as well, bankrupt – and a bad guest was on par with a petty thief (which made an odd sense, Isabel decided: guests did eat your food and take your time). There were entire books written on host/guest etiquette, the most seminal of which – *Rules for Guests of Good Lineage* – had been the go-to for over a hundred standards. Isabel had skimmed a few opening paragraphs and left the rest of the tedious tome unread. Using her own alienness as a social buffer, she figured her Good Host status was assured by providing a non-poisonous meal on clean plates in friendly company.

She hoped so, anyway.

TESSA

Tessa approached the playground, a box of piping hot cricket crunch in hand. 'Aya!' she called. No heads turned on the swings, nobody paused on the obstacle course. She looked over to the scrap heap, where a pack of youngsters were hauling otherwise-unusable sheets of fatigued metal – edges sanded smooth, of course – in an attempt to assemble . . . something. A shelter, maybe? In any case, her daughter wasn't there, either. 'Hey, Rafee,' she said to a kid running toward the construction project with a bucket of pixel paint.

The boy stopped. 'Hey, M Santoso,' he said, glancing at his comrades. This crew was on a tight schedule.

'You seen Aya around?'

He turned and pointed. 'I saw her in the tank,' he said before running off, hauling his cargo two-handed in front of his chest.

Tessa made her way to the small plex dome. Inside, about a dozen or so kids of varying ages enjoyed the freedom of disabled artigrav nets. The tank was, in concept, intended as a place where kids could learn how to do tasks in zero-g. There was a panel on the wall covered with buttons, knobs, and blocks that needed to be placed in similarly shaped holes. A tiny girl was attentively working on the block problem. A slightly older boy was running at break-neck speed over the tank's inner walls with a pair of cling boots, looping upside down and sideways and backwards, over and over and over. The rest of the kids were engaged in a classic – the only thing you really used the tank for – seeing who could kick off the wall and do the most flips in a row. Tessa's personal best had been four.

She watched as a familiar head of choppy black hair launched forward, curled inward, and flipped, flipped, flipped. Tessa counted. *One. Two. Three. Four.* She grinned. *Five.*

That's my kid.

Tessa stepped forward and knocked on the plex. Aya displayed the surprise all kids did when they saw an adult outside their expected context. Teachers lived in schools, doctors lived in clinics, parents could be found at work or home. *Why are you here?* Aya's expression said. It wasn't an accusation, just genuine enquiry.

Tessa held up the box of cricket crunch and gave it a tempting shake. She couldn't hear the kids behind the plex, but Aya's mouth formed the words: 'What? *Yes!*'

With a quickness Tessa could barely remember having, Aya made her way to the tank exit, grabbing soft support poles to pull herself along. She worked her way down to the floor, then stepped out the airlock, tripping over herself as gravity took hold again. Tessa had never gotten the hang of that, either.

Aya fetched her shoes from a nearby cubby, slipped her socked feet inside, and began to tie them with dogged concentration. As she did, Tessa watched unsurprised as the cling boot kid paused in his circuit and casually threw up. The other kids' faces contorted in laughter, disgust, and unheard shouts. A cleanerbot undocked itself from an upper corner, its gentle boosters propelling it through the air toward the floating mess. Tessa rapped on the plex again. 'You okay?' she called to the kid, mouthing the words as clearly as possible.

The kid gave a weak nod, holding the sides of his head.

Tessa flashed him a thumbs-up. They'd all been there.

Aya ran over as soon as the shoe-tying was complete. She put out both hands with a broad smile, her twin rows of teeth checkered with empty spaces. 'Yes, please.'

Tessa gave her the box. 'Careful, it's hot.'

Aya tucked into the sugar-fried bugs without hesitation. Tessa caught a wince as her daughter burned her tongue. Neither commented on it.

'Come on, it's our family's night to cook,' Tessa said. They began to walk together.

'I know,' Aya said. She frowned. 'I'm not late, right?'

'No, you're not late.'

'Then how come you came to get me?' She looked at the snack box in her hands, the realisation dawning that she'd been given a sweet treat *before* dinner. 'How come I get cricket crunch?'

'Just 'cause,' Tessa said. 'I guess I'm feeling sentimental.'

Aya tucked a mouthful into her cheek. 'What's sentimental?'

'It's . . . caught up in your feelings. The way you feel when you're thinking a lot about the people or things you care about.'

Tessa had stopped looking at her daughter, but she could feel her staring back. 'You've been weird today,' Aya said.

Tessa didn't want to have the conversation, and she knew there were parts she'd have to tread extra carefully around for Aya's sake. But Pop would bring it up the second they were home, so: 'You're right, I have been. I'm sorry. Something happened you should know about. Everything's okay. That's the first thing you should know.'

Aya listened intently, still chewing.

'You know how Uncle Ashby went to build a new tunnel?'

'Yeah.'

'Well, there were some sapients there who weren't very nice' – she wasn't sure Aya was ready for *Ashby was on the business end of the first shot in what looks like a territory war* – 'and they damaged his ship.'

Aya's face went rigid. 'Are the bulkheads okay?'

Tessa put her hand on Aya's shoulder. She knew why the question was being asked. Despite counselling, despite patience, despite everybody's best efforts and five more years of growing up, Aya still crumbled at the idea of any breach between *in here* and *out there*. She remained uncomfortable around airlocks, she avoided cupolas as if they were on fire, and *bulkheads* were a matter she fixated on to a concerning degree. 'His ship's stable,' Tessa said. 'He wrote to me this morning, and he's okay. There are a lot of repairs to do, but everyone is safe.'

Aya processed that. 'Is he coming here?'

'Why would he come here?'

'For repairs.'

'There are plenty of spaceports he can do that in. But you should know, before we get home, your grandpa's pretty shook up.'

'How come?'

'Because Ashby's his kid, and parents can't help but worry about their kids.' She tousled Aya's hair. 'So be extra nice to Grandpa tonight, okay?'

'Did they use a gun on Ashby's ship?'

Guns were another subject of fixation – an exotic, abstract danger Aya knew of from sims and news feeds and whatever kids talked about among themselves. 'Yes,' Tessa said.

'What kind?'

'I don't know.'

Aya crunched and crunched. 'Was it Aeluons?'

Tessa blinked. 'Was what Aeluons?'

'The aliens who broke his ship.'

'No. Why would it be Aeluons?'

Crunch crunch crunch. 'They have the biggest guns and go to war all the time.'

'That's—' Tessa struggled to unpack that technically accurate statement. 'The Aeluons have a big military, that's true. But they're our friends. They've done a lot of good things for us in the Fleet, and they wouldn't hurt Ashby.'

'Have you ever met one?'

'An Aeluon? Yes. I've done work with a few Aeluon merchants, a long time ago. They were all very nice. Well, except one. You gotta remember, baby, other sapients are people just like us. There are good people and bad people and everything in between.'

Crunch crunch. 'Then who shot at Uncle Ashby?'

'A species called the Toremi.'

'What do they look like?'

'I don't actually know. I don't know much about them. We can look it up on the Linkings when we get home.'

'Have you met one?'

'No. How could I have met one if I don't know what they look like?'

'Why were they mad at Uncle Ashby?'

'I don't know. I don't think it was about *him*, just the GC in general.'

'Why—'

'I don't know, honey. Sometimes . . . sometimes bad things just happen.'

The crunching had stopped. 'Will they come here?'

'No,' Tessa said with a firm voice and a reassuring smile. 'They're very far away. The Fleet's a safe place. It's one of the safest places you can be.'

Aya said nothing. Her mother was sure she was thinking of bulkheads and damaged hulls.

SAWYER

Everybody had a home, and nobody went hungry.

That was one of the foundational ideas that had first drawn Sawyer in when he'd started reading about the Fleet. Everybody had a home, and nobody went hungry. There was a practical necessity in that, he knew. A ship full of people fighting over food and space wouldn't last long. But there was compassion, too, a commitment to basic decency. Too many people back on Earth *had* been hungry and cold. It was one of the copious problems the first Exodans had vowed not to take with them.

Sawyer stood in a home now – one of the empties left behind by a family that had gone planetside, now opened to travellers like himself. The grass was always greener, he supposed, but he couldn't understand why anyone would travel in the opposite direction he had. Colonies had hungry people. They had people without homes. He'd seen both plenty of times back in Central space – sapients picking through trash or carrying everything they owned. The GC tried, they really did, but planets were big and settlements were vast and taking care of everyone was hard. Things were better in sovereign territories, but in neutral colonies like Mushtullo, where trade was the primary drive and nobody could agree on whose rules they should follow . . . well, it was easy for people to fall through the cracks. Sawyer had been mugged twice in the past standard, once by some messed-up woman with a badly installed headjack, then again by someone he never even saw. Just a pistol in his back and a hand he couldn't identify twisting his arm around to scan his patch and drain his credits. The bank got the creds back, but that wasn't the point. Someone had been willing to kill for the sake of . . . what? Some new clothes? A few tendays of groceries? That had been the last straw for Sawyer. That had been the moment he decided he was leaving.

He set his bag on the floor and looked around. An entry-and-storage room, a common room, a bathing room, and four more bedrooms, all the same size and shape as the others, all window-less, all spread out around the circular hatch that led down to the family cupola. The home was tidy and filled with basic furniture, all signs of previous ownership erased by cleanerbots. There were tables and chairs, a couple of couches. Cupboards for food and belongings. Empty planters waiting for seedlings and a guiding hand. It looked like a package home, like something that popped out of a box. There was no sign that anyone else had ever lived there – except one. Sawyer walked with reverence toward the wall in the common room, the one the cleanerbots had known to leave alone. It was covered with handprints, pressed in paint of every colour. Big handprints, little handprints, smudged infant feet. *Belkin,* someone had painted above it – the name of the first family that had lived here, and the name that every other family who lived there after had taken, regardless of genetics. This was one of the many Exodan customs he admired. When born, you took your parents' name. When you grew up and started a family of your own, you took the name of the home you settled in. In a lot of cases, your name didn't change at all, not if you kept living with your parents and grandparents and so on. If you settled in the home of your partner, you took your partner's family name. If you both decided to live in a separate home entirely, apart from both of your families, you'd both get the name of whoever'd taken care of that home before you. Sawyer liked that.

He looked up at the bold, painted letters above his head. He wasn't a Belkin. It wasn't his custom yet, and this placement was temporary. He ran his hand along where others had been. 'Wow,' he whispered. He didn't need to count the prints to know that there were at least nine generations represented here, all the way back to the first. He crouched down, looking toward where the wall joined the floor. The prints there were faded, and covered with others, but their shapes were clear as day: six adults, three children, one baby. He tried to imagine what they must have felt, watching their planet fade away through a window in the floor, pressing painted hands to an empty wall with the hope that one day the wall would be full.

Sawyer put his hand over the tiny footprint. That kid had grown up never having known the ground. That kid had grown old and died in this ship, and all xyr kids besides. The enormity of it almost made him dizzy.

He straightened back up and looked around the room. The wall was full, but the home was empty. So empty. It was a space meant to house three generations at least, where kids could run around and adults could relax and everyone would be together. But right then, it held only him. Just him in a big room full of ghosts. There were families outside, in the homes the Belkins had shared a hex with. Sawyer knew the kitchen was for his use as well, and the digestive punishment of Jojo's ninth day special had faded enough for him to be hungry again. But he wasn't sure about going out there. When he'd gone to the housing office, he'd hoped to be put in a home with another family – a spare room, like he'd read about. When he'd gone to the hex number he'd been given, he'd hoped for a big welcome, with shaken hands and big smiles, introductions all around. Granted, he'd gotten his hand shook and a few names and nods, but the smiles had been hit or miss and mostly confused, and everybody seemed too busy for him. There were kids to chase, vegetables to chop. They all looked at him, though, with questioning eyes and words whispered out of earshot. He got it. He was a stranger, the new neighbour, the guy who'd just moved in. They had their own days to get about, and ice-breaking would come soon enough. And truth be told, Sawyer was tired. It had been a long haul, and a long day. One adventure at a time.

He stuck his head in each of the bedrooms, trying to determine a favourite. Each was the same as the last. He settled on the middle-left, and sat on the edge of the bed. The air filter whirred quietly. He could hear a faint rushing in the pipes below the floor, the odd click in the walls. But other than that, nothing. No drunk idiots out on the street, no skiffs zipping past at every hour, no delivery vehicles rumbling along. It was nice. It was odd. It would take getting used to.

His stomach growled. He reached into his bag and pulled out the bean cake he'd bought on his way. He was used to wrappers that crunched and rustled, but even the throw-cloth was silent. He took a bite. It was just a cheap sweet, but his taste buds bloomed with gratitude for something sugary. Take that, pickle bun.

Sawyer sat alone and ate his snack. Okay, so it wasn't the first day he'd imagined, but hey, the sentiment held true. Everybody had a home, and nobody went hungry.

KIP

There was a delicate balance to getting the dishes done fast. Do it too quick, and a parent or a hexmate would make him do it over. Too slow, though, and . . . well, then you were still cleaning dishes. Nobody wanted to be in those shoes.

He picked up a plate from the eternal stack and scraped the food remnants into the compost bucket. Crumbs, flecks, whatever oil and sauce hadn't been soaked up by quickbread. Kinda gross, but he supposed it could be worse. He remembered one time watching this crime-solving vid set on Titan – *Murder on the Silver Sea* – where some characters were at a fancy restaurant having this crazy smart conversation where the investigator and the informant both think the other one's the killer and they were saying it but they're not really *saying* it – and also they kind of wanted to bang each other? That scene had *layers*, seriously – and when the conversation was done, they just . . . left their food. Like, let the server come get it while they walked out of the place. The scene would've made sense if one of them wasn't hungry or had a stomach ache or something, but if that were the case, then the other one would've reached over and eaten the leftovers. But no. *Both of them left*. They left half-plates of food on the table. It was the weirdest shit. He couldn't imagine what cleaning dishes was like in a place like that. Dealing with half-eaten food sounded disgusting.

Scraps bucketed, he picked up the compressed air canister you could find in any kitchen and blasted away everything that wasn't plate. He'd kind of liked that part when he was little. He remembered it being satisfying. But that had been about, oh, eleven

73

billion dishes ago, and blasting away food bits had long since lost its charm. He looked over at Xia, who was helping him that night. She was seven, and hadn't yet realised that getting to do grown-up things like dishes and pruning and floor cleaning was super boring. She stood attentively at his side, waiting for each plate he handed her, placing each one *just so* in the sanitiser. He had to admit, it was kind of cute.

He handed off the blasted dish to Xia, then picked up another dirty one, and scraped, and blasted, and handed off, and started again. Beyond the kitchen counter, everybody else from his hex was sitting in the same spots at the same tables, as they always did, having the same conversations they always had.

'The new algae pumps everybody's using, they're no good,' Grandma Ko said. 'You can feel it on the ferry. Anytime we push past the slow zone, there's this hum that starts up . . .' Grandma Ko – Kip's great-grandma, but that took too long to say – had been a freighter pilot back in the day and thought any tech that had been invented past, like, thirty standards ago was garbage.

'I'm telling you, we're going about the water budget all wrong,' M Nguyen said, on a tear about some political thing like always. 'If the other guilds got together and unanimously pushed for the growers to overhaul the farms, the growers would have to give in, and the council would *have* to fund it. But that'd mean the guilds doing something efficiently together, and we all know *that's* not going to happen.' Seriously, there was nothing more boring than politics.

'Did you see that new planter they've set up over in 612?' M Marino said. Kip took a wild guess that the next sentence would include the word *imports* or *creds*. 'Imported seedlings, all of it.' Bingo. 'They've even got jorujola in there. It's incredible – have you seen it? Those bio-luminescent leaves? But I don't know where they get the creds—' Double bingo.

'I hear Sarah's moved back in with the Zhangs,' M Sousa said in an excited hush to Kip's mom. 'Now, it's none of my business, but this isn't exactly the first time she's had things go south with a partner, and you have to wonder—' Kip's mom gave a nod that didn't really confirm anything, and she threw in an 'mmm' here and there for good measure. Kip knew she didn't care, and she didn't even like M Sousa much, but she pretended to, because that's how hexes worked.

'That reminds me of the time me and Buster let a whole tank of hoppers out,' laughed Kip's dad, talking to the Mullers. 'Have I told you this one before?' Stars, Dad. Yes, everybody had heard this one before. Everybody had heard this story twelve thousand times.

Kip thought about Solan restaurants, where people talked about murder and sex and left dishes full of food for someone else to deal with. He thought about the university exams looming on the horizon. He thought about his score on the last practice exam. Ras had told him it was no worries, that he'd do better next time. But Kip knew what was what. He was going to fail, and he'd live here in the same hex forever, cleaning dishes and listening to his dad tell the same jokes over and over until one of them died.

Stars, he was stuck. He was so, so stuck.

Kip scraped and blasted faster now, knowing he'd left bits less than clean but hoping the heat of the sanitiser would burn away the evidence.

'You missed some,' Xia said, holding up the dish she'd been handed, pointing at a swatch of oily crumbs.

Kip sighed and took the plate back. 'Guess I did,' he said, giving the plate another scrape. How come lunch breaks never lasted this long?

At last, at fucking last, the stack of dishes ended. Xia looked satisfied; Kip was relieved. They both washed their hands. As they did so, a few bubbles appeared in the big clear cistern by the herb planters. Kip remembered one time when he was really little letting the water run and run because he liked the bubbles so much. His mom had given him a strong talking-to for that.

He looked at Xia, counting the seconds under her breath as she washed up, hurriedly turning off the faucet once she hit *fifteen.* Looked like somebody'd given her the same talking-to.

Kip started to head for home, but his mom stopped him, dead interrupting M Sousa. 'Kip?' she called, leaning away from the table. 'Did you empty the bucket?'

Kip shut his eyes. 'No.'

'Well?'

Kip sighed again, trudged back to the kitchen, picked up the forgotten bucket of crumbs and bug husks and veggie stems, lugged it to the garden, and dumped it into the hot box. He could feel Mom watching him the whole way.

'I don't understand why he can't come sit with us,' he heard Dad mumble. Dad never mumbled as quiet as he thought.

'He will when he wants to,' Mom said.

Kip did not want to. He wanted to go home, so he did just that. The front door slid closed behind him, and he exhaled. He kicked off his shoes and headed to his room, letting that door close behind him, too. A double barrier. He flopped down on his bed and shut his eyes. *Finally.*

He heard the sound of his scrib dinging, muffled under . . . something. He sat up and looked around his bed. Nothing. He rolled over, found his satchel on the floor, and dug around. Nothing. He rolled over the other way. There it was – on the floor, sticking out from the jacket he'd been wearing earlier. He picked it up, and found a blinking alert from Ras.

Ras (17:20): do you have any tethering cable

Kip (18:68): uh no

Kip (18:68): why

Ras (18:69): I have something really cool for us to do

Kip (18:70): what

Ras (18:70): it's a surprise

Kip (18:70): what kind of surprise

Ras (18:71): a tech project

Ras (18:71): trust me, it's going to be awesome

Ras (18:71): I can get the parts in a few tendays

Ras (18:72): so long as you're not studying

This was code. Kip's parents didn't read his scrib, as far as he knew, but Ras' had once, and they'd found out he and Rosie Lee snuck a couple bottles of kick out of Bay Twelve and got shit-faced together, and it had been a ridiculous mess. Like, completely ballistic. So now, if there was something Ras wanted to talk about but didn't want to put in writing, he said 'so long as you're not studying' instead of 'it's a secret, I'll tell you in person.' Studying was the perfect cover for anything. What was that if not respon-sible? What parent would read that and worry?

Okay, maybe Ras' parents. Ras never studied.

EYAS

Hopping between homesteaders was a beautiful thing. She'd taken the ferry more times in her life than she could count, and yet every time, she looked forward to those twenty minutes or so spent in transit. She could view the space outside anytime she pleased from a cupola, but it was easy to lose track of the fact that reality did not end with a bulkhead, that the starry black outside was not just a pretty picture framed below your feet. It was in passing beyond the hull, in travelling through the gap, that she was reminded of the true scope of things. The view out the window beside her passenger seat was a busy one (the window *beside her*, that was important – the confirmation that space existed not just below but *above* and *beside*). She could see public ferries, family shuttles, cargo ships, mail drones, nav markers, harvesting satellites. There were spacewalkers, out doing repairs or for the sheer joy of it, separated from the ship lanes by rows of self-correcting buoys. Behind it all was their adoptive sun, Risheth – a white sphere that deceptively looked to be about the size of a melon, shining softly through the ferry's filtered windows, scattering light among the dense plane of floating rock that gravity would gather up in time. No planets to speak of, though. Risheth didn't have any orbital bodies big enough to build on (hence why the Aandrisks hadn't felt much loss in shrugging off their claim to the system). Eyas had been planetside twice in her life, both times on short vacations, both times wonderful, yet nothing she needed to repeat. Planets were imposing. Impressive. Intimidating. Eyas preferred the open. It was easier for her to wrap her brain around. Even though it was dangerous. Even though she'd seen it at its worst. But that wasn't something she needed to dwell on right then. No point in spoiling the view.

The ferry docked at the *Ratri*, and Eyas took her place in the exiting shuffle. Most people had made the trip for trade or friendly visits, and carried goods or luggage accordingly. Eyas was there for neither, and so carried neither. She had only a satchel of personal effects and the clothes on her back – the latter of which she wouldn't need for long.

Eyas hadn't had sex on her home ship since her thirtieth birthday, two standards prior. It had been even longer since she'd done so with anyone who wasn't a professional. The combination of those decisions was the best thing she'd ever done for herself (well, second maybe to moving out of her mother's home and in with friends). People got weird around caretakers. That was part and parcel of the job, and she'd long been accustomed to it. But it did get in the way of relationships, especially the kind where clothing was optional. Whenever she told a potential partner what she spent her days doing, the reaction was either one of stumbling deference – which invariably led to the exhausting business of guiding them to the conclusion that she was just an ordinary person who wanted an honest, uncomplicated hookup – or discomfort, which shut the whole thing down. Her choices were then either her peers – and yes, the caretaking profession was pretty incestuous that way, but she didn't have any workmates she thought of in those terms – or the tryst clubs. She'd learned that her use of the latter benefited from a bit of distance. The last time she'd visited a club on her own homesteader, the host whose room she'd been sent to had been one of the family members present at a laying-in she'd conducted the tenday prior. He'd realised who she was before they'd gotten much of anywhere, and she'd spent the next two hours helping him tearfully talk through the death of his uncle. Not an activity she minded, but definitely not the one she'd been after. Since then, she visited clubs off-ship, where nobody knew her face or what she spent her days doing, and nobody would start crying when she took her pants off (she knew the crying hadn't been in response to her lack of pants, but still).

She took the exit ramp to the dockway, the dockway to the transport deck, and the transport deck to the plaza, which led her, at last, to the club. All clubs had fanciful names – Daydream, Top to Bottom, the Escape Hatch. The establishment she entered now was called the White Door; she'd never been to this one before (she was pleased to note the door matched the name). She left the dimming artificial light of the plaza for a very different kind of illumination: dim, yes, but with a welcoming warmth as opposed to a sleepy absence. The decor was classy and simple, like the others. She'd noticed supposedly similar establishments on her one teenage trip to Mars, but she hadn't been able to get past their appearance: windowless shop fronts that popped up around bars and shuttledocks, painted slippery red and emblazoned with disembodied mouths and muscles. She had a hard time imagining anybody finding such a place appealing, let alone *paying creds* for it. Creds weren't part of the exchange in the tryst clubs, nor was barter. They provided a service, not goods, and their hosts fell into the same broad vocational category she did: *Health and Wellness*. The clubs were an old tradition, a part of the Fleet practically since launch, one of many ways to keep everybody sane during a lifelong voyage. Hosts took that tradition seriously, as seriously as Eyas did her own. Plus, they were often some of the loveliest folks she'd ever met. It went without saying that to work in a club, you had to *really* like people.

The hallway opened into a large lounge, filled with flowering vines, hovering globulbs, and comfortable furniture. A welcome desk stood at the entrance, staffed by a friendly-looking woman with ornately braided, electric blue hair. Eyas approached the desk, feeling a crackle against her skin as she passed through the privacy shield that blocked any conversation from those outside its radius. One of the many touches Eyas appreciated.

'Welcome,' the woman said with a kind smile. 'I haven't seen you here before, have I?'

'No,' Eyas said. 'I'm from the *Asteria*.'

'Oh, well then, doubly welcome, neighbour!' She gestured at the discreetly shielded pixel projector in front of her. 'You'll be in your ship's system, then?' The woman nodded toward the patch scanner bolted to the edge of the desk. 'Do the thing, and I'll get your info transferred over. Just needed a change of pace?'

Eyas swiped her wrist. 'Yes.'

'I hear that,' the woman said as she assessed the new pixels conjured up by Eyas' patch. Some of the information there Eyas had submitted herself – what she liked, what she didn't, that kind of thing – but she imagined there was more in her file than that. Health records, probably. Maybe some kind of note that she'd always followed the rules. 'All right. Are you looking to take a chance, or for a sure thing?' This was the option always given at the entrance. Were you interested in meeting a fellow visiting stranger and seeing where the night took you, or . . .

'The latter,' Eyas said. Not that it was a *sure thing*. The host could decline service, for any reason, and she could leave at any time. Neither party was pressured to do anything, and mutual comfort was paramount. But being matched with another walk-in would've defeated the entire purpose of her being there.

A polite nod, a bit of gesturing. 'Are you interested in a single partner, or multiples?'

'Single.'

'Any changes to your usual preferences?'

'No.'

'And how long of a visit would you like? Overnight, a few hours . . . ?'

'I'll take a half night.' Long enough to make the trip worth it, but with plenty of time to get back home and sleep in her own bed. And that, right there, in addition to everything else she'd been asked, was why the *sure thing* was the better option by far. She saw so many similarities between this kind of work and her own, polar opposites of the life experiences spectrum though they were. She, too, had strangers' bodies placed in her care. They couldn't speak, but they'd been assured their whole lives that when the time came, they'd be treated with gentleness and respect. Nobody would find them odd or ugly. Nobody would do anything unkind. They'd be handled by someone who understood what a body was, how important, how singular. Eyas undressed those bodies. She washed them. She saw their flaws, their folds, the spots they kept hidden. For the short time they had together, she gave them the whole of her training, the whole of her self. It was an intimate thing, preparing a body. An intimacy matched only by one other. So when she placed her own body in someone else's hands, she wanted to know that her respect would be matched. You couldn't make guarantees like that with a stranger at a bar. You couldn't know from a bit of conversation and a drink or two whether they understood in their heart of hearts that bodies should always be left in a better way than when you found them. With a professional, you could. And you'd know, too, that their imubots were up to date, that the kind of sex that could lead to pregnancy carried no such risk, that there wouldn't be any dancing around whether or not to stay the night or see each other again or if it *meant* something. Of course it always meant something. But you couldn't know if that something was the same. In Eyas' opinion, going to a club was the safest way to have sex, both physically and emotionally. The alternative was a minefield.

The pixels behind the counter filtered themselves as the blue-haired woman entered Eyas' answers. 'Okay,' she said. 'I've got eight guys free this evening who fit the bill. Would you like to go through the list, or—'

Eyas realised, in that moment, that she didn't want to make any more decisions. She hadn't thought about it when she'd headed out for the *Ratri*, but she was *tired*, tired in a quiet way that had become an everyday thing for reasons she couldn't point to. The tenday hadn't been bad, but it had been long, and she'd grown weary of decisions. 'Surprise me,' she said. She paused in thought. 'Whoever you think the nicest of them is.'

'Ha! You're going to get me in trouble.' The woman tapped her lips, then made a definitive gesture at the pixels. 'All right, you'll be in room fourteen. Your host will be there in about twenty minutes. You're welcome to wait in there, or you can relax in the lounge. If you feel the need to clean up, there are showers to the right of the bar. You're welcome to go there with your host as well. If you don't go straight to your room, we'll call you when it's time.' She gave Eyas an amused smile. 'And do *not* tell him how I picked him, or I will never hear the end of it.' Eyas thanked her, and walked on through. The lounge was inviting, and the aforementioned bar was laden with colourful bottles of kick, a menu of snacks, and short, clear jars displaying varieties of redreed and smash. Another time, she would've treated herself to something spicy to snack on and something sweet to drink. She would've chatted with the bartender, contemplated the clientele (which, as always, was as varied as varied could be), maybe played a round of flash with someone else waiting their turn. But Eyas looked at the crowd, and all she wanted was to be behind a door.

She found room fourteen, waved her wristwrap over the lock, and entered. Just the sight of the room felt like she'd taken a sip of water after several hours without. Everything looked soft – the bed, the couch, even the table, somehow. There was a thumpbox for music, a chill box for drinks, a storage compartment full of other things the host could introduce if desired. All clean, all inviting. All for her.

She sat down on the couch, closed her eyes, and let twenty minutes slip by. She barely felt them.

There was a soft chime at the door before it opened. A man entered, carrying a bottle of something amber brown. He was tall, but not too tall. Fit, but not too fit. His hair was thick and his eyes were kind. 'Hey,' he said. 'I'm Sunny.'

Of course you are, Eyas thought. 'I'm Eyas.'

'Eyas,' he repeated, the door closing behind him. 'I haven't heard that one before.'

Her mouth gave a scrunch as it prepared to offer an explanation given a million times. 'It's an old word for a hawk.'

Sunny leaned against the bedframe. 'What's a hawk?'

'Earthen bird. Bird of prey, apparently. Very striking, very fast. My mother' – she tried to find a tactful way to explain the most incongruous person in her life – 'she's a romantic.'

'Clearly. That's a poetic name.'

'Yes. Granted, she didn't dig deep enough into the language files to figure out that an eyas is a *baby* hawk, not a hawk hawk. So, I'm a scruffy baby bird that hasn't learned to fly. Not the best sentiment to carry around as an adult.'

Sunny laughed. 'You're not the only one with a name like that. I know a guy named Walrus.'

'I don't know what that is.'

'You know what a wolf is?'

Eyas thought back to school trips to the Archives. 'It's a . . . oh, I know this.' She frowned, rifling through neurons that hadn't been needed in a while. 'Some kind of carnivore, right? Or am I thinking of something else?'

'No, you're right. Like a wild dog. Beautiful, powerful, all that good stuff. That's what his parents were going for. Only, they got mixed up and didn't double-check, and went with Walrus.'

'And what's a walrus?'

Sunny raised a finger and pulled his scrib from his belt holster. He gestured at the screen, then turned it her way. The Archives helpfully displayed his friend's namesake – a sack-like water beast with ludicrous tusks and unfortunate whiskers.

Eyas laughed. 'Okay, that's worse than mine.'

The host chuckled as he set his scrib on the table. 'Hey, if it's any consolation, I don't like my given name, either.'

'You mean it's not Sunny?' Eyas said with a smirk.

The host winked. 'So, I heard you've had a long day.'

Eyas raised her eyebrows. 'Did you?'

'That was Iana's guess, at least. Did she get that wrong?'

Assuming Iana was the blue-haired woman, Eyas mentally gave her a few points for perception. 'No. It has been a long day.'

Sunny held up the bottle. 'Do you like sintalin?'

'I've never had it.' She considered the name. 'Aeluon?'

'Laru. It's . . . well, it's what I pour myself on long days.' He picked up two glasses, asking her a silent question. She nodded. He poured.

Eyas examined the glass placed in her hand. The liquid within had a caramel warmth, and the colour got darker and darker the deeper the glass went. It smelled unlike anything she'd ever had. A good smell, at least. A rich, spiced smell. She took a sip, and shut her eyes. 'Wow.'

'It's something, right?' Sunny sat next to her on the couch – close, but not too close. Close as good friends might sit, and just as easy. He took a sip from his own glass.

'That's . . . wow.' She laughed.

'I've got a friend who's a cargo runner, makes a lot of stops in Laru space. She always brings me a case of this when she's back home.'

'This isn't from the bar?'

'Nah, this is my stash.'

Another point to Iana. It was entirely possible Sunny pulled this bit with everybody who came to room fourteen, but even if it was fiction, it was very nice.

Sunny looked at her seriously. 'Eyas, I'm here to give you a good night, and that can be whatever you need it to be. If you need to just talk, have some drinks, chill out – that's fine. I'm happy with that.'

Eyas was sure he'd said those words before, but she also got the sense that he meant them. She studied his face. His lips looked soft. His beard was perfect, almost annoyingly so. 'No,' she said. She put her hand on his chest. She set her glass down, ran her palm up his throat, over his neck, into his hair. Stars, it felt good in her fingers. 'If it's okay by you,' she said, as his hand greeted her thigh, 'I'd rather not talk much at all.'

ISABEL

Dinner had been chaos, as per usual, and at one time in Isabel's life, this would have aggravated her. She would've wanted to put on a good face for an academic guest, particularly an alien one. But Isabel loved the nightly feeding frenzy, and at this point, she wouldn't have wanted it any other way. They hadn't done anything special, not even shifted the cooking order. Ninth day was her cousin's family's night to cook, and cook they did (albeit with some quiet instruction from Isabel, who'd sent them a list of common ingredients Harmagians could not digest – heavy salt being the trickiest one). There had been kids running around everywhere, a misunderstanding about how gravy worked (namely: not as a drink), a broken dish, a few translation errors, a bombardment of questions in both directions, and three dozen people tripping over themselves to look good in front of a fancy visitor. It was real. It was honest. It was so very Exodan.

Her hex was quiet now. Ghuh'loloan had departed for her guest quarters – not for sleep, as her species did not have that need, but to take comfort in a space designed for Harmagian merchants and diplomats, rather than incompatible Human physiology. The kids, in contrast, were (mostly) sleeping, and the grown-ups had retreated to the sanctuary of their homes. It was always such a sharp change, the switch between daytime and night-time. Not that the view outside changed. But the lights did, and the clocks did, and as much as Isabel seized upon the bright energy of the bustling hours, she always cherished restful dark.

She made her way through the courtyard, a mug of tea in each hand as she passed through her well-worn environment. In structure, every hex was the same, but once you got past the standard kitchen-garden-cistern setup, the hex was whatever you made of it. Isabel and her neighbours liked plants and they liked kids, so their shared space was a haven for both. They had an herb garden, where her wife's parents and *their* neighbours had grown vegetables once. The current eldest generation was content to leave farming to farmers, though there was a patch of climbing beans studiously tended by her grand-nephew Ollie, age six. He was much more at ease tending his tiny crop and whispering secret stories to his toys than joining in with the rest of the roaring, shrieking, giggling pack. Whenever his harvest was ready, he went from home to home, hand-delivering bundles tied with bits of string – usually no more than ten beans in a bunch. Isabel always treated this occasion with the same seriousness he did. She would unwrap each bundle, snap a bean between her teeth, chew thoughtfully, and after a moment of consideration, inform Ollie that this was, without a doubt, his best batch yet. This was not always true, but what kind of monster would say otherwise?

Aside from the herbs and Ollie's bean farm, the other greenery in the hex was decorative, from the blankets of vines encasing the walkways, to the orderly flower pots arranged around front doors. Isabel never had time for gardening, but Tamsin's brother did enough of that for everyone. That was the best thing about having hexmates. Everybody had tasks they were good at and ones they weren't, chores they didn't mind and chores they loathed. More often than not, it balanced out. Everybody pitched in, leaving plenty of time for rest and play. Humans were, after all, a social species – even the quiet Ollies, or the thoughtful, shy types that gravitated toward work in the Archives. There was a difference between being shy and being sequestered. Rarely in history had things turned out well for people who chose to lock themselves away.

Beyond the plants was the workshop – a three-sided area framed by workbenches and filled with larger shared tools. Isabel knew without asking that she'd find Tamsin there. She was seated in the back corner, at ease in the big soft chair their hexmates had jointly given her for her birthday. The years had been hard on Tamsin's body, and workstools didn't suit her like they used to. She'd been a zero-g mech tech once – life support maintenance, specifically – and like so many of her profession, the cumulative decades spent in a different realm of physics had played hell with her skeleton. She walked with a cane now, and had left her previous career to younger bones. Her days were now spent leading classes at the neighbourhood tech shop, where she taught basic everyday systems repair, or at home, where she'd make metal art or fix too-loved toys – anything that kept her hands occupied. Like Isabel, she was happiest when busy. It was why they'd hit it off so well, over fifty years before.

'What've you got there?' Isabel asked, entering the inner sanctum.

Tamsin had a box of fabric at her feet and a sewing kit perched on the closest shelf. She held up a small pair of trousers. 'Sasha wore the knees out.'

'Again?'

'Again.' Tamsin picked up her needle and resumed patching. 'She's an active kid.'

There was no argument there – of their five grandkids, Sasha was the biggest handful, always bruised or bleeding or stuck in a storage cabinet somewhere. *Menace* wasn't the right word for her. She was too agreeable for that. *Scamp*. That fit the bill. Sasha was an absolute scamp, and though Tamsin showered all the grandkids and hex kids with equal amounts of teasing and candy, Isabel knew she had a special soft spot for the little cabinet explorer. Tamsin had never said so, but she didn't need to. Isabel knew.

She set Tamsin's mug of tea within easy reach, pulled up a workstool facing her, and sat. 'You should've made Benjy do it. He's started stitching, he could use the practice.'

'Yeah, but then she'd be running around with lame practise

patches.' Tamsin spoke, as always, flat and factual, the kind of voice that hid its owner's perpetual good humour beneath a dry disguise. 'You get patched-up duds from *me*, you're gonna look real cool.'

Isabel laughed into her tea. 'So, tonight went well.'

'It did.'

Tamsin said the words in a neutral tone, but there was a line between her eyes that made Isabel ask: 'But?'

'No buts. Tonight went well.'

'*But?*'

Tamsin rolled her eyes. 'Why are you pushing?'

'Because I can tell.'

'You can tell *what?*'

Isabel poked the spot in question. 'You've got that crease.'

'Oh, stars, you and your magical crease. I don't have a crease.'

'Yes, you do. You're not the one who looks at you every day.'

Tamsin squinted at Isabel as she knotted a thread. 'And what does the magical crease tell you?'

'That there's something you want to say.'

'If I wanted to say something, I would've said it.'

'Something that you're *not* saying, then.'

'You're such a pain,' Tamsin sighed. 'It just . . . felt kind of . . . I don't know. I don't know what I'm saying. It was fine, you're right.'

Isabel sipped her tea, watching, waiting.

Tamsin set down her stitching. 'She's condescending.'

'You thought so?' This came as a genuine surprise.

'Didn't you?'

'No, I—' Isabel replayed the events of the evening as quickly as she could. Ghuh'loloan had been delighted to meet the hex. She'd brought gifts and stories and a wealth of patience. Isabel had thought it a rousing success on both sides of the exchange, right up until now. 'I had a really good time. It felt like we got things off to a great start.'

'See, and that's why I didn't want to say anything. This is your work, your friend. I don't know her like you do, and I don't want to ruin this for you.'

'You're not. This is your home – our home – and if something in it bothers you, you have to say.'

'Can I tell our neighbours to knock off their brewing experiments then? That scrub fuel they cooked up last time was *awful*.'

'Tamsin.'

Tamsin picked up her tea. 'She just came across so . . . so sugary. Everything was *wonderful* and *fascinating* and *incredible*.'

'That's just how Harmagians are. Everything's couched in hyperbole.'

'Yeah, but it makes it hard to trust them, y'know? If *everything* is wonderful and fascinating . . . I mean, everything *can't* be those all the time.'

'But it is to her. This is her . . . her passion. She's curious. She wants to learn about us.'

'I get that, I do. And I don't want this to sound like a bigger deal than it is. It's . . . I just felt like I was on display. Like some kind of exhibit she's visiting.' She shook her head. 'I don't know. I'm probably being unfair.' She paused. 'I know this isn't a nice thing to admit,' she added slowly, 'but it's hard to have her here saying these sugary things, poking our tech, touching our kids, and not remember how it was.'

Isabel didn't need to ask what she meant. She remembered. She remembered being not much older than Sasha and hearing the adults in her hex talking about the growing push for GC membership. She remembered the news feeds, the public forums, the pixel posters with their catchy slogans. She remembered being a little older, when the Fleet and the Martian government were in the thick of smoothing out relations so as to join as a unified species, and everything felt like it was one spark away from a flash fire. She remembered being in her teens and watching the parliamentary hearings, listening to the galaxy's most powerful debate whether her species had merit enough to go from tolerated refugees to equal citizens. She remembered the hopes everybody had pinned on it – Grandpa Teyo, with his medical clinic badly in need of new tech and proper vaccines, Aunt Su, with her merchant crew hungry for new trade routes. Everybody who had ever been to a spaceport and felt like they were a subcategory, a separate queue, an other. And she remembered the Harmagian delegation in those hearings, fully split on the issue of whether Humans were worth the bother, unable to vote in consensus. They hadn't been the only species with objections, but that wasn't the point. Every voice that got up there and spoke against Humanity stung as if the words were being said for the first time.

Isabel laid her hand on her wife's knee. 'That was such a long time ago,' she said. 'So much has changed.'

'I know.'

'Ghuh'loloan wasn't around for any of that. She wasn't even born yet.'

'I know.' Tamsin thought. 'They're born underwater, right?'

'Yes.' Isabel smirked. 'I'm sure she'd be happy to answer your questions about it. Seeing as how you're curious about her species.'

Tamsin stuck out her tongue. 'It's not that I don't understand curiosity. It's that . . . it's like you said. She wasn't even born yet. She missed out on all of that ugliness, and yet we're kind of *quaint* to her, it feels like. Yeah, it was forever ago, but those Harmagians who said those things are still around, right? They had kids, and those kids would've learned—'

'They don't raise kids like we do.'

'Well, *somebody's* raising them, right? Somebody's teaching them, somebody's telling them how the galaxy works. So what was your pal Ghuh taught about us? What do they say about us when we're not around? In some ways, they were right. We *don't* have much to offer. We build off their tech, and we get the planets they've decided are too crummy to live on. And *our* kids see that. They all want to go to Central space and mod their bodies and get rich. Did you hear Terra at dinner tonight?'

'You'll have to be more specific.'

'She was talking about the ferry ride she went on last tenday, and she said, "we flew past a big *yelekam*". I asked her what the word was in Ensk. She didn't know. She didn't know the word for *comet*.'

Isabel blinked. The younger generation, she knew, was mixing Klip and Ensk in ways hers never had, and they tended to lean heavily on the galactic language when speaking among themselves. But Terra was five years old. She would've barely started being taught Klip at school. Clearly, she'd been learning elsewhere. 'Languages adapt.' Isabel exhaled. 'That's the way of it.'

'Stars, you are the worst person to sympathise with about change being scary,' Tamsin said with a crooked smile. She set both stitching and mug aside, and leaned in to Isabel, lacing the hand on her knee into her own. 'I'm not saying I hated it tonight, or that I don't want her here. I'm saying I felt like I was on display, and it was weird. I expect that if I'm elsewhere. I don't expect that here. That's all.'

Isabel cupped Tamsin's face with her free hand and leaned forward to kiss her. 'I'm sorry you felt that way,' she said after their lips parted. 'That isn't fair to you.'

Tamsin rested her forehead against Isabel's for a long moment, the kind of moment that made everything else hold still. She pulled back just a touch. 'So since I've been so emotionally wounded in my own home—'

'Oh, stars.' Isabel sat back, letting the roll of her eyes lead the way.

'Can you go fetch the leftover custard out of the stasie?' She gave her lashes an out-of-character flutter.

Isabel sighed in acquiescence. 'Did you not get any at dinner?'

Her wife looked at her seriously. 'I am seventy-nine years old. If I want dessert twice . . . I get dessert twice.'

TESSA

This was a battle of wills, and Tessa was going to win. She was sure of that, sure in her bones, even though the scene before her was a daunting one.

'Ky,' she said. 'You need to lie down now.'

Her toddling son stood atop his cot in her room, all tummy and gravity-defying curls. He was the cutest thing in the universe, and she would've given anything for him to be someone else's kid right then.

'No,' Ky said with simple conviction. 'Up now.'

'It's not time to be up,' Tessa said. 'It's time for sleep.'

'No.'

'Yes.'

'No.' His knees wobbled, but they held steady. Ky presented his argument: 'Mama up now. Aya up now.' He raised his voice. 'Ky up now! All fixed!'

'Your sister is not up, either. She's asleep.'

'No!'

Tessa looked over her shoulder, across the living room toward Aya's door. It was closed, but . . . *but*. A new uncertainty needled at her. She wondered what little ears could hear that hers couldn't. Tessa ran her hand through her hair and let out a terse sigh. She looked Ky in the eye as she started to exit the room. 'When I come back, you need to be lying down.'

'No!'

Tessa crossed the living room, trading one battle for another. She opened Aya's door, and – well, she had to give the kid credit.

93

She was tented under her blanket, which would have hidden the light of her scrib were it not for one traitorous hole created by an errant foot.

'Hey,' Tessa said sternly.

Her daughter froze, an *oh shit* rigor that might've been funny if Tessa hadn't been so sick of this. 'I was just—' Aya began.

'Bed,' Tessa said. That would've been that, were it not for a creeping suspicion. She pulled the blanket up and away. Aya scrambled to shut off her scrib, but she was too slow. An image of neon weapon blasts and campy explosions lingered in the empty air.

Tessa frowned. 'What were you watching?'

Her daughter pouted at the bed.

'Aya.'

' . . . *Cosmic Crusade.*'

'Are you allowed to watch *Cosmic Crusade*?'

'No,' Aya said, mumbling so low her lips barely moved.

'No,' Tessa said. Stars, but she was over fighting to keep that Martian trash out of her kid's head. She took the scrib.

The protest was immediate and indignant. 'Mom! That's not *fair*!'

'It's totally fair.'

'When do I get it back?'

'You're not really in a negotiating position here, kiddo.'

'When?'

'When I say so.' She pointed. '*Bed.*'

She heard her daughter let out a long-suffering sigh as the door closed. One down. Tessa forged ahead, back to her room. She walked through the open door and . . . she blinked. 'Ky, where are your pajamas?'

Her naked son slapped his torso with twin palms. 'All fixed!'

Everything was *all fixed!* with him these days, and she had no idea where he'd picked it up from, no more so than she could figure out where his pajamas had gone. She looked around the bed, beside it, under it, under blankets, under pillows, feeling ridiculous at being outwitted by a two-year-old who was placidly watching her with a finger up his nose. This was one single room. How many places could there . . . she paused. It wasn't one room, technically. She walked the short distance to the attached lavatory, and opened the door. The light switched on. Tessa closed her eyes. 'Come here, please.'

Silence.

'Ky, *come here.*'

Ky padded over. He looked at her with his lips pulled inward, rocking slightly as he stood in place. It was an expression that would have been the same on any person of any age – the unmistakable dread of someone who knew they'd fucked up but wanted to see how it would play out.

Tessa put her hands on her hips. 'Why are your pajamas in the toilet?' she asked.

'Don' know.'

'You don't know? Who put them there?'

'Daddy.'

Tessa bit back a laugh. 'Your daddy's not here.'

'Yes, he – he put 'jamas. And – and then bye. Bye Ky, bye Aya, bye Mama.' He put his hand on his mouth and made kissing sounds. 'No 'jamas. No way.'

'I don't think so,' Tessa said, tugging the discarded footies away from the vacuum pulling them toward the sewage line. 'I think you put them here.'

'No, I don' think so,' he repeated while giggling. 'You – you put them here.'

Tessa imagined, as she put her kicking, now-crying boy back into another pair of pajamas, this same script playing out in this same room with herself and her parents. It had been their room once, and their parents' before that, and their parents' before that, and on and on. Generation after generation of wriggling toddlers and weary adults. She remembered waking in what was now Aya's room and hearing tiny, tubby Ashby shriek with laughter across the way. It was fair, she supposed, this cycle of aggravation. Payback for the days when you threw your own jammies in the toilet.

After two more false starts, three sung rounds of 'Five Baby Bluefish', and ten minutes of hand holding and hair stroking, the kid was down. Tessa tiptoed out of the room, holding her breath. She didn't exhale until the door closed behind her and she had waited long enough to confirm that the sound had fallen on unconscious ears. *Whew*.

Usually, she didn't fly solo for bedtime. But Pop was out that evening – off at the waterball game with his cronies, like he did every pair of tendays. He'd be home in a few hours, tipsy and ornery and no help whatsoever. She could've asked the Parks for a hand. They didn't have any kids, and they often helped out around the hex in terms of bathing and bedtime stories, but both Paola and Jules were going through that temporary period of punkiness everyone went through after bot upgrades, and Neil had had a rough shift at work – yet another water main was about to bust, he'd said at dinner – so Tessa hadn't wanted to bother any of them. No, better to brave bedtime alone and savour the reward of a few sweet, sweet moments all to herself.

She surveyed the living room. It was a wreck, as always, a carnage of toys and laundry and stained furniture even the cleanerbots couldn't keep up with. She considered the nearly-full bottle of kick sitting on the shelf, a gift from her workmates the standard prior. A few warm sips before bed sounded awfully nice, but . . . nah. If Ky woke up, she wanted to be clear-headed, and these days, even one drink was enough to make her start the next day with a headache.

Somewhere within, her teenage self was screaming in horror.

She poured herself a glass of water instead, and sat on the sofa, letting her body fall back like a bot that'd had its signal cut. Her head sank blissfully into the balding fabric. She closed her eyes. She listened. Quiet. Beautiful, sweet quiet. Nobody crying, nobody complaining, nobody needing her for anything. Just air filters sighing from above and the distant whoosh of greywater pipes below. She'd go to bed before long, but first, she was going to just *sit*. She was going to sit and do n—

Her scrib pinged. Somebody was making a sib call. If it had been anybody else, she would've thrown the thing across the room, but when she saw the name, she relented. With a sigh, she hauled herself up, sat back down at the ansible desk, and answered.

'You just missed 'em,' she said.

On screen, George sighed. 'Yeah, I thought I might've. Damn.' He was unsurprised, but still disappointed. Tessa couldn't help but smile. His skewed frown looked just like Ky's.

If you'd told eighteen-year-old Tessa that she'd have kids with George one day, she would've thought you were insane. George had been the friendly guy, the low-key guy, the guy you might trade a word or two with at a party before you each went off with your respective friends. George was nothing like gorgeous Ely, with a body straight out of a sim and the emotional intelligence of fish spawn, or charismatic Skeet, whose ambitious dreams were so easy to become smitten with until you realised there was no work ethic to back them up. It wasn't until she and George were both in their thirties that something clicked. He was on leave from his latest mining tour, Tessa was the bay worker who noticed the discrepancy on his formwork. Not exactly the most romantic of reunions, but it had led to drinks, which led to bed, which led to days of more of the same, which led to a fond and noncommittal farewell, which led to two idiots having a panicked sib call – 'Wait, did you not get dosed?' 'I figured you had!' – which led, in turn, to Aya.

At first, George had talked about leaving his job for something that would keep him around, but asteroid mining was valuable work, and Tessa hadn't seen any reason to disrupt things more than a kid already would. George made sure he was around the first half-standard of Aya's life, then went off again to the rocky orbital edges, with the baby in Tessa's care and the hex looking after both. Mining tours were long hauls, so Tessa and George conducted themselves how they liked during the interim, each keeping their own schedules and having the occasional fling (the highs and lows of which were always shared with the other). They were, in most ways, their own people with their own lives. But whenever George's ship came home with a haul of ice and metal, he stayed in the Santoso home, wrestling with Aya, chatting with the neighbours, sharing Tessa's bed. They always got their doses now, except for that one time three years prior, when they'd decided the first accident was worth repeating. They'd also decided, without much fuss, that since the whole arrangement suited them both fine, they might as well get married – nothing fancy, no big party or anything. Just ten minutes with an archivist and a nice dinner at the hex. None of it was love as her younger self had imagined. It was so much better. There was nothing frantic or all-consuming about her and George. They were grounded, sensible, comfy. What more could you ask for?

George's on-screen image crackled with distance. 'Well, if they're down, that means more time for us,' he said. 'Though you look pretty tired.'

'I *am* pretty tired. But I've always got time for you.'

'Aww,' he simpered.

'Aww,' she repeated, making a face. 'So? How's the edge?' This was always her first question.

George shrugged, looking around his cabin. 'Y'know. Rocks. Dark. The usual. We've got a big ol' ore ball we're headed for now. Take us about two tendays to get there. Should be a good haul.'

'Teracite?'

'Iron, mostly, looks to be. Why? You going into comp tech?'

'Not me. Everybody else, though. I can't tell you how many queries we get about teracite stores.' She leaned her jaw on her palm. 'How's the ship?' This was always her second question, the one spacers were forever asking each other.

'Fine, fine,' he said. His eyes shifted away from the screen. 'Still kicking.'

Tessa squinted. 'Don't bullshit me, George.'

'It's nothing, and definitely nothing you need to worry about.'

'You know that's a great way to make someone worry, right?'

'We had a minor – *minor,* Tess – hiccup in life support today. Air not filtering right, CO2 got a little high for a couple hours.'

That *was* minor, in the grand scheme of things. But the *Rockhound* was an old ship even by Exodan standards, and this wasn't the first time there'd been 'hiccups' in their patched-up life support. 'Did Garren get it fixed?' Their mech tech.

George gestured to his door. 'Would you like me to get him up here?' he asked with a teasing look. 'Have him walk you through it?'

Tessa eyed the screen flatly. 'I'm just saying, Lela' – his captain – 'should talk to the mining guild about replacing it already.'

'You know as much as anyone there's a list as long as my leg for ships that need upgrades, and we are not at the top, I assure you.' He smiled in a way that was meant to soothe. 'Worst case, we'll head home if we start coughing.' His smile went wistful, and Tessa could see the tangent at work. An unexpected trip home meant he could hug the kids sooner, which meant they'd have grown a little less since the last time he saw them. 'How're they doin'?' he asked.

'Your son—'

'Uh oh.'

'—stuffed his pajamas down the toilet and told me you did it.'

George guffawed. 'No! I'm innocent, I swear!'

'Don't worry. You have a solid alibi.'

'That's a relief. My own son, throwing me out the hatch like that.'

Tessa shook her head. 'It's like family means nothing.' She paused. 'He's on this kick lately – "all fixed". He says it *constantly*. Any idea where he got it?'

George stroked his thick beard. 'I dunno.' He squinted at the ceiling. 'Isn't that a Big Bug thing?'

Tessa had never been into *The Big Bug Crew* as a kid, and she hadn't played any of the new ones with her daughter. 'Is it?'

'Maybe I'm remembering it wrong, but I swear it's Big Bug. Whenever something on the ship breaks down and you repair it, there's this, like . . . fanfare and confetti, and the kids yell, "All fixed!"'

'But he hasn't—' Tessa stopped. Ky wasn't old enough to be playing sims yet, not by a long shot. Anybody who'd only figured out his knees a standard ago didn't yet have the mental chops to distinguish between virtual reality and *reality* reality. She knew this. Aya knew this. Aya had been *told* this. And yet, Aya had also recently been deemed responsible enough to look after her brother unsupervised for a few hours. There'd been a few of those afternoons where Tessa had come home to find Ky wound up like she'd never seen. She'd chalked it up to his sister's overly liberal forays into the cookie box, or him just being excited about time spent playing with the coolest person in his little world. But Tessa put herself back in her childhood big sister shoes. She remembered the times her parents left her alone with Ashby. She remembered how annoying he'd been sometimes, how impossible to please. She remembered trying to find something, *anything* that would keep him occupied for more than ten minutes. She wondered, if they'd had a sim hub at home then, if she might've stuck a slap patch on his head, leaned him into a corner of the couch, and pumped sims into his brain while she did whatever she fancied. Watched forbidden Martian vids, maybe.

'Uh oh,' George said again.

'What?'

'Your face.' He made a circular hand motion around his own. 'It went super scary.'

She glared at him. 'I don't have a scary face.'

'You do. You do, sometimes, have a scary face.'

'If I have a scary face, it's because *your daughter*—'

'Ohhhh, boy.'

'—is in big trouble.' And stars, was she ever. Tessa had half a mind to wake her up right then. She would've, too, if getting her to sleep hadn't been such an odyssey.

'Sounds like everybody's in trouble. Am *I* in trouble? I swear to you, Tess, I didn't have anything to do with the toilet thing.'

She rubbed one of her temples and gave half a laugh. 'I still have to review the evidence on that. You're not out of the open yet.'

'Shit,' George said, with a sad shake of his head. 'Maybe it'd be best if I *didn't* come home early.'

Tessa looked at him – his broad chest, his big beard, his perpetually sleepy eyes. He was greyer than he'd been once, and fuller, too. He was a kind-looking man. A normal-looking man. George wasn't the sort of guy she'd once dreamed about. George was just George, and George never changed.

She knew that wasn't true. Nothing was permanent, especially out in the open. But when she was with George, even just on opposite ends of a sib call, it was nice to pretend, for a little bit, that this one thing would never end. It didn't matter that it wasn't perfect, or wasn't always exciting. It was hers. There was one thing in this universe that was wholly, truly *hers*, and always would be.

It was the cosiest lie she knew, and she saw no reason to stop telling it.

. . . .

Part 2

WE HAVE WANDERED

Feed source: Reskit Institute of Interstellar Migration (Public News Feed)
Item name: The Modern Exodus – Entry #4
Author: Ghuh'loloan Mok Chutp
Encryption: 0
Translation path: [Hanto:Kliptorigan]
Transcription: 0
Node identifier: 2310-483-38, Isabel Itoh

[System message: The feed you have selected has been translated from written Hanto. As you may be aware, written Hanto includes gestural notations that do not have analogous symbols in any other GC language. Therefore, your scrib's on-board translation software has not translated the following material directly. The content here is a modified translation, intended to be accessible to the average Kliptorigan reader.]

———

At the heart of every district is a four-story cylindrical complex, stretching through the layered decks like a dowel stuck into a disc. The complex is made of metal, like everything else, and has no windows. The exterior is covered in muted murals of varying age, the details often obscured by the climbing vines growing from planters that encircle the base of the building. There are two entry-points at the neighbourhood level – an unobtrusive door used by the people who work there, and a larger archway used by those going through the most difficult days of their lives.

The complex is, in function, a corpse composting facility. Exodans do not call it that. They call it, simply, the Centre.

I admit I felt trepidation as I passed through the archway. This is an area of Exodan custom I was unschooled in, and I was unsure what I would find. I braced myself for the sight of rotting flesh, the air of decay. I found neither. The Centre does not feel like a place of death.

The lights are kind. There are planters everywhere, but they are tame and controlled, just as the entire process within this place is. The air surprised me the most: a slight hint of agreeable humidity, coupled with an utterly pleasant warmth (in truth, it was the most comfortable environment I've been in since arriving in the Fleet). There's a strange feel to it, yes, but it is inoffensive, reminiscent of a forest after a rain. I wondered if Humans – with their notoriously poor olfactory sense – could detect it at all.

The professionals who tend this place are known as caretakers, and one named Maxwell met me near the entrance. I knew his clothing was ceremonial, but you would never know it, dear guest, if you had not been told in advance. He wore no ornamentation, nothing that communicated pomp or importance. Just loose-fitting garments made of undyed fabric, cinched around his forearms and ankles to prevent dragging in the dirt. The outfit was a reminder that my visit that day was on a strict schedule. Maxwell was to conduct a burial – a 'laying-in', they call it – and though I was welcome to see the preparation, I would not be permitted to attend the ceremony itself. It was a 'family matter', he said, and studying the events from the sidelines would not be well received. Exodans tend to express strong emotions quite freely – brashly, even – but I have observed a general (though not universal) dislike of doing so around strangers. I struggle with this idea, but I respect it all the same.

'So,' my host said, gesturing to the chamber before us. 'This is the main event.'

The space we occupied was as tall as the exterior suggested. Stretching up before us was an enormous cylinder, unchanged since the days of the Earthen builders. A ramp spiralled around the cylinder, all the way to the top, wide enough for several Humans to walk side-by-side. At the base were several well-sealed hatches, from which the final product could be retrieved. Another caretaker was engaged in this very activity, filling metal canisters with what could easily be mistaken for nothing more extraordinary than dark soil. I was immediately filled with questions, but Maxwell had other ideas. 'We'll come back to this,' he said. 'We can't go out of order.' He paused, studying me. 'Are you comfortable seeing bodies?'

I answered honestly. 'I don't know. I have never seen one.'

He blinked – a response that indicates surprise. 'Never? Not one of your own kind?'

I gestured in the negative before I realised he wouldn't understand. 'No,' I said. 'I'm not in a medical profession, and am lucky enough to have never witnessed serious violence. I have lost connections, and have grieved them with others in a ceremonial sense. But we do not grieve with a corpse present. We do not see the body that remains as the person we have lost.'

Maxwell looked fascinated, as one could rightly expect from one of his profession. 'What do you do with them, then?'

'They're cleanly disposed of. Some still practise the old way of leaving them just beyond the shoreline, where the waves cannot reach them. Mostly, though, corpses are dissolved and flushed away.'

'Just . . . with wastewater?'

'Yes.'

Maxwell visibly wrestled with that. 'Right. That sounds . . . efficient.' He gestured for me to follow him. 'Well, if you *do* feel uncomfortable, just let me know, and we'll leave.'

I followed him through a staff door and down a corridor until we reached his preparation room. The difference between this place and the main chamber could not have been starker. My tentacles reflexively curled with chill, and the air was irritatingly dry.

It is difficult for me to distill all I felt as we entered the room. If I were to describe the moment with pure objectivity, I stood at a table looking at a dead alien. She was old, her body withered. I related to nothing of her anatomy, laid bare and unshrouded. I realised my declaration to Maxwell that I had never seen a dead body was untrue. I have seen dead animals. I have eaten them. I have walked past them in food markets. I have fished expired laceworms out of my beloved swimming tank at home. In some ways, observing the Human corpse on the table was no different than that. Please understand, dear guest, I do not mean that I believe Humans are equivalent to lesser species.

What I mean is that what lay before me was a species other than myself, and so any connection to my own mortality, my own eventual fate, was at first safely distant.

But then I began to think of the dead animals I have seen and disposed of and consumed, the ended lives I did not grieve for because I did not understand them fully. I did not see myself in them, and therefore it did not matter. I looked to this former Human – this former sapient, with a family and loves and fears. Those things I *could* understand, even though the body was something I could not. Nothing in the room was moving, nothing was *happening*, and yet within me, I felt profound change. I grieved for the alien, this person I had never known. I grieved for my pet laceworms. I grieved for myself. Yet it was a quiet grief, an everyday grief, a heaviness and a lightness all at once. I was overwhelmed, yet there was no way to express that beyond silence.

I do not feel I am explaining this experience well, dear guest, but perhaps that is appropriate. Perhaps none of us can truly explain death. Perhaps none of us should.

———

TESSA

Tessa stood in the doorway to her workroom, lunch box in one hand, the other hanging at her side. She'd had a bad feeling since the moment she'd discovered that the staff door opened for her despite the lock being offline. In the workroom, poor Sahil lay with his head on the desk, snoring and drooling without a care in the world. She looked out to the endless shelves. Everything appeared just as it had when she'd left the day before. She knew it wasn't. Somewhere, something was missing. Probably a lot of things were missing.

She did not need this today. She really, really did not.

She crouched down beside her colleague. 'Sahil?' she said, giving his shoulder a shake. 'Sahil? Dammit.' She gave him a once-over, just to make sure nothing was bloodied or broken, then turned to the vox. 'Help,' she called.

The connection was instant. 'Patrol dispatch,' a voice said. 'Is this an emergency?'

Tessa was pretty sure she knew the speaker. 'Lili?' she said. 'It's Tessa, down in Bay Eight.'

'Ah, jeez.' Definitely Lili. 'Again?'

Tessa wasn't sure whether to laugh or sigh, so she did both. 'Again.'

'Anybody hurt?'

'No, but looks like they hit my coworker's bots.' It was a mean but easy exploit, if you could get your hands on a med scanner. Trigger the imubots' suppression protocol, like a doctor would before a minor surgery, and say goodnight. 'I think he's just asleep, but—'

'Yeah, I gotcha. You've got two patrollers and a medic headed your way. Ten minutes, tops.'

'Thanks, Lili.'

'You got it. If you come by Jojo's tonight, I'll get you a drink.'

Tessa laughed dryly. 'I just might take you up on that.' The vox switched off. Tessa sat on the desk. She set her lunch down and studied Sahil, her hands folded between her legs. His sinuses roared. She thought about wiping up the drool, but no. She did enough of that kind of thing at home.

She glanced up at the clockprint on the wall. *Ten minutes, tops*, dispatch had said. So, rounding up to ten, that meant it was in her best interest to wait five minutes before calling Eloy, who would take twelve to get from home to work. Technically, she was supposed to call the supervisor the second something like this happened, but Tessa found the idea of delaying the inevitable headache until she had patrollers there much more palatable. Eloy was easier to deal with if another person of authority was there to balance him out.

One minute passed. Tessa opened her lunch box and removed the cake she'd packed for the afternoon. It was only eighth hour. It was warranted.

Four minutes passed. The cake had been pretty good. A little stale, but then, it was two days old. She brushed the remaining crumbs off her knee. Sahil snored.

Five minutes passed. She took a breath. '225-662,' she said to the vox.

A second went by. Two. Three. 'Yeah,' Eloy's marginally awake voice said. Great. Just great. This was the start of his day.

'Eloy, it's Tessa,' she said. 'We've had a break-in.'

'Ah, *fuck*,' he snapped. She could practically hear him rubbing his hands over his face. 'Fucking again?'

Sahil shifted in his sleep, his lips folding unflatteringly against the desk. 'Fucking again,' Tessa said.

ISABEL

When dealing with other sapients, issues of compatibility were difficult to anticipate. Isabel's go-to example of this was the first meeting between Exodans and Aeluons. The Exodans, overjoyed by what felt like a rescue, exhilarated by the confirmation that their species was not alone, predictably assembled in their festive best, and decorated the shuttledock in streamers, banners, bunting. There were recordings of the scene in the Archives – an overwhelming array of every colour the dyeworks could cook up, hung and layered like confetti frozen in time. To Exodan eyes, the display was ebullient, effusive, a celebration like no other (not to mention an extravagant use of cloth). To the chromatically communicative Aeluons, it was the equivalent of opening a nondescript door and finding a thousand screaming people on the other side. The Aeluons, well familiar with the more colourful habits of other species, dealt with it as gracefully as they could, but as soon as some Klip/Ensk translation wrinkles had been ironed out, a gentle request was made to please, *please* put the flags away.

Such misalignments were unpredictable, and blameless. Nothing that could've been foreseen. Nothing that could've been prevented. Isabel told herself that as she stood helplessly at the transport pod platform as . . . *something* nearby kept shutting down Ghuh'loloan's cart. She'd been fine on the elevator, fine as they crossed the platform. As soon as she approached the transport pod, though, the cart stopped in its tracks, as if someone had thrown a switch. Isabel had tugged her backward, and the cart had come back to life. But as soon as Ghuh'loloan drove herself across some invisible line, the wheels froze and the engine audibly slumped. None of her colleague's increasingly agitated flicking of switches had any effect.

'Weird,' the transport attendant said in schoolroom Klip. He scratched his head. 'It's got to be . . . I don't know.' He switched over to Ensk and gave Isabel an apologetic shrug. *'Some kinda signal interference from the pod. I'm sorry, M, I don't know where to start.'*

Isabel glanced around as she mentally scrambled for a solution. A small crowd had gathered, because of course they had. They kept their distance – out of respect and wariness in equal measure, no doubt – but their interest was unapologetic, and anything but subtle. How often did you get to go home and tell the dinner table about the alien you saw stuck on the transport deck? Isabel was aware that they were watching herself as well, the obvious responsible party, the one who would come up with something clever.

She did not.

'I do not hold you at fault,' Ghuh'loloan said to the attendant. 'Nor you, dear host. These things happen!' Her tone was bright, but her tentacles still flicked switches in fading hope. She pulled in her tendrils, and her eyestalks shut for a moment. 'M Transport Attendant,' she said, perking back up. She had yet to get a proper hold on honorifics, and the overdone result was often charming. 'Do you think you are capable of carrying my cart? It weighs approximately sixteen kems.'

The transport attendant – clearly tickled at being called 'M' by an alien visitor – nodded. 'Yes, I can lift. But, um . . .' He paused, searching for words. 'I'm not sure I can carry it and you same. Together?'

'Together,' Isabel said.

He nodded again. 'It and you together.'

'Oh, you won't need to worry about that,' Ghuh'loloan said. 'Isabel, would you—?' She gestured at her cart, and Isabel caught on. She grabbed the edge of the cart and dragged Ghuh'loloan a short ways backward. Right on cue, the cart hummed to life again. Ghuh'loloan pressed a few controls, and a compact ramp extended slowly from the side.

Understanding her colleague's intent, Isabel looked at the floor. Smooth, dry metal plating, just like everywhere else. Clean, but hard to say what had been on it, or what it had been cleaned *with*. A bit of solvent residue, a bootprint with traces of fertiliser, or an unseen patch of spilled salt were all enough to make a Harmagian itch for the rest of the day. Isabel frowned with concern. 'I'm sure one of us can carry you.'

'No,' Ghuh'loloan said. 'You can't.' She angled her eyestalks toward Isabel's bare forearms. *Right*, Isabel thought. Soap. Skin oil. Lotion. And you couldn't forget the clothes, either, undoubtedly still dusted with detergent. Stars, but Humans made a mess of getting clean.

Isabel looked to the crowd. *'Does anyone have any water with them?'* she called out in Ensk. *'A canteen, or . . . ?'*

The faces in the crowd looked surprised to be addressed, as if they'd just discovered they were playing a sim instead of watching a vid. But they responded to the question, opening satchels and digging through backpacks. Bottles, bags, and canteens were raised up.

'I'm sorry to ask this,' Isabel said. *'But we need to rinse off a path for her.'*

Ghuh'loloan wagged her facial tendrils. 'What are you saying?'

'I'm asking them to clean off the floor for you.'

'Oh, dear host, I'll be all right, really—'

'Don't be silly,' Isabel said, and turned again to the crowd. *'Any volunteers? Clean water only, please, no tea or anything flavoured.'*

Isabel hadn't expected differently, but was pleased to see everybody with water come forward to help. She knew a good deal of the motivation was self-serving – not only did they see an alien in a pinch on the platform, *but they got to help*. Still, the unquestioning willingness to pitch in made her proud. The onlookers emptied their drinks, tossing the water in forward-moving splashes.

One small girl upended her equally small cup straight down in front of her. It did little for the task at hand – most ended up on the girl's shoes – but she got the point. Every bit counted.

After a minute or two, a glistening path stretched from the Harmagian cart to the Exodan pod. '*Thank you, friends*,' Isabel said. '*And thank your families for us, too*.' That water had come from many, after all.

'Yes, yes,' Ghuh'loloan said, having caught a familiar word. Her dactyli unfurled like waking leaves. Had she continued in Klip, she likely would have delivered a truly Harmagian declaration of gratitude, but instead, she exercised one of the few Ensk phrases she knew: '*Thank oo mutsch.*'

The crowd was delighted.

Ghuh'loloan's eyestalks shifted to the ramp. 'Now, if you will forgive me further, this will take some time.'

And with that, Ghuh'loloan began to crawl.

There were a few muffled sounds from the crowd – a smothered gasp, a nervous laugh. Isabel looked sharply to them, giving everyone the same look her grandkids got if reaching for something forbidden. But in truth, she was one with the crowd, choking back her own instinctive yelp. She'd never seen a Harmagian leave xyr cart. She knew, logically, that vehicle and rider were two separate entities, but the visual confirmation was cognitively dissonant. She had imagined, given the Harmagian lack of legs, that Ghuh'loloan would simply slide, like the recordings she'd seen of slugs, or perhaps snakes. But instead, Ghuh'loloan's smooth belly began to . . . stars, what was the word for it? Grab. Pull. It was as if Ghuh'loloan's stomach was covered with a thick swath of fabric – several bedsheets, maybe – and behind the bedsheets there were hands, and the hands pushed against the sheets, curling, grasping, dragging the rest of the body forward. *Dough*, Isabel thought. *Putty*. There was no symmetry to it, no pattern easily discernible to a bipedal mind. And the result *was* slow, as Ghuh'loloan had intimated. Isabel imagined trying to walk alongside her like this. She'd have to take two short steps, then wait two beats, then two steps, then two beats, on and on. This was why Harmagians had spent so much of their evolutionary history enjoying the quickness of the sea before adapting for the riches of the land. It was why they'd invented carts. It was why their tech was so incredible. It was why they'd become so good at defending themselves – and at taking from others.

Ghuh'loloan heaved herself forward, a lumbering mass inching across the wet patch of already clean floor that had been rinsed with pure water for the sake of fussy, fragile skin. Isabel watched, and marvelled.

The former conquerors of the galaxy.

EYAS

'Need a hand?'

Eyas stopped spreading compost and turned her head. A man was there – younger than her, but not a kid, either. She looked him in the eye, thrown by his question. 'Sorry, what?'

'Do you need a hand?' he asked again in an accent she couldn't place. It was rough and bright and thick as pudding. He gestured to her cart. 'Looks like you have a lot to get through. I can't say I've ever really gardened, but I'm sure I could chuck dirt around.'

Eyas slowly brushed off her gloves and stood up. 'I'm—' She tried to straighten out her baffled brain. 'You know this is compost, right?'

'Yeah,' he said.

They stared at each other. 'You know what compost *is*, right?'

'Sure.' His face suggested he was starting to doubt that.

'Are you a trader, or—?'

The man laughed. 'No. The accent gave me away, huh?'

'Yeah,' she said. *That, and other things.* She knelt back down to the compost she'd been distributing, waiting for him to leave.

He did not. 'Do you sell it?'

'Do I *what*?'

'Do you sell this stuff? Or is it just something you make at home?'

Eyas lidded her canister, walked to the edge of the planter, and looked seriously at the man. 'These are Human remains,' she said in a low voice. 'We compost our dead.'

The man was mortified. 'Oh. Wow, I'm . . . jeez, I'm sorry.'

He looked at the cart full of canisters. 'These are all . . . people? Like, individual people, or . . . oh man, are they all mixed together?'

'If you have questions, I'm sure someone at the Centre would be happy to give you a tour.'

'The Centre. That's where you . . .' He gestured vaguely to the canisters.

'Yes.'

'And that's . . . your job.'

'Yes.' She threw a pointed glance back at the plants. 'Which I am not doing.'

The man held up his palms. 'Right. Sorry. Really sorry.' He turned to leave.

Eyas turned back to the plant and began to crouch down. For reasons unknown, she turned back. 'Where are you from?'

The man stopped. 'Mushtullo.'

'And you're not a trader.'

'No.'

She squinted. 'Do you have family here?'

'Heh, everybody asks that. No, I'm just trying something new.'

Oh, stars, he was one of those. She'd heard others complaining about said same, but never encountered it herself. Young grounders had made a thing of showing up on the Fleet's door-step hoping to find kin or connection or some other such fluff, succeeding at little except treating everyone's home like a zoo before learning there wasn't any romance in it and heading back to cushier lives where every problem could be answered with creds.

Except here was this one, standing there with his hands in his pockets and an irritatingly eager smile. She should have let him walk away, but . . . he'd asked to help. He'd offered to help.

'Do you have work?' she asked.

'Not yet,' the man said. 'I went to the job office and everything, but they said the only openings they had were for sanitation. And not to be picky, but—'

'But you were picky.'

The man gave a guilty shrug. 'I'm just hoping something else will open up. I'm good with code, I'm good with customers, I could—'

Eyas removed her gloves, folded them over her belt, and sat at the edge of the planter, bare hands folded between her legs. 'Do you understand why they tried to give you a sanitation job?'

'They said—'

'I know what they said. There were other openings, I promise you.' Lots of them, she knew. 'That's not the point. Do you understand why they tried to give you *that* job?'

The last traces of his easy grin evaporated. 'Oh.'

Eyas sighed and ran her hand through her hair. He thought this was a matter of bigotry. 'No, you still don't get it. They tried to give you a sanitation job because *everybody* has to do sanitation. Everybody. Me, merchants, teachers, doctors, council members, the admiral – every healthy Exodan fourteen and over gets their ID put in a computer, and that computer randomly pulls names for temporary, mandatory, no-getting-out-of-it work crews to sort recycling and wash greasy throw-cloths and unclog the sewage lines. All the awful jobs nobody wants to do. That way, nothing is out of sight or out of mind. Nothing is left to *lesser people*, because there's no such thing. So you, coming in here at – how old are you?'

'Twenty-four.'

'Right. You've got ten years of potential sanitation shifts to make up for. You're here eating the food we grow, sleeping inside a home somebody worked hard to maintain, drinking water that is carefully, carefully managed. The people at the job office knew that. They wanted to see if you were actually willing to live like us. If you were more than just a tourist. They wanted to know if you were serious.'

The man straightened up. 'I'm serious.'

'Well, then, go muck out a sewer like the rest of us have to. Do that, and they might let you put some code to use.' Eyas was sure they would. There was need for that kind of skillset, no question. It just needed to be in the hands of someone with the right principles.

'Okay,' the man said. 'Yeah, okay. Thank you. Thanks very much.' The smile returned. 'I'm Sawyer, by the way.'

She gave him a polite nod. 'I'm Eyas.'

'Eyas. That suits you.'

'No.' She got to her feet and put her gloves back on. 'It really doesn't.'

KIP

'Trust me,' Ras said. 'This is totally safe.'

Kip wasn't so sure. His friend was smiling his usual smile, but he had a bunch of weird shit spread out on the floor between them – a patch scanner, some complicated cables, an info chip labelled 'BIRTHDAY.' All of it looked hand-hacked, and none of it was anything Ras had ever given any indication he knew how to use. 'Where'd you get this stuff?' Kip asked.

'Mail drone. I had some creds saved up.'

'Yeah, but from *where*?'

'You remember that job I worked for M Aho—'

'Not the creds. This . . . hackjob stuff.'

Ras lowered his voice, even though they were safe in his room. His mom had ears like you would not believe. 'Have you heard of this feed called Picnic?'

'No.'

'It's like . . . *serious* black market modder shit. Implants, code, ships even. You name it. Whatever you want, somebody there has it, or knows where to get it. And it's totally off the map. You can't find Picnic in public searches.'

Kip wasn't super comfortable with the sound of that, but he didn't want to look like a wuss. 'So how'd *you* find it?'

'Toby told me about it. It's where his sister gets all the gear she needs to make smash.'

'Wait, Una? She makes smash?'

'Do you not know that? I thought everybody knew that. How

do you think she bought her own skiff? Anyway, the supplier I
got this from, xe told me—'

'Who?'

'What?'

'Who's the supplier?'

'Just . . . you know, it's anonymous, everybody's got codenames
and—'

Kip leaned forward. *'Who?'*

Ras cleared his throat. 'Xe's called fluffyfluffycake.'

'Fluffyfluffycake.'

'Xe really knows xyr shit, man, I'm telling you—'

'You bought a hack kit from somebody called *fluffyfluffycake.*'

Ras rolled his eyes and pulled back his wristwrap, exposing
the implant beneath. 'Look, I already did me.' He picked up the
patch scanner – definitely hand-hacked, there were two different
colours of casing fused together – and swiped it over his wrist.
He turned the scanner screen toward Kip so he could read the
ID data it had just pulled. 'See?'

Kip read, blinked, raised his eyebrows. 'Huh.'

'Yeah, *huh.*'

'And it's . . . okay?' Kip remembered the standard before, when
the *Newet* had gone under quarantine because somebody came
back from some neutral market with a bot virus – Marabunta,
they called it. Hijacked your imubots and gave you seizures, then
hopped to anybody you brushed your patch against, whether it
was a hug or a handshake or a crowded transport car or whatever.
Kip remembered seeing pictures of the victims on the news feeds
– folks tied down in hospital beds, mouths strapped shut so they
wouldn't break their own teeth. Everybody'd been really freaked
out. At school, they'd gotten a big long boring talk about how
you should never, ever get unlicensed bots and you should never,
ever go to an unlicensed clinic. He could hear that lecture playing
dimly in the back of his head, but the reality of his friend sitting
in front of him was much louder. 'You feel okay?' Kip asked.

'Stars, I get us something awesome, and you turn into my mom. Yes, I feel fine. I did it yesterday before I asked you over. What, did you think I was gonna test it out on you first? C'mon, I'm not *that* much of an asshole.'

Kip's pulse thudded in his ears. If Ras'd done it, and he was okay, and the hack hadn't messed up his bots or anything, then . . . it was okay, right? He stared for a second, then pushed up his own wristwrap – blue and green triangle print, frayed around the edges. The one his dad had given him last Remembrance Day. 'All right,' he said.

Ras grinned. 'Only takes a sec.' He connected one end of the cable to Kip's patch, then the other end to his scrib. He popped the info chip in an empty port and gestured at the screen. 'You want to keep your actual birthday, yeah? Easier to remember.'

'Yeah,' Kip said. He shifted his weight as Ras worked. 'What if somebody we know sees us?'

'Well, if we're not stupid about it, they won't. We can go to one of the other districts and it'll be fine.' He waved his hand, and the scrib made a completed *ding*. 'All right, let's see what we got.'

'That's it?' Kip asked.

'That's it,' Ras said, picking up the scanner. 'I told you, fluffy-cake knows xyr shit.' He swiped the scanner over Kip's wrist, gave a nod, then handed the scanner over.

Kip took it and looked down at the screen.

GC citizenship record:
ID #: 9836-745-112
GC designated name: Kristofer Madaki
Emergency contact: Serafina Madaki, Alton Madaki
Next of kin: Serafina Madaki, Alton Madaki
Local name (if applicable): Kristofer (Kip) Madaki

Locally required information:
Ship: *Asteria*, Exodus Fleet
Address: 224-324
Standard date of birth: 23/292
Age: 20

'There we go!' Ras said. 'Damn, *finally* you look like you're having fun.'

Kip couldn't help but smile. He could get in so much trouble for this, and yet . . . yet he felt like he'd cut the line, like he'd been granted a reprieve from the agonising wait between birthdays. 'Do I look twenty, though?'

Ras pursed his lips and nodded. 'Totally.' He cocked his head. 'Maybe don't shave.'

Kip didn't have much to shave yet except his upper lip and a patch on his chin, but he didn't feel like sharing that. 'So, now what?' he said. Now that the scary part was over with, the lack of plan felt kind of anticlimactic. 'We could go get some kick, or . . . redreed? Do you wanna get some redreed?' Kip had tried it once and didn't like it, but he could get it now, and that was the important thing.

But Ras shook his head. 'I have a way, way better idea.'

SAWYER

Compared to the brightness and bluster of the rest of the plaza, the job office was a rather humble spot. Still, it was welcoming in its own way. There were benches outside where people could skim through listings on their scribs, and calming plants in neat boxes, and pixel posters cheering the reader on. *Need a change? We can help!*, read one, the letters glowing above a loop of a relieved-looking man setting aside a vegetable-gathering basket and picking up a stack of fabric instead. Another poster featured a teenage girl standing in a semblance of a hex corridor, surveying doors printed with various symbols – a leaping fish, a magnified imubot, a musical instrument, a shuttle in flight. *You never know where a job trial will take you*, the pixels read.

Sawyer took a seat on the bench beside the girl with four lives ahead of her. He'd just left the office, and done what the compost woman had suggested. Going back in armed with advice had put a spring in his step. Coming back out . . . he wasn't sure what he felt. He hadn't talked to the same clerk as before, so he'd missed out on the satisfaction of returning to say *aha, look, I have passed your test!* Learning that there was an expected order of vocational initiation had felt significant to Sawyer. The clerk hadn't conveyed the same, but why should he? What was *significant* about filling out the same formwork he probably filled out dozens of times a day? What had Sawyer expected? A knowing nod? An approving smile?

That's exactly what he'd wanted, he knew, and he felt stupid about it. But then again, he'd been given no next step, no direction beyond 'thank you, we'll contact you when a shift becomes available.' When would that be? Tomorrow? A tenday? More? In principle, Sawyer didn't mind downtime, especially when he didn't have to worry about food or a roof, but the idea of rattling around that big empty home until some nebulous point in the future arrived didn't sit well.

He set his jaw. Getting down about everything he didn't know yet wouldn't do any good. Maybe he could try making inroads with his hex neighbours again. Maybe they'd be more than distantly polite if they knew he was going to clean up the same messes everybody else did. Maybe he'd go out there at dinnertime today instead of going to a cafe or hiding out insecurely in his room. He'd never really cooked before, but he could chop stuff, at least. He could help. He could—

'Working up some courage?' a friendly voice said.

Sawyer found the speaker: a stocky man with an infectious smile and a mech arm. Such implants were common among Humans back home, but Sawyer hadn't seen many in the Fleet. 'I've already been in,' he said.

'Needing some comfort, then, judging by your face.' The man raised up a canteen, signalling the intent to share. 'Want some in liquid form?'

Sawyer smiled and put up his hands. 'I better not,' he said. 'I'm kind of a lightweight.'

'Then you've got nothin' to fear here,' the man said. He waggled the canteen. 'Just tea. Lil' sugar boost, that's all.'

Sawyer's smile grew, and he nodded. 'All right,' he said, joining the man. 'That's very kind.'

'I've been in your shoes,' the man said. He filled the canteen lid and handed it over. 'Not a comfy thing, having idle hands, huh?'

'No,' Sawyer said, nodding in thanks as he took a sip of tea. Stars, but this guy wasn't kidding about the sugar. He could already feel it clinging fuzzily to his teeth.

The man stuck out his hand. 'I'm Oates,' he said.

Sawyer returned the handshake, a kick of happy adrenaline coursing through him. 'Sawyer,' he said.

'And where are you from, Sawyer?' He pointed toward Sawyer's mouth. 'We don't grow Rs like those in the Fleet.'

Sawyer laughed. 'Mushtullo.'

'Long way from home.' Oates pulled a redreed pipe and a tiny bag out of his jacket pocket. Sawyer knew what was coming next: 'You got family here?'

'Nah.' He had the reply down pat by now. 'Just trying something new.'

Oates nodded as he filled his pipe – redreed in the hand he'd been born with, bowl in the one he'd chosen. 'Good for you.' He hit his sparker and took one puff, two puffs, three. The smoke rose steady. 'You been here long?'

'Two tendays.'

'How's it treating you so far?'

'Great,' Sawyer said, a little too fast, a little too loud. 'Yeah, it's . . . it's been great.'

Oates eyed him through the pipe smoke. 'Bit different than home, huh?'

Sawyer took another sip of the sickeningly sweet tea. 'Still finding my footing, I guess. But that's normal, right?'

'I'd say so,' Oates said. He offered his pipe; Sawyer declined. 'So what kind of work did they hook you up with?'

'I put my name in for sanitation.' Sawyer tried to look casual as he said it, but he was keen to see how that answer was received.

Oates did not disappoint. 'Sanitation,' he said with a favourable look. 'A time-honoured gig.' He took a long drag and let the smoke curl slowly from his nose. 'That's good of you. But tell me honestly, now that we're tea buddies and all – that's not really what you *want* to be doing, right?'

'Well . . .' Sawyer laughed. 'Does anybody?'

Oates chuckled. 'No. That's why the good ol' shit lottery exists in the first place. What kind of jobs did you do back on Mushtullo?'

'Lots of stuff – uh, let's see . . . I've worked at a cafe, a fuel depot, a stasie factory—'

'So, you can lift stuff and follow directions and be nice to people. Good, good. What else?'

'I can write code.'

'No kidding.' Oates looked interested. 'What kind of code?'

'I'm not a comp tech or anything. I didn't go to school for it. But I can write Siksek and Tinker, and—'

'Tinker, huh?' Oates rolled his pipe between his metal fingers. 'What level?'

'Four.'

Oates studied Sawyer. 'Listen, I know we've known each other for all of three minutes, but I can tell you're a good dude. If you really want to start with the sewers, I won't bother you further. But if you're interested in something more . . . *dynamic*, I'm on a salvage crew, and we're looking for some extra hands. Specifically, someone who knows Tinker. I've stopped a few others today, and you're the first I've chatted with who's got that skill.'

Sawyer had started to take another sip of tea, but the cup froze halfway there.

'Now, lifting shit and following directions is the main part of the job,' Oates went on. 'But we use Tinker more often than not. You know how it is with busted tech – sometimes you can't get a panel to work or a door to open, and it's always faster when we've got people who can just get in there and force code the thing. That sound like something you could handle?'

'Yeah, definitely,' Sawyer said, loud and fast again. 'I've never done it before, but—'

'If you're level four, it'll be cake.' Oates folded his lips together and nodded. 'All right, well, if you're interested, come meet me tonight at shuttledock twelve, after twenty-half. I'll take you to meet my boss.'

Sawyer's heart was in his throat. This was it. A friend. A *crew*. Holy shit, the compost woman had been right! Five minutes out of the job office, and just putting his name on that list had changed things. 'I mean—' Sawyer stammered, 'that would be awesome. I can just go find the listing, if that's easier, I don't want to take up any more of your time—'

'Not at all,' Oates said. 'Besides, my boss doesn't use listings. Personal recommendations only. She's a face-to-face kind of person.' Smoke escaped from between his smiling teeth. 'Great judge of character.'

TESSA

There had been a time, once, when Eloy hadn't been a bad boss. Or maybe he always had been, but he just hadn't yet been given the opportunity to let that quality shine. In any case, he'd been Tessa's vote for Bay Eight supervisor last standard, when Faye stepped down and left for the independent colonies. Tessa missed Faye. She got shit done, but you could go have a drink with her at her hex in off-hours and forget that she was in charge. Tessa had never been buddies with Eloy, but he was a reliable worker, and absurdly organised. He had that no-nonsense edge you needed when you had to go speak for everybody else at cargo guild meetings. But as soon as he got his stripe, he turned into one of those people who equated *being in charge* with *being outwardly stressed out*. He hadn't broken any rules or disrupted workflow enough to justify the workers voting him out yet, but it was coming. Tessa knew it was coming, and it was going to be ugly, but . . . well. That was the way stuff worked.

Eloy paced around the workroom, fingers tapping against his pockets. 'And you guys have no idea who's responsible for this yet,' he said, tossing the words at the patroller without looking at her.

The patroller – Ruby Boothe, from the Santosos' neighbourhood – was keeping it cool, but her patience was visibly running thin. 'That's why—'

'Because this is the fourth,' Eloy said. 'The fourth theft since I took this job. The sixth in a standard. And you haven't caught anyone. Not a one.'

'That's why we're asking questions,' Ruby said, her grip on her scrib tightening *ever* so slightly. 'And why we're out there inspecting the scene.' She pointed with her stylus toward the storage racks, where her volunteer second was walking with the now-awake Sahil – no worse for wear – trying to figure out what had been taken.

'Questions.' Eloy shook his head. 'You'd think with all the questions, you'd have some damn answers by now.'

'Eloy, come on,' Tessa said. She knew he wouldn't like her taking the patroller's side – and the terse look he threw her confirmed that – but this wasn't helping. 'How many people do you know who could do with some extra scrap to melt?' She nodded at the patroller. 'She's got a hell of a list to narrow down.'

The patroller gave her a thankful glance. 'Precisely,' she said. 'And there's no telling if the culprits are the same as the previous times. Nothing we've found here so far can tell us if this is an organised group, or a copycat, or a first-timer. Someone hit your worker's bots, and they made off with some scrap. That is not a lot to go on, but we're doing our best here.'

'Yeah, well, while you're doing your best, we're falling behind. I have to go to *my* supervisors and make excuses for why you can't keep this from happening to us.' Eloy gestured at Tessa. 'She can't do any of the shit she needed to do today because of this.'

Tessa rankled at Eloy using her as fuel for berating the patroller, but there was a kernel of truth in there she couldn't argue with. The crime at hand had a stupid irony: someone had been impatient enough with cargo bay processing times that they'd resorted to theft, thus setting the processing schedule back further for everyone. That was the part that really pissed Tessa off, more than falling behind in her work, more than finding Sahil knocked out, more than having to spend what should've been a quiet morning listening to Eloy take things out on people who didn't deserve it. The theft benefited the thief, and maybe the thief's friends or family, but that was it. They'd taken things out of the hands of people who *also* needed them, who had grit their teeth and followed the rules and made do without.

Sahil and the volunteer patroller came back. Eloy looked over. 'What'd they get?' he asked.

Tessa squinted. 'You feeling okay?' she asked.

Sahil was still looking a bit rough from his bot hack – dark around the eyes, paler in the cheeks. But he nodded. 'Just groggy,' he said, giving her a faint smile. 'Medic said it'd be like this for a few hours.' He turned his attention to the boss. 'So, teracite, mostly. Looks like they grabbed a few handfuls of sixtops, too, but not much. Just whatever they could put in their pockets as they left, I guess.'

'How much teracite?' Eloy said.

'A good amount,' Sahil said. 'I'd say . . . about a hundred kems, give or take.'

'Oh, fucking hell,' Eloy snapped. Tessa said nothing, but she felt the same. A lot of good things could've been done with that. Medical equipment. School computers. Shuttle upgrades. But instead, somebody was either going to melt it down for home use – personal smelters were everywhere these days – or sell it for creds. She hoped the thieves would go for the former option. The idea of somebody using the stolen stuff to repair their hex was easier to stomach. The latter meant luxuries that were nice but not necessary, and that . . . that was worth an Eloy-style rant or two.

'They'd need an autocart for a haul that size,' Ruby said, tapping her chin with her stylus. She looked to her second. 'What does that tell you?'

'A merchant,' the volunteer said. Tessa had missed his name, but he was older, and had the look of someone who had been excited to get his name pulled for this job. She didn't blame him. Tagging along after full-time patrol to keep them honest beat the pants off sewer duty. 'Either that, or someone who had access to bay-to-bay transport.'

'Yup,' Ruby said.

Eloy frowned. 'That is not much to go on.'

'No,' the patroller said, gathering her gear bag. 'But it's something, and it's more than we had when we walked in here.' She picked up the empty tea mug resting on the desk beside her. 'Where should I . . .'

'Just leave it,' Tessa said. 'I'll take care of it.' She smiled – the kind of smile you gave someone when the circumstances sucked but you appreciated them being there. 'Thanks for the help.'

The patrollers said their goodbyes and left. A silence sat uncomfortably in the workroom.

'I'm sorry, Eloy,' Sahil said. 'If I'd—'

Eloy put up his hand. 'Shit happens,' he said.

Tessa frowned. 'It wasn't your fault,' she said, speaking the words *someone else* should have. 'You sure you're okay?'

'I'm okay. Really.'

'I'm gonna come check up on you at home later.'

'Fine, fine,' Sahil chuckled. 'Eloy, do you need anything else from me?'

Eloy was somewhere else. He gave Sahil's question a half-hearted headshake. He seemed to have barely registered it.

'What's up?' Tessa asked.

Eloy let out a sigh that frayed around the edges. 'I was going to bring this up at the next bay meeting, but you might as well know now. The board's talking about AIs.'

Sahil looked confused. 'AIs for what?'

'For us,' Eloy said. 'AIs instead of us.'

'Wait, what?' Tessa said.

'They think it'd do away with the *Oxomoco* backlog. Sort through everything we've been trying to, get it recycled faster, have it done in a fraction of the time, keep it from happening again.'

Tessa laughed. 'We don't have the infrastructure for that. Do you have any idea the . . . the heavy duty gear you need to run one of those?' Her brother had one on his ship, and it was one of the most expensive things he had to maintain. Had to hire a separate tech to look after it and everything. AIs were long-haul stuff, big-creds stuff. There were AIs in the Fleet, sure, but they weren't the thinking kind. Just public safety systems, the kind who could recognise fire or turn off gravity if you fell a long way. Not the kind that watched everything and were programmed to sound like people. Not the kind that could do a Human job.

Eloy stuck his hands in his pockets and shrugged tersely. 'Yeah, well, apparently labour oversight has been on their ass about our processing times, and the idea's been floated that the cost of building a . . . I don't know what the terminology is here – building the shit you'd need to run a bunch of AIs – is less of a pain in the ass than doing things like we do them now. So they say.'

'That's . . .' Tessa shook her head. It was insulting, to say the least. 'They're not serious, are they?'

'I don't know,' Eloy said. The words indicated nothing, but the look on his face said he'd be worrying about it.

'They can't be,' Sahil said. 'There are so many higher-priority projects floating around. They'd never tag the resources for it.'

Tessa stared off into the cargo bay. She remembered, when she'd been in her teens, how M Lok next door had left one morning to go test the oxygen mix and came home that afternoon having been told that, thanks to the new monitoring systems his super-visors were going to install, he wouldn't need to do it anymore. The job office got him new training and a new profession, of course, but it was a hard switch for a man of forty-five, and all the harder because he didn't like his new career in aeroponics the way he had his old one. He was still at it, to this day. She wondered if he still thought about taking air samples in life support.

'Sahil, go home,' Tessa said. 'Get some rest.'

'I had plenty of that already,' Sahil said with a grim smile.

She laughed. 'Some real rest.' She looked to Eloy. 'And if it's all the same to you, boss' – she looked out to the overflowing racks of things people needed, the dormant liftbots awaiting her command – 'I need to get to work.'

KIP

Kip remembered how to speak, but it took him a minute or two to get there. 'I don't know,' he said slowly.

Ras placed a hand on his shoulder. 'Aw, come on,' he said. 'Don't be nervous.'

In front of them stood a doorway like any other. A panel. A frame. Plants and globulbs arcing up around it. But the sign on the door . . . that made all the difference.

THE NOVA ROOM
Age 20 and over

Kip swallowed. His palms started to sweat. This was Ras' grand plan, why he'd saved up those creds, why he'd found some random modder to help him hack his patch. Ras wanted to go to a tryst club. And being the good dude that he was, he'd brought his best friend along. Kip should've felt grateful. He should've felt excited – and he did, maybe? But it wasn't excited like finding a plate of jam cakes in the kitchen or trading in your old clothes for some crisp new ones. This was the other kind of excited. *Broken artigrav* excited. *Rattle in the shuttlecraft wall* excited. The kind of excited that occurred when the chances were good that everything would be okay, but you were still going to hold your breath until said okayness was a done deal.

'I don't know,' Kip said again. 'I— I haven't showered, I—'

'They've got places you can clean up,' Ras said.

'How do you know?'

'Omar told me. He goes to the one in our district, like, every day.'

Kip looked at his friend, all confidence and smile (and fresh shirt, too). His hair still had too much goo in it, but he at least looked like he *belonged* in a place like this. Ras'd had sex before – once with Britta, who he couldn't even be in the same room with now, and lots with Zi before her family moved to Coriol and Ras moped around for, like, ever. Kip had . . . well, Alex had kissed him at that party that one time, and he'd . . . um . . .

He hadn't.

Ras gave him a friendly slap on the chest. 'Trust me,' he said. 'You're gonna have a good time.' He strolled through the door, hands in his pockets, looking like he'd done this a million times.

Kip stood frozen. 'Shit,' he whispered, and hurried after.

The hallway beyond the door was nice – like, *really* nice. Little lights, big flowers, and something that smelled *awesome*. He'd seen places like this in vids and sims and stuff, but this was the real thing, and . . . and stars, he felt out of place. He could feel every stray hair on his chin, every zit on his face. He knew the clubs were a public service and all, but would anybody even *want* to have sex with him? He thought about the guy he'd seen staring back in the bathroom mirror that morning. That skinny torso. That beard that wasn't. *Nobody* would have sex with that.

Ras was already at the front desk, chatting with the receptionist. 'Two hours each for me and my buddy,' he was saying. 'Not together, I mean. We're not together.'

The receptionist looked between them, squinted, then craned his head toward the patch scanner without taking his eyes away.

Moment of truth. Ras swiped his wrist.

The scanner chirped, and the pixels in front of the receptionist rearranged themselves. His eyes moved as he read, but his face didn't change. 'And you?' the receptionist said, eyes flicking up toward Kip.

Kip felt like he might throw up. He could get in so much trouble, and he wasn't even sure he wanted to go in, but – but

Ras had done this for him, and spent all those creds, and if he just stood there and did nothing, then they'd *definitely* be in trouble. He swiped his wrist. The scanner chirped. The receptionist read, paused, and smiled.

'Okay, gentlemen,' he said. 'I've got some good news for you. Since it's your first time visiting us, we've got an extra special welcome package for you. If you'll follow me, we'll set you up with free drinks in the lounge, then send over some of our most requested hosts to take care of you this evening.'

'Ha! All right!' Ras said, grinning at Kip.

Kip managed a weak smile. Was this happening? Was this his life?

'Don't we need to fill out a survey or something, so you know who to send?' Ras asked the receptionist. 'I like ladies, and he—' He turned to Kip. 'Which way you wanna go tonight?'

'We'll take care of the preference questionnaire in the lounge,' the receptionist assured him. He stood and gestured toward a door. 'If you'll come this way?'

Ras followed the receptionist. Kip followed Ras.

The lounge was, no doubt, the coolest place Kip had ever been to. He turned this way and that as he walked, taking it all in. The ceiling was painted like a sunset – or at least, what he was pretty sure a sunset looked like. There were crazy drinks stuffed with fruit and leaves and flowers, and floating globulbs shining through the dim. There were all kinds of people in there – people alone, people together, people waiting, people headed elsewhere. There were some old people, too, which he hadn't imagined at all and thought was kind of weird, but all right, okay. At the bar, he saw a super fit dude in a too-tight shirt and perfect trousers murmuring to a lady wearing short-sleeved coveralls like they did down at the farms. The dude touched her hair. He pressed his palm against the small of her back. The woman laughed and ran her hand down the dude's chest as he whispered, down his stomach, down to – holy shit. She squeezed, and Kip tripped, running into an unseen table, rattling the flowery drinks perched on top, startling the kissing couple on the other side. 'Sorry,' he said. 'Uh – sorry.'

Ras glanced back. *What the fuck are you doing?* his face said.

Kip hurried after. Cool. He was already looking stupid.

'Right here, if you would,' the receptionist said. He held out a gracious palm toward a table next to a fountain with a trio of globulbs slowly dancing above it.

'Thanks very much,' Ras said brightly, as if he went to places like this all the time. He sat. Kip joined him. The receptionist left toward the bar. Ras turned toward Kip, triumph written across his face. 'Worth. Every. Cred.' He glanced out at the room, and his mouth went slack. 'Holy *hell*,' he said, gaping at a pair of women at the bar. 'Stars, they're hot.' He elbowed Kip. 'See anybody you like?'

Kip didn't know how to answer that. He saw lots of people that yeah, he did like the look of, but the idea of having *actual sex* with any of them was making his foot tap and his mouth dry.

The receptionist came back with a drinks tray. 'Oh, nice!' Ras said, and Kip had to agree with the sentiment. The drinks were . . . what even *were* they?

'Two tropical twelves,' the receptionist said, placing a tall, thin glass in front of each of them. Kip inspected the contents – layered greens and yellows, ice spheres *that were glowing*, a rim of sparkling sugar around the top, a blue and flowery plume crowning the whole thing.

Ras raised his drink. 'Cheers, buddy.'

They clinked glasses, and sipped. 'Wow,' Kip said. Whatever was in a tropical twelve was pretty damn incredible. Kick usually tasted terrible, but there wasn't anything bitter or rough about this. Just sweet and cool. If it hadn't come from a bar, Kip would've sworn it was just juice.

Ras slapped Kip's arm. '*Finally* you look like you're enjoying yourself.' He took another sip. 'Damn, that's good. Seriously, that's the best drink I've ever had.'

The receptionist beamed. 'I'm so glad. Now, you might have a bit of a wait ahead of you. We're a little busy tonight. But we'll send over some snacks, and if you need another round or two, we'll keep them coming. Just wave at the bartender.' He turned and waved at the lady behind the bar, who did the same. She was laughing about something. A conversation they couldn't hear, Kip figured.

'Thanks very much,' Ras said. 'And no worries, we've both got free days tomorrow.'

That wasn't even remotely true. Ras had another round of shuttle licence practice, and Kip had math class. *Shit*, Kip thought. Did he have practice problems he was supposed to do? If he did, he hadn't done them. Shit.

But he looked at Ras, leaning back so chill in his chair. He looked at the receptionist, bowing his head to both of them like he was there for no other reason than to make their lives easy. He looked at the fancy drink, the fancy room. He looked at the polished people milling around, leaving in twos or occasional threes, holding hands or other things as they headed down mysterious hallways. Kip set his jaw. Okay. He could do this. He could be Kip Madaki, age 20, drinker of tropical twelves and expert at sex. He could have sex. He was *going* to have sex. Yeah. *Yeah.* He ran his hand through his hair, trying to knock it into something . . . good. 'Do I look okay?' he asked.

Ras gave him a thumbs-up and a nod. 'You look real cool.'

'You sure?'

'One hundred percent.'

They drank their drinks, ate a bowl of spicy fried peas, got more drinks, and . . . they waited. They waited and waited and waited.

'Should we go ask what's up?' Kip asked.

'Relax,' Ras said. 'He said they were busy.'

More time passed. More drinks were consumed, and more snacks, too. The novelty of the place wore off, and Kip's worries gave way to boredom. Even Ras looked unimpressed after a while.

Two women approached their table. Kip and Ras straightened up. The women passed them by for the next table over, and the boys slumped back down, returning to their drinks. A man headed toward them. They straightened up. He went elsewhere. They slumped. The pattern repeated, again and again. Straighten, slump, sip a drink. Straighten, slump, sip a drink.

The lift at the far end of the room opened, and Kip saw the woman in the farm coveralls walk out. Her hair was different. She was alone. She was smiling.

'How much longer, do you think?' Kip asked.

Ras shrugged. Kip could tell he was trying to look casual about it.

Kip swirled his glass. The ice had melted into the last sips, and the cool layers had fallen into each other and gone kinda pale. It didn't even really taste good anymore. 'Do you feel drunk?' he asked. He didn't feel drunk at all.

Ras shrugged again. 'I've got a high tolerance.'

'Do you think they forgot about us?'

'They've been bringing us drinks.'

'Yeah, but like—'

Kip felt a hand drop hard on his shoulder. He saw the same happen to Ras. They turned, and— oh no. Oh *no*.

'Fuck,' Ras groaned.

'So!' boomed Ras' dad, loud enough that half the lounge turned to look. 'You boys lookin' to get laid, huh?'

It wasn't just Ras' dad. It was his mom, and Kip's mom, and the swift, cataclysmic end of Kip's entire life.

ISABEL

'Buzz buzz,' Tamsin said, sticking her head through the open doorframe.

Isabel looked up over the cacophony of pixel displays and data tables wallpapering the air above her desk. 'What are you doing here?'

'What are *you* doing here?' Tamsin ambled in, cane in one hand, cloth bag in the other. 'Did you forget about your other home?'

What time was it? Isabel tapped the control bar on the side of her hud, bringing a clock up. She blinked. How was it twenty-half? She shut her eyes and shook her head. 'I'm so sorry, I—' She gestured wordlessly at the desk.

'I figured,' Tamsin said. She plunked the bag on the table and herself in a chair. 'That's why I brought dinner.'

Isabel peeked into the bag. A couple small storage boxes and a fork lay waiting. 'You sweetheart,' she said.

'Crispy fish, bean salad, and a slice of melon for after. It's not the best.' Tamsin leaned back and folded her arms over her belly. 'It was the Thompsons' night to cook. You know how Dek is about spices.'

'You mean, he forgets them?'

Tamsin winked. 'But, y'know. Food.' She eyed the pixels. 'I thought your minions were taking care of things while you're busy with M Tentacles.'

'Don't call her that.'

'Why? Is she here?'

'That's not the point.'

'You're ignoring my question.'

Isabel sighed. 'Everybody else *has* been taking care of things, but there's a question of recategorising that's come up.'

'Oh, stars,' Tamsin said knowingly. 'Uh oh.'

If you were to ask someone of another profession what archivists spent the most time fretting about, the assumption might've been restoring old corrupted files, or maintaining backup systems. But no. No, there was nothing nearer and dearer to the average archivist's heart than *categorising*, and it seemed like every standard an argument broke out over some file that belonged to too many categories, or too few, or some visitor who hadn't found what they were looking for because the tags weren't responsive or efficient or thorough enough, and nobody could get anything done until the matter of *everything being in the right place* was settled. Isabel opened her mouth, about to detail the issue – this one had to do with Earthen historical eras, which was always a thorny thing to delineate – but she took one look at Tamsin and changed her mind. Her wife's face was one of *look interested at all costs*, and she appeared to be bracing herself for an onslaught of archival minutiae. 'I'll spare you the details,' Isabel said.

Tamsin smiled. 'Big project,' she suggested.

'Big project,' Isabel confirmed.

'The kind of thing you're gonna get done in one night?'

The projected data tables stared imposingly down at Isabel. 'No,' she sighed, tucking an errant lock behind her ear. 'No, I suppose not.'

Tamsin cocked her head. 'I kinda miss you at home.'

'I'm sorry,' Isabel said. 'She'll only be here for a few more tendays, and then—'

'No, no.' Tamsin put up her hand. 'What you're doing with M— with Ghuh'loloan is good, and I know you're excited about it. And I know this kind of thing' – she pointed to the desk – 'is *your thing*, and that it's important. I care. It's good. You're doing cool stuff. But, also, I miss you.'

Isabel reached her foot beneath her desk and found one of Tamsin's. 'I miss you, too.'

Tamsin scrunched her lips so high, they nearly touched her nose. 'Wanna go do the Sunside?'

The suggestion came from out of nowhere and was the last thing Isabel expected to hear that day. She couldn't help but laugh.

'Come on,' Tamsin said with a grin. 'I'm serious. We could make the night flight if we go right now.'

'We haven't done that in ages.'

'And?'

'And I'm still working.'

'And?'

'And you just brought me dinner.'

'Psh,' Tamsin said, narrowing her eyes. 'Put it in the stasie, have it for lunch. I'll get you a stuffer on the way.' She patted the side of her jacket. 'I got a whole pocket of trade, and all you've got is weak excuses.' Her grin spread wider. Every line in her face took part.

Isabel was incredulous, but enchanted, too. The latter won out. 'All right,' she said, throwing up her hands. 'All right, let's go.'

'Ha!' Tamsin said, clapping her hands together and collecting her cane. 'I thought you'd punk out on me.' She extended her hand once she'd made it to her feet. Isabel took it without even thinking. The best kind of habit.

'Deshi,' Isabel called as they left her office. The junior archivist looked up from his desk. 'Please let everyone know I'm leaving the pre-spaceflight project until tomorrow. I'm—'

'She's being kidnapped,' Tamsin said, marching them toward the exit. 'Better call patrol.'

Deshi laughed and nodded. 'I dunno, M,' he said. 'I saw the one who did it, and she looked like bad news.'

Tamsin gave a deep, short chuckle. 'Smart man,' she said. She gave him a threatening squint worthy of any festival actor. 'Nobody likes snitches.'

Isabel rolled her eyes. 'Have a good night,' she said.

They made their way to the shuttledock as the globulbs began to dim. They made a short stop at the closest marketplace, where Tamsin made good on her word and traded a round of striped ribbon for two big pocket stuffers – toasted golden on the outside, packed with spicy shreds of red coaster meat and sweet onions. Isabel's stomach growled in anticipation as she raised it to her mouth. It was hardly a balanced meal, and had she seen any of her grandkids trying to argue the same for dinner, she'd have foisted a few vegetables on them first. But stars, it was good. The dough crunched at first bite, then bloomed into airy fluff, then gave way to the fiery centrepiece. Perfect.

She glanced over at Tamsin, who tore into her own stuffer as they walked. 'Did you not have dinner?' Isabel asked.

Tamsin swallowed. ''Course I did,' she said. 'But why should you be the only one to benefit from my good idea?' She took a large bite, *mmm*-ing appreciatively.

They continued their walk, relaying the events of the day between bites of bun until they arrived at their destination. The shuttledock stretched out before them, less crowded than in earlier hours. Beyond the entryway, a team of sanitation volunteers swept the floor, gaining nods and *thank you*s and short bursts of applause from the few passersby.

'Hi there.' A dock attendant appeared – a young teen, probably new to the job. He was short and well-groomed, and his polite alertness made it apparent that he took his role seriously. 'Can I help you find any particular vessel?'

'Have we missed the Sunside?' Tamsin asked.

The kid looked surprised, but recovered quickly. 'Let me check, M.' His eyes darted and blinked with practised purpose as he accessed information on his hud. 'You've still got time. Leaves in ten minutes.' He looked between the two old women before him, a slight anxiety creeping in. 'Have you done the Sunside before?'

Tamsin *tsked*. 'Kid, I was there for the *first* Sunside.' She smiled wickedly. 'And that was before they put in seatbelts.'

That last detail wasn't a bit true, but Isabel didn't dare call her out. The look on the kid's face was too hilarious. She leaned in. 'Is it still dock thirty-seven?'

The attendant gave a smart nod. 'Dock thirty-seven, yes, M.' He pointed the way with a flat, business-like hand. Isabel could feel him watching them leave with the air of someone who'd had their sense of balance thrown slightly askew. She couldn't help but smirk. Tamsin had always had a flair for ruffling strangers.

Dock thirty-seven was empty, save for the skiff waiting at the ready and a young woman leaning against the safety rail outside, playing a pixel game on her scrib. She was the pilot, as the multiple certification patches stitched onto her jacket indicated, and her uniformed appearance was every bit that of her profession, from her practical bamboo-fibre slacks to the resource-heavy boots that had probably belonged to another pair of feet first. But there were other details that would've been out of place on a pilot back when Isabel had been her age. The hypnotically shifting bot tattoos that danced up and down her forearms, for one. The thick Aandrisk-style swirls painted on her nails. The tiny glittering tech ports embedded near her temples, whose purpose Isabel could only guess at. She was an Exodan pilot, yes. But also . . . more.

The pilot glanced up as Isabel and Tamsin approached. 'Hey, M Itoh and M Itoh!' she said. 'How's it going?'

Isabel didn't know the girl well, but she knew her name, that she was from neighbourhood five, and that she sometimes came into the Archives to look at records of old Earth architecture. Isabel had done the naming ceremony for her niece earlier that standard. 'Hello, Kiku,' she said warmly. 'Are you our pilot this evening?'

Kiku looked delighted. 'You two here for the Sunside?'

'It appears that way,' Isabel said, throwing a look in Tamsin's direction.

Tamsin looked around the empty walkway. 'Do we have it to ourselves?' she asked, pleased with the possibility.

Kiku switched off her game, and the pixels scattered away. 'Not many folks go for a night flight on a work night,' she said, holstering her scrib and stepping toward the shuttle door. 'Just kids on dates, mostly.' She winked at them, and politely gestured toward the door. 'Come on in.'

The shuttle had six pairs of passenger seats in a straight line, and a clear, domed roof that began at seat level and arched all the way around. Walking through the door, you could tell the roof was as thick and sturdy as any bulkhead, but sitting next to it, you'd never know it was there.

'Anywhere you'd like,' Kiku said.

'What about that one?' Tamsin pointed at the pilot seat, serious as could be.

Kiku played right along. 'Can't have that one,' she said without cracking a smile.

'You sure?'

'Super sure.'

'*Tsk*,' Tamsin said, shaking her head. 'Well, this was a bust.' She started to head back toward the door, then chuckled, scrunched her nose at Kiku, and picked the second row behind the pilot's seat. Far enough to not be crowding the pilot, but close enough to give her a hard time.

Kiku started her prep, and Isabel took the seat beside her wife. Tamsin leaned over, speaking in a low whisper. 'Y'know, if she's used to kids on dates, I bet she won't mind if we make out.'

Isabel smothered a laugh and slapped Tamsin's leg. 'We'd traumatise the poor kid.'

'What? No. We're gorgeous.' Her eyes narrowed in thought. 'Didn't we make out on the Sunside once?'

A very old memory dusted itself off: a pair of women, younger than their pilot was now, drunk on bartered kick and eyes full of nothing but the other, cosied up in the back row of a shuttle as if no one else was there. 'That was the ferry, not the Sunside,' Isabel said.

'You sure?'

'I'm sure.'

'Okay. You're the archivist.'

Isabel leaned a little closer. 'How would you make out on the Sunside anyway? You'd knock your teeth in.'

Her wife snorted. 'But if you didn't, you'd be a legend. I'm surprised that's not a thing.'

'What? Go to town as long as you can without needing medical attention?'

'Yeah,' Tamsin laughed heartily. 'The Sunside challenge.'

The sounds of conspiratorial merriment made Kiku look back. 'You two gonna be trouble?'

Tamsin sat up straight and folded her hands across her lap. 'No way, M,' she said, like a school kid caught with cheat codes. 'No trouble here.'

'Mmm-hmm,' the pilot said, returning to her switches and buttons.

Isabel reached over and held Tamsin's hand. 'No trouble from me, anyway,' she said.

'Traitor,' Tamsin said. She gave her fingers an affectionate squeeze.

Kiku slipped on a navigation hud. 'Oh,' Isabel said. She reached up to her face, remembering that she'd been wearing her own hud since work. She removed it, and gave Tamsin a facetious glare as she slipped the device into a pocket. 'How long were you going to let me run around wearing this?'

Tamsin shrugged. 'Until now, I guess.'

The engines outside whirred, their ion jets starting to glow. 'All right,' the pilot said. 'Everybody ready?' She paused. 'I assume you two don't need the safety lecture, yeah?'

Tamsin tugged on her fastened seat restraint in response. 'Sit down, strap in, hang on.'

'And let the pilot do her job,' Isabel added.

Kiku pointed a finger back toward Isabel as she began to pull out from dock. 'I like that bit,' she said. 'I'm adding that bit.' She switched and pressed and made adjustments. 'You two want grav or nah?'

Isabel raised her eyebrows. 'You're allowed to switch it off?'

Kiku gave a mischievous shrug. 'Not officially.'

'We'll stick with grav,' Tamsin said. 'I like to feel like I'm actually upside down.'

'You got it,' Kiku said. She leaned into the vox. 'Sunside One, requesting a spot in line.'

'Granted, Sunside One,' the traffic controller replied. 'Have fun.'

The skiff pulled out and headed for the nearest airlock exit. A queue of private shuttles and long-haul transports each waited their turn. 'It'll be about half an hour until we reach the course,' Kiku said, easing into the queue. 'So just kick back and relax.' She took a hand away from the controls and dug around in a storage box strapped to the side of her seat. 'Either of you like salt toffee?'

Tamsin and Isabel spoke in tandem: '*Yes*.' Kiku grinned, retrieved a tin, and gestured at her controls. A cleanerbot deployed itself from its dock in the corner of the craft, its tiny stabiliser jets firing friendly green. It hummed over to Kiku, who balanced the tin on its flat housing. 'Second row,' she commanded, and the bot complied, uncaring of the extra cargo.

'Now that's a creative use for a cleanerbot,' Tamsin said, retrieving the tin from the idling machine.

'Works, yeah?' Kiku said.

'Sure does.' Tamsin looked at Isabel as she opened the tin. 'I'm never getting up to fetch you something ever again.'

The queue moved forward without much wait, and the skiff entered the airlock. One gate slid shut behind them, another opened ahead. Metal made way for space and starlight. Tamsin held her hand a little tighter, and Isabel didn't need to look at her to know she was smiling. She shared the feeling. The open was always beautiful.

And so they made their way to that old classic: the Sunside Joyride. A break-neck, full-throttle, sun-facing jaunt through whichever designated patch of rock the Fleet was orbiting closest to. A just-for-fun extravagance unveiled after GC citizenship expanded trade routes, and maintained by private donations after it became obvious that resources weren't as freely flowing as hoped. The courses were safe, obviously. They were mapped out well in advance, and every rock was equipped with proximity alarms and *backup* proximity alarms and stabilisation thrusters that kept them from straying into the track. The pilots were exhaustively trained, and traffic control back home watched their every move on the tracking map. But none of that changed the way it felt to be strapped into a small craft, looping and leaping in three dimensions, the clear wall around you playing the convincing trick that there was nothing between you and open sky. Some people hated it. Some people tried it once and decided they preferred keeping their lunch down.

Some people were no fun.

'What course are we hitting tonight?' Isabel asked.

'The Ten-Drop Twister,' Kiku said.

Tamsin looked at Isabel. 'I don't remember that one.'

'It's new,' Kiku said. 'Replaced the Devil Dive.'

'Aw, really? That one was *great*.'

The pilot nodded with sympathetic agreement. 'Yeah, but they found tungsten in that one.'

'Hard to argue that,' said Tamsin.

'Don't worry,' Kiku said. She put on a pair of pilot's gloves, the kind you only wore for manual control. Isabel's heart raced with anticipation. 'The Ten-Drop's a real kick in the pants. You won't be disappointed.'

The skiff pulled up to an asteroid patch, filled with tell-tale lights and markers. A big circle of light buoys wreathed the entrance point, blinking in an assortment of colours. Kiku activated her hud. The engines burned loud and hot. 'You two strapped in?'

Isabel tugged on her restraints, and her wife did the same. This had scared Tamsin the first time, Isabel remembered. She remembered a row of painful semi-circles embedded in her palm, where Tamsin had gripped tightly in fear. She remembered rubbing her then-girlfriend's back as she threw up on the dock the second they left the skiff. And she remembered the next day, when she awoke to find Tamsin's open eyes looking back from the pillow beside her, a who-cares grin in her voice as she asked Isabel if she wanted to go again.

Isabel had. From then on, if Tamsin was there, she'd be right alongside.

The engines roared, and the skiff ripped forward. 'Ohhhhhh nooooo!' Tamsin yelled, the last vowels blooming into a cackling yelp. Isabel yelled too, a screaming, living laugh as their skiff ducked and slid and jived.

'Faster!' Tamsin called.

'Faster!' Isabel echoed.

From behind, Isabel could see Kiku's cheeks pull into a huge smile. 'You got it,' she said, and they went faster, louder, upside down and circling sharp. Giant rocks floated beyond the windowed walls, looming one moment, then behind them in a blink. Stars flew by in a confettied blur. Tamsin was laughing so hard she was crying, and it was impossible not to laugh along. Isabel could feel nothing but motion, joy, heartbeat. It was as good as it'd been the first time, as good as it had always been. She shut her eyes, and she cheered.

EYAS

A canyon rose up around her, arches crumbling and rocks stained red. The sky was so far away, a swath of intangible blue beyond the grass-tufted clifftops. Below, birds nested in whatever cracks and crevices they could find. They darted around the shady space with breathtaking speed, turning to catch beakfuls of the insects that filled the hot air.

Presumably hot air, that is. The theatre did not include sensory input beyond sound and sight. This wasn't a sim. The theatre pre-dated that technology – or, to put it more accurately, pre-dated contact with species willing to share that technology. Every Exodan district had a theatre, and they still used the same antiquated tech, patched up a thousand times over, and the same recordings, taken by Eyas' ancestors' ancestors when it became clear that collapse was unavoidable. It was an old tradition, viewing the last scraps of a living Earth. There had been a time when going to the theatre was something you did every tenday – every *week*, then – or more. Every day, for some. You and your hexmates put on comfortable clothes, you brought some floor pillows, and you sat alongside other families on the floor beneath the projector dome, surrounded by all-encompassing images of a canyon, a beach, a forest. It was time made for reflection, for reminding. People laughed, sometimes, or wept, or sang quietly, or had whispered conversations. Anything beyond that was frowned upon. The theatre was a sacred place. A quiet place, even when any given day found it packed from end to end.

Eyas had never seen a theatre that crowded. The need to

acquaint oneself with what a planet looked like had faded more with each generation after the real thing had been found. She'd never seen more than ten people in a theatre at once, and not all the theatres were in use anymore. They weren't a vital system, and they didn't get resource priority unless the surrounding district voted otherwise. Hers always had. Eyas sympathised with people who wanted their stores to go to more practical uses, but she was glad the majority of her neighbours shared her view that practicality became dreary if you didn't balance it out properly.

Her primary reasoning for loving the theatre was selfish, and she knew it. She could've cited tradition and culture – and no one would've questioned her, given that her work embodied said same – but no, Eyas was glad to have a functional theatre nearby because it was one of the few places she could just *think*. Her work might've seemed quiet to some, but there were always families involved, and supervisory meetings like everyone else had. And even on the days when her only company was someone dead, she was focused on the task at hand. As for home – home was a place of rest, sure, but more chiefly distraction. Chores to do, friends to chat with, conversations leaking through closed doors. There weren't many places in the Fleet you could be alone. While she very much enjoyed being around the living, sometimes her own thoughts were noise enough. The theatre wasn't private. It was as public as could be. But it was a different kind of public, the kind of place where you could be alone around others.

She lay down on the floor, resting her head against the cushion she'd brought from home. The ghost of a wind rustled the scrappy canyon plantlife, and she imagined she could feel it coasting over her skin. She had no strong yearnings for wind and sky, but they were fun to think of anyway. Imagine: the intense vulnerability of an unshielded space. The wild chaos of atmosphere. Such thoughts were soothing and thrilling in equal measure.

Eyas folded her hands over her stomach, letting them rise and fall with each breath. She let her mind drift. She thought about the laundry she needed to do at home. She thought about her mother, and knew she should summon the fortitude to visit her one day soon. She thought about Sunny, and a hidden place inside her kicked with remembrance. She thought about dinner, and her empty stomach growled. She thought about work the next day, and she felt . . . she felt . . . she wasn't sure.

She shifted her weight, the floor now less comfortable than it had been a few breaths before. There it was again – that tiredness, that nameless tiredness. It wasn't lack of sleep, or overwork, or because anything was wrong. Nothing was wrong. She was healthy. She had a good home with good friends, and a full belly when she remembered to feed it. She had the profession she'd wanted since she was a little girl, and it was a valuable thing, a meaningful thing, a thing she believed in with all her heart. She'd worked hard for that. She had the life she'd always wanted, the life she'd set out to build.

Maybe . . . maybe that was the problem. So many years of training and study, always striving, always chasing the ideal at the end of the road. She'd reached that end by now. She had everything she'd set out to do. So now . . . what? What came next? Maintaining things as-is? Do well, be consistent, keep things up for however long she had?

She pressed her back into the metal floor, and felt the faint, faint purr of mechanical systems working below. She thought of the *Asteria*, orbiting endlessly with its siblings around an alien sun, around and around and around. Holding steady. Searching no more. How long would it stay like that? Until the last ship finally failed? Until the last Exodan left for rocky ground? Until the sun went nova? Was there any future for the Fleet that did not involve keeping to the same pattern, the same track, day after day after day until something went wrong? Was there any day for *her* that would not involve the same schedule, the same faces, the same tasks? What was better – a constant safeness that never grew and never changed, or a life of reaching, building, striving, even though you knew you'd never be completely satisfied?

A bang broke the stillness, startling everyone present. The

canyon gave a seizing shake, froze, and went dark. The audience collectively held their breath. Someone turned on a handlight and ran around the theatre's edge.

'Sorry, folks,' the theatre attendant called out, to a chorus of disappointment (but also, relief). 'Looks like we've bust a projector. I'll get the techs up here right now.'

Eyas got to her feet and picked up her pillow, knowing maintenance had a thousand more important things to fix *right now*. Besides, her stomach was growling louder. She'd never solve anything hungry.

KIP

This was, hands down, the worst night of Kip's life.

He sat in the living room, opposite his parents at the low table. Grandma Ko was doing whatever in the background. Messing with plants. He didn't care.

'We're not mad, Kip,' Dad said.

'I'm mad,' Mom said. She stirred a steaming mug of tea.

'Okay, your mom's mad. I think it'd be a good idea—'

'No, wait, he needs to understand why he's in trouble.' She set down her spoon. 'It's not because you went to a club. It's really important that you understand that.'

'That's right.' Dad did that dorky pointing thing with his index finger that he always did when he thought he was saying something smart. 'We're not mad because you wanted to have sex.'

Kip would've given anything in that moment – anything – for an oxygen leak, a stray satellite, a wormhole punched in the wrong place. Anything that would swallow him up and bring a merciful end to this conversation.

But instead, Mom *kept talking*. 'That part's okay. That's normal.'

'Absolutely,' Dad said. 'I remember what it was like to have all those hormones going around, all those urges – I couldn't stay out of the clubs when I turned twenty.'

'Me neither,' Mom said. 'Twice a day, sometimes.'

Kip buried his face in his hands. 'Can we . . . maybe . . . not?'

Grandma Ko looked over from her plants and laughed. 'It's not like you and your friends invented sex, kiddo,' she said. She pointed back and forth between his parents with her gardening clippers. 'You wouldn't be here otherwise.'

A rogue comet. A Rosk battlecruiser. A face-eating alien plague. *Anything*.

'The reason you're in trouble,' Dad said, 'is because you lied and you broke the rules.'

'He broke the *law*, Alton,' Mom said. 'Not just Fleet law. GC law.' She looked at Kip with that look that meant the next tenday or so was really going to suck. He could already picture the lengthy list of chores that was going to appear on his scrib after this. 'The only reason you're talking with us and not a patroller right now is because that host at the club cut you and Ras a break. Tampering with your patch is not a joke, Kip.'

'I know,' Kip mumbled. The faster he agreed with them, the faster this might be over.

'That hack you boys used could've uploaded *anything*. It could've carried a virus that messed with your bots. You know that's what happened to those people on the *Newet*, right?'

'I know, Mom.'

'One person went to an unlicensed mod vendor, and the next thing you know—'

'My patch is fine,' Kip said. 'You made me scan it, like, five times.'

'That's not the point,' Mom said. 'The point is, you did something illegal and dangerous. You got *lucky*.'

'Not in the way he was hoping,' Grandma Ko laughed.

'Grandma,' Mom said. 'Please.'

Grandma Ko put up her hands in surrender and kept working. '*Tika lu*, okay?' Kip said.

The look on Mom's face somehow got even frostier. 'In Ensk.'

Oh, stars, was she really going to get on his ass about *that*? Fine. Fine, whatever it took to get him out of there. 'I'm sorry. All right? I don't know how many times you want me to say *I'm sorry*.'

'We know you're sorry,' Dad said, 'and we also know you want to get out of here. But you need to know the score, son.'

'I get it,' Kip sighed. 'I do, okay? I get it.'

Mom tapped her fingers against her mug. 'When do you start your next job trial?'

Ah, shit, Kip thought. He mumbled a response under his breath.

'What was that?'

'I haven't signed up for one yet.'

The look on Mom's face got worse. Kip could see three more to-dos being added to his list. 'You were supposed to sign up for another before your last one ended,' she said.

'I forgot.'

'Kip, we talked about this,' Dad said.

'Okay, so, first thing tomorrow, you're signing up for a job trial,' Mom said. 'And until it starts, you come straight home after school so you can help your hex. No sims, no cafes, no hanging out wherever it is you hang out. There are a lot of projects in the neighbourhood that need some extra hands right now.'

Kip reeled. 'But I probably won't start another trial for a tenday.'

'Yep,' Mom said.

No way. *No way.* 'That's not fair!'

'You're home instead of in detention. You don't get to complain about *fair* right now.'

Dad put his hands flat on the table. 'All we're asking is for you to clear your head and get focused,' he said, his voice irritatingly mellow. He often did this thing where he wanted to sound all reasonable and cool even though he was just agreeing with Mom. It drove Kip nuts.

He tried to negotiate. 'Ras and I are going to the waterball game on second day. We have plans.'

Mom's mouth tightened. 'We think a break from Ras might be a good idea, too.'

That did it. Kip exploded. 'This wasn't his fault!' he said. It was totally Ras' fault, but that wasn't the point. 'Stars, you guys are *always* hating on him.'

'I don't hate Ras,' Mom said. 'I'm just not sure he's—' She looked up at the ceiling, thinking. 'It'd be wise for you both to take some time to think about the kinds of choices you've been making.'

'This is bullshit,' Kip muttered.

'Hey,' Dad said.

'No, it is,' Kip said, getting louder. 'It *is* bullshit. Look, I'm sorry I messed up tonight, but the only – the only reason I went along – the only reason we went there is because *there's nothing to do.* It sucks here. What am I supposed to do? Go to school, do chores, learn how to do a job that's basically more chores?'

'Kip—'

'And now you don't even want me to have *friends.*'

'Oh, come on, Kip.' Mom rolled her eyes.

'Of course we want you to have friends,' Dad said. 'We just want you to have friends that bring out the best in you.'

'You guys don't understand,' Kip said. 'You don't understand at all.' He pushed away from the table and walked off.

'Hey, we're not done,' Mom said.

'*I'm* done,' Kip said. He went into his room and punched the door switch behind him.

'Kip,' Dad called through the metal wall.

Kip ignored him. Stars, fuck this place. Fuck these stupid rules and stupid jobs and fuck being sixteen. He was getting *out.* The day – no, the *second*, the very second the clock hit his twentieth birthday, he was hopping on a transport, and he'd be *gone,* university or not. He'd find a job somewhere. He didn't care where or what. Anything was better than this. Anything was better than Mom's lists and Dad's stupid voice. Anything was better than here.

Behind his door, he could hear them still talking. Kip knew listening in would only make him madder, but he put his ear up anyway.

'Maybe I should go talk to him,' Dad said. 'Y'know, just me and him.'

'He doesn't want to talk to either of us,' Mom said. 'Or were you not here for this conversation?'

'But—'

'Let him be,' Grandma Ko said.

Mom sighed. 'He's so impossible right now.'

'Yes, well,' Grandma Ko said. 'You were a dipshit at that age, too.'

Kip snorted. 'Love you too, Grandma,' he grumbled. He flopped down onto his bed and buried his face in his pillow, wishing he could erase the entire day. *Dammit, Ras*, he thought, but he wasn't mad at him. Well . . . kind of. But not, like, a forever kind of mad. He knew Ras hadn't meant for it to go wrong.

He rolled over onto his side and groaned. Seriously. Zero hour on day 23, standard 310. Once that hit, he was *out*.

SAWYER

'Nervous?' Oates asked as they headed down the walkway.

Sawyer gave a sheepish smile. 'It's a job interview. Have you ever *not* been nervous at one?'

Oates chuckled and clapped Sawyer's shoulder with his mech hand. 'Don't worry. The boss is gonna love you. I mean, unless she hates you.' He winked. 'She'll tell it to you straight if she does.'

They continued along. Ships of varied size coasted slowly by. The shuttledock was a complicated stack of layers and levels, all built over a century prior, once Exodans found themselves with *other places to go*. Sawyer felt as if he were standing in the middle of the sea, watching creatures migrate past – little lively ones, modest middling beasts, and ponderous behemoths everything else made way for. He remembered his mom taking him to the planetside docks on Mushtullo, making up stories about where each ship had gone and was going. The memory came with a familiar sting, but it was a hurt he'd long ago learned to shelve.

Oates led him to a dock designated for mid-size ships – merchant vessels and small cargo, mostly. They walked past thick bulkheads, slim atmospheric fins, hand-hacked tech upgrades, every design as different as the last. Sawyer eyed the names with enjoyment. *Out of the Open. Take-A-Chance. Good Friend. Quick and Easy. The Better Side of Valour.*

'Here we are.' Oates gestured Sawyer ahead. 'Home sweet home.'

Sawyer looked up at a nondescript freighter – dull grey plating, big engine, somewhat rough around the edges. It wasn't as flashy or added-to as some. It didn't stand out. But to Sawyer, that was a good thing. Flashy tech would've been intimidating, and too much of a penchant for modding would've worried him. This ship appeared solid, functional, and looked-after. All you wanted in a spacecraft, really.

He spotted the ship's registry info, printed by the open entry hatch.

THE SILVER LINING
Registration No. 33-1246
Asteria, Exodus Fleet

'Do you live on this ship?' Sawyer asked.

'Pretty much,' Oates said. He walked through the hatch; Sawyer followed. 'I see my folks when we're docked, but it's easier to keep all your stuff in one place, y'know? Nyx, though – that's our pilot – she splits her time between this home and a home-home. Her ex's hex. They hate each other, but they've got a kid, so. Y'know. You don't have kids, right?'

'Uh, no,' Sawyer said. He ducked, avoiding a low string of festival flags stretched across a doorway. The internal structure of the *Silver Lining* was as standard as the outside suggested, but it was crammed to the gills with crates, boxes, and barrels, sealed and stamped with the same multilingual export permits you'd find on any goods that had to cross a territory or two. On top of that, this ship was unmistakably a home, with all the weird decor and knick-knacks that implied. There were pixel posters of musical acts he'd never heard of, globulb strands wrapped around doorways, failing herbs planted in old snack tins and struggling up toward a grow lamp. It wasn't a mess, exactly, but it was a *lot*. 'What do you guys trade in?'

'Oh, a little of this, a little of that. We're not picky. If it'll fetch good creds, we'll haul it.' He rounded a corner, and ran smack into the tallest, burliest woman Sawyer had ever seen.

Whoa, Sawyer thought. Was this the boss? Was *this* who he'd have to impress?

'Whoops!' Oates said with a laugh. 'Sorry about that, Dory.'

Dory squinted wordlessly at him with her one organic eye. The plex lens in the other audibly clicked into focus. Her head was only about a hand's length away from the ceiling, and her broad arms looked as though they resented what short amount of sleeve they'd had to push themselves through. Sawyer waited for her to smile, to offer her own cheerful apology, to do *something* resembling friendly Human behaviour. But no, instead, she moved her eye – and only her eye – to Sawyer. The squint evolved into a full frown.

'This is Sawyer,' Oates said. 'He's here about our empty spot. Sawyer, this is Dory. She's terrifying.'

Dory let out . . . not so much a laugh, but a short chuff. And that was it. She pushed past them and continued on her way.

'A real bundle of sunshine,' Oates said. 'Come on, let's find some better company.' He went a short way further, and they entered a kitchen. Three people were present there, two in conversation across a table. A clean-shaven man leaned against a storage cabinet, eating a large jam cake. He, too, was broad and muscled, but something about his stature – or maybe the sticky pastry he held – made him look far more approachable than his one-eyed crewmate. He nodded congenially at Oates, then continued to watch as the other two spoke.

'You said nine hundred last time,' one said in a testy tone. She was around Sawyer's age – twenty, tops, he guessed.

The other was at least twice that, and cool as rain in her reply. 'Last time, you brought me better merchandise. Nine hundred is what you get for quality. Not for this.' She gestured dismissively at an opened box on the table between them.

Sawyer no longer wondered who was in charge here.

'That's not *fair*,' the girl said. 'We made a *deal*.'

'Yes, and you're the one who isn't delivering, Una, not me. You can either take three hundred a pop now, or come back with something better. Or find another buyer, if you really feel you're being treated unfairly.' Her eyes flicked over to Sawyer and Oates. 'My next meeting is here, so I'll let you settle this with Len.' She gestured to the cake-eating man. 'He'll let me know your decision.'

The man – Len, apparently – folded the last of his pastry into his mouth, brushed the crumbs from his hands with a neat *one-two*, and stepped forward to escort the young woman elsewhere. The woman sulked, but she grabbed her box of . . . whatever it was, and followed.

The boss put her hands on her hips and sighed at Sawyer with the sort of knowing smile he might expect if they'd already met. 'Business,' she said. She waved him over. 'You must be Sawyer.'

Sawyer approached the table. 'And you must be the boss.'

She laughed – a rich, honest sound. 'Muriel,' she said. She looked to Oates. 'I like this one already.' She made a short tipping gesture toward her mouth as a means of request. Oates went about fetching some mugs. 'I have to say, it's a trip hearing that accent on this side of the galaxy. Central space, Oates said?'

'That's right.' Sawyer took a seat. 'Mushtullo.'

'I haven't been myself, but I have a friend who's done business there. A bit rough, is what I heard.'

The words came across as a question. 'A bit,' Sawyer answered.

Muriel leaned back in her chair. 'So. You're here after Livia's job.'

Sawyer was confused. 'Sorry, I don't—'

Oates leaned over from the counter, where he was pouring water from a kettle. 'I don't think I mentioned Livia.'

'Ah,' Muriel said. 'Livia was – let me back up. How much has Oates already told you about this job?'

'I know it's a salvage job,' Sawyer said. 'Recovering scrap, that kind of thing.'

Muriel gave a thoughtful nod. Despite her friendly demeanor, Sawyer couldn't help but feel that every word that left his mouth was being weighed, measured, and scored. 'Exactly,' she said. 'And the trick with wrecked ships is, sometimes both they and their cargo pose challenges that require a bit of code.' She turned her palm to Sawyer, silently adding: *and that's why you're here.*

Oates handed both her and Sawyer a mug overflowing with spicy steam. 'Thanks,' Sawyer said, setting it down before his fingers scalded. 'What kind of challenges?'

'Let's say . . .' Muriel considered. 'Let's say we're talking about a cargo ship. Medical supplies, going from here to there. Now, any merchant worth xyr salt is gonna have xyr crates locked up, and xe's not going to hand over the key code until creds are exchanged. But our poor merchant met the mean side of an asteroid patch, and now xe and xyr crew are dead, and nobody knows the cargo key.'

'Ah.' Sawyer got it. 'You need somebody who can open doors so the rest of you can do your job.'

'Bingo. Because otherwise, nobody can get those goods to where they were going.'

'I see.' This sounded like kind of a cool job, now that Sawyer thought about it. Opening doors, salvaging goods, making sure nothing went to waste. Nothing went to waste in the Fleet.

'So Livia.' Muriel's eyes rolled. 'She did stupid during our last planet stop.' She waved her hand. 'Not worth getting into. Kick and poor decisions. Anyway, her dumb ass is now in an Aandrisk jail, and I'm stuck here without a comp tech.' She sighed at Oates.

'I hear Aandrisk jails are nice,' Oates said over the rim of his mug. 'Y'know, far as jails go.'

'She doesn't deserve it,' Muriel said dryly.

A flicker of concern shot through Sawyer. 'Just to be totally up front,' he said, 'I'm not a comp tech. I'm not certified or anything, and I don't have a ton of experience. I just know mid-level Tinker.'

'So Oates told me,' Muriel said. 'Though I appreciate your honesty. Certifications don't concern me. What I care about is skill, and a willingness to learn. You have a scrib on you?'

Sawyer reached for his holster. 'Yeah.'

Muriel reached elsewhere, and came back with a lockbox. 'Think you could get this open?' She slid the box across the table.

Sawyer picked up the box and wet his lips. 'I've never done locks before.'

'What have you done?'

'Input pads, gesture relays, that kind of thing.'

Muriel looked less than impressed, but she shrugged and tossed over a tethering cable. 'Hook it up, take a look. And take your time thinking about it.' She blew over the top of her tea. 'I'm in no rush.'

You can do this, Sawyer thought. He connected scrib to cable and cable to lock jack. He gestured at his scrib, and a flurry of code appeared. *All right*, he thought. He spoke this language. He understood these puzzles. *If, then*. He scrolled through, minutes ticking by. Every second that passed pressed down on his neck. He could feel Muriel watching him as she sipped her cooling tea. He wondered if this was part of the test, too, if he was taking too long, if the bit of sweat forming on his brow was giving her second thoughts. But all he could do was his best. He'd been honest with her. He had to expect the same. She said take time to think about it, so he did. It was, in a way, not too different than his trips to the commerce square back home, demonstrating his skills for judgey Harmagians, impressing by doing rather than writing the right words. Only, this was so much better. This wasn't a judgey Harmagian watching him work. This was a cool lady and a nice guy who were as Human as he was and didn't hold it against him. These were people who wanted him to succeed. His nerve steadied as he realised that, and, at last, words and strings began to reveal themselves to him.

Sawyer pieced the logic together. He tweaked here, added there.

The box stayed shut.

He glanced up. Muriel was nearly through her mug of tea. *Shit.*

He grit his teeth, and he wrote, and he read, and he wrote some more, and—

There was a sound – a dull click. It wasn't much of a sound, but to Sawyer, it was sweet victory. He pulled the lid open and swung its empty inside around to Muriel.

The boss nodded with a quiet smile. 'Found him outside the job office?' she said to Oates.

Oates gave a happy shrug. 'It's a talent, what can I say.'

'I don't pay you enough.'

'I know.'

Muriel studied Sawyer. 'I'd want you to do that faster. But now that you've done it once, you have a better idea of what to do next time, right?'

'Right. I can practise before the job, no problem. I mean . . . if I got the job.'

Muriel smirked. 'Let's talk about the job. We're heading to the *Oxomoco*.'

'Wow,' Sawyer said. 'Okay. Wow.'

Muriel leaned forward and rested her chin on her laced fingers. 'What does that mean to you?'

'Well . . . jeez, everybody heard about that. What happened to it, I mean. That was a huge thing. And horrible. Really horrible.' He processed this new info. 'Must be a ton of scrap that needs sorting, huh?'

The captain considered him in silence. Something satisfied her, and she sat back up. 'It's a trial run, you understand. Right now, all you and I have is one gig we're going to work together. If either of us is unhappy with how it goes, we walk away, no hard feelings, and no further obligations. But if it goes well . . .' She made a *let's see* motion with an opened palm. 'I do have an empty set of quarters open to the right person.'

Sawyer wasn't sure when he'd last felt so determined. He was the right person for this, he knew it. He was going to rock this job. He was going to give it one hundred percent. One hundred and *ten*.

A part of him, though, was hesitant. This wasn't what he'd imagined. He'd imagined a hex, an address in the Fleet. But then again . . . A warm thought cut through the caution. This was the Fleet, too. He'd read the Litany they recited at ceremonies. *We are the homesteaders*, yes, but also: *We are the ships that ferry between*. Well, here he was, on a ship, ready to do some spacer recycling. That sounded pretty Exodan to him.

Muriel reached her hand across the table. 'We got a deal?'

Sawyer took her hand and shook it firmly. 'We got a deal.'

Part 3

TO THIS DAY,
WE WANDER STILL

Feed source: Reskit Institute of Interstellar Migration (Public News Feed)
Item name: The Modern Exodus – Entry #6
Author: Ghuh'loloan Mok Chutp
Encryption: 0
Translation path: [Hanto:Kliptorigan]
Transcription: 0
Node identifier: 2310-483-38, Isabel Itoh

[System message: The feed you have selected has been translated from written Hanto. As you may be aware, written Hanto includes gestural notations that do not have analogous symbols in any other GC language. Therefore, your scrib's on-board translation software has not translated the following material directly. The content here is a modified translation, intended to be accessible to the average Kliptorigan reader.]

———

It is without question that there are many ways in which Exodans have benefited from GC influence. Imubots, artigrav, algae fuel, tunnel access – and of course, mek, which Exodans drink in quantities on par with the rest of the galaxy. But cultural exchange is never without its disruptions, and while the elder Exodan generation frowns over the younger's preference for Klip and penchant for Harmagian charthump (why that genre of music in particular, I can't say), I submit that there is one introduced factor more divisive than any other: the Galactic Commons Commerce Credit.

To understand the conundrum created by the humble cred, you must first understand how Exodans manage labour and resources – and indeed, how they have done so for centuries. To begin, the basics: if you are physically present within the Exodus Fleet, you receive lodgings, food, air, and water. You have access to all public services, and you are granted the same sapient rights as any. No exceptions, no questions asked. There are limits to how much an individual can receive, of course – finite stores within a closed system can only be stretched so far. But Exodan life support capacity has been greatly expanded by the upgrades they've implemented over the standards (again, thanks to GC tech), and they take careful count of each person who enters the majestic homesteader shuttledocks. Were Fleet systems or supplies to become taxed, all but citizens would be systematically deported. This has yet to become an issue. In fact, if anything, the decrease in Exodan population since their admission into the GC has made the Fleet more capable of welcoming others.

You may be wondering, dear guest, as I did, how labour is compensated if your base needs are met. This is the part that's hard for many – non-Exodan Humans included – to understand: it's not. Nor do some professions receive more resources than others, or finer housing, or any such tangible benefits. You become a doctor because you want to help people. You become a pilot because you want to fly. You become a farmer because you want to work with growing things, or because you want to feed others. To an Exodan, the question of choosing a profession is not one of *what do I need?* but rather *what am I good at? What good can I do?*

Of course, some professions are more glamorous than others – a pilot, it's safe to argue, has more dynamic days than a formwork clerk – but this ultimately comes down to personal preference. Not everyone *wants* a busy, exciting profession that requires long hours and special-ised training. Many are content to do something simple that fulfils the desire to be useful but also allows them plenty of opportunity to spend time with their families and hobbies. This is why professions that *do* require rigorous schooling – or pose inherent risk, either physically or emotionally – are so highly respected within Exodan society. I witness this often in the company of my dear host, Isabel, who receives gifts and deference wherever she goes (you may be wondering how *gifts* work in a society with no native currency; I will come to that). I have seen this behaviour as well with caretakers, miners, and council members. This is not to say that other professions are unvalued – far from it. There is no such thing as a meaningless job in the Fleet. Everything has a purpose, a recognisable benefit. If you have food on your plate, you thank a farmer. If you have clothing, you thank a textile manufacturer. If you have murals to brighten your day, you thank an artist. Even the most menial of tasks benefits someone, benefits *all*.

Perhaps it is their very lack of planetary scale that makes this kind of inclusive thinking possible. Societal machinations and environmental stability are not abstract concepts for the Exodans. They are an immediate, visceral reality. This is why it is rare for able adults to eschew a profession entirely (though this does happen, to considerable scorn), and why youths are under intense scrutiny from their elders as to which line of work they will apprentice in. A job is partly a matter of personal fulfilment, yes, but also – and perhaps chiefly – *social* fulfilment. When an Exodan asks 'what do you do?', the real question is: 'What do you do *for us*?'

This is not a wholly communal society, however. The concept of personal belongings (and living space) still exists, and is quite important. A canister of dried beans, for example, is a public resource, until said canister is allotted to a family. The family trades nothing for this item, as access to it is their right as citizens. But once the canister crosses from storeroom to home, it now belongs to the family in question, and another family taking it would be a punishable act of theft (not to mention unnecessary, as the thieves would have their own beans to start with). Let's now imagine that a member of this family decides to become a baker. Xe takes xyr family beans, makes them into dough, and creates delicious confections (or so I am told; as with so many Human foods, bean cakes are one of the many staples I cannot consume). Unless this individual is extremely generous, xe will not distribute these goods for free, as this is food now absent from the family pantry. Xe will instead engage in that most Exodan of traditions: bartering. Were I an Exodan with want of cake, I could offer vegetables from my home garden, or a selection of spare bolts, or any such offering that both the baker and I deemed a fair and acceptable trade.

If the baker is successful enough in bartering xyr wares, xe will have a surplus of bartered items that can then be traded with the public food stores in exchange for surplus allotments of beans, at which point the herbs and bolts and whatnot re-enter the realm of public resource and become available to the general populace. Or, the baker can simply hang onto xyr bartered items in lieu of having a full cupboard at home, if the family decides they prefer bolts to beans. So even though all resources are rigidly controlled and meted out on a public level, there is profound freedom in what each family decides to do with their share.

Perhaps it has already become obvious how this delicate balance was disrupted the moment Exodan forebears crossed paths with an Aeluon research probe. Exodans are not impoverished (a misconception I encounter constantly back home). They are healthy and housed, and experience no extraordinary stress. But it is true that if you were to pick up an Exodan home and place it in the middle of, say, Sohep Frie or the residential edges of Reskit, that home would appear jarringly meagre. It is not that Exodans are lacking; it's that the privileged of us have so much more. A canister of dried beans is well and good, but it's not as nutrient-packed as jeskoo, not as tasty to a Human palate as snapfruit, not as exciting as *something new*. Yes, an Exodan might say, the shuttle engines built in Fleet factories are perfectly adequate, but have you seen what the Aandrisks are flying these days? Have you seen the latest sim hubs, the latest implants, the latest redreed hybrids? Have you seen what wonders our alien friends have?

I should note, in case you're getting the wrong idea, that Exodans have been steadily innovating and inventing throughout their history. The Fleet is one enormous tinkerer's workshop, and the equity with which goods are accessible means that anybody with a new idea – mechanical, scientific, artistic, what have you – has the resources to bring it to life. The only limit to what an Exodan can create is what xe has on hand. The fact that Humanity has been liberally implementing GC tech (and building off of it in ingenious, locally specialised ways) does not mean that the Fleet has been technologically stagnant since leaving Earth, nor does it mean their system of labour management is insufficient in driving creative minds to improve upon the old. Dear guest, I cannot impress strongly enough how important it is that we understand the current Exodan state of affairs. It is not that the Exodans were standing still. It is that the rest of us were so far ahead.

Which brings us to those who keep the treasures the average Exodan cannot resist: GC merchants. Non-Human species in residential areas are so rare as to be effectively hypothetical, but the merchant-facing shuttledocks are relatively diverse. Multilingualism is a job requirement for today's import inspectors, as is interspecies sensitivity training. But while the Exodans working the docks have made efforts to adapt to alien custom, the merchants they so eagerly welcome have neglected to adapt in one crucial respect: payment. This is hardly surprising, nor is it unfair. A GC trader has no use for beans or bolts. Xe wants creds, plain and simple. If the Exodans want their imports (and they badly do), they must pay up.

On a galactic scale, a unified currency makes sense. The alternative would be madness. But in a society as small as the Exodus Fleet, the mixture of creds and barter has yet to gel. The Exodus Fleet produces virtually no trade goods of outside interest, which means creds can only come from elsewhere. For generations, more and more Exodans have left to do work in other systems, in search of wealth, adventure, or simply a broader variety of occupational options. These individuals are Exodan through and through, however, and they do what any community-minded citizen would: they send creds home. Who wouldn't do this? Who wouldn't want their families to eat better, to be more comfortable, to have more conveniences and delights? How could this act of sharing be born of anything but kindness?

Imagine now that our baker has been given some creds. Now xe no longer needs to wait for beans to become available, or to carefully save up the right number of bolts. Xe can instead put in an import order for suddet root – not the same as beans, but usable in the same way, and more valuable for its exoticism. The creds then leave the Fleet, nothing re-enters the public stores – beans, bolts, or otherwise – and other bakers who once comfortably traded bean cakes in nearby neighbourhoods now find their customers making longer walks elsewhere for the sake of alien novelty. A seamless harmony that was maintained for centuries has been thrown off-key, and it remains unclear how the song will end.

This is not a new problem. The Fleet has been struggling with creds since the days of first contact. At first, participation in the galactic economy was perceived as a harmful acquiescence to foreign values – not alien, interestingly, but *Martian*. Contact with the GC in turn enabled Fleet contact with the Sol system for the first time since the Exodans left, and the reunion was not a cordial one. Much has been written on this topic elsewhere, so in the interest of brevity, I will mention only that in the early days of the post-contact Fleet, anything coded as Martian – money, war, extreme individualism – was understood to be dangerously incompatible with Exodan morality. This sentiment still lingers (unwaveringly so in military affairs), but in matters of economy, there has been a slow, steady shift. There are Exodan merchants who, to this day, steadfastly refuse to accept creds out of cultural pride, and there is a social righteousness I've observed in individuals who, in turn, choose to only interact with such establishments. But these principled people live next door to others who *do* have the newest implants and the trendiest food. While our resolute barterers may not be tempted by flash and fashion, while they may be content to live with amenities that are *suitable* and *adequate* and *just enough* . . . their children are still making up their minds.

SAWYER

Sent message
Encryption: 0
Translation: 0
From: Sawyer (path: 7466-314-23)
To: Eyas (path: 6635-448-80)

Hi Eyas,

I hope you don't mind me sending you a note. I found your scrib path in the ship's directory (you're the only one with your name!). Anyway, I wanted to thank you again for your advice the other day. I'd just signed up for sanitation work when I met somebody outside the job office looking to hire workers for a salvage project. It's just a gig right now, but it might be more. Plus, this crew's been the only group of people other than yourself to offer to show me the ropes. They seem like fun folks. So I'm on board with them now, but don't worry! My name's still in the sanitation lottery. I took what you said seriously, and I'll help out when I'm needed. Thanks for steering me in the right direction.

Sawyer

———

He should've been sleeping. Sleep was the smart thing, the responsible thing. He was worried about not screwing things up that day, and he knew that if he was smart, he'd still be in bed, because being well-rested would help him actually accomplish that. But instead, he was up during the artificial dawn, standing in his bedroom in the otherwise unoccupied home, turning this way and that in front of the mirror, cycling through the five shirts he owned and liking none of them. They didn't look like what Exodans wore. They were too bright, too crisp. They lacked that degree of sincere, inoffensive wear that Exodan clothing always had, that reminder that new cloth only came around every so often. His clothes, cheap though they'd been, simple though he'd thought them, were made too well. He hadn't known that when he'd packed his bags back on Mushtullo, but he knew it now, just like he knew that his accent put people off, and that even though he shared the same DNA as everybody else here, they saw him as something other.

I should've bought new clothes, he thought irritably as he pulled off his shirt with a sigh. He'd meant to, but he'd been so busy brushing up on Tinker that he'd run out of time. He backed up to the edge of his bed and sat down, holding the garment in his hands. Red and brown threads, woven together in a breezy fashion, perfect for the sticky days back home. He'd bought this shirt at Strut, one of his favourite shops down in Little Florence. He'd been with friends at the time – Cari and Shiro and Lael, blowing their creds and getting drunk in celebration of yet another payday at the shitty stasie factory.

Of all the things he'd anticipated in leaving Mushtullo, homesickness hadn't been one of them. He didn't feel it with a pang, but with an ache – a dull, keening ache, the kind of thing you could ignore at first but that grew less tolerable every day. There was a lot about his homeworld he didn't miss. The crowds. The grime. The triple dose of daylight that made shirts like the one he held a necessity. But he missed the people. He missed Lael, with her incessant puns. He missed Cari, always good for the latest gossip. He even missed Shiro, the cranky bastard, garbage taste in music and all.

He'd left for good reasons, he told himself. He'd left for the *right* reasons. What was there for him on Mushtullo, beyond working jobs he didn't care about so he could buy drinks he'd piss away and shirts he wouldn't like later? What was there beyond a drab studio in a drab residence block, in a neighbourhood where people shoved guns in your back and took your creds? What meaning was there in that? What good?

Even so, he missed his friends. Stars, he missed having friends.

He wondered, cautiously, if he'd made a mistake. If he was still making one. Maybe Eyas had been right. Maybe the folks at the job office had been trying to tell him that he didn't have the right stuff to become part of the Fleet. He knew where the transport dock was. He only had five shirts. It wouldn't take him long to pack.

Sawyer shook his head. What was wrong with him? He was starting a job today! A job! With people! With Oates, who'd liked him! Muriel seemed to like him, too, and Len seemed all right, and . . . okay, Dory was scary, but maybe she'd come around. Maybe he was what they were looking for. Maybe they'd welcome him in.

Sawyer realised that was what was scaring him. He was afraid of getting his hopes up, of putting too much stock into this new thing. He'd learned, in the past few tendays, that deciding ahead of time how a thing was going to go was setting yourself up for a faceplant.

So, fine, he didn't know how it would go . . . but he knew what he wanted from them. A posse. A crew. A real crew, like he'd seen in vids and sims. People who looked after each other. People who were messy sometimes, but could pull together when stuff got tough. People who would laugh at his jokes, and give him a nickname, maybe, who would knock on his door late at night because they knew where they could go with their problems. People who always had a spot at the table for him. People to whom he mattered.

It was too big of an expectation to put on one job offer, he knew that. But he looked at himself in the mirror, and he felt some confidence creep back in. If it was a matter of either getting

his hopes up or glooming himself to the edge of going home –
well then, hopes up it was. He took a breath and put on his shirt.
His clothes were fine. They would do. The crew of the *Silver
Lining* would like him. He'd do a good job. He'd use the last of
his creds and buy everybody a drink after. He'd be cool and
funny, and they'd want him to come back again.

Sawyer stood and examined himself. *Red looks good on you*,
he could hear Cari saying, the payday kick making her loud. *You
should definitely buy that.*

He nodded. He smiled. He was gonna do great.

TESSA

'Aren't you supposed to be at work?' Pop grumbled, slumped and spread-legged in the clinic waiting room. They were the only ones there, thank goodness. The last thing this ridiculous to-do needed was an audience.

'Nope, I'm here,' Tessa said, idly scrolling through a news feed on her scrib. Stars, was there ever a day when the news was good?

'Don't you have a shift?'

'I swapped with Sahil for the afternoon.'

Out of the corner of her eye, Tessa saw his arms cross and mouth scowl. 'I would've gone,' Pop said.

'You haven't gotten a checkup in six tendays. You're supposed to go every three.'

'I'm *fine*.'

Tessa's eyes shifted to the wall across from them. 'Can you read that sign?'

'What sign?'

She nodded at the assertive yellow notice on the wall, informing people about the new imubot models that had become available. '*That sign.*'

'Oh, so *you're* my doctor now?'

'Pop.'

'Sorry, but only a medical professional can ask me those kinds of questions.' He looked her up and down. 'And I don't see your credentials.'

A twinge appeared in Tessa's left temple. He was acting infant-
ile, but she was also fairly certain he *couldn't* read the sign, and
that meant she had to stick this out.

The office door opened, thank goodness, and Dr Koraltan
stood waiting with a broad smile. 'M Santoso, at last!' he said
in a tone that suggested he knew exactly what the score was. 'I
was beginning to think you didn't like us.'

Pop stood; Tessa did the same. 'You're not coming with me,'
Pop mumbled.

'Oh, yes, I am.' She put her scrib in its holster and gestured
toward the door. 'After you.'

Dr Koraltan's smile grew larger. 'Nice to see you as well, Tessa.
How's your back?'

'Behaving,' she said, following her defeated father onward to
the examination room. 'Amazing how not twisting my spine while
lifting my toddler has helped.'

The doctor laughed as he waved the exam room door closed.
'Up on the table, please, M. Tessa, make yourself comfortable.'
He gestured at his scrib. 'All right, M, it looks like it's been . . .
wow, almost nine tendays since you were last here.'

Tessa's head snapped to her father. 'Nine, huh.'

Pop scowled at the floor. He looked for all the world like Aya
when she'd gotten into something she shouldn't. It might've been
funny if it weren't so damned embarrassing.

Dr Koraltan cleared his throat. 'I really do recommend coming
by every thirty days, M. I know it's not fun, but—'

'I'm not having another surgery,' Pop blurted out. 'I'm fine.'

The doctor exchanged a glance with Tessa. 'Do you think you
need one?' he asked.

Pop was quiet a beat too long. 'How should I know?' he said.

The twinge in Tessa's temple made its way to her eye socket.

'Well, let's see if I can settle the matter,' the doctor said. He
wheeled over a bot scanner; Pop placed his wrist in habitually.
For all his protesting, he was entirely compliant as the doctor
performed the exam. Tessa had seen this play out many times,

but there was always something disquieting, something sad about watching Pop submit to the pokes and prods. In childhood, he'd been awesome, invincible, the guy who could pick you up and spin you around and make your fears melt away. Superhuman, him and Mom both. It had been an eternity or two since Tessa had thought of Pop like that, but he was, after all, still her dad. And while her mother's too-soon death had been a brutal confirmation of mortality, it had also been fairly quick. Watching someone succumb to an unexpected disease over the course of a few tendays wasn't the same as standing witness to decades of decline. Pop wasn't ill or anything. He'd be a pain in everyone's ass for a good while yet. But she looked at him now, wrinkles and spots and hunched shoulders, here because of problems that kept coming around. She thought of her back, which *was* better, but still woke her up in the night sometimes. There were lines in her face that weren't getting shallower. Grey highlights were taking over her black curls. She looked at Pop, entropy incarnate, and wondered if his present would be her future. She wondered which of her kids would sit in the extra chair in the exam room and lament the days when she'd been awesome.

Dr Koraltan studied the live feed from the imubots reporting within Pop's eye, and he sat back with a neutral look. Tessa held her breath. Their doctor was an affable sort, and the only time he didn't show his cards was when the news was going to suck. 'I'm sorry to say it, M,' he said. 'But the growth around your cornea's come back.'

Pop didn't look overly surprised, but his mouth twisted. He said nothing.

'This is the trouble with Kopko's syndrome,' the doctor said. 'We can remove the errant tissue, we can have your bots clean out the remnants, but this is about your genes. You didn't get the prenatals that your kids did, and performing gene therapy on someone your age is often too much of a system shock. It's not worth the risk.'

'We got new lights at home,' Pop said. 'The good ones.'

The doctor looked sympathetic. 'Modern globulbs do decrease the risk of Kopko's coming back. But it's a *decrease*, not a guarantee. You – and I see this in so many patients your age – you spent decades rolling the dice with the old sun lamps down at the farms. Once that switch gets flicked, it's so hard to turn off. We can try, but . . .' He sighed. 'I'm sorry, M. Kopko's is a bastard.'

'So, he needs another surgery,' Tessa said.

'I'm afraid not,' Dr Koraltan said. 'And I'm sure *you're* happy to hear that, M, but . . .' He pressed his lips together.

Uh oh, Tessa thought. This really wasn't good.

'Every time we go in there to clean things out, we do damage. Tissue scars. Things wear out. Can't be helped. We've gotten to the point where your eye can't take much more.'

Tessa frowned. 'What are our options, then?'

The doctor made an empty-handed gesture. 'We either do nothing, and he loses sight in that eye, or we do another surgery, and there's a good chance that he loses sight in that eye. Honestly, I don't think the modest chance of benefit is worth the trouble of surgery.' He nodded at Pop. 'But that's up to you.'

'What about an optical implant?' Tessa said.

The doctor looked at her with interest. 'Is that on the table?'

Pop stared. 'We can't afford that.'

Tessa braced herself, knowing what she was about to say wouldn't go over well. 'Ashby sent me some creds, specifically so we could order you an implant.'

Pop glared as he realised he'd been ganged up on. 'If he's sent you creds, you should spend them on the kids.'

'The kids aren't our only family, Pop.'

'M Santoso,' Dr Koraltan said seriously. 'I understand that this isn't what you want to hear. I also can't force you to receive treatment. But replacing your eye with an optical implant would solve the problem. No more surgeries after installation. If repairs need doing, we can undock the main attachment without any pain. I know the implants back in your day were unreliable, but modern biotech is incredibly comfortable and easy to maintain. Your vision would be good as ever. *Better* than ever.'

'And I'd look like one of those modder freaks,' Pop said. 'No thanks.'

The doctor was careful with his words. 'Getting used to the look of a new implant can take some adjustment, yes,' he said. 'Especially if it's on your face. But you *would* adjust.'

Pop looked at the floor. He was quiet for a moment. 'I don't want to lose my eye.'

A sliver of sympathy pushed past Tessa's frustration – not enough to erase it entirely, but she did *care*. She wouldn't want to lose an eye, either.

Dr Koraltan's voice was gentle, but direct. 'M Santoso, if something doesn't change, you're going to lose your eye one way or the other. It'll still be in your head, but it won't work. I'm sorry. We did everything we could do with what we have here.' He gestured at his scrib. Pop's scrib dinged in response. 'I've sent you some reference docs on implants. They're good, M. If you have the means, I really do recommend it.' He stood and gestured toward the door. 'Go home, take some time to think about it. Let me know what you decide.'

Pop exited the room without a word.

Tessa sighed, and stood. Stars and fire, he was such a child. 'Thank you,' she said on her way through the door. He gave her an understanding nod.

Her father was old, but he was still fast, and already out into the courtyard by the time she got out of the clinic. 'Hey,' she called. She quickened her pace until she fell into step beside him. 'Where are you going?'

'I'm goin' to Jojo's,' he said. His face was grim, but he strode forward purposefully. 'It's second day, and that means fish rolls. If I get there before eleventh, they'll still be warm.'

'Pop.'

'Plus, Micah owes me trade. We bet lunch over flash last tenday, and he hasn't made good yet.'

'*Pop.*' She took his arm.

Pop shrugged her off and kept walking. 'You've got two kids at home,' he said. 'I'm not one of 'em.'

Tessa stopped, a swell of anger ballooning in her chest. She'd switched her shift for this. She'd upended her *whole day* for this, and . . . and . . . what a stupid, stubborn jackass. *Fine.* Fine, he could go to Jojo's, and play his stupid games, and let his eye kill itself. It was his fucking life. She was only the one who had to live with him.

She turned away and stormed off toward the transport deck, where she could catch a pod to Bay Eight. *Someone* had to be an adult that day.

ISABEL

'So it's true, then,' Ghuh'loloan said with delighted disgust. 'You expel organs during live birth.'

Isabel laughed as they made their way down the ramp to the viewing area. 'We expel *one* organ, yes. But it's a disposable one. We don't have it the rest of the time, and we only need it during pregnancy.'

The Harmagian's tentacles rippled. 'You'll forgive me, dear host, but to me, the idea is . . .'

'Horrifying?'

'*Yes.*'

'You're not alone in that. Explaining the business to kids always results in a raised eyebrow or two.'

'A raised . . . ah, yes, yes. Is it not painful?'

'. . . giving birth, not raising eyebrows, correct?'

Ghuh'loloan laughed. 'Correct.'

'It is. But not the . . . the discarding of an organ. That part's not so bad, or so I hear. Everything else is, though.' She spread her arms as they came to the end of the ramp. 'Here we are,' she said. They'd come to a broad platform, fitted with benches and picnic tables, guarded with a waist-high railing around the edge. Below the platform lay a fibre farm, overflowing with thickets of bamboo standing in orderly rows under a ceiling painted with blue sky. The tall plants had plenty of room to stretch up and up and up until finally bowing under their own leafy weight. Farmers made themselves busy in the walkways between, some harvesting, some testing the soil, some planting new seedlings. A caretaker was at work as well, pulling her heavy wagon behind her.

Isabel kept waiting for something that did *not* elate her colleague, but that moment had yet to arrive. 'Oh, marvellous!' Ghuh'loloan cried. 'Stars, look at them! What curious trees!'

'Grass, in fact,' Isabel said.

'No!'

'Yes. That's what makes it a much better crop for us. It reaches full height quickly.'

Ghuh'loloan's dactyli undulated in a gesture Isabel had come to learn meant *appreciation*. 'A grass forest,' she said. 'Ahh, I can smell the new oxygen. Wonderful.'

Isabel sat on a nearby bench and considered the Harmagian's phrasing. 'Does your species have a sense of smell?' She could've sworn she'd heard they didn't.

Ghuh'loloan parked alongside her, so they were both facing the farm. 'Well caught, dear host,' she said. 'We do not, not in the same manner as you. You know that we do not breathe, yes?'

Isabel turned that statement over. She'd never thought about it before, but . . . but yes, other than their mouths, Harmagians didn't have visible breathing holes. 'Then . . . how . . .' She searched for the right words. 'You're *speaking*.'

Had she not been in alien company for several tendays, what happened next might've sent Isabel running – and even so, she had to steel herself through it. To say that Ghuh'loloan opened her mouth wide was an understatement. There was no word Isabel knew that could properly describe what she saw. Not a gape, not a yawn, but an unfolding, an expanding, a hideous extension of empty space. Ghuh'loloan pointed one of her tentacles toward her gullet, and with a smothered shiver, Isabel understood. Ghuh'loloan wanted her to look inside her throat. And so Isabel did, with all the grace she could muster, leaning forward – not into her mouth, of course, there were limits – and spotting an unfamiliar structure at the back. A large, fleshy sack, unconnected to what was presumably Ghuh'loloan's oesophagus (or equivalent thereof), every bit as yellow as her exterior.

Thankfully, Ghuh'loloan closed her mouth, and Isabel leaned back. 'Now watch carefully,' Ghuh'loloan said, pointing at her mouth again. She formed each word that came next with exaggerated precision, as a teacher might speak to a child. 'Watch – what – is – happening – in – my – throat.'

Isabel could see it, though she wasn't sure that she wanted to. The oesophagus did not move, but the sack did, expanding to give the words life, contracting to push them out. 'So you don't . . . you don't use that to breathe.'

'No,' Ghuh'loloan said, speaking normally now. 'It is my *kurrakibat*, a wholly self-contained organ. An airbag, in essence. It pulls in air and it makes sounds. That is all.'

Isabel tried to imagine how she was going to relay this part of her day to Tamsin when she got home, and came up empty. 'Then how do you breathe?'

'Through my skin. All over, front to back. And in the same manner, I can detect chemicals in the air around me, and this produces . . . it is difficult to explain. In Hanto, the word is *kur'hon*.' She considered. '"Air-touch" is a rudimentary translation, but it does not envelop the full meaning.'

'I understand.'

Ghuh'loloan curled her front tentacles. 'It is a full-body sensation, and much like smell – or, that is, what I understand of smell – it can be pleasurable or distasteful. It is easier, then, for us to use words like *smell* or *scent* in Klip, as the end effect is the same.'

'I see.' A question arose in Isabel's mind, a childish thing she wasn't sure she wanted the answer to. 'I have . . . I have heard that other species often . . .' She sucked air through her teeth with an embarrassed smile. 'I have heard that other species sometimes find the way Humans smell to be . . . unpleasant.'

Ghuh'loloan's entire body gave way to a mighty laugh. 'Oh, dear host, do not ask me this!'

Isabel laughed as well. 'I'm so sorry.'

'Do not be,' Ghuh'loloan said, her skin rippling with mirth. 'And please do not take offence.'

'I won't.'

'If it is any consolation, I stopped noticing it within a few hours of arriving.'

Isabel groaned. Poor Ghuh'loloan. 'You got used to us, eh?'

'Well . . .' Ghuh'loloan gave a quieter laugh. 'Stars, this is a horrible thing for a guest to say. But in the interest of cultural exchange: the Human *kur'hon* in these ships is so overpowering that not only have I become numb to it, but I cannot "smell" much of anything else.'

'Oh, dear.' Isabel put her palm to her cheek. 'On behalf of my species, I apologise.' She paused. 'But you could smell – you could—' She wrapped her lips around the unfamiliar word. '*Ker-hone*.'

'You are very close. *Kur*. Our word for both air and vapour. *Kurrrrr'hon*.' The Harmagian gave the R a mighty, over-exaggerated trill.

Isabel couldn't duplicate the sound, but she gave it a valiant attempt. '*Ker'hon*.' That would have to do. 'You could . . . you detected the oxygen here.'

'Yes, it is very strong here, and it's wonderful. I could stay here all day.'

Isabel had no argument there. The fibre farms were peaceful, and sitting on a bench and discussing differences of biology sounded like a marvellous way to spend an afternoon – provided Ghuh'loloan did not invite her to inspect her innards again. Isabel's disquiet from the experience was still ebbing away, and she found herself with an impish desire to return the favour. 'So you were asking about Human birth.'

'Yes, indeed.'

'Do you know,' Isabel said with a grin, 'that during late pregnancy, sometimes you can see the baby's features pressing through the mother's skin?'

The Harmagian's eyestalks gave a slight pull downwards. '. . . not the face.'

'Sometimes the face.'

Ghuh'loloan made a sound of good-humoured revulsion. 'My dear Isabel, I really do recommend that your species try spawning like normal people do. It is far, far less disturbing.'

SAWYER

The vox snapped on with a loud scratch, waking Sawyer with all the courteousness of being dropped into a pond. 'One hour to go time,' Oates announced. 'Up and at 'em, folks.'

Sawyer processed the message, processed his surroundings, and processed the fact that he felt wholly like shit. 'Ugh, stars,' he moaned, rubbing his face with his palms. He was hungover, and how. Len had presented two bottles of Whitedune after dinner the night before, and every memory Sawyer had retained after that point was hazy at best. A bellyful of corrosive kick should've been enough to make him sleep through the night, but it turned out that Oates, who had the room next to his, snored with a vigour and volume that could pull even the drunkest punk into a queasy, half-awake limbo for cumulative hours.

And yet, in between the heavy pulses in his temples, he remembered other things. He remembered the table cracking up at his lousy imitation of a Martian accent. He remembered Len jamming on his lap drum and cheering loudly when Sawyer proved he could sing along to 'Go Away Away' – the Exodan pop song of the standard – in its entirety. He remembered Dory roaring with laughter and thumping him across the back after he choked on one shot too many and felt it exit his throat by way of his nose. He remembered Muriel saluting him with a raised glass.

They like me, he thought as he threw up in the washbasin. He spat, smiled, and half-laughed at himself. What a great look for his first day. He'd laugh in full about this, at some point, that first job on the *Silver Lining* when Len got everybody shitfaced the night before. Yeah, that was the kind of story you'd tell fondly a few days down the road.

He washed himself up and found his last clean shirt. It had been four days since they'd left dock and headed into the open. He could make out the Fleet in the distance, just barely – a bright cluster of lights that didn't match the stars. But he couldn't see the *Oxomoco* yet. He didn't know much about navigation, granted, but he was kind of confused by the direction they were heading. He thought he'd heard that the wreck had been put into orbit in such a way that it and the Fleet were always on opposite sides of the sun, so nobody would have to look at it. If he could still see the Fleet, then . . . then maybe he'd got that wrong. He'd misunderstood. Wouldn't be the first time.

He headed to the kitchen. No one else was there, but some saintly person had put out a big hot pot of mashed sweet beans, a bowl of fruit, and – best of all – an open box of SoberUps. He availed himself of everything, plus a giant mug of water.

'Hey hey, grounder,' Nyx said, entering the room. The pilot delivered the dig with a friendly grin, then spotted the items on the counter. 'Oh, thank fuck,' she said, reaching into the box of SoberUps. She had a packet open and its contents crunched between her teeth in seconds flat. Nyx grimaced. 'I hate the taste of these.'

'Me too,' Sawyer said.

She flipped the packet over and squinted at the label. 'Snapfruit flavoured, my ass. More like . . . snapfruit's ghost. Like a really sad ghost.'

Sawyer navigated a chuckle around his mouthful of mash. The magic combo of carbs and medicine was already doing its trick, and his temples throbbed less forcefully now.

Nyx helped herself to breakfast. 'You ready for the hop?'

Sawyer wasn't sure what she meant. A tunnel hop? That couldn't be right. He was pretty sure they weren't anywhere near the Risheth tunnel, and they couldn't have got there in four days anyway. Besides, they weren't leaving the system for this job, so

– hmm. Whatever. He chose ignorance over sounding stupid, and replied: 'Yeah, totally.'

'Good good,' she said, fetching herself a spoon and heading for the door. 'You can ride it out anywhere you like. Bed's best for it, though, if you're not flying. Doesn't take long, but most folks like to lie down.'

'Okay, cool,' Sawyer said, having even less of an idea of what was going on now. 'Is there . . .' He had no idea what they were talking about, much less what to ask. 'Is there anything I can do to help?'

'Nah,' Nyx said, grabbing a spoon. 'Muriel or Oates'll call you when it's your time to shine. Go put your feet up.' She winked. 'Let the snapfruit ghosts do their job.'

Sawyer chuckled and nodded, feeling utterly lost as she left the room. Well, it was his first day. Feeling lost came with the territory, right?

He headed back to his room and lay down, as instructed. His body sank into the bed with gratitude. SoberUps were great and all, but he still felt like he was balancing his brain on stilts. A bit of rest, and he'd be good to go.

He passed the time quietly, skimming through feeds on his scrib and letting the helpful drugs smooth out his edges. He'd almost forgotten about all his questions until another one appeared: *What's that sound?*

It was a sound he knew, but he couldn't place it. A mechanical sound. An engine sound. Something that had been activated. Something . . . different. He started to sit up, but the vox stopped him. 'Hop time, everybody,' Oates said. 'Sit down or lie back.'

Sawyer lowered himself back down. His heart quickened. His head puzzled. And then – *oh fuck*.

Space disappeared. Time disappeared. For how long or how far, nobody could say, because neither of those things meant anything anymore. Everything doubled, tripled, folded in on itself. Sawyer tried to look out the window, but his vision swam and his head begged to hold still, *hold still, everything's wrong.*

Then, just as abruptly, everything was fine.

Sawyer sat bolt upright and held onto the edge of the mattress. Nausea – a whole fun new version of nausea – pushed at him in waves. He knew that feeling. Not well, but he knew it. He'd felt it once on a trip to Hagarem, when his sedatives hadn't quite kicked in before the deepod got going. That's what had happened. That's what the sound had been.

They'd punched through the sublayer. The *Silver Lining* had a pinhole drive.

Sawyer knew, as any kid who'd taken a shuttle licence lesson did, that pinhole drives were dead-ass dangerous, that making tiny collapsing holes in the space between space was risky business, that doing so outside of designated transport lanes was illegal in the GC. He frowned. Well, it was illegal in Central space, anyway. Was it in the Fleet? He didn't know.

There was nothing to worry about, he told himself. These folks were professionals. They had a clean ship, a registry number, kids and families back home. Besides, he didn't know jack about scavenging. He didn't know—

Something tugged at the edge of his vision. He looked up. He froze. Slowly, he got to his feet and approached the window. 'Stars,' he whispered. In the blackness hung what was left of the *Oxomoco*. A shell. A corpse. A ruin clasped in a sphere of flotsam. He'd seen pictures. He'd known where Muriel and her crew were taking him that day. None of that had prepared him for it. Nothing had made him ready for the tangible presence of this once-mighty homesteader, torn to shreds by something so seemingly simple as one moment of air meeting vacuum. Sawyer stood at the window, awed and shaken.

What was he doing here?

The sound of the vox switching on made him jump. 'All right everybody,' Oates said. 'You know what to do. Sawyer, meet us at the airlock. Time to suit up.'

Sawyer didn't waste a moment. He headed down the walkway, getting his head on straighter with every step. This was new, and he was just nervous. Time to shove that aside. He had a boss to impress. A crew to join, maybe. There'd be plenty of opportunity for questions later. For now, he had a job to do, and dammit, he was going to do it right.

KIP

Kip knew, theoretically, that things weren't always going to be like this. He knew that he wasn't going to be sixteen forever, that exams would be a memory one day, that if other people lived away from their parents, he could, too. He *would*.

But right then, it sure as shit felt like life was never, ever gonna change.

Bored wasn't even the word for it anymore. There was something biting inside him, something shouting and endless sitting right at the bottom of his rib cage, pressing heavy with every breath. He wanted . . . he didn't know *what,* even, but he was always reaching, always waiting, and not knowing how to fix it was making him crazy. He thought about the vids he watched, where everyone was cool and clever and knew how to dress. He thought about the sims he played, where jumping meant flying and punches exploded. He thought about the spacers he'd see in the shuttledock sometimes, coming home with armfuls of expensive shit for friends and fam, handing their belt guns over to patrol before crossing that invisible line between *out there* and *in here*. Squish all of that together, and that's what he wanted. He wanted aliens to nod hello to him when he walked through spaceports. He wanted to look in the mirror in the morning and think something other than *well, I guess that's as good as it gets.* He wanted. He *wanted*.

Yet he knew, as he made his way to his usual bench after trading for his usual lunch, that he was full of it. He was still seething at his parents after the whole patch thing – which, of course, had gotten around school, too, and was doing such fucking wonders for his social life – but deep down, there was some snivelling, traitorous part of him that . . . *ugh* . . . that had been glad, kind of. Glad that his parents had showed up at the Nova Room. Glad that he'd been given an out. And that was his whole problem, really, more than parents or job trials or the slow crawl between birthdays. The problem was that what he wanted, more than anything, was to fuck someone or fight something, and he knew – from experience, now – that if given the opportunity, he'd be too scared to do either.

Cool. Real cool.

A group of his schoolmates walked by, on their way to Grub Grub for hoppers of their own. He didn't look at any of them, but he could hear whispers, giggles, a pack passing him by.

Stars, he sucked. Everything sucked.

He saw Ras approach out of the corner of his eye. He had a spring in his step, a look that said *I've got an idea.* Kip took a long sip of his choko and sighed. He was still kind of pissed at Ras, but at the same time, there was nobody else coming over to sit with him.

'*Tek tem*, man.' Ras took his place on the bench and reached for Kip's drink. 'You look like shit.'

Kip let the bottle go without a fight. 'Yeah, well, I spent my night boxing up all the food compost in the whole fucking hex, so . . .' He let a shrug serve as the end of the sentence.

Ras winced. 'They are really on your ass about this, huh?'

'Are yours not?'

Ras shook his head as he drank. 'They keep giving me shit, but I'm not in trouble-trouble.' He handed the bottle back over. '*Tika lu*, man. I feel kinda responsible.'

Kip looked at his friend and felt some irritation slip away. Ras cared, and that . . . that felt pretty good. 'Nah,' Kip said. 'It's cool. *Semsem.*'

The smile returned to Ras' face. 'To make sure that it is, I wanna make it up to you. You think they'll let you come out soon?'

Kip considered. It had been a tenday since it had all gone down, and Mom was being more reasonable. 'Maybe. I got a job trial—'

'Where at?'

'Tailor shop. Y'know, stitching socks, whatever.'

Ras rocked his head, trying to look positive but undoubtedly unimpressed. 'Cool.'

Kip gave a short laugh. 'It's not.' He took another sip.

'Well, here,' Ras said, handing over his satchel. 'You'll feel even better about this, then.'

Kip looked at the bag, then looked at Ras.

'Open it, dumbass.' Ras turned his head toward another group from school. 'Hey, Mago!' he called cheerfully. '*Porsho sem!*' *Nice ink.*

'Go fuck yourself,' came the inevitable reply. Mago had gotten a cheap bot tattoo on vacation and it looked straight up *dumb*. Like, the lines didn't even move at the same time.

Kip unclasped Ras' satchel as the sparring continued. Just school stuff, it looked like. Scrib, stylus, some pixel pens, a bag of candy, a lunch tin, an info chip, a— *wait.* He rifled back to the bag of candy. He wasn't sure that it *was* candy.

'Dude,' Kip said, starting to lift the bag out of the satchel. 'Is this—'

Ras pushed Kip's hand down into the satchel without looking. 'Stay stylish, man,' he called after Mago's back. Ras snapped to Kip. 'What the hell,' he whispered, more amused than mad. 'Don't let people see.'

That clinched it. This was *not* candy. Kip dropped his voice to match Ras', his heartbeat kicking up several notches. 'Where did you get this?'

'Toby's sister, remember? I told you.'

Kip looked at the clear pack, full of non-threatening bundles, each wrapped in a colourful bit of throw-cloth. He'd never smoked smash before, but he knew what it looked like. He'd played sims. Smash wasn't illegal or anything – not in the Fleet, anyway – but you could only get it and use it in special cafes with bouncers at the door and patrol always hanging around outside. It was also yet another one of those things locked away behind the *When You Turn Twenty* seal, and he didn't know any adults who were into it. His mom definitely wasn't. She said it was 'a waste of time, trade, and self-respect.'

'Don't worry.' Ras gave him a reassuring look. 'It only lasts a few hours, and it's not like we'll be sitting around your kitchen. We'll go park ourselves in a garden somewhere after lights out, and it'll be a real good time. And besides, Una makes solid stuff.'

'Have you tried it?'

'Well . . . no, but everybody says. You should've heard her explaining it to me as she packed it up. It's some serious science. Look, if you don't want to, it's cool—'

'Nah,' Kip said. He closed the satchel definitively. 'Let's do it.'

Ras blinked, then laughed. 'All right, man!' He clapped Kip on the shoulder. 'I thought you were gonna take more convincing than that.'

Kip swallowed the last of his choko, heart still quick but head as steady as could be. He shrugged again, as if he did this every day. 'Something to do, right?'

TESSA

Somewhere in her head, she knew that she'd left the cargo bay, that she'd found someone to cover for her, that she'd taken a transport pod, that she'd walked (and run, in spurts) through the crowded plaza and into the entry doors of the primary school. She'd felt nearly none of it. Nothing but a furious blur existed between getting a vox call at work and her bursting into the admin office, where Aya sat sobbing on the couch, untouched tea and cookies on the table in front of her, a pair of concerned adults on either side.

'Tessa, I am so sorry,' one of them said, standing to make way for her. M Ulven, Aya's teacher. 'I don't know how they got away from the group, it happened so fast—'

In the same distant part of her head that held the memory of getting from there to here, Tessa knew that the teacher wasn't to blame, that field trips were frantic and kids were unpredictable, that her daughter would be okay. But all of that was shadowed behind a raw animal fury, something that wanted to roar at everyone who'd let this happen.

She took her place beside Aya and pulled her close. Aya trembled, her face burning red and her nose pouring down her lip. There was a throw-cloth clutched in her hand, unused. Some part of her head was distant, too.

Tessa glared at the people who were supposed to keep her kid safe. 'Give us a moment,' she said from behind her teeth.

M Ulven started to say something, but the head teacher laid her hand on his arm. He nodded guiltily – *good* – and they exited the office. Aya clutched Tessa's shirt as the door slid shut, sobbing all the harder.

'It's all right, honey,' Tessa said, hugging, rocking. The girl in her arms was so big, and yet still so small. 'Here, blow your nose.' A sizable portion of Tessa's shirt was already soaked with snot. No matter. Ky had done the same to another corner that morning. Her definition of *clean* hadn't been the same since the moment a night-shift doctor had placed a blood-smeared newborn in her arms.

Tessa took the throw-cloth from Aya's hand and pressed it to the kid's face. 'Blow.'

Aya did as told, and continued to sob. 'I was so scared.'

'I would've been, too.' Tessa rubbed her daughter's back with the palm of her hand for a few minutes, waiting for Aya to quiet a bit. The sobs slowed, hiccuping out weakly every few seconds. 'M Ulven told me what happened, but I want to hear it from you. Tell me how it went.'

Aya sniffed. 'Am I in trouble?'

'No.' Under different circumstances, she would have been, but that was a bridge too far right then.

Aya swallowed hard and began to speak. 'Everybody age nine went on a field trip to water reclamation today.'

'Mmm-hmm,' Tessa said, handing her the wet cloth. That part she hadn't needed a recap of, but okay.

'And Jaime, he – he said – it wasn't my idea, Mom—'

'You guys snuck off on your own,' Tessa said. A pack of four or five of them, was what she'd gotten over the vox.

'Yeah.'

'Yeah,' Tessa echoed. She was sure that her daughter had leapt at the chance to abandon a dull field trip for a de facto obstacle course. That was a talk for another day. 'And then what?'

Aya's lower lip quivered. She wiped her nose with the back of her hand.

'Use the cloth, please.'

Aya gave her nose a perfunctory rub. 'I don't know why they

– why they – I *hate* Opal. I hate her!' Her words were ragged now. Angry.

Tessa raised her eyebrows. 'Opal was involved in this?' She didn't even try to keep the edge out of her voice.

Aya nodded hard. 'Palmer, too. I hate him also.'

Aya's most frequent playmates – or they had been, before this. Their parents were going to get hell incarnate on their doorsteps before the day was out, but for the time being, Tessa put her arm around her daughter's shoulders and squeezed. 'Tell me what they did,' she said.

'Opal told everybody that I'm scared of – that I'm scared of outside. Etty told me that was stupid, and Palmer said I was a baby, and – and they kept being mean, and I told them to stop it but they didn't, and then—' The sobs started again.

Tessa put both her arms around Aya now, and let her cry. She knew what had come next. The little bastards had shoved her in a cargo drone port, closed the door, and made her think they were going to pop the hatch. They didn't have the auth codes for it, but Aya didn't know that. Her screaming was what brought one of the nearby mech techs running.

'I hate them,' Aya said again. 'I'm not going to school anymore.'

That . . . okay, *that* wasn't on the table, but Tessa didn't think it was the time to argue. 'They did a horrible thing to you, honey,' she said. 'I am so, so sorry.'

'Why did they *do* that?' It was a genuine question, brittle with betrayal.

'I don't know. Sometimes . . . sometimes kids think it's funny to be mean to each other.' Tessa reached back to the times she'd been teased, to the times she'd teased in response or for no reason at all. 'I don't know why.'

'It wasn't funny.'

'No, it most definitely was not funny.'

'And I hate living on a ship.'

Tessa blinked. This turn wasn't entirely unexpected, but it surprised her nonetheless. 'I know you're scared of outside, but our home is so good. Yeah? It's safe here. You're safe with me, and your grandpa, and our hexmates, and our friends—'

'I *hate* it.'

'You know those kids couldn't have opened the hatch, right? There are codes that—'

'I don't want to live on a ship anymore. I want to live on a planet.'

Tessa sighed. 'Planets have dangerous things, too.'

Aya wiped her nose with her sleeve. She pulled close to her mother, away from the walls, away from the emptiness outside. 'Not like here.'

Tessa searched for the right response, the right comfort, some of that motherly instinct bullshit you were supposed to just *have*. She found nothing.

Aya sniffled mightily and said: 'Can I say a swear word?'

Tessa remembered a couple tendays prior, when she'd knocked a mug of mek onto her workbench while repairing a cleanerbot. A cascade of profanities had exited her mouth before she'd noticed the kids had entered the room. *Don't say stuff like that*, Tessa had told them at the time. *I only said it because I was mad*. She'd spent several days after trying to make Ky stop glee-fully chanting 'son of a *bitch*' – and had won that particular skirmish – but hadn't realised Aya sponged up a lesson from the exchange, too. 'Yes,' Tessa said. 'This is a time when a swear word is entirely appropriate.'

Aya took a breath. 'I fucking hate them,' she said. 'I'm gonna kick all their asses.'

Tessa smothered the laugh pressing against her lips. She gave a serious nod. 'That was two swear words.'

'Well, I'm really mad.'

'And you know fighting solves nothing, right?'

'Ugh, Mom.' Aya rolled her bloodshot eyes. 'I didn't mean like that. I just meant . . . I meant . . .'

'I know.' Tessa put her arm around her daughter and kissed the top of her head. 'I want to kick all their asses, too.'

EYAS

Sunny had become a habit, and Eyas didn't know what to make of that. It wasn't romance, she knew that much. Romance had never been her thing. She watched him as he traced the path back from the bed to where his pants had ended up. He picked up the rumpled pair and dug around in a pocket. 'Do you mind if I . . .?' he asked, holding a retrieved redreed pipe and an accompanying tin.

Eyas shook her head. 'Not at all.' He'd never done this before, and she found it endearing. This wasn't part of a seductive script. There was nothing in this *for her*. The man wanted a smoke. On the clock though he was, something had shifted enough for him to feel comfortable not spending every second entertaining her. They were just . . . hanging out now. She liked that.

He returned to bed, leaving the pants where they'd been. 'Do you want some?'

'Not really my thing.' She reached for his bottle of Laru kick, an ever-present part of these evenings. 'This, however, is.'

Sunny nodded as he filled his pipe. 'Help yourself.'

He puffed; she poured. They sat side by side, leaning against propped pillows, close enough to feel the warm brush of the other's bare skin but nowhere in the realm of a cuddle. Eyas felt perfectly at ease. No pretence, no bullshit. No 'M.' She felt like herself, nothing more or less. Judging by the content neutrality on Sunny's face, he felt the same.

It was really nice.

'Is this what you always wanted to be?' Eyas asked, cupping

her glass in the palm of her hand. Sintalin benefited from a bit of warmth, she'd learned.

Sunny exhaled. The smoke twisted up toward the air filter above. 'You mean, a host?' His face shifted into a far-away smile. 'Not my first choice. I was going to be a Monster Maker.'

'A what now?'

'A Monster Maker! Didn't you play that sim?'

'Oh, stars.' Eyas shut her eyes and laughed. 'I'd forgotten about that. Where you go around the galaxy scanning different animals to . . . collect their DNA, or something.'

'Yeah! And then you smash them together to make hybrids!'

'This was for some superficially educational purpose, right?'

'Yeah, yeah, you did it to solve *problems*. Say, like – say you've got to cross a flooded area. You've got DNA scans for something with long legs, and scans for something that can move through water. You punch 'em both into your Monsteriser—'

'Your—'

'Your *Monsteriser*. Eyas, please, this is serious technology we're discussing.'

'Of course, I'm sorry.' She swallowed her smile. 'Please explain how a Monsteriser works.'

'Well . . . I can't, but that's beside the point. The point is, it makes a monster. It is the most crucial tool a Monster Maker has.' He bowed his head. 'It was a very, very hard day when my dad broke the news that none of it was real.'

Eyas patted his shoulder. 'My condolences.'

Sunny scrunched his face into a parody of grief. 'Thank you.'

'So once you got over the shock,' she said, 'you decided the only thing left for you was a life of getting people off.'

Smoke shot out of Sunny's nose as he laughed. 'There were a few more steps between that and this. I bounced around for a while. I thought about being a doctor, but I'm a lazy student. I spent some time in one of the festival troupes—'

'You play music?'

'No, I sing. It was fun, but . . . I dunno. Wasn't what I wanted to do forever, y'know? Then one of my friends, she started her host training, and she was telling me about it – not just the physical side of it, but all the ethos and whatnot. I was like, hey, that sounds pretty cool. And it was, and here I am.'

Eyas sipped her drink. 'You found something that incorporates everything else you tried. You perform, you make people feel better.' She took another sip and smiled. 'And maybe sometimes you help people with their monsters.'

Sunny's pipe paused on the way to his mouth. 'Huh,' he said, seeming pleased. 'Huh.' He took a drag and angled himself toward Eyas. 'So what about you? I mean, seems fair to ask, but I know you don't like talking about work, so it's cool if—'

'No, I don't mind,' she said. *I don't mind talking about it with you*, she meant. It was different with Sunny. Backwards. Usually, people had to get past what she did in order to get to know her. Sunny had come at it the other way around. Explaining her work wasn't a chore with him. She wasn't teaching; she was sharing. 'I always wanted to be a caretaker. Seriously. I went to my aunt's laying-in when I was six. She died very suddenly. Exosuit accident.'

'Stars. I'm sorry.'

Eyas nodded in acknowledgement. 'The caretaker who conducted the ceremony, he was so kind and so . . . *impressive*. I was upset and confused, and the adults around me were a mess, but he was this . . . this *calm* in the centre of it. I remember watching him, watching the ritual, absorbing everything he explained to me – me, directly – about the science of it. It was beautiful. Magic, almost. That was it for me. That was what I wanted to do.' She took a pensive sip.

Sunny watched her even though she wasn't looking at him. 'And?' he asked.

'And, nothing. It's what I always wanted to do.'

'Is it exactly what you'd thought it would be?'

She glanced at him. 'Perceptive,' she said, surprised but unbothered.

'Literally part of that training I mentioned.'

Eyas leaned her head back into the pillows, taking her time. 'The caretaker I encountered that day, he was a . . . a symbol to me. This symbol of fearlessness, of . . . harmony. He took a terrifying thing I barely understood and he showed me it was okay. It was normal. And that feeling was reinforced by the way adults treated him. They didn't pull away. They weren't repulsed. They embraced him – in both senses of the word. He was life and death walking as one, and they wrapped their arms around him and gave him gifts, and by extension, showed me I did not have to be afraid of our reality.' She paused again. She'd never talked about this with someone outside of her profession, and certainly not to this degree. 'I am that, now. I am that symbol to others. It's exactly what I wanted, what I worked for. But there's this other side to it I didn't expect. I'm a symbol, yes, but a symbol wearing my face and my name. Myself, but also not. Mostly not. People know, when I walk through my district, who I am, what I do. Doesn't matter if I've got my wagon or am wearing my robes. They know. And so I always have to be Eyas the symbol, the good symbol, because I never know who's looking at me, who needs to see that thing I saw in a caretaker when I was six. It doesn't matter if I'm having a bad day, or if I'm tired, or if I'm feeling selfish. They look to me for comfort. I have to be that. And that *is* me, in a sense. That is a genuine part of me. But that's just it – it's a part. It's not—'

'It's not the whole,' Sunny said.

Eyas nodded. 'And that aspect of my work, I wasn't ready for. I never thought about who my aunt's caretaker was when he went home.'

Sunny held the bowl of his pipe in his palm. The smoke ascended as if he were conjuring it. 'Sounds lonely.'

Eyas weighed that word. *Lonely*. Was she? She pursed her lips. 'Not exactly. It's not like I work alone, or live alone. It's more that I feel . . . I feel . . . incomplete. Or stuck, maybe. Like I can only ever be this one thing. Like this is the only side of myself I'll be able to express. Like there's something more I could be doing.' She shrugged and sipped. 'But then, I've never wanted to do anything else, so I have no idea what it is I want to change.' She paused, her mouth twisting.

'What?'

'That's not entirely true.'

'What's not?'

Oh stars, was she really going to tell him this? *Why not*, she thought. She was already naked as naked could be. Eyas looked away with an embarrassed smile. 'There was a brief period in my teens when I went off on a Gaiist kick, but *other than that—*'

'Wait, wait, wait.' Sunny laughed. 'You can't fly past that. You. You went on a Gaiist kick.'

Eyas laughed right along with him. 'I did. Drove my family crazy.'

Sunny was gleeful. 'Were you going to go to Earth, or . . .'

'No, it's so much worse than that.' She made an exaggerated grimace. 'See, I got this info chip at a spaceport—'

He cracked up. 'Oh, stars, you were going to be a *missionary*. Oh, fuck. That's so much dumber than Monster Makers.'

Eyas flicked his thigh. 'Shut up,' she said. 'I was fifteen.'

'And that's why it's forgivable,' he said. He took a deep breath. '*Hoo*. Congrats on growing out of it.'

She raised her glass in salute.

'So what steered you away from that truly amazing life goal?'

'I don't know. Not one specific thing.' She pursed her lips. 'The problem with Gaiist philosophy is . . . well, my work.'

He spread out his hands, inviting her to continue.

Eyas considered. 'You're fine with me digging into what I do? It won't ruin the mood?'

'Yeah, it's cool.' He rearranged himself on the mattress, facing her fully now. 'It's interesting. Just . . . part of life, right?'

Eyas studied him. 'Yeah.' She smiled. 'Okay. So. Gaiist philosophy. "Our souls are tied to our planet of origin." That's their central tenet, yeah? Our souls are tied to Earth, and they essentially get sick if we go elsewhere. Since there's no hard-and-fast definition of *soul* anywhere, we'll go with what I interpret that to be: the quality of being alive. The thing that separates us from rocks or machines. By my definition, every organic thing has a soul – it's not just for sapients.' She gestured around the room. 'According to Gaiists, the Fleet should be a place chock-full of diseased, malnourished souls. This is as far from organic as it gets. We live inside machines. We've replicated the systems on Earth. There is no wind to move our air, there is no water cycle, there is no natural source for photosynthesis. This is a lab experiment. A biologist could make no real conclusions about our natural behaviour. They'd have to add the caveat "born in captivity" to everything they recorded.'

'That's . . . oof. Okay.'

'See, I told you I was going to ruin the mood.'

'You haven't, but I would like some of *that*,' he said, nodding at the bottle. 'Seriously, I want to hear this.'

'Okay.' Eyas poured him a glass. 'I promise things look up from here.'

He nodded. 'I trust you.'

Eyas inwardly noted that, and kept going. 'So, despite everything about our environment, there *is* a natural cycle that remains, and it's one that we can't escape, that we couldn't leave behind. It's completely beyond our technological grasp to alter or replicate.'

'You mean death.'

'I mean life *and* death. Can't have one without the other. If my work has taught me anything, it's that death is not an end. It's a pattern. A catalyst for change. Death is recycling. Proteins and nutrients, 'round and 'round. And you can't stop that. Take a living person off Earth, put them in a sealed metal canister out in a vacuum, take them so far away from their planet of origin that they might not understand what a *forest* or an *ocean* is when you tell them about one – and they are *still* linked to that cycle. When we decompose under the right conditions, we turn into soil – something awfully like it, anyway. You see? We're not detached from Earth. We turn *into* earth. And it's an entirely organic process. We can't substitute anything artificial. I can't make a corpse compost without adding batches of bamboo chips to get the carbon–nitrogen ratio right. If I don't remove the corpse's bots, they'll disrupt the bacteria the entire process relies on. Likewise, I have to take out any implants or mods the person had installed, or they'll contaminate the finished product.'

'But isn't the core artificial, too? I'm not being contrary, I'm just trying to understand.'

'It is,' Eyas said. 'But think about it: it's an artificial system set up to accommodate something *that would happen without it*. We would still die and rot if the core wasn't there. We'd rot *differently*, yes, but you could say that about someone who died in a desert versus someone who died in a swamp. In both cases, rot is inevitable. So all we've done is provide conditions that encourage the kind of rot we want, and facilities that ensure we're not tripping over corpses all day. Sorry for the visual.'

'That's okay.'

Eyas nodded. 'Despite growing up in an environment that is utterly artificial, we default to the rawest, purest state at the end. So you can't tell me that our souls are sick and broken when they're inextricably linked to a force that powerful. Whatever soul we got from Earth – whatever that even means – we took it with us when we came out here. And that's why I do what I do. Yes, I'd love to see a forest, a real forest. I'd love to stick my hands down into the humus and touch saplings growing out of stumps. I'd love to see a system of decomposition and growth that just *happened* without any need for Human tending. But the system we built here *does* need tending, and that means it needs caretakers who understand the magnitude of that.'

'It needs you.'

Eyas paused, considering the line between hubris and honesty. 'Yes,' she said. 'It needs me. And I do believe that. I do love what I do. So I don't know what this . . . this discontent is. I don't know why I'm conflicted about it lately.'

Sunny swished his drink around. 'Can I ask you a weird question? And I'm not trying to be disrespectful or negative, honestly. I just want to pick your brain.'

'Go ahead.'

Her companion shifted his jaw in thought. 'Is it the most efficient thing? Composting, I mean. In terms of resources, is it still the best thing for us to be doing?'

Eyas had been preparing herself for a question about funeral preparation, or states of decay, or what bodily functions a corpse can still perform. Those questions, she was used to. This, she was not. 'What alternatives are there? You want to just space them?'

'Of course not. You could fly people into the sun, though, right? Like we did after the *Oxomoco*. Wouldn't that be easier? Less work?'

Eyas continued to feel thrown. She remembered the announcement that the *Oxomoco* victims would be flown *en masse* into their sun, and the second grieving that decision had prompted – the disbelief, the backlash, the endless requests for personal exceptions, the crowded lines at counselling clinics and emigrant resource centres and neighbourhood bars, the exhaustion, the resignation, the popular justification that the bodies would fuel the sun, and the sun fuelled their ships, so a similar end would be achieved. And now here they were, just a few standards later, talking about that recourse as matter-of-fact as could be. 'You're forgetting resources,' she said, speaking words she'd never thought an Exodan would need to be reminded of.

'That was true for old folks,' Sunny said. 'That's why we did composting while we were still drifting around the open. It's different now.'

'We . . . we still have to manage metal and fuel. They're less rare than before contact, yes, but the . . . the need to be frugal hasn't changed. You can't fly bodies anywhere without metal and fuel.'

'But does the math work out that way? Is it *actually* less of a drain on resources anymore to keep the Centres working than it would be to kit out a busted old skiff sometimes?'

Eyas stared at him. That wasn't math she'd ever done, ever *considered* doing. She had a dozen polished responses to the question of *why* the tradition she oversaw existed. But Sunny wasn't asking *why*, he was asking *why now*, and that . . . that she didn't know how to answer. She emptied her glass down her throat and tried to think.

Sunny cringed apologetically. 'So, what I was *trying* to do was push you into some kind of epiphany and help you untangle this thing . . . but it looks like I maybe messed you up further.'

She sputtered. 'How was this supposed to help?'

'You were *supposed* to say that the math doesn't matter. Because you love it, and because it's our way, and that's reason enough. And then, see, you'd feel like your *job* was enough, and you wouldn't feel conflicted anymore.'

'You asked me a practical question!' She hit him with a pillow. 'Not an emotional question! Those two never have the same answers!'

'Well, fuck, sorry!' he laughed, fending off her attack, holding his pipe well out of harm's way. 'You called me perceptive, and I got cocky.'

Eyas shook her head with a smile. 'That's the last time I pay you a compliment.'

'Probably for the best.' Sunny gave a low whistle. 'Stars, I am sooooo glad I picked an easy job. I am not used to getting this existential.'

She chuckled. 'I wouldn't call your job easy.'

He gestured to his reclining, naked frame. 'I am in the middle of a shift, right now.' He took a long drag of his pipe. 'I am on the clock.' He sipped the last of his drink and swallowed with an indulgent exhale. 'Oh, what a difficult profession.' He set the pipe and glass aside and rolled over onto her, far more goofball than alluring, and planted his face smack between her breasts. 'Look at me, serving the greater good,' he said, nuzzling appreciatively. He sat back as Eyas laughed. 'I guess I kinda am, huh?' he said, his voice more serious. He gestured at her. 'You're the literal greater good here.'

Eyas raised an eyebrow. 'Do you get this sappy with all your clients?'

Sunny grinned broadly. 'I wouldn't have gotten very far in this job if I didn't.' His eyes softened – not worryingly so, but enough to make her stop teasing. 'I meant it, though.'

Eyas held his eyes for a moment. She squeezed his hand, and poured them both another drink.

SAWYER

'Boss, we got a problem.'

Everybody in the airlock paused their suiting up. 'Do tell,' Muriel said, continuing to wake the four empty autocarts that would be joining them.

Nyx cleared her throat over the vox. 'We've got company. The *Neptune*.'

Muriel paused. 'How long?'

'Three hours, maybe four.'

Sawyer stood awkwardly, helmet in hands, not sure what that meant or why the mood in the airlock had changed. 'Ah, shit,' Oates said. He frowned at everyone present. 'Who got drunk and told someone where we were going today, hmm?' His eyes lingered on Sawyer.

Sawyer swallowed. He was pretty sure he hadn't said anything to anybody other than that he had a salvage job. He hadn't known he wasn't supposed to talk about it, but who would he even have talked to?

'It doesn't matter,' Muriel said. She fastened her suit latches in sequence, one, two, three. Methodical. Matter-of-fact. 'Is what it is.' She looked around at her crew. 'This just became a rush job. Grab and carry first. Tear-downs if you can.'

Sawyer cleared his throat. 'I'm sorry, I don't— what's going on?'

Muriel clicked her helmet into place, and the vox below the seam switched on. 'We've got competition. Another salvage crew. Think of it like a race.'

A competition. Sawyer hadn't planned on that. 'Do you guys – do the salvage crews not keep a schedule?'

Dory laughed and shook her head, walking toward the hatch.

'Salvage is a more . . . independent line of work,' Oates said. 'First come, first serve.'

The airlock remained tense, so Sawyer decided to save the rest of his questions for later. Still, his list was growing. If retrieving salvage was competitive, there must be some kind of special compensation given by the Fleet to salvage crews, but that didn't mesh with . . . well, with how everything else worked. Maybe it was dangerous, or messy? You could say the same about asteroid mining, though, or zero-g mech work, or sanitation. Sanitation. Maybe he *should* have stuck with that, started there. He didn't understand enough about anything else yet. Maybe . . . maybe the race Muriel mentioned was purely a matter of pride. A race to see who could bring the best stuff back home. Yeah, that made sense. He put on his helmet and got ready to follow.

That is, he *thought* he was ready. He'd been outside before, tethered and on a guided walk, but that was different; he wasn't floating now. He could feel the sudden lightness of everything in and around him, but his cling boots held his feet firmly to the ruined shuttledock they walked out onto. He'd never worn cling boots before, and he found them . . . not uncomfortable, exactly, but more challenging than the others made them look. A little like walking through wet sand. It'd take practice, he assured himself. After all, this crew had probably been wearing them since they were kids. One step at a time.

Sawyer looked up from his feet and met the *Oxomoco*. He shuddered. He swallowed. Around them were the same features he'd seen in the *Silver Lining's* dock four days prior – walkways, railings, directional signs – but this was a fever dream, a rent and twisted mirror image. The vacuum occupying the space around them glittered with dust and dreck. It would've been almost pretty, were it not for the violently wrenched metal everywhere else.

Sawyer turned to look around, and even in the regulated warmth of his exosuit, the sight made him go cold.

There was no wall on the other side of the dock. Just a gaping hole into empty space, the edges surrounding it bent outward. He knew the decompression had been quick, but stars, he hoped it had felt that way, too.

'All right, three hours,' Muriel said. 'We should split up. Oates, head to the hexes. Dory and Len, let's go to cargo. It's bound to be even more picked over than the last time we were here, but we gotta give it a shot. Sawyer, you're with Oates. More code that'll need tweaking where he's headed. Nyx, you'll keep us posted?'

'You know it,' Nyx's voice said inside their helmets.

Muriel nodded at the group. 'Let's move.'

They split as directed, autocarts trailing after. Sawyer followed Oates, and tried his best to look nonchalant.

He failed at that, apparently. 'Don't worry,' Oates said, pushing his big bag of tools along. 'Fucks everybody up the first time.'

Sawyer felt embarrassed at that, but relieved, too. 'I've seen pictures, but—'

'Yeah, pictures don't cut it. I always need a good, stiff drink to get me to sleep after we make a run here. Speaking of – you holding up okay?'

The slightest echo of a headache was all that remained of Len's Whitedune. 'Yeah,' Sawyer said. 'I'm good.'

Oates gave him a solid pat on the back, his thick glove landing dully against an even thicker oxygen canister. 'See, you'll be great. We got about an hour's walk there, and if we've gotta be back in three, we need to keep a good pace if we're gonna have any time to actually work. If you gotta piss, well – you've worn a suit before, right?'

Sawyer hadn't ever used that particular exosuit feature, but nodded.

Oates grinned. 'It's a fancy job, what can I say.'

The walk was tiring, thanks to the boots, but Oates made for good chatter. After an hour and change, as had been predicted, they arrived in a residential corridor. 'Okay, a lot of these will be empty already,' Oates said. 'I'll know a good one when I see it, though.'

Oates' quarry was found a few minutes later, though Sawyer couldn't see what had drawn him to this particular spot. The centre of the hex was empty. No toys or tools littered the floor. No dishes lined the table. No plants remained in the hollowed planters. Everything that wasn't bolted down had been sucked away through a gash in the floor that split the hex in two. Sawyer could see the remaining edges of the sewage deck below and the stars beyond.

'Hmm,' Oates said, as if he were picking apart a pixel puzzle. He eyed the front doors. 'That one. We'll start there.' He pointed to a door that was open about a hand's width, on the other side of the gash.

Sawyer hesitated. 'How do we . . .'

'Ah,' Oates said. 'Here, I'll show you.' He reached down and hit the cling boot controls on his ankles. With a low buzz, Oates was unanchored. 'Okay? And then—' His suit thrusters activated, and he flew forward at a cautious speed, drifting over the tear in the floor, then reactivated his boots once he reached the other side. 'See? Nothin' to it.'

Sawyer repeated each step. Detach, thrusters, forward, anchor. There wasn't anything to it, now that he'd done it, but he felt pleased anyway.

The autocarts flew themselves across the gap as well, and the small party stood at the cracked-open door. Oates reached into his tool bag and retrieved a power pack and a pair of cables. He popped open a service panel by the doorframe, connected the pack, and gestured at the door. Nothing happened. He ran his hand inside the open space between door and frame. 'Nothing blocking it,' he said. He rattled the door itself. 'And it's not off-track. It's just locked itself in a weird spot.' He nodded at Sawyer. 'This is where you come in.'

On cue, Sawyer hooked up his scrib to the control panel and dove into the code. It was a different setup than the lockbox code, naturally, but the territory was more familiar now. He tweaked and teased, coaxing the commands to do what he wanted. Sure enough, five minutes in, the door slid open.

'Hey, hey!' Oates said. He rubbed his hands together as he entered the home. 'We're in business. Nice work.'

A smile briefly formed on Sawyer's lips, then disappeared. Eerie as it was to see a hex without any stuff in it, a home still full to the brim with belongings was worse. Free of gravity, every piece of furniture and everything that had been on them was afloat, drifting in a bizarre jumble. Oates pushed things out of his path as he walked through, like a parody of a man wading through water. The objects tumbled into each other, set in motion by the intrusion.

A sock floated past Sawyer's face. He saw a fork, a kettle. A frozen, dilapidated piece of fruit. A horrible thought struck him. 'Are there any . . . um . . . there aren't still . . .'

Oates looked at him. 'What?'

Sawyer wet his lips. 'Bodies.'

'Oh, stars, no.' He made a face. 'Couldn't pay me enough to come here if there were. No, after it happened, the Aeluons, they've got these . . . I dunno what they're called. Some kind of bots that detect whatever organic form you tell 'em to look for. They use 'em to retrieve their dead after battles in zero-g. You know what I'm talking about?'

'No.'

'Well, anyway, the Aeluons gave us a bunch for clean-up. They can bore through walls and whatnot, so if you're in a closed-off space like this and you don't see a big hole in the wall, it means there was nobody in here, and nobody's been in since.'

There was nobody in here. A small comfort, but Sawyer took it.

'Okay,' Oates said. 'Cloth and metal, those are always good to grab. Anything that can be made into textiles or melted down.'

He grabbed a floating storage crate, put it beneath one boot, and began to pry the lid up. 'Tech takes priority over everything. Broken is fine, intact is better, functional is best. We can't grab everything, so use good judgment. Find things people can make use of.'

Sawyer looked around. Everything in there had had a use, once. Everything in there had been brought in for a purpose. He shook his head. Job. He had to do his job. *Okay*, he thought. He reached out and grabbed the floating kettle. 'Like this?'

'Yeah. Someone can smelt it, if nothing else. Remember, we're on the clock. Grab and go.'

Sawyer grabbed. Utensils, tech bits, blankets. He brought handful after handful to one of the autocarts, steadily filling its enclosed compartments. The grimness of the place was starting to ebb into the background. Instead there was just the work, the task at hand. There were creds to be made, and crew to win over, and – he paused. He'd opened a decorative box – no, not a box. An old cookie tin someone had painted. The contents inside drifted up to greet him. Sawyer's chest went tight. There wasn't much in the box, nothing that Oates would want, nothing that was of any use. There were kitschy figurines, a pair of Aandrisk feathers, an info chip, a handful of yellow stones washed smooth by an alien sea. He took the info chip, which had a name printed on it. *Myra*, it read. He turned his attention to the wall of painted handprints, which he'd been steadfastly ignoring since the moment they walked in. *Okoro*, it read. The hands reached nearly to the ceiling. He wondered which of them was Myra's. He wondered where she'd been during the accident, if she hadn't been here. He wondered if she'd made it.

'Hey,' Sawyer said. 'What about things like this?' He gestured to the floating mementos.

Oates was busy carving hunks of stuffing out of the sofa with his knife. 'Like what?' He looked over. 'Just junk. Leave it.'

'It's got a name on it. If she's still around, she'd be in the directory, yeah? Doesn't weigh much, and I bet she'd be happy to get her stuff back.'

Oates paused. He lowered his knife. 'We're here for salvage,' he said. 'Not lost and found.'

'But—'

Oates' voice changed. Sawyer couldn't put his finger on what it was, but he didn't like it. 'On the clock, remember?' Oates said. 'You pick up every piece of junk you find, and we'll be here forever.'

Sawyer frowned. An uneasiness filled him, the same feeling he'd gotten after the tunnel hop, the same he'd gotten in the airlock when competition arose. Competition. He looked at Oates, speedily tearing away hunks of fibre as if someone might take it away at any moment.

'Oates,' Sawyer said slowly. His tongue felt thick. He knew what he wanted to ask, and he knew how stupid it was. He knew he'd sound like an idiot, that it was probably nothing to worry about, that this might take him down a few points in the eyes of the man who'd picked him out of a crowd. But the needling grew stronger, and his stomach felt sour, and . . . and he had to. 'Are we allowed to be here?'

Oates sighed, his helmet angling toward the floor. 'Can we have this talk once we get back to the ship?'

'Um—' Sawyer shook his head, a bright panic growing in his chest. 'No, I want to talk about this now. Are we allowed to be here?'

Oates gave him a look of pure exasperation, then returned his attention to the sofa. 'You're a grounder, so you'll understand this analogy. Imagine you're with a bunch of people wandering out in the desert. I mean a *real* desert, nothin' anybody can use. There are jungles nearby, but you can't go there. The jungle will eat you up. You'll get lost in there. You'll disappear. Now, some-times, the people in the jungles will throw you a bag of food, but it ain't much. Not like you'd get if you actually lived in there. But you're desert people, and you're not goin' anywhere. One day, you stumble across a big, dead animal. Like a . . . I dunno, I was never good at animals. What's a big one?'

'I—'

'A horse. That's big, right? You stumble across a dead horse. Biggest horse you've ever seen, and it's freshly dead. You could cut it up and eat it right now. It's there for the taking. But the leaders of your group, they say, no, no, we need to talk about this. We can't do this now. We need to talk about how to do this fairly. We have to make sure everybody's getting the exact same amount of horse. We're going to cut just a *little* bit of horse off, but oh, wait, no, now we need to reorganise all our satchels so we have room for the horse bits. And while we're doing that, we should really talk about which of us could use some horse more. So everybody sits in the sand, doing fuck all but talk about the horse instead of actually using it. Meanwhile, everybody's hungry, and they're getting hungrier. Your *family* is getting hungrier, and that horse isn't getting any better as the days go on. So some of your group, they decide to just cut up the damn horse already, because the people in charge are going to talk forever anyway, and you can feed a few mouths in the meantime.' He shoved an armful of sofa stuffing into the nearly-full autocart. 'What's the harm in that?'

Sawyer stared at him. 'That's . . . this isn't a horse. The *Oxomoco* isn't rotting. And nobody's starving. Nobody's gonna die without . . . without . . .' He gestured emptily at the cart.

Oates opened a closet and began working his way through the floating clothing. 'I didn't say it was a perfect analogy. But we're getting people the things they need. We're not hurting anybody. We're helping. If the council's gonna sit on its ass, somebody else is gonna step in.'

'But you're . . . you're . . .' Sawyer tried to work some moisture back into his mouth. 'You're stealing.'

Oates laughed. 'You've filled half this cart yourself, kid.'

Sawyer's head swam. He pulled his fingers into his gloved palms. 'I – if I'd known—'

Oates' expression grew serious. 'You heard the boss. If you're not happy, you walk away after this. *After this*. We are your ride home. We put food in your mouth and air in your lungs.' He took a step forward, knife still in hand. 'Right now, you owe us.' He smiled as if nothing were wrong. 'Now, we've eaten up a good chunk of time with this. To make up for it, I want you to take the other cart and check out the other homes while I finish up here.' He clapped Sawyer's shoulder. 'Are we good?'

Sawyer would've given anything in that moment to be a stronger person. A smarter person. He wanted to tell Oates to fuck off, he wanted to run out of the room, he wanted to get back to the ship and into an escape pod and beat them back to the Fleet, where he could tell patrol what had happened, and they'd understand, they'd know he hadn't known, they'd be reasonable and fair and . . . and . . . would they? Or would they scoff at him for being stupid? Would they lock him up? Would they kick him out?

The moral high ground didn't look any safer. What would happen if Sawyer simply did nothing, if he refused to help any further with this? Would they leave him? Would they . . . He looked at Oates' knife. Stars, they wouldn't, would they?

Would they?

Sawyer couldn't see any path of refusal that ended well. He didn't have any clue what he'd do when they got back to the Fleet, but Oates was right. They were his ride home. He had four more days with these people. There wasn't much else he could do.

He looked at the floor, and nodded.

'Good,' Oates said. He handed Sawyer his satchel of tools. 'Go quick, and holler if you need a hand.'

Sawyer gestured for the cart to follow. He left the home. He walked to the next home over. There was nothing else he could do. Nowhere else he could go.

The front door was firmly sealed, and as unresponsive as the first had been. There was no big hole made by Aeluon bots. No one had opened this place up since the accident.

Sawyer stood motionless for a moment. He didn't want to do this. He didn't want to be there. *Sanitation*, he thought. That's where he should be. Maybe he'd tell that to patrol when he got back. Maybe if he mentioned that he was in the sanitation lottery, they'd go easy on him, they'd see that he was serious about being there, that he hadn't come all this way to cause trouble. Or would he go to patrol? Maybe it was better to do like Muriel had said – shake hands, walk away, no problem, never speak of it again.

'Shit,' he said. He leaned his forehead against the inside of his helmet and shut his eyes. He had to do this. He had to get back home. Back to the Fleet, anyway. He wasn't sure he had a home. At the moment, he wasn't sure he deserved one.

Sawyer reached into Oates' satchel and found another power pack. He gestured. Nothing happened. He connected his scrib, like he had before. He went through the code, like he had before. This one was the same as the other had been, and he blazed through it in a blink. It was keyed differently, that was all. Keyed for someone else. Another family. Another wall full of hands.

Focus, he thought. *C'mon, don't fuck this up even more.*

He punched in the last command.

Sawyer would never be sure of what came next. The sealed door slid open, and with it came force, and fear, and pressure, and Sawyer was in the air – no, that wasn't right, there wasn't air in space, there was – there *was* air, all the air that had been behind the door, and it was carrying him, and the contents of the home, all the things Oates wanted, all the things that family had needed, rushing, rushing, flying, thudding, falling. Then there was a bulkhead, and a split second of pain, pain everywhere, an inescapable shatter. But that was all. He didn't have time to process what dying felt like.

Part 4

BUT FOR ALL OUR TRAVELS

Feed source: Reskit Institute of Interstellar Migration (Public News Feed)
Item name: The Modern Exodus – Entry #11
Author: Ghuh'loloan Mok Chutp
Encryption: 0
Translation path: [Hanto:Kliptorigan]
Transcription: 0
Node identifier: 2310-483-38, Isabel Itoh

[System message: The feed you have selected has been translated from written Hanto. As you may be aware, written Hanto includes gestural notations that do not have analogous symbols in any other GC language. Therefore, your scrib's on-board translation software has not translated the following material directly. The content here is a modified translation, intended to be accessible to the average Kliptorigan reader.]

――

Where would you begin, dear guest, if you wanted to venture out into the galaxy? Would you talk to a friend? A trusted person who had made the journey before? Would you reach for a Linking book, or test the waters with a travel sim? Would you study language and culture? Update your bots? Purchase new gear? Find a ship to carry you?

Every one of these options are on offer at the emigrant resource centre, a relatively new fixture you can find in most homesteader districts. Some are set up at existing schools, others fill unused merchant space. All serve the same purpose: to prepare GC-bound Exodans for life beyond the Fleet.

Scroll through a workshop listing for any centre, and you will find an exhaustive array of topics. Here is a sampling of the current menu at the resource centre my dear host Isabel took me to visit yesterday:

- *Conversational Klip: What You Didn't Learn In School*
- *Interspecies Sensitivity Training 101*
- *Weather, Oceans, and Natural Gravity: Overcoming Common Fears*
- *A Guide to Human-Friendly Communities*
- *Trade Licence Advice Forum (ask us anything!)*
- *The Legal Do's and Dont's of Engine Upgrades*
- *How to Choose the Right Exosuit*
- *Introduction to the Independent Colonies*
- *Those Aren't Apples: Common Alien Foods You Need To Avoid*
- *Imubot and Vaccination Clinic (check calendar for your desired region)*
- *Ensk Six Ways: Making Sense of Humans from Elsewhere*
- *Ground Environment Acclimation Training (sim-based)*
- *Ground Environment Acclimation Training (non-virtual discussion)*
- *Tunnel Hopping for Beginners*

The list goes on.

I sat in on 'A Guide to Human-Friendly Communities.' Neutral market worlds were prominently mentioned, as were Sohep Frie and, I was pleased to note, my own adopted home of Hashkath. Harmagian territories, depressingly but unsurprisingly, were presented as hit-or-miss. Quelin space was vehemently discouraged, to no one's surprise.

'People's biggest fear is getting kicked to the margins,' said Nuru, the course instructor, who graciously took time to speak with me afterward. 'Everybody's got a great-aunt or uncle sitting around the hex, grumbling about how their parents were sidelined when they made market hops in the pre-membership days. Everybody hears horror stories about Human slums or whatever, and they come in here with exciting ambitions but a huge fear of ending up homeless or mistreated. Life outside the Fleet isn't like that anymore, not if you're smart about it. Times have changed. There are rough places in the galaxy, yeah, but that's what my class is for. That's what this whole centre is for. We want to give people the best start we possibly can.'

I asked Nuru why he spends his days training people for life elsewhere when he himself lives in the Fleet. 'I lived on Fasho Mal for ten years,' he said. 'I loved it, every second. I loved the sky, the open space, the dirt, all of it. But I came home when my mom got sick last standard. Our hex was taking good care of her, but . . . how could I not? So, now I help people get ready for *their* lives on Fasho Mal, or wherever it is they're headed. It's the next best thing to being there myself. At least someone gets to go, right?'

Not everyone agrees with that sentiment. The majority of my time spent in the Fleet has been a delight, but I have, on rare occasion, encountered individuals less approving of my presence. I crossed paths with one of these on my way to the resource centre – not an elderly person, as you might have expected, but a man somewhere in his middle years.

'We don't need you,' he shouted at me as Isabel and I approached the centre. It was clear from the way my skin puckered as he came close that he was intoxicated.

At first, I was not sure if he was addressing me. In hindsight, Isabel knew, as she began to walk more quickly, but in my ignorance, I stopped my cart to make sense of the situation. 'Are you speaking to me?' I asked.

The man did not answer my question, but continued on as if that point were obvious. 'We're Exodans. We belong *here*. You get that? You're not like us. You don't understand what we need.'

Isabel tried to get me to move away, but I assured her I was fine. 'I want to hear what he has to say,' I said. I gestured my willingness to listen to the man, even though he would not understand, even though I believe it only agitated him more. 'I do not understand why you are angry at me.'

'Whatever you're here to teach, take it home,' he said. 'Take it home. We don't need you.'

'I'm not here to teach,' I said. 'I'm here to learn.'

The clarification confused the man, and I admit that I cannot relay what his reply was, for the remainder of it did not make much sense. The underlying intent was anger, though. That much I can say for certain.

'You're embarrassing yourself,' Isabel said curtly. 'Go sober up.' My host is gracious and kind, dear guest, but even to my alien ears, she can be quite assertive when the situation calls for it. I thought it best to follow her into the resource centre at that point, as it was clear nothing else of value would be gained from the exchange. Isabel apologised for the encounter (which was hardly her fault or that of her people, but I understood her embarrassment all the same). I told her it was nothing. I have weathered far worse in academic review. But the exchange did colour my time at the resource centre, and I was thinking of it still as I spoke with Nuru later on. I asked him if this was a sentiment he encountered often.

He replied, with weariness, that it was. 'I get told that I don't deserve the food in my mouth and the walls around me,' he said, 'because I'm taking away instead of giving back. I'm taking away the people who grow the food and maintain the walls, is how they see it. Look – there's no denying that more Exodans are leaving than coming back, but we're hardly in danger of dying out. Farms are still working. Water's still flowing. The Fleet is fine. The people I teach, they'd leave whether or not classes were available to them. But if they left without taking a class or two, they won't know what's what out there. That way lies trouble. All we're doing is giving them the tools they need to stay safe. Exodans helping Exodans. Isn't that what we're supposed to be about?'

I asked Isabel her opinion of the centre once we had left – as an elder, as someone who had watched friends leave and trends unfold across decades. My host was noncommittal.

'Knowledge should always be free,' she said. 'What people do with it is up to them.'

———

KIP

Everything was tingly. Kip had thoughts beyond that one, amazing thoughts that people probably needed to hear. Toes were weird – like *really* weird, if you thought about it. Thinking was weird, too. He could think about what he was thinking about. Did that mean that there was a separate part of him? A thinking part and a . . . thinking thinking part? That was a super good idea, but first: cake. Man, he loved cake. He wished he had a cake. He imagined a cake so big he could put his face down into it and the frosting would rise up and up around him, like the waves of seafoam in the theatre vids, only thick, dense, enveloping him, taking the place of air, sliding in closer and closer and – and no, no, that was scary. He didn't like cake. Cake needed to stay small and manageable and away from his nostrils.

Kip had those thoughts, and more besides, but as soon as they'd bubble up, they were drowned out, washed away by the thought – The Thought – that dominated all others.

Everything was really, really tingly.

'Do you ever wonder,' Ras said. He was tapping the tip of his nose with the tip of his finger, drumming, pulsing. Kip watched him do so for a short eternity. Tap. Tap. Tap. 'Do you ever wonder about, like – okay, you're sitting here.'

'Yeah.'

'And I'm sitting here.'

'Yeah.'

'We're sharing this . . . this moment.'

'Yeah.'

'But *are we really?*' Ras looked deeply concerned. 'Because think about it. I'm seeing *this*, right?' He gestured at the oxygen garden, tracing angled lines outward from his eyes. 'But you – you're seeing *this*.' He touched the sides of Kip's face and drew a different set of lines.

'Whoa,' Kip giggled. 'Your hands are so *weird*.'

'Dude, listen, this is – this is important. What you see is different from what I see. And nobody's ever seen this before. Nobody's ever seen the oxygen garden exactly like I'm seeing it, but it's – it's not like you're seeing it. Kip, we're – we're not sharing anything. Nobody has ever shared anything.'

Kip looked at Ras for a long time – or maybe a short time? A time. He looked at him for a time. He blinked. He laughed, but quietly, because he remembered they were supposed to be quiet, and that part was very important. 'I have no idea what you just said.'

Ras stared at Kip, and he started laughing, too. 'You're such an idiot.'

Kip shut his eyes and nodded, still laughing. He fell back into the grassy bed. He could feel every blade of grass, bending to hold him like a million caring hands. They were in the centre of the garden, the best place in the garden, the quietest, tallest, most hidden place, the place where you could actually *lie down* surrounded by bushes and little trees and leaves leaves leaves. Plants were good. Plants were so good. He loved plants, and he loved smash, and he loved Ras, and he loved life. He loved himself. Wow. He loved *himself*. Everything was . . . was so . . . tingly.

Ras grabbed Kip's shirt. The move was intense and hurried, out of place among the grassy hands and quiet laughter. Kip didn't like it. 'Someone's coming,' Ras whispered.

Kip sat up, abandoning the grass. 'Are you sure?'

They froze. Everything froze. Everything except the unmistakable sound of footsteps. Movement. Invasion.

'Fuck,' Ras whispered. 'I think it's patrol.' He scrambled. 'C'mon!'

They scurried behind a large bush, and everything was bad now, loud heartbeat and metal muscles and screaming edges. The footsteps got closer. With every step, Kip willed himself to be more still, more invisible. He would turn into stone, and they'd never find him. They couldn't find him. Shit, they couldn't find him. They couldn't.

He wished the tingles would go away for a minute.

He could feel Ras beside him. They weren't actually touching, but he could *feel* him, buzzing like a living thing. Ras was wrong. They *were* sharing this. It wasn't a good thing to share, but it was better than being alone.

Someone was in the grass now, the sounds told him. Someone was standing in the grass, turning in a careful circle, looking around. Someone was sitting down, coughing, opening a bottle, drinking. Staying put. Kip was sure the someone would know he and Ras were there, that xe'd hear their breath, their blood. But the someone surprised him. The someone didn't notice. The someone waited.

Then, all at once, there were two someones. The new one spoke. 'Looks like you've been hitting that hard,' she said.

'I'm surprised you haven't,' the first someone said – a male someone.

The woman sat. 'I know this shit's been rough—'

'Rough? *Rough?* Rough is when you haven't been laid in a while, or when your engine breaks, or . . . I fucking killed that kid, Muriel.'

Kip and Ras looked at each other. The ground fell away. Everything was wrong.

'Keep your voice down,' the woman said calmly.

'There's nobody here.'

'Still,' she said. 'Keep it down.' She sighed. 'How could you have guessed he'd do something that stupid? Stars, my niece knows not to open a sealed door in a vacuum, and she's *six*.'

'I should've said something, I was distracted, I—'

'You should've, yes. But it was an accident. Accidents happen.'

'Somebody ever accidentally die on you?' There was a long pause. 'Yeah. I thought not.'

'Oates. It happened. It's done. All we can do is clean up and move forward.'

Kip felt like the giant cake was back, only now it was the air itself, pressing in and smothering. 'Is this real?' he mouthed to Ras.

Ras said nothing, which said everything.

Beyond the bush, the bottle glugged. 'You got everything ready?'

'Yes,' the woman said. 'Food, fuel, every favour I had. We can be out of here this time tomorrow.'

'Thank fuck. Every time I see a patrol, I nearly shit myself.'

'Just keep your head down and your mouth shut, and it'll be fine.'

The bottle glugged again. 'Where'd Dory put him?'

'Do you care?'

'Yes.'

The woman was silent a little too long. 'We didn't have great options.'

'*Where?*'

'Cloth processing. Bottom of the pile.'

'Cloth processing? Are you fucking high? They'll find him in a—'

'—in several days, which is all we need to get gone. Look, where could we have put him where they *wouldn't* find him? We couldn't space him or leave him there without those fuckers on the *Neptune* finding him – and you know they wouldn't hesitate to use that against us one way or another. We couldn't risk a second punch, especially a blind one. We couldn't keep him on the ship, because there's no chance import inspection would overlook a body, no matter how many creds we sent their way. The gardens aren't deep enough, he's too big for a hot box chute without us getting disgusting about it, the foundry's always got people there, cargo bay's too closely patrolled these days – and where do you get off, anyway? We clean up, and you complain about the details?'

'I'm sorry. I just—' The man's voice broke. 'I didn't mean it. I really didn't—'

'I know. And that is why we're doing this for you. Because you're crew, and shit happens. If you'd *meant* to hurt that kid, we wouldn't be busting our asses to make this right.'

'I'm sorry. I'll make it up to you, I—'

'I know.' There was a touching sound, a friendly pat. 'Now are you going to share that kick, or what?'

Kip shut his eyes. He tried to ignore the voices. He tried to ignore everything. He wanted to go back to the grass and the weird toes, but that was gone now. Lost. Now everything was sharp and hot, and – and he didn't want this. He didn't want his brain to be like this anymore, but he was pretty sure he was stuck this way forever, and someone had *died*, and oh stars, what if *he* died? What if he was going crazy and then something went wrong in his brain and he *died*? He looked down at the dirt he was crouching in, the dirt smeared across his palms, the dirt staining his knees. There were dead people in that dirt. Lots and lots of dead people. They were dead, and he'd be dead, and he'd be dirt, too. He didn't like smash anymore. He didn't want to feel like this. He wanted to be okay. He wanted to live. He wanted to live so badly.

TESSA

She heard him, despite his best efforts. Stars, he really was giving it his best. She heard the rustle of his sheets as he tossed them aside, then a slow, deliberate crossing of the floor and ascent of the mattress. He wiggled under her sheet. She did not respond. He thought she was sleeping, and she wanted to see where that would lead. With what must've been agonising self-control, Ky lay alongside her, touching but only barely, silent except for his breathing. He held himself with a two-year-old version of stillness – a tortured rigidity that gave way to a stray twitch and wiggle every few seconds or so.

He was trying – trying *very hard* – to snuggle without waking her up.

Tessa scooped the kid up and covered his tangled scalp with kisses.

'You 'wake!' he squealed.

'Yes, buddy,' she said between one kiss and another. 'I've been awake a while.'

'Good morning!'

'Good morning, Ky.' She waved at the bedside lamp, and a soft glow spread through the room. Ky's hair was a portrait of chaos, and deep pillow lines crossed one of his chubby cheeks. Tessa sat up with her boy in her arms and caught a glimpse of herself in the wall mirror. Her hair and face weren't in much better shape than his, and she didn't have the free pass of toddler-hood. But who cared, at this hour? Certainly not her son, who had inserted a finger a worrying ways into his ear canal.

'Mama, no breakfast,' Ky said. He raised his voice in a shout: 'No breakfast!'

'Shh,' Tessa whispered, pulling his twisting hand away from his head. 'We don't want to wake everybody up. Okay? Can you be quiet? Can you whisper?'

'*Yes.*' Ky's whisper could've been heard from the opposite side of the room, but it was an improvement.

'Do you want to go see the stars?'

'No.'

Everything was *no* these days. He'd put precisely zero effort behind this particular one, so Tessa paid it no mind. 'I think you do. Let's go see the stars.'

Ever-growing boy on her hip, Tessa walked into the living room. A few nightlights and the emergency arrow pierced the darkness, but otherwise, it was pitch dark. She could hear Pop snoring, and nothing from Aya's room. Good. Tessa tiptoed forward, anticipating the couch, the table, the— '*Motherf—*' Tessa hissed, and swallowed the rest in a muffled groan. She hadn't anticipated the stray toy that had found its way into the bare sole of her foot.

'Shh!' Ky breathed loudly. 'Quiet!'

'Yes, thank you,' Tessa said. *Smartass*, she thought.

She reached the ring of tiny floor lights that marked the edge of the shaft down to the family cupola. She'd thought, once, that the reason homes had cupolas in common spaces was because the architects had tried to parcel out window resources as economically as they could. That was true, but only the half of it. Apparently, the shared portal was an intentional design. Her ancestors had worried that if people could lock themselves away and look outside in solitude, they'd lose a few screws. They'd get scared, lose hope. It was a mixed bag, the view of the open. Breathtaking beauty and existential dread all mixed together. Far easier to focus on the former and avoid the latter, the thinking went, if you sat at the window with friends ready to hold your hand or listen or just share company with. That, Tessa thought dryly, or you'd go buggy as a group. Either way, you weren't alone.

Her eyes adjusted to the negligible light. She opened the railing gate, sat on the bench with kid firmly in grasp, and pushed the down button. Home slid away, and for a second or two, the only sounds were the pulley turning and her son sucking his fingers. Then: a rushing, strangled roar behind thick walls. 'Ky, can you tell me what that sound is?'

'Don' know.'

'Yes, you do. What goes through the deck under ours?'

Even in the dim, Tessa could see her son's blank stare.

'Water,' she said. 'Remember? All the water we use goes through big pipes in the floor.' She'd save *filtration tanks* and *settlement ponds* for another year.

'Can have cookie?'

Tessa looked forward to the day when linear conversations became a thing. 'Not for breakfast.'

'What 'bout . . . what 'bout cookie to lunch?'

'*Maybe* if you're good this morning, Grandpa will give you a cookie at lunch.'

Ky looked around as the background noise changed. 'Where water?'

So he *was* paying attention. 'It's up above us now. We're about to stop.'

'Oh boy, get ready!' he said.

'Get ready,' Tessa said with a laugh. 'Aaaaand – stop!'

The bench settled into place. At their feet was a shallow window sticking into the empty space outside. It was different than the one her family'd had when she was a kid. They'd had one of the old ones then, polygonal in shape, made of thick glass as old as the Fleet itself, the view cut in segments by thick metal frames. Ashby had bought them one of the nice new plex ones after his first tunnelling gig – no angles, no inner frame. He was always doing stuff like that. She'd once worried that he was treating them at the expense of getting things for himself, but once he'd bought his own ship, she didn't feel as bad about it. She was just glad he kept them in mind.

She thought about how much she liked the things he sent them – the plex window, the sim hub, a box of spices from some alien port. A guilty, toxic idea surfaced, the same one that had awoken her hours before. Tessa shoved it away before it could make itself plain. She focused on her son.

She slid off the hanging bench onto the cupola seating area. It wasn't much, just a shelf around the edges. The view wasn't much either – at least, not compared to the big, broad starscapes you got at the plazas. But this was her own corner of sky, and she liked that. She'd always liked that.

Ky wriggled against her grasp. She let him go. He toddled out onto the plex, brown feet against black sky. He sat, all at once, unceremoniously. 'Stars!' he said, looking down through the gap between his bent knees.

'Yep,' Tessa said.

He pointed a chubby finger. 'Is five stars.' With his other hand, he held up two fingers and a thumb.

'It's a bit more than five, baby.'

The stars darkened as a hefty transport shuttle sailed past, docking lights blinking, hull crusty with tacked-on tech and repurposed siding. Ky shrieked with glee. 'Oh man!' He looked to her, his eyes and mouth perfect circles. 'Mama, did you see?'

'Yeah!'

'Wow! Did you – did you see?'

'Yeah, I saw.'

'Dat's my ship.'

'Wow, that's *your* ship? Cool.'

''s my ship. 's all fixed.'

Aya had lost dessert privileges for a tenday over the origin of *all fixed*, but even though the illicit sim babysitting sessions had ended, the vocabulary addition remained. Tessa sighed, hoping her eldest hadn't irrevocably mixed up the younger's brain.

She let him play on the window, automatically responding with stock affirmations as he babbled on and on (he was on about . . . pillows? She'd lost the plot, and so had he, it seemed). Her mind was on the sky at her feet, which was to say she wasn't thinking about much at all. Something about that view always set her right, even though she'd seen it a million times. She thought back to the first time she'd been planetside, on a family trip to Hashkath. Ashby hadn't been much older than Ky. Mom was still with them. Their first night, Pop called Tessa out to the courtyard by their bunkhouse. 'Look at that, kiddo,' he'd said. She'd tilted her head up to match his. As an adult, she remembered how different the stars looked in that moment, how muted, how fuzzy. Her father had wanted to share something special with her, she knew in hindsight, but her immediate impression then was one of fear. There was no plex, no frame between her and that sky. She felt that any second, someone would switch the gravity off, and she'd float up and up, out forever. She'd stayed outside for all of two seconds before running back in and clinging fast to her bewildered mother, sobbing that she wanted to go home.

That experience still lingered on the few subsequent vacations she'd taken in adulthood, even though she knew nobody could turn off a planet's gravity, even though she knew her walls were less reliable than grounders' atmospheres. She knew that at home, she wasn't really looking *down*. She was up, sideways, all around. She was looking in the direction the artigrav nets told her to look, the same direction the old centrifuges made her ancestors look (and their view, of course, had always been spinning). But she could know that and still feel in her gut that stars lived below her feet. That was normal. That was where they belonged.

She thought, though, of visitors she'd had from somewhere else. The last time Ashby had been there with his crew – Ky had been tiny then, she reflected, remembering him kicking his untrained legs in her brother's arms – those two odd techs and the Aandrisk had parked themselves in the cupola for hours, sitting on the floor like Ky was now, freaked out and fascinated, never tiring of the novelty. A person's view of the stars was, ultimately, a matter of perspective. Of upbringing.

Tessa wondered how Aya would do with a planetside sky. She never came down to the family cupola – or any cupola, for that matter. These days, wherever she was in a room, she strategically placed herself as far from walls as she could manage. Would she mind being close to a wall if her feet were always held fast to the ground? Would she look out windows if she could trust them to not suck her through?

As for Ky, he was small. The sky was just another constant to him, like cookies and pajamas and family. He wouldn't care one way or the other for a few years yet. He'd absorb whatever environment you stuck him in. *All fixed.*

The guilty idea began to surface again, and Tessa knew it was time to get about her day. 'Come on, baby,' she said, gathering Ky, wiping his spit off the plex where he'd been licking it. 'I gotta get to work.'

They returned to the bench and headed upward. He looked up, watching the cable carry them. Tessa looked down just in time to see the stars darken again. 'Hey, Ky, look! There's a skiff!'

Ky nearly threw himself out of her arms, doubling over at the waist, pointing his head toward the cupola. But he was too late. The ship had already passed.

'Aw, bummer,' Tessa said. 'It's gone now.'

Her son looked at her, stricken, betrayed. His eyes widened. His lip trembled. The entirety of his face collapsed into itself, and he wailed with bitter injury.

Dammit. Well. Time for everybody else to wake up anyway.

ISABEL

Isabel hurried through the door as soon as she saw Ghuh'loloan through her office window, patiently waiting in front of her desk. 'Good morning,' Isabel said. She tapped her hud to bring up the time. 'I'm sorry, were we supposed to meet early?' She didn't recall that they'd arranged that, but then, she had so much on her plate that things were starting to fall off the edges.

'No, no,' Ghuh'loloan said. She stretched her dactyli reassuringly. 'I simply had much on my mind and wished to speak with you.' She pointed a tentacle at Isabel's desk, where two mugs of mek stood waiting. 'I managed to brave that contraption of yours, but I'm afraid I was too cowardly to try for a brew as hot as you make.'

'That's not cowardly.' Not at all, Isabel thought, considering the Ensk-labelled temperature dial and smooth knobs built for human hands. 'That was very kind.' She rather disliked starting her day with mek, but she wasn't about to turn down a drink made by someone who'd risked a nasty burn. She sat, and sipped. Stars, but Ghuh had made it strong. 'So, what brought you here?' She put her scrib on the table, ready for whatever questions about musical traditions or food storage or toilet technology her colleague had today.

But the Harmagian surprised her. Ghuh'loloan did not have her own scrib out, and she did not launch forth with a ravenous barrage of queries. Instead, she did something Isabel had never seen: she hesitated. 'Dear friend, I'm not sure how to begin,' Ghuh'loloan said. Isabel took immediate note of the change in address. Not *dear host*. *Dear friend*. 'The topic I wish to discuss is positive, but I worry it may cause difficulty, or worse, insult.'

Isabel set down her mug. She knew Ghuh'loloan understood smiling, and so she smiled. 'Dear friend,' she said, hoping her echo of the phrase came across as sincere. 'I very much doubt you'd insult me, especially since you've told me at the outset that it's not your intent. You trust me to be honest with you, right?'

Ghuh'loloan's tentacles relaxed. 'Indeed. Still, if my profession has made me aware of anything, it is that cultural bruising is often worst when done accidentally.' Her body quivered from front to end – her species' equivalent of a shrug. 'But now, at least, if insult occurs, you will know it was not by design.'

Isabel sipped her lukewarm mek and nodded, patiently awaiting the end of the Harmagian song and dance.

There was a great sucking sound as Ghuh'loloan filled her airsack. 'You know my writings of my time here have gained a sizable audience.'

'Yes.' Isabel didn't know how she could've responded otherwise. Ghuh'loloan had been downright euphoric over the messages she'd received from her readers. Modern life in the Fleet, it seemed, had struck a chord in the niche world of ethnography, and her colleague was happily spending her sleepless nights responding to as many questions as she could until Isabel woke up.

Ghuh'loloan forged ahead. Her friendly concern was absent now, having given way to matter-of-fact explanation. If there was one thing a scholar was good at, it was laying out a case. 'There has been a particularly strong reaction to my mentions of the Fleet's technical capabilities and resulting challenges. I'm sure you can imagine the sort I mean.'

Isabel gave a tight smile. 'They think we're a little backward, hmm?'

'To some, yes. Please do not take it personally. Cultural arrogance is depressingly universal, particularly among my people.' Ghuh'loloan paused, waiting.

It took Isabel a moment to catch on. 'I don't take it personally,' she said. 'Not to worry.'

The Harmagian was satisfied. She continued. 'Those responses, I pay no attention to. But there are others . . .' The hesitance returned. 'Others who wish to help. Not because you are incapable of helping yourselves,' she added quickly, 'but out of a real desire to provide resources that would be of benefit.'

Isabel leaned back in her chair. 'We're still a charity case,' she said. She felt that twinge of ego once more.

'Again, to some. But I wouldn't look at it as an act of pity. For many, it's out of a genuine wish for you to gain equal footing.' She wrapped a tentacle around her own neglected mug of mek. 'The reason I have decided to share this with you is that I have had a few letters that offer some intriguing possibilities.'

'Such as?'

Ghuh'loloan conducted the retract-face-open-mouth-pour-liquid manoeuvre, then cradled the mug against her porous bulk. 'Such as oshet-Tasthiset esk-Vassix as-Ishehsh Tirikistik isket-Haaskiset.'

Isabel blinked. Full Aandrisk names were nothing if not a mouthful. 'Who's . . . that?'

'Have you heard of Ellush Haaskiset?'

'No.'

'It's a comp tech developer, based in Reskit. Their entire managing council is comprised of a single feather family, and they represent a staggering amount of wealth. Tirikistik is one of the more public faces in their circle. She's also an amateur enthusiast of alien cultural study, and I've seen her in attendance at various symposiums at the Institute. It was quite exciting to receive a letter from her directly.'

Ghuh'loloan paused again, and Isabel took the cue to compliment her on a prestigious happening. 'That does sound exciting,' Isabel said. 'It speaks well of your work.'

Her colleague twisted her dactyli with pride. 'Thank you,' she said. 'Tirikistik has read all my writings on the Fleet to date, and she is understanding of the problem creds have created. She said she initially considered opening a trade line here, but my piece on your economic imbalance made her reconsider.'

Isabel gave a slight frown. Was Ghuh'loloan's work inadvertently discouraging outside trade? Were alien merchants reading her essays and becoming concerned that their business was doing more harm than good? The creds-or-barter issue required some serious ironing out, yes, but . . . but they did *need* that stuff. She wondered, with a sudden heaviness in her midsection, if this cultural exchange would hurt them in the end.

Ghuh'loloan continued her thread. 'Instead, she's interested in making a donation.'

'What kind of donation?'

'Well, she mentioned ambi storage facilities—'

'That wouldn't be of much use here.'

'That's what I said. I suggested that rather than her deciding what would be of help from an outside perspective, I could perhaps open a line of communication to the Fleet itself to see what would be of most use.'

'I can tell you exactly what the labour guilds' consensus would be,' she replied. 'Exodan problems require Exodan solutions. They'll say we've already relied too much on alien charity.'

'Charity from the GC parliament, and from Aeluons collectively. But this is a representative of a civilian business offering what amounts to a personal gift. A potentially enormous gift, but a gift nonetheless.' Ghuh'loloan took another disquieting gulp from her mug. 'The thing about gifts is, with correct, careful phrasing, they can always be turned down. Plus, you have me as an . . . an ambassador of sorts. I can easily deflect her if this offer would be poorly received. But I felt obligated to, if nothing else, pass the message along.'

Isabel tapped her fingertips together as she thought. A personal gift. Yes, *that* might open some doors. 'I could set up a meeting with the resource oversight council,' she said. There was no harm in a conversation, right? Like Ghuh'loloan said, they could always say no. But you couldn't know what you were declining until the option was at least on the table.

'Splendid,' Ghuh'loloan said. 'I'll hold off on my reply to Tirikistik, then.' She raised her mug in a mimicry of a Human cheer.

Isabel returned the gesture with a smile. As she drank, she thought of the artigrav nets beneath her feet, the solar harvesters orbiting outside, the limited-cognition AIs installed in public corridors for safety's sake. All gifted in decades past by species who couldn't imagine life without such things. Now, it was her own species who couldn't imagine life without them. She wondered what else could — and would — be replaced. What essentials would disappear.

KIP

Kip (10:13): are you awake

Ras (10:16): yes

Kip (10:16): can we meet up

Kip (10:16): I need to talk

Ras (10:20): I can't, I have chores

Kip (10:20): I really need to talk

Ras (10:21): there's nothing to talk about

Kip (10:21): uh yes there is

Ras (10:21): no

Kip (10:21): Ras come on

Kip (10:22): this is serious

Ras (10:23): I have to study

Ras (10:23): like actually study

Kip (10:23): okay fine I can come over

Kip (10:23): we could study together

Kip (10:25): and I could help with chores

Kip (10:30): Ras?

Kip (10:42): come on man

Kip (10:48): stop ignoring me

Kip (10:54): stop

Kip (10:54): ignoring

Kip (10:54): me

Kip (10:75): Ras please I just want to talk

Bastard.

Kip had hoped Ras would change his tune after they'd both slept and sobered up – both of which had been a profound fucking relief. Or at least, it *had* been a relief, until Kip had awoken enough to realise that everything that had happened really *happened*, and that the conversation they'd overheard wasn't a dream or a trip or anything so convenient.

Somebody had hid a body. It wasn't exciting, like it was in vids. This was terrifying. This was real.

As soon as the garden had cleared out, Ras had made it clear that he got how fucked up this was, but that they weren't going to say anything. They didn't know who those people were, and if they told someone, those same people might come after them. They might end up down in cloth recycling, too. Ras had left no room for argument. End of discussion. *They didn't hear anything.*

Except they had. They *had* heard it, and there was no forgetting it. There was no wishing it away, no matter how hard Kip tried.

He lay in bed, staring at the ceiling. He was starving, and his mouth was so dry his tongue felt sticky. But he hadn't left his room, even though he'd been awake for hours. The thought of facing family was too much. He couldn't put on an easy face. There was no pretending with something like this.

He was really hungry, though. Like, really hungry. He had a weird headache, too, and he felt tired to his bones. He was never doing smash again, he decided. Not fucking worth it.

Maybe somebody's already found him, he thought. Yeah. Yeah, that was comforting. If those people had stuck the – stars – the body down in cloth recycling . . . well, there were lots of people who worked there, right? Somebody would have to find him. Even the people who'd put him down there knew that. Yeah, somebody else would find him – had found him already, probably. Somebody had found him, and the patrols would take care of it, and Kip didn't have to worry about it. Nobody would know that he knew.

He wondered if someone was looking for whoever it was. His hex had to have noticed that he hadn't come home. The dead guy had been a bad dude, if he was working for those folks. But . . . he'd been someone, right? He'd been someone. They'd called him 'kid'. Someone else had to be looking.

Kip dug around the clothes lying by his bed and found his scrib. He did a skim through the news feeds. Bot upgrades, council meetings, Aeluons at war, Toremi at war, boring Human politics, boring alien politics – nothing about a body down in cloth recycling.

Shit.

He rubbed his face. Maybe they just hadn't found it *yet*. They'd find it today, though, definitely. Kip thought back to the time he'd won the shit lottery and spent two tendays in the recycling centre. He'd been on food compost, not cloth, but he'd walked through there, and seen all the folks washing and folding and stitching, all the folks walking by the . . . the . . . the giant piles of cloth. The piles you'd never get through in one day.

Kip thought about what it would be like to pick up an armload of everyday laundry and discover something horrible shoved underneath. A dead face lying silent. Cold eyes staring still. He wondered how it would be – how it would *look* – if the body lay there for a few days. His empty stomach knotted. He didn't want to think about that. He didn't want to, but now that he'd started, he couldn't stop.

Someone else would find the body, yeah. Someone else would find it, and xe wouldn't expect it, and it'd be the worst day of xyr life.

And those people he'd heard the night before . . . they were gonna get away. Throw a person away like it was nothing and hop to some planet where no one would ever find them. That wasn't okay. That wasn't right.

That wasn't right.

Kip thought about what Ras had said – how those people in the garden might come after them. He thought a lot about that. That thought made his stomach hurt, too. But he also thought about the opposite: what if they went after someone else? What if they did this again? Could he sit with that? How would his stomach feel if he read the feeds one day and . . . and . . . 'Fuck it,' he muttered. He sat up and searched for some trousers. His head tightened, the last remnants of smash sleep still making him feel crunchy around the edges. His heart hammered, too, but *that* wasn't because of the smash. That, he'd done on his own.

He stood at his bedroom door for a while before waving it open. Mom and Dad were in the living room, reading their scribs, drinking tea. The scene was so normal, so boring. So comforting. His heart beat harder, and even though there was nothing in his stomach, he wanted to throw up.

'You came home late,' Mom said. Her voice was annoyed, and her face was, too, right until she looked at Kip. The lines around her eyes let go. 'Kip, what's wrong?'

Kip had barely realised that he'd started crying. Stars, he was such a fuck-up. His parents were dumb, but they *cared*, in their own dumb way, and they'd *always* cared, and then he went and did shit like this. He stood there stupidly, hands in his pockets, trying to pull the tears back. He failed. Fine. He failed at everything else anyway.

He cleared his throat and frowned at the floor. 'I need to tell you guys something.'

EYAS

Eyas sat in her chair and stared at Sawyer's corpse, lying ready on her worktable. This was a typical sight, an everyday tableau, and the tasks ahead were normal as could be. But nothing about this body was normal. Nothing about this was okay.

She sat for half an hour before she finally got to her feet. She walked to her cabinet, opened the top drawer, and took out a belongings bag. The bag was made of throw-cloth, clean and well-stitched. A neutral way to contain objects that were anything but. She turned to the body, hesitant like she'd never been. Knowing him in life wasn't what troubled her. She'd prepared corpses of people she'd known, and known far, far better than a one-time acquaintance such as this. Hexmates' family members. Her favourite childhood school teacher. Her grandfather, which had been bitterly difficult. No, her reticence came from elsewhere. This wasn't a heartbreak. This was a desecration.

Her nose itched beneath her heavy breathing mask. She rarely wore a mask at work, not even when the person had been old or the death had been gruesome. But then, she'd never worked with a corpse in this state. It wasn't dangerous, of course – it had gone through a decontamination flash on arrival like all the rest. However, it *was* in the early stages of unchecked decay, and neither Eyas nor any of her colleagues encountered that regularly. This corpse hadn't been brought to the Centre on the day of death, accompanied by a grieving family and sombre medical staff. This corpse had been brought in by a patrol team, still retching and moaning over what they'd found hidden away.

Are you sure you want to take this one? her supervisor had asked. They'd been assembled that morning, every caretaker and apprentice, sitting in shock as it was explained what had been left for them.

I'm sure, Eyas said. She'd volunteered, and no one had argued. Everyone knew it was right. She was the one who'd gasped when the patroller displayed a picture of the corpse's face. She was the one who'd known the deceased's name.

Someone had thrown Sawyer away. Like garbage. Like a thing unwanted, used up. The thought filled Eyas with silent rage. The feeling smouldered in her chest as she removed a soiled shirt, a pair of thick socks, a trinket ring of alien make. It rattled her hands as she washed the body and saw flecks of trash floating down the drain. It wrenched her jaw as she reset visibly bent bones. She hoped whatever happened had been quick. Stars, she hoped it had been quick.

Sawyer was just one death, but the indignity, the aberrance, the slackness brought on by improper storage made her think of the tendays following the *Oxomoco*. She remembered cleaning body after body after body, laid out not in the seclusion of her workroom, but in the chill of a repurposed food storage bay. She remembered the day spent aboard the *Oxomoco* itself, when it had been her turn to take a shift cleaning out the abandoned Centres. She remembered learning what bodies looked like when they'd only composted halfway, remembered the smell that lingered on her exosuit in the airlock, remembered spending a standard afterward hand-grinding bones that hadn't disintegrated properly after exposure to air.

That time had been worse than this. An exponential amount worse. And yet, tame as Sawyer's corpse was in comparison, she knew the details of this day were going to bolt themselves to a similar spot in her mind. She didn't know this man, really, but he'd . . . he'd trusted her. Blindly trusted her, just like he'd blindly trusted the people who had led him to this table. If she'd been more patient with him, if she'd answered his letter and become his friend, if she'd given him a few more than five minutes of her time, would he – no, no, no. She knew better than to get dragged along by *if*s in situations like these, and she shut that line of questioning down. The guilt lingered, even so. Ghosts were imaginary, but hauntings were real.

She turned over the corpse's right arm, studying the hole where his wristpatch had been. The removal had been rushed and clumsy, and there wasn't much she could do about the damage. She wrapped it with a cloth bandage, for decency's sake. She'd read about patch thieves who prowled the grittier sides of spaceports, but – even though she had no experience with such things herself – her gut said this wasn't that. She'd never heard of that flavour of crime in the Fleet, and she doubted, under the circumstances, that someone had jumped on that particular bandwagon *now*. No, someone didn't want anybody to know who this corpse had been. But she knew. She'd given patrol a name, a place of origin, and a scrib path. *We can work with that*, the patroller had said, visibly grateful. That was a shred of comfort, at least. That was something.

She lifted the corpse's arm and inserted a length of thin, fluid-filled tubing connected to a bot reclaimer. She hit the switch and heard a mechanical hum as the reclaimer activated Sawyer's imubots, directing them to parade up the tube and into the soon-to-be-sealed receptacle. Eyas would then send them along to the hospital, where they'd be sterilised and reset and injected into someone else. Nothing went to waste in the Fleet.

She looked at the thrown-away corpse, the skin bruised and blue. Nothing was *supposed* to go to waste.

The reclaimer finished its task. Sawyer's body was ready for storage. Eyas wheeled it into the stasis chamber and shut the door. The corpse was gone, but she could still feel it in the room with her, a mess that would never be clean. She looked at the bag she'd put the clothes and trinkets in. There was a delivery label printed on the front of it, waiting for a name and family address. She found a heat pen, and wrote the only piece of information she had. She hoped the patrollers would fill in the rest.

She removed her mask, washed herself as hastily as good hygiene would allow, and left the room in a hurry, taking the belongings bag with her. She passed colleagues in the hall, but didn't meet their eyes.

'Eyas?' someone called. 'You okay?'

Eyas said nothing. She continued to the main chamber and took the elevator down to the cupola. She kept everything placid, everything *inside*, just in case there were any families down there, seeking the same quiet she was.

The elevator came to rest. Thankfully, thankfully, Eyas found herself alone.

She sat on one of the benches surrounding the domed window in the floor. Stars spilled out beneath her feet. The Centre wasn't sunside, but it was right on the cusp. Bright fingers of light teased past the thick windowsill, upstaging the delicate glitter beyond. The constellations changed as the *Asteria* continued its unending orbit, but the view from this spot always felt the same. The constancy was a comfort, a reminder that whatever unpleasant-ness you'd just been through was only a moment, only a blink within a vast, slow splendour.

Or it *was* a comfort, most days. All Eyas could feel now was the smouldering, the shaking, the wrenching. Assured of her solitude, she did something she hadn't done in a long time, not where bodies were concerned. She held the belongings bag in her lap, and she wept.

Part 5

· ·

WE ARE NOT LOST

Feed source: Reskit Institute of Interstellar Migration (Public News Feed)
Item name: The Modern Exodus – Entry #14
Author: Ghuh'loloan Mok Chutp
Encryption: 0
Translation path: [Hanto:Kliptorigan]
Transcription: 0
Node identifier: 2310-483-38, Isabel Itoh

[System message: The feed you have selected has been translated from written Hanto. As you may be aware, written Hanto includes gestural notations that do not have analogous symbols in any other GC language. Therefore, your scrib's on-board translation software has not translated the following material directly. The content here is a modified translation, intended to be accessible to the average Kliptorigan reader.]

Before I was Ghuh'loloan, my body belonged to someone else. Some*thing* else. By definition, I cannot remember this time, but I can tell you, from having visited my own offspring while they were in development, what it would've been like. The Being That Was Not Ghuh'loloan had no name, no identifying distinction beyond parentage. Xe was a polyp, an unfeeling mass anchored to a rock face alongside a hundred or so siblings. That being had the beginnings of the tentacles I do now – tiny buds waving in the simulated tides, pulling in the nutrient mix the minders routinely pour into the nursery pools. All Harmagians begin this way. For the first ninety tendays before we become ourselves, the polyps do nothing but hold fast and eat while engaged in the taxing business of growing a brain.

When the brain is sufficiently formed, the polyp detaches from the rock. Xe floats freely in the water for another tenday at least, wriggling constantly and without direction. Slowly, slowly, the new brain masters locomotive control, and the swimmer becomes strong enough to navigate around the pool. It is marvellous, dear guest, to watch the near-instantaneous shift from hapless writhing to purposeful experimentation. The child – for it is a child, now – does not have fully formed eyes or dactyli yet, nor is xyr gut developed, nor will xe venture out of the water for another eight tendays. But xe has control. That is when a Harmagian begins life. That is when I became Ghuh'loloan.

Biologically, I find that other species understand this phase of transition quite readily. What they do not understand is that culturally, we consider the moment of the polyp's detachment to be a death. To a Harmagian, this is obvious. What else could it be? The form and behaviour of a polyp are so different from that of a mature Harmagian that they can only be seen as separate entities. How could I have been Ghuh'loloan if I did not have a brain to understand what Ghuh'loloan was? How could I claim that polyp as a part of myself if I have not even the faintest recollection of that experience? (I do of swimming in the nursery pools: a hazy memory of a dash around a very tall rock, an image of an adult's enormous tentacle reaching underwater to fix an oxygen filter). Remember, we are a species that does not sleep. Our lives are defined by the aggregate of all that happens during the waking.

I used to assume, when I first began to study the lives of my sapient neighbours, that perhaps sleep would better prepare those species for death. Sleep sounds quite like death to me, a strange temporary death, complete with an afterlife of surreal visions. I have heard both a Human and an Aandrisk, on separate occasions, posit that death must feel like nothing more than a 'dreamless sleep'. You would think, then, that these species are less fearful of the inevitable end. If one experiences oblivion daily – and for an enormous portion of the day, at that – should it not be familiar territory?

I was wrong about this, of course. Some species have a more passive reaction to death than others – I am thinking here of the Laru, with their total lack of funerary customs – but sleep or no, all fear it. All spend lifetimes trying to outstretch its grasp.

In a highly social species such as my Human hosts, a death is keenly felt, even if it is that of a stranger. Certainly, I have been moved by the end of those I did not know – please read my fourth essay on this feed, dear guest, if you have not already – but Humans habitually react in a way that members of my own species might find extreme. A single death, regardless of relation, can dominate conversation for tendays upon tendays. It takes over news feeds, workplace chatter, decisions about the day. A death always fixates Humans in one direction or the other. They either talk about it at any given opportunity, or doggedly avoid the topic. I did not have a good hypothesis as to why this might be until I joined my dear host Isabel for dinner at her hex tonight. There has been an unusual death in the Fleet – accidental or purposeful, no one yet knows – and the families could speak of little else. All species emote around death, but there is an intensity of mood here I am unaccustomed to. I cannot stop pondering it.

As I sat witness to this behaviour tonight, two individuals caught my eye: Isabel and Tamsin's son, Miguel, holding his young daughter Katja on his lap. His embrace was snug, and he was stroking her hair as the others spoke and argued. At first, I thought the gesture was in order to calm or reassure her. Perhaps consciously, that is why he did it. But Katja was paying no attention to the conversation. She was fully engrossed in building a fortress out of mashed vegetables on her plate. If she registered the topic at hand, I do not think she understood much of it. But still, her father held, and stroked, and the longer the conversation went on, the more affectionate he became. I thought then of the means of Human reproduction. It is an intense process, an internal process. Even though her father did not go through this process himself, he was close audience to it (as is commonly the case, he is romantically partnered with Nina, Katja's mother). Human infants are famously frail, and the amount of time they remain dependent on adults for needs as basic as eating or locomotion makes me wonder how the species didn't give up on the whole prospect millennia ago.

Perhaps I am completely wrong about linking these two behaviours, dear guest, but I find it likely that there is a connection – even if only a tenuous one – between Humans' heavy parental involvement in child-rearing and how socially unsettled they become around death. Were I among my own kind and had someone met a sad end, it would be discussed, certainly. If I knew the deceased, I would visit their family to recite my praise of their life, as is proper. But I would not think of my offspring in that time. This would not occur to me. My offspring are not the ones who have died. I would know them to be well. Depending on age, I would know them to be swimming safely in their ponds, or being mindfully reared by their tutors, or living in homes of their own. I would not imaginatively transfer the misfortune of another onto them. I would not worry about them unless given reason.

Human parents always worry. Their offspring developed while attached not to rocks, but to themselves. And unlike Harmagians, who bid farewell to polyps and welcome new children in their stead, their progeny have but once to die.

———

TESSA

There was never a day when Tessa's home wasn't a mess, but the one she walked in on now was of a different kind. Cupboards were open, drawers were empty, and things she was sure she'd tidied up had found their way elsewhere. She might've thought the break-ins at work had moved to her home, were it not for Pop sitting on the couch in the middle of it, smoking his pipe and observing.

'What is going on?' Tessa asked warily, hanging her satchel by the door. Elsewhere in the home, she could hear industrious movement.

Pop raised his chin. 'Aya,' he said, 'is packing.'

Tessa had long ago stopped trying to predict anything that was likely to be waiting for her at home. She might as well write a bunch of nouns on some strips of cloth, add an equal number of verbs, shake them up in a box, pull two of each out, and pair them with her kids' names. *Ky eating paint. Aya breaking bots.* That system would be closer to the mark than anything she could come up with on her own.

Still. *Packing.* That was new.

She made her way to Aya's room and leaned against the open doorframe. Yes, indeed, there was her daughter, sitting by several old storage crates and everyday satchels stuffed with clothes and sundries – a pack of dentbots, Tessa could see, and a tin of tea as well. Her son was present too, kneeling on Aya's bed and trying his darnedest to put on one of her shirts. He was attempting to stick his head through the sleeve, but hey, points for effort.

Tessa surveyed the goings-on. 'Hey,' she said. 'What's all this?'

Aya looked up from her concentrated work. She took a large breath. 'Mom,' the nine-year-old said in a serious voice. 'I know this might be hard for you to hear.'

Tessa kept her face as straight as possible. 'Okay.'

'I'm moving.'

'Oh,' Tessa said. She gave a thoughtful nod. 'I see. Where are you moving to?'

'Mars. I know you don't like it there, but it's better than here.'

'Sounds like you've made up your mind about this.'

Aya nodded and resumed emptying her dresser into one of the crates.

Tessa watched for a moment. 'Can I help?'

Her daughter considered, then pointed. 'You can put my toys in this box here.' She pointed again.

As directed, Tessa sat on the floor and began to gather figurines and model ships. 'So, how are you getting to Mars?'

'I wrote to Uncle Ashby,' Aya said. 'He's going to pick me up and take me there.'

'Really,' Tessa said. 'Did he say that to you, or is that what you asked him?'

'That's what I asked him. He hasn't replied yet, but I know it'll be fine.'

'Hmm. You know, he's pretty far away right now. Why not take a transport from here?'

'I don't have trade good enough for a ticket.'

'Ah. Yeah, that's a problem.'

Ky wriggled his way off the bed and marched over to the boxes. 'I help!' he said. He grabbed a battery pack out of one of the crates, put it on the floor, then reached for something else to remove.

'Ky, stop it,' Aya said, not a trace of patience in her voice.

'No,' Ky said. He threw a bundle of socks with a laugh. 'No!'

'Mom,' Aya whined. 'Make him quit it.'

Tessa pulled her son into her lap. 'Ky, come on, don't throw,' she said. She handed him the least fragile of the toy ships in order to keep him busy. 'Aya, be nice to your brother.'

'He's so annoying,' her daughter muttered.

'You were annoying when you were little, too.'

'Was not.'

Tessa laughed. 'All toddlers are annoying, baby. It's the way of the universe.' She kissed her son's hair as her daughter continued packing. 'So, once Ashby drops you off on Mars, what's your plan?'

'They have bunkhouses at the docks,' Aya said. 'I can stay there until I make enough creds for a house.'

Tessa smothered a smile. Whatever vids Aya had picked up *dockside bunkhouses* from hadn't driven home the fact that nobody on Mars would give her a room *without* creds. She was from the Fleet, through and through. She wondered what other facts about grounder life her daughter hadn't gleaned. 'You know Martians don't live under open air, right?' She said the words strategically, trying not to scare *too* much.

Aya paused. 'Yeah, they do.'

'They don't. Humans can't breathe the outside air on Mars. Every Martian city is under a big shield dome.'

'What? No.'

'Yep. Here,' Tessa said, handing Aya her scrib. 'You can look it up on the Linkings.'

Ky dropped the toy ship and reached for the device as it was handed off. 'Mine!' he said.

'That's definitely not yours,' Tessa said. 'And your sister's using it now.' Ky started to fuss, so she grabbed the pair of socks he'd thrown earlier and put it in his stubby hands. 'Here, show me how fast you can make this into two socks.'

Ky plucked at a random patch of fabric. He'd be at it a while.

Aya, meanwhile, was frowning in a way that said she expected parental trickery. She looked down at the scrib and made a few practised gestures. The screen responded with pictures of Florence, Spirit's Rest, Perseverance. All glittering, all metropolitan, all . . .

corralled behind barriers against the harsh red dust outside. Aya visibly wilted. Tessa felt a little sorry for her. Adventures were a hard thing to let go of.

'Did something happen at school?' Tessa asked. The bullying had ended – as far as she knew – but Aya had been playing solo since then.

'No,' Aya said, annoyed at the question.

'You sure?'

'*Yes.*'

'Okay.' Tessa raised her palms. 'Why do you want to move, then?'

Her daughter's bravado was shrivelling before her eyes. 'I don't know,' she mumbled.

'That's not what you told me,' Pop said. Tessa craned her head back to find him standing in the doorway. How long had he been watching? 'Go on, bug,' he said kindly.

Aya said nothing. She fidgeted.

Pop looked to Tessa. 'She's upset about that grounder they found.'

'Oh, honey,' Tessa said. A pang of jealousy blossomed in her, and she hated it, but she couldn't shake it, either. Why had Aya shared that with Pop over her?

Ky fell quiet, understanding as far as his baby brain could that something was up with the grown-ups. Pop reached over and picked him up, making distracting nonsense sounds, leaving nothing to get between mother and daughter.

'I'm upset about that, too,' Tessa said. 'Everybody's upset about it.' That was true, and how could they not be? Some grounder thief, murdered and tossed away. Murdered. In the Fleet. Was there anyone who wasn't rattled by that news, who wasn't still wrestling with the idea of something like that happening *here*? There wasn't much to the story yet, but that didn't stop everybody from talking endlessly about it. Tessa scolded herself for not bringing it up with Aya before now. She hadn't thought it was anything a little kid needed to concern herself with, but clearly, it was. Sometimes, she lost sight of how easy it was for children to absorb the things adults whispered about. 'That was an awful thing that happened,' she said. 'A really terrible thing. But the patrols are on it. They're gonna find the bad guys who did it, and it won't happen again.'

'How do you know that?' Aya said. It was a direct challenge, a question that demanded an answer.

'I—'

'She doesn't,' Pop said. 'She wants you to feel better.'

Tessa glared at her father. 'How is that helping?'

He shrugged. 'She wants the truth, Tess. She's old enough to understand what happened, so she's old enough for – hey, hey, quit it, buddy.' He turned his attention to his grandson, who was pulling hard at his remaining hair.

His refuting her in front of her daughter was irritating, but he was – all the more irritatingly – right. Tessa folded her hands together and spoke to her daughter, who was growing up too fast. 'I *don't* know that it won't happen again. I'm bothered by it, and I'm scared, too. But I also know that . . . that kind of thing isn't normal here. Our home is a safe place, Aya. It really is.'

'That's not—' Aya struggled. She understood so much, and yet, not quite enough to pick apart her feelings. 'I'm not scared about it happening again.'

'Then what?'

'I'm not scared.' She frowned harder. 'You said we can't go live on a planet because bad stuff happens there. But – but bad stuff *does* happen here. I don't understand why we can't live on the ground if bad stuff happens here, too. If it happens every-where, then . . . then it's everywhere.'

Aya's words were clumsy, but Tessa understood. Every lesson she'd tried to impart was based in principle, rather than practi-cality. *No, we can't move planetside, because it's too dangerous. No, you can't have creds, because you need to learn to trade. No, you can't watch Martian vids, because they solve every problem with violence, and that's not our way. No, you can't keep all the cookies to yourself, they belong to the hex, and you have to share, because we share. That's what we do. That's who we are.*

But now there was one news story, one unpleasant headline, that had thrown all that out of whack. There was danger in the Fleet, and it came from people who hadn't cared about trade, who hadn't minded violence – and those people were Exodan. That was the part that bothered Tessa the most. Everybody was so focused on the grounder, they sidestepped the one sentence that had shaken her: the patrols were pretty sure the dead guy's crew was Exodan, and would anybody who knew anything please come forward?

She looked at her daughter, bags packed, brow furrowed. Her daughter, who didn't understand that rooms cost money, who had unabashedly called on extended family for help when she lacked the ability to trade. Fear was the primary driver for Aya wanting to be elsewhere, despite how *not scared* she claimed to be. But maybe there was more to it than that. Maybe it wasn't that Aya didn't want to be Exodan. She was Exodan already.

Maybe, in her daughter's eyes, it was the Fleet that wasn't Exodan anymore.

'I think,' Tessa said, getting to her feet, 'I think we could do with something out of the ordinary this evening. How about . . . fish fry for dinner?'

Aya looked suspicious. 'We only do that on birthdays.'

'Well, I want to treat my kid. Is that allowed?'

Tessa watched her daughter wrestle between a nagging existential problem and the promise of greasy, crispy, calorie-laden food. 'Can we go to the waterball game, too?' she said.

'Is there a game tonight?' Tessa asked her father.

He nodded. 'Fast Hands versus Meteors,' he said. 'Just a scrimmage, not a qualifier.'

'Still, that sounds fun,' Tessa said. She wasn't much for waterball, but for her kid, she'd put up with a scrimmage. She smiled. 'Sure. We can go to the game.'

'Looks like it's you and me tonight, buddy,' Pop said to Ky, who was dozing off on his shoulder.

'No,' Tessa said. 'No, we should all go.' She took in her family, the mess, the room that had been hers. 'It's more fun if we go together.'

EYAS

Eyas hurried into the Centre, her heart a touch lighter. Her supervisor hadn't said anything over the vox except that patrol was there and wanted to talk to the grounder's caretaker. That had to mean progress. The stasis chamber holding the corpse had been left undisturbed since she'd cleaned the body over a tenday ago. Finally, *finally* patrol had found something. They'd found someone to take him home.

She headed to one of the family waiting rooms, where she'd asked for patrol to wait for her. The door swung open at her gesture, and a woman wearing a distinctive shoulder patch sat on one of the couches inside.

The patroller stood. 'Hello, M. I'm Patroller Ruby Boothe,' she said. 'I understand you're the one looking after Sawyer Gursky.' She was full-time, her patch indicated, but oddly, she didn't have a volunteer second with her. Under any other circumstances, Eyas would've reported her, but in this case, she got the impression the absence was for discretion's sake. Perhaps the patroller didn't want to stoke the gossip further. If so, Eyas respected that.

The addition of a last name to Sawyer's first should've kept Eyas' mood aloft, but the grim look on the woman's face prompted a spike of concern. 'You found his family?'

The twitch of Patroller Boothe's mouth said otherwise. She gestured for Eyas to sit, then pulled out her scrib. 'Sawyer Gursky,' she read. 'Twenty-four Solar years of age, born on Mushtullo, no siblings. We had to do some digging, but he's a descendant of the Arvelo family on the *Al-Qaum*. Housing records say they left to grab some ground right after contact.'

'No relations here, then?' This wasn't a surprise, given what Sawyer had said during their brief interaction, but she'd been hoping she remembered wrong.

'No.' Boothe cleared her throat. 'We don't have much communication with anybody in Central space, so it took a while to find the proper folks to talk to. Local law enforcement helped us out in the end.' She was dancing around something. Whatever it was, it bothered her. 'There was an outbreak of saltlick fever that tore through the Human district on Mushtullo about thirteen standards ago.'

'I don't know saltlick fever.'

'Neither did I. One of those wildfire mutations you hear about from time to time. Some minor alien thing that jumps species and fucks everyone over for a few tendays until imubots can be updated. I'll spare you the details. It was . . . well, it was bad. He lost his whole family. Grandparents, parents, everybody. Sawyer was the only one that made it.'

Eyas converted standards to Solars. 'He would've been . . . what? Six?'

''Round about.'

'Stars.' She frowned. 'Why did he remain on Mushtullo, then? He must have had relatives elsewhere.'

The patroller shrugged. 'I have no idea. Maybe they weren't close. Maybe they didn't know. Maybe they didn't care. Grounders, y'know?'

Eyas didn't care for that assumption. She gave a noncommittal 'mmm' and waited for Boothe to get to the point.

'Anyway, we couldn't find much about him, but based on his bank records and known addresses, it looks like he bounced around until adulthood – some kind of foster home setup, or friends, maybe. I don't know. He worked a bunch of odd jobs, then he wound up here.'

Eyas sighed. *Trying something new.* 'So who'd he record as his next of kin?'

'That's the shitty bit,' the patroller said. She tossed her scrib onto the table between them. 'He didn't.'

Eyas stared. 'His emergency contact, then.'

'Nope.'

'All GC records have them. It's right there for you to fill out when you update your patch.'

'Yeah, well, apparently he missed that bit. Didn't think he'd need it, or something.'

How could you miss that bit? Eyas thought incredulously. *How could you—* She shook her head, ending the loop between scorn and pity. 'There has to be someone.'

The patroller shifted in her chair. 'I'm telling you, M, we tried. We tried to get on the local news feeds, we tried to get law enforcement to put out a notice or something. But they're not Human, and they don't get it. The way they see it, somebody with no family and no emergency contact is dead and has been identified, and their job is done. If he has friends, all we can do is hope they read Exodan news, because we don't know who to—'

'Are you saying,' Eyas broke in, 'that nobody's coming for him?'

Patroller Boothe nodded. She cleared her throat again. 'We might hear from someone. I don't know. I can't predict that. Could be tomorrow, could be next standard. But I also know that the, um . . . the stasies you guys use here aren't built for long-term storage. So you might . . .' She trailed off.

Eyas understood. 'I might want to take care of it sooner rather than later.'

'Yeah.'

The room fell quiet. Nobody was coming for him. Nobody was coming for him, and there was nothing more to say.

KIP

Feed source: The Thread – The Official News Source of the
Exodan Fleet (Public/Klip)
Item name/date: Evening News Summary - Galactic - 130/306
Encryption: 0
Translation path: 0
Transcription: [vid:text]
Node identifier: 8846-567-11, Kristofer Madaki

————

Hello, and welcome to our evening update. I'm Quinn Stephens. We begin tonight's headline summary with news from the Fleet.

The investigation into the body discovered aboard the *Asteria* last tenday is still unfolding. Five suspects have been apprehended and detained in connection with the untimely death of Sawyer Gursky, a Central space immigrant who recently took up residency in the Fleet. The crew of the *Silver Lining*, a registered Exodan cargo ship captained by Muriel Saarinen, are believed to have hired Gursky to assist with looting aboard the *Oxomoco*. Large stores of stolen and illegally obtained goods were found aboard the *Silver Lining*, in addition to drugs and small weapons. All five crew members have been charged with theft, smuggling, illegal salvage, possession of firearms, and unlicensed possession of a pinhole drive. No murder charges have been reported yet. Jannae Green, a member of the traffic control guild, has been arrested as well. Green allegedly accepted credits from the thieves in exchange for disabling the

Oxomoco's proximity alert system for several hours while salvaging took place.

The supervisory council for the Fleet Safety Patrol reminds all citizens that illegal salvage is a serious crime, and is punishable by imprisonment. Patrol also encourages any persons aware of such activity to make an anonymous report, and wants to remind the public that without such a report having been filed, today's arrests would not have been made so quickly.

———

There was a buzz at the door. Kip put his scrib down and raised his head up from the pillow. 'Yeah?'

The door spun open. His dad entered, wearing a dorky smile and carrying a shopping bag. 'Know what time it is?'

Kip shook his head. Shit, was he supposed to be somewhere?

'Almost three. You blazed right through lunch, buddy.' He lifted the bag. 'Hungry?'

A tantalising, familiar smell drifted its way to Kip's nose. He sat up. 'Yeah.'

The dorky smile intensified, and his dad produced the bag's contents: a wrapped-up hopper and a frosty bottle of choko. He tossed both to Kip, one at a time.

Kip turned the warm bundle over after he caught it. The order was quick-printed on the cloth. *2x pickle. Fried onion. Extra hot sauce. No greens. Toasted bun.* 'How'd you know?'

'M Rajan knows your order, apparently.' His dad shook his head. 'I weep for your stomach lining.'

Kip managed a small smile. 'Thanks, Dad.'

The meal had been exchanged, and Kip was grateful, really, but his dad just stood there awkwardly, hands in his pockets, bag hanging around his wrist. 'So . . . tailoring didn't work out, huh?'

Kip rubbed his face. Stars, but he did not want to talk about job trials. 'Please don't lecture me.'

'No lectures,' Dad said, holding up his hands. 'Just . . . curious as to what you're up to.' He paused. 'Any fun plans today?'

'No.'

'Nothing with Ras?'

Kip looked away. 'No.' He didn't want to hang out with Ras. Ras had been pissed at first that Kip talked to patrol, but once time went by and no trouble came with it, Ras started straight-up *bragging*. Everybody at school was talking about the body, and Ras was telling them, yeah, he'd overheard the scavengers who did it, they were a buncha mean motherfuckers, you should've heard the way they laughed about killing that dude. Kip hadn't talked to Ras since he heard him doing that, and he hadn't responded to any of his scrib messages, either. 'I don't want to talk about it.'

'Okay.' Dad nodded like he understood. Kip didn't know if he actually did or not. 'You know that if you ever do want to talk – about Ras, or work, or . . . or . . . you know your mom and I are here, right?'

Kip picked at the hopper wrapper. Dad going to Grub Grub was nice and all – like, really nice – and he knew Dad wanted him to talk. But Kip wanted to be alone. Alone was easier. Alone was safe. He didn't know what to say. He didn't know what he was feeling. The wanting was still there, but it was different now. It wasn't him and Ras wanting more together. It was just Kip, wanting alone. 'Yeah. Thanks.'

His dad nodded. He seemed disappointed, but he didn't push. 'I'll be in the hex if you need anything,' he said. He started to leave, then turned back. 'You know, might feel good to get out for a while. I can give you some extra trade. Y'know, if you want to go play a sim or pick up some vid chips or something. I heard there's a new vid out with – oh, what's his name, that Martian actor you like – Jacob something.'

Kip rolled his eyes. 'Jasper Jacobs,' he mumbled.

'That's right,' Dad said. 'He's not my type, but I get it, I really do. He's got those . . . those big arms, and—'

Kip's chest began to cave in on itself. Stars, of all the things he didn't feel like talking with his dad about, Jasper Jacobs' arms were in the top three.

Dad cleared his throat. 'Anyway, let me know if you want to do something fun.'

Kip squinted. 'I spent all my tenday trade already.'

'I know.'

His suspicion grew. 'Mom doesn't let me have more after that.'

Dad winked. 'Mom doesn't have to know.' He gave a half-wave. 'In the hex. Just holler.' The door slid shut behind him.

Kip sat cross-legged on his bed, gifted lunch in his lap, guilt gnawing at his empty gut. Dad was trying to be his friend, and he knew that. He sighed, unwrapped the hopper, and tucked in. '*Mmmmph.*' The moan was reflexive. He *was* hungry. He tore into the meal like somebody was going to take it away. M Rajan had made it perfect, like always. The fried grasshopper meal was satisfyingly crunchy, the twice-round pickle felt like a salty, sour hug, and the hot sauce skirted that line between *ow, this hurts, please stop* and *I want to eat this forever*. He swore she put more hot sauce on each time, like she was training him or something.

The knot in his stomach grew. He thought about M Rajan, who knew his order when he wasn't even there, and Dad, who'd thought to go pick it up for him, and Grandma Ko, who'd been offering to take him for 'an unofficial Sunside' even though she one-hundred-percent did not have a shuttle licence anymore – and even Mom, who hadn't given him any shit when he pulled out of the trial at the tailor shop.

He shoved the last of his hopper into his mouth. He kind of wanted another one, and he did kind of want to go out. Not to the sims or the vid shop or anything. He popped open the choko and washed the burn away from his mouth. He'd had a weird thought for the past tenday or so, one he couldn't shake and couldn't share. It wasn't bad or anything. It was just . . . weird. A weird thing he wanted to do, one he couldn't have explained to Dad or Ras or anybody. Definitely not to himself.

Kip folded the wrapper and picked up his scrib. He stared at it for a moment. Maybe this was stupid, but . . . nobody would know, right?

'Public feed search,' he said. 'Saved parameters.'

The scrib chirped and did as told. He'd run this search probably a dozen times by now, but this time, a new result popped up. It wasn't much – just three lines. He read them a couple times over. He took another swig of his drink, then thought for a minute, then took another. He noted the date (tomorrow) and the time (eleventh hour). He looked down at himself, wearing a holey shirt and pajama pants. He got up, opened his closet, and sighed. Most of what belonged in there was on the floor. Bit by bit, he gathered shirts and trousers and underwear, and threw them into the basket that often stood empty.

His dad – who hadn't made it to the hex yet – looked surprised as Kip exited his room with laundry in tow.

'Hey,' he said, sounding confused. 'You . . . doing laundry?'

'Yup,' Kip said.

'Need any help?'

'Nope.' He headed to the hex's wash machines without another word. If he was going to do this weird thing, he was gonna do it right.

ISABEL

Funerals were never an easy affair, but Isabel was hard-pressed to think of one as uncomfortable as this. Not in a personal way. That distinction belonged to the funerals of her parents, her sister, Tamsin's parents, close friends. This was a different sadness. A social sadness. It was a natural feeling to have when attending – or even hearing of – a funeral for someone you didn't know. But this . . . this was exceptional.

In attendance were herself, of course, to make record, and Tamsin, who insisted on joining her for this one. Eyas Parata was the caretaker that day. Isabel had done ceremonies with her before, and she knew her to be the sort of compassionate guide a grieving family would benefit from. But there was no family today. There were no friends. Just three strangers, a body that had been thrown away, and a story that elicited plenty of public thrill but little sympathy. People had been horrified by the discovery of the body, and satisfied when the culprits were caught. There was a general buzz in the air that something had gone too far, something had to be done.

When it came to the victim himself, however, feelings changed. Isabel had heard everything from apathy to blame to indignation. The victim was an outsider. A leech. *He'd come into their home*, the party line went. *He'd eaten their food. He repaid their welcome by attempting to steal.* There was more to it than that, Isabel knew, but that was the story being told over tables. Sawyer Gursky had become an abstraction, an evidence file for whatever societal shift you hoped for. You want to encourage your kids to lock down a profession instead of heading elsewhere? Look at that poor dead boy, born of people who'd left Exodan values behind. He hadn't had the sense to find honest work. You want resource management reform? Look at that guy who died on the *Oxomoco*. He wouldn't have been there at all if there wasn't demand on the black market. You want to tighten up entry requirements for non-citizens? Look at that thieving bastard who got himself killed. Why should we let people like that into our homes?

'Round and 'round the chatter went, at hundreds of tables with hundreds of families. Yet none of them seemed to care about the indisputable truth: a Human being was dead, and no one had come to mourn him.

Isabel and Eyas stood together in the privacy of the shrouding room, side by side next to the body. Neither said a word. Tamsin had pulled up a chair. Her legs were giving her extra trouble that day, so she was saving herself – 'preserving her batteries,' as she put it – for the walk up the ramp.

'This is so . . .' Eyas began. She shook her head. 'I know how to do this with families. I've done this a thousand times.'

'I know,' Isabel said. 'I'm feeling lost, too.'

They were quiet again, and still.

'Can I see him?' Tamsin asked, nodding toward the body.

'Are you sure?' Eyas said. In preparation, she'd made an under-standable break with tradition: the body was already shrouded. Usually, that was part of the ceremony – the family lovingly wrapping the cloth together. In this case, though . . . 'He's not in the best of shape.'

Tamsin pursed her lips. 'Is it bad?'

'Not—' Eyas' face twisted as she thought, perhaps weighing the difference between what was 'bad' to her and what it was to people who didn't do this every day. 'Not gruesome. There's no blood or disfigurement. But we didn't receive him right away. He'd started to decay before I got him into stasis. I did my best with him, but he . . . doesn't look like they usually look.'

Tamsin took in that information. 'I'd like to see him.'

Eyas stepped forward and pulled the shroud from his face. She'd done her best with him, that much was clear. He was clean. He was peaceful. But yes, he was different, different enough to give Isabel a stab of adrenaline, a shiver of disgust. This wasn't right.

'Oh, stars,' Tamsin said. 'He's just a kid.' Isabel laid her hand on Tamsin's shoulder. Her wife grabbed it. 'I'm sorry,' she said, brushing at her cheeks.

'Don't be,' Eyas said. 'I'm glad someone's crying for him.' She paused. 'I did, too.'

Tamsin nodded. Her tears continued to flow. She stopped wiping them away.

'Do you want to read the Litany?' Eyas said. 'I wasn't sure which of us should do it, so if—'

The door to the shrouding room opened, and they all turned to look. A boy stood there, a teenage boy in fresh-pressed clothes that didn't fit quite right. Isabel didn't know him. It didn't appear that Eyas did, either.

'Are you lost?' Eyas said.

The boy's eyes fell to the body, and he stared. 'I, um—' He cleared his throat. 'I asked outside where to go, and uh, they said I should go here, and— I didn't know you'd already started—'

'Are you a friend of his?' Eyas said, her words rising with a sliver of hope. 'Did you know him?'

The boy continued to stare. 'No. I just, um, y'know, I heard about it, and I—' He tugged at the edge of his shirt. '*Tika lu*— I mean, I'm sorry, this is stupid, I—'

Eyas gave a puzzled frown. 'You're welcome to join, if you want, but—'

Two pieces clicked together in Isabel's mind – a sliver of gossip and an inexplicable hunch. 'Are you the one who told patrol?'

The boy swallowed, and nodded. Isabel watched him with interest. His eyes had yet to leave the table. Had he been to a funeral before? Had he seen a body? To him, the face on the table would not be young, but older and respectable, an ideal he could grow into, a stage he aspired to, a promise cut short.

'What's your name?' Isabel asked.

The boy finally made eye contact with someone other than the corpse. 'Kip,' he said. 'Uh, Kip Madaki.'

Madaki, Madaki. Her brain tossed the name around, seeking connection. 'Does someone in your family work in water?'

'My Grandpa Griff did.'

Another piece clicked. 'Yes, I remember him. Not well, but I remember.' Old memories surfaced. She remembered being an assistant, an extra pair of hands at a naming. 'He had twin girls?'

'Yeah. My mom and aunt.'

Her brain was satisfied. 'Well, then. Kip Madaki.' She nodded with confirmation. 'I'm Isabel, and this is Eyas and Tamsin. We're glad you're here.'

'Would you like a seat?' Tamsin asked, pointing toward the other chairs.

'I'm good,' Kip said, shuffling closer to the table. 'Thank you.'

Isabel continued to study him. 'How did you know this was happening today?'

The boy moved as if he didn't know where to put his limbs. Stars, Isabel didn't miss that age. 'I've, um, been checking,' he said.

'Ceremony schedules? The public feed?'

'Yeah.'

'You mean, since they found him?'

The boy shrugged.

Isabel felt her spirits rise. 'Kip, before you came in, we were discussing who should read the Litany for the Dead. Would you like to?'

Kip was taken aback. 'Me? Um . . . I dunno, I've never—'

'Is this your first laying-in?' Eyas asked gently.

'No,' Kip said, 'but – I've never read the . . . that.'

'It's up to you,' Isabel said. 'But you helped this man. You helped the right people find him. You're the closest thing he has to a friend.'

Eyas extended her scrib. Kip took it. 'I don't know,' he said.

'You can do it,' Eyas said with the sympathetic smile that went hand-in-hand with her profession.

He cleared his throat, then licked his lips, then cleared his throat again. He began to read. 'From the stars, came the ground. From the ground, we stood. To the ground, we return.'

Isabel bowed her head as he spoke, one hand on his shoulder, the other holding Tamsin's. This still wasn't right. But it was better. It was a little better.

'Here, at the Centre of our lives, we carry our beloved dead. We honour their breath, which fills our lungs. We honour their blood, which fills our hearts. We honour their bodies, which fuel our own. We honour you, son of, um . . .' Kip stopped. 'What's his homeworld?'

Isabel turned the question over a few times. She'd never heard this portion of the Litany for the Dead said with anything other than a homesteader name. She wasn't so rigid in her traditions that the idea of inserting the name of an alien planet bothered her, and yet . . . and yet. 'He's still Exodan,' she said. 'Just more distantly.'

The boy looked unsure. 'So . . . should I say the *Asteria*, or . . .'

'The *Al-Qaum*,' Eyas said. She looked at Isabel and nodded. 'Patrol said that's where he was descended from.'

Kip started again. 'We honour you, son of the *Al-Qaum*. From death, you took life, and from your death, we now live. Here you will stay, until we rejoin the stars once more.'

Isabel took her cue and gestured at her scrib. 'We record the laying-in of Sawyer Gursky, age twenty-three. His name will be remembered. For so long as the Archives remain, so shall he.'

Eyas turned to Kip. 'Will you help me with him?'

Kip nodded, his face unreadable, his heart unknowable. But he took his place at the head of the stretcher. He shared the caretaker's weight. He accompanied the stranger on the long walk up the ramp. He did these things, and it said all that needed to be said about him.

Isabel followed, Tamsin leaning on her arm. All unoccupied caretakers had gathered, as they always did, standing vigil along the pathway, each holding an item of their choosing – a globulb, a flower, a dancing ribbon, a gnarled root, a bowl of water.

'Thank you,' they murmured to the body as it passed by. 'Thank you.' *Thank you for what you will become*, they meant. *Thank you for what you will give us*.

They came at last to the top of the ramp, and reached the covering bed. To the untrained eye, it was nothing more than a flat layer of bamboo mulch, but Exodans knew better. There were walking paths raked by the caretakers around the unmistakable mounds. There were painted flags stuck in patches recently filled. There were shallow craters over patches ready to be filled again. And there was the warmth – a thick, earthy heat rising from the ground, almost too hot. A suggestion not of death, but of life, of energy, of birth.

Eyas led the way to an unmarked patch, then set down her end of the stretcher. Kip set down his as well. A set of shovels lay waiting. They both took one, and Isabel did as well, though she knew she wouldn't get as far as the other two. That wasn't the point. Everyone who was able had to turn the soil. Tamsin stood by the body, resting her weight on her cane, eyes closed as she whispered the Litany from memory, for no one's comfort but her own.

Isabel dug as best she could, and as she did so, her heart filled with a complicated tangle. Sorrow for Sawyer, whose time had been stolen. Anger for Sawyer, who'd been led astray. Respect for Eyas, and all of her profession. Respect for Kip, too, who dug vigorously, even as his face became covered in silent tears. Love for Tamsin. Love for her living family. Love for her dead family. Fear of death. Joy for life.

It was, in the end, a proper funeral.

They set aside their shovels and lifted Sawyer's body. Slowly, carefully, they laid him in. He was cold now, and heavy, but those things would soon change. He'd followed his ancestors. He'd rejoined their ancient cycle. They would keep him warm.

Part 6

. . . .

WE FLY
WITH COURAGE

Feed source: Reskit Institute of Interstellar Migration (Public News Feed)
Item name: The Modern Exodus – Entry #18
Author: Ghuh'loloan Mok Chutp
Encryption: 0
Translation path: [Hanto:Kliptorigan]
Transcription: 0
Node identifier: 2310-483-38, Isabel Itoh

[System message: The feed you have selected has been translated from written Hanto. As you may be aware, written Hanto includes gestural notations that do not have analogous symbols in any other GC language. Therefore, your scrib's on-board translation software has not translated the following material directly. The content here is a modified translation, intended to be accessible to the average Kliptorigan reader.]

———

Imagine, for a moment, a Harmagian shoreline village of old. It is a busy place, but a simple one. The people there do little more than gather – river mud for building, ocean sand for resting, smaller creatures for eating. There is a world outside this tiny territory, but the villagers know next to nothing of it. There is no need for them to think beyond home and dinner.

Well past the beach, there is a wooded marsh, and in the marsh lives an animal. The villagers have never seen it, but they have heard its call – a strange hooting that pierces the dawning hours. There are many stories about the sound. Some say it is a monster that will prey on any children foolish enough to leave the safety of the village. Some say it is a being made of dead Harmagians, the amalgamation of each body left to disappear under the heat of the sun. But there are some who doubt these stories. How, they wonder, can you speak of what a thing is if you have never seen it with your own eyes?

One day, quite by accident, the question of the animal is answered. Its corpse washes downstream, and comes to rest in the very spot where the villagers gather mud. No one has seen anything like it before. This is a creature adapted not to water, but to trees. It is covered in hair – a feature no Harmagian has seen before. Much debate takes place over what to do with it, and, perhaps inevitably, one question dominates all others: *Can we eat it?*

When the beast is cut apart, a discovery is made. The poor thing's stomach is full of metal slag, which the villagers routinely dispose of in an out-of-sight heap on the edges of the beach. Undoubtedly, this was the cause of death. *Why was the animal eating this?* the villagers wonder. *Why did it continue to eat this?*

Why?

And so, they make the leap from people of superstition to people of science. A group of the village's bravest set out for the marsh, in search of the animal's kin. They discover much more than that, of course, and a frenzy takes hold of the explorers, a mad passion for wanting to unlock every secret the marsh holds. More expeditions are launched. Base camps are built, so they may journey farther and farther still. Trading posts are built near rivers, so as to not waste any time in back-tracking to replenish supplies. Their intentions are born of the purest curiosity, a trait no one can fault them for. But their quest for knowledge has an unfortunate side effect. The animal they were seeking – bal'urut, they have named it – is comprised of a devastating combination of traits. It is skittish to the extreme, instinctively afraid of anything travelling in a pack (thanks to the prowling kressrols, a predatory species our villagers will encounter in due time). If the bal'urut becomes scared enough, its drive for survival will cause it to flee the area – with or without the lengthily gestated young it has been caring for in its den.

The bal'urut is also a specialist. It eats only a specific type of insect that nests in a specific type of tree in this specific corner of the world. Migration to more tranquil territory is not an option, not in the time it would take their guts to evolve for more varied fare.

By the time the explorers realise their presence is what is driving the very creature they wish to understand to abandon its offspring, it is too late. Infant mortality has skyrocketed to the point that the species can no longer sustain itself. Within a Harmagian lifetime, the bal'urut is no more. Other species fall in its wake. Our plucky explorers have the dubious distinction of making the first Harmagian record of a trophic cascade.

If you have studied any scientific discipline through Harmagian instruction, dear guest, you already know the story of the bal'urut. It is one of our most enduring cautionary tales. Many a professor has relished frustrating students with the ethical quandary at its core. If the villagers had not ventured into the marsh to better understand the bal'urut, then its breeding behaviour would not have been disrupted. But had the villagers stuck to their beach and their narrow view, they would've continued to pile slag at the marsh's edge, and the bal'urut would've kept dying from eating it (archaeological studies suggest that bal'uruts found the salt deposits left behind in the metalworking process irresistible). My own research methodology professor phrased this concept succinctly: learn nothing of your subjects, and you will disrupt them. Learn something of your subjects, and you will disrupt them.

The bal'urut has been on my mind as of late. As an ethnographer, my role is to be a neutral observer. I cannot judge, I cannot suppose, I cannot fill in blanks with my own biases (as much as this is possible). And yet, my presence here has prompted change. I have not done anything harmful, to my knowledge. All I have done is talk. I ask questions, I give answers, I make connections. This is not much, and yet, I of all people should know that this can be everything.

I am being vague, dear guest, and for that, I apologise. I have set events in motion that will bring new technologies into the Fleet – namely, improved medical equipment, and sentient AI installations to facilitate resource management. I believe – or I sincerely hope, at least – these will be of great benefit to my hosts here. Given the letters I have received from many of you, I feel confident in assuming that you would agree. Indeed, I am humbled by the generosity that has made these donations possible. Truly, the name of our Galactic Commons was chosen well.

Still, I cannot ignore the fact that I came here to document the Exodan way of life, and as I near the end of my visit, that way of life is changing. This should not surprise me. I have ventured into the marshlands. I know this story well.

———

Received message
Encryption: 0
Translation: 0
From: Tessa Santoso (path: 6222-198-00)
To: George Santoso (path: 6159-546-46)

Well, they actually did it. Cargo bay jobs are going away. Not today. Not for a while. But they're going to install sentient AIs here on the *Asteria* as a pilot programme, and, if it goes well, kit out the rest of the Fleet as well. I would've told you differently a couple tendays ago, but today, my gut says that pilot programme is going to catch on quick. People love these things. My brother just had to get a replacement for his old one, and he's being very weird about it. It's like he lost a pet or something. I don't get it, but I've never worked with one, so who knows. Easier to deal with something that's always cheerful and there to help than with us slow, cranky people, I suppose.

Me and a few others have been asked to work with the incoming comp techs to figure things out or set things up or however it works. Teach the machines what we're doing so they can do it better. I've also been advised to start talking to the job office now, so I can figure out where I might want to go. Y'know, make time for classes. Make time to apprentice. Stars, George. I've been running job trials all standard, and now I'm the one who needs one.

I'm mad about it, and I know it's stupid. It's not like managing cargo is the most exciting job there is. But it was *my* job, and all I can think about are the projects I'm not going to finish and the systems I worked out and felt proud of that don't matter anymore. I don't know if this will make sense, but I keep wondering where we're going to draw the line. Nobody's talking about replacing pilots or bug farmers or teachers, even though AIs could do all of those, because those are *fun* jobs. Jobs that mean something, right? But *I* liked my job. There were things in it that I found fun. I thought what I did was meaningful. I thought I was doing something good. Who decides that? What if we decide that flying shuttles and raising red coasters aren't actually all that fun, and we get rid of those jobs, too? What do people do, then? I went for a drink with Sahil after we got the news, and I asked him that question. He thought it'd be great. He said he'd go be a perma-student at some university and learn all he could. But why? Why learn anything if you're not going to do something with it? Why learn anything if everything worth knowing is in the Linkings anyway, and you can ask your pet AI?

Sorry, I know I'm rambling. I just don't know where I want to go from here. Right now, I'm not sure I want to be here at all.

———

EYAS

Eyas fidgeted in the corridor outside the unfamiliar hex. What if this was a bad idea? What if this screwed things up? She'd entertained both those possibilities, and was entertaining them still, but this was the only course of action that didn't leave her feeling restless. This was the only thing, right then, that made sense.

She walked forward into the common area. Eyas had thought, on her way here, that she'd have to approach a stranger, introduce herself, bring a third party into this exchange. But her timing was perfect. Sunny was kneeling right there in a planter square, a gardening apron tied around his neck and waist, a palette of leafy starters abandoned by his knees, a young boy clinging to his back and wrestling him from behind. Sunny could've easily thrown the kid off, but he swayed and moaned in mock defeat.

'Oh, no!' Sunny yelled. 'Oh, no, you've got me! Help, someone help, there's a monster, a horrible monster's got me—'

The kid giggled. 'I'm not a monster,' the boy said. 'I'm a lion. I'm from Earth!' He made a . . . well, he made a sound. Whether it was actually lion-like was anyone's guess.

'I'm very sorry, I should have realised,' Sunny said. 'Please, M Lion, don't eat me.'

'I *am* gonna eat you!' the kid said, noisily play-biting Sunny's shoulder.

Sunny gave a wicked grin. 'Or maybe . . . I'm gonna eat *you*!' In one fluid sequence, he grabbed the kid, hauled him around to his front, pinned him down, and made chomping sounds as he mercilessly tickled the now-shrieking boy's tummy. 'Oh, no, a dramatic reversal! Nom nom nom nom nom—' His eyes flicked up and saw Eyas for the first time.

Eyas had her knuckle against her mouth, a smile spreading behind it. She gave a little wave.

Sunny was surprised, no question, but took it in stride. The ticklefest ended abruptly. 'We gotta take a break, buddy. We've got company.' The kid looked over as Sunny stood up. 'This is my friend Eyas,' Sunny said, cocking his head. 'Hi.' It was a question.

'Hi,' Eyas said. She smiled at the boy. 'What's your name?'

The kid scrutinised her. 'Kirby.'

'My nephew,' Sunny said, pushing his own hair back into place, brushing his hands on his apron. Was he self-conscious? Did he mind her seeing him like this – unshowered, dirty palms, ratty work clothes? Had she crossed a line? Having sex was one thing; entering someone's home was another. Maybe this was an intimacy she shouldn't have assumed.

'I'm sorry,' Eyas said, 'I hope I'm not—'

'No.' He meant it. 'No, not at all. Please.' He gestured to one of the dinner tables. She followed.

'Hi there!' someone called. Eyas turned. An elderly woman had stuck her head out the front door of her home, no doubt curious about the newcomer. She waved as if they were fast friends.

'Hello,' Eyas called back.

'Friend of mine,' Sunny said. 'From the *Asteria*.'

'Oh, welcome!' the old woman said. She nodded with approval – approval of *what*, Eyas could only guess at – then went back into her space.

'That's M Tsai,' Sunny said, sitting at the table. 'She's very sweet, and very nosy.'

Eyas laughed as she sat opposite him. 'I gathered.' She looked around the hex. Kirby had abandoned lioning and was now digging haphazardly through Sunny's neat planter rows. If Sunny noticed, he didn't seem to mind.

'So.' Sunny looked at her, the question unanswered.

'Right,' she said. She'd had the entire ferry ride to think about this, but now she didn't know where to start. 'I was hoping I could – that is, if you have the time to talk—'

'Yeah, I'm not— hey, Kirby, you can play in the dirt all you want, but leave the shears alone, yeah? – sorry.'

'Don't be. Kids are kids.'

'I'm not busy, is what I was saying.'

'Cool. Okay, well . . . I've been stuck on this idea, and I thought—'

Her attempt was derailed by M Tsai, who had reappeared with offerings in hand. 'I thought you two might like some iced tea,' M Tsai said, setting down a full pitcher and a pair of glasses. 'My own special recipe. I always keep some around in case guests show up.' She filled Eyas' glass. 'Are you one of his clients?'

'M, you know you can't ask that,' Sunny said. 'That's confidential.'

'It's okay,' Eyas said. She smiled at M Tsai. 'I am.'

'But she's my friend, too,' Sunny said. He locked eyes with Eyas. Something passed between them. He'd seen her every which way, and yet, somehow, *this* – a shared pitcher of tea, a confirmation of friendship, a secret smile – this was the most vulnerable she'd ever felt around him.

'How nice,' M Tsai said. 'And what's your profession?'

Sunny transmitted an apology through his eyes.

'I'm a caretaker,' Eyas said.

'Oh! Oh, my goodness. Well.' She looked at the now-filled glasses, trying to find an excuse to stay now that her previous one had ended. 'You know . . . biscuits. I got a packet of quick dough as trade a few days ago, and a bunch of herbs in my home that aren't going to last much longer. I think this kind of company deserves a proper snack, don't you?'

'M,' Sunny said, 'that's really—'

'It's no trouble!' M Tsai said, already on her way. 'It won't take long!'

Sunny gave an apologetic sigh as soon as M Tsai's door shut. 'I'm sure this isn't why you came by.'

'Not quite,' Eyas said.

He folded his arms on the table. 'Start at the beginning.'

'I'm still thinking about Sawyer.' She'd reserved a whole night with Sunny after the funeral, instead of the usual half. Neither of them had commented on it, or needed to. She'd taken care of someone else. He'd done the same for her.

Sunny folded his mouth sympathetically. 'That had to be pretty . . . I dunno. Traumatic.'

'Not his body. It was . . . unpleasant, yes. But I don't mean that. I mean *Sawyer*. I mean the man I spoke with for five minutes.' She frowned. 'I wasn't very patient, and I wasn't very kind. But he was so grateful for what flimsy advice I gave him. He looked so happy. He wrote me a letter. I think I may have been more patient and kind to him than most, and that's . . . that's why he's dead. He got taken advantage of. He didn't know how things worked. But he *wanted* to. I know I only had that one short conversation, but . . . I think his heart was in the right place.' Eyas sipped her iced tea and paused. 'This is delicious.'

Sunny nodded. 'M Tsai is a legend in the kitchen. Used to work in imports, so she's got all kinds of spices and stuff. I'm honestly stoked she's making biscuits.' He sipped his own drink. 'But again, not why you're here.' He looked at her with kind eyes. 'It makes sense that you're still upset about it.'

Eyas shook her head. He was getting the wrong idea. 'I'm not here because I'm upset. If I needed a counsellor, I'd go see a counsellor.'

'Talking to friends is okay, too, y'know.'

'I didn't mean – I know. And I appreciate it. But I don't want to sit around and be sad. I want to do something about it.'

'Okay.' He leaned back thoughtfully. 'What'd you have in mind?'

'You know the emigrant resource centres, right? With their workshops and such. How to speak proper Klip, how to live alongside aliens. Everything you need to know before you move planetside. That's what our ancestors were trying to prepare us for, right? That's why the Fleet *exists*. Except that's *not* the point of the Fleet anymore, not entirely. I'm not here to shepherd people along to new planets. I care for the ones who made their lives here. And you – you're the same, only in present tense. We both want to make life good for the people who choose to stay. So . . . why don't we have the opposite?'

'The opposite of what?'

'Classes. Workshops. Resources for grounders who want to live in the Fleet. We have nothing for them right now. We have homes standing empty, and jobs unfilled, and we're . . . what? Hoping that the next generation will want to stick around more than the last? Look, if it was a matter of everybody wanting to leave here, fine. But that's not the case. People aren't just staying in the Fleet. They're *coming back*. We have such disdain for outsiders who come and act like this is a museum, but what about the Sawyers? What about the people who *don't* have a place out there, who think that our way of life has some appeal? We look at them and we say, oh, stupid city kids, stupid Martians, they don't know how things are. They don't understand how life works out here. So, let's teach them. Let's teach them, instead of brushing them off and laughing behind their backs. Let's bring them in.'

Sunny took that in. 'Huh,' he said. He took a long sip of his tea, looked over his shoulder to verify that his nephew had indeed left the shears alone, then set his drink back down. 'Huh. That is . . . not a terrible idea.' He paused. 'That's a great idea, actually.'

'Thank you.'

'You could totally get council support for it, too. They'd be all over it, especially given your . . .' He gestured. 'What you do.'

'My thinking exactly.' Some of the *Exodan resources for*

Exodan problems types might be harder to sway, but – come on. Who could argue with a caretaker who wanted some resource allotments in the name of *preserving tradition*?

He nodded. 'And you want to teach?'

'Not full-time, and not alone. Think about the resource centres. Most of those people put in an hour here, a day there. All sorts of different professions helping out. It has to be that way, if the centres want to give people a proper toolkit. So, we'd need to do the same. Get people with jobs you don't find elsewhere in the galaxy to explain what it is we do and why.'

'"We".'

'Yes. I want you to do it with me, if you're interested.'

'Wow, okay. Um . . . hmm. I'm not sure I'd be much of a teacher.'

'Why not?'

'I was an awful student. I've told you. The laziest.'

'Academic prowess and base intelligence are two separate things.'

'See? I could never make a sentence like that on the fly.'

'So? That's ideal, actually. That was a boring sentence, and the last thing we want to be is boring. You're charismatic. You know how to talk to people. You'd be great at this.'

'You're serious.'

'Completely.'

'Okay.' He crossed an arm over his stomach and scratched his chin with the other. 'Well . . . can I think about it a bit?'

'Of course. Take some time, see how it sits.'

'In the meantime, can I give *you* something to think about?'

'Always.'

Sunny stared up at the ceiling for a moment, as if the words he was looking for were up there. 'Obviously, I don't have plans on going anywhere soon, and I know we live on different ships, but whenever my time comes – how would you feel about . . . y'know. Taking care of me.'

Eyas set down her glass. 'Yes, absolutely. You can put in a

request for a specific caretaker at your deck's Centre. We're all part of the same guild, so they'd contact me.'

He laughed. 'So you *don't* need to think about that one.'

She paused. 'Sorry, I treated that like a practical question, didn't I?'

'Yep.'

She laughed as well. 'Sorry.' Stars, here he'd asked her something profound and she'd responded like a formwork header.

He folded his hands on the table. 'Treat it like an emotional question.'

She looked down at her drink. 'I'd be honoured,' she said. 'That means a lot to me, that you want that.'

Sunny smiled. 'And it would mean a lot to *me* to know that the person who will take care of me is a *whole* person. Not just a symbol.' He stopped, and his smile grew. 'You'll be happy to know we can stop being corny now, because I have some great news.'

'What's that?'

He gave a dramatic sniff and pointed at the air. 'Biscuits.'

ISABEL

Of all the places Isabel might've guessed Ghuh'loloan would want to make a repeat visit to, her hex was at the bottom of the list. The First Generation murals, perhaps, or a musical performance, or the plaza oxygen garden. But no, this distinguished academic from an equally distinguished species wanted to spend one of her final days in the Fleet in hex 224-613's common area. She was in their far more humble garden now, surrounded by shrieking kids. Shrieking, laughing, soaking-wet kids.

'Again! Do it again!' one of the relatively older kids cried in Klip. The others echoed him in tiny accents: 'Again! Again!'

'Again?' Ghuh'loloan said, her tentacles dancing with amusement. 'Are you quite sure?'

'Yes!'

'As you wish.' She gestured to her cart, and the kids flailed with knowing anticipation as a panel opened. Out flew Ghuh'loloan's mistbot, a floating globe filled with cool water, designed to refresh Harmagian skin whenever the need arose. Nothing about Ghuh'loloan's face approximated Human expression, but nonetheless, Isabel could discern the unbridled glee her colleague felt as she directed the bot to deploy itself, for the fifth time now, over the kids' heads. They screamed and giggled, running aimlessly in the steady drizzle.

'Again! Again!'

'I'm afraid that will have to do, dear children,' Ghuh'loloan said, 'or I will have none left.'

Isabel stepped in, venturing into the splash zone. *'That's enough now,'* she said in Ensk. *'Let's give Ghuh'loloan a break, hmm?'*

There was some mild protesting, but the kids were too wound up now to hang around doing nothing. They dispersed in bits and pieces, running off to play with toys or raid the kitchen or shake their soggy hair at their parents.

'It is a truly singular experience,' Ghuh'loloan said, 'living alongside your offspring *and* your offspring's offspring.'

Isabel took a seat on a nearby bench. 'An experience you wish you'd had?' she asked.

The Harmagian let out a rolling laugh. 'Oh, stars, no. This is madness. Wonderful, too, dear host, but I enjoy it for the novelty. I could not do this every day. I admire your species for its stamina in this regard. And your patience.'

'Oh, we run out of patience plenty,' Isabel said. She glanced aside. Tamsin was seated nearby, out of earshot, but within plain sight. Isabel had thought she'd been watching the mistbot shenanigans, but though they had ended, she remained, her hands busy with a broken vox, her eyes on the alien. Isabel caught her wife's gaze, waved her over, and continued speaking to Ghuh'loloan. 'You don't miss them? Your children, I mean. When they're growing up.'

'It is not the same for us,' Ghuh'loloan said. She bowed her eyestalks in acknowledgement as Tamsin joined Isabel on the bench. 'It is not an experience we have, so there is nothing to miss. Children are kept in nursery pools, tutelage villages, and universities. I was never in the homes of either of my parents until I was an adult, and I never lived there. It would not have occurred to me to want that.' She looked around the hex. 'You would think a communal home would not feel so strange to me, as I live in an Aandrisk city. But their homes are not like yours. You are different, dear hosts. You are unique.'

Tamsin leaned forward. 'But are we worth it?' She spoke the words without hesitation, as if they'd been sitting on her tongue for tendays.

Isabel knew they had been, and she couldn't believe they'd been let out. '*Tamsin.*'

Her wife was as unconcerned as could be. 'It's just a question.'

Ghuh'loloan looked puzzled. 'Forgive me, but I do not understand.'

'Do you think we're worthy of the rest of the galaxy's time?' Tamsin said. 'GC membership, donated tech, this star you gave us. Do you think we're worth it?'

Isabel looked away in embarrassment. She wasn't going to fight in front of a guest, but oh, it was happening later.

The Harmagian fanned her dactyli in thought. 'I am here, am I not? But that is not what you are asking. You are not asking if the Reskit Institute finds you worthy of study. You are asking what I, Ghuh'loloan, think of you.'

'Yes,' Tamsin said.

'That is a risky thing to ask, dear host, but I would not insult you with a dishonest answer.' Ghuh'loloan's eyes blinked and widened. 'Very well. You are a species of slim means. You produce nothing beyond extra bodies to perform labour, and you have contributed nothing to the technological progress of the GC at large. You value being self-reliant, and you were, once, but now you eat our food and harvest our suns. If we kicked you out now, it would be difficult for you to sustain yourselves as you did before. And even with our help, the age of these vessels means you are constantly, irresponsibly courting a disaster like the one you've already weathered. These are the facts. Now, let us discuss the facts of my own species. We are the wealthiest species alive today. We want for nothing. Without us, there would be no tunnels, no ambi, no galactic map. But we achieved these things through subjugation. Violence. We destroyed entire worlds – entire species. It took a galactic war to stop us. We learned. We apologised. We changed. But we can't give back the things we took. We're still benefiting from them, and others are still suffering from actions centuries old. So, are *we* worthy? We, who give so much only because we took so much? Are you worthy, you who take without giving but have done no harm to your neighbours? Are the Aeluons worthy? Are the Quelin? Show me the species that has never wronged another. Show me who has always been perfect and fair.' She flexed her body, her alien limbs curling strong. 'Either we are all worthy of the Commons, dear Tamsin, or none of us are.'

Tamsin said nothing for a moment. 'The first Harmagian I ever saw was on a news feed, talking about how Humans didn't belong.'

'The membership hearing.'

'Yeah.'

Ghuh'loloan stretched the dactyli around her mouth. 'The first Human I ever saw was at a spaceport, in the process of being arrested for selling unlicensed scrub fuel.'

Tamsin gave a short chuckle. 'Great first impressions, huh?'

'Indeed.'

Isabel looked between the two, still thrown by the turn the conversation had taken. Would Ghuh'loloan ever have said anything like this to her on one of their carefully chosen field trips, in one of their polite academic chats? Would her dear guest have been this candid if, for a moment, Isabel had stopped worrying about being a good host?

'You can't shake hands, right?' Tamsin gestured vaguely. 'I can't touch your tentacle with my hand, right?'

Ghuh'loloan reached for one of the storage compartments on her cart. 'If you give me a moment, I believe I have some sheaths with me . . .'

'Some what?'

'It's like a glove,' Isabel said.

'Oh, no, don't go to that trouble,' Tamsin said. 'How would . . . do you know what shaking hands means?'

'Yes,' Ghuh'loloan said. 'In essence.'

'Do you . . . have an equivalent of that? How would you communicate something like that to me?'

'It would help if I knew the specifics of what you wish to communicate.'

Tamsin looked at Ghuh'loloan seriously. 'Respect.'

The Harmagian rose up on her cart, holding her body like a wave frozen in time. Her tentacles shuddered, curling and unfolding in strange symmetry. 'Respect,' she said.

Tamsin took in the display, and gave a satisfied nod. 'Right back at you.'

TESSA

Received message
Encryption: 0
Translation: 0
From: George Santoso (path: 6159-546-46)
To: Tessa Santoso (path: 6222-198-00)

Tess,

I know you're running around like a headless hopper these days, but I've got a surprise for you. Go to our bench after dinner, or whenever you can manage. Leave the kids with the hex. It might take a while. And no, I won't tell you what it is. I think you'll like it, though.

George

——

Tessa would never disparage her husband for being cute, but stars, she didn't have time for this today. Aya needed help with her schoolwork – she was struggling with reading, just like her father had – Ky needed a bath, Pop needed . . . stars, what *didn't* he need. A swift kick in the butt was what he needed. Besides which, the laundry needed doing, the herb garden was wilting, and the cleanerbot had glitched out *again*. Whatever George was up to was probably very sweet, but did it have to be *today*?

She stepped off the transport pod and headed for the big plaza oxygen garden, not needing to follow the signs. She took a breath and tried to shift her mood. She was being ungrateful. Since that cargo guild meeting a tenday ago, she'd written George a half-dozen or so letters that amounted to nothing more than emotional ejection. He hadn't had the time to respond to any of them, which she'd expected. He was busy, and had never been one for writing. She hadn't really wanted a back-and-forth, to be perfectly honest. She'd wanted a recycling bin, a compost box, somewhere she could throw the junk cluttering her brain. But now he'd gone and arranged something to make her feel better – *what*, she had no idea. She considered the possibilities as she entered the garden and wound her way along the lush, familiar paths. A present dropped off by a friend, maybe. She hoped it was nothing performative. That wasn't his style, but then, he wasn't in the habit of sending her cryptic messages and making her trek through the district on a school night, either. She was being a jerk about the whole thing, she knew, but she hoped whatever it was was worth the bother. She hoped—

Tessa froze, mid-stride. There, on a bench, with his back toward her, was George. George. Her husband, George.

His head turned slightly at the sound of her, just a touch, no eye contact needed. 'There's room for two,' he said.

She walked up and faced him. 'What—' Her mouth could form no other words, and her brain was stuck on one thought and one thought alone. George. George was *here*. 'What—'

George looked around. 'Well, this is a canteen,' he said, lifting the container resting beside him. He patted the space to his left. 'And this is a bench.'

Tessa rolled her eyes. 'What are you doing here?' He wasn't supposed to be back for another three tendays, at least.

George took the lid off the canteen. A ribbon of steam unfolded as if it were alive. He filled the lid with tea and gestured for Tessa to sit. 'I got your letters.'

Tessa sighed and sat. 'Stars, George. I'm fine.'

'You didn't sound fine.'

'All right, fine, I'm *not* fine, but I've been not fine before without you – you running back home. You could've got on the sib.'

He handed her the cup. 'This seemed like it should be a face-to-face conversation.' He reached into his pocket, produced a flat packet of throw- cloth, and unwrapped two big spice cookies.

Tessa accepted both cookie and tea, but consumed nothing yet. She leaned back against the bench, a hand's-width apart from George, not ready to be closer until she'd processed the full scope of things here. He smelled great, though. He always smelled great. 'I don't know if I meant any of it,' she said. 'I was just . . . y'know. Mad. I don't know why you took it so seriously.'

'The way I read it, Tessa Santoso is considering the *mere possibility* of leaving the Fleet. That seems pretty damn serious to me.'

Thick steam drifted from the cup, but she braved a sip anyway. 'Is this your dad's blend? He added something.'

'Don't change the subject.'

'What is that? Cinnamon?'

'Don't—' He frowned and took the cup, taking a timid sip of his own. 'Huh. Yeah, I think that is cinnamon. Where'd he get cinnamon?'

'See,' she said. 'That's why I don't mean what I said.'

'I'm not following.'

'Why I don't mean what I said about leaving.' Tessa looked at the tea and shook her head. 'Your dad, your mom, my dad. Your brother—'

'You've got a brother, too. He left, and it was fine.'

'Yeah, and that's why I can't. One of us needs to be here.'

'Why?'

She looked him in the eye, disbelieving. 'Are you seriously saying I should?'

'No,' he said, taking a large bite of his cookie. 'I'm just asking questions.' He swallowed, sipped the tea, and handed the cup back. 'I don't believe for a minute that the sole reason you're here is because Ashby left and you feel obligated. That's never been the case.'

'I'm not saying it is. I'm just . . . I'm just saying. With the exception of Ashby, our family is here. Aya and Ky's family is here.'

'So then explain the letters you wrote me. Explain why you're entertaining this.'

'I already told you.'

He waved his hand. 'Tell me again. Tell me so I can hear how you sound when you say it. Come on, I'm missing out on cleaning drill bits for this.'

She snorted. 'You're having tea and cookies.'

'I've got both tea and cookies back on my ship. And honestly, scrubbing off ore bits is easier than getting anything out of you sometimes.'

Tessa ignored the comment and drank the tea. The added cinnamon was growing on her. She sat, thinking. She wasn't sure what to say.

A moment passed. George leaned forward and folded his hands together. Tessa knew that pose, the George Is Being Serious pose. 'How much of this is about the job?' he asked.

She relented. 'I was thinking about it – about leaving – before that. The job was just . . . I don't know, the last fucking straw, I guess.'

'So, this isn't solely because you don't want to learn a new job.'

'No. Well—' She sighed impatiently. 'There's a part of me that's scared about learning something new. Not because I don't think I can do it, but because this has been my job for twenty years. I hadn't ever pictured doing anything else. Not because it's my favourite thing in the world, but because I'm good at it, and because it's got things that are weirdly satisfying, and because I know – I *knew* what every day was going to look like. At least, as far as work went.'

'You liked the stability.'

'Yeah.'

'And now you're staring down a whole mess of instability and you're like, eh, fuck it, let's see how much of that I'm comfortable with.'

Tessa laughed. 'I guess.' Her face fell. 'It's the kids, mostly. I . . . I don't know. This doesn't feel like the same Fleet you and I grew up in.'

'That's been true with every generation.'

'I know, but . . . this is different. In my gut, this is different. We've had six break-ins in my bay in the past standard. Six. And that's just my bay. Then that whole business with that grounder – stars, *nothing* like that ever happened when we were kids.'

George flexed his eyebrows in acknowledgement. 'Break-ins, sure—'

'Not this many.'

'True.'

'And nobody died.'

'Also true. But bad shit happens everywhere.'

'That's what I told Aya, and she turned it around on me.' A weight pressed against Tessa's chest. 'She's not doing any better. She's getting worse, if anything. Those little bastards at school—'

'Have they kept at it?'

'No, but she's playing by herself.'

George frowned. 'That's not like her.'

'She's scared of them, George. She's scared of them, and she's scared of our home. And I don't know how to help her. I know we thought she'd grow out of it, and she's had counselling, but . . .' Tessa felt her eyes well up, and given the company, she didn't feel the need to hide it. 'She doesn't feel safe here. Do you know how awful that must be, to be a kid and not feel safe at home?'

George slid closer to her and put his arm around her shoulders. 'Almost as awful as being the parent who can't make that kid feel safe, huh?'

'Stars,' Tessa said, taking a shaky breath. 'I'm such a shit mom.'

'Oh, come on. You are not.'

'My mom – she always knew what to do. Whenever I got scared, all she had to do was *be there* and I knew I'd be okay.'

'Your mom didn't have to walk you through seeing a home-steader blown to shit.' He sighed. 'And you also had a dad who was around all the time.'

They both fell quiet.

George spoke, slow and kind. 'Let's say you did leave. Where would you go? Central space? Sol?'

Tessa gave him a sharp look. 'George Santoso, if you seriously think I'd raise our children on Mars, we are getting a divorce.'

Her husband guffawed. 'Well, hey, I didn't want to presume.'

'Sol,' Tessa snorted. 'I'm not freaking out *that* much.' She took another sip of tea. 'Honestly, I – and this is hypothetical—'

'Sure.'

'For the sake of argument.'

'One hundred percent.'

Tessa chewed the inside of her lip. 'The independent colonies. We know people who've gone there. I keep thinking about Seed.'

George made a thoughtful sound. 'Where Ammar went.'

'Yeah.' Ammar and his husband Nick had lived one hex over until three standards prior, when they'd packed up and headed for ground. Tessa had been friends with him through school, and though they weren't close, he was the type of person she imagined would be happy to hear about her moving nearby.

Hypothetically.

'They could definitely put someone with bot-wrangling experience to work in a place like that,' he said.

'That they could,' Tessa said noncommittally. 'If not cargo, then map drones, or . . .' She shrugged. 'I have to learn a new job either way, right?'

'True,' George said. 'I hear it's kinda rough out there, though. Terraforming's a long-game deal.'

'Yeah,' Tessa said, with a nod. 'But . . . is it so different from here? It's not as clean, sure. It's not as established. They're still figuring it out. But they have to ration their water and mind their food stores, and . . .' She shrugged. 'I don't know, I think I'd fit much better in a place like that than a city, or . . . a market stop, or something.'

'Stars, no, I couldn't see you in a market stop.'

She looked askance at him. 'But you could see me on Mars?'

'I didn't say – you're not going to let this go, are you?'

'Never.' She leaned into him, releasing some of her weight, taking on some of his warmth. 'But I love it here. I do. I love how we do things, and why we do them. I love Remembrance Day. I love the Bug Fry Festival. I love the gardens. So many people who left, they wanted *more*. I don't want more. I'm good with what I have. I don't need land or . . . or open sky, or whatever. So many people have left for the wrong reasons.'

George pulled in his lips, folding mustache into beard as he thought. 'Maybe that's why you *should* go. Go for the right reasons. Go for the reason the first of us left Earth – to find a better place for your family. Honestly, Tess, you're the best kind of person to join a colony, because you'd bring all those right reasons with you. You believe in our way of life here? Cool. Implement those ways planetside. Make sure people don't forget. Make sure people remember that a closed system is a closed system even when you can't see the edges.'

Tessa said nothing for a while. 'I don't want to leave you, either. Or take the kids away.'

'What makes you think you would?'

She shut her eyes. 'Don't be ridiculous. I couldn't – that is too much to ask.'

'So . . . what, I'm not allowed to want to do this with you if I think it's an okay idea?'

Tessa pulled back. 'I couldn't ask you to do that.'

George scoffed. 'I go where my family goes. End of discussion.'

'You have a job here. You have a life—'

'I have a skillset I can apply anywhere, and my life is ongoing until the universe says otherwise. I go where you and our kids go. And if you think you can give them a better life on the ground than you can here, then I believe you. You're with them every day. You spend more time with them than I do. There's no question in my mind that you know what's best for them.' He stroked his beard. 'And maybe . . . maybe it would be a good thing for me that way, too. Maybe if we found somewhere I could work planetside instead of hopping rocks all the time, maybe I could be a better dad. A better husband, too.'

'You're good at both of those.'

'If you say so. But I'm not an *always around* kind of guy, am I? I don't have any regrets about how we've been doing things, but it would be nice to . . . I don't know, not be surprised when Aya's grown a hand-length since I saw her last.'

'That'll surprise you even if you see her every day.'

'You know what I mean. I'm not saying this is what I want, definitively. I'm saying that if this is what *you* want . . . I might not be opposed, either.'

'You can't put this all on me.'

'I'm not. I'm asking you if you really – I mean, really, really, really – want to do this. And if you do, then we need to sit down and talk about it.'

Tessa took inventory of their situation. 'We're already sitting down and talking.'

George gave her a knowing glance.

Tessa thought about the letters she'd sent, full of cagey phrasing and danced-around ideas. She thought about the nights she'd lain awake, the long hours spent looking down at the stars. She thought about the whisper she'd been trying to ignore, the one that got a little louder every time she read the news, every time she patched up her home, every time she watched her kids. And here was George, calling the whisper out in plain speech, telling her what she already knew.

'Shit,' she said. She put her face in her palms. 'Oh, stars.'

KIP

System log: device unlocked
Node identifier established: 8846-567-11, Kristofer Madaki

———

Ras (18:62): tek tem dude

Ras (18:62): I know you're not talking to me or whatever, but I
wanted you to know exam scores are out

———

**Feed source: The Human Diaspora Centre for Higher Education
Student Portal**
Encryption: 0
Translation: 0
Transcription: 0
Password: accepted

Thank you for using the Human Diaspora Centre for Higher Education
student portal!

Your most recent exam was: HDCHE entrance qualification exam
Your score was: 803 (out of possible 1000)

Congratulations! You have qualified for admission into any Tier 2 member institution of the HDCHE.

Your options are as follows:

- Red Rock University (Spirit's Rest, Mars)
- College of the Rings (Silver Sea City, Titan)
- The Jovian School for Future Technicians (Jupiter Station, Jupiter)

The following schools require at least an 875 to attend. Should you wish to attend one of these schools, you will need to retake the entrance qualification exam.

- Alexandria University (Florence, Mars)
- The Solan Institute of Reconstructive Biology (Hamilton Junction, Luna)

If you accept admission to any of the schools listed here, you will still need to complete placement tests for any given academic track. Some academic degree programmes require an additional qualification test.

If you are interested in attending a school outside of Human territory, there are many GC educational institutions with reciprocal admission agreements with the HDCHE. Admission conditions vary greatly, so please contact an HDCHE adviser for information specific to your desired school.

Based on your listed location, your nearest source for HDCHE informational meetings is:

- *Asteria* Emigrant Resource Centre, Deck 2, Plaza 16

We highly encourage you to attend an informational meeting. All questions are welcome.

Happy studies!

———

Ras (18:80): how'd you do?

Ras (18:81): I got a 908

Ras (18:81): going to mars, baby

Ras (18:81): big cred time

Ras (18:94): dude will you please talk to me

Ras (19:03): whatever

Ras (19:12): I don't get why you're being such an asshole

———

Node identifier disconnected
System log: device deactivated

ISABEL

Isabel rarely went to the theatre in the dark hours, so she couldn't say what the usual crowd was during that time. There were a few people in the audience who were easy to predict. Old folks like her, scattered around the mostly empty hall. A young father, dozed off on the floor, his tiny child asleep on his chest, the exhausted conclusion to what had likely been a long night of walking the mostly vacant public corridors with a crying infant. But there was one member of the audience she did not expect. She sat down next to him, as she would with an old friend.

'Hello, Kip,' she whispered. 'Mind if I join you?'

Kip was taken aback. Wherever he'd been, he hadn't expected *her* to rouse him. 'Uh . . . yeah, sure, M.'

Isabel folded her arms across her lap and took in the view. The projected environment was a rich tapestry of thick reeds, waving sheets of grass, protective trees, scummy water, and the calls of chittering birds with pointed opinions. 'Wetlands,' she said. 'I haven't been to a wetlands recording in a while. I tend to favour deserts. This is a nice change.'

Kip was quiet – not a contemplative quiet, but the unsure kind of quiet that kids his age sometimes fell into when addressed by an adult. Maybe he was just shy. Maybe he wanted to be left alone.

Isabel kept talking anyway. 'Why aren't you asleep, Kip?'

Kip shifted. 'Why aren't you?'

She chuckled. 'Fair. My wife has a bad pair of legs. They wake her up a lot, and that woke *me* up enough times tonight that there wasn't any going back from it.'

'That sucks,' Kip said.

'That it does.'

He was quiet, again. The recorded trees rustled. The water lapped. 'I haven't slept great since . . . y'know,' Kip said.

'Understandable. Have you talked to someone about it?'

Another long pause. 'My parents won't *stop* talking to me about it. And I get they're just trying to help, but like . . . sometimes I *don't* want to talk about it.'

'Yes,' Isabel said, with a nod. 'I get that.'

Kip shuffled, as restless as the reeds. 'Sorry.'

'No, no, I asked. I appreciate you being honest.' She watched as a great grey and white bird – some kind of predator – glided past on motionless wings. 'So why here? Why not the sim hub, or the Linkings, or . . . ?'

'I dunno. It's . . . it's quiet. I like that.' He shifted again. 'I like pretending I'm somewhere else.' Isabel would've changed the subject at that, had he not continued: 'That's what the theatre's for, right?'

Isabel turned her head toward Kip, his face silhouetted against the bright muddy green. 'Is it?' she asked.

'Well, and so we know what it's like to live on planets. So the ancestors wouldn't freak out if they made it to the ground. They'd know what the sky looked like and . . . and yeah.'

Isabel looked back to the blue sky – that edgeless blue, streaked with clouds and birds whose names few knew off-hand. 'Do you have somewhere to be anytime soon?'

'Uh . . . no?'

'Come on,' she said, giving his arm a definitive pat. 'I want to show you something.' She stood. He hesitated. 'There's a bean cake in it for you.'

Kip got up.

The Archives were on the same side of the plaza as the theatre, so getting there took little time. Isabel swiped her patch over the locked entrance. Doors opened and lights bloomed awake. She looked around. None of her colleagues were there. Good. They would've gotten a scolding about still being up if they had been. No Ghuh'loloan, either, who was likely packing her things and preparing her goodbyes. Isabel and the boy were alone.

'You spend much time in the Archives?' Isabel asked as they took the lift down to the lowest level of her place of work.

Kip shrugged. 'Namings and stuff. Sometimes for school.'

'But never just to look, hmm?'

'Uh, not really. When I was little, I guess.'

That wasn't a surprise to Isabel. Why paw through boring old memories when you could go out and make your own?

The lift came to a halt, and Isabel led the way into the centre of the data room. Seemingly endless towers of globular nodes spiralled out around them, each pulsing with the soft blue light that meant all was well. Isabel smiled proudly. 'Beautiful, isn't it?'

Judging by Kip's expression, he was making a valiant effort to be polite – or maybe he just really wanted that bean cake. 'It's cool, yeah.'

Isabel folded her hands in front of herself and continued to admire their surroundings.

Kip waited. He shuffled. He stopped waiting. 'I've been down here before, M.'

'I'm sure you have. School visit?'

'Yeah.'

'Mmm. I'm sure you got a very technical explanation of how it all works, like I'm sure you did with water reclamation and engine tech and solar harvesters.' She sighed. 'Kip, what's the most important cargo the Fleet carries?'

'Um . . . food?'

'Wrong.'

He frowned. 'Water. Air.'

'Both wrong.' She pointed to the racks. 'This.'

Kip was unconvinced. 'We'd die without air, M.'

'We die one way or another. That's a given. What's *not* is being remembered after the fact. To ensure that, you have to put in some effort.' She reached out and touched one of the racks, feeling the warring balance of cold metal and warm energy. 'Without this, we're merely surviving. And that's not enough, is it?' Isabel looked at the boy, who was still confused. She patted the rack and began to walk. 'Our species doesn't operate by reality. It operates by stories. Cities are a story. Money is a story. Space was a story, once. A king tells us a story about who we are and why we're great, and that story is enough to make us go kill people who tell a different story. Or maybe the people kill the king because they don't like his story and have begun to tell themselves a different one. When our planet started dying, our species was so caught up in stories. We had thousands of stories about ourselves – that's still true, don't forget that for a minute – but not enough of us were looking at the reality of things. Once reality caught up with us and we started changing our stories to acknowledge it, it was too late.' She looked around at all the lights, all the memories. 'It is easy to remember that story here, in the Fleet. Every time you touch a bulkhead, every time you tend a garden, every time you watch the water in your hex's cistern dip a little lower, you remember. You know what the story is here. But *outside* of here, there's a different story. There's sky. There's ground. There are cities and money and water you can take for granted. Are you following?'

'Uh . . . I think so.'

Isabel nodded and went on. 'Comforts are not bad things, not by base. There's nothing wrong with wanting to make life easier. The Gaiists on Earth would have you think otherwise, but they're also dying of diseases that can be easily cured and leaving imperfect infants out to freeze, so no, I don't think technology is the greater evil here. The comforts we've invented – or that our neighbours have invented – can *become* bad if you don't always, always ask what the potential consequences could be. Many of our people skip that step. Many – not all, but many – leave here and are too eager to change their story. There's not just one planet with organic resources anymore. There are thousands. Hundreds of thousands. And if that's true, you don't need to worry so much, right? You don't need to be so careful. Use one up and move on to the next. The Harmagians were like that, once, until the rest of the galaxy got tired of their story. They changed. They learned. And that's why their society, and the Aandrisks, and the Aeluons, and everybody else – that's why they look so appealing to us. We're coming in at their happy ending and not stopping to think about how they got there. We want to take on their story. And we can, if we want to. But I worry about those who think adopting someone else's story means abandoning their own.' She turned to face the boy. '*That's* why the theatres are here, Kip. That's why we keep Archives, why we paint our hands on the wall. It's so we don't forget. We're our own warning. That's why the Fleet needs to remain. Why it *has* to remain. Without us out here, the grounders will forget within a few generations. We'll become just another story, and not one that seems relevant. Sure, we broke Earth, but we won't break *this* planet. We won't poison *this* water. We won't let *this* invention go wrong.' She shook her head. 'We are a longstanding species with a very short memory. If we don't keep record, we'll make the same mistakes over and over. I think it is a good thing that the Fleet is changing, that our people are spreading out. That's what we were meant to do. That's what our species has always, always done. But we must remember.' She contemplated Kip, as if he were a file that needed categorising. 'What are your plans for the future? Have you chosen a profession yet?'

Kip shifted his weight. 'I'm gonna leave the Fleet.'

Isabel waited for some specificity. None came. 'And do what?'

'I dunno.'

'Where will you go?'

'I . . . I'm not sure.'

'Are you going to university? Are you looking for work?'

'I don't know. I don't know yet.'

'Then why,' Isabel asked without judgment, 'do you want to go?'

Kip shrugged with agitation. 'I just . . . I need to get out of here.'

'Why?'

She'd hit the crack in the boy's patience. 'Because there's no point to any of this!' Kip blurted out, finally speaking with something other than a guarded drone. 'Seriously, what is the point to orbiting here forever? So we remember stuff? Why? For what? What are we *for*?'

'A fair question. You think you'll find the answer to that planetside?'

'It's . . . that's where we're supposed to be.'

Isabel laughed. 'That's a slippery slope you'll never see the end of. Head down the path of "how we're supposed to be", what we *evolved* to be, and you'll end up at "hunting and gathering in grassy plains". Maybe the Gaiists are right, and that is how we're *supposed* to be. I don't know. But if everything has to have a point: what's the point of hunting and gathering? How is that more meaningful than any of this?'

'I'm not talking about hunting and gathering, M.'

'Oh? Why?'

'Because . . .' He struggled. 'That can't be all there is, either.'

'So what you're saying is Humans aren't really *supposed* to do anything in particular, and we get to choose the kind of lives we have. But that doesn't mean any of it has a point, son. You think people born planetside don't wonder what the point of it all is? You don't think they know that their cities will fall and their houses will rot, and that somewhere down the line, their planet will get swallowed up by its sun? Spacers and grounders, we're riding the same ship. We both depend on fragile systems with a million interconnected parts that can easily be damaged and will eventually fail. Yes, we built the Fleet. The Fleet didn't just *happen* the way a planet does. But why does that matter? The only difference between our respective ecosystems is scale and origin.

Otherwise, it's the same principle.' She studied him. 'Have you ever gone through any of the Archives from the first days of Human spaceflight?'

'No.'

'I'd be surprised if you had. It's archaic stuff, and the Ensk translations aren't the best.' Yet another project, she thought, to keep some future archivist happy. 'Do you know why people – why Humans started heading out into the open? Oh, there was lots of military posturing involved, no mistake, but the true believers, the ones who couldn't bear the thought of *not* going out there – that's where they thought they'd find answers. They said, hey, we haven't got the context right. We need a sample size bigger than one lonely planet if we're ever going to understand any of this. And in many ways, they were right. We found other people out here, so that question got answered. We found out that life isn't rare. We've learned exponentially more about how planets work and how physics works, and the technology we have today would've blown their minds. We understand the galaxy in a way we never could have if we hadn't left. But the big question – the end-all, be-all question – well, that's still up for discussion. *Why?* What's the *point?* Kip, there isn't a sapient species living or dead that hasn't grappled hard with that. It scares us. It makes us panic, just like you're panicking now. So if the lack of a point is what's bothering you, if it's making you want to kick the walls and tear your hair out, well, welcome to the party.'

'But—'

Isabel put up her palm. 'Your ancestors thought they would answer the big question in space. Now here you are, out where they longed to go, looking back at the planets, trying to answer the same damn thing. You won't. You need to reframe this frustration you're feeling. If what you're saying is that you don't see a life for yourself here, that the kind of work you want to do or the experiences you want to have aren't available in the Fleet, then by all means, go. But if the only reason you want to do it is because you're looking for a *point*, you're going to end up miserable. You'll float around forever trying to make peace with that.'

Kip looked lost, but an entirely different kind of lost than he had moments before. 'I have no idea what kind of life I want,' he said at last. 'I don't know what I want to do.' He fell quiet, the blue glow of the data nodes highlighting his face.

Stars, he was young. He had so far to go.

'What do you like to do?' Isabel asked. 'What interests you?'

Kip gave a brittle laugh. 'Nothing.'

'There must be *something*. What do you do with your day?'

'Nothing important. Sims, vids, school.'

Isabel let the implication that school wasn't important slide. 'Job trials?'

The heaviest sigh in the world escaped the boy's lips. 'Yeah.'

'And nothing's stuck?'

'Nothing's stuck.'

'And you think something will out there?'

He looked at her as if that were obvious. 'Why else would so many people leave and not come back?'

'Again, that's fair. You're waiting for something to grab you, then. Something that feels like it's got a *point*.'

'Yeah.' Kip looked at her. 'What do you think I should do?'

'Oh, I can't tell you that,' Isabel said. 'I can only tell you what I *want* you to do, and that's based on my shallow impression of who you are and how I'd like your story to go. You can't operate by that. You're the only one who can think about what you *should* do.'

'Okay,' Kip said. 'Then what do you *want* me to do?'

Isabel paused. 'I'll only tell you if you understand that when a person tells you what they want of you, they're not deciding for you. It's their opinion, not your truth. Got it?'

'Yeah.'

'All right.' Isabel didn't need to think about what she was going to say next. She'd wanted to say it since the moment they'd started digging a burial trench together. With a sure step, she began to walk back out of the data chamber the way they'd come. 'I want you to apprentice with me.'

She could practically hear the kid blink. 'What?' he said.

'Not a job trial. A proper apprenticeship. Stripes and all.'

'Um.' Kip hurried after and fell alongside. 'Why?'

'Because of what you did for Sawyer.'

'What does—'

'—that have to do with anything? You tell me. Why wasn't it enough for you to simply report what you heard to patrol and have them deal with it?'

'I – I don't—'

'Yes, you do,' Isabel said firmly. 'Why?'

'It just . . . it bothered me.'

'Him being alone.'

'Yeah.'

'Him being thrown out. Him not getting a real funeral.'

'Yeah.'

'But you didn't just pay your respects. You weren't a passive mourner. You carried his body. You read the Litany for the Dead. You care about our ways, Kip, even if you think you don't. The idea of them not being performed shook you so hard, you had to do them yourself. And *that* – that's the kind of love the Archives needs. We won't survive without that.' She sorted her thoughts. 'I know that in this moment, you hate it here. I'm not belittling that. That's why I don't want you to apprentice for me *right now*.'

Kip was the picture of confusion. 'M, I'm sorry, but I . . . I really don't get it.'

Isabel smiled. 'I want you to leave the Fleet, Kip. For a little while. If you decide to stay wherever you land forever, so be it. But you can't apprentice with me until you see what's out there.'

'I don't—' Kip gave his head a short shake. 'You don't know me, M. You don't know me at all. I'd suck working here. I'm not smart.'

'What makes you say that?'

'I'm . . . I'm *not*. I suck at school, and—'

'What'd you get on your entrance exams?'

'803.'

Not amazing, true, but hardly a suggestion of *not smart*. 'That's an entirely decent score, Kip. That'll get you into everything but the top-tiers.'

'I barely made it, though. I busted my ass, and I got *entirely decent*. I'm not like . . .' He frowned. 'Like people who ace all their tests.'

Isabel gave a single nod. 'Good! Stars, the last thing I want is some cocky gifted kid who's never had to break a sweat. Give me someone who wants it and had to work for it any day.'

'But I don't know if I *want* to work here, M. I— I dunno, I've never thought about it.'

'You don't have *anywhere* you want to work, so having at least one option on the table can't hurt, hmm?'

'Wait, so . . . why would I have to leave first?'

'It's simple. If you never leave, you'll always wonder. You'll wonder what your life could've been, if you did the right thing. Well . . . scratch that. You'll *always* wonder if you did the right thing, no matter what the decision is, big or small. There's always another path you'll wonder about. But that wondering is less maddening if you know what the other path looks like, at least. So. You should go. Go to Hashkath. Go to Coriol. Go to Earth, even. Go wherever calls to you. And maybe you'll find out that life out there is good, that it suits you. Maybe you'll find that thing you're missing. Maybe not. What you *will* find, no question, is perspective. What that perspective is, I have no idea. But you'll find one. Otherwise, you'll only ever think about other people in the abstract. That's a poisonous thing, thinking your way is all there is. The only way to really appreciate *your* way is to compare it to somebody else's way. Figure out what you love, specifically. In detail. Figure out what you want to keep. Figure out what you want to change. Otherwise, it's not love. It's clinging to the familiar – to the comfortable – and that's a dangerous thing for us short-term thinkers to do. If you stay, stay because you want to, because you've found something here worth embodying, because you *believe* in it. Otherwise . . . well, there's no point in being here at all, is there? Better for everybody to leave, in that case.' She pushed the button to call the lift. 'Go out there and see what it's like to be the alien. Eat something weird. Sleep somewhere uncomfortable. Then, *if* you come back, and *if* you want to apprentice here, I want you to look me in the eye and tell me exactly why.'

Kip frowned. 'I don't know, M. This is kind of a lot.'

'Of course it is!' The lift arrived, and she stepped in. 'I wouldn't want anything to do with you if it felt otherwise.'

TESSA

The scene at home was the last thing she expected to find. Instead of discarded clothes and messy toys, there was only Pop, sitting on the couch in a tidied-up living room, a bottle of kick and two empty glasses on the table. He had been waiting, elbows on his thighs, hands folded between his knees. He smiled when she entered the front door.

Pop picked up the bottle. 'Don't worry about waking the kids. They're spending the night next door. Been a while since this home had only grown-ups in it, huh? Not since Aya was born.' He examined the label. He squinted, holding it at length, then up close, then farther out, trying to find the spot that fit his eyes best. 'You know, they don't make this stuff anymore.' He rotated the bottle for her to see: a bluefish, leaping its way into the stars. 'Farmer's Friend,' he said. 'They used to make it out of the fruit that wasn't good enough for the stores. Stopped making it after M Nazari died – must've been . . . well, let's see now . . . I guess forty-some years ago. She was the one who made the stuff. Sweet old lady, always nice to me and my brother. Whenever we'd go down to trade with her, she'd always hand us a bunch of fruit or something after the barter was done. And we'd always say, aw, c'mon, M, we didn't give you enough for that, here, take a couple extra chips. But she'd always say, no, no, and tell us we were her favourite customers. I think she said that to everybody, but she made you feel like it was true. After she went, though – well, none of her kids were much into brewing, so, the kick went, too.'

Tessa sat down, the back of her neck tingling, her stomach uneasy. She'd been holding the conversation with George in her stomach the whole way home, and the added uncertainty of wherever this conversation was going made her . . . not scared, exactly. But time had slowed, and she felt *awake*. *Present*. There was gravity centred around the table. Real gravity, not the conjured stuff in the floor. 'I remember the label,' she said. An old memory came back to life. 'You kept a few bottles on the shelf, over there.' She pointed. There weren't bottles there now, but tins of seeds and tech bits.

Pop nodded. 'For fun and company,' he said, pouring two generous fingers into the glasses. 'That's how your mother always put it. And you two weren't supposed to touch that shelf. You did once, though.'

'Oh, stars.' Tessa laughed. 'Oh, no. I forgot about that.'

'When your mother and I were going on a market trip—'

'The shuttle broke down half a day out, and you had to come home early.'

'Yeah, we came home to you two dipshits, puking your guts into a blanket.'

'Hey, that was Ashby, not me. *I* found a sink.'

Her father gave her a look that told her how little that distinction mattered. 'Couple of dumb teenagers who couldn't handle themselves.'

'I maintain that playing charthump all the next day was an asshole move.' Full volume drums, for hours and hours. She felt an echo of nausea from memory alone.

Pop laughed heartily. 'That was your mother's doing, and you deserved every second of it. Here.' He handed her a glass. 'For grown-ups.'

They clinked glasses and sipped. The kick was rough, but once she got past the edges, it warmed her all the way through. She didn't remember the taste – she didn't remember much of that adolescent night, honestly – and yet, somehow, it made her feel at home.

'Ahhhhh,' Pop said. 'Stars, that's fun.' He took another sip. 'Do you like it?'

'I do,' Tessa said honestly. She eyed the bottle. 'It's half empty,' she said.

'That it is.'

'I've never seen you drink this.'

'I've been saving it. Wasn't sure if I'd ever get to have any again.'

Tessa waited patiently. Pop didn't always make sense on the first go.

'I first opened this bottle,' he said, 'when your brother told me there was something he needed to talk about.' He briefly met her eyes over the rim of his glass. 'Would've been a good number of years ago now.'

Nobody said anything for a moment. 'You kept the other half for me,' Tessa said quietly.

'Yep,' Pop said. He drained his glass and exhaled appreciatively. 'Just in case. I didn't think I'd bring it out again, but – well, kids have a way of surprising you.'

Tessa stared into her glass, held with both hands low in her lap. She watched sediment drift and swirl in the decades-old kick. She raised the glass and tossed it back in one smooth swallow. 'We haven't made a decision yet.'

He refilled both their glasses. 'Uh huh,' he said. He left the bottle uncorked. 'Is George with his folks right now?'

'Yes,' she said.

'So, you've decided between yourselves, then.'

Tessa shook her head. She couldn't believe they were having this conversation. She couldn't believe anything about this at all. 'I don't know.'

'You don't know . . . what? Where you two left things?'

'No, I – I don't know. I don't know how to have this conversation.'

Pop sipped and exhaled, same as he had every sip before. 'One word in front of the other is how I do it.'

'Me and him and the kids . . . that's not our only family.'

'Obviously.'

'And we can't do this without talking to everyone else.'

'Define "this". Tessa, if you can't say it, you've got no business doing it.'

She shoved the words out. 'We're thinking about going planetside.' There. They were out now, out in the open, somewhere between treachery and relief.

Pop did nothing but nod. 'Colonies?'

'Yeah.'

'Good. It's hard work out there, and hard work keeps you honest. Keeps your head on straight.'

She waited for him to say more than that. She waited for him to get mad, to scoff, to tell her every reason why this was stupid, to be the outward confirmation of all the guilt and fear she felt within.

He did not.

'Is that all you have to say?' Tessa said incredulously.

'What do you want me to say? That I don't care? Of course I care. I'll miss you and the kids like hell. Or do you want me to get pissed and tell you no way, no how are you leaving home? That kind of thing didn't work when you were a teenager, and it sure as shit won't fly now.' He laughed. 'You're an adult. You know what you're about. Whatever you decide, I'm not gonna tell you otherwise. I'm too old for making big decisions. Had my fill of those.'

'But—' She scrambled, trying to find the trigger for the reaction she'd expected. 'But what about—'

'You know *I'm* not going, girl. I'll visit. But I'm not going anywhere.' He reached across the table and patted her hand. 'You don't have to worry about me. I got a good hex and the best friends a person could ask for.' His face scrunched into a worryingly pleased grin. 'Y'know Lupe from neighbourhood four?'

An image appeared in Tessa's mind: a tiny, white-haired old

woman, arguing with her son behind the seed shop counter. One of Pop's lunchtime cronies. 'Yeah.'

Pop replied with a waggle of his eyebrows.

The other shoe dropped, and Tessa recoiled. 'Ugh, Pop, I don't need to know.'

'It's nothing serious,' he said, relishing her discomfort. 'Just some casual fun—'

'Pop. I don't. Need. To know.'

Her father laughed and poured them both another drink. 'Here, I have something else to show you.' He unholstered his scrib, gestured at the screen, and slid it across the table.

M Santoso,

This is a confirmation for your ocular implant installation this upcoming second day.

Please arrive at the clinic at 10:00.

On a personal note, I'm very happy you've made this decision. I think you're going to be pleased with the results.

Dr Koraltan

'See,' Pop said, bringing his glass to his mouth. 'You don't need to worry about me.' He sipped and exhaled loudly. 'Though you are gonna have to send me those creds.'

Tessa truly, genuinely didn't know what to say.

Pop's gaze lingered on the wall of painted hands, reaching from floor to ceiling. 'Y'know, my great-granddad – we called him Great-pa, he thought that was funny – I didn't know him long, but I knew him.'

Tessa knew this much already, but she didn't interrupt.

'He remembered contact,' Pop said. 'He told me so often about that day when the Aeluons arrived. He was always pushing me to go. "Get out there, boy," he'd say. "That's what we're meant to do." I wondered, when I got older, why *he* didn't go, if he felt that way. I thought maybe he'd been scared, or set in his ways. But now I think it's because he knew that wasn't for him. Some of us have to go, yes. But some of us have to stay and kick the others out. Otherwise . . .' He scratched his chin. 'Otherwise all we know is the same place. My great-pa, he was right. We're meant to go. And we're meant to stay. Stay and go, each as much as the other. It's not all or nothing anymore. We're all over the place. That's better, I think. That's smarter.' He nodded. 'That's how we'll survive, even if not all of us do.' He looked up. 'You're gonna do great out there. I know you will.'

Tessa's first instinct was to protest. They hadn't made a decision yet, and here he was, talking like it was a done deal. But she looked again at the bottle, kept half full for her sake, an offering for a future her father had prepared himself for decades before she'd considered said same. She closed her eyes for a moment. She got up from her chair, sat down on the floor, and rested her head against her father's leg like she used to when she was small, like she used to when he was huge and handsome and knew everything there was to know. He pressed his palm into her curls, and she closed her eyes. 'I love you, Pop.'

'I love you, too, Tess.'

Part 7
· · · · · · · · · · · · · · · · · · ·

AND WILL UNDYING

Feed source: Reskit Institute of Interstellar Migration (Public News Feed)
Item name: The Modern Exodus – Entry #20
Author: Ghuh'loloan Mok Chutp
Encryption: 0
Translation path: [Hanto:Kliptorigan]
Transcription: 0
Node identifier: 2310-483-38, Isabel Itoh

[System message: The feed you have selected has been translated from written Hanto. As you may be aware, written Hanto includes gestural notations that do not have analogous symbols in any other GC language. Therefore, your scrib's on-board translation software has not translated the following material directly. The content here is a modified translation, intended to be accessible to the average Kliptorigan reader.]

———

When their planet could no longer sustain them, the waning Humans dismantled their cities. Down came the shimmering towers of glass and metal, beam by beam, bolt by bolt. Some of it was repurposed, but most was melted in noxious foundries hastily constructed on barren farmland. The Humans who did this knew they would not live to see the end result. Their years were almost universally cut short by famine and disease, but even if they had been as healthy as their ancestors, the work was too great for one lifetime alone. The scavengers made way for the builders, who poured and welded for the sake of children they would likely not live to see grown. Their completed efforts were launched into low orbit, and assembled there into thirty-two ships, each a city unto itself.

'A city made of cities,' my host told me during our first day. 'We took our ruins with us.'

I keep thinking of this now that I have returned to my own

adoptive city of Reskit. I look out at this sprawling architectural triumph, and I cannot imagine a Hashkath where this does not exist. I cannot imagine how this land looked when Aandrisks first arrived. I cannot imagine how it will look after they – and I – are gone.

Strange as it is to be back, I have slid effortlessly back into my usual patterns. I missed the length of a Hashkath day, the warmth of a brighter sun. I appreciate the open sky as I never have before, and will never again complain of days that are too windy. I spent an entire afternoon swimming at the Ram Tumma'ton Aquatic Park, and at one point, I could not help but sing for joy.

And yet, though I have travelled far from Risheth, I have brought the Fleet with me. There is no place I can go, no activity I can engage in without thinking of them. I can't see a garden without thinking of how theirs differ, nor can I watch a sunset without thinking of the mimicked rhythms of their abandoned sun.

'Night-time' in the Fleet is a curious thing. This is a people who have never lived on a planet – for some, never even *visited* a planet – yet they still follow an artificial semblance of a rotational day. I have experienced this environmental arrangement within long-haul ships built by a variety of species, but these have all been among crews with at least passing familiarity with life on the ground. Consider that the only generation of Exodans that would have truly needed an Earth-like environment would have been the first. It was they who needed night-time, who needed gravity, whose moods would've benefited from being surrounded by plant life rather than cold metal alone. And yes, the original intent of the Fleet was to seek out a terrestrial home, and they believed their progeny would adapt to that better if they were already accustomed to planetary norms. In that context, Exodan adherence to Earthen patterns is quite logical.

But imagine the alternative. Imagine if the Earthen builders had known their descendants would choose to remain in space, that this transitory life satisfied them even when empty ground lay within reach. What would the Human species look like today were that the case? Evolution is often thought of as a glacial process, but we know from countless examples that this is not always true. Rapid environmental change can prompt rapid physical change. What if the first Exodans had left their ornamental gardens behind? What if their lights did not dim? What if they had built homes designed for zero-g instead of gargantuan centrifuges filled with unsecured objects?

The first generation would have been miserable, no doubt. Health problems, both mental and physical, would have been rampant, especially when coupled with the unfathomable stress of leaving their planet for the unknown. But what of the second generation? What of the third, the fourth, the tenth? It is possible – likely, even – that my Exodan friends would look quite different today. Currently, there are small physical differences in modern Humans based on region. Centuries-old Solan populations based around the sun-starved Outer Planets are distinctively pale. Exodans, Martians, and independent colonists can sometimes tell each other apart (I have yet to grasp that nuance). So, imagine an Exodan people who had gone without gravity, without scheduled darkness. I find it likely that we would already see hereditary changes in bone mass, digestive process, eye structure. We would be present for the first days of a new species. Instead, we have space-dwelling Humans who get irritable if malfunctioning environmental lights prolong day or night beyond its time. They love their gardens, even if they have not seen wild plants. Chaos breaks out if local grav systems fail.

I must stress, dear guest, that I do not view the idea of a separate Exodan species as a missed opportunity – merely an intriguing road untravelled. I myself am bound by the pulse of bygone generations. I mist myself constantly, because my skin still requires an approximation of the steady sea breeze my people have not lived in since primitive times. I cannot digest the absurdly broad variety of foodstuffs that my sapient counterparts can, even though Harmagians have lived alongside such delicacies for centuries. For all my species' vast travels, our skin has not hardened, and our guts have not diversified. We, too, took the ways of our planet with us. And so, too, go the Exodans, a spaceborn people who balk at abandoning an environment inspired by a planet that, to most, may as well be myth.

Humans will never leave the forest, just as Harmagians will never leave the shore.

——

EYAS, HALF A STANDARD LATER

Every fourth day, she reviewed her lesson plans and practised her explanations, and every fifth day, she went to the spare classroom she'd reserved at the technical school, where no one but the other instructors – the other people *she'd asked* to do this – were waiting. Fifth day had become the most depressing day out of ten. Her usual work included.

She stepped off the transport pod, and, as she walked through the plaza, she did the necessary preparation of keeping her expectations low. *Nobody will be there*, she told herself. Maybe nobody ever would. Ten tendays, she'd told her assorted volunteers. If they tried this for ten tendays and nobody showed up, they'd call it quits. Well, this was the ninth tenday, and that meant she only had to sit around an empty classroom two more gruelling times before she could go back to her life and forget this whole idea. Just forget this whole thing ever—

Her interest piqued as she saw Sunny running out of the school and across the plaza toward her. He stopped a few feet in front of her, eager as a kid who'd flown his first shuttle. 'There's *people*,' he said.

Eyas' jaw dropped. 'What? No. Really?' She hurried along the way he'd come. 'How many?'

'*Three.*'

'Are you serious?'

'Dead serious. I guess those pixel posters Amad keeps putting up at the docks worked.'

Eyas tried to get her wits about her as they entered the school and walked down the corridor. Three people! It wasn't much, but it was a start. Finally, at last: a start.

'Oh, no,' she said. She came to a halt before they entered the classroom door.

'What's up?'

Eyas paused. 'We've never *had* people before.'

Sunny laughed. 'Are you scared?'

She cuffed him. 'Of course not. I'm just . . .' She took a breath. He squeezed her shoulder. 'Okay. People.'

The door spun open, and sure enough, there they were: a young woman, a middle-aged man, and . . . She turned and gave Sunny a secret, surprised look. An *Aeluon*.

Sunny raised his eyebrows and gave a nod of *yeah, I know*.

The other instructors turned to look at her, each as excited as she was. Eyas took a breath, and walked up to the teacher's station at the front of the room. The others sat in the chairs lined up alongside her, like they'd practised. 'Hello, everybody,' Eyas said to the attendees. 'Thank you so much for coming to our workshop.' She gestured at the assembled volunteers. 'We're the Exodan Cultural Education Collective.' She gave a slight pause, half expecting at least one of the attendees to realise they were in the wrong place and leave. None did. She smiled. 'Right. So.' This was harder than she'd anticipated. At the Centre, there were Litanies and traditions, set ceremonies to follow. She'd planned this class out, sure, but that didn't change the fact that she had made this whole thing up, and was making it up still.

She glanced over at Sunny. He winked. She steadied. 'This is a whole-day workshop, but if you need to leave at any time, feel free. We're hoping, at some point, to split this into individual classes – and more advanced classes as well – but we're new, and we're learning, too, so for now, you get all of us at once.' She paused, the presence of an alien prompting the realisation of something she should've thought of ahead of time. 'Does everyone here speak Ensk?'

The middle-aged man nodded. The Aeluon wiggled her hand.

'Yes,' the young woman said in some staggeringly thick fringer accent. 'But not much well.'

Eyas shifted linguistic gears. '*Klip remmet goigagan?*'

Everyone nodded, including the Aeluon. She'd clearly spent time around Humans. Eyas turned to the row of instructors. 'That okay with you guys?' she asked in Ensk.

'Mine's not great,' Jacira said. She was older, maybe fifty or so.

'That's okay,' Eyas said. 'Just do it in Ensk, and one of us will translate.' She switched back to Klip. 'This better? Okay, good. Our goal here today is to give you a good starting point for finding the resources and assistance you need to begin a life in the Fleet. We're going to cover a huge range of topics and services, and there will be plenty that we won't have time for. We're not here to teach you everything, but our hope is that you'll leave here knowing where to find the right answers. Let me introduce you to your instructors. Some of these professions won't be things you're familiar with. Others will be, and they're here to highlight some of the differences between our way of doing things and the ways you might be more used to. I'll start with myself, and we'll go down the line. My name's Eyas. I'm a caretaker for the dead. I conduct funeral rites and . . . well, I'll explain the specifics of it later.' She turned to the other volunteers. 'Let's focus on the living for now, yeah?'

'Hi, I'm Ayodeji,' the first said. 'I'm a doctor at a neighbourhood clinic. I'll be answering your questions about basic medical care.'

'Hi, I'm Tohu. I'm a ferry pilot. I'm gonna explain how to get around, both inside a homesteader and in between.'

'I'm Jacira. I'm a bug farmer, and I'll be talking to you about food stores and water management.'

'Hey there, I'm Sunny.' He smiled with all the confidence in the world. 'I'm a sex worker, and I'll be explaining where to go if you want to get laid.'

The young woman stared. The man laughed. The Aeluon looked at him, confused as to what was funny.

The instructors continued – a mural artist, a mech tech, a trade-only merchant – until there were no more names to give. Eyas turned to the class. 'Now, I'd like you three to introduce yourselves as well. Who are you, where are you from, and what brings you here?'

The students sat in silence for a moment, like all groups of strangers did. The man spoke first. 'I'm Bruno,' he said. 'I'm a spacer. From Jupiter Station originally, but that was a long time ago. I haul cargo – foodstuff, mainly. The Fleet's been one of my stops for six standards now, and I'm considering putting an end to all the back and forth. I like the people here, but I'm . . . I'm not quite sure yet.' He gestured to the instructors. 'I was hoping you could give me a better idea of what I'd be in for.'

Eyas smiled. 'We'll certainly try.'

'I'm Lam,' the Aeluon said. 'I am sure you weren't expecting me.'

The room chuckled. 'Not exactly,' Eyas said kindly.

'I'm from Sohep Frie, and I'm a textile merchant,' Lam said. 'I'm not going to relocate here, but I would like to understand the Exodans I work with better. They make great effort to make me comfortable. I'd like to be able to do the same.'

Eyas hadn't considered that other species might find value in a Exodan cultural crash course. Something to add to the workshop description, she supposed. Out of the corner of her eye, she saw Amad, the poster maker, already making a note on her scrib. 'That's wonderful,' Eyas said. 'We're delighted to have you here.' She looked to the woman. 'And what about you?'

The young woman swallowed. Eyas could tell she was shy. 'I'm Anna,' the woman said. 'I don't really . . . I guess I'm . . . I dunno. I guess I'm trying something new.'

There wasn't an encompassing word for what Eyas felt then. Tightness. Warmth. Pain. Clarity. She thought of the top of the cylinder, of one particular sunken crater she'd refilled with bamboo chips some tendays before now. She thought of the canisters that had rattled in her cart some tendays after then.

She thought of dirt, dark and shapeless, and of sprouts, tender and new.

Why now? Sunny had asked of her profession, right before giving her the answer she'd always had: *Because you love it, and because it's our way, and that's reason enough.* There wasn't maths or logic or any ironclad measure of efficiency to back it up. There didn't need to be. If *trying something new* was valid, then *keeping something old* was, too. No, this wasn't the same Fleet as that of their ancestors. Yes, things had changed, and would keep changing. Life meant death, always. But by the same token, death meant life. So long as people kept choosing *this* life, Eyas planned to be there – for as long as she could – guiding them through both sides of the equation.

Eyas looked Anna in the eye. She smiled, and said what she should've said the first time she'd heard a grounder speak those words. 'Welcome. Whatever questions you have, we're happy to help.'

KIP, ONE STANDARD LATER

Ever since he'd arrived on Kaathet, Kip had encountered so many things he'd never seen before that the phrase 'I've never seen anything like this' had almost stopped feeling like something worth pointing out. Nothing was like what he knew, not the food, not the crowds, and definitely not the school, which was the complete opposite of school back home in that *everything* was fun and interesting (and that was a whole new problem, because it was all so good, he didn't know what concentration to pick). To say 'I've never seen anything like this' was the same as saying 'I got up today'.

That said: he'd never seen anything like the Osskerit Museum, one of the biggest repositories of Arkanic artefacts in the GC. The inside of the building was decorated to look like one of their long-gone grand temples – or, at least, somebody's best guess as to how they looked. It was hard to say anything hard and fast about a sapient species that had gone extinct long before any of the ones around today had woken up. Still, if their buildings looked anything like the Osskerit, the Arkani had been damn impressive. Everything inside and out was harsh angles and reflective surfaces, a sharp, stabbing fractal of shimmering light. The visual effect felt violent, almost, and was nowhere Kip would want to live. He was wowed all the same.

'Hey, come look at this!' Tuumuu said. The Laru's body was facing a display, but her limb-like neck was stretched back around her foreleg so she could face the others. Kip was still getting used to that. He was also still getting used to having whole conversations in Klip all day every day, which he was getting better at. He wore a translation hud to fill in the gaps.

The rest of the group came over to Tuumuu's side, and Kip left the fossils he'd been looking at to drift their way. They were inseparable, the five of them, all first-year students, all inter-stellar transfers, all taking Introduction to Historical Galactic Civilisations. They were each from *somewhere else*, and even though the homegrown students at the Kaathet Rakas school were friendly (mostly), somehow it felt natural for the outsiders to stick together. Even if they were total weirdos.

Dron leaned toward the display, his cheeks swirling speckled blue. 'Huh,' he said.

Viola pointed at Dron's face. 'What's that one mean?'

The Aeluon gave Viola a tired look. 'Stars, you are not going to let this go, are you?'

'How else am I supposed to know what's up with you if you don't explain your colours? See, now there's some yellow in there. What's yellow mean?'

'Yellow means lots of things.'

'What's *this* yellow mean?'

'Annoyed. It means I'm annoyed.'

Viola cuffed the innocent Laru. 'Jeez, Tuumuu, stop bugging Dron. Can't you see he's yellow?'

'Kip,' Dron called. 'Will you please get over here and make your cousin behave?'

'And will you all please shut up?' Kreshkeris said from a bench nearby. She was taking furious notes on her scrib, like always. 'Some of us would like to actually do well on this assignment.' She was a lifelong spacer, too, and always acted like she had to prove herself to the grounder Aandrisks they went to school with. Some things weren't that different.

Kip walked up to Viola with his hands in his pockets. 'Hey, cousin,' he said. 'Behave.' He could hear his accent, his impre-cise words. But it was cool. With this group, he knew it was cool.

Viola smirked at the joke. Their first day at school, Dron had asked if she and Kip were related, which was hilarious, because Viola came from Titan, and they looked nothing alike. At least, they didn't think so. Everybody else did. *'Bug-fucking spacer,'* Viola said in her weird, flowy Ensk.

'Cow-licking Solan,' Kip shot back.

'That's for Martians, you idiot. There aren't any cows in the Outers.'

'I dunno, I'm looking at one right now.'

They both grinned.

'They're talking shit about us again,' Dron said in the others' general direction.

'You have no idea what we're saying,' Kip said.

An elaborate explosion of colour danced across the Aeluon's face. 'And neither do you.'

'Oh, *come on*,' Viola said.

'You guys,' Tuumuu said, the fur on her neck waving in the air as her big funny feet danced impatiently. 'Look at this.'

They leaned in to see what had gotten their fuzzy history nerd so excited. On the pedestal before them rested an ancient lump of metal, smashed in on itself, worn down by time.

'It's a star-tracker,' Tuumuu gushed. 'It's what they used to study the sky. Think about it! They were trying to find people out there, too. Only . . . only we showed up too late.' Her head sagged. 'Stars, that's sad.'

They leaned in closer. 'Doesn't look like much,' Dron said.

'That's 'cause it's old, dummy.'

'How'd it work?' Viola asked.

Kip cocked his head. 'Looks like there was a switch here.' He reached out and picked up the star-tracker.

Everything went batshit at once. An alarm went off. Previously unseen lights started flashing. His friends yelled in unison.

'Kip, what the fuck?!'

'Dude, what are you—'

'Put it back!'

A shout in Reskitkish came from behind. A line of translation shot across Kip's hud: *Put the object down.*

He turned to see an Aandrisk security guard standing behind him. She was about two heads taller than he was, and had a stun gun at the ready.

Kip stammered. 'I – what—'

The Aandrisk repeated herself in hissing Klip: 'Set the item down.'

Kip looked down at the lump of metal he was still holding stupidly. He had no idea what he'd done wrong, but he did as told. 'I – I wasn't stealing—'

The guard glared at him, and everyone else. She looked straight at Kreshkeris as she walked away. *'Mind your foreign friends,'* she said.

Kreshkeris got up from her bench and stormed over to Kip, her feathers on end. She was tall, too. 'What were you *thinking*?'

Kip looked at his friends – Tuumuu an anxious puff from front to back, Dron red as a bruise, Viola laughing with her forehead in her palm. What was he thinking? He had a better question: what had he *done*? 'I wasn't stealing,' he said again.

'Kip, you – you know you can't touch stuff at a museum, right?' Dron said.

Kip blinked. 'Why not?'

'Oh, stars,' Viola said, laughing harder.

Tuumuu stepped in. 'These are priceless things,' she explained. Her fur started to settle. 'This star-finder might be the only one left. If you break it, that's . . . that's it. There are no more, and we can't learn anything.'

'If you break it, why not fix it?' Kip frowned. 'You can't learn anything like – like this.' He gestured to the trouble-making metal. 'You can't learn how it works if it's broke.'

'I – well – you should take an archeology class,' the Laru said, her tone brightening. 'Professor Eshisk is great. You'd learn all about restoration techniques, and preserving context, and—'

'The point, Kip,' Kreshkeris said, 'is that you can't touch. That's the rules.'

'Okay.' Kip put his palms up. 'Okay, that's the rules. I'm sorry.' He surrendered the argument, but he didn't understand. He tried to imagine the same situation playing out back in the Fleet. *This is a First Generation telescope, and you can't attempt fixing it, you can't recycle the metal and glass, and you definitely can't touch it. We're just going to put it here on the shelf, spending space and fuel on something nobody can use.*

Tuumuu seemed to read his mind. She fell alongside him as the group continued through the hall, walking on four legs and keeping her neck down so as to match his height. 'Don't you have museums in the Exodus Fleet? You obviously don't have *buildings*, but collections or . . . or museum *ships* maybe, or . . .'

'No,' Kip said. 'We have the Archives, I guess.'

'What's that?'

'They're like a library. All on servers though, no paper or tablets or anything. Just recordings of . . . of . . .' The Archives were such a basic thing to him, such an everyday given. He'd never had to sum them up before. 'Of everything. Earth, the Fleet, families. Seriously everything. We don't need to carry museum stuff around.'

'But you – you don't have any physical artefacts of your history. None at all.' She looked bothered by that idea. Tuumuu lived and breathed for artefacts.

Kip started to say no, but realised that wasn't true. He thought about his hex, where he'd watched Mom melt down old busted tools, where he'd watched Dad refit an exosuit that was still good and sealed after three generations. He wondered how Tuumuu would react to that. If she freaked out over him just *picking up* an old thing, she'd lose her mind at a neighbourhood smelter. 'We . . . use stuff,' Kip said. 'If we can use it, we use it, and if we can't, we make something else.' He thought for a moment. 'I guess everything is an artefact, kind of. Like . . . I dunno, a plate. A plate wasn't always a plate, see. It could've been a bulkhead once, or . . . or flooring, or something. Or maybe it *was* a plate all along, and my great-great-great-great-great-grandparents ate off of it. I'm still going to use it.'

Tuumuu got that cute fold in her face that happened when she was putting ideas together. 'And that plate would've been something else down on Earth first. A machine, or a house, maybe.'

'A house?'

'Well, because of the metal foundries, right? Where they took apart the cities.'

'I guess so,' Kip said. The Laru beside him had a better grasp on Earthen history than he did, and he was kind of embarrassed about it. He'd been meaning to get a Linking book.

'Wow,' Tuumuu said. 'Wow. So you *can* touch everything. You're touching your artefacts all the time.' She let out one of her weird alien chuckles. 'So that star-tracker, you would've just . . .'

Kip shrugged. 'Made a plate.'

'Made a plate,' she repeated, disbelieving. She pushed her face a little closer to his. 'Can I come visit some time? Can I stay with your family?'

Laru, Kip had learned, didn't find it rude to ask for exactly what they wanted, be it a favour or part of your lunch or, apparently, a cross-galaxy trip to stay with your parents. 'Yeah, sure,' he said, and as he said it, he realised that he really, weirdly, *did* want Tuumuu to visit. He thought about the Fleet through her eyes, and it wasn't the same Fleet he knew at all. He thought about the murals he walked past every day without a second thought, the theatres he went to because it was something to do, the farms that were just farms until you saw farms on the ground. He imagined how Tuumuu would see those things, what they'd mean to someone who never shut up about *artefacts*. He imagined saying, 'Go ahead, touch anything you want.' He imagined her fur fluffing and her big feet bouncing and her face folding and folding until she exploded from excitement. He thought, for a second, about taking her to the Archives so she could meet M Itoh, who would totally be able to tell Tuumuu anything she wanted . . . but that imagining wasn't as good. *He* wanted to be the one to tell her. He wanted to know stuff, like Tuumuu knew stuff. He wanted to hang out in his district with her and have the neighbours come stare. He wanted to teach her things. He wanted his alien friend to think the Fleet was cool.

And maybe . . . maybe it was.

'Hey, hurry up!' Dron called back to them. The rest of the group was rounding a corner. 'I'm not coming back if you get lost.'

Kip followed along. He moved through the museum, passing intangible history and thinking of home.

TESSA, TWO STANDARDS LATER

The sun spike was a weird plant. Not quite a succulent and not quite a tree, it rose from the desert sand on its spindly trunk, an improbable support for the pod-like leaves and bright orange fruit that puffed out from its upper arms. The sun spikes weren't native to Seed; they were an introduced species, just as the Humans who tended them were.

Tessa watched the sun spikes go by in neat rows as she flew the low-hovering skiff down the orchard road and back toward the village. 'What'd I tell you?' she said to her passenger. She threw a glance over her shoulder to the bed of the skiff, full to the brim with bushels of fat fruit.

Ammar raised his calloused palms. 'You win,' he said. 'I'll never question your pollinator maps again.'

Tessa nodded, satisfied. Drawing up a new rotation for the pollinator bots hadn't been hard. Geometry and logic, that was all. Move this shape here, fill that gap there, and hey presto, you've got more efficient field coverage. That part had been a cinch. The hard part was convincing the settlers who'd been there far longer than her – people who didn't trip over their own feet when looking up at the sky, who didn't freak out over bugs that weren't food, who no longer stared at the unending horizon until they felt dizzy – that her suggestion had a good chance of boosting the next harvest. That part had been hard, too – waiting. Seasons on their world moved fast, but still, she couldn't just grab a few spare aeroponics parts and put her plan into action. She'd drawn up the map in winter, waited until spring to actually do anything, and crossed her fingers until late summer in the hopes that she'd be right.

And she had been. She couldn't help but feel a bit smug about it. It was a good way to feel.

Ammar reached back, plucked a choice sunfruit from their haul, and took a huge bite. '*Mmm*. Stars, I love these.'

'Hey,' Tessa said, slapping his knee. 'What is that, your fourth?'

'If I pick 'em, I eat 'em,' Ammar said. He took another bite, his lips already stained from the previous three. '*Mmm mmm mmm*.' He looked down at Tessa's arm. 'Did you forget your jacket again?'

A bit of the smugness faded. 'I'm fine,' she said tersely.

Ammar laughed. 'You are goosebumps from shoulder to wrist. Tess, you gotta remember that weather exists.'

Tessa stuck her tongue out at him as she flew around the construction site for the new water reclamation building. Days on Seed were hot, and it was easy to remember to dress cool when you woke up with blankets kicked to the floor. The bit she kept forgetting was that the sun going down meant the warmth went with it. A lifetime of disconnect between *light* and *air temperature* was a tough thing to shake.

The sky was a hazy pink by the time they got home, and Tessa was starting to shiver. She warmed up quick, though, as she and Ammar and the villagers who saw them approach worked to get the fruit into the storehouse before dark. The liftbots – which had lain unused and in disrepair before Tessa's arrival – accepted their new inventory, emptying the heavy bushels into stasis crates, carrying their burdens silently. In contrast, the busy Humans unleashed a loud chorus of chatter. Tessa heard people talking about the size of the fruit, the colour, how it compared to the year before, and the year before that, and the year before that. They talked about who was going to make jam, and who was going to make kick, and how the suddet root should be coming up soon. Simple talk. Harvest talk. She'd never had interest in the farms back home – back on the *Asteria*, that is. This was different, somehow. Something about the dirt, maybe, or the added chaos of wild bugs and desert chickens (which weren't actual *chickens*, of course – they weren't much like Earthen birds at all – but you made do with the words you had). She wasn't entirely sure what the reason was, but she liked being part of the farm crew here. To her unending surprise, she liked it.

A herd of kids ran over, the eldest and fastest at the front, the little ones trailing dutifully. They were followed by two elderly folks – the childminders. Their careful eyes were belied by their unfussed stroll and minimal interference. The kids waited the barest of seconds to get an approving nod from an adult, then swarmed upon the fruit. They took them into their hands, gnawed in starting points, then scraped out the sweet pulp with whatever stage of teeth they had. Tessa saw Ky, shadowing Alerio as usual. His idol was an impressive *six and a half*, and everything five-year-old Ky wanted to be. But though Alerio always generously put up with his devotee, he failed to notice that Ky couldn't reach the top of the bushels.

Tessa made her way over and crouched down behind Ky. She put her hands over her son's eyes. 'Guess who,' she said.

Ky ducked down out of her hands and spun around. 'Mom, don't *do* that,' he giggled.

'Oh, I'm very sorry.' She raised her eyes to the out-of-reach sunfruit. 'Do you want one?'

'Yes!'

'Yes, what?'

Ky bounced up and down. 'Yes, *please*.'

She stood, picked him up around his midsection, and lifted him within reach. Stars, he was heavy. Ky made a move for a fruit that was about half the size of his head. 'You're never gonna finish that one, bud,' Tessa said. 'I think you should get one you can pick up with one hand.'

Ky grabbed a more moderately sized one with both hands. 'I can finish this one.'

'All right,' Tessa said. Compromise had been found, in a way, and besides, her back couldn't take much more of him deciding. She set Ky down, and he wasted no time in running back toward the pack. Tessa called after him. 'What do you say?'

'Thank you!' Ky shouted in motion.

'You're welcome,' she said, even though she was sure he'd stopped listening. She scanned her eyes over the kids, looking for a tall head of choppy black hair.

Where was Aya?

Ammar was leading the charge with harvest storage, and there were more than enough hands, so Tessa had no qualms about walking home in search of her errant kid. It was properly dark by then, and she hurried along with hands in her pockets and bare arms pressed to her sides. She passed the school, the fuel depot, the med clinic. She passed the gathering hall, still decked with bunting from Remembrance Day. She passed the sculpture of a homesteader standing in the middle of a growing wreath of desert plants, the plaque below inscribed with heat-etched words:

In honour of all who carried us this far.

She arrived, at last, at a mud-and-metal home, not particularly different from the others. This one, though, had a painted sign beside the door. *Santoso*, it read, underlined by four handprints – two big, two small. She relaxed as she saw a familiar red scoot-bike tossed unceremoniously onto the front porch. Aya was home. She'd be receiving yet another talking-to about putting her things away properly, but still – she was home.

The warm air inside made Tessa melt with relief, and a wonderful smell met her nose. George stuck his head out of the kitchen doorway. His beard and belly were streaked with flour, and he wore a pair of oven mitts. 'You are about fifteen minutes away from a kickass desert chicken soup and what is, I believe, my best bread yet,' he said. He looked her up and down. 'Did you forget your jacket again?'

Tessa rolled her eyes. 'What's so special about this bread?' she asked as she pulled off her boots.

'Nuh uh,' he said, ducking back into the kitchen. 'A chef never reveals his secrets.'

Tessa shook her head with a smile. The previous winter – their first on Seed – when there'd been little to do but stay warm and go bonkers, George had discovered a previously unknown love for baking. He was honestly talking about quitting the construction crew to open up a shop. George. Her husband, George. Tessa privately thought he could do with a few more loaves that weren't gooey on the inside before he made the leap, but she wasn't about to squash his enthusiasm, and besides, she was happy to eat her way through as many experiments as it took.

Stars, but it was nice having him around.

'Where's Aya?' she asked.

'Talking to your dad,' he said.

Tessa raised her eyebrows and made her way to the living room. There indeed was her daughter, covered in dirt from head to toe, having an animated discussion with Pop on the sib.

'And *then*,' Aya said, 'Jasmin was like, I bet you can't jump that ditch, and I said, yeah, I can, and I *did*. I crashed when I landed, though. Look, see.' She raised up her elbows toward the screen. 'I've already got crazy bruises.'

'Yikes,' Pop said. Light glinted off his ocular implant as he nodded approvingly. 'Those are impressive.'

'Yeah, tomorrow we're gonna go off the dock into the lake. Tommy built a ramp, and it's fine, the water's real deep.'

Pop laughed from way deep in his chest. 'You'll have to show me when I come visit.'

'When are you coming?'

'Early next standard. Takes a long time to get there. Think you can find a scoot-bike for me?'

Aya giggled. 'I dunno.' She turned her head. 'Mom's here, do you want to talk to her?'

'Nah,' he said. 'Don't have time.'

Tessa raised her voice. 'Thanks, Pop.'

Pop leaned toward his screen confidentially. 'Tell your mom I can't talk because I've got a hot date.'

Aya craned her head back. 'Grandpa says he can't talk, he's got a hot date.'

'Oh, stars,' Tessa said. She pinched the bridge of her nose, then walked into frame. 'Lupe?'

'Psh,' Pop said. 'Old news. I'm meeting Marjo at Top to Bottom.'

'And I'm sorry I asked,' Tessa said. She gave a sarcastic wave. 'Have fun.'

'Bye, Grandpa,' Aya said.

Pop was still waving and smiling as the screen went dark.

Tessa put her hands on her hips. 'So speaking of scoot-bikes . . .'

'Oops.' Aya gave her a charming smile.

Tessa was not swayed. She plucked at her daughter's shirt. 'Have you been strolling around this house in this nasty shirt?' She moved her hand to Aya's scalp. 'Stars, *your hair*.' Crusty bundles of dirt clung to her daughter's locks.

Aya looked down as if seeing her clothing for the first time. 'Oops,' she said again.

Tessa brushed the transferred crud off her palm, wondering just how much of Seed was now coating the inside of her home. 'Kiddo, you have got to remember that dirt exists.'

'And *you* have to remember to bring a jacket.'

Tessa ignored the poorly smothered laugh from the kitchen. She narrowed her eyelids. 'Shower. Clean clothes. Now.' Aya made a face, but she obeyed, and received a gentle swat on the shoulder from Tessa as she went.

Tessa sighed and surveyed her wreck of a living room. Toys, tools, visible footprints. She bent over and started tidying up, knowing her efforts would be made futile by tomorrow. Her limbs were sore from the day spent in the field, and she knew that while the next day would be less strenuous, it'd be just as busy.

They had to start covering the roots before the first fall frost hit, and the pollinators needed to be cleaned before they got packed away. Plus, there was laundry that needed doing, and globulbs that needed replacing, and a draughty wall that needing patching, and . . . stars, it never ended, did it?

'Hey,' George called. 'You're not cleaning, are you?'

'I'm just tidying up.'

'Tessa. It's not hurting anybody, and I can do it in the morning. Sit down, have some kick, warm up.'

She opened her mouth to protest, but then . . . why not? The mess *wasn't* hurting anybody, it wasn't going anywhere, and there'd just be another one tomorrow. She picked up the bottle of Whitedune and an accompanying glass from the top of one of the shelves. She sat on the couch, pretending she didn't see the puff of dust that rose up when she sat down. She poured herself a splash. She didn't need more than that. Just five minutes of a warm throat and stillness. That would do nicely.

She thought, as she closed her eyes, about home. Seed was a good place, better than she'd expected. But it wasn't *home* yet, and she worried, sometimes, about whether it ever would be. There were nights when she lay awake, missing the hex so much she could hardly breathe, or when she was so unaccustomed to the luxury of having George home all the time that she went and slept on the couch for the familiarity of sleeping alone. Sometimes she snapped at the kids when they didn't deserve it. Sometimes she got sad over silly things – the oxygen garden, her old mek brewer, even the stupid cargo bay. It was hard, life on the ground. Yes, homesteaders had to worry about water and crops, too, but if one of those systems failed, if your ship fell apart, there were others you could go live on. It wasn't like that out here. Leaving Seed meant leaving the system, travelling for tendays, figuring life out again. Part of her still couldn't believe that she'd done this. Part of her was still unsure. Maybe part of her always would be.

She opened her eyes. Something was off. With a sigh, she

realised – she hadn't heard any sounds of showering. She hadn't even heard the water turn on yet. She got up, walked to the bathroom, pushed the door open, and – the scolding died on her lips. Aya was in there all right, still clothed, still filthy. But she had the window propped open, and she was halfway out of it, twisting her torso to look up at the sky. Her dirty hair swayed in the evening breeze. Her face was turned toward the biggest moon, shining bright and beautiful overhead. She hadn't noticed her mother come in, and was talking to herself. Whatever the words were, Tessa could not hear. Some story, perhaps. Some idea she didn't want to forget. But while her words were lost, the expression on her face was unmistakable. She was curious. She was unafraid.

Tessa stepped back out, taking care to lean the door shut silently. She made her way to the kitchen. George was facing away from her, transferring his precious bread from oven to cooling rack. She walked up behind him, wrapped her arms around his middle, and rested her cheek between his shoulder blades.

'Hey, you,' he said.

'Hey,' she said.

'I think I fucked up this bread,' he sighed.

She laughed and shut her eyes, soaking up the warmth of him. The bread, fucked up or not, smelled great. So did he. He always did. 'That's okay,' she said. She held him tight. 'You'll make another one.'

ISABEL, THREE
STANDARDS LATER

The assembly hall was decorated as it always was – cloth flags, metal stars, shining ribbons. There were differences, of course. Some of the other archivists had been fed up with the worn flags they'd dragged out standard after standard and took it upon themselves to make a batch of new ones (Isabel had to admit, they were much better). The seedlings on the favour table weren't sky vine anymore, but four-toes, which had come back into fashion (she'd found their fussy flowers so old hat when she'd been in her youth). But details didn't matter. It was still a Naming Day, and she never tired of those. They were the best kinds of days.

She felt someone looking at her, and she glanced over from her out-of-the-way corner to Tamsin, who'd tagged along for this one. The Mitchell family from hex 625 was the one getting an extra name record that day, and their cooking was legendary throughout the neighbourhood. Tamsin had taken a chair off to the side of the room, and very much looked the part of an innocent old woman who needed to rest her legs. Isabel knew her too well for that. Her wife had chosen a strategic spot that would put her right at the front of the buffet line once the formalities were over. Tamsin locked eyes with her, and gave a purposeful tilt of her head toward a man setting down a giant bowl of noodles mixed with crispy fish, a rainbow of vegetables, and all sorts of tasty bits Isabel couldn't make out at a distance. Tamsin held her hands close to her stomach and gave Isabel two secretive thumbs up.

Isabel smothered a laugh and looked elsewhere. She had to be respectable today. Tamsin didn't always make that easy, but then, that was part of the fun.

The young family arrived, hanging back in the hallway. Isabel made eye contact with the musicians, and they began to play. The crowd parted. The couple approached, baby in tow. They stopped at the podium, as they knew to do. But Isabel did not move. Instead, she looked to another, and nodded.

Isabel watched her new apprentice as he took his place. He'd filled out well in the years that he'd been away. He'd grown into himself. He had a full beard, and his voice had settled steady and low. He'd completed an academic track in Post-Unification History, which he'd passed by the skin of his teeth. He spoke spaceport Reskitkish, and his arm sported a swirling bot tattoo he'd picked up from some market stop, like you do. He'd gained a soft spot for snapfruit tarts. He liked letting ocean waves run over his toes. But he drank his mek hot and his kick ice cold, and found no meal as comforting as a hopper topped with twice-round pickle. He peppered his Klip with Ensk, his Ensk with Klip, and thought Martian accents were the funniest thing there was. He knew that the sky was best viewed below his feet. And he'd told her, when she'd demanded to know why he was back, that seeing so many singular things had made him realise he came from somewhere singular, too, and even if it was ass-backwards and busted – his words – it was *theirs*, and there was nothing else like it. The Fleet was priceless. The only one. If it was gone, there wouldn't just be nothing for other Humans to learn from. There'd be nothing for *him* to learn from.

She'd put in an order for his robes right then, the same robes he wore handsomely now – bright yellow with a white apprentice's stripe on the shoulders. He was nervous, she could tell, more than his face gave away. Of course he was. She'd been nervous her first time, too.

She looked out at the crowd waiting for him to begin. They

smiled warmly at him. They understood. They had his back. He was one of theirs.

Kip cleared his throat and gave a brave smile. 'We destroyed our world,' he said, 'and left it for the skies. Our numbers were few. Our species had scattered. We were the last to leave. We left the ground behind. We left the oceans. We left the air. We watched these things grow small. We watched them shrink into a point of light. As we watched, we understood. We understood what we were. We understood what we had lost. We understood what we would need to do to survive. We abandoned more than our ancestors' world. We abandoned our short sight. We abandoned our bloody ways. We made ourselves anew.' He spread his hands, encompassing the gathered. 'We are the Exodus Fleet. We are those that wandered, that wander still. We are the homesteaders that shelter our families. We are the miners and foragers in the open. We are the ships that ferry between. We are the explorers who carry our names. We are the parents who lead the way. We are the children who continue on.' He picked up his scrib from the podium. 'What is his name?'

'Amias,' the man said.

'And what name does your home carry?'

'Mitchell,' said the woman.

'Amias Mitchell,' Kip spoke to the scrib. A blue square appeared on screen. He took the baby's foot and attempted to press it to the square. The baby kicked mightily, and for a moment, Kip looked intimidated by the person a fraction of his size. A quiet laugh rippled through the crowd. Kip laughed, too, and with the help of the child's father, got the foot in order. The scrib chirped. Record had been made.

'Amias Mitchell,' Kip said. 'Born aboard the *Asteria*. Forty Solar days of age as of GC standard day 211/310. He is now, and always, a member of our Fleet. By our laws, he is assured shelter and passage here. If we have food, he will eat. If we have air, he will breathe. If we have fuel, he will fly. He is son to all grown, brother to all still growing. We will care for him, protect him, guide him. We welcome you, Amias, to the decks of the *Asteria*, and to the journey we take together.' He spoke the final words now, and the room joined him. 'From the ground, we stand. From our ships, we live. By the stars, we hope.'

ACKNOWLEDGEMENTS

This book had the unusual experience of starting with one editor and ending with a different one. This is the sort of thing that would make a writer panic (and there may have been a bit of that), but my luck on both sides of this equation has been amazing. Thanks forever to Anne Perry, who pulled me out of the weeds and gave me a place to lay down roots, and to Oliver Johnson, who helped me find the rhythm of the whole thing. Thanks, too, to Sam Bradbury, Jason Bartholomew, Fleur Clarke, Becca Mundy, and the entire team at Hodder.

On the science side, the Exodan caretaking tradition was inspired by real-world efforts to establish human composting as a funerary practice. Big thanks to Katrina Spade of the Urban Death Project and Recompose for taking the time to chat with me and answer my questions. Additional thanks to Mom and Dad for letting me bug them about gravity.

As always, I'd be nowhere without my posse: my family, my friends, and Berglaug the incredible. Much love to all of you.

WANT MORE?

If you enjoyed this and would like to find out about similar books we publish, we'd love you to join our online Sci-Fi, Fantasy and Horror community, Hodderscape.

Visit hodderscape.co.uk for exclusive content form our authors, news, competitions and general musings, and feel free to comment, contribute or just keep an eye on what we are up to.

See you there!

HODDERSCAPE
NEVER AFRAID TO BE OUT OF THIS WORLD

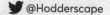 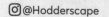